THE ENCYCLOPEDIA OF
Ethnic Groups in Hollywood

THE ENCYCLOPEDIA OF ETHNIC GROUPS IN HOLLYWOOD

JAMES ROBERT PARISH

Associate Editor
ALLAN TAYLOR

Facts On File, Inc.

The Encyclopedia of Ethnic Groups in Hollywood

Facts On File, Inc.
132 West 31st Street
New York NY 10001

Library of Congress Cataloging-in-Publication Data

The Encyclopedia of Ethnic Groups in Hollywood/[edited by] James Robert Parish and Allan Taylor.
p. cm.
Includes bibliographical references and index.
ISBN 0-8160-4604-2
1. Minorities in motion pictures—Encyclopedias. 2. Minorities on television—Encyclopedias. 3. Minorities in the motion picture industry—United States—Encyclopedias. 4. Minorities in television broadcasting—United States—Encyclopedias. I. Parish, James Robert. II. Taylor, Allan.
PN1995.9.M56 M85 2002
791,43′6520693—dc21 2002004376

Facts On File books are available at special discounts when purchased in bulk quantities for businesses, associations, institutions, or sales promotions. Please call our Special Sales Department in New York at (212) 967-8800 or (800) 322-8755.

You can find Facts On File on the World Wide Web at
http://www.factsonfile.com

Text design by Erika K. Arroyo
Cover design by Nora Wertz

Printed in the United States of America

VB Hermitage 10 9 8 7 6 5 4 3 2 1

This book is printed on acid-free paper.

To Film and Television Talent of All Races

Contents

Acknowledgments

With special appreciation to Allan Taylor, associate editor of this project.

Many thanks to the Academy of Motion Picture Arts and Sciences' Margaret Herrick Library, Richard Baer (Hollywood Film Archive), Larry Billman (Academy of Dance on Film), Billy Rose Theater Collection of the New York Public Library at Lincoln Center, Michael Buering (Museum of Television and Radio), John Cocchi (JC Archives), Stephen Cole, Bobby Cramer, Ernest Cunningham, Steve Eberly, Echo Book Shop, Prof. Jim Fisher, Alex Gildzen, Bill Givens, Beverly Gray, Ken Hanke, Jane Klain (Museum of Television and Radio), Frederick Levy, Andy Mangels, Doug McClelland, Alvin H. Marill, Jim Meyer, Martin Norden, Michael R. Pitts, Barry Rivadue, Jerry Roberts, Jonathan Rosenthal, Brenda Scott Royce, Barry Saltzman, Arleen Schwartz, Nat Segaloff, Sam Sherman, André Soares, Vincent Terrace, Gerry Waggett, Tom Waldman, and Elaine Woo.

My especial gratitude to my agent, Stuart Bernstein, and to my editor, James Chambers, for making this project a reality.

Introduction

The five groups (African Americans, Asian Americans, Hispanic Americans, Jewish Americans, and Native Americans) presented and discussed in this volume are certainly not the only ethnic minorities who found themselves disfavored in the United States during the past centuries and today. Some of the groups not included in this book have also suffered and continue to suffer discrimination to varying degrees, whether they be Poles, Hindus, or Irish.

Even the English were not spared. There were segments of the twentieth-century American public (which Hollywood movies often reflected) that took every available opportunity to poke fun at these "foreigners" with their peculiar way of speaking English, their apparent fascination with titles and royalty, their perceived emotional frigidity, and their alleged horrendous cooking.

Earlier, when the Irish had sought refuge in America against famine and poverty, they also were looked down upon, ridiculed as strange-talking folks with an unquenchable thirst for spirits, conversations that were laced with blarney, and it was assumed, an unhealthy interest in things fantastic. Later, as the Irish adapted more to the American culture, they were generally accepted as Americans. And so the cycle goes.

In examining and presenting the history of the five selected ethnic minorities in relation to American motion pictures and television programming during the twentieth century, the entries and accompanying text in each of the five chapters reflect not only how each group was represented or *not* represented on the screen but also how the U.S. entertainment industry dealt with talent from each of these minority communities. What emerges from the material is that often the exclusionary practices, the derogatory presentation of presumed ethnic characteristics, and the belittling of a particular cultural heritage as "naturally" inferior were based on ingrained prejudices passed down from generation to generation (with new or old groups substituted as the latest targets to be demeaned). As a result, some individuals practiced (or practice) such discrimination without conscious awareness that they were (or are) doing so. Even if they should be cognizant of their bigotry, they were (or are) comforted by their skewed, deep-rooted beliefs that these practices were/are based on logic, tradition, and practicality.

Illustrations of this unenlightened view of some Americans can be viewed in almost any patriotic wartime movie made by Hollywood in the early 1940s. Whether on the battlefield or on the home front, almost inevitably in such a picture, one of the characters (or a voice-over) insists that America is fighting the war against the Axis so that everyone, everywhere can enjoy equality as exemplified by the United States. Yet, within some of these very same movies, when the camera pans over a battalion of servicemen, there are no African Americans represented. Similarly, if a scene takes place in, say, a New England town, only WASP types are presented as townsfolk. An insidious aspect of discrimination was—and is—that it can sometimes become an unconscious mode of behavior.

Bad traditions, wrongful habits, or deliberate persecution of members of the five groups profiled did not occur overnight in the United States, nor have or will they end in short order. In the treatment of each of the five groups highlighted in this book, the reasons for their being considered "lesser" Americans have often differed, sometimes based on greed, or smugness, or, perhaps, jealousy or fear of what the other culture might have to offer. Conversely, the reactions to discrimination during the twentieth century of each of these put-upon groups were not the same, and their unique responses to persecution and disdain in turn caused a new set of counterresponses. The complex cycles of such behavior were, and are, not easy to break, nor is the history and heritage of such bigotry easy to forget, forgive, or understand.

Each of the five ethnic groups treated in this book has its own particular history of abuse at the hands of the American majority. For example, many African Americans are descended from African peoples who were brought to America as slaves. Even after their emancipation was substantiated by America's bloody Civil War in the 1860s, they were still treated by many Americans for decades thereafter as second-class individuals who were not entitled to equality, opportunities of advancement, or the right to mingle with whites.

Many Asian Americans came to the United States in the nineteenth century when cheap labor was needed to build the railroad and other industries and agriculture. Others immigrated to find greater freedom in a country not bound by the burdensome traditions of their homelands. But when, for example, World War II began, even the most acculturated Japanese Americans were suddenly considered enemies by many other Americans—resulting in their property being confiscated and their being shipped to detention camps where they were treated as the enemy for the duration of the war. Prison camps were not exclusively a foreign phenomenon during World War II.

Later generations of Americans easily forget that much of the American Southwest was settled early on by the Spaniards and the Mexicans before European settlers other than Spaniards moved westward to claim the land for themselves. Later, when so many Mexicans, Cubans, Puerto Ricans, and others from Central and South American countries immigrated to the United States—legally or otherwise—they were looked upon by many Americans, or stereotyped, as uneducated foreigners who were in the new land as a drain on the economy. They were branded en masse as people who could not, or who refused to, speak English.

Many Jews came to America in the late nineteenth and early twentieth centuries to escape the pogroms of Eastern Europe and other kinds of discrimination. Many of those who arrived in New York City remained in the vicinity, seeking, during generations, to balance assimilation with a retention of valued religious and ethnic traditions. These customs created especially strong emotional and mental turmoil for them during the time of the Holocaust in Nazi Germany and the later fight for the statehood of Israel—ramifications that still are felt today.

It is also difficult for present-day Americans to justify somehow the treatment of Native Americans who were on the North American continent long before the Europeans settled in what became the United States and Canada. How could one expect these long-time residents not to react with anger, fury, and bloodshed when they were pushed off their land simply because newcomers wanted it for themselves. (Later, these white settlers were the first to cry foul when former owners attempted to retrieve these lands. These outraged newcomers roared that they were being pushed off "their" land!)

Exclusion was, and is, a most pervasive way of rejecting ethnic groups. For decades (even into the twentieth century) many states had laws against miscegenation that made interracial marriage a criminal offense. This unfortunate doctrine of purity was aimed against blacks, Native Americans, and Asians, in particular, and its consequences were felt for years after such laws were repealed or found unconstitutional. Making laws to keep races separate was one kind of exclusion; another was the doctrine of invisibility. Such was the exclusion applied to Jews by the entertainment industry for many years. In their case, it was generally their traditions—not their skin color—that separated them from the American majority. The greater irony was that the film and TV business was heavily populated with Jews. However, these Jewish people in power, who could have presented Jewish characters on screen or allowed Jewish performers to be visible to the public as Jews, refused to do so. These industry leaders were so anxious to acculturate into the American establishment that reminders of the past and their association to it was anathema to them. Thus, the Jewish moguls adopted a policy by the early 1930s not to present Jews on screen, to have Jewish performers change their names, and/or to modify their features to look less ethnic. This practice worked so well that, for years (as was the case with presenting gays and lesbians), the only way to tell that a character or a theme on screen was Jewish was by indirection. Styles in costuming and personal effects or the hint of an accent could alert the cognoscenti that Jews or Jewish topics were being suggested on camera.

The entertainment industry's ongoing oppression of ethnic minorities encompassed excluding stories or plot lines dealing with their cultural heritage, refusing to allow actors of such ethnic background to be on camera (unless in a demeaning role), or forcing them to disguise themselves as part of the mainstream. Thus generations of filmgoers and TV watchers were seldom exposed to these cultures, and when exposed, it was mainly to negative stereotypes of the particular groups.

Another effect of this ethnic-minority exclusion (or, at best, limitation in types of roles) was to deprive many performers from any meaningful participation in the American entertainment industry, either in front of or behind the camera. This vicious cycle kept such ethnic minorities from gaining exposure in their profession, thus preventing them from succeeding in the career of their choice. Insult was added to injury as the industry, for many years of the twentieth century, insisted on using apparently cultural-mainstream actors to "play" blacks, Asians, warrior braves, Jews, or Latinos. (One rationale for using these performers to play ethnic minorities was to avoid repercussions caused by members of different races involved, for example, in a love story, thereby violating contemporary miscegenation laws, censorship codes, or traditions of discrimination.)

Another example of the irony of discrimination occurred during World War II's sudden demand for Asian-American performers to enact Japanese enemy or Chinese ally roles. Because most West Coast Japanese Americans were confined to relocation camps, Chinese-American actors suddenly had to act as Japanese villains or Korean Americans might be called upon to play Chinese nationals. (This charade was based largely on the conceit that most mainstream American moviegoers never bothered to, or could not, distinguish between Asians of different countries.)

Another effect of World War II was the fascination with things Hispanic, exotic, exciting, and acceptable because of the U.S. government's fostering of a "Good Neighbor Policy" with South America. Rapidly, such dances as the rumba and the conga, the heavily accented Carmen Miranda, and the rhythms of bandleader Xavier Cugat became popular. Even the screen cliché of the lazy Latino peasant was suddenly regarded as quaint by American moviegoers. However, by the early 1950s this wartime U.S. (and Hollywood) fad favoring some Latinos had reversed itself back to the old clichés and disparagements.

Another strange twist in stereotyping and/or oppressing show-business ethnic minorities was cinema fabrications of heroes or popular characters who were supposed to be representative of a given cultural heritage. Hispanics had to endure decades of American portrayals of the Cisco Kid or Zorro on screen; Asian Americans were patronized by that quaint, pidgin-English-speaking detective Charlie Chan or the dastardly Fu Manchu, the latter supposedly representative of the typical "Yellow Peril." For Jews it was to endure yet another screen version of *Oliver Twist* with its sinister Fagin or the money-grasping Shylock from *The Merchant of Venice*, both considered to be penultimate anti-Semitic characters. It was not long before black males were portrayed as drug pushers and gangbangers and it was assumed that most African Americans aspired to be pimps like the Mack or Superfly. Native Americans had to cope with all those westerns that depicted Indian warriors, such as Geronimo or Sitting Bull, as bloodthirsty savages who had no real reasons for going on the warpath against the whites, or Native Americans as weak-willed victims of firewater and individuals and who were unable to say more than "how" or "ugh." (Digging the knife of bigotry in deeper, Hollywood chose to have members of any race other than Native Americans play Native Americans.)

For years active pressure groups represented the interest of ethnic minorities, pushing to gain more fair and more objective depiction of their people on screen. Typically, the battle for equality would gain a few degrees of advancement, acceptance, and participation with the Hollywood establishment, only to suddenly have that establishment pull back. For example, in the wake of 1960s civil-rights legislation on behalf of African Americans—emphasized by riots of discontent in pockets of the United States—a sudden development in the 1970s was a new black cinema. Although confined mainly to black action (blaxploitation) cinema, still it provided acting opportunities for previously marginalized talent, and black moviegoers also suddenly had a cinema that was directed to them, about them, and performed by members of their race. This splurge lasted through much of the 1970s. However, by the end of the decade, a subtle backlash lead to the curtailing of black topics and the presence of black performers on screen.

The canvas of the twentieth-century entertainment industry and its depiction and use of ethnic minorities is complex and frustrating, but it is a strong fiber in the history of American cinema and television.

About the Organization of This Book

Each chapter is self-contained in that words in the text that appear in small capital letters are cross-references to headwords for individual topics discussed within the given chapter. Conversely, because a surname, film or TV series title, or word topic is not placed in small capitals in a particular chapter does not imply that the person, film, TV show, or topic is not given an entry in the book. For ease, the general index directs the reader to the appropriate chapter(s) where the subject is discussed.

One of the other ways that the Hollywood mainstream marginalized ethnic minorities over the decades was either to place such cast members low in the cast credits or to omit their names from the screen credits altogether. To remedy this situation, after listing the major players/characters related to a given entry, the ethnic actors/characters in the film or television series being discussed are listed. Examples of genre titles, individuals, themes, and so on provided within the text of an entry are a representative sampling. They are not meant to be inclusive of all illustrations of the point being made in the entry.

In essays for movies, telefeatures, and TV series, wherever possible, the title, author, and date of the original source of the production is included. This should be of assistance to those readers who wish to examine the original property to determine for themselves how much the screen adaptation was true to its source.

It should be noted that the criteria for inclusion of films, TV series, and so on in this book was primarily that the production or coproduction, at least, must be American. In film credits, "b&w" stands for *black and white.* For silent films, generally the footage (e.g., 7,238′) is given, rather than the running time, unless a credible contemporary source provides the running time.

—James Robert Parish

African Americans

A

***Across 110th Street* (1972)** United Artists, color, 102 minutes. **Director:** Barry Shear; **Screenplay:** Luther Davis; **Cast:** Anthony Quinn (Capt. Frank Mattelli), Yaphet Kotto (Detective Lieutenant Pope), Anthony Franciosa (Nick D'Salvio), Antonio Fargas (Henry Jackson), Marlene Warfield (Mrs. Jackson).

At the time of its release, this slickly made major studio film was an innovative entry in the emerging BLACK ACTION film genre. It helped to establish the plot formula of Harlem's African-American underworld competing with the Mafia in Lower Manhattan's Little Italy for control of the rackets. The premise had solid appeal to many filmgoers because it showed African Americans (albeit gangsters here) standing up against Caucasians. It also reflected a trend throughout American life of the new guard (i.e., the upstart Harlem hoods) opposing the old establishment (i.e., the long-entrenched Italian mob). Made for $1.3 million, this action-packed movie earned nearly $13 million in domestic film rentals.

Within the fast-paced, violent story, three African-American men disguised as cops rob a Harlem numbers bank of $300,000, and, in the process, kill several syndicate members and two actual cops. The city's Italian underworld orders Nick D'Salvio to go uptown to regain control of the rackets. Meanwhile, the police investigators—the old-line politically incorrect Captain Mattelli and the college-educated politically correct Detective Lieutenant Pope—battle between themselves about police methodology and department politics as they hunt the culprits.

Several of the cast, including Kotto and Fargas, became stalwarts of Hollywood's blaxploitation movie cycle.

Adventures of Huckleberry Finn See *HUCKLEBERRY FINN*.

***Ali* (2001)** Columbia, color, 154 minutes. **Director:** Michael Mann; **Screenplay:** Stephen J. Rivele & Christopher Wilkinson and Eric Roth & Mann. **Cast:** Will Smith (Cassius Clay/Muhammad Ali), Jamie Foxx (Drew "Bundini" Brown), Jon Voight (Howard Cosell), Mario Van Peebles (Malcolm X), Angelo Dundee (Ron Silver), Jeffrey Wright (Howard Bingham), Mykelti Williamson (Don King), Jada Pinkett Smith (Sonji), Giancarlo Esposito (Cassius Clay Sr.).

Born in 1942, Cassius Clay went on to become an Olympic gold medalist in 1960 as a light heavyweight boxer. Later, Clay, an African American, turned professional and won the world heavyweight title in 1964, 1974, and 1978. Outgoing, idiosyncratic, and with a charismatic personality, he was the darling of sports commentators, columnists, and enthusiasts. Having converted to Islam and changed his name to Muhammad Ali, the athlete was stripped of his heavyweight title, suspended from boxing, and sentenced to five years in prison when he refused to be drafted into military service on the grounds of conscientious objection. The highly controversial matter was resolved when the U.S. Supreme Court overturned his conviction in 1971. In later years, the former champion was in ailing health, which seemed only to enhance his appeal with fans and the public at large.

A movie about Ali would have to balance carefully between being a paean to the legendary sports star and presenting a viable biography in terms that would appeal to moviegoers. When the long-in-the-works and highly anticipated feature was released in late 2001, the picture received mixed reviews, everyone agreeing it was not the new millennium's answer to Martin Scorsese's *Raging Bull* (1980). The *Los Angeles Daily News* (December 25, 2001) summed up: "While the movie boasts the great one-two punch of Mann's impressionistic direction and WILL SMITH's thrilling performance as the Champ, *Ali* the movie remains as elusive as its subject was in the boxing ring. It has plenty of great moments, but sorely lacks the cohesiveness needed to connect the dots into a satisfying portrait." British *Sight and Sound* magazine (March 2002) agreed that while Smith captured the routines and mannerisms of the celebrity boxer, it was a "tricky proposition" because the subject was so well known and remembered by the public. Regarding the boxer's private life, the publication judged that the biopic and its chief players were not so successful. The magazine's reviewer observed, "At times Smith seems constrained, unwilling to risk anything that might be deemed disrespectful to such an icon" (especially as the film has been endorsed by Ali himself).

Made at a cost of $107 million, the picture grossed a less than stellar $58 million in domestic distribution. *Ali* received two Oscar nominations: Best Actor (Smith) and Best Supporting Actor (Voight). It won two NAACP Image Awards: Outstanding Motion Picture and Outstanding Supporting Actor (Foxx) and received three additional Image Award nominations: Outstanding Actor (Smith), Outstanding Supporting Actor (Van Peebles), and Outstanding Supporting Actress (Jada Pinkett Smith)

Other performers who played Muhammad Ali on screen have included: Chip McAllister as the Young Ali (*The Greatest*, 1977), Darius McCrary (*Don King: Only in America*, 1997—a cable TV movie), and David Ramsey (*Ali: An American Hero*, 2000—a TV movie).

***Alice Adams* (1935)** RKO, b&w, 99 minutes. **Director:** George Stevens; **Screenplay:** Dorothy Yost and Mortimer Offner; **Cast:** Katharine Hepburn (Alice Adams), Fred MacMurray (Arthur Russell), Fred Stone (Mr. Virgil Adams), Evelyn Venable (Mildred Palmer), Frank Albertson (Walter Adams), Ann Shoemaker (Mrs. Adams), Hattie McDaniel (Malena Burns).

Unlike the silent-movie adaptation (1923) of Booth Tarkington's 1921 novel about snobbish social mores in small-town America, the Hepburn screen edition offers a happy ending. In the 1935 release, reluctant suitor Arthur Russell perceives the virtues of well-meaning Alice despite her unsophisticated parents, her thieving brother (Albertson), and a dinner party from hell hosted by her parents. The leisurely paced movie was a surprise hit, winning two Oscar nominations: Best Actress (Hepburn) and Best Picture.

The film's most cited sequence occurs when unpretentious Virgil Adams and his social-climbing wife (Shoemaker) invite Russell, the matrimonial catch of the decade, to a formal dinner. Under the tutelage of socially ambitious but naïve Alice, the Adamses turn a simple meal into a gauche formal affair. At the center of the hilarious dining maelstrom is Malena Burns, the family's part-time cook, who is commandeered to cook the special meal and act as the family's supposed household maid for the night. The gum-chewing Malena displays obvious disdain at being a pretend domestic. When not battling her ill-fitting uniform, a grumpy Malena serves the inedible meal peppered with disrespectful comments and mocks the pretentious dinner-table conversation she overhears.

Until *Alice Adams*, rarely had Hollywood films presented a domestic—especially an African-American one—as defiant toward her employers. HATTIE MCDANIEL's Malena openly rebels at being the stereotypical docile maid and McDaniel was impressive in this landmark screen role.

***Amistad* (1997)** Dreamworks/HBO, color, 152 minutes **Director:** Steven Spielberg; **Screenplay:** David Franzoni and Steven Zaillian; **Cast:** Morgan Freeman (Theodore Joadson), Nigel Hawthorne (Martin Van Buren), Anthony Hopkins (John Quincy Adams), Djimon Hounsou ("Cinque"—Sengbe), Matthew McConaughey (Roger Baldwin), Razaaq Adoti (Yamba).

Having scored so effectively with *SCHINDLER'S LIST* (1993), which portrays the Holocaust, filmmaker Spielberg turned to a nearly forgotten chapter of African-American history as his next movie epic about inhumanity.

Off the coast of Cuba in 1839, aboard the Spanish slave ship *Amistad*, an African American named Cinque leads fifty-two other slaves in a bloody revolt against their captors. Two of the slave traders—who promise to steer the vessel back to Africa—are spared. Instead, the white men sail the ship to New York Harbor where the mutineers are imprisoned. Theodore Joadson and others hire attorney Roger Baldwin to represent the prisoners. He proves victorious, but the appeals eventually lead to former U.S. president John Quincy Adams arguing the case before the Supreme Court. Adams is victorious and the once-slaves are returned to their African homes.

Many commentators cited Spielberg's overly cerebral approach to the topic of slavery for the lack of viewer enthusiasm. Although the lavishly detailed narrative included graphic flashbacks depicting extreme brutality toward Africans as they were rounded up and shipped to America in slavery, too much of the talky film was filled with courtroom rhetoric about economical and political causes behind the support by U.S. individuals of slavery. On the plus side, the movie, which could easily have become mawkish and melodramatic, benefited greatly from West African–born Hounsou's performance.

Made for $40 million, *Amistad* grossed more than $44 million in domestic distribution. It received Oscar nominations for Best Cinematography, Best Costume Design, Best Original Dramatic Score, and Best Supporting Actor (Hopkins).

***Amos 'n' Andy* (1951–1953)** CBS-TV series, b&w, 30 minutes. **Cast:** Alvin Childress (Amos Jones), Spencer Williams Jr. (Andy [Andrew Hogg Brown]), Tim Moore (the Kingfish [George Stevens]), Ernestine Wade (Sapphire Stevens), Horace Stewart (Lightnin' [Nick O'Demus]), Amanda Randolph (Ramona Smith—Sapphire's mother), Lillian Randolph (Madame Queen).

This long-considered politically incorrect TV series was an adaptation of a long-running radio show that was first known as *Sam 'n' Harry*, which began in 1926 on WGN radio in Chicago. Retitled *Amos 'n' Andy* by March 1928 it debuted the next year on the NBC radio network, gaining a tremendous following throughout the United States. Although strange that the black community-themed show was created by and starred two white actors (Freeman Gosden and Charles Correll), it was customary in that era for white performers to play African-American roles in BLACKFACE. Detailing the many misadventures of Amos Jones and Andrew H. Brown, the radio show flourished on NBC until 1948 when it moved to the CBS radio network; it lasted there, in differing formats, until 1960. (Gosden and Correll also lent their voices to a projected series of theatrical cartoon shorts based on their hit radio characters. Two entries were produced in 1934 by RKO before the property was dropped because of audience disinterest in this animated version of the ongoing radio success.)

In the early years on radio, all the roles (many of them exaggerated stereotypes with thick "funny" accents and "quaint" ideas about survival) were played by Gosden and Correll. By 1943, however, black performers—including Ernestine Wade and Amanda Randolph who would both make the transition to the TV version of *Amos 'n' Andy*—had joined the supporting cast. Although Gosden and Correll performed their roles in blackface for the 1930 feature film *CHECK AND DOUBLE CHECK*, by 1950 it was decided to cast the TV series with all black talent.

As soon as the upcoming CBS-TV edition had been announced, the NAACP renewed its long-running condemnation of the program as a negative stereotype of blacks as lazy, dishonest, inferior, and so on. Nevertheless, the TV series debuted as scheduled, ran for two years, and was repeatedly shown in reruns. A new outburst against *Amos 'n' Andy* flared up in 1963 when CBS Films touted that it had sold rerun rights in Kenya and Western Nigeria. Soon thereafter a Kenyan official proclaimed that the offensive TV program would *not* air in his country. An outcry in 1964 from black PRESSURE GROUPS against a Chicago TV station's rerunning *Amos 'n' Andy* caused CBS Films to acknowledge the declining sales of this controversial series and withdraw the program from TV distribution.

The legend of the politically incorrect *Amos 'n' Andy* has since grown so large that it is impossible to judge today the old TV series with any objectivity. In actuality, the production values (typical for the early 1950s) were primitive, the characterizations were often way over the top, and several characters acted childishly and connivingly to win their way from episode to episode. On the other hand, *Amos 'n' Andy* did present a well-honed ensemble of experienced black talent who knew how to milk laughs from the scripts and who worked in tandem to the best effect.

Set in Harlem, the TV series of *Amos 'n' Andy* revolves around George Stevens, the Kingfish, a schemer who always seeks to make easy money. Although he is president of the Mystic Knights of the Sea Lodge, his unscrupulous ways keep him at odds with many acquaintances and especially with his shrewish wife Sapphire and her intimidating mama. Of the other lead characters, Andy Brown, a susceptible soul, is easily tricked into being the patsy and often the target of grand hustler Kingfish. (Andy's girlfriend is Madame Queen and Andy's favorite expression is "Holy mackerel, Andy!") As for Amos Jones, a philosophical, relatively low-key taxi driver, he is often a subordinate character in the proceedings who often narrates the events transpiring within the weekly episode.

A decade after *Amos 'n' Andy* came to TV, its creators Gosden and Correll packaged an animated series for ABC-TV based on a "new" idea, the premise of *Calvin and the Colonel* (1961–62) being that several animals from the South relocated to a large Northern metropolis. The colonel was a tricky fox; Calvin, his pal, was an endearing but not-so-bright bear. Another series regular was a lawyer named Oliver Wendell Clutch, a weasel. With *Calvin and the Colonel*, Gosden and Correll found a way to repeat their *Amos 'n' Andy* formula without offending assorted pressure groups.

Anderson, Eddie "Rochester" (1906–1977) While of short stature, Anderson was a big talent who could sing, dance, and do sly comedy. With his gravelly voice and a devil-may-care sparkle in his eyes, he exuded great independence, even when playing—his most famous role—Rochester, comedian Jack Benny's butler, on radio, in films, and on TV. With his smarts and a touch of guile, it was questionable whether it was Rochester who worked for Benny or the other way around. In an era before racial integration became meaningful in the United States, Anderson generally sidestepped being pushed into demeaning, stereotypical, complacent servant roles that so many others had been forced to play to work.

Born in Oakland, California, the son of show-business parents, Anderson's father was a minstrel; his mother was a circus tightrope walker. The young teenager began to perform in all-black revues and then, teamed with his older brother Cornelius, had a song-and-dance act that toured the circuits for years. By the early 1930s Eddie was based in Los Angeles and made his screen debut playing a butler in *What Price Hollywood?* (1932). It was his role as Noah in *THE GREEN PASTURES* (1936) that made him noticeable to audiences. In March 1937 he appeared on Benny's popular radio show, first as a Pullman porter then as Benny's quick-witted valet, who was replete with amusing quips. His gruff voice and comic delivery made Rochester a mainstay of the weekly show. Anderson was also part of the proceedings when Benny made such feature films as *Man About Town* (1939) and *Buck Benny Rides Again* (1940). In *Star-Spangled Rhythm* (1942) Eddie did a jitterbug with Katherine Dunham. The next year, in the all-black musical *CABIN IN THE SKY*, Anderson was at his best as the gambling, shiftless Joe, the trouble-prone husband of Ethel WATERS.

In the 1950s Anderson was primarily a TV performer, especially on Jack Benny's sitcom. One of his final acting assignments was as the voice of Bobby Joe "B. J." Mason on the early 1970s TV cartoon series *The Harlem Globetrotters*.

animation—shorts and feature films From 1930 to 1938 a series of cartoon shorts featured Bosko the Talking Kid, a variation of a black minstrel character. In 1934 Hollywood released two cartoon shorts as part of a projected *AMOS 'N' ANDY* animated series, based on the hit radio show, but the highly ethnic venture did not catch on with the public. During the years several established cartoon series (e.g., Bugs Bunny, Tom and Jerry) incorporated occasional black characters (usually blatant caricatures, later determined to be politically incorrect), and sometimes individual cartoons showed characters involved in escapades in Africa where native figures were utilized. (Example of these stereotyped images occurred in such entries as 1935's *Mickey's Man Friday*, 1937's *Uncle Tom's Bungalow*, and 1943's *Coal Black and de Sebben Dwarfs.)*

Walt Disney's *SONG OF THE SOUTH* (1946), part live-action, part animation, was Hollywood's first feature-length effort at incorporating African-American characters with white figures. This adaptation of Uncle Remus tales also proved to be one of the industry's controversial entries, due to the portrayal of characters by James Baskett and HATTIE McDANIEL.

In the 1970s, the black action-film vogue reflected the growing influence of ethnic minorities on mainstream cinema. Controversial filmmaker Ralph Bakshi turned out several adult-rated animated features that pushed boundaries in their presentation of ethnic and social minorities. His well-crafted output included *Fritz the Cat* (1972), *COONSKIN* (1975), and *Hey, Good Lookin'* (1982).

For *Bebe's Kids* (1992), an animated musical derived from the life of the late comedian Robin Harris, most of the characters were blacks, as were the performers (e.g., Faizon Love, Nell Carter, and Vanessa Bell Calloway). In 1994's box-office mega-hit, *The Lion King*, the animated feature used several well-known black performers (e.g., WHOOPI GOLDBERG, Robert Guillaume, and JAMES EARL JONES) to provide voices for some of the jungle characters. The same year's *The Pagemaster*, a mix of live action and animated sequences, featured black talents (e.g., Goldberg and Dorian Harewood) as voiceovers for characters. The imaginative *Antz* (1998) had among its voice cast DANNY GLOVER. *Mulan* (1998) used, as one of its principal voices, comedian EDDIE MURPHY, who would also be a voiceover on the big 2001 hit, SHREK. Glover also provided a voice for the biblical musical tale, *The Prince of Egypt* (1998), and Goldberg spoke a character's role in *The Rugrat Movie* (1998). More recently, Goldberg and Glover participated in the animated feature *Our Friend Martin* (1999), dealing with Martin Luther King Jr. Goldberg also was involved with *Monkeybone* (2000). Eartha Kitt was a key voice in *The Emperor's New Groove* (2000). CHRIS ROCK and LAURENCE FISHBURNE were voices in 2001's *Osmosis Jones*, a part animation, part live-action comedy feature. *Recess: School's Out* (2001) featured further adventures of the ethnically diverse primary school pupils from the TV series *Recess* (1997–2001).

animation series—television Just as live-action TV series basically ignored African-American characters and themes for much of the 1950s and 1960s, cartoon series did likewise. One of the few exceptions, *Calvin and the Colonel* (1961–62), was created and voiced by Freeman Gosden and Charles Correll who had conceived and acted in radio's black-themed *AMOS 'N' ANDY* from the late 1920s onward. The new offering had several animal characters from the South relocating to the North and coping with the new living situation. By disguising the figures as animals, this unsubtle variation on *AMOS 'N' ANDY* avoided stirring up racial problems.

From 1970 to 1973, the animated children's series *The Harlem Globetrotters* recorded the exploits of that legendary basketball team. *The Jackson Five* (1971–73) presented comic (mis)adventures of the sibling Motown recording group with the actual Jacksons, including Michael, providing voices for their animated alter egos. *Kid Power* (1972–74), based on the *Wee Pals* newspaper cartoon strip created in 1965 by Morrie Turner, had a multicultural cast of youngsters. One of the decade's most popular kid shows, *Fat Albert & the Cosby Kids* (1972–84), was created by stand-up comedian Bill Cosby, who provided several of the voices in these recollections of his childhood pals in North Philadelphia. When the live-action *STAR TREK* (1966–69) was adapted to a Saturday morning cartoon format, it utilized the voices of the original cast, including black actress Nichelle Nichols as Lt. Uhura.

A mixture of adventure and comedy, *I Am the Greatest: The Adventures of Muhammad Ali* (1977–78) had the flamboyant ex-heavyweight boxing champ providing his own voice for this children's series. A regular feature of the omnibus cartoon series *The Plasticman Comedy-Adventure Show* (1979–84) was a segment entitled "Rickety Rocket," which dealt with a quartet of black teens. *The Super Globetrotters* (1979–80) brought back the Harlem Globetrotters basketball team, this time showcased as superheroes fighting crime.

The 1982 TV movie *The Kid with the Broken Halo* had starred GARY COLEMAN as an angel in the making. The cartoon series adaptation, *The Gary Coleman Show* (1982–83), continued his adventures on Earth as he tries to do good deeds to please those above. He provided his own voice. Ex-boxer Mr. T was scoring as one of TV's *The A-Team* (1983–87) when he provided the voice for the animated show *Mister T* (1983–86) playing a gym owner who was helped by several multicultural youths to solve a weekly mystery. Trading on the hit movie *Ghostbusters* (1984), the animated show *The Real Ghostbusters* (1986–92) had as "fearless" fighters of the supernatural, a quartet among whom was Arsenio Hall's voice as Winston Zeddmore. (After the first season, Edward J. Jones took over this assignment.). A short-lived TV series in the later 1980s was *Bionic Siz* (1987).

In 1995, *Spider-Man* returned to the airwaves, having been an animated series from 1967 to 1970 and then again from 1981 to 1986. In the new production, veteran black actor Roscoe Lee Browne provided the voice of the Kingpin, a mob boss. The adult cartoon show, *South Park* (1997–) was set in a Rocky Mountains community and dealt with a group of crudely precocious youngsters. Disney's *Recess* (1997–2001) followed the (mis) adventures of a multicultural group of primary school kids. One who watched over them was the Chef, with the voice provided by musician/actor

Isaac Hayes. *The PJs* (1999–2001) was a high-profile cartoon series with EDDIE MURPHY providing a lead voice. Also in 1999, Bill Cosby tapped into his North Philadelphia childhood once again for a new project, this time an animated children's series entitled *Little Bill*. *Downtown* (1999) was a short-lasting MTV cable series devoted to life in Manhattan below 14th Street. Two more recent young adult oriented animated shows were *Static Shock* (2000–), based on an African-American superhero comic book, and *The Proud Family* (2001–), a big hit on cable's Disney Channel.

***Anna Lucasta* (1958)** United Artists, b&w, 97 minutes. **Director:** Arnold Laven; **Screenplay:** Philip Yordan; **Cast:** Eartha Kitt (Anna Lucasta), Frederick O'Neal (Frank), Henry Scott (Rudolph Slocum), Rex Ingram (Joe Lucasta), Georgia Burke (Theresa Lucasta), Alvin Childress (Noah), John Proctor (Stanley Lucasta), James Edwards (Eddie), Sammy Davis Jr. (Danny Johnson).

Originally written by Yordan in 1936 as a drama about a Polish-American family, the revised work was staged as an all-black play by Harlem's American Negro Theater in mid-1944. Later that year it became a huge Broadway hit. Many of the cast (including O'Neal, Childress, and Proctor) repeated their stage roles in this the second screen version of *Anna Lucasta*. (The earlier movie adaptation of 1949 featured a white cast.)

Having been thrown out of her parents' Los Angeles home, Anna Lucasta earns her living as a prostitute in San Diego. A request to the Lucastas from an old family friend from the South states that the man's son, Rudolph Slocum, is coming to California and asks whether they could find him a wife. Meanwhile, Theresa and Joe allow Anna to return home. When Rudolph arrives, he secures a teaching post at a local junior college and falls in love with Anna. They marry, but the possessive Joe undermines their happiness. Thereafter, Danny Johnson, a cocky young sailor who knew Anna in San Diego, arrives to steal the bride away. Later, as Joe is dying, he reconciles with Anna. Thereafter, she renounces the irresponsible Danny and is reunited with her grateful spouse.

Unlike earlier major studio dramas (e.g., 1949's *PINKY* and *LOST BOUNDARIES*), which dealt with African Americans interacting with whites, *Anna Lucasta* was focused entirely within the black community and, for a change, not a stereotypical sitcom approach to the ethnic minority but an intense domestic drama. For audiences of the day, it was controversial because the heroine was a prostitute (not because she was black) and also because of its hints of incipient incest in Joe's possessive relationship with his daughter. Much of the uproar over the 1958 film (as had been the case even with the far tamer 1949 movie version) revolved around the moviemakers' exploration of the drama's sexual content, despite the era's strict industry production codes. That aside, the 1958 release was not a cohesive drama nor was its cast effective in their characterizations. As a result, it was not a box-office success.

***Any Day Now* (1998–2002)** Lifetime, color, 60 minutes. **Cast:** Annie Potts (M.E. [Mary Elizabeth] O'Brien Sims), Lorraine Toussaint (Rene Jackson), Chris Mulkey (Collier Sims), Olivia Friedman (Kelly Sims), Calvin Devault (Davis Sims), Donzaleigh Abernathy (Sara Jackson), Mae Middleton (Mary Elizabeth—as a child: 1998–2001); Shari Dyon Perry (Rene—as a child: 1998–2001).

One of the more affecting recent dramas, this focused on interracial friendships and the emerging power of two strong-willed women. Jumping back and forth from present-day Birmingham, Alabama, to the 1960s (when the city was a hotbed of racial tension), the show traces the ongoing friendship between white Mary Elizabeth O'Brien and black Rene Jackson. The former, a housewife struggling with her contractor husband to make ends meet, finally achieves her goal of writing a book. Jackson, a high-powered attorney, returns home to take up the mantle of her late father, a civil-rights litigator. The cultural blend continues into the next generation when Mary Elizabeth's daughter Kelly becomes pregnant by her African-American boyfriend, weds him, and raises their child with him.

At times overly sincere and preachy, the program never shied away from discussing (or recreating in the flashbacks) strong issues of racial contention.

***Arena, The* (aka: *Naked Warriors*) (1973)** New World, color, 85 minutes. **Director:** Steve Carver; **Screenplay:** John Corrington and Joyce Hooper Corrington; **Cast:** Margaret Markov (Bodicia), Pam Grier (Mamawi), Lucretia Love (Deidre), Paul Mueller (Lucilius), Daniele Vargas (Timarchus).

The R-rated *The Arena* may have lacked the intricate special effects of the lavish *Gladiator* (2000) or the intelligent script of Kirk Douglas's *Spartacus* (1960), but this American-Italian coproduction, produced by prolific B-movie filmmaker Roger Corman, had its own virtues. It boasted statuesque GRIER who was fast-becoming the leading BLACK EXPLOITATION film-cycle figure. It also used its story of (female) slaves arising from bondage as a parallel to the plight of African Americans emerging from the yoke of the white majority in the mid–twentieth-century United States.

In 44 B.C. recent prisoners of the Roman Empire include blond Bodicia, a Druid high priestess from Brittany, voluptuous black Mamawi from Nubia, and the cunning Deidre. Besides being forced to "entertain" their captors with sexual favors, the women are trained to become gladiators and to fight to the death in the arena. Eventually Mamawi, the strongest among them, leads the surviving women gladiators in revolt against their sadistic masters and to eventual freedom.

Made for an economical $75,000, *The Arena* was a popular box-office attraction.

***Arsenio Hall Show, The* (1989–1994)** Syndicated TV series, color, 60 minutes. **Cast:** Arsenio Hall (host), Burton Richardson (announcer), Michael Wolff and Band (themselves).

When this program debuted, the late-night TV talk-show arena was dominated by white hosts Johnny Carson and David Letterman; both appealed largely to a middle-aged audience. This all changed with the arrival of African-American standup comic HALL who already had on-air experience with the talk-show format. The difference in Hall's new forum was not in format (much the same as other genre shows) but in his ability to provide a hip opening monologue, to attract a wide array of untypical gab-show guests (especially those who were young, trendy, and ethnic), and to preside over his telecast like the smart-mouthed host of a cool party. This breath of fresh air in the increasingly stale talk-show arena, appealed to a mix of the young, the up-to-date crowd, and African Americans. In the months before Hall ended his series in May 1994, he often featured controversial black personalities (e.g., SPIKE LEE).

***Atlanta Child Murders, The* (1985)** CBS-TV, color, 250 minutes. **Director:** John Erman; **Teleplay:** Abby Mann; **Cast:** Jason Robards (Alvin Binder), James Earl Jones (Major Walker), Rip Torn (Lewis Slaton), Morgan Freeman (Ben Shelter), Calvin Levels (Wayne Williams), Lynne Moody (Selena Cobb), Ruby Dee (Faye Williams), Martin Sheen (Chet Dettlinger).

Between 1979 and 1981, several African-American young people were killed in Atlanta, Georgia. This highly controversial feature for two nights telecast the case and the trial of black music promoter Wayne Williams, the alleged murderer. What upset some critics and viewers alike was the unsubtle attempt of this telefeature to examine minutely the American judicial system and to suggest the possibility that the defendant was not guilty.

Lewis Slaton is the sinister-seeming prosecuting attorney in the case against Williams, the latter defended by a courtly old Southerner (Robards). Others involved in the sensational prosecution are the accused murderer's mother (DEE), the insensitive police chief (JONES), the well-meaning white liberal newspaperman (Sheen), and the very objective police investigator (FREEMAN).

Neither documentary nor pure fiction, this upsetting and at times blatantly subjective retelling of the serial killing spree in Georgia drew much viewer attention. The two-part made-for-television movie won three Emmy nominations: Outstanding Supporting Actor (Sheen and Torn), and Outstanding Hair Styling.

A more recent made-for-cable movie about the decades-old slaying was *Who Killed Atlanta's Children?* (2000) in which magazine reporter James Belushi has concerns about the "accepted" findings in the investigation of the case.

***Autobiography of Miss Jane Pittman, The* (1974)** CBS-TV, color, 100 minutes. **Director:** John Korty; **Teleplay:** Tracy Keenan Wynn; **Cast:** Cicely Tyson (Jane Pittman), Odetta (Big Maura), Josephine Premice (Madame Gautier), Ted Airhart (Sheriff Guidry), Sidney Arroyo (Tee-Bob), Richard Dysart (Master Bryant), Rod Perry (Joe Pittman), Thalmus Rasulala (Ned), Arnold Wilkerson (Jimmy).

Based on Ernest J. Gaines's 1971 book, this landmark telefeature opens in 1962 in Bayonne, Louisiana, as 110-year-old Jane Pittman recounts her lengthy life, which began in pre-Civil War days. Her memories include her husband Joe, their adopted son Ned (who became an educator), and young Jimmy (whom Jane helped to raise), now a civil-rights worker in town. Not letting her advanced age stop her, Jane participates in the 1960s fight for racial equality.

Bolstered by TYSON's captivating performance, this movie was a huge award winner. Its star won two Emmys (Outstanding Actress in a Drama and Actress of the Year in a Special). Other Emmys went to the production for: Outstanding Costume Design, Outstanding Directing in Drama, Outstanding Makeup, Outstanding Special, and Outstanding Writing in Drama (Adaptation). Filmmaker Korty also won an award from the Directors Guild of America, and scripter Wynn earned one from the Writers Guild of America. The show was also bestowed with the prestigious Christopher Award.

Along with the miniseries *ROOTS* (1977), *The Autobiography of Miss Jane Pittman* did much to educate TV viewers to African-American history and the minority's servitude, which did not end with their emancipation in the 1860s.

B

***Baby Boy* (2001)** Columbia, color, 129 minutes. **Director/Screenplay:** John Singleton; **Cast:** Tyrese (Jody), Taraji P. Henson (Yvette), Omar Gooding (Sweetpea), Tamara LaSeon Bass (Peanut), Candy Ann Brown (Ms. Herron), Adrienne-Joi Johnson (Juanita), Ving Rhames (Melvin).

In this R-rated URBAN DRAMA, SINGLETON returns to the locale he understood so well—the inner city in general and the black community in particular. Like his debut screen project (*BOYZ N THE HOOD*, 1991), the characters here reflect an insider's point of view of the neighborhood, not the outlook of a filmmaker who is focusing from outside the environment. If the impassioned film has any major flaw, it is Singleton's impatience to communicate his particular message (i.e., that the cumulative effect of racism has caused young African Americans to remain juvenile in adulthood, leading them to avoid self-sufficiency and responsibility in their lives). As a result, the narrative frequently becomes pedantic, distracting from the drama's flow.

Twenty-year-old Jody, an ex-convict but essentially a decent person, has a baby by one of his girlfriends (Bass); he has just accompanied another (Henson) to have an abortion. Jody sees nothing wrong with the status quo in which he is supported by his single mother (Johnson). He has no job ambitions or plans to grow up emotionally. He enjoys his casual existence and hanging out with such friends as Sweetpea (who is hoping to get back in tight with his former gang). The situation alters when his mother, only in her thirties, finds romance with a landscaper named Melvin. Jody fears that their growing relationship may force him out of the house. Moreover, Melvin, who admits to having made mistakes in life, sees through Jody's toughness and calls him to task for it.

Made on a $16 million budget and filmed in Los Angeles's South Central neighborhood, *Baby Boy* was a raw and sexy excursion, with very explicit dialogue. It grossed a mild $28.7 million in domestic distribution.

***Backstairs at the White House* (1979)** NBC-TV miniseries, color, 450 minutes. **Director:** Michael O'Herlihy; **Teleplay:** Gwen Bagni-Dubov and Paul Dubov; **Cast:** Olivia Cole (Maggie Rogers), Leslie Uggams (Lillian Rogers Parks), Louis Gossett Jr. (Levi Mercer), Robert Hooks (John Mays), Leslie Nielsen (Ike Hoover), Cloris Leachman (Mrs. Jaffray), Paul Winfield (Emmett Rogers Sr.).

Based on (and expanded from) the 1961 book *My Thirty Years Backstairs at the White House* by Lillian Rogers Parks and Francis Spatz Leighton, this acclaimed miniseries detailed the life and times of Lillian Rogers Parks, a crippled seamstress/maid, who devoted fifty-two years (some with her mother) as a White House domestic for eight administrations of U.S. presidents.

In distinct contrast to movies of Hollywood's golden age, showing black servants through the viewpoint of their white employers, *Backstairs at the White House* reverses this viewpoint by depicting a series of twentieth-century American-history events and personages as seen through black domestics' eyes. In particular, this is the narrative of stern Maggie Rogers and her daughter Lillian, seen both at the White House and at their living quarters. Mrs. Jaffray is the bigoted head housekeeper at the White House.

Among the eleven Emmy Award nominations for this well-received entry were: Outstanding Actress (Cole), Outstanding Limited Series, and Outstanding Teleplay (part I).

***Bamboozled* (2000)** New Line, color, 135 minutes. **Director/Screenplay:** Spike Lee; **Cast:** Damon Wayans (Pierre Delacroix), Savion Glover (Manray/Mantan),

Tommy Davidson (Womack/Sleep 'n' Eat), Michael Rapaport (Dunwitty), Sarah Jones (Dot).

At the ratings-plagued CNS TV network in New York City, Ivy League college-educated Pierre Delacroix is ordered by his dumb Caucasian boss (Rapaport) to devise a new trend-setting series. When the network refuses Pierre's concept for a BILL COSBY-type sitcom, the frustrated executive suggests a bizarre idea—revive the old minstrel-show format. Delacroix's gimmick is not to utilize the traditional white actors in BLACKFACE but to have African-American performers cavort in even blacker faces. To his astonishment, the tasteless foray *(Mantan—The New Millennium Minstrel Show)* becomes a nationwide hit. However, the successful entry triggers tragic repercussions for many concerned.

While praised by some reviewers, many other critics dismissed the offering as lacking the technical finesse or entertainment values to support successfully its hard-hitting message: the media stereotyping of African Americans during the past century. Utilizing archival footage (e.g., 1915's *THE BIRTH OF A NATION* and both Judy Garland and Bugs Bunny in black face), LEE's thesis in this outrageous satire was that essentially little had changed in the media's treatment of the black minority and that complacent African Americans were partly responsible for having allowed it to continue. The film's title derived from a speech given by Malcolm X, and the movie was dedicated to Budd Schulberg who wrote the screenplay for *A Face in the Crowd* (1957), a savage media satire that Lee has long admired.

Bamboozled grossed an extremely weak $2.2 million in its domestic distribution.

***Barefoot in the Park* (1970–1971)** ABC-TV series, color, 30 minutes. **Cast:** Scoey Mitchell (Paul Bratter), Tracy Reed (Corie Bratter), Thelma Carpenter (Mabel Bates), Nipsey Russell (Honey Robinson), Harry Holcombe (Mr. Kendricks).

As "Black Is Beautiful" became the theme of Hollywood during its 1970s BLACK ACTION FILM onslaught, the television networks wanted to capitalize on this profitable trend.

One gimmick used in this period in movies was to take past works featuring white characters and remake them with a predominantly African-American cast. One such experiment on TV was *Barefoot in the Park*, derived from Neil Simon's Broadway success (1963) and the hit movie adaptation (1967). However, stretching Simon's premise into a protracted story arc spread through weekly television episodes diluted the original narrative punch and diminished the novelty of the ethnic cast. The show went off the air after less than four months.

A similar experiment was tried a decade later with another Simon vehicle (based on a Broadway play that had become a movie and then a TV series). *The New Odd Couple* (1982–83) starred Demond Wilson as sportswriter Oscar and Ron Glass as finicky photographer Felix. It was a remake of TV's *The Odd Couple* (1970–75) which featured Jack Klugman as Oscar and Tony Randall as Felix. The black version of the sitcom lasted but a season, suffering from its revamped lead characters displaying a lack of ethnic identity or cultural heritage, the unembellished gimmick of race-changing wearing out its welcome quickly.

Bassett, Angela (1958–) Intense, dramatic, and striking are among the qualities of five-feet, four-inch Bassett who reached the ranks of Hollywood's top serious performers. Some of her more remarkable screen appearances occurred portraying real-life people, ranging from the forceful mother of the Jackson Five *(The Jacksons: An American Dream*, 1992 TV movie), Dr. Betty Shabazz wed to the martyred civil-rights leader *(MALCOLM X*, 1992), and star Tina Turner *(WHAT'S LOVE GOT TO DO WITH IT?*, 1993) and Rosa Parks *(THE ROSA PARKS STORY*, 2002).

Bassett was born in New York City but grew up in St. Petersburg, Florida. Thanks to the prodding of a high school teacher, she applied to Yale University where she spent an additional three years in postgrad theater work. Stage acting led to her first movie, the telefeature *Doubletake* (1985), in which she played a prostitute. By the early 1990s she had acted in several TV movies, ranging from *In the Best Interest of the Child* to an athletic part in *The Heroes of Desert Storm* (1992). She won an Image Award as Outstanding Supporting Actress in a Motion Picture for *Malcolm X* for playing Betty Shabazz, and was Oscar-nominated for her interpretation of trouble-plagued Tina Turner in *What's Love Got to Do With It?* She was again Betty Shabazz in a cameo for *Panther* (1995), joined WHITNEY HOUSTON in *Waiting to Exhale* (1995), and tried the sci-fi genre in *Contact* (1997). In a rare major Hollywood film devoted to an upper-middle-class black love story, she and the younger TAYE DIGGS portrayed lovers in *HOW STELLA GOT HER GROOVE BACK* (1998).

More recently, Bassett joined with DANNY GLOVER in an apartheid-era study of a domestic relationship in *Boesman and Lena* (2000), participated in the heist entry *The Score* (2001), with Robert De Niro cast as her lover, and in 2002, she was cast in the TV movie *The Rosa Parks Story* and the ensemble big-screen drama *Sunshine State.*

Beavers, Louise (1902–1962) In the first version (1934) of *IMITATION OF LIFE* Beavers gave a touching performance as the broken-hearted mother whose daughter (FREDI WASHINGTON) wants to be part of the white world. It was a characterization worthy of an Oscar nomination, if (1) there had been a Best Supporting Actress Category at the time and if (2) racial discrimination had been less virulent in that era. Unlike another famous black actress, HATTIE McDANIEL, who did win such an Oscar for *GONE WITH THE WIND* (1939), Louise usually played sympathetic, soft-spoken types. It was not her nature to perform the sassy, at times overbearing, celluloid domestics that became McDaniel's forte. Beavers's restraint did not indicate subservience or phony politeness but was a heartfelt interpretation of persons whose lives had been limited by racial intolerance.

Beavers was born in Cincinnati, Ohio. She and her family moved to California when she was eleven. Her mother hoped that she would use her fine voice on the concert stage, but Beavers opted to work with an all-female minstrel show. During a career lull in the early 1920s, she became the personal maid to silent star Leatrice Joy, which led, as of 1924, to Beavers doing film walk-ons and the like. After the landmark *Imitation of Life*, unfortunately, it was back to playing the typical faithful on-camera servant. An exception was Beavers's part as Toinette, who raised a white orphaned boy (Bobby Breen) in the movie musical *Rainbow on the River* (1936). She also shone as Bing Crosby's wise housekeeper in *HOLIDAY INN* (1942), which was the actress's favorite screen part. Her performance as the baseball star's mother in *The Jackie Robinson Story* (1950) was touching.

In the early 1950s, along with ETHEL WATERS and Hattie McDaniel, Beavers took her turn playing the leading role in the TV comedy series BEULAH. Later in the decade, she made her legitimate stage debut in *Praise House* (1957), but the show faded in San Francisco. Her final movies were 1960's *All the Fine Young Cannibals* (a drama in which Pearl Bailey had the key African-American role) and *The Facts of Life* (with Bob Hope and Lucille Ball).

Belafonte, Harry (1927–) Handsome, sexy, and black was not a combination that Hollywood was used to in the racially unintegrated 1950s. Adding to the situation, singer/actor Belafonte—known for his calypso beat, husky singing voice, and provocative costuming—marched to his own beat in the filmmaking industry, as much as the system would allow him. He was uncomfortable being a smoldering matinee idol and turned quickly to playing character leads instead, while devoting much of his time in the 1960s and thereafter to the Civil Rights movement.

He was born Harold George Belafonte in the Harlem section of New York City of mixed-blood forebears. Before he was six his father had deserted the family. Belafonte spent part of his youth in Kingston, Jamaica, with his mother and younger brother. He dropped out of high school in 1944 to join the World War II Navy. Later, he gravitated to stage work with the American Negro Theater and then turned, successfully, to singing in clubs, appearing in a Broadway revue, and recording for a major label. In the fall of 1949 he was part of a black cast TV variety show *(SUGAR HILL TIMES)*.

Belafonte was brought to Hollywood to costar with DOROTHY DANDRIDGE in *Bright Road* (1953), a small MGM movie that did not allow for much chemistry between the two beautiful actors. The duo were reunited for the musical *CARMEN JONES* (1954) where Harry was overshadowed by his sultry colead. He was embarrassed by his role in the tawdry *Island in the Sun* (1957) but was touted for his on-camera romancing of a white star (Joan Fontaine). This led Belafonte—who continued to be popular on stage, in clubs, on records, and on TV—to turn to nontraditional lead roles such as *ODDS AGAINST TOMORROW* (1959). He earlier rejected the costarring part in the musical *PORGY AND BESS* (1959) because he thought it demeaning.

After years away from films, Belafonte returned as narrator of the documentary: *King: A Filmed Record* (1970). He teamed with long-time friend SIDNEY POITIER for *BUCK AND THE PREACHER* (1972) and *UPTOWN SATURDAY NIGHT* (1974). More recently, his occasional movies included *White Man's Burden* (1995), an allegory about an America where blacks were affluent and in charge, as well as the TV movie *Swing Vote* (1999) and the Robert Altman feature film *Voltage* (2003).

***Beloved* (1998)** Touchstone, color, 174 minutes. **Director:** Jonathan Demme; **Screenplay:** Akosua Busia, Richard LaGravenese, and Adam Brooks; **Cast:** Oprah Winfrey (Sethe), Danny Glover (Paul D), Thandie Newton (Beloved), Kimberly Elise (Denver), Beah Richards (Baby Suggs), Lisa Gay Hamilton (Younger Sethe), Albert Hall (Stamp Paid), Irma P. Hall (Ella).

Shortly after Toni Morrison's acclaimed novel *Beloved* (1987) was published, WINFREY acquired the screen rights. More than a decade later the much-anticipated feature debuted to resounding critical and filmgoer disappointment. It was a laudably meticulous but unfortunately overly literal and ponderous adaptation. It failed to capture the book's magic in which the narrative created a metaphor for the legacy of slavery that clung to generations of postemancipation African Americans. In the film, the anguish of slavery was summoned up, but there was no real catharsis for either the characters or the viewers regarding the plight of African Americans during and after slavery.

In Ohio, some years after the Civil War, Paul D locates his old friend Sethe, another former slave. He moves in with her and her daughter Denver. Before long, the strange Beloved arrives on the scene. Once she is taken into Sethe's household, bizarre occurrences begin to take place as the childlike newcomer has a strong effect on both Sethe and Denver. Sethe reexamines her horrific past, and Denver reaches a new maturity. Paul D, who has left town, is drawn back to care for the now-devastated Sethe, a woman chained to her slave past.

Made on a $53 million budget, *Beloved* grossed almost $23 million in domestic distribution. It received an Oscar nomination for Best Costume Design. GLOVER received an Image Award as Outstanding Lead Actor in a Motion Picture.

***Benson* (1979–1986)** ABC-TV series, color, 30 minutes. **Cast:** Robert Guillaume (Benson DuBois), James Noble (Gov. James Gatling), Missy Gold (Katie Gatling), Inga Swenson (Gretchen Kraus), René Auberjonois (Clayton Endicott III: 1980–86).

On the outrageous TV sitcom *Soap* (1979–84), the crazy Tate household boasted one relatively sane individual, Benson, the precise African-American butler. After two years as the popular, outspoken character, Guillaume earned an Emmy and was given his own spin-off series *(Benson)*. In the new format he is the gilt-edged servant to a widowed governor (Noble) and must deal with the man's bright youngster (Gold) and the rigid German housekeeper (Swenson). As time progresses the efficient, often prissy Benson proves such a great confidant to his employer that he is appointed to public office and eventually is made lieutenant governor. (In the show's final episodes, he runs for the governorship itself.)

As amusing as Guillaume was in the pivotal assignment, there was a strange dichotomy in his small-screen characterization. Here was a self-sufficient man who had more common sense and political smarts than his employer, yet he was willing (comfortably) to still serve his white employer. Obviously, American TV networks were not yet ready to take the premise one step further and have an African-American character rise to political power and not still be attached—one way or another—to white bosses.

Berry, Halle (1968–) Like other Hollywood beauties through the decades, Berry suffered the problem of few starring screen roles being written for women. This difficulty was compounded by her being biracial, which sometimes—but not always—ruled out her chances for appearing in a love story opposite a white actor. The lack of viable acting jobs led her more recently to producing her own projects to ensure new roles. Constantly pushing her acting limits, she won a Best Actress Oscar in March 2002, the first African-American woman to do so.

She was born in Cleveland, Ohio. Her black father had been a hospital attendant; her Caucasian mother was a former psychiatric nurse. Although brought up mainly by her mother, Berry has always considered herself black. She first came to public notice when she was victorious in the Miss Teen All-American Pageant. The next year she was the prime runner-up for the Miss USA Pageant. Her subsequent modeling work—a career in past generations not available in the United States to black women—led to her being cast in the short-lived TV sitcom *Living Dolls* (1989). Her early screen roles of note were playing a crack addict/prostitute in SPIKE LEE's *JUNGLE FEVER* (1991), enacting EDDIE MURPHY's feisty vis-à-vis in *Boomerang* (1992), and emoting in the lead of the melodramatic TV miniseries *Queen* (1993). Next, she moved from juvenile comedy *(The Flintstones*, 1994) to heavy drama *(Losing Isaiah*, 1995). After thankless assignments in *Why Do Fools Fall in Love?* and *Bulworth* (both 1998), Berry triumphed as a tragic singer/Hollywood movie star in *INTRODUCING DOROTHY DANDRIDGE* (1999), winning much favorable notice and many industry awards. In John Travolta's heist drama *Swordfish* (2001), Halle had a topless scene. She received many trophies—including an Academy Award—for *Monster's Ball* (2002), teaming with Billy Bob Thornton in this interracial love story set in the Deep South.

***Beulah* (1950–1953)** ABC-TV series, b&w, 30 minutes. **Cast:** Ethel Waters (Beulah: 1950–52), Hattie McDaniel (Beulah: 1952), Louise Beavers (Beulah: 1952–53), Butterfly McQueen (Oriole: 1950–52), Ruby Dandridge (Oriole: 1952–53), Percy "Bud" Harris (Bill Jackson: 1950–51), Dooley Wilson (Bill Jackson: 1951–52), Ernest Whitman (Bill Jackson: 1952–53).

The character of the heart-of-gold black maid Beulah (with the famous catchphrase "Somebody bawl for Beulah?") originated in 1944 on radio as part of the series *Fibber McGee and Molly* (1935–56) and performed initially by a white actor (Marlin Hurt), using a falsetto voice. He was given his own series *The Marlin Hurt and Beulah Show* in 1945. After his death in 1946, the radio program was revived as *Beulah* in 1947 with first another Caucasian performer (Bob Corley) in the lead and then played by a succession of black actresses (HATTIE McDANIEL, LOUISE BEAVERS, and Lillian Randolph) until the show left the airwaves in 1952.

The popular vehicle—especially among white audiences—translated to TV as the first sitcom to feature a black lead character, albeit a servant and a subservient, compliant soul. In the white middle-class household where she works, faithful Beulah is the busy domestic who always puts her employers' needs first and devotes herself to keeping them out of trouble. After WATERS left the role in the spring of 1952, McDaniel took over the assignment, but she became ill and was replaced by Beavers. For home viewers of the era, it was an excellent opportunity to see three stalwarts of Hollywood films play the same role. McQUEEN (and then Dandridge) was on hand as Beulah's girlfriend/neighbor Oriole, while several actors, including WILSON (of *CASABLANCA* fame) played Bill Jackson, Beulah's relaxed boyfriend who always had a new "reason" for not wedding his good-hearted best girl.

It would not be until *JULIA* (1968–71), starring DIAHANN CARROLL, that another black actress would have the lead in an American network TV sitcom.

***Beverly Hills Cop* (1984)** Paramount, color, 105 minutes. **Director:** Martin Brest; **Screenplay:** Daniel Petrie Jr.; **Cast:** Eddie Murphy (Axel Foley), Judge Reinhold (Det. Billy Rosewood), John Ashton (Sgt. John Taggart), Lisa Eilbacher (Jenny Summers), Ronny Cox (Lt. Andrew Bogomil), Steven Berkoff (Victor Maitland).

Today this landmark film seems formulistic and somewhat trite (because of all the imitations after its release), but when this action entry debuted stand-up comic MURPHY'S fresh take on the cop/buddy genre was warmly greeted by critics and moviegoers alike. The star's Axel Foley was a new step forward for African Americans in Hollywood cinema, especially important given the retrenchment period that followed the 1970s cycle of black action pictures. In *Beverly Hills Cop* Murphy took up RICHARD PRYOR's mantle as the ultra smart-mouthed African American who constantly and blatantly turned the tables on his white confreres. Axel's (seeming good-natured) slyness appealed to many segments of filmgoing audiences.

Detroit law enforcer Axel Foley is determined to solve the murder of an ex-convict friend. Taking a leave of absence from the Motor City police force, cagey Axel follows the trail to Beverly Hills. There the unamused local police assign Det. Billy Rosewood and Sgt. John Taggart to trail Foley. Before long this untraditional law enforcer—an ex-slum boy—proves that his street smarts work effectively in dealing with criminals ensconced among Los Angeles society and its gaudy materialistic splendor.

Made for an estimated $14 million, *Beverly Hills Cop* grossed a staggering $235 million in domestic distribution. The movie was Oscar nominated for Best Original Screenplay. It led to the less satisfying *Beverly Hills Cop II* (1987) and the flabby *Beverly Hills Cop III* (1994). More importantly, as a result of Murphy's Axel Foley, no longer would/could African-American cop characters be *always* relegated to subservient or near-invisible roles in Hollywood movies.

***Bird* (1988)** Warner Bros., color, 161 minutes. **Director:** Clint Eastwood; **Screenplay:** Joel Oliansky; **Cast:** Forest Whitaker (Charlie "Yardbird" Parker), Diana Venora (Chan Richardson Parker), Michael Zelniker (Red Rodney), Samuel E. Wright (Dizzy Gillespie), Keith David (Buster Franklin).

At first blush, Eastwood, most noted for his Dirty Harry Callahan bloody cop pictures, did not seem the appropriate director for this sensitive project. However, Eastwood, a lifelong jazz fan, proved adept in translating this screen drama—based in part on the unpublished memoir of the musician's common-law wife Chan Parker—to the screen. Although the real-life Parker (1920–55) suffered a great deal of racial discrimination in his professional/private life, the screen biography did not emphasize this aspect, nor did it become exploitive or judgmental in treating the talent's drug addiction that led to his early death. Rather, *Bird*, which used actual Charlie Parker solo performances remastered for the soundtrack, devoted itself to a depiction of the man's complexities. It wove its way through Parker's life without reaching for pat explanations to his self-destructive behavior or attempting to explain his musical genius.

In the course of this downbeat, perceptive biography of the great alto saxophonist, the highlights were his playing at jazz clubs on New York's 52nd Street, his shaky relationship with the white Chan Richardson, and the traumatic repercussions to him and Chan when their daughter dies. The narrative captures his tour of the South, his successful play dates in Paris, his performances with fellow musician Dizzy Gillespie on the West Coast, and his shock in his last years at how rock 'n' roll music was submerging audiences' interest in jazz.

Made at a cost of $10 million, *Bird* unfortunately grossed only slightly more than $2 million in domestic distribution. It received an Oscar for Best Sound, and Eastwood received a Golden Globe Award as Best Director of a Motion Picture. Along with *ROUND MIDNIGHT* (1986), *Bird* was one of the best American films about jazz and its great African-American musicians.

***Birth of a Nation, The* (aka: *The Clansman*) (1915)** Epoch Producing Corp, b&w, 175 minutes. **Director:** D. W. Griffith; **Screenplay:** Griffith and Frank E. Woods; **Cast:** Lillian Gish (Elsie Stoneman), Mae Marsh (Flora Cameron), Henry B. Walthall (Col. Ben Cameron), Miriam Cooper (Margaret Cameron), Mary Alden (Lydia Brown), Ralph Lewis (the Hon. Austin Stoneman), Elmer Clifton (Phil Stoneman), Robert Harron (Tod Stoneman), George Siegmann (Silas Lynch), Walter Long (Gus), Jennie Lee (mammy), Tom Wilson (Stoneman's servant).

Cinematically, *The Birth of a Nation* was the apogee of Kentucky-born Griffith's career as a movie pioneer. Culturally and historically, this blatantly racist silent feature was an embarrassment. In exaggerated terms, it depicted African-American and mulatto carpetbaggers as the scourge of the Reconstruction era after the Civil War and the white-sheeted Ku Klux Klan as the valiant savior of the devastated South. Later, just as when first shown, this biased epic still raised strong feelings among filmgoers. Griffith's saga was based on Thomas Dixon's novel *The Clansman: An Historical Romance of the Ku Klux Klan* (1905) and his play adaptation (1906). In addition, the movie relied on Dixon's book *The Leopard's Spots: A Romance of the White Man's Burden: 1865–1900.*

In the nineteenth century, Phil and Tod Stoneman, the sons of abolitionist leader and U.S. congressman Austin Stoneman, visit Phil's school chum, Ben Cameron, and his family in Piedmont, South Carolina. Phil romances Ben's sister Margaret. Later, when President Abraham Lincoln declares war between the North and South, Phil and Tod enlist. During a subsequent battle both Phil and Ben's brother—fighting on opposite sides—are killed. Meanwhile, Ben meets Phil's sister Elsie, now a nurse, and they fall in love. After the war, the elder Stoneman becomes powerful in Congress, while back home in the South, Ben inaugurates the Ku Klux Klan to redress the wrong being done by carpetbagging African Americans and mulattos. Following an encounter between black troops and the KKK, the latter emerges victorious. The African Americans are disenfranchised. With "peace" restored, Margaret and Phil, as well as Elsie and Ben, marry. An epilogue depicts Christ's resurrection and a new millennium where nations live in harmony and brotherhood.

At the time of initial release—and whenever the picture was reissued through the years—*The Birth of a Nation* led to protests (especially by the NAACP) in many cities throughout the United States and Canada, and the film was banned in many jurisdictions. Nevertheless, the feature made at a cost of $100,000 went on to gross more than $18 million. One of the dramatic "highlights" of this highly controversial picture was the death leap of Marsh's character who chose to die rather than to submit to the advances of Gus, the African-American renegade.

The film was filled with racial stereotypes that lasted for decades: the resilient, big-sized mammy, the loyal household servant, the anxious mulatto caught between two cultures/races, the vicious African-American troublemaker, and the humorous black character (i.e., the "coon"). These successors to similar types in literature, theater, and early short films were generally played by white performers made up in BLACKFACE, while African Americans were relegated, at best, to tiny roles.

A short screen adaptation of Dixon's *The Clansman* had been produced in 1909 by the Kinemacolor Company. It starred Linda Arvidson, the actress wife of Griffith. It had been shelved because of technical problems with the photography.

As a direct reaction of *The Birth of a Nation*, African-American filmmakers such as OSCAR MICHEAUX arose in the American cinema to make movies from the minority's point of view.

black action films This genre of Hollywood movies became enormously popular in the early 1970s. However, by the end of that decade, the specie had almost totally faded due to marketplace oversaturation as well as a subtle backlash by the white majority against the temporary emergence of a strong ethnic cinema. Although there had already been occasional mainstream dramas featuring (all) black casts (e.g., *BRIGHT ROAD*, 1953; *ANNA LUCASTA*, 1958; *A RAISIN IN THE SUN*, 1961; *NOTHING BUT A MAN*, 1964), they were mostly specialty, art offerings about an ethnic minority that made little impact on the general moviegoing public. These entries were generally set in black ghettos and rarely, if ever, depicted interaction between blacks and whites.

In contrast, the black action films, while geared to their target ethnic audiences, broke the "rules" by using African-American performers in action stories that once had been the province of white-focused cinema. These films showed proud, often boisterous characters who not only challenged the white man but also generally won out in the confrontations. For black Americans, spurred on by the strides in integration made possible by civil-rights legislation and riots during the 1960s, this brand of cinema was salutary. Many of these pictures featured gutsy, flavorful characters (e.g., Shaft, Superfly, Foxy Brown, and the Mack) who provided role models of sorts for the black community (despite some of the same community who found that such exaggerated figures, often operating outside the law, created negative stereotypes of African Americans).

The late 1960s had seen the emergence of ex-football star JIM BROWN as a viable Hollywood presence in major American films, often with a (then daring) interracial love interest detailed on screen. Brown broke through the racial barriers within the action picture field as Sidney Poitier had in the 1950s and 1960s in the dramatic and romance movie categories. In 1971 came two trend-shaking pictures: *SWEET SWEETBACK'S BAADASSSSS SONG* and *SHAFT*. The former, an independently made venture directed by African-American moviemaker MELVIN VAN PEEBLES, is a strong tale of a black individual from the ghetto rebelling against whites (i.e., "the man") in general and the racist police in particular. It proved to be enormously successful, as did *Shaft*, directed by GORDON PARKS SR. *Shaft* told of a cool dude, a black New York City private investigator, who had a way with firearms and women. *Shaft* was also notable for being released by a major Hollywood studio.

The popularity of *Sweet Sweetback* and *Shaft* led Hollywood to embark on a binge of blaxploitation films. Many, such as *HAMMER* (1972) and *HELL UP IN HARLEM* (1973), were imitations of these two pathfinding movies. Others traded on the novelty of presenting a mainly black cast in screen genres once reserved for white performers. Thus, there were black versions of horror movies (e.g., *BLACULA*, 1972; *Blackenstein*, 1973), westerns (e.g., *THE LEGEND OF NIGGER CHARLEY*, 1972, and *Adios Amigos*, 1975), karate fests (e.g., *Black Belt Jones*, 1974, and *Black Samurai*, 1977), detective yarns (e.g., *Black Gunn* 1972, and *Death Journey*, 1975), sex comedies (e.g., *Black Shampoo*, 1976), mafia tales (e.g., *The Black Godfather*, 1974), and animated features (e.g., *COONSKIN*, 1975). Another gimmick was to remake previously white-cast pictures with black talent (e.g., 1950's *The Asphalt Jungle* became 1972's *Cool Breeze*). Even on television, which had strict censorship guidelines of what could be aired, thus precluding much of the violence, sexuality, raw language, and racial hatred that comprised typical blaxploitation entries, a few film series surfaced (e.g., *Shaft* and *TENAFLY*, both 1973–74). However, they were so watered down for home viewer consumption that they had little appeal.

Most of these entries, as in white Hollywood, starred males, but the black action cinema gave rise to two powerhouse female talents—PAM GRIER and Tamara Dobson. The cinema escapades of Grier (e.g., *Black Mama, White Mama*, 1973; *FOXY BROWN*, 1974) and Dobson (e.g., *CLEOPATRA JONES*, 1973) not only satisfied blaxploitation genre enthusiasts but also reflected the rising feminism movement and created female role models for any race.

So many black action entries (often poorly constructed) having been cranked out during the 1970s, the genre became a near-rarity in the 1980s (e.g., *Action Jackson*, 1988). It later led to screen spoofs of the once so popular, lucrative black action movies (e.g., *I'm Gonna Git You Sucka*, 1988; *Original Gangstas*, 1996). By 2000, JOHN SINGLETON felt the black action genre could be reinvented, and he did a revamping of *Shaft* (1971). The next year, director ERNEST DICKERSON made *Bones*, which had rapper Snoop Doggy Dogg playing the ghost of a numbers racket boss who returns to his turf to seek vengeance on his killers.

***Blackboard Jungle, The* (1955)** Metro-Goldwyn-Mayer, b&w, 100 minutes. **Director/Screenplay:** Richard Brooks; **Cast:** Glenn Ford (Richard Dadier), Anne Francis (Anne Dadier), Louis Calhern (Jim Murdock), Margaret Hayes (Lois Judby Hammond), Sidney Poitier (Gregory W. Miller), Vic Morrow (Artie West), Dan Terranova (Belazi), Rafael Campos (Pete V. Morales), Jameel Farah [Jamie Farr] (Santini).

Evan Hunter's 1954 novel was effectively dramatized in this uncompromising—for its era—study of juvenile delinquency in the urban school systems. "Rock Around the Clock," as sung under the film's credits by Bill Haley and His Comets, promulgated the then current theory that rock 'n' roll and youthful antiestablishment behavior went hand in hand.

Former serviceman Richard Dadier takes a teaching job at New York City's North Manual High, a high school filled with conflicting ethnic minorities. The soft-spoken Dadier must deal with disruptive student Artie West, a gang leader, and his many belligerent followers. Following several experiences, harrowing for Dadier and the other teachers, the new instructor stands up to Artie, and the punk later quits school.

As played by POITIER, Gregory W. Miller, a bright but extremely alienated student, is not the constantly angry African American of subsequent Hollywood movies about troublesome teenage students; rather this skeptical young man is a complex, emotionally bruised character who can be just as sensitive as he is explosive about the world's mistreatment of ethnic minorities. Despite his charismatic presence, Poitier's Gregory remains frequently on the story's sidelines until the film's climax. (His subordinate role was another example of Hollywood's racial relegation of African Americans to the sidelines.) At film's finish, Gregory challenges the discouraged Dadier to remain teaching, and he promises to continue as a student.

The influential *The Blackboard Jungle*—which dated rather quickly—was nominated for several Academy Awards: Best Art Direction, Best Cinematography (Black and White), Best Film Editing, and Best Screenplay.

***Black Caesar* (1973)** American International, color, 94 minutes. **Director/Screenplay:** Larry Cohen; **Cast:** Fred Williamson (Tommy Gibbs), Phillip Roye (Joe Washington), Gloria Hendry (Helen), Julius W. Harris (Mr. Gibbs), Val Avery (Sal Cardoza), Minnie Gentry (Mama Gibbs), Art Lund (John McKinney), D'Urville Martin (Reverend Rufus).

As the BLACK ACTION genre accelerated in 1970s Hollywood, many such entries followed the useful plot mold, established by *ACROSS 110TH STREET* (1972), in which African-American hoodlums in Harlem combat the Italian mob in New York's Little Italy for control of the metropolis's lucrative rackets. Rarely was the formula executed in such an effective manner as in this chronicle of Tommy Gibbs, who grows up to become an underworld kingpin uptown and then confronts the downtown criminal organization run by Sal Cardoza. The ruthless Gibbs seems unstoppable as he upstages his Italian "partners" in lower Manhattan. But Tommy's rise to power is lonely. His true love—Helen, a singer—has married Gibbs's best friend (Roye). Before the criminal mastermind is finished, he has rubbed out many of his enemies and, in the final confrontation, the badly wounded Tommy makes it back to the ghetto to die at home.

What helped to make the ultraviolent *Black Caesar* so impressive was its tapestry of supporting characters, ranging from the bogus Reverend (Martin) to the tough, self-sufficient Mama Gibbs, to Tommy's long-absent father who returned and became part of his son's reckless life. Providing the film's conscience were Gibbs's longtime friends, Helen and Joe Washington.

Audiences responded favorably to this smart, sexy, and powerful "dude" who was tough and clever enough to take on "the Man" and emerge—for a time—victorious. Whatever Tommy's shaky morals, this vigilante was embraced as an African-American screen hero. As played by athletic, handsome WILLIAMSON (a substitute for first-choice actor SAMMY DAVIS JR.), here was a new-breed role model, asserting his independence from the establishment.

Made inexpensively, this gangster melodrama—reminiscent of mainstream Hollywood's *Little Caesar* (1931) and *Scarface* (1932)—earned more than $2 million in domestic film rentals. It led to *Hell Up in Harlem* (1974). The sequel resuscitates Tommy Gibbs (again played by Williamson) as he and his gang battled the city's Mafioso. This equally violent film accumulated $1.55 million in domestic rentals. Another planned follow-up never materialized.

blackface In nineteenth- and early-twentieth-century minstrel shows, it was common for white actors to perform in blackface. This convention also was used in vaudeville by such stars as Al Jolson and Eddie Cantor and carried over to the stage where, if an important character was to be an African American, it was performed by a white actor with black makeup. This "tradition" also was used by the silent cinema in its first decades (e.g., George Siegmann's Silas Lynch in *THE BIRTH OF A NATION*, 1915). Jolson, who became the talking pictures' first big star with the release of *The Jazz Singer* (1927), carried on the tradition in several movies (e.g., *Mammy*, 1929; *Big Boy*, 1930; *Wonder Bar*, 1934), as did Cantor (e.g., *Kid Millions*, 1934; *The Story of Will Rogers*, 1952), though the practice was found increasingly offensive by the black community. When the late 1920s hit radio series *AMOS 'N' ANDY* was translated to the screen, the two white stars of the audio show donned blackface to play their characters in *CHECK AND DOUBLE CHECK* (1930).

The use of blackface continued—infrequently—into the 1950s, by which time such mainstream Hollywood performers as Mickey Rooney, Betty Grable, June Haver, Fred Astaire, Judy Garland, Martha Raye, Bob Hope, Bing Crosby, Marjorie Reynolds, Larry Parks, Keefe Brasselle, Joan Crawford, Doris Day, Ava Gardner, and even the cartoon character Bugs Bunny had appeared on film in variations of blackface. Even some westerns had incorporated minstrel numbers into their horse-opera plots (e.g., *Oklahoma Renegades*, 1940; *Boss of Rawhide*, 1943). (To be noted, in scattered entries such as 1964's *BLACK LIKE ME* and 1986's *SOUL MAN*, the white characters became "black" *not* because they were performing a show business act within the movie but for plot points.) An indictment of this demeaning show-business practice was at the heart of SPIKE LEE's *BAMBOOZLED* (2001), a film that lambasted whites for doing it and scolded blacks for allowing it to perpetuate.

A variation of the blackface business occurred in *WATERMELON MAN* (1970) and *The Associate* (1996) where, respectively, black performers Godfrey Cambridge and WHOOPI

GOLDBERG performed in whiteface as part of the plot. In *COTTON COMES TO HARLEM* (1970), two characters (played by black actors Raymond St. Jacques and Cambridge) darkened their complexion further as a disguise. In the musical *Funny Lady* (1975), African-American entertainer Ben Vereen used blackface to portray stage great Bert Williams as did Savion Glover in *BAMBOOZLED* (2000).

***Black Girl* (1972)** Cinerama, color, 97 minutes. **Director:** Ossie Davis; **Screenplay:** J. E. Franklin; **Cast:** Brock Peters (Earl), Leslie Uggams (Netta), Claudia McNeil (Mu' Dear), Louise Stubbs (Mama Rosie), Gloria Edwards (Norma), Loretta Greene (Ruth Ann), Ruby Dee (Netta's mother).

When BLACK ACTION entries flooded the movie marketplace, this modest, thoughtful drama, based on Franklin's play, offered an opposing type of African-American cinema. It was one steeped in the traditions of such character-driven films a *A RAISIN IN THE SUN* (1961).

Matriarch Mama Rosie feels that she has failed in raising her own daughters (Edwards and Greene) and turns to nurturing her foster child, Netta, prompting the jealous ire of her offspring, a situation with which Rosie and her spouse (Peters) must deal. Meanwhile, the grandmother (McNeil) is shocked to see the next generation repeating her own past domestic errors.

DAVIS was still a budding filmmaker, and the resultant *Black Girl* was technically flawed and often dramatically gauche. But the performances of the cast, including Davis's wife, actress DEE, compensated for the movie's many flaws. *Black Girl* was not financially successful, as audiences were still caught up in the popular blaxploitation fare.

***Black Like Me* (1964)** Continental, b&w, 107 minutes. **Director:** Carl Lerner; **Screenplay:** Gerda and Carl Lerner; **Cast:** James Whitmore (John Finley Horton), Dan Priest (bus driver), Walter Mason (Mason), John Marriott (Hodges), Clifton James (Eli Carr), Roscoe Lee Browne (Christopher).

Relying on John Howard Griffin's 1961 novel, this film borrowed the gimmick of the movie *Gentleman's Agreement* (1947), in which a member of the white majority masquerades as a Jew to learn about anti-Semitism. *Black Like Me* focuses on white Southern journalist John Finley Horton who darkens his skin so he can live like an African American and write a series of magazine articles about his revealing experiences. In the process, Horton undergoes harrowing encounters—both with whites and with African Americans—as he travels throughout the South. The pressures of his undercover work lead him to a near nervous breakdown. Once back in his own environment Horton wonders if his forthcoming articles will have beneficial effects.

Reversing the more frequent ploy of an African American passing as white (e.g., *PINKY*, 1949), this low-budget exploitation picture lacked technical finesse but proved surprisingly effective—thanks largely to Whitmore's well-modulated performance.

As was true of *Gentleman's Agreement*, the plot premise contained a major flaw. The lead character could only approximate what it felt like to be a full-time member of the minority for he could always return to the safe establishment world. The "passing" gimmick of *Black Like Me* turned up again in the comedic *SOUL MAN* (1986) starring C. Thomas Howell.

***Blacula* (1972)** American International, color, 93 minutes. **Director:** William Crain; **Screenplay:** Joan Torres and Raymond Koenig; **Cast:** William Marshall (Mamuwalde [Blacula]), Vonetta McGee (Tina/Luva), Denise Nicolas (Michelle), Thalmus Rasulala (Dr. Gordon Thomas), Gordon Pinsent (Lieutenant Peters).

During the rash of 1970s BLACK ACTION FILMS, inventive Hollywood filmmakers adapted the blaxploitation idiom to nearly every genre, including, creatively, the horror story. Shakespearean actor Marshall proved a good choice to inhabit a screen part associated in the past with Hungarian-born Bela Lugosi.

While visiting Transylvania in 1790, African prince Mamuwalde is cursed for eternity to be a vampire. Jumping ahead to present-day Los Angeles, when several victims die mysteriously, Dr. Gordon Thomas concludes that Blacula is on the prowl. Meanwhile, the vampire is drawn to Tina, whom he thinks is the reincarnation of his long-ago murdered wife. Eventually, the police corral the villain at his lair. Forced out into the sunlight, Blacula disintegrates into dust . . . or does he?

Deliberately campy and without a strong directorial touch, *Blacula* nevertheless found devotees among moviegoers hungry for films presenting minority performers and among those who thrived on any type of horror pictures. Earning $1.2 million in domestic film rentals, the entry inspired *Scream Blacula, Scream* (1973), which also starred Marshall, and such poor offshoots as *Abby* (1974) and *Dr. Black, Mr. Hyde* (1976).

blaxploitation films See BLACK ACTION FILMS.

***Blue Collar* (1978)** Universal, color, 110 minutes. **Director:** Paul Schrader; **Screenplay:** Paul Schrader and Leonard Schrader; **Cast:** Richard Pryor (Zeke), Harvey Keitel (Jerry), Yaphet Kotto (Smokey), Ed Begley Jr. (Bobby Joe), Harry Bellaver (Eddie Johnson), George Memmoli (Jenkins).

Centering on disaffected Detroit auto assembly-line workers, this superior, often overlooked film deals with three married pals (PRYOR, Keitel, and Kotto) who rob their local union's office safe. Their haul nets them only $600 in cash, but they discover that they have also taken confidential papers from the safe. When the union later tells everyone that it was robbed of $10,000, the provoked trio blackmails the union's branch office.

Within *Blue Collar*, the humdrum lives of the auto workers are never sufficiently delineated, nor is the friendship between the two African Americans (Pryor and Kotto) with their white pal (Keitel) mined for its full potential. Nevertheless, in this movie Pryor offers one of his best screen performances, while Kotto, like Pryor a veteran of many BLACK EXPLOITATION screen actioners, created a strong presence.

Filled with crude but realistic dialogue, this R-rated feature effectively touched on the despairing, hopeless life of its lead figures, with each receiving equal screen time. It was a step forward in having Hollywood present an intelligent, integrated screen drama in which African Americans emerged as major characters.

***Body and Soul* (1925)** Micheaux Film, b&w, 9 reels. **Director:** Oscar Micheaux; **Cast:** Paul Robeson ("Jeremiah the Deliverer" [Rev. Isaiah Jenkins]/Sylvester), Marshall Rodgers (the businessman), Lawrence Chenault (Yellow-Curley Hands of Atlanta), Chester A. Alexander (Deacon Simpkins) Walter Conick (Brother Amos), Lillian Johnson (Sis Ca'line), Madame Robinson (Sis Lucy).

In Tatesville, Georgia, an escaped prisoner takes on the guise of Rev. Isaiah Jenkins and, along with another criminal (Chenault), plans to defraud the congregation.

The always impressive ROBESON made his screen debut in this silent photoplay in dual roles: as the devious preacher (a favorite target of filmmaker Micheaux) and as Sylvester, the middle-class hero. Because of censorship problems, especially in the state of New York, the "offensive" portrait of the shifty clergyman determined to take advantage of his congregation was altered so that it became a bad dream endured by the heroine. In the revised, jumbled continuity, the finale became an optimistic climax to the narrative.

A remake directed by George Bowers, written by and starring Leon Isaac Kennedy, was released in 1981.

***Boyz N the Hood* (1991)** Columbia, color, 107 minutes. **Director/Screenplay:** John Singleton; **Cast:** Larry [Laurence] Fishburne (Furious Styles), Ice Cube (Doughboy), Cuba Gooding Jr. (Tre Styles), Nia Long (Brandi), Morris Chestnut (Ricky Baker), Tyra Ferrell (Mrs. Baker), Angela Bassett (Reva Styles).

This remarkably realistic study of ghetto life in South Central Los Angeles is far removed from the fantasy urban action dramas of 1970s Hollywood's BLACK ACTION cycle. Here, the characters were victims of their harsh environment: The potentially bad individuals have been hardened by their tough lives, while the virtuous escape their likely fate only with great effort. The film's two noticeable flaws were making the noble characters (e.g., Furious Styles) too righteous and allowing the movie's climactic scenes to be preachy.

In the (neighbor)hood, Tre Styles and Ricky Baker grow up as the good kids, while Ricky's brother Doughboy becomes the leader of a troublesome group. Tre is guided on the righteous path by his divorced, honorable father Furious. Tre's future includes eventual marriage to his neighborhood sweetheart Brandi, once they both have graduated college; all-American athlete Ricky, however, dreams of a sports scholarship to UCLA. When Ricky is killed by a gang from another turf, Furious pressures Tre not to be part of the inevitable retaliation; instead, Doughboy hunts down and eliminates his brother's murderers. Thereafter, Tre and Doughboy are left to their individual fates.

For a rare change, the stereotype of the fatherless African-American household was altered, with Furious being the single parent in charge of his teenage son, and while the characters were specific to the contemporary L.A. ghetto, they had universal traits, thereby broadening the film's message.

In his debut as a filmmaker, twenty-three-year-old SINGLETON was Oscar nominated as Best Director. The film was also nominated as Best Picture. Made at a cost of less than $7 million, *Boyz N the Hood* grossed $57.5 million in domestic distribution. This screen debut of rap star Ice Cube led to a rash of URBAN DRAMAS (e.g., *South Central* and *Juice*, both 1992 releases).

***Brian's Song* (1971)** ABC-TV, color, 100 minutes. **Director:** Buzz Kulik; **Teleplay:** William E. Blinn; **Cast:** James Caan (Brian Piccolo), Billy Dee Williams (Gale Sayers), Jack Warden (Coach George Halas), Shelley Fabares (Joy Piccolo), Judy Pace (Linda Sayers), Bernie Casey (J.C. Caroline).

This effective tearjerker sprang from the true story of Brian Piccolo, running back for the Chicago Bears football team, who died of cancer at age twenty-six. (The telefeature was adapted from the 1970 book *I Am Third* by Gale Sayers with Al Silverman.) In the era of such buddy pictures as *Butch Cassidy and the Sundance Kid* (1969), this movie provided an added twist by having the friendship be interracial.

When Piccolo joins the Chicago Bears' squad, he is befriended by fellow player Sayers even though they are both competing for the same team position. The two athletes, each of whom is married, become roommates on the road, and it is Piccolo who urges Sayers on to recovery when the latter is injured on the gridiron. Later, the career of overachieving Brian is cut short when he develops testicular cancer. It is Gale and his spouse Linda who provide the fortitude for their dying friend and his wife Joy.

This highly regarded telefeature, which drew huge audience ratings and set the mold for buddy sports stories to come, won an Emmy Award as Outstanding Program, for its teleplay, and for Warden (Outstanding Supporting Actor in a Drama). Handsome WILLIAMS, who received an Emmy nomination in the category of Outstanding Single Performance by a Lead Actor, made a strong impression on viewers. In 2001, *Brian's Song* was remade for TV, with Mekhi Phifer as Gale Sayers and Sean Maher as Brian Piccolo. The reprise lacked the emotional punch of the original.

***Bright Road* (1953)** Metro-Goldwyn-Mayer, b&w, 68 minutes. **Director:** Gerald Mayer; **Screenplay:** Emmet Lavery; **Cast:** Dorothy Dandridge (Jane Richards), Philip Hepburn (C. T. Young), Harry Belafonte (Mr. Williams), Barbara Ann Sanders (Tanya Hamilton), Robert Horton (Dr. Mitchell), Vivian Dandridge (Miss Nelson).

Reaching for a new maturity on screen, MGM made this low-budget drama, based on the 1951 short story "See How They Run" by Mary Elizabeth Vroman and notable for being one of the first Hollywood nonmusical productions to feature a predominantly African-American cast.

As a new fourth-grade teacher at a small African-American elementary school in the South, Jane Richards takes a particular interest in one student, C. T. Young, a well-mannered but distracted child. Soon Jane awakens an interest in learning within the bored youngster, but he suffers an emotional setback when his classmate/friend Tanya dies of pneumonia. The distraught C. T. becomes incorrigible in the classroom, and it takes all Jane's patience and ingenuity to bring him back into the right path.

This relatively short, yet leisurely drama benefited greatly from the presence of DANDRIDGE and BELAFONTE, each on the verge of screen stardom. While MGM was "daring" in making this specialized story for the general marketplace, it still was too conservative to allow the comely teacher and the handsome school principal to have a romantic relationship on camera. (Then too, to hedge its bet, the studio spent little on the production.) The picture received only spotty distribution because of its interracial theme and was often relegated to the bottom half of double bills. It was not a money earner for the studio.

***Broken Strings* (1940)** International Road Shows, b&w, 60 minutes. **Director:** Bernard B. Ray; **Screenplay:** Carl Krusada; **Additional Dialogue:** Clarence Muse and David Arlen; **Cast:** Clarence Muse (Arthur Williams), Sybil Lewis (Grace Williams), William Washington (John Williams), Tommie Moore (Mary), Matthew "Stymie" Beard (Dickey Morley), Pete Webster (Gus Stevens).

Made outside the Hollywood mainstream, this obvious melodrama allowed veteran actor MUSE to break his mold of playing on-camera servants. Here, he is a professional man—a respected concert violinist—with ample opportunity during the narrative to deal with his character's problems rather than to enact his typical good-natured movie domestic subservient to his white employers.

Famed violinist Arthur Williams is injured in an auto accident and must abandon his career. He becomes a music instructor, with Dickey Morley his favorite student. In contrast, William's twelve-year-old son Johnny, also a dedicated violinist, prefers to play swing music, which upsets his father. Meanwhile, Arthur's daughter, Grace, arranges for her dad to have special surgery on his injured hand. Johnny and Grace enter a radio talent show, hoping to win the prize money to pay for the medical treatment. Because two of the strings snap on his violin, Johnny is forced to play a swing number rather than a planned classical one. Johnny is delighted to win the contest but even happier when later his now-cured parent acknowledges his son's talent as a swing artist.

Beard had gained fame as a member of the Our Gang short subjects in the 1930s.

***Bronze Buckaroo* (1939)** Hollywood Productions, b&w, 57 minutes. **Director/Screenplay:** Richard C. Kahn; **Cast:** Herbert Jeffrey (Bob Blake), Lucius Brooks (Dusty), Artie Young (Betty Jackson), F. E. Miller (Slim Perkins), Spencer Williams (Pete), Clarence Brooks (Buck Thorne).

This is one of several all-black westerns that singer Herb Jeffries—then using his real name of Herbert Jeffrey—made in the late 1930s. These low-budget sagebrush entries had special appeal for minority audiences, as the engaging hero looked dashing and could sing, ride, and handle his six-shooter as dexterously as his white counterparts on screen. The story concerns Bob Blake who is out to avenge the death of Betty Jackson's dad.

Filmed near Victorville, California, at an African-American dude ranch, this production contrasts light-skinned Jeffrey and Young with the dark-skinned villain (Williams) and hero's sidekick (Brooks). (The filmmakers were reflecting the bigoted view that the lighter skinned a black person, the closer he/she was to being white and thus a good person.)

Black westerns in the 1920s included such independently made, specialty-audience films as *The Bull-Dogger* (1922) starring Bill Pickett.

Bronze Venus, The See *DUKE IS TOPS, THE*.

***Brother from Another Planet, The* (1984)** Cinecon International, color, 110 minutes. **Director/Screenplay:** John Sayles; **Cast:** Joe Morton (the Brother), Darryl Edwards (Fly), Steve James (Odell), Leonard Jackson (Smokey), Bill Cobbs (Walter), Dee Dee Bridgewater (Malverne), David Strathairn and John Sayles (men in black).

This morality tale in the guise of a sci-fi adventure finds an escaped black alien (Morton) from another planet crash-landing his spacecraft near Manhattan's Ellis Island. On Earth seeking freedom and adventure, he makes his way to Harlem where he is pursued by two white aliens determined to take him back to captivity on their planet. With his tattered clothing, this mute experiences a spectrum of ghetto life: a brief liaison with a local singer (Bridgewater) and a display of great healing powers with his hands (including the repair of video games). Eventually, the locals come to the alien's aid, leading the bounty hunters to self-destruct.

Episodic and made cheaply with tacky special effects by rising independent filmmaker Sayles, the film benefits greatly from Morton's performance as the extraterrestrial, instilling continuity into the meandering movie. Some commentators praised the film as an astute allegory of contemporary ethnic minority life; others took issue with the Caucasian filmmaker presenting such an ethnic story and having the lead character never speak.

Made at a cost of $300,000, *The Brother From Another Planet* grossed $5 million in domestic rentals. Fledgling cinematographer ERNEST R. DICKERSON emerged in the 1990s as a film director.

***Brothers* (1977)** Warner Bros., color, 104 minutes. **Director:** Arthur Barron; **Screenplay:** Edward Lewis and Mildred Lewis; **Cast:** Bernie Casey (David Thomas), Vonetta McGee (Paula Jones), Ron O'Neal (Walter Nance), Rennie Roker (Lewis), Stu Gillam (Robinson), Owen Pace (Joshua Thomas).

In many ways this impassioned drama was an intelligent outgrowth of Hollywood's fading BLACK ACTION picture vogue, which included such prison entries as *RIOT* (1969) and *The Slams* (1973), both featuring JIM BROWN. *Brothers* was based on real-life people: fiery activist/college professor Angela Davis and black militant convict George Jackson who pursued their romance while he was in San Quentin penitentiary for bank robbery. (Later, she was tried but acquitted for allegedly helping to plan Jackson's breakout effort, during which his younger brother and a judge died at the Marin County, California, courthouse. Still later, Jackson would be killed during another supposed prison breakout attempt.)

This heated entry was buoyed by convincing performances from the leads, especially Casey as the hot-headed young convict who learns the need of education from his prison cellmate (O'NEAL). The film highlights the abusive treatment of African-American prisoners (especially by the white guards) and how David Thomas's life spirals out of control. Paula Jones takes an interest in his legal case and falls in love with him. Their growing love remains unconsummated and ends in tragedy.

The jail sequences were filmed at the North Dakota State Penitentiary.

Brown, Jim (1935–) A former gridiron hero, in the late 1960s Brown became Hollywood's first black star in major Hollywood action pictures, helping to pave the way for

Jim Brown, one of the kings of Hollywood's black action film cycle in a dangerous moment from *Three the Hard Way* (1974). (JC ARCHIVES)

the BLACK ACTION FILM cycle of the 1970s. Silent, burly, and graceful of movement—with penetrating eyes—he later became a frequent star of blaxploitation films.

Brown was born on St. Simons Island, Georgia, attended Syracuse University, and then played professional football for the Cleveland Browns from 1957 onward. He made his feature film debut in the Western *Rio Conchos* (1964) and, by the time of *The Dirty Dozen* (1967), *THE SPLIT* (1968), and *RIOT* (1969), he was a major name. Ironically once the black action film onslaught began, his films (e.g., *SLAUGHTER*, 1972; *The Slams*, 1973; *Three the Hard Way*, 1974) did not showcase him to the same advantage as such peers as RICHARD ROUNDTREE, FRED WILLIAMSON, and Ron O'Neal.

After being out of the acting limelight for much of the 1980s, Brown returned in featured character roles in such action entries as *L. A. Heat* (1989) and *Twisted Justice* (1990). Although he parodied his past image in the genre satires *I'm Gonna Git You Sucka* (1988) and *Original Gangstas* (1996), he had more serious parts in SPIKE LEE's *He Got Game* (1998) and the football-oriented feature *Any Given Sunday* (1999). In 2002, the athlete/actor was the subject of Spike Lee's full-length documentary, *Jim Brown: All American*. It covered both his professional careers as well as his often-troubled private life.

***Buck and the Preacher* (1972)** Columbia, color, 102 minutes. **Director:** Sidney Poitier; **Screenplay:** Ernest Kinoy; **Cast:** Sidney Poitier (Buck), Harry Belafonte (Preacher [Rev. Willis Oakes Rutherford]), Ruby Dee (Ruth), Cameron Mitchell (Deshay), Denny Miller (Floyd), James McEachin (Kinston), Clarence Muse (Cudjo).

Among the merits of this comedic tale are the screen-directing debut of star POITIER and the marvelous opportunity given BELAFONTE to play a multidimensional leading man. Unlike many of the "soul westerns" (e.g., *THE LEGEND OF NIGGER CHARLEY*, 1972), which focused on antiwhite militarism, this entry told its story as a boisterous sagebrush adventure, also depicting the joining of two minorities (African Americans and Native Americans) in the old West to combat their common enemy—marauding whites.

Buck, a former Union Army cavalryman, has become a wagon-train guide for African Americans who migrate westward, seeking freedom on the frontier. This exodus of cheap labor upsets Louisiana farmers; they hire bounty hunter Deshay and his thugs to drag back the latest group of ex-slaves. Meanwhile, con artist Preacher encounters Buck and his newest wagon train and is impressed by their bravery against Deshay and his men. The conniving Preacher joins them as they prepare to move through dangerous Native American country. Because the ex-slaves' money was stolen by Deshay and his followers—now mostly dead—Buck, the Preacher, and Ruth (Buck's lady love) rob a nearby bank and then rejoin their wagon train as it heads to Colorado.

As part of the new Hollywood cinema of the 1970s that allowed African Americans to emerge triumphant over Caucasians, *Buck and the Preacher* found a receptive audience both in its targeted ethnic marketplace and with many white filmgoers. The PG-rated film earned $3.1 million in domestic film rentals.

***Bucktown* (1975)** American International, color, 94 minutes. **Director:** Arthur Marks; **Screenplay:** Bob Ellison; **Cast:** Fred Williamson (Duke Johnson), Pam Grier (Aretha), Thalmus Rasulala (Roy), Tony King (T. J.), Bernie Hamilton (Harley), Art Lund (Chief Patterson), Carl Weathers (Hambone).

Uniting two stalwarts (WILLIAMSON and GRIER) of the BLACK ACTION FILM genre, this slapdash feature won no plaudits from the critics. For example, *Variety* (July 9, 1975) opined, "AIP's blaxploitation mill grinds out films that are merely flimsy excuses for prolonged violent confrontations between protagonists, usually black and white. This Fred Williamson topliner veers slightly from the formula only in the fact that blacks beat up as much on other blacks as they do white."

Filmed in Kansas City and Platte City, Missouri, this entry chronicles the chaotic way of life in Buchanan (somewhere in the South) where crooked police, gambling joints, and whorehouses are the prime attractions. Duke Johnson comes to town to bury his brother and remains to reopen the family gambling salon as well as to pursue a romance with the immoral Aretha. To even the odds against the corrupt Chief Patterson and his white henchmen, Duke summons his tough Philadelphia pal Roy and the dude's even tougher underlings (including Weathers). Although they topple the crooked cops, a bloody battle develops between Duke and Roy, with the victorious Duke claiming the complacent Aretha.

What was strange about this violent entry is the extreme passivity of Grier's world-weary character in comparison to her usual zesty tough-babe film performances. Notably, this picture presented one of the strongest on-screen clarifications of what truly motivated these amoral black action "heroes." As Roy said within *Bucktown:* "Respect comes from knowin' how it is in the street. What you have to do to get by and doin' it." As the street smart kid Stevie (played well by Tierre Turner) insisted, "I'm just trying to grow up fast in a fast town." Such were the guidelines driving these genre folk.

C

***Cabin in the Sky* (1943)** Metro-Goldwyn-Mayer, b&w, 98 minutes. **Director:** Vincente Minnelli; **Screenplay:** Joseph Schrank; **Cast:** Ethel Waters (Petunia Jackson), Eddie "Rochester" Anderson (Little Joe Jackson), Lena Horne (Georgia Brown), Louis Armstrong (the trumpeter), Rex Ingram (Lucius/Lucifer Jr.), Kenneth Spencer (Reverend Green/the General), John W "Bubbles" Sublett (Domino Johnson), Oscar Polk (the Deacon/Sgt. J. Fleetfoot), Mantan Moreland and Willie Best (idea men), Butterfly McQueen (Lily), Ruby Dandridge (Mrs. Kelso).

It had been fourteen years since Hollywood produced full-scale African-American musicals (1929's *HALLELUJAH* and *Hearts of Dixie*). In 1943, during the height of World War II when the U.S. government was fostering a "better" sense of brotherhood between the white majority and ethnic minorities, the studios released two such pictures: this and Twentieth Century-Fox's *STORMY WEATHER*. The buoyant song-and-dance fest *Cabin in the Sky* was based on the 1940 Broadway musical (book by Lynn Root, lyrics by John Latouche, music by Vernon Duke) that featured WATERS and Ingram.

Hard-working Petunia Jackson is forever coping with her gambling, lazy husband, Little Joe. Although he repeatedly promises to give up his vices, he is drawn to the local casino where slinky Georgia Brown performs. Joe is shot in a scuffle at the club. As he lays in perilous health and Petunia prays for his recovery, the forces of Heaven and Hell fight over Joe's soul. He awakens from his nightmare determined to repent and become a better man.

Several contemporary reviewers faulted this musical fable as a disservice to African Americans because it ignored the reality of ethnic minorities' daily struggle in its depiction of such a fanciful parade of characters, but others then, and more later, reveled in this vibrant—and rare—showcase opportunity for so many African-American talents (which also included the Hall Johnson Choir and Duke Ellington and his Orchestra). In many ways this movie was a passing of the star mantle from veteran performer Waters to relative Hollywood newcomer HORNE.

Made for a relatively low cost ($662,142), *Cabin in the Sky* was to be the first of three all African-American musicals that the studio planned at the time. None of the other genre pieces were forthcoming because the studio lost interest in its experimentation with such fare as movie theaters in the South refused to show such ethnic product. Its song "Happiness Is Just a Thing Called Joe" (sung by Waters) was Oscar nominated.

Ethel Waters and Eddie "Rochester" Anderson, the costars of *Cabin in the Sky* (1943). (JC ARCHIVES)

***Carbon Copy* (1981)** Avco Embassy, color, 92 minutes. **Director:** Michael Schultz; **Screenplay:** Stanley Shapiro; **Cast:** George Segal (Walter Whitney), Susan St. James (Vivian Longhurst Whitney), Jack Warden (Nelson Longhurst), Denzel Washington (Roger Porter), Paul Winfield (Bob Garvey).

In retrospect, this fitful farce (executed in TV-sitcom style) was more embarrassing than entertaining. It presumed the superiority of the white (gentile) race and treated its African-American characters (and people of Jewish background) as if they were temporary, annoying inconveniences.

Middle-aged, white executive Walter Whitney is a successful California businessman who has hidden a few facts along the way. Then one day his WASP-oriented world collapses: A black seventeen-year-old shows up, insisting that he is the product of Walter's romance years ago with a black woman now dead, and he wants to be recognized by his father. (It also is revealed that Whitney is Jewish, a fact hidden from his corporate world.) Once these two revelations leak out, Whitney loses his job, his wife, his friends, and the rest of his comfortable life. He is forced to do manual labor to survive. In the end, clean-cut Roger, who initially wanted revenge on this man who deserted his mother, has a positive effect on Walter. The latter not only "accepts" his offspring but also gains a fresh perspective on life.

As in the later *SOUL MAN* (1986), this floundering comedy—with pretenses of white liberalism—attempted to view the world strictly through the eyes of the white mainstream while being condescending to minorities.

***Carmen Jones* (1954)** Twentieth Century-Fox, color, 107 minutes. **Director:** Otto Preminger; **Screenplay:** Harry Kleiner; **Cast:** Harry Belafonte (Joe), Dorothy Dandridge (Carmen Jones), Pearl Bailey (Frankie), Olga James (Cindy Lou), Joe Adams (Husky Miller), Brock Peters (Sergeant Brown), Diahann Carroll (Myrt).

Heralded as Hollywood's first all African-American musical in eleven years, the film, nevertheless, drew the concern of Walter White, the executive secretary of the National Association for the Advancement of Colored People (NAACP), because his organization was committed to integration. Costar BELAFONTE had strong doubts that this production would in and of itself lead to more African Americans being employed in mainstream films. He told the *New York Times* (October 24, 1954): "I think it will provide some help symbolically. It proves there's no corner of human drama that Negroes cannot play. However, I don't think Hollywood, as a whole, is geared to pioneering of this sort."

Based on the 1943 musical play *Carmen Jones*, with music by Georges Bizet and book/lyrics by Oscar Hammerstein II, the movie is set in Florida as Joe prepares to enter military flying school during World War II. He is led astray from his goal and his relationship with Cindy Lou by the sensuous Carmen Jones, a parachute-plant worker. His chance to marry Cindy Lou is ruined when Joe goes AWOL from the army. Later, in Chicago, the flirtatious, grasping Carmen, believing the death card in her fortune, desperately enters a relationship with boxer Husky Miller. Joe follows her to the fight stadium where he strangles the unfaithful woman.

Directed by Austrian-born Preminger, *Carmen Jones* boasted a fine roster of African-American talent, but none of the lead players (except for Bailey) were allowed to do their on-screen singing. Similarly in this stylized, gaudy musical, the actors emerged as mannequins rather than full-bodied, passionate individuals—more a fault of the antiquated stage book. If Belafonte, in particular, was made to appear restrained on camera (reflecting Hollywood and America's then supposed fear of the virile black male), DANDRIDGE, nevertheless, proved to be vibrant and sexy; Bailey, deliberately raucous, bordered on the vulgar.

Carmen Jones, made for a relatively modest $750,000 in the CinemaScope widescreen process, was a box-office success. Dandridge was nominated for a Best Actress Oscar, and Herschel Burke Gilbert was nominated in the Best Scoring category. The film should have led Dandridge to a successful mainstream movie career, but discrimination policies in the movie industry and the star's personal demons stymied her career moves.

In 2001, ROBERT TOWNSEND directed the made-for-cable movie *Carmen: A Hip Hopera* in which Beyoncé Knowles and Mekhi Phifer starred in an update of the story with contemporary music.

Carroll, Diahann (1935–) She had a rags-to-riches show business success story, one that should have endeared her to the public much more than it did, but Carroll's acting was often stiff and her manner protectively defensive. Nevertheless, she was a show business survivor (as she was of breast cancer) who achieved many high points in her lengthy entertainment career.

She was born Carol Diahann Johnson in the Bronx, New York, the daughter of a subway conductor father and a nurse mother. As a youngster she was a member of the Tiny Tots choir at Adam Clayton Powell's Abyssinian Baptist Church. By age fifteen she was attending the High School of Music and Art, was modeling, and had appeared on a TV talent show. Long conflicted about her ethnic roots, she saw show business as a means for assimilation into the mainstream. She had already appeared as a singer in swank Manhattan clubs when she made her film debut in a small role in *CARMEN JONES* (1954). On Broadway she was in *House of Flowers* (1954) and returned to pictures for *PORGY AND BESS* (1959). With SIDNEY POITIER, costar of that musical, Carroll, who was still wed to her white first husband, had an off-camera relationship, and they reunited for the movie *PARIS BLUES* (1961). For her lead role in *No Strings* (1962), the Broadway musical about interracial love, she won a Tony Award.

Long a guest performer on TV, Carroll starred as *JULIA* (1968–71), a sitcom that helped to integrate further black talent into mainstream television programming. For her performance in the romantic comedy *CLAUDINE* (1974), she was Oscar nominated. In between club work, she made such dramatic ethnic TV fare as I KNOW WHY THE CAGED BIRD SINGS (1979). Then she was showcased as the ultra-upscale Dominique Deveraux in the classy nighttime soap opera *Dynasty* from 1984 to 1987.

In 1996, her fourth marriage, to singer Vic Damone, ended in divorce. More recently, Carroll appeared in such movies as *Eve's Bayou* (1997) and as the subject's mother in the telefeature *Livin' for Love: The Natalie Cole Story* (2000). In spring 2002, Carroll was an ensemble regular on *The Court*, a TV series about U.S. Supreme Court justices starring Sally Field.

***Carter's Army* (1970)** ABC-TV, color, 78 minutes. **Director:** George McCowan; **Teleplay:** Aaron Spelling and David H. Kidd; **Cast:** Stephen Boyd (Capt. Beau Carter), Robert Hooks (Lt. Edward Wallace), Susan Oliver (Anna), Rosey Grier (Big Jim), Moses Gunn (Doc), Richard Pryor (Jonathan Crunk), Glynn Turman (George Brightman), Billy Dee Williams (Lewis).

This minor TV movie, another World War II combat entry, boasted a stalwart cast of African-American talent. It also featured a relatively innovative (for national TV consumption) plot point. A bigoted white army captain (Boyd) is suddenly put in charge of a novice, all African-American rear-line service detachment. Set on the road to Berlin in mid-1944, Carter and his inexperienced men must stave off the Germans at a key dam site. After the ensuing skirmish, the officer learns to respect his men for their courage and not their skin color.

***Car Wash* (1976)** Universal, color, 97 minutes. **Director:** Michael Schultz; **Screenplay:** Joel Schumacher; **Cast:** Franklyn Alaye (T. C.), Bill Duke (Dwayne), Antonio Fargas (Lindy), Melanie Mayron (Marsha), Garrett Morris (Slide), Clarence Muse (Snapper), the Pointer Sisters (the Wilson Sisters), Richard Pryor (Daddy Rich), Tracy Reed (Mona).

This was a madcap, if shallow, panorama of African-American life from the point of view of workers at, and visitors to, a Los Angeles car wash. Made with verve and filled with soundtrack songs, director Schultz turned these meandering vignettes of ethnic life into an engaging tapestry. Nonetheless, rather than present its ethnic minority characters in a realistic narrative, the film always opted for the comedic and the exaggerated.

One of the comedy's highlights is the arrival of bogus preacher Daddy Rich (delightfully overplayed by PRYOR) and his entourage (including the Pointer Sisters) in his ostentatious vehicle. Duke as the sensitive young revolutionary provides the strongest characterization in this pastiche, while the romantic pining of car wash worker T. C. for Mona the waitress gives the proceeding a conventional break from its pseudo-hip skit sequences.

***Casablanca* (1942)** Warner Bros., b&w, 102 minutes. **Director:** Michael Curtiz; **Screenplay:** Julius J. Epstein, Philip G. Epstein, and Howard Koch; **Cast:** Humphrey Bogart (Richard "Rick" Blaine), Ingrid Bergman (Ilsa Lund Laszlo), Paul Henreid (Victor Laszlo), Claude Rains (Capt. Louis Renault), Conrad Veidt (Maj. Heinrich Strasser), Sydney Greenstreet (Señor Ferrari), Peter Lorre (Ugarte), Dooley Wilson (Sam).

Now considered a classic of Hollywood's golden age, *Casablanca* was one of three 1942 features (along with *HOLIDAY INN* and *IN THIS OUR LIFE*) that provided African-American talent with screen roles of respect and near equality with their pictures' leading Caucasian characters.

Casablanca was set in the intrigue-filled North African city occupied by the Nazis during World War II. There, American Rick Blaine runs a popular nightclub. He remains in business because of his supposed neutrality in the global situation and, as such, has established a rapport with Louis Renault, the French local prefect of police. Blaine's confidant is African-American pianist/singer Sam, who had previously worked with Rick at his Paris venue. As Rick's friend, Sam is caught in the middle when Ilsa Lund—wife of freedom fighter Victor Laszlo—shows up in Casablanca begging Rick to provide her with the two letters of transit that he holds. During Rick and Ilsa's reunion (which eventually leads Blaine to become noble), both parties beg Sam to play/croon their song, "As Time Goes By." (Ironically Wilson could not play the piano, and his keyboard work had to be dubbed.)

At the time of release, most everyone was so caught up in the film's impressive love story, intermingled with wartime intrigue, that relatively little was made of Sam's near-equal status with Rick. Although Sam often called Blaine "boss," it was a reflection of the duo's fine working rapport, not their standing as pals. The film demonstrated that a black screen character did *not* always have to be the servant of the white master but could have a connection with the person of (near) equal footing. As such, *Casablanca*, which won Oscars for Best Director, Best Picture, and Best Screenplay (and earned five other Academy Award nominations), was a milestone in the history of African-American integration on camera.

In the 1955–56 TV series of *Casablanca*, CLARENCE MUSE played Sam to Charles McGraw's Rick. In the 1983 *Casablanca* TV show, Scatman Crothers was Sam to David Soul's Rick.

***Change of Mind* (1969)** Cinerama Releasing, color, 103 minutes. **Director:** Robert Stevens; **Screenplay:** Seeleg Lester and Dick Wesson; **Cast:** Raymond St. Jacques (David Rowe), Susan Oliver (Margaret Rowe), Janet MacLachlan (Elizabeth Dickson), Leslie Nielsen (Sheriff Webb).

This exploitation entry gained currency when released because of a growing interest—due to civil-rights legislation, ethnic rioting, and so on—in the United States about the world of African Americans. *Change of Mind's* gimmick was really similar to that employed in *Gentleman's Agreement*, the 1947 movie in which gentile reporter Gregory Peck passed for Jewish and "experienced" anti-Semitism. It was a safe way of handling a potentially explosive bigotry issue in post-

World War II America because the hero was really part of mainstream America.

In *Change of Mind*, a respected Caucasian district attorney, David Rowe, is dying of cancer. His brain is transplanted into the body of a recently deceased black man. Even when he can legitimize that he is *still* David Rowe but in a new body, his wife (Oliver), his professional associates, and others cannot adjust to his new skin color. Rowe finds temporary comfort with the widow (MacLachlan) of the person whose body he now inhabits, but even she—understandably—is uneasy dealing with him. Eventually, disgusted with the prejudice surrounding him, Rowe leaves town.

Less responsible than the earlier *BLACK LIKE ME* (1964), *Change of Mind* was only a few degrees better than the tasteless *The Thing with Two Heads* (1972) in which a dying racist (Ray Milland) had his head grafted onto the body of another—which turned out ironically to be that of a burly black man (Rosey Grier).

***Check and Double Check* (1930)** RKO, b&w, 71 minutes. **Director:** Melville Brown; **Screenplay:** J. Walter Ruben; **Cast:** Freeman F. Gosden (Amos), Charles J. Correll (Andy), Sue Carol (Jean Blair), Irene Rich (Mrs. Blair), Ralf Harold (Ralph Crawford), Russ Powell (Kingfish), Roscoe Ates (Brother Arthur), Duke Ellington and His Cotton Club Orchestra (themselves).

When the hugely popular radio show *AMOS 'N' ANDY* was transferred to the screen, its two white costars donned BLACKFACE to interpret their parts as co-owners of the Freshair Taxicab Company. Portions of the film's pedestrian plot are devoted to the two Harlem men spending a night in a haunted house to fulfill a task for their lodge. More of the story line, however, focuses on the trite quandary of Caucasian debutante Jean Blair, who must choose between two white suitors—one rich, the other not. Obviously, the studio wanted to cash in on radio's well-liked *Amos 'n' Andy* but hesitated to devote too much screen footage to ethnic minority figures as that would disinterest mainstream filmgoers.

The *Motion Picture News* reported (October 4, 1930) of this crudely constructed comedy: "In only one scene are the two classes [i.e., blacks and whites] shown together, and then with no familiarity. Southern cities, where racial feelings may be pronounced, will find nothing in the picture to cause objection."

In addition to largely positive reviews, *Check and Double Check* earned a $260,000 profit. In 1934 Gosden and Correll provided the voices for a series of animated shorts based on their famed radio characters. After two entries, RKO dropped the property.

***City of Angels* (2000)** CBS-TV series, color, 60 minutes. **Cast:** Blair Underwood (Dr. Ben Turner), Michael Warren (Ron Harris), Hill Harper (Dr. Wesley Williams), Vivica A. Fox (Dr. Lillian Price), Phil Buckman (Dr. Geoffrey Weiss), T. E. Russell (Dr. Arthur Jackson).

Blair Underwood as the lead physician in the TV medical drama *City of Angels* (2000). (ECHO BOOK SHOP)

This was another creation from the TV production factory of industry veteran Steven Bochco (*Hill Street Blues*, *L. A. Law*, *NYPD Blue*). The gimmick of this standard medical series was to feature a predominantly black cast in all levels of hospital health care from administrator (Warren), to hotshot surgeon (Underwood) to young resident (Harper); it included female medical personnel (Fox). That said, there was nothing to distinguish this entry from more established genre pieces like *ER* (1994–), which already had cornered the market in viewership. Adding to the problems of this offering was that its ethnic cast (especially Underwood and Fox) took their soap opera–type roles far too seriously. Even with cast changes in its fall 2000 second season, the show proved too weak and was off the air before year's end.

Clansman, The See *BIRTH OF A NATION, THE.*

***Claudine* (1974)** Twentieth Century-Fox, color, 92 minutes. **Director:** John Berry; **Screenplay:** Tina Pine and

Lester Pine; **Cast:** Diahann Carroll (Claudine), James Earl Jones (Roop), Lawrence Hilton-Jacobs (Charles), Tamu (Charlene), David Kruger (Paul), Yvette Curtis (Patrice).

If *Claudine*'s plot line had been performed by a white cast, it would have been just another big-screen romantic comedy using a hackneyed sitcom plot. However, as delivered by JONES, CARROLL, and her six on-camera kids, the movie emerged as a revealing study of a contemporary African-American woman coping with unemployment, single parenthood, and the desire for a fulfilling love life. It was a refreshing change from the 1970s BLACK ACTION FILMS and ethnic minority message pictures.

Harlem-based Claudine keeps her household together with part-time work as a domestic and welfare. When she meets an unlikely suitor—hulking, jovial sanitation worker Roop—her hip, street-smart offspring are suspicious that he will disappoint their mom. As Claudine and Roop struggle toward mutual commitment, she copes with her militant son Charles while daughter Charlene encounters the pain of romantic love.

Rather than relying on heavy drama to explicate the characters and move on the plot, *Claudine* used (slapstick) comedy. Despite the often contrived nature of the humor, it worked, and, along with the well-etched lead performances (especially by Carroll), this ghetto story proved to be entertaining. Carroll was Oscar nominated as Best Actress.

***Cleopatra Jones* (1973)** Warner Bros., color, 89 minutes. **Director:** Jack Starrett; **Screenplay:** Max Julien; **Cast:** Tamara Dobson (Cleopatra Jones), Bernie Casey (Reuben Masters), Shelley Winters (Mommy), Brenda Sykes (Tiffany), Antonio Fargas (Doodlebug), Bill McKinney (Officer Purdy).

Along with PAM GRIER, ex-model Dobson proved to be the other powerhouse female star of 1970s Hollywood BLACK ACTION FILMS. Tall (six feet, two inches), slinky, and aggressive with her karate kicks, Dobson was an ideal choice to play this ultimate African-American fantasy heroine. As a narcotics agent for the CIA, her mission is to clean up the ghettos and save the children from substance abuse and the crime it engenders. Thus when crooked cops raid the halfway house run by Cleopatra's boyfriend (Casey), she flies back to Los Angeles to put matters right. She comes up against Mommy, the vicious Caucasian lesbian who operates a drug-pushing organization.

Not only did *Cleopatra Jones* showcase a memorable new action heroine, but it also presented a chaotic world in which men were meek or disloyal or corrupt or bigoted (or all of the above). At the top of the power heap—on opposite sides of the law—were self-sufficient Cleopatra and her arch foe, the butch (and campy) master criminal Mommy. Their final tussle in a junkyard was a delicious sight. (Most of the film's stunts were performed by Ernest Robinson and the Black Stuntmen's Association.) The finale had the black heroine emerging victorious over the white villain.

Cleopatra Jones earned a solid $3.25 million in domestic film rentals, and its soundtrack album by J. J. Johnson sold more than 500,000 copies. The movie's success led to the less-satisfying *Cleopatra Jones and the Casino of Gold* (1975), which also featured the striking Dobson.

Coleman, Gary (1968–) As a result of a severe kidney ailment, he grew no taller than three feet, eight inches for much of his childhood. It enabled him to remain cast as a precocious youngster on the hit TV comedy series *DIFF'RENT STROKES* (1978–86) well into his teens. The situation was great for his then thriving show business career but had repercussions on his complex private life. Coleman's enormous popularity led to the brief rise of another diminutive African-American child star, Emmanuel Lewis, on the TV sitcom *WEBSTER* (1983–87).

Coleman was born in Zion, Illinois. By 1973 he had had his first kidney transplant (his second came in 1984). Appearances in local TV commercials in the mid-1970s impressed TV-series creator Norman Lear, who wanted him to star in a TV version of *The Little Rascals*, a series that never came to be. Instead, Lear packaged the sitcom *Diff'rent Strokes*, which made Gary a star, along with his castmates (the black Todd Bridges and the white Dana Plato). To expand his image beyond his TV character, Gary starred in such telefeatures as *The Kid with the Broken Halo* (1982) and *Playing with Fire* (1985), the last a serious study of a young pyromaniac crying for love.

With the end of *Diff'rent Strokes*, the now adult Coleman, at four feet, eight inches, kept leaving and returning to show business, mostly in cameos or talk-show appearances. There

Conrad Bain (left) and Gary Coleman—two of the stars of the TV sitcom *Diff'rent Strokes* (1978–86). (JC ARCHIVES)

was a nasty lawsuit against his parents for alleged misappropriation of his trust fund and a long-running court battle with a fan whose desire for Coleman's autograph led to a reported altercation between the two.

***Color Purple, The* (1985)** Warner Bros., color, 152 minutes. **Director:** Steven Spielberg; **Screenplay:** Menno Meyjes; **Cast:** Danny Glover (Albert), Whoopi Goldberg (Celie), Margaret Avery (Shug Avery), Oprah Winfrey (Sofia), Willard Pugh (Harpo), Akosua Busia (Nettie), Adolph Caesar (Old Mister), Rae Dawn Chong (Squeak), Desreta Jackson (Young Celie), Larry [Laurence] Fishburne (Swain).

Alice Walker's 1982 novel *The Color Purple* won the Pulitzer Prize and nearly unanimous acclaim from critics and the public. In contrast, the film adaptation was highly controversial from the day it was announced that Jewish, Caucasian Spielberg—rather than a filmmaker of color—had dared to acquire the screen rights to this acclaimed narrative of African Americans in the South from the 1900s to the 1940s. When the picture was completed, the NAACP and other PRESSURE GROUPS lambasted the movie version as racist for its one-dimensional negative presentation of African-American men, with no male character emerging as a positive figure. The detractors also felt that the movie (naïvely) depicted its African-American figures as caricatures (as in *SONG OF THE SOUTH*, 1946) who scamper through a fantasy landscape that was completely unlike the real South of the period. The nationwide maelstrom continued when *The Color Purple* was nominated for eleven Oscars (including GOLDBERG for Best Actress, WINFREY and Avery for Best Supporting Actress, and the film for Best Picture). Later, the Academy Award festivities in March 1986 in Los Angeles were picketed by the movie's detractors. (*The Color Purple* did *not* win a single Oscar.)

In the deep South of the 1900s, young Celie is twice impregnated by her stepfather. Her children are given away for adoption, and Celie is made to marry the much older Albert (known as Mr.). Because Albert covets Celie's sister Nettie despite her rejection, he persuades Celie's stepfather to separate the two sisters. Years pass and Celie never hears from Nettie because Mr. has hidden all the letters Nettie sent from Africa, where she is a missionary and is bringing up Celie's offspring. By getting to know Mr.'s mistress, the sensitive singer Shug, Celie comes out of her shell. She asserts herself and breaks away from Mr. Meanwhile, Nettie returns from Africa with Celie's children, and the two sisters have a joyous reunion.

In *The Color Purple*, film newcomers Goldberg and Winfrey (as the spunky wife of Mr.'s son) provide sterling characterizations of women who deal differently with the chaos of their punishing lives. On the other hand, the picture was criticized for many alleged faults, including veering from the popular novel (i.e., deleting Celie's lesbian relationship with Shug, and making the character of Mr. undergo only mild changes) as well as sugar-coated characterizations, situations, and settings.

Despite being the white establishment's fantasy of the old South, *The Color Purple* drew in moviegoers. Made on a $15 million budget, it earned almost $50 million in domestic film rentals.

combat dramas—feature films and television Although some blacks had participated with the colonists during the American Revolutionary War fought against England, they were not depicted as having done so on the Hollywood screen until Mel Gibson's *The Patriot* (2000). Likewise, African Americans had fought for both the North and (ironically) the South during the Civil War. However, this point was not registered effectively on screen in such entries as *THE BIRTH OF A NATION* (1915), *So Red the Rose* (1935), *GONE WITH THE WIND* (1939), and *North and South, Book II* (1986—TV miniseries). It remained for *GLORY* (1989) to make that fact clear to moviegoers, as did such later productions as the lengthy *Gettysburg* (1993).

The lack of black characters in World War I dramas made by American moviemakers about the fight against the Germans reflected a general reality. However, there were many African-American troops in the Second World War, though still generally segregated from the white soldiers. This truth was casually reflected in such World War II-era film fare as *Bataan* (1943), where the character played by black actor Kenneth Spencer was part of the valiant group of Americans caught in a losing campaign against the Japanese. Later, *HOME OF THE BRAVE* (1949) showed James Edwards's character not only as part of the fighting force but also as suffering from the pressure of racial prejudice. *RED BALL EXPRESS* (1952) featured SIDNEY POITIER as a member of an army transportation corps that had several black participants. JIM BROWN was among *The Dirty Dozen* (1967) and part of the *Pacific Inferno* (1979), doing World War II duty. The TV movie *CARTER'S ARMY* (1969) depicted a group of black soldiers fighting in the European theater of war, while the made-for-cable feature *The Tuskegee Airmen* (1995) was a strong presentation of black American pilots doing their patriotic duty against the Axis. By the time of *Pearl Harbor* (2001), it was considered essential (for political correctness) to have a few black characters in noteworthy military roles (e.g., the part played by Cuba Gooding Jr.). *Hart's War* (2002) encompassed discrimination against blacks among allied prisoners at a Nazi POW camp. Conversely, most of the few TV series (e.g., *Combat Sergeant*, 1956; *Combat!* 1962–67; *McHale's Navy*, 1962–66; *Baa Baa Black Sheep*, 1976–78) devoted to World War II exploits did not highlight black characters. A rarity was *Roll Out* (1973–74), which dealt with the same transportation unit that was featured in the movie *RED BALL EXPRESS*.

America's participation in the Korean War of the early 1950s was covered in several dramas of the time (e.g., *The Bridges at Toko-Ri* and *Men of the Fighting Lady*, both 1954), but it was not until Alan Ladd's *All the Young Men* (1961) that a black trooper (played by Poitier) was depicted in any meaningful way.

By the time of the Vietnam War in the later 1960s and early 1970s, Hollywood had become more integrated, and ethnic minority figures played a greater part in the proceedings (e.g., *The Green Berets*, 1968; *Apocalypse Now*, 1979; *A Rumor of War*, 1980—TV movie; *Platoon*, 1986; *Good Morning, Vietnam*, 1987; *We Were Soldiers*, 2002). The few TV series (e.g., *Tour of Duty*, 1987–90; *China Beach*, 1988–91) devoted to the unpopular Vietnam War featured "representative" black characters.

When America went to war with Iraq over its invasion of Kuwait in 1991, U.S.-made features (e.g., *The Heroes of Desert Storm*, 1992—TV movie; *Courage Under Fire*, 1996; *Three Kings*, 1999) that dealt with those strike forces included black characters as major participants, reflecting the reality of the combat situation.

comedies—feature films In the early silent film era when most major black character roles were played by whites in blackface, African Americans were a rarity on screen, let alone in leading comic roles. Famous vaudeville/stage star Bert Williams was an exception, making such silent shorts as *Darktown Jubilee* (1914) and *Natural Born Gambler* (1916). By the 1920s black performers—if they were children—had found a small place in the realm of silent-film comedy series. Ernest Frederick Morrison (aka "Sunshine Sammy" Morrison) so impressed comedy filmmaker Hal Roach that he signed the boy to a two-year contract in 1919, one of the first long-term agreements ever made for a black performer in burgeoning Hollywood. Morrison had his own series *(The Pickaninny)* in 1921 and was an original member of the Our Gang comedy shorts, which began in 1922. When he left the ongoing series—which ran well into the 1940s—he was followed by such other young black talent as Allen Clayton Hoskins Jr. (as Farina), Matthew Beard Jr. (as Stymie), and William Thomas Jr. (as Buckwheat).

By the late 1920s when talkies had come into their own, black performers increasingly were used not only to fulfill the need for on-camera domestics but also to provide comedy relief, thereby reinforcing demeaning, negative stereotypes. By the early 1930s such performers as STEPIN FETCHIT, Willie Best, HATTIE McDANIEL, LOUISE BEAVERS, and later EDDIE "ROCHESTER" ANDERSON were frequently on hand as servants to provide "humor" to the main story about white characters. During the 1940s African-American MANTAN MORELAND, who had played comedic roles in both Hollywood mainstream productions and "race" movies made for black audiences, took on the role of Birmingham Brown, the superstitious, garrulous chauffeur in the Charlie Chan movie series while continuing to perform in all-black films (e.g., *Mantan Messes Up*, 1946).

By the 1950s it was a rarity to have a sassy black maid character on the big screen, an exception being Pearl Bailey in Bob Hope's *THAT CERTAIN FEELING* (1956). The same held true in the 1960s where, although the era of the wise-mouthed black domestic had finally passed, there were occasional black figures used for comedy relief or satire (e.g., *The Busy Body*, 1967; *Putney Swope*, 1969).

As BLACK ACTION FILMS became a major part of the American film industry in the early 1970s there arose black-themed comedies, often with a (nearly) all-black cast: *COTTON COMES TO HARLEM* (1970), *UPTOWN SATURDAY NIGHT* (1974), *CAR WASH* (1976), *NORMAN . . . IS THAT YOU?* (1976), *California Suite* (1978). African Americans in these entries included RICHARD PRYOR, BILL COSBY, and REDD FOXX. In another avenue, reminiscent of the 1930s and 1940s movies made for the black cinema circuit, highly ethnic comedies played almost exclusively in black neighborhoods (e.g., Rudy Ray Moore in *Dolemite*, 1975).

Although performers such as Pryor continued as major players in black-themed Hollywood comedies of the 1980s, the arrival of TV comedian EDDIE MURPHY marked the decade with a series of highly successful features, all containing strong comedic ingredients: *TRADING PLACES* (1983), *BEVERLY HILLS COP* (1984), *Eddie Murphy Raw* (1987), and *Coming to America* (1988). Occasionally there was a black-themed satire (e.g., *HOLLYWOOD SHUFFLE*, 1987) or an entry that had blacks poking fun at the bygone blaxploitation pictures (e.g., *I'm Gonna Git You Sucka*, 1988).

In the 1990s a new crowd of African-American comedians emerged on the Hollywood scene, often in highly ethnic comedies that were geared for mainstream audiences: Christopher Reid's *House Party* (1990) and its several sequels; MARTIN LAWRENCE with *You So Crazy* (1994—his stand-up comedy act); and such comedies as *Nothing to Lose* (1997), *Blue Streak* (1999), *Big Momma's House* (2000), and *Black Knight* (2001); WHOOPI GOLDBERG in *SISTER ACT* (1992) and its 1993 sequel, plus *Call Me Claus* (2001, TV movie); Damon Wayans in *Mo' Money* (1992), *Major Payne* (1995), *Goosed* (1999), *BAMBOOZLED* (2000), and *Marci X* (2003); Chris Tucker in *Friday* (1995), *RUSH HOUR* (1998), *Rush Hour 2* (2001), and *Mr. President* (2002); Jamie Foxx in *Booty Call* (1997), CHRIS ROCK in *Down to Earth* and *Pootie Tang* (both 2001); Marlon and Shawn Wayans in *Scary Movie* (2000) and *Scary Movie 2* (2001); and the revitalization of Murphy's career with such funny entries as *The Nutty Professor* (1996), *Doctor Dolittle* (1998), and *Doctor Dolittle 2* (2001). Another success was SPIKE LEE'S concert film of *THE ORIGINAL KINGS OF COMEDY* (2000), featuring four black comedians. One of the more offbeat new comedic entries was *Punks* (2001), which the *Los Angeles Times* (November 16, 2001) labeled "a groundbreaking black gay male romantic comedy. . . ."

comedy series—television See SITUATION COMEDY SERIES—TELEVISION.

***Conrack* (1974)** Twentieth Century-Fox, color, 107 minutes. **Director:** Martin Ritt; **Screenplay:** Irving Ravetch and Harriet Frank Jr.; **Cast:** Jon Voight (Pat Conroy), Paul Winfield (Mad Billy), Hume Cronyn (Skeffington), Madge Sinclair (Mrs. Scott), Tina Andrews (Mary), Antonio Fargas (Quickfellow).

Based on Pat Conroy's 1972 book *(The Water Is Wide)* of his actual experiences, *Conrack* follows the life of an idealistic young schoolteacher (Voight) who takes a post on a small island off the South Carolina coast, where the African-American children have been deprived of an education. Using every conceivable commonsense method he can think of, the teacher whom his pupils call "Conrack" (they mispronounce his name, strives to enlighten these underprivileged youths. Not only must he break through their barrier of illiteracy (and in some cases mental retardation), but he is also opposed continuously by the snobbish white school superintendent (Cronyn) and the arrogant black principal (Sinclair). (A subplot has Conroy dealing with Mad Billy, the island's hermit.) In the film's ironic ending, hardly has Conroy succeeded with his classroom charges than he is fired from his position.

Despite its overabundance of winning optimism and earnestness *Conrack* suffers from too much white righteousness as the liberal Caucasian teacher tends munificently to the African-American unfortunates. For more sensitive viewers, this sapped the well-intentioned picture of some of its strength.

***Cooley High* (1975)** American International, color, 107 minutes. **Director:** Michael Schultz; **Screenplay:** Eric Monte; **Cast:** Glynn Turman (Preach), Lawrence-Hilton Jacobs (Cochise), Garrett Morris (Mr. Mason), Cynthia Davis (Brenda), Corin Rogers (Pooter), Maurice Leon Havis (Willie).

Just as *American Graffiti* (1973) so aptly explored the world of white high school students, so *Cooley High* focused on African-American teenagers who experience good and bad times as they cope with emerging adulthood. (The picture was scripted by Monte who had created the Chicago-set sitcom, GOOD TIMES, 1974–79.)

In 1964 Chicago three pals (Turman, Rogers, and Jacobs) skip school one Friday. They visit the zoo, play basketball, flirt with girls, get into a brawl, and take a joyride in a stolen car. Thereafter, two of the group are nearly arrested for auto theft but one of their teachers (Morris) intervenes. Later, after Cochise is beaten to death. Preach goes to the funeral, privately reading a farewell poem he has composed.

To provide period flavor and give the narrative more momentum, the film's soundtrack used a series of Motown Records hits. The well-regarded feature, with dimensional characters that appealed to filmgoers of different backgrounds, earned $2.6 million in domestic film rentals. *Cooley High* served as inspiration for the TV sitcom WHAT'S HAPPENING!! (1976–79).

***Cool World, The* (1963)** Cinema 5, b&w, 1963. **Director/Screenplay:** Shirley Clarke; **Cast:** Hampton Clayton (Richard "Duke" Custis), Yolanda Rodriguez (LuAnne), Bostic Felton (Rod), Gary Bolling (Littleman), Carl Lee (Priest), Gloria Foster (Mrs. Curtis), Georgia Burke (grandma), Clarence Williams III (Blood).

Well-respected cinema vérité director Clarke turned to the urban ghetto in this controlled, nonexploitive film. As source material, she utilized Warren Miller's 1959 novel and the 1960 Broadway play adaptation by Miller and Robert Rossen.

This semidocumentary focuses on Duke Custis, an African-American teen struggling to survive in the rough world of Harlem with his life-weary mother (Foster) and grandma (Burke). Duke's local role model is Priest, who has become a hoodlum. Duke feels he needs a gun to prove that he can be the leader of his local gang, the Royal Pythons. His romance with LuAnne, the gang's whore, dissipates and a scuffle with a rival group leads to his knifing one of the enemy. Retreating to his family's apartment, he is captured by brutal law enforcers.

Variety (September 11, 1963) championed the movie as a "telling look at Harlem and probably one of the least patronizing films ever made on Negro life." Other sources thought the filmmaker was trying to present too big a canvas in her celluloid depiction of the Harlem ghetto. Nonetheless, this sturdy drama contained a haunting portrayal of a life-scarred, downtrodden youth searching for meaning in his seemingly futile existence.

***Coonskin* (aka: *Street Fight*) (1975)** Bryanston, color, 82 minutes. **Director/Screenplay:** Ralph Bakshi; **Cast:** Barry White (Samson/Brother Bear), Charles Gordone (Preacher/Brother Fox), Scatman Crothers (Pappy/Old Man Bone), Philip [Michael] Thomas (Randy/Brother Rabbit).

One of the most controversial films of the mid-1970s, this R-rated, part live action, part animation feature—a satire of the Walt Disney film SONG OF THE SOUTH (1946)—was made by the Jewish, Brooklyn-born Bakshi who had previously helmed such raunchy R-rated cartoon features as *Fritz the Cat* (1971) and *Heavy Traffic* (1973).

Coonskin was completed in 1974 but, after a screening, CORE (Congress of Racial Equality) denounced the movie as racist and insulting, suggesting that the film presented African Americans as slaves, hustlers, whores, and so on. The movie's distributor (Paramount) withdrew, and it was several months before *Coonskin* found release through an independent company. Some reviewers were impressed with Bakshi's depiction of Harlem life. Other critics found that while the film mildly stereotyped blacks, it was much more clichéd in dealing with white women and gays. Still others noted that the animation medium caused a heightened use of stereotypes—that characters emerge unsubtly without the possibility of softening human touches that a live-action production allows.

One night, Pappy and Randy, two African Americans in a Southern prison, wait in the exercise yard for an escape car to arrive. To make the time pass more quickly, Pappy tells his confederate a fable, a modernizing of Uncle Remus tales. It involves a hip rabbit, a bewildered bear, and a weak-willed fox who head north. In Harlem they overcome Mafia figures and crooked cops and end by taking over the uptown rackets. During the course of their adventures, they encounter a bigoted white Southern sheriff, an African-American garbage picker, the drag-queen son of the New York godfather, and the voluptuous "Miss America," a sinister blonde who lures several African-American men to their doom.

***Cornbread, Earl and Me* (1975)** American International, color, 94 minutes. **Director:** Joe Manduke; **Screenplay:** Leonard Lamensdorf; **Cast:** Moses Gunn (Ben Blackwell), Rosalind Cash (Sarah Robinson), Bernie Casey (Atkins), Madge Sinclair (Leona), Keith Wilkes (Cornbread), Tierre Turner (Earl), Antonio Fargas (One Eye), Larry [Laurence] Fishburne III (Wilford Robinson).

This impressive 1970s URBAN DRAMA seethes with the frustration of ghetto life, but it also presents an even-handed depiction of African Americans coping with the white man's system. Ironically, that objectivity robbed the grim film of some of its dramatic heat, defusing various characters' anger and/or bigotry.

Two weeks before an earnest ghetto youth (Wilkes) is to start college on a basketball scholarship, he is shot dead in error by two policemen (one white, one black). The dead teen's mother (Leona) wants to clear her son's name. The one witness to the mishap is young Wilford, who is traumatized by the tragedy. Leona persuades attorney Ben Blackwell to represent her/the dead boy at the police-department inquest. Urged on by his mother (Cash), Wilford takes the witness stand and tells the true facts of the shooting.

This well-acted PG-rated feature, based on the book *Hog Butcher* (1966) by Ronald L. Fair, earned about $2 million in domestic film rentals.

Cosby, Bill (1937–) An enormously successful stand-up comic, comedy album headliner, TV series star, and author, Cosby did a great deal to break down racial barriers in the American entertainment field. As costar of the television series *I SPY* (1965–68), he was the first African American to star with a Caucasian actor on a weekly network show. Two decades later, he made his mark again, this time with his sitcom *THE COSBY SHOW* (1984–92). On the hit series he depicted a rarity on American television—a professional black man and his family living an upscale life. Meanwhile, as a performer, Cosby won several Emmy Awards for his unique contributions to the medium.

He was born William Henry Cosby Jr. in Philadelphia, the oldest of four boys. The family struggled financially, especially because of his father's drinking. When Cosby was ten, his dad disappeared altogether. Besides the constant economic struggle, the youngster—who had to supervise his three younger siblings while his mother worked—also had to deal with racial discrimination at school. Later, to escape his environment, he joined the navy. Thereafter, he continued his education, winning an athletic scholarship to Philadelphia's Temple University.

During his sophomore college year, Cosby worked part time as a bartender and discovered he had a gift for joke telling and mimicry that led to his performance debut at the club where he worked. By 1962, he was being featured at comedy venues in Greenwich Village and chose to quit college. Within the next few years his reputation as a comedian rose, and during a Los Angeles gig he met a TV producer who thought he would be right for an upcoming adventure/espionage series. Cosby auditioned for *I Spy* and won the part of Rhodes scholar Alexander Scott who travels the globe as the trainer for a tennis player (played by Robert Culp), the duo working undercover for the U.S. government.

When *I Spy* went off the air, Cosby returned to club work, recorded several popular comedy albums, and did more TV series (this time sitcom, variety formats, and children's programming). He made his feature film debut in the western *Man and Boy* (1972), but his greatest success on the big screen came when he teamed with SIDNEY POITIER for several comedies: *UPTOWN SATURDAY NIGHT* (1974), *Let's Do It Again* (1975), and *A PIECE OF THE ACTION* (1977). Cosby also starred in one-man comedy shows both in concerts and films (e.g., *Bill Cosby: Himself*, 1982).

By the early 1980s there was a new guard of hip young black comedians—especially RICHARD PRYOR and EDDIE MURPHY—and the older Cosby found himself better known to TV viewers as a product spokesman than as a cutting-edge performer. That changed with the hit *Cosby Show*, from which entrepreneur Cosby spun off another successful TV sitcom, *A Different World* (1987–93). Less successful, however, were his 1992–93 revival of the classic TV game show *You Bet Your Life* and his sleuthing series *The Cosby Mysteries* (1994–95). He did far better with a new TV comedy project, *Cosby* (1996–2000), this time playing a cantankerous, retired blue-collar worker who is always getting himself and his family into scrapes. By now the star was listed in *Forbes* magazine as one of the richest Americans, with a net worth of well over $300 million. In 2002, he starred in *The Cosby Reunion*, a TV movie reuniting his sitcom family from the 1980s.

Besides his trio of Emmy Awards for *I Spy*, Cosby earned two Golden Globes for *The Cosby Show* and received many other professional accolades.

***Cosby Show, The* (1984–1992)** NBC-TV series, color, 30 minutes. **Cast:** Bill Cosby (Dr. Heathcliff "Cliff" Huxtable), Phylicia Rashad (Clair Huxtable), Sabrina Le Beauf (Sondra Huxtable Tibideaux), Lisa Bonet (Denise Huxtable Kendall: 1984–91), Malcolm-Jamal Warner (Theodore Huxtable), Tempestt Bledsoe (Vanessa Huxtable), Keshia Knight Pulliam (Rudy Huxtable).

Veteran stand-up comic/actor COSBY struck pay dirt with this beloved TV sitcom, that focused on a black household and was uniquely different from what had been seen previously in the medium. Rather than a stereotypical single black parent scraping by in the projects, this on-camera African-American couple was upscale and professional (he an obstetrician/gynecologist; she an attorney). At college age, each of their children went on to higher learning. Having full creative control of the series, Cosby utilized the child-rearing and educational principals he had absorbed when acquiring his doctorate (in education) in the 1970s.

Top row: Tempestt Bledsoe, Malcolm-Jamal Warner, and Phylicia Rashad; bottom row: Lisa Bonet, Keshia Knight Pulliam, Bill Cosby, and Sabrina Le Beauf make up the TV family in the sitcom *The Cosby Show* (1984–92). (JC ARCHIVES)

The show's novelty and the warm family-oriented episodes (mostly eschewing the usual sitcom situations) appealed to many. However, there were commentators and viewers who argued that the program was unrealistic in its glorified presentation of a "typical" black (supposedly middle-class) household. Such sources also noted the relative lack of interaction between blacks and whites on the program. (One of the few Caucasian characters on the show was Peter Costa, cast as Rudy's little classmate.) *The Cosby Show* was nominated for and won several Emmys over its long run.

In decided contrast was the far more conventional *Cosby* (1996–2000), which reunited the star with his sitcom colead Phylicia Rashad. In the new, far less successful series, he is a cranky, unemployed New Yorker who had worked for an airline for decades. His wife and her best friend (played by white actress Madeline Kahn) run a business together in their Queens neighborhood. (The show was based on the British TV series *One Foot in the Grave.)*

***Cotton Comes to Harlem* (1970)** United Artists, color, 97 minutes. **Director:** Ossie Davis; **Screenplay:** Davis and Arnold Perl; **Cast:** Raymond St. Jacques (Coffin Ed Johnson), Godfrey Cambridge (Grave Digger Jones), Calvin Lockhart (Rev. Deke O'Malley), Judy Pace (Iris), Redd Foxx (Uncle Bud), Frederick O'Neal (Casper), Cleavon Little (Lo Boy).

Based on Chester Himes's 1965 novel, this well-crafted feature was made by a mainstream Hollywood studio on a sizeable $2.2 million budget. It provided many firsts: the first of Himes's mystery novels to be filmed, celebrated actor DAVIS's bow as a motion picture director, and the first really successful BLACK ACTION FILM, earning a substantial $25.4 million in domestic film rentals. (The movie avoided any ghetto message directed at the white "Man.")

Unapologetically filled with stereotypes, this fanciful and zany entry deals with Harlem-based plainclothes cops Gravedigger Jones and Coffin Ed Johnson, who are pursuing the robbers of $87,000 that had been gathered by Rev. Deke O'Malley from locals for his "Back to Africa" boat. The unorthodox law enforcers think that O'Malley is responsible for the heist and has the money; O'Malley is convinced that his white partner (J. D. Cannon) is the culprit and has the cash. In actuality, as the police partners learn, the stolen money fell off the robbers' getaway truck and was found by old junk dealer Uncle Bud, who spends it on himself. Wanting to make things right for the Harlem community, Jones and Johnson blackmail a downtown Mafia chieftain into replacing O'Malley's funds.

The film so successfully mixed the comedy and crime genres—and in the milieu of an ethnic minority—that two years later came the sequel *Come Back, Charleston Blue* (1972) with St. Jacques and Cambridge repeating their characterizations. The characters of Grave Digger and Coffin Ed also turn up, in far lesser roles, in 1991's *A RAGE IN HARLEM*, based on another Himes novel.

crime, detective, and police drama—feature films Although black characters—usually individually—had been used to portray criminal wrongdoers (e.g., *NATIVE SON*, 1951) or juvenile delinquents (e.g., *THE BLACKBOARD JUNGLE*, 1955), only occasionally was a drama filled with groups of black lawbreakers (e.g., *Underworld*, 1937). With the advent of the 1970s BLACK ACTION FILM trend, this ethnic group was strongly and repeatedly displayed as participants in organized crimes: In such features as *SHAFT* (1971), *ACROSS 110TH STREET* (1972), *Shaft's Big Score!* (1972), *SUPERFLY* (1972), *Willie Dynamite* (1973), *Gordon's War* (1973), *The Black Godfather* (1974), *BUCKTOWN* (1975), and *The Avenging Godfather* (1979), African Americans were depicted as mobs themselves, often in conflict with other criminal organizations such as the white-controlled Mafia. After the blaxploitation movie craze fizzled, it was not until the 1990s that African Americans were noticeably featured again as organized crime lords (e.g., *The Return of Superfly*, 1990; *NEW JACK CITY*, 1991; *Sugar Hill*, 1993; *Hoodlum*, 1997; *Romeo Must Die*, 2000; and *SHAFT*, 2000).

In the detective drama, *Shaft* (1971) was among the first to have an African-American sleuth on the Hollywood screen. As part of the black action film cycle a slew of movies suddenly appeared about prowling black private eyes, including BILL COSBY in *Hickey and Boggs* (1972), Peter De Anda in *Cutter* (1972—TV movie), Yaphet Kotto in *Friday Foster* (1974), PAM GRIER in *Sheba, Baby* (1975), and FRED WILLIAMSON in *Death Journey* (1975). Williamson was so enamored of playing detective Jesse Crowder that he returned to this characterization several times thereafter (e.g., *No Way Back*, 1976; *Blind Rage*, 1978; *The Last Fight*, 1982). (Williamson went to Europe in the 1980s to make such American-set detective entries as *Black Cobra*, 1986, and *Black Cobra 2*, 1989.) In the telefeature *Cocaine and Blue Eyes* (1982), an unsold series pilot, O. J. SIMPSON was the gumshoe. DENZEL WASHINGTON evolved into a private eye in the period piece *Devil in a Blue Dress* (1995), based on a Walter Mosley novel (1990), the aborted start of an ongoing film series. In the 2000 remake of *Shaft*, SAMUEL L. JACKSON inherited the key role of hip sleuth John Shaft.

In police movies, SIDNEY POITIER as Philadelphia law enforcer Virgil Tibbs was drawn into a murder case in his Southern hometown for *IN THE HEAT OF THE NIGHT* (1967). (He replayed the character in *They Call Me MISTER Tibbs*, 1971, and *The Organization*, 1972.) JIM BROWN was a law enforcer in the Deep South in *. . . tick . . . tick . . . tick* (1970), and OSSIE DAVIS had a similar chore in a California town in *The Sheriff* (1971—TV movie), as did BILLY DEE WILLIAMS in *The Take* (1974). Two other memorable African-American law enforcers of the period were Coffin Ed Johnson and Grave Digger Jones (played respectively by Raymond St. Jacques and Godfrey Cambridge) in *COTTON COMES TO HARLEM* (1970). They repeated their roles in the screen adaptation of another Chester Himes novel in *Come Back, Charleston Blue* (1972).

The 1980s saw a backlash in Hollywood against the black action film vogue of the past decade; and EDDIE MURPHY broke through new barriers as a smart-mouthed cop in the huge box-office hit *BEVERLY HILLS COP* (1984), which led to two sequels (1987 and 1994). Later in the decade, Danny Glover co-starred in another cop-movie franchise, *LETHAL WEAPON* (1987), which had him as the straight man for the wild shenanigans in crime solving of his partner (played by Mel Gibson). This led to three follow-up entries (1989, 1992, and 1998). Meanwhile Lynn Whitfield was a federal law-enforcement agent in the telefeature *Johnnie Mae Gibson: FBI* (1986), Carl Weathers was the unorthodox Detroit law enforcer in *Action Jackson* (1988), and Denzel Washington investigated a childhood buddy in Jamaica in *The Mighty Quinn* (1989).

By the 1990s—except for the aforementioned movie franchises—having African Americans play police law enforcers at any level of authority was not a novelty, but generally they remained subordinate characters (e.g., the Coffin Ed and Grave Digger Jones characters in *A RAGE IN HARLEM*, 1991). Shaking up the genre stereotype in this decade was WHOOPI GOLDBERG as an off-the-wall cop in *Fatal Beauty* (1987) and in *The Player* (1992) where she stood out as the witty and observant investigator. On a far gentler note, she was a sympathetic detective in the drama *The Deep End of the Ocean* (1999). Another black star who made a specialty of law enforcers in the 1990s was Washington in *Ricochet* (1992), *Virtuosity* (1995), *Fallen* (1998), *The Siege* (1998), *The Bone Collector* (1999), and *Training Day* (2001, for which he won an Academy Award). LOUIS GOSSETT JR. starred as a postal inspector in the telefeature *The Inspectors* (1998) and its sequel *Inspectors 2: A Shred of Evidence* (2000).

crime, detective, and police series—television Most early TV police drama shows (e.g., *Naked City*, 1958–63; *The Untouchables*, 1959–63), when portraying organized crime, focused on the Mafia as the principle underworld organization. By the time television series became more integrated in the casting in the 1970s (e.g., *The Blue Knight*, 1975–76; *Delvecchio*, 1976–77), the mobs depicted were of several races. This holds true with more-recent entries *Law & Order* (1990–) and *NYPD Blue* (1993–).

In detective series, although *Mannix* (1967–75) featured a Caucasian as the lead detective, African-American Gail Fisher played his right-hand helper in the office. As black action films were exploding on screen, television tried a TV version (1973–74) of the movie *SHAFT* (1971), with RICHARD ROUNDTREE recreating his role of hip and cool New York City private eye John Shaft. However, the proceedings were so diluted from the gritty big-screen version that the series was unsuccessful. The gimmick in *Tenspeed and Brown Shoes* (1980) was that one of the coleads was a black ex-convict (played by Ben Vereen) who found legitimate employment as a detective, partnered with a straight-arrow white man (performed by Jeff Goldblum).

On the Hawaii-set *Magnum, P.I.* (1980–88), one of the helpers assisting Tom Selleck's lead character was T. C., the owner of a local helicopter service, played by black actor Roger E. Mosley. On the light-hearted *Tucker's Witch* (1982–83), the husband-and-wife detective agency employed a secretary (played by ALFRE WOODARD) who helped to a degree in their sleuthing capers. Another offbeat detective offering was *Double Dare* (1985), which featured BILLY DEE WILLIAMS as a thief-turned-undercover detective, doing assignments for the San Francisco Police. In the brief-running *Half Nelson* (1985) FRED WILLIAMSON ran a Beverly Hills private security/surveillance firm. On *Spencer: For Hire* (1985–88) the Boston private eye (played by Robert Urich) relied on his mysterious pal Hawk (played by Avery Brooks) to help him solve capers. (In 1989 Brooks had a spinoff series set in Washington, D.C., where he was again the tough hombre, settling scores and solving mysteries for clients, in *A Man Called Hawk*.) On *Outlaws* (1986–87) Roundtree was one of the 1890s Texas outlaws catapulted in time to present-day Texas, where he and his cohorts opened a detective agency. On *Matlock* (1986–95), starring Andy Griffith as an attorney in Atlanta, Georgia, among his support staff to solve capers on behalf of their clients was Tyler Hudson (played by black actor Kene Holliday), who was the office legman from 1986 to 1989. He was replaced by another black legman (played by Clarence Gilyard Jr.) from 1989 to 1993 and thereafter by a white character. MR. T turned up as a well-dressed private detective in *T and T* (1988–90). Mario Van Peebles operated his detective agency out of a phone booth, and his expertise was being a master of disguise in *Sonny Spoon* (1988).

In the 1990s, *South Beach* (1993) featured a Miami, Florida, detective agency for which Jamaican Eagle-Eye Cherry (played by Vernon Charday) was a legman. Also, there was *Diagnosis: Murder* (1993–) in which black actress Victoria Rowell was always helping a fellow physician (played by Dick Van Dyke) solve crimes. LOUIS GOSSETT JR. was a restaurant owner moonlighting as a PI in the 1994 TV movie *Ray Alexander: A Menu for Murder.* He was a different type of sleuth—a U.S. postal investigator—in the made-for-cable movies *The Inspectors* (1998) and *Inspectors 2: A Shred of Evidence* (2000). On *Baywatch Nights* (1995–97) Gregory Alan-Williams was partnered in a detective agency run by David Hasselhoff (in a continuation of his Mitch Bucannon characterization from *Baywatch*). *Total Security* (1997) was another teleseries about a high-tech surveillance/security firm that had an African-American member, Neville Watson (played by Flex), on the Los Angeles-based squad.

As for police series, one of the earliest to feature a black performer (i.e., Don Mitchell) as a regular cast member was *Ironside* (1967–75) starring Raymond Burr. On *THE MOD SQUAD* (1968–73), Clarence Williams III was the African-American member of this undercover cop team. *The Rookies* (1972–75) featured Georg Stanford Brown as one of the young cops. *Get Christie Love!* (1974–75) boasted black actress Teresa Graves as a Los Angeles Police Department special unit cop. *Caribe* (1975) offered Carl Franklin playing a black cop with a white partner in Miami and the Caribbean. While he was not a policeman, Huggy Bear (played by Antonio Fargas) was the ever-helpful informant for the cops on *Starsky and Hutch* (1975–79). For the comedy *Barney Miller* (1975–82), Ron Glass played the black detective at the Greenwich Village precinct. On the sitcom *Carter Country* (1977–79), Kene Holliday played the black sergeant who worked for a bigoted white boss. JAMES EARL JONES was a police captain in *PARIS* (1979–80).

By the 1980s it was a matter of format and political correctness to have black members of the on-camera police department in TV series. Among the multicultural squad in *Hill Street Blues* (1981–87) was Michael Warren as Officer Bobby Hill. For the Manhattan-set *Cagney & Lacey* (1982–88), Carl Lumbly played African-American Detective Mark Petrie. For *Simon & Simon* (1981–88) Tim Reid was cast as Detective Marcel "Downtown" Brown (1983–87). On *MIAMI VICE* (1984–89), Philip Michael Thomas costarred as the black partner of a white detective (Don Johnson). Carl Weathers was ex-cop turned enforcer for a mayor on *Fortune Dane* (1986), while on *21 Jump Street* (1987–90) Holly Robinson was one of the youthful-looking undercover cops. On the gritty *The Street* (1988), set in New Jersey, Michael Beach was one of the rugged young cops. The character of Virgil Tibbs played by SIDNEY POITIER in 1967's *IN THE HEAT OF THE NIGHT* and two follow-up pictures was revived by HOWARD E. ROLLINS JR. in the TV series version, which starred Carroll O'Connor and ran from 1988 to 1994. Rollins left the show in 1993 and was replaced by a new police character played by Carl Weathers.

In the 1990s and thereafter most every police series featured African-American characters, often in a position of authority. Among such entries were *Nasty Boys* (1990), *Law & Order* (1990–), *Silk Stalkings* (1991–93; 1993–99), *Sirens* (1993), *NYPD Blue* (1993–), *HOMICIDE: LIFE ON THE STREET* (1993–99), *New York Undercover* (1994–98), *The Cosby Mysteries* (1994–95), *Law & Order: Special Victims Unit* (1999–), *The District* (2000–), *The Division* (2001–), *The Job* (2001–2), *Law & Order: Criminal Intent* (2001–), *UC Undercover* (2001–2), and *The Shield* (2002–).

***Cry, the Beloved Country* (1995)** Miramax, color, 111 minutes. **Director:** Darrell James Roodt; **Screenplay:** Ronald Harwood; **Cast:** James Earl Jones (Rev. Stephen Kumalo), Richard Harris (James Jarvis), Charles S. Dutton (John Kumalo), Vusi Kunene (Priest Msimangu), Leleti Kumalo (Katie), Dambisa Kente (Gertrude Kumalo), Eric Miyeni (Absalom Kumalo).

Alan Paton's powerful and dramatic 1948 novel, set in South Africa during the worst period of apartheid, made a strong impact on readers, as did the 1951 British-made film that featured a young SIDNEY POITIER and veteran talent Canada Lee. (The novel was also the basis of a 1949 Broadway musical, *Lost in the Stars*, which was filmed in 1974 and featured Brock Peters and Melba Moore.) Although well photographed and ably acted (especially by JONES and Harris), this well-intentioned adaptation was hindered by the change in the political climate in South Africa. With the near end of apartheid, the story lost much of its immediacy and gave an unneeded historical sense to the proceedings.

In South Africa, Rev. Stephen Kumalo, a Zulu Christian pastor, arrives in Johannesburg from the Natal Province in search of his ailing sister (Kente). He discovers that she has become a prostitute, that his brother (Dutton) has abandoned Christianity and is enmeshed in antiapartheid activism, and that his son Absalom—who has a girlfriend and baby—has become a thief. Later, a white and wealthy farmer, James Jarvis, also from Kumalo's village, comes to Johannesburg to claim the body of his son who was killed in a robbery. Absalom and two others are put on trial for the crime, and he is sentenced to hang. The two fathers meet and discover that, although they come from different cultures, they both are dedicated family men and religious. They exchange words of sympathy and regret (which gives the film its upbeat tone of potential racial harmony). After Absalom's death, the grieving reverend prays for understanding.

Cry, the Beloved Country received three Image Award nominations: Outstanding Lead Actor in a Motion Picture (Jones), Outstanding Picture, and Outstanding Supporting Actor in a Motion Picture (Dutton).

D

Dandridge, Dorothy (1922–1965) Like Marilyn Monroe, Dandridge was beautiful, sensitive, and tormented; like Marilyn, Dorothy's life climaxed in a tragic early death, ending her long-frustrated dreams of breaking through the racial barriers that limited her chances of success as movie star or club chanteuse in the white establishment world.

She was born in Cleveland, Ohio, the daughter of hopeful actress Ruby Dandridge. As a youngster she and her older sister Vivian toured the South, performing at churches and social functions. By 1937, she, her mother, and her sister were in Los Angeles, and the siblings had bits in *A Day at the Races* and *It Can't Last Forever* (both 1937).

By the early 1940s Dorothy was playing in Soundies musical shorts and had married her first husband, Harold Nicholas, part of the famous dancing brothers act. (That their daughter was born with brain damage tormented Dandridge for the rest of her life.) Meanwhile, efforts to obtain screen roles beyond bit parts led nowhere, mostly because of racial barriers. She turned to club engagements on both the West and the East Coast and made a reputation as a sultry songstress in swanky venues. She was forced to be a tribal queen in *Tarzan's Peril* (1951), but had the lead in *BRIGHT ROAD* (1953), which revealed her dramatic abilities. She played the title role in *CARMEN JONES* (1954) and was Oscar nominated; however, a lack of decent acting options thereafter led to such screen trash as *Tamango* (1957) and *The Decks Ran Red* (1958). Her last major film assignment was costarring with SIDNEY POITIER in the musical *PORGY AND BESS* (1959).

In her final years Dorothy returned to club work but kept chasing that elusive comeback screen vehicle. It never came because of racial discrimination, her drinking problem, bad financial management, and the passing years. At a low ebb, Dandridge committed suicide in her West Hollywood apartment, dying of barbiturate poisoning.

In 1999 HALLE BERRY starred in a made-for-cable biography of Dorothy's unhappy life: *INTRODUCING DOROTHY DANDRIDGE*.

Davis, Ossie (1917–) In his many decades of performing, Davis amassed numerous credits on stage, in films, and on TV. Along with his actress wife RUBY DEE, he was a potent force in the emerging role of black entertainers in integrating American show business, all the while participating in the growing Civil Rights movement. In his later years, he was considered the elder statesman of African-American actors.

He was born Raiford Chatman Davis in Cogdell, Georgia. (Supposedly, his mother's dialectal pronunciation of his initials "R. C." sounded like "Ossie," which became his professional first name.) He was educated at both Howard and Columbia Universities and apprenticed at the Rose McClendon Players in Harlem. After serving in the World War II army, he made his Broadway debut in *Jeb Turner* (1946), where he met his future wife, Dee. His screen debut came in *NO WAY OUT* (1950) with SIDNEY POITIER.

It was still difficult to find decent roles in any medium for a black performer in the 1950s, but by the 1960s Ossie had guest roles on several network TV series. By the time of the feature films *The Hill* (1965) and *THE SCALPHUNTERS* (1968), he was providing a commanding presence on screen.

A long-time playwright, Davis's self-written satiric farce *Purlie Victorious*, in which he and Dee co-starred on Broadway (1961), became a 1963 film (*Gone Are the Days!*) and also a 1970 Broadway musical (*Purlie*). He turned to movie directing with *COTTON COMES TO HARLEM* (1970) and the violent BLACK ACTION FILM *Gordon's War* (1973). In the miniseries *KING* (1978), he was cast as Martin Luther King Sr., and in the TV production of *ROOTS: THE NEXT GENERATION* (1979), he was Dad Jones.

Ossie's working relationship with filmmaker SPIKE LEE encompassed such movies as *SCHOOL DAZE* (1988), *JUNGLE FEVER* (1991), and *MALCOLM X* (1992). With his pal Burt Reynolds, Davis costarred in the TV series *B. L. Stryker* (1989–90) and later in the sitcom *Evening Shade* (1990–94). More recently, he was in such feature films as *Doctor Dolittle* (1998) and *Bubba Hotep* (2002), and such TV movies as *A Vow to Cherish* (1999) and *Finding Buck McHenry* (2000—for which he won a Daytime Emmy Award).

A two-time winner of Image Awards, Davis received a Life Achievement Award in 2001 from the Screen Actors Guild. He and Ruby Dee were named to the NAACP Image Awards Hall of Fame in 1989.

Davis, Sammy, Jr. (1925–1990) He was a twentieth-century show-business legend, a multitalented performer who gained additional publicity for his much-vaunted swinging lifestyle, his close association with Frank Sinatra and the Rat Pack, and, more importantly, for his efforts in his earlier performing years in helping to tear down the color barriers in American show business.

He was born in Harlem, New York City. His father was a lead dancer in Will Mastin's "Holiday in Dixieland" troupe; his mother was the act's primary chorine. After his parents separated, Sammy, age two and a half, was brought up by his dad. The boy soon became part of his dad's vaudeville act. Sammy made his film debut in 1933 in a short subject with ETHEL WATERS. As part of the Will Mastin Trio, Davis continued to play vaudeville. Drafted into the World War II army in 1943, Sammy experienced severe discrimination. After the war, the trio continued their club work, and Sammy made successful recordings. A near-fatal car accident in 1954 cost Davis his left eye. The ordeal inspired him to convert to Judaism.

A success in the clubs, in recordings, and on TV variety shows, Davis starred on Broadway in *Mr. Wonderful* (1956). The Will Mastin Trio broke up in 1958, and Sammy became a solo act. He made his TV dramatic debut that year and also played the jive-talking Danny Johnson who lusts for *ANNA LUCASTA* (1958). He was the dope-dealing Sportin' Life in *PORGY AND BESS* (1959), the all-black opera brought to the large screen as a musical.

Hip beyond hip, Davis joined the Rat Pack for such films as *Ocean's Eleven* (1960) and *Robin and the Seven Hoods* (1964), was dramatically sound in the shaky screen drama *A Man Called Adam* (1966), and teamed with Caucasian Peter Lawford for the spy spoof *Salt and Pepper* (1968) and its sequel, *One More Time* (1970). Having starred in TV specials, Sammy had his own television variety show in 1966. He was back on Broadway in the musical *Golden Boy* (1964) and turned out more hit albums.

In the mid-1970s as both Sammy and his career slowed down, he had briefly his own syndicated variety TV series (*Sammy and Company*). He was back on stage for *Sammy on Broadway* (1974) and returned for *Stop the World, I Want to Get Off* (1978). Davis won a Daytime Emmy in 1979 for his guest-starring role on the daytime soap opera, *One Life to Live*. Later, he did a cameo in Burt Reynolds's silly *The Cannonball Run* (1981) and its foolish 1984 sequel. What proved to be his final movie was *Tap* (1989), starring Gregory Hines and a slew of tap-dancing greats from the past. *Why Me?* (1989) was Sammy's book follow-up to his popular first autobiography (*Yes I Can*, 1965). Not long before his death from cancer at age sixty-five, Sammy was the subject of a lavish TV tribute.

Dee, Ruby (1924–) A distinguished performer in all mediums, Dee built her reputation over many years, often appearing in tandem with her actor husband OSSIE DAVIS. A consummate professional, many of her first decades of acting were relegated to minor roles—the only ones open then to black players—especially in playing the lively, helpful wife.

She was born Ruby Ann Wallace in Cleveland, Ohio, the daughter of a waiter/railroad porter and a schoolteacher mother. The family moved to Harlem when she was still an infant. While attending Hunter High School in New York City, she decided to become an actress; simultaneous to studying Romance languages at Hunter College, she apprenticed at the American Negro Theater. Her Broadway debut was as a native girl (a walk-on) in the 1943 drama (not the famous musical) *South Pacific*. After graduating college she was in the Broadway drama *Jeb* (1946) and two years later wed its leading man, Davis. Dee assumed the lead part in the Broadway hit *Anna Lucasta* in 1946 and later acted with Ossie in the play's national tour. Participating in such plays as *The World of Sholom Aleichem* (1953) raised Dee's social consciousness further. On radio, she had the nonblack lead in the daytime soap opera *This Is Nora Drake*. (Later, in the mid-1970s, she and her husband cohosted radio's *The Ossie Davis and Ruby Dee Story Hour*.)

On the big screen Dee appeared in such entries as *NO WAY OUT* and *The Jackie Robinson Story* (both 1950), as well as *EDGE OF THE CITY* (1957), *Virgin Island* (1958), and *A RAISIN IN THE SUN* (1961), all three with SIDNEY POITIER. She had the recurring role of Martha Frazier in the daytime TV series *The Guiding Light* in 1967 and in 1968–69 she played Alma Miles on the nighttime TV drama *Peyton Place*. She was on camera in such entries as *UPTIGHT* (1968) and *Countdown at Kusini* (1976).

Repeatedly teamed professionally with her husband, she joined him for the TV series *With Ossie and Ruby* (1981–82) and played with him in such SPIKE LEE movies as *DO THE RIGHT THING* (1989). Earlier, she had enacted the mother in an all-black production of *Long Day's Journey into Night* on TV, receiving a CableACE Award. She won an Emmy in 1991 for her supporting role as the housekeeper in *Decoration Day* (1991) on *Hallmark Hall of Fame*. Ruby was part of the short-lasting sitcom *Middle Ages* and joined in the miniseries *Stephen King's The Stand* (1994). Her more recent TV movie appearances included *Having Our Say: The Delany Sisters' First 100 Years* (1999), *A Storm in Summer* (2000), and *Taking Back Our Town* (2001). On the children's cable TV animated series, *Little Bill* (1999–) conceived by BILL COSBY, Dee provided the voice of Alice the Great.

Among her other accomplishments, Dee wrote a collection of stories and poems, entitled *My One Good Nerve* (1987), and several juvenile books. Her several awards include the 1972 Operation PUSH Martin Luther King Jr. Award and Actors Equity's Paul Robeson Citation (which she shared with her husband) "for outstanding creative contributions both in the performing arts and in society at large." Dee received the National Medal of Arts from President Clinton in 1995. She and Davis were elected to the NAACP Image Awards Hall of Fame in 1989.

***Defiant Ones, The* (1958)** United Artists, b&w, 1958. **Director:** Stanley Kramer; **Screenplay:** Nathan E. Douglas and Harold Jacob Smith; **Cast:** Tony Curtis (John "Joker" Jackson), Sidney Poitier (Noah Cullen), Theodore Bikel (Sheriff Max Muller), Charles McGraw (Capt. Frank Gibbons), Lon Chaney Jr. (Big Sam), Cara Williams (the woman).

This was another landmark film by Kramer who had made the earlier antiracism entry, 1949's *HOME OF THE BRAVE*. In a movie full of strong social messages—for its time—on racial tolerance, POITIER made a major impact on audiences. Here the African American received costar billing with Caucasian Curtis, which brought desegregation another step further in the American film industry.

Southerner Noah Cullen has a great deal of pent-up anger, the result of a lifetime of suffering from racism. When he hits a white man, he is arrested and put on a chain-gang detail. Another prisoner is John "Joker" Jackson, an illiterate redneck bully, who had been conditioned by society to scorn "niggers." One day, as their work detail is being driven back to prison, the truck crashes. The two men escape, bound together at the wrist by a three-foot chain. As they survive one harrowing experience after another, their forced togetherness brings on a grudging acceptance of one another. At a farmhouse, a lonely, sex-starved woman (Williams) provides a tool for them to cut their chain. She suggests that Jackson go away with her and her son, leaving Cullen as the scapegoat for the pursuing sheriff (Bikel) and his posse. By now the bigoted Joker has come to respect Noah and refuses. Later, the two escapees reach the railroad tracks. Cullen jumps onto a freight car as it rumbles by. He reaches out to grab his partner's hand. However, Jackson, too weak from a prior gunshot wound to make the leap, falls to the ground. Noah chooses to tumble after his friend. As the sheriff approaches, Cullen, cradling the injured Jackson, stoically sings the anthem "Long Gone."

Contemporary critics praised this highly charged, thought-provoking film and lauded the superior acting of its coleads. A few sources then and more in retrospect wondered why in 1958 when African Americans were emerging into activism (e.g., protests) Poitier's character sank into passive resistance at the finale.

The Defiant Ones won Academy Awards for Best Cinematography (Black and White) and Best Story and Screenplay. It received Oscar nominations for Best Actor (Curtis and Poitier), Best Director, Best Film Editing, Best Picture, Best Supporting Actor (Bikel), and Best Supporting Actress (Williams).

Nearly thirty years later, in 1985, *The Defiant Ones* was remade as a TV movie starring Robert Urich as Joker and Carl Weathers in Poitier's role. Although much of the drama was the same, there were a few subtle differences in the new edition, such as having a fine African-American actor, Thalmus Rasulala, play a deputy sheriff, in the posse hunting the two escapees. The new version did not measure up to the original, nor did it have the same impact on viewers.

Detroit Heat See *DETROIT 9000*.

***Detroit 9000* (aka: *Detroit Heat; Police Call 9000*) (1973)** General, color, 108 minutes. **Director:** Arthur Marks; **Screenplay:** Orville Hampton; **Cast:** Alex Rocco (Lt. Danny Bassett), Hari Rhodes (Det. Sgt. Jesse Williams), Vonetta McGee (Roby Harris), Ella Edwards (Helen), Scatman Crothers (Reverend Markham), Herbert Jefferson Jr. (Ferdy).

Although this R-rated entry was filled with the gore and violence so common to BLACK ACTION FILMS, it had many intriguing ingredients. Besides the presence of a sterling cast (especially Rocco, McGee, and Crothers), the movie made several statements about race. One African American tells another "You've got to realize not every black man is your brother." When the Native American member of a heist gang accidentally wounds himself in the leg, one of his cohorts, an African American, observes, "No wonder they always lost [against the troopers and cowboys]." Within this film there is also a good deal of bigotry displayed by the African Americans regarding the social classes within their own race. Also, by the end of *Detroit 9000*, the African Americans and the Caucasians have racked up equal points for good and bad members depicted on camera—this was a rarity in such genre movies.

In Detroit, during a banquet honoring a black congressman, masked robbers steal $400,000 in jewelry and valuables donated by the African-American guests for the politician's gubernatorial campaign. Assigned to the case is Caucasian Lt. Danny Bassett and his black partner, Sgt. Jesse Williams. By the time the heist (motivated by greed, not racism as believed at first) is solved, Bassett is dead. Williams ponders whether his late partner died trying to recover the loot or had been planning to abscond with it.

Detroit 9000 earned $1.2 million in domestic film rentals.

***Devil in a Blue Dress* (1995)** TriStar, color, 102 minutes. **Director/Screenplay:** Carl Franklin; **Cast:** Denzel Washington (Easy Rawlins), Tom Sizemore (DeWitt Albright), Jennifer Beals (Daphne Monet), Don Cheadle (Mouse), Maury Chaykin (Matthew Terrell), Terry Kinney (Todd Carter), Mel Winkler (Joppy), Lisa Nicole Carson (Coretta James).

Made on an elaborate scale, this period crime drama is a deliberate throwback to the film noir movies of the 1940s. As in Walter Mosley's original book (1990), the detective and many lead performers are played by African Americans in a story line that swirls through both upscale-white and ghetto parts of Los Angeles and encompasses a great deal of realism. The chief ingredient left out in the translation from the novel was the passionate interracial affair between Easy Rawlins and Daphne Monet.

In post–World War II L.A., decorated combat hero Easy Rawlins has lost his airplane factory job. Through bad luck, he finds himself becoming a private eye, hired to track down the Caucasian Daphne, who has a yen for African-American men and who is the fiancée of a wealthy mayoral candidate (Kinney). As the mystery deepens and people are beaten up and/or killed, the perplexed Easy asks his mentally disturbed pal Mouse to help him solve the caper. By case's end, the disillusioned Rawlins is a sadder man.

Whether it was WASHINGTON'S glum on-camera persona or Franklin's slow pacing of the sleuthing, the visually impressive *Devil in a Blue Dress* did not have great appeal for filmgoers. (Cheadle as the muscle received the most critical attention.) The movie grossed only about $16 million in domestic distribution. This entry was to have led to a series of whodunit features, based on Mosley's books and the Easy Rawlins character.

Dickerson, Ernest [R.] (1952–) Like others (e.g., Haskell Wexler) before him, Dickerson began his career as a cinematographer, displaying a striking eye for imagery and the ability to capture passion on film. From 1983 to 1992 he photographed feature films for such black directors as SPIKE LEE, MICHAEL SCHULTZ, and ROBERT TOWNSEND. Thereafter, Dickerson made his debut as a movie director with the urban drama *Juice* (1992).

He was born in Newark, New Jersey, and attended Howard University, majoring in architecture. By this time already interested in cinematography, his first work in the field was recording a surgery on film at Howard. Matriculating at New York University's film school, Ernest became friendly with Lee and served as cinematographer for the budding director's *Joe's Bed-Stuy Barbershop: We Cut Heads* (1983). Next, John Sayles hired Dickerson to photograph his science fiction allegory *THE BROTHER FROM ANOTHER PLANET* (1984), followed by the musical *Krush Groove* (1985) for Schultz. Thereafter, for Lee, Ernest photographed such features as *SCHOOL DAZE* (1988), *DO THE RIGHT THING* (1989), *JUNGLE FEVER* (1991), and *MALCOLM X* (1992). Meanwhile he photographed segments of TV's *Law & Order* (1990–) and music videos for Bruce Springsteen, Miles Davis, and others.

Dickerson's *Juice* was followed by such diverse fare as *Bulletproof* (1996) with Adam Sandler and Damon Wayans, *Blind Faith* (1998) with Charles S. Dutton and Courtney B. Vance, the made-for-cable movie *Strange Justice* (1999) about the Anita Hill harassment case, the supernatural thriller *Bones* (2001) with Snoop Doggy Dogg and PAM GRIER, *Monday Night Mayhem* (2002), a cable movie drama dealing with TV sports announcers in the 1970s, and *Big Shot: Confessions of a Campus Bookie* (2002), another cable film.

Diggs, Taye (1971–) As ethnic minority barriers in the American entertainment industry further dissolved in the late 1990s, five-feet, nine-inch Diggs enjoyed "sudden" career prominence based more on his clean-cut good looks than his show business versatility. By the time *People* magazine named him one of the "50 Most Beautiful People in the World" in spring 1999, he had already made a striking film debut in *HOW STELLA GOT HER GROOVE BACK*. Thereafter, he became one of the busiest young black performers in Hollywood movies.

He was born Scott Diggs in Essex County, New Jersey, the eldest of five children. (His acquired new first name came about because friends called him "Scottaye," which he shortened to Taye.) He and his siblings grew up in Rochester, New York, where he attended the High School of the Arts. He later earned a B.F.A. degree from Syracuse University where he was a member of a rock band. By then the former bespectacled geek had muscled up, thanks to weightlifting and modern-dance classes. He made his Broadway debut in 1995 in a revival of *Carousel* and the following year played the nasty landlord in another musical, *Rent*. (Along the way Diggs spent more than six months performing in a Caribbean-themed show at the Adventureland stage at Disneyland Tokyo.) In 1996 Taye had acting spots on two TV series (*New York Undercover* and *Law & Order*) and the next year won the recurring role of Adrian "Sugar" Hill on the daytime TV drama, *Guiding Light*, which lasted until 1998.

In the steamy *How Stella Got Her Groove Back*, Diggs had the beefcake role of a twenty-year-old Jamaican who fell in love with an older woman (ANGELA BASSETT). While he was but one of the ensemble in the movie *Go* (1999), in two of his other 1999 releases (*The Best Man* and *The Wood*), both of which dealt with the African-American community, Taye had a focal role. He then participated in a horror film remake (*House on Haunted Hill*, 1999) and was a bad guy in the violent crime tale, *The Way of the Gun* (2000). During this period he appeared off-Broadway in *The Wild Party*. In the spring of 2001 he was seen as a new member of the Boston law firm on the TV series, *Ally McBeal*. Later feature-film credits included the sci-fi thriller *Equilibrium* (2001) and *Chicago: The Musical* (2002) the latter an adaptation of the hit Broadway show from the 1970s.

directors of African-American-themed motion pictures Hollywood long discriminated against black talent in the entertainment industry both in front of and behind the cameras. Although in the late 1920s and thereafter ethnic minority actors gained occasional screen roles, it was almost impossible for a person of color to become a film director within the movie establishment. Thus African Americans had to direct films as independent ventures, something very costly and difficult to achieve in the 1910s and 1920s. Nevertheless film pioneer OSCAR MICHEAUX rose to the challenge and directed his first feature, the silent entry *The Homesteader*, in 1919, and his last endeavor, *The Betrayal*, in 1948. During the 1920s and 1930s he was the most famous of African Americans directing features outside the Hollywood studio system.

It was not until 1969 that a black moviemaker directed a feature film for a major Los Angeles film company. The man was GORDON PARKS SR., and his vehicle was the semi-autobiographical *THE LEARNING TREE*. Two years later Parks turned out *SHAFT*, a black-themed detective action yarn for MGM, and it was a huge success. Also in that year, MELVIN VAN PEEBLES released his independently made feature *SWEET SWEETBACK'S BAADASSSSS SONG*, the odyssey of an angry black man. That too made a sizable profit and helped, along with *Shaft*, to set Hollywood on the BLACK ACTION FILM cycle of the 1970s. One of the more talented black filmmakers to emerge in that decade was MICHAEL SCHULTZ, who helmed such works as *Cooley High* (1975) and *CAR WASH* (1976). A maker of gritty, tough films, Jamaa Fanaka debuted with *Welcome Home Brother Charles* (1975) and *Emma Mae* (1976) but had his most notable success with *PENITENTIARY* (1979) and its two sequels (1982 and 1987).

Multitalented Charles Burnett, director of *Killer of Sheep* (1977), went on to make such entries as *To Sleep With Anger* (1990) with DANNY GLOVER, *The Glass Shield* (1994), *Selma, Lord Selma* (1999—made-for-cable movie); *Finding Buck McHenry* (2000—made for cable movie), the latter with OSSIE DAVIS and Ruby Dee. Also in the 1970s, black actors such as SIDNEY POITIER and Ossie Davis used their newfound industry clout to direct projects. Davis turned out such pictures as *Cotton Comes to Harlem* (1970), *Black Girl* (1972), and *Countdown at Kusini* (1976); Poitier helmed such entries as *BUCK AND THE PREACHER* (1972), *Let's Do It Again* (1974), and *Stir Crazy* (1980).

Another filmmaker of note was Zeinbabu Irene Davis. Her first picture was the short *Filmstatement* (1982), which she also wrote and produced. Thereafter, she made such documentaries as *Recreating Black Women's Media Image* (1983) and *Sweet Bird of Youth* (1986), often focusing on the "invisibility" of African Americans. The short *Cycles* (1989) was followed by her first feature, *A Powerful Thang* (1993). The latter revolved around an African-American couple and the scope of their relationships. Next came *Mother of the River* (1995) and *Compensation* (1997), both of which she produced.

A major new force emerged in the 1980s with the young SPIKE LEE, who was articulate, controversial, and confrontational. He gained tremendous publicity for his projects, which improved his bankability. He ranged from romantic comedy (*SHE'S GOTTA HAVE IT*, 1986) to a satirical musical (*SCHOOL DAZE*, 1988) to raw urban drama (*DO THE RIGHT THING*, 1989). He continued onward in the 1990s and thereafter with such fare as *JUNGLE FEVER* (1991), *MALCOLM X* (1992), *Crooklyn* (1994), *He Got Game* (1997), *Summer of Sam* (1999), *BAMBOOZLED* (2000), *A Huey P. Newton Story* (2001, a made-for-cable movie), and the documentary *Jim Brown, All American* (2002). Already a director of TV series episodes, Bill Duke turned to features with the TV movie *The Killing Floor* (1984) and went on to direct such items as *A RAGE IN HARLEM* (1990) and *Hoodlum* (1997).

Actor/writer ROBERT TOWNSEND debuted with *HOLLYWOOD SHUFFLE* (1987) and went on to helm such features as *THE FIVE HEARTBEATS* (1991), *B*A*P*S* (1997), and *Little Richard* (2000—made-for-cable movie). A friend and collaborator of Townsend was KEENEN IVORY WAYANS who made his feature film directing debut with the spoof *I'm Gonna Git You Sucka* (1988), leading him to such other full-length productions as *A Low Down Dirty Shame* (1994), *Scary Movie* (2000), *Scary Movie 2* (2001), and *The Incredible Shrinking Man* (2003).

Julie Dash who had made earlier films was noticed for her *Daughters of the Dust* (1991) and her later made-for-cable movie *Funny Valentines* (1999) and *THE ROSA PARKS STORY* (2002). JOHN SINGLETON exploded on the movie scene with *BOYZ N THE HOOD* (1991) and such subsequent work as *Poetic Justice* (1993), *Rosewood* (1997), *SHAFT* (2000), and *BABY BOY* (2001). ERNEST R. DICKERSON, who had photographed several of Lee's movies, turned to directing himself in 1992 with *Juice*, followed by such items as *Bulletproof* (1996), *Ambushed* (1998), and *Bones* (2001). Carl Franklin, who had been an actor (e.g., *Five on the Black Hand Side*, 1973), turned to directing with the short *Punk* (1986) but hit his stride with such 1990s features as *Laurel Avenue* (1993—made-for-cable movie) and *DEVIL IN A BLUE DRESS* (1995). Other black filmmakers of the 1990s included Matty Rich (e.g., *Straight Out of Brooklyn*, 1991), Allen and Albert Hughes (e.g., *MENACE II SOCIETY*, 1993), Reginald Hudlin (e.g., *House Party*, 1990), actor Mario Van Peebles (e.g., *NEW JACK CITY*, 1991), director/writer Leslie Harris (*Just Another Girl on the I.R.T.*, 1992), veteran performer FOREST WHITAKER (e.g., *WAITING TO EXHALE*, 1995), and newcomer Lee Davis (e.g., *3 A.M.*, 2001—made-for-cable movie). One of the most promising of the new black female talent was Kasi Lemmons, a former actress, who made her directing debut with the self-written feature *Eve's Bayou* (1997). This was followed by *The Caveman's Valentine* and *Dr. Hugo* (both 2001). Antoine Fuqua built his reputation on hard-hitting actioners such as *The Replacement Killers* (1998), *Bait* (2000), and *Training Day* (2001). In the latter, its star, Denzel Washington, won a Best Actor Academy Award among other trophies for his performance in Fuqua's picture.

***Do the Right Thing* (1989)** Universal, color, 120 minutes. **Director/Screenplay:** Spike Lee; **Cast:** Danny Aiello (Sal), Ossie Davis (Da Mayor), Ruby Dee (Mother Sister), Richard Edson (Vito), Giancarlo Esposito (Buggin' Out), Spike Lee (Mookie), Bill Nunn (Radio Raheem), John Turturro (Pino), Joie Lee (Jade), Rosie Perez (Tina), Samuel L. Jackson (Mister Señor Love Daddy).

Cinematically, LEE took a giant step forward with this highly controversial comedy/drama, inspired by actual events in the Howard Beach section of Queens, New York. It reasserted the power of cinema to make political statements, this time focusing on African Americans. This major studio release—

the first of Lee's movies to have noticeable white characters—put Lee at the front ranks of minority independent filmmakers. Compared to his earlier films, many characters were more fully developed, as is the film's technical style. Lee raised the racially charged question: What degree of activism is required to give African Americans equality in the United States? With many on-screen figures representative of ethnic-minority stances (e.g., militancy, passivism), the movie's central theme is what is "doing the right thing."

On summer's hottest day in Brooklyn's Bedford-Stuyvesant section, Buggin' Out, a local activist, buys a slice at Sal's Pizzeria. The customer asks the fiercely proud Italian American why there are no African Americans on his photo wall of fame. With the question posed, the day proceeds as the camera follows Sal's helper, Mookie, on his delivery rounds. As the temperature rises, so do tempers in the culturally diverse neighborhood, leading eventually to a physical showdown between riled Sal and staunch activist Radio Raheem. The scuffle moves out into the street where the cops "accidentally" kill Raheem and arrest Buggin' Out (who is pummeled in the back of the squad car). The usually laid-back Mookie becomes so angered that he throws a garbage can through Sal's window. This leads to a riot in which the pizzeria is burned. The next day, Sal collects on his insurance, but he and Mookie remain deadlocked in their opposing views.

Made on a $6.5 million budget, *Do the Right Thing* grossed $27.5 million in domestic distribution. The film received two Oscar nominations: Best Original Screenplay and Best Supporting Actor (Aiello).

With Lee as the leader of the pack, Hollywood's URBAN DRAMAS were becoming cogent. No longer mere showcases for violence, they were serving as a forum for political statements, especially on African-American matters and rights.

Spike Lee and Danny Aiello in a tense moment from *Do the Right Thing* (1989). (JC ARCHIVES)

***Down in the Delta* (1998)** Miramax, color, 111 minutes. **Director:** Maya Angelou; **Screenplay:** Myron Goble; **Cast:** Alfre Woodard (Loretta), Al Freeman Jr. (Earl), Mary Alice (Rosa Lynn), Esther Rolle (Annie), Loretta Devine (Zenia), Wesley Snipes (Will).

For her screen directing debut, acclaimed novelist/poet Angelou chose to make this earnest drama that examines the heritage of African Americans as well as the responsibilities of family members to one another in the present. Of key importance in ethnic-minority-film history is that the production was helmed by an African-American woman—a double rarity even in today's Hollywood.

Because single-parent Loretta is crack addicted, her mother (Alice) pawns a family heirloom so that she can send her daughter and two grandchildren away from the Chicago ghetto to stay with her brother Earl in rural Mississippi. Once there, Loretta becomes a waitress at her uncle's chicken restaurant and begins to order her life. She is inspired by watching Earl tend his Alzheimer-ridden wife (Rolle) and seeing how her own autistic girl is responding to his attention to her. By film's end Loretta better appreciates her cultural roots and seeks to pass on the heritage to her children.

The film grossed almost $6 million in its limited domestic distribution. Both WOODARD (who co-produced the venture) and the film were nominated for Image Awards.

***Duel at Diablo* (1966)** United Artists, color, 105 minutes. **Director:** Ralph Nelson; **Screenplay:** Marvin H. Albert and Michael M. Grilikhes; **Cast:** James Garner (Jess Remsberg), Sidney Poitier (Toller), Bibi Andersson (Ellen Grange), Dennis Weaver (Willard Grange), Bill Travers (Lt. Scotty McAllister), John Hoyt (Chata), Armand Alzamora (Ramirez).

This extremely violent feature was based on Marvin H. Albert's novel *Apache Rising* (1957) in which the Toller character was *not* African American. However, Poitier was eager to play an on-screen cowboy and accepted the second lead in this Garner vehicle. Its director, Nelson, had guided Poitier through his Oscar-winning performance in *LILIES OF THE FIELD* (1963).

In the post–Civil War West, scout Jess Remsberg rescues Ellen Grange from the Apaches. (His own wife, a Comanche, was killed by an unknown white man.) When Ellen's bigoted husband rejects her as tainted by the savages, she returns to the warriors' camp. Meanwhile, Jess guides Lieutenant McAllister and his cavalry recruits to Fort Concho. Also joining the group is Grange and ex-cavalryman Toller, who tames horses for the army. After several encounters with the warring Apaches, only Jess, Toller, Ellen, and a few soldiers remain alive.

This offbeat western was filled with venomous hate between several whites and the Native American characters; in fact, even the dandified Toller, himself an ethnic minority, joins the Caucasian majority in their hatred and killing of warrior braves. Although this was one of the first *major* studio Hollywood westerns to feature an African American in a lead role (*SOUL SOLDIERS* was still four years away), there is much evidence of many such ethnic minority members in the Old West. Only six years thereafter, Poitier starred in and directed *BUCK AND THE PREACHER* in which he and the other African-American characters worked in cooperation with Native Americans, while a group of dastardly whites were their common enemy.

***Duke Is Tops, The* (aka: *The Bronze Venus*) (1938)** Million Dollar Productions, b&w, 72 minutes. **Director:** William Nolte; **Screenplay:** Phil Dunham; **Cast:** Ralph Cooper (Duke Davis), Lena Horne (Ethel Andrews), Lawrence Criner (Doc Dorando), Monte Hawley (George Marshall), Neva People (Ella).

Making her feature film debut in this independently produced, all-black musical, HORNE was understandably awkward as an actress. However, the budding legend radiated personality, looks, and vocal talent.

This distillation of *The Broadway Melody* (1929) finds Ethel Andrews abandoning her manager and boyfriend, singer Duke Davis, to take a big-time show business job in New York City. While Ethel's career initially accelerates, Duke's professional standing declines and, in desperation, he takes a job with Doc Dorando's traveling medicine show. Later, when Ethel has a professional setback, Duke rushes to Manhattan to bolster her spirits and to showcase her in a new production.

After Horne gained popularity at MGM in the 1940s, *The Duke Is Tops* was reissued in 1944 as *The Bronze Venus* with Horne billed over the title. Lena's co-star Cooper had been a bandleader and initiated Million Dollar Productions, which made African-American films from the 1930s through the 1940s.

E

***East Side/West Side* (1963–1964)** CBS-TV series, b&w, 60 minutes. **Cast:** George C. Scott (Neil Brock), Elizabeth Wilson (Frieda Hechlinger), Cicely Tyson (Jane Foster).

This highly realistic dramatic series involved a dedicated young social worker (Scott) trying to make a difference in New York City's slums. The tone was earnest; the stories were grim and left viewers feeling downbeat about the often overwhelming problems of urban life.

On a positive note, this was the first network dramatic series to feature an integrated cast of regulars, although the talented TYSON was stuck in the unrewarding role of the office secretary.

***Edge of the City* (1957)** Metro-Goldwyn-Mayer, b&w, 85 minutes. **Director:** Martin Ritt; **Screenplay:** Robert Alan Aurthur; **Cast:** John Cassavetes (Axel North), Sidney Poitier (Tommy Tyler), Jack Warden (Charlie Malik), Kathleen Maguire (Ellen Wilson), Ruby Dee (Lucy Tyler).

With this drama, Hollywood took another (belated) major step forward in presenting on screen interracial themes set in inner city slums. The story was based on a 1955 episode ("A Man Is Ten Feet Tall") aired on TV's *Philco Playhouse.* POITIER repeated his TV role, with Aurthur adapting his original drama to the big screen.

Morose army deserter Axel North is bothered by his AWOL status and his belief that he caused his brother's death in an accident. North hires on to work at a freight-yard loading dock and becomes friendly with coworker Tommy Tyler, who tries to draw out his new acquaintance. Meanwhile, their bigoted boss, who has a nasty reputation, goads North, whom he is blackmailing (for being a deserter). Later, when North and Malik argue heatedly, Tommy steps in, enraging the bigot, and in the ensuing fight between Malik and Tyler, the latter is killed. When the police arrive, everyone claims to have seen nothing. Tyler's angry wife (Dee) tells Axel that he betrayed his dead friend by not telling the police the truth. North later confronts Malik and, after beating him up, drags the man off to the law.

Although this politically liberal film was cited by cinema historians as a milestone for presenting an African American as a fully integrated citizen who interacts at work/socially with whites, given the times in which it was made, it was still a too idealistic representation of real life. Then too, some viewers—then and later—wondered why Poitier's character so willingly sacrificed himself for his Caucasian pal, let alone spent time with this less-than-engaging deserter.

Edge of the City helped to elevate Poitier into a major film stardom.

***Education of Sonny Carson, The* (1974)** Paramount, color, 104 minutes. **Director:** Michael Campus; **Screenplay:** Fred Hudson; **Cast:** Rony Clanton (Sonny Carson), Don Gordon (Detective Pigliani), Joyce Walker (Virginia), Paul Benjamin (Pops), Thomas Hicks (young Sonny Carson), Mary Alice (Moms), Ram John Holder (preacher), Jerry Bell (Lil' Boy).

Not every African-American-themed picture of the 1970s was part of the BLACK ACTION FILM onslaught. This thoughtful drama, set in the Brooklyn slums, was based on the 1972 autobiography of Sonny Carson (Mwina Imiri Abubadika) and was directed by Campus, who had helmed the blaxploitation genre classic *SUPERFLY* (1973). The movie's lead actor, Clanton, had been the focal performer in *THE COOL WORLD* (1973), under the acting name of Hampton Clanton.

Using a cinema vérité approach, this insightful movie concerns a prize-winning school boy in Brooklyn's Bedford-

Stuyvesant who is thrown into jail for having committed burglaries. Once back on the streets, the toughened Sonny battles his way into becoming a gang leader. His participation in serious crimes leads to a prison sentence. Having an epiphany about his thus-far wasted life, Mwina Imiri Abubadika (his new name) now yearns to become a community leader. Among those involved in Sonny's tumultuous life are his girlfriend (Walker), who sinks into drug addiction, an energetic preacher (Holder), and Lil' Boy, who dies in a gang tussle.

Too episodic and exploitive of the violence, degradation, and despair of the ghetto, *The Education of Sonny Carson* was not a profitable release. Nevertheless, this perceptive screen study was a sterling example of thought-provoking cinema and the potential for exploring in depth a minority group's culture.

***Emperor Jones, The* (1933)** United Artists, b&w, 80 minutes. **Director:** Dudley Murphy; **Screenplay:** DuBose Heyward; **Cast:** Paul Robeson (Brutus Jones), Dudley Digges (Smithers), Frank Wilson (Jeff), Fredi Washington (Undine), Ruby Elzy (Dolly), Rex Ingram (court crier).

When Eugene O'Neill's provocative drama *The Emperor Jones* opened on Broadway in 1920 starring Charles Gilpin, for the first time a major black role was played by an African American on the New York stage. In 1924 when the play was revived, ROBESON took over the lead; he did so for the film, which was made independently on the East Coast and released by a major studio (United Artists). In its review, *Variety* (September 26, 1933) predicted that white moviegoers in the South would not see the film and that cinemas catering to African Americans might have problems because of the use of the word *nigger* in the dialogue. (The studio deleted the offensive word from prints targeted for ethnic theaters but kept to the original release cut for other engagements.)

While on the job, arrogant Pullman porter Brutus Jones overhears information that leads to his making a sum of money in the stock market. Living high, he fights with his old friend Jeff and accidentally kills the man. Later, he escapes from prison en route to Jamaica, is taken prisoner by a dictator, and is sold to a white trader/gunrunner (Digges). Eventually Jones maneuvers himself into being ruler of the country and promptly becomes a tyrant. When his subjects rebel, Brutus flees into the forest where he is shot by his former guards.

This was a noteworthy entry in African-American cinema—albeit a rather technically crude and stagy production—because it presented an ethnic minority as proud and disdainful, ready at an instant to stand up to the white man. It represented a 360-degree turn from the stereotypical shuffling, polite servants in Hollywood movies of the period. Although this film contains one of Robeson's best screen performances, the star never cared for the role because it presented an African American as a killer and scoundrel.

Enterprise See *STAR TREK*.

***Ethel Waters Show, The* (1939)** NBC-TV series, b&w, 60 minutes. **Cast:** Ethel Waters (hostess), George Hicks (announcer).

Before World War II put a temporary halt to the spread of commercial TV in the United States, the New York City–based NBC network was among those experimenting with the broadcasting of a few test programs. The fare was aired to a limited local audience equipped with television sets. Among the early test shows presented was this variety hour featuring famed club, stage, and recording artist WATERS. As the hostess of this program of songs and music, she was the first African-American performer to star in an American TV show.

Among her guests were Georgette Harvey, Georgia Buck, Joey Faye, and Philip Loeb.

F

***Fame* (1982–1987)** NBC (then Syndicated) TV series, color, 60 minutes. **Cast:** Debbie Allen (Lydia Grant), Erica Gimpel (Coco Hernandez: 1982–83), Carol Imperato (Danny Amatullo), Valerie Landsburg (Doris Schwartz: 1982–85), Gene Anthony Ray (Leroy Johnson), Janet Jackson (Cleo Hewitt: 1984–85), Nia Peeples (Nicole Chapman: 1984–87).

The successful movie *Fame* (1980) traced the lives of eight students at New York City's multiethnic High School for the Performing Arts. (The film's joyful title song won an Academy Award.) The premise was next translated into a TV series with Allen (as the superstrict dance teacher) and Ray (as a talented dancer from the ghetto) recreating their roles. The youth-oriented show balanced drama (the hopes and aspirations of the students and teachers) with musical interludes. Other African-American characters on the show included Coco Hernandez, a driven dancer-singer anxious to break into show business. Jackson was highly promoted in her one-year stint on the series, while Peeples, as an attractive black dancer/singer, ended her three seasons on the series when her character died in a car accident.

Allen, a dynamic force on the series, was Emmy nominated several times in both acting and choreographing capacities, finally winning an Emmy in the latter category for her 1984–85 season work.

Filled with ethnic minority characters, *Fame* was a positive illustration of individuals with divergent cultural backgrounds who work together in relative harmony.

Fetchit, Stepin (ca. 1902–1985) He was a talented entertainer who, in the late 1920s, took the then-rare opportunity for a black man to succeed in the Hollywood film business. To do so, he played the movie stereotype of the slow-moving, dimwitted African American. Although his deliberately exaggerated screen image (i.e., "coon" antics) was viewed with amusement by white audiences of the day, for blacks then and especially in retrospect, it seemed a very demeaning screen type. In later years his show-business image caused Fetchit great pain: He was disheartened (and sometimes angered) that his career breakthrough, which had helped to open the movie industry to black talent, should have been so badly regarded by most of his own race.

He was born Lincoln Theodore Monroe Andrew Perry in Key West, Florida, where his father was a cigar maker. His parents died when he was young, and he was adopted by one of his seamstress mother's customers. By his midteens he gravitated into minstrel-show work. When he entered vaudeville with his partner Ed Lee in a comedy/dance act, their names were "Step" and "Fetchit." (The name was allegedly inspired by a race horse Fetch It; another legend has it that his stage name derived from a song Perry wrote called "The Stepin Fetchit, Stepin Fetchit Turn Around.")

His first film role of note was in MGM's *In Old Kentucky* (1927), where, for a rare change, a black man was played on screen by an African American, not by a Caucasian in BLACKFACE. It was at Fox Films, in early talkies, that Fetchit found his berth in *The Ghost Talks* and *HEARTS IN DIXIE* (both 1929). On loan to Universal, he was Joe in the part-talking 1929 version of *Show Boat.* That same year he was in John Ford's *Salute* (1929). By 1931 Fetchit, who was living relatively well, came to a parting of the ways with Fox, which found him too meddlesome on the set. He returned to vaudeville.

By 1934, Stepin was back at Fox with a new contract and a supposed promise to "behave." He displayed his song-and-dance versatility in *Stand Up and Cheer* (1934). The studio teamed him with Caucasian humorist Will Rogers in *David Harum* (1934); they worked so well together—albeit Fetchit doing his shuffling, stammering, subservient lazy-man routine—that the actors were reteamed for *JUDGE PRIEST* (1934),

The Country Chairman (1935), and *Steamboat 'round the Bend* (1935—Rogers's last film before his fatal plane crash). Fetchit's final movie for the time being was 1939's *Zenobia,* in which HATTIE McDANIEL was also featured. By this point, he had become the object of ridicule by several black civil-rights groups.

After stage work failed to revive his career, the once well-to-do Fetchit filed bankruptcy in Chicago in 1945. Following a role in the all-black *Miracle in Harlem* (1948), he next turned up in bits in two 1952 Hollywood releases. He had a featured role in John Ford's *The Sun Shines Bright* (1953), a remake of *Judge Priest.*

Through his Hollywood years, Fetchit's off-camera exploits (e.g., car accidents, reputed brawls, extravagant spending) were well recorded by the press, a rarity regarding a black performer in those days. His sad decline was also documented. In 1970 he sued a TV network for defamation of character for showing clips of his movies (out of context) in a history of blacks on the screen. Fetchit made a few brief film appearances in the mid-1970s (e.g., *Won Ton Ton, the Dog Who Saved Hollywood*), but by then he was a shell of the man he once was. He suffered a stroke in 1976 and lost the ability to speak. He died at the Motion Picture Country House in Woodland Hills, California, a symbol to many of his race of a screen type well left in the unpleasant past.

Fishburne, Larry See FISHBURNE, LAURENCE.

Fishburne, Laurence (aka: Larry Fishburne) (1961–) This strong, often dour-looking dramatic actor grew up in show business, displaying a keen talent from an early age. He matured into a solid performer who was at his best in roles that required a powerful inner rage or heightened intensity. As such, he was impressive in his Oscar-nominated part of musician Ike Turner in the musical biography *WHAT'S LOVE GOT TO DO WITH IT* (1993).

He was born Laurence Fishburne III in Augusta, Georgia, where his father was a corrections officer and his mother was a math teacher. When he was still young, the family relocated to New York City. His parents separated when he was three. His first acting was in the second grade, by which point he already stood out from other children with his booming voice. His first professional work came in 1971 in an off-Broadway play, and the next year he was in an episode of the prestigious TV show, *ABC Theater.* From 1973 to 1976 he appeared on the daytime soap opera *One Life to Live.* Having already been in the URBAN DRAMA *CORNBREAD, EARL AND ME* (1975), his next screen role was Mr. Clean in *Apocalypse Now* (1979). Still a teenager, the part in this prestigious movie—not to mention bad habits picked up on the long location jaunt in the Philippines—turned him into a troubled adult.

After drifting through screen roles in the early 1980s, he began to reclaim his career in *THE COLOR PURPLE* (1985). But when further worthwhile acting jobs did not materialize, he signed on in 1986 as Cowboy Curtis on TV's *Pee-wee's Playhouse* starring Pee-wee Herman. It was his appearances in serious stage work as well as in SPIKE LEE's *SCHOOL DAZE* (1988) and then JOHN SINGLETON's *BOYZ N THE HOOD* (1991) that put Fishburne back on the acting map. For starring on Broadway in August Wilson's *Two Trains Running* (1992), Fishburne won a Tony Award. That same year's film *Deep Cover* was his first starring role after seventeen years in pictures. He won an Emmy in 1993 for his guest-starring part in the TV drama series *Tribeca,* and proved impressive in the lead role of *Othello* (1995), a feature film in which Kenneth Branagh played his nemesis, Iago.

In the later 1990s, Fishburne was among the ensemble of black actors in the made-for-cable movie *The Tuskegee Airmen* (1995), joined ALFRE WOODARD in the TV production of *Miss Evers' Boys* (1997) for which he won an Image Award, and took part in the big sci-fi entry, *Event Horizon* (1997). He wrote, directed, and starred in the crime drama *Once in the Life* (2000), based on his 1994 play *Riff Raff.* As the hulking, agile Morpheus, Fishburne was a key player in the hugely successful virtual reality movie *The Matrix* (1999), which led to two sequels in 2003.

***Five Heartbeats, The* (1991)** Twentieth Century-Fox, color, 121 minutes. **Director:** Robert Townsend; **Screenplay:** Townsend and Keenen Ivory Wayans; **Cast:** Robert Townsend (Duck), Michael Wright (Eddie), Leon (J.T.), Harry J. Lennix (Dresser), Tico Wells (Choirboy), Diahann Carroll (Eleanor Potter), Harold Nicholas (Sarge), John Canada Terrell (Michael "Flash" Turner), Chuck Patterson (Jimmy Potter).

Although it grossed only about $9 million in domestic distribution and won no awards, the well-mounted *The Five Heartbeats* was a resilient drama that overrode the clichés of musical biographies. It presented the rise and fall of a singing quintet of young African-American men, without letting the music or the industry horror stories overshadow the distinctive characterizations. The creative verve of this unheralded entry was a testament to the multitalented TOWNSEND and his adept screenplay collaborator WAYANS, two major players in the new Hollywood.

In flashback, Duck, now middleaged, recalls the Five Heartbeats 1960's rough climb to success, all the while coping with personal problems that range from drugs to relationships. Once they are famous, an unscrupulous promoter convinces lead singer Eddie to have the group drop their manager (Patterson), not knowing that the "removal" means the man's ruination. A saddened Eddie quits the group and is replaced by Michael "Flash" Turner, and the five vocalists go on to bigger fame. At that point, several egocentric members pull out of the group to go solo. Back in the present, the Five Heartbeats reunite for an impromptu concert for their families and friends.

***Flip Wilson Show, The* (1970–1974)** NBC-TV series, color, 60 minutes. **Cast:** Flip Wilson (host), the Jack Rogers Dancers and the George Wyle Orchestra (themselves).

Other more-celebrated black entertainers (e.g., Nat "King" Cole, SAMMY DAVIS JR.) headlined earlier TV network variety series, but it was outrageous comedian WILSON who came along at just the right time—thanks to civil-rights legislation and black militancy—to wow home viewers with his high-energy, far-out comedy/variety series. As the emcee and star of this trend-setting series, he was the first black performer to attain great success in the genre.

Wilson's most vivid creation was sassy Geraldine Jones, a hip, party-happy doll with a boyfriend named Killer and zany outfits that heightened his drag routine. Among his other comedy persona were Danny Danger, a rugged private eye; Herbie, the happy-go-lucky ice-cream man; and the Reverend Leroy, a gospel preacher from the Church of What's Happening Now. Although the show appealed to both white and black audiences, there were some commentators who felt Wilson's alter egos—especially Geraldine—were somewhat racially stereotypical and allowed white viewers to derive some of their pleasure from feeling superior to the entertainment being provided.

Wilson often featured black talent on his show, ranging from LENA HORNE to RICHARD PRYOR to Mahalia Jackson. During the show's run, Flip received a Golden Globe Award as Best TV Actor: Musical/Comedy.

***48 Hrs.* (1982)** Paramount, color, 96 minutes **Director:** Walter Hill; **Screenplay:** Roger Spottiswoode, Hill, Larry Gross, and Steven E. de Souza; **Cast:** Nick Nolte (Jack Cates), Eddie Murphy (Reggie Hammond), Annette O'Toole (Elaine), Frank McRae (Haden), James Remar (Albert Ganz), David Patrick Kelly (Luther).

There had been dramatic (and essentially polite) interracial buddy films before (e.g., *THE DEFIANT ONES*, 1958; *PARIS BLUES*, 1961), but this was a male bonding comedy that used a barrage of racial epithets that are now considered hip and true-to-life. This box-office hit (it earned more than $30 million in domestic film rentals) also established TV's *Saturday Night Live* cast member MURPHY—in his big-screen debut—as a major new movie star. (Murphy was a replacement for RICHARD PRYOR in this project.)

When Albert Ganz escapes from prison and heads to San Francisco, all hell breaks loose. Local law enforcer Jack Cates is confronted with several homicides and the further embarrassment of Ganz still being at large. To hasten the killer's capture, Cates arranges a forty-eight-hour pass for Reggie Hammond, a former member of Ganz's gang, who still has six months to serve on his prison sentence. The hard-nosed Cates and the flip-mouthed Hammond make an unlikely law-enforcement duo, but Reggie proves useful in tracking down Ganz and his henchmen. With Cates agreeing to watch over a stash of money that Reggie claims from his past dealings with the now-dead Ganz, Hammond returns briefly to jail.

Throughout this fast-paced mayhem, Cates, Hammond, and others engaged in a verbal slugfest, spewing forth racial slurs. For many, the highlight of this boisterous action comedy occurs when the brazen Reggie strides into a country-western bar filled with rednecks. Sizing up the situation and the odds of making a fast getaway, Hammond cracks to the tough crowd: "I'm your worst fuckin' nightmare, man. I'm a nigger with a badge." With that said, this film opened the floodgates for an anything-goes attitude in studio films regarding the verbalization of clichés that bigots (on both sides of the fence) loved to use in the safety of their own kind. The constructive take was that if characters on screen could speak out what they felt, a lot of racial friction would evaporate, and the world could move on to the next step toward greater racial harmony.

Murphy and Nolte reunited for the less-successful *Another 48 Hrs.* in 1990.

Foxx, Redd (1922–1991) From a raunchy club act as a stand-up comic, Foxx built a popular reputation with his equally crude routines on his comedy albums. (He was a predecessor to the wicked humor of RICHARD PRYOR and EDDIE MURPHY.) Redd's spate of albums proved a springboard to major success on TV with his sitcom *SANFORD AND SON* (1972–77). Using his raspy voice and crabby attitude to maximum value, he became a pop-culture icon, an amazing career jump for a poor boy who began his career entertaining on street corners.,

He was born John Elroy Sanford in St. Louis, Missouri. By age four, his dad had vanished, leaving him, his older brother, and their mother to survive on their own. After his mother departed to be with a hoodlum boyfriend, the boys were taken in by their grandmother, a full-blooded Native American who lived in the black ghetto. By the time Sanford was twelve, he had joined with neighborhood pals in creating a washtub band. They went to New York in 1939, performing on subways and street corners.

During this apprentice period, Sanford acquired the nickname of "Chicago Red" because of his light skin color and his hair. His new surname came from a then-popular baseball player as well as to connote that Redd himself was a "foxy" dresser. He performed on the Chitlin' (black club) Circuit in the East and teamed with Slappy White in vaudeville.

By 1951 Foxx was based in Los Angeles. When he could not find show-business work (because of racial discrimination), he worked as a sign painter. He started making his party albums of raucous routines, gaining him an underground reputation. Redd leaped into the big time when he played Las Vegas showrooms in the 1970s. His scene stealing as the grouchy junk dealer in the movie *COTTON COMES TO HARLEM* (1970) led to his being cast as Fred Sanford in TV's *Sanford and Son.* After the series and its follow-up, *Sanford* (1980–81) ended, he returned to the Las Vegas club circuit. Thereafter followed much grief due to problems with the Internal Revenue Service.

Eddie Murphy, who had long admired Foxx, cast him in the gangster comedy *Harlem Nights* (1989) and then, in his capacity as executive producer, signed Foxx (opposite Della Reese) for a new TV sitcom, *The Royal Family*, debuting in

September 1991. It had been on the air for only a few weeks when Redd suffered a fatal heart attack and the show folded.

***Foxy Brown* (1974)** American International, color, 92 minutes. **Director/Screenplay:** Jack Hill; **Cast:** Pam Grier (Misty Cotton [Foxy Brown]), Antonio Fargas (Link Brown), Peter Brown (Steve Elias), Terry Carter (Michael Anderson [Dalton Ford]), Kathryn Loder (Katherine Wall), Bob Minor (Oscar).

As a follow-up to her successful *Coffy* (1973), GRIER reunited with filmmaker Hill for a fourth and final time in this zesty BLACK ACTION FILM fantasy. It contained all the ingredients that the star's fans had come to love: violence, gore, rough talk, gaudy costumes, nudity, and the deification of this avenging woman. The movie was trashy, extremely episodic, and highly exploitive (of both the star and the genre), but it entertained its targeted audiences mightily (earning more than $2 million in domestic film rentals).

In *Foxy Brown* and others of her blaxploitation entries, Grier provided a rare role model for females of all races: In these action pictures, the heroine was no longer an exploited victim and subservient to males; instead, she was the butt-kicking aggressor. Most likely, it was the sort of feminism that the women's movement might not have appreciated, but it vicariously satisfied many distaff viewers.

When gangsters liquidate Foxy Brown's government-agent lover, she vows revenge. Learning their whereabouts from her stoolpigeon brother (Fargas), she goes undercover, using an alias to become a call girl for Katherine Wall, the queen bee of the rackets, and the latter's lover/enforcer, Steve Elias. With the assistance of Oscar, who heads a ghetto neighborhood antidrug group, Foxy mows down several of Katherine's gang. Her ultimate act of defiance is to capture Elias and have him castrated, later tossing the extracted parts in front of the horrified Wall. Next, she tells the deposed crime lord: "Death is too easy for you, bitch. I want you to suffer!" With that, statuesque Foxy and Oscar stalk off.

Although hastily assembled features such as *Foxy Brown* pandered to ethnic minority and action-hungry audiences, they also established new ground rules in mainstream cinema. Now, not only could African Americans be equal to white characters on camera, but they could also be the top honchos and victors at plot's end.

***Frank's Place* (1987–1988)** CBS-TV series, color, 30 minutes. **Cast:** Tim Reid (Frank Parrish), Robert Harper (Sy "Bubba" Weisburger), Daphne Maxwell Reid (Hannah Griffin), Francesca P. Roberts (Anna-May), Frances E. Williams (Miss Marie), Virginia Capers (Mrs. Bertha Griffin-Lamour), Tony Burton (Big Arthur).

The talented and low-keyed Tim Reid starred in this offbeat comedy that featured an unusual setting (a small Creole restaurant in New Orleans), a predominantly black cast playing eccentric characters, a Dixieland music score, and no canned laughter.

Frank Parrish, a history professor in Boston, inherits a dining spot from his late father whom he had not seen since he was a youngster. Not only must he adjust to life in the Big Easy, but also he has to deal with a frequently contentious restaurant staff and an assortment of peculiar clientele, which ranges from the flim-flam Reverend Deal to the daughter of the local funeral-parlor owner (played by Reid's actual wife, Daphne).

While *Frank's Place* became a critical favorite, the viewing public was perplexed by the unorthodox proceedings, and the quality show did not last even a season.

Freeman, Morgan (1937–) In contrast to the norm, Freeman's career expanded in later middle age, providing the six-feet, two-inch actor with character lead roles that were unavailable to him in his earlier professional years because of racial bigotry. Despite the quantity of his quality work, the dignified Freeman—with his mellifluous voice and carefully controlled body movements—never had a romantic lead or a female love interest in any of his movie assignments because of happenstance, as well the limitations frequently still placed on black performers in Hollywood films.

Freeman was born in Memphis, Tennessee. At age eighteen he joined the air force; five years later he began to act while at Los Angeles City College. After years of struggle, he gained a role in the Pearl Bailey all-black edition of *Hello, Dolly!* on Broadway in 1968. Subsequently, he earned national TV exposure as Easy Reader on the PBS network's *The Electric Company* (1971–76). Thereafter, he started to appear in telefeatures (e.g., *Attica*, 1980; *THE MARVA COLLINS STORY*, 1981) and made an impression in feature films (e.g., *Death of a Prophet*, 1981—as Malcolm X). From 1982 to 1984 he was Dr. Roy Bingham on the daytime TV soap opera, *Another World.* On stage the accomplished performer earned Obie Awards in 1980 for playing off-Broadway in *Coriolanus* and *Mother Courage*, in 1986 for *The Gospel at Colonus*, and in 1988 for *Driving Miss Daisy.*

It was the movie *Street Smart* (1987), in which he played a sadistic pimp, that turned the tide for Freeman. He was Oscar nominated as Best Supporting Actor and was again nominated in the Best Actor category for *Driving Miss Daisy* (1989). (He won a Golden Globe for his role as the even-tempered chauffeur in this film.) With his versatility he was seen on screen in several genres: costumed adventures (e.g., *GLORY*, 1989; *Robin Hood: Prince of Thieves*, 1991; *Moll Flanders*, 1996), westerns (e.g., *Unforgiven*, 1992), and thrillers (e.g., *Se7en*, 1995; *Outbreak*, 1995). Meanwhile, he directed the apartheid drama *Bopha!* (1993), a film starring DANNY GLOVER, and earned another Academy Award bid for his leading role in the prison drama *The Shawshank Redemption* (1994). Freeman played Dr. Alex Cross in the serial-killer thriller *Kiss the Girls* (1997) and repeated his well-liked characterization in *Along Came a Spider* (2001). Freeman was part of the historical entry *AMISTAD* (1997), the U.S. president in the sci-fi movie *Deep Impact* (1998), and a sinister killer in the satire *Nurse Betty* (2000). Later film assignments included the spy thriller *The Sum of All Fears* (2002) with Ben Affleck and

Tusker (2003), joining Jodie Foster in providing voices for this animated feature.

Over the years, the much-nominated Freeman won two Image Awards: Outstanding Supporting Actor for *Amistad* and for *Deep Impact*. The Philadelphia Festival of World Cinema presented him with a Lifetime Achievement Award in 2001.

***Fresh Prince of Bel Air* (1990–1996)** NBC-TV series, color, 30 minutes. **Cast:** Will Smith (Will Smith), James Avery (Philip Banks), Janet Hubert-Whitten (Vivian Banks: 1990–93), Daphne Maxwell Reid (Vivian Banks: 1993–96), Alfonso Ribeiro (Carlton Banks), Karyn Parsons (Hilary Banks), Tatyana M. Ali (Ashley Banks), Joseph Marcell (Geoffrey, the butler), Jeff Townes (Jazz [D.J. Jazzy Jeff]).

In some ways this TV sitcom, coproduced by musician Quincy Jones, is an updating of *THE JEFFERSONS* (1975–85), only this time it is WILL SMITH from the 'hood of West Philadelphia who goes upscale when he migrates to plush Bel Air, California, to live with his Uncle Philip and Aunt Vivian. Not only must the rambunctious teenager make a major readjustment to residing in a splashy mansion, but he must also cope with his relatives' pretensions, especially those of his preppie cousin Carlton. Adding to the cartoonlike ambiance of the series is Geoffrey, the *very* proper black British butler to the Banks, who proves to be a major ally of the newcomer.

What made the series work so well was the infectious personality of real-life rap star Smith in the lead role. (His professional rap partner, D.J. Jazzy Jeff, was a recurring guest on the show.) The buffoonery of the Banks clan is seen through Smith's eyes as he attempts to enjoy, exploit, and sometimes lampoon his wealthy relatives. This funky young man was far removed from J.J., the teenage con artist, as played by Jimmie Walker on *GOOD TIMES* (1974–79).

Along with (to a lesser extent) *THE COSBY SHOW* (1984–92) and Damon Wayans's *My Wife and Kids* (2001–), this series was one of the few American TV programs, especially in the sitcom genre, to present the African-American upper middle class to home viewers.

G

ghetto dramas—feature films See URBAN DRAMAS—FEATURE FILMS.

***Ghost Dog: The Way of the Samurai* (1999)** Artisan Entertainment, color 115 minutes. **Director/Screenplay:** Jim Jarmusch; **Cast:** Forest Whitaker (Ghost Dog), John Tormey (Louie Bonacelli), Cliff Gorman (Sonny Valerio), Henry Silva (Ray Vargo), Isaach de Bankolé (Raymond), Tricia Vessey (Louise Vargo), Camille Winbush (Pearline).

Quirky, bloody, funny, and at times pretentious, this art-house film revolved around an extremely sensitive performance by Whitaker as Ghost Dog, a mob employee. This American is a hit man who is guided by the samurai code *(Hagakure)*, keeps pigeons, and lives a solitary life. His only friends are Raymond, a Haitian ice-cream seller, and a youngster (Winbush) whom he encounters in the park. When a contract assignment goes amiss, the mobsters put a hit out on Ghost Dog. After killing several of the mob's thugs, Ghost Dog gives away his prize possessions to Pearline and Raymond. Then, following his code, he allows himself to be killed by the gangster's underlings.

If it seemed incongruous for a twentieth-century American to be living by ancient Japanese samurai codes, it was even more so having the bulky but precise African-American Ghost Dog so enveloped in Asian ways. But that was only part of the mix as iconoclastic filmmaker Jarmusch meshed the cultures of African Americans with Italian Americans intermingled with Japanese philosophy. The leisurely moving feature veered discordantly from comedy to sentiment to violence but was centered by Whitaker's soulful characterization.

It was not surprising that this offbeat feature grossed only slightly more than $3 million in domestic distribution.

***Gimme a Break* (1981–1987)** NBC-TV series, color, 30 minutes. **Cast:** Nell Carter (Nellie Ruth "Nell" Harper), Dolph Sweet (Chief Carl Kanisky: 1981–85), Kari Michaelson (Katie Kanisky: 1981–86), Lara Jill Miller (Samantha "Sam" Kanisky), Telma Hopkins (Addy Wilson: 1984–87), Rosetta LeNoire (Maybelle Harper: 1986–87).

Carter brought great exuberance to her TV sitcom role of a former club singer turned black housekeeper to a white widower—a cranky police chief—and his three daughters. Much like the lead character in *BEULAH* three decades earlier, Carter completely commits herself to her duties, often sacrificing her own life to take care of her charges. When she does take time off, it is usually to gallivant about town with her equally man-crazy pal Addy. LeNoire made several appearances as Nell's sour-faced mama from Alabama.

By the start of the show's fifth season, Chief Kanisky has died, and Nell is the head of the household, making her character seem less like the old mammy-type character of 1930s movies. In the final year on the air, Nell moves herself and her "family" to New York City and finds work at a publishing house. She has finally become a contemporary, liberated woman.

***Glory* (1989)** TriStar, color, 122 minutes. **Director:** Edward Zwick; **Screenplay:** Kevin Jarre; **Cast:** Matthew Broderick (Col. Robert Gould Shaw), Denzel Washington (Private Trip), Cary Elwes (Maj. Cabot Forbes), Morgan Freeman (Sgt. Maj. John Rawlins), Jihmi Kennedy (Pvt. Jupiter Sharts), Andre Braugher (Cpl. Thomas Searles), Raymond St. Jacques (Frederick Douglass).

While the 1970s BLACK ACTION FILMS largely exploited the African-American condition, they rarely provided historical perspective on the race. In the wake of that genre came *Glory*, a superior historical spectacle that not only focused on African Americans but also revealed (and explained) a little-publicized aspect of the Civil War—the ethnic minority troops who bravely fought and died for the North during the 1860s. Relying on letters of the actual Colonel Shaw, plus the books *Lay This Laurel* (1983) by Lincoln Kirstein and *One Gallant Rush* (1965) by Peter Burchard, *Glory* was a testament to the unheralded minority soldiers. As such this antiwar film was light years away from the theatrical Civil War depicted in *THE BIRTH OF A NATION* (1915) and *GONE WITH THE WIND* (1939).

During the Civil War, young Col. Robert Shaw—a wealthy New Englander—leads the 54th Regiment of Massachusetts Volunteer Infantry, the first regiment of African Americans to fight against the Confederacy. His ragged recruits are composed of runaway slaves and freed men, many of them illiterate and shoeless. They follow Shaw to training camp eager to fight, even though the South promises to enslave captured blacks and to execute caught African Americans who wear Northern uniforms. Among Shaw's regiment is ex-gravedigger John Rawlins, who displays leadership qualities, and runaway slave Trip, who is rebellious, tough, and a bully.

The recruits undergo grueling training while suffering racial discrimination in pay, equipment, and respect from bigoted white soldiers. Later, Shaw and the 54th are finally sent against the Confederacy at Fort Wagner (South Carolina). Badly outnumbered by the enemy, the men are slaughtered as they storm on foot their impregnable objective. The fallen troops and their white officers are buried in a common grave by Southerners. With more than half of the 54th Regiment dead, the fort remains in enemy hands.

Grossing almost $27 million in domestic film rentals, *Glory* won three Oscars: Best Cinematography, Best Sound, and Best Supporting Actor (WASHINGTON). It received additional Academy Award nominations for Best Art Direction/Set Decoration and Best Film Editing.

Glover, Danny (1947–) Although he did not begin to act until he was thirty-three, this sturdy, muscular character actor/lead quickly made up for lost time. A reliable performer on stage, film, and TV, his greatest success proved to be as Det. Sgt. Roger Murtaugh, the constantly harassed cop/buddy "partner" of Mel Gibson in the *Lethal Weapon* movie franchise (1987, 1989, 1992, and 1998). Equally at home in serious ethnic drama, Glover shone in such presentations as *A Raisin in the Sun* (1989—TV movie) and *Bopha!* (1993).

He was born in the Haight-Ashbury district of San Francisco, the eldest of five children; his parents were U.S. postal workers. After high school and before attending San Francisco City College, he lived in a commune. On the SFCC campus he joined the Black Student Union and became an activist. He earned an economics degree and then worked in the city-planning department. However, he found true satisfaction by moonlighting in acting assignments, which led to studies at the local Black Actors Workshop. He made his movie debut in a bit in Clint Eastwood's *Escape from Alcatraz* (1979).

In early 1980 Danny was off-Broadway in *Blood Knot* and then again on stage in *Master Harold . . . and the Boys* (1982). After bit parts on TV, he was seen to advantage in the film *Places in the Heart* (1984) as the itinerant farm worker. The six-feet, four-inch Glover was a murderous cop in *Witness* (1985) and was "Mister," the abusing farmer, in *THE COLOR PURPLE* (1985). For his role as the stressed cop/family man in *LETHAL WEAPON*, Danny received the NAACP Image Award (the first of three thus far). That same year, he interpreted the title role in the made-for-cable movie *Mandela*.

Always an activist, Glover spoke out against South Africa's Apartheid policy, was a spokesperson for the National Association for Sickle Cell Anemia, and participated in NAACP conferences. He was coexecutive producer and star of the low-budget feature *To Sleep with Anger* (1990), a drama in which he exuded chilling meanness. Also in 1990, Glover was inducted into the Black Filmmakers Hall of Fame and starred in the actioner *Predators*.

In typical fashion, he alternated between heavy drama (e.g., *The Saint of Fort Washington*, 1993), comedy (e.g., *Angels in the Outfield*, 1994), and western adventure (*The Buffalo Soldiers*, 1997—TV movie). He played opposite OPRAH WINFREY in *BELOVED* (1998) and was the voice of Jethro in the animated feature *The Prince of Egypt* (1998). Glover was part of *Freedom Song* (2000—TV movie), dealing with the 1960s Civil Rights movement, and costarred with ANGELA BASSETT in the personal drama *Boesman and Lena* (2000). Later projects included the cable TV movie *3 A.M.* (2001), which deals with the lives and dreams of New York City taxi drivers (a job Glover once held in his early years), and the hit comedy *The Royal Tenenbaums* (2001) with Gene Hackman.

Goldberg, Whoopi (1955–) From mortuary cosmetologist to welfare mother to Best Supporting Actress Oscar winner (*Ghost*, 1990) to the screen's new singing nun (*Sister Act*, 1992) to Academy Award host (1994 and 1996) and on to being the star/producer of TV's revived *Hollywood Squares* (1998–2002), Goldberg—famed for her dreadlocks and big smile—seemingly did it all professionally. What made her multimedia success all the more astounding was that she had to overcome three big obstacles in the white male-dominated American entertainment industry: She was female, black, and unconventional looking.

She was born Caryn Johnson in 1955 (some sources list 1949) in New York City and raised in a housing project by her nurse mother after the father abandoned the family. She began to act at age eight in a local children's theater. As part of the Hippie generation, she became drug dependent but broke the substance abuse and wed her drug counselor. After divorcing her spouse, she and their daughter moved to San Diego, California. There, between very odd jobs, Caryn worked in improvisational theater and adopted her professional name of Whoopi Goldberg. Relocating to San Francisco she performed a one-woman production (*The Spook*

Show), which eventually was mounted on Broadway (1984), made into a TV special, and recorded as an album. Now a bona-fide celebrity, the unusual-looking Goldberg became the media's darling. An Academy Award nomination for her sensitive lead role in *THE COLOR PURPLE* (1985) transformed Whoopi into a much-in-demand Hollywood star.

Goldberg floundered in such unworthy celluloid vehicles as *JUMPIN' JACK FLASH* (1986), *Fatal Beauty* (1987), and *The Telephone* (1988). She did much better in her recurring role as Guinan the starship lounge host on TV's *STAR TREK: THE NEXT GENERATION* (1988–93). After her Oscar-wining *Ghost*, she alternated between heavy drama *(The Long Walk Home*, 1990), interracial romantic comedy (e.g., *Made in America*, 1993), interracial romance (e.g., *Corrina, Corrina*, 1994), embarrassing farce (e.g., *Theodore Rex*, 1995), and astute drama (e.g., *Boys on the Side*, 1995). Meanwhile, Whoopi became the first woman to solo host the Academy Awards (1994, 1996, 1999, and 2002), and she continued with her fundraising efforts in the *Comic Relief* TV specials.

A series of movie flops in the mid-1990s (e.g., *Bogus* and *The Associate*, both 1996) led to Goldberg switching to film character leads (e.g., *HOW STELLA GOT HER GROOVE BACK*, 1998, for which she won an Image Award; *The Deep End of the Ocean*, 1999; *Girl, Interrupted*, 1999) and an assortment of large cameo assignments on TV specials (e.g., the Cheshire Cat on *Alice in Wonderland*, 1999). The outspoken, high-energy Goldberg found renewed popularity as the star of the TV panel show *Hollywood Squares* in the late 1990s. A workaholic, her more recent projects included the animated feature *Monkeybone* (2001), the ethnic family drama *Kingdom Come* (2001), the comedy *Rat Race* (2001), and repeating her role as Guinan in the feature film *Star Trek: Nemesis* (2002).

Whoopi Goldberg in *The Long Walk Home* (1990). (JC ARCHIVES)

***Goldie and the Boxer* (1979)** NBC-TV, color, 100 minutes. **Director:** David Miller; **Teleplay:** David Debin and Douglas Schwartz; **Cast:** O. J. Simpson (Joe Gallagher), Vincent Gardenia (Sam Diamond), Ned Glass (Al Levinsky), Gordon Jump (Alex Miller), Madlyn Rhue (Marsha Miller), Phil Silvers (Wally), Melissa Michaeleen (Goldie Kellog).

Years before SIMPSON became involved in the infamous Los Angeles double homicide case, he starred in this pleasing TV movie. When her boxer father dies, ten-year-old Goldie Kellog finds herself being cared for by her dad's sparring partner, Joe Gallagher. Before long, the precocious white child is managing the black pugilist.

Coy and saccharine as it may be, the telefeature pleased many viewers and led to the sequel *Goldie and the Boxer Go to Hollywood* (1981). Nevertheless, there was some dissent among reviewers who found this entry about having a little white youngster guiding the tall adult's life patronizing to African Americans. These made-for-TV movies were produced by Simpson's own production company.

***Go, Man, Go!* (1954)** United Artists, b&w, 82 minutes. **Director:** James Wong Howe; **Screenplay:** Arnold Becker; **Cast:** Dane Clark (Abe Saperstein), Pat Breslin (Sylvia Saperstein), Sidney Poitier (Inman Jackson), Edmon Ryan (Zack leader), Ruby Dee (Irma Jackson), the Harlem Globetrotters (themselves).

The famed basketball team had already appeared in another low-budget entry, *The Harlem Globetrotters* (1951), which featured DOROTHY DANDRIDGE. This new drama revolved around the formation of the hoops squad, prized for their humorous shenanigans and prowess on the court. Because the segregation line in sports had already been breached by this time, it was a way to present minority figures on screen (i.e., retelling how the team came to be). As so often was true in American movies of the 1950s and even for decades later, at the nub of the black characters' achievement was a well-intentioned white figure. Without him, it was inferred, the African Americans would have never triumphed. Few commentators took notice of the condescending premise at the time of this film's release.

In the 1930s, Jewish sports coach Abe Saperstein encounters a group of blacks playing basketball in their ghetto. Determined to have them succeed, he tutors them and takes them on a barnstorming tour, where they must deal with discrimination. The crucial big game in this chronicle finds the Globetrotters matched against an outstanding white team where victory will mean more than just a sports win.

Expert cinematographer Howe made his directorial debut here, and the programmer featured the young, slender POITIER as one of the team players with DEE as his wife. Blended into the proceedings was actual footage of the Globetrotters at work.

***Gone with the Wind* (1939)** Selznick-MGM, color, 220 minutes. **Directors:** Victor Fleming, and uncredited Sam Wood and George Cukor; **Screenplay:** Sidney Howard; **Cast:** Clark Gable (Rhett Butler), Vivien Leigh (Scarlett O'Hara), Olivia de Havilland (Melanie Hamilton), Leslie Howard (Ashley Wilkes), Thomas Mitchell (Gerald O'Hara), Hattie McDaniel (Mammy), Oscar Polk (Pork), Butterfly McQueen (Prissy), Everett Brown (Big Sam, the foreman)

Regarded by many as Hollywood's greatest film, this sweeping epic of the South before, during, and after the Civil War earned eight Academy Awards (plus five other nominations), grossed more than $200 million in domestic distribution since its original release, and caused various reactions over the decades among African-American audiences regarding its depiction of the black slave characters.

Although much of *Gone with the Wind* focused on willful Scarlett O'Hara, the belle of Tara plantation, her abiding love for genteel Ashley Wilkes (whom she loses to Melanie Hamilton), and her growing passion for the macho rogue Rhett Butler, screen time was devoted to a few (representative) African-American characters. Most notable in the proceedings was Mammy, a no-nonsense Tara house slave who never thought of herself as subservient to her white masters, especially not headstrong Scarlett. Whether squeezing her mistress into a tight corset or directing her on the proper etiquette for eating and flirting, Mammy was a refreshingly feisty individual—strong, resourceful, chipper, and not a stereotype. Then there was the unforgettable Prissy, Scarlett's black maid in Atlanta, a scatterbrained young woman who was easily shocked into fluttering her hands wildly and screaming in high-pitched hysteria. Further on in the screen saga, after the South had lost the Civil War, there was a key sequence in which Scarlett rode out from Atlanta, alone in her carriage. Recklessly, she drove too close to a shantytown and was nearly molested by randy white scavengers. She was miraculously saved by the sudden arrival of Big Sam, formerly a Tara field foreman.

All three of these black characters were particularly intriguing images on the Hollywood screen of the late 1930s. MCDANIEL's impudent and resilient Mammy was a sassy prototype of the black servant so frequently played by McDaniel or LOUISE BEAVERS on the screen, the type who loved her white employer (usually a headstrong young woman) and was not about to let her go astray, even if it required mouthing off to her boss. She was also a woman of vanity, especially flattered when Rhett Butler remembered to buy her a bright red petticoat, revealing that she was as feminine and self-confident as any white woman. MCQUEEN's Prissy represented a continuation of Hollywood (reflecting other media) using the ethnic minority as comedy relief—a silly woman fearful of real and unreal dangers—but one nevertheless who stuck to her job as best she could. She too had impressive allegiance to Scarlett in the face of (actual) danger. In addition, Brown's physically powerful Big Sam displayed loyalty and courage in rescuing his former plantation owner, Scarlett. He was rewarded with reassurances that he would not suffer repercussions from the reconstructionists and other whites for his special act of bravery.

At the time of the film's release, the movie was picketed by members of the black community around the country and attacked by the NAACP and other organizations as perpetuating negative stereotypes of African Americans. In more recent years, the black characters presented in *Gone with the Wind* emerged—in the viewpoint of black audiences—as largely positive images of representational figures from the times of slavery. No longer, as in the late 1930s or the more militant 1960s and 1970s, were these African-American screen performances considered embarrassing because their characters showed compassion for their (former) white owners. Then too, more recent generations of blacks generally look with pride at McDaniel's commanding portrayal of Mammy for which she won a Best Supporting Actress Academy Award. After all, she was the first black performer to win an Oscar.

With significantly lesser results, Margaret Mitchell's 1936 best-selling novel was also adapted into a stage musical (1970), and the book sequel, *Scarlett* (1991) by Alexandra Ripley, became a 1994 TV miniseries. In that 360-minute (inferior) television production, ESTHER ROLLE was Mammy, while PAUL WINFIELD took over the part of Big Sam, now a lumber-mill entrepreneur. (The roles of such black characters as Prissy and Pork were deleted from the proceedings.)

Good Day to Die, A See *CHILDREN OF THE DUST*.

Gooding, Cuba, Jr. (1968–) One of the few African-American performers to thus far have won an Academy Award—in his case, for Best Supporting Actor for his performance in *Jerry Maguire* (1996). Gooding's intensity on camera is his trademark, although he can be comedic, as in the light-hearted western *Lightning Jack* (1994), in which he was the mute sidekick of Australia's Paul Hogan.

Born in the South Bronx, Gooding Jr., the son of a musician, was exposed to the creative arts from an early age. His father was the lead singer of the Main Ingredient. The group had great success with their hit "Everybody Plays the Fool," and for a time there was financial stability in the Gooding household. Then Cuba Sr. departed, and his wife and children had to go on welfare. After Cuba quit high school, he worked as a busboy and a construction worker. His first professional gig was at the 1984 Olympics in Los Angeles, where he did break dancing for Lionel Richie's act. His first TV part was on the sitcom *Amen* in 1986. His movie debut (as a youth getting a haircut) was in EDDIE MURPHY's *Coming to America* (1988).

The cast of TV's *Good Times* (1974–79) in 1978: Ralph Carter, Janet Jackson, Esther Rolle, BerNadette Stanis, Ben Powers, Ja'net DuBois, and Jimmie Walker (JC ARCHIVES)

He was in the TV adventure series *MacGyver* several times between 1989 and 1991, but it was his presence in the URBAN DRAMA *BOYZ N THE HOOD* (1991) that made Hollywood take notice of him. He appeared in *A Few Good Men* (1992), the suspense thriller *Outbreak* (1995) with Dustin Hoffman, and *The Tuskegee Airmen* (1995—cable TV movie), about a group of African-American pilots in World War II who overcome racial prejudice and serve their country in combat.

His character's demand ("Show me the money!") to his sports agent (Tom Cruise) in the box-office hit *Jerry Maguire* became a national catchphrase. After that, Academy Award winner Gooding seemed to suffer the Oscar jinx in his career. He was active in films (e.g., *As Good As It Gets*, 1997; *What Dreams May Come*, 1998; *A Murder of Crows*, 1999), but his presence in these entries did not elevate him professionally. He had more-focused roles in the thriller *Instinct* (1999) and the actioner *Chill Factor* (1999) and was in fine form conflicting with tough officer/bigot Robert De Niro in *Men of Honor* (2000). In the overblown epic *Pearl Harbor* (2001), Cuba was Petty Officer Dorie Miller. Later roles included the thriller *In the Shadows* (2001) with James Caan and the comedy *Boat Trip* (2002) with Vivica A. Fox.

Gooding's younger brother Omar also became an actor (e.g., *Ghost Dad*, 1990; *BABY BOY*, 2001).

***Good Times* (1974–1979)** CBS-TV series, color, 30 minutes. **Cast:** Esther Rolle (Florida Evans: 1974–77, 1978–79), John Amos (James Evans: 1974–76), Jimmie Walker (J.J. [James Evans Jr.]), Ja'net DuBois (Willona Woods), Ralph Carter (Michael Evans), Janet Jackson (Penny Gordon Woods: 1977–79).

This TV comedy, a spin-off from *Maude*, which was a spin-off from *All in the Family*, was noteworthy as the first black family sitcom of the 1970s. As conceived, the show was designed to showcase a lower middle-class black couple (ROLLE and Amos) and their three children who live in a run-down ghetto high-rise building on Chicago's South Side. Florida is a bedrock of strength, while her well-meaning husband, constantly in and out of work, struggles to provide for his family. (After two seasons, Amos left the show and his character was killed off.)

As time progressed, Rolle's role was downplayed to that of J.J., her eldest child. The latter, who referred to himself as the "Ebony Prince," attends a trade school but is consumed with chasing girls, borrowing money from a loan shark, and looking for the next get-rich-fast scheme. With his double talk, his double takes, and his endless use of the expression "Dy-No-Mite," he soon became the show's most popular character. Although J.J. found work, he became increasingly mindless as a person, emerging as a foolish caricature.

In a well-publicized walk-out, Rolle quit *Good Times* for one season (1977–78), angered that the program was presenting negative images of young blacks by focusing so much on smart-mouthed, empty-headed J.J. By the time she returned, her character's new husband (seen in 1977 episodes) had magically vanished, and the program had already lost its vogue. It soon was yanked from the network lineup.

Watched today, *Good Times* seems tremendously dated. Its much-hyped original intention of presenting topical racial and economic issues became, in reality, nothing more than occasional declamations by a single character with little to no plot follow-through.

Gossett, Lou See GOSSETT, LOUIS, JR.

Gossett, Louis See GOSSETT, LOUIS, JR.

Gossett, Louis, Jr. (aka: Lou Gossett; Louis Gossett) (1936–) Impressive in height (six feet, four inches), this lanky actor is also noteworthy for his sterling acting performances, often playing prideful African Americans who mask their warm interiors. In fact, it was this character trait in much of his work that stopped sinewy Gossett from partaking in the BLACK ACTION FILM bonanza of the 1970s. After a long apprenticeship on stage, film, and TV—including a brief career as a member of a doo-wop singing group—the commanding Gossett won an Academy Award as the Best Supporting Actor for *AN OFFICER AND A GENTLEMAN* (1982). Louis is also notable for his role as Fiddler in the TV miniseries *ROOTS* (1977—for which he won an Emmy Award) and for starring in the popular *Iron Eagle* film franchise (1986, 1988, 1992, and 1995).

He was born in Brooklyn, New York, the son of a porter and a maid. After a leg injury temporarily halted his high school basketball career, he turned to acting, making his Broadway debut in 1953 in *Take a Giant Step.* He attended New York University on an athletic scholarship, while pursuing stage and TV acting jobs. Although later drafted by the New York Knickerbockers pro basketball team, he turned down the offer to continue his acting career. He acted in both the stage (1959) and film (1961) editions of *A RAISIN IN THE SUN.* Despite the limited scope of jobs open to African-American actors on TV, he appeared on assorted TV series. He was explosive in the overlooked ethnic feature *THE LANDLORD* (1970). In 1977, the same year as his exceptional performance in *Roots*, he was stuck as a nondimensional villain in the exploitive film *The Deep.* He went on to star in the brief-lasting TV series *THE LAZARUS SYNDROME* (1979) and was effective in the dramatic TV movie, *A Gathering of Old Men* (1987).

Louis was in a rash of TV movies in the 1990s and thereafter including *Ray Alexander: A Taste for Justice*, 1994; *To Dance with Olivia*, 1997; *Strange Justice*, 1999; and *For Love of Olivia*, 2001. (He also joined with Jonathan Silverman as investigating postal inspectors in the telefeatures *The Inspectors*, 1998; *The Inspectors 2: A Shred of Evidence*, 2000.) Gossett often supplied his sonorous voice for narration of TV specials (e.g., *Story of a People*, 1993) and continued making feature films: *Curse of the Starving Class* (1994); *Managua* (1996); *Legend of the Mummy* (1997), and so on.

***Grambling's White Tiger* (1981)** NBC-TV, color, 100 minutes. **Director:** Georg Stanford Brown; **Teleplay:** Zev Cohen, Louis A. Potter, and William A. Attaway; **Cast:** Harry Belafonte (Eddie Robinson), Bruce Jenner (Jim Gregory), Dennis Haysbert (James Shack Harris), Bill Overton ("Fat Rabbit" Manning), Deborah Pratt (Jennifer Johnson), LeVar Burton (Charles "Tank" Smith).

This telefeature has an intriguing premise. California high school graduate Jim Gregory, a white gridiron star, wants to become a professional football player after attending college. To get the sports training he needs, and to further his education, he attends Grambling College in Louisiana—an all-black institution. This reverse-type minority narrative was based on a true story, as recounted in *My Little Brother Is Coming Tomorrow* (1971).

BELAFONTE, in his TV dramatic bow, played Coach Eddie Robinson, the tough football instructor on campus, with Jenner, an Olympic decathlon gold medal winner in 1978, as the white student who coped with antiwhite discrimination from his African-American classmates at Grambling.

***Greased Lightning* (1977)** Warner Bros., color, 96 minutes. **Director:** Michael Schultz; **Screenplay:** Kenneth Vose, Lawrence DuKore, Melvin Van Peebles, and Leon Capetanos; **Cast:** Richard Pryor (Wendell Scott), Beau Bridges (Hutch), Pam Grier (Mary Jones), Cleavon Little (Peewee), Vincent Gardenia (Sheriff Cotton), Richie Havens (Woodrow), Noble Willingham (Billy Joe Byrnes), Julian Bondli (Russell).

Demonstrating his acting acumen, PRYOR starred in this biography of America's first black championship race-car driver. Covering a twenty-five-year period, the film traces Wendell Scott's track career, which began after the World War II veteran returned to Danville, Virginia, in the mid-1940s. He weds Mary Jones and purchases a taxicab, hoping one day to have a garage repair shop. To earn extra money he runs moonshine, but his luck runs out and he is put in jail. However, the conniving sheriff (Gardenia) is prompted by a race-car prompter (Willingham) to enter Wendell in a local stock race. On the track, Scott, a novelty in the white track world, must cope with racial discrimination. Despite the bigotry, he pursues his career, building a team of helpers (including Bridges and Little) in the process. Eventually, Wendell enters the Grand National Championship and, despite past injuries and his being middle-aged, wins.

A bit more serious than Pryor's earlier *The Bingo Long Traveling All-Stars and Motor Kings* (1976)—which also dealt with sports (baseball) in a period setting—this production provided a then-rare celluloid instance of a black man as a positive role model.

During production, coscripter Van Peebles was replaced as director by Schultz, who had worked with Pryor in *CAR WASH* (1976). The reason why BLACK ACTION FILM icon Grier took a conventional, subordinate assignment here was that she was engaged to Pryor at the time. Made for approximately $3.2 million, the PG-rated *GREASED LIGHTNING* grossed a relatively mild $7.6 million in domestic film rentals.

***Great White Hope, The* (1970)** Twentieth Century-Fox, color, 102 minutes. **Director:** Martin Ritt; **Screenplay:** Howard Sackler; **Cast:** James Earl Jones (Jack Jefferson), Jane Alexander (Eleanor), Lou Gilbert (Goldie), Joel Fluellen (Tick), Chester Morris (Pop Weaver), Marlene Warfield (Clara), Beah Richards (Mama Tiny), Moses Gunn (Scipio).

A few years after Sackler's play won the Pulitzer Prize and Tony Award, JONES, Alexander, and Warfield repeated their Broadway roles on camera. The drama was a semifictionalized account of Jack Johnson (1878–1946), the world's first African-American heavyweight champ. At the time, the sporting world was still agog over heavyweight boxing star Muhammad Ali (aka: Cassius Clay), and many found parallels between Ali's life and this picture.

Having won the boxing title and overinflated by fame, Jack Jefferson abandons his lover (Warfield) to romance a white divorcée (Eleanor). This daring act and white envy over his fame leads to his being arrested, with the court determined to punish this "uppity nigger." Later, he escapes from jail and flees to Canada with Eleanor. After years abroad, where he is humiliated by bigots in and out of the sports world, a U.S. agent offers to reduce Jefferson's prison sentence if he will take a dive in a boxing match in Cuba. The champ refuses. Later, after the distraught Eleanor has killed herself, Jack agrees to the Havana competition. Part way through the bout, the badly mauled Jefferson changes his mind, but it is too late and the victory goes to his white opponent.

Instead of an idealized SIDNEY POITIER-type of character as the key figure, the robust Jones presented a raw, powerful sexual magnet. Like the emerging stardom of JIM BROWN, Jones's character presented a new (threatening to whites) ingredient for the Hollywood screen, especially in an interracial romance. The film also clarified how the price of fame was even heavier for a minority individual in a white world and how each race expected/demanded different things from the champ.

***Green Pastures, The* (1936)** Warner Bros., b&w, 93 minutes. **Directors:** Marc Connelly and William Keighley; **Screenplay:** Connelly and Sheridan Gibney; **Cast:** Rex Ingram (De Lawd, Adam/Hezdrel), Oscar Polk (Gabriel), Eddie Anderson (Noah), Frank Wilson (Moses), George Reed (Mr. Deshee), Abraham Gleaves (Archangel), Myrtle Anderson (Eve), Edna M. Harris (Zeba).

Connelly's Broadway original (1930) won a Pulitzer Prize and ran for 1,779 performances. It had been seven years since Hollywood had produced a major film with an all-African-American cast and everyone was so self-congratulatory about this picturization that, at the time, little heed was paid to the underlying conceit of this biblical drama/fable: that is, the amusement of having ethnic minorities portray Old Testament figures and speak the Scriptures in quaint ethnic slang, performing their parts in childlike wonderment. Despite this veiled bias, the piece offered many talented players an opportunity to play something on screen other than one-dimensional domestics, and they acquitted themselves with dignity. In the course of the movie, the famed Hall Johnson Choir sang portions of twenty-five spirituals.

In Louisiana, Mr. Deshee instructs his Sunday School class in Bible studies, telling them about God and Heaven in terms they can relate to—a Southern fish fry. He tells them of the creation of Earth, of Adam and Eve, Noah and his ark, the Israelites and Moses leading them out of Egypt, and of Jesus Christ who suffered for humanity's sins. With class over, the youngsters go out into the countryside, which resembles greatly the Heaven they have just heard about.

Well received by most critics, *The Green Pastures* was ranked among the year's top ten films by the *New York Times*, *Film Daily* trade paper, and the National Board of Review. Not distributed in many Southern communities, this "daring" film was banned in several European countries and severely edited for its British release. The property was later adapted for a 1957 TV production featuring William Warfield and Earle Hyman.

Grier, Pam (1949–) So impressed was filmmaker Quentin Tarantino when he auditioned Grier for a role in *Pulp Fiction* (1994) (which went to Rosanna Arquette) that he wrote *Jackie Brown* (1997) as a starring screen vehicle for her. He had discovered what others knew for decades: that five-feet, eight-inch Grier was not only a striking beauty but also an extremely sturdy performer. Far more than Tamara Dobson (e.g., *CLEOPATRA JONES*, 1973), Grier symbolized the BLACK ACTION FILM cycle of the 1970s with vivid performances in such entries as *Coffy* (1973) and *FOXY BROWN* (1974). Her blaxploitation movie leads also made her an icon of the women's movement, as no one was more liberated than Grier's butt-kicking heroines. In the late 1980s, she overcame cancer, which added to her status as a survivor role model.

She was born Pamela Suzette Grier in Winston-Salem, North Carolina, the daughter of an air force mechanic and a nurse. As a UCLA student, she found time to sing backup for singer/composer Bobby Womack. Later, Pamela, the cousin of football player-turned-actor Rosey Grier, went from film-company switchboard operator to movie actress, once executives noted her voluptuous figure and chiseled features. She had a bit in *Beyond the Valley of the Dolls* (1970), but it was the exploitive programmer *Women in Cages* (1971) that started her rise to Queen of the Bs. This part of the upsurge of blaxploitation movies led to *The Big Doll House* (1971) and *Black Mama, White Mama* (1972). Her title role in *Coffy* inaugurated her reign as the tough action heroine who triumphed over male opponents in several movies, including *Friday Foster* (1975) and *Sheba, Baby* (1975). As a change of pace, she was sedate in *GREASED LIGHTNING* (1977), starring her then boyfriend, RICHARD PRYOR.

Pam had small but memorable assignments in the TV miniseries *ROOTS: THE NEXT GENERATION* (1979) and the movie *Fort Apache, the Bronx* (1981) and a recurring guest role as Philip Michael Thomas's New York cop girlfriend in *MIAMI VICE* (1985). Before, during, and after her cancer battle, she kept busy with stage, TV, and film roles, including *Posse* (1993), *Serial Killer* (1995), and *Original Gangstas* (1996—a satire on the 1970s black action-picture craze). Along with Tim and Daphne Reid, she was part of the cable TV series *Linc's* (1998–2000). Thereafter, she continued making a stream of big-screen pictures: *Fortress 2* (1999), *Snow Day* (2000), *Wilder* (2000), *Bones* (2001), and the sci-fi action comedy *The Adventures of Pluto Nash* (2002) with EDDIE MURPHY. She joined DANNY GLOVER in the made-for-cable feature *3 A.M.* (2001).

In 1999 she received a Career Achievement Award from the Acapulco Black Film Festival.

***Guess Who's Coming to Dinner?* (1967)** Columbia, color, 108 minutes. **Director:** Stanley Kramer; **Screenplay:** William Rose; **Cast:** Spencer Tracy (Matt Drayton), Sidney Poitier (Dr. John Prentice), Katharine Hepburn (Christina Drayton), Katharine Houghton (Joey Drayton), Cecil Kellaway (Monsignor Ryan), Roy E. Glenn Sr. (Mr. Prentice), Beah Richards (Mrs. Prentice), Isabel Sanford (Tillie).

At the time of release, this was considered a highly controversial film—one that bravely tackled the issues of interracial love and marriage. In retrospect, this hugely idealistic tale is no more than a visually appealing, conventional screen romance buttressed with politically liberal platitudes that skirt most key points. Its chief contribution to the history of ethnic minorities in the American cinema was to make filmgoers *think* they were being liberal merely by watching this contrived drama. Thereafter, it was a bit easier for filmmakers and audiences alike to take the next tiny steps in accepting real racial minority issues and characters on camera.

In San Francisco, liberal newspaper publisher Matt Drayton and his broadminded wife (who operates a chic art gallery), a successful white couple, have their progressive viewpoints put to the test when their daughter (Houghton) returns from a Hawaiian vacation with her new beau (POITIER). They must react to the situation quickly because Joey wants to marry the man right away as he is scheduled to leave almost immediately for Switzerland to work for the esteemed World Health Organization. On one hand, the prospective groom is a high achiever (a much-lauded physician), handsome, considerate, and polite. But, the problem is that John Prentice is African American. Before long the groom-to-be's working-class parents arrive from Los Angeles, and they have their own reactions to the potential union.

This movie greatly stacked the decks by making Poitier's character a highly desirable black man—a successful professional man who is handsome and thoughtful. In contrast, the comely white bride-to-be had not achieved much beyond growing up in a pampered lifestyle and is now indulging her whim to wed a person she has known for only ten days. Her looks and her white nobility (willing to wed outside her race) are all that she brought to the love match. The many ramifications to the couple's pending marriage are hardly discussed, for example, the discrimination the couple (as well as their mixed-blood children) will certainly face in the future. Dismissed along the way is the life of subservience that laboring class Mr. Prentice must certainly have endured in the white world, a situation that is hardly hinted at in his interaction with his so laudable offspring.

Despite its flaws, *Guess Who's Coming to Dinner?* released after Tracy's death, was a huge box-office winner, earning more than $25 million in domestic film rentals. It won two Academy Awards: Best Actress (Hepburn) and Best Screenplay. It earned Oscar nominations for Best Actor (Tracy), Best Art Direction/Set Decoration, Best Director, Best Film Editing, Best Picture, Best Scoring, Best Supporting Actor (Kellaway), and Best Supporting Actress (RICHARDS).

H

***Hallelujah* (1929)** Metro-Goldwyn-Mayer, b&w, 100 minutes. **Director:** King Vidor; **Screenplay:** Wanda Tuchock and Ransom Rideout; **Cast:** Daniel L. Haynes (Zeke), Nina Mae McKinney (Chick), William Fountaine (Hot Shot), Harry Gray (Parson), Fannie Belle DeKnight (Mammy), Victoria Spivey (Missy Rose), Dixie Jubilee Singers (themselves).

Given that MGM knew that *Hallelujah* would be denied release in much of the Deep South, it was a brave gesture to make this, one of the first all-African-American features by a major Hollywood studio. (It was directed by the white filmmaker Vidor, who had experienced black culture while growing up in Texas.) Shot on location in Tennessee as a silent, sound was added in postproduction.

The simplistic narrative concerns tenant farmer Zeke who is led astray by a mulatto dance-hall siren (McKINNEY). His downfall includes accidentally killing his younger brother, becoming a preacher, reuniting with the tragic temptress (who later dies in a buggy accident), and killing her recurrent lover (Fountaine). Thereafter, Zeke serves a sentence on a chain gang and then returns home to his loyal woman (Spivey).

Vidor embellished this melodrama with ethnic music (especially spirituals), dancing, and culture, which were the chief virtues of this primitive entry. McKinney was especially vibrant as the mixed-blood miss who was portrayed (due to her background) as bound to be trouble. Vidor received an Oscar nomination in the Best Director category.

***Hearts in Dixie* (1929)** Fox, b&w, 71 minutes. **Director:** Paul Sloane; **Additional Director:** A. H. Van Buren; **Screenplay:** Walter Weems; **Cast:** Clarence Muse (Nappus), Eugene Jackson (Chiquapin), Stepin Fetchit (Gummy), Bernice Pilot (Chloe), Clifford Ingram (Rammey), A. C. H. Billbrew (voodoo woman)

In the post-Civil War South, elderly Nappus still works his farm. His hard-working daughter Chloe is wed to shiftless Gummy. When Chloe and their daughter are taken ill, instead of having the white doctor attend them, Gummy summons a voodoo woman. Both patients die. This prompts Nappus to sell his farm and his mule. He uses the money to send his grandson north to become a doctor, praying that the boy will one day return home to help his people.

Released several months before *HALLELUJAH*, another all-African-American musical, *Hearts in Dixie* was part of Hollywood's experimental craze in which the new talkie medium almost guaranteed a willing audience. While MUSE was the film's star, this primitive song-and-dance fest (featuring the sixty-member Billbrew Chorus) really showcased FETCHIT, whose patented shuffling walk and slow speech was already attracting moviegoers and would make him a major studio star in the early 1930s. His caricature also created a stereotype that became increasingly offensive to African Americans. In addition, this movie also catered to other types expected of plantation life including "singing darkies," "carefree pickaninnies," and "superstitious blacks" caught up in voodoo ritual.

To bolster its reception by mainstream audiences not used to seeing ethnic minorities dominate a film, *Hearts in Dixie* had a two-minute prologue asking the audience's indulgence for this tale of the Old South and its quaint people.

Hernandez, Juano (1896–1970) This respected performer with the imposing presence and ever-searching eyes was part of Hollywood's post–World War II new breed of black talent. Like James Edwards and, later, SIDNEY POITIER, Hernandez was *not* a singing, dancing, or comedic diversion to the film's main plot line but a serious actor who performed with sensitivity. Juano's professional achievements within the still-segregated movie industry made possible the later rise of such stars as Poitier, MORGAN FREEMAN, and DENZEL WASHINGTON.

Born Huano G. Hernandez in San Juan, Puerto Rico, the son of a seaman, in his peripatetic youth, he sang on the streets of Rio de Janeiro, Brazil, to earn food money. Later, he did a stage acrobatic act and became involved with circuses, vaudeville, and radio (often as a scriptwriter). At one point, under the name Kid Curley, Hernandez was a boxer in the Caribbean. He was on Broadway in *Show Boat* (1927) and began his film career with such all-black movies as *Harlem Is Heaven* and OSCAR MICHEAUX's *The Girl from Chicago* (both 1932). In the 1940s he was back on the New York stage in *Strange Fruit* (1945) and *Set My People Free* (1948).

Hernandez made a major breakthrough in films when he went to Hollywood to play an innocent man, Lucas Beauchamp, accused of killing a white southerner in *INTRUDER IN THE DUST* (1949). Juano was a musician in *Young Man with a Horn* (1950)—dispensing advice to the confused Kirk Douglas—and, that same year, was in the solemn western *Stars in My Crown* starring Joel McCrea. In MGM's *TRIAL* (1955) Hernandez was the African-American judge presiding over the trial of a Mexican youth charged with murder. (This entry was a major leap forward for racial integration on the screen, casting a black performer in the role of the presiding authority in a white majority courthouse.)

Although Juano's screen career should have leaped forward after *Trial*, thanks to the slowness of racial integration and his ordinary looks, his movie roles were generally unsatisfying subordinate assignments: *St. Louis Blues* (1958), *SERGEANT RUTLEDGE* (1960), *Hemingway's Adventures of a Young Man* (1962), *The Pawnbroker* (1965), *The Reivers* (1969) and his final movie, Poitier's *They Call Me MISTER Tibbs!* (1970).

***Holiday Inn* (1942)** Paramount, b&w, 100 minutes. **Director:** Mark Sandrich; **Screenplay:** Claude Binyon and Elmer Rice; **Cast:** Bing Crosby (Jim Hardy), Fred Astaire (Ted Hanover), Marjorie Reynolds (Linda Mason), Virginia Dale (Lila Dixon), Walter Abel (Danny Reid), Louise Beavers (Mamie).

Not only was this an excellent cavalcade of Irving Berlin tunes—including "White Christmas," which won an Oscar as Best Song—but this Crosby–Astaire showcase did what few Hollywood movies had yet done: It presented an African-American character as a (near) equal to her Caucasian coplayers. Although veteran actress BEAVERS was once again cast as a domestic, she did not overcompensate for her celluloid servant's status by being a caricature of the loyal "mammy" type. Instead, she was a three-dimensional, thoughtful housekeeper to Crosby's bachelor character. It is she who gives him the sage advice of how to pursue his lady love (Reynolds) with honesty. In a scene vital to the progression of ethnic minorities in American films, the hero listens to her counsel as equal-to-equal. He displays no flippancy or condescending attitude to "compensate" for taking an employee's advice.

Fed up with the rigors of show business, easygoing song-and-dance man Jim Hardy retires to a New England farm. When the discovers the difficulties of being a gentleman farmer, he converts his place into a hotel/supper club that will be open only on national holidays. His former partner, dapper Ted Hanover, appears at the inn and is immediately attracted to ambitious Linda Mason, part of Jim's new show. This leads to an ongoing contest between Jim and Ted to win Linda's hand as a dance and life partner.

This picture was made in the same year as *CASABLANCA* and *IN THIS OUR LIFE*, each of which also progressed the cause of equality for African-American performers on film. *Holiday Inn* was a huge money earner and was nominated for two additional Oscars: Best Original Screenplay and Best Scoring for a Musical.

The musical number "Abraham," performed as the Lincoln Birthday celebration, found Crosby, Reynolds, and the club's serving staff working in BLACKFACE. It also featured Beavers and her two on-camera children. Years later, when the climate of political correctness had improved, this sequence was often excised from TV showings of *Holiday Inn* because many viewers found the blackface routine offensive.

***Hollywood Shuffle* (1987)** Samuel Goldwyn, color, 82 minutes. **Director:** Robert Townsend; **Screenplay:** Townsend and Keenen Ivory Wayans; **Cast:** Robert Townsend (Bobby Taylor), Anne-Marie Johnson (Lydia), Starletta Dupois (Bobby's mother), Helen Martin (Bobby's grandmother), Craigus R. Johnson (Stevie, Bobby's brother), Paul Mooney (NAACP president), Keenen Ivory Wayans (Donald/Jerry Curl).

The humor was scattershot and the filming often amateurish, but first-time moviemaker TOWNSEND proved himself a talent in this independent production. This satire focused on Bobby Taylor, an African American who is anxious to break into Hollywood movies and desperate to win a role in a new BLACK ACTION FILM—the only venue for a novice minority talent. As he prepares for his audition as a jive-talking, street-mean dude—coached by his hip younger brother (Johnson) and chided by his grandmother (Martin) for wanting such a demeaning role—he fantasizes about various aspects of white-controlled show business and the ridiculous images created for African Americans to play. Although he wins the coveted screen part, his conscience won't let him accept it.

Ironically, in this attempt to satirize the "accepted" image of African Americans on screen, the film poked fun at grasping Jews, mincing gays, and other "types."

Shot during a three-year period for $100,000, *Hollywood Shuffle* grossed more than $5 million in domestic film rentals. It was nominated for an Independent Spirit Award as Best First Feature. This entry launched Townsend as a force within the entertainment industry.

***Home of the Brave* (1949)** United Artists, b&w, 88 minutes. **Director:** Mark Robson; **Screenplay:** Carl Foreman; **Cast:** Douglas Dick (Major Robinson), Steve Brodie (Corp. T. J. Everett), Jeff Corey (doctor), Lloyd Bridges

(Finch), Frank Lovejoy (Mingo), James Edwards (Peter Moss).

In Arthur Laurents's 1945 Broadway play—on which this landmark film was based—the central figure had been Jewish. Producer Stanley Kramer reasoned that two breakthrough movies (1947's *Crossfire* and *Gentleman's Agreement*) had already dealt with anti-Semitism and shrewdly switched the character to be African-American.

During World War II, when soldier Peter Moss is examined at a military hospital, there seems to be no physical reasons for his partial paralysis and amnesia. Administered drugs to release repressed memories, Moss recounts a recent reconnaissance mission. During the dangerous assignment to a Pacific isle, the white soldiers treat Moss like an outsider. What especially hurts is that Finch, with whom Peter plans to open a bar/restaurant after the war, reveals his true racial feelings during a crisis. When the Japanese open fire, the injured Finch must be left behind so that the others can escape. Hearing the enemy torture/kill Finch leaves Moss guilt stricken and paralyzed. Awakening from his trance, Moss is told the reason for his problem. To provoke the man into walking, the doctor riles him by saying, "Get up, you dirty nigger." The plan works.

Promoted as "THE FIRST MOTION PICTURE OF ITS KIND! . . . Here is Hollywood's greatest blow at racial hatred," the independently made *Home of the Brave* was a critical and financial success. A still-potent drama when viewed today, the film's chief failing was the "happy" ending that found a white soldier (Lovejoy) suggesting to the now-recovered Moss that they open a bar together. It indicated that once again the African American was dependent on the kindness of a Caucasian.

***Homicide: Life on the Street* (1993–1999)** NBC-TV series, color, 60 minutes. **Cast:** Ned Beatty (Det. Stanley Bolander: 1993–95), Richard Belzer (Det. John Munch), Daniel Baldwin (Det. Beau Felton: 1993–95), Melissa Leo (Det./Sgt. Kay Howard: 1993–97), Andre Braugher (Det. Frank Pembleton: 1993–98), Yaphet Kotto (Lt. Al Giardello).

If *Hill Street Blues* (1981–87) provides a benchmark for a superior TV police drama, for many viewers the Baltimore-set *Homicide: Life on the Street* is an even grittier genre piece. It too presents a grim view of life on the street and uses a multiethnic cast to show its array of good guys, bad guys, and civilians. However, *Homicide* is more expansive in its coverage of black cops, ranging here from dedicated, overworked Lt. Al Giardello to persistent, hypercharged Det. Frank Pembleton. Not only are these figures shown on the job, but also their personal lives are more fully explored. This ranges from Giardello's estranged son (played by Giancarlo Esposito), a FBI agent trying to get close to his dad, to Giardello's wife (played by Ami Brabson), wanting to live a more normal life, one not engulfed in her husband's dangerous, thankless job. In such delineation, each of these African-American characters becomes a full-rounded figure (thanks to the fine acting of such talent as Kotto and Braugher), far from the token black characters of TV programming in the 1960s and 1970s.

Horne, Lena (1917–) With her husky, earthy voice, Horne became one of the great song stylists of the twentieth century. As a proud and determined African American, she made great strides in breaking down the color barrier in the Hollywood film industry and in clubs throughout the United States. As a beautiful, sensuous woman, she provided a remarkable presence in such movies as *CABIN IN THE SKY* (1943) and *Till the Clouds Roll By* (1946).

Horne was born in Brooklyn, New York. Her parents divorced when she was very young, and she was brought up by her grandparents. Later reunited with her mother, an aspiring actress, she traveled a good deal with her. Back in Brooklyn, she quit school as a teenager and found her first stage job—dancing (and later singing) at Harlem's famed Cotton Club. She was on Broadway in 1934's *Dance With Your Gods*, playing a quadroon girl, and soon began to record. Her movie debut was in the all-black movie musical, *THE DUKE IS TOPS* (1938), and the next year Horne returned to Broadway *(Blackbirds of 1939)*. After touring with Charlie Barnet's all-white band, she became a club chanteuse in New York City in the early 1940s. About this time she became active in pro-black causes.

Signed by the lofty MGM studio, her contract allowed her to reject stereotypical roles (e.g., the maid in Jeanette MacDonald's *Cairo*, 1942, which ETHEL WATERS accepted). The next year, Lena was a femme fatale in the studio's *CABIN IN THE SKY* and moved to Twentieth Century-Fox for another all-black song-and-dance fest, *STORMY WEATHER* (1943). Mostly at MGM she was stuck in films (e.g., *Panama Hattie*, 1942) doing specialty numbers, songs that could be sliced from release prints distributed in the South. Her greatest disappointment was losing the long-promised role of Julie in MGM's remake of *Show Boat* (1951). Her second marriage (undertaken secretly in 1947, publicly known in 1950) to white film music composer Lennie Hayton resulted in much hate mail from both blacks and whites.

Horne quit films in 1950 to return to club work, recordings, TV special appearances, and to a starring vehicle on Broadway (*Jamaica*, 1957). In the 1960s she became involved increasingly in the Civil Rights movement. She made another try at movies in the western *Death of a Gunfighter* (1969), in which her character was wed to a Caucasian. Horne was Glinda the Good Witch in the unsatisfying screen musical *THE WIZ* (1978), and she was a host in the documentary *That's Entertainment! III* (1994). Her one-woman show, *Lena Horne: The Lady and Her Music* (1981), became Broadway's longest running show of that type.

Capping the many tributes bestowed on Horne during the years, she received the Kennedy Center Honors in 1984 and a Grammy Lifetime Achievement Award in 1989. In 1996, PBS-TV aired a documentary: *Lena Horne: In Her Own Voice.* New and compilation albums of Horne's vocals continued to be released into the new millennium.

Houston, Whitney (1963–) Her performance career as a singer has been full of amazing statistics of hit songs and albums, awards, and her debut feature film, *The Bodyguard* (1992), which grossed more than $400 million worldwide. On the other hand, Houston—especially after her marriage to bad-boy rap singer Bobbi Brown—has amassed an unenviable array of bad press concerning marital spats, alleged possession of drugs, and her ongoing displays as a high diva.

She was born in Newark, New Jersey, the daughter of a staffer on the city's planning board and a mother, Cissy, who was a well-regarded gospel and rhythm-and-blues singer. Her aunt was Dionne Warwick, and such legendary singers as Aretha Franklin were frequent visitors in her home. By age nine, Houston was singing in the gospel choir at the local church. Thereafter, she and her mother performed together in clubs and on recordings. As a teenager, Whitney became a popular fashion model. While she auditioned and lost the role of Sondra on TV's THE COSBY SHOW (1984–92), she was signed by Arista Records and began an extensive recording career.

She had made a few acting appearances on TV shows (e.g., *Silver Spoons*) and in film bits, but *The Bodyguard* (which provided her with another hit album) launched her screen career. Her follow-up, *WAITING TO EXHALE* (1995), was a well-engineered tale of contemporary black women balancing the score with the men in their lives. Less entertaining was *THE PREACHER'S WIFE* (1996) in which her gospel singing, not her acting or the cumbersome romantic tale, was the highlight. For the multiethnic TV movie *Cinderella* (1997), Houston played the Fairy Godmother, while young songstress Brandy had the lead. In mid-2001, Whitney signed a new megamillion-dollar recording deal.

***How Stella Got Her Groove Back* (1998)** Twentieth Century Fox, color, 121 minutes. **Director:** Kevin Rodney Sullivan; **Screenplay:** Terry McMillan and Ron Bass; **Cast:** Angela Bassett (Stella), Whoopi Goldberg (Delilah), Taye Diggs (Winston Shakespeare), Regina King (Vanessa), Suzzanne Douglas (Angela), Michael J. Pagan (Quincy).

Two primary ingredients elevated *How Stella Got Her Groove Back* from the usual Hollywood romantic fluff: (1) It dealt with (upscale) African Americans, and (2) it told of an older woman (BASSETT) bedding a younger man (DIGGS). Based on McMillan's 1996 popular novel, this celluloid fantasy switched the clichés of a white-establishment love tale. For a refreshing change, the on-screen African-American heroine is allowed to be successful, fashionable, and responsible. Her problem: She is forty, divorced, mother of one, and makes no time for love. This changes when she vacations in Jamaica and is drawn to a handsome, well-educated stud. Their sexual idyll turns to love, but, as his parents and her relatives constantly remind her, he is half her age and has no real career. Eventually, in true Hollywood tradition the couple ignore the obstacles and cement their love bond.

If the story was not grounded in reality, and if many of the subordinate characters (especially GOLDBERG as her wisecracking, dying friend and King as her sister) seemed over the top, this wish-fulfillment narrative allowed minority players to function away from the standard cinema ghetto turf and to reflect other spectrums of African-American social classes.

Made on a $20 million budget, this romantic drama/comedy grossed almost $38 million at the box office in domestic distribution. At the Acapulco Black Film Festival, Bassett won as Best Actress.

***Huckleberry Finn* (aka: *Adventures of Huckleberry Finn*) (1939)** MGM, b&w, 88 minutes. **Director:** Richard Thorpe; **Screenplay:** Hugh Butler; **Cast:** Mickey Rooney (Huckleberry Finn), Walter Connolly (the "King"), William Frawley (the "Duke"), Rex Ingram (Jim), Lynn Carver (Mary Jane), Elizabeth Risdon (Widow Douglass), Victor Kilian ("Pop" Finn).

Mark Twain's (Samuel L. Clemens) book *The Adventures of Tom Sawyer* (1876) had focused on mischievous Tom and, to a lesser extent, on his social outcast pal, Huck Finn, as they experienced life in pre-Civil War Hannibal, Missouri. In *The Adventures of Huckleberry Finn* (1885), Twain made the rambunctious Huck the central character. That novel featured Jim, an escaped slave who befriends Huck on their wild adventures, both of them developing a strong bond in the process. Both volumes became literary classics and inspired many film adaptations. The most successful screen version of *Huckleberry Finn* came in 1939 with nineteen-year-old movie magnet Rooney in the understated lead assignment and veteran talent INGRAM as the respectful, often comical runaway slave.

When his drunken father (Kilian) reappears on the scene, irrepressible young teen Huck escapes on a river raft down the Mississippi, accompanied by Jim. Along the way, they encounter two con artists (Connolly and Frawley), and Huck is later bitten by a rattlesnake. When Jim is caught by authorities and refuses to reveal the whereabouts of the recuperating Huck, the slave is charged with murdering the youth. Only Finn's timely appearance saves Jim from being hanged.

The book original had depicted Jim as superstitious, ignorant, and gullible, but according to Huck, he was levelheaded "for a nigger." The 1939 movie edition presented Jim as a somewhat humorous and always subservient figure. Later screen versions of Huck Finn's misadventures revealed Jim as more dimensional and sympathetic, but always as a minority character who knew his place in the white world.

Other Hollywood big-screen versions of *Huckleberry Finn*—and the actors who played the slave Jim—include: 1920 (George Reed), 1931 (CLARENCE MUSE), 1960 (Archie Moore), 1974 (PAUL WINFIELD), and 1993 (Courtney B. Vance). There have been four American-made TV movies about *Huck Finn* and Jim: 1975 (Antonio Fargas), 1981 (Brock Peters), 1985 (Samm-Art Williams), and 1990 (Paul Winfield). In the TV movie *Rascals and Robbers—The Secret Adventures of Tom Sawyer and Huck Finn* (1982) the character of Jim the slave did not appear.

I

***I Know Why the Caged Bird Sings* (1979)** CBS-TV, color, 100 minutes. **Director:** Fielder Cook; **Teleplay:** Leonora Thuna, Ralph B. Woolsey, and Maya Angelou; **Cast:** Paul Benjamin (Freeman), Diahann Carroll (Vivian), Ruby Dee (Grandmother Baxter), Roger E. Mosley (Bailey Sr.), Esther Rolle (Momma), Madge Sinclair (Miss Flowers), Constance Good (Maya), John M. Driver II (Bailey).

Angelou's reminiscences of growing up in 1930s Arkansas during the Depression provided the basis for this prestigious drama, which lost some of its eloquence in the well-intentioned translation to TV. The memory piece focuses on teenage Maya and her beloved brother (Driver II) growing up with their steadfast grandmother (ROLLE), Maya's awe at her glamorous, irresponsible mother (CARROLL), the teenager's coping with being raped by one of her mother's friends, and the impression that her strong teacher (Sinclair) makes on her.

Despite the diminution of Angelou's poetic prose in the conversion to more standard small-screen fare, this still-powerful entry, like the book, opened many people's eyes to the perspective of the ethnic minority and how it differed from that of white America.

***Imitation of Life* (1934)** Universal, b&w, 106 minutes. **Director:** John M. Stahl; **Screenplay:** William Hurlbut; **Cast:** Claudette Colbert (Beatrice "Bes" Pullman), Warren William (Stephen Archer), Ned Sparks (Elmer), Louise Beavers (Delilah Johnson), Rochelle Hudson (Jessie, at age eighteen), Fredi Washington (Peola, at age nineteen).

Fannie Hurst's popular 1933 novel became a glossy soap opera movie, a well-produced showcase for star Colbert. But it was also the first Hollywood feature film to dare to suggest that there were racial problems in America. As such it was, and is, a landmark in U.S. cinema.

Widowed white Beatrice Pullman, who has a young daughter named Jessie, operates a small maple-syrup business. Beatrice hires a black housekeeper, Delilah Johnson (who has a light-skinned daughter named Peola). Soon Beatrice is marketing Delilah's pancake mix and, before long, the two have achieved great success. Delilah is reluctant to accept even a percentage of the business and remains living with/serving her white friends. Time passes, and Delilah's grown daughter Peola, determined to have the advantages accorded to whites, leaves home and tells her mother to avoid making contact with her. Meanwhile, Beatrice is being courted by eligible Stephen Archer. Later, a heartsick Delilah searches for her daughter who has quit college and finds her working as a "white" cashier in a segregated restaurant in Virginia. The schism with her child leads to Delilah's death. Peola returns home in time for her mother's funeral.

During the making of *Imitation of Life* the film industry's production-code board was much concerned that the word *nigger* not be used in the movie, that the issue of miscegenation that led to the birth of the light-skinned Peola be downplayed (the picture suggested that the girl was a full-blooded black who happened to have fair skin), and that the racial issue be handled by the studio very carefully.

When released, *Imitation of Life* was a tremendous hit with, among others, both BEAVERS and WASHINGTON receiving laudatory reviews from many critics. (Some African-American groups and reviewers were displeased with the film's presentation of the black characters as secondary citizens and Beavers's Delilah as being too meek to the whites.) The performances of Beavers and Washington often outshine those of the others, particularly in the scenes where the two women are interacting together.

More obvious in retrospect, the film was full of its own built-in racial inequalities. Even as Beatrice and Delilah's fortunes escalated, Delilah chose to remain serving her white friend, living in far lesser/segregated quarters in the house. Although much was said in the film about "passing for white," the implications of the character's reasons to do so were left in a vacuum. In actuality, having seen firsthand the advantages that whites enjoy inside and outside the home, Peola wants the same options in life, not to be hemmed in with the few choices and secondary status that had been her mother's fate.

The extremely sentimental *Imitation of Life* received three Oscar nominations: Best Assistant Director, Best Picture, and Best Sound. Sadly and ironically neither Beavers nor Washington were even considered for Oscar nominations. Twenty-five years later, the film was remade.

***Imitation of Life* (1959)** Universal, color, 125 minutes. **Director:** Douglas Sirk; **Screenplay:** Eleanore Griffin and Allan Scott; **Cast:** Lana Turner (Lora Meredith), John Gavin (Steve Archer), Sandra Dee (Susie Meredith, at age sixteen), Susan Kohner (Sarah Jane Johnson, at age eighteen), Robert Alda (Allen Loomis), Juanita Moore (Annie Johnson), Mahalia Jackson (choir soloist).

In the mid-1950s producer Ross Hunter planned a musical movie remake of the classic tearjerker, *Imitation of Life* (1934), with Shirley Booth and Pearl Bailey costarred; instead, he turned out this superglossy production as a Lana Turner showcase. Because of changing times in which racial integration had become—to a degree—more acceptable in America, plot alterations were made to Fannie Hurst's 1933 novel.

As revised for the 1959 film, the heroine, Lora Meredith, is a young widow seeking an acting career in 1947 New York. She and her daughter Susie meet African-American Annie Johnson (who has no particular talents) and her light-skinned daughter Sarah Jane at Coney Island. Before long, Annie (with her daughter in tow) is working for and living with the two Meredith women in a small apartment. Soon Lora's show business career takes off, and within years she becomes a great success. In the process she ignores her materially pampered daughter, who has been brought up by the selfless Annie. As for Sarah Jane, on learning that she can pass for white, she seeks romance with Caucasian men and later, again pretending to be white, seeks a show business career in Los Angeles. After Sarah Jane rejects her self-sacrificing mother one more time, the grief-stricken Annie dies. At Annie's elaborate funeral in Harlem, a grieving Sarah Jane returns, begging forgiveness. She is reunited with Lora and Susie, as is Lora with her faithful suitor, Steve Archer.

In a dazzling egocentric performance, Turner's self-involved Lora battled for career success, pushing away romance and her child in the process. But at the heart of the drama was the conflict between the black domestic and her ambitious daughter. Moore's Annie was not the entrepreneurial whiz LOUISE BEAVERS's Delilah was in the 1934 film, but she, nevertheless, made her character dimensional (with little help from the script or from egocentric Turner), desiring the most for her daughter but not wanting her to deny her forebears or culture. In this screen version, the light-skinned black daughter was played by a Caucasian-Hispanic actress (Kohner)—not by a black performer as was the case with FREDI WASHINGTON in the 1934 film. As such the filmmakers were more inclined to have the character seen in an interracial romance with a white man.

The elaborate and gaudy finale of the 1959 rendition allowed for a special appearance by the great spiritual singer Jackson, who performed "Trouble of the World"; the film's theme song was sung over the opening credits by another African-American singer, Earl Grant. Interestingly, the black mother and daughter, as in the first screen adaptation, lived in an ethnic vacuum, having no African-American friends (that is, until the grand finale of the 1959 movie in which the screen was mobbed with dark-skinned extras).

The weepy *Imitation of Life* was again a major box-office success. Both Moore and Kohner were nominated for Best Supporting Actress Oscars.

***In Living Color* (1990–1994)** Fox-TV series, color, 30 minutes. **Cast:** Keenen Ivory Wayans: 1990–92, Jim Carrey, Tommy Davidson, David Allan Grier, Damon Wayans: 1990–92, Kim Wayans: 1990–93, Shawn Wayans: 1990–93, and Marlon Wayans: 1992–93 (regulars).

This no-holds-barred comedy/variety series was assembled by multitalented KEENEN IVORY WAYANS and featured four of his siblings in various on-camera capacities. Producer-writer-actor-comedian Keenen Ivory took the satirical thrust and style of *Saturday Night Live* (1975–) and adapted it to the black idiom. (As such, he helped to redefine ethnic humor on TV.) Among the show's recurring skits were "Men on Film" (featuring two gay movie critics), "Hey Mon" (a soap-opera send-up about an industrious West Indian family), "The Home Boys" (two con-artist crooks), and "Homey" (the mean-spirited clown).

After two successful seasons, Keenen Ivory left the program in a dispute with the network; by the end of the third season his family members had quit too. This left white comedian Jim Carrey as the show's star, now joined by black comic CHRIS ROCK. Marlon and Shawn Wayans returned to TV as costars of the sitcom *The Wayans Bros.* (1995–99).

For the first season, *In Living Color* won an Emmy in the category Outstanding Variety, Music, or Comedy Program.

***In the Heat of the Night* (1967)** United Artists, color, 109 minutes. **Director:** Norman Jewison; **Screenplay:** Stirling Silliphant; **Cast:** Sidney Poitier (Virgil Tibbs), Rod Steiger (Sheriff Bill Gillespie), Warren Oates (Sam Wood), Quentin Dean (Delores Purdy), James Patterson (Purdy), Lee Grant (Mrs. Leslie Colbert), Beah Richards (Mrs. Bellamy [Mama Calebal]).

Some months before the release of the supposedly daring *GUESS WHO'S COMING TO DINNER?* (1967), which dealt idealistically with interracial love, came this tough drama told in the guise of a police procedural story. Both films featured Oscar-winner POITIER who, in each entry, was forced—by a timid Hollywood—to play an unrealistically near-perfect individual, one whose high professional abilities were matched by his great integrity of character. While *Guess Who's Coming to Dinner?* then and now leaves a great deal to be desired in its presentation, *In the Heat of the Night* allowed the black star to be much more of a real person, one who registered somewhat believable emotions, given the circumstances and the times.

In fact, Poitier's screen character was allowed to show genuine grit during *In the Heat of the Night.* This occurred in the scene where an angered, haughty white southern "gentleman" slapped Poitier's Virgil Tibbs and he—certainly a first in a major Hollywood picture—responds to the unwarranted assault by slapping the man back! For African-American audiences of the day, emboldened by slowly emerging racial integration (which was still so tentatively registered on the screen), this was an astounding (and satisfying) on-camera interaction.

In the small town of Sparta, Mississippi, a northern industrialist is murdered. This leads to a black stranger at the train station being arrested. The recently appointed sheriff, the redneck Bill Gillespie, is embarrassed to learn that the detained man is not only a police officer from Philadelphia (visiting relatives in Sparta) but that he also earns $200 more a month in salary than Gillespie. Overcoming his racial bias and knowing that this case requires Tibbs's expertise, the sheriff unofficially puts the visitor on the case. As Virgil and Bill work together, they each gain a grudging respect for one another, while Tibbs must cope with both the local white bigots and the astounded blacks of Sparta who don't know what to make of this seemingly uppity northerner. With the case eventually solved, Tibbs leaves town, with Gillespie even carrying Virgil's bag to the station.

Based on John Dudley Ball's 1965 novel, the film earned a powerful $11 million (approximate) in domestic film rentals. It won five Academy Awards: Best Actor (Steiger—Poitier was not even nominated!), Best Editing, Best Picture, Best Screenplay, and Best Sound. It received Oscar nominations for Best Direction and Best Sound Effects. Poitier returned to the role of Virgil Tibbs in two sequels, each a lesser effort than the one before: *They Call Me MISTER Tibbs!* (1970) and *The Organization* (1971).

Twenty-one years after the original feature film, Carroll O' Connor starred in a NBC-TV movie: *IN THE HEAT OF THE NIGHT* (1988). The plot found Tibbs (HOWARD E. ROLLINS JR.) and his wife (Anne-Marie Johnson) returning to Sparta for his mother's funeral. Soon, Chief Gillespie asks him to become the town's chief detective. This inaugurated a weekly TV series a few weeks later that lasted till 1994.

***In the Heat of the Night* (1988–1994)** NBC-TV (then CBS-TV) series, color, 60 minutes. **Cast:** Carroll O'Connor (Chief/Sheriff Bill Gillespie), Howard Rollins Jr. (Chief of Det. Virgil Tibbs: 1988–93), Anne-Marie Johnson (Althea Tibbs: 1988–93), Alan Autry (Sgt./Capt. Bubba Skinner), David Hart (Dep./Sgt. Parker Williams), Hugh O' Connor (Dep./Lt. Lonnie Jamison), Lois Nettleton (Joann St. John: 1988–89), Denise Nicholas (Harriet DeLong: 1989–94), Carl Weathers (Chief Hampton Forbes: 1993–94).

Twenty-one years after the successful *IN THE HEAT OF NIGHT* feature film, the weekly TV series adaptation of the original movie debuted. Cast in the lead as law-enforcer Bill Gillespie, a southerner and a bigot by birth, was O'Connor, famed for playing television's arch racist Archie Bunker on *All in the Family* (1971–83), but in the TV edition, reflecting the slowly improving status of racial integration and the need to have a more appealing lead character, Gillespie is not depicted as such a diehard segregationist. Gillespie's attitude toward Virgil Tibbs is cautious, just as much because he is an adopted northerner as because of his race. Besides, Gillespie is suspicious that this newcomer (forced on him by the mayor who wants to woo the black constituency of Sparta, Mississippi) might someday want his post. Before long, Gillespie (relying on years of experience) and Tibbs (who knows the latest scientific criminology techniques) are working together fairly harmoniously, skirting around the bigots on the police force and in town to solve the latest case.

Virgil Tibbs's home life in Sparta allowed for his on-camera wife (Johnson) to appear briefly from time to time, providing a small dollop of displayed black domestic life. As for previously wed Gillespie, in the show's second season he became interested in black councilwoman Harriet DeLong. Often, she was part of his case work, and, despite their different backgrounds, they began to date. By the 1991–92 season, they were having an affair that almost led to his ouster from office.

After the series switched networks, things changed for Gillespie. The city council did not renew his work contract, hiring instead African-American former FBI agent/Memphis police official Hampton Forbes to replace him. Thereafter, Gillespie became the sheriff of Newman County, working with the Sparta law enforcers when cases fell into their mutual jurisdiction. (By now, Rollins Jr., having had a spate of highly publicized personal problems, was no longer a series regular. According to the story line, he had started law school and only occasionally appeared on the show.)

In the spring of 1994—the series' last season—Gillespie and Harriet DeLong finally wed, causing further consternation among the citizens of Sparta.

By the fadeout of the popular TV series, the Gillespie-Tibbs rapport had undergone a tremendous change from the original concept of John Dudley Ball's 1965 novel and the classic 1967 feature film adaptation.

Of the *In the Heat of the Night* TV cast, only O'Connor was Emmy nominated, winning in the category Outstanding Lead Actor in a Drama Series for the 1988–89 season.

***In This Our Life* (1942)** Warner Bros., b&w, 97 minutes. **Director:** John Huston; **Screenplay:** Howard Koch and Huston; **Cast:** Bette Davis (Stanley Timberlake), Olivia de Havilland (Roy Timberlake), George Brent (Craig Fleming), Dennis Morgan (Peter Kingsmill), Charles Coburn (William Fitzroy), Hattie McDaniel (Minerva Clay), Ernest Anderson (Parry Clay).

Ellen Glasgow's Pulitzer Prize-winning novel (1941) was the basis of this overblown Davis–de Havilland melodrama set in the contemporary South. Of particular interest is the subplot of Parry, the son of Minerva Clay, the African-American maid to the Timberlake family. Bright and industrious, he works in Craig Fleming's law offices to earn funds to attend law school. Later, when reckless Stanley Timberlake kills a child in a hit-and-run accident, she places the blame on innocent Parry. Remaining dignified, the jailed Parry protests his innocence. Eventually, Stanley's scheme is shattered, and she dies in a car crash eluding the police.

In the more socially responsible era of World War II, Hollywood was slowly becoming more politically correct. There had been brief signs in the 1939 movie *Of Mice and Men* in which Leigh Whipper's minority character was treated more respectfully than the usual stereotype. By the time of *In This Our Life*, the era of the caricatured African American (e.g., the shiftless male, the selfless domestic, the giggling mammy) was beginning to disappear. This movie, along with the same year's *CASABLANCA* and *HOLIDAY INN*, helped to integrate further African Americans into white establishment movies as dimensional human beings—some good, some bad, as in any race.

Warner Bros. was listed on the Honor Roll of Race Relations of 1942 for presenting the Parry Clay character in such a dignified fashion. (Ironically the studio had cut some scenes featuring Parry because they feared adverse reaction when the movie was distributed in the South.) In 1943, the Office of Censorship, based in Washington, D.C., refused to classify the film for general export because it had so many inferences/statements that an African American could be accused and perhaps convicted merely on the charge of a white person.

***Introducing Dorothy Dandridge* (1999)** HBO cable, color, 115 minutes. **Director:** Martha Coolidge; **Teleplay:** Shonda Rhimes and Scott Abbott; **Cast:** Halle Berry (Dorothy Dandridge), Brent Spiner (Earl Mills), Klaus Maria Brandauer (Otto Preminger), Obba Babatundé (Harold Nicholas), Loretta Devine (Ruby Dandridge), Cynda Williams (Vivian Dandridge), LaTanya Richardson (Auntie), Andre Carthen (Harry Belafonte).

For years, there had been discussion about making a movie of the turbulent life of famed black singer/actress DOROTHY DANDRIDGE (1923–65), more recently as a project for Janet Jackson, ANGELA BASSETT, or BERRY. It was Berry who won out, starring in this better-than-average depiction of the life of a famed (and troubled) singer. In crowding so much of Dandridge's life into the confines of the biography format, such elements as the flavor of past decades, the extreme racial tension in the years Dorothy grew up, and her frustrated efforts to break through the racial barriers in American show business all received short shrift. Then, too, because the beautiful Berry could not approximate the truly sultry voice (talking or singing) of her subject—let alone that haunted, frightened look that lurked beneath Dorothy's seemingly confident demeanor—it was hard for today's viewers to appreciate the degree of magnetism the talented Dandridge possessed.

Based on the 1970 biography of Dandridge by her manager Earl Mills, the made-for-cable feature won Halle an Emmy, a Golden Globe, and an Image Award as Best Actress, with the show itself winning Golden Globe and Image trophies and the entry winning four other Emmys and six other Emmy nominations.

***Intruder in the Dust* (1949)** Metro-Goldwyn-Mayer, b&w, 87 minutes. **Director:** Clarence Brown; **Screenplay:** Ben Maddow; **Cast:** David Brian (John Gavin Stevens), Claude Jarman Jr. (Chick Mallison), Juano Hernandez (Lucas Beauchamp), Porter Hall (Nub Gowrie), Elizabeth Patterson (Miss Eunice Habersham), Elzie Emanuel (Aleck).

As part of Hollywood's emerging new post-World War II maturity, it tackled William Faulkner's 1928 novel and filmed it on location in the then-segregated town of Oxford, Mississippi. The movie (like the book) daringly challenged mainstream audiences to accept the major character first as a man—self-reliant, ornery, and unyielding—before considering the fact that he was not white. Within *Intruder in the Dust*, the bigoted white townsfolk did the opposite.

When a Caucasian lumberman is murdered in a small southern town, African-American property owner Lucas Beauchamp is suspected of the crime and dragged to jail. Young white Chick Mallison who had been saved from drowning by Lucas and still feels uncomfortably beholden to this different type of man, nevertheless persuades his lawyer uncle (Brian) to take the case. When Beauchamp refuses to name the white lumberman who is the likely killer, Chick, the attorney, the sheriff, and others ferret out the truth in time to save Lucas from being lynched and to trap the actual criminal.

Puerto Rican–born HERNANDEZ proved extremely effective in his role as the proud loner caught in the trap of a town's bigotry and envy. Despite the high praise for Hernandez's performance and for the film itself, neither he nor the picture received any Academy Award nominations.

***I Passed for White* (1960)** Allied Artists, b&w, 91 minutes. **Director/Screenplay:** Fred M. Wilcox; **Cast:** Sonya Wilde (Lila Brownell [Bernice Lee]), James Franciscus (Rick Leyton), Pat Michon (Sally Roberts), Elizabeth Council (Mrs. Leyton), Isabelle Cooley (Bertha), Lon Ballantyne (Chuck Lee).

Unlike such earlier Hollywood dramas as *PINKY* and *LOST BOUNDARIES* (both 1949) that dealt with mixed-blood African

Americans "passing" for Caucasian, this low-budget and lower-caliber entry sensationalized the subject matter. It was based on Mary Hasting Bradley's 1955 novel.

Virginia-born Bernice Lee, a light-skinned African American—her grandmother had had an interracial marriage—calls herself Lila Brownell when she moves to New York to start a new life. She pretends to be white at work and when dating Caucasian Rick Leyton. Despite her better judgment, she marries Rick, fearing that he will learn about her racial background. Her confidant becomes her African-American maid (Cooley). Bernice's concerns escalate when she becomes pregnant and worries what the color of her infant's skin will be. In the trauma of her baby being stillborn, her bigoted husband learns his wife's secret. Bernice leaves the marriage and returns home.

The producers claimed that they could not find an experienced, light-skinned African-American actress to play the lead, so they hired Caucasian Wilde. The *Hollywood Reporter* (March 1, 1960) noted: "The treatment of Negroes is dignified and respectful, but unfortunately one of the plot points unwittingly perpetuates an old wives' tale about genetic dominance. For much of the picture, she lives in fear of giving birth to a dark child."

When first released, several U.S. media outlets refused to advertise the film, and many theater circuits (North and South) ignored booking the picture. After successful drive-in theater engagements, the movie was accepted into several previously bypassed venues.

***Island in the Sun* (1957)** Twentieth Century-Fox, color, 120 minutes. **Director:** Robert Rossen; **Screenplay:** Alfred Hayes; **Cast:** James Mason (Maxwell Fleury), Joan Fontaine (Mavis Norman), Dorothy Dandridge (Margot Seaton), Joan Collins (Jocelyn Fleury), Harry Belafonte (David Boyeur), Michael Rennie (Hilary Carson), Stephen Boyd (Evan Templeton), John Justin (Denis Archer).

Alec Waugh's 1955 best-seller featured interracial romance, which was touted as a titillating key ingredient of *Island in the Sun*. The multistory drama was set on the imaginary British West Indies isle of Santa Mara and shot in glorious widescreen color on the islands of Barbados and Grenada.

As wealthy Englishman Maxwell Fleury prepares to run for political office against black union leader David Boyeur, the Briton learns that he may have mixed blood. This does not bother him (he thinks that it will help his political chances), but it concerns his younger sister (Collins) who hopes to wed the governor's son (Boyd). Meanwhile, Britisher Denis Archer is carrying on clandestinely with dark-skinned Margot Seaton; Boyeur is drawn to aristocratic lily-white Mavis Norman.

Although DANDRIDGE was given little opportunity to shine in her abortive characterization, let alone declare her love on camera to her British suitor (Justin), and although the highly touted passion between Fontaine and BELAFONTE's characters never materialized, the cagily conceived film created a storm of controversy because it cast white and African-American leads to play opposite each other. Beyond relegating the Oscar-nominated star of *CARMEN JONES* (1954) to the sidelines, it demoted Belafonte to a cardboard character who was barely allowed to touch his lady love.

Expectedly, southern movie theaters threatened not to exhibit the film, and in South Carolina a proposed bill (which did not pass) would have fined any theater $5,000 for showing the movie. The hullabaloo helped the picture (which cost more than $2 million to make) gross $8 million in domestic distribution.

***I Spy* (1965–1968)** NBC-TV series, color, 60 minutes. **Cast:** Robert Culp (Kelly Robinson), Bill Cosby (Alexander Scott).

This watershed series was the first dramatic show on American TV to give an African-American talent a leading role. Its premise of white Kelly Robinson and black Alexander Scott, two U.S. government agents traveling on undercover assignments around the world, made this the first example of interracial male bonding on an American TV show.

Of course, being the 1960s, Culp was top billed as the supposed tennis champ (his cover); second-billed COSBY was established as his trainer/traveling companion. Highly promoted for its integrated lead cast, the show, nevertheless, was careful to set the action largely outside the United States so as not to have any sticky plot-line questions such as: Would U.S. hotels be discriminatory toward black guests?

Throughout the adventure/espionage series, Cosby was forced to walk a fine line: On one hand, he could not downplay his character's equality to the white coplayer or he would have been considered an "Uncle Tom" to black home viewers; on the other hand, *I Spy* made sure that Cosby's Alexander Scott matched but never outdid his on-air partner in the areas of fashionable clothes, smart dialogue, or attracting women. As to socializing, Alexander Scott always dated black women, for, in the 1960s, interracial romance would have been too much for many viewers to accept.

By the time of *I Spy Returns* (1994), the program's reunion telefeature, it was clear how dated the show had become and that its once chief novelty, the integrated lead cast, was no longer enough to disguise the ordinariness of the proceedings. In 2002, EDDIE MURPHY, joined by Owen Wilson, took on the roles of Alexander Scott and Kelly Robinson in the big-screen edition of *I Spy*.

J

Jackson, Samuel L. (1948–) Although he was effective as the supercool and "righteous" private eye in the *SHAFT* remake (2000), he has been best known in his prolific career for his menacing celluloid villains. In the latter category, Jackson was Oscar nominated as Best Supporting Actor for playing hitman Jules Winnifield in *Pulp Fiction* (1994).

He was born Samuel Leroy Jackson in Washington, D.C. By the third grade, he was playing musical instruments and was in the school orchestra. He attended Morehouse College in Atlanta, Georgia, where he participated in a student protest against the administration and was expelled in 1969 but later returned to graduate. (He did, however, continue his interest in the black student movement.) Having gravitated into acting, Samuel relocated to New York City where he worked with the Negro Ensemble Company (with MORGAN FREEMAN). As a struggling actor, one of his many jobs during the years was as a doorman at a Manhattan high-rise building where many subsidized actors and artists resided.

Six-feet, three-inch Jackson made his film debut in Michael Schultz's drama, *Together for Days* (1972). A decade later, he was still stuck with small roles, such as playing a lowly gang member in *Ragtime* (1981) and being a hold-up man in EDDIE MURPHY's *Coming to America* (1988). For three years in the 1980s, he served as stand-in for BILL COSBY on *THE COSBY SHOW* (1984–92). Things finally improved for the actor when he began to work for filmmaker SPIKE LEE: *SCHOOL DAZE* (1988), *DO THE RIGHT THING* (1989), *MO' BETTER BLUES* (1990), and *JUNGLE FEVER* (1991). Ironically, Samuel, who openly acknowledged having had a drug problem, had just abandoned substance abuse when Lee cast him as crackhead Gator Purify in *Jungle Fever.*

With his heightened professional visibility, Jackson worked nonstop, including *Juice* (1992), *Jurassic Park* (1993), *MENACE II SOCIETY* (1993), and *Assault at West Point: The Court-Martial of Johnson Whittaker* (1994—TV movie).

Following his *Pulp Fiction* success, Samuel's screen credits ranged from heavy drama (*Losing Isaiah*, 1995) to gangster melodrama (*Kiss of Death*, 1995) to action entries like *Die Hard: With a Vengeance* (1995) and *The Long Kiss Goodnight* (1996).

With his high show-business profile, Jackson produced and starred in the southern Gothic entry *Eve's Bayou* (1997). He was back to on-screen meanness in *Jackie Brown* (1997) with PAM GRIER and was on hand in the rampaging sharks entry *Deep Blue Sea* (1999). In the *Star Wars* blockbuster *The Phantom Menace* (1999), Jackson appeared as Jedi knight Mace Windu, a part he repeated in George Lucas's next installment (2002) of the major sci-fi series. Jackson joined with Bruce Willis in the supernatural *Unbreakable* (2000) and shared screen time with Tommy Lee Jones in the military politics drama *Rules of Engagement* (2000). As executive producer of the drama *The Caveman's Valentine* (2001), Jackson cast himself as the man out to catch the killer of a homeless boy. The star was producer and star of the action entry *51st State* (2001) and Jackson teamed with Ben Affleck for *Changing Lanes* (2002), a story of road rage.

Jackson won an Image Award as Outstanding Supporting Actor in a Motion Picture for *A Time to Kill* (1996) and received a Career Achievement Award at the 1999 Acapulco Black Film Festival.

***Jeffersons, The* (1975–1985)** CBS-TV series, color, 30 minutes. **Cast:** Sherman Hemsley (George Jefferson), Isabel Sanford (Louise Jefferson), Mike Evans (Lionel Jefferson: 1975, 1979–81), Damon Evans (Lionel Jefferson: 1975–78), Roxie Roker (Helen Willis), Franklin Cover (Tom Willis), Marla Gibbs (Florence Johnston), Zara Cully (Mother Olivia Jefferson: 1975–78).

For the first four years (1971–75) of the TV sitcom *All in the Family*, George and Louise Jefferson and their son Lionel lived in Queens next door to archbigot Archie Bunker (and his family). The Jeffersons were a thorn in Archie's white side because they were black and not meek. (Conversely, George's brother Henry—played by Mel Stewart—was even more opinionated about whites than outspoken George.) So popular were the Jeffersons that in early 1975 they were given their own TV show, with the Jeffersons "movin' on up" to a luxury high-rise apartment on Manhattan's East Side. Adding to the mix was the Jeffersons' new neighbors, the Willises, he being white, and she black. (They were American TV's first interracial couple.)

In the show's initial seasons, diminutive firecracker George—complete with an Afro—was so ego inflated by the success of his dry cleaning business that he was an outrageous motor mouth. He sounded off unfavorably about "honkies," his dislike of the Willises and their biracial daughter whom he warns his son Lionel—to no avail—to stay away from. But the bickering did not stop there. George and wife Louise ("Weezie") are constantly at odds over his contentious behavior and his braggart ways. George must also deal with his acidic mother (Cully) and his biggest adversary, the Jeffersons' tart-mouthed black maid Florence, who, unlike a TV maid like *BEULAH* (but similar to the comedic domestics of 1930s films), preferred idleness and speaking her mind.

As the seasons wore on, pompous George and somewhat pretentious Louise became more assimilated and far less ethnic, but observant Florence remained her sarcastic, unpretentious self—relishing her confrontations with blustery George.

During the long run of the series—which received several Emmy and Golden Globes Awards nominations—*The Jeffersons* lost its sharp satirical edge. In the program's early years, many commentators thought that the comedy show was too stereotypical of a middle-class, bickering, black household. In the sitcom's declining seasons, several reviewers wondered where all the entry's ethnic edge had gone to.

***Jo Jo Dancer, Your Life Is Calling* (1986)** Columbia, color, 97 minutes. **Director:** Richard Pryor; **Screenplay**: Rocco Urbisci, Paul Mooney, and Pryor; **Cast:** Richard Pryor (Jo Dancer/alter ego), Debbie Allen (Michelle), Art Evans (Arturo), Fay Hauser (Grace), Barbara Williams (Dawn), Carmen McRae (grandmother), Paula Kelly (Satin Doll).

Because the real-life stand-up comedian PRYOR experienced approximations of many of the events depicted in this drama, it was hard not to take this piece—which he produced, directed, coscripted, and starred in—as not at least semiautobiographical (although he has claimed otherwise). As choreographer Bob Fosse did in his quasi-life story film *All That Jazz* (1979), Pryor used a life-threatening situation (here a drug-related accident) to reevaluate his existence. Through flashback, the narrative traces his childhood years with his grandmother (McRae) who ran a bordello and his mother (Diahnne Abbott) who was a prostitute. It passes quickly to his struggling years as a comic before he becomes a temperamental major star. In the process he has had several wives (e.g., Hauser and Allen), including a white spouse (Williams). Eventually, his substance abuse leads to near death, where he concludes that he will combat his many demons.

This relatively honest, edgy screen biography confused Pryor's fans, who expected another of his typical slapstick movie comedies; reviewers criticized the film's technical shortcomings (especially the narrative pacing and the star's reluctance to present his alter ego on camera in a dimensional manner). Other commentators noted that the picture's women were generally undeveloped pawns and that not enough was made of the ethnic ambiance surrounding his meteoric rise to fame. *Jo Jo Dancer* grossed about $18 million in domestic distribution.

Jones, James Earl (1931–) In whatever he played, and whether on stage, film, or TV, this man with an imposing presence and resounding voice (developed to overcome a childhood stutter) made himself the focus of attention. Having won a Tony as the ferocious boxer in Broadway's *THE GREAT WHITE HOPE* (1969), he received an Oscar nomination for recreating the showy part on film (1970). After that, Jones's commanding mien and rumbling voice was everywhere—sometimes grappling with roles for which he was not best suited. Jones was also noted for providing the booming voice of Darth Vader in the *Star Wars* movie trilogy (1977, 1980, and 1983).

Jones was born in Arkabutla, Mississippi, the son of a boxer who had turned to acting. Raised mostly by his maternal grandparents on their Michigan farm, Jones dropped plans to study medicine to concentrate on acting at the University of Michigan. Following army service, he enrolled at the American Academy of Dramatic Arts in New York City. His Broadway bow came in 1957, and during the next few years he played in a variety of new and classic roles, including several seasons with Joseph Papp's New York Shakespeare Festival. His movie debut was in *Dr. Strangelove* (1964), followed by a recurring role in the mid-1960s as a doctor on the daytime TV soap opera *The Guiding Light*

After *The Great White Hope*, Jones, by then stouter and, as an actor, broader, tackled a range of acting jobs, including the first black U.S. president in *The Man* (1972), DIAHANN CARROLL'S sanitation-worker lover in *Claudine* (1974), the robust pal of a pirate in *Swashbuckler* (1976), Malcolm X in *The Greatest* (1977), the title role in *Paul Robeson* (1978—TV movie), author Alex Haley in the TV miniseries *ROOTS: THE NEXT GENERATION* (1979), Father Divine in *Guyana Tragedy: The Story of Jim Jones* (1980—TV movie), and the heavenly Gabriel in *Amy and the Angel* (1981—TV movie). By then he had already starred in the brief-lasting TV cops series (PARIS, 1979–80). He was back on Broadway for *Fences* (1986), which earned him another Tony.

Jones ventured into more TV series (*Me and Mom*, 1985; *Gabriel's Fire*, 1990–92; and *UNDER ONE ROOF*, 1995). He was effective as the reclusive writer in *Field of Dreams*

(1989) and played Admiral James Greer in two actioners (*Patriot Games*, 1992; *Clear and Present Danger*, 1994), based on Tom Clancy novels. James's trademark voice was much in demand for voiceovers on TV specials and in cartoon features (e.g., Mufasa in *The Lion King*, 1994 and its sequel *The Lion King II, Simba's Pride*, 1998). His later feature work included *Gang Related* (1997), *Undercover Angel* (1999), *Finder's Fee* (2000), and the science fiction animated feature, *Magic* 7 (2002).

Along the way, Jones won a Daytime Emmy Award for Outstanding Performer in a Children's Special (*Summer's End*, 1998). Earlier he earned an Emmy as Outstanding Supporting Actor in the 1990 miniseries *Heat Wave*.

***Josephine Baker Story, The* (1990)** HBO cable, color, 129 minutes. **Director:** Brian Gibson; **Teleplay:** Ron Hutchinson; **Cast:** Lynn Whitfield (Josephine Baker), Rubén Blades (Count Giuseppe Pepito Abatino) David Dukes (Jo Boullion), Louis Gossett Jr. (Sidney Williams), Craig T. Nelson (Walter Winchell), Luis Reyes (Josephine's father).

Caught in the confines of a standard and often trite screen biography, this made-for-cable feature struggled to contain its unwieldy narrative of the complex, crowded life of St. Louis-born Baker (1906–75), 1930s star of Paris's Folies-Bergère. Told mostly in flashback, it endeavored to reveal the uniqueness of this highly emotional expatriate artist (famed for her exotic dancing and risqué outfits) who gained fame abroad, including film. Whitfield was commanding as the celebrity dancing/singing talent (although her vocals are dubbed by Carol Dennis) who found racism and rejection in her homeland. With Blades as the chief man in her life, this lavish production was filmed in Budapest.

In the cable TV movie *Winchell* (1998) about the New York journalist who had a contretemps with Josephine, Victoria Platt played Baker.

***Judge Priest* (1934)** Fox, b&w, 79 minutes. **Director:** John Ford; **Screenplay:** Lamar Trotti; **Cast:** Will Rogers (Judge William "Billy" Priest), Henry B. Walthall (Rev. Ashby Brand), Tom Brown (Jerome Priest), Anita Louise (Ellie May Gillespie), Hattie McDaniel (Aunt Dilsey), Stepin Fetchit (Jeff Poindexter), George H. Reed (servant).

This leisurely, episodic piece of Americana was adapted from the Judge Priest character created by Irwin S. Cobb in many short stories and was the first of four studio films to team world-famous humorist/actor Rogers with African-American character star FETCHIT. At the time, lanky Fetchit was a leading purveyor of the sleepy-eyed, shuffling, black man stereotype, typically, as here, a seemingly dimwitted servant who is oblivious to his employers' demands and exists in his own special space. On the other hand, Fetchit's Poindexter jumps to attention at any order issued by dynamic MCDANIEL, playing another of her many high-voltage celluloid domestics. Forced into a racist mold, these two talents (and many other African Americans) tried their best to shine in their demeaning niche during Hollywood's pre-politically correct era.

In 1890 in a small southern town, Judge Priest is involved in the trial of a Civil War veteran. The defendant had protected the honor of an orphan girl (Louise), a young woman whom the Judge's lawyer nephew (Brown) wants to marry but dares not because of her supposed illegitimacy. While the jurist resolves the sticky matter and regains the town's faith in him and vice versa, the soft-spoken Priest takes alleged chicken thief Poindexter into his household. The unlikely duo fish at Jeff's favorite spot, share confidences, and so on.

Just as many of director Ford's westerns are biased toward Native Americans, so the filmmaker follows the "custom" of the day in treating the black minority characters here as secondary citizens always in subordinate roles to the whites. On the other hand, there was great on-camera rapport between Rogers and Fetchit, which frequently bypassed the interracial aspect of their association, a distinct novelty of the times.

Originally, there was to have been a scene in the film in which the Judge saves Jeff from a lynch mob who think he is a murder suspect because he has blood on his hands (actually beef liver blood) and because he resembles the alleged culprit (another minority man). When Ford remade this feature as *The Sun Shines Bright* (1953), Fetchit recreated his role of Jeff Poindexter.

***Juke Joint* (1947)** Sack Amusement, b&w, 68 minutes. **Director:** Spencer Williams; **Screenplay:** True T. Thompson; **Cast:** Spencer Williams (Whitey Vanderbilt [Bad News Johnson]), July Jones ("Cornbread" Green), Inez Newell (Louella "Mama Lou" Holiday), Leonard Duncan ("Papa Sam" Holiday), Dauphine Moore (Honey Dew Holiday), Melody Duncan (Melody Holiday), Katherine Moore (Florida Holiday).

One of the last of the several independent features (e.g., *Dirty Gertie from Harlem, U.S.A*, 1946) directed by and starring veteran performer Spencer Williams, technically crude and filled with many inept performances, this boisterous film—brimming with ethnic stereotypes—captured the flavor of a bygone era and types of African-American entertainment/comedy.

Con artist Bad News Johnson and his not-so-smart crony (Jones) arrive in Dallas, Texas, where they persuade "Mama Lou" Holiday to take them in as boarders. To make himself indispensable to his landlady, Johnson offers to tutor her daughter Honey Dew for an upcoming beauty contest. Meanwhile, Mama Lou's shiftless husband is sidetracked at the local juke joint, where he happily plays poker while the establishment's married owner sweet talks his daughter Florida. Before long, everyone arrives at the raucous juke joint, including an angered Mama Lou.

***Julia* (1968–71)** NBC-TV, color, 30 minutes. **Cast:** Diahann Carroll (Julia Baker), Lloyd Nolan (Dr. Morton

Chegley), Betty Beaird (Marie Waggedorn), Marc Copage (Corey Baker), Paul Winfield (Paul Cameron: 1968–70), Fred Williamson (Steve Bruce: 1970–71).

Three years earlier, NBC-TV had gained a tremendous amount of coverage for debuting *I SPY* (1965–68), the first dramatic series to have a white and a black colead. Now the network drew a lot of attention for starring stage/club/movie actress CARROLL in a sitcom. Not only was she the first female African-American lead in a major TV comedy series since the era of *BEULAH* (1950–53), but her role was not as a servant but as a professional.

Pretty young widow Julia Baker moves with her son to Los Angeles, where she becomes a nurse for Caucasian doctor Dr. Morton Chegley. She and her boy (Copage) live in a fully integrated apartment building. Outside Carroll's and Copage's skin color, there is little to identify these characters as part of the contemporary African-American community. Although Julia dates black men (first Paul Cameron, then Steve Bruce), the bulk of the episodes involve normal sitcom plots, whether at the office, at home, or out socializing. Little reference is made to any of the ethnic issues so much in the news at the time. In the opening segment, Julia does tell her would-be employer in a phone conversation that he should know that she is a woman of color, but he is unfazed, as are most of Corey's playmates about the racial issue. For this persistent lack of topicality, the sitcom was criticized by both black and white reviewing sources.

During the show's run, Carroll was once Emmy-nominated as Outstanding Actress in a Comedy Series but lost to Hope Lange (*The Ghost and Mrs. Muir*). Years later, Carroll told of the huge pressure of responsibility she felt on *Julia* as a representative of her race.

***Jumpin' Jack Flash* (1986)** Twentieth Century-Fox, color, 100 minutes. **Director:** Penny Marshall; **Screenplay:** David H. Franzoni, Patricia Irving, and Christopher Thompson; **Cast:** Whoopi Goldberg (Terry Doolittle), Stephen Collins (Marty Phillips [Peter Kane]), Carol Kane (Cynthia), Annie Potts (Liz Carlson), Roscoe Lee Browne (Archer Lincoln), Jonathan Pryce (Jack).

Then as now, Hollywood seemed unable to harness the massive talents of comedian GOLDBERG. Near the start of her film career, she was starred in this major studio comedic vehicle, but no one had any progressive ideas of how to deal on camera with this star who was unconventional looking *and* African American. As had happened with HARRY BELAFONTE and EDDIE MURPHY in their early films, a charismatic personality received a neutered screen alter ego.

In Manhattan, kooky computer operator Terry Doolittle works in the international department of a bank. One day, on her computer, she intercepts a message for help from someone named "Jumpin' Jack Flash." Soon she is engulfed in deadly encounters with Soviet agents.

This film cannot decide whether its heroine is an eccentric white working girl (e.g., the tone of her outfits, her apartment, her white associates) or if this bizarrely dressed woman with dreadlocks is a (black) fish out of water. (Examples include scenes where a bigoted cop assumes automatically that she is a lawbreaker because of her skin color, when she crashes an Embassy ball by pretending to be a soul sister and lip-synching a song, and where she dares to have a facial at Elizabeth Arden's fancy salon.) To enliven the narrative, Goldberg resorts to manic physical humor, ranging from ethnic-style double takes to stumbling down the street like a buzzed-out druggie (actually she's been injected with truth serum).

Saddest of all, the film did not permit Goldberg physical contact with her fantasy love, the Caucasian (Pryce) whose life she saved. They meet briefly with a polite exchange, and the film quickly ends. (The same situation occurred with the heroine's white coworker [Collins] who was an undercover agent. If both she and the latter were of the same race, they would have had romantic clinches.)

Made for $15 million, *Jumpin' Jack Flash* earned $11 million in domestic film rentals.

***Jungle Fever* (1991)** Universal, color, 132 minutes. **Director/Screenplay:** Spike Lee; **Cast:** Wesley Snipes (Flipper Purify), Annabella Sciorra (Angie Tucci), Spike Lee (Cyrus), Ossie Davis (the Good Reverend Doctor Purify), Ruby Dee (Lucinda Purify), Samuel L. Jackson (Gator Purify), John Turturro (Paulie Carbone), Lonette McKee (Drew), Anthony Quinn (Lou Carbone), Halle Berry (Vivian).

There was nothing subtle about LEE's examination of interracial romance in this highly charged film. If one did not accept the outspoken filmmaker's thesis that the lust between races was surface deep only and was inspired by the novelty of trying something different, then this drama lost some of its point. On the other hand, as Lee had become increasingly adept as a filmmaker, the director's technique allowed the characterizations to stand out even more effectively. Whereas his *DO THE RIGHT THING* (1989) was criticized by some commentators for not presenting the drug influence as part of the ghetto scene, Lee made amends in this gritty presentation.

Although Flipper Purify, an upcoming African-American architect in New York City, is married and has a family, he begins a fling with office temp worker Angie Tucci, an Italian American. Hardly has Flipper told his pal Cyrus of his affair than Flipper's wife (McKee) learns of the situation and throws her spouse out of the house. In contrast, Angie is more discreet and therefore must remain silent as her father attempts to fix her up with a local Italian boy (Turturro), who in actuality has a crush on a black woman. Meanwhile, Flipper's dope-addicted brother (JACKSON) attacks his mother (DEE) for drug money and is shot to death by his clergyman father (DAVIS). Eventually, Angie and Flipper exhaust their romance and tire of dealing with the repercussions among family and friends, and he attempts to reconcile with his wife.

In this drama, BERRY played a controversial cameo as a wasted druggie/prostitute, which gave the film an even higher profile.

Made for $14 million, *Jungle Fever* grossed more than $32 million in domestic distribution.

***Just Another Girl on the I.R.T.* (1993)** Miramax, color, 96 minutes. **Director/Screenplay:** Leslie Harris; **Cast:** Ariyan Johnson (Chantel Mitchell), Kevin Thigpen (Tyrone), Ebony Jerido (Natete), Chequita Jackson (Paula).

As a rare distaff voice in African-American cinema, writer/director Harris made her debut with this feature shot in seventeen days for $130,000. Despite its plot line flaws, the intriguing film (which insisted it was giving us "the real deal") presented a nonstereotypical URBAN DRAMA heroine, a smart, aggressive, generally responsible young black woman.

Chantel Mitchell, a high school junior from the Brooklyn projects, plans to graduate early and to go to college and med school. When not studying, she has a part-time job, cares for her younger siblings, and finds free moments to date. She meets Tyrone at a party, and they soon become intimate. (For a bright girl, however, she is woefully uninformed about proper birth-control or AIDS-prevention methods.) When she becomes pregnant, she hides the fact from her mother and boyfriend—for a time. After giving premature birth, the hysterical Chantel orders Tyrone to get rid of the infant. However, he does not, and she must now deal with being a mother.

This film won a Special Jury Prize at the Sundance Film Festival.

K

Killing Affair, A **(1977)** CBS-TV, color, 100 minutes. **Director:** Richard C. Sarafian; **Teleplay:** E. Arthur Kean; **Cast:** Elizabeth Montgomery (Viki Eaton), O. J. Simpson (Woodrow York), Rosalind Cash (Beverly York), John Mahon (Shoup), Priscilla Pointer (Judge Cudahy), Dean Stockwell (Kenneth Switzer), Todd Bridges (Todd York).

This telemovie received a good bit of attention, not for its pedestrian script or acting but for its study of an interracial romance.

College-bred Woodrow York, a black police officer in Los Angeles, is a loose canon who is assigned to work with feisty, patronizing veteran police detective Viki Eaton, who is white. Their big case of the moment is following through on a psychotic killer (Stockwell) who was released from jail on a technicality. Before long, the married York and the cultivated Eaton have an affair, which causes intense repercussions, especially for York, who has earned the enmity now of both white and black cops. Eventually York returns to his wife (Cash) and son (Bridges), not because of interracial concerns but because of his guilt about being an adulterer.

Because the network was so timid about dealing with the white-black issues, this potentially meaningful forum is wasted on a meandering story that is full of cop jargon and clichéd, bigoted responses to the romance between members of different races.

King **(1978)** NBC-TV miniseries, color, 300 minutes. **Cast:** Paul Winfield (Martin Luther King Jr.), Cicely Tyson (Coretta King), Roscoe Lee Browne (Philip Harrison), Lonny Chapman (Chief Frank Holloman), Ossie Davis (Martin Luther King Sr.), Cliff DeYoung (Robert F. Kennedy), Al Freeman Jr. (Damon Lockwood), Dick Anthony Williams (Malcolm X).

This was one of the major black-themed properties that followed in the wake of the hugely successful miniseries *ROOTS* (1977). In this chronicle of the man (1929–68) who believed in nonviolent demonstration to attain racial equality for blacks and who won the Nobel Peace Prize in 1964, the miniseries focused on King's years as a Baptist minister in the South of the 1950s until his assassination in Memphis, Tennessee, in 1968. WINFIELD gave a glowing, insightful performance as the famed leader, not just a good impersonation. The score for *King* won an Emmy Award; among the seven other Emmy nominations were Outstanding Actor (Winfield), Outstanding Actress (TYSON), and Outstanding Supporting Actor (DAVIS). Originally HARRY BELAFONTE was to have played Malcolm X.

L

***Lady Sings the Blues* (1972)** Paramount, color, 144 minutes. **Director:** Sidney J. Furie; **Screenplay:** Terence McCloy, Chris Clark, and Suzanne De Passe; **Cast:** Diana Ross (Billie Holiday), Billy Dee Williams (Louis McKay), Richard Pryor (Piano Man), James Callahan (Reg Hanley), Paul Hampton (Harry), Virginia Capers (Mama Holiday), Scatman Crothers (Big Ben).

Although a distortion of the life and often bad times of famed jazz singer Billie Holiday (1915–59), this film proved a sensational screen debut for former Supremes singing star ROSS. (It was a new and exhilarating experience for moviegoers to be able to see such a lushly mounted, fully developed screen love story with two such attractive African-American coleads.) *Lady Sings the Blues* also demonstrated that a heavily romantic love story between African-American coleads could succeed at the box office. (This movie brought in almost $10 million in domestic film rentals.) It also earned five Oscar nominations, including Best Actress (Ross) and Best Original Screenplay, which made use of the 1956 autobiography *Lady Sings the Blues* by Holiday and William Duffy.

Following a rags-to-fame formula, this slick entry smoothly traces the teenage Holiday leaving Baltimore after being raped, working for a time in a New York brothel, and then finding emotional and artistic release as a sultry, distinctive jazz singer in clubs (although always discriminated against because of her race). She finds great love with Louis McKay, but the pressures of career and the injustices heaped on her and her race lead her into drug addiction, a habit that prompts repeated brushes with the law, the downfall of her career, and her early death at age forty-four.

Not only did Ross prove herself a dynamic screen presence and a superior song stylist, but also Williams (as the handsome, high-stepping man in her life) and PRYOR (as the feisty piano player who is beaten to death by drug dealers) were impressive. Although both glossy and formulistic, this movie nevertheless translated well the screen musical-biography idiom to an ethnic minority sensibility. It also presented jolting moments of vile bigotry, as when Billie, on tour in the South, witnesses a black man being lynched, or the assorted humiliations foisted on this famous talent because of her race.

In *MALCOLM X* (1992), Miki Howard had a brief cameo as the legendary Billie Holiday.

***Landlord, The* (1970)** United Artists, color, 112 minutes. **Director:** Hal Ashby; **Screenplay:** William Gunn; **Cast:** Beau Bridges (Elgar Enders), Pearl Bailey (Marge), Diana Sands (Fanny), Louis Gossett [Jr.] (Copee), Lee Grant (Mrs. Enders), Melvin Stewart (Professor Duboise).

This unheralded feature, written by African-American Gunn, had a lot to say on the state of the ethnic minority. His forceful tale of interracial love was directed with perspicacity by Caucasian Ashby using satire, comedy, and heated drama to present the narrative. Reflecting its story from *both* racial points of view, the movie boasted superior (but overlooked) performances by SANDS, GOSSETT, and Bailey.

Elgar Enders, the unemployed twentysomething scion of a napalm/insecticide/deodorant tycoon purchases a tenement building in Brooklyn's black ghetto. He intends to gentrify it for his own use but must first evict the tenants. These include boisterous Marge, a whiz at making soul food, segregationist school instructor Duboise, and Fanny—a past Miss Sepia—who has a jealous spouse (Gossett) and a twelve-year-old son. After developing a conscience, Elgar makes repairs and takes up residence in the building's now-vacant basement. He soon gets Fanny pregnant and is later nearly killed by her ballistic mate. At the finale, Enders takes the baby, leaves the building to Fanny and her family, and heads off to restore his relationship with a black art student he had once dated.

***Last Dragon, The* (1985)** TriStar, color, 109 minutes. **Director:** Michael Schultz; **Screenplay:** Louis Venosta; **Cast:**

Taimak (Leroy), Vanity (Laura), Christopher Murney (Eddie Arkadian), Julius J. Carry III (Sho'Nuff), Faith Prince (Angela).

Taking advantage of the renewed interest in the kung fu craze generated by *The Karate Kid* (1984), Berry Gordy, the founder of Motown Records, concocted this ethnic-flavored excursion. It was an effective blend of martial arts, street gang action in the hood, and music videos. By this point, Hollywood knew well how to exploit effectively ethnic culture for the moviegoing masses.

African-American teen Leroy has grown up in Harlem with his family and hopes to become a martial arts master. Because of his absorption in Asiatic culture, his friends call him Bruce Leroy. Leroy's popularity bothers local black bully Sho'Nuff, who intends to snuff out the competition. Meanwhile, downtown, white gangster Eddie Arkadian kidnaps Laura, the hostess of a popular music-video TV show, intending to make her air the untalented Angela's videos. It is Leroy who comes to Laura's rescue, not only winning her love but also outsmarting Sho'Nuff.

This shrewdly concocted ethnic mix, which cost $10 million to make, grossed $30 million in domestic distribution.

***Law & Order* (1990–)** NBC-TV series, color, 60 minutes. **Cast:** Christopher Noth (Det. Mike Logan: 1990–95), Jerry Orbach (Det. Lennie Briscoe: 1992–), Dann Florek (Capt. Donald Cragen: 1990–93), S. Epatha Merkerson (Lt. Anita Van Buren: 1993–), Michael Moriarity (Asst. D.A. Ben Stone: 1990–94), Richard Brooks (Asst. D.A. Paul Robinette: 1990–93), Steven Hill (D.A. Adam Schiff: 1990–2000), Sam Waterston (Asst. D.A. Jack McCoy: 1994–).

One of TV's most popular series ever, *Law & Order* combined the elements of a police action series with that of legal drama, essentially splitting the story focus of each week's episode into two parts. Set in New York City, with its accounts of crimes and punishments, the show featured a multiethnic cast of characters. Similarly, but to a lesser degree, so did the ensemble of figures playing the lead series roles.

During the first three seasons of *Law & Order*, black performer Richard Brooks appeared as the subordinate assistant district attorney, directed by white superiors (played by Moriarity and Hill). During one of the series' frequent cast turnovers, Brooks left the proceedings (returning occasionally as a private attorney), and that fall, African-American actress Merkerson came aboard to be the police detectives' new superior. She replaced the Caucasian Capt. Donald Cragen. By adding Merkerson to the cast roster, the show solved two problems at once: having more ethnic representation on the program and adding another female to the male-dominated talent lineup. To be noted, neither of the above-mentioned black performers was given dimensional roles in which to work. On the other hand, for once, the lead black characters' private lives were touched upon briefly, as were those of the Caucasian leads. Unlike some other law-enforcement series (e.g., *NYPD Blue*, 1993– , and *HOMICIDE: LIFE ON THE STREET*, 1993–99), less was made of the principals' private lives than the various plot lines of their professional lives—at least until later in its series run.

Lawrence, Martin (1965–) Somewhere between the outrageous comedic tradition of RICHARD PRYOR and EDDIE MURPHY lay the humorous talent of Lawrence, the round-faced stand-up comic with a bent for controversial, sharp-witted material. More so than many of his contemporaries (e.g., CHRIS ROCK, Jamie Foxx, Steve Harvey, and the younger Wayans brothers), Lawrence's abilities were often overshadowed by his news-making escapades, which included such events as: 1994—after a considered-tasteless appearance on NBC-TV's *Saturday Night Live*, he was banned from all of that network's shows; 1996—being arrested at the Burbank, California, airport for alleged possession of a loaded gun in his baggage; 1997—in March being detained by the police outside a Hollywood club when a man claimed that Lawrence had hit him; 1997—in September, being required to undertake community service as a consequence of March incident; 1999—collapsing from heat exhaustion while jogging, lapsing into a coma, and then recovering in a hospital.

Born in Frankfurt, Germany, Lawrence graduated from public high school in Landover, Maryland. His apprentice years found him as a street performer in New York City's Washington Square Park; working in a Queens, New York, department store; and performing at open-mike night at Manhattan's Improv comedy venue. Lawrence made his first show business mark by appearing in the TV series *WHAT'S HAPPENING NOW!!*, joining the cast for its 1987–88 season as Maurice, a high school student who worked part time at the local diner. In the same period he won the stand-up comedy competition

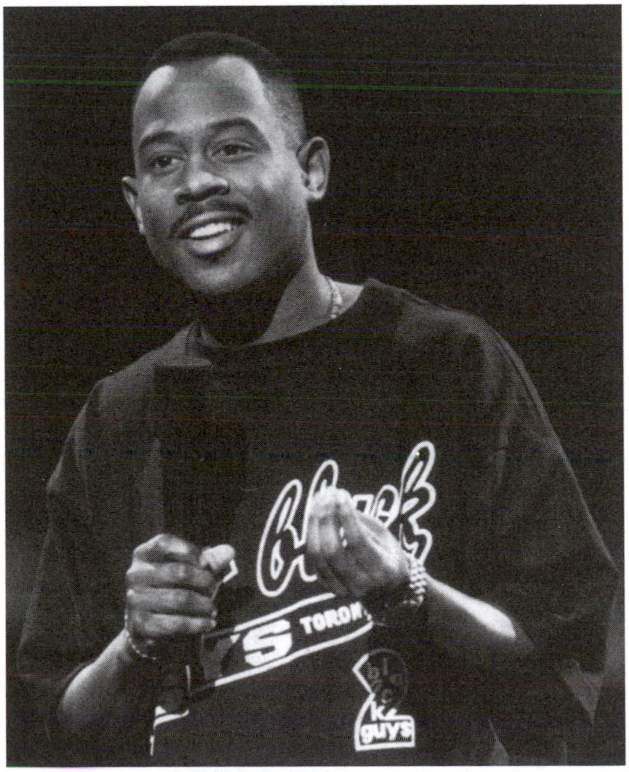

Martin Lawrence hosting *Russell Simmons' Def Comedy Jam* on cable TV in 1999. (JC ARCHIVES)

on TV's *Star Search* talent show. Martin had a small role in SPIKE LEE's *DO THE RIGHT THING* (1989) and performed the recurring role of Bilal in the screen comedy *House Party* (1990) and *House Party 2* (1991). He was a host from 1992 to 1997 on *HBO's Def Comedy Jam* show and began his own TV network sitcom series, *MARTIN*, in 1992, toning down somewhat his one-step-too-far comedy manner. (He won an Image Award in 1996 for his lead performance on the show.) During the program's last season (1996–97), costar Tisha Campbell (who played Lawrence's on-camera girlfriend-then-wife) left the show, reportedly claiming sexual harassment from the star, returning only for the series's last episode.

Lawrence joined with equally fast-rising WILL SMITH for *Bad Boys* (1995), an action/buddy picture in which they were Miami cops, searching for $100 million in heroin stolen from the police lock-up. From that big hit movie, Lawrence tackled *A Thin Line Between Love and Hate* (1996) as producer/director/star/scenarist/music supervisor. This poorly paced parody of *Fatal Attraction* (1987) was rated crude and unfunny by most commentators. Martin matched well with Eddie Murphy in *Life* (1999), a semiserious study about two con artists framed for murder and how they became good friends when stuck on a southern prison farm for the rest of their days. Then, Lawrence was executive producer of his next two comedies *Big Momma's House* (2000) and *What's the Worst That Could Happen?* (2001), the former a funnier farce than the latter; in it, he was a FBI operative who went undercover disguised as a fat old woman. Later came the action comedy *National Security* (2001), *The Black Knight* (2001—a takeoff on *A Connecticut Yankee in King Arthur's Court*), and *Blue Streak 2* (2002), a follow-up lark to *Blue Streak* (1999) in which he played an unrepentant jewel thief. This was followed by *Bad Boys 2* (2003), in which Lawrence was teamed again with Will Smith.

***Lazarus Syndrome, The* (1979)** ABC-TV, color, 60 minutes. **Cast:** Louis Gossett Jr. (Dr. MacArthur St. Clair), Ronald Hunter (Joe Hamill), Sheila Frazier (Gloria St. Clair), Peggy Walker (Virginia Hamill), Peggy McCay (Stacy).

In the late 1970, in the wake of the BLACK ACTION FILM cycle, both theatrical releases and TV productions reflected a great lessening in the number of ethnic performers utilized on camera. One of the few new series of that time to feature an African American was this medical drama.

The show's tone was supposed to be deliberately contentious: Dr. St. Clair is chief of cardiology at Webster Memorial Hospital. Helping him—as well as opposing him—in his battles to overcome the red tape is Caucasian Joe Hamill. Meanwhile at home, the dedicated St. Clair is there too infrequently or is too tired to be a real member of the household, all of which upsets his wife. The show's title refers to the theory that physicians can be miracle workers.

After a month on the air, this series was pulled, leaving the network lineup even more bereft of black talent, especially of African-American characters who are well educated and sensitive. A similar fate later befell *Gideon's Crossing* (2000–01), a medical drama featuring black talent Andre Braugher as a caring big-city physician.

***Leadbelly* (1976)** Paramount, color, 126 minutes. **Director:** Gordon Parks (Sr.); **Screenplay:** Ernest Kinoy; **Cast:** Roger E. Mosley (Huddie Ledbetter), Paul Benjamin (Wes Ledbetter), Madge Sinclair (Miss Eula), Alan Manson (prison chief guard), Albert P. Hall (Dicklicker).

When this little-seen entry was released, esteemed filmmaker/photographer PARKS complained that the studio had not given his picture proper distribution. He was also upset that the movie's promotional material suggested that the picture was *just* another BLACK ACTION entry, rather than the thoughtful biography it actually was. Ironically, in picturizing the hazardous life of Huddie Ledbetter (1885–1949), better known as blues singer Leadbelly, Parks, abetted by cinematographer Bruce Surtees and self-effacing leading player Mosley, presented a prettified version of the famed singer's chronicle. Had they been grittier and more rough-edged, as was their subject material, the film would have fared much better in the marketplace.

Ledbetter, a man of great strength and bottled anger, who frequently lets his temper explode with disastrous results, spends much of his adulthood on chain gangs, in prison, or just surviving. Told largely through flashbacks, the film recounts the violent escapes in Huddie's life—exacerbated by the intense southern racism of the times—that leads to his hellish existence. It traces his growing love of music and how this budding blues talent uses his art as an outlet for his enormous frustrations. Weaving in and out of his life is his sharecropper father (Benjamin), a Louisiana madam (Sinclair) who becomes his great love, and the complex prison guard (Manson). Hi Tide Harris dubbed the vocals for the film's soundtrack.

Learn, Baby, Learn See *LEARNING TREE, THE.*

***Learning Tree, The* (aka: *Learn, Baby, Learn*) (1969)** Warner Bros., color, 107 minutes. **Director/Screenplay:** Gordon Parks; **Cast:** Kyle Johnson (Newt Winger), Alex Clarke (Marcus Savage), Estelle Evans (Sarah Winger), Dana Elcar (Sheriff Kirky), Mira Waters (Arcella Jefferson), Joel Fluellen (Uncle Rob).

Relying on his own biographical novel (1963), multitalented PARKS (who also produced and provided the film's music) tells a touching account of a sensitive African-American teen growing up in the mid-1920s in a small Kansas town. As Newt's daily life is depicted—which includes both indoctrination into sex by the local prostitute and the death of his mother (Evans)—viewpoints of *both* black and white townsfolk are presented. Newt's emerging adulthood is crystallized when he witnesses the killing of a white man by a black fellow, the latter the father of his former friend, Marcus. Despite his fears of the repercussion in town, the youth reveals the true facts at the murder trial. Thereafter, when Marcus is shot in the back by the sheriff, Newt is so upset by the growing racism and violence in town that he goes to another town to live with an aunt.

The well-regarded *The Learning Tree* was the first major-studio Hollywood release to be directed by an African American. Years later, it was among the first twenty-five features included in the National Film Registry at the Library of Congress.

Lee, Spike (1957–) Regarded as a new breath in the independent film movement of the late 1980s, Lee also gained a reputation as an outspoken, frequently contentious spokesperson for the African-American point of view (as well as for being a fanatic New York Knicks basketball team fan). Lee's directorial abilities, especially in his earlier years, were often overshadowed by his high-profile status as a prickly maverick. A filmmaker who often acted in as well as wrote and produced his own projects, Lee's scope of screen topics expanded greatly as he gained further experience in his craft.

He was born Shelton Jackson Lee in Atlanta, Georgia, the son of a jazz musician/composer father and a schoolteacher mother. The oldest of five children, his mother gave him the nickname "Spike" for being a "tough baby." By 1959, the Lees were living in Brooklyn. The youngsters had a strict upbringing, in which the parents rationed their TV watching, insisted on their children learning about black culture, and had each child learn to play an instrument.

At Morehouse College in Atlanta, Georgia, Spike became interested in filmmaking, hoping one day to make pictures geared to black moviegoers. Thereafter, at New York University's film school, he made *Joe's Bed-Stuy Barbershop: We Cut Heads* (1980) as his master's thesis film. The picture won a Student Award from the Academy of Motion Picture Arts and Sciences. His 1984 efforts to make a semiautobiographical film (*The Messenger*) did not materialize. However, he did make the R-rated, low-budget *SHE'S GOTTA HAVE IT* (1986), a sex comedy with an all-black cast (including Spike and his sister Joie). When not directing music videos or writing books about the making of each of his new films, Lee completed the controversial musical *SCHOOL DAZE* (1988), which explored, among other ethnic topics, antiblack blacks. His own production company (40 Acres and a Mule) produced the angry *DO THE RIGHT THING* (1989), a highly explosive study of race relations in the Bedford-Stuyvesant section of Brooklyn, for which he received his first Oscar nomination for Best Original Screenplay.

Taking a page from his father's life as a jazz musician, Spike turned out *MO' BETTER BLUES* (1990), the first of his features to star DENZEL WASHINGTON. *JUNGLE FEVER* (1991) is his passionately felt study concerning theories about whites and blacks romancing the opposite race. After a long maturation, Lee directed *MALCOLM X* (1992), an expansive screen biography of the Black Muslim militant (Washington); the resultant movie, however, was a commercial and (for many reviewing sources) artistic disappointment.

After that, Lee's movies were a mixed bag, ranging from the perceptive *Clockers* (1993), about life on the mean streets, to the lesser *Girl 6* (1996), which focused on a frustrated actress (Theresa Randall) who becomes a phone-sex operator. He was on target directing the documentary *4 Little Girls* (1997) about the ramifications of a racist hate bombing in 1965 of a Birmingham, Alabama, church. (It was Oscar nominated for Best Documentary.) *He Got Game* (1998) reteamed Lee again with Washington in a finely executed drama about a convict dad and his high-school-basketball hotshot son. Another documentary, *THE ORIGINAL KINGS OF COMEDY* (2000) was well received, while Lee's overdone satire, *BAMBOOZLED* (2000—for which he also wrote the screenplay), was widely panned. Later came his cable TV movie *A Huey P. Newton Story* (2001), the TV miniseries *The Blues* (2002), and the feature-length documentary *Jim Brown: All American* (2002)

Among Lee's core workers over the years, such talents as African-American cinematographer ERNEST R. DICKERSON, went on to become an established filmmaker.

***Legend of Nigger Charley, The* (1972)** Paramount, color, 98 minutes. **Director:** Martin Goldman; **Screenplay:** Larry G. Spangler and Goldman; **Cast:** Fred Williamson (Nigger Charley), D'Urville Martin (Toby), Don Pedro Colley (Joshua), Gertrude Jeanette (Theo), Marcia McBroom (Julia).

Unlike the high-caliber *BUCK AND THE PREACHER* (1972), this scatter-shot feature lacked humanity. It was solely focused on creating a bloody western in which the white characters are the (deserved) victims of the carnage. On the plus side, WILLIAMSON and the resourceful, underrated Martin give an earnestness to the proceedings.

Although freed by his dying plantation owner, circumstances force Nigger Charley, along with two other slaves (Martin and Colley), to flee west. On the frontier, attracted to a married half-breed, he helps her white husband defeat a vicious group of Caucasian whites. Then, Charley and Toby ride off into the sunset.

Made at a cost of $400,000, this production earned $3 million in domestic film rentals and led to *The Soul of Nigger Charley* (1973). Neither movie matched the quality of the earlier genre piece, *SOUL SOLDIER* (1970).

***Lethal Weapon* (1987)** Warner Bros., color, 110 minutes. **Director:** Richard Donner; **Screenplay:** Shane Black; **Cast:** Mel Gibson (Det. Sgt. Martin Riggs), Danny Glover (Det. Sgt. Roger Murtaugh), Gary Busey (Mr. Joshua), Tom Atkins (Michael Hunsaker), Mitchell Ryan (Gen. Peter McAllister), Darlene Love (Trish Murtaugh), Traci Wolfe (Rianne Murtaugh).

When first released, this interracial buddy-cop picture was a fresh and different genre entry with a lot to recommend it. For a change, the loose cannon of the two was *not* the African American (Roger Murtaugh): He was fifty, a responsible family man, and nearing career retirement. The lethal weapon is his new police partner, the Caucasian Martin Riggs, who, since his wife's death, has been nearly over the edge and totally reckless on the job. The two men become involved in a drug-trafficking organization run by ex-Vietnam mercenaries and headed by Gen. Peter McAllister. In the showdown, the gang's sadistic henchman (Busey) is prevented from killing Murtaugh's wife (Love) and daughter (Wolfe).

Beyond its well-paced action sequences, what made this police story so successful was the uneasy camaraderie between the two law enforcers. Out-of-control widower Riggs, who values nothing in life anymore, begrudgingly gains a fresh perspective from his seasoned, older black partner. The scenes at Murtaugh's middle-class, wholesome home have a warmth not often found in mainstream films. The effect of interaction with the Murtaugh clan somewhat softened the brittle, bitter Riggs and added richness to the movie.

Made for $15 million and grossing more than $65 million in domestic distribution, *Lethal Weapon* earned an Oscar nomination for Best Sound. It led to three sequels (1989, 1992, and 1998), none of which matched the debut entry. By the time of the mechanical *Lethal Weapon IV* it was African-American CHRIS ROCK and Asian Jet Li who gave the proceedings its juice.

***Liberation of L. B. Jones, The* (1970)** Columbia, color, 102 minutes. **Director:** William Wyler; **Screenplay:** Stirling Silliphant and Jesse Hill Ford; **Cast:** Lee J. Cobb (Oman Hedgepath), Anthony Zerbe (Willie Joe Worth), Roscoe Lee Browne (L. B. Jones), Lola Falana (Emma Jones), Yaphet Kotto (Sonny Boy Mosby), Arch Johnson (Stanley Bumpas), Zara Cully (Mama Lavorn), Fayard Nicholas (Benny).

This was one of Hollywood's last-produced social-consciousness pictures about African Americans *before* the industry began to churn out profitable BLACK ACTION FILMS. Shot on location in Humboldt, Tennessee, it was directed by three-time Academy Award winner Wyler and based on Ford's 1965 novel. This entry turned out to be alternately ponderous and steamy/violent but not as trashy or pointless as the later *The Klansman* (1974) with Richard Burton and Lee Marvin.

Militant Sonny Boy Mosby returns to Somerton, Tennessee, to exact revenge on a bigoted white cop (Johnson) who beat him as a child. In town, white attorney Oman Hedgepath agrees reluctantly to handle the divorce case of wealthy black funeral director Lord Byron Jones, whose randy wife, Emma, has been carrying on with a local white policeman Willie Joe Worth. After the latter learns of the suit, he batters Emma and warns Jones to see reason. Jones refuses, is arrested, escapes, and then is shot and castrated in a confrontation with Worth. Although the guilty policemen admit their crimes against Jones, they are not prosecuted. Later, Mosby shoves Willie Joe into a harvester and then leaves town.

A key theme of this melodrama was the two opposing camps of present-day African Americans. On one hand, there were the well-mannered, intellectual blacks (represented by L. B. Jones) who sought to assimilate to the whites' standards. They were called Uncle Toms by the opposition, the latter being the new breed of militant blacks (e.g., Sonny Boy Mosby) who believed that force and not conciliatory words is the only approach in dealing with whites.

Life with the Erwins See *STU ERWIN SHOW, THE.*

***Lilies of the Field* (1963)** United Artists, b&w, 94 minutes. **Director:** Ralph Nelson; **Screenplay:** James Poe; **Cast:** Sidney Poitier (Homer Smith), Lilia Skala (Mother Maria), Lisa Mann (Sister Gertrude), Isa Crino (Sister Agnes), Francesca Jarvis (Sister Albertine).

Made on a $240,000 budget and shot in and around Tucson, Arizona, this heartwarming feature not only became a charming, commercially successful feature but it also occasioned the first Academy Award won by a black performer (POITIER) in the Best Actor category. The memorable movie also earned Oscar nominations for Best Cinematography (Black and White), Best Picture, Best Screenplay, and Best Supporting Actress (Skala). The picture was based on William E. Barrett's 1962 novel.

In the narrative, ex-GI Homer Smith roams around the Southwest doing odd jobs to pay for his wanderings. One day the African American stops near the desert's edge at a small farm run by five German nuns, whose order inherited the land. The persuasive Mother Maria convinces Homer to help repair the farmhouse's leaky roof and to do other manual chores. Next, she prevails on Smith to clear away the rubble from a dilapidated barn. Thereafter, to his amazement, it is suggested that he construct a new chapel. Despite the many potential obstacles, Homer is so impressed with the refugee nuns' determination that he agrees. Meanwhile, he works for a local contractor to earn money to help feed the nuns and in his "spare" time teaches them English. With his work done and the bishop about to arrive to dedicate the chapel, Homer quietly leaves the farm.

As much as this movie was praised by many commentators for its fine performances and uplifting message, there were African-American publications and groups who were unhappy with *Lilies of the Field.* They found the star's role as the overly obliging black man to be demeaning and a step backward for their race. (In retrospect, it was seen as a sad precursor of Poitier's future benign, subservient film parts.)

In 1970 Shirley Booth starred as the mother superior with Al Freeman Jr. cast as Homer Smith in *Look to the Lilies*, a short-lasting Broadway musical adaptation of *Lilies of the Field.* In 1979, Nelson, who had directed the original movie, wrote and helmed a telefeature sequel to it entitled *Christmas Lilies of the Field.* BILLY DEE WILLIAMS was showcased as Homer Smith with Maria Schell as the Mother Superior.

***Little Colonel, The* (1935)** Fox, b&w and color, 80 minutes. **Director:** David Butler; **Screenplay:** William Conselman; **Cast:** Shirley Temple (Lloyd Sherman), Lionel Barrymore (Colonel Lloyd), Evelyn Venable (Elizabeth Lloyd Sherman), John Lodge (Jack Sherman), Hattie McDaniel (Mom Beck), Bill "Bojangles" Robinson (Walker).

This magnolia-drenched, rose-tinted version of the Old South—where the Civil War seemed to have changed nothing—was another song-filled comedy drama starring the Queen of 1930s Hollywood, little Miss Temple. Here she was joined by veteran stage and vaudeville performer ROBINSON, and the two created magic and cinema history in their wondrous dance up and down the magnificent staircase at her grandfather Lloyd's home. It was such a marvelous sequence then (and now) that it *almost* makes the saccharine story (based on the 1895 novel by Annie Fellows Johnston) and the demeaning/patronizing treatment of the "darkies"—even by the Little Colonel—fade somewhat into the background.

In the 1870s, while her ex-Yankee soldier husband is off prospecting for gold, Elizabeth Lloyd Sherman returns to her Kentucky hometown, despite the fact that her ex-Confederate-colonel father (Barrymore) disowned her when she wed a northerner (Lodge). She is accompanied by her youngster Lloyd, who quickly ingratiates herself with most of the town, including her grumpy grandfather, his household cook (McDANIEL), and his servant (ROBINSON), as well as several young black playmates. The crotchety colonel eventually accepts his son-in-law, and harmony is restored at the manse.

At one point, McDaniel (projecting her usual strong-minded mammy) and Bojangles took Shirley for a walk about town, and they came across a Hollywood version of an old-fashioned revival meeting. This allowed for wide-eyed Temple to be amazed by this energetic ethnic (exotic for white folks) display.

So popular was *The Little Colonel* that later in 1935, the studio reunited Temple and Robinson in *The Littlest Rebel*. This entry was set during the Civil War with Bojangles as Uncle Billy, a house slave at the plantation owned by Shirley's family. Temple and Robinson would make two further movies together in the late 1930s.

***Long Walk Home, The* (1990)** Miramax, color, 97 minutes. **Director:** Richard Pearce; **Screenplay:** John Cork; **Cast:** Sissy Spacek (Miriam Thompson), Whoopi Goldberg (Odessa Cotter), Dwight Schultz (Norman Thompson), Ving Rhames (Herbert Cotter), Dylan Baker (Tunker Thompson), Erika Alexander (Selma Cotter).

This was one of several Hollywood entries (e.g., *MISSISSIPPI BURNING*, 1988) made in this period regarding U.S. civil-rights issues *not* told by the increasing number of African-American filmmakers but by white moviemakers with a politically liberal viewpoint. *The Long Walk Home* was quietly effective in recreating the mid-1950s of Montgomery, Alabama, where Dr. Martin Luther King Jr. led the bus boycott. On the down side, this movie still utilized a Caucasian as its first-billed star, and the white household (not the key black characters) was the central focus in this moving account of minority discrimination.

Only gradually does Alabaman Miriam Thompson realize how privileged a life she and her family live. Long oblivious to the discriminatory and financial hardships of her faithful black maid Odessa Cotter, who has her own family to tend to as well, Miriam slowly begins to see her servant as a flesh-and-blood person. As the racial/political situation in Montgomery heats up and Odessa becomes an active boycott supporter, Miriam—whose husband is part of the racist white citizen's council—makes a moral stand and actively assists the African Americans in their nonviolent resistance against the bigots.

GOLDBERG provided a well-modulated performance, especially in the scenes (unfortunately subordinated to the story) of her home life in a part of town far removed from the upscale world of her employer. The critically liked, but little seen feature earned only little more than $4 million in domestic film rentals.

***Lost Boundaries* (1949)** De Rochemont/Film Classics, b&w, 99 minutes. **Director:** Alfred L. Werker; **Screenplay:** Virginia Shaler, Eugene Ling, Charles A. Palmer, and Furland de Kay; **Cast:** Beatrice Pearson (Marcia Carter), Mel Ferrer (Dr. Scott Carter), Richard Hylton (Howard Carter), Susan Douglas (Shelley Carter), Canada Lee (Lieutenant Thompson), Rev. Robert Dunn (Rev. John Taylor), Leigh Whipper (janitor).

In its day, this was considered a courageous production, daring to address the U.S. racial problem at a time when most of Hollywood, like America, was still ignoring the escalating issues of racial discrimination. Like the same year's *PINKY*, *LOST BOUNDARIES* featured white actors as the story's light-skinned Africans Americans, reasoning that Caucasian filmgoers would thus better relate to the narrative. Despite that major compromise, as well as the contrived screenplay (based on a real-life incident), *Lost Boundaries* was and remains an important entry in the evolving minority cinema.

When the blacks in a Georgia community reject the newly arrived young Dr. Scott Carter and his wife (Pearson) because they are fair skinned (i.e., "high yallar"), the demoralized couple move back up north and eventually settle in a New Hampshire town where they pass for white. Twenty years later, their secret is revealed when Scott and his son Howard want to join the military during World War II and a background check reveals the Carters' racial heritage. At first rejected by the townsfolk who had been their "friends," the plea of a local minister (Dunn) brings about a reconciliation between the community and the "outsiders."

Told in a now-dated pseudodocumentary style, the movie maintained a degree of objectivity in its presentation.

***Lost Man, The* (1969)** Universal, color, 122 minutes. **Director/Screenplay:** Robert Alan Aurthur; **Cast:** Sidney Poitier (Jason Higgs), Joanne Shimkus (Cathy Ellis), Al Freeman Jr. (Dennis Laurence), Michael Tolan (Hamilton), Leo Bibb (Eddie Moxy), Paul Winfield (Orville).

Eager to translate the black experience to the screen, Hollywood during the 1970s remade past films that had featured white casts. Usually, the conversions failed because what had been appropriate to the original characters did not work when overlaid with the sensibilities of another culture. *The Lost Man* was based on the 1945 novel (*Odd Man Out*) by Frederick Lawrence Green, a story of Irish freedom fighters. It had been made into a highly regarded 1947 British movie starring James Mason.

When police break up a peaceful demonstration by African Americans outside a Philadelphia plant, Jason Higgs and his pals rob the factory to fund the families of now-jailed demonstrators. During the heist, there are killings, and Higgs takes refuge with a white social worker (Shimkus) with whom he has recently fallen in love. In the end, the pursuing police kill both of them.

Many commentators then, and more later, cited that POITIER's involvement on camera in an interracial romance is a cop-out and a distraction. This fumbling picture was not well liked. An annoyed Charles Champlin of the *Los Angeles Times* (June 25, 1969) assessed, "*The Lost Man* is a notably offensive work, . . . The realities of ghetto misery and the earnest sacrifices of genuine leaders are cheaply made to serve the ends of what in its own terms is a trivial and derivative little charade."

M

***Mack, The* (1973)** Cinerama, color, 110 minutes. **Director:** Michael Campus; **Screenplay:** Robert J. Poole; **Cast:** Max Julien (John "Goldie" Mickens), Don Gordon (Hank), Richard Pryor (Slim), Carol Speed (Lulu), Roger E. Mosley (Olinga), Dick Williams (Pretty Tony).

A major complaint about the exploitive BLACK ACTION FILMS of 1970s Hollywood was that in their eagerness to depict African Americans, the moviemakers (usually whites) mostly focused on—and accentuated—the corrupt underbelly of the minority community because it allowed for vibrant characterizations and slam-bang action. Few of this type were as vivid as *The Mack*, a celluloid drama about pimps and their stable of prostitutes. What bolstered the proceedings was the talented and charismatic Julien as well as a solid performance by feisty PRYOR as the lead's friend who is killed by crooked cops.

Technically haphazard like many of these hastily assembled blaxploitation pieces, the picture detailed the rise and fall of John "Goldie" Mickens who builds a career in the white-controlled world as a mack (i.e., a pimp). He has to contend with the conflicting influence of a white prostitute (Sandra Brown) and his own brother (Mosley), the latter intent on cleaning up the neighborhood. As usual in such proceedings, the hero must cope with corrupt white cops, as well as the Mafia.

The Mack was made on location in Oakland, California, and utilized scenes of the Players Ball (a fancy get-together for Bay area pimps). Poole's script rang true as he had served a prison term for having been a pimp. *The Mack* grossed an impressive $3 million in domestic film rentals.

***Malcolm X* (1992)** Warner Bros., color, 201 minutes. **Director:** Spike Lee; **Screenplay:** Lee, Arnold Perl, and James Baldwin; **Cast:** Denzel Washington (Malcolm X [Malcolm Little]), Angela Bassett (Betty Shabazz), Albert Hall (Baines), Al Freeman Jr. (Elijah Muhammad), Delroy Lindo (West Indian Archie), Spike Lee (Shorty), Theresa Randle (Laura), Kate Vernon (Sophia), Lonette McKee (Louise Little).

One of the most anticipated motion pictures of the early 1990s, even in preproduction this screen biography was highly controversial as LEE passionately staked his claim to filming subject matter that had long intrigued him: the life and times of Malcolm X (1925–65), the political activist who vigorously campaigned for black rights. When Malcolm X was assassinated, the martyred leader became an enduring symbol of ethnic pride.

Angela Bassett and Denzel Washington in Spike Lee's *Malcolm X* (1992). (ECHO BOOK SHOP)

To Lee's credit, the moviemaker remained largely objective through much of this lengthy, complex chronicle. Some reviewers felt that what was missing from *Malcolm X* was the obvious ardor that had fueled Lee's *DO THE RIGHT THING* (1989), regarded by many critics as Lee's best movie to date. Occasionally the filmmaker's fervor/bias came forward, as in the movie's opening moments with its images first of African-American motorist Rodney King being beaten by the Los Angeles police and then of an American flag incinerated into an "X," or in the film's closing moments with its polemics.

During Malcolm Little's childhood, his minister father was murdered by the KKK, and his mother went mad and was committed to an asylum. By the early 1940s, living in the black ghetto of Roxbury, Massachusetts, he takes a white lover (Vernon) and hangs with his friend Shorty (Lee). Later, in Harlem, he works for a numbers gang; when he cheats his boss, he flees back to Boston where he is soon arrested on burglary charges. In prison he encounters Baines, who tells him of the teachings of the Honorable Elijah Muhammad, the leader of the Nation of Islam. By 1952, when he leaves prison, he is known as Malcolm X and becomes a Nation of Islam spokesperson, coming under the supervision of Elijah Muhammad. Malcolm X weds Betty Shabazz, a Muslim nurse, and continues to preach vehemently against the white race. As Malcolm X becomes a national media figure, he raises the suspicion of Elijah Muhammad. By 1964, Malcolm X leaves the Nation of Islam and makes a pilgrimage to Mecca. Now calling himself El-Hajj Malik El-Shabazz, he returns to the United States, having abandoned his separatist viewpoint and now believing in the unification of blacks and whites. In 1965 Malcolm X is assassinated by assumed followers of the Nation of Islam.

Made on a $34 million budget, *Malcolm X* grossed more than $48 million in domestic distribution. The stirring film received two Oscar nominations: Best Actor (WASHINGTON) and Best Costume Design. BASSETT won an Image Award for Outstanding Supporting Actress. The screenplay was based on an earlier one by the late James Baldwin, and, in turn, *The Autobiography of Malcolm X* (1965) by Malcolm X and Alex Haley.

With strong performances by Washington and Freeman Jr., *Malcolm X* was an important entry in the history of African Americans in Hollywood films, without being the masterpiece or final word on ethnic history that Lee strove to make.

Freeman Jr. had played Malcolm X in the TV miniseries *ROOTS: THE NEXT GENERATION* (1979). Another Freeman, Morgan, portrayed Malcolm X in *Death of a Prophet* (1981) which examined the man's last day alive. In *The Greatest* (1977), about Muhammad Ali the boxer, JAMES EARL JONES was Malcolm X. For the TV movie *Ali: An American Hero* (2000), Joe Morton was seen as Malcolm X. In the telefeature *King of the World* (2000), Gary Dourdan was Malcolm X. Mario Van Peebles played the leader in *ALI* (2001).

***Mama Flores' Family* (1998)** CBS-TV, color, 140 minutes. **Director:** Peter Werner; **Teleplay:** David Stevens and Carol Schreder; **Cast:** Cicely Tyson (Mama Flora), Erika Alexander (Young Flora), Blair Underwood (Willie), Queen Latifah (Diana), Mario Van Peebles (Luke), Hill Harper (Don).

After the death of Alex Haley (1921–92), the Pulitzer Prize winning author of *ROOTS: THE SAGA OF AN AMERICAN FAMILY* (1976), Stevens completed the novel *Mama Flores' Family* (1998), which was loosely based on Haley's household, tracing events from the late nineteenth century into the next one. The episodic telefeature that is based on the book boasts a strong cast of contemporary African-American talent. The story is held together by TYSON's riveting performance as the aging matriarch who suffers a great deal in her lifetime. The chronicle traces the tragedies that marked her life: becoming pregnant and having to relinquish her child; her marriage and the murder of her husband, along with the burning of their property; the struggles of her children and grandchildren as they endure racial discrimination and become angry adults, resentful of their treatment in America.

By now such dramatic, ethnic-oriented chronicles on TV and in films were no longer the total rarity they had been in the days of *A RAISIN IN THE SUN* (1961); moreover, such works no longer glossed over past and present mistreatment of African Americans, discriminatory situations that so strongly affected the lives of the characters depicted in this wide-reaching narrative.

Mama Flores' Family won two Image Awards: Outstanding Lead Actor (Underwood) and Outstanding Lead Actress (Tyson). It was nominated for two other Image Awards: Outstanding Lead Actress (Latifah) and Outstanding Television Movie, Mini-Series or Drama Special.

***Mandingo* (1975)** Paramount, color, 126 minutes. **Director:** Richard Fleischer; **Screenplay:** Norman Wexler; **Cast:** James Mason (Maxwell), Susan George (Blanche), Perry King (Hammond), Richard Ward (Agamemnon), Brenda Sykes (Ellen), Ken Norton (Mede), Ji-Tu Cumbuka (Cicero), Paul Benedict (Brownlee).

At the height of the 1970s BLACK ACTION FILM trend, Hollywood offered such tawdry entries as this, which explored—in highly exploitable terms of sexuality and brutality—the world of pre–Civil War South where downtrodden slaves are bedded by their masters and mistresses and are physically tormented. Trashy films like *Mandingo* exploited both races. This movie was based on the 1957 novel by Kyle Onstott, a book that was adapted into a short-lasting Broadway play (1961) with Franchot Tone and Dennis Hopper.

In 1832, bigoted Alabama plantation-owner Maxwell insists that his reckless son Hammond marry Blanche so they can have a child to carry on the dynasty. Oversexed Blanche has had a relationship with her brother, while randy Hammond has a yen for slave Ellen. To revenge herself on her wayward spouse, Blanche later beds rugged slave Mede, resulting in her giving birth to their illegitimate child who is done away with—as is Mede (in a sadistic sequence).

Despite bad reviews, *Mandingo* was a sufficiently lurid potboiler to appeal to moviegoers (of various races). The sizable hit led to *Drum* (1976), a stinker also featuring boxer-turned-actor Norton.

***Mannix* (1967–1975)** CBS-TV series, color, 60 minutes. **Cast:** Mike Connors (Joe Mannix), Joseph Campanella (Lou Wickersham: 1967–68), Gail Fisher (Peggy Fair: 1968–75), Robert Reed (Lt. Adam Tobias: 1969–75), Ward Wood (Lt. Art Malcolm: 1969–75).

Best known for the many brawls tough Joe Mannix slugged his way through in the course of any given TV season, this long-running detective series also was noteworthy for featuring black actress Fisher. Starting with the show's second season, she played Peggy Fair, secretary/girl Friday/confidante to rugged Mannix. Along with CICELY TYSON in the short-lasting *EAST SIDE/WEST SIDE* (1963), Fisher was one of the first African-American actresses to be featured as a lead regular on an integrated network TV series

***Martin* (1992–1997)** Fox-TV series, color, 30 minutes. **Cast:** Martin Lawrence (Martin Payne/Sheneneh), Tisha Campbell (Gina Waters), Carl Anthony Payne II (Cole Brown), Thomas Mikal Ford (Tommy Strong), Garrett Morris (Stan Winters: 1992–94), Jonathan Gries (Shawn: 1992–94).

Raucous, unbridled, and always sporting a devilish look in his eyes (that belied his sad-sack appearance), LAWRENCE rose through the ranks as a stand-up comic, which in turn led to movies and to this series. On the sitcom, he proved to be a mixture of FLIP WILSON, RICHARD PRYOR, and EDDIE MURPHY with a few dashes of CHRIS ROCK thrown in.

To define and lampoon the contemporary African-American male and his role in the dating/bedding/marriage game, Lawrence plays chauvinistic, smart-mouthed talk-show host Martin Payne, who reigns on Detroit radio station WZUP. His girlfriend (later wife) is Gina Waters, a marketing executive who copes with his "bad-ass" attitudes because she truly loves the nice soul buried within his loutish exterior. Cole and Tommy are Martin's two pals who spend a great deal of time hanging around their friend's apartment. Living across the hall from wisecracking Martin is Sheneneh (also played by Lawrence), a gaudy bigmouthed airhead. (In his gallery of characterizations on the show, Lawrence also played—from time to time—his mama, a hippie pal from the hood, and security guard Otis.)

As the series progressed, many of the sharp edges and heightened caricatures were toned down, while off-camera the apparently troubled star was exhibiting increasingly erratic behavior and gaining many tabloid headlines in the process. Eventually, Fox TV, one of the prime network homes of black talent, canceled the series, despite its loyal following among African Americans.

***Marva Collins Story, The* (1981)** CBS-TV, color, 100 minutes. **Director:** Peter Levin; **Teleplay:** Clifford Campion; **Cast:** Cicely Tyson (Marva Collins), Morgan Freeman (Clarence Collins), Roderick Wimberly (Martin Luther Jones), Mashuane Hardy (Cindy Collins), Brett Bouldin (Patrick Collins).

This high-minded, well-executed telefeature was based on an actual Chicago schoolteacher of the 1970s who achieved impressive results with minority children who were considered unteachable. She succeeds by using unorthodox teaching methods—much to the chagrin of traditional educators and the suspicion of community parents. Helping her overcome the obstacles is her staunch husband (FREEMAN).

TYSON, who, in the same year, made the exceedingly light-hearted *Bustin' Loose* with RICHARD PRYOR, was forceful here in her characterization of the determined educational pioneer who helps ghetto children. (She received an Emmy nomination in the Outstanding Actress category.) This telefilm was everything that DOROTHY DANDRIDGE's *BRIGHT ROAD* (1953) could have been but that the Hollywood of that era would not allow.

McDaniel, Hattie (1895–1952) The first African-American performer to win an Academy Award—a Best Supporting Actress Oscar for portraying Mammy in *GONE WITH THE WIND* (1939)—but stifled by the racial inequities prevalent in Hollywood's golden era, McDaniel was limited to playing an onslaught of celluloid domestics. However, they were ones that stuck in viewers' minds because she imparted to her roles her own inimitable touches of impertinence and performed her scenes with such a commanding presence.

She was born in Wichita, Kansas, the daughter of a Baptist minister and his wife, a singer of spirituals. At age fifteen, McDaniel won a drama prize and soon began her show business career, first as a songstress in minstrel shows and later as vocalist for George Morrison's Melody Hounds (with whom she performed also on radio). By 1924, she was a vaudeville headliner. As a result of the stock market crash of 1929, work became hard to get, and for a time, she found employment as a washroom attendant. As of 1931 she relocated to Los Angeles, hoping to work in films and on radio. (Her brother Sam, already working in pictures, persuaded Hattie to come to the West Coast. Another sibling, Etta, would also enter movies.)

McDaniel's Hollywood film debut was in 1932, the year she made such movies as *Washington Masquerade* and *The Golden West.* With her bulky figure, round face, and deep throaty laugh, she soon exhibited authority in executing her subordinate roles and, as such, her small parts registered with filmgoers. As the grumpy domestic in *ALICE ADAMS* (1935), she stole the limelight from the white stars in their joint scenes. She was in the fine 1936 musical *SHOW BOAT,* along with PAUL ROBESON. It became traditional in McDaniel's screen appearances that she dominated the on-camera men in her characters' lives, bossing them around verbally and punctuating her orders with her typical imposing look. Also

Hattie McDaniel in one of her innumerable roles as a maid, here in *Soldiers of the Storm* (1933) with Barbara Barondess. (JC ARCHIVES)

during the 1930s, she performed on radio on *AMOS 'N' ANDY* and Eddie Cantor's show.

She capped the 1930s with her memorable playing of Mammy, the crabby but always wise household slave at Tara who reined in willful Scarlett O'Hara. (Her great scene, telling Melanie of the death of Rhett and Scarlett's child, was a highlight of the film.) McDaniel delivered a thoughtful acceptance speech at the Academy Awards but was forced to sit in the back of the nightclub where the ceremonies took place. By this period she had been targeted by the National Association for the Advancement of Colored People (NAACP) as a negative example of a black performer playing into the hands of white Hollywood by performing such stereotypical "mammy" roles. Her argument that these were the only type of roles offered to her and that she sought to give these clichéd parts dimension did not stop the outcry from the NAACP and from members of the black community.

McDaniel continued as a movie domestic in such 1940s features as *They Died with Their Boots On* (1941), *Since You Went Away* (1944), *SONG OF THE SOUTH* (1946), and *Family Honeymoon* (1948). (Interestingly, her screen maids in the new decade became less hyper, less authoritative, and much more humane, in the tradition of her peer, LOUISE BEAVERS. It was perhaps establishment Hollywood's own effort to veer away from Hattie's stereotypical "mammy" roles of the past.) One of the actress's standout movie performances in the 1940s was her "Ice Cold Katie" song/dance number in the all-star picture revue, *Thank Your Lucky Stars* (1943).

On radio, Hattie headlined as *BEULAH* from 1947 until early 1952, later taking over the role from ETHEL WATERS in the TV version in 1952, but after doing a few episodes she left the comedy due to ill health. She died months later of breast cancer. McDaniel, who had been married four times, was the first black person to be buried in Los Angeles' Rosedale Cemetery. In August 2001, the made-for-cable documentary *Beyond Tara, The Extraordinary Life of Hattie McDaniel*, examined the struggles and triumphs of Hattie's life.

McKinney, Nina Mae (1912–1967) The star of Hollywood's first all-black musical (HALLELUJAH, 1929), McKinney quickly discovered that the segregated film industry of the 1930s did not welcome an African-American leading lady.

Born in Lancaster, South Carolina, she relocated to New York City, where she eventually found work in Lew Leslie's *Blackbirds of 1928*. Discovered there and cast as the tragic Chick in *Hallelujah*, and despite glowing reviews, she found further work in films hard to come by. McKinney did an uncredited bit in *They Learned About Women* (1929) and had a small role in the redeemed prostitute drama, *Safe in Hell* (1931). She joined with the Nicholas Brothers in the all-black musical short *Pie, Pie Blackbird*.

Discouraged by the lack of significant work available to her in America, she went to Europe, working there in clubs and cabarets. In England her films included *Sanders of the River* (1935) with PAUL ROBESON. Back in the United States, McKinney, known as the Black Garbo, found screen work in all-ethnic films (e.g., *The Black Network*, 1936; *Straight to Heaven*, 1939; *Swanee Showboat*, 1940; *Mantan Messes Up*, 1946). There were occasional mainstream features but only insignificant parts as maids (e.g., *Dark Waters*, 1944; *The Power of the Whistler*, 1945). She had a subordinate role in PINKY (1949) in which the white actress Jeanne Crain played the mulatto lead. By now, the once svelte, beautiful Nina Mae looked worn, plump, and cynical. Her last film was a bit in the Hedy Lamarr western, *Copper Canyon* (1950). The next year she played one of her last noteworthy performances—as the prostitute Sadie Thompson in a Brooklyn stage production of *Rain*.

McQueen, Butterfly (1911–1995) Her high-pitched voice, eccentric mannerisms, and unusual style of arcane clothing were sufficient to make this intriguing African-American player stand out from the crowd. However, she was indelibly linked with the screen role of the scatterbrained Prissy, the flighty domestic in *GONE WITH THE WIND* (1939). The memorable characterization should have furthered her career greatly, but, instead, because of racial bigotry at the time, she was stuck in an acting rut playing similar scatter-brained screen characters—that is, when she could find work.

She was born Thelma McQueen in Tampa, Florida, the offspring of a stevedore and his wife, a domestic. For a time she lived in Augusta, Georgia. Later, she and her mother moved to New York City where the parent worked as a cook. Soon, thirteen-year-old McQueen joined a Harlem theater group. As a performer in *A Midsummer Night's Dream*, she was part of the butterfly-ballet segment, which led to her nickname. Later, the determined, always genteel actress won a role in the Broadway play *Brown Sugar* (1937), and its producer, George Abbott, used her in *Brother Rat* (1937) and *What a Life* (1938).

After her noteworthy screen bow as the fragile soul in *Gone With the Wind*, Butterfly was wasted in several Hollywood productions: *Affectionately Yours* (1941), *Mildred Pierce* (1945), and *Duel in the Sun* (1946)—typically cast as a weepy, whiny domestic. (She had a larger role in the all-black musical, *CABIN IN THE SKY*, 1943, and was in the all-black film *Killer Diller*, 1948.) On radio, Butterfly was heard on the *Danny Kaye Show* in the mid-1940s and was Oriole on the comedy *BEULAH* (1947—52). From 1950 to 1953 on TV's *Beulah*, McQueen repeated her role as the star's neighbor, another domestic.

Never having fitted into the Hollywood system (both because of her race and her unconventional manner), she moved back to New York. It was tough sledding, and in between rare stage assignments, she often worked at menial jobs. Later, even more discouraged by life, the still unmarried McQueen returned to Augusta, Georgia. There, for a time, she had her own radio show and was in the restaurant business.

After years out of the limelight, McQueen reemerged in 1969 in the off-Broadway production of *Curley McDimple*, followed by mounting her own one-woman show and, later, a nightclub act. She turned up in a few movies (e.g., *The Phynx*, 1970; *Amazing Grace*, 1974) and occasionally on TV (e.g., *The Adventures of Huckleberry Finn*, 1981). She was in Harrison Ford's movie *The Mosquito Coast* (1986). Her final appearance was as Miss Priss in *Polly* (1989), a TV movie adaptation of the classic *Pollyanna*.

In 1980 Butterfly had created headlines when she sued a bus company, claiming their security guards had mistreated her and alleged that she was a pickpocket. Likewise, her tragic death made news: She died from burns suffered when her makeshift room heater malfunctioned.

***Member of the Wedding, The* (1952)** Columbia, b&w, 91 minutes. **Director:** Fred Zinnemann; **Screenplay:** Edna Anhalt; **Cast:** Ethel Waters (Berenice Sadie Brown), Julie Harris (Frankie Addams), Brandon De Wilde (John Henry), Arthur Franz (Jarvis), Nancy Gates (Janice), James Edwards (Honey Camden Brown).

Based on Carson McCullers's 1946 novel and her hit Broadway play adaptation (1950), WATERS, as well as Harris and De Wilde, were recreating their stage assignments. This sensitive drama provided the now hefty, white-haired Waters with one of her best screen roles—a riveting performance that was overlooked (expectedly, given the era) in the Academy Awards competition. Like the later *THE LONG WALK HOME* (1990) and many other dramas of the South, it detailed the complex relationship between a strong black woman and whites, often at a point when the latter are waking up to the real world. What also made this screen adaptation special—especially considering the times—was the (brief) footage devoted to the touching relationship of Waters's character with her restless foster brother (EDWARDS). The latter was a man at loose ends in the confining black world, who found partial escape through his career as a musician.

In a southern town, Frankie, a twelve-year-old motherless tomboy, insists that she will join her brother (Franz) and his bride (Gates) on their upcoming honeymoon. Her wise housekeeper, Berenice Sadie Brown, who has experienced a lifetime of sorrow, tries to warn the youngster that she is asking for a big disappointment to have such expectations. Later, the distraught girl runs away briefly. Meanwhile, her little cousin (De Wilde) takes sick and dies. Thereafter, when Frankie's family moves to smaller quarters and no longer needs Berenice's ministering, the now maturing Frankie becomes so infatuated with a new neighbor boy that she carelessly ignores staunch, saddened Berenice.

The film's best moments were reserved for Waters as she reminisced about her late first husband and when she tried to help her brother, Honey Camden Brown.

Harris received a Best Actress nomination for her performance as Frankie Addams. *The Member of the Wedding* was twice remade as a TV movie: in 1982 with Pearl Bailey (Berenice) and HOWARD ROLLINS JR. (Honey Brown) and again in 1997 with ALFRE WOODARD. (The character of Honey Brown was written out of the 1997 production.)

***Menace II Society* (1993)** New Line Cinema, color, 90 minutes. **Directors:** Allen Hughes and Albert Hughes; **Screenplay:** Tyger Williams; **Cast:** Tyrin Turner (Kaydee "Caine" Lawson), Larenz Tate (O-Dog), Samuel L. Jackson (Tat Lawson), Glenn Plummer (Pernell), Khandi Alexander (Karen Lawson), Jada Pinkett (Ronnie).

This entry was the feature filmmaking debut of the Hughes brothers, twenty-year-old twins. Although not offering any fresh perspective on the black URBAN DRAMA either in plot or nonstereotypical characters, the picture presented its sad narrative of hellish ghetto life with remarkable fluidity. (Lisa Rinzler won the Independent Spirit Award for her cinematography.)

In the Watts section of Los Angeles, eighteen-year-old Caine—whose father died in a bad drug deal and his mother from a heroin overdose—lives with his very religious grandparents (Jackson and Lawson). Caine is on hand when his reckless, macho pal O-Dog robs a convenience store and kills the Korean owners for a supposed insult. Meanwhile, Caine impregnates a casual date but refuses to take responsibility. He does, however, find a meaningful relationship with Ronnie, a single parent. Just as he prepares to leave town with her, he is killed by a cousin of the pregnant girl.

With its rap score preaching inner city violence, the film graphically depicted just that on all levels—among the youths, between races, and between the cops and their suspects. It was predicted, as so often had happened with other such films, that *Menace II Society*, which seemed to celebrate the characters' rough lives, would create riots when shown. The forecast proved groundless. Made for $3.5 million, it grossed about $28 million in domestic distribution.

Men of the Tenth See *RED, WHITE, AND BLACK, THE*.

***Miami Vice* (1984–1989)** NBC-TV series, color, 60 minutes. **Cast:** Don Johnson (Det. James "Sonny" Crockett), Philip Michael Thomas (Det. Ricardo Tubbs), Edward James Olmos (Lt. Martin Castillo), Saundra Santiago (Det. Gina Navarro Calabrese), Olivia Brown (Det. Trudy Joplin).

With its display of designer fashions, fast cars, hip rock music soundtracks, and MTV-style cinematography, *Miami Vice* came to represent everything that was trendy, glitzy, and one-dimensional about the me-generation of the materialistic, conformist decade of the 1980s. Starring in this showy, calculated TV ensemble are two handsome lead actors (Johnson and Thomas) as well as the city of Miami. The resort town, making a comeback as a celebrity Mecca, is usually highlighted on episodes with two contrasting locales: the wealthy homes and haunts of the well-to-do establishment set, and the lavish abodes and lairs of the corrupt drug world. (Rarely are the tawdry, downbeat ghettos of Miami featured on this extremely popular series because, presumably, that would have spoiled the airy mood of this seemingly topical, relevant police series.) Also part of the program's ongoing success is its multicultural cast that ran from white, brash Johnson to blank-faced, African-American Thomas to pouting, Hispanic Olmos as the detectives' boss. The quirky lineup of guest stars ranged from singers Little Richard and Phil Collins to such guest stars as Pam Grier and such celebrities as boxing promoter Don King and Watergate participant G. Gordon Liddy.

In this interracial cop/buddy series, both leads played ciphers. Little is known about their pasts. (Crockett is separated from his wife and son; he lives on a sailboat and drives a Ferrari. Tubbs is an ex-vice cop from New York City who is great at donning disguises for his undercover assignments.) Regardless, one of the progressive elements of this show is that initially both members of the duo are equals, with no trace of the Tubbs character being subordinate to his white partner. This enlightened presentation makes the show more relevant to socially conscious viewers. (Ironically this ingredient lessened as the seasons went on and the segments focused increasingly on egocentric Crockett and his yen for fast cars, women, and cool clothes, while sensitive, moody Tubbs was pushed progressively more onto the sidelines.)

Adding immeasurably to the blend are the cool, high-living thugs and lowlifes who often ended being mowed down in artistically staged gunfire or blown up in their fancy cars or on their plush yachts.

For his role on *Miami Vice*, Thomas was nominated for a Golden Globe for Best Performance in a TV Series—Drama for the 1985–86 season.

Micheaux, Oscar (1884–1951) He was the first African American to produce a feature film (*The Homesteader*, 1919) and, similarly, was first to make a sound feature (*The Exile*, 1931). One of the most original of American film pioneers, this prolific African-American moviemaker turned out more than forty movies in his lengthy career, all of which reflected his concern for the upward mobility of his race in a white-dominated society. His independently made features were crudely made, low-budget affairs with often dreadful production values, but the filmmaker's concerns (e.g., a lynch mob in 1920's *WITHIN OUR GATES*, the future of a black college graduate in a racist business world in 1939's *Birthright*—a remake of his 1924 silent) were always evident. Sometimes Micheaux employed negative ethnic images on screen to contrast with the worthy prototypes of the black community he was depicting. (A great believer in the moderate point of view, Oscar was most interested in dealing with members of the black middle class, *not* slum/ghetto dwellers.) As with D. W. Griffith (the creator of 1915's *THE BIRTH OF A NATION*), the world of cinema eventually passed Micheaux by, but he was the father of inspiration to such later black filmmakers as MICHAEL SCHULTZ, GORDON PARKS SR., and SPIKE LEE.

Micheaux was born in Metropolis, Illinois, the son of freed slaves. Growing up in poverty, he had little structured education. At age seventeen, he left home and thereafter held a variety of jobs (including train porter, shoeshine man, laborer) before becoming a homesteader on a South Dakota farm. His debut novel (*The Conquest: The Story of a Negro Pioneer*, 1913) was somewhat autobiographical but was published anonymously. A black-operated movie company sought to acquire his third book, *The Homesteader* (1917). When the deal fell through, the ambitious, daring Oscar made the movie himself, raising the money by traveling from town to town to find small investors. (He formed the Oscar Micheaux Corp., which lasted from 1918 to 1948.) Made for $15,000, *The Homesteader* brought only in $5,000. Despite the financial setback, Micheaux was now a full-time moviemaker.

During the years, many of his films were distributed independently to black theaters, often with Micheaux engineering down payments on rental fees. (A good many of the director's screen works were lost over the years, thus leaving a scattered legacy of his actual work.) Often Micheaux used titillating sexual scenes in his plot to keep the audience's interest. Sometimes, because of his themes about racism, theaters in the South refused to show his movies; even in the more liberal North, local censor boards would cancel his latest release for fear that it might incite race riots. Most importantly, throughout his years in the film industry, the moviemaker was always operating outside the Hollywood establishment, proceeding audaciously in his own sphere—the world of ethnic minorities. (Nevertheless, in having to deal with the real world, he was subjected to racial and class bias all his life.)

In 1925, Micheaux directed PAUL ROBESON as a young clergyman in the silent photoplay *Body and Soul.* It remains Oscar's best-known silent. Often, the director took established Hollywood genres and adapted them to the black idiom. For example, *Daughter of the Congo* (1930) was a jungle adventure tale; *Underworld* (1937) dealt with Chicago's underbelly. Because of his prodigious output, Oscar assembled a stock company of sorts, with his leading players often paralleling popular Hollywood personalities, for example, Lorenzo Tucker (billed as the "black Valentino") and Ethel Moses (known as the "black Harlow"). In a few of his films, the quite dark-skinned Oscar played cameo roles (e.g., 1932's *Ten Minutes to Live*, 1935's *Murder in Harlem*).

Throughout the 1930s Micheaux—with his screen portraits of an idealized ethnic minority world—continued to produce product for black audiences: *Harlem After Midnight* (1934), *Temptation* (1935), *Swing!* (1938), and *Lying Lips* (1939). After 1940's *The Notorious Elinor Lee*, he made only one more feature, 1948's *The Betrayal.* By then it seemed that African Americans had lost interest in watching race movies, much preferring the slicker product of Hollywood, particularly as it was beginning to use its ethnic minority talent for more than on-screen domestics. He died of a heart attack in Charlotte, North Carolina, at age sixty-seven.

In 1986, the Directors Guild of America posthumously awarded a Golden Jubilee Special Award to Micheaux. The next year, Oscar belatedly received a star on Hollywood Boulevard's Walk of Fame. The telefeature *You Must Remember This* (1992) cast Robert Guillaume as a Michaeaux-type film director who is so discouraged by breaking into the Hollywood establishment as a moviemaker that he becomes a barber, hiding his past creative efforts from his family.

***Minstrel Man* (1977)** CBS-TV, color, 100 minutes. **Director:** William A. Graham; **Teleplay:** Richard A. Shapiro and Esther Shapiro; **Cast:** Glynn Turman (Harry Brown Jr.), Ted Ross (Charlie Bates), Stanley Clay (Rennie Brown), Saundra Sharp (Jessamins), Art Evans (Tambo), Gene Bell (Harry Brown Sr.).

In searching for more black topics to convert into television movies, the network came up with this history of black minstrelsy as seen through the eyes of two siblings. One (Turman) is conservative and aspires to be innovative as a song writer; the other (Clay) is entrepreneurial and wants to own a real minstrel troupe, not one featuring Caucasians in BLACKFACE. The brothers are managed by the sneaky Charlie Bates, while Jessamins is the woman in the boys' lives. Before the finale, one of the siblings is lynched by a white mob.

Minstrel Man received an Emmy nomination for Outstanding Music Score.

***Miracle in Harlem* (1948)** Screen Guild, b&w, 69 minutes. **Director:** Jack Kemp; **Screenplay:** Vincent Valentini; **Cast:** Hilda Offley (Aunt Hattie), Sheila Guyse (Julie Weston), Stepin Fetchit (Swifty), Kenneth Freeman (Jim Marshall), William Greaves (Bert Hallam), Sybil Lewis (Alice Adams), Creighton Thompson (Reverend Jackson), Lawrence Criner (Albert Marshall), and the Juanita Hall Choir.

Filmed in New York City, this was another of distributor Herald Pictures' all-African-American movies. The production values and the script were flimsy, and FETCHIT still did his shuffling, dimwitted-man routine. However, this slight murder mystery depicted ambitious, upwardly mobile, and entrepreneurial black characters. Coming in the late 1940s, this unsophisticated production was avant-garde and progressive.

In Harlem, Aunt Hattie operates a candy-making business from her kitchen. Her protégée is her niece, Julie Weston. Ex-serviceman Bert Hallam, who is preparing for the ministry, loves Julie. Meanwhile, Jim, the son of candy manufacturer Albert Marshall, returns home. Albert tricks Hattie out of control of her business and puts Jim in charge while he romances Julie. Later, both Marshalls are murdered, and the chief suspect seems to be Hattie. When all is resolved, Julie and Bert pursue their romance.

***Mission: Impossible* (1966–1973)** CBS-TV series, color, 60 minutes. **Cast:** Steven Hill (Daniel Briggs: 1966–67), Peter Graves (James Phelps: 1967–73), Barbara Bain (Cinnamon Carter: 1966–69), Martin Landau (Rollin Hand: 1966–69), Greg Morris (Barney Collier), Peter Lupus (Willie Armitage), Leonard Nimoy (Paris: 1969–71).

Compared to the big-screen feature-length updates (1996 and 2000) of this series, the original *Mission: Impossible* episodes were tame, quaint, and filled with primitive technology. But in its day this series was an audience-grabber, mixing its espionage themes with exciting capers, frequent disguises and con games by the undercover government team, and dastardly villains. Although Bain won three Emmys for her performance on the series, Morris as the electronics expert Barney Collier quietly make some viewers take note—he was black. In the troublesome 1960s when civil-rights demands, riots, and integration were a hot issue, the show wanted to be quietly relevant but make no particular comment about the character's racial background. For some viewers, this was doing the cause of integration an injustice, for they felt that Barney Collier should have been given dialogue, motivation, and so on that reflected his cultural heritage. On the other hand, the integration of the cast showed the Collier character interacting in a white world peacefully and responsibly and being treated with respect. It was a small advancement for racial integration on TV.

When the once-popular series was revived (1988–90) on ABC-TV, the role of Grant Collier, Barney's son, was played by Morris's real-life offspring, Phil Morris. In the two feature film versions (1996 and 2000) African-American actor Ving

Rhames played a former CIA operative who helps the hero (Tom Cruise).

***Mississippi Burning* (1988)** Orion, color, 128 minutes. **Director:** Alan Parker; **Screenplay** Chris Gerolimop; **Cast:** Gene Hackman (Rupert Anderson), Willem Dafoe (Alan Ward), Frances McDormand (Mrs. Pell), Brad Dourif (Deputy Pell), R. Lee Ermey (Mayor Tilman).

The shocking 1964 Mississippi killings by the Ku Klux Klan of three civil-rights workers (one African American and two Jewish men) led to several picturizations. They ranged from the exploitive, low-budget *Murder in Mississippi* (1965) to the much more elaborate and thoughtful TV movie, *Murder in Mississippi* (1990). Somewhere in the middle was this 1988 entry by British filmmaker Parker, a fictionalization of the case told in terms of the cop/buddy genre.

On one hand is hot-headed civil-rights advocate Alan Ward, a by-the-book FBI agent who regards this investigation as a crusade. In contrast, former southern sheriff Rupert Anderson, an older FBI operative who has been inured by years in law enforcement, uses his ability to communicate with southerners to amass needed information quietly. When Ward brings in a FBI task force, there are outbreaks of racism. Later, an informant (McDormand) with whom Anderson has become infatuated is brutalized by her KKK spouse (Dourif). Thereafter, the enraged Anderson pushes Ward into joining him in illegal methods to learn the truth. After the culprits are caught, they are charged with civil-rights violations because a murder case would be a local jurisdictional matter and the defendants would likely receive favorable court treatment.

At times, in its efforts to appeal to mainstream audiences, this film tended to tell its story from a white perspective and thus deemphasized the plight of the civil-rights workers involved, as well as that of African Americans in general.

Mississippi Burning won an Oscar for Best Cinematography and received six other Academy Award nominations: Best Actor (Hackman), Best Director, Best Film Editing, Best Picture, Best Sound, and Best Supporting Actress (McDormand). It grossed more than $34 million in domestic distribution.

Mr. T (1952–) Hollywood's answer to Muhammad Ali, Mr. T was in great vogue in the 1980s. With his bald pate, burly five-feet, ten-inch figure, the boxer-turned-actor spoke flavorfully, acted outrageously on and off camera, and punctuated his massive presence by wearing an overabundance of gaudy gold jewelry. If Mr. T had not been such an engaging self-promoter, he might have been taken as black comedy relief. Instead this flavorful character—who, in his heyday, was merchandized in cereals, dolls, and cartoon series—emerged a beloved icon to school children.

He was born Lawrence Tureaud on Chicago's rough Southside, the tenth of a family of twelve children. His older brother encouraged the boy to bulk up to survive in the ghetto. (He later took up martial arts.) Always athletic, Tureaud played football and wrestled in high school and won a sports scholarship to a Texas college. He dropped out (or was dismissed) after a year, surviving by working as a gym instructor and a bouncer. His tough demeanor soon qualified him to be a bodyguard for such celebrities as Muhammad Ali and Michael Jackson.

Mr. T's appearance on a TV game show led to his being cast as Clubber Lang, the vicious boxer who opposed Sylvester Stallone in the ring in *ROCKY 3* (1982). Despite being nominated for a Razzie Award (in the Worst New Star category), this movie role snowballed into his featured part as Sgt. Bosco "B. A." Baracus, the menacing mechanic on the TV adventure series *The A–Team* (1983–87). In addition he also made movies, including *D.C. Cab* (1983). Meanwhile, Mr. T provided his voice for the cartoon series *Mister T* (1983–86), penned his autobiography (*Mr. T: The Man with the Gold*, 1984), and, having become a pro wrestler in 1985, appeared on TV's *WrestleMania* that year, briefly the tag-team partner of Hulk Hogan. He abandoned the sport for a time (until his return in 1994) and starred in the detective series *T. and T.*, which was syndicated between 1988 and 1991. Despite being diagnosed with T-cell lymphoma in 1995, he still managed a few film appearances later on: *Inspector Gadget* (1999), *Apocalypse IV: Judgement* (2001).

***Mo' Better Blues* (1990)** Universal, color, 127 minutes. **Director/Screenplay:** Spike Lee; **Cast:** Denzel Washington (Bleek Gilliam), Spike Lee (Giant), Wesley Snipes (Shadow Henderson), Giancarlo Esposito (Left Hand Lacey), Robin Harris (Butterbean Jones), Jolie Lee (Indigo Downes), Bill Nunn (Bottom Hammer), Cynda Williams (Clarke Bentancourt).

Loosely based on the life of LEE's musician father Bill, who has written the scores for many of his son's features, this relatively uncontroversial feature focuses lengthily on jazz trumpeter Bleek Gilliam (and is a showcase for WASHINGTON's acting acumen). Thanks to a dominating mother, self-centered Bleek makes music his life's priority. As such, he keeps at arm's length both women he is dating: school teacher Indigo (played by Lee's sister Jolie) who wants a permanent relationship, and would-be band vocalist Clarke Bentancourt. Ambivalent about so much, Bleek allows his gambling-addicted manager Giant to make a bad club contract for the group. Also involved is ambitious saxophonist Shadow Henderson, who wants to take over the band and Clarke. Later, when Bleek helps trouble-prone Giant, the trumpeter is beaten up and left with a mangled face by thugs. After attempting a comeback in Henderson's band, he finds that he can no longer perform. Bleek retires, weds Indigo, and later teaches their child to play the trumpet. As for Giant, he is reduced to being a club doorman.

While focusing on the world of black jazz musicians and suggesting how the white world has denigrated them, Lee presented a wealth of jazz music, some composed and played by Branford Marsalis. At the time of release, some reviewers, as did the B'nai Brith Anti-Defamation League, perceived negative portrayals in the roles of the Jewish club owners (played by the Turturro brothers, John and Nicholas).

Mo' Better (a reference to sexual coupling) *Blues* grossed more than $16 million in domestic distribution.

***Mod Squad, The* (1968–1973)** ABC-TV series, color, 60 minutes. **Cast:** Michael Cole (Pete Cochran), Clarence Williams III (Linc Hayes), Peggy Lipton (Julie Barnes), Tige Andrews (Capt. Adam Greer).

This precursor series to *21 Jump Street* (1987–90) had the gimmick of three young-looking law enforcers as the lead characters. They were known as "hippie cops" because they each had dropped out from traditional society and each had their unpleasant past encounters with the law. Not only did this series appeal to the expanding youth culture, but also it dealt (to a small degree) with the racial issues of the day. While two of the young stars were white (Cole and Lipton), the third was an Afro-haired, tall black dude (Williams III). With this combination of generational and quasi-racial relevance, the show was quite successful.

As the special unit of the Los Angeles Police Department, the trio investigates and infiltrates suspect organizations that the ordinary police cannot penetrate. While engaged in their dangerous activity, the three young converts attempt to straighten out their lives and sort out their identities. (Linc's character was raised in the Watts ghetto of Los Angeles in a large family; he was arrested for participating in the Watts riots.) The actor trio made appearances in the weak reunion TV movie: *The Return of the Mod Squad* (1979). In the big-screen fizzle remake of the series, *The Mod Squad* (1999), African-American actor Omar Epps inherited the role of Linc(oln) Hayes.

***Moonrise* (1948)** Republic, b&w, 90 minutes. **Director:** Frank Borzage; **Screenplay:** Charles Haas; **Cast:** Dane Clark (Danny Hawkins), Gail Russell (Gilly Johnson), Ethel Barrymore (Grandma), Allyn Joslyn (Sheriff Clem Otis), Rex Ingram (Mose Johnson), Henry Morgan (Billy Scripture), Lloyd Bridges (Jerry Sykes).

This morose minor film was notable for its film-noir ambiance and for the appearance of veteran African-American actor Ingram in a well-handled character role as one of the town's outcasts. (Another oddball in this southern town was deaf mute Billy Scripture.) It was based on Theodore Strauss's 1946 novel.

In a small Virginia town, Danny Hawkins grows up being ridiculed as the son of a killer: Years before, his father had murdered a local doctor who failed to save Mr. Hawkins's wife and had been hung for his crime. Now an adult, Danny kills Jerry Sykes, the banker's son, in a scuffle; there are no witnesses, but Danny is convinced that he will be found out. Later, Danny becomes friendly with schoolteacher Gilly Johnson, who had been the dead man's girlfriend. Increasingly guilt-ridden, Hawkins visits another of the town's outsiders, Mose Johnson, a black man who lives in a shack near the swamp. The older man, who gives Danny advice on life, is the one who later finds Sykes's body. As the sheriff (Joslyn) pieces together the clues, the evidence leads to Danny. Eventually he gives himself up to the pursuing lawmen.

Moonrise received an Oscar nomination for Best Sound.

Had this film been made some decades later (after attitudes changed), Ingram's Mose might well have been given more importance in the script and his wisdom given more credence in the town.

Moreland, Mantan (1901–1973) In his day, Hollywood utilized this solidly built actor to play the stock role of the comic-relief black man. He was great at double takes, rolling his eyes, and playing the superstitious sort who, when panicked, would shout out in shaking fright "Feets, do you' stuff!" As such he was tremendously in demand by Hollywood film studios. (He made well more than 100 movies.) However, in retrospect, his stereotype parts were considered demeaning to his race, a caricature of the near-illiterate, credulous soul, a sidekick to do the white man's bidding. His alternate performing career was in black films, where he often played the boastful ladies' man.

He was born in Monroe, Louisiana. At age twelve, he left home to join a circus. Later, he was in vaudeville for years. At one point he did a comedy act with F. E. Miller as his partner. Later, he joined with Tim Moore for a stage routine. (Further on, in the late 1940s and early 1950s, he worked with comedian REDD FOXX.) Moreland made his screen bow in *That's the Spirit* (1933). He had a minor bit (as an angel) in *THE GREEN PASTURES* (1936). He also played in several black-cast movies of the period: *Harlem on the Prairie* (1937) and *Two Gun Man from Harlem* (1938). Mostly he played chauffeurs, cooks, elevator operators, train porters, etc., but in *CABIN IN THE SKY* (1943), he played the First Idea man.

Mantan Moreland, as Charlie Chan's chauffeur Birmingham Brown, is about to perform one of his famous comedic double takes in *The Jade Mask* (1945). (JC ARCHIVES)

Mantan gained his greatest recognition as Birmingham Brown, the trouble-prone, fearful chauffeur of the great detective in fifteen films of the Charlie Chan detective film series (from 1944's *Charlie Chan in the Secret Service* to 1949's *The Sky Dragon*). Meanwhile, Moreland continued to make race films, often top-featured: *Mantan Runs for Mayor* and *Mantan Messes Up* (both 1946). In the mid-1950s the actor was in a trio of low-budget rock 'n' roll features (including 1956's *Rockin' the Blues*). By the late 1960s, the game actor was reduced to playing bit parts: *The Comic* (1969), *The Biscuit Eater* (1972), and *The Young Nurses* (1973). His TV credits included guest appearances on such shows as *Adam 12* and *The Bill Cosby Show*.

Murphy, Eddie (1961–) In the early 1980s, audacious, acid-tongued Murphy was the quick-witted young turk in the world of black entertainers; the older BILL COSBY was considered a conservative establishment figure whose public image and foibles were a ripe target for aggressive Eddie. Jumping ahead twenty years, Murphy was now a Cosbylike figure, appealing more—who would have believed?—to the establishment and to family audiences. Meanwhile, snapping at Eddie's heels were such younger black comics as Chris Tucker (considered by some commentators to be the Eddie Murphy of the new millennium).

Edward Regan Murphy was born in Brooklyn, New York, to a transit authority policeman father and a telephone operator mother. The youngster was three when his parents separated (and later divorced). His mom became seriously ill in 1964 causing Eddie and his older brother Charles to be placed in a foster home. In 1969 the recuperated Mrs. Murphy remarried, and Eddie's stepfather moved his new family to Roosevelt, Long Island. By age fifteen, smart-mouthed Murphy had found his forte—class clown. He translated this into his first gig as emcee at a local youth center. He developed a raunchy act, modeled after his stand-up comedy idol RICHARD PRYOR. By the fall of 1979 he was making the round of New York City comedy clubs, learning by watching others and through his own riffs.

Murphy dropped college plans when he was hired to join the cast of TV's *Saturday Night Live* in the fall of 1980. He soon became a star of the show and developed a repertoire of satirical characters: "Dion" (a gay hairdresser); a tongue-tied singer; a TV huckster named "Velvet Jones"; "Rascal Buckwheat"; and "Solomon," a Jewish senior citizen. By 1981 Eddie was extremely popular with viewers and had recorded a comedy album. The next year, he made his movie debut in *48 HRS.*, proving that he had great screen charisma. This was confirmed by *TRADING PLACES* (1983) in which his tart ghetto-style remarks displayed a slight meanness beneath their jovial exterior. His marquee value rose still higher with *BEVERLY HILLS COP* (1984), the first of three entries in that action series. Meanwhile, he performed cable TV stand-up comedy specials and had already unleashed the first of his concert movies. In these unbridled filmed ventures he displayed sexist and antigay attitudes that caused a mild furor, but he was too entrenched as a big name for it to make a difference—at least, at that time.

Eddie Murphy as *The Distinguished Gentleman* (1992). (ECHO BOOK SHOP)

For Murphy, the descent from on high was relatively rapid. *Harlem Nights* (1989), a period gangster yarn that Murphy produced, directed, scripted, and starred in, was not appreciated. Follow-up sequels to earlier hits (e.g., *Another 48 Hrs.*, 1990; *Beverly Hills Cop III*, 1994) displayed a lethargic, stale side to the star, and the misconceived *Vampire in Brooklyn* (1995) was neither funny enough nor sufficiently horrific. Also, the public lost interest in and became appalled at the reported indulgences of his posse of friends, as well as Murphy's own bloated lifestyle.

Nonetheless, Eddie rebounded in a remake of an old Jerry Lewis screen comedy: This new edition of *The Nutty Professor* (1996) gave the star ample opportunity to play several characters within the film and to be relatively inoffensive on camera. (Its popularity led to a successful sequel in 2000.) If an action entry (1997's *Metro*) and the feckless *Holy Man* (1998) were relative commercial disappointments, family audiences approved of *Doctor Dolittle* (1998). Its whopping box-office success prompted a follow-up entry (2001).

Expanding on his renewed popularity, he provided one of the voices for the animated TV series, *The PJs*, which began in 1999. Along the way, he turned in solid performances in two 1999 releases: the drama *Life* with MARTIN LAWRENCE and the comedy *Bowfinger* starring Steve Martin. Eddie also did the voice of the Donkey, a supporting character in the popular animated feature, *Shrek* (2001). Later films for Murphy included a spoof of buddy cop movies, *Showtime* (2002), which teamed him with Robert De Niro, and the sci-fi entry *The Adventures of Pluto Nash* (2002). Murphy took over Bill Cosby's role of Alexander Scott in the big-screen edition (2002) of the TV series *I SPY* and then starred in a remake of *The Incredible Shrinking Man* (2003).

Muse, Clarence (1889–1979) A law-school graduate, Muse was nevertheless caught in the rut of playing the only type of parts that the Hollywood film studios offered to black performers in the 1930s and 1940s. With his cultured background, Muse often found himself at odds with the semiliterate, blue-collar characterizations he had to essay. He became reserved on camera, a man with a mellifluous voice who enunciated his diction well and a frustrated creative artist who spent time composing songs for films and sometimes helping to create his own dialogue for movie assignments.

He was born in Baltimore, Maryland, and attended law school at Dickinson College. By the 1920s he had shifted professions to the theater. Moving to New York City, he was part of the Lincoln Players in Harlem and helped to found the Lafayette Players. He went to Hollywood for the all-black screen musical *HEARTS IN DIXIE* (1929), being paid a then princely sum of $1,250 a week for his key assignment. In *Huckleberry Finn* (1931), he was seen as Jim, the escaped slave.

Like so many of his race, solid screen performances did not guarantee a productive future. Thereafter, Muse was pigeonholed in tiny parts as celluloid working men: coach driver (*White Zombie*, 1932), shoeshine man (*Flying Down to Rio*, 1933), chauffeur (*The Wrecker*, 1933), and janitor (*The Public Menace*, 1935). Because of his fine singing voice, he occasionally was on camera—quite briefly—as a vocalist (e.g., *Big City Blues*, 1932; *Frisco Jenny*, 1933; *Follow Your Heart*, 1936). He sporadically contributed songs he had written for movies in which he appeared (e.g., *High Hat*, 1937; *Spirit of Youth*, 1938). For *Way Down South* (1939), he both wrote songs and coauthored the screenplay. During this decade, Muse's most offbeat assignment was in *So Red the Rose* (1935), a Civil War tale in which he played Cato, an aggressive, angry slave.

In the 1940s Clarence continued to take the subservient screen bits that he was allowed. Years earlier, he had written a pamphlet on the plight of the African-American actor in the United States, and he continued to speak out on the need for racial integration in the movie industry and elsewhere. Throughout the decade, he played a string of train porters (e.g., *The Thin Man Goes Home*, 1944). In 1950, filmmaker Frank Capra, who had used Muse in several films including *Broadway Bill* (1934), cast Clarence in the musical remake *Riding High*, in which he had a musical interlude with star Bing Crosby.

In the pallid TV series version (1954–55) of *CASABLANCA* (1942), Muse took on the role of Rick's friend/piano player, a part handled in the classic movie by DOOLEY WILSON. He was in some of the *Swamp Fox* episodes on TV's *The Wonderful World of Disney* in the late 1950s. His final big screen entries included *CAR WASH* (1976) and *The Black Stallion* (1979).

For his many contributions to show business, Muse was inducted into the Black Filmmakers Hall of Fame in 1973.

musicals—feature films In Hollywood's most famous part-talkie film, *THE JAZZ SINGER* (1927), there were no black main characters, but the star of the musical—Al Jolson—performed in BLACKFACE, a practice he continued in several subsequent films (e.g., *The Singing Fool*, 1928, *Say It With Song*, 1929). A later part-talkie, *Show Boat* (1929), based on the Edna Ferber novel, had a prologue in sound that featured Jules Bledsoe and Tess "Aunt Jemima" Gardella singing songs from the stage version. Within the silent main story, STEPIN FETCHIT had the role of Joe, the dock worker (who on stage sang "Ol' Man River").

Also in 1929, ETHEL WATERS performed specialty numbers within the revue musical *On with the Show* but was not integrated into the story line. In that year of the musical film craze, Hollywood made two all-black song-and-dance pictures: *HEARTS IN DIXIE* and *HALLELUJAH*, experiments that would not be repeated for another fourteen years. During the rest of the 1930s, scattered appearances by blacks in musicals performing specialty numbers were isolated from the main story line; for example, CLARENCE MUSE sang a jungle number ("I Go Congo") that he co-wrote in *High Hat* (1936), a musical about radio broadcasting; musician/singer Louis Armstrong provided musical interludes in such items, among others, as *Pennies from Heaven* (1936), *Artists and Models* (1937), and *Every Day's a Holiday* (1938); a promising entertainer such as the very young SAMMY DAVIS JR. starred in a short subject (*Rufus Jones for President*, 1933); LENA HORNE, before joining MGM in the 1940s, made her screen debut in the all-black independent production, *THE DUKE IS TOPS* (1938); Duke Ellington and his Band made some short subjects and feature film appearances (e.g., *Symphony in Black*, 1935; *Hit Parade of 1937*, 1937).

In contrast, LOUISE BEAVERS in *Rainbow on the River* (1936), HATTIE McDANIEL in *Can This Be Dixie?*, and PAUL ROBESON in *SHOW BOAT* (1936) were integrated into the stories of these mainstream productions but were cast—as were all blacks at the times—in roles as slaves or domestics. Such was also the case with the legendary dancing great, BILL "BOJANGLES" ROBINSON, who made his greatest impression on moviegoers when teamed with little Shirley Temple in several 1930s musicals (e.g., *The Little Colonel*, 1935). Following the wake of singing cowboy movies made by the establishment film industry, black performer Herb Jeffries starred in several such all-black sagebrush offerings (e.g., *Harlem on the Prairie*, 1937), made independently for the black movie-theater circuit.

Although Hollywood and America were undergoing a Latin American craze in the 1940s (due to the World War II diplomatic gesture to win friends in South America), black performers continued to appear largely as specialty numbers in studio movies, such as the renowned tap-dancing Nicholas Brothers and singers DOROTHY DANDRIDGE (e.g., *Sun Valley Serenade*, 1941) and Hattie McDaniel (e.g., *Thank Your Lucky Stars*, 1943). In 1943, Hollywood made two new all-black musicals (*CABIN IN THE SKY* and *STORMY WEATHER*), both co-starring Horne. However, generally she was sandwiched into a product by her home studio (MGM) where she had separate song interludes (e.g., *Thousands Cheer*, 1943) that could be deleted from release prints when shown in the South. African-American talent continued to appear in short subjects for theatrical release or in Soundies used in moviola-type machines in entertainment arcades. The post-World War II era witnessed the last hurrah of the black independent cinema, and several musicals were released (e.g., *Harlem Is Heaven* and *Sepia Cinderella*, both 1947).

By the early 1950s, Hollywood was awakening to the vibrancy of African-American musical talent but still did not know how to present them without "offending" viewers when they integrated them into the story lines. The third version of *Show Boat* (1951) played down some of the stereotyping of the ethnic minority characters but still segmented William Warfield's Joe from much of the main action; once again, the role of Julie the mulatto was played by a white performer (Ava Gardner) as the studio feared casting an African-American talent such as Horne in such a key role might hurt the box office take in the South. In such low-budget potpourri grab fests of song-and-dance as *Disc Jockey* (1951), talents such as Sarah Vaughn were used for specialty numbers. *CARMEN JONES* (1954) and *PORGY AND BESS* (1958) both starred Dandridge and used a great many black musical talents, but these films were considered isolated examples and all right for mainstream consumption because they derived from Broadway productions.

In the mid-1950s, Satchmo Armstrong was recognized around the world for his musical talent, but most of America was still segregated, so this talented performer was still a band-playing specialty number even in his friend Bing Crosby's *High Society* (1956). More integrated into the proceedings but still as an isolated character was Johnny Mathis who was dragged into a nonmusical (*A Certain Smile*, 1958) or Pearl Bailey who provided the only levity with her wisecracks and musical moments in Bob Hope's *That Certain Feeling* (1956). (Nat "King" Cole, never a relaxed actor, was starred in *St. Louis Blues*, 1958, the life of W. C. Handy, a low-budget studio musical that used largely black performers.)

As Hollywood and the world submitted to the thudding beat of rock 'n' roll in the 1950s, several cheaply assembled offerings (e.g., *Rock Around the Clock*, 1956; *Rock Baby, Rock It*, 1957) showcased black performers (e.g., Little Richard in 1956's *Don't Knock the Rock* and 1957's *Mr. Rock and Roll*). Because these films were little more than strung-together specialty numbers tied very loosely by a vague plot, there was no concern about upsetting biased filmgoers.

By the 1960s musicals were a dying format in Hollywood and those that were made—Elvis Presley entries aside—were based largely on Broadway shows. *Sweet Charity* (1969), starring Shirley MacLaine, included Sammy Davis Jr. in a guest specialty but did manage to retain Paula Kelly's character in the main plot as a dance-hall friend of the star, as in the play.

Diana Ross made her feature film debut in *LADY SINGS THE BLUES* (1972), a popular interpretation of the life of singer Billie Holiday that seemed to prepare Ross for follow-up musicals. Instead, she made the melodramatic *Mahogany* (1976) and ended the decade with the disappointing *THE WIZ* (1978), an all-black production based on the Broadway musical, which, in turn, derived from the film *The Wizard of Oz* (1939). Meanwhile, on TV there were a few black-themed musical movies: *Cindy* (1973), *MINSTREL MAN* (1977), and *Scott Joplin: King of Ragtime* (1977).

Within 1984's *The Cotton Club*, director Francis Ford Coppola failed to recreate the magic of the old Harlem glamour spot, despite the presence of Gregory and Maurice Hines and other black personalities. When he was still known as Prince, the diminutive rock star had great success with his outré musical *PURPLE RAIN* (1984) but ran amuck with *Under the Cherry Moon* (1986). *Fame* (1980), dealing with the famous High School of the Performing Arts in New York City, had made a star of Irene Cara, but most of the cast was of other ethnic backgrounds. Later in the decade, Blair Underwood headlined the musical *Krush Groove* (1985), while another dramatic actor, Mario Van Peebles, starred in *Rappin'* (1986). But it was SPIKE LEE who turned out *the* black musical of the decade with the satirical *SCHOOL DAZE* (1988).

Lee began the 1990s with another musical tale, this time of a self-centered trumpeter (played by DENZEL WASHINGTON) in *MO' BETTER BLUES*. Multitalented ROBERT TOWNSEND created the screen biography of a 1960s rock group, *THE FIVE HEARTBEATS* (1991), and Lynn Whitfield starred in the made-for-cable biography, *THE JOSEPHINE BAKER STORY* (1991). WHOOPI GOLDBERG joined the screen adaptation of *Sarafina!* (1992) which dealt with apartheid in South Africa. The 1992 animated musical feature, *Bebe's Kids*, concerned the life of the late comedian Robin Harris. Rocker Tina Turner provided the vocals for her life story (*WHAT'S LOVE GOT TO DO WITH IT*, 1993) starring ANGELA BASSETT and LAURENCE FISHBURNE as Tina and Ike Turner. WHITNEY HOUSTON had made her feature film starring debut as a diva in Kevin Costner's *The Bodyguard* (1992), and she again tried to act and sang gospel numbers in *THE PREACHER'S WIFE* (1996). She was finally in a full musical in the TV production of *Cinderella* (1997). Rounding out the decade, HALLE BERRY was in the made-for-cable entry *INTRODUCING DOROTHY DANDRIDGE* (1998). There was a multiethnic cast in *Can't Stop Dancing* (1999) about a dance troupe in the Midwest. Wood Harris, Vivica A. Fox, and Dorian Harewood headlined *Hendrix* (2000), a made-for-cable biography of famed rock musician Jimi Hendrix. Adopting the story of Carmen to a modern idiom, Townsend directed the made-for-cable movie *Carmen: A Hip Hopera* (2001) in which Beyoncé Knowles and Mekhi Phifer starred.

N

Naked Warriors See *ARENA, THE.*

***Native Son* (1951)** Classic Pictures, b&w, 91 minutes. **Director:** Pierre Chenal; **Screenplay:** Chenal and Richard Wright; **Cast:** Jean Wallace (Mary Dalton), Richard Wright (Bigger Thomas), Nicolas Joy (Henry Dalton), Gloria Madison (Bessie Mears), Charles Cane (Britten), George Rigaud (Farley), George Green (Panama), Willa Pearl Curtiss (Hannah), Gene Michael (Jan Erlone).

Wright's powerful novel had been published in 1940, and the next year Orson Welles directed a Broadway adaptation by Wright and Paul Green, with Canada Lee starred. After years of trying fruitlessly to get a movie version made in the United States, African-American Wright agreed to this Argentinean-based project that he coadapted with French filmmaker Chenal. This English-language movie was geared for the U.S. market and used a largely American cast.

In the overcrowded Chicago black ghetto in the 1930s, Hannah lives in a tiny apartment with her three children. Her eldest, Bigger, a twenty-five-year-old with a troubled past, gets a chauffeur's job for the Daltons, a wealthy white family. Later, his nightclub-working girlfriend Bessie is jealous of Bigger's interest in the Daltons' daughter Mary. One night, a drunken Mary orders Biggers to carry her to her room. While trying to quiet her babbling, he accidentally suffocates her. He disposes of her body and then puts the blame on Mary's labor radical friend, Jan Elone. When the police suspect Bigger, he hides out with Bessie. He murders her when he thinks she is attempting to betray him to pursuing lawmen. Thereafter, as Bigger is about to be executed in prison, he tells his lawyer that he hopes his misfortunes do not befall another ghetto boy.

The ineffectual film production, which interpolated stock footage of Chicago into the narrative, also suffered from Wright playing the lead, a character almost half his age. Unlike such then recent Hollywood films as *PINKY* (1949), which as a gentle plea for racial tolerance, *Native Son* was a blatant indictment of the American system that fostered and bred racial tension. Its subject matter proved too strong for most mainstream filmgoers of the day. Thirty-five years later it was remade, this time within the United States.

***Native Son* (1986)** Cinecom, color, 122 minutes. **Director:** Jerrold Freedman; **Screenplay:** Richard Wesley; **Cast:** Carroll Baker (Mrs. Dalton), Akousua Busia (Bessie), Matt Dillon (Jan), Art Evans (Doc), John Karlen (Max), Victor Love (Bigger Thomas), Elizabeth McGovern (Mary Dalton), John McMartin (Mr. Dalton), Oprah Winfrey (Mrs. Thomas).

Thirty-five years after the failed first screen version of the late Richard Wright's novel (1940), this new economy production was mounted. Although well intentioned and craftily assembled to make it as visually authentic in its 1930s setting as possible, it failed to convey the author's powerful message that the rage that had turned Bigger Thomas into an unsympathetic, explosive killer was the end result of centuries of ugly treatment of African Americans by the white majority. In contrast, this adaptation sought to make Bigger more empathetic by deleting his premeditated murder of his girlfriend Bessie and by emphasizing his being played for a fool by the impulsive Mary Dalton and the patronizing communist radical (Dillon). Ironically, by making this presentation more accessible to mainstream audiences, this version distorted Wright's original intent. Despite the subtle performance of newcomer Love and WINFREY's torment as his mother, the new *Native Son* was unsuccessful. Made at a cost of $2.4 million, it earned only $1.3 million in domestic film rentals.

***Nat "King" Cole Show, The* (1956–1957)** NBC-TV, b&w, 15 (then 30) minutes. **Cast:** Nat "King" Cole, the Boataneers: 1956, the Herman McCoy Singers, the Randy Van Horne Singers: 1957, the Cheerleaders: 1957, and Nelson Riddle and His Orchestra (themselves).

For five weeks in the fall of 1949, CBS-TV network had aired *Sugar Hill Times*, a musical variety series (one of the cast members was the fast-rising HARRY BELAFONTE), a brief effort to showcase African-American talent. The next year, Trinidad-born beauty Hazel Scott, a black singer/pianist who had a vogue in clubs/stage/movies, had her own showcase, again briefly.

In the politically conservative 1950s, *The Nat "King" Cole Show* was a rare network TV outing because it featured a black lead performer. He was the first major star of his race to star in a network variety series. Because of the show's time constraints, Cole usually had time only to sing a few songs and perhaps to introduce a guest vocalist. Not only was the show unable to attract a large viewership, but it also had difficulty attracting sponsors (supposedly due to low ratings, but primarily because of disinterest in sponsoring a show starring a black).

The entertainment industry was well-aware of Cole's plight and struggled to keep the show going, leading many performers—blacks and whites—to appear on his program for minimum salaries. Among his guests were SAMMY DAVIS JR., Ella Fitzgerald, Peggy Lee, Tony Martin, Cab Calloway, Mahalia Jackson, and Frankie Lane.

***New Jack City* (1991)** Warner Bros., color, 97 minutes. **Director:** Mario Van Peebles; **Screenplay:** Barry Michael Cooper and Thomas Lee Wright; **Cast:** Wesley Snipes (Nino Brown), Ice-T (Off. Scotty Appleton), Allen Payne (Gee Money), Chris Rock (Pookie), Mario Van Peebles (Detective Stone), Michael Michele (Selina), Bill Nunn (Duh Duh Duh Man), Russell Wong (Park), Judd Nelson (Off. Nick Peretti).

Released in the same year as the much superior *BOYZ N THE HOOD*, this slickly assembled, well-budgeted, major studio feature was a pastiche of past white- and black-made urban action dramas. Generally well cast, it effectively showcased SNIPES (as a criminal overlord of the crack drug scene), gangsta rapper Ice-T (as a politically incorrect roughneck cop), and comedian CHRIS ROCK (as a crackhead killed for betraying the local crime boss). However, filmmaker VAN PEEBLES goes overboard in glorifying his screen alter ego, a supergood, well-dressed lawmaker determined to eliminate low-life drug dealers, among others. More ineffective is Nelson as the bigoted brought-back-on-the-job cop who screws things up for everyone.

Set in late 1980s New York, *New Jack City* depicts ambitious Nino Brown's rapid rise to power from street-gang member and cocaine pusher to drug kingpin. His nemesis is Detective Stone who goes to any length to bring down this arch lawbreaker. Ironically, that feat is ultimately accomplished by an old man.

When released there was much hype about this movie supposedly glorifying drugs and criminal activity because of the several riots that occurred at theaters showing the picture. (Actually the film was clearly antidrugs.) *New Jack City* grossed more than $47 million in domestic distribution, making Van Peebles a favorite of the film industry establishment.

The film received an Oscar nomination for Best Screenplay.

***Norman . . . Is That You?* (1976)** Metro-Goldwyn-Mayer, color, 91 minutes. **Director:** George Schlatter; **Screenplay:** Ron Clark, Sam Bobrick, and Schlatter; **Cast:** Redd Foxx (Ben Chambers), Pearl Bailey (Beatrice Chambers), Dennis Dugan (Garson Hobart), Michael Warren (Norman Chambers), Tamara Dobson (Audrey), Vernee Watson (Melody).

On Broadway (1970) this simplistic sex comedy lasted only twelve performances, but it later became a favorite in summer/dinner theater venues. The plot was overstuffed with homosexual stereotypes, and the dialogue contained nearly every imaginable cliché about how the nongay community reacts to such a minority.

For the film version, the studio altered the lead characters from white/Jewish to African-American/gentile. This allowed for veterans FOXX and Bailey, as the battling parents, to discover that not only is their sole offspring (Warren) gay but also that his lover (Dugan) is Caucasian. The statuesque Tamara Dobson (*CLEOPATRA JONES* [1973]) is the radiant prostitute hired to make a man of Norman but who ends up bedding randy Ben Chambers.

Originally R-rated, the classification for this vulgar, low-brow exercise was altered to PG on appeal. (Nevertheless, it was still condemned by the National Catholic Film Office for its insensitive treatment of gay and nongay love.) Nonetheless, the film offered a showcase for Foxx and Bailey to parade their patented high-energy shtick. Then too, in the hasty conversion of the screenplay for a predominantly black cast, nothing was made of their racial background. Thus, by accident, *Norman . . . Is That You?* became one of the first Hollywood films to present an African-American clan on camera without making any issue of their color.

***Nothing but a Man* (1964)** Cinema V, b&w, 95 minutes. **Director:** Michael Roemer; **Screenplay:** Roemer and Robert Young; **Cast:** Ivan Dixon (Duff Anderson), Abby Lincoln (Josie Dawson), Gloria Foster (Lee), Julius Harris (Will Anderson), Yaphet Kotto (Jocko), Stanley Greene (Reverend Dawson).

Made by well-intentioned white liberals, this independent production often went overboard in its aim to present the African-American characters as sensitive and dimensional. These figures emerged as overly solemn, without any sense of humor or optimism.

In Alabama, a railroad worker abandons his "carefree" life to wed the schoolteacher daughter (Lincoln) of a minister (Greene). Duff becomes a laborer at the local sawmill, but when he refuses to placate his racist white employers, he is fired. Even working at a gas station, he is harassed by the locals. The frustrated Duff takes it out on his wife Josie, beating her in the process. Later, after witnessing the death of his alcoholic father (Harris), Anderson reconsiders his life and returns to Josie, hoping to make a fresh start on a more mature basis. He brings with him his son from a past relationship.

Shot on a $230,000 budget during a twelve-week period, *Nothing But a Man* boosted a marvelous cast of rising talent. It was a rare opportunity in 1960s films for African Americans to portray full-bodied characters with complex relationships. Because it featured a largely minority cast, the movie had a lot of trouble finding distribution beyond the art-house circuit, but those who saw the film then or later applauded its superior presentation.

***No Way Out* (1950)** Twentieth Century-Fox, b&w, 106 minutes. **Director:** Joseph L. Mankiewicz; **Screenplay:** Mankiewicz and Lesser Samuels; **Cast:** Richard Widmark (Ray Biddle), Linda Darnell (Edie Johnson), Stephen McNally (Dr. Daniel Wharton), Sidney Poitier (Dr. Luther Brooks), Mildred Joan Smith (Cora Brooks), Ruby Dee (Connie), Ossie Davis (John).

Having tentatively explored racial issues in *PINKY* (1949), Twentieth Century-Fox took a leap forward with this more controversial picture, concerning contemporary blacks and the price they pay daily to exist in a white-dominated world. Reflecting the post–World War II race riots that had hit America, this film depicted the explosive belligerence between whites and blacks, with the latter attacking first and winning. In his feature film debut, POITIER's character was both heroic and perfect, as if only in that way could an African American compete successfully with whites. It was a script ploy that Hollywood reused for years in Poitier's films.

African-American Dr. Luther Brooks is a resident at a big city hospital. When he treats two wounded hoodlum brothers caught by the police, one dies during the medical procedure. The other, the racist Ray Biddle, blames Brooks for his sibling's death. The only way the self-doubting Brooks can prove that his treatment was proper is to have himself arrested on an alleged murder charge so that an autopsy will be performed. Meanwhile, Ray orders his sister-in-law Edie to have Ray's bigoted white friends start a race riot to get even for his brother's "murder." In a later shootout, Ray wounds Luther, but the latter still insists on treating the criminal.

Although the script was overly contrived, it succeeded in presenting a small sampling of the humiliations an African American endured in the professional world (e.g., at the hospital a woman told Luther to get his "black hands" off her son). In its attempts to be mature, the movie showed life in an African-American household, suggesting that they were no different from their white counterparts. The dialogue—daring for its day—had the city's ghetto referred to as "Niggertown" by racist whites, while the finale found heroic Luther treating the dying Roy. (In the original script, Luther's character died, but it was considered too downbeat an ending.)

As predicted, *No Way Out* was not released in most southern cities, and in the North it underwent (temporary) bans in such cities as Chicago. Other venues demanded cuts in the narrative (especially showing the African Americans preparing for and winning the encounter with the racist whites).

O

***Odds Against Tomorrow* (1959)** United Artists, b&w, 96 minutes. **Director:** Robert Wise; **Screenplay:** John O. Killens [fronting for blacklisted Abraham Polonsky] and Nelson Gidding; **Cast:** Harry Belafonte (Johnny Ingram), Robert Ryan (Earl Slater), Shelley Winters (Lorry), Ed Begley (Dave Burke), Gloria Grahame (Helen), Kim Hamilton (Ruth), Cicely Tyson (Fra).

This was a superior film noir produced by BELAFONTE'S production company, dealing with two-way racial tensions between whites and blacks, referencing such derogatory slang as a Caucasian calling an African American "boy" and the latter referring to a white person as "ofay."

Ex-cop Dave Burke hires two men to help him rob a bank in upstate New York: bigoted southerner Earl Slater, a tough ex-convict, and African-American Johnny Ingram, a club entertainer with a gambling addiction, who is being pressured by a mobster to pay off his money debt. As the mismatched trio map out their strategy, Slater incites Ingram with racial slurs while Burke referees between the two. The bank job goes amuck. Burke is killed, and the other two—furious with one another—flee on foot. The enraged Johnny chases Slater to the top of an oil tank. As they shoot at one another, their gunfire ignites the refinery. Later, when the pursuing police examine the corpses, they are charred beyond recognition. "Which is which?" asks one lawman. Another says, "Take your pick."

Not only did this feature explicate a microcosm of racial prejudice, but also it presented—rare for the time—a reflection of a middle-class African-American home, that of Johnny's ex-wife Ruth and their daughter. Unique for its time was the scene when Johnny visited Ruth, she in the midst of a PTA meeting, with the living room filled with a mix of whites and blacks.

***Officer and a Gentleman, An* (1982)** Paramount, color, 126 minutes. **Director:** Taylor Hackford; **Screenplay:** Douglas Day Stewart; **Cast:** Richard Gere (Zack Mayo), Debra Winger (Paula Pokrifki), David Keith (Sid Worley), Robert Loggia (Byron Mayo), Lisa Blount (Lynette Pomeroy), Louis Gossett Jr. (Sgt. Emil Foley).

The part of tough Marine Sgt. Emil Foley was originally written for a white performer, and when GOSSETT won the key role, no ethnic changes were made to the characterization.

Zack Mayo abandons the slums and his alcoholic father (Loggia) to start the tough regimen necessary to become a naval officer/flyer. The grueling training is supervised by Sergeant Foley, who brooks no excuses from his charges, especially not from unresponsive Mayo. During the course of learning to become officers and gentlemen, one of their number (Keith) commits suicide when he and his millworker girlfriend (Blount) break up. As for Zack, whom Foley pushes nearly to a breaking point, he eventually realizes the worth of his love (Winger) and carries her off from her mill job. With Mayo's group now graduated to the next level of their training, tough Foley is already breaking in and weeding out the next group of trainees.

This hugely popular film grossed about $130 million in domestic distribution and won two Academy Awards: Best Supporting Actor (Gossett) and Best Song ("Up Where We Belong"). The film received other Oscar nominations for Best Actress (Winger), Best Film Editing, Best Original Score, and Best Original Screenplay. Gossett was only the third African American to win an Oscar, following HATTIE McDANIEL (1939) and SIDNEY POITIER (1963).

Even in the early 1980s when *An Officer and a Gentleman* was released, this was a rare Hollywood film to feature an African American in the position of structured authority within the system, a man in charge of white (and other ethnic) subordinates.

***Once Upon a Time . . . When We Were Colored* (1995)** IRS Releasing, color, 113 minutes. **Director:** Tim Reid; **Screenplay:** Paul W. Cooper; **Cast:** Al Freeman Jr. (Poppa), Phylicia Rashad (Ma Ponk), Leon Robinson (Uncle Melvin), Paula Kelly (Mama Pearl), Salli Richardson (Miss Alice), Bernie Casey (Mr. Walter), Isaac Hayes (Preacher Hurn), Richard Roundtree (Cleve), Willie Norwood Jr. (Cliff—age ten to eleven), Damon Hines (Cliff—age seventeen).

Utilizing Clifton Taulbert's memoirs (1989), actor and first-time director Reid presented a marvelously textured, nostalgic account of a young African American growing up in 1950s Mississippi. Reid employed humor and optimism, rather than a downbeat narrative, to put across his message: With fortitude and the support of family and community, minority people can not only survive their bleak existence in a white-dominated world but can also help to close the gap of inequality between the races. The flaws in Reid's presentation included a tendency to make his characters' lives seem more joyful than reality would have dictated and, conversely, to make the film's serious sequences excessively weighty.

In a small segregated town in the Delta, the parentless Cliff grows up in "Colored Town," first with his great-grandfather (Freeman Jr.) and then with his great aunt, Ma Monk. Now an impressionable teen, he is influenced by Uncle Melvin's account of a better life for blacks in Detroit, where he lives. Later, Cliff hears more about the wonders of the North and big-city life from a circus dancer visiting town. In the early 1960s, the black townsfolk are frightened into using a white-operated ice company rather than the one owned by a member (Roundtree) of their community. In protest, the once-meek locals quit their jobs picking cotton, and now the white cotton grower is without laborers. Times are changing.

The film grossed more than $3 million in domestic distribution.

***Original Kings of Comedy, The* (2000)** Paramount, color, 115 minutes. **Director:** Spike Lee; **Cast:** Steve Harvey, D. L. Hughley, Cedric the Entertainer, and Bernie Mac (themselves).

This documentary was filmed by LEE in Charlotte, North Carolina, in February 1999 during the "Kings of Comedy" tour in which a quartet of popular African-American stand-up comics deliver their jokes about families, sex, the human condition, and, of course, race (more observational than from a point of anger). The viewer is taken behind-the-scenes of their performance (for interviews with the four comics), which enhances the on-stage presentation as the performers successfully bring down the house with their individual approaches to humor.

Although not exciting in terms of motion picture technique, the raucous show well depicted four contrasting black funsters and their rapid-fire takes on contemporary life. As such, it was a valuable document on the perspective of African Americans in today's United States.

Made on a $3 million budget, this production—initially envisioned as a cable TV special—yielded a strong $38 million in domestic distribution. Its success was an endorsement of black comedians and the validity of their ethnic humor/observations. *The Original Kings of Comedy* received an Image Awards nomination for Outstanding Motion Picture.

P

***Palmerstown, U.S.A.* (1980–1981)** CBS-TV series, color, 60 minutes. **Cast:** Jonelle Allen (Bessie Freeman), Bill Duke (Luther Freeman), Star-Shemah Bobatoon (Diana Freeman), Jermain Hodge Johnson (Booker T. Freeman), Beeson Carroll (W. D. Hall), Janice St. John (Coralee Hall), Michael J. Fox (Willy-Joe Hall), Brian Godfrey-Wilson (David Hall).

Based on the memories of coproducer Alex Haley, who had great cachet with network TV because of his hit miniseries *ROOTS* (1977), this dramatic series is a visual scrapbook of Haley's childhood. Two nine-year-old boys, the black Booker T. Freeman and the white David Hall, grow up in the small rural town of Palmerstown in the South during the 1930s Depression. Booker's dad is the local blacksmith; David's father is the town's grocer. As a result of the youngsters' friendship, their respective families develop ties. Because the series wanted to be relevant drama, the weekly episodes feature some aspect of a racial problem that involves various townsfolk. This formula, along with its pat resolutions and soft-edged characters, resulted in few plaudits for the series.

***Paris* (1979–1980)** CBS-TV series, color, 60 minutes. **Cast:** James Earl Jones (Woody Paris), Lee Chamberlain (Barbara Paris), Hank Garrett (Dep. Chief Jerome Bench), Cecilia Hart (Stacey Erickson), Mike Warren (Willie Miller).

Statistically, this entry was another ethnic first: the debut network dramatic series to star a black actor. There was nothing mild mannered about JONES in the title role: He boomed his way through the proceedings as the cultured, highly moral African-American police captain in the Metro Division of the Los Angeles Police Department. As if not busy enough with his job, and to make the lead character even more of a superhuman creature (all in the name of racial equality), Woody Paris teaches a criminology course at night at a local university.

To balance out the drama, there are scenes that feature Paris's wife, Barbara, a nurse. Their respectable, middle-class, and ethnically rooted home life adds flavor to the weekly episodes, making liberal white viewers feel that they are getting to know better another race. With a paucity of decent ratings, *Paris* was canceled in less than four months.

***Paris Blues* (1961)** United Artists, b&w, 98 minutes. **Director:** Martin Ritt; **Screenplay:** Jack Sher, Irene Kamp, and Walter Bernstein; **Cast:** Paul Newman (Ram Bowen), Joanne Woodward (Lillian Corning), Sidney Poitier (Eddie Cook), Louis Armstrong (Wild Man Moore), Diahann Carroll (Connie Lampson), Barbara Laage (Marie Seoul).

A travelogue with great music could sum up *Paris Blues*, a lethargically directed vehicle in which the lead characters mouth idealistic chatter about racial issues and the purity of the jazz idiom. The film's saving graces were ARMSTRONG's exciting jazz renditions and Duke Ellington's score. Then, too, the picture was an early Hollywood illustration of two African-American characters as the equals of their white friends. The movie focused—albeit not enough—on the romance of the black coleads and has Eddie discuss the scope of racial intolerance in the United States that led to his being based in far more racially liberal Paris.

Trombonist Ram Bowen and African-American saxophonist Eddie Cook are jazz musicians and American expatriates living in Paris. Ram left the United States to avoid distractions that would compromise his music composing; Eddie fled America to avoid the racial problems he constantly encountered. Two American tourists, Lillian Corning and her black friend Connie Lampson, are on a two-week vacation in France. Before long, Ram is dating Lillian and

Eddie is romancing Connie. Later, despite the temptation, Ram bids goodbye to Lillian to remain in Paris to pursue his composing. In contrast, Eddie is on the brink of accepting Connie's challenge to return home, marry her, and fight racial bigotry.

Many critics of the time chided this entry for not giving more screen time to the secondary (in the plot) Eddie–Connie romance and for not exploring more fully the racial issues that drove the saxophonist to Paris.

Paris Blues received an Oscar nomination for Best Scoring of a Musical Picture.

Parks, Gordon, Sr. (1918–) Like fellow black filmmakers OSCAR MICHEAUX and MELVIN VAN PEEBLES, Parks was a pioneer in the history of African-American integration into mainstream Hollywood filmmaking. When Parks helmed the autobiographical coming-of-age drama *THE LEARNING TREE* (1969) for Warner Bros., he was the first black man to direct a feature for a major American movie studio. The movie was a critical success. Two years later, Parks switched to a new screen genre with *SHAFT;* along with Van Peebles's *SWEET SWEETBACK'S BAADASSSSS SONG* (1971) the two films greatly responsible for the BLACK ACTION FILM cycle that swept Hollywood in the early 1970s.

He was born in Fort Scott, Kansas, the youngest of 15 children in an impoverished farm family. By his young teens, Parks was working in Chicago as a busboy. Thereafter, his varied means of livelihood included piano playing in a Minnesota bordello, becoming a dope runner in Harlem, and then playing professional basketball. By the post–World War II years, he had developed a strong interest in photography and, in 1948, began a 20-year association with *Life* magazine, working for them as a photographer/reporter. In 1964, he directed his first film, a documentary short, *Flavio.*

While living in Paris in the 1960s, Parks authored two autobiographical books—one of them was adapted to the screen as *The Learning Tree.* (Years later, the movie was one of the initial 25 movies included in the National Film Registry of the Library of Congress.) After the huge success of *Shaft,* Parks directed *Shaft's Big Score!* (1972). However, a dispute with the producing studio, MGM, over salary and artistic control ended in his not directing the follow-up *Shaft in Africa* (1973). Instead, Parks helmed *The Super Cops* (1974), dealing with a pair of extraordinarily talented law enforcers combating drug dealers in Brooklyn's black neighborhood. More effective was his *LEADBELLY* (1976), a sensitive biography of the famed trouble-prone blues singer.

Having had a public dispute with the releasing studio of *Leadbelly* about the marketing of the movie, Parks was subsequently ignored by mainstream film companies. It was not until 1984 that he directed another feature, this time a movie made for PBS-TV. *Solomon Northup's Odyssey* was based on a true story about a free black man (Avery Brooks) in pre–Civil War times who is sold into slavery. In bondage, he has great difficulty convincing people of the truth and finding the means to return to his family.

The multitalented Parks composes not only music for his films but also works to be performed in concert halls. He also pens novels and poetry. In 2000, he was the subject of the cable TV documentary *Half Past Autumn: The Life and Works of Gordon Parks,* which focused on the Renaissance man's professional and personal life.

Parks's son, Gordon Parks Jr. (1934–79), was also a film director, with such credits as *SUPERFLY* (1972), *Three the Hard Way* (1974), and *Aaron Loves Angela* (1975). His career was cut short when he died in a plane crash while location scouting for a new film to be shot in Africa.

***Passenger 57* (1992)** Warner Bros., color, 90 minutes. **Director:** Kevin Hooks; **Screenplay:** David Loughery and Dan Gordon; **Cast:** Wesley Snipes (John Cutter), Bruce Payne (Charles Rane), Tom Sizemore (Sly Delvecchio), Alex Datcher (Marti Slayton), Bruce Greenwood (Stuart Ramsey), Robert Hooks (Dwight Henderson).

After the fadeout of BLACK ACTION FILMS in the late 1970s, action films—especially big-budgeted ones—largely became the domain of such Caucasian stars as Sylvester Stallone, Bruce Willis, Arnold Schwarzenegger, Clint Eastwood, Harrison Ford, Mel Gibson, and Jean-Claude Van Damme. (An exception was DANNY GLOVER who had a changed status because he costarred with Gibson in 1987's *LETHAL WEAPON;* Oscar winner DENZEL WASHINGTON tread water in several big-budgeted action entries.) Changing that trend was SNIPES, who had excelled the previous year as the power-crazed drug lord in *NEW JACK CITY.*

Having just quit his career as an antiterrorist specialist, John Cutter boards a plane headed for Los Angeles. Another passenger is Charles Rane, being escorted to the coast to stand trial on terrorist bombing charges. Rane's henchmen hijack the plane, leaving it to enterprising Cutter, with the help of African-American flight attendant Marti Slayton, to release the plane's fuel, forcing the craft to land in Louisiana. The climactic shootout occurs at a local country fair, which leads to another passenger–hostage situation. With the villain finally dispatched, cool Cutter escorts Marti to the fair.

Filled with high-tech special effects, typical illogical happenings, and prefabricated characters, the film let Snipes display a strong aptitude for such athletic shenanigans, and it led to more such roles for him. The picture was directed by African-American actor Kevin Hooks and featured his performer father, Robert, who had begun his film career in the late 1960s.

Passenger 57 grossed more than $44 million in domestic distribution.

***Patch of Blue, A* (1965)** Metro-Goldwyn-Mayer, b&w, 105 minutes. **Director/Screenplay:** Guy Green; **Cast:** Sidney Poitier (Gordon Rolfe), Shelley Winters (Rose-Ann D'Arcy), Elizabeth Hartman (Selina D'Arcy), Wallace Ford (Ole Pa), Ivan Dixon (Mark Rolfe).

In Elizabeth Kata's novel *Be Ready with Bells and Drums* (1961), on which this film was based, the plot line was far more staggering: The blind girl heroine was a bigot, and when she learned that her friend from the park was African American, she rejected him, which, in turn, led to his death.

On screen, five-year-old Selina D'Arcy loses her eyesight, the result of an accident engendered by an argument with her prostitute mother. For the next thirteen years, she remains in her tenement apartment, cared for mostly by her grandfather (Ford), never being educated or even learning Braille. One day, Ole Pa takes Selina to the park where she meets congenial young Gordon Rolfe. Their friendship grows into love, although he has yet to tell her of his racial background. When her mother Rose-Ann learns of the relationship—which will spoil her plans to turn her daughter into a prostitute—she beats her offspring and reveals the truth about Gordon. Unmoved, the gentle Selina still wishes to marry Gordon. He arranges for her to enter a school for the blind, insisting that she must adjust to the adult, real world before they can pursue a real relationship.

This supposedly liberal film offended many of both races and further frustrated Poitier about the taboos of American society/cinema that restricted him to playing such a demeaning role (i.e., cast as an African American too ashamed to reveal his heritage). As the *Newsweek* (December 27, 1965) critic noted, Poitier's role reduced him to "part Romeo and part Annie Sullivan" and added, "no other film has managed to simultaneously insult the Negroes and the blind."

Despite the negative feedback from many, especially from black America, *A Patch of Blue* was a profitable release. The picture won an Oscar for Best Supporting Actress (Winters) and won four other Academy Award nominations: Best Actress (Hartman), Best Art Direction/Set Decoration (Black and White), Best Cinematography (Black and White), and Best Musical Score.

***Pelican Brief, The* (1993)** Warner Bros., color, 140 minutes. **Director/Screenplay:** Alan J. Pakula; **Cast:** Julia Roberts (Darby Shaw), Denzel Washington (Gray Grantham), Sam Shepard (Thomas Callahan), John Heard (Gavin Verheek), Tony Goldwyn (Fletcher Coal), James B. Sikking (FBI Director F. Denton Voyles), Robert Culp (U.S. President).

In John Grisham's 1992 best-seller thriller, there was a romance between the Tulane Law School student and the savvy Washington, D.C., investigative reporter. However, in the film translation, the attractive heroine and the handsome, smart hero—who were apparently smitten with one another—never fulfilled their romance. Why? Because she was white and he was black, and Hollywood did not wish to break the still existent taboo of interracial romance on camera in such an expensive production with two high-profile stars.

In New Orleans, bright law student Darby Shaw is involved with her professor Thomas Callahan. After two Supreme Court justices are murdered, Darby develops a brief that the two deaths might be the work of a secretive oil multimillionaire who wants oil rights to a Louisiana bayou, the home to endangered brown pelicans. Her wild theory leads to Callahan's death and to her teaming with hotshot reporter Gray Grantham. Darby ends hidden away in a Caribbean retreat, while Grantham goes public with the evidence to prosecute the bad guys.

Despite all its faults, *The Pelican Brief* grossed more than $100 million in domestic distribution. WASHINGTON was nominated for an MTV Movie Award in the Most Desirable Male category.

***Penitentiary* (1979)** Jerry Gross, color, 99 minutes. **Director/Screenplay:** Jamaa Fanaka; **Cast:** Leon Isaac Kennedy (Martel "Too Sweet" Gordone), Thommy Pollard (Eugene T. Lawson), Hazel Spears (Linda), Donovan Womack (Jesse Amos), Floyd Chatman (Hezzikia "Seldom Seen" Jackson), Wilbur "Hi-Fi" White (Sweet Pea).

Besides borrowing ingredients from Sylvester Stallone's *Rocky* (1976) franchise, *Penitentiary* incorporated elements from prison pictures and BLACK ACTION FILMS. What gave this film its punch was the combination of charismatic Kennedy (an ex-disc jockey and radio talk-show personality) and relatively new filmmaker Fanaka, who had already directed such entries as *Welcome Home Brother Charles* (1975). These two African Americans turned the clichéd *Penitentiary* into a box-office winner, grossing more than $13 million in domestic distribution on a cost of $250,000. What made the feat even more impressive was that it occurred a few years after Hollywood had judged the blaxploitation film cycle moribund.

As a result of a fracas in which a biker dies, Martel Gordone is sent to prison, where his love of candy earns him the nickname "Too Sweet." The feisty Martel becomes involved in prison tournament boxing and proves a winner. His ring success eventually leads to his being released and taking up professional boxing. Filled with an array of offbeat characters, lots of violence, and much blood in the ring and elsewhere, *Penitentiary* was a raunchy rags-to-riches tale focused on a personable leading man.

The film's success led to two sequels (1982 and 1987), each less intriguing and successful than its predecessor. Kennedy also starred as another boxer in *Body and Soul* (1981), an ill-focused remake of John Garfield's 1947 classic.

***Piece of the Action, A* (1977)** Warner Bros., color, 134 minutes. **Director:** Sidney Poitier; **Screenplay:** Charles Blackwell; **Cast:** Sidney Poitier (Manny Durrell), Bill Cosby (Dave Anderson), James Earl Jones (Joshua Burke), Denise Nicholas (Lila French), Hope Clarke (Sarah Thomas), Tracy Reed (Nikki McLean).

As a follow-up to their popular *UPTOWN SATURDAY NIGHT* (1974) and *Let's Do It Again* (1975), POITIER and COSBY reunited for their third crossover comedy. It not only appealed to African Americans as wholesome family fare but also drew white audiences. For those viewers who were tired of BLACK ACTION FILMS, this feature—which played like an extended TV sitcom—provided an antidote. In typical fashion, director Poitier drew the limelight away from his character and generously showcased his costars, which led to relaxed performances, even from stentorian JONES.

In Chicago, two con-artist criminals, Dave Anderson and Manny Durrell, are brought together by police detective, Joshua Burke. The latter, who blackmails them anonymously, gives them a choice: Donate their time to a southside community improvement center operated by Lila French or go to jail. With Lila in charge, their mission is to help thirty ghetto youngsters become useful citizens in short order. Meanwhile, the duo track down their blackmailer's identity. In the end, Anderson and Durrell emerge victorious over a local mobster and give their young charges a real future.

***Pinky* (1949)** Twentieth Century-Fox, b&w, 102 minutes. **Director:** Elia Kazan; **Screenplay:** Philip Dunne and Dudley Nichols; **Cast:** Jeanne Crain (Patricia "Pinky" Johnson), Ethel Barrymore (Miss Em), Ethel Waters (Dicey Johnson), William Lundigan (Dr. Thomas Adams), Basil Ruysdael (Judge Walker), Kenny Washington (Dr. Canady), Nina Mae McKinney (Rozelia), Frederick O'Neal (Jake Waters).

Along with two other 1949 Hollywood releases (*HOME OF THE BRAVE* and *LOST BOUNDARIES*) about racial discrimination, *Pinky* reflected the so-called new maturity within the American film industry. But the advances made by this trio of films were qualified ones. Beyond dictating illustrations of contemporary racial injustices, the three movies did *not* provide, by example or dialogue suggestion, any progressive, concrete answers to troublesome integration issues. The most affecting of these pictures was *Pinky*, an emotional excursion that was further compromised by having a Caucasian actress play the lead role of the tragic mulatto character. Pinky was based on the 1946 novel *Quality* by Cid Ricketts Sumner.

Having been brought up in the North where she passes for white and becomes a nurse, light-skinned Pinky Johnson returns to her small southern town. Her hardworking grandmother urges Pinky to be proud of her race and to be part of her community. Through a scuffle with Rozelia, the wife of a black man (O'Neal) who has cheated Pinky and her grandmother, Pinky is arrested by the police, who are told that she is black. Later freed, she is attacked by two drunk Caucasians. Badly upset, she decides to return North and to her white doctor boyfriend. Her grandmother convinces her to remain long enough to tend the ailing white lady, Miss Em. Pinky agrees and comes to respect the astute old woman. After the latter dies, she leaves Pinky her home and land, which leads to a court battle with Miss Em's relatives. Against all odds, Pinky wins the case. By now her doctor boyfriend has arrived and urges Pinky to come away with him up North where she can again pass for white. However, Pinky sends him away and opens Miss Em's Clinic and Nursery School for the African-American community.

In the genesis of making this film, the studio sought advice from diverse African-American groups, as well as from the movie industry censors. From these often-contradicting sources, it was suggested that (1) the movie not show any interaction between the white and the black lead character and that (2) the story depict the black characters/community going beyond just protecting the status quo. Neither advice was taken by Twentieth Century-Fox (although the studio did drop the concluding episode from the original book in which the KKK burned down Miss Em's school, and the studio also omitted the black northern newsman/agitator who came to town during the trial).

Despite fears that southern exhibitors would not show the movie, the film made its successful debut in Atlanta, Georgia (with black patrons restricted to balcony seats), and thereafter in other southern cities. When an East Texas town formed a censorship board to prohibit the planned showing of *Pinky* in town, the ensuing court case eventually reached the U.S. Supreme Court. There, in 1952, the high court struck down the censorship ordinance.

Pinky grossed more than $4 million in domestic distribution. It received three Oscar nominations: Best Actress (Crain) and Best Supporting Actress (Barrymore and WATERS).

Poitier, Sidney (1927–   ) On his broad shoulders sat the responsibility of representing a race, as he singlehandedly (seemingly) changed how Hollywood and moviegoers regarded black America. Certainly, later megastars (e.g., RICHARD PRYOR and EDDIE MURPHY) made more money at the box office, but no other individual had such impact on how African Americans were regarded in the cinema than Oscar-winning Poitier, the American screen's first prominent major black star. It was a daunting situation in which he was thrust for years, one that affected the shape of his career, not always for the best.

He was born in 1927 (some sources list 1924) in Miami, Florida, the youngest of seven children of poor tomato growers from the Bahamas who were visiting the mainland at the time. He grew up on Cat Island in the Bahamas, quitting school at age thirteen. A few years later, he went to stay with a brother in Miami and then moved on to New York City. There he had assorted menial jobs. For a brief time he was in the army, working at a veteran's hospital. Through happenstance he auditioned for the American Negro Theater in Harlem but was rejected by its director, Frederick O'Neal. That failure spurred him on, and six months later he reauditioned (having lost his Bahamian accent) and was accepted in the group, which included HARRY BELAFONTE, RUBY DEE, and OSSIE DAVIS. By 1946, Poitier had made his Broadway debut in an all-black production of *Lysistrata* (1946).

After appearing in the documentary *From Whence Cometh My Help* (1949), he was cast in the major Hollywood studio film *NO WAY OUT* (1950) as an unsure young doctor caught in a heated racial situation. In contrast to past stereotypes encouraged on the Hollywood screen, Sidney's clean-cut character was intelligent, articulate, and most of all had a sense of racial pride. He then moved from the apartheid drama *Cry, the Beloved Country* (1951) to a World War II combat drama (*RED BALL EXPRESS*, 1952) that involved racial bigotry. His most vivid role of this period was as the defiant high school student in *THE BLACKBOARD JUNGLE* (1955).

It was his performances in the URBAN DRAMA *EDGE OF THE CITY* (1957) and the interracial buddy film, *THE DEFIANT ONES* (1958), that demonstrated the range of Sidney's dramatic talent—able to be likeable but also to explode from inner rage about racial inequality. The latter picture, for which he was Oscar nominated, established a key ingredient for future Poitier movies—that of the noble black man. He seemed out of his element in the musical *PORGY AND BESS* (1959) but was on target in the touching drama of hope and despair—*A RAISIN IN THE SUN* (1961). For *LILIES OF THE FIELD* (1963), he won an Academy Award—the first black performer to win in the Best Actor category. (Some commentators then and later felt that Sidney's character of the accommodating black man persuaded to help German nuns construct a chapel put his screen figure in the same selfless category as past movie domestics who did everything for white people without having their own identities or lives.)

There were negative feelings by a segment of the black community about *A PATCH OF BLUE* (1965) in which his character was apparently ashamed of admitting to the blind white girl that he was African American. He had the tougher role in the landmark film *IN THE HEAT OF THE NIGHT* (1967), but it was Rod Steiger as the bigoted white sheriff who was nominated and won the Oscar. For a rare change, *GUESS WHO'S COMING TO DINNER?* (1967) provided Poitier's character with a love life (something missing from most of his earlier movies), but this time there was another taboo subject for Poitier to explore—interracial love. What offended some moviegoers was that Sidney's screen alter ego had to be an incredibly exemplary man (a doctor, a potential Nobel Prize winner, handsome, and polite) to merit a Caucasian woman who was nowhere near his equal in life.

By the early 1970s, Poitier was turning out such derivative works as *They Call Me MISTER Tibbs!* (1970) and *THE ORGANIZATION* (1971), rehashing his Virgil Tibbs character from *In the Heat of the Night*. Meanwhile, Hollywood was caught up in a slew of BLACK ACTION FILMS that made Poitier's screen roles/image appear out of touch with the black community. Trying to reshape his career by developing and/or directing his own vehicles, he helmed the western *BUCK AND THE PREACHER* (1972), which appealed to his core audience of African-American moviegoers. It led to his directing/starring in several more pictures, including three comedies with BILL COSBY: *UPTOWN SATURDAY NIGHT* (1974), *Let's Do It Again* (1975), and *A PIECE OF THE ACTION* (1977). They were nonsensical and slapstick and somewhat regressive but found a niche in the movie marketplace.

For much of the 1980s, Poitier abandoned acting to helm more movies, none of them distinguished. They included *STIR CRAZY* (1980), *HANKY PANKY* (1982), and *Ghost Dad* (1990), the latter a turkey starring Cosby. By the time he returned to movie acting, the newer generations of filmgoers were no longer his previous fans. He was with River Phoenix in the insipid thriller *Little Nikita* (1988), part of Robert Redford's ensemble in the heist caper *Sneakers* (1992), and made a sequel to an earlier hit, *To Sir With Love 2* (1996—TV movie).

Sidney Poitier in *The Slender Thread* (1965). (JC ARCHIVES)

In several telefeatures, Poitier played prestigious characters, in line with his position as the elder statesman of black cinema. He was a Supreme Court justice in *Separate But Equal* (1991) and Nelson Mandela in *Mandela and de Klerk* (1997—for which he received an Emmy nomination). He acted with his daughter Sydney in the made-for-cable drama *Free of Eden* (1999). He was a ninety-one-year-old carpenter fighting to save his property from developers in *The Simple Life of Noah Dearborn* (1999—for which he won an Image Award), and in the telefeature *The Last Brickmaker in America* (2001), he was a lost soul who found comfort helping a bewildered thirteen year old.

In 1969 the Golden Globes awarded Poitier a trophy as World Film Favorite—Male; in 1982 they presented him with their Cecil B. DeMille Award. In 1992, Sidney accepted a Life Achievement Award from the American Film Institute. In the year 2000, the superstar received a Life Achievement Award from the Screen Actors Guild. Two years later, he was bestowed an Honorary Oscar for lifetime achievement at the March 2002 Academy Awards.

Police Call 9000 See *DETROIT 9000.*

***Porgy and Bess* (1959)** Columbia, color, 146 minutes. **Director:** Otto Preminger; **Screenplay:** N. Richard Nash; **Cast:** Sidney Poitier (Porgy), Dorothy Dandridge (Bess), Sammy Davis Jr. (Sportin' Life), Pearl Bailey (Maria), Brock Peters (Crown), Leslie Scott (Jake), Diahann Carroll (Clara), Clarence Muse (Peter).

Unlike the earlier *CARMEN JONES* (1954), also starring DANDRIDGE and directed by Preminger, *Porgy and Bess* remains a museum piece, best appreciated as an opportunity to see several legendary talents performing on screen. The film was also noteworthy for the controversy caused before and during its making.

In 1925, DuBose Heyward wrote *Porgy,* a novel about vibrant characters in Charleston's Catfish Row. Two years later, he and his wife fashioned the successful Broadway play adaptation, also called *Porgy.* In 1935, Heywood joined with George and Ira Gershwin to create the folk opera, *Porgy and Bess,* which was an artistic but not a commercial success. Later, in revival, it became a popular work, but there were always black critics and viewers who felt the show was demeaning to their race.

When producer Samuel Goldwyn first decided to film the property in the mid-1950s, he wanted HARRY BELAFONTE to star, but the actor refused, thinking the role and the show itself debased his race. Goldwyn next decided on POITIER, who had similar misgivings over the role and later claimed to have been pressured into accepting the lead. Even before shooting began, there was unfavorable reaction from African-American PRESSURE GROUPS who thought the movie would emerge with negative racial stereotypes. In mid-1958 when the film's set mysteriously burned to the ground, the required delay led to more eruptions. While Goldwyn was replacing film director Rouben Mamoulian with Preminger, black actor Leigh Whipper, the president of the Negro Actors Guild of America, announced in early August 1958 that he was withdrawing from the movie because of Preminger, claiming that the director was unsympathetic to African Americans. This led to counterattacks by film cast members who defended Preminger. By late September 1958, filming began. The singing of several lead performers (including Poitier, Dandridge, and CARROLL) was dubbed for artistic reasons.

On Catfish Row, crippled Porgy drives a goat cart and is content to have "plenty of nothin'." He falls under the spell of seductive Bess who has been living with the vicious Crown. The latter kills a man during a dice game but is chased into hiding from the police by Bess. Meanwhile, drug-pusher Sportin' Life attempts to seduce Bess who now lives with Porgy and is drug free. Later, in a fight with Crown, Porgy kills him. The police take the fearful cripple to identify the dead man. By the time he returns to Catfish Row, Bess, thinking that Porgy won't be back, accepts Sportin' Life's drugs and leaves with him for New York. Porgy heads after her in his goat cart.

The very expensive movie emerged as a static stage piece, and Poitier, in particular, looked extremely glum as the carefree Porgy. Having so many of the leads' vocalizing dubbed, further distanced audiences from whatever artistic values lay within the folk opera. Not a commercial success, and not distributed in some parts of the South, the overly ambitious movie won a token Academy Award: Best Scoring. The picture also received Oscar nominations for Best Cinematography (Color), Best Costume Design (Color), and Best Sound.

***Preacher's Wife, The* (1996)** Buena Vista, color, 124 minutes. **Director:** Penny Marshall; **Screenplay:** Nat Maudlin and Allan Scott; **Cast:** Denzel Washington (Dudley), Whitney Houston (Julia Biggs), Courtney B. Vance (Rev. Henry Biggs), Gregory Hines (Joe Hamilton), Jenifer Lewis (Marguerite Coleman), Loretta Devine (Beverly).

Robert Nathan's novella, *The Bishop's Wife* (1928), was the source of a saccharine but quite successful romantic screen fantasy in 1947 starring Cary Grant, Loretta Young, and David Niven. Nearly 50 years later, it was translated into an African-American remake, starring WASHINGTON, HOUSTON, and Vance in the parallel roles. In addition, the Yuletide film became a musical and, to give it more relevance, was relocated to an eastern America inner city.

The angel Dudley is dispatched to Earth to help the Biggs family. Minister Henry Biggs is so concerned about saving his church from financial ruin and possible demolition that he has become distant with his wife Julia (who leads the church choir) and has little time for their young son. Henry is considering an offer from a greedy developer (Hines) in which the latter would take over the church. When Dudley appears—in answer to the minister's prayers for heavenly guidance—and reveals his assignment to Henry, the clergyman is skeptical. Nevertheless, the charming angel insinuates himself into the household and does his (clumsy) best to straighten out the Biggses' disharmony. Eventually, with Julia and Henry reunited and the church spared, Dudley vanishes, with only the Biggses' son Jeremiah able to remember the angel's special visit.

Despite the topical updating, the ethnic relevancy of the setting, and the bolstering help from Lewis (as the smart-mouth mother) and Devine (as Henry's overemotional secretary), the overlong film did not work for most viewers. There appeared to be little chemistry between debonair Washington and haughty Houston, and Vance meandered in a flavorless role. In addition, the supposed hipness and topicality of the subplots only prolonged the narrative, which also featured too many gospel numbers (and surprisingly no appropriate Christmas favorites).

The costly *The Preacher's Wife* grossed an unimpressive $48 million in domestic distribution. The film received an Oscar nomination for Best Original Score.

pressure groups Organizations (beyond such broad-based groups as the American Civil Liberties Union and Common Cause) involved in specifically trying to protect the rights of African-American talent and helping to integrate further the entertainment media have included: African-American Cultural Alliance (AACA) African-American Life Alliance (AALA), Association for the Preservation and Presentation of the Arts (AAPA), Black American Cinema Society (BACS), Black Awareness in Television (BAIT), Black Filmmaker Foundation (BFF), Black Rock Coalition (BRC), National Association for the Advancement of Colored People (NAACP), National Black Media Coalition (NBAC), National Negro Congress, and the Rainbow Coalition.

***Pressure Point* (1962)** United Artists, b&w, 87 minutes. **Director:** Hubert Cornfield; **Screenplay:** Cornfield and S. Lee Pogostin; **Cast:** Sidney Poitier (doctor), Bobby Darin (patient), Peter Falk (young psychiatrist), Carl Benton Reid (chief medical officer), Mary Munday (bar hostess).

Hollywood continued fumbling in its efforts to present African Americans on screen, trying to find ways that would not divert less-liberal white filmgoers from the box office. The industry's current token black star, POITIER, was featured again as a doctor who interacts with whites (on a professional basis only) but who seemingly has no personal life. And to make the proceedings less guilt-inspiring to more open-minded Caucasians, Poitier's character reveals that a black man can have racist feelings as well (albeit here a reaction to virulent bigotry on another's part).

Based on Robert Mitchell Lindner's 1955 story "Destiny's Tot," this screen account of a racist is put safely in the past by having a doctor (Poitier) recalling for a young psychiatrist (Falk) a case he had during World War II when he was on the staff at a federal prison. At that time, the physician had to deal with an American Nazi (Darin), imprisoned for subversion. From their sessions, the doctor learns about the man's troubled childhood, adolescent rejections, and so on. As such, the healer uncovers the reasons why the tormented man became a dangerous Aryan sympathizer who hates Jews and blacks. Despite his need for professional objectivity in the case, the doctor finds himself angered by this racist and worried that his feelings may have swayed his decision that the man should not be released. Nevertheless, prison authorities countermand his evaluation and free the individual, who later kills a man and then, in turn, is executed for the homicide.

Pryor, Richard (1940–) A man of immense potential with a sharp eye and a candid (if foul) mouth for depicting black street life and the absurdities and cruelties of racial bias, Pryor's groundbreaking comedy club act was raw and raucous, but unlike the earlier REDD FOXX, his contentious persona was fueled by racial and social ills, not snide, crude sexual anecdotes. He was immensely popular in the 1970s and early 1980s (despite being in a slew of bad movies), and his influence inspired many other later comedians such as EDDIE MURPHY. Thereafter, the continual onslaught of personal problems, bad breaks, and life-threatening ailments left the much-married Pryor a shell of his former self with little influence.

He was born in Peoria, Illinois, and claims to have spent his early years living at his grandmother's brothel where his mother worked and his father took her money. He was a school dropout, spent two years in the U.S. Army, and then joined the show-business ranks. He learned his craft the hard way through crummy club engagements filled with hostile audiences. But he observed while he worked, shaping his life observations to become fodder for his frantic, rough comedy patter. During much of the 1960s—by which time he had literally cleaned up his act—he played establishment, integrated, upscale clubs in the United States and appeared on TV variety shows. By 1970 he had an epiphany that he was not being true to himself or his race, so he dropped out of public life for many months. When he returned to the club world, he presented a manic observational humor act that knew no boundaries of good taste. His routines were filled with black pride and anger at the white establishment.

Pryor had already acted in a few episodes of TV series (e.g., *The Wild, Wild West*, 1966; *The Partridge Family*, 1971) and had been in a few feature films (e.g., *The Busy Body*, 1967; *Wild in the Street*, 1968; *CARTER'S ARMY*, 1969—TV movie). He became a staff writer for the television variety series, *THE FLIP WILSON SHOW* in the early 1970s. With his excess energy, he turned up everywhere, playing a dramatic role in Diana Ross's *LADY SINGS THE BLUES* (1972) and participating in BLACK ACTION FILMS such as *THE MACK* (1973) and *Adiós Amigo* (1975) before going mainstream. Teaming with Caucasian comic actor Gene Wilder in *SILVER STREAK* (1976), the movie was so popular that the duo was rematched for *STIR CRAZY* (1980), *See No Evil, Hear No Evil* (1989), and *Another You* (1991). Pryor starred in the auto-racer biography *GREASED LIGHTNING* (1977) and took on the title role in the unsuccessful screen musical *THE WIZ* (1978). Meanwhile, his inventive and unusual comedy/variety TV series *(The Richard Pryor Show)* lasted only five weeks in the fall of 1977 as he had pushed the limits of the network censors.

The "real" Richard Pryor was on view in *RICHARD PRYOR: LIVE IN CONCERT* (1979), the first of several exhilarating and exhausting stand-up comedy performance movies. (The fifth and last of these was *Richard Pryor: Live and Smokin'*, 1985.) Watching the progression of Richard's far-out persona and his deteriorating personal health during the span of these live-event movies, one witnessed his descent into hell. In 1980 he set himself on fire while freebasing (i.e., ingesting a cocaine mixture). Suffering third-degree burns over half his body, he was lucky to have survived and later acknowledged that the accident was likely a suicide attempt.

After making a miraculous recovery, Pryor continued at his usual frantic pace, turning out movies that ranged from *Bustin' Loose* (1981), a feel-good comedy with CICELY TYSON, to playing the villain in *Superman III* (1983) and stumbling through the dreary *Brewster's Millions* (1985), the black remake of a hoary old comedy. A new TV comedy series

(*Pryor's Place*) expired after one season (1984–85). The star went philosophical in *JO JO DANCER, YOUR LIFE IS CALLING* (1986), an uninspired biographical movie that he wrote, produced, directed, and starred in. By the time of *Harlem Nights* (1989), Pryor was playing support to one of his disciples, Eddie Murphy.

Bad luck plagued Pryor in the early 1990s. He endured triple bypass surgery and then was diagnosed with multiple sclerosis. The debilitating disease left him so physically weak and emaciated that his personal appearances before the public were severely limited. He made occasional token walk-ons in movies (e.g., *Mad Dog Time*, 1996; *Lost Highway*, 1997) and became the subject of heartfelt testimonials, sometimes aired on TV (e.g., *The Mark Twain Prize: Richard Pryor*, 1999). Meanwhile, he received a 1996 Emmy nomination for guest-starring on an episode of TV's *Chicago Hope*.

In 1993 Pryor accepted a Lifetime Achievement Award in Comedy from the American Comedy Awards. Three years later, he was bestowed the Lifetime Achievement Image Award and received a similar award from the New York Comedy Festival in 1997.

***Purple Rain* (1984)** Warner Bros., color, 111 minutes. **Director:** Albert Magnoli; **Screenplay:** Magnoli and William Blinn; **Cast:** Prince (the Kid), Apollonia Kotero (Apollonia), Morris Day (Morris), Olga Karlatos (Mother), Clarence Williams III (Father), Jerome Benton (Jerome).

When the Artist Formerly Known as Prince was still known to the public as Prince, the diminutive and egocentric rock star made a much-heralded feature film debut in this quasi-autobiographical musical.

Set midst the Minneapolis music scene, the Kid is the product of an interracial marriage (Williams III and Karlatos), a union in which his black father, a former musician, constantly beats his masochistic white mother. The Kid's bad home life carries over into his singing career and in his romantic pursuit of performer Apollonia. Meanwhile, she is drawn to the more manly Morris, a lead singer in his own rock group. Both men promise Apollonia fame, but each abuses her emotionally and physically. After saving his father from suicide, the Kid finds some of his dad's old music, which he takes to the club to perform. Thanks to his new heartfelt approach to music and Apollonia's declared love for him, the Kid is a redeemed soul.

Although Prince—described by some observers as a mix of Little Richard and Liberace for the rockin' 1980s—was definitely an acquired taste, the negative portrayal of women in *Purple Rain* drew adverse commentary. Some observers noted that the film perpetuated the tradition of the unhappy mulatto with its similarly light-skinned leads (Apollonia and Day).

Already a star of record albums and music videos, Prince's different look and bizarre outfits and the presentation of several musical numbers translated into almost $32 million in domestic film rentals. The movie won an Academy Award for Best Original Song Score. The soundtrack album won a Grammy. Two years later Prince's vanity movie, *Under the Cherry Moon*, filmed in arty black and white, was not successful.

R

***Rage in Harlem, A* (1991)** Miramax, color, 115 minutes. **Director:** Bill Duke; **Screenplay:** John Toles-Bey and Bobby Crawford; **Cast:** Forest Whitaker (Jackson), Gregory Hines (Goldy), Robin Givens (Imabelle), Zakes Mokae (Big Kathy), Danny Glover (Easy Money), Stack Pierce (Coffin Ed), George Wallace (Grave Digger).

Back in the 1970s, Chester Himes's crime novels, featuring Coffin Ed and Grave Digger's misadventures in Harlem, had provided the basis for two (*COTTON COMES TO HARLEM* and *Come Back, Charleston Blue*) flavorful and full-bodied entries in the BLACK ACTION FILM cycle. In this adaptation of Himes's book *For Love of Imabelle* (1957), set in the mid-1950s, those two characters take a back seat to Jackson, a nerdy accountant for a funeral home, and his half-brother, a con artist named Goldy. This duo seek the luscious Imabelle and the horde of gold she has brought to Harlem from a heist scene in Natchez, Mississippi. Also involved in this brutal caper is transvestite Big Kathy and unscrupulous Easy-Money.

Forest Whitaker and Robin Givens in *A Rage in Harlem* (1990). (JC ARCHIVES)

While the earlier screen translations of Himes's fiction had been gaudy, comical, and generally fast paced, this new addition came at a time in American filmmaking where having vibrant "characters" from jivey Harlem's underbelly no longer guaranteed a novelty factor to draw filmgoers. Perhaps that is why former actor and TV director Duke, an African-American talent, in his feature film directing debut, chose to emphasize the violence, the anatomy of shapely Givens, and sexual encounters to push along the protracted plot.

Featuring a who's who of contemporary African-American talent, *A Rage in Harlem* grossed little more than $10 million in domestic distribution.

***Raisin in the Sun, A* (1961)** Columbia, b&w, 127 minutes. **Director:** Daniel Petrie; **Screenplay:** Lorraine Hansberry; **Cast:** Sidney Poitier (Walter Lee Younger), Claudia McNeil (Lena Younger), Ruby Dee (Ruth Younger), Diana Sands (Beneatha Younger), Ivan Dixon (Asagai), Louis Gossett Jr. (George Murchison).

In 1959, this heartfelt play, the first by an African-American woman to be staged on Broadway, won the Drama Critics Circle Award. Two years later, many of the original cast, including McNeil, POITIER, and SANDS, recreated their highly emotional roles for the screen adaptation. In this era it was still a rarity—even for such a prestigious project—for a story focusing almost entirely on African-American characters to become a major American movie production.

Set in a bleak three-room tenement apartment in the Chicago ghetto, dignified matriarch Lena Younger rules the constrained household, which includes her chauffeur son Walter, his wife Ruth, and their son, as well as Lena's daughter Beneatha, a medical school student who has two suitors (DIXON and GOSSETT). Suddenly, their despair-filled lives take on a new dimension and fresh problems: Lena receives $10,000 from her late husband's insurance policy. She insists that $3,500 be used as a down payment for a little house in the white suburbs. Explosive Walter begs for the money to open a liquor store, while outspoken Beneatha requires help with medical school tuition. Without permission, Walter takes $6,500 for his store and is quickly swindled out of the money. Horrified at what his dreams and frustrations led him to do, he urges the family to sell back the house to the neighborhood association, which is willing to pay a higher price to avoid having African Americans move into their district. Again, Lena remains firm in her dreams and decisions: The family will relocate to the suburbs, despite the sacrifices it will entail.

In 1989, Bill Duke directed a TV movie remake of *A Raisin in the Sun*, starring ESTHER ROLLE (Lena), DANNY GLOVER (Walter Lee), and Kim Yancey (Beneatha).

***Red Ball Express* (1952)** Universal, b&w, 83 minutes. **Director:** Budd Boetticher; **Screenplay:** John Michael Hayes; **Cast:** Jeff Chandler (Lt. Chick Campbell), Alex Nicol (Sgt. Ernest "Red" Kalleck), Charles Drake (Pvt. Ronald Partridge), Hugh O'Brian (Private Wilson), Sidney Poitier (Cpl. Andrew Robertson), Bubber Johnson (Pvt. Taffy Smith), Robert Davis (Pvt. Dave McCord).

During World War II, the 371st Quartermaster Truck Company of the Army Transportation Corp—known as the Red Ball Express—was charged with rushing fuel, ammunition, and other supplies through enemy territory to supply Gen. George Patton's tanks. The division had many African-American soldiers (segregated to their own quarters), although the leaders were all white. This potentially exciting premise was converted into a standard combat drama. Nonetheless, Chandler and POITIER provided grit in their performances, and, in fact, this was another tiny step forward in integrating Hollywood screen fare.

Lt. Chick Campbell is in charge of the Red Ball Express, which includes many disgruntled soldiers, including Sgt. Red Kalleck who blames Campbell for a trucking accident in the United States where his brother died. When Cpl. Andrew Robertson, one of the ethnic minority soldiers attached to the group, is called "black boy," racial tension explodes and a fist fight ensues. Robertson asks to be transferred, but Campbell refuses. Eventually the newly formed group becomes a cohesive, efficient whole, and the men come to respect their hard-nosed leader. Even Robertson adjusts to his outfit and withdraws his transfer request.

Rather than having several/many of the Red Ball Express group be African Americans, as was the actual case, there are only a few scattered representational ones seen in the on-camera convoy. Although relative film newcomer Poitier is the bristling young soldier who (rightly) saw racism at every turn, there was, for contrast, his black tent mate Pvt. Dave McCord, who not only defends Campbell as a nonracist but also dies when the enemy blows up his truck.

Poitier had a similar role as the token African-American symbol of forthcoming integration in the bland Alan Ladd Korean War combat film, *All the Young Men* (1960). The TV sitcom series *Roll Out* (1973–74) featuring black actors (e.g., Mel Stewart and Garrett Morris) dealt with the same World War II transportation unit that figured in *Red Ball Express.*

***Red, White, and Black, The* (aka: *Men of the Tenth; Soul Soldier; Soul Soldiers*) (1970)** Hirschman-Northern, color, 103 minutes. **Director:** John Cardos; **Screenplay:** Marlene Weed; **Cast:** Robert DoQui (Trooper Eli Brown), Janee Michelle (Julie), Lincoln Kilpatrick (Sergeant Hatch), Rafer Johnson (Private Armstrong), Cesar Romero (Colonel Grierson), Barbara Hale (Mrs. Grierson), Isabel Sanford (Isabel), Robert Dix (Chief Walking Horse).

This gory entry led to a rash of violent BLACK ACTION westerns and was a precursor to such postblaxploitation tales as *Posse* (1993) and the TV movie, *CHILDREN OF THE DUST* (aka *A Good Day to Die*) (1995). For many viewers—especially young minority filmgoers—movies like this proved to be not only informative (i.e., they acknowledged the fact of black soldiers in the Old West) but also heightened their racial pride (e.g., the black man succeeding over white oppressors). In addition, this entry featured two ethnic minorities (African American and Native American) struggling against predatory whites. This auxiliary racial aspect of the movie was overlooked or ignored by many reviewers.

In 1871, at Fort Davis, Texas, Caucasian Colonel Grierson is in charge of the all-black Tenth Cavalry. Among the troopers are newcomers Eli Brown and Hatch, who are competing for the attention of the post's seamstress, Julie. When Chief Crazy Horse complains about white men having stolen his people's horses, Private Armstrong, who is friendly with the chief, and several men are dispatched against the wrongdoers. Later, Indian warriors attack marauding whites. After the troopers defeat Crazy Horse's men, the prisoners are brought back to the fort. The black cavalrymen find it ironic that they have been pitted against another persecuted minority.

***Richard Pryor: Live in Concert* (1979)** Special Events Entertainment, color, 78 minutes. **Director:** Jeff Margolis; **Screenplay:** Richard Pryor; **Cast:** Richard Pryor (himself).

Many reviewers regarded this, one of several concert films featuring the inimitable PRYOR performing full throttle on stage, as the comedian's best. No longer restrained by someone else's movie script, he let loose with a high-energy showcase that was arresting in its range of topics (e.g., drug use, police problems, car accidents, heart attack) and the breadth of his talent through monologue, impersonations, mime, and so on. Pryor drew the viewer into his view of the hectic world in which even the most serious event had a humorous aspect.

Racy and at times vulgar, Pryor also included his impression of whites, parodying their speech patterns, habits, attitudes—sort of a turnabout from the decades of stage performers poking fun at parallel aspects of African Americans. His very successful concert films paved the way for the more outrageous ones by EDDIE MURPHY in the 1980s.

Richards, Beah (1920–2000) Quietly resourceful as an actress (stage, films, and TV), she occupied her own special acting space, never becoming melodramatic, even when her characters grew agitated. After a lengthy and prolific career, she was best known for her role as SIDNEY POITIER's mother in *GUESS WHO'S COMING TO DINNER?* (1967), a part for which she was Oscar nominated. She also proved impressive—again serene and dignified even though angered—in a 1984 episode of TV's *ST. ELSEWHERE.* Called to task for practicing medicine although only a midwife, she informed the interfering resident (played by DENZEL WASHINGTON) that in her lifetime she had delivered more than 2,000 babies and had lost only seven. With that, and without missing a beat, she tossed her shawl over her head and marched out of Boston's St. Eligius Hospital. It was a great acting moment between two generations of African-American performers.

Richards was born in Vicksburg, Mississippi. She came to New York City in 1950 but did not gain a noteworthy acting role until she was cast in a 1956 off-Broadway revival of *Take a Giant Step.* Without using stage makeup, she was convincing as the octogenarian grandmother. In 1965 she appeared as an evangelist in James Baldwin's *The Amen Corner,* directed by Frank Silvera. In addition to acting, Richards also wrote poetry and plays. Among her early TV roles were episodes of *The Big Valley* (1965) and *I SPY* (1967). BILL COSBY, the co-star of *I Spy,* gave Richards a regular role (1970–71) on his TV comedy series *The Bill Cosby Show.* In 1972, she had the ongoing part of Aunt Ethel on *SANFORD AND SON.*

On the big screen, Richards's credits included *THE GREAT WHITE HOPE* (1970), *The Biscuit Eater* (1972), and *Drugstore Cowboy* (1989), while she was in such telefeatures as *Outrage* (1983), *Just an Old Sweet Song* (1976), *A Christmas Without Snow* (1980), and *Capital News* (1990). In the miniseries *ROOTS: THE NEXT GENERATION* (1979), Beah was Cynthia Palmer. On John Ritter's TV sitcom *Hearts Afire,* the actress was seen (in 1992) as Miss Lulu, a contemporary mammy. During 1994–95 she performed on TV's *ER* as the ailing mother of Eriq LaSalle's doctor character.

Her last feature film was OPRAH WINFREY's *BELOVED* (1998); her final (TV) appearance was on an April 2000 segment of *The Practice.* For that latter performance, she received an Emmy Award as Outstanding Guest Actress in a Drama Series. By then Richards was already dying of emphysema, and the prize had to be delivered to her in Vicksburg, Mississippi, where she passed away in mid-September 2000.

At the 2000 Los Angeles Pan African Film Festival, Beah Richards received a Lifetime Achievement Award.

***Riot* (1969)** Paramount, color, 97 minutes. **Director:** Buzz Kulik; **Screenplay:** James Poe; **Cast:** Jim Brown (Cully Briston), Gene Hackman (Red Fletcher), Ben Carruthers (Joe Surefoot), Mike Kellin (Bugsy), Gerald S. O'Loughlin (Grossman).

In the 1967 book by ex-convict Frank Elli, the Cully Briston character had been a white convict. However, to make this latest prison genre action entry more topical—and to take advantage of the box-office clout of former football star BROWN—the character became African American. With his solemn demeanor, muscular presence, and handsome look, Brown had already been exploited as a crossover star whose appeal extended to both ethnic majority *and* minority audiences.

Beyond the excesses of violence, and homosexual characters (including one who makes a pass at Briston), the most unique aspect of this turgid exploitation entry was Brown's Cully being one of the ringleaders, not just a follower/stooge, in the prison breakout. In fact, of those who instigate the breakout, Cully is the only one to make it to freedom. This plot outcome said a great deal about changing Hollywood, even if Briston's macho character was quite brutal.

Robeson, Paul (1898–1976) Decades after his death, Robeson still remains an impressive, intriguing, and controversial figure. The passions of this cultured and articulate man went far beyond acting and included his continual criticism of the social injustices (especially racial) in America. His rhetoric so upset factions of the government and public alike that he was persona non grata in his homeland for many years. Early to earn recognition as a stage and film actor and concert singer, he gained a high position (almost mythical) in the echelon of U.S. black talent of the century.

He was born in Princeton, New Jersey, the son of a Presbyterian minister (who had once been a runaway slave). Growing up with a love of music and excelling in school in debate and sports, he won a full scholarship to Rutgers University. While playing on the college gridiron, and participating in other sports, he was named to the All-American football team. After graduating class valedictorian, he entered Columbia University Law School in 1920. To earn extra money, he took up professional singing, appearing at Harlem's Cotton Club where he used his rich baritone voice to advantage.

Robeson made his professional acting debut in *Simon the Cyrenian* on Broadway in 1921. He took another Broadway play, *Taboo* (1922), in which he daringly costarred with a white actress, on tour abroad. After receiving his law degree in 1923 and trying the practice of law, he went into acting full time. He played the leads in two Eugene O'Neill plays (including *THE EMPEROR JONES*).

His feature film debut was in OSCAR MICHEAUX's all-black *BODY AND SOUL* (1925). That same year he gave a concert in Greenwich, Connecticut, the first such recital to be comprised entirely of black spirituals. Paul made recordings and, in the late 1920s, moved with his family to London. In

Paul Robeson in *The Emperor Jones* (1933). (JC ARCHIVES)

1932 he was back on Broadway playing Joe (and singing "Ol' Man River") in a revival of *Show Boat*, a role he repeated in the 1936 Hollywood feature. Robeson also starred in an independent film of *The Emperor Jones* (1933).

Robeson had a larger following abroad than in the United States and was back in England to film such entries as *Sanders of the River* (1935), *Song of Freedom* (1936), *King Solomon's Mines* (1937), and *Proud Valley* (1939). During this productive period, he made trips to Russia where he was impressed by the communist system. Yet again on Broadway, he had a big success with his *Othello* (1942). He was politically active (especially pro-Soviet) throughout the 1940s, while finding time to record and do concerts. His only Hollywood picture of the decade was 1942's multipart *Tales of Manhattan*. Thereafter, he announced he was through making movies until there were substantially better roles available for blacks. He made no more films. Some of Robeson's highly charged statements continued to upset Americans (both white and black). He was one of those denounced by the House Un-American Activities Committee in the late 1940s.

An outspoken opponent to the U.S.'s involvement in the Korean War, Robeson found his passport revoked and his acting/lecture/concert opportunities in America at an end. His right to travel aboard was restored by the U.S. Supreme Court in 1958. He played *Othello* for the final time in 1959 at Stratford-on-Avon in England. After living in Russia for a time, he came back to the United States in 1963 in poor health. He soon retired and later became reclusive. He died in Philadelphia; his tombstone read: "The artist must elect to fight for freedom or slavery. I have made my choice. I had no alternative."

Over the years, several actors (e.g., JAMES EARL JONES, Bennet Guillory, and Avery Brooks) portrayed Robeson in dramatic works on stage. In the 1999 documentary *I'll Make Me a World*, John Henry Redwood was seen as the great performer.

***Robin Hood: Prince of Thieves* (1991)** Warner Bros., color, 143 minutes. **Director:** Kevin Reynolds; **Screenplay:** Pen Densham and John Watson; **Cast:** Kevin Costner (Robin Hood [Robin of Locksley]), Morgan Freeman (Azeem), Mary Elizabeth Mastrantonio (Maid Marian), Christian Slater (Will Scarlett), Alan Rickman (Sheriff of Nottingham), Michael McShane (Friar Tuck), Sean Connery (King Richard).

This revisionist, politically correct version of Robin Hood and life in the Middle Ages has scant resemblance to the famed Errol Flynn screen version of *The Adventures of Robin Hood* (1938). This new edition boasts a feminist Maid Marian, a band of merry men that includes several women, and a plumpish leader who is a thinker not a doer. With all that, the presence of one more startling ingredient did not seem so strange to filmgoers: casting African-American FREEMAN as the Muslim Moor Azeem, who helps Robin of Locksley break free from prison in the Holy Land and returns with him to England. There they find that the sinister Sheriff of Nottingham has taken control of the countryside and that Richard the Lionhearted remains in exile. Robin, Azeem, and others join together to form the band of rebels in Sherwood Forest to combat the dastardly sheriff who plans to force Maid Marian into marriage so that he will have royal ties. Thanks to a warm performance by Freeman, his Azeem seemed more at ease in Robin's camp than the more familiar characters of Will Scarlett, Friar Tuck, or Little John.

Despite the competition of a TV movie on *Robin Hood* (which had no parallel ethnic minority character to Freeman's Azeem) that aired that year just before Costner's theatrical release, *Robin Hood: Prince of Thieves* grossed more than $165 million in domestic distribution. It earned an Oscar nomination for Best Song: "(Everything I Do) I Do It for You."

Robinson, Bill "Bojangles" (1878–1949) On a par with famed Caucasian dancer Fred Astaire, Robinson was an important role model for African Americans. In a time when segregation infected every part of American life, Robinson did the near impossible: He was exceedingly popular with both black and white audiences. The fact that, in his several films, he usually played a servant subordinated to whites was overlooked by his race because of his infectious style of superb tap dancing. (Interestingly, offstage, the life-hardened Bojangles was not the docile, sweet person he portrayed in front of audiences; he was argumentative, always ready for a fight, and carried a pistol.)

He was born Luther Robinson in Richmond, Virginia, later taking his new first name from his brother William. He quit school by age seven and, in the next year, began to dance professionally. He gained the nickname Bojangles for his joyful, carefree stage manner. Sometimes in his earlier career, he was matched with a partner (as the team of Butler and Robinson in 1908), but he soon developed a single act in vaudeville where he displayed his world-famous tap dancing and his trademark stair tap routine. As the King of Tap Dancers he won several national dance contests in the late 1920s. He made his feature film bow in the musical *Dixiana* as a specialty dancer. Dancing roles followed in *Harlem Is Heaven* (1932), an all-black independent film, and the musical short, *King for a Day* (1934). *In Old Kentucky* (1935) joined him with humorist/actor Will Rogers in a tale of horseracing.

THE LITTLE COLONEL (1935) found tall, dapper Bojangles teamed with the country's favorite tyke, Shirley Temple, in a sentimental post-Civil War tale. So successful was their rapport and their display of tap dancing together that they were reunited on camera three further times: *The Littlest Rebel* (1935), *Rebecca of Sunnybrook Farm* (1938), and *Just Around the Corner* (1938). (For one of Temple's films—1936's *Dimples*—in which he was not featured, Robinson provided the choreography.) When not moviemaking, Robinson, who was known as the Honorary Mayor of Harlem, did major club and stage work (e.g., *Brown Buddies*, 1930; *The Hot Mikado*, 1939). Bojangles's final movie was the all-black musical *STORMY WEATHER* (1943), loosely suggested by his life story. He made an occasional foray onto television in the late 1940s, appearing on Milton Berle's variety hour.

When Robinson died in November 1949, thousands lined the streets to pay their respects at his funeral. In 1989, Congress designated the star's birth date (May 25) as National Tap Dancing Day. In the Showtime cable movie *Bojangles* (2001), Gregory Hines played the star.

Rock, Chris (1966–) In the highly competitive world of stand-up comedy, Rock stood out from the crowd with his brash, no-holds-barred brand of comedy shtick in which he mixed charm and rage, classiness and uncouthness. Some commentators thought of him as the younger version (by five years) of motor-mouth comedian/movie star EDDIE MURPHY. Like Murphy, Rock also spent time (1990–93) as a resident clown on TV's *Saturday Night Live*, which he used as a springboard to further his screen acting and TV comedy-specials career.

He was born in Georgetown, South Carolina, but was raised in the Bedford-Stuyvesant section of Brooklyn, New York. The oldest of six children (there was also a stepbrother from his dad's first marriage), he gained an early reputation as a wise-mouthed individual. Intrigued with the world of stand-up comedy, he studied the work of such pros as BILL COSBY, RICHARD PRYOR and Sam Kinison and of such 1980s rappers as Public Enemy and N.W.A. He made his professional debut at Manhattan's comedy club Catch a Rising Star in 1985.

By 1987 Chris had made his screen debut in Murphy's *Beverly Hills Cop II*, on screen briefly as a parking valet. He graduated to playing a rib-joint customer in KEENEN IVORY WAYANS's comedy, *I'm Gonna Git You Sucka* (1988). In *Comedy's Dirtiest Dozen* (1988), Rock and Tim Allen were among the twelve stand-up comics who did their act on camera. After three years with *Saturday Night Live* where he gained tremendous exposure, he spent a season on *IN LIVING COLOR* during its 1993–94 final season. Meanwhile, he was impressive in a small role in the URBAN DRAMA, *NEW JACK CITY* (1991). By the mid-1990s he was appearing in such screen comedies as *Sgt. Bilko* (1996) and *Beverly Hills Ninja* (1997). From 1997 to 2000, he headlined his own cable-TV comedy series, *The Chris Rock Show*, for which he received trophy nominations from the American Comedy Awards, the Emmys, and the Image Awards.

Greatly interested in politics, he brought his observation to the forum of TV's *Politically Incorrect* (1994), where he was "Indecision '96 Correspondent." Chris did several TV specials (e.g., *Chris Rock: Bring the Pain*, 1997—the show won two Emmys; *Chris Rock: Bigger & Blacker*, 1999—for which he won an American Comedy Award for Funniest Male Performer in a TV Special). On the big screen, he played a thug accomplice of MORGAN FREEMAN in *Nurse Betty* (2000) and the next year wrote, starred in, and produced *Down to Earth* (2001), a remake of Warren Beatty's *Heaven Can Wait* (1978). Chris produced and starred in the crude and generally unfunny *Pootie Tang* (2001), provided the voice for the title character in the comedy animation feature *Osmosis Jones* (2001), and, among other movie vehicles, played a CIA agent with Anthony Hopkins in the action comedy *Bad Company* (2002). For *Head of State* (2003), Rock starred in and directed this comedy.

***Rocky III* (1982)** Metro-Goldwyn-Mayer, color, 99 minutes. **Director/Screenplay:** Sylvester Stallone; **Cast:** Sylvester Stallone (Rocky Balboa), Carl Weathers (Apollo Creed), Mr. T (Clubber Lang), Talia Shire (Adrian Balboa), Burt Young (Paulie), Burgess Meredith (Mickey).

In the Academy Award-winning picture *Rocky* (1976), the inarticulate South Philadelphia underdog Rocky Balboa lost his title match to hulking, handsome Apollo Creed, the African-American champ. In the follow-up, *Rocky II* (1979), the tide turned with Balboa the victor against Creed in the ring. For the next entry, *Rocky III*, moviemaker Stallone made his opponent another black athlete, this time the highly contentious Clubber Lang played by the vibrant ethnic personality, MR. T. Giving the plot additional ethnic twists, Apollo agrees to coach Rocky for the bout if he will train in Los Angeles's black ghetto at the local gym where Apollo works out. There, says Creed, there are many black fighters—in the mold of Clubber—who are really anxious to give a white opponent a big bruising. (The first trio of Rocky movies each featured a barely disguised racial contest between white Rocky and his African-American opponent.) Thanks to the tutoring of Apollo, who has developed a strong friendship with Balboa during the years, Rocky emerges the champion—in a bit of cinematic wish fulfillment—against Clubber, who towers over him in the ring.

Rocky III grossed about $123 million in domestic distribution.

Rolle, Esther (1922–1998) Stocky and serious of face, Rolle rose to fame in the 1970s playing smart-mouthed Florida Evans, first on *Maude* (1972–74), then on her own spin-off sitcom, *GOOD TIMES* (1974–77, 1978–79). While at the height of her show business fame, Esther, a proponent of improving her race's media image, spoke out against the unflattering buffoonish stereotype played by her *Good Times* on-camera son (Jimmie Walker). To show she meant business, she quit the series for a time.

She was born in Pompano Beach, Florida, graduated from Spelman College in Atlanta, Georgia, in 1942, and later moved to New York to pursue her interest in acting. A charter member of the Negro Ensemble Company, she was a dancer with Shogala Obola Dance Company. She was off-Broadway in such productions as *The Blacks* (1961), toured with *Purlie Victorious* in 1962, and appeared on Broadway in *Blues for Mister Charlie* (1964), *The Amen Corner* (1965), and *Don't Play Us Cheap* (1972). Her film debut came with *NOTHING BUT A MAN* (1964). In 1971, she took over for Lillian Hayman for a while in the role of Sadie Gray on the daytime TV soap *One Life to Live*.

While still involved with *Good Times*, Esther was featured in the TV movie *Summer of My German Soldier* (1978), winning an Outstanding Supporting Actress Emmy for it. Other acting assignments included *A Raisin in the Sun* (1989—TV movie), *Driving Miss Daisy* (1989), *The Mighty Quinn* (1989), *The Kid Who Loved Christmas* (1990—TV movie), and *To Dance with the White Dog* (1993—TV movie). She co-starred with Harold Gould in the short-lived, clash-of-cultures TV series, *Singer & Sons* (1990). On *Scarlett* (1994), the miniseries sequel to *GONE WITH THE WIND*, Esther was Mammy. Her last big-screen roles included *ROSEWOOD* (1997), *DOWN IN THE DELTA* (1998), and the posthumously released *Train Ride* (2000).

In 1975, she received a NAACP Image Award as Best Actress in a Television Series. The television union AFTRA presented her with a Human Rights Award in 1983.

Rollins, Howard See ROLLINS, HOWARD, JR.

Rollins, Howard, Jr. (aka: Howard Rollins) (1951–1996) Sadly, this handsome performer with a once-promising career (he received both Oscar and Golden Globes nominations for his Best Supporting Actor role in *Ragtime*, 1981) ended his life in a mire of tabloid headlines exploiting his personal problems, which included substance abuse and run-ins with the law for driving while under the influence of drugs and/or alcohol. Like many talented actors before him, a good deal of Rollins Jr.'s frustrations over the years were caused by the limited options for African-American players in U.S. show business.

He was born in Baltimore, Maryland. He attended Towson State College (now University) in Baltimore and pursued an acting career. His first performance of note was playing Andrew Young in the TV miniseries *KING* (1978). In another miniseries, *ROOTS: THE NEXT GENERATION* (1979), he was George Haley. Even after Howard's burst of fame with *Ragtime* as Coalhouse Walker—the young black revolutionary—his career did not take off as expected. He accepted the role of Ed Harding on the daytime TV soap *Another World* (1982) and then played Honey Brown in the Pearl Bailey version of *The Member of the Wedding* (1982—TV movie). In *For Us, the Living* (1983—TV movie), he was civil-rights martyr Medgar Evers. As with *Ragtime*, after the actor's well-reviewed assignment as Captain Davenport, the restrained, nonmilitant black man in *A Soldier's Story* (1984), his career should have soared. But it was back to TV with the brief western series *Wildside* (1985) and such telefeatures as *The Children of Times Square* (1986).

Rollins Jr.'s career was salvaged when he was hired to take on the colead role in the TV series version (1988–94) of the movie *IN THE HEAT OF THE NIGHT* (1967). Six-foot Howard was to play Philadelphia lawman Virgil Tibbs, the part made famous by SIDNEY POITIER, while top-billed Carroll O'Connor was portraying Sheriff Bill Gillespie of Sparta, Mississippi. The two actors worked well together and the show was a moderate hit. Then in the early 1990s, stories began leaking out to the public about Howard's erratic behavior on and off the set. As the supermarket newspapers probed deeper, the accounts grew more repellent. Throughout the ongoing ordeal, O'Connor supported keeping Rollins Jr. on the series. But by 1993, when matters had gotten worse and the actor was in and out of court, jail, and substance-abuse programs, it was decided to shunt Howard to the sidelines. Carl Weathers was brought in to play a parallel role for the series' last season (1993–94).

Rollins Jr.'s final screen work was a role in the ensemble drama *Drunks* (1995). He played an alcoholic attending a twelve-step support group, having guilt over his son's death, caused by his drunk driving. In December 1996 Rollins died in New York from complications from lymphoma.

***Room 222* (1969–1974)** ABC-TV series, color, 30 minutes. **Cast:** Lloyd Haynes (Pete Dixon), Denise Nicholas (Liz McIntyre), Michael Constantine (Seymour Kaufman), Karen Valentine (Alice Johnson), Judy Strangis (Helen Loomis), Heshimu (Jason Allen), Ivor Francis (Ken Dragon), Eric Laneuville (Larry).

In the late 1960s as the United States went through a transition regarding the explosive issue of racial integration, so did American network TV. One of the programs to help the racial situation quietly was this school drama, based on, and sometimes filmed at, the 3,000-student Los Angeles High School.

Not only did the drama have a racially mixed cast of teacher and student characters, but also its lead figure was the good-natured Pete Dixon, the black teacher in charge of

American history and whose homeroom was 222. School counselor Liz McIntyre was Pete's African-American girlfriend. In the multicultural Walt Whitman High School, the students—black and white—come to thoughtful and low-keyed Dixon to sort out their problems—academic and otherwise. (It was a refreshing change from most TV shows that always had the students, white or black, going to their Caucasian instructors for help.)

Nicholas was twice nominated for a Golden Globe for her work on *Room 222* in the category of Best Supporting Actress—Television Drama.

***Roots* (1977)** ABC-TV miniseries, color, 570 minutes. **Directors:** David Greene, John Erman, Marvin J. Chomsky, and Gilbert Moses; **Teleplay:** William E. Blinn, Ernest Kinoy, James Lee, and M. Charles Cohen; **Cast:** Maya Angelou (Nyo Boto), Ji-Tu Cumbuka (wrestler), Moses Gunn (Kintango), Thalmus Rasulala (Omoro), Harry Rhodes (Brima Cesay), William Watson (Gardner), Ren Woods (Fanta), LeVar Burton (Kunta Kinte), Cicely Tyson (Binta), Edward Asner (Capt. Thomas Davies), O. J. Simpson (Kadi Touray), Ralph Waite (Slater), Louis Gossett Jr. (Fiddler), Robert Reed (William Reynolds), Lorne Greene (John Reynolds), Lynda Day George (Mrs. Reynolds), John Amos (Toby—Kunta Kinte as an adult), Madge Sinclair (Bell), Beverly Todd (Fanta—as an adult), Raymond St. Jacques (the Drummer), Lawrence-Hilton Jacobs (Noah), Leslie Uggams (Kizzy), Richard Roundtree (Sam Bennett), Ben Vereen (Chicken George), Brad Davis (Ol' George Johnson), and Todd Bridges (Bud).

In 1976, Alex Haley's book *Roots: The Saga of an American Family* was a monumental success in its sweeping chronicle of the history of slaves brought to the United States from Africa. The text told how each generation thereafter coped with slavery and then, in the 1860s, with freedom. Haley's popularization of a race's cultural heritage, which was inspired by his efforts to trace his own roots, won a Pulitzer Prize. It led the ABC-TV network to package this twelve-hour (with commercials) miniseries, shown for eight consecutive nights. Building on the fame of the best-selling book, the TV series drew an audience of more than 130 million viewers. Most importantly, the book, and especially the miniseries, created a new consciousness among blacks and other races of the torment and struggle African Americans have endured in America, the supposed land of the free. It became a living history of their race.

Beyond the exploration of the African tribespeople and how they were captured, chained, and cruelly shipped to the United States under deplorable conditions, one of the most revealing aspects of the TV adaptation of *Roots* was its comprehensive depiction of how slaves existed when they were not in their masters' cotton fields or working in the plantation homes. This provided a fuller, much more stark picture than what moviegoers had seen in the movies of the Old South such as *So Red the Rose* (1935) or *GONE WITH THE WIND* (1939). (The later *North and South*, 1985—TV miniseries, also played to the stereotypes of pre-Civil War times in the South.)

On the other hand, an irony of the making of this miniseries was that the majority of the guiding creative forces were white and were extremely concerned about attracting a viewing audience that went beyond the African-American marketplace. As such, in adapting the book, several white characters and new incidents were added to the story line, and some Caucasian figures were deliberately made into sympathetic souls (e.g., Asner as the slave-ship captain who turns remorseful) so that white viewers could better relate to the miniseries. In typical miniseries procedure, the $6 million chronicle became an extended grand soap opera, filled with an alternating mix of tragedy, small joys, victories and defeats, and sexuality.

Generally, the Caucasian performers in *Roots* were well-known TV figures who were geared to draw in viewers; the black talents covered the range of experienced ethnic minority talent. The miniseries provided substantial roles to black actors, many of whom had been limited previously to small, one-dimensional parts because of continuing racial inequality in show business.

The wildly successful *Roots* won thirty-seven Emmy nominations. Among the Emmy prizes the show claimed were: Outstanding Actor (GOSSETT JR.), Outstanding Director (David Greene—Part 1), Outstanding Limited Series, Outstanding Supporting Actor in a Limited Series (Asner), Outstanding Supporting Actress in a Limited Series (Cole), as well as two for scripters (Kinoy and Blinn—Part 2), and the Music Score for Part 1 by Quincy Jones and Gerald Fried. Among the other actors nominated for Emmys were: Amos, Burton, Gunn, Sinclair, Reed, TYSON, Uggams, and Waite.

The follow-up to *Roots* was *ROOTS: THE NEXT GENERATIONS* (1979). In 1988, there appeared *Roots: The Gift*, a ninety-four-minute TV movie based on Haley's characters. It was set at Christmas time of 1770 and traced how Kunta Kinte (LeVar Burton) and Fiddler (Lou Gossett Jr.) attempted to escape from their lives of slavery in the South. Their efforts led to other fellow slaves winning their freedom. The production was directed by Kevin Hooks.

In 2002 Burton hosted the TV documentary, *Roots: Celebrating 25 years.*

***Roots: The Next Generations* (1979)** ABC-TV miniseries, color, 685 minutes. **Directors:** John Erman, Charles Dubin, Georg Stanford Brown, and Lloyd Richards; **Teleplay:** Ernest Kinoy, Sydney A. Glass, Thad Mumford, Daniel Wilcox, and John McGreevey; **Cast:** Georg Stanford Brown (Tom Harvey), Olivia de Havilland (Mrs. Warner), Henry Fonda (Col. Frederick Warner), Paul Koslo (Ear Crowther), Avon Long (Chicken George), Lynne Moody (Irene Harvey), Greg Morris (Beeman Jones), Richard Thomas (Jim Warner), Brian Mitchell (John Dolan), Ja'net DuBois (Sally Harve), Stan Shaw (Will Palmer), Irene Cara (Bertha Palmer), Ossie Davis (Dad Jones), Ruby Dee (Queen Haley), Dorian Harewood (Simon Haley), Hal William (Aleck Haley), Bernie Casey (Bubba Haywood), Pam Grier (Francey), Percy Rodriguez

(Boyd Moffatt), Brock Peters (Ab Decker), Beah Richards (Cynthia Palmer), Paul Winfield (Dr. Horace Huguley), Debbie Allen (Nan Branch Haley), Damon Evans (Alex Haley—ages seventeen to twenty-six), Diahann Carroll (Zeona—Mrs. Simon Haley), Della Reese (Mrs. Lydia Branch), Marlon Brando (George Lincoln Rockwell), Claudia McNeil (Sister Will Ada), Al Freeman Jr. (Malcolm X), Howard Rollins Jr. (George Haley), James Earl Jones (Alex Haley).

As a companion to the much-lauded miniseries *ROOTS* (1977), this sequel cost $18 million and lasted fourteen hours (with commercials) for seven nights. Also based on Haley's 1976 book *Roots: The Saga of an American Family*, its narrative opens in 1882 (where the original miniseries ended) and goes through the 1960s when Alex Haley (played by JONES) is a writer.

Of the cast from the first TV *Roots* only Brown and Moody—playing the great-great-grandparents of the writer Haley—continued their roles. Receiving the most publicity for his guest role was Brando as American Nazi leader George Lincoln Rockwell, an individual whom Haley had actually interviewed for *Playboy* magazine in the 1960s. Having covered the larger dramatic historical issues in the earlier entry, the new *Roots* was a more sedate chronicle with lower-keyed acting, as the cast depicted changing events in the United States, such as African-American soldiers serving overseas in World War I, blacks trying to integrate into an American capitalist system that ignored them, and the emerging civil-rights acts, protests, and riots of the 1960s. Interwoven with this history of black America in the twentieth century were assorted romances that propelled the story forward to the present.

Roots: The Next Generations won Emmys for Outstanding Limited Series and Outstanding Supporting Actor (Brando). Among the other five Emmys nominations were Outstanding Supporting Actor in a Limited Series (Freeman Jr. and WINFIELD) and Outstanding Supporting Actress in a Limited Series (DEE).

Rosa Parks Story, The* (2002)** CBS-TV, color, 100 minutes. **Director:** Julie Dash; ***Teleplay: Paris Qualles; **Cast:** Angela Bassett (Rosa McCauley Parks), Peter Francis James (Raymond Parks), Tonea Stewart (Johnnie Carr), Van Coulter (E. D. Nixon), Dexter Scott King (Dr. Martin Luther King Jr.), Cicely Tyson (Leona McCauley), Charde' Manzy (young Rosa).

On December 1, 1955, African-American Rosa Parks (1913–   ), an activist with the National Association for the Advancement of Colored People (NAACP), refused to relinquish her bus seat to a white man in Montgomery, Alabama. Parks's arrest precipitated the resultant local bus boycott and NAACP protest, and the repercussions thereafter helped to advance racial equality and integration in the United States.

ANGELA BASSETT, who had lent fire and authenticity to her portrayal of Tina Turner in *WHAT'S LOVE GOT TO DO WITH IT* (1993) performed her pivotal role in this small-screen biography of the civil rights icon with quiet authority, as did CICELY TYSON in her small role as Rosa's mother. *Daily Variety* (February 22, 2002) described this docudrama as "a tasteful and stylish biopic as much about love and inspiration as it [is] about the birth of the Civil Rights Movement. . . . [It] should be considered required viewing." On the other hand, the *New York Times* (February 22, 2002), while praising the telefeature's ambitions and its cast, concluded "There's very little that's insightful or surprising in the film." The *Hollywood Reporter* (February 22, 2002) pointed out, "Bassett invests great emotion in the part but, ultimately, is limited by a script that tightly confines her character, revealing human frailties only to the extent that they heighten her heroism."

***Rosewood* (1997)** Warner Bros., color, 141 minutes. **Director:** John Singleton; **Screenplay:** Gregory Poirier; **Cast:** Jon Voight (John Wright), Ving Rhames (Mann), Don Cheadle (Sylvester Carrier), Bruce McGill (Duke), Loren Dean (James Taylor), Esther Rolle (Sarah Carrier), Elise Neal (Scrappie), Michael Rooker (Sheriff Walker).

This film recreated the tragic event in 1923 Florida where the white citizens of a neighboring town destroyed the black community of Rosewood, massacring many of its citizens. The rednecks in this narrative, directed with understandable passion by SINGLETON, emerged as despicable racists, especially in contrast to the super people of Rosewood, the African-American community. Added into the mix was the fictitious character of Mann, a black stranger who rides into Rosewood before the trouble brews. Later, he became the rallying force, along with white shopkeeper John Wright, against the sinister bigots. In this lengthy feature, there is a last-minute train rescue of the victims which, while exciting, strained credulity.

The mysterious Mann comes to Rosewood where he is helpful to the Carrier household (mother Sarah, her married son, Sylvester, and her teenaged daughter Scrappie). A contentious situation arises between Mann and white shopkeeper John Wright when both bid on a piece of local property, but they grow to respect one another. Later, in the nearby town of Sumner, a woman hides her adultery by insisting she was attacked by a black man, assumed to be an escaped convict. The law enforcer and the husband (Dean) of the supposed victim lead an unruly mob to Rosewood where they lynch and shoot people and burn many houses. The surviving townsfolk are saved by the nick-of-time train ride. Thereafter, the mysterious Mann rides off accompanied by the thought-dead Sylvester.

Made on a budget of $31 million, *Rosewood* grossed only slightly more than $13 million in domestic distribution.

***Round Midnight* (1986)** Warner Bros., color, 133 minutes. **Director:** Bertrand Tavernier; **Screenplay:** Tavernier and David Rayfiel; **Cast:** Dexter Gordon (Dale Turner), François Cluzet (Francis Borier), Gabrielle Haker (Berangere), Sandra Reaves-Phillips (Buttercup), Lonette McKee

(Darcey Light), Herbie Hancock (Eddie Wayne), Bobby Hutcherson (Ace), Martin Scorsese (Goodley)

The superlative *Round Midnight*, a French-U.S. coproduction, was obviously superior to earlier Hollywood films on expatriate black jazzmen. Using an actual jazz musician, Gordon, French director Tavernier creates a captivating, sad account of African-American talent Dale Turner (an amalgam of the lives of Lester Young and Bud Powell), a disillusioned, haunted tenor saxophonist. He leaves New York in 1959 and relocates to Paris, a jazz center and a sophisticated city where racial bigotry is not an issue as in America. Ill, alcoholic, and perhaps a past drug addict, Gordon works at the Blue Note jazz club, watched over by Buttercup. He comes into contact with young Frenchman Francis Borier, a commercial artist without much funds. Borier, a devotee of jazz music, is a single parent with a daughter and is a devotee of jazz music. He idolizes Turner, and they soon become friends, eventually sharing an apartment. For a time, Turner fares better and returns to New York to perform there, see his family and friends, and live music. A few weeks later, he dies.

Filled with recorded live jazz music by greats such as Hancock, this special movie explicates the ethnic minority who are forced to leave their homeland but are forever homesick. *Round Midnight* received an Academy Award for Best Original Music Score, and Gordon was Oscar nominated in the Best Actor category. The film grossed more than $3 million in domestic distribution.

Roundtree, Richard (1942–) In spite of appearing in dozens of feature films after gaining movie fame, Roundtree remained indelibly identified with his memorable screen role of sharp-dressing ladies' man John Shaft, the rugged Manhattan private eye of *SHAFT* (1971) and its two sequels. For many, Roundtree, FRED WILLIAMSON, and JIM BROWN were *the* icons of the BLACK ACTION FILM marathon of 1970s Hollywood.

He was born in New Rochelle, New York, and later attended Southern Illinois University on a football scholarship. But six-feet, two-inch, clean-cut Roundtree soon developed an interest in acting and dropped sports and college. He worked for a time as a janitor and then toured as a model with the Ebony Fashion Fair. In 1967 he enrolled in a workshop program at the Negro Ensemble Company. He had a bit in the candid camera big-screen excursion *What Do You Say to a Naked Lady?* (1970). Next, Richard won the lead in *Shaft*. (At one point, MGM demanded that Roundtree shave his mustache for the part, a command he refused, insisting that it was part of his identity as a black man.) While making the movie, the newcomer honed his craft from director GORDON PARKS SR. The movie was a surprising big hit, resulting in Roundtree starring in two sequels and a TV series (1973–74). (In typical discriminatory fashion, the studio paid Richard pittance for the two follow-up entries, assuming that as a black man he should be grateful for whatever modest salary he received.) Following his *Shaft* period, Richard was in such major movies as *Earthquake* (1974) and *Diamonds* (1975). In the ROOTS (1977) TV miniseries, he played Sam Bennett.

Thereafter as the blaxploitation movie craze died down in the later 1970s so did Roundtree's acting career. He had small parts in big pictures (e.g., *City Heat*, 1984) and larger parts in junk entries (e.g., *The Big Score*, 1983). Richard was in the TV detective series *Outlaws* (1986–87) and settled into a routine of making three to four small-budgeted action pictures a year. He was on the daytime TV soap opera *Generations* from 1989 to 1991. Later TV series included *413 Hope Street* (1997–98) and *Rescue* 77 (1999). When SHAFT (2000) was remade with SAMUEL L. JACKSON as the star, Roundtree was on hand to play Uncle John Shaft. In the popular cable series *Soul Food* (2000–), the actor played the senior citizen Mr. Lester for several episodes.

***Rush Hour* (1998)** New Line, color, 94 minutes. **Director:** Brett Ratner; **Screenplay:** Ross LaManna and Jim Kouf; **Cast:** Jackie Chan (Det. Insp. Le), Chris Tucker (Det. James Carter), Tom Wilkinson (Griffin/Juntao), Elizabeth Peña (Johnson), Tzi Ma (Consul Han).

By the late 1990s, Hollywood gave a new twist to the pairing of different ethnic minority coleads by teaming African Americans with Asian Americans. One such profitable example was *Rush Hour*, made on a $35 million budget and grossing more than $141 million in domestic distribution. It smartly united motor-mouth comedian Tucker with agile, congenial, but often taciturn Hong Kong martial arts star Chan in a buddy-cop movie.

Consul Han orders Hong Kong Detective Inspector Lee to Los Angeles to retrieve the diplomat's kidnapped daughter. The FBI have the Los Angeles Police Department assign a liaison to keep this foreigner out of their way. Carter is annoyed to be stuck with the foreigner, and he embarks on solving the case himself while keeping his charge preoccupied. However, it is astute Lee, bolstered by his amazing martial art skills, who uncovers that British businessman Griffin is at the crux of the case. Working with the now friendly Carter, Lee and his American "partner," along with LAPD Officer Johnson, resolve the caper satisfactorily.

Rush Hour won an MTV Award for Best On-Screen Duo (Chan and Tucker). It led to a sequel, *Rush Hour 2* (2001), with Chan and Tucker reprising their roles. Set in Hong Kong, the picture grossed $226 million in domestic distribution.

S

***St. Elsewhere* (1982–1988)** NBC-TV series, color, 60 minutes. **Cast:** Ed Flanders (Dr. Donald Westphall), Norman Lloyd (Dr. Daniel Auschlander), William Daniels (Dr. Mark Craig), Ed Begley Jr. (Dr. Victor Ehrlich), David Morse (Dr. Jack Morrison), Howie Mandel (Dr. Wayne Fiscus), Christina Pickles (Nurse Helen Rosenthal), Cynthia Sikes (Dr. Annie Caverno: 1982–85), Denzel Washington (Dr. Phillip Chandler), Kim Miyori (Dr. Wendy Armstrong: 1982–84), Eric Laneuville (Orderly Luther Hawkins), Byron Stewart (Orderly Warren Coolidge: 1984–88).

As a bridge between earlier TV medical shows such as *Medic* (1954–56), *Dr. Kildare* (1961–66), *Ben Casey* (1961–66), and the much later *Chicago Hope* (1994–2000) and *ER* (1994–) was *St. Elsewhere.* Unlike the earlier doctor dramas cited, *St. Elsewhere* was far grittier, faster paced, and much more: It also had a few cast regulars who were black.

In this acclaimed series, which sought after realism and not idealistic self-sacrificing medicos who saved every patient, the setting is St. Eligius Hospital in Boston. It is a seedy establishment but with a top-notch staff full of ethnic types. Among the residents is Dr. Phillip Chandler, an African American. To give his character dimension, WASHINGTON—still formulating his on-camera persona and technique—played it straight. His Chandler is sincere, cynical, and hard working. Interestingly, compared to the other residents and doctors featured on the series, little is revealed about Phillip's past or his current life outside the hospital. When he is depicted pursuing a woman for possible romance, conventions of the time demanded that she must be black. Mostly, Washington's Dr. Chandler supplied a dose of clean-cut, handsome masculinity in the drama.

Much more ethnic and far less conventional on the show is orderly Luther Hawkins. He is a manipulator who is out to play the angles, but he is the first to sacrifice his time and energy to help an underdog. Unabashedly self-confident about himself, he has no qualms about speaking back to his superiors (e.g., the officious, bigoted Dr. Craig). In later seasons, he had an on-site confederate in orderly Warren Coolidge, a hulking African American who relied on his short black cohort, Luther, to make their decisions. Just the physical disparity between the two created humor, but their activities together lapsed into stereotypical ethnic comedy, in which they were often in situations over their heads. Above all, they were subordinated to the white main characters.

***St. Louis Blues* (1958)** Paramount, b&w, 93 minutes. **Director:** Allen Reisner; **Screenplay:** Robert Smith and Ted Sherdeman; **Cast:** Nat "King" Cole (W. C. Handy), Eartha Kitt (Gogo Germaine), Pearl Bailey (Aunt Hagar), Cab Calloway (Blade), Ella Fitzgerald (herself), Mahalia Jackson (Bessie May), Ruby Dee (Elizabeth), Juano Hernandez (Charles Handy), Billy Preston (W.C. Handy—as a boy).

In the year that W. C. Handy (1873–1958), the well-known composer of blues tunes, died, this low-budget musical biography of the African-American talent was released. In simplistic, saccharine terms, it traced the life of the artist whose minister father (HERNANDEZ) disapproved of his son's wicked music. Later, W. C. must choose between wholesome Elizabeth back home and the city-smart Gogo Germaine, as well as coping with the loss and regaining of his sight. Stuck in a B movie plot, Cole was ineffectual. The other ethnic stars were mostly wasted in this pedestrian effort.

Sandwiched in between the high caliber *CARMEN JONES* (1954) and *PORGY AND BESS* (1959), *St. Louis Blues* suggested that Hollywood was embarking on a new cycle of minority musicals, but such was not to be the case.

***Sanford and Son* (1972–1977)** NBC-TV series, color, 30 minutes. **Cast:** Redd Foxx (Fred G. Sanford), Demond Wilson (Lamont Sanford), Slappy White (Melvin: 1972), Don Bexley (Bubba Hoover), Hal Williams (Officer Smith: 1972–76), Beah Richards (Aunt Ethel: 1972), La Wanda Page (Aunt Esther Anderson: 1973–77), Whitman Mayo (Grady Wilson: 1973–77).

Unheralded at the time, *Sanford and Son*, full of crude humor and curmudgeonly characters bursting with invectives, did much to change the face of TV. It set the stage for such upcoming African-American-themed TV sitcoms as *GOOD TIMES* (1974–79), *THE JEFFERSONS* (1975–85), and *WHAT'S HAPPENING!!* (1976–79). The program was based on the successful British TV comedy series, *Steptoe and Son*.

At the heart of *Sanford and Son* was rascally Fred Sanford—a role that stand-up comic FOXX was born to play and a part that was tailored to his well-honed talents—a self-indulgent, childish old man running a junkyard. Sixty-five-year-old Fred controls his grown bachelor son Demond, has his buddies (White, Bexley, and Wilson), and constantly squabbles with domineering Aunt Esther, his late wife's sister, who operates the Sanford Arms rooming house adjacent to the junkyard. Sanford's character is typified by a wide array of peculiarities, such as parading around all hours of the day unshaven and still in his bathrobe, adding trinkets to the mess inside his rundown home and in the yard, and doing his fake heart attack routine (to gain sympathy), calling to his late wife Elizabeth that he is coming to join her.

Life at 9114 South Central in Los Angeles was never dull, and the show drew a huge following, both black and white home viewers. Unlike other black-oriented TV fare it didn't try to present or resolve racial issues, but at the same time it showcased all aspects of the scalawag Fred Sanford.

When both FOXX and Wilson left the series at the end of the 1976–77 season, the show continued without them, retitled *The Sanford Arms*, but this spin-off with most of the same supporting cast lasted only a month in the fall of 1977. In March 1980, FOXX returned as the cantankerous Los Angeles junk dealer in *Sanford*, joined by two associates (played by Dennis Burkley and Nathaniel Taylor), pals of Sanford's son Lamont, the latter away working in Alaska on the pipeline. It was on and off the air three different times before fading for good in July 1981.

FOXX won a Golden Globe Award for his work on *Sanford and Son* for the 1972–73 season in the category Best TV Actor—Musical/Comedy.

***Scar of Shame, The* (1927)** Colored Players Film Corp., b&w, 8,023′. **Director:** Frank Peregini; **Screenplay:** David Starkman; **Cast:** Harry Henderson (Alvin), Lucia Lynn Moses (Louise), Ann Kennedy (the landlady), Norman Johnstone (Louise's father), William E. Pettus (Spike), Pearl MacCormick (Ann Hathaway), Lawrence Chenault (Mr. Hathaway).

In the convoluted plot line for this melodramatic silent photoplay, Alvin, a serious music student of classical music, weds Louise, the daughter of a lower-class, abusive drunk (Johnstone). The union is doomed to failure because the snobbish man is ashamed of his wife's background. Thus, it is not difficult for Spike, a crony of Louise's father, to break up Louise's marriage and make her his companion. Thereafter, Alvin is sent to jail for accidentally wounding Louise in a skirmish with Spike. Alvin soon escapes and starts a new life as a piano teacher. Later, he reencounters Louise who asks that they reconcile. When he refuses, she kills herself. As for Alvin, he pursues a romance with one of his students (MacCormick).

Produced in Philadelphia, *The Scar of Shame* was directed and written by white talent. Nevertheless, it presented its ethnic minority characters with relative objectivity and a degree of sensitivity, making it a rarity for its era.

***School Daze* (1988)** Columbia, color, 120 minutes. **Director/Screenplay:** Spike Lee; **Cast:** Larry [Laurence] Fishburne (Vaughn "Dap" Dunlap), Giancarlo Esposito (Julian "Big Brother Almighty" Eaves), Tisha Campbell (Jane Toussaint), Kyme (Rachel Meadows), Joe Seneca (President McPherson), Ossie Davis (Coach Odom), Spike Lee (Half-Pint).

LEE's *SHE'S GOTTA HAVE IT* (1986) and ROBERT TOWNSEND's *HOLLYWOOD SHUFFLE* (1987) helped to instigate a fresh wave of (independent) African-American filmmakers. With high-profile Lee positioned as the movement's forerunner, his next work came under intense scrutiny. It proved to be quite controversial (causing a change of film distributors, a change of site for filming on an Atlanta college campus, etc.). Lee's quasi musical offended some because of its focus on division within the minority race, bored others because of its rehashing of fraternity/sorority antics seen in several prior films, and annoyed some reviewers for its unresolved dramatic theme at the film's finale.

Made on a sizable budget ($6.5 million), the narrative focuses on a weekend at Atlanta's Mission College, a black institution. Militant Vaughn "Dap" Dunlap is mounting a protest against the administration's financial ties to South Africa, and his chief opposition is Julian "Big Brother Almighty" Eaves, leader of the Gamma Phi Gamma fraternity. (The former represents the "Jigaboos," the dark-skinned students who want to better their race; the latter speaks for the "Wannabees," the light-skinned classmates who seek to be upscale, mimicking the white world.) As these two factions collide, other students are caught in the middle, engulfed in humiliating antics.

Filled with a wide range of blossoming ethnic talent, *School Daze* was least successful when it reverted to its "musical" numbers, among them "Straight 'n' Nappy." The film grossed more than $14 million in domestic distribution.

Schultz, Michael (1938–) During the 1970s when Hollywood was churning out slapdash BLACK ACTION FILMS, Schultz directed three of the most affecting black-themed movies, including the highly regarded *COOLEY HIGH* (1975) and *CAR WASH* (1976). Later, quietly and efficiently, he helmed movies, TV series episodes, and so on in a wide variety of genres.

He was born in Milwaukee, Wisconsin, and attended the University of Wisconsin. By 1966 he had debuted as a stage director in Princeton, New Jersey. Thereafter, he joined the Negro Ensemble Company where, in the late 1960s, he directed many of its productions. By 1969, he was directing on Broadway and received a Tony nomination for his work on *Does a Tiger Wear a Necktie?* He helmed a TV adaptation of *To Be Young, Gifted and Black* (1972) featuring RUBY DEE, Al Freeman Jr., and Claudia McNeil. That same year he made his movie debut, directing the drama *Together for Days* (1972), which provided actor SAMUEL L. JACKSON with his feature film debut. Schultz's *Honeybaby, Honeybaby* (1974) was a comic spy thriller starring Diana Sands in her final movie work. During the mid-1970s Michael directed episodes of TV series such as *Baretta* and *The Rockford Files.*

After the touching *Cooley High*, Schultz made *Car Wash*, his first of four projects with RICHARD PRYOR, which also included *Which Way Is Up?* (1977), *Greased Lightning*, and his uncredited work on the comedy *Bustin' Loose* (1981).

On TV, Schultz directed the drama *Benny's Place* (1982) featuring CICELY TYSON and LOUIS GOSSETT JR. and did the telefeature about civil-rights activist Medgar Evers (*For Us, the Living* [1983]). He helmed the slick *THE LAST DRAGON* (1985), which melded a story of two diverse ethnic minorities: African Americans and Asian Americans.

In the 1990s, Michael was directing episodes of such teleseries as *Chicago Hope* and *Promised Land* and then guided segments of such very mainstream TV shows as *The Practice, Ally McBeal*, and *Family Law.* Schultz later directed episodes of the black-themed medical drama *CITY OF ANGELS* (2000) and the ethnically diverse *Boston Public* (2000–).

science fiction—feature films Because science fiction movies were often set in the future, it was felt that moviegoers could more easily adjust to an integrated cast in this genre, even though the mingling of ethnic groups was not occurring in the present days. Thus, this feature-film genre was a recurrent one for mixing casts of different cultural heritages.

Years before the *STAR TREK* TV series (1966–69) introduced a black character (Lieutenant Uhura) on an Earth craft in outer space, the little-seen movie *Five* (1951), a postapocalypse drama, featured a black figure. Directed by Arch Oboler the programmer dealt with a quintet of survivors—including a black bank cashier (played by Charles Lampkin)—who cope with staying alive in the wake of the devastation. A later drama with a similar premise was *The World, The Flesh and the Devil* (1959) starring HARRY BELAFONTE.

In *Beneath the Planet of the Apes* (1970), Don Pedro Colley was among the participants, while Hari Rhodes was aboard *Conquest of the Planet of the Apes* (1972). When *Star Trek: The Motion Picture* (1979) was released, it featured the original cast from aboard the USS *Enterprise*, including Nichelle Nichols as Lt. Nyota Uhura. (She also appeared in the next five feature films based on the series, released in 1982, 1984, 1986, and 1989.) Aboard the spacecraft helping Sigourney Weaver fight the horrendous stowaway in *Alien* (1979) was Yaphet Kotto. For *Alien³* (1986) Charles S. Dutton was involved with Weaver's Ripley as they combat the regenerated outer space beast. Meanwhile, in 1980, BILLY DEE WILLIAMS joined the Star Wars franchise, playing Lando Calrissian in the intergalactic *The Empire Strikes Back* (1980) and *Return of the Jedi* (1983).

The intriguing *Iceman* (1984), a sci-fi fantasy about the discovery of a frozen prehistoric man, had DANNY GLOVER among the cast. For the low-budget genre piece, *THE BROTHER FROM ANOTHER PLANET* (1984), director John Sayles hired Joe Morton to play the outer space visitor who comes to New York City's Harlem. The elaborate but unappreciated *Enemy Mine* (1985) featured a contest between two space enemies—one of them played by LOUIS GOSSETT JR., hidden behind extensive lizard makeup. Michael Winslow was the crew's radar technician on Mel Brooks's irreverent *Spaceballs* (1987).

WESLEY SNIPES was Sylvester Stallone's mortal enemy in 2036 Los Angeles in the fanciful *Demolition Man* (1993). *Cosmic Slop* (1994), a sci-fi movie with three stories (a la *Twilight Zone*), featured Brock Peters in one of its segments. In *Stargate* (1994), an interstellar teleportation device allows for entry onto a planet beyond the ordinary dimensions. Among those involved was the character played by Djimon Hounsou. FOREST WHITAKER participated in *Species* (1995) in which scientists tamper with DNA samples, causing great problems. In the virtual reality/futuristic drama *Strange Days* (1995), ANGELA BASSETT's character has an interracial romance with the huckster, played by Ralph Fiennes.

LeVar Burton interpreted the blind Lt. Geordi La Forge on the TV series *STAR TREK: THE NEXT GENERATION* (1987–94), and WHOOPI GOLDBERG was the lounge hostess Guinan from 1988–93. As such, they both participated in the big-screen entry *Star Trek Generations* (1994) and *Star Trek: Nemesis* (2002); Burton was also among the crew of *Star Trek: First Contact* (1996) and *Star Trek: Insurrection* (1998).

PAUL WINFIELD appeared in the futuristic entry *White Dwarf* (1995) while LAURENCE FISHBURNE was a lead player in the big-budget sci-fi thriller, *Event Horizon* (1997).

WILL SMITH was among those involved in *Independence Day* (1996), while PAM GRIER, JIM BROWN, and PAUL WINFIELD were trapped in the sci-fi comedy, *Mars Attacks* (1996). Blair Underwood joined in for adventure in the "near future" in *Gattaca* (1997); the same year, ANGELA BASSETT was among those in *Contact.* Smith returned to the genre in the highly successful *Men in Black* (1997), which led to *Men in Black 2* (2002). *Blade* (1998) was a futuristic horror film with SNIPES as part man, part vampire, a gore fest that led to *Blade 2* (2002). Samuel L. Jackson was featured in *Star Wars: Episode I—The Phantom Menace* (1999) as Mace Windu, a role he repeated in the next *Star Wars* episode in 2002. Ice Cube was part of the cast of John Carpenter's *Ghosts of Mars* (2001).

Other later genre pieces featuring black characters included *Deep Impact* (1998—MORGAN FREEMAN), *Futuresport* (1998—Snipes), *Battlefield Earth* (2000—Whitaker), *Supernova* (2000—Bassett), *Equilibrium* (2001—TAYE DIGGS), *Planet of the Apes* (2001—Michael Clark Duncan), *Evolution* (2001—Orlando Jones), *The One* (2001—Delroy Lindo), *The Breed* (2001—Bokeem Woodbine), and the animated feature *The Adventures of Pluto Nash* (2002—voice of EDDIE MURPHY).

science fiction series—television Just as the American science fiction movie was a relatively "early" genre to integrate its casts to a degree with black talent, so it was true in the TV medium. The pathfinding show was *STAR TREK* (1966–69), which had Lt. Nyota Uhura aboard the starship USS *Enterprise* to show that in the future—in outer space—racial integration and harmony were possible. A decade later *Battlestar Galactica* (1978–80), a well-mounted genre entry set in the seventh millennium, had Herb Jefferson Jr. as Lt. Boomer for its first season. *The Power of Matthew Star* (1982–83) found LOUIS GOSSETT JR. cast as the guardian of Peter Barton, an alien visiting Earth and disguised as a high school student. *STAR TREK: THE NEXT GENERATION* (1987–94) was set in the twenty-fourth century. This new USS *Enterprise* had both a new captain and a new crew. Among the latter was LeVar Burton as Lt. Geordi La Forge, the blind helmsman who was able to see/navigate thanks to a special visor. Also aboard (for assorted episodes between 1988 and 1993, was WHOOPI GOLDBERG as the humanoid lounge hostess/bartender who had amazing perceptions, as well as Michael Dorn as Lieutenant Worf, the Klingon officer aboard. On *SuperForce* (1990–92) set in the year 2020, Larry B. Scott was F. X. Spinner, a computer whiz helping the ex-astronaut hero (played by Ken Olandt) protect Metroplex against crime.

On the syndicated *Babylon 5* (1992–99), situated aboard a space station in the year 2258, Richard Biggs played Dr. Stephen Franklin, the caring chief doctor. *seaQuest DSV* (1993–95), set some twenty-five years in the future, had a multicultural crew, including Don Franklin as Comdr. Jonathan Ford. *STAR TREK: DEEP SPACE NINE* (1993–99) had an African American (Avery Brooks) as Comdr. Benjamin Sisko of the space station Deep Space Nine that was orbiting around the planet Bajor. Among those at the station with the widower was his teenaged son (played by Cirroc Lofton). The premise of *M.A.N.T.I.S.* (1994–95) found lead player Carl Lumbly as a scientist who had been paralyzed in a shooting ambush and who could function when he wore a special suit that gave him superhuman strength. In *Tattooed Teenage Alien Fighters from Beverly Hills* (1994–95), a distillation of the Mighty Morphin Power Rangers daytime kids show that began in 1993, black performer Rugg Williams was the nerdy kid among the group of youths fighting aliens. For *Earth: Final Conflict* (1994–95), Hari Rhodes was among the cast of regulars on this series, which was set 2,000 years in the future. On *STAR TREK: VOYAGER* (1995–2001), Tim Russ appeared as Security Chief Tuvok, a Vulcan, on the crew, with Kate Mulgrew as Capt. Kathryn Janeway. The next *Star Trek* series, *Enterprise* (2001–), featured African-American Anthony Montgomery as Ensign Travis Mayweather.

Other more-recent genre series featuring black talent included *Sliders* (1995–97; 1999–2000) with Cleavant Derricks, *Seven Days* (1998–99) with Franklin, *Now & Again* (1999) with Dennis Haysbert, and *Jeremiah* (2002) with Malcolm-Jamal Warner. On the fantasy/science fiction drama *The X-Files* (1993–2002) in 1998 James Pickens Jr. joined the cast as FBI Assistant Director Alvin Kersh; in another fantasy genre outing, *G vs. E* (1999), Richard Brooks played a heavenly hitman from the 1970s called to help protect the streets of Hollywood from corrupt forces.

***Sergeant Rutledge* (1960)** Warner Bros., color, 111 minutes. **Director:** John Ford; **Screenplay:** James Warner Bellah; **Cast:** Jeffrey Hunter (Lt. Thomas Cantrell), Constance Towers (Mary Beecher), Billie Burke (Mrs. Cordelia Fosgate), Woody Strode (1st Sgt. Braxton Rutledge), Juano Hernandez (Sgt. Matthew Luke Skidmore), Willis Bouchey (Col. Otis Thornton Fosgate), Mae Marsh (Nellie).

After years of politically incorrect treatment of ethnic minorities in his movies, veteran filmmaker Ford made an about-face in this western. Importantly, it was Hollywood's first mainstream sagebrush tale to revolve around a black character. Resourceful STRODE, still a fledgling actor, played the lead with great dignity. His sterling performance (as well as HERNANDEZ's soulful performance) almost compensated for the movie's stiffness. (Initially, the studio had wanted SIDNEY POITIER or HARRY BELAFONTE—already established at the box office—to play the lead role, but Ford objected that they were not tough enough to portray Rutledge.)

In 1881 at Fort Linton in the Arizona Territory, a major and his teenage daughter are found murdered in their quarters. An African-American officer, 1st Sgt. Braxton Rutledge of the all-black Ninth Cavalry, is accused of the crimes and placed on trial. The presiding judge (Bouchey), as well as his wife (Burke) and others in attendance at the court-martial, are prejudiced against Rutledge because of his race. Even such witnesses as Mary Beecher (who was protected from marauding warrior braves by Rutledge) and Lt. Thomas Cantrell (who claims to be a friend of the accused and who was his commander for six years), although attesting to the defendant's good character and actions, have moments when they question the man's innocence due to subconscious racial bias. Rutledge speaks eloquently in his own defense, and soon thereafter, the real culprit is unmasked.

While *Sergeant Rutledge* itself was claustrophobic, with too much of its focus on the courtroom sequences, the movie, nevertheless, presented a strong, warm portrait of the all-black cavalry, a group termed by their Native American adversaries as "Buffalo Soldiers." Because of its subject matter and the lack of overall excitement to this western picture itself, *Sergeant Rutledge* grossed only a meager $784,000 in domestic distribution.

Jeffrey Hunter, Woody Strode, and Carleton Young in *Sergeant Rutledge* (1960). (JC ARCHIVES)

It would be another decade before such films as the actionful and violent *THE RED, WHITE, AND BLACK* (aka: *Soul Soldiers*) (1970) made black westerns a popular commodity at the box office.

***Set It Off* (1996)** New Line, color, 126 minutes. **Director:** F. Gary Gray; **Screenplay:** Kate Lanier and Takashi Bufford; **Cast:** Jada Pinkett (Stony), Queen Latifah (Cleo), Vivica A. Fox (Frankie Scott), Kimberly Elise (Tisean), John C. McGinley (Detective Strode), Blair Underwood (Keith).

Gray, who directed the rap comedy *Friday* (1995), showcases four African-American lead actresses in a conventional heist yarn. Although some reviewers wished that the female talents could have been utilized for a less-hackneyed format, most sources applauded the cast, especially LATIFAH, for giving the proceedings grit and depth.

Four working-class young women from South Central Los Angeles are at an impasse on improving their lives. They include ex-bank teller Frankie Scott, ex-convict Cleo, single mother Tisean (whose son was taken away by social services), and Stony (whose collegiate brother was killed accidentally by the police). They embark on a series of bank heists, but their loot is confiscated by a third party. They try one more big bank robbery that ends with three of the robbers dying, while the fourth, Stony, flees to Mexico.

Latifah, as the film's hard-drinking lesbian, was nominated at the Independent Spirit Awards as Best Supporting Actress. Made on a $9 million budget, *Set It Off* grossed more than $36 million in domestic distribution.

***Shaft* (1971)** Metro-Goldwyn-Mayer, color, 98 minutes. **Director:** Gordon Parks Sr.; **Screenplay:** John D. F. Black and Ernest Tidyman; **Cast:** Richard Roundtree (John Shaft), Moses Gunn (Bumpy Jonas), Charles Cioffi (Lt. Vic Androzzy), Christopher St. John (Ben Buford), Gwenn Mitchell (Ellie Moore).

This movie burst onto the scene at just the right time. Its mix of slam-bang action, flashy characters, a handsome lead figure full of black pride, and the film's enormously popular Isaac Hayes soundtrack combined to make this picture a big crossover hit with filmgoers. Its tremendous success solidified Hollywood's growing acceptance of and interest in African-American-themed films. It led to the explosion of BLACK ACTION FILMS that was very prominent in the American film industry in the 1970s. Ironically it was directed by PARKS SR. who had previously helmed the thoughtful, low-key *THE LEARNING TREE* (1969).

John Shaft, a tough New York City private investigator, is hired by an uptown underworld figure (Gunn) to find his kidnapped daughter. The trail leads initially to black militant Ben Buford. However, it is actually the downtown Mafia who have the girl, using her as leverage to regain more control of the Harlem rackets. In the bloody showdown, Shaft, aided by Buford and his men, free the girl, killing several Mafia goons in the process.

John Shaft had enormous attraction for many filmgoers: He was a fearless investigator, a snappy dresser, and a great ladies' man who had supercool living quarters. Most of all, he was a self-sufficient African American speaking up not only for himself but also for his race as he challenged and beat the Italian underworld. More than the ground-breaking action characters played on screen in the 1960s by JIM BROWN, ROUNDTREE's Shaft was an impressive soul brother who did not mingle in the white world. He either tolerated it or worked against it and always came out ahead

Made for about $1.5 million, *Shaft* earned more than $7 million in domestic film rentals. "Theme from Shaft" won an Academy Award, while Hayes's soundtrack was Oscar nominated.

This box-office bonanza, besides inspiring a horde of celluloid imitations, led to Roundtree starring in *Shaft's Big Score!* (1972) and *Shaft in Africa* (1973). The actor, in a much-tamer mode, headlined a quite watered-down TV series version of *Shaft* (1973–74) that was unsuccessful. Twenty-nine years later came a new screen adventure of *SHAFT* featuring SAMUEL L. JACKSON.

***Shaft* (2000)** Paramount, color, 99 minutes. **Director:** John Singleton; **Screenplay:** Richard Price, Singleton, and Shane Salerno; **Cast:** Samuel L. Jackson (John Shaft), Vanessa Williams (Carmen Vasquez), Jeffrey Wright (Peoples Hernandez), Christian Bale (Walter Wade Jr.), Busta Rhymes (Rasaan), Dan Hedaya (Jack Russell), Richard Roundtree (Uncle John Shaft), Toni Collette (Diane Palmieri).

Rather than remake the classic 1971 *SHAFT*, this new *Shaft*—which used an updated Isaac Hayes score—established the screen hero in a new posture (as a New York police detective) and gave him a fresh Big Apple adventure. But unlike the original that helped to formulate its own Hollywood genre, the glossy latest entry was no industry trendsetter. It wavered between being a flaccid big action adventure and a moody but clichéd piece about a NYPD law enforcer who feels that his color and his job place him in a no-man's land, accepted by neither his police-force peers nor by his own race.

New York police detective John Shaft turns in his badge but continues to investigate—as a vigilante—the murder of a young African American. The likely suspect, Walter Wade Jr., the scion of a white billionaire, jumps bail and flees to Europe. Meanwhile, a waitress, the one witness to the crime, disappears. Two years later, Wade returns to Manhattan to face the homicide charge. He hires drug lord Peoples Hernandez to find and eliminate the troublesome waitress. Having quit the police force, Shaft still follows through on the case. He eventually kills Hernandez and his thugs in a shootout. Although Wade does stand trial, the vengeful mother of the man he once killed provides the final justice.

Charismatic Jackson was unable to elevate sufficiently this pedestrian big-budgeted feature that director SINGLETON divested of most of its ethnic-root ties to the original *Shaft*. (ROUNDTREE made a brief appearance as the original John Shaft, uncle of the new crime crusader, while GORDON PARKS SR., who had directed the original *Shaft*, had a cameo in the remake as a barroom customer.) Made for $46 million, *Shaft* grossed more than $70 million.

Shakur, Tupac (aka: 2Pac Shakur) (1971–1996) In the late 1980s and thereafter, several rap stars crossed over from the world of music to film acting, including Queen Latifah, WILL SMITH, and Ice Cube. One of the most controversial personalities to transcend both creative worlds was Shakur. Besides his on-the-edge lifestyle, in his relatively short life he brought an intriguing presence to his screen work and demonstrated an impressive flair for acting.

He was born in New York City in 1971. His mother, Afeni Shakur, was a member of the Black Panthers, who had been arrested with others of the group in 1969 for an alleged conspiracy to bomb buildings in the Big Apple. In 1971, the pregnant Afeni was still incarcerated in a Greenwich Village jail. One month after she was acquitted, she gave birth to Shakur.

As a youngster, Tupac and his parent relocated several times within Harlem and the Bronx. Later, the restless teenager found creative release by writing poetry. He made his acting debut in a Harlem theater group in a fundraiser production of *A Raisin in the Sun*. After he and his mother moved to Baltimore, Maryland, he studied dance and acting at the local School for the Arts. It was there that he composed his first rap number. Next, he and Ms. Shakur moved to Marin City, California, where he became further involved in dangerous gang and street life.

By 1990, the musically inclined talent had joined the Bay Area rap ensemble Digital Underground. He toured with them as well as making his recording debut with the group. His first solo album, *2Pacalypse Now* (1991)—filled with violent anti-Establishment lyrics—was followed that same year by his movie debut with Digital Underground in the film *Nothing But Trouble*. However, it was in Ernest Dickerson's *Juice* (1992) that Shakur really displayed his acting mettle.

During the next few years, as Shakur's popularity grew, so did his controversial reputation for assorted bad-boy deeds he was alleged to have committed. Meanwhile, he received upbeat reviews for his appearance in JOHN SINGLETON's *Poetic Justice* (1993), matched on-camera with Janet Jackson, and for his performance in the basketball movie *Above the Rim* (1994). (In this period Shakur got into a dispute with filmmaker Allen Hughes when the latter fired him from 1993's *MENACE II SOCIETY* for being a problem on the set. As a result of that altercation, Shakur spent fifteen days in jail.) With his own music group, Thug Life, Shakur released the album *Thug Life: Volume One* (1994). In late 1994 he was shot and robbed in Manhattan but was well enough later to attend his sentencing hearing for his reputed involvement in the sexual abuse of a woman. He was sentenced to up to four and a half years of prison time. (While in prison, Shakur married a college student.)

Shakur was released after eight months behind bars and soon thereafter was a victim in a drive-by shooting rumble in Las Vegas. After three operations and being in a coma for six days, he died on September 13, 1996. Even after his death his show business career continued with the release of several albums that sold well. His two last films were released posthumously: *Gridlock'd* and *Gang Related* (both 1997). He was the subject of several documentaries that sought to analyze the life of the talented performer: *Tupac Shakur: words never Die* (1997), *Tupac Shakur: Before I Wake* (2001), and *Biggie and Tupac* (2002). Still revered by a large coterie of devout fans, Shakur was a prime and tragic example of rap's "gangsta" era.

Shakur, 2Pac See SHAKUR, TUPAC.

***She Done Him Wrong* (1933)** Paramount, b&w, 66 minutes. **Director:** Lowell Sherman; **Screenplay:** Mae West, Harvey Thewe, and John Bright; **Cast:** Mae West (Lady Lou), Cary Grant (The Hawk [Captain Cummings]), Owen Moore (Chick Clark), Gilbert Roland (Serge Stanieff), Noah Beery Sr. (Gus Jordan), Louise Beavers (Pearl), Rafaela Ottiano (Russian Rita).

It is in *I'm No Angel* (1934) that farceur West tells her African-American maid the classic line, "Beulah, peel me a grape." However, in the earlier *She Done Him Wrong*, based on West's self-penned 1928 Broadway vehicle, West plays Bowery siren Lou and has great rapport with her black domestic, Pearl. The latter is played with zest by BEAVERS.

Although Pearl may work for the cagey siren, she was treated with a relative degree of respect—given the lack of political correctness in the 1930s and taking into account that Lou slammed everyone in her path. Within this comedy set in 1890s New York, the two women have amusing interchanges that are less put-downs of Pearl herself than sly joshings of Hollywood's stereotypes of black servants. For example, when Lou summons Pearl, the helper responds in deliberate clichéd ethnic minority slang of the day: "I'se comin'. I'se comin'," to which wisecracking Lou retorts, "You're comin', your head is bendin' low. Get here before winter." When the plump Pearl finally reaches her impatient mistress, Lou rejoins, "Here you is, here you is. What're you doing' eight ball, workin' for me, or sleepin' for me?" (Since an eight ball in pool is traditionally black, this is Lou's nickname of the moment for her employee, who, like the eight ball in pool, can be troublesome.)

West, who had a great affinity for African Americans on and off camera, presented filmgoers with black characters who did not kowtow to their white bosses but were often trusted confidants of their employer.

***She's Gotta Have It* (1986)** Island, b&w and color, 84 minutes. **Director/Screenplay:** Spike Lee; **Cast:** Tracy Camila Johns (Nola Darling), Tommy Redmond Hicks (Jamie Overstreet), John Canada Terrell (Greer Childs), Spike Lee (Mars Blackmon), Raye Dowell (Opal Gilstrap), Joie Lee (Clorinda Bradford), [S.] Epatha Merkinson (Dr. Jamison), Bill Lee (Sonny Darling).

LEE's debut professional feature positioned him as the bright new hope of (black) independent cinema in the United States. Shot in Brooklyn for less than $200,000 and grossing more than $7 million in domestic distribution, this romantic comedy won Lee the Young Cinema Award at the Cannes Film Festival and the Best First Feature prize at the Independent Spirit Awards.

On the surface, this entry concerns attractive Nola Darling, a graphic designer who has trouble deciding between the three men currently in her life: conventional, dependable Jamie Overstreet; narcissistic, handsome Greer Childs; and nerdy, but amusing Mars Blackmon. In reality, the movie focuses on how much each of the trio wants to bed Nola and how they as males view this female.

In contrast to Lee's later movies, this entry did not define particular ethnic history, causes, or stances. On the other hand, it was a rare minority-populated mainstream feature that allowed its black cast to develop their characters fully in a romantic-comedy setting (in contrast to the BLACK ACTION FILMS of the 1970s or such highly dramatic message films as 1961's *A RAISIN IN THE SUN*). It did not present Nola as a "ho," but rather as a self-sufficient bachelor gal who wanted her share of fun just like a playboy would (especially in onscreen offerings).

Although Lee still had a lot of polishing to learn as a filmmaker, he acquitted himself well as an actor. He also used his sister (Joie) and his father (Bill) as subordinate screen characters.

***Show Boat* (1936)** Universal, b&w, 115 minutes. **Director:** James Whale; **Screenplay:** Oscar Hammerstein II; **Cast:** Irene Dunne (Magnolia), Allan Jones (Gaylord Ravenal), Charles Winninger (Cap'n Andy Hawks), Paul Robeson

(Joe), Helen Morgan (Julie LaVerne), Helen Westley (Parthy Hawks), Hattie McDaniel (Queenie).

Edna Ferber's popular novel *Show Boat* (1926) was adapted for the Broadway stage in 1927 with music by Jerome Kern and lyrics by Oscar Hammerstein II. Its lyrical tale of marital strife and miscegenation on a Mississippi river boat—including the character of the mulatto Julie LaVerne—became a big hit and was often revived. The racially mixed Julie, the penultimate unhappy woman seen in so many media presentations, furthered the clichéd image of mulattos as being despondent, restless creatures. (This was much the same as stereotypical associations tied to half-breeds—i.e., those of part Native American heritage.)

In 1929 there was an unspectacular part-talkie Hollywood screen version of *Show Boat* that boasted a special sound prologue with members of the original Broadway cast, including Helen Morgan (as Julie), recreating their most popular song numbers. In the largely silent movie, the black servants were played by STEPIN FETCHIT (Joe) and Gertrude Howard (Queenie).

Seven years later, the same studio, Universal, remade the property, this time adhering more closely to the stage musical. Among the key ethnic minority characters for this *Show Boat* were Morgan (again as Julie), ROBESON as dock-worker Joe, and McDANIEL as Queenie, his sassy servant wife. Although there was controversy over casting a white performer (Morgan) to portray Julie, her experience in the role on Broadway and in the earlier film counterbalanced the criticism, and she performed well the classic numbers "Can't Help Loving Dat Man of Mine" and "Why Was I Born." Her interpretation of the unhappy, mix-blood woman was a strong interpretation of the role, just as Robeson's deep-voiced singing of "Ol' Man River" lent great dignity to that number (despite the hackneyed screen montage superimposed over his image on the screen).

In MGM's fictitious biography (1946's *Till the Clouds Roll By*) of composer Jerome Kern, there was a staged excerpt from *Show Boat.* With LENA HORNE playing the tragic Julie, this was the first time on the American screen that an African American performed the mulatto role. She effectively sang "Can't Help Lovin' Dat Man of Mine." In addition, Caleb Peterson (as Joe) did a strong version of "Ol' Man River."

By the time of the 1951 MGM remake of *Show Boat*, the stereotypical comic antics of Queenie (Frances Williams) and Joe (William Warfield) were greatly downplayed. However, the role of Julie, which Horne long wanted to perform in a full screen version, was instead given to Caucasian actress Ava Gardner.

***Silver Streak* (1976)** Twentieth Century-Fox, color, 113 minutes **Director:** Arthur Hiller; **Screenplay:** Colin Higgins; **Cast:** Gene Wilder (George Caldwell), Jill Clayburgh (Hilly Burns), Richard Pryor (Grover Muldoon), Patrick McGoohan (Roger Devereau), Ned Beatty (Sweet [FBI Agent Stevens]).

In this wacky tribute to Alfred Hitchcock movies, Wilder and PRYOR teamed for the first time and turned this romantic comedy/murder mystery into a big hit, grossing more than $30 million in domestic distribution. The slapstick highlight has Wilder being taught how to "act" black so that the duo can escape detection from the villains and police. With talented Pryor at the helm and wide-eyed Wilder as his nervous student, the sequence was hilarious, but some viewers found the scene demeaning to African Americans.

Riding the luxury train *Silver Streak* from Los Angeles to Chicago, meek book editor George Caldwell meets Hilly Burns, the attractive private secretary to an elusive art historian. Later, George sees her boss pushed from the fast-moving train, but no one believes him. The killers, Roger Devereau and his helpers, are now out to eliminate Caldwell. En route, George unwillingly leaves the train and finds himself paired with car thief Grover Muldoon. Between the two, they not only protect Hilly but also outwit Devereau and survive the impact when the luxury train smashes into the Chicago railroad terminal.

The interracial comedic team of Wilder and Pryor made three additional features together, including *STIR CRAZY* (1980).

Simpson, O. J. (1947–) Before the 1994 homicide of his ex-wife Nicole Brown Simpson and her friend Ronald Goldman—and the highly controversial criminal and civil trials thereafter—Simpson had been known as the ex-gridiron star who had acted in movies and on TV for more than two decades. Similar to other black athletes (e.g., WOODY STRODE, JIM BROWN, and FRED WILLIAMSON), clean-cut, six-feet, two-inch Simpson had used his fame in the sports world—where black stars were accepted before Hollywood—to prolong his celebrity status by becoming an actor. If not in the ranks of a DENZEL WASHINGTON, Simpson had a pleasant public persona that translated well on camera.

Born Orenthal James Simpson in San Francisco, as a youngster he hung out with the street "gang," the Persian Kings. At the University of Southern California, he excelled in football and track. After graduating in 1969, "Juice" (or O. J.) as he was known, signed on with the Buffalo Bills professional football team. He left them in 1977 and spent his two final gridiron seasons with the San Francisco 49ers.

Simpson began his acting life with small roles (between 1968 and 1973) on episodes of such TV series as *Dragnet 1967*, *Medical Center*, and *Here's Lucy.* His big-screen debut came with the blockbuster film *The Towering Inferno* (1974), in which he was the chief security guard. Too mainstream to get down-and-dirty, he remained on the fringes of the BLACK ACTION FILM cycle, appearing instead in such establishment pictures as *The Klansman* (1974), *The Cassandra Crossing* (1976), *A KILLING AFFAIR* (1977—TV movie), and *Firepower* (1979). On the TV miniseries *ROOTS* (1977), he was Kadi Touray. His popular telefeature *GOLDIE AND THE BOXER* (1979) led to a sequel two years later.

Simpson had been a sports announcer since 1969 on the major TV networks. His telefeature *Cocaine and Blue Eyes* (1983) was a pilot for an unsold detective series. From 1985 through 1991, he played T. D. Parker on the HBO cable TV series *1st & Ten* about a fictional (the California Bulls) football squad. As Los Angeles police detective Nordberg in the genre spoof *The Naked Gun: From the Files of Police Squad!* (1988) and in its two sequels (1991 and 1994), the actor won a Razzie Award as Worst Supporting Actor for the third entry, *Naked Gun 33 1/3: The Final Insult* (1994).

Since the fateful 1994 turning point in his life, Simpson's TV appearances have largely been media coverage of his still-controversial private life and past. However, others have played him in TV dramatic fare: Bobby Hossea (*The O. J. Simpson Story*, 1995—TV movie), Raymond Forchion and the voice of Rodney Saulsberry (*American Tragedy*, 2000—TV movie), and Chad Coleman (*Monday Night Mayhem*, 2002—TV movie).

Sinbad (1956–) Some personalities are such constant performers in the entertainment field for so many years that they are taken for granted. Such is the case with Sinbad who, since 1984, has been perfecting his craft as stand-up comic and/or actor in comedy clubs, on TV, in films, and on the comedy concert circuit. Less raucous than other black comedians such as Chris Tucker, MARTIN LAWRENCE, and CHRIS ROCK, Sinbad was more of a new-generation BILL COSBY but with vinegar in his comedic mix.

He was born David Adkins in Benton Harbor, Michigan. He attended the University of Denver and later was in the U.S. Air Force, where his behavior (playacting at being officers and organizing his own days) led to a tug-of-war between the military and the enlistee. (While in the service, he toured with the air force's Tops in Blue program that showcased talent from the military at bases around the world.) Although the six-feet, five-inch Adkins had once dreamed of being a pro basketball player, his quirky sense of humor and joy in making others laugh won out as a career choice after he returned to civilian life.

With a professional name of Sinbad, he plied the comedy-club circuit and in the mid-1980s was a finalist on Ed McMahon's *Star Search* TV talent contest. On the brief-enduring sitcom *The Redd Foxx Show* (1986), Sinbad was among the cast of regulars. He was also part of the 1987 TV variety program *Keep on Cruisin'*. Thereafter he joined *A Different World*, where from 1987 to 1991 he played Coach Walter Oakes at Hillman College, a largely black institution. For the 1993–94 TV season, he was headlined in his own TV sitcom that dealt with several generations of an African-American extended family.

Sinbad had already been in feature films (e.g., *That's Adequate*, 1989; *Coneheads*, 1993; *The Meteor Man*, 1993), but it wasn't until 1995's *Houseguest* that he had the lead role. He proved likable as a man who went undercover to avoid troublesome money collectors. He served as executive producer and top-billed performer in *First Kid* and *The Cherokee Kid* (both 1996), the latter a comedic western made-for-TV movie. He was one of those supporting Arnold Schwarzenegger in *Jingle All the Way* (1996), for which Sinbad won the Blockbuster Entertainment Award as Favorite Supporting Actor—Family Film. From 1997 to 1998, he hosted the syndicated talk/music late-night program *Vibe*. In the family-themed telefeature *Ready to Run* (2000), the comedian provided an off-camera voice. For *Crazy as Hell* (2002) Sinbad was one of the ensemble in the drama starring and directed by Eriq La Salle.

Singleton, John (1968–) He was part of the cinema's new wave of African-American filmmakers in the 1990s. Singleton gained immediate attention in his directorial debut with *BOYZ N THE HOOD* (1991) for which he received two Oscar nominations: Best Director and Best Original Screenplay. His struggle for success in a formerly all-white filmmaking community was eased by such past trailblazers as OSCAR MICHEAUX, GORDON PARKS SR., MELVIN VAN PEEBLES, MICHAEL SCHULTZ, and, later, SPIKE LEE.

He was born in Los Angeles to unwed teenage parents. (His father later became a mortgage broker, and his mother became a sales executive for a pharmaceutical company.) John spent his first five years with his mother living in working-class suburbs of greater Los Angeles; thereafter, he commuted back and forth between his parents. When he was twelve he moved in with his father. Already determined to become a filmmaker one day, Singleton entered the University of South California on a scholarship from the Black Alumni Association. His writing skills led to his winning writing awards and earning representation from a major talent agency (while he was still a sophomore). One off-campus job was working as a production assistant on TV's *Pee-wee's Playhouse*. There Singleton became friendly with struggling actor LAURENCE FISHBURNE who was a regular on the children's show.

A month after graduation from USC's film school in 1990, John had a pact with Columbia Pictures to direct his script of *Boyz N the Hood* (1991). This coming-of-age tale set in violence-ridden South Central Los Angeles made a big impression on critics and filmgoers alike. Thereafter he directed music videos and helmed *Poetic Justice* (1993), costarring the music world's Janet Jackson and TUPAC SHAKUR. That film was regarded as pretentious and slow moving, and it was two years before his next picture emerged. In that entry, *Higher Learning*, set on a college campus where racial unrest was brewing, Fishburne was cast as a faculty member. The end product was gritty but often diverged from its themes of racism, self-identity, and idealism. Two years later came *ROSEWOOD*, but this time Singleton dealt with the well-established African-American community in Florida that was destroyed by whites in 1923.

Keeping to ethnic topics, Singleton directed a remake (2000) of the classic *SHAFT* (1971). With SAMUEL L. JACKSON as the cool private eye, the new edition was more graphically violent but did not have the punch of the original. *BABY BOY* (2001), the third of John's screen trilogy of the 'hood, concerned young black men in the community who refused to grow up. Again the filmmaker, who also wrote, directed, and produced this often preachy vehicle, was criticized by several commentators for the picture's dramatic contrivances. The movie, which featured Tyrese, had been written some years back for Tupac Shakur.

***Sister Act* (1992)** Touchstone, color, 96 minutes. **Director:** Emile Ardolino; **Screenplay:** Joseph Howard; **Cast:** Whoopi Goldberg (Deloris Van Cartier), Maggie Smith (Mother Superior), Kathy Najimy (Mary Patrick), Wendy Makkena (Mary Robert), Mary Wickes (Mary Lazarus), Harvey Keitel (Vince LaRocca).

When singer/comedian Bette Midler rejected the lead part here, Goldberg took over the role in this smash comedy hit that grossed more than $139 million in domestic distribution. Veering toward slapstick comedy and bypassing plot logic and real characterization, it was, nevertheless, Goldberg's most successful movie assignment since *THE COLOR PURPLE* (1985). But in this farce, Whoopi's character operated in her own world (as in 1986's *JUMPIN' JACK FLASH*). She had no romantic scenes because Hollywood still was unsure how to present this unconventional-looking African American to filmgoers. At least in *Sister Act*, the plot provided reasons for her "isolation" and for her acting/reacting to the other characters, rather than with them.

When Deloris, a lounge singer in Reno, Nevada, accidentally witnesses her gangland thug lover (Keitel) murder a stool pigeon, she goes undercover at a San Francisco convent. The only one to know that "Sister" Deloris is not a nun is the Mother Superior. To occupy her time, Deloris takes over the convent choir and turns it into a hip rockin' group who sing pop favorites (such as "My Guy") altered into religious numbers. This draws crowds to the once ignored services and allows Deloris and the sisters to provide better help to the depressed neighborhood. The convent's sudden popularity, however, leads her former gangland associates to attempt again to terminate Deloris.

This movie's popularity led to *Sister Act II: Back in the Habit* (1993) also starring Goldberg.

situation comedy series—television In the early 1950s, at a time when Hollywood was not producing big-screen comedies with black themes (let alone using black talent in any significant way on camera), the emerging commercial TV industry had an occasional ethnic show—always comedies in the early years. *BEULAH* (1950–53) was a transfer of a radio hit about a folksy black domestic who works for a white family. In the same year, radio's *AMOS 'N' ANDY* (1951–53) moved into the new medium, using a full black cast (in contrast to the radio production that featured white lead actors) and quickly won condemnation from increasingly powerful black-action groups who were angered by its exaggerated stereotypes. Some early 1950s sitcom series reverted to the 1930s/1940s practice of having on-camera black domestics to provide sass and/or subservient deference to the white characters. This was a facet of such shows as *THE STU ERWIN SHOW* (aka: *The Trouble with Father*) (1950–55), *My Little Margie* (1952–55), *The Danny Thomas Show* (aka: *Make Room for Daddy*) (1953–71), and *Father of the Bride* (1961–62).

A breakthrough on American TV occurred with DIAHANN CARROLL's *JULIA* (1968–71), the first sitcom since *Beulah* to have its lead character be black. Soon BILL COSBY was starring in *The Bill Cosby Show* (1969–71), and in 1970–71 came *BAREFOOT IN THE PARK*, an all-black version of a previous white-cast play/movie. Playing off the current success of the blaxploitation film cycle in which the action swirled around black characters living in ethnic neighborhoods, the 1970s saw the birth of *SANFORD & SON* (1972–77) with REDD FOXX, *GOOD TIMES* (1974–79) with ESTHER ROLLE and Jimmie Walker, and *WHAT'S HAPPENING!!* (1976–79). On the other hand, *THE JEFFERSONS* (1975–85) was set on Manhattan's upper East Side and had a mix of black and white characters. Also in that mode was *Diff'rent Strokes* (1978–86), which utilized the premise of two black youths living in an upscale New York City neighborhood.

In *BENSON* (1979–86), a spin-off of *Soap* (1977–81), Robert Guillaume was the proper black butler who went to work for a white governor and later moved into the political arena himself. Funnyman Cosby returned with *The Cosby Show* (1984–92), a black-themed vehicle that took a different tack: It showed an upscale African-American household in New York City in which the husband was a physician, and the wife (played by Phylicia Rashad) was an attorney; as such it appealed to a greater crossover audience.

In contrast, *GIMME A BREAK* (1981–86) was from the old school of Hollywood comedy, which had a black domestic (played by Nell Carter) sacrificing her time, energy, and love for a Caucasian household. *Square Pegs* (1982–83) featured a multicultural mix of students at Weemowee High School. Similarly "old-fashioned" was *227* (1985–90), which spotlighted the tenants of an apartment house in a black section of Washington, D.C., and rarely showed any white people in the episodes. By the end of the 1980s, there were two main types of sitcoms involving blacks. Some (e.g., *Designing Women*, 1986–93; *She's the Sheriff*, 1987–89; *Living Dolls*, 1989) had merely token ethnic representation with rarely more than one black performer in the cast of regulars. Others, such as *Different World* (1987–93), a spin-off from *The Cosby Show*, showcased an almost all black cast.

By the early 1990s some of the independent American TV networks were featuring a heavy line-up of black-cast comedies, most of which were geared to undemanding viewers: *Hangin' with Mr. Cooper* (1992–97), *Martin* (1992–97), *The Sinbad Show* (1993–94), *Living Single* (1993–98), *Sister, Sister* (1994–99). This pattern continued throughout the rest of the decade with the likes of *The Parent' Hood* (1995–99), *The Wayans Bros.* (1995–99), *The Jamie Foxx Show* (1996–2001), *The Steve Harvey Show* (1996–2002), *Malcolm & Eddie* (1996–2000), *The Hughleys* (1998–2002), *My Wife and Kids* (2001–) and *Bernie Mac* (2001–). In comparison, the major TV networks opted for sitcoms that featured a predominantly white cast, but with the few black players included on such projects now given more importance in the proceedings: *Spin City* (1996–2002), *Smart Guy* (1997–99),

Veronica's Closet (1997–2000), *Sports Night* (1998–2000), *Becker* (1999–), *King of Queens* (1999–), *DAG* (2000–2001), *Scrubs* (2001–), and *Leap of Faith* (2002).

***Slaughter* (1972)** American International, color, 92 minutes. **Director:** Jack Starrett; **Screenplay:** Mark Hanna and Don Williams; **Cast:** Jim Brown (Slaughter), Stella Stevens (Ann Cooper), Rip Torn (Dominick Hoffo), Don Gordon (Harry Bastoli), Cameron Mitchell (Insp. A. W. Price).

With the huge success of *SHAFT* (1971), Hollywood turned out a rash of black action movies filled with mindless mayhem and illogical plots. While rising action star FRED WILLIAMSON was starring in such violent entries as *HAMMER* (1972), BROWN stalked through sadistic fare like *Slaughter*. It was a comeback for the star who had made a success in the 1960s playing the "good black man." Now he was following the suit of other genre stars: being the tough African-American dude.

The murder of his gangster father and his mother leads ex–Green Beret Slaughter to commence a one-man crusade against the culprits. After retaliating against some of those responsible, the trail leads Slaughter to Mexico City and to underworld kingpin Dominick Hoffo. When not pursuing his prey, Slaughter romances Hoffo's girlfriend, Ann Cooper. In the showdown, Slaughter incinerates Hoffo in his overturned vehicle.

Although Brown's character is supposed to be accepted by filmgoers as heroic, it is hard to side with a man who uses such brutal tactics. On the other hand, Brown is an imposing presence as this taciturn, cool leading man, a macho sort who occasionally engages in droll dialogue.

Shot in Mexico City for about $750,000, *Slaughter* earned $1.2 million in domestic film rentals. It spawned *Slaughter's Big Rip-Off* (1973).

***Slaves* (1969)** Continental, color, 110 minutes. **Director:** Herbert J. Biberman; **Screenplay:** Biberman, John O. Killens, and Alida Sherman; **Cast:** Stephen Boyd (Nathan MacKay), Dionne Warwick (Cassy), Ossie Davis (Luke), Robert Kya-Hill (Jericho), Barbara Ann Teer (Esther), Julius Harris (Shadrach), Aldine King (Emmeline).

Even at the time of its release, this was an overwrought melodrama, a badly acted excursion that highlighted an interracial romance. It was another precursor to the soon-to-explode BLACK ACTION FILM craze. Some commentators saw a parallel between this exploitive study of the pre-Civil War South and the rash of racial riots that broke out in the United States during the 1960s. This was singing star Warwick's feature-film debut.

In the 1850s, Mississippi plantation owner and former slave-ship captain Nathan MacKay purchases new slaves, including Luke, Jericho, and young Emmeline. MacKay has a slave mistress, Cassy, whom he showers with material items but treats in a demeaning manner. After a slave woman dies (because cruel MacKay will not summon a doctor), Luke adopts the baby, insisting that she will not grow up in slavery. Later Luke arranges for Cassy, Emmeline, and the baby to escape but has to hide them, temporarily. The angered MacKay tortures Jericho to learn their whereabouts, but he will not tell. When Luke refuses to reveal any information, MacKay flogs him to death. His killing incites the plantation slaves to revolt and creates a diversion so that Cassy, Emmeline, and the infant can make their getaway.

While Davis lent dignity to his performance, at age fifty-two he was too mature to be playing the fiery young man.

***Slender Thread, The* (1965)** Paramount, b&w, 95 minutes. **Director:** Sydney Pollack; **Screenplay:** Stirling Silliphant; **Cast:** Sidney Poitier (Alan Newell), Anne Bancroft (Inga Dyson), Telly Savalas (Dr. Coburn), Steven Hill (Mark Dyson), Indus Arthur (Marion).

Based on the true-life case reported by Shana Alexander in her 1964 article "Decision to Die," which appeared in *Life* magazine, this entry united two recent Oscar winners (POITIER and Bancroft). In a much-touted ploy, the film made no reference to Poitier's race, which was supposed to be regarded as a step forward in Hollywood's effort to integrate the cinema. However, in his constricted role, Poitier was turned into a near-invisible voice dealing with the outside world. In short, the star was once again the token African American in a Caucasian-oriented feature.

Alan Newell is an anthropology student at the University of Washington. He volunteers at a Seattle suicide crisis clinic. He is on duty alone when Inga Dyson calls saying she has just taken an overdose of sleeping pills. While he frantically keeps her talking on the line so that she will not fall into a deadly coma, he manages to initiate a top-priority trace on her call. Gradually, he learns from the distraught caller that her fishing-boat skipper husband (Hill) has learned that he is not the father of their son and will not forgive her. As others arrive at the crisis center, Newell creatively keeps his contact (i.e., the slender thread) with the fading woman. Eventually, the police track her to a motel room and find her still alive. Both relieved and overjoyed, the exhausted Newell takes the next crisis call.

The manipulative *The Slender Thread* earned Academy Award nominations for Best Art Direction/Set Decoration (Black and White) and Best Costume Design (Black and White).

Smith, Will (1968–) There was a long tradition of singers (e.g., Frank Sinatra) making a successful crossover to motion pictures; in more recent years, the movies tapped the world of rappers (e.g., Queen Latifah, Ice T, and TUPAC SHAKUR) for screen parts. However, none made the tremendous mainstream success attained by Smith. But then, few of the black musicians who transferred into the film world had such a clean-cut act to start with, a quality that made six-feet, two-inch Will stand out from the majority of the hip-hop crowd. At the time, he was partnered in a team known as DJ

Jazzy Jeff (Jeffrey Townes) and the Fresh Prince, and they were the first team to win (in 1989) a Grammy in the freshly established rap category.

He was born Willard Smith in Wynnefield, Pennsylvania, the second of four children of a refrigeration engineer and his wife, a school-board employee. Despite coming from a black, middle-class part of outer Philadelphia, Smith went to predominantly white parochial schools but after classes hung out with his black friends in the neighborhood. Long interested in rap music, he was performing in local rap groups by the time he was in his early teens. In 1986, he remet Townes, whom he had known slightly years before. They formed a rap act and in 1987 had their debut album released. By eighteen, Will had acquired a hefty bank account, and he went on a nonstop spending spree. As royalties rolled in from his second and third albums, he continued spending freely. By the time Will was twenty-two, he had frittered away more than $1 million; the reality of it all made him reevaluate his life.

A chance meeting with an industry figure in Los Angeles led Will to musician/producer Quincy Jones who packaged the sitcom *FRESH PRINCE OF BEL AIR*, which debuted in September 1990 and proved to be a big success; much of the show relied on the charm, versatility, and easy-going manner of its young star. During the hit series' six seasons on the air, Smith made several films, ranging from *Made in America* (1993), a comedy with WHOOPI GOLDBERG, to the heavily dramatic *Six Degrees of Separation* (1993), where he played a homosexual con artist. He had an action hit with *Bad Boys* (1995) and did extremely well in the sci-fi spoof *Independence Day* (1996). He racked up another major hit with *Men in Black* (1997). Will worked with Gene Hackman in the action thriller *Enemy of the State* (1998) and took on the role of Capt. James West in the big-screen version (1999) of *The Wild Wild West* (1965–70), a classic TV series that had featured a white actor in that role. After *The Legend of Bagger Vance* (2000) with Matt Damon, Smith trained rigorously to take on the role of Cassius Clay/Muhammad Ali in the boxing biography *ALI* (2001) for which he received an Oscar nomination. The star reunited with Tommy Lee Jones for *Men in Black 2* (2002) and MARTIN LAWRENCE for *Bad Boys 2* (2003).

Will Smith in *Six Degrees of Separation* (1993). (AUTHOR'S COLLECTION)

Nominated for several Image Awards over the years, Smith won a Special Image Award in 1999 as Entertainer of the Year.

Snipes, Wesley (1962–) He emerged in the early 1990s as one of the new breed of African-American leading men, more at home on screen in the urban ghetto than in the upscale suburbs. In dramatic vehicles, he was as intense as DENZEL WASHINGTON or the earlier PAUL WINFIELD but had more grit and inner violence. Not since the 1970s blaxploitation film trend had any African American starred in action pictures with such muscular punch, and the five-feet, ten-inch actor proved to be an equal of Caucasian Bruce Willis and others in headlining such mainstream genre pieces.

He was born in Orlando, Florida, one of seven children of an aircraft-engineer father and a teacher's-aide mother. His parents divorced when Wesley was less than a year old. While the dad took four of the offspring with him to South Carolina, Wesley, along with two of his sisters, went with his mother to live in the South Bronx where she had relatives. When not learning survival lessons on the mean streets, he discovered acting when he was a young teen. He was in Manhattan's High School of Performing Arts when his mother returned to Florida with her children. After graduating public high school in Orlando, he attended college at the State University of New York at Purchase. While there, he studied acting and also became exposed to the works of Malcolm X, which reshaped his life and priorities, putting a focus on ethnic pride.

Snipes made his Broadway bow in 1985's *The Boys of Winter*. His movie debut occurred in *Wildcats* (1986) as one of the football squad coached by Goldie Hawn's character but playing a bad guy in Michael Jackson's music video *Bad* (1987) provided Wesley with great exposure. Having turned down a role in SPIKE LEE'S *DO THE RIGHT THING* (1989) for a bigger part in the baseball comedy *Major League* (1989), the actor worked for Lee in both *MO' BETTER BLUES* (1990) and *JUNGLE FEVER* (1991). Mario Van Peebles used Snipes as the ferocious drug lord in *NEW JACK CITY* (1991). After such dramas as *The Waterdance* (1992), Snipes starred in a major action film, *PASSENGER 57* (1992), acquitting himself well. In subsequent years he alternated between thrillers, such as *Drop Zone* (1994) and *U.S. Marshals* (1998), romantic fare (*WAITING TO EXHALE*, 1995; *DOWN IN THE DELTA*, 1998), and offbeat parts (e.g., one of a trio of transvestites in *To Wong*

Foo, Thanks for Everything, Julie Newmar, 1995). One of his most commercial vehicles was *Blade* (1998), which found him cast as a half-human, half-vampire in a grotesque urban tale. (It led to a sequel, *Blade 2;* 2002). Snipes's more recent releases included *The Art of War* (2000), *Zigzag* (2001), and *Liberty Stands Still* (2002).

soap opera series—television It took from the late 1940s, when soap operas began on U.S. commercial television, until 1965 for barriers against casting black performers in featured roles on daytime dramas to break down. (Reportedly, in the early 1960s, *Guiding Light,* which began in 1952, used African-American actors as extras playing doctors and nurses.) The first to be hired was Micki Grant on *Another World* (1964–) She was seen as Peggy Harris Nolan, a doctor's secretary, until 1973. (Originally the role had been planned for a white performer, but Grant won out at the audition.)

One Life to Live (1968), created by Agnes Nixon and set in a suburb of Philadelphia, was planned to exhibit ethnic diversity, including: one African-American family, one Jewish household, one middle-class Polish Catholic clan, and one wealthy WASP household. The Gray family was the black group, with established performer Lillian Hayman playing the mother from 1968 to 1986 (with a brief interruption in 1971 when ESTHER ROLLE took over the role temporarily). The daughter Carla, played by Ellen Holly, was light skinned enough to pass for white, which she did by denying her mother. For a time on her story arc (which went from 1968 to 1981 and then from 1983 to 1985), she dated a white physician, but eventually she wed a black police lieutenant and they adopted a child. On *Days of Our Lives* (1965–), in 1977, the show inaugurated an interracial romance between a white man and a black woman. However, when there was negative reaction from viewers, the plot arc was dropped.

Generations (1989–91) was set in Chicago, and to herald the new program that focused on two major households (one white, one black), the network promoted the show with "Black and White—In Color." Both families were wealthy, and their lives soon intertwined. The program dealt with such topical issues as racism but soon evolved into more of a (campy) crime-and-spy adventure show. As such in 1990, it introduced RICHARD ROUNDTREE (of *SHAFT,* 1971, fame) as a doctor accused of a homicide that occurred years before.

During the decades, many noted black performers found work on daytime soaps, including MORGAN FREEMAN and HOWARD E. ROLLINS JR. (*Another World*), JAMES EARL JONES, RUBY DEE, BILLY DEE WILLIAMS, and Kristoff St. John (*The Young and the Restless*), and TAYE DIGGS (*Guiding Light*), and Al Freeman Jr. and LAURENCE FISHBURNE (*One Life to Live*). SAMMY DAVIS JR. made recurring appearances on *One Life to Live* as a con artist/blackmailer named Chip Warren and was nominated for a Daytime Emmy for his guest role.

By the early twenty-first century, most of the daytime dramas had African-American characters as integral to the ongoing plots, often presenting them as mixed-blood figures who are caught between two worlds. They ranged from *Guiding Light* in which the character Vicky Brandon was the black niece of the ultrawealthy, white Spaulding clan, thanks to an affair Brandon Spaulding had years back with a black woman on a distant island. Meanwhile, Vicky had a black police-officer boyfriend named David Grant, he from a well-to-do physician's family. Another example was *As the World Turns* (1956–), which in more recent times featured Denise Maynard Dixon, an ex-stripper. Her offspring, Hope, from Denise's relationship with white photographer Andy Dixon, had been switched with a white couple's child and passed off as white. Finally, on *Days of Our Lives* (1965–), there was Abe and Lexie Carver. He is the police chief in town, and his wife is a physician, her dad the white criminal kingpin Stefano Dimera, and her black mother, Celeste, a psychic. On *The Young and the Restless* (1973–), Shemar Moore played Malcolm Winters from 1994 to 2002. His character was the brother of Neil Winters played by Kristoff St. John since 1991.

In the field of nighttime drama, black performers received relatively little representation during the decades. *Soap* (1977–81), a genre spoof, had for its first two seasons the irrepressible, insulting butler Benson (played by black talent Robert Guillaume). When Guillaume left to star in *BENSON* (1979–86), he was replaced on *Soap* by Roscoe Lee Browne, playing a snooty butler. *Dynasty* (1981–89) received a great deal of publicity when it hired DIAHANN CARROLL to join the cast as singer Dominique Deveraux from 1984 to 1987. She proved to be Blake Carrington's secret half-black sister. The unique aspect of Carroll being on the series was having her play a very glamorous, albeit bitchy, African-American character. While on the series, Carroll's character was involved—for a time—with her record-mogul husband Brady Lloyd (played from 1984 to 1985 by Billy Dee Williams.

Knots Landing had gone on the air in 1979, but this nighttime drama set in southern California did not integrate its cast until 1988 when the Williams family, involved in the Witness Protection Program, relocated to the "quiet" community of Knots Landing. The mother was played by Lynne Moody (who in 1979 had integrated the cast of *Soap* when she joined the program as a widow who had a romance with Ted Wass's character Danny, a one-time gangster-widower). Moody's character was killed off on *Knots Landing* in 1990 by a drunken neighbor. Her daughter (played by Kent Masters-King) had her share of adolescent problems, while the father (played by Larry Riley), once a widower, began to date the attractive Debbie Porter (performed by HALLE BERRY) in 1991.

On *Falcon Crest* (1981–90), Roscoe Lee Browne was involved in a seventh-season story arc in 1988 as a key member of a group of unscrupulous multimillionaires involved in a cartel. By the end of the season, he had been disposed of, and life in the Napa Valley, California, vineyards went on as before.

In the fall of 1991, Vivica A. Fox played the daughter in a black family that moved into the neighborhood on *Beverly Hills 90210* (1990–2000). However, after one episode these characters disappeared from the storyline, as did, at another point in the ongoing plot, the African-American boyfriend of one of the series regulars, the Jewish Andrea Zuckerman (played by Gabrielle Carteris). On another southern California–set show, *Melrose Place* (1992–99), the "other" Vanessa Williams was a series regular when this nighttime drama went on the air. She was Rhonda Blair, an aerobics instructor who found romance, was married off, and disappeared from the show before the start of its second season.

***Some Kind of Hero* (1982)** Paramount, color, 97 minutes. **Director:** Michael Pressman; **Screenplay:** James Kirkwood; **Cast:** Richard Pryor (Eddie Keller), Margot Kidder (Toni Donovan), Ray Sharkey (Vinnie DiAngelo), Ronny Cox (Colonel Powers), Lynne Moody (Lisa Keller), Olivia Cole (Jessie Keller).

Prolific, comedic, and audacious PRYOR returned to the serious screen format of his earlier *BLUE COLLAR* (1978). For this underdeveloped venture, author Kirkwood adapted his 1975 novel into a screenplay fitted to its star. Nevertheless, the picture was a jumble of conflicting moods, undecided whether to be starkly realistic or surreally humorous. Once again, with his range of acting talent, Pryor rescued a muddled vehicle. (Thanks to Pryor's large fan following, the picture grossed more than $20 million in domestic distribution.)

The irony of *Some Kind of Hero* was that its lead character had served heroically in the unpopular Vietnam War but was accorded no respect or other considerations when he returned to civilian life. With Pryor in the lead assignment, there was another aspect to the discrimination and humiliation he endured once back in the United States—he was African American.

After six years as a Viet Cong prisoner, demobilized soldier Eddie Keller returns to Los Angeles. He finds that his wife (Moody) is now living with another man, his bookstore business is defunct, his ailing mother is in an expensive nursing home, and he is denied military service back pay because he signed a confession for the enemy (hoping to save a dying buddy). The final blow occurs when Keller's bank loan is denied because he has no collateral. By accident, the frustrated man becomes involved in robbing banks, which leads to his grabbing a haul of cash and U.S. Treasury bonds. After outmaneuvering underworld figures who want the spoils, he takes off with a high-class hooker (Kidder) whom he met earlier. Before departing, he returns the stolen bonds to the bank and sends some of the money to ensure his mother's nursing care.

***Song of the South* (1946)** RKO, color, 94 minutes. **Directors:** Harve Foster (live action) and Wilfred Jackson (cartoons); **Screenplay:** Dalton Raymond, Morton Grant, and Maurice Rapf; **Cast:** Ruth Warrick (Sally), James Baskett (Uncle Remus/voice of Brer Fox), Bobby Driscoll (Johnny), Luana Patten (Ginny Favers), Lucile Watson (Miss Dosby), Hattie McDaniel (Aunt Tempy), Erik Rolf (John), Glenn Leedy (Toby), Anita Brown (Chloe), Nicodemus Stewart (voice of Brer Bear).

In the era before the Walt Disney Studio began to make live-action, mature-themed pictures, one did not associate that film lot—the home of Mickey Mouse, Donald Duck, and Pluto—with controversial movie fare. But such was the case with *Song of the South*, based in part on *Uncle Remus: His Songs and Sayings, the Folk-Lore of the Old Plantation* (1881) by Joel Chandler Harris. Long in the works, this pet project of studio founder Disney met with resistance even before filming of the part live-action, part-animated picture began on a ranch in Phoenix, Arizona. Many African-American PRESSURE GROUPS expressed concern that to reactivate the Uncle Remus tales on screen would emphasize anew negative stereotypes of black Americans. The film industry's own self-censorship organization advised Disney that, at the opening of the movie, it should be made clear to viewers that the story was set in the *post*-Civil War period and was not a representation of the slavery period in the old South. Disney ignored this request.

Within the narrative, in an unspecified period of the nineteenth century, newspaperman John and his wife Sally take their son Johnny to visit her mother (Watson) at her plantation outside of Atlanta. They are accompanied by Johnny's nursemaid, Aunt Tempy. John returns to Atlanta, while the others remain at the manse. One day Johnny meets Uncle Remus, renowned as a storyteller. Over succeeding weeks, the elderly African American, an ex-slave, tells Johnny many wonderful stories about Brer Fox, Brer Rabbit, and others, which provide the youngster with useful morals to apply to his life. However, Johnny's snobbish mother, who disapproves of Uncle Remus's influence on her son, constantly rebukes the old man, which upsets her boy. Later, Johnny is injured by a bull, and his recovery brings his arguing parents back together. Thereafter, Uncle Remus is on hand to see Johnny and his friends, the white neighbor girl (Patten) and a young black house servant (Leedy), happily playing with a rescued puppy.

When released, many reviewers approved of the film's imaginative cartoon sequences but thought that many of the live-action segments were old fashioned and poorly acted, except for Baskett's Uncle Remus. Many African-American publications strongly criticized the movie's minority figures' subordination to their white employers and being presented in costume, dialogue, and action as caricatures. Walter White, executive secretary of the NAACP, complained (November 27, 1946) on behalf of his organization, that "in an effort neither to offend audiences in the North or South, the production helps to perpetuate a dangerously glorified picture of slavery" and that the movie "unfortunately gives the impression of an idyllic master-slave relationship which is a distortion of the facts." Many U.S. movie theaters showing *Song of the South* were picketed by the National Negro Congress and other PRESSURE GROUPS.

Song of the South won an Academy Award for Best Song ("Zip-A-Dee-Doo-Dah"), and an Oscar nomination for Best Scoring of a Musical Picture. Baskett, who was touted for an Oscar, was not even nominated. (He and the other African-American talents in the picture had not been invited to the film's premiere, which was held in the then still-segregated

Atlanta.) However, in 1948, some months before he died at age forty-four, he received an Honorary Oscar for his "able and heart-warming characterization of Uncle Remus in *Song of the South*, friend and storyteller to the children of the world." He was the first African-American male performer to receive an Academy Award.

Despite continued controversy over *Song of the South* during the decades, the movie was periodically reissued through the mid-1980s, by which time it had earned more than $29 million in domestic film rentals. Ralph Bakshi's R-rated, live-action/animated feature, *COONSKIN* (1975), satirized *Song of the South*. On Showtime cable, in 1996, DANNY GLOVER narrated an animated short feature of *Brer Rabbit & Boss Lion*. Earlier, in the screwball comedy, *Twentieth Century* (1934), African-American actor George Reed played Uncle Remus in a play-within-the-movie.

***Sonny Spoon* (1988)** NBC-TV series, color, 60 minutes. **Cast:** Mario Van Peebles (Sonny Spoon), Terry Donahoe (Asst. D.A. Carolyn Gilder), Joe Shea (Lucius DeLuce), Jordana Capra (Monique), Bob Wieland (Johnny Skates), Melvin Van Peebles (Mel).

This detective drama, seen sporadically in 1988, was an offbeat showcase for the talented, handsome black actor Mario Van Peebles. Here he plays a hip private eye whose specialty is going undercover in disguise, which might range from a preacher to an Arab terrorist. He also had an assortment of pals to help him with his case load: newsstand owner Lucius, double amputee Johnny Skates (whose transportation of choice was a skateboard), and prostitute Monique. When he needed added assistance, there was always Mel (played by VAN PEEBLES's famous father), the bar owner, or Carolyn Gilder, a most receptive assistant district attorney.

Sonny's character was so slick and slippery and the show so off-key and quirky in its attempt to be different that it failed to attract an audience. The same fate had befallen the earlier *Fortune Dane*, an ABC-TV hour-long police drama in February–March 1986, with African-American actor Carl Weathers as a police detective turned troubleshooter.

***Sophisticated Gents, The* (1981)** NBC-TV, color, 200 minutes. **Director:** Harry Falk; **Teleplay:** Melvin Van Peebles; **Cast:** Sonny Jim Gaines (Coach Charles "Chappie" Davis), Paul Winfield (Richard "Bubbles" Wiggins), Bernie Casey (Shurley Walker), Rosey Grier (Cudjo Evers), Thalmus Rasulala (Kenneth "Snake" Dobson), Robert Hooks (Ezzard "Chops" Jackson), Raymond St. Jacques (Dartagnan Parks), Ron O'Neal (Clarence Henderson), Melvin Van Peebles (Walter Moon [Silky Porter]), Dick Anthony Williams (Ralph Jopkin), Rosalind Cash (Christine Jackson).

After the huge success of the miniseries *ROOTS* (1977), the TV networks were more receptive to presenting black-oriented dramas. In 1979, this lengthy adaptation of John A. Williams's novel *The Junior Bachelor Society* (1976) was produced, based on a script by VAN PEEBLES. But the network lost faith in the completed product and it sat for two years before being aired in three installments, which diminished the work's cumulative power.

To celebrate the upcoming seventieth birthday of Chappie Davis, nine athletes—all part of a black group who have known one another for twenty-five years—get together. Davis was the coach who perceived the greatness within each of the men and encouraged them in their athletic activities. Among the middle-aged attendees at the reunion are Richard "Bubbles" Wiggins, the group's president; Dartagnan Parks, a vocalist who has been hiding the fact that he is gay; successful playwright Ralph Jopkin; California college professor Clarence Henderson; magazine editor Ezzard "Chops" Jackson; city commissioner Kenneth "Snake" Dobson; and Walter Moon. The latter, better known as Silky Porter, is a pimp who has committed a homicide and is in great trouble. Many of the men have come with their wives. Before long, the reunion turns into emotional chaos thanks to two cops—one black, one white.

Donald Bogle noted in *Blacks in American Films and Television* (1988) that "This is a sophisticated race movie: fiercely determined to tell a story to a black audience, . . . What makes it all work, of course, are the actors, who are comfortable with their dialogue and their attitudes and are invigorated by the jazzy, sexy style of the script."

***Soul Food* (1997)** Twentieth Century Fox, color, 114 minutes. **Director/Screenplay:** George Tillman Jr.; **Cast:** Vanessa L. Williams (Teri Joseph), Vivica A. Fox (Maxine Joseph), Nia Long (Bird Joseph), Michael Beach (Miles), Mekhi Phifer (Lem), Jeffrey D. Sams (Kenneth), Irma P. Hall (Mother Joe), Brandon Hammond (Ahmad).

Following in the wake of the successful *WAITING TO EXHALE* (1995), this was another refreshing change from despairing urban ghetto dramas and mindless ethnic comedies. This flavorful production featured an impressive array of attractive ethnic talent. The film's chief structural fault was subjugating the female point of view to a male one: Based on the childhood experiences of filmmaker Tillman, the picture was seen through the eyes of Maxine's young son, Ahmad, who was the movie's narrator.

For decades Mother Joe has held her divisive family together, using their traditional Sunday dinner to anchor the clan. When the matriarch falls seriously ill, her daughters—attorney Teri, homemaker Maxine, and beauty-shop owner Bird—begin to bicker more than usual with one another, especially as to whether they should sell mama's house after she passes on. During this tense period, Maxine catches her husband (Beach) cheating on her with her cousin. Bird's ex-convict husband needs a job, and Bird causes problems when she asks an ex-boyfriend to help out. Just before Mama expires, she instructs her beloved grandson Ahmad to restore somehow family harmony. The perceptive boy tricks his relatives into coming for Sunday dinner, and there they repair their relationships. All ends on an upbeat note when it is discovered that mama had hidden away a bundle of money.

Made for $7.5 million, *Soul Food* grossed more than $43 million in domestic distribution. At the Acapulco Black Film Festival, the much-nominated picture was named Best Picture, and Fox was selected Best Actress. The production claimed several Image Awards: Best Actress (Williams), Best Supporting Actress (Hall), Outstanding Picture, and Outstanding Youth Actor/Actress (Hammond). In 2000, Showtime cable began a weekly comedy/drama series (*Soul Food*) based on the film with some of the cast from the original repeating their characterizations.

***Soul Man* (1986)** New World, color, 101 minutes. **Director:** Steve Miner; **Screenplay:** Carol Black; **Cast:** C. Thomas Howell (Mark Watson), Arye Gross (Gordon Bloomfeld), Rae Dawn Chong (Sarah Walker), James Earl Jones (Professor Banks), Melora Hardin (Whitney Dunbar), Jonathan "Fudge" Leonard (George Walker).

Two decades earlier, Hollywood had made *BLACK LIKE ME* (1964), a serious/exploitive approach to the ramifications of a white man passing for African American. In the mindless comedy *Soul Man*, Mark Watson, a white UCLA senior, is accepted to Harvard Law School. Mark's well-to-do parents, however, decide he should earn his own way through grad school. Watson discovers that there is a law-school scholarship available for a needy black student from the L.A. area. Gobbling dosages of an experimental suntan pill, Mark's skin darkens sufficiently so that, with a nappy wig, he passes for being African American and receives the financial aid. At Harvard, he finds that single-parent Sarah Walker, a qualified, hardworking black woman, lost out on the law school scholarship because of him. As the increasingly guilt-ridden Mark continues his charade, he becomes the love object of WASPy Whitney Dunbar who has a yen for African-American men. Also enmeshed in the proceedings is law professor Banks (played in self-mocking stentorian fashion by JONES) who sets the unmasked Mark on a more socially responsible course.

This lighthearted fare aspired to social relevance, but the plot was so farfetched that it lost credibility. To execute his masquerade, Mark (and the filmmakers) trotted out many stereotypical traits of black men (e.g., being good at sports, superior at lovemaking, overloaded with rhythm). Although the film grossed a hefty $28 million in domestic distribution, it created a backlash in some quarters (including the NAACP and the Black American Law Students Association at UCLA) for its politically incorrect postures.

Soul Soldier See *RED, WHITE, AND BLACK, THE.*

Soul Soldiers See *RED, WHITE, AND BLACK, THE.*

***Sounder* (1972)** Twentieth Century-Fox, color, 105 minutes. **Director:** Martin Ritt; **Screenplay:** Lonne Elder III; **Cast:** Cicely Tyson (Rebecca Morgan), Paul Winfield (Nathan Lee Morgan), Kevin Hooks (David Lee Morgan), Carmen Mathews (Mrs. Boatwright), Taj Mahal (Ike), Janet MacLachlan (Camille Johnson).

In the midst of the expanding BLACK ACTION FILM cycle—full of quickly made, exploitive action entertainment—there were occasional quality films such as the drama *Sounder*. This highly professional production about full-bodied African-American characters was an insightful presentation of the daily pressures and frustrations minority individuals suffer at the hands of the white majority. Because the story was set decades earlier (during the Depression), it distanced for white viewers the discomforting situation in which blacks in a white world must hold their emotions in check and maintain their "place" to survive. Nonetheless, it was a potent tale, saying a lot about both races. Moreover, *Sounder* goes one step further—still relatively rare in 1970s Hollywood. It carefully delineated the Morgan family's home life and how they maintained their dignity and hope in the face of severe obstacles.

In 1930s Louisiana, impoverished farmer Nathan Lee Morgan steals a ham to feed his hungry family. He is arrested and sent to a work camp. This leaves his wife to keep the farm going and to watch over her three children. The eldest offspring, David Lee, sets out to find his dad. Unsuccessful, he heads home, taking refuge one night with a black schoolteacher (MacLachlan). The next day at her school, he is amazed to see that the minority students are full of racial pride and appreciate what education can do for them. Back at home, he joins the family in welcoming back Nathan Lee who has been released early because he was a victim of an "accident." It is Nathan Lee who encourages David to accept the teacher's offer of attending her school, even though it means he won't be able to help with the farming.

Sounder grossed almost $10 million in domestic distribution and was nominated for four Academy Awards: Best Actor (WINFIELD), Best Actress (TYSON), Best Picture, and Best Screenplay. (Ironically, it received average or quasi-negative reviews from many white establishment publications.) *Sounder, Part 2* (1976) was a rich but lesser film, with none of the leads recreating their roles.

***Sparkle* (1976)** Warner Bros., color, 98 minutes. **Director:** Sam O'Steen; **Screenplay:** Joel Schumacher; **Cast:** Philip Michael Thomas (Stix), Irene Cara (Sparkle), Lonette McKee (Sister), Dwan Smith (Dolores), Mary Alice (Effie), Dorian Harewood (Levi), Tony King (Satin).

More fable than realistic account, this precursor to the 1980s Broadway musical *Dreamgirls* dealt with the rags-to-riches story of a hit singing group. (The film was promoted with the catchphrase "From Ghetto to Superstars.") It boasted a fine music score by Curtis Mayfield.

Three spirited sisters from Harlem embark on a meteoric career in the music business. At first, it seems that the hip and beautiful Sister will be the one to really succeed, but she is self-defeated by her drug addiction and her attachment to a louse (King). Later, it is not racial activist Dolores who takes over the limelight but the youngest sibling, the innocent Sparkle. The latter's well-meaning boyfriend (Thomas) borrows money from an unscrupulous white man to pave the way for Sparkle's successful Carnegie Hall showcase. Stix's naïve folly with this underworld figure almost costs him his life and Sparkle's future.

Despite the Lapses and clichés in plot and characterization, *Sparkle* remained an insightful study of minorities in the show-business world and boasted a trio of fine female performances.

***Spenser: For Hire* (1985–1988)** ABC-TV series, color, 60 minutes. **Cast:** Robert Urich (Spenser), Avery Brooks (Hawk), Barbara Stock (Susan Silverman: 1985–86, 1987–88), Richard Jaeckel (Lt. Martin Quirk: 1985–87), Ron McLarty (Sgt. Frank Belson), Carolyn McCormick (Asst. D.A. Rita Fiori: 1986–87).

Robert B. Parker's long-running, superior detective book series (which began in the early 1970s), featuring an erudite Boston private eye, came to television in this well-produced offering. Although some commentators found Urich too genteel as the rugged ex-boxer and former Beantown cop, there was no disputing the rapport between him and Hawk, the latter operating on both sides of the law. The two first met in the boxing ring and soon developed a friendship. Since then, Hawk (who usually slipped from the shadows calling out "Spen—SAH!") often acted as the detective's contact to the meaner elements in town and was a collaborator and backup on tougher cases requiring muscle and firearms. Hawk was not merely an offshoot of a typical 1970s black action-movie character—although he did resemble John Shaft of *SHAFT* (1971) to a degree. Rather, he was an impeccably dressed, cultured, and intellectual soul whose talents as an enforcer for hire were highly prized by a wide spectrum of clients. Although Hawk was known to be a great success with women, rarely was this side of his life shown in the series. He did have a lighthearted rapport with Susan Silverman, Spenser's girlfriend.

The bond between Caucasian Spenser and African-American Hawk was one of the best-delineated interracial buddy setups that had appeared on American TV. It exceeded the gimmicky relationship presented in the four-to-date *Lethal Weapon* movie series between the two cop leads.

After *Spenser: For Hire* went off the air, Brooks continued his Hawk persona in the series *A Man Called Hawk* (1989), set in the character's hometown of Washington, D.C., where he righted wrongs with his scowl, his powerful fists, and his trusty .357 Magnum gun. In mid-1990, Urich and Brooks reunited for four TV movie adventures of Spenser and Hawk. In the late 1990s, Joe Mantegna took over as Spenser in a fresh batch of made-for-cable capers. In the first, *Spenser: Small Vices* (1999), Shiek Mahmud-Bey played Hawk, while in *Walking Shadow* (2001), Ernie Hudson portrayed the tall black man.

***Split, The* (1968)** Metro-Goldwyn-Mayer, color, 90 minutes. **Director:** Gordon Flemyng; **Screenplay:** Robert Sabaroff; **Cast:** Jim Brown (McClain), Diahann Carroll (Ellie), Julie Harris (Gladys), Ernest Borgnine (Bert Clinger), Gene Hackman (Lt. Walter Brill), Jack Klugman (Harry Kifka), Donald Sutherland (Dave Negli).

Originally planned as a starring vehicle for Lee Marvin, this violent heist caper was considered a novelty at the time of its release because it boasted two African-American leading players. As part of the emerging BLACK ACTION filmmaking trend, it showcased ex-football star BROWN—reaching his peak as the frontrunner of the exploding genre cycle—as the tough, silent antihero. He was the dude who not only could attract cool, beautiful CARROLL but also had the smarts to outwit and survive his gang of Caucasian accomplices.

Professional thief McClain shows up in Los Angeles and convinces his ex-wife Ellie to let him stay with her. Along with his criminal pal Gladys, McClain plans to rob the receipts from a championship Rams football game at the Los Angeles Coliseum. To help him execute his plan, he assembles a squad (Borgnine, Sutherland, Oates, and Klugman) whom he leads through a brutal training period. The daring robbery is successful, but Ellie, who is safekeeping the money, is killed by her wacko landlord who grabs the loot. This leads the survivors to fight among themselves, a situation inflamed by a dishonest cop (Hackman). By the finale, McClain and the policeman have become uneasy partners, with McClain heading to Mexico. He wonders if he can keep his promise to Ellie about going straight.

Star Trek In the 1960s, it was still rare to have an integrated cast on U.S. network television. Occasionally, a black performer had a subordinate part on a mostly white TV series (e.g., *EAST SIDE/WEST SIDE*; *MANNIX*) and even less occasionally a colead assignment (e.g., *I SPY*; *MISSION: IMPOSSIBLE*). In the latter category was also *Star Trek* (1966–69), which provided for many African Americans the first real TV role model in the characterization of Lieutenant Uhura. (Being the major female lead among a mostly all-male cast also gave Uhura significance in the women's liberation movement.)

In this classic sci-fi series, set aboard the starship USS *Enterprise* in the twenty-third century, Uhura, as communications officer, was an integrated equal among the crew (albeit a smaller role in the proceedings—part of the chauvinistic approach to TV series at the time). As home viewers were quick to note, generally with approval, the intergalactic craft also contained an Asian-American character, Sulu, the physicist turned helmsman. With such a diverse representation aboard the *Enterprise*, this futuristic series gave assurance that in the future, at least, racial and sexual discrimination was a thing of the past.

Nichols would provide the voice of Uhura on the cartoon version of *Star Trek* (1973–75) as well as appearing in the first six *Star Trek* feature films (1980–91). Just as Nichols had been an inspiration to actress WHOOPI GOLDBERG when she was growing up, so Goldberg, in turn, would provide a role

***Star Trek* series**
Major African-American Characters

Avery Brooks	Played Comdr. Benjamin Sisko, commander of the space station Deep Space Nine *(Star Trek: Deep Space Nine).*
LeVar Burton	Played Geordi La Forge, chief engineer aboard starship *Enterprise-D (Star Trek: The Next Generation).*
Michael Dorn	Played Worf, the first Klingon to serve on a starship *(Star Trek: The Next Generation)* and then security officer of the space station Deep Space Nine *(Star Trek: Deep Space Nine).*
Whoopi Goldberg	Played Guinan, bartender on the starship *Enterprise-D,* a member of an alien race, the El-Aurians, or Listeners. She became a confidante of Capt. Jean-Luc Picard of *Enterprise-D.*
Cirroc Lofton	Played Jake Sisko, son of Comdr. Benjamin Sisko of the space station Deep Space Nine *(Star Trek: Deep Space Nine).*
Anthony (A. T.) Montgomery	Plays Ensign Travis Mayweather, helmsman of the Starfleet ship *Enterprise* on the latest series entry, *Enterprise.*
Nichelle Nichols	Played Uhura, communications officer on the starship *Enterprise* (*Star Trek:* the original series).
Tim Russ	Played Tuvok, the Vulcan security officer on USS *Voyager (Star Trek: Voyager).*

***Star Trek* series/feature films**
Additional African-American Characters

Felicia Bell	Played Jennifer Sisko, the wife of Comdr. Benjamin Sisko *(Star Trek: Deep Space Nine).*
Brooker Bradshaw	Played Doctor M'Benga, physician aboard the original *Starship Enterprise* (*Star Trek:* the original series). (He was on two separate episodes.)
Ron Canada	Played Martin Benbeck in one episode *(Star Trek: The Next Generation)* and as Ch'Pok in one episode *(Star Trek: Deep Space Nine).*
Bernie Casey	Played Calvin Hudson, a Maquis leader *(Star Trek: Deep Space Nine).*
Penny Johnson	Played Kasidy Yates, civilian freighter captain with whom Comdr. Benjamin Sisko fell in love *(Star Trek: Deep Space Nine).*
William Marshall	Played Dr. Richard Daystrom on one episode (*Star Trek:* the original series).
Brock Peters	Played Admiral Cartwright (in the fourth and sixth *Star Trek* films: 1986's *Star Trek IV: The Voyage Home* and 1991's *Star Trek VI: The Undiscovered Country*). Also played Joseph Sisko, the father of Comdr. Benjamin Sisko, in several episodes *(Star Trek: Deep Space Nine).*
Madge Sinclair	Played Silva La Forge, the mother of Geordi La Forge *(Star Trek: The Next Generation).*
Ben Vereen	Played Calvin Hudson, a Maquis leader *(Star Trek: Deep Space Nine).*
Paul Winfield	Played Captain Clark Terrell in the second *Star Trek* film (1982's *Star Trek II: The Wrath of Khan*).
Alfre Woodard	Played Lily Sloane, an aerospace engineer in the eighth *Star Trek* film (1996's *Star Trek: First Contact*).

model to later generations of TV viewers in her assignment as Guinan, the humanoid host/bartender in charge of the spaceship's recreation lounge on *STAR TREK: THE NEXT GENERATION* (1987–94). In addition, a variety of other African Americans were used as regulars in the first four *Star Trek* series—along with guest appearances by other black American acting talent in various episodes and the assorted feature film spinoffs of the first two series. (The other two *Star Trek* series were: *STAR TREK: DEEP SPACE NINE*, 1993–99; and *STAR TREK: VOYAGER*, 1995–2001.)

In 2001–2002, a new *Star Trek* series was started. *ENTERPRISE* was a sort of prequel to the classic first *Star Trek.* Set in the mid-22nd century—2151—about 100 years *before* Captain James T. Kirk and the USS *Enterprise,* this new show introduced the pioneering days of space exploration when interstellar travel on the part of the human race was still in its infancy. The series explores both the crew's sense of awe and wonder at the strange experiences they undergo and also the intergalactic upheaval that eventually leads to the forging of the Federation. Among the members of this first starship, the *Enterprise,* is African-American Ensign Travis Mayweather (played by Anthony Montgomery, a young actor originally from Indianapolis). Also, in keeping with the international standard represented in other *Star Trek* series, there is a Japanese communication officer, Ensign Hoshi Sato (played by Linda Park).

STAR TREK—TV SERIES

***Star Trek* (1966–1969)** NBC-TV, color, 60 minutes. **Cast:** William Shatner (Capt. James T. Kirk), Leonard Nimoy (Mr. Spock), DeForest Kelley (Dr. Leonard McCoy), George Takei (Mr. Haraku Sulu), Nichelle Nichols (Lieutenant Uhura), James Doohan (Eng. Montgomery Scott), Walter Koenig (Ens. Pavel Chekov: 1967–69), Majel Barrett (Nurse Christine Chapel).

See *STAR TREK* essay.

***Star Trek: The Next Generation* (1987–1994)** Syndicated, color, 60 minutes. **Cast:** Patrick Stewart (Capt. Jean-Luc Picard), Jonathan Frakes (Exec. Off. William T. Riker), Brent Spiner (Data), LeVar Burton (Chief Eng. Geordi La Forge), Michael Dorn (Worf), Gates McFadden (Dr. Beverly Crusher), Marina Sirtis (Counselor Deanna Troi), Wil Wheaton (Wesley Crusher), Denise Crosby (Natasha Yar).

See *STAR TREK* essay.

***Star Trek: Deep Space Nine* (1992–1999)** Syndicated, color, 60 minutes. **Cast:** Avery Brooks (Comdr. Benjamin Sisko), Rene Auberjonois (Odo), Alexander Siddig (Dr. Julian Bashir), Terry Farrell (Science Off. Jadzia Dax), Cirroc Lofton (Jake Sisko), Colm Meaney (Eng. Miles O'Brien), Armin Shimerman (Quark), Nana Visitor (First Off. Kira Niris), Michael Dorn (Worf).

See *STAR TREK* essay.

***Star Trek: Voyager* (1995–2001)** UPN-TV, color, 60 minutes. **Cast:** Kate Mulgrew (Capt. Kathryn Janeway), Robert Beltran (First Officer Chakotay), Roxann Biggs-Dawson (Chief Eng. B'Elanna Torres), Robert Duncan McNeill (Lt. Thomas Paris), Jennifer Lien (Kes), Ethan Phillips (Neelix), Robert Picardo (Emergency Medical Hologram), Tim Russ (Security Off. Tuvok), Garrett Wang (Ens. Harry Kim).

See *STAR TREK* essay.

***Enterprise* (2001–)** Syndicated, color, 60 minutes. **Cast:** Scott Bakula (Capt. Jonathan Archer), Jolene Blalock (Sub Commander T'Pol), Connor Trinneer (Comdr. Charles "Trip" Tucker III, Engineer), Dominic Keating (Lt. Malcolm Reed, Munitions Officer), Linda Park (Ensign Hoshi Sato, Comm. Officer), Anthony (A.T.) Montgomery (Ensign Travis Mayweather, Helmsman), John Billingsley (Doctor Phlox).

See *STAR TREK* essay.

***Stir Crazy* (1980)** Columbia, color, 111 minutes. **Director:** Sidney Poitier; **Screenplay:** Bruce Jay Friedman;

Gene Wilder and Richard Pryor in *Stir Crazy* (1980). (AUTHOR'S COLLECTION)

Cast: Gene Wilder (Skip Donahue), Richard Pryor (Harry Monroe), Georg Stanford Brown (Rory Schultebrand), JoBeth Williams (Meredith), Miguel Angel Suarez (Jesus Ramirez), Craig T. Nelson (Deputy Ward Wilson).

Building on their screen chemistry in *SILVER STREAK* (1976), the interracial comedy team of Wilder and PRYOR reunited for this wacky prison tale. As directed by POITIER, the episodic, at times meandering, proceedings were more slapstick, less biting, and more benign than the team's previous outing. Nevertheless, the public, if not the critics, adored the antics and the R-rated film grossed more than $101 million in domestic distribution.

En route to California from New York, fledgling playwright Skip Donahue and would-be actor Harry Monroe accidentally become involved in an Arizona bank robbery and are sentenced to long prison terms. At the penitentiary, they come up against a variety of (stereo)types, including gay Rory Schultebrand. Through happenstance, the warden enters Skip into a rodeo competition with another prison. During the big day, Skip and Harry engineer an escape, and Donahue confesses his love for the female attorney (Williams) who represents him and Monroe. Meanwhile, the real bank robbers have been captured, and the two innocents will soon be free men.

Even with Poitier at the helm, Caucasian Wilder emerged as the top banana in the shenanigans, reducing Pryor to being his ethnic cohort. The highlight of the feature borrowed from a similar scene in *Silver Streak.* It had hip Pryor teaching his wide-eyed friend how to "get bad" and act real black in this domain run by the tough African-American prisoners.

A TV series adaptation of *Stir Crazy* aired in September 1985, starring Larry Riley (as Harry) and Joseph Guzaldo (as Skip). Very loosely based on the hit movies, much of the weekly episodes followed the goofy duo as they continued their flight from the law and pursued the actual killer for whose crime they were sentenced to a chain gang. The feckless sitcom had vanished by January 1986.

***Stormy Weather* (1943)** Twentieth Century-Fox, b&w, 77 minutes. **Director:** Andrew Stone; **Screenplay:** Frederick Jackson, Ted Koehler, and H.S. Kraft; **Cast:** Lena Horne (Selina Rogers), Bill "Bojangles" Robinson (Corky Williamson), Cab Calloway and Band (themselves), Katherine Dunhan and Her Troupe (themselves), Fats Waller (Fats), the Nicholas brothers (themselves), Ada Brown (herself), Dooley Wilson (Gabe Tucker).

In the same year as MGM's all-black musical *CABIN IN THE SKY*, this cavalcade of African-American performing talents was packaged at a rival studio, presenting over seventy minutes of music. Its slim story—which allows for plenty of breaks for song and dance numbers—revolves around a salute to veteran entertainer Corky Williamson and flashes back on his musical career between 1911 and 1936. It features his on-off-and-on-again romance with entertainer Selina Rogers. (ROBINSON was four decades older than HORNE, and the latter disliked the tap-dancing legend because she felt he was an "Uncle Tom" kowtowing to the white world.)

Most importantly, this all-black song-and-dance fest was a parade of legendary performers, who each had superb opportunities to exhibit their specialities. Fox reasoned that if this all-ethnic cast production was treated as mostly a series of extended musical specialities—similar to a big vaudeville show—and racial discussions and interracial activity was avoided in the plot, the film would likely appeal to entertainment-hungry filmgoers of the World War II era—whether the movie audience be black or white.

Among the impressive performances are: Horne (singing "Stormy Weather," "I Can't Give You Anything But Love," and more), Waller (performing "Ain't Misbehavin'"), the Nicholas Brothers (doing their astoundingly limber dance steps to "Jumpin' Jive"), Katherine Dunham and Her Troupe (dancing to "Stormy Weather"), and, of course, tap dancing and singing Robinson ("Rhythm Cocktail," "Rang Tang Tang," etc.). *Stormy Weather* provided the last film performances of both Robinson and Fats Waller.

Street Fight See *COONSKIN*.

Strode, Woody (1914–1995) He helped to break the color barrier in American football and went on to become a character actor in both American and foreign movies. At six-feet, four-inches and weighing more than 200 pounds, the muscular Strode had the innate talent—as he proved with his key role in *SERGEANT RUTLEDGE* (1960)—to have become a versatile Hollywood player, but racial discrimination limited his choice of roles for many years. One of his best-remembered parts was as the bald, powerful gladiator who battled Kirk Douglas in *Spartacus* (1960).

Woodrow Wilson Strode was born in Los Angeles and later attended UCLA where he was a football star. Along

Bill "Bojangles" Robinson, Lena Horne, and Cab Calloway in a publicity pose from *Stormy Weather* (1943). (JC ARCHIVES)

with black teammate Kenny Washington (who also became a film actor), Strode played in the National Football League, they being the first African Americans to do so. Thereafter, he joined the Calgary Stampeders of the Canadian Football League. By the 1950s, Woody had become a professional wrestler.

Square-jawed Strode made his film debut in a tiny role as a tribal cop in *Sundown* (1941) and was in the Eddie "Rochester" Anderson sketch in *Star-Spangled Rhythm* (1942). When Woody returned to pictures in 1951, he was trapped into playing jungle natives (e.g., *The Lion Hunter*, 1951) or West Indians (e.g., *Caribbean*, 1952). He was a gladiator in *Demetrius and the Gladiators* (1954) and the king of Ethiopia (and also doubled as a slave) in *The Ten Commandments* (1956). After his breakthrough role in John Ford's *Sergeant Rutledge*, Woody worked for the famed director in *Two Rode Together* (1961), *The Man Who Shot Liberty Valance* (1962), and 7 *Women* (1966).

Finding more popularity and acceptance abroad than at home, Woody made several Italian westerns (*Black Jesus*, 1968; *Boot Hill*, 1969; *The Devil's Backbone*, 1971) and Italian actioners (*Hired to Kill*, 1973; *The Million Dollar Fire*, 1976). Occasionally he worked in American movies (*The Cotton Club*, 1984; *Lust in the Dust*, 1985). Active almost to the end (he died of lung cancer), he appeared in the Hollywood westerns *Posse* (1993) and *The Quick and the Dead* (1995).

***Stu Erwin Show, The* (aka: *Life with The Erwins; The Trouble with Father*) (1950–1955)** ABC-TV series, b&w, 30 minutes. **Cast:** Stu Erwin (himself), June Collyer (June Erwin) Sheila James (Jackie Erwin), Ann Todd (Joyce Erwin: 1950–54), Willie Best (Willie).

Unlike such early TV sitcoms as *Father Knows Best* (1954–60) and *Leave It To Beaver* (1957–63) in which the father figure was indeed wise, this show focused on bumbling, good-natured dad. Erwin was the principal of Hamilton High School, where he occasionally got himself into a pickle, but usually it was at home where his well-meaning efforts translated into household fiascos—all in the name of innocent comedy. His real-life wife Collyer played his on-camera spouse, Todd was his well-mannered daughter, and James was the younger offspring, a rambunctious tomboy.

Among the supporting cast was Best as handyman Willie. This veteran African-American character actor was famed for his stereotypical screen specialty of the slow-moving, overly accommodating, celluloid domestic who was forever being amazed by life and doing exaggerated double takes. He did the same here, fostering the negative image he had made so popular. Meanwhile, in Best's other small-screen assignment of this same era, he was the bug-eyed, subservient elevator-operator/handyman on the classic sitcom *My Little Margie* (1952–55), starring Gale Storm and Charles Farrell.

***Superfly* (1972)** Warner Bros., color, 96 minutes. **Director:** Gordon Parks Jr.; **Screenplay:** Phillip Fenty; **Cast:** Ron O'Neal (Youngblood Priest), Carl Lee (Eddie), Sheila Frazier (Georgia), Julius W. Harris (Scatter), Charles McGregor (Fat Freddie), Polly Niles (Cynthia).

In the BLACK ACTION FILM era, a certain few of the genre created cult figures of their lead characters (e.g., Shaft, Foxy Brown, and the Mack). Near the top of this pantheon was the title figure of *Superfly*. He was a crafty fabrication that glorified a rugged Harlem drug lord who strutted the streets in his sweeping, long coats, wide-brim hats, and tousled long hair. As his celluloid adventures amply demonstrated, this tough dude was not to be messed with. Best of all, he was a Brother. The film was a mix of authenticity (shooting on the streets of Harlem), realism (the drug scene), and the fantastic (the supercool Super Fly).

Youngblood Priest's underlings push dope (mostly to white people) on the streets of New York City. He takes no nonsense from his stooges or from testy clients. The snazzy dresser has his choice of women, who range from beautiful black Georgia to his comely white woman (Niles). When Priest decides to quit the racket, he wants to make one last big score (which will, by the way, "stick it to the Man"). As anticipated, he backstabs his Caucasian confederates and grabs his stash of money.

Thanks to O'Neal's charismatic performance, the atmospheric backdrops, and Curtis Mayfield's score, *Superfly* received critical endorsements. It grossed more than $6 million in domestic distribution and led to the sequel *Superfly T.N.T.* (1973) with O'Neal (who also directed). Seventeen years later, Sig Shore, who produced the original two features, produced/directed *The Return of Superfly* featuring Nathan Purdee as the famed Superfly with Margaret Avery and SAMUEL L. JACKSON in support. Critically roasted, the 1990 reprise failed at the box office.

***Sweet Sweetback's Baadasssss Song* (1971)** Cinemation, b&w, 1971. **Director/Screenplay:** Melvin Van Peebles; **Cast:** Melvin Van Peebles (Sweetback), Simon Chuchster (Beetle), Hubert Scales (Mu-Mu), John Dullaghan (commissioner), Rhetta Hughes (old girl friend).

This landmark film, along with *SHAFT* (1971), helped to define and establish the emerging BLACK ACTION FILM genre. While Hollywood had been toying tentatively with the concept for a few years, this picture by VAN PEEBLES dared to depict blatantly the anger of African Americans with the white establishment (i.e., "the Man"). The story also reflected the growing sense of black pride that paralleled the Civil Rights movement of the 1960s. Despite being technically crude and structurally episodic, *Sweet Sweetback* showed Hollywood that not only was there an audience for such outspoken, ethnic-oriented film fare but also that it could be quite profitable.

The movie opens with a title card that reads, "This film is dedicated to all the Brothers and Sisters who have had enough of The Man." Even as an adolescent, African-American Sweetback had a reputation as a great lover. Now that he is an adult, he is a pimp in southern California. One day he is asked to accompany two white vice-squad cops for an interrogation at the precinct. En route, the racist police brutalize a black man whom they encounter. This so enrages Sweetback that he beats the law enforcers to death. Now on the run, and always just one step ahead of the police, he finds shelter with assorted street friends and past lovers, all of whom have had problems with the cops. He eventually crosses the border into Mexico and safety. The final title card alerts, "Watch out. A baadasssss nigger is coming back to collect some dues."

Directed, written, scored, produced, and starring the iconoclastic Van Peebles, the pioneering filmmaker initially had great difficulty in finding distributors for his movie. Eventually, he prevailed, and the violent, X-rated feature earned more than $4 million in domestic film rentals—an amazing feat.

The raw and crude *Sweet Sweetback*, despite all the imitators over the years, remains a powerful viewing experience.

T

***Take a Giant Step* (1959)** United Artists, b&w, 100 minutes. **Director:** Philip Leacock; **Screenplay:** Louis S. Peterson and Julius J. Epstein; **Cast:** Johnny Nash (Spencer Scott), Estelle Hemsley (Gram Martin), Ruby Dee (Christine, the maid), Frederick O'Neal (Lem Scott), Ellen Holly (Carol), Pauline Meyers (Violet), Beah Richards (May Scott).

Made for $300,000 and based on a 1953 off-Broadway play by Peterson, this "pathfinding" drama was considered amateurish by most reviewers and inept in its efforts to present a realistic account of the pain of being African American in a white-controlled society.

Seventeen-year-old African-American Spencer Scott is expelled from his predominantly white high school for having stormed out of class when his history teacher made disparaging remarks about southern blacks. After being comforted by his ailing grandmother (Richards), he visits a black neighborhood where he meets a trio of prostitutes and expresses his interest in having a sexual adventure. Still a virgin, he returns home where he is reassured by his grandmother's caregiver (Dee) and argues with his parents about a minority person's role in the white world. Following his grandmom's death, he patches up his relationship with his parents and admits he understands better now the limits of integration into white society that he can expect.

Badly dated, this early screen depiction of racial inequality was criticized by several ethnic sources at the time because some of the black characters advocated a complacent attitude toward dealing with white suppression. The static film did win two prizes at the Locarno (Switzerland) Film Festival—one for the film and another for Nash (a pop singer in real life) for "the humanity and intensity" of his performance.

talk shows—television For decades, this small-screen format was the special province of white hosts such as Steve Allen, Jack Paar, Johnny Carson, Merv Griffin, Mike Douglas, Dick Cavett, David Frost, Dinah Shore, Virginia Graham, David Letterman, and Phil Donahue. However, by the mid-1980 OPRAH WINFREY had emerged on the Chicago talk-show scene and within a few years became the queen of that special medium. She led the way for several other African Americans to join the field, ranging in personalities from comedians Byron Allen and especially Arsenio Hall (with *THE ARSENIO HALL SHOW*, 1989–94), to former teenage actress Tempestt Bledsoe (of *THE COSBY SHOW*, 1984–92), to movie star WHOOPI GOLDBERG. One of the most effective of all such hosts was former marine drill sergeant Montel Williams, who began his syndicated talkfest in 1991 and consistently proved to be a keen moderator of the human condition. Other later African-American personalities who had TV talk shows included Queen Latifah, Amanda Jewis, and Tavis Smiley.

***Tenafly* (1973–1974)** NBC-TV series, color, 90 minutes. **Cast:** James McEachlin (Harry Tenafly), Lillian Lehman (Ruth Tenafly), Paul Jackson (Herb Tenafly), Rosanna Huffman (Lorrie), David Huddleston (Lt. Sam Church).

During the 1970s vogue for BLACK ACTION FILMS, American network TV followed suit but in a much diluted fashion, not wishing to offend its home viewers with too much "ethnicity," too much violence, or too much sex. As such, the entries used to showcase African-American life lost the exaggerated zesty, flamboyant characters and the heightened violent action that so identified blaxploitation pictures. As a result, none of these genre shows (e.g., *Shaft*, 1973–74) succeeded. *Tenafly* was another such entry, a ninety-minute format that alternated every fourth week on the anthology series *NBC Wednesday Mystery Movie*.

In this detective drama, Harry Tenafly, a black detective, lives in Los Angeles and has a happy home life with his wife Ruth and their son Herb. Following the pattern of mainstream American entertainment that interpreted and/or linked black culture through white authority figures, Tenafly's contact and helper at the LAPD is Caucasian Lt. Sam Church. With such a benign lead character—neither chasing or being pursued by lovelies nor being enmeshed in the film-noir world of the usual on-screen private eye—the bland *Tenafly* soon disappeared from TV screens.

***Tenspeed and Brown Shoe* (1980)** ABC-TV series, color, 60 minutes. **Cast:** Ben Vereen (Tenspeed [E. L. Turner]), Jeff Goldblum ("Brown Shoe" [Lionel Whitney]).

This high-concept detective drama emphasizes comedy rather than hard-boiled activity. Two mismatched individuals become partners in a Los Angeles detective agency. African-American Tenspeed, an ex-convict with a knack for disguises, has a yen to charm the people he is hustling. His partner in private-eye work is naïve, romantic, square "Brown Shoe" (i.e., slang for a straight type) who thinks detective work should be like that about which he reads in old whodunit novels. Produced by the prolific Stephen J. Cannell, the show was greatly hyped, and much was made of its interracial buddy theme. In actuality, racial issues had little or nothing to do with the faltering series, which lasted only a few months on the air.

***10,000 Black Men Named George* (2002)** Showtime-cable, color, 100 minutes. **Director:** Robert Townsend: **Teleplay:** Cyrus Nowrasteh; **Cast:** Andre Braugher (Asa Philip Randolph), Charles S. Dutton (Webster), Mario Van Peebles (Totten), Brock Peters (Leon Frey), Carla Brothers (Lucille Randolph), Ernestine Jackson (Mrs. Randolph).

Aired in February 2002 as part of Black History Month, this high-profile, made-for-cable feature, geared as a history lesson, was based on the actual facts in the unionization of the black railroad porters working for the Pullman Company. The narrative, which begins in the 1920s, is focused on Asa Philip Randolph, a socialist (who publishes a radical magazine in Harlem) and pioneering champion of the Civil Rights movement. Propelling the chronicle are the efforts of the degraded African-American railroad workers to combat their villainous employers who seek to break up the unionizing of their industry. The cast of characters also includes Milton Webster, a union organizer; Ashley Totten, an early member of the brotherhood who is almost murdered by Pullman company henchmen; and porter Leon Frey who is an ex-slave.

The *Hollywood Reporter* (February 22, 2002) complimented director ROBERT TOWNSEND for his "sure hand for the dramatic tension" and rated the offering "fairly entertaining." The trade paper detailed further: "the characters are engaging, though you can pretty much guess where the story is going."

***That Certain Feeling* (1956)** Paramount, color, 103 minutes. **Directors:** Norman Panama and Melvin Frank; **Screenplay:** Panama, Frank, I. A. L. Diamond, and William Altman; **Cast:** Bob Hope (Francis X. Dignan), Eva Marie Saint (Dunreath Henry), George Sanders (Larry Larkin), Pearl Bailey (Gussie, the maid), Jerry Mathers (Norman Taylor).

Jean Kerr's popular Broadway comedy, *The King of Hearts* (1954), received a mediocre screen adaptation in its conversion to a Hope vehicle. In the hackneyed presentation, Francis X. Dignan "ghosts" for celebrated cartoonist Larry Larkin, who has lost his magic professional touch. Making it more difficult for neurotic Dignan, his ex-wife Dunreath is now engaged to snobbish Larkin.

The bright spot in the stale proceedings was the casting of Bailey, then gaining great fame as a club singer. Her role was the type of outdated Hollywood convention that mostly had disappeared by the end of World War II. But the studio revived the patronized species to "showcase" sassy Bailey as the dedicated, chipper maid who cannot resist telling the white lady (Saint) how to win back her man. (When Dunreath does not take her advice, Gussie tricks the former spouses into a loving situation and lets nature take its course.) The movie also had wisecracking Bailey sing both the title tune and "Zing Went the Strings of My Heart."

***. . . tick . . . tick . . . tick* (1970)** Metro-Goldwyn-Mayer, color, 96 minutes. **Director:** Ralph Nelson; **Screenplay:** James Lee Barrett; **Cast:** Jim Brown (Jimmy Price), George Kennedy (John Little), Fredric March (Mayor Jeff Parks), Lynn Carlin (Julia Little), Don Stroud (Bengy Springer), Janet MacLachlan (Mary Price), Bernie Casey (George Harley).

By 1970 Hollywood was dealing more frequently with racial issues on camera, but the major studios still treated the subject gingerly. This overblown, prefabricated drama—which came before the BLACK ACTION FILM cycle overwhelmed Hollywood in the early 1970s—was intended to be a big, important message picture but was an artistic mess.

Jimmy Price is the first African-American sheriff in Colusa County, Mississippi, his election helped by northern organizers. Everyone advises Price on how to handle himself in office in a town rampant with Ku Klux Klan members. Trying to be impartial racially, low-keyed Price does his duty. He arrests a black militant who has raped a young girl, and takes into custody a wealthy young white man, Bengy Springer, for vehicular manslaughter. When a Caucasian contingent threatens to storm the jail to free Bengy, the white ex-sheriff (Kennedy) rallies to Price's side, and soon, other whites join them to stand off the mob.

Brown, the leading African-American action star of the period, was still playing the "good black man" on camera. His image would change within a few years to keep in pace with the onslaught of the new breed of rough, ready, and proud "heroes" of the blaxploitation movie trend.

***Touched by an Angel* (1994–)** CBS-TV series, color, 60 minutes. **Cast:** Roma Downey (Monica), Della Reese (Tess), John Dye (Andrew), Valerie Bertinelli (Gloria: 2001–), Paul Winfield (Special Agent Angel Sam: 1995–).

Reminiscent of Michael Landon's *Highway to Heaven* (1984–89), this fantasy series focused on how angels Monica and her superior Tess, with the latter monitoring the former on Earth, interact with mortals and try to improve their lives. As Tess, Reese evoked ETHEL WATERS in her later years—the heavy-set lady with years of wisdom and much heart.

Never recalling the deliberate caricatures of *THE GREEN PASTURES* (1936), the show had as ballast Reese's portly Monica. Whenever *Touched by an Angel* exuded too many feel-good moments leading to the expected tearjerking finale, Reese's Monica was on hand to ground the scenes, giving commonsense advice, and moving on to the next "case." This was not a subservient, mammy-type figure from Hollywood's past, but a relevant albeit here ethereal creature who was benevolent toward all people (of whatever race).

Reese was twice-nominated for an Emmy Award in the Outstanding Supporting Actress—Drama Series category. For her work on this program, Reese earned several Image Awards in the category of Outstanding Actress in a Drama Series.

Townsend, Robert (1956–) Like fellow African-American comedian, director, actor, writer, and producer KEENEN IVORY WAYANS, Townsend used his sharp perceptions as an ethnic minority to create a variety of forums (comedy clubs, films, and TV) in which to explore the humor and pathos of the contemporary black man. (Sometimes his overoptimistic attitude blunted his comic wit.) *HOLLYWOOD SHUFFLE* (1987), Townsend's debut as a moviemaker, set the benchmark for his satirical barbs (focused in that picture on the white majority stereotyping blacks in the entertainment business). Thereafter, his output was uneven but prolific and wide ranging.

He was born in Chicago, Illinois, and later matriculated at Illinois State University. By then he realized he had a funny bone and eventually became part of Chicago's famed Second City improvisational troupe. He had made his film debut in a bit in *COOLEY HIGH* (1975) and had more substantial roles in *Willie and Phil* (1980) and in *A Soldier's Story* (1984). By then, he had experienced the racial prejudice within the film industry that limited opportunities for ethnic minorities. He used these observations and his anger to create *Hollywood Shuffle.* The low-budget film was a surprise success.

Now a recognized talent, he helmed EDDIE MURPHY's stand-up comedy concert (*Eddie Murphy Raw,* 1987). To utilize his energies while awaiting other directing assignments, he acted in films (e.g., *The Mighty Quinn,* 1989) and guested on TV (e.g., *The Carol Burnett Show,* 1991). He served many functions on the underrated *THE FIVE HEARTBEATS* (1991), a chronicle of a 1960s singing group. His next feature was the corny superhero spoof *The Meteor Man* (1993). On TV his *Townsend Television* (1993), a comedy/variety series, tried to expand the genre format but failed to win over viewers. A more traditional sitcom, *The Parent 'Hood* (1995–99) followed, in which Suzzanne Douglas played his TV wife.

Now limiting himself mostly to directing vehicles, Robert turned out the middling comedy *B*A*P*S* (1997) in which a black American princess (HALLE BERRY) headed to Los Angeles to find love and riches. In the TV movie format, he helmed such items as *Up, Up, and Away!* (2000), a family-oriented comedy/fantasy in which he played a role, and two musical biographies, *Little Richard* and *Livin' for Love: The Natalie Cole Story* (both 2000). Robert turned serious with the telefeature *Holiday Heart* (2000) with Ving Rhames and ALFRE WOODARD, about a drag queen who took in a mother and her daughter. Switching directions, Townsend directed MTV cable's *Carmen: A Hip Hopera* (2001), a variation on the *Carmen* story. Again pivoting back to drama, Robert helmed the Showtime cable movie *10,000 BLACK MEN NAMED GEORGE* (2002) with Andre Braugher, Charles S. Dutton, and Mario Van Peebles. He made occasional acting appearances as in the comedy *Book of Love* (2002).

***Trading Places* (1983)** Paramount, color, 106 minutes. **Director:** John Landis; **Screenplay:** Timothy Harris and Herschel Weingrod; **Cast:** Dan Aykroyd (Louis Winthorpe III), Eddie Murphy (Billy Ray Valentine), Ralph Bellamy (Randolph Duke), Don Ameche (Mortimer Duke), Denholm Elliott (Coleman), Jamie Lee Curtis (Ophelia).

Heralded at the time as a great interracial buddy comedy, and a great follow-up vehicle to *48 HRS* (1982) for fast-rising screen comedian MURPHY, this well-mounted production left much to be desired in the name of racial equality. The premise has two elderly Philadelphia Main Line duffers (Bellamy and Ameche) betting on the importance of heredity versus environment. To prove their point, they rescue recently arrested con artist Billy Ray Valentine and place him into a good life. Simultaneously, they take established commodity broker Louis Winthorpe III and displace him from his job, home, and friends. In the end, Billy Ray and Louis bond and turn the tables on the old meddlers.

Harmless as this variation of Mark Twain's *The Prince and the Pauper* (1882) might have *seemed,* it had a nasty underbelly. There were sequences where the suddenly elevated Billy Ray invited his old down-and-dirty pals to his new fancy pad for a splashy party. As the unrestrained invitees created mayhem, much to the consternation of the suddenly upscale Valentine, there was little doubt that the film's point of view was far from impartial regarding these wild (and primitive) African-American party guests. Then too, while the reclaimed Winthorpe found romantic satisfaction with a pleasing prostitute named Ophelia, there was no woman in the script waiting for Murphy's Billy Ray at the finale. (The same unbalanced situation occurred in the two earlier teamings of Gene Wilder and RICHARD PRYOR in 1976's *SILVER STREAK* and 1980's *STIR CRAZY.*)

The hugely popular *Trading Places* grossed more than $40 million in domestic distribution and earned an Oscar nomination for Best Scoring.

***Trial* (1955)** See entry in Hispanic Americans chapter.

***Trouble Man* (1972)** Twentieth Century-Fox, color, 99 minutes. **Director:** Ivan Dixon; **Screenplay:** John D. F. Black; **Cast:** Robert Hooks (Mr. T), Paul Winfield (Chalky Price), Ralph Waite (Pete Cochrell), William Smithers, (Capt. Joe Marks), Paula Kelly (Cleo), Julius W. Harris (Mr. Big).

Promoted with the tagline "Mr. T is cold hard steel! He'll give you peace of mind . . . piece by piece!" this violent drama was directed by African-American Dixon, who next helmed the impressive *Gordon's War* (1973), which also featured WINFIELD. Made as the BLACK ACTION craze was jumping into full gear, it was violent escapist fare that adhered to the genre's formula. Scripter Black had earlier written the trend-setting *SHAFT* (1971).

As competing Los Angeles gaming syndicates escalate their competition over their roving crap games, extra-tough, sharp-dressing Mr. T—who considers himself a black Robin Hood—steps into the messy situation to settle the score. On one side is Chalky Price and his white partner (Waite), and on the other is his rugged adversary, Mr. Big. Also involved in the vicious caper is confused police detective Capt. Joe Marks, as well as the sensuous club singer Cleo, who is Mr. T's woman.

Interestingly, the upwardly mobile, aggressive Mr. T was an avid advocate of the white capitalist system and emulated high-steppers with his fancy pad and wardrobe.

Trouble Man boasted a fine Marvin Gaye score, with Gaye singing the film's theme song

Trouble with Father, The See *STU ERWIN SHOW, THE.*

***227* (1985–1990)** NBC-TV series, color, 30 minutes. **Cast:** Marla Gibbs (Mary Jenkins), Hal Williams (Lester Jenkins), Alaina Reed-Hall (Rose Lee Holloway), Jackee Harry (Sandra Clark), Regina King (Brenda Jenkins), Helen Martin (Pearl Shay), Paul Winfield (Julian Barlow: 1989–90).

While most contemporary urban black stories on the screen dealt with the downside of life (drive-by shootings, drugs, prostitution, etc.), this sitcom, set in a black neighborhood in Washington, D.C., focuses on the humorous activities of tenants at building #227. The center of activity is Mary Jenkins, a housewife, her engineer husband (Williams), and her teenage daughter (King). Other tenants at 227 include sexy Sandra Clark, who has an eye for men, and nosy old Pearl Shay, who never misses anything that goes on in the busy neighborhood. The favorite spot for many of the building's inhabitants is the front stoop. During the show's final season, Rose Lee Holloway, who owns #227, sells it to Julian Barlow, a man of much pretension.

In the program's early episodes, the characters were real-to-life ethnic individuals. As the series progressed, they became more one dimensional, going for the easy laughs. Gibbs was surprisingly restrained in her lead role, only occasionally reverting to the tart-mouthed, no-nonsense lady that she had played so well on *THE JEFFERSONS* (1975–85).

Tyson, Cicely (1933–) As a prolific, tenacious, and effective actress, she spent years delineating meaningful characters on stage, screen, and TV, all of them elucidating different aspects of black Americans with dignity. Because, relatively early in her lengthy career, she created such an indelible characterization in her dual Emmy Award-winning role as the 110-year-old in *THE AUTOBIOGRAPHY OF MISS JANE PITTMAN* (1974), viewers were surprised thereafter when she played characters far closer to her actual age.

She was born in New York's Harlem, the youngest of three children of a couple who had emigrated from the West Indies. Her carpenter/painter father sometimes sold fruits

Cicely Tyson and Robert Hook in "Just an Old Sweet Song," a 1976 episode of *GE Theater.* (JC ARCHIVES)

from a pushcart to make ends meet. Cicely helped out at age nine by selling shopping bags to neighbors. Her devoutly religious mother took her girl to church, where Cicely sang in the choir and played piano and organ. After high school graduation, Tyson worked as a secretary for the American Red Cross. She got into modeling by chance, but, by the mid-1950s, the very attractive woman was a top black model in the United States. She later studied acting and made her Broadway stage debut in *Talent '59*. Her subsequent plays included *The Cool World* (1960), *A Hand Is On the Gate* (1966), *Carry Me Back to Morningside Heights* (1968), and *To Be Young, Gifted and Black* (1969).

Tyson's debut film, *The Spectrum*, started in the late 1950s, was never completed, but *The Last Angry Man* (1959) was, and she was seen as a ghetto girl. In the 1960s there were few roles available to black women, and those that were often were prostitutes or criminals. Refusing these stereotypes left Tyson with meager opportunities, but she was in such fare as *A Man Called Adam* (1966), *The Comedians* (1967), and *The Heart Is a Lonely Hunter* (1968). Her first major screen role was *SOUNDER* (1972) for which she was Oscar nominated. It led to good parts (e.g., *The River Niger*, 1976, and *A Hero Ain't Nothin' But a Sandwich*, 1977) but also to celluloid junk (e.g., *The Blue Bird*, 1976; and *The Concorde—Airport '79*, 1979).

On U.S. television, Tyson made a breakthrough for all African Americans with her continuing featured role on *EAST SIDE/WEST SIDE* (1963–64). Although cast as a secretary, it was the first time that a black actress was allowed a regular role on a network drama series. It was on TV that Cicely was most often allowed to shine: as Kunta Kinte's mother in the miniseries *ROOTS* (1977), as the mother of Olympic track star Wilma Rudolph in *Wilma* (1977), as Coretta Scott King in the miniseries *KING* (1978), and as former slave Harriet Tubman in *A WOMAN CALLED MOSES* (1978).

In the 1980s, Tyson appeared in such TV outings as *THE MARVA COLLINS STORY* (1981), *Playing with Fire* (1985), and the miniseries *The Women of Brewster Place* (1989). Her 1990s credentials included the telefeatures *Heat Wave* (1990—for which she won a CableAce Award), *House of Secrets* (1993), and the miniseries *Oldest Living Confederate Widow Tells All* (1994—for which she won an Emmy as Outstanding Supporting Actress). She costarred with Melissa Gilbert in the TV series *Sweet Justice* (1994–95) as a southern lawyer. She earned an Image Award for her appearance in the made-for-TV movie *MAMA FLORA'S FAMILY* (1998). Her more recent TV movies included *The Price of Heaven* and *Ms. Scrooge* (both 1997), as well as *Aftershock: Earthquake in New York* (1999), *Jewel* (2001), and a featured role in *The Rosa Parks Story* (2002).

Once wed to jazz musician Miles Davis, Tyson was a cofounder of the Dance Theater of Harlem. She received many awards, including presentations from the NAACP and the National Council of Negro Women.

U

***Under One Roof* (1995)** CBS-TV series, color, 60 minutes. **Cast:** James Earl Jones (Neb Langston), Joe Morton (Ron Langston), Vanessa Bell Calloway (Maggie Langston), Essence Atkins (Charlotte "Charlie" Langston), Ronald Joshua Scott (Derrick Langston), Monique Ridge (Ayesha Langston), Merlin Santana (Marcus).

Although black sitcoms flourished on TV in the 1990s, dramatic series revolving around African-American characters were few and far between. When they were shown, and despite their quality (such as this entry starring veteran JONES), they floundered in the ratings and usually went off the air quickly. It *seemed* to substantiate the theory that the majority of home viewers—no matter their race—were not interested in serious fare with ethnic emphasis.

In this well-crafted series, Neb Langston is a widowed Seattle law enforcer whose home in the suburbs is filled with his family. Neb's son Ron, having retired from the marines, is now running a lumber and hardware store with a Caucasian partner. Ron's wife Maggie, a college graduate, is returning to the workforce, now that her children (Atkins and Scott) are teens. Also present is Ayesha, Neb's offspring who has just returned to the roost, as well as Marcus, Langston's foster son.

The thrust of the weekly episodes was the interaction among the generations of this African-American household and how love—with big dollops of understanding—can help the characters through their problems.

***Uptight* (1968)** Paramount, color, 104 minutes. **Director:** Jules Dassin; **Screenplay:** Dassin, Ruby Dee, and Julian Mayfield; **Cast:** Raymond St. Jacques (B. G.), Ruby Dee (Laurie), Frank Silvera (Kyle), Roscoe Lee Browne (Clarence), Julian Mayfield (Tank Williams), Janet MacLachlan (Jeannie), Max Julien (Johnny Wells), Richard Anthony Williams (Corbin).

This film reflected the accelerating civil-rights debates, legislation, and riots that were so much a part of 1960s America. *Upright* was the first major Hollywood feature—after the assassination of nonviolent leader Dr. Martin Luther King Jr.—to deal with contemporary African-American revolutionaries who used violent methods to assert their rights. The movie was based on Irishman Liam O'Flaherty's 1925 novel *The Informer* and the classic 1935 feature film *The Informer* directed by John Ford. As so often happened when white-themed properties were converted into ethnic screen pieces, the transformation left troublesome plot and character gaps.

In Cleveland, a few days after the 1968 assassination of Dr. Martin Luther King Jr., the city is bracing for riots. Meanwhile, a trio of men, including Johnny Wells, rob an ammunition arsenal. Their steelworker pal Tank Williams was to have been part of the heist but had been drunk at the time. As a result, African-American militant leaders B. G. and Corbin remove Williams from their revolutionary group. Later, a police informer (Browne) suggests to the bewildered Tank that if he helps the law capture Wells, he will be rewarded financially, and his police record will be expunged. As his life snowballs out of control, Williams becomes isolated from his ghetto brethren as well as from his prostitute girlfriend (DEE). After the pursuing police shoot the fleeing Wells, it becomes evident that Tank had a part in the betrayal. Thereafter, he is shot by his one-time friends.

This preachy misfire won no plaudits from reviewers or filmgoers. Interestingly, the confrontations shown on screen occur between the assorted black ghetto groups, *not* between blacks and whites.

***Uptown Saturday Night* (1974)** Warner Bros., color, 104 minutes. **Director:** Sidney Poitier; **Screenplay:** Richard Wesley; **Cast:** Sidney Poitier (Steve Jackson), Bill Cosby

(Wardell Franklin), Harry Belafonte (Geechie Dan Beauford), Flip Wilson (the Reverend), Richard Pryor (Sharp Eye Washington), Rosalind Cash (Sarah Jackson), Roscoe Lee Browne (Congressman Dudley Lincoln), Paula Kelly (Leggy Peggy), Lee Chamberlain (Mme. Zenobia), Calvin Lockhart (Silky Slim).

As his third directorial assignment, superstar POITIER presented this anecdote to the snowballing number of violent, mindless BLACK ACTION FILMS. Although he gathered together a marvelous ethnic cast, dramatic actor Poitier seemed ill-at-ease in the unoriginal lowjinks that propound two unpromising theories: (1) When left to their own devices, men will be chauvinistic boys, and (2) within the African-American culture there are no real class levels.

Cabbie Wardell Franklin and his bored buddy, factory worker Steve Jackson, hightail it to Madame Zenobia's illegal club to drink, gamble, and dally with shapely women. In the midst of their partying, the club is raided by crooked Silky Slim's men. Later, Jackson realizes that his confiscated wallet contains a lottery ticket worth $50,000! Determined to regain the precious voucher, the desperate pair hire inept private investigator Sharp Eye Washington, who proves to be of no use. Soon, the trail leads them to snooty and unscrupulous Congressman Dudley Lincoln, gaudy Leggy Peggy, and ghetto crime boss Geechie Dan Beauford (with BELAFONTE providing a zesty takeoff of Marlon Brando from 1972's *The Godfather*). By the hectic finale, the two buddies have jumped into a river to grab their lottery ticket from a suitcase tossed over a bridge by the fleeing Silky Slim.

Made for more than $3 million, *Uptown Saturday Night* earned more than $7 million in domestic film rentals and led Poitier and COSBY to reunite—in similar wide-eyed roles—for the equally slapstick, unimaginative, but quite profitable *Let's Do It Again* (1975) and *A PIECE OF THE ACTION* (1977).

urban dramas—feature films In the 1910s and 1920s there had been an entire category of silent screen dramas (e.g., *Children of the Ghetto*, 1915; *Rose of the Tenement*, 1928) that reflected life among the Jews in their neighborhood on New York City's Lower East Side. It took more decades before mainstream cinema began to explore the lives of African Americans living in the urban tenement enclaves to any meaningful degree because the industry chose to deal largely only with black characters as slaves or hired help to white characters in narratives that took place in white neighborhoods.

Twentieth Century-Fox's *One Mile from Heaven* (1938), which starred Claire Trevor and featured black actress FREDI WASHINGTON in a secondary role, set part of its social drama in a black neighborhood where Washington lived. One of the first American movies to deal with a black neighborhood in a focal way was *Take My Life* (1942), an independent feature made by Million Dollar Productions and geared for the black movie marketplace. It centered on the Harlem Tuff, a crime-prone group that was, in some ways, parallel to the white cinema's Dead End Kids/East Side Kids movies. The mainstream cinema took up the topic of juvenile delinquents and urban gangs in the 1950s, and one of the first to really feature a black character (SIDNEY POITIER) was *THE BLACKBOARD JUNGLE* (1955), although the settings were mostly around the inner-city high school. (Earlier, in 1950's *NO WAY OUT*, Poitier had played a young doctor in a big city hospital, and the story touched on riots in the black part of town.) Two years later, Poitier costarred in the bleak drama *EDGE OF THE CITY* (1957), which was a meatier treatment of African Americans caught in the unrelenting rut of trying to make ends meet in the big city.

In the 1960s, as Hollywood, like the rest of America, was being forced to acknowledge blacks in a more meaningful way, more films began to focus on African Americans. Adapted from the 1959 Broadway play, *A RAISIN IN THE SUN* (1961) played out its drama in an urban surrounding. Even grittier was *THE COOL WORLD* (1963), which portrayed its young New York City lead character's descent into crime. Another stark drama set in the Big Apple was *The Pawnbroker* (1965), set in Harlem and featuring a mix of ethnic characters. Based on the 1935 movie *The Informer* (set in Ireland), *UPTIGHT* (1968) told its tale in the Cleveland black ghetto.

The 1970s saw an increase of such dramas as the BLACK ACTION FILM cycle began in earnest. *COTTON COMES TO HARLEM* (1970) and its follow-up *Come Back, Charleston Blue* (1972) were period studies of uptown New York City where crime, humor, and romance intermeshed. Many of the blaxploitation dramas took place on the gritty inner-city streets of black neighborhoods: *SHAFT* (1971), *The Final Comedown* (1972), *THE MACK* (1973), *THE EDUCATION OF SONNY CARSON* (1974), and *CORNBREAD, EARL AND ME* (1975). On a more serious note, later in the decade, there were such stark entries as *The River Niger* (1976), *A Hero Ain't Nothing but a Sandwich*, and *Killer of Sheep* (both 1977).

The early 1980s witnessed a rash of urban dramas (e.g., *Fighting Back*, 1982; *Vigilante*, 1983) focusing on good citizens overcoming the criminal elements, but these typically involved multicultural neighborhoods. Much more black-oriented were SPIKE LEE's *Joe's Bed-Stuy Barbershop: We Cut Heads* (1983), and other directors' *South Bronx Heroes* (1985), *Street Smart* (1987), and *Crack House* (1989). The decade ended with Lee's *DO THE RIGHT THING*, which explored the interracial tension within a Brooklyn neighborhood during a hot summer.

By the 1990s—which found more black talent in front of and behind the camera—mainstream cinema was dealing with tensions in the inner cities and reflecting the reality of confrontations and riots that were occurring around the United States. *Common Ground* (1990—TV movie) provided a perspective on racial tension in Boston in the 1970s. *Heat Wave* (1990—TV movie) concerned race riots in the Watts section of Los Angeles. The outburst of such urban dramas in 1991 included Mario Van Peebles's *NEW JACK CITY*, Lee's *JUNGLE FEVER*, JOHN SINGLETON's *Hangin' with the Homeboys*, John Sayles's *City of Hope*, and Matty Rich's *Straight Out of Brooklyn*. Cinematographer ERNEST R. DICKERSON made his feature film directing debut in 1992 with *Juice;* like many of his black peers, he chose to focus on the spectrum of society and the array of problems (unemployment, drugs, street gangs, drive-by shootings, etc.) found in urban ghettos, including the black ones. Other similar pictures were *South Central* (1992), *MENACE II SOCIETY* (1993), and *Fresh* (1994). In fact, there were so many of this subgenre being produced that it led to the satirical *Don't Be a Menace to South Central While Drinking Your Juice in the Hood* (1996), written by and starring Marlon and Shawn Wayans.

Other less violent but equally serious dramas about black urban neighborhoods that appeared in the 1990s and thereafter included *Higher Learning* (1994), *Raising the Heights* (1997), *He Got Game* (1998), *Summer of Sam* (1999), *Harlem Aria* (1999), *Waterproof* (1999), *Once in the Life* (2000), *BABY BOY*, *MacArthur Park*, and *The Visit* (all 2001).

Another more contemporary offshoot of the urban drama deals with more upscale African Americans and included such entries as *The Woods* (1999), *The Best Man* (1999), and *The Brothers* (2001).

V

Van Peebles, Melvin (1932–) A Renaissance man with boundless talents that moved in several directions, his *SWEET SWEETBACK'S BAADASSSSS SONG* (1971), along with the same year's *SHAFT*, kick-started the BLACK ACTION FILM explosion. Always a renegade—especially from the white entertainment establishment—Van Peebles spent years battling to do artistic projects his way and thus setting a provocative example for later ethnic moviemakers.

He was born in Chicago, the son of a tailor. After graduating from Ohio Wesleyan, he joined the U.S. Air Force, where he spent three years as a B-47 navigator. Returning to civilian life, he was blocked by racial discrimination from getting a relevant job with a commercial airline. Instead he became a cable-car brakeman in San Francisco. By the late 1950s he was making his own film short subjects: *Three Pickup Men for Herrick* and *Sunlight* (both 1957). When he could not turn his moviemaking experience into a Hollywood job, he moved his family to Holland, where he did graduate studies at the University of Amsterdam. He also acted with the Dutch National Theater. Moving to Paris, Van Peebles panhandled on the streets to get by financially. Finding racial bigotry in France, which prevented him from joining the directors union, he learned that a published writer could direct his own work. He churned out five novels, one of which, *La Permission*, became a film in 1967. Shown at the San Francisco Film Festival as a French entry, the picture gave Melvin a great deal of publicity, which led, in turn, to his directing the mainstream offering, *WATERMELON MAN* (1970).

Upset by the confining studio system and the racist attitudes he had to confront, Melvin made his next movie, *Sweet Sweetback's Baadasssss Song*, independently. He used perseverance and marketing savvy to get the movie distributed, and it became a sizable hit. Van Peebles was hailed by the media as a hero of his race.

Trying Broadway, he put on two black-themed shows: *Ain't Supposed to Die a Natural Death* (1971) and *Don't Play Us Cheap* (1972). The latter featured ESTHER ROLLE, and although he also filmed it, he had problems finding distribution. Emerging a few year later as the author of the TV script *Just an Old Sweet Song* (1976), he next filmed his ambitious TV movie *THE SOPHISTICATED GENTS* (1979) for which he was scripter, director, composer, actor, and associate producer. The telefeature finally aired in 1981.

Van Peebles directed two off-Broadway shows, *Bodybags* (1981) and *Waltz of the Stork* (1982); for the latter, he wrote the words and the music and costarred with his son Mario. In yet another career turnabout, Melvin Van Peebles became a trader on the floor of the American Stock Exchange—the only black one. He acted again with Mario in the film *Jaws: The Revenge* (1987), appeared on his son's TV series *SONNY SPOON* (1988), began to direct short subjects again (e.g., *Vroom Vroom Vroom*, a segment of the movie *Erotic Tales*, 1996), and wrote the novel *Panther* (1995), which he adapted into a screenplay that his son filmed that year. Then Van Peebles helmed the TV movie *Gang in Blue* (1996) starring Mario and directed the French-Dutch coproduction *Le conte du vente plein* (2000). His more recent screen acting assignments included *Love Kills* (1998) and *Smut* (1999). In 2002 he taught filmmaking as a writing professor at Hofstra University in Hempstead, New York.

At the 2000 Acapulco Black Film Festival, Van Peebles won the Trailblazer Award.

W

***Waiting to Exhale* (1995)** Twentieth Century Fox, color, 121 minutes. **Director:** Forest Whitaker; **Screenplay:** Terry McMillan and Ronald Bass; **Cast:** Whitney Houston (Savannah "Vannah" Jackson), Angela Bassett (Bernadine "Bernie" Harris), Loretta Devine (Gloria Matthews), Lela Rochon (Robin Stokes), Gregory Hines (Marvin King), Dennis Haysbert (Kenneth), Mykelti Williamson (Troy), Michael Beach (John Harris Sr.), Wesley Snipes (James Wheeler).

McMillan's popular 1992 novel was transformed into a surprisingly commercial motion picture—a glossy soap opera with an upbeat finale. As with the original book, it had broad appeal to women in general for asserting the strength of female bonding and the rejection of men when they proved to be negative forces. More importantly, *Waiting to Exhale* provided a welcome change of movie fare for black women by providing on-screen role models with whose domestic/career problems they could relate. For other viewers, it was a refreshing situation to have African-American actresses showcased in key leading roles and *not* entrapped as negative ghetto stereotypes (e.g., whores, druggies, or downtrodden housewives).

Four upper middle-class black women, who are supportive pals, have men troubles. Bernadine Harris's husband (Beach) abandons her for his white office worker. Her friend Savannah Jackson, a TV news producer, is unhappily dating a married man (Haysbert). The older Gloria Matthews is hopeful that her new neighbor (Hines) may be the right man for her and her seventeen-year-old son. As for peppy Robin, she has been socializing with a string of losers and now finds herself pregnant by one of them. Buoyed by each other, the four women cope with their dating issues positively.

Made for $15 million, *Waiting to Exhale* grossed more than $66 million in domestic distribution. It won Image Awards for Outstanding Lead Actress in a Motion Picture (BASSETT), Outstanding Motion Picture, Outstanding Soundtrack Album, and Outstanding Supporting Actress in a Motion Picture (Devine). It received Image Award nominations for Outstanding Lead Actor in a Motion Picture (Hines), Outstanding Lead Actress in a Motion Picture (Houston), and Outstanding Supporting Actress in a Motion Picture (Rochon). This was the second directorial assignment for WHITAKER, who proved amazingly sensitive and adept in showcasing his diverse female cast.

Washington, Denzel (1954–) Clean-cut, strikingly handsome, and possessing a strong sexual presence, Washington evolved into a mainstream Hollywood movie star in the 1990s. This status afforded him almost the same range of roles as white stars such as Mel Gibson or Tom Cruise. Having won a Best Supporting Actor Oscar for *GLORY* (1989), the six-feet-tall Washington spent the next several years in a variety of leading roles, alternating between ethnic-oriented pictures (e.g., *MO' BETTER BLUES*, 1990; *MALCOLM X*, 1992; *DEVIL IN A BLUE DRESS*, 1995; *THE PREACHER'S WIFE*, 1996; *He Got Game*, 1998) and integrated projects where his race or the cultural heritage of his coplayers was not an emphasized plot issue (e.g., *THE PELICAN BRIEF*, 1993; *Virtuosity*, 1995; *Courage Under Fire*, 1996; *The Bone Collector*, 1999). Thanks to the change in the racial/political climate in Hollywood and the United States, Denzel had a much different movie-star experience than did SIDNEY POITIER decades earlier. Unlike standard-bearer Poitier, Washington could mostly practice his craft successfully without having to make race a key factor in his screen image or in the choice of acting assignments.

He was born Denzel Washington Jr. in Mt. Vernon, New York, the second of three children. His father was a Pentecostal minister, and his mother was a gospel singer turned beautician. He grew up in a multicultural neighborhood and was guided by his mother's wish that he become a doctor. By the time he was fourteen, his parents had divorced, and he was raised by his mother; in the process Washington became a rebellious teenager. To straighten out her son, Mrs. Washington sent him to boarding school in upstate New York. At a YMCA-sponsored summer camp, he performed in a talent show and discovered that he had acting talent. This observation was reinforced when he was a sophomore at Fordham University. He played in *The Emperor Jones* and *Othello* on campus and decided on an acting career. In his last year of college, he was spotted by a talent scout and given a role in the TV movie *Wilma* (1977).

After graduation, Washington spent a year at the American Conservatory Theater in San Francisco. Later, back in New York City he scrounged for acting assignments on stage. Late in 1979, he had a supporting role as a boxer in the TV movie *Flesh and Blood;* next came playing Malcolm X in the Negro Ensemble Company's off-Broadway production of *When the Chickens Come Home to Roost;* another high point was performing in the off-Broadway production of *A Soldier's Play* and winning an Obie Award in the process. (He repeated his role as the self-righteous serviceman killer in the film adaptation, *A Soldier's Story*, 1984.)

Washington's first big-screen project was the often condescending farce *CARBON COPY* (1981). He was a regular on the TV medical series *ST. ELSEWHERE* (1982–88), but his role as a resident was one-dimensional. (ALFRE WOODARD was introduced on the show in the fall of 1985 as a potential love interest for Denzel's character, but it did not improve Washington's dour persona on the show.)

In *Cry Freedom* (1987) Washington enjoyed one of his first meaningful screen roles. He was Steve Biko, the nonviolent leader of the Black Consciousness Movement in South Africa. The part earned him a Best Supporting Actor Oscar nomination. Two years later, he won the Academy Award (and a Golden Globe Award) as Best Supporting Actor for *Glory*, dealing with an all-black Northern regiment during the Civil War.

His career jumped ahead when he began to work on camera with SPIKE LEE. Their first collaboration was *Mo' Better Blues* in which he was the egocentric musician. Next, the team made *Malcolm X*, for which Washington received an Oscar nomination in the Best Actor category. (Lee and the star joined forces again in 1998 for *He Got Game.*) If Washington stumbled in the sloppy action movie *Ricochet* (1991), he also looked appropriately bored when forced to play a nonromantic pal of heroine Julia Roberts in the big-budgeted *The Pelican Brief* (1993). Similarly, as the bigoted anti-gay attorney who developed compassion for his homosexual client in *Philadelphia* (1993), Washington's performance was overshadowed by Tom Hanks's. Then, Denzel did box-office service for the thriller *Crimson Tide* (1995) and the same year's *Virtuosity.* For many reasons, the complex and somber *DEVIL IN A BLUE DRESS*, a period whodunit with a black cast, did not work. There was little the star could do with his roles in *THE PREACHER'S WIFE* (where he and WHITNEY HOUSTON displayed no on-screen chemistry), *Fallen*, or *The Siege* (all 1998 and all meaningless cinema).

Washington probably enjoyed the challenge of emoting as a bedridden cripple in the thriller *The Bone Collector*, but he definitely excelled as the black boxer railroaded on a murder charge in 1999's *The Hurricane* (for which he won an Image Award and a Golden Globe in the Best Performance category). Next, he was the coach experiencing racial tension in the college-football yarn entitled *Remember the Titans* (2000—for which he won both the Black Entertainment and Image Award as Best Actor). His more recent movies include the police drama *Training Day* (2001), for which he won his second Oscar; the thriller *John Q* (2001), with Anne Heche; and *The Antwone Fish Story* (2002), in which he starred and made his directorial debut.

Washington, Fredi (1903–1994) This beautiful mulatto performer remained best known for her role as the tragic light-skinned Peola, a woman of mixed race who wanted to pass for white in *IMITATION OF LIFE* (1934). Fredi was pretty and talented, but Hollywood was not prepared then to cast this ethnic minority performer in the leading roles she deserved. Too attractive to play stereotypical domestics on film or stage, her promising show business career floundered.

She was born Fredericka Carolyn Washington in Savannah, Georgia. After her mother's death, she and her sister Isabel were sent to a convent school in Pennsylvania that educated black and Native American youngsters. Later, after a period back home, Fredi moved to New York City, where her grandmother lived and her divorced sister was a dancer. Fredi had modest jobs (e.g., bookkeeper at Black Swan Records) and then was hired to dance on Broadway in *Shuffle Along* (1922). She teamed with Charles Moore for a dance act that toured Europe. Back on Broadway she played opposite PAUL ROBESON in *Black Boy* (1926) as a woman who wants to pass for white.

She was in two 1929 musical shorts: *St. Louis Woman* with Bessie Smith and *Black and Tan* with Duke Ellington. On stage Fredi joined her sister in *Singin' the Blues* (1931). In Robeson's film version of *THE EMPEROR JONES* (1933), Washington was Undine. Her movie career break should have been *Imitation of Life*, but she made only one more Hollywood feature—*One Mile from Heaven* (1937), in which she was again chasing dreams (she wants to keep a white baby she finds).

With no screen roles available to her, Washington returned to New York. She acted on Broadway with Ethel WATERS in *Mamba's Daughters* (1939) and was in such later stage productions as *Lysistrata* (1946), *A Long Way Home* (1948), and *How Long Till Summer* (1949).

Washington was one of the founders of the Negro Actors Guild and served as its first executive secretary in the late 1930s.

***Watermelon Man* (1970)** Columbia, color, 97 minutes. **Director:** Melvin Van Peebles; **Screenplay:** Herman Raucher; **Cast:** Godfrey Cambridge (Jeff Gerber), Estelle Parsons (Althea Gerber), Howard Caine (Mr. Townsend), D'Urville Martin (bus driver), Mantan Moreland (counterman), Kay Kimberly (Erica).

This film's creative premise could have been translated into a biting satire, but it wavered between broad farce and needling pathos, leaving its supposed hero unsympathetic to indifferent viewers. (Part of the movie's alternating tone was due to the production controversy between VAN PEEBLES and the studio as to the film's "proper" approach.) On the plus side, the talented African-American Cambridge responded well to the acting challenge, although his white-face makeup in the opening scenes is never convincing.

One day, white bigot Jeff Gerber, a married insurance man, wakes up to discover that his skin is now black. Unable to eradicate the color change, the baffled man learns firsthand what it is like to be a minority figure in a white world. His doctor, family, and neighbors shun him, and his calculating boss (Caine) wants to connect him with a potentially lucrative ghetto clientele. Even Gerber's secretary, a Swedish bombshell (Kimberly) who had no interest in him before, is suddenly sexually aroused by his new ethnic identity. Fed up with the rejection and the reverse bigotry, Gerber, whose family has deserted him, relocates to a black neighborhood, planning to open a local insurance agency. Now one of the minority, he enrolls in a self-defense class for African Americans.

Van Peebles, who also wrote the picture's score, used his salary from this effort to make the trendsetting, important *SWEET SWEETBACK'S BAADASSSSS SONG* (1971).

Waters, Ethel (1896–1977) This remarkable entertainer never had a singing lesson, but she became a major blues singer. In her era, most blues vocalists were black and sang in a rough-hewn manner. In contrast, Waters had a smooth, distinctive tone that allowed her to cross over into many forms of mainstream entertainment, where she was a pathfinder for racial integration. However, she was not an activist, and preferred to focus on her career.

She was born in 1896 in Chester, Pennsylvania, the daughter of an unwed, raped thirteen-year-old. Ethel was raised by her grandmother, sometimes living in her hometown or in Philadelphia but always in slums. To escape her impoverished childhood, she wed when she was thirteen, but her husband turned out to be a brute. While doing menial jobs to help support the household, she practiced her singing and dancing as outlets to help her forget her trouble. She first sang professionally on her fifteenth birthday in a Philadelphia club, and it launched her career. Because she was so scrawny, she was billed as Mama Stringbean. She later toured the black club circuit. By the 1920s, she was recording for the ethnic Black Swan label and performing at the better venues (e.g., Harlem's Cotton Club). Waters made her Broadway bow in *Africana* (1927).

In her screen debut, Ethel appeared in an-all variety revue, *On with the Show* (1929). But there were few roles available to her in Hollywood unless she played comic-relief domestics. As she did not want to do that, she returned to Broadway for *Blackbirds of 1930*, *Rhapsody in Black* (1931), *As Thousands Cheer* (1933), and *At Home Abroad* (1935). Reaching a career peak, she gave a Carnegie Hall recital in 1938 and the following year starred in a brief experimental TV program, *THE ETHEL WATERS SHOW*. She made her dramatic acting bow on Broadway in *Mamba's Daughters* (1939).

The no-longer-svelte Waters headlined the all-black Broadway musical *Cabin in the Sky* (1940). When LENA HORNE rejected the maid's role in MGM's *Cairo* (1942), Ethel accepted the job and stayed at the studio to recreate her role of Petunia in *CABIN IN THE SKY* (1943). Because of Waters's rivalry with Horne and her growing outspokenness about the studio hierarchy, Ethel's movie career stalled again.

Waters made her film comeback in *PINKY* (1949) and was Oscar nominated. She was the understanding housekeeper on Broadway in *The Member of the Wedding* (1950) and wrote her autobiography (1951's *His Eye Is on the Sparrow*). As part of the public's renewed interest in her, she starred in the TV series, *BEULAH*, repeating her 1940s radio success, but left the popular TV program to recreate her role in the film of *THE MEMBER OF THE WEDDING* (1952).

In the early 1950s, Ethel, now quite heavy, went broke because of problems over back taxes and unwise past investments. Rediscovering God in 1957, she began to work with evangelist Billy Graham on his crusades. Occasional guest spots on TV in the 1950s and a religious film (*The Heart Is a Rebel*, 1956) led to a featured role in the Hollywood movie *The Sound and the Fury* (1959), playing once again a family maid. A TV pilot, *Professor Hubert Abernathy* (1967), failed to sell. Her second memoir, *To Me It's Wonderful*, was released in 1971. She continued to sing with Billy Graham Crusades up to 1976, months before she died of cancer.

Wayans, Keenen Ivory (1958–) Several of his younger siblings (Damon, Kim, Shawn, and Marlon) went into show business, but it was Keenen who pioneered the family name into the world of entertainment. He was in the vanguard of the 1980s African-American talents (including Arsenio Hall, EDDIE MURPHY, and ROBERT TOWNSEND) who jump-started their careers in stand-up comedy and moved into TV and movies. In his self-created TV series *IN LIVING COLOR* (1990–94) and the movies he directed (e.g., *I'm Gonna Git You Sucka*, 1988; *A Low Down Dirty Shame*, 1994), Wayans displayed a heightened perspective about the black man's place in contemporary society, making his observations through broad, often tart satire. By the 1990s, Keenen was a guiding force in Hollywood's African-American filmmaking community.

He was born in New York City in 1958 the first of ten children. The father, a Jehovah's Witness, was a supermarket manager. A few years later, the family moved downtown from Harlem to a housing project in the city's Chelsea section. In his new multicultural environment, he discovered that comedy often diffused the racial bigotry he encountered locally. After graduating high school in 1975, Wayans attended Tuskegee Institute in Alabama on a scholarship as an engineering major but quit college to enter show business. He performed at the Improv in Manhattan and other comedy-club venues.

By the early 1980s, Wayans and his pal Townsend were in Los Angeles working the comedy clubs. He made an unsold TV pilot (*Irene*, 1981) and appeared on episodes of various TV series, as well as having a featured role on the briefly aired television drama series *For Love and Honor* (1983). In these years, he experienced firsthand how few opportunities there were for black entertainers in the white-controlled show business. He networked with African-American pals to create projects. This led to his cowriting *HOLLYWOOD SHUFFLE* (1987) with

Townsend. Wayans packaged and wrote sketch material for *Eddie Murphy Raw* (1987), a stand-up comedy concert film; wrote, directed, and acted in *I'm Gonna Git You Sucka*, his spoof of BLACK ACTION FILMS; and was the guiding force behind the innovative black sketch/variety show *IN LIVING COLOR*, also acting in many of the show's skits. After leaving the hit series due to a dispute with the network, he wrote, directed, and performed in another movie satire, *A Low Down Dirty Shame* (1994), followed by his producing and acting in *Don't Be a Menace to South Central While Drinking Your Juice in the Hood* (1996), a broad send-up of the URBAN DRAMA genre. Then, he performed in *The Glimmer Man* (1996) and *Most Wanted* (1997—which he also wrote and produced).

Wayans was considered a natural to host a late night TV talk program, but *The Keenen Ivory Wayans Show* lasted only one season (1997–98). He was more successful when he produced and directed *Scary Movie* (2000), which featured his brothers Marlon and Shawn and in which Keenen had a cameo role. The positive response (it grossed $157 million in domestic distribution) to this spoof of slasher movies led to *Scary Movie 2* (2001) and *Scary Movie 3* (2002) both of which Keenen directed. He next helmed a remake of *The Incredible Shrinking Man* (2003) starring Eddie Murphy.

***Webster* (1983–1987)** ABC-TV series, color, 30 minutes. **Cast:** Emmanuel Lewis (Webster Long), Alex Karras (George Papadapolis), Susan Clark (Katherine Calder-Young Papadapolis), Henry Polic II (Henry Silver), Eugene Roche (Bill Parker: 1984–86).

Following in the wake of *DIFF'RENT STROKES* (1978–86), Webster also spotlighted a young lead character who was black and precocious. At age twelve, the real-life Lewis was only forty inches tall (he suffered from a genetic predisposition to be small) when he began this series. He played a child nearly half that age, who finds himself thrust into the Chicago household of a newlywed white couple: the groom (Karras) a former pro football player and now a sportscaster and the bride (Clark—wed to Karras in real life) a skittish socialite (later a psychologist) who works as a consumer advocate. According to the premise, Webster's father was a gridiron teammate of George, and Papadapolis had impetuously agreed to be the boy's godfather. Now, the seven-year-old is an orphan and needs a place to live.

Cute as Lewis was, this derivative comedy suffered from the underlying concept of benevolent white figures caring for the needy black youngster. The show concentrated on the white world, and other blacks hardly made an appearance. This sitcom structure upset many ethnic minority viewers, who found the show demeaning to African Americans. Nevertheless, the show attained a degree of popularity.

westerns—feature films In the early years of the American cinema, there were rarely black characters included in the proceedings, even as slaves or servants. A few exceptions were *The Crimson Skull* (1921) and *West of the Pecos* (1935). However, in the late 1930s as part of the independent black-filmmaking trend, singer/performer Herb Jeffries starred in several all-black sagebrush tales (e.g., *Harlem on the Prairie*, 1937; *Bronze Buckaroo*, 1939). In 1948, black talent Louis Jordan starred in *Look-out Sister*, a combination western and musical.

The turning point for presenting African Americans out West in mainstream pictures occurred with John Ford's *SERGEANT RUTLEDGE* (1960), which featured WOODY STRODE as a member of the all-black Ninth Cavalry who was accused of murdering whites. This resolute study blended into the decade's experimenting with using black lead performers in mainstream cowboys-versus-"redskins" pictures: JIM BROWN in *Rio Conchos* (1964), SIDNEY POITIER in *DUEL AT DIABLO* (1966), OSSIE DAVIS in *The Scalphunters* (1968), and Brown in *100 Rifles* (1969) and *El Condor* (1970).

In 1970, as part of the emerging blaxploitation cycle, came *THE RED, WHITE, AND BLACK* (aka *Soul Soldiers*) with Rafer Johnson in the focal role of a tale that showed a growing understanding between African Americans and Native Americans, both exploited by the white troopers and settlers. More vocal in its message was *BUCK AND THE PREACHER* (1972) and especially the angry *THE LEGEND OF NIGGER CHARLEY* (1972). Other genre pieces of the decade include *Adios Amigo* (1975), *Take a Hard Ride* (1975), *Joshua* (1976), and *Boss Nigger* (1977). More subtle integration of black characters with the western ambiance occurred in *The Skin Game* (1971) and the TV movie *Sidekicks* (1974), which was based on the former.

By the 1980s with the western genre dying, one of the few sagebrush pieces made by Hollywood was Kevin Costner's *Silverado* (1985), which featured DANNY GLOVER as a major participant, as Clint Eastwood's later *Unforgiven* (1992) gave prominence to MORGAN FREEMAN's role. Mario Van Peebles directed and starred in the violent western actioner *Posse* (1993), which used a largely black cast as the group hunting a racist officer and a vicious sheriff. The offbeat western comedy *Lightning Jack* (1994), starring Australia's Paul Hogan, had CUBA GOODING JR. as his black, mute sidekick. The comedian SINBAD was featured in the amiable western comedy *The Cherokee Kid* (1995); in contrast, Poitier starred in *Children of the Dust* (aka: *A Good Day to Die*), a violent western of blacks out west, as well as *The Buffalo Soldiers* (1997). In 1999's *Wild, Wild West*, based on the 1960s TV series, black WILL SMITH starred as a government agent who was teamed with a white inventor (played by Kevin Kline) on a mission out west for President Grant. Not much was made of Smith's ethnic background within the leaden proceedings.

western series—television Although the 1950s was filled with TV western series, the first black to have a regular role on such a genre show was Raymond St. Jacques on Clint Eastwood's *Rawhide* (1959–66) and that was not until the last season (1965–66) of the series when he was brought on to play Solomon King, a culinary worker on the cattle drives. Meanwhile, on *The Travels of Jaimie McPheeters* (1963–64), based on Robert Lewis Taylor's 1958 Pulitzer Prize–winning novel, the program dealt with a wagon train heading westward in 1849. Vernett Allen III played Othello, a black valet to one of the pioneers. *The Outcasts* (1968–69) revolved around a man of the gentry turned gunman (played by Don Murray) and a freed slave (played by Otis Young), the latter now a bounty hunter in post–Civil War days. The duo—who were constantly at odds with one another—were partnered in tracking down criminals.

In the short-lasting western show *Wildside* (1985) HOWARD E. ROLLINS JR. appeared as an explosives expert, part of a group that was bound to keep the law in their part of the world. DANNY GLOVER played Joshua Deets on the miniseries *Lonesome Dove* (1989). *Dr. Quinn, Medicine Woman* (1993–98), set in 1860s Colorado, found the transplanted Boston doctor (portrayed by Jane Seymour) fighting for racial equality for both African Americans and Native Americans who live in or pass through the growing town. On *Lonesome Dove: the Series* (1994–96), for the first season, DIAHANN CARROLL was one of the settlers in the Dakota Territory of the 1870s who had a young white man (played by Scott Bairstow) as a partner in her hotel business because the local bank refused to finance a black-run business.

***What's Happening!!* (1976–79)** ABC-TV series, color, 30 minutes. **Cast:** Ernest Thomas (Raj [Roger Thomas]), Fred Barry (Rerun [Freddie Stubbs]), Haywood Nelson (Dwayne Clemens), Mabel King (Mrs. Thomas), Danielle Spencer (Dee Thomas), Shirley Hemphill (Shirley Wilson), Thalmus Rasulala (Bill Thomas: 1976–77).

Three black high-schoolers—Raj, Rerun, and Dwayne—pal around at school and often, after classes, at Rob's, a local diner where Shirley Wilson is a waitress. Raj, a good student, who is often lost in clouds of thought, has frequent run-ins with his hard-nosed mother (Mrs. Thomas) and clashes with his smart-mouthed young sister (Spencer). Sometimes, his divorced father (Rasulala) shows up, but he is no role model. By the 1978–79 season, Raj and Rerun have graduated high school and moved into an apartment together, with Raj going to college and Rerun stuck in a job.

As with such earlier black-themed sitcoms as *That's My Mama* (1974–75) and *Good Times* (1975–79), the overbearing mother—who had become a staple of ethnic minority TV sitcoms—was a major force on the series. Here, the no-nonsense Mrs. Thomas works as a maid to support her single-parent household.

Following in the wake of such young audience-oriented series as *Happy Days* (1974–84), *What's Happening!!* had a large youth following. In the mid-1980s, the series returned to the air as *What's Happening Now!!* (1985–88), showcasing much of the same cast: Ray, a writer, is now married; Dwayne is a computer programmer, and Rerun has a become a used-car salesman.

What's Happening!! derived from the theatrical film *COOLEY HIGH* (1975).

***What's Love Got to Do with It* (1993)** Touchstone, color, 120 minutes. **Director:** Brian Gibson; **Screenplay:** Kate Lanier; **Cast:** Angela Bassett (Tina Turner), Laurence Fishburne (Ike Turner), Jenifer Lewis (Zelma Bullock), Phyllis Yvonne Stickney (Alline Bullock), Rae'ven Kelly (young Anna Mae), Vanessa Bell Calloway (Jackie).

Born Anna Mae Bullock, she survived an impoverished and troubled childhood in Tennessee to emerge as Tina Turner, one of America's great rock vocalists and a black artist who received worldwide acclaim. With Kurt Loder, Turner wrote her haunting autobiography, *I Tina* (1986), recounting her rise to rock 'n' roll fame with singer Ike Turner and the years of extreme abuse she endured as his wife. As graphic and intense as was Tina's memoir, the film pulsated with the performances of BASSETT (whose vocals were dubbed by Tina Turner) and FISHBURNE (who did his own singing) as the performing duo whose personal relationship is accentuated by Ike's substance abuse and fierce temper. In a burst of self-preservation, Tina flees from her abusive spouse and reinvents herself as a tremendously successful solo star. (The film—whose title comes from one of Tina's song hits—concludes with the actual Tina Turner performing the title song in concert.)

This was not a standard show-business screen biography of an emerging black artist, such as the TV movie *Little Richard* (2000). Rather, it ranked with *LADY SINGS THE BLUES* (1974), another graphic account of a black American talent (Billie Holiday). Even more than that earlier film, the ambitious *What's Love Got to Do With It* was a dimensional account of the onstage and offstage life of an ethnic minority performer who dealt with tremendous personal and professional odds. The narrative benefited greatly from the intensity of the coleads' energetic performances and the effectively staged musical numbers. The well-received movie grossed more than $39 million in domestic distribution and received two Oscar nominations: Best Actor (Fishburne) and Best Actress (Bassett). Bassett won an Image Award as Outstanding Lead Actress in a Motion Picture, while one of the film's songs ("I Don't Wanna Fight") was nominated for a Grammy.

Whitaker, Forest (1961–) Hefty and six feet, two inches in height, he had the same baby face as comedian/actor MARTIN LAWRENCE; however, Whitaker was a serious actor (e.g., *Bird*, 1988) who also proved to be an efficient film director (e.g., *WAITING TO EXHALE*, 1995; *Hope Floats*, 1998). He frequently appeared in offbeat movies (e.g., *The Crying Game*, 1992; *GHOST DOG: THE WAY OF THE SAMURAI*, 1999) that utilized his sensitivity as an actor to display black sensibilities. Never a major star, he was a reliable movie character lead who easily stole scenes, as well as a perspicacious director behind the camera.

Whitaker was born in Longview, Texas, attended Pomona College, and then majored in music at USC, planning a career in that field. Instead, he became interested in acting. After stage work, he debuted on screen in *Fast Times at Ridgemont High* (1982), thereafter, showing up in the Civil War era TV miniseries *North and South* (1985) and repeating his role of Cuffey in the sequel, *North and South II* (1986). His next acting credentials included such diverse fare as *Platoon* (1986), *Bloodsport* (1988), *Downtown* (1990), and *Diary of a Hit Man* (1991). By then he had given a superior performance in the key role of jazz musician Charlie Parker in *Bird* and had played the lead male assignment in the black-focused *A RAGE IN HARLEM* (1990). Whitaker was back to major supporting parts in such features as *Blown Away* and *Jason's Lyric* (both 1994).

Drawing much attention in the mid-1990s when he directed the high-profile black women's vehicle *Waiting to Exhale*, three years later he directed a Caucasian love story,

Hope Floats, with Sandra Bullock and Harry Connick Jr. (Whitaker's first directorial chore had been the TV movie *Strapped*, 1993.) Thereafter, he was among the cast that sank in the sci-fi muck *Battlefield Earth* (2000) but performed well in the British-made thriller *The Fourth Angel* (2001) and joined Jodie Foster in the suspense drama *The Panic Room* (2002). He teamed with Colin Farrell for the thriller *Phone Booth* (2002).

For *Green Dragon* (2001), about Vietnamese refugees coming to the United States in 1975, Whitaker produced and costarred (with Patrick Swayze) as he did with *Feast of All Saints* (2001). The latter was a telefeature based on the 1979 Anne Rice book about the dazzling "Free People of Color" in nineteenth-century New Orleans. Other African Americans in the cast included PAM GRIER and Jasmine Guy.

White Shadow, The **(1978–1981)** CBS-TV series, color, 60 minutes **Cast:** Ken Howard (Ken Reeves), Ed Bernard (Jim Willis: 1978–80), Joan Pringle (Sybil Buchanan), Thomas Carter (James Hayward: 1978–80), Kevin Hooks (Morris Thorpe), Eric Kilpatrick (Curtis Jackson: 1978–80), Timothy Van Patten (Salami [Mario Pettrino]), Ken Michelman (Abner Goldstein: 1978–80), Ira Angustain (Ricky Gomez: 1978–80), Byron Stewart (Warren Coolidge).

The TV series concept of a high-school gym teacher/coach and his problem-prone teenage charges was not new. BILL COSBY had played one in *The Bill Cosby Show* (1969–71) and Joe Namath, more recently, in the short-lasting *The Waverly Wonders* (1978). In *The White Shadow*, Ken Reeves is a former professional basketball player who has retired because of a knee injury. He joins the faculty of Carver High in Los Angeles as its basketball coach; located in the inner city, the crowded school has a racially mixed student body. As Reeves adapts to instructing the sport, he also learns how to relate to these street-savvy students, who include several African Americans (Hooks, Carter, and Stewart).

Some sources cited this teleseries as being built on a demeaning premise—that is, the shining white knight again helping needy African-American minority students gain a better future. On the other hand, within its series format, *The White Shadow* did showcase young black talent, and in its sympathetic depiction of student problems, it reflected some of the turmoil of growing up an ethnic minority while residing in a tough, sometimes hostile, urban neighborhood. Most of all, the program avoided the ethnic stereotyping of such other shows as *GOOD TIMES* (1974–79) or *Welcome Back, Kotter* (1975–79).

Williams, Billy Dee (1936–) He had been acting already for many years when he became a movie star in the 1970s, regarded as the first African-American screen lover. Whereas SIDNEY POITIER had been noted for his idealistic, dramatic movie roles and HARRY BELAFONTE had been stiff in his leading man movies, the handsome Williams created a new type of romantic black icon. His screen type appealed to women filmgoers, especially those in the black community.

Born William December Williams in New York City, the son of a maintenance man, he began to appear in plays when he was seven. In 1947, his mother, an elevator operator in a Manhattan theater building, learned of a casting call for a new play. The boy auditioned and made his Broadway debut in *The Firebrand of Florence* (1947). He studied acting at the New York High School of Music and Art and later at the National Academy of Fine Arts. (He had a penchant for painting, an avocation that he continued through the years, with gallery showings, etc.) Thereafter, Williams was on the Broadway stage in such projects as *Take a Giant Step* (1956), *A Taste of Honey* (1960), *The Blacks* (1962), and *Hallelujah Baby!* (1967).

Williams made his movie debut in *The Last Angry Man* (1959) as a tough ghetto youth and, in 1966, played a physician on *The Guiding Light*, a daytime TV soap opera. He was seen as a black soldier in the telefeature *CARTER'S ARMY* (1969) and made a big impression as the football player whose gridiron buddy (James Caan) died in the TV movie *BRIAN'S SONG* (1971). Williams's stardom was consolidated when he played the cool object of Diana Ross's hysterical affections in *LADY SINGS THE BLUES* (1972). (The two reunited for the less successful *Mahogany* in 1975.) Now a box-office name, he starred in such action entries as *Hit!* (1973) and *The Take* (1974) and played the famed ragtime musician in *Scott Joplin* (1977). Later, he was Homer Smith in *Christmas Lilies of the Field* (1979), the role that had won Poitier an Academy Award in *LILIES OF THE FIELD* (1963).

In his midforties Williams's career was reinvigorated by his being the lively Lando Calrissian in two of the *Star Wars* sci-fi entries: *The Empire Strikes Back* (1980) and *Return of the Jedi* (1983). Later in the decade, his parts ranged from enacting DIAHANN CARROLL's lover on TV's *Dynasty*, to budget action movies (e.g., *Number One with a Bullet*, 1987), to TV productions like *The Jacksons: An American Dream* (1992), in which he was cast as record mogul Berry Gordy. More recent assignments included *The Prince* (1996), *The Contract* (1998), *Code Name: Eternity* (1999—TV series), *The Visit* (2000), *Very Heavy Love* (2001), and *Undercover Brother* (2002)

Williamson, Fred (1938–) For sheer volume this actor-producer-scripter-director was a one-man exponent of the BLACK ACTION FILM cycle. While his blaxploitation era peers (e.g., JIM BROWN, Ron O'Neal, and RICHARD ROUNDTREE) fell on tougher professional times after the fad ended in the late 1970s, Williamson continued to churn out low-budget actioners. He often produced (through his Po Boy Productions) and/or directed his own programmer vehicles. His genial persona was always as the macho ladies' man. If his acting style was frequently stiff and his exaggerated manly veneer at times too calculated, he played his rough-and-ready parts with earnestness.

He was born in Gary, Indiana, and received his B.A. from Northwestern University in 1959. (He later became a trained architect.) An excellent athlete, for the next decade he played professional football (where he was known as "The Hammer"). Following the lucrative lead of another ex-gridiron star, Jim Brown, Williamson became an actor. At six feet, three inches and personable, the slick athlete began his entertainment career with an episode guest role in *Star Trek* in 1969. More vital to his career, he played DIAHANN CARROLL's boyfriend from 1970 to 1971 on the TV sitcom *JULIA.* Meanwhile, Williamson performed in such mainstream films as *M*A*S*H* and *Tell Me That You Love Me, Junie Moon* (both 1970).

With the black action-movie bonanza under way, Williamson starred in a blaxploitation western, *THE LEGEND OF NIGGER CHARLEY* (1972), and did his variation of *SHAFT* (1971) with *Hammer* (1972). His violent entry *HELL UP IN HARLEM* (1973) led to the sequel *Black Caesar* (1973). In *Death Journey* (1975), which he produced and directed, Williamson starred as rugged private eye Jesse Crowder, a favored character that he would play several times again. His debut scripting credit was for *Adiós Amigo* (1975), a western that had RICHARD PRYOR as his sidekick. Williamson's initial producing credit had been the prior year's *Boss Nigger,* another sagebrush tale.

In the midst of his moviemaking, Williamson joined Howard Cossell on *NFL Monday Night Football* (1974) as a commentator. Several of Fred's quickie movies were filmed abroad (e.g., *Three Tough Guys,* 1974; *Deadly Mission,* 1977). Sometimes, he teamed on screen with his genre rivals Jim Brown (e.g., *Three the Hard Way,* 1974; *One Down, Two to Go,* 1983) and Richard Roundtree (e.g., *The Big Score,* 1983), Jim Kelly (e.g., *Take a Hard Ride,* 1975). Williamson did episode TV as well: *ChiPs* (1979), *Lou Grant* (1981), and *The Equalizer* (1985). He was featured in the detective TV series *Half Nelson* (1985).

Throughout the 1990s, the mustached actor continued making action entries (e.g., *Black Cobra III,* 1990; *Deceptions,* 1992; *Silent Hunter,* 1995). He was in the blaxploitation-genre spoof *Original Gangstas* (1996), appeared in Quentin Tarantino's *From Dusk Till Dawn* (1996), was part of John Woo's *Blackjack* (1998—cable TV movie), and, in 2001, added *Deadly Rhapsody* and *Carmen: A Hip Hopera* (cable TV movie) to his resume.

Wilson, Dooley (1894–1953) Once he made the film *CASABLANCA* (1942), Wilson earned a special place in American movie history and with nostalgia buffs. His screen character was not a black servant or employee—the typical roles given to African-American performers of the era—but rather a piano player treated as an equal by the Caucasian leading man (Humphrey Bogart). It was the start of Hollywood's path to racial integration in the movies.

Born Arthur Dooley Wilson in Tyler, Texas, by age twelve he was performing with the "Rabbit Foot" Minstrels and next went to Chicago to join the Pekin Stock Company; later, he was in vaudeville. Following World War I, Wilson joined James Reese's musical group, which toured Europe and following that, formed his own quintet that played in London and Paris (where he opened his own club). By 1930 Wilson was back in the United States, having ended his career as a singing drummer. Turning to stage work, later in the decade he worked in productions with the Federal Theater and other companies (including playing *Booker T. Washington* in Harlem and at the New York World's Fair of 1939).

Wilson began the new decade as Little Joe Jackson opposite ETHEL WATERS in the all-black Broadway musical *Cabin in the Sky* (1940). During this period, he was on the executive board of the newly formed Negro Actors Guild of America. He made his screen debut in a small role in *Cairo* (1942), in which Waters was Jeanette MacDonald's maid; that same year, the black actor shone as the hero's stoic pal in *Casablanca.* (Cast as a singing pianist, he vocalized fine, but his piano playing had to be dubbed.) Part of the all-black musical film extravaganza *STORMY WEATHER* (1943), he was then stuck with stereotypical small movie assignments in Frank Sinatra's *Higher and Higher* (1943) and the feckless comedy *Seven Days Ashore* (1944). Returning to Broadway, Wilson performed in the musical *Bloomer Girl* (1944) singing "The Eagle and Me" and "I Got a Song."

He made five more pictures between 1948 and 1951, the best of which was *Come to the Stable* (1949) with Loretta Young.

Winfield, Paul (1941–) As a dramatic actor, he possessed the versatility, intelligence, and range to play a variety of movie leading roles; however, even after his Oscar nomination for *SOUNDER* (1972), Hollywood frequently relegated him to subordinate parts with less-talented Caucasian actors in the lead parts. Winfield turned to television, where there were a few more casting options, such as the focal role of civil-rights leader Dr. Martin Luther King Jr. in the TV miniseries *KING* (1978) or guesting as Judge Harold Nance in two fall 1994 episodes of the small-screen drama series *Picket Fences,* which earned him an Emmy. (Winfield was also active on the stage, especially in regional productions such as *An Enemy of the People* in 1980 Chicago or *Checkmates* in 1987 Los Angeles.)

Born in Los Angeles, after attending a local community college, Winfield transferred to UCLA, where he received his B.A. in theater arts. While acting with L.A. stage groups, he made his TV debut in 1965 on a segment of *Perry Mason.* From 1968 to 1970 Winfield was DIAHANN CARROLL's boyfriend on the sitcom *JULIA,* replaced by FRED WILLIAMSON for the show's last season. Among Paul's first movies were two with SIDNEY POITIER, *THE LOST MAN* (1969) and *Brother John* (1971).

Sounder did not provide the anticipated career break for Winfield. He accepted the lead in the ultra violent BLACK ACTION entry *Gordon's War* (1973) and was baseball player Roy Campanella in the telefeature *It's Good to Be Alive* (1974). *CONRACK,* which had a similar flavor to *Sounder,* found him as Mad Billy in support of Jon Voight. Winfield was in the screen musical of *Huckleberry Finn* (1974) as Jim Watson, the runaway slave. (He recreated the part in the telefilm *Back to Hannibal: The Return of Tom Sawyer and Huckleberry Finn,* 1990.) Winfield ended the decade with viable roles in two TV miniseries, *BACKSTAIRS AT THE WHITE HOUSE* and *ROOTS: THE NEXT GENERATIONS* (both 1979).

White Dog (1982), in which Winfield was effective as the animal trainer dealing with a killer dog geared to attack blacks, had only limited release. By now, he was in his forties, and a younger generation of (black) actors were getting the acting jobs he once might have claimed (e.g., the lead in the TV movie *For Us, the Living*—it was HOWARD ROLLINS JR. who played civil-rights activist Medgar Evers, while Winfield portrayed a subordinate character). During the late 1980s, he had a regular role on TV's *Wiseguys* and was on the TV sitcom *227* during its final season (1989–90).

One of Winfield's best roles in the 1990s was as the judge in Harrison Ford's *Presumed Innocent* (1990). The veteran actor was not above playing a silly role in the blaxploitation spoof *Original Gangstas* (1996) nor taking a supporting assignment in the short-lived TV comedy *Built to Last* (1997). From being the campy "Auntie Miriam" in the gay-themed *Relax . . . It's Just Sex* (1998), he segued to *Strange Justice* (1999), a TV movie about the Anita Hill case, in which he was Supreme Court Justice Thurgood Marshall. In *Catfish in Black Bean Sauce* (2000), he and his wife (Mary Alice) raised two Vietnamese siblings who later are reunited with their mother. Then it was back to action fodder for Winfield, playing a police detective in *Second to Die* (2001).

Winfrey, Oprah (1954–) If SIDNEY POITIER was the African-American community's representative of hope in the 1950s and 1960s regarding the integration of the U.S. entertainment industry, Winfrey became the black people's dream later in the twentieth century. Here was an individual from an impoverished and troubled childhood who became one of America's most respected individuals, a media mogul with great influence on the public through her TV talk show, her film and TV acting/producing, and her charitable work.

She was born out of wedlock in Kosciusko, Mississippi, to Vernita Lee, a domestic, and Vernon Winfrey, a barber. Before her first birthday, she was sent to live with her maternal grandmother on a farm near Jackson, Mississippi. When she was six, Winfrey was given her first pair of shoes; also that year she went to Milwaukee, Wisconsin, to be with her mother, her younger half-sister Patricia, and her younger half-brother, Jeffrey. Near age ten, she was sexually molested by a cousin but told no one about the traumatic incident for years. This shocking episode led her to becoming sexually promiscuous. Vernita could not cope with her rebellious daughter, now thirteen, and sent her to stay with her father and his wife in Nashville. At the time Oprah was pregnant. (She gave birth prematurely; the baby boy died soon thereafter). Once under her father's strict guidance, Winfrey abandoned her wild phase.

Winfrey's first media-industry job was a summer position in 1971 as a news reporter for a Nashville (black) radio station. At Tennessee State University, besides her class regi-

Oprah Winfrey, TV talk-show host in action in 1992. (AUTHOR'S COLLECTION)

men, she entered several ethnic beauty pageants and worked at the local CBS-TV affiliate (where she was the first African-American news coanchor). She ended her college life in 1976 a few courses short of earning her diploma (later awarded via an honorary B.S. degree in communications in 1987) to join the news team of a Baltimore TV station as a coanchor and reporter. During this period when the station sought to remold her physical image to mirror Caucasian counterparts in the industry, the frustrated, five-feet, seven-inch Oprah turned to food and blossomed to more than 190 pounds. (Her roller coaster ride regarding her weight became a lifelong problem that earned her great empathy with the American public.) Because of her new physical size, the station eventually demoted her to handling a morning talk program; she found that she liked the format far better than doing news. Now happier, she ventured into participating on stage in a local Black Theater Festival. In 1983 she was hired to host a Chicago talk show; before long Winfrey's ratings were on a par with Phil Donahue's Chicago-based talk program.

While Winfrey was establishing herself as a talk show success, she made her big-screen debut playing the proud Sophia in *THE COLOR PURPLE* (1985), for which she won a Best Supporting Actress nomination in both the Academy Award and the Golden Globe competitions. The next year, she founded her film/TV production company, Harpo Productions, took her talk show into national syndication, and appeared in the movie remake of *NATIVE SON*. Her income in that breakthrough year of 1986 was estimated at about $11 million. In 1986 she won the first of several Daytime Emmys as Best Host of a Talk Show. Winfrey produced and starred in the two-part TV movie *The Women of Brewster Place* (1989), dealing with seven African-American women struggling in the ghetto. The popular telefeature was turned into a short-lasting TV series *(Brewster Place)* in 1990 with Winfrey again playing her role of Mattie Michael, which had won her an Image Award in 1989.

Not content with having "just" an interesting TV talk show, she found ways to enhance the program while educating her home viewers (e.g., her book-reading club, which had enormous influence on the public). She became an active advocate against child abuse and was heavily involved in ethnic causes. Winfrey began to write her autobiography but stopped the project because of its traumatic effect on her and because she concluded that it would not be an empowering experience for readers. In *There Are No Children Here* (1993—TV movie) Winfrey returned to acting (replacing Diana Ross), with distinguished black poet Maya Angelou cast as her mother. In 1997 she acted in the made-for-TV drama *Before Women Had Wings*, and the following year, she brought Toni Morrison's best-seller *BELOVED* to the screen. The latter was not a hit. Her Harpo Productions produced several TV movies, including *David and Lisa* (1998) with Poitier and *Tuesdays with Morrie* (1999) starring Jack Lemmon. In 1999 she and her longtime boyfriend Stedman Graham taught a course in the "Dynamics of Leadership" to grad students at Northwestern University. Meanwhile in 1996, she coauthored with Bob Greene the book *Make the Connection: Ten Steps to a Better Body—and a Better Life;* the next year she made a tied-in video *(Oprah: Make the Connection)*. All the proceeds from these two ventures were donated to charity.

By the end of the twentieth century, Oprah was one of the richest women in America and was ranked by *Entertainment Weekly* as one of the most important people in the entertainment industry. She is the only woman, and the only African American, to have made that ranking list thus far.

In 1989 the NAACP Image Awards named her Entertainer of the Year, and in 1998 the Emmys bestowed on Oprah a Lifetime Achievement Award.

***Within Our Gates* (1920)** Micheaux Film Co./Quality Amusement, b&w, 8 reels. **Director/Screenplay:** Oscar Micheaux; **Cast:** Evelyn Preer (Sylvia Landry), Flo Clements (Alma Prichard), James D. Ruffin (Conrad Drebert), Jack Chenault (Larry Prichard), William Smith (Philip Gentry), Charles D. Lucas (Dr. V. Vivian).

This silent photoplay by prolific African-American filmmaker/pioneer MICHEAUX had more than enough plot and melodrama to fill several motion pictures. It centers on Sylvia Landry, a black woman who comes north to visit her divorced cousin, Alma Prichard. After the jealous Alma breaks up Sylvia's romance with Conrad Drebert, a dejected Sylvia returns south and finds employment at a school for impoverished minority children. To help the institution locate a benefactor, Sylvia journeys to Boston, where she is successful in her mission. Back at the school, its director proposes to Sylvia, but she loves Dr. Vivian whom she met up north. Eventually, even after learning Sylvia's troubled background, the enamored Vivian still asks her to be his wife.

Filled with subplots of miscegenation, lynching, and racial strife, *Within Our Gates* caused considerable controversy at the time of its distribution and led to many of the debated sequences and themes being deleted from release prints. Part of the film's message, encapsulated by the too-restrained Vivian character, is that African Americans should not focus so much on past injustices in the United States but be proud of their contributions to the country's growth and be good citizens. Some commentators found contrasting parallels between this Micheaux entry and D. W. Griffith's *THE BIRTH OF NATION* (1915).

***Wiz, The* (1978)** Universal, color, 133 minutes. **Director:** Sidney Lumet; **Screenplay:** Joel Schumacher; **Cast:** Diana Ross (Dorothy), Michael Jackson (Scarecrow), Nipsey Russell (Tinman), Ted Ross (Lion), Mabel King (Evillene), Theresa Merritt (Aunt Em), Thelma Carpenter (Miss One), Lena Horne (Glinda the Good), Richard Pryor (the Wiz).

This expensive failure (made for more than $24 million, it grossed only $13.6 million in domestic film rentals) did much harm to the future of black filmmaking. Its colossal failure kept many of the major studios, for several years to come, from funding African-American themed movies. Ironically, as a 1975 Broadway musical, *The Wiz* had run for 1,672 performances and won several Tony Awards. It derived from L. Frank

Baum's children's novel, *The Wonderful Wizard of Oz* (1900) as permutated into the 1939 MGM movie musical classic starring Judy Garland and then adapted for Broadway with a book by William F. Brown and music and lyrics by Charles Smalls.

Among the film's many problems was having Lumet, a director of serious urban stories, helm the picture and to have another Caucasian (Schumacher) write the screenplay. The duo had no flair for the ethnic idiom, and the resultant film seemed detached from contemporary African-American life. Another key fault was casting thirty-four-year-old ROSS as the ingenue lead (now a sheltered Harlem schoolteacher who discovers all about life by a magical trip to Munchkinland, another part of New York City). PRYOR, as the Wizard of Oz, was also off his mark. (In contrast, Jackson as the Scarecrow was effective, as were King—from the Broadway cast—as the Wicked Witch and HORNE—the former mother-in-law of Lumet—as Glinda.)

With sloppy choreography, a lack of joy in most aspects of the film, and a naïve heroine who, seemingly, has learned nothing from her adventures in the big world, *The Wiz* was a big disappointment to most critics and viewers. (The best moments in the film were Jackson and Ross dueting "Ease on Down the Road," Horne joining with Ross in "Believe In Yourself," and King performing "Don't Bring Me No Bad News.")

The lackluster *The Wiz* won four Oscar nominations: Best Art Direction-Set Decoration, Best Cinematography, Best Costume Design, and Best Original Song Score and/or Adaptation.

Woman Called Moses, A **(1978)** NBC-TV, color, 200 minutes. **Director:** Paul Wendkos; **Teleplay:** Lonne Elder III; **Cast:** Cicely Tyson (Harriet Ross Tubman), Will Geer (Thomas Garrett), Robert Hooks (William Still), James Wainwright (Andrew Coleman), Jason Bernard (Daddy Ben Ross), Clifford David (Doc Thompson), Dick Anthony Williams (John Tubman).

With the momentum generated from the miniseries *ROOTS* (1977), the networks were more willing to air black-themed programming. One such entry is this lengthy telefeature based on the life of Harriet Tubman (ca. 1820–1913), a slave in Maryland who escapes in 1849—thanks to the Underground Railroad. After receiving what she claims are messages from God, she makes several trips back to her home state to lead several hundred slaves to freedom.

The most poignant part of this often too-contrived drama details the many humiliations endured by Tubman while the "property" of her white master: beatings, separation from her sister, being forced to pull a wagon like a mule, and so on. Slowly, she saves to buy her freedom, only to have her money stolen by her husband (Williams), thus forcing her to start the saving all over again.

In the pivotal role, TYSON provides a strong performance with her interpretation of this legendary historical figure. Strangely, the telefeature does not include any of the intriguing events in the subject's later life, such as Harriet spying for the North during the Civil War, becoming a suffragist, and so on.

Woodard, Alfre (1953–) More so than CCH Pounder, another contemporary, versatile black actress, Woodard projected great vulnerability and could also be believably comedic; in fact, she seemed capable of tackling most types of roles on stage, film, or TV. It could only be speculated what she would have done with the part of Celie in the movie *THE COLOR PURPLE* (1985), a cherished role that she lost to WHOOPI GOLDBERG.

Woodard was born in Tulsa, Oklahoma, the youngest of three children. Reportedly, she gained her unusual first name when her godmother saw a vision with the letters *Alfre* spelled out in gold. During high school, Woodard became interested in acting and pursued her craft at Boston University. She then worked at the Arena Theater in Washington, D. C., and at the Mark Taper Forum in Los Angeles. (Her later off-Broadway credits included *Two by South* and *Map of the World.*) The actress's movie debut was in *Remember My Name* (1978). On TV she was in such telefeatures as *THE SOPHISTICATED GENTS* (1981), *For Colored Girls Who Have Considered Suicide/When the Rainbow Is Enuf* (1982), and the quick-failing sitcom *Tucker's Witch* (1982).

Woodard's professional breakthrough occurred in *Cross Creek* (1983), where she played Geechee to Mary Steenburgen's lead. Oscar nominated as Best Supporting Actress (the first time a black woman had been nominated in that category since BEAH RICHARDS for 1967's *GUESS WHO'S COMING TO DINNER?*), and despite her celebrityhood, she still had to deal with the paucity of roles offered her. In 1984 she won an Emmy for Outstanding Supporting Actress in a Drama Series for her appearance on *Hill Street Blues*, in 1985 was Geena Davis's best friend on a silly sitcom, *Sara*, and then played Dr. Roxanne Turner for two years (1985–87) on *ST. ELSEWHERE*. (Woodard was nominated for an Emmy for her work on that series; she had won an Emmy for her guest role on the pilot of *L. A. Law* in 1986.)

After playing the rich role in *Mandela* (1987—TV movie) of the wife of the South African leader (DANNY GLOVER), she and Glover reunited for *Grand Canyon* (1991) and *Bopha!* (1993). Meanwhile Woodard joined John Sayles's *Passion Fish* (1992) as the nurse/companion of a white ex–soap-opera star. Woodard won an Image Award as Outstanding Actress for her starring performance in the telefeature *The Piano Lesson* (1995) and an Emmy Award, as well as the CableACE Award and an Image Award for Best Actress in a Movie or Miniseries, for *Miss Evers' Boys* (1997—TV movie). That same year, she was nominated for a CableACE Award for Best Supporting Actress in a Movie or Miniseries for playing Berenice Sadie Brown in *The Member of the Wedding*.

Woodard was coproducer of *DOWN IN THE DELTA* (1998) and executive producer of *Funny Valentines* (1999—TV movie), the latter entry teaming her with Pounder and Loretta Devine (with both of whom she reunited for *Baby of the Family*, 2001). She received an Image Award as Outstanding Supporting Actress for her role in the movie *Love & Basketball* (2000) and provided the voice of Plio in the animated feature *Dinosaur* (2000). Next, she supported Kevin Spacey and Jeff Bridges in the fantasy *K-PAX* (2001), as well as providing a voice in *The Wild Thornberrys* (2002) and acting in the sci-fi film, *The Core* (2002).

Asian Americans

A

action and adventure series—television Because these genres of TV programming often took their protagonists to the exotic Far East, occasionally recurring roles became available to Asian Americans, but the characters were not always played by Asian Americans. One of the earliest such entries was *Ding Ho and the Flying Tigers* (1950) with Richard Denning as Ding Ho, commander of the Flying Tigers in pre-World War II China. The cast featured RICHARD LOO and VICTOR SEN YUNG. The syndicated *Terry and the Pirates* (1952), based on Milton Caniff's comic strip, showcased the pilots of Air Cathay who battled sinister villainess Lai Choi San, better known as the Dragon Lady, played by Gloria Saunders. Another such entry was *China Smith* (1952–55); Dan Duryea's China Smith was a con artist/private eye based out of a Singapore bar. Caucasian Myrna Dell played Shira, nicknamed "Empress," a very Eurasian type of figure. *Hong Kong* (1961) dealt with an American journalist operating out of the British crown colony. His first houseboy was Fong (played by Harold Fong in 1960); Ling (played by Gerald Jann from 1960–61) succeeded him. At the local club where the reporter hung out, hostess Ching Mei was played by Mai Tai Sing. *THE GREEN HORNET* (1966–67) offered BRUCE LEE as KATO, the resourceful manservant of the white lead (played by Van Williams). *Big Hawaii* (1977), set on a large ranch on the island of HAWAII, had a mix of Asian-American and Caucasian characters, including Moe Keale as the son of the housekeeper (played by Elizabeth Smith). Another Hawaiian-set series, *The MacKenzies of Paradise Cove* (1979), concerned Caucasian orphans who adopt a fishing boat operator as their surrogate father and featured several Asian Americans playing Hawaiians (e. g., Moe Keale as Big Ben Kalikini).

Tales of the Gold Monkey (1982–83), set in pre-World War II days, had John Fujioka as Todo, the commander of a private army for the exotic Princess Koji. *The Master* (1984) centered on a Westerner (played by Lee Van Cleef) who, after World War II, became a NINJA master. Back in America, he and a young pal set out on adventures while being pursued by Ninja assassins, including Okada (played by Sho Kosugi). *Bring 'Em Back Alive* (1982–83), inspired by the hit feature film *Raiders of the Lost Ark* (1981), was set in pre-World War II Malaya, with Clyde Kusatsu as the helper of the show's hero, and George Lee Cheong as Chaing, the bartender at the local watering hole. A favorite canine star, Rin Tin Tin returned to television in *Rin Tin Tin K-9 Cop* (1988–93) in which one of the police officers, Ron Nakamura, was enacted by Denis Akiyama.

On *KUNG FU: THE LEGEND CONTINUES* (1993–97), DAVID CARRADINE was back playing the grandson of the Chinese-American kung fu expert (the star character of *KUNG FU*, 1972–75). A recurring figure in this show was the elderly Lo So (known as "the Ancient"), performed by Kim Chan. A parallel series was *VANISHING SON* (1995), starring RUSSELL WONG as a martial arts expert come to the United States from China.

MYSTERY FILES OF SHELBY WOO (1996–99) offered PAT MORITA as the grandfather of an adventurous girl involved in crime solving. *Wind on Water* (1998), which lasted two weeks on the air, was set on the big island of Hawaii and presented Bo Derek as the widowed clan ruler and cattle-ranch owner. One of her two sons had a surfing pal named Kai (played by Matthew Stephen Liu).

Baywatch, which began in 1989, was originally set in Los Angeles/Malibu Beach. In 1999 the show relocated the plot to the U.S.'s fiftieth state and became known as *BAYWATCH HAWAII*. Among the new lifeguards who joined the cast of regulars were Stacy Kamano as Kekoa Tanaka, Jason Mamoa as Jason, and Kala'i Miller as Kai. *Baywatch Hawaii* left the air in spring 2001. *Poltergeist: the Legacy* (1995–) dealt with a secret society based in the San Francisco area that opposed evil spirits such as demons. One of the group was Alexandra "Alex" Moreau, played by Robbi Chong. *V.I.P.* (1998–2002) involved the Vallery Irons Protection firm and starred Pamela Anderson Lee. One of the partners in the security firm was Nikki Franco, played by Natalie Raitano. *The Relic Hunter* (1999–) presented a professor—with a black belt in karate—as a globe-trotting finder of lost relics. The role was played by Hawaiian-born Tia Carrere. On *Higher Grounds* (1999–2000), which dealt with troubled youths who were sent to a special boot camp to reform, one of the subordinate "inmate" characters was Annie played by Benita Ha. The adventure series, *Level 9* (2000–2001) had among its multiethnic cast, Susie Park as Joss Nakano.

***Adventures of Fu Manchu, The* (1956)** Syndicated TV series, b&w, 30 minutes. **Cast:** Glen Gordon (Dr. Fu Manchu), Lester Matthews (Sir Dennis Nayland-Smith), Clark Howat (Dr. John Petrie), Carla Balenda (Betty Leonard), Laurette Luez (Karamanch), John George (Kolb).

Sax Rohmer's memorable literary characterization of the fiendish Far Easterner, DR. FU MANCHU, had been adapted for feature films, a serial, and a radio version. In 1950 a pilot had been made for a TV series to feature John Carradine as Dr. Fu Manchu and Sir Cedric Hardwicke as Dennis Nayland-Smith, but the show did not sell. Finally this new syndicated rendition was launched, once again with a Caucasian playing the dastardly Fu Manchu. It was one of the few television programs at that time to star a villain. The series presented the remarkable scientist as a vengeful force, operating from his home in Macao or other exotic sites in the Orient. In sending out his operators to do his evil biddings, the racial angle was deemphasized, thus playing down the old concept of the "Yellow Peril" against the Caucasian free world.

Sir Dennis Nayland-Smith of Scotland Yard was on hand once again as Fu Manchu's long-standing nemesis as was Dr. John Petrie.

Ahn, Philip (1905–1978) Despite his more than 110 feature film roles, this Korean American was best remembered for his portrayals of sadistic Japanese officers in World War II movies, where he was often cofeatured with RICHARD LOO, but Ahn was sometimes cast as a goodly Chinese. Very frequently, his assignments were slight, but his face was so well known to moviegoers that even a quick flash of him on screen established an image immediately.

Born in Los Angeles, he almost made his screen debut in Douglas Fairbanks's *The Thief of Bagdad* (1924), but his mother did not think acting was a proper occupation for her son. He attended the University of Southern California where he studied foreign commerce and acting. One of his early screen parts was in the low-budget thriller *A Scream in the Night* (1935). He was a revolutionary captain in *THE GOOD EARTH* (1937). That same year he was Prince Chung in *Thank You, Mr. Moto* (1937) and joined another Asian sleuth series for *CHARLIE CHAN IN HONOLULU* (1938).

By the early 1940s, Ahn was already being cast frequently as a Japanese soldier/officer: *THEY MET IN BOMBAY* (1941), *BEHIND THE RISING SUN* (1943). He was still alternating in feature films between being an evil Nipponese or benevolent Chinese in the 1950s and 1960s, by which time he had a recurring role on the *Mr. Garlund* (1960–61) adventure TV series. Later, he was Master Kan on *KUNG FU* (1972–75) and appeared as Wong in *Portrait of a Hitman* (1977), a year before he died. Ahn's brother Philson also appeared in many movies.

***All-American Girl* (1994–1995)** ABC-TV series, color, 30 minutes. **Cast:** Margaret Cho (Margaret Kim), Jodi Long (Katherine Kim), Clyde Kusatsu (Benny Kim), B. D. Wong (Stuart Kim), J. B. Quon (Eric Kim), Amy Hill (Grandma).

This series was promoted as the first mainstream network sitcom to deal with a Korean-American family. Following its demise after one season, stand-up comic CHO rehashed the rise and fall of the series in her comedy act, gaining renewed coverage for this television-show misfire.

In *All-American Girl*, hip Margaret Kim is extremely acculturated. She attends college, works at the cosmetic counter of a San Francisco department store, and spends a good deal of time arguing with her tradition-bound mother. Katherine, who owns a bookstore with her compliant husband Benny, wants her daughter to date Korean-American men; Margaret prefers Caucasians, especially the biker types. Her older brother, Stuart (a cardiologist-in-the-making and engaged to a Korean girl), is no consolation to her, as he does everything to please his traditional parents. Margaret receives better support from her younger sibling Eric and from the aged grandma who always speaks her mind.

The powers that be on *All-American Girl* kept Americanizing the series, sanitizing its ethnic flavor. The scenes at the Kims' townhouse and the family bookstore revealed almost nothing of the owners' cultural heritage. In addition, many sequences were set at the department store where Margaret worked. As this show progressed, Cho's character became like any other nondescript sitcom lead.

All-American Girl generated controversy among the Korean-American community in Los Angeles, some of whose members felt the show was unrealistic in its hodgepodge of ethnicities, its unauthentic accents, and its stereotypical presentation of what Korean Americans wore, ate, or said.

In the spring of 1995, the network aired a revamped version of the show in which Cho's TV screen alter ego moved out of her parents' home and roomed in an apartment with three guys.

***Ally McBeal* (1997–2002)** Fox-TV series, color, 60 minutes. **Cast:** Calista Flockhart (Ally McBeal), Greg Germann (Richard Fish), Lisa Nicole Carson (Renee Raddick: 1997–2001), Jane Krakowski (Elaine Bassell), Peter MacNicol (John Cage), Lucy Liu (Ling Woo: 1998–2001, 2002).

When it premiered, *Ally McBeal* quickly proved it was more than just another legal drama/comedy and that its roster of characters could often be totally bizarre. The show soon became noted for its offbeat fantasy sequences.

Self-indulgent, whimsical attorney Ally works at an extremely quirky Boston law firm, famous for its weird senior partner John Cage, for its mercenary founding lawyer Richard Fish, and for its unisex bathroom. As cast members came and went, a second season arrival was Asian-American "dragon lady" Ling Woo. At first she was merely one of the firm's more aggressive clients, a superbright woman who delighted in suing others, but she soon began to date the self-absorbed Fish. Later, she revealed she was an attorney and thereafter became a litigating member of the firm, and eventually moved on to become a judge on a TV reality show.

As in her feature film appearances (e.g., *Charlie's Angels*, 2000), the attractive LIU displayed a smart-mouth behavior on *Ally McBeal*. Whether manipulating the will of the others, making a brief lesbian pass at Ally, or voicing her strong views, she proved to be atypical of western culture's stereotype of a submissive Asian-American female.

Amazing Chan and the Chan Clan, The **(1972–1974)** CBS-TV series, color, 30 minutes. **Voices:** Brian Tochi (Alan Chan), Leslie Kumamota (Anne Chan: 1972), Jodie Foster (Anne Chan: 1972–74), Keye Luke (Charlie Chan), Jay Jay Jue (Flip Chan: 1972), Gene Andrusco (Flip Chan: 1972–74), Robert Ito (Henry Chan).

In this bland children's animated TV series, LUKE, who had played #1 son Lee in the 1930s CHARLIE CHAN film series, portrays the great Chinese detective. The format is geared to the 1970s (with shades of *The Partridge Family*, 1970–74). Saddled with ten rambunctious offspring, Chan and the children drive about in their van, are a performing rock group, and have a family canine, Chu-chu. During the early weeks of its run, the bulk of the Asian-American talent providing the children's voices were replaced because of concerns that their speech was too accented. The show was produced/directed by William Hanna and Joseph Barbera.

American Geisha **(1986)** CBS-TV, color, 100 minutes. **Director:** Lee Philips; **Teleplay:** Judith Paige Mitchell; **Cast:** Pam Dawber (Gillian Burke), Richard Narita (Kangoro), Stephanie Faracy (Katy), Robert Ito (Mr. Hasimoto), Dorothy McGuire (Ann Suzuki), Clare Nono (Yoshiko), Beulah Quo (Kangoro's mother), Takayo Fischer (Okaasan).

Based in part on Liza Dalby's book *Geisha* (1983), the contrived telefeature *American Geisha* attempted to explain (as had the 1963 movie comedy *MY GEISHA*) that a geisha was *not* a prostitute but a highly trained and respected provider of light entertainment to male customers.

American Gillian Burke is writing her anthropology doctorate thesis on the traditions of the geisha and intends to study the subject firsthand. In Tokyo, she is introduced to Okaasan who operates a tea house for geishas in the city of Kyoto. He helps Gillian through the complex training rituals to become a geisha. In the process she makes friends with one peer (June Angela) and earns the enmity of another (Nono). She falls in love with Kangoro, a Kabuki theater star, but his mother (Quo) convinces her that such an intermarriage would be disastrous. She returns to the United States, eventually marries, and has children.

American Guerrilla in the Philippines, An **(1950)** Twentieth Century-Fox, color, 105 minutes. **Director:** Fritz Lang; **Screenplay:** Lamar Trotti; **Cast:** Tyrone Power (Ens. Chuck Palmer), Micheline Presle (Jeanne Martinez), Tom Ewell (Jim Mitchell), Bob Patten (Lovejoy), Tommy Cook (Miguel), Robert Barrat (Gen. Douglas MacArthur), Chris de Varga and Eduardo Rivera (Japanese officers).

Officially World War II ended in 1945, but Hollywood continued restaging its bloody battles. Derived from Ira Wolfert's 1945 novel, which, in turn, was based on the actual wartime experiences of navy Lt. I. D. Richardson in the Philippines, this combat entry—in glamorized terms—captured the grittiness of Ensign Palmer and his men, who refuse to surrender after Bataan falls to the Axis in 1942. Instead, Palmer and his group join with local resistance leaders to evade/undermine the Japanese and to support the Allied invasion of Leyte under General MacArthur.

By 1950, the Philippines was a republic and no longer a satellite U.S. possession. Thus, a greater effort was made by the film studio to reflect the actual participation and bravery of the locals, rather than have the American characters grab all the on-camera glory. Nevertheless, bowing to convention and convenience, some of the Filipino characters were played by Caucasian Americans (e.g., Cook), and the focal enemy officers (played by de Varga and Rivera) were *not* Japanese.

animation—feature films During the World War II era, several of the ongoing Hollywood movie-studio cartoon series—frequently those of Walt Disney—had their lead characters (e.g., Donald Duck, Mickey Mouse) involved in combat activity against Axis forces, with the latter depicted in stereotypical caricatures. Some training films for the armed forces during World War II also utilized animated characters to represent vicious Japanese troops or pilots involved in combat activity against the brave Allied forces.

Disney's 1955 feature, *Lady and the Tramp*, featured singer/actress Peggy Lee as the voices of Si and Am, the Siamese cats, who sang the catchy number (written by Lee) "We Are Siamese If You Please." In 1959 came the theatrical release of a new big-screen short subject series featuring Hashimoto, a Japanese house mouse, who was a martial arts expert and had wonderful memories of his homeland and its cultural traditions. The entries were produced by Terrytoon. Also involved in these episodes (released between 1959 and 1963) were his wife, Hanaoka, and their offspring, Yuriko and Saburo. These animated shorts about Hashimoto were also utilized on the TV series *The Hector Heathcote Show* (1963–65)

MULAN, the 1998 feature film produced by Walt Disney, dealt with the elaboration of a Chinese fable and featured a large cast of Chinese characters. Its sequel, *Mulan 2*, was set to appear in 2003. The hit Broadway musical, *The King and I* (1951), based on the movie *Anna and the King of Siam* (1946), was translated into a 1956 screen musical and was remade as an animated feature film in 1999. In this condensing of the classic song-and-dance fest, several well-known songs in the score were deleted, while animal characters were added into the mix. Many of the characters' voices were provided by Caucasians (e.g., Miranda Richardson, Ian Richardson, Darrell Hammond, and Adam Wylie). In the translation to a cartoon format, several of the Siamese figures became stereotypical, including the king's evil minister and his dastardly (slapstick-prone) sidekick.

In *Titan, A. E.* (2000), a sci-fi animated feature set a millennium into the future, there are some Asian characters, and a few Asian-American performers were used for some of the lesser figures (e.g., TSAI CHIN as the Old Woman). What made *Final Fantasy: The Spirits Within* (2001), a U.S./Japanese coproduction based on a popular interactive video game, so unique was the use of a full cast of computer-generated characters. In this sci-fi entry, MING-NA provided the voice of lead character Dr. Aki Ross. *Lilo & Stitch* (2002) was an animated feature about a five-year-old Hawaiian girl (voice of Daveigh Chase) with a passion for helping animals in need.

animation series—television One of the earliest TV programs to utilize Asian characters was *The Hector Heathcote Show* (1963–65) series, which made use of the Terrytoon theatrical-release short subjects (1959–63) revolving around the character Hashimoto, the judo-expert house mouse. John Myhers provided the voices for the central figures of Hashimoto, his wife, and their two children. *THE AMAZING CHAN AND THE CHAN CLAN* (1972–74), with the voice of KEYE LUKE as the Chinese sleuth, focused on the Chinese detective CHARLIE CHAN and his several offspring who helped him to solve cases. *Kid Power* (1972–74) was another Saturday morning program based on cartoonist Morrie Turner's *Wee Pals* newspaper strip that began in 1965. The multicultural series featured several ethnic minority representatives.

STAR TREK (1973–75), based on the cult TV series (1966–69), featured representations of the original cast, including the voice of GEORGE TAKEI as Lieutenant Sulu, the helmsman of the USS *Enterprise*. In *Hong Kong Phooey* (1974–76), about a superhero dog combating evil, the switchboard operator was played by Kathy Gori. *Wolf Rock TV* (1984) was a short-lived entry that showcased radio deejay Wolfman Jack (based on his real-life personality), who mentored three teenagers at his TV station. One of them, Sunny (voice of Siu Ming Carson), was Asian American. *TEENAGE MUTANT NINJA TURTLES* was based on the cult comic book that first appeared in 1983. This animated TV series (1987–95), about four oversized turtles who talked and walked erect, featured the villainous Shredder, who wore a mask of Japanese-style armor. *THE KARATE KID* (1989–90), a Saturday morning cartoon-series entry, derived from the hit 1984 movie and utilized the voices of Robert Ito (Miyagi Yakuga), Joe Dedio (Daniel), and Janice Kawaye (Taki). Hong Kong action star JACKIE CHAN, having made a name at the American box office, supplied the voice for an animated series *Jackie Chan Adventures* (2000–), which presented not only his exploits in today's aggressive world (accompanied at times by his eleven-year-old niece) but also had a segment devoted to young fans asking the star questions about his martial arts skills, and so on. *Samurai Jack* (2001–) focused on a Japanese warrior from the past thrust into the future, where he battles the wizard Aku (voice of MAKO).

***Anna and the King* (1999)** Twentieth Century Fox, color, 147 minutes. **Director:** Andy Tennant; **Screenplay:** Steve Meerson and Peter Krikes; **Cast:** Jodie Foster (Anna Leonowens), Chow Yun-Fat (King Mongkut), Ling Bai (Tuptim), Tom Felton (Louis Leonowens), Syed Alwi (the Kralahome).

At tremendous expense and effort, this production, filmed in Malaysia, sought to recreate the splendor of 1860s Siam (today's Thailand) as a lush backdrop to the battle of wills between the hired British schoolmarm (Foster) and the totalitarian ruler (CHOW) as they explore the virtues of each other's culture and the emotional similarities between men and women. For a change, the Asians were not played by Hollywood Caucasians, the tempestuous king's 58 children did not steal the limelight, and Yun-Fat's progressive monarch was charismatic and *almost* erased memories of Yul Brynner in *THE KING AND I* (1956) and Rex Harrison in *ANNA AND THE KING OF SIAM* (1946). Unfortunately, Foster was obviously ill at ease as the widowed mother attracted to the dynamic ruler, and the film lost believability. The PG-13-rated movie was nominated for two Academy Awards: Best Art Direction/Set Decoration and Best Costume Design.

Yet another rendition of the Anna Leonowens adventures arrived with the release of the elaborate animated feature-length musical, *The King and I* (1999), which was geared for youngsters. It featured the voices of Miranda Richardson (Anna—talking), Christiana Noll (Anna—singing), Martin Nidvovic (the king), and Ian Richardson (the Kralahome).

Classic as this tale of the nineteenth-century English tutor's experience in Siam had become, there were those who found its account of the "barbaric" ruler an embarrassing stereotype of what the general public thought of Siam/Thailand in that unsophisticated (i.e., not Westernized) bygone era.

***Anna and the King of Siam* (1946)** Twentieth Century-Fox, b&w, 128 minutes. **Director:** John Cromwell; **Screenplay:** Talbot Jennings and Sally Benson; **Cast:** Irene Dunne (Anna Owens), Rex Harrison (the King), Linda Darnell (Tuptim), Lee J. Cobb (the Kralahome), Gale Sondergaard (Lady Thiang), Mikhail Rasumny (Alak), Dennis Hoey (Sir Edward), Tito Renaldo (Prince—grown up).

After World War II, Hollywood was more focused on world cultures, even if the "exotic" locales were still created on studio back lots. Relying on two works (1870 and 1872) by Britisher Anna Leonowens that provided source data for Margaret Landon's book, *Anna and the King of Siam* (1944), this intricate production introduced filmgoers to the feisty widow who, in the 1860s, tamed the ruler of Siam while he simultaneously punctured her British hauteur. What with the English Harrison, Russian Rasumny, Russian-American Jew Cobb, Texas-born Darnell, Minnesota-reared Sondergaard, Hispanic Renaldo, and so on, this film was a United Nations of talent. Playing up the "barbaric" aspects of "uncivilized" Siam, the movie was presented strictly from the point of view of American/British filmgoers.

The elaborate *Anna and the King of Siam* won Academy Awards for Best Art Direction/Set Decoration (Black and White) and Best Cinematography (Black and White), as well as three other Oscar nominations, including Best Supporting Actress (Sondergaard).

This much-praised movie provided the basis for the 1951 Broadway musical *THE KING AND I* (1951), which was, in turn, picturized in 1956 by the same studio. The original screen drama was essentially remade in 1999 as *ANNA AND THE KING*, while another adaptation of the musical *The King and I*—this time as an animated feature geared for children—appeared in 1999. A short-enduring TV series, *Anna and the King*, aired in 1972 starring Yul Brynner (the king) and Samantha Eggar (Anna) and featured KEYE LUKE (the Kralahome) and Lisa Lu (Lady Thiang).

B

***Bachelor Father* (1957–1962)** CBS (later NBC and ABC) TV series, b&w, 30 minutes. **Cast:** John Forsythe (Bentley Gregg), Noreen Corcoran (Kelly Gregg), Sammee Tong (Peter Tong), Bernadette Withers (Ginger Farrell/Loomis Mitchell), Jimmy Boyd (Howard Meechim: 1958–61).

This early situation comedy featured Forsythe as a well-to-do show business attorney who lives in Beverly Hills. Others in the household of this ladies' man are his orphaned niece Kelly, whose parents were killed in an auto accident, and houseman Peter Tong. As the perpetually good-natured domestic (following in the tradition of African-American actors), SAMMEE TONG played the part as a constantly smiling employee. He attends night school to sharpen his knowledge of America but, as a responsible servant, always has dinner ready for his employer at seven nightly and is willing to be straight man to his white employer's jokes.

Several of Peter Tong's on-screen relatives show up on the series, including Grandfather Ling (Beal Wong), a "seventy-year-old juvenile delinquent" with a vocabulary limited to "Hello, Joe" and "nice." (Although many Caucasians appreciated such clichéd characterizations, Asians/Asian Americans did not appreciate the trite representations.) Also seen frequently was Cousin Charlie Fong (VICTOR SEN YUNG), a con artist and family beatnik whose wild schemes usually backfired.

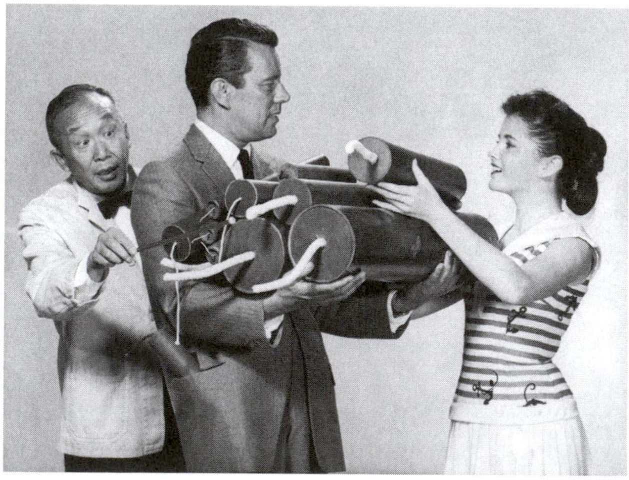

Sammee Tong, John Forsythe, and Noreen Corcoran in the TV sitcom *Bachelor Father* (1957–62). (VINCENT TERRACE)

***Back to Bataan* (1945)** RKO, b&w, 97 minutes. **Director:** Edward Dmytryk; **Screenplay:** Ben Barzman and Richard Landau; **Cast:** John Wayne (Col. Joe Madden), Anthony Quinn (Capt. Andres Bonifacio), Beulah Bondi (Miss Bertha Barnes), Fely Franquelli (Dalisay Delgado), Richard Loo (Major Hasko), Philip Ahn (Colonel Kuroki), Abner Biberman (Japanese captain/Japanese diplomat).

Thanks to the demands of Wayne and producer Robert Fellows, this patriotic World War II feature did *not* end with Colonel Madden singlehandedly leading the Filipinos to victory against the Japanese as the Allies under General MacArthur prepared to land troops at Leyte. Instead, the revised script focused on the regenerated Captain Bonifacio, the grandson of a respected Philippine leader, inspiring his men to continue the good fight.

Within this rousing combat drama based on true events, actual survivors of the Japanese prisoner-of-war camp at Cabanatuan appeared in news clips and newly staged footage, but much of the cast was composed of familiar Hollywood

Richard Loo, Philip Ahn, Abner Biberman, Leonard Strong, and Michael Mark (right) in *Back to Bataan* (1945). (JC ARCHIVES)

talent. It was the presumption of the era that moviegoers would readily accept Mexican-born Quinn as a Filipino or Wisconsin-reared Biberman as a Japanese. The role of Dalisay Delgado was, however, interpreted by a Filipina. Veteran actors AHN and LOO appeared here as nasty Axis officers.

***Bad Day at Black Rock* (1955)** Metro-Goldwyn-Mayer, color, 81 minutes. **Director:** John Sturges; **Screenplay:** Millard Kaufman; **Cast:** Spencer Tracy (John J. MacReedy), Robert Ryan (Reno Smith), Anne Francis (Liz Wirth), Dean Jagger (Sheriff Tim Horn), Walter Brennan (Dr. T. R. Velie Jr.), Ernest Borgnine (Coley Trimble).

This was one of Hollywood's more gripping studies of racial bigotry. Set in the small, rundown Arizona town of Black Rock, the movie was framed within the format of a western, although the narrative took place in 1945. A one-armed stranger, John J. MacReedy, arrives and asks the whereabouts of Mr. Komoko. The locals suddenly turn vague and/or hostile. As the situation heats up, MacReedy fears for his life but refuses to leave. It develops that several of the citizens—including Reno Smith and Coley Trimble—in the "patriotic" heat of hating anything Japanese, badgered and killed farmer Komoko and buried his corpse in an unmarked grave. It turns out that MacReedy is in Black Rock to deliver a medal of honor to Komoko on behalf of his son who died fighting in the U.S. Army during World War II (and had in fact saved MacReedy's life in combat).

Astutely developing its theme of abstract bigotry and fear against an entire race, *Bad Day at Black Rock* harkened back to *Crossfire* (1947). In that landmark film, a bigot (also played by Ryan) murdered a Jew out of a blanket hatred for an ethnic minority that had nothing to do with the specific victim. *Bad Day at Black Rock* was based on a 1947 short story ("Bad Time at Honda") by Howard Breslin. The picture received three Academy Award nominations: Best Actor (Tracy), Best Director, and Best Screenplay.

***Barbarian and the Geisha, The* (1958)** Twentieth Century-Fox, color, 1958. **Director:** John Huston; **Screenplay:** Charles Grayson; **Cast:** John Wayne (U.S. Consul Townsend Harris), Eiko Ando (Okichi), Sam Jaffe (Henry Heusken), Soh Yamamura (Tamura), Norman Thomson (ship captain), Morika (prime minister).

A decade after World War II, Hollywood was experiencing a minicycle of Japanese-themed movies (e.g., *SAYONARA*, 1957) that explored the culture of its former battlefield enemy. Filmmaker Huston, who could be so accomplished, ran amuck here in creating a viable story about the little-known nineteenth-century American diplomat and his efforts to open up Japanese trade with America. Huston was inspired by the visual beauty of the Japanese-made *Gate of Hell* (1953), so the focus in his wide-screen drama was on the cinematography.

Chosen because his oversized presence would contrast nicely with the more diminutive Asian figures, Wayne was properly unsophisticated as the naïve American matching wits with the subtle Japanese, but he was far from the romantic figure that the screenplay suggested. Japanese traditions were showcased only to a minor degree in this overly simplistic handling of the age-old culture clash of East vs. West.

***Barney Miller* (1975–1982)** ABC-TV series, color, 30 minutes. **Cast:** Hal Linden (Capt. Barney Miller), Abe Vigoda (Det. Phil Fish: 1975–77), Gregory Sierra (Det. Sgt. Chano Amenguale: 1975–76), Maxwell Gail (Det. Stanley "Wojo" Wojohowicz), Jack Soo (Det. Nick Yemana: 1975–78), Ron Glass (Det. Ron Harris), Steve Landesberg (Det. Arthur Dietrich: 1976–82).

The Twelfth Precinct of the New York Police Department, as portrayed in this classic TV comedy series, was depicted as a true United Nations of ethnic types. The crew of the rundown precinct (with its faulty toilets) included Jewish Barney Miller and Detective Fish, African-American Detective Harris, Hispanic-American Detective Baptista, Puerto Rican Detective Sergeant Amenguale, Detective Wojohowicz (of eastern European heritage), Detective Dietrich (of German descent), and Japanese-American Detective Yemana, the latter addicted to horse racing and gambling. Yemana, who was born in Omaha, Nebraska, was characterized as the philosophical one but also the law enforcer who was always making (dreadful) coffee for the others. Here, for a change on TV, an Asian American was portrayed as one of the accepted crowd, a positive role model.

As played by SOO, Yemana became one of the offering's most beloved characters. By the start of the 1978–79 series Soo was suffering from cancer and his last appearance on the series was in October 1978. Soo died in January 1979 at the age of sixty-three. In May 1979, the series devoted a special episode to him. The tribute included clips from past segments and reminiscences by the regular cast. At the finale, the cast members raised their coffee cups in salute to their departed comrade.

***Batman, The* (1943)** Columbia, b&w, 15-chapter serial. **Director:** Lambert Hillyer; **Screenplay:** Victor McLeod, Leslie Swabacker, and Harry Fraser; **Cast:** Lewis Wilson (Batman [Bruce Wayne]), Douglas Croft (Robin, the Boy Wonder [Dick Grayson]), J. Carrol Naish (Dr. Daka), William Austin (Alfred), Shirley Patterson (Linda), Charles C. Wilson (Captain Arnold), Charles Middleton (Ken Colton); **Chapters:** (1) The Electrical Brain, (2) The Bat's Cave, (3) The Mark of the Zombies, (4) Slaves of the Rising Sun, (5) The Living Corpse, (6) Poison Peril, (7) The Phony Doctor, (8) Lured by Radium, (9) The Sign of the Sphinx, (10) Flying Spies, (11) A Nipponese Trap, (12) Embers of Evil, (13) Eight Steps Down, (14) The Executioner Strikes, (15) The Doom of the Rising Sun.

Perhaps in no arena of 1940s Hollywood moviemaking were racial stereotypes so exploited as in the action-packed cliffhangers that were standard fare as part of children's Saturday matinees. During the height of World War II, filmmakers created some of their most rampant ethnic types to represent the dastardly Yellow Peril—the Japanese. This fifteen-installment serial features the caped crusader (who appeared in *Detective Comics* and *Batman* comic magazines as first conceived by comic book talent Bob Kane in 1939).

Once again, playboy Bruce Wayne and his helper Dick Grayson don their disguises as the masked Batman and his assistant Robin, the Boy Wonder, to fight the evil forces. Their target this time is dastardly Dr. Daka, who maintains his extraordinary power by converting people into zombies. Now he is working for the Axis and using his evil genius to steal Gotham City's radium supply. A pawn in the battle between Good and Evil is Bruce Wayne's girlfriend Linda, whom Daka kidnaps. Later, Daka has an untimely encounter with reptiles in his alligator pit.

Indicating the tenor of this mechanical, patriotic serial, the titles for this chapter play were biased (e.g., "Slaves of the Rising Sun") or had negatively ethnic-tinged episode names (e.g., "A Nipponese Trap").

***Baywatch Hawaii* (1999–2001)** Syndicated, color, 60 minutes **Cast:** David Hasselhoff (Lt. Mitch Bucannon: 1999–2000), Michael Newman (Michael "Newmie" Newman), Brooke Burns (Jessica "Jessie" Owens), Jason Brooks (Sean Monroe), Stacy Kamano (Kekoa Tanaka), Jason Mamoa (Jason), Kala'i Miller (Kai).

This fluffy, long-running TV series was originally set at Malibu Beach, California, where then-youngish Lt. Mitch Bucannon was in charge of a frequently rambunctious crew of lifeguards. The popular but critically drubbed series was often called "Bodywatch" because of its emphasis on barely clad females and bare-chested hunks, jogging on the beach, jumping into the surf, or sprawling on the hot sands.

In the often changing cast, executive producer Hasselhoff was a constant until near the end of the series' run. By 1999 the veteran show had changed its locale to HAWAII and was known as *Baywatch Hawaii*. Taking advantage of the gorgeous tropical landscape of the fiftieth state, it added Hawaiian-born actors to its stable of regulars, including Mamoa, Kamano, and Miller.

***Beach Red* (1967)** United Artists, color, 105 minutes. **Director:** Cornel Wilde; **Screenplay:** Clint Johnston, Donald A. Peters, and Jefferson Pascal; **Cast:** Cornel Wilde (Captain MacDonald), Rip Torn (Sergeant Honeywell), Burr de Benning (Egan), Jean Wallace (Julie MacDonald), Genki Koyama (Colonel Sugiyama), Dale Ishimoto (Captain Tanako).

This was one of several feature films produced, starring, and directed by former swashbuckling actor Wilde. It made a strong antiwar plea. Reminiscent of *All Quiet on the Western Front* (1930), which treated the once-enemy (Germans) as human beings, so *Beach Red* was not merely just another bloody tale of World War II carnage in the South Pacific. It tried to present objectively the affect of war on both a marine battalion and their adversaries, the Japanese. Thus, it showed both American soldiers daydreaming about their home life and their Axis counterparts recalling their civilian existences.

This presentation (which also included extremely graphic combat sequences) was a dramatic change from the World War II pictures produced in the United States during the flag-waving 1940s and 1950s by virtue of its relative impartiality and in its use of authentic Nipponese performers. (If anyone evolved as inhumane in the movie, it was sadistic Marine Sergeant Honeywell.) Based on the 1945 book by Peter Bowman, *Beach Red* was filmed on location in the Philippines and in Japan.

***Behind That Curtain* (1929)** Fox, b&w, 91 minutes. **Director:** Irving Cummings; **Screenplay:** Sonya Levien and Clarke Silvernail; **Cast:** Warner Baxter (John Beetham), Lois Moran (Eve Mannering), Gilbert Emery (Sir Frederic Bruce), Claude King (Sir George Mannering), Philip Strange (Eric Durand), Boris Karloff (Sudanese servant), E. L. Park (Charlie Chan).

Based on the CHARLIE CHAN novel by Earl Derr Biggers serialized in the *Saturday Evening Post* in 1928, Fox Films took control of screen rights to the famed sleuth. They hired the British actor Park to play Chan, but, as in the past two films involving Chan, the Asian detective was *not* a major force in the proceedings. It was part of Hollywood's belief then that, with rare exceptions, most filmgoers did *not* wish to watch a movie starring a Chinese character—let alone have the part be played by an actual ethnic.

Wealthy Eve Mannering has married a fortune hunter named Eric Durand but leaves him when she learns that he may have killed the investigator hired by her uncle, Sir George Mannering, to examine the son-in-law's background. Sir Frederic Bruce of Scotland Yard takes an interest in the case when a pair of Chinese slippers are found near the victim's corpse. The trail leads from England to India to San Francisco. Chan makes a short appearance as the law enforcer who helps to stop the gun-wielding Durand.

This Charlie Chan entry, was Park's only appearance as Chan. KARLOFF returned to the Chan series in *CHARLIE CHAN AT THE OPERA* (1937).

***Behind the Rising Sun* (1943)** RKO, b&w, 88 minutes. **Director:** Edward Dmytryk; **Screenplay:** Emmett Lavery Sr.; **Cast:** Margo (Tama), Tom Neal (Taro Seki), J. Carrol Naish (Reo Seki), Robert Ryan (Lefty), Gloria Holden (Sara), Don Douglas (Clancy O'Hara), Leonard Strong (Tama's father).

Having successfully fanned the flames of patriotism with *Hitler's Children* (1942), the filmmaking team of Dmytryk and Lavery turned to the Land of the Rising Sun for their next exploitation effort. Although filled with 1940s stereotypes of barbaric Japanese World War II butchers, the movie centered much of its narrative on Japan in the late 1930s and how the pending war and battle fever transformed many peace-loving civilians into fanatic militarists. The focal character is Taro Seki, the American-educated engineer son of a Japanese publisher (Naish). The latter, appointed minister of propaganda, convinces his offspring to become a member of his country's zealous air corps. After his son's death in combat, Seki realizes the folly of his country's wartime ambitions and commits hara-kiri, hoping that his demise will shake his people's faith in the old order.

Imaginatively made on a relatively low budget, this feature drew its inspiration from a 1941 book by James R. Young, who spent thirteen years as a news correspondent in prewar Japan. To its credit, the picture distinguished between the victimized Chinese and the imperialist Japanese, the latter subdivided into the pampered elite and the exploited lower classes. In standard Hollywood fashion, however, actors of all nationalities impersonated the Japanese characters—from New York-born, swarthy-complexioned Naish to Mexican-born Margo.

Better Luck Tomorrow* (2002)** Hudson River Entertainment/Cherry Sky Films, color, 101 minutes. **Director:** Justin Lin; ***Screenplay: Ernesto M. Foronda, Lin, and Fabian Marquez; **Cast:** Parry Shen (Ben Manibag), Jason Tobin (Virgil Hu), Sung Kang (Han), Roger Fan (Daric Loo), John Cho (Steve Choe), Karin Anna Cheung (Stephanie), Jerry Mathews (biology teacher).

This low-key but effective drama focuses on a high-achieving Asian-American student (Shen) at a southern California high school in Orange County who slowly is drawn into street-gang activities. By the time he realizes what his once praiseworthy life has become, he is involved in a criminal caper that leads to tragic results. The surviving teens have their own perspective on the import of the dire situation. *Daily Variety* (January 16, 2002) reported of the low-budget feature: "Deliberately designed to be provocative in its morally ambiguous stance toward the boys' amoral and illegal activities, Justin Lin's nicely turned out picture . . . provides a generally absorbing look at a slice of society normally taken for granted, both in life and onscreen." A pleased *Hollywood Reporter* (January 16, 2002) said, "Filmmaker Justin Lin's expressive storytelling fits his darkly ironic theme, and the performances are nicely fleshed-out and edgy."

***Big Hawaii* (1977)** NBC-TV series, color, 60 minutes. **Cast:** Cliff Potts (Mitch Fears), John Dehner (Barrett Fears), Lucia Stalser (Karen "Keke" Fears), Bill Lucking (Oscar Kalahani), Elizabeth Smith (Lulu Kalahani), Moe Keale (Garfield Kalahani), Remi Abellira (Kimo Kalahani).

This short-duration adventure series is set at the expansive Paradise Ranch on the big island of HAWAII. The spread is operated by domineering Barrett Fears, who is later joined by his only son, Mitch. The latter is a free-spirited soul in constant conflict with his traditional dad. The foreman of the spread is local-born Oscar Kalahani. Although Oscar was played by a Hollywood-based Caucasian, at least two other members of the Kalahani clan were played by Hawaiians (Keale and Abellira).

One of the themes weaved into this offering was how the inroads of "progress" were altering the time-honored Hawaiian lifestyle.

***Bitter Tea of General Yen, The* (1933)** Columbia, b&w, 88 minutes. **Director:** Frank Capra; **Screenplay:** Edward Paramore; **Cast:** Barbara Stanwyck (Megan Davis), Nils Asther (General Yen), Gavin Gordon (Dr. Robert Strike), Lucien Littlefield (Mr. Jackson), Toshia Mori (Mah-Li), Richard Loo (Captain Li), Walter Connolly (Jones), Moy Ming (Dr. Lin).

According to the *Variety* review (January 17, 1933), "Seeing a Chinaman attempting to romance with a pretty and supposedly decent young American white woman is bound to evoke adverse reaction." Such was the trade paper's prognosis for this controversial mainstream feature. The movie evoked complaints from Chinese officials (about its depiction of the treatment of war prisoners in China), proselytizing agencies (about its representation of blundering missionaries), and other sources (about the presentation of the grasping financial adviser, Jones).

At heart, this was another of Hollywood's fantasy concoctions, based on a 1930 novel by Grace Zaring Stone, about the inscrutable East clashing with the forthright and crass West. The sincere young Americans—the missionary Dr. Strike and his fiancée Megan Davis—are naïve souls whose well-meaning deeds often cause disaster for others. In contrast, the worldly warlord, General Yen (portrayed by Swedish-born Asther), is fully attuned to the subtleties of human nature, whether it be his avaricious American adviser (Connolly), his duplistic concubine (Mori), or the unsophisticated Megan. The latter finds herself drawn to the Chinese man and he to her, but it is an impossible romance. By the finale, Yen's life is ruined and, to salvage his honor and to compensate for the futility of his love for the Westerner, he drinks poisoned tea. The tragedy leaves Megan wistful, knowing that some day in the future, she will be reunited with him in heaven.

The grossly negative images presented of most of the story's non-Caucasians were standard fare of this period.

***Black Camel, The* (1931)** Fox, b&w, 67 minutes. **Director:** Hamilton McFadden; **Screenplay:** Barry Conners and Philip Klein; **Cast:** Warner Oland (Insp. Charlie Chan), Sally Eilers (Julie O'Neil), Bela Lugosi (Tarneverro [Arthur Mayo]), Dorothy Revier (Shelah Fane), Victor Varconi (Robert Fyfe), Robert Young (Jimmy Bradshaw), Otto Yamaoka (Kashimo).

According to CHARLIE CHAN of the Honolulu Police Department, "Death is a black camel that kneels unbidden at every gate," and it certainly does at the Royal Hawaiian Hotel where Hollywood movie star Shelah Fane is murdered.

In his second outing as the estimable Chinese police inspector, OLAND had the benefit of superior production values and had as his comedy foil a Japanese character used by author Earl Derr Biggers in his 1929 Chan novel on which this film was based As played by Yamaoka, this sidekick (who constantly shouted "Clue!") was far more interfering and agitated than any of the police detective's later on-screen helpers (usually one of Chan's offspring). As was true within Biggers's books, here was an early illustration of a non-Caucasian being depicted as intellectually superior to his Caucasian associates and those involved in the murder caper. On the other hand, the movie sequence revealing Chan breakfasting with his hovering wife and brood of energetic children was played for (condescending) laughs.

***Black Rain* (1989)** Paramount, color, 125 minutes. **Director:** Ridley Scott; **Screenplay:** Craig Bolotin and Warren Lewis; **Cast:** Michael Douglas (Nick Conklin), Andy Garcia (Charlie Vincent), Ken Takakura (Masahiro Matsumoto), Kate Capshaw (Joyce Kingsley), Yusaku Matsuda (Sato), Tomisaburo Wakayama (Sugai).

With renewed interest in cop/buddy pictures after the huge success of *Lethal Weapon* (1987)—which teamed a white and a black cop—this slickly made feature offered its own twist on the buddy formula. Ruthless New York police detective Nick Conklin is under investigation for allegedly having dipped into confiscated drug money to finance his divorce and plush lifestyle. Soon, he and his partner (Garcia) fly to Japan to return a recently captured Yakuza murder suspect (Matsuda) to the authorities. After being tricked out of their prisoner, rogue cop Conklin so annoys the Tokyo authorities that he must rely on a Japanese underworld figure (Wakayama) to track the missing man.

What gave grist to this stylishly lensed if predictable picture was its depiction of the hectic Tokyo underworld. Here, in contrast to U.S.-set movies, the Americans were the fish out of water as they dealt with the smart, tough Japanese hoodlums. Far more impressive than the scowling Douglas or the sensitive Garcia were Wakayama as the growling hoodlum and Takakura as the Tokyo police liaison. Grossing more than $45 million in domestic distribution, *Black Rain* was nominated for an Academy Award for Best Sound.

***Blood on the Sun* (1945)** United Artists, b&w, 98 minutes. **Director:** Frank Lloyd; **Screenplay:** Lester Cole; **Cast:** James Cagney (Nick Condon), Sylvia Sidney (Iris Hilliard), Porter Hall (Arthur Bickett), John Emery (Baron Giichi Tanaka), Robert Armstrong (Colonel Tojo), Wallace Ford (Ollie Miller), Rosemary DeCamp (Edith Miller).

As World War II ended, filmmakers sought fresh gimmicks to intrigue moviegoers satiated by all the combat and espionage pictures dealing with the global conflict. *Blood on the Sun* turned back history to 1929 in its fictionalized account of the real-life Baron Giichi Tanaka, the statesman/general who in the 1920s advocated Japanese imperialism through expansion. He had been the nation's minister of war and, in 1927, became its prime minister. In 1929, he resigned his post and died that same year. The baron had earlier written a detailed plan proposing the conquest of Manchuria, China, and it was given to Emperor Hirohito. When a copy of the scheme was published surreptitiously in China, Tanaka insisted it was a forgery.

Parading through this rough'-em-up espionage drama is tough Nick Condon, the editor of an English-language newspaper in 1929 Tokyo. He gets hold of the Tanaka Plan, which leads Colonel Tojo, Captain Oshima, and others of the Japanese military/police to pursue him relentlessly. Tossed into the mix is Eurasian Iris Hilliard, who has been working for Tojo.

Like earlier exploitational dramas, *Blood on the Sun* relied almost exclusively on Caucasian actors to enact the Japanese villains—as well as the Eurasian heroine—which created a studied artificiality to the film. Nonetheless, it was hoped that the slam-bang action would maintain viewers' attention. *Blood on the Sun* was not one of Cagney's bigger hits.

***Blue Hawaii* (1961)** Paramount, color, 101 minutes. **Director:** Norman Taurog; **Screenplay:** Hal Kanter; **Cast:** Elvis Presley (Chad Gates), Joan Blackman (Maile Duval), Nancy Walters (Abigail Prentice), Roland Winters (Fred Gates), Angela Lansbury (Sarah Lee Gates), Flora Hayes (Mrs. Manaka), Frank Atienza (Ito O'Hara), Lani Kai (Carl).

This Presley musical used HAWAII's lush settings to enliven its formula plot and presentation of stock songs (e.g., "Rock-a-Hula Baby"). Here Chad Gates, fresh from army duty, vetoes working for the pineapple business owned by his dad (Winters) and instead becomes a tour guide with his buddies. He devotes much of his time to courting Maile Duval and avoiding romantically inclined schoolteacher/client Abigail Prentice.

The by-the-numbers plot allowed for impressive visual jaunts about the tropical paradise—geared to making moviegoers envy the locals who lived there. With the exception of a beach luau and a colorful Hawaiian wedding sequence, the film treated its Asian-American characters as merely part of the passing scenery. Presley returned to the tropics in *Paradise, Hawaiian Style* (1966), a weak variation of *Blue Hawaii*.

***Breakfast at Tiffany's* (1961)** Paramount, color, 114 minutes. **Director:** Blake Edwards; **Screenplay:** George Axelrod; **Cast:** Audrey Hepburn (Holly Golightly), George Peppard (Paul Varjak), Patricia Neal ("2E"), Buddy Ebsen (Doc Golightly), Martin Balsam (O. J. Berman), Mickey Rooney (Mr. Yunioshi).

Even in this sanitized rendition of Truman Capote's 1958 book, *Breakfast at Tiffany's* emerged as an offbeat romance. The love-struck duo consisted of an aspiring writer/gigolo (Peppard) and a madcap young woman (Hepburn) whose feline is named "Cat" and who adores window shopping at the expensive Tiffany's store. Holly earns rent money for her East Side Manhattan brownstone apartment from the large tips that her gentleman escorts provide and from her weekly trip to Sing Sing prison to visit a former mobster. Although Holly can gather the courage to send her much older ex-husband (Ebsen) back home after a surprise visit, she can't so easily dismiss her upstairs neighbor, Mr. Yunioshi. As played by Rooney, this Japanese gentleman emerges as an over-the-top caricature, complete with buck teeth and very wide-open eyes behind oversized, thick-lensed spectacles. Rooney's overdone slapstick and Asian imitation is an embarrassment.

Breakfast at Tiffany's won two Academy Awards for composer Henry Mancini: Best Original Dramatic Score and Best Song ("Moon River"). The film was also nominated for three other Oscars: Best Actress (Hepburn), Best Adapted Screenplay, and Best Art Direction/Set Decoration (Color).

***Bridge on the River Kwai, The* (1957)** Columbia, color, 161 minutes. **Director:** David Lean; **Screenplay:** Pierre Boulle, and uncredited Michael Wilson and Carl Foreman; **Cast:** William Holden (Shears), Alec Guinness (Colonel Nicholson), Jack Hawkins (Major Warden), Sessue Hayakawa (Colonel Saito), James Donald (Major Clipton), Geoffrey Horne (Lieutenant Joyce), Ann Sears (nurse).

First translated into English from the French in 1954, Boulle's novel was adapted into a classic antiwar thesis on the insanity of war. It was based on the real-life events of the Japanese railroad construction from Bangkok to Rangoon in 1942, which used Allied prisoners as slave/death labor. The epic traces the descent into madness of English Colonel Nicholson who, with his regiment, has surrendered to the enemy in 1943 Burma. At the jungle prison camp, Colonel Saito taunts and tortures the egotistical Nicholson into accepting the near-impossible challenge of building a bridge over the high canyon of the River Kwai. As the structure reaches completion, an escaped American prisoner, Shears, returns with a team of British guerrillas to blow up the bridge and the enemy. The insane Nicholson spots the dynamite

Alec Guinness and Sessue Hayakawa in *The Bridge on the River Kwai* (1957). (JC ARCHIVES).

charges and attempts to prevent the detonation. Suddenly, he snaps back into sanity and although severely injured sets off the bridge's destruction.

Beyond the fascination of watching the intricate railroad trestle become a reality against overwhelming odds were the striking characterizations of the British and Japanese colonels. In fleshing out his role, HAYAKAWA provided a complex portrait, a man bound by tradition, pride, and determination—in many ways the alter ego of the equally arrogant and tenacious British Colonel Nicholson.

With World War II years in the past, Hollywood was now willing to go beyond cardboard portrayals of America's once-enemies. It was another progression in the slow emergence of Nipponese screen characters from combat stereotypes to full-bodied human beings in American-made movies.

The Bridge on the River Kwai, produced at a cost of $3 million, grossed more than $30 million in its first three years of distribution. It received seven Academy Awards: Best Actor (Guinness), Best Adapted Screenplay, Best Cinematography, Best Director, Best Film Editing, Best Picture, and Best Score. Hayakawa was nominated for a Best Supporting Actor Oscar. This was the motion picture famous for its whistled theme song ("Colonel Bogey March").

***Bridges at Toko-Ri, The* (1954)** Paramount, color, 102 minutes. **Director:** Mark Robson; **Screenplay:** Valentine Davies; **Cast:** William Holden (Lt. Harry Brubaker, USNR), Fredric March (Rear Adm. George Tarrant), Grace Kelly (Nancy Brubaker), Mickey Rooney (Mike Forney), Robert Strauss (Beer Barrell), Keiko Awaji (Kimiko).

Paralleling its literary source (James A. Michener's 1953 best-seller), this antiwar combat movie sought to be different in two major ways: It presented a reluctant warrior, jet pilot Brubaker, who felt that he had already done his patriotic duty during World War II and that he should not be dragged away from his family and law practice to active service during the Korean War, and then there were the scenes of the flier's wife (Kelly) in Japan waiting for and occasionally rendezvousing with her jet pilot husband. (If this had been World War II, she would have remained at home in the United States, not based overseas to be closer to her spouse.) Nancy resides among the former enemies of her country and husband, people with whom she now interacts and whose culture she is experiencing. These aspects gave this somewhat conventional movie its unusual twists, along with the wide-screen VistaVision cinematography. *The Bridges at Toko-Ri* was Oscar nominated for Best Editing.

***Bridge to the Sun* (1961)** Metro-Goldwyn-Mayer, b&w, 112 minutes. **Director:** Etienne Perier; **Screenplay:** Charles Kaufman; **Cast:** Carroll Baker (Gwen Harold Terasaki), James Shigeta (Terry [Hidenari Terasaki]), James Yagi (Hara), Tetsuro Tamba (Jiro), Sean Garrison (Fred Tyson), Ruth Masters (Aunt Peggy).

Earnest and low-keyed, this drama was based on the real-life of Gwen Harold Terasaki whose 1957 book related her unusual interracial love story. In 1930s Washington, D.C., Gwen, a southerner, meets and weds Hidenari "Terry" Terasaki, a Japanese diplomat, in spite of her family's racial bigotry. After the bombing of Pearl Harbor, the Terasakis (including daughter Mako) are ordered to Japan in exchange for the release of American diplomats there. Gwen (because of her being an enemy foreigner) and Terry (due to his opposition to the warmongers at home) are treated badly there. After the war ends, Terry, suffering from a fatal ailment, sends his wife and daughter back to the United States.

Because of its controversial interracial subject matter, *Bridge to the Sun* was shot inexpensively in black and white to lessen potential box-office losses. Hawaiian-born SHIGETA had much better success that same year with the screen musical *FLOWER DRUM SONG*. A reverse side to this narrative had been presented earlier in *JAPANESE WAR BRIDE* (1952).

***Broken Blossoms* (1919)** United Artists, b&w and tinted sequences, 90 minutes. **Director/Screenplay:** D. W. Griffith; **Cast:** Lillian Gish (Lucy Burrows), Donald Crisp ("Battling" Burrows), Arthur Howard (the boxer's manager), Richard Barthelmess (the Yellow Man), Edward Peil (Evil Eye), Norman Selby (a prize fighter).

While Japanese-born SESSUE HAYAKAWA was already an established American movie star in the late 1910s, there was no equivalent Chinese actor in U.S. films whom director Griffith considered appropriate for this elaborate project. Instead, he selected Caucasian Barthelmess, whom he placed under contract and who became a star as the result of appearing in this poignant silent photoplay.

The depiction of the inscrutable Asian as stereotype rather than as a person was evident even in the title of Thomas Burke's 1916 short story ("The Chink and the Child") on which *Broken Blossoms* was based. (Griffith's movie adaptation was intended originally to be called *Broken Blossoms or The Yellow Man and the Girl.*) The film's bias was obvious in its portrayal of the unassuming Asian-born shopkeeper hero as a second-class citizen who must remain with his own kind and *not* intrude upon the superior white world.

A devout Chinese Buddhist seeking to make Westerners more peaceful leaves his homeland. Some years later, he has become a discouraged shopkeeper in London's Limehouse district. He encounters Lucy, the abused daughter of boxer "Battling" Burrows. When the frail waif returns to his shop after suffering another beating from her crude father, the Yellow Man cares for her, and she responds to his kindness. Further on, however, her sadistic dad murders her. The brutal pugilist, in turn, is killed by the Yellow Man, who then commits hara-kiri.

Broken Blossoms proved to be one of Griffith's most-praised artistic productions. Nonetheless, this feature did much to solidify Hollywood's categorizing of men from the Far East as individuals who lived only to covet white women.

In 1936, the British remake of *Broken Blossoms* starring Dolly Haas and Emlyn Williams would receive far less acclaim than the original. By then, the overly dramatic story of the Cockney and the Asian mystic seemed overly quaint. The spoken dialogue of the new edition only emphasized how dated the melodramatic story had become.

Brotherhood of the Yakuza See YAKUZA, THE.

C

Carradine, David (1936–) The son of legendary screen character actor John Carradine (1906–88) was born in Hollywood, California. This lanky, somber-looking Caucasian actor was acting in such mid-1960s features as *Bus Riley's Back in Town* (1965) before he starred in the western TV series, *Shane* (1966). His interest in martial arts and Far Eastern philosophy expanded when he starred as Chinese-American Kwai Chang Caine in *KUNG FU* (1972–75). That cult series led eventually to the telefeature continuation of Caine's adventure in *KUNG FU: THE MOVIE* (1986) and thereafter to *KUNG FU: THE LEGEND CONTINUES* (1993–97), in which he appeared as Caine's grandson in a contemporary setting. Carradine's more recent features included *ZOO* (1999), *Nightfall* (2000), *Warden of Red Rock* (2001—TV movie), and *Wheatfield with Crows* (2002).

Chan, Charlie Earl Derr Biggers's marvelous literary creation enjoyed a long life in assorted media for many decades. The Chinese detective first came to the screen in a ten-chapter Pathé silent serial of 1926 entitled *The House Without a Key*. Chan, not a major character of the chapterplay, was enacted by Japanese actor George Kuwa. Two years later he reappeared in *The Chinese Parrot* (1928), based on the 1926 Biggers novel. This time, Japanese actor KAMIYAMA SOJIN played Chan. In the third—and first talkie—film project involving Chan, *BEHIND THAT CURTAIN* (1929), the Asian sleuth was entrusted to British actor E. L. Park. Even in this Fox Films entry, Charlie Chan was still a subordinate character.

Fox Films (by 1935, Twentieth Century-Fox) waited two years before producing its next Chan installment, this time hiring Swedish-born WARNER OLAND to be the Honolulu-based Chinese sleuth—the portly gentleman with an overabundance of offspring and aphorisms. The first entry was *CHARLIE CHAN CARRIES ON* (1931) and proved successful. It led to *THE BLACK CAMEL* the same year. There followed: 1932: *Charlie Chan's Chance*, *Charlie Chan's Greatest Case;* 1934: *Charlie Chan's Courage*, *Charlie Chan in London;* 1935: *Charlie Chan in Paris*, *Charlie Chan in Egypt*, *Charlie Chan in Shanghai;* 1936: *Charlie Chan's Secret*, *Charlie Chan at the Circus*, *Charlie Chan at the Racetrack*, *CHARLIE CHAN AT THE OPERA*; 1937: *Charlie Chan at the Olympics*, *Charlie Chan on Broadway;* 1938: *Charlie Chan At Monte Carlo.*

Oland died in 1937 while making *Charlie Chan at the Ringside*. Footage from that uncompleted entry, which also featured KEYE LUKE as Charlie's #1 son Lee (a role he had been playing since *Charlie Chan in Paris*) was incorporated into *Mr. Moto's Gamble* (1938).

To fill the void left by the late Oland, Twentieth Century-Fox contracted Missouri-born SIDNEY TOLER to take over as the Chinese detective, with no consideration given for hiring an Asian-American performer for the pivotal part. Luke had already departed the Chan series, and the recurring role of the helpful Chan offspring went to Chinese-American VICTOR SEN YUNG, who was assigned to be Chan's #2 son, Jimmy. He and Toler debuted in *CHARLIE CHAN IN HONOLULU* (1938). Thereafter they were in: 1939: *Charlie Chan in Reno*, *Charlie Chan at Treasure Island*, *Charlie Chan in the City in Darkness;* 1940: *Charlie Chan in Panama*, *Charlie Chan's Murder Cruise*, *Charlie Chan in the Wax Museum*, *Murder over New York;* 1941: *Dead Men Tell*, *Charlie Chan in Rio*, 1942: *Castle in the Desert.*

At this point, Twentieth Century-Fox dropped the property. But the series' star, Toler, acquired the screen rights to Chan from the widow of Earl Derr Biggers, and the property moved over to low-budget Monogram Pictures. Besides the economy production values, the new ingredients included the introduction of Charlie's #3 son Tommy (played by Chinese-American BENSON FONG through the entry *Dark Alibi)* as well as African-American chauffeur Birmingham Brown (played for exaggerated comedy by Mantan Moreland). The first such entry (which also included Marianne Quon as Charlie's daughter Iris) was *CHARLIE CHAN IN THE SECRET SERVICE*. It was followed by: 1944: *Charlie Chan in the Chinese Cat, Charlie Chan in Black Magic;* 1945: *The Jade Mask, The Scarlet Clue, The Shanghai Cobra;* 1946: *Dark Alibi, Shadows over Chinatown, Dangerous Money;* 1947: *The Trap.*

With the death of Toler in 1947, Monogram turned to Massachusetts-born ROLAND WINTERS to take over as the latest Charlie Chan. Fong had left the series already, and Sen Yung had returned—as of 1946's *Shadows over Chinatown*—as the criminal investigator's #2 son Jimmy. (He left the series after 1948's *The Golden Eye.*) Birmingham Brown remained as the series' comedy relief. The first Winters Chan entry was *THE CHINESE RING* (1947). This was followed by: 1948: *Docks of New Orleans, Shanghai Chest, The Golden Eye, The Feathered Serpent;* 1949: *The Sky Dragon.* For the final two entries of the Winters/Monogram run, Luke reemerged as Jimmy Chan.

While the lengthy film series was being produced, Charlie Chan had become a radio program. It debuted in 1932, first as a fifteen-minute entry and later in a thirty-minute format on the NBC Blue network. It lasted through 1948, with several changeovers of network and a gap between ABC network's 1944–45 installments and Mutual network's 1947–48 new adventures. Chan was played during the years by Walter Connolly, Ed Begley, Santos Ortega, and William Rees. Charlie's #1 son Lee was interpreted by Leon Janney and then by Rodney Jacobs.

In 1957, a British-produced TV series, *THE NEW ADVENTURES OF CHARLIE CHAN* appeared. It featured Brooklyn-born J. Carrol Naish in the lead role and had Chan based in London and working with Scotland Yard. Nearly twenty years later, a TV cartoon series—made for Saturday morning children viewers—debuted. *THE AMAZING CHAN AND THE CHAN CLAN* (1972–74) featured the voice of Luke, the one-time #1 son of the Chan movies, as Charlie Chan. In another property offshoot, Ross Martin was an undistinguished Chinese sleuth in the telefeature *The Return of Charlie Chan.* Made in 1970, it first aired on British TV in mid-1973 as *Happiness Is a Warm Clue.* It finally was shown in the United States in 1979.

Neil Simon concocted *Murder by Death* (1976), a comedy feature with satirical characterizations of some famous detectives of literature and film. Peter Sellers was on hand in an oversized unfunny presentation of Charlie Chan, herein called Sidney Wang, with Richard Narita as his son Willie Wang. The spoof *Charlie Chan and the Curse of the Dragon Queen* arrived in 1981. This lackluster comedy featured British-born Peter Ustinov as a rather droll Chan, with Richard Hatch as his addled grandson and David Hirokani as Charlie's #1 son Lee. Angie Dickinson was cast as the Dragon Queen. At the time of release of *Charlie Chan and the Curse of the Dragon Queen,* there was much objection from Asian-American groups, who were unhappy with the portrayal of ethnic minorities in the film. (In earlier decades there had been protests against the showing of Charlie Chan movies on television, and for several years they were not aired.)

Warner Oland, the most enduring of the actors to play Charlie Chan on screen. (JC ARCHIVES).

In 1996 Miramax Pictures planned a new Charlie Chan big-screen adventure to star RUSSELL WONG. The project never materialized.

Chan, Jackie (aka: Jacky Chan, Yuen-lung Chan, Long Cheng, Sing Lung) (1954–) Rising from stuntman to premier leading man of Hong Kong martial arts movies, the five-feet, nine-inch Chan with the bangs haircut became one of the world's most popular screen performers. Some thought him adorable for his comedy fantasies; others judged his creative but dangerous movie stunt wizardry—which he insisted on doing himself—as foolhardy exhibitionism. But in the final decades of the twentieth century, he proved to be one of the movie business's most bankable talents, a fact reconfirmed when he went to the United States to make such features as *RUSH HOUR* (1998) and *SHANGHAI NOON* (2000).

He was born Chan Kong-sang in Hong Kong, the only child of impoverished parents who had fled China before their boy's birth. Things improved when the parents found work as domestics at the French Embassy. Unable to care for their child when they got a job overseas, they apprenticed the six-year-old to the Chinese Opera Research Institute in Hong Kong. The training was very difficult and highly regimented.

When a visiting filmmaker offered young Jackie a chance to do stunts in a film, he accepted, doing work in such BRUCE LEE movies as *Fist of Fury* (1971) and *ENTER THE DRAGON* (1973). It eventually led to a position as a stunt coordinator and then as a second-unit director. Chan was among the many who, following the death of martial-arts film king Bruce Lee in 1973, wanted to assume his crown. Chan felt he had to be different and proved his point in his solo directorial debut: *Shi di chu ma* (1980). In this and many subsequent features, the broad-nosed leading man mixed slapstick-type humor with ultraenergetic martial-arts action. (One of his trademarks was the use of unique props for his fight scenes—lamps, ladders, chairs, etc.) As the years passed, his breath-stopping stunts grew increasingly dangerous and often proved perilous to the star. He usually produced and wrote his projects, as well as directing and starring in them. Among his most popular entries were: *Project A* (1983), *Wheels on Wheels* (1984), *Police Story* (1987), *Miracles* (1990), and *Crime Story* (1993).

Chan's first attempts to become a crossover American star (including 1980's *The Big Brawl* and 1985's *The Protector*) proved to be box-office disappointments in the United States. In contrast, one of his Hong Kong produced movies, *Rumble in the Bronx*, was dubbed into English and reedited to make it more appealing to the English-language market. It did more than adequately in U.S. distribution in 1996. A few years later, Chan returned to America to costar with Chris Tucker in the comedic cop/buddy picture *Rush Hour* (1998), which led to a sequel, *Rush Hour 2* (2001), and plans for *Rush Hour* 3 in 2004. His cowboy movie spoof, *Shanghai Noon*, showed that the ebullient Chan had learned how to appeal to western audiences with his blend of sly humor and athletic stunts. (It too led to a sequel in 2002.) Adding to the mix, Jackie was the voiceover star of a Saturday morning cartoon series entitled *Jackie Chan Adventures* (2000–). Next came his 2002 feature films *Highbinders* (2002) and *Shanghai Knights* (2003).

Chan, Jacky See CHAN, JACKIE.

Chaney, Lon (1883–1930) Born Leonidas Chaney in Colorado Springs, Colorado, to deaf-mute parents, he became legendary in silent features as the "Man of a Thousand Faces." He was renowned for the meticulousness of his makeup and the painful body manipulations he underwent to alter his appearance on screen. His long list of distinguished, varied film roles included Fagin in *Oliver Twist* (1922), *The Hunchback of Notre Dame* (1922), *The Phantom of the Opera* (1925), and *Laugh, Clown, Laugh* (1928). His final feature, *The Unholy Three* (1930), was his first talkie feature and a remake of his 1925 silent.

One of Chaney's movie specialties was portraying Asian characters, a pursuit that lasted through much of his film career: *OUTSIDE THE LAW* (1920), *Bits of Life* (1921), *Shadows* (1922), *The Road to Mandalay* (1926), and his most remarkable such cinema role, *MR. WU* (1927).

***Chan Is Missing* (1982)** New Yorker, b&w, 80 minutes. **Director:** Wayne Wang; **Screenplay:** Wang, Isaac Cromin, and Terel Seltzer; **Cast:** Wood Moy (Jo), Marc Hayashi (Steve), Laureen Chew (Amy), Judi Nihei (lawyer), Peter Wang (Henry, the cook), Presco Tabios (Presco), Frankie Alarcon (Frankie), Ellen Yeung (Mrs. Chan).

This entry was significant as the first American feature film fully made by an Asian-American cast and crew. This deceptively simple comedy was created by Hong Kong-born WANG on a $22,000 budget. It became a surprise hit.

In San Francisco's Chinatown, two cabbies (Moy and Hayashi) search for the elusive Chan Hung who has taken their hard-earned $4,000.

Chao, Rosalind (1949–) She became familiar to TV viewers playing Keiko Ishikawa, married to (Transportation Chief, later Chief Operations Officer) Miles O'Brien on TV's *Star Trek: The Next Generation* (1991–93) and *Star Trek: Deep Space Nine* (1992–97). She was born in Anaheim, California, and her Chinese name was Chao Jyalin. On the TV series *Anna and the King* (1972) set in Siam, she was Princess Serena, and Rosalind played Rose in *THE JOY LUCK CLUB* (1993). Later films included *To Love, Honor, and Deceive* (1997), *What Dreams May Come* (1998), *Enemies of Laughter* (2000), *I Am Sam* (2001), and an uncredited role as a newscaster in the sci-fi thriller *Imposter* (2002).

***Charlie Chan at the Opera* (1937)** Twentieth Century-Fox, b&w, 68 minutes. **Director:** H. Bruce Humberstone; **Screenplay:** Scott Darling and Charles S. Belden; **Cast:** Warner Oland (Charlie Chan), Boris Karloff (Gravelle), Keye Luke (Lee Chan), Charlotte Henry (Mme. Kitty), Thomas Beck (Phil Childers), Margaret Irving (Mme. Lilli Rochelle), Gregory Gaye (Enrico Barelli), William Demarest (Sergeant Kelly).

Pitting CHARLIE CHAN against KARLOFF, the king of screen horrors, was a smart casting gimmick that led to several exciting moments in *Charlie Chan at the Opera.* Both actors knew how to milk a scene for maximum effect. That this most popular of all the Charlie Chan entries had plot loopholes, disjointed transitions, and borrowed ideas from *The Phantom of the Opera* (1925) did not concern admirers of this entry. The picture was also noteworthy for its operatic sequences, all part of a specially created faux opera *(Carnival)* with music by Oscar Levant and libretto by William Kernell.

A running gag of this movie was handed to the not-so-bright Sergeant Kelly, who had a strong prejudice against Chan. Kelly asked his boss, "You haven't called 'Chop Suey' in on the case, have you, chief?" Later this dunce insisted, "No Chinese cop is gonna show me up!" But, of course, Chan did so repeatedly. By the finale, even the bigoted Kelly was impressed when Chan solved the tough case. The cop acknowledged, "You're all right. Just like chop suey. A mystery, but a swell dish."

Meanwhile, Charlie's son (Luke) had several on-camera moments that made his character more a typical young man, not just an exotic "foreigner." Ever anxious to help his renowned dad, he enthusiastically goes undercover at the opera house and proves astute at ferreting out clues. To be noted, BENSON FONG, who would play Chan's #3 son Tommy in several Monogram Pictures Charlie Chan entries, had a bit here as an extra in a theater sequence.

***Charlie Chan Carries On* (1931)** Fox, b&w, 76 minutes. **Director:** Hamilton MacFadden; **Screenplay:** Philip Klein and Barry Conners; **Cast:** Marguerite Churchill (Pamela Potter), John Garrick (Mark Kenaway), Warner Oland (Charlie Chan), Warren Hymer (Max Minchin), Marjorie White (Sadie Minchin), C. Henry Gordon (John Ross), George Brent (Capt. Ronald Keane), Peter Gawthorne (Inspector Duff).

Having already appeared as the arch villain FU MANCHU in several films, Swedish-born OLAND debuted as the celebrated Honolulu policeman—now chief of detectives—CHARLIE CHAN. Based on a 1930 Charlie Chan novel by Earl Derr Biggers, the film presented the Asian sleuth in full dimension, providing all the character traits that would make the Oland/Chan entries so well liked by filmgoers. As delineated, the sleuth was generally modest, always astute, and occasionally short-tempered when his priorities were not met by others. As in the book original, Chan did not appear till well into the case, which built suspense for his arrival. That the well-educated Charlie spoke in broken English was a concession of the day to what a Chinese person "should" sound like. On the other hand, Charlie's passion for aphorisms revealed him to be a sharp observer.

So well liked was *Charlie Chan Carries On* that it led to a host of subsequent entries, fifteen of which would star Oland before his death in 1937. This entry would be remade as *Charlie Chan's Murder Cruise* (1940) with SIDNEY TOLER as the legendary detective.

***Charlie Chan in Honolulu* (1938)** Twentieth Century-Fox, b&w, 65 minutes. **Director:** H. Bruce Humberstone; **Screenplay:** Charles Belden; **Cast:** Sidney Toler (Charlie Chan), Phyllis Brooks (Judy Hayes), Victor Sen Yung (James Chan), Eddie Collins (Al Hogan), John King (George Randolph), Claire Dodd (Mrs. Carol Wayne [Mrs. Elsie Hillman]), Layne Tom Jr. (Tommy Chan).

Following the death of WARNER OLAND in 1937, Missouri-born TOLER, a veteran actor, was signed to take over as the Chinese police sleuth, CHARLIE CHAN. Because KEYE LUKE, who had played Chan's #1 son, Lee, was in a contract dispute with Twentieth Century-Fox, SEN YUNG was brought in to play #2 son, Jimmy, with Tom Jr. as another of the Chan clan, the young Tommy.

Chan is supposed to investigate a murder aboard the freighter *Susan B. Jennings*, docked in Honolulu. But he has rushed to the hospital with his wife and his son-in-law, Wing Foo, to await the birth of his first grandson. Meanwhile, Chan's #2 son, Jimmy, is goaded by younger brother Tommy to take on the investigation himself—which he does with enthusiasm if not expertise.

Despite its excessive comedy sequences, this was a relatively fast-paced installment in the Chan series and one that allowed for the proper introduction of the new actor playing the popular Chinese sleuth. Toler added his own layers of subtle interpretation to his portrayal of the cinema's most eminent Asian character.

Charlie Chan in the Chinese Ring See CHINESE RING, THE.

***Charlie Chan in the Secret Service* (1944)** Monogram, b&w, 65 minutes. **Director:** Phil Rosen; **Screenplay:** George Callahan; **Cast:** Sidney Toler (Charlie Chan), Mantan Moreland (Birmingham Brown), Arthur Loft (Jones), Gwen Kenyon (Inez Aranto), Marianne Quon (Iris Chan), Benson Fong (Tommy Chan), Lelah Tyler (Mrs. Winters).

It had been two years since *Castle in the Desert* (1942), the last CHARLIE CHAN adventure to be made at Twentieth Century-Fox. After that studio dropped the screen series, star TOLER had purchased the rights to the Chan character from the widow of its creator, Earl Derr Biggers. This was the first of a new batch of celluloid entries, produced at the poverty-row studio Monogram Pictures. A fresh ingredient to the property was the introduction of loquacious Birmingham Brown, a superstitious chauffeur, played with pop-eyed stereotypical excess by black actor Moreland. No longer aboard were either Chan's #1 (Lee) or #2 (Jimmy) sons to help solve the capers; instead, there was #3 son Tommy played by FONG, and thrown into the mix was Iris, one of Chan's several daughters.

The three Chans fortuitously happen to be in Washington, D.C., sightseeing when Charlie is called in to investigate the death of the inventor of a secret torpedo needed for the World War II effort. While he determines who is the killer, Charlie must deal with the dizzy socialite Mrs. Winters and her driver, Birmingham Brown.

Despite the threadbare plots and the economy production values, the new group of Chan adventures proved winning enough at the box office to continue onward for a few more years.

***Cheat, The* (1915)** Paramount, b&w, 5 reels. **Director:** Cecil B. DeMille; **Screenplay:** Hector Turnbull and Jeanie McPherson; **Cast:** Fannie Ward (Edith Hardy), Sessue Hayakawa (Hishuru Tori), Jack Dean (Dick Hardy), James Neill (Jones), Utaka Abe (Tori's Valet), Dana Ong (District Attorney).

Twenty-three-year-old HAYAKAWA received notoriety as the costar of this risqué society drama. The Japanese-born actor had been making movies for only a few years in America when he was cast as Hishuru Tori, an affluent Japanese curio dealer who is part of the Long Island rich set. He takes a fancy to the married Edith Hardy. After Edith loses funds belonging to a Red Cross charity in the stock market, she borrows replacement money from Tori. As part of the deal, she must submit to him the next night. By then, she has secured cash to repay the loan, but Tori demands she keep to their bargain. When she refuses, he brands her shoulder with his seal. She shoots him, but he survives, only to be castigated in court when the full story is revealed.

The built-in prejudices of this film's plot premise were many. For starters, a wealthy non-American, especially a non-Caucasian, was shown as able to have intimate relations with a coveted white woman only through blackmail, and only a bestial foreigner would brand his possessions. Then it was pointed out how an American jury registered shock at the heroine's fate, not so much because it occurred but that it was accomplished by an Asian to an (American) white woman.

Some weeks after this film debuted, the Japanese Association of Southern California registered a formal protest with the Los Angeles City Council to prohibit showings of the movie. When Paramount reissued the silent film in late 1918, Hayakawa's character was changed to be a Burmese. *The Cheat* was remade in 1923 (where the villain was a phony South American) and in 1931 (where the rogue was an American who had spent years in the Orient). In 1937, Hayakawa recreated his role in the French remake of *The Cheat* entitled *Forfaiture.*

Chen, Joan (1961–) In the early 1980s, radiant teenager Chen made several movies in China including *Youth* (1977) and *The Little Flower* (1980). Her performances not only won the attractive youth the billing of "China's Elizabeth Taylor" but also earned her a Golden Rooster Award, the equivalent of an Oscar. Thereafter, in pictures made in Hollywood and abroad, Chen developed an international reputation as a superior thespian, not just a fine Asian actress. Later, she would add TV series work (*Twin Peaks,* 1990–91) and film directing to her résumé, making her an important figure on the global movie scene.

She was born Chen Chong in Shanghai, the second of two children of Chinese doctors. During the Cultural Revolution, when her parents were sent away for "reeducation" programs, she and her brother were brought up by their grandparents. When she was fourteen, she made her first film, a two-line part as a young guerrilla in a Shanghai-filmed movie. This led to more cinema roles as part of a government-supervised training program.

Chen's parents came to the United States in the late 1970s, and in 1981 their daughter joined them. After two years at California State University in the film studies program, Joan started to win small roles on such American TV series as *Miami Vice* and *MacGyver.* She also had a tiny part in *DIM SUM: A LITTLE BIT OF HEART* (1984) as a young mahjongg player. When she was signed for a major role in *TAI-PAN* (1986), she had to return to her homeland, where her screen character as a concubine to a foreigner (Pierce Brosnan) was not appreciated. However, her portrayal of Wan Jung in *The Last Emperor* (1987) won her acclaim, and in Oliver Stone's *HEAVEN & EARTH* (1993), her character was required to transform from youngish woman to one of old age.

Long-interested in directing, Joan made *Xiu Xiu: The Sent-Down Girl* (1998), filmed on the sly in China and earning her the enmity of its government because of the movie's reflection of living conditions and politics there. The internationally well-received movie provided Chen with, among other tributes, the Best Foreign Feature prize at the inaugural Ammy Award in the fall of 2000. (The Ammys were established to recognize the year's brightest achievements by Asians and Asian Americans in film and television.) Chen continued to act on camera (*WHAT'S COOKING?*, 2000; *Avatar,* 2002) and to helm other movies (*Autumn in New York,* 2000).

children's series—television In addition to animated TV programming with Asian-American themes (see ANIMATION SERIES—TELEVISION), there was *The New Mickey Mouse Club* (1977), which featured Curtis Wong as one of the Mousketeers. Within *The New Voice* (1981), a PBS-TV series about students who wrote for the newspaper at Boston's Lincoln High School, class members included Ken Mochizuki (Ken) and Kiko McKee (Kiko). There was also *Mighty Morphin Power Rangers* (1993–96), featuring five teenagers who had the power to transform into Power Rangers to fight evil alien invaders. One of the quintet was Trini, the Yellow Ranger (played by Thuy Trang from 1993 to 1994). Later there was Tonya, the Yellow Ranger (played by Nakia Burrise in 1996). (The program was adapted into the 1995 feature film, *Mighty Morphin Power Rangers.*) *CityKids* (1993–94) concerned six youths involved with the CityKids Foundation in New York. One of their number was played by Hassan Elgendi.

Ghostwriter (1992–95) was a PBS-TV series aimed at youngsters to encourage their interest in reading. The multicultural cast included Tram-Anh Tran as Tina Nguyen, with Richard Eng and Ginny Yang as her parents. *Rugrats,* the Nickelodeon cable network's animated series, had begun in 1991 and dealt with the world from an infant's point of view. In 2000, it added new characters to expand the ethnic mix. Introduced on the series were Kira Watanabe-Finster and Kimi Watanabe-Finster (voices of Julila Kato and Dionne Quan, respectively). *Third Rumble,* a magazine format series, began in November 2001, geared to Asian-American youths and their lifestyles.

Chin Tsai (1937–) Born Irene Chow in Shanghai, China, the daughter of Peking Opera star Zhou Xinfang, Chin left China as a teenager. Her parents, who remained behind, were later killed in the Cultural Revolution. Chin was the first Chinese woman to study at the Royal Academy of Dramatic Art in London, where a classmate was Glenda Jackson. In a series of British-made DR. FU MANCHU movies, she played Lin Tang. A veteran of stage and TV as well, she made her greatest impressions as Aunt Lindo in *THE JOY*

LUCK CLUB (1993) and as Chairman Xu in *RED CORNER* (1997). Later film roles included *My American Vacation (1999)*, *Titan A.E.* (2000—as the voice of the Old Woman in this animated feature), and *Gold Cup* (2000).

***China* (1943)** Paramount, b&w, 78 minutes. **Director:** John Farrow; **Screenplay:** Frank Butler; **Cast:** Loretta Young (Carolyn Grant), Alan Ladd (David Jones), William Bendix (Johnny Sparrow), Philip Ahn (Lin Cho—first brother), Iris Wong (Kwan Su), Victor Sen Yung (Lin Wei—third brother), Marianne Quon (Tan Ying), Richard Loo (Lin Yun—second brother).

Geared to strike every emotional chord available in pro-Allied moviegoers, this patriotic World War II movie stars Ladd as a cold-hearted American profiteer in 1941 China, selling oil to the Japanese. He and his partner, Johnny Sparrow, become involved with flinty Carolyn Grant, an American schoolteacher born in China, who is shepherding female Chinese college students to safety from the advancing Japanese forces. By the finale, as Carolyn and Johnny and the surviving students drive to safety, they (and the audience) have experienced a full microcosm of wartime adversities. As the latecomer to the fight for freedom, Ladd's mercenary character dies, protecting the others against the enemy.

This efficiently made war film used a full contingent of Hollywood's available Asian-American actors. It was one of many early-to-mid-1940 features set in war-torn China and contrived to arose the sympathy of American filmgoers for the Chinese against the Japanese.

***China Gate* (1956)** Twentieth Century-Fox, b&w, 96 minutes. **Director/Screenplay:** Samuel Fuller; **Cast:** Gene Barry (Brock), Angie Dickinson (Lucky Legs), Nat "King" Cole (Goldie), Paul DuBov (Captain Caumont), Lee Van Cleef (Major Cham), Neyle Morrow (Leung), Warren Hsieh (the boy).

Years before the escalated U.S. involvement in Vietnam, and at a time when the French still controlled that country, this low-budget but effective action drama was made by Fuller. Brock is an American soldier of fortune who finds himself involved with his estranged spouse, a Eurasian political activist known as Lucky Legs, on a mission to take out a Chinese Communist ammunition supply dump. Brock's command includes members of the French Foreign Legion, one of whom is the emotionally drained Goldie.

Dickinson would portray another Far Easterner in the would-be comedy, *Charlie Chan and the Curse of the Dragon Queen* (1981).

***China Girl* (1942)** Twentieth Century-Fox, b&w, 95 minutes. **Director:** Henry Hathaway; **Screenplay:** Ben Hecht; **Cast:** Gene Tierney (Haoli Young), George Montgomery (Johnny Williams), Lynn Bari (Captain Fifi), Victor McLaglen (Maj. Bull Weed), Alan Baxter (Jones), Bobby Blake (Chinese boy), Philip Ahn (Dr. Young).

Like many of the Hollywood-made wartime dramas, this one features a tough-as-nails American—Montgomery—who is caught on the wrong part of the globe as World War II broke out and who suddenly realizes his patriotic duty to the United States.

Johnny Williams is a newsreel cameraman in Luichow, China, in November 1941. The area is controlled by the Japanese, who detain the American, demanding that he film for them the building of the Burma Road. To ensure his cooperation, they put operatives (McLaglen and Bari) to work on him, but Williams finds himself attracted to a beautiful woman (Tierney) who proves to be a Vassar College-educated Eurasian.

Resolving the issue of an interracial love match—at the time still considered a shocking subject by Hollywood film studios, the industry production-code board, and the public—was easier to accomplish in war action entries. Here, Haoli Young is killed while rescuing orphans from the Japanese onslaught.

Tierney had previously played an Eurasian in *THE SHANGHAI GESTURE* (1940). She captured the part's exotic look and emotional reserve but conveyed little of the blending of the two cultures.

***China Girl* (1987)** Vestron, color, 88 minutes. **Director:** Abel Ferrara; **Screenplay:** Nicholas St. John; **Cast:** James Russo (Alberto "Alby" Monte), Richard Panebianco (Tony Monte), Sari Chang (Tyan-Hwa), David Caruso (Johnny Mercury), Russell Wong (Yung-Gam), Joey Chin (Tsu-Shin).

With the increased acculturation of Asian Americans into all facets of U.S. society, it was only a matter of time before filmmakers depicted the turf wars between Chinese street gangs and those of other cultures. *China Girl* was one such violent example.

In New York City's Little Italy, a Chinese restaurant opens in what used to be a cappuccino shop. Thus, bad feeling between a local Italian street gang and a Chinese one (known as a TONG) accelerates. Caught in the middle of the culture clash are Tony Monte and Tyan-Hwa who have fallen in love but are ordered by bigoted relatives and friends to break their relationship. Meanwhile, the Italian and the Chinese underworlds unite to crush the escalating war before it destroys their lucrative tourist traffic.

In this slick distillation of the *Romeo and Juliet (West Side Story)* theme, one of the more diehard racists was played by Caruso. Cast as the brother of the Asian-American girl in love was WONG, soon to become a major film and TV name.

***China Seas* (1935)** Metro-Goldwyn-Mayer, b&w, 90 minutes. **Director:** Tay Garnett; **Screenplay:** Jules Furthman and James Kevin McGuinness; **Cast:** Clark Gable (Capt. Alan Gaskell), Jean Harlow ("China Doll" Portland),

Wallace Beery (Jamesy MacArdle), Lewis Stone (Tom Davids), Rosalind Russell (Sybil Barclay), Soo Yong (Yu-Lan), Hattie McDaniel (Isabel McCarthy), Willie Fung (cabin boy).

In Crosbie Garstin's 1931 novel, on which this project was based, China Doll was Chinese and her past affair with Alan Gaskell had resulted in an illegitimate child. To appease the film industry's censorship board, the character of China Doll was considerably changed. She lost her ethnicity and became a brassy blond Caucasian entertainer with a questionable past. That aside, this exciting feature bristled with atmosphere of the exotic Far East, merciless Chinese pirates, and unscrupulous opium-den habitués.

Aboard the China Seas steamer *Kin Lung*, bound from Hong Kong to Shanghai, are the China Doll, Captain Gaskell's sharp-mouthed tart; her wisecracking African-American maid Isabel; and Sybil Barclay, an aristocratic British widow whom Gaskell once loved. Also included are disgraced third officer Tom Davids, rascally China Sea trader Jamesy MacArdle, and a mysterious cargo.

Before the vessel reaches Shanghai, there is a ravaging typhoon, and Malay pirates board the ship. At the end, China Doll faces a maritime trial for her involvement in the cargo hijacking scheme, but Gaskell will stand by her.

If the character of China Doll bore a resemblance to another "China Coaster" (i.e., prostitute) named Shanghai Lily from *SHANGHAI EXPRESS* (1932), that was because screenwriter Furthman participated in both projects. In addition, Furthman was a scribe on *THE SHANGHAI GESTURE* (1941), which featured other unprincipled Shanghai-based women.

***Chinatown Charlie* (1928)** First National, b&w, 6,365′. **Director:** Charles Hines; **Screenplay:** Roland Asher and John Grey; **Cast:** Johnny Hines (Charlie), Louise Lorraine (Annie Gordon), Harry Gribbon (Red Mike), Fred Kohler (Monk), Kamiyama Sojin (the Mandarin), Anna May Wong (the Mandarin's sweetheart), George Kuwa (Hip Sing Toy).

In the waning day of silent features, this modest movie used a Chinatown backdrop for quick and easy exotic flavoring to intrigue filmgoers. Playing one of the Chinese was Japanese-born Kuwa, who was the American screen's first CHARLIE CHAN in the ten-chapter serial *The House Without a Key* (1926). Another Japanese-born actor in the cast, SOJIN, had played Charlie Chan in *THE CHINESE PARROT* (1927). As would so often happen in Hollywood's casting of Oriental roles, it made no difference to the casting directors (or the American filmgoing public) whether a Chinese character was portrayed by a Japanese or Chinese—or Caucasian in makeup.

Chinatown tour-guide Charlie comes to the rescue of one of his passengers, Annie Gordon, when thieves attempt to steal her ring (which is supposed to have magical powers). Later, the action moves to a local Mandarin's estate to which Annie is kidnapped, again in hope of grabbing the ring.

***Chinatown Nights* (1929)** Paramount, b&w, 88 minutes. **Director:** William A. Wellman; **Screenplay:** Ben Grauman Kohn; **Cast:** Wallace Berry (Chuck Riley), Florence Vidor (Joan Fry), Warner Oland (Boston Charley), Jack McHugh (the shadow), Jack Oakie (the reporter), Tetsu Komai (Woo Chung), Frank Chew (the gambler), Mrs. Wong Wing (the maid).

Based on Samuel Ornitz's short story "Tong War" (publication undetermined), this part-talkie featured a resilient cast in a standard story (with a few plot twists) of San Francisco's Chinatown.

When socialite Joan Fry is left behind when her tourist bus hastily departs the Chinese section of San Francisco, a TONG war erupts. She is rescued by Chuck Riley, the Caucasian leader of one tong faction. Before long, she is so attracted to the rough character that she lives with him. Their romance is rocky, and one night, when he forces her to leave their home, she is picked up by Boston Charley, the Chinese rival of Riley. He gets the distraught woman inebriated and then redelivers her to Riley with an embarrassing note attached. This prompts the gruff Irishman to depart the district, taking Joan with him.

This film took hackneyed situations (e.g., tong wars and mystifying Chinatown) and stock characters (e.g., the sinister Oriental) and used them to advantage as brooding atmosphere. But instead of having the white heroine fall in love with an Asian or half-caste and the romance be doomed (on then current movie industry and real-life moral grounds that forbade interracial romances), the scenario used the tong-war setting for maximum effect but had the tong leader be Caucasian so that a "happy" ending was feasible.

In this same year, Swedish-born OLAND played the first of his DR. FU MANCHU screen roles.

***Chinese Parrot, The* (1927)** Universal, b&w, 7,304′. **Director:** Paul Leni; **Screenplay:** J. Grubb Alexander; **Cast:** Marian Nixon (Sally Phillimore), Florence Turner (Sally Phillimore—the older woman), Hobart Bosworth (Philip Madden/Jerry Delaney), Edward Burns (Robert Eden), Kamiyama Sojin (Charlie Chan), George Kuwa (Louie Wong), Anna May Wong (Nautch dancer).

Based on Earl Derr Biggers's 1926 novel, this was the second filmed CHARLIE CHAN entry. Like the prior one—the serial *The House Without a Key* (1926), which had George Kuwa as the fictional sleuth—this silent entry featured a Japanese *not* a Chinese performer in the lead. This casual casting rationale was part of the condescending American conceit of the time that all Asians looked alike to the average moviegoer, no matter what their heritage.

In *The Chinese Parrot*, one of the few Chan movies of which no known print survives, Chan, the Chinese detective, is hired to guard valuable pearls that have been sold at auction. Before the jewelry reaches its rightful new owner, it is stolen several times. Helping Chan with his investigation is a Chinese parrot who has witnessed a kidnapping.

This was SOJIN's only appearance as the famed detective. For the next installment, *BEHIND THAT CURTAIN* (1929), a British actor, E. L. Park, inherited the role.

***The Chinese Ring* (aka: *Charlie Chan in the Chinese Ring*) (1947)** Monogram, b&w, 68 minutes. **Director:** William Beaudine; **Screenplay:** W. Scott Darling; **Cast:** Roland Winters (Charlie Chan), Warren Douglas (Sgt. Bill Davidson), Mantan Moreland (Birmingham Brown), Louise Currie (Peggy Cartwright), Victor Sen Yung (Tommy Chan), Philip Ahn (Captain Kong), Jean Wong (Princess Mei Ling).

The last Monogram Pictures entry in their CHARLIE CHAN film series to feature SIDNEY TOLER as the intrepid Chinese sleuth was 1947's *The Trap*. With Toler's death that same year, the role was inherited by Massachusetts-born WINTERS. Although not the most likely candidate to headline this declining screen property, he proved surprisingly authentic in the part, although he hardly looked Chinese. SEN YUNG (sometimes spelled *Young* on screen credits) was now Tommy Chan, formerly the detective's #3 son but here called #2 son. Starting with this entry, Chan was based in San Francisco and had the benefit of a laboratory at home. Also the "new" Chan did not suffer fools happily.

In actuality, *The Chinese Ring* was a remake of *Mr. Wong in Chinatown* (1939), an entry in the inexpensive Monogram series that had starred BORIS KARLOFF as MR. WONG. A mysterious Chinese princess visits Chan in his San Francisco home, and before she is murdered, she gives Chan's butler (Moreland) an antique ring. It develops she came to the United States to purchase war planes for her brother's army in the Far East. When the princess's maid is murdered, a deaf mute boy provides a clue that leads to Armstrong, the banker. Others involved in the case include news reporter Peggy Cartwright and police sergeant Bill Davidson.

Cho, Margaret (1968–) She had the distinction of being the first Asian American to star in her own U.S. TV series (*ALL-AMERICAN GIRL*, 1994–95). Her sitcom was not a success but, as she was doing in her stand-up comedy act, it highlighted Korean-American culture. Such showcases helped to break down stereotypes associated with her ethnic minority group, and it made her the highest-profile Asian-American stand-up comic in the United States.

Cho was born in San Francisco to parents who had come from Korea to the United States in 1964 to complete their college education. (Her mother had broken with traditions when she refused to accept an arranged marriage, engineered by her own father, a Methodist minister who ran an orphanage in Seoul during the Korean War.) Cho's liberal yet religious parents bought a bookstore in the Haight-Ashbury district of San Francisco, and it was there that she and her younger brother were raised. After graduating from the local High School of Performing Arts, Cho attended, for a time, San Francisco State University as a theater major. It was in this period that she turned to stand-up comedy to express her dissatisfaction with the limited acting roles available to Asian and Asian-American women. Many of her comedy routines—which poked fun at her own generation—she developed while working in her parents' bookstore. (Her father later became a comedy writer, authoring joke books.)

By 1992, Cho had relocated to Los Angeles and was entering comedy-club competitions. One such win led to her being on the same bill with Jerry Seinfeld. She made the rounds of stand-up comedy venues and was on several cable-TV comedy showcases, which led a network to shape a TV sitcom around her. (When the show failed, Cho admitted publicly, it sent her into an emotional tailspin that involved substance abuse.) Her subsequent acting assignments included roles in *The Doom Generation* (1995), *It's My Party* (1996), a small assignment in the JOHN WOO-directed *Face/Off* (1997), and a co-lead in *Can't Stop Dancing* (1999), a comedy about a Kansas fun park dance troupe.

Recovering from her addictions and the medical problems engendered by the quick weight loss needed to do *All-American Girl*, she began to appear again in comedy clubs. She developed a new one-woman show, *I'm the One That I Want*, a witty showcase that was recorded as a full-length film (2000) and came out in book format (2001) as a comedic autobiography about her life lessons. Other recent films included *The Tavern* (1999), *$pent* (2000), the TV documentary *Miss America* (2002), and another concert film, *Notorious C.H.O.* (2002), more raw and raunchy than her prior one.

Chow Yun-fat (1955–) Initially lumped together with JACKIE CHAN and JET LI as one of the most bankable of the Hong Kong MARTIAL ARTS movie stars, handsome and stylish Chow displayed an intriguing versatility, dramatic acumen, and genuineness in his debut English-language features in the late 1990s. (His roles more often called for him to wield a gun than flying fists and feet.) In one of them, the cop/crime thriller, *THE CORRUPTOR* (1999), he was brooding and complex—and handled a gun quite well. In another, *ANNA AND THE KING* (1999), he proved that he had sexual charisma as the chauvinistic nineteenth-century Siamese ruler, King Mongkut. These performances were followed by another entry, made for the Asian movie market and not dubbed into English, *CROUCHING TIGER, HIDDEN DRAGON* (2000), in which he was the moody but resourceful warrior on a mission to redeem his honor, a characterization he imbued with layers of complexity.

Chow was born on Lamma Island, Hong Kong, the third of four children. His childhood was spent helping his vegetable farmer mother scrape together a living. (His father was an oil-tanker seaman who was rarely at home and who died in 1974.) At age seventeen, he left school and found work as a salesman and bellboy before starting acting lessons at TVB, the largest of Hong Kong's TV studios. From 1973 onward, Chow appeared in several of the company's projects and became a favorite with viewers. By the early 1980s, his fame was expanding, and by then he was making feature films; one of his early favorites was *The Story of Woo Viet* (1981). In 1982 he reportedly attempted suicide after a failed romance with a Chinese actress.

He gained true popularity with his performance in the JOHN WOO–directed *A Better Tomorrow* (1986) in which the actor played a top-level gangster. This led to several sequels, also blending a mix of drama, comedy, and action. Taking advantage of his growing popularity, in 1988 alone he made twelve feature films. Several of his shoot-'em-up movies have been directed by Ringo Lam.

The six-feet, one-inch Buddhist made his American movie debut in *The Replacement Killers* (1998) as the hit man who refused to carry out an assignment and thereby became the target of hired assassins. In the course of eighty-six minutes, the body count ran high, but the by-the-book plot/direction didn't allow the star much leeway to demonstrate the range of his skills. The next year's *The Corruptor*, which teamed him with Mark Wahlberg, was much better received. Although Jodie Foster was the major star of *Anna and the King*, it was Chow who earned positive critical notice. Chow next made *Bulletproof Monk* (2002) teamed with Seann William Scott.

Chung, Connie (1946–) On network television, Chung is one of the more prominent distaff reporters and one of the few of Asian heritage. Born in Washington, D.C., she graduated from the University of Maryland and became a political reporter for CBS-TV in 1971. In the late 1970s she rose to recognition as coanchor of the early and late evening news. A rising name in the newscast world in the 1980s, she anchored *NBC Weekend News* and the public affairs show *1986*, hosted *SATURDAY NIGHT WITH CONNIE CHUNG* (1989–90), and became coanchor of *20/20* news magazine in 1998. (Her pathfinding work paved the way for such personalities as Lisa Ling who joined the TV newsmagazine *The View* in 1999.) In early 2002 Chung left ABC-TV to move to CNN cable to anchor a new one-hour show in primetime, entitled *Connie Chung Tonight*.

***City of Dim Faces* (1918)** Paramount, b&w, 4,219′. **Director:** George Melford; **Screenplay:** Frances Marion; **Cast:** Sessue Hayakawa (Jang Lung), Doris Pawn (Marcell Matthews), Marin Sais (Elizabeth Mendall), James Cruze (Wing Lung), Winter Hall (Brand Matthews), Togo Yama (Foo Sing).

This turgid drama was created for Japanese-born HAYAKAWA, who was becoming a major name with his U.S.-made feature films.

Years before, Elizabeth Mendall had wed a Chinese merchant, Wing Lung. When their son Jang is born, she wants the boy to be raised in the Christian faith. Refusing to agree, Wing Lung imprisons her in the cellar, and she goes mad. Years later, Jang Lung falls in love with Marcell Matthews, a college classmate. They plan to wed in his home town of San Francisco, but after visiting Chinatown, she has second thoughts. This enrages her fiancé, who hands Marcell over to a marriage broker. Later, Jang learns about his mother and, now remorseful, tries to rescue Marcell. In the process, he is fatally wounded, but before he expires he reconciles with his parent and with Marcell.

This was one of seven 1918 silent features starring Hayakawa. The miscegenation issue in the story was resolved by having Hayakawa's character die heroically so that the interracial love tale could end on a "happy" spiritual note without offending filmgoers.

Clark, Mamo (1914–1986) As Maimiti, a Tahitian beauty in *Mutiny on the Bounty* (1935), she became the on-camera mate of Clark Gable. It was the screen debut for the actress, who was born on Maui, Hawaii. Clark was active in the late 1930s, playing tropical screen lovelies who were sometimes Hawaiian, sometimes Tahitian, sometimes pure Hollywood fantasy: *Robinson Crusoe of Clipper Island* (1936—serial), *The Hurricane* (1937), and *HAWAII CALLS* (1938). In *One Million B.C.* (1940) she was a prehistoric miss; in her final release, *The Girl from God's Country* (1940), she was cast as an Eskimo.

combat dramas—feature films The bulk of American-made war films involving Asian Americans dealt with twentieth-century hostilities. Ironically, these clashes between nations—especially World War II, the Korean War, and the Vietnam War—provided work of a type for Asian-American actors in Hollywood. In such movies, they were often cast as friendly villagers, local troops, resistance operatives, or, in contrast, the enemy. (Ironically, because the U.S. government, after the Pearl Harbor attack, shipped most Japanese Americans to inland detention camps for the duration of World War II, most Japanese roles in Hollywood-made World War II era dramas were played by non-Japanese Asians or Asian Americans.)

One of the few World War I dramas turned out by U.S. filmmakers to deal with Asian Americans was *The Lost Battalion* (1919). This silent drama highlighted the 308th Regiment's Seventh Division, drawn from New Yorkers of diverse backgrounds. Among the group were two soldiers from opposing TONG factions in Chinatown. Once in France and in the thick of battle, they fought the common enemy—together.

As the world became engulfed in a swamp of war in the 1930s and the Japanese military machine expanded, the escalating hostilities between Japan and China saw the former grabbing chunks of the latter. This unrest in China was expressed in such Hollywood films as *SHANGHAI EXPRESS* (1932), *THE GENERAL DIED AT DAWN* (1936), *Shadows over Shanghai* (1938), *Exiled to Shanghai* (1937), and *North of Shanghai* (1939). As America had not entered the war officially but was unofficially on the side of China, studios began to produce screen accounts of U.S. volunteers who fought on behalf of the Chinese cause. Such entries—sometimes recapping what had happened a few years earlier—included *THE FLYING TIGERS* (1942), *CHINA GIRL* (1942), *CHINA* (1943), and *China Sky* (1944).

Once the United States declared war against Japan following the attack on Pearl Harbor in December 1941, some later Hollywood films looked back to this period and what had "actually" been transpiring in Japan *prior* to that time.

Entries of this type were *BEHIND THE RISING SUN* (1943) and *BLOOD ON THE SUN* (1945). One of the more atmospheric pictures dealing with Japanese espionage in the western world before Pearl Harbor was *Across the Pacific* (1942). An early low-budget entry on Axis fifth columnists at work in Los Angeles was *LITTLE TOKYO, U.S.A.* (1942).

Once the United States had declared against Japan, many feature films detailed the heroics of Americans in combat with the Axis enemy. These flag-rousing entries were packed with representations of the sinister and sadistic Japanese forces. Typical of this genre were *Corregidor* (1942), *WAKE ISLAND* (1942), *Bataan* (1943), *OBJECTIVE, BURMA!* (1945), *They Were Expendable* (1945), and *BACK TO BATAAN* (1945). Two of the most memorable pictures reflecting women's courage on the battlefront—as nurses—were *SO PROUDLY WE HAIL* and *CRY HAVOC*, both 1943. Painting a picture of the grueling life of American soldiers caught behind Japanese lines was the thesis of *THE PURPLE HEART* (1944), *THIRTY SECONDS OVER TOKYO* (1944), and *FIRST YANK IN TOKYO* (1945). Depicting the Japanese propaganda machine at work was the focus of *TOKYO ROSE* (1946).

Once World War II ended in 1945, a few years passed before Hollywood felt itself or the American public ready to refight the war in the Pacific on screen. The new surge of patriotic battle dramas included *SANDS OF IWO JIMA* (1949), *AMERICAN GUERRILLA IN THE PHILIPPINES* (1950), *Halls of Montezuma* (1950), and *Operation Pacific* (1951). A graphic account of women trapped in Japanese POW camps was the thesis of *THREE CAME HOME* (1950) starring Claudette Colbert (as a prisoner) and SESSUE HAYAKAWA (as her captor). A positive account of Japanese Americans in the World War II Army was the basis of *GO FOR BROKE!* (1951).

As the 1950s progressed Hollywood continued to turn out World War II films but on a lesser scale: *The Purple Plain* (1954), *Hellcats of the Navy* (1957), *The Gallant Hours* (1960), *HELL TO ETERNITY* (1960), *Merrill's Marauders* (1962), *No Man Is an Island* (1962) *PT-109* (1963—based on John F. Kennedy's wartime experiences), *The Thin Red Line* (1964), *KING RAT* (1965—Allied soldiers in a Japanese POW camp), and *None But the Brave* (1965). One of the most bloody World War II-themed films was *BEACH RED* (1967), which, uniquely for its time, suggested both sides' point of view in the war. *HELL IN THE PACIFIC* (1968) did the same on a much smaller scale.

With the 1970s came a new type of film looking back to the big battles of World War II. *TORA! TORA! TORA!* (1970), made in conjunction with Japanese talent, recalled the events leading up to the Pearl Harbor attack as well as the actual attack and its most immediate aftermath. *MIDWAY* (1976) focused on that decisive battle in the Pacific, and *MacArthur* (1977) depicted the determined American general. Just as *The Beginning or the End* (1947) had traced the building of the atomic bombs to use against Japan, so the 1980 TV movie *Enola Gay* focused on the dropping of the bomb on Hiroshima. The miniseries *Pearl* (1978), written by Stirling Silliphant and featuring Angie Dickinson, was another account of events on the Hawaiian island before the Japanese surprise attack.

Steven Spielberg's *EMPIRE OF THE SUN* (1987) followed the plight of British civilians and others caught behind Japanese lines when Shanghai fell and they were then placed in prisoner camps for the duration. The elaborate, star-studded remake (1998) of *The Thin Red Line* (1964) turned the taking of Guadalcanal in 1942 into an artistic tapestry, and the epic *Pearl Harbor* (2001) once again treated the Japanese sneak attack on HAWAII—this time on an even more massive scale of recreation.

While Hollywood was still refighting World War II in the early 1950s, the real world was coping with the Korean conflict. Among the first U.S. features about the Korean War were *One Minute to Zero* (1950), *The Steel Helmet* (1951), *A Yank in Korea* (1951), *Korea Patrol* (1951), and *Retreat, Hell!* (1952). Others followed, including *Prisoner of War* (1954), *THE BRIDGES AT TOKO-RI* (1954); after the war concluded came *Battle Hymn* (1956), *The Hunters* (1958), and *All the Young Men* (1960). The exuberant but quite cynical *M*A*S*H* (1970) was a far different take on medics in the front lines of the Korean War than had been the much earlier *Battle Circus* (1953).

As America's presence in Vietnam in the 1960s turned into major warfare in Asia, it caused great controversy in the United States. Hollywood quickly turned to this new type of war where there were no clearly defined good guys. *The Lost Command* (1966) showed the build-up to the hostilities. This was followed by John Wayne's *The Green Berets* (1968) and such other entries as *Twilight's Last Gleaming* (1977), *The Boys in Company C* (1978), *THE DEER HUNTER* (1978), *Go Tell the Spartans* (1978), and the highly controversial *Apocalypse Now* (1979).

Once again, there was a gap there between the late 1970s and the mid-1980s before Hollywood launched a new offensive against the Vietcong with such gritty Vietnam war dramas as *PLATOON* (1986), *Full Metal Jacket* (1987), and *Hamburger Hill* (1987). Other aspects of the Vietnam horror were covered in such films as *Hanoi Hilton* and *Good Morning, Vietnam* (both 1987), *The Green Dragon* (2001) and *We Were Soldiers* (2002), or TV movies such as *The Children of An Lac* (1980), *Fly Away Home* (1981), *China Beach* (1988—the pilot to the TV series), and *Siege of Firebase Gloria* (1989).

Gene Hackman's *Uncommon Valor* (1983), Chuck Norris's *Missing in Action* (1984)—which prompted two sequels—and *Rambo: First Blood Part II* (1985) started a cycle of Hollywood movies that dealt with American soldiers missing in action during the Vietnam War and commando campaigns to retrieve them.

Steven Spielberg's massive, graphic, and touching *Saving Private Ryan* (1998), starring Tom Hanks, Edward Burns, and Matt Damon, was a return to World War II combat dramas on a grand scale set in the European theater of war. Its success led in 2001 to the Michael Bay-directed *Pearl Harbor*, a lavish supposed recreation of the surprise attack by the Japanese forces in 1941. It was more noteworthy for its action sequences and special effects than for its pat story line, cardboard characters, and gross factual inaccuracies.

In addition, during the decades there were several cold-war movies—especially after the breakup of the Soviet

Union—where China became the new culprit. These ranged from *THE MANCHURIAN CANDIDATE* (1962) to *The Chairman* (1969) to action themes presented within the more recent James Bond escapades (e.g., *Tomorrow Never Dies*, 1997), and such film entries as *Red Corner* (1997) with Richard Gere.

combat series—television There were many reasons why dramatic series about war were so rare on TV: Showing graphic fighting scenes to home viewers was considered distasteful, sponsors did not want to be associated with somber-themed shows, it was assumed women would not watch such bloody action, and the cost of staging or utilizing stock footage was prohibitive. A majority of the combat series on TV revolved around World War II fighting in Europe (e.g., *Combat!* 1962–67; *Combat Sergeant*, 1956). An exception was *Baa Baa Black Sheep* (1976–78) set in the World War II Pacific Theater of War. It featured Robert Conrad as Maj. Gregory "Pappy" Boyington, who was in charge of Squadron 214, which was composed of unruly fliers. It was a variation of *The Dirty Dozen* (1967) movie theme. One of the misfits was Capt. Tommy Harachi, played by Byron Chung for the 1976–77 season.

TOUR OF DUTY (1987–90) was a gritty combat series set during the Vietnam War. One of the members attached to Company B was Pvt. "Doc" Randy Matsuda (played by Steve Akahoshi). This Japanese American was one of the two cast members killed off in action during the show's first half-year on the air. In the episodes of battles with the enemy, when sometimes the Vietcong enemy were depicted, Asian-American performers were utilized. This was also true of *China Beach* (1988–91), which was less graphic than *Tour of Duty* and focused more on the personal lives of the Vietnam combatants and the (female) support staff at the base.

A two-part TV movie dealing was the Vietnam conflict was *A Rumor of War* (1980), based on the 1977 book by Philip Caputo recounting his wartime experiences. It starred Brad Davis as the idealistic college youth who became a battle-tough marine, and thereafter a disillusioned veteran. Scenes of South Vietnam featured Asian-American actors (e.g., David Chow as the mayor of Danang), as did those scenes dealing with the Vietcong enemy.

***Combination Platter* (1993)** Arrow Releasing, color, 84 minutes. **Director:** Tony Chan; **Screenplay:** Chan and Edwin Baker; **Cast:** Jeff Lau (Robert), Colleen O'Brien (Claire), Lester "Chit-Man" Chan (Sam), Colin Mitchell (Benny), Kenneth Lu (Andy), Thomas K. Hsiung (Mr. Lee), Jia Fu Liu (Dishwasher), Juliet Leong (Michelle).

This joyful independent feature examined the lives of blue-collar workers among the Asian community of New York City. Robert, recently arrived from Hong Kong, is hired as a waiter at the Szechwan Inn in Queens. It becomes his world as he interacts with the staff and customers, learns about American ways from watching the courtship of an interracial couple, contemplates marriage to an American-Chinese girl (Leong) to get his green card, copes with Sam (a crude waiter who is stealing tips from other workers), and absorbs more American culture with his pal Andy. A constant presence is the ongoing fear of Robert and other illegal workers at the restaurant of being caught in a raid by the Department of Immigration. As the days pass, Robert's relationship with the retiring Claire ends when he reveals his ulterior motive (i.e., to gain his citizenship) for dating her.

Made on a budget of less than $250,000 and using his family's restaurant after hours for his set, Chan presented a glimpse into the lives of American-based Asians from contrasting areas (such as Hong Kong and Taiwan) and different cultural/intellectual backgrounds. It provided a smorgasbord of broad types and cameos. However, the depiction of Caucasians was generally unflattering.

comedies—feature films In the silent movie era, Asian characters were utilized largely for ambiances of intrigue, mystery, and violence, and rarely as subjects of amusement. (In contrast, POLYNESIAN figures through the decades were depicted in generally nonhumorous, romanticized, or dramatized images. A rare exception was the Bloody Mary character of *SOUTH PACIFIC*, 1958.) Occasionally, Japanese and especially Chinese characters were subordinate figures in the background of amusing happenings involving the lead Caucasian characters, as in *After Five* (1915), *In High Gear* (1923), *The Cameraman* (1928), and *CHINATOWN CHARLIE* (1929). When the sound era commenced, new possibilities opened up to utilize heavily accented Asian characters to display a lack of communication and a seemingly foolish nonmainstream presence compared to "normal" Americans. Frequently, in 1930s features, haranguing Chinese individuals, often seen talking rapidly at bazaars, marketplaces, and so on, lent moments of amusement to the montage of urban life. Other times there were brief on-camera bits of Asians as domestics, coping with or tolerating the strange behavior of their employers or making jokes in their own tongue without their bosses knowing what was being said. Such character actors as WILLIE FUNG made a specialty of this type of movie role. In several of the CHARLIE CHAN screen adventures, the sight gag of the respected sleuth being outmaneuvered or overwhelmed by his offspring or merely the size/demands of his clan were enough to cause audiences to giggle.

Once the trauma of World War II ended, Hollywood developed a penchant for presenting amusing culture clashes between Americans and Japan. Frequently, these were service comedies that had the advantage of avoiding audience bigotry by showing that the Americans were in charge of the conquered Japanese. But as the comedies—some drawn from Broadway hits—demonstrated, the reality was often the opposite, or at best a draw: *TEAHOUSE OF THE AUGUST MOON* (1956), *Joe Butterfly* (1957), *THE GEISHA BOY* (1958), *A MAJORITY OF ONE* (1961), *Cry for Happy* (1961), and *MY GEISHA* (1962). A much later comedy, *Volunteers* (1984), had two Caucasian Americans (Tom Hanks and John Candy) join the Peace Corps and create great trouble in Thailand.

Woody Allen started his film career taking a Japanese film and dubbing it into English with dialogue that poked fun at the Nipponese characters. Released in the United States as *What's Up Tiger Lily?* (1966), it was a profitable exercise for the distributor. *The Bad News Bears Go to Japan* (1978) and another sports comedy, *Mr. Baseball* (1992), traded on the humor of the athletic prowess of Americans versus the physically smaller Japanese. (A more subtle story line was the true story of an American schoolteacher studying with a martial arts expert in *Iron & Silk*, 1990.)

On the opposite side, *GUNG HO* (1986) showed Japanese executives "conquering" small-town America. *COMBINATION PLATTER* and *THE WEDDING BANQUET* (both 1993) found healthy amusement in Asian visitors/immigrants to the United States dealing with the American culture and/or Asian-American ways. Later in the 1990s, Hong Kong martial-arts star JACKIE CHAN went Hollywood to prove that culture clash comedy worked in the cop/buddy (*RUSH HOUR*, 1998; *Rush Hour 2*, 2001) and western (*SHANGHAI NOON*, 2000) formats. *Kung Pow: Enter the Fist* (2002) was a sloppy satire of martial arts films using footage from a 1976 Chinese feature in tandem with new bridging sequences.

On the periphery of these Asian-American themed comedies were the drug culture movies of Cheech and Chong (born Asian Canadian), which began with *Up in Smoke* (1978). In reality, World War II Japanese tourists inadvertently helped develop the stereotype of the bespectacled visitor to the United States with clicking camera and a pack of children in tow. Perhaps the nadir of such stereotyping was the buck-toothed impersonation of a "funny" Japanese by Mickey Rooney in *BREAKFAST AT TIFFANY'S* (1961) and the lowbrow buffoonery of Peter Sellers (an Englishman) in *Murder by Death* (1976—as a Charlie Chan–like detective) and in *The Fiendish Plot of Dr. Fu Manchu* (1980—as a villainous Asian mastermind). Sellers was also involved with another negative stereotyping of a Japanese character with his karate-wielding manservant Kato (Burt Kwouk) in several of the Pink Panther series entries (e.g., *The Pink Panther Strikes Again*, 1976). Not to be overlooked was the clichéd Asian-American houseman Ito played by Yuki Shimoda in Warner Bros.' *Auntie Mame* (1958) and by George Chiang in the studio's musical version, *Mame* (1974).

comedies—television See SITUATION COMEDY SERIES—TELEVISION.

***Come See the Paradise* (1990)** Twentieth Century-Fox, color, 138 minutes. **Director/Screenplay:** Alan Parker; **Cast:** Dennis Quaid (Jack McGurn), Tamlyn Tomita (Lily Kawamura), Sab Shimono (Mr. Kawamura), Shizuko Hoshi (Mrs. Kawamura), Stan Egi (Charlie Kawamura), Ronald Yamamoto (Harry Kawamura).

With rare exceptions such as *HELL TO ETERNITY* (1960) to one side, American films scarcely dealt with the disgraceful subject of the World War II internment camps in the United States that were created during the hysteria after the bombing of Pearl Harbor to incarcerate Japanese Americans. Stripped of their constitutional rights, these Americans had to abandon their homes and property and suffer through the war in bleak relocation centers. British filmmaker Parker examined the topic in this leisurely and too character-crowded feature that excited little interest at the box office (it grossed a paltry $847,000 in domestic distribution).

In the mid-1930s, hotheaded New York union organizer Jack McGurn flees the law to Los Angeles, where he becomes a projectionist in a Little Tokyo movie theater. He falls in love with the owner's daughter Lily, and, much against her father's wishes, they wed in Seattle, Washington. When World War II comes, the Kawamura family are among the thousands of Japanese Americans shipped to relocation camps. Meanwhile, McGurn, who had been separated from his wife and child, reconciles with them, and joins the army. Later, he goes AWOL to visit her at the detention camp. As for the Kawamuras, one son dies in combat duty for the United States, another is deported to Japan, and the father eventually commits suicide. At war's end, McGurn serves a prison term, but, finally, he is reunited with his wife and child who now are migrant fruit workers in California.

***Confessions of an Opium Eater* (aka: *Secrets of a Soul; Souls for Sale*) (1962)** Allied Artists, b&w, 85 minutes. **Director:** Albert Zugsmith; **Screenplay:** Robert Hill and Seton I. Miller; **Cast:** Vincent Price (Gil de Quincey), Linda Ho (Ruby Low), Philip Ahn (Ching Foon), Richard Loo (George Wah), June Kim (Lotus), Victor Sen Yung (Wing Yung).

Utilizing the title and other exploitational items from Thomas De Quincey's *Confessions of an English Opium-eater* (1821), this cheaply made feature mixed the exotica of San Francisco's Chinatown with a drug-induced romance and a TONG war.

In the early 1900s, slave girls are being smuggled into the Golden Gate city to be sold at auction. Newspaper editor George Wah, a tong leader, tries to stop the practice but only creates warfare between the local tong gangs. Meanwhile, adventurer Gil de Quincey comes to Wah's rescue by persuading Ruby Low, leader of a rival tong faction, to help Wah.

Even as late as the 1960s the allure of the mysterious—to Occidental Americans—tong gangs and the happenings in the Chinatown ghetto of any major city gave this film its marketing gimmick—along, of course, with the marquee value of Price and the bevy of "slave" girls pictured in the proceedings.

***Conqueror, The* (1956)** RKO, color, 111 minutes. **Director:** Dick Powell; **Screenplay:** Oscar Millard; **Cast:** John Wayne (Temujin), Susan Hayward (Bortai), Pedro Armendáriz (Jamuga), Agnes Moorehead (Hunlun), Thomas Gomez (Wang Kahn), Richard Loo (captain of Wang's guard).

Temujin (1162–1227) founded the Mongol Empire. He adopted his name Genghis Kahn—meaning "ruler of all"—

in 1206. He united the Mongol tribes, and his grandson, Kublai Khan, finished the conquest of China. Little of this came across in the hokey *The Conqueror*. It's hard to imagine anyone less suited to the role of this great fighter than Wayne, but this project was made at a time when Hollywood would never have considered an actual Asian American to play the key role. (In point of fact there were no Asian-American film actors with any sort of marquee name that *could* have been considered. Hollywood, in this period, had chosen not to develop any.)

Wayne's phony Mongol guise (complete with pointed helmet and goatee) was matched by the pidgin, inane dialogue he spouted. The rest of the unfortunate cast, ranging from Brooklyn-born redhead Hayward to Mexican-born Armendáriz and Hispanic-American Gomez, were equally ill at ease in this misguided narrative, which was filled with clichéd verbiage and posturing. Hawaii-born LOO, having played stereotypical roles, usually as a sinister Japanese officer in World War II movies, had a slight change of pace in this nonepic as the head of Wang's guards.

cooking series—television One of the areas where Asian Americans made a small but noticeable inroad on television was in the area of cooking shows. Because variations of Asian foods (especially the American version of "Chinese food") were long popular in the United States, it seemed natural that audiences would be drawn to demonstrations of how to prepare such cuisine properly. It was also assumed that if the chefs hosting such specialized cooking shows were Asian Americans, they would have built-in credibility with viewers.

One of the earliest such network and/or syndicated shows was *Yan Can Cook* on PBS-TV, beginning in 1983. Martin Yan, who was born in Guangzhou, China, in 1950, studied the art of cooking in Hong Kong and then moved to Canada and later to the United States. In the early 1980s he began a San Francisco-based TV cooking show that was famous for not only for the speed of his precision dicing and slicing but also for his verbal instructions. In the mid-1990s his series was re-run on cable TV's Food Network.

Ming Tsai is another well-known TV chef. He was born in Dayton, Ohio, in 1964. While completing a degree in mechanical engineering at Yale University, he pursued his cooking interest during summers at the Cordon Bleu in France. He then attended the hotel school at Cornell University, and, after serving as executive chef at various U.S. establishments, he opened his own bistro in the Boston area. After appearances on various Food Network shows, he was asked to head his own Food Network program, *East Meets West with Ming Tsai*, which premiered in 1998. The thrust of his program was to demystify Asian cuisine.

Another increasingly popular show, *Iron Chef*, began to air on Japanese-language TV stations in the United States in 1993. Produced by Fuji-TV in Japan, each episode was a fiercely competitive contest between an Iron Chef (a master in his field) and a challenger. The show was hosted by actor Kaga Takeshi.

***Corruptor, The* (1999)** New Line, color, 109 minutes. **Director:** James Foley; **Screenplay:** Robert Pucci; **Cast:** Chow Yun-Fat (Nick Chen), Mark Wahlberg (Danny Wallace), Ric Young (Henry Lee), Paul Ben-Victor (Schabacker), Andrew Pang (Willy Ung), Byron Mann (Bobby Vu), Elizabeth Lindsey (Louise Deng).

Following on the heels of JACKIE CHAN, YUN-FAT adapted his Hong Kong action flick format to the American scene in this cop/buddy movie with the added ingredient of various racial issues. Teamed with former rap singer-turned-underwear-model-turned-actor Wahlberg, *The Corruptor* studied the Asian-American underworld in New York City, making its own statements about ethnic and cultural differences in the process. Not having much comedy to lighten the formula (as did, for example, *RUSH HOUR*, 1999), the film grossed a disappointing $15.2 million in domestic distribution.

Nick Chen, of the NYPD's Asian Gang Unit, is given a new partner, Danny Wallace. The Asian American and the Caucasian (the only one in the group) bring their own racial biases to the union. As the duo deal with the turf war among the TONGS, a triad family, and the Fukiense Dragons, each lawman grudgingly develops more respect for the other—or so it seems. It turns out that Wallace is working undercover for the Internal Affairs Department on an investigation of Chen.

Yun-Fat displayed a steely charisma in his athletic performance and demonstrated why he was becoming a favorite with North American filmgoers. Young, as tough hoodlum Lee, the corruptor, proved effective in his key assignment.

***Courageous Coward, The* (1919)** Robertson-Cole, b&w, 5 reels. **Director:** William Worthington; **Screenplay:** Frances Guihan; **Cast:** Sessue Hayakawa (Suki Iota), Tsuru Aoki (Rei Oaki), Toyo Fujita (Tangi), George Hernandez (Big Bill Kirby), Francis J. McDonald (Tom Kirby), Buddy Post (Cupid).

When HAYAKAWA was not starring in Hollywood-made vehicles about the romances of miscegenation, he was often featured in love stories in which the leading lady was played by his real-life wife, actress Aoki.

Suki Iota, a Japanese-American law student, is attracted to Rei Oaki, who has recently arrived from Japan to become a singer. When Iota enrolls at an East Coast law school, Rei is convinced that her beloved could care only for an American-style woman, so she persuades Tom Kirby, whose father has great power in Chinatown, to instruct her in "American ways." Later, when Iota returns home, he is upset that Rei has abandoned her traditional ways. Meanwhile, he is appointed assistant district attorney and prosecutes a case involving Kirby, whom he suspects of being Rei's lover. Later, to protect Rei's reputation, he withdraws from the proceedings, seemingly making him a coward. Eventually, the matter is resolved, and Iota and Rei rebuild their romance.

crime, detective, and police dramas—feature films In pre-World War II Hollywood, features occasionally utilized the lurking shadows of Chinatown to give ambiance to their narratives of criminal activity. In the silent era, these included such entries as *The Midnight Patrol* (1918), *Outside the Law* (1929), *Tearing Through* (1925), *Shadows of Chinatown* (1926), and *Ransom* (1928). Similar examples occurred in the early decades of sound moviemaking: *DAUGHTER OF SHANGHAI* (1932), *Secrets of Chinatown* (1935), *Shadows of the Orient* (1937), *King of Chinatown* (1939), *Rubber Racketeers* (1942), and *Half Past Midnight* (1948). By the 1950s, with the rift between the United States and Japan mending, occasional Japanese-themed underworld tales were set in Japan: *HOUSE OF BAMBOO* (1955), *THE YAKUZA* (1975), and *BLACK RAIN* (1989). In *RISING SUN* (1993), the influence of criminal activities on an American-based Japanese corporation was explored.

In contrast, there were several movie series devoted to the exploits of crime-solving Asian detectives; typically, these sleuths were played on screen by Caucasian actors. The first Hollywood property was that of Honolulu-based Chinese police detective (later private sleuth) CHARLIE CHAN, which began with a 1926 ten-chapter serial, *The House Without a Key*. The most frequent performers of the screen role created originally in novels by Earl Derr Biggers were WARNER OLAND, SIDNEY TOLER, and ROLAND WINTERS. The MR. MOTO series, based on the fiction of John P. Marquand, revolved around a Japanese businessman turned amateur sleuth. The subject of an eight-film series in the late 1930s, he was played by Peter LORRE and, in an attempted revival of the series in 1965, by actor Henry Silva.

Created as competition to the Charlie Chan and Mr. Moto series, the MR. WONG detective series evolved in 1938 in which BORIS KARLOFF starred. He was featured in five entries, with KEYE LUKE taking over the franchise for one installment in 1940, playing the Chinese detective's son. A nonseries entry was *The Peacock Fan* (1929), which had Lucien Prival as Dr. Chang Dorfman, a Chinese-American detective who solved the murder of a curio collector who had in his possession a legendary peacock fan.

The prejudices of Hollywood filmmakers allowed for the novelty of Chinese detectives solving crimes, but it was another matter when it came to having Asians as members of the American police in the pre-1960s. Although, in the initial Charlie Chan entry, the wise Chinese investigator was a member of the Honolulu Police Department and later worked in conjunction with police departments of various cities and countries, Chan was an exception. This held true also for James Wong, another Chinese detective with associations to the American police department but not a typical member of its staff. One of the first clear examples that portrayed an Asian-American police enforcer working on mainland United States was *THE CRIMSON KIMONO* (1960) with JAMES SHIGETA as the Nisei detective. Thanks to changing senses of political correctness and the examples of TV's *HAWAII FIVE-0* (1968–80) and *OHARA* (1987–88), American-set feature films such as *The Choirboys* (1977), *KINJITE: FORBIDDEN SUBJECTS* (1989), and *Rising Sun* had Asian-American police in their story lines, albeit not always prominently displayed.

crime, detective, and police series—television A carry-over from literature and films dealing with Sax Rohmer's creation of dastardly DR. FU MANCHU was the TV series *THE ADVENTURES OF FU MANCHU* (1956) starring Glen Gordon as the Asian peril. Frequently, on TV series based in San Francisco (e.g., *The Streets of San Francisco*, 1972–77; *Nash Bridges*, 1996–2002) or HAWAII (e.g., *HAWAII FIVE-0*, 1968–80—especially with its character of Wo Fat, a criminal genius, played by KHIGH DHIEGH) or New York City (e.g., *Law & Order*, 1990–), where there were heavily populated Asian-American communities, there were recurrent underworld characters of Asian-American heritage.

Fighting on the side of the law was not restricted to police law enforcers. Film actress ANNA MAY WONG had a brief, early television series, *THE GALLERY OF MME. LUI-TSONG* (1951), in which she played an art-gallery owner. It featured her fighting and solving crimes. Utilizing a literary property that had been the basis of film and radio series, *THE NEW ADVENTURES OF CHARLIE CHAN* (1957), a British-packaged syndicated series, starred J. Carrol Naish. From 1972 to 1974 a Saturday-morning TV animated cartoon series was titled *THE AMAZING CHAN AND THE CHAN CLAN*. On the fantastic side, superhero *THE GREEN HORNET* (1966–67) presented Japanese manservant Kato (played by BRUCE LEE) as the assistant of the newspaper publisher hero.

Occasionally, private detective characters on TV series were Asian-American. *Mysteries of Chinatown* (1949–50) was devoted to the exploits of Dr. Yat Fu, the owner of a curio shop in San Francisco's Chinatown, played by Caucasian Marvin Miller and his associate, Ah Toy, by Gloria Saunders. On *HAWAIIAN EYE* (1959–63), an unofficial helper of the lead characters in solving crimes was Hawaiian-American taxi driver Kazuo Kim (played by Poncie Ponce). *KHAN!* (1975) with Khigh Dhiegh as a private eye in San Francisco's Chinatown, also featured the hero's son and daughter, who were involved in his cases. The TV movie *Blade in Hong Kong* (1985) starred Terry Lester as a San Francisco private eye who flew to Hong Kong to be with his adoptive dad, a wealthy Chinese businessman. *Murphy's Law's* (1988–89) George Segal was an insurance investigator whose live-in girlfriend, the Eurasian Kimiko Fannuchi (played by Maggie Han), sometimes helped with his cases.

Series featuring Asian-American police detectives included *Hawaii Five-O* (1968–80), *Jigsaw John* (1976), *QUINCY, M.E.* (1976–83), *21 JUMP STREET* (1987–90), *MAGNUM P.I.* (1980–88), *Hawaiian Heat* (1984), *SIDEKICKS* (1986–87), *OHARA* (1986–87—in the third format for the series, Ohara retired from the police force and became a private eye), *Nasty Boys* (1990), *One West Waikiki* (1994), *Nash Bridges* (1996–2002), and *MARTIAL LAW* (1998–2000). Sometimes the Asian-American police were part of a comedic series, such as JACK SOO's Det. Nick Yemana on *BARNEY MILLER* from 1975 to 1978. *Tropical Punch* (1993), a spoof of *Hawaii Five-O*, featured two Asian-American characters. In

2001, B.D. WONG joined *Law & Order: Special Victims Unit* (1999–) as police psychiatrist George Huong.

***Crimson Kimono, The* (1959)** Columbia, b&w, 92 minutes. **Director/Screenplay:** Samuel Fuller; **Cast:** Victoria Shaw (Christine Downes), Glenn Corbett (Det. Sgt. Charlie Bancroft), James Shigeta (Det. Joe Kojaku), Anna Lee (Mac), Paul Dubov (Casale), Jaclynne Greene (Roma).

In this production, one of several movies made by filmmaker FULLER involving Asian characters/themes, the director pushed hard on racial tolerance between Asian Americans and Caucasian Americans. *Motion Picture Herald Production Digest* (September 12, 1959) observed that "For the first time an American film tells a story in which a Japanese boy wins the white girl."

Los Angeles police detective Charlie Bancroft and Joe Kojaku, roommates, are assigned to a stripper's homicide in the Little Tokyo neighborhood. The clues lead them to Christine Downes, an art major at the University of Southern California, as well as to a thug named Shuto and a wigmaker (Greene). During the investigation, which climaxes during the Nisei Week parade in the Japanese part of town, Bancroft is drawn to Christine, but she responds to Kojaku.

This meandering production was filled with the atmosphere of Japanese-American culture and especially of Little Tokyo in Los Angeles to educate (American) filmgoers about the traditions of other races. It also encompassed martial arts sequences, a topic that would become explosive in the late 1960s and thereafter, thanks to the likes of BRUCE LEE.

The Crimson Kimono jump-started the career of SHIGETA who was making his feature film debut.

***Crouching Tiger, Hidden Dragon* (aka: *Wo hu zang long*) (2000)** Sony Classics, color, 120 minutes. **Director:** Ang Lee; **Screenplay:** Hui-Ling Wang, James Schamus, and Kuo Jung Tsai; **Cast:** Chow Yun-Fat (Li Mu Bai), Michelle Yeoh (Yu Shu Lien), Zivi Zhang (Jen Yu), Chen Chang (Lo), Sihung Lung (Sir Te), Pei-Pei (Jad Fox).

One of the more transcendent film productions of recent years, based on a book by Du Lu Wang, the film combines the martial arts and fantasy genres with a lacing of romance and philosophical underpinnings. Beautifully photographed, this international coproduction captured amazing flights of fancy. Its narrative revolves around the disappearance of Green Destiny, a magical sword of jade, which Li Mu Bai, a disillusioned Wudan school swordsman, has entrusted to warrior Yu Shu Lien to pass along to Sir Te. The search to recover the special weapon involves master criminal Jade Fox and the noble lady Jen.

Made on a budget of $35 million, it grossed more than $128 million in its U.S. distribution. This remarkable entry by LEE elevated not only his professional status but also that of costars YUN-FAT and YEOH. In the United States, the movie was shown in the original-language Chinese with English-language subtitles. It won four Academy Awards (Best Art Director/Set Decoration, Best Cinematography, Best Foreign Language Film, and Best Original Score) plus six other Oscar nominations.

***Crow, The* (1994)** Miramax, color, 100 minutes. **Director:** Alex Proyas; **Screenplay:** David J. Schow and John Shirley; **Cast:** Brandon Lee (Eric Draven), Michael Wincott (Top Dollar), Rochelle Davis (Sarah), Ernie Hudson (Albrecht), David Patrick Kelly (T-Bird), Angel David (Skank), Bai Ling (Myca).

This production was geared to make a full-fledged film star of BRANDON LEE, son of the legendary BRUCE LEE. It did create a cult status for Asian-American Brandon because the handsome, muscular actor died in an on-set accident during filming, but *The Crow* was also a well-crafted, grim fable with an underlying sensitivity in a narrative of enduring love.

Based on the comic-book and comic-strip series by James O'Barr, *The Crow* relates the murder of would-be rock star Eric Draven and his girlfriend (Shinas). A year later, on Devil's Night, Draven returns from the grave—with a crow as his guide—to revenge the killings done by vicious T-Bird, Skank, Tin Tin, and Funboy. Draven accomplishes his mission and then, after eliminating the evil twosome who controlled the quartet of lowlifes, returns to his grave.

With his face painted a clown's white, his hair in disarray, and wearing a punk rocker outfit (a mix of leather and chrome), Lee was an eerie antihero, one bound to intrigue young filmgoers. Add to that the movie's murky, nighttime settings in bleak Detroit and the high level of violence (which garnered the picture an R-rating). *The Crow* was extremely successful (made for $6 million, it grossed more than $50 million in domestic distribution) and prompted the sequels *The Crow 2: City of Angels* (1996) and *The Crow: Salvation* (2000). In addition, a TV movie pilot (*The Crow: Stairway to Heaven*, 1998) led to the 1998–99 syndicated TV series, both of which featured Mark Dacascos (born in Honolulu, Hawaii) as the new Eric Draven.

***Cry Havoc* (1943)** Metro-Goldwyn-Mayer, b&w, 98 minutes. **Director:** Richard Thorpe; **Screenplay:** Paul Osborn; **Cast:** Margaret Sullavan (Lt. Mary "Smitty" Smith), Ann Sothern (Pat Conlin), Joan Blondell (Grace Lambert), Fay Bainter (Capt. Alice Marsh), Marsha Hunt (Flo Norris), Ella Raines (Connie Booth).

Along with *SO PROUDLY WE HAIL* (1943) starring Claudette Colbert, *Cry Havoc* was one of the most stirring examples of a Hollywood combat movie focusing almost exclusively on its female characters.

In *Cry Havoc*, based on the play *Proof Through the Night* (1942) by Allan Kenward, two army nurses (Sullavan and Bainter) are part of the Allied contingent at Marivèles, Bataan Peninsula, the Philippines. Needing additional nurses to tend the wounded from the battles with the Japanese, Smitty instead receives nine civilian women evacuated from Manila. As the enemy approaches, the surviving army troops are ordered to dig in, but the nurses and their volunteer helpers are free to depart for safer quarters. Instead, the brave females elect to remain to tend to the wounded. Finally the women's underground bunker is surrounded by Japanese troops, and they await a grim fate.

What made this drama—filled with sympathetic character types—so spine chilling was the approaching presence of the unseen Japanese soldiers and the assumption that death would be the only outcome for these courageous women. It was a plot set-up that was bound to leave a lasting impression, as well as to increase filmgoers' hatred of the Japanese, an intentional result by Hollywood.

Typical of these World War II entries set in the Philippines, there were always a few subordinate roles of villagers and/or domestic help included for local color. Here they were played by, among others, Billy Cruz and Roque Espiritu.

D

***Dangerous to Know* (1938)** Paramount, b&w, 70 minutes. **Director:** Robert Florey; **Screenplay:** William R. Lipman and Horace McCoy; **Cast:** Anna May Wong (Madame Lan Ying), Akim Tamiroff (Stephen Recka), Gail Patrick (Margaret Van Kase), Lloyd Nolan (Inspector Brandon), Harvey Stephens (Philip Easton), Anthony Quinn (Nicolia "Nicky" Kusnoff).

This "B" picture, based on a 1930 play by Edgar Wallace that had been novelized in 1932, had WONG repeating her role from the Broadway production as the mistress of a big city gangster (Tamiroff). The latter has been involved in several murders and now has become intrigued with socialite Margaret Van Kase, a situation that arouses Lan Ying's jealousy. Unmindful, Recka implicates Margaret's boyfriend Philip Easton in a crime to get him out of the way. Lan Ying saves Easton but realizes that Recka is still infatuated with Margaret.

Wong gave credibility to her role of an inscrutable woman who takes matters into her own hands when she loses her worthless loved one to a Caucasian lady. At the time, Wong was still Hollywood's *only* Asian-American leading lady.

***Dark Delusion* (1947)** Metro-Goldwyn-Mayer, b&w, 90 minutes. **Director:** Willis Goldbeck; **Screenplay:** Jack Andrews and Harry Ruskin; **Cast:** Lionel Barrymore (Dr. Leonard Gillespie), James Craig (Dr. Tommy Coalt), Lucille Bremer (Cynthia Grace), Jayne Meadows (Mrs. Selkirk), Warner Anderson (Teddy Selkirk), Alma Kruger (Molly Byrd), Keye Luke (Dr. Lee Wong How).

In the last of the Dr. Gillespie hospital series, LUKE's Dr. Lee Wong How had a more subordinate role than before. The thrust of this plot deals with Dr. Tommy Coalt, a surgeon at Blair General Hospital in New York, who is assigned to take over the small-town practice of a doctor who will be away for several weeks. He endures the tribulations of adjusting to the suburban setting and helping his new patients while Dr. Lee fills in for him at Bayhurst during an emergency. Meanwhile, Dr. Gillespie is asked to assist on the complex situation involving Cynthia Grace, who, it develops, suffers from a blood clot near her brain.

This was the sixth time that Luke played Dr. Wong How. As such, he helped to formulate a new image for Asian Americans as they were being given more mainstream professions when depicted in Hollywood movies.

***Daughter of Shanghai* (1938)** Paramount, b&w, 67 minutes. **Director:** Robert Florey; **Screenplay:** Gladys Unger and Garnett Weston; **Cast:** Anna May Wong (Lan Ying Lin), Charles Bickford (Otto Hartman), Larry "Buster" Crabbe (Andrew Sleete), Cecil Cunningham (Mrs. Mary Hart), Anthony Quinn (Harry Morgan), Philip Ahn (Kim Lee).

With the ongoing success of the CHARLIE CHAN detective series at another studio, Paramount made this budget entry, utilizing WONG as an amateur sleuth. It was one of several she made on the lot during the late 1930s.

When her father, an importer of Oriental antiques, is murdered, Lan Ying Lin vows to find his killers. (She has no faith that police detective Kim Lee will solve the case, which is tied to the smuggling of illegal aliens into San Francisco.) The search takes Lan Ying to the Central American town of Port O'Juan, where Otto Hartman operates a nightclub.

Filled with action presented in the style of an old-fashioned movie serial, this programmer had a flavorful cast, including Cunningham, as a family friend of Lan Ying's. For whatever reasons, Paramount decided against pursuing a series of sleuthing movies featuring the agile Wong.

***Daughter of the Dragon* (1931)** Paramount, b&w, 72 minutes. **Director:** Lloyd Corrigan; **Screenplay:** Corrigan and Monte M. Katterjohn; **Cast:** Anna May Wong (Princess Ling Moy), Warner Oland (Fu Manchu), Sessue Hayakawa (Ah Kee), Bramwell Fletcher (Ronald Petrie), Frances Dade (Joan Marshall), Holmes Herbert (Sir John Petrie), Tetsu Komai (Lao), George Kuma (Sing Lee).

For his fourth and final appearance as the infamous DR. FU MANCHU, OLAND teamed with two popular and enduring Asian (American) performers, WONG and HAYAKAWA. The overtly racist vehicle was based on Sax Rohmer's novel, *Daughter of Fu Manchu* (1931).

Princess Ling Moy, an exotic Chinese dancer, is the toast of London. She encounters Ronald Petrie and quickly falls in love with him, despite his having a fiancée, Joan Marshall. Meanwhile, the nefarious Fu Manchu, long thought dead, arrives in England to carry out his revenge on the Petrie family, whom he blames for the demise of his wife and son. Ah Kee, a Chinese detective, alerts Scotland Yard to the deadly threat to the Petries. Later, Fu Manchu, who has just killed Sir John Petrie, is fatally wounded by Ah Kee. As Fu Manchu dies, he informs Ling Moy that she is his daughter and must carry out his revenge.

In this convoluted plot filled with secret tunnels and inscrutable Asians, the theme of interracial love was again explored but resolved quickly by Ling Moy's death. Again, the stereotype of villainous Orientals lurking in the shadows, seeking revenge was the main element of this crime drama.

For Wong, who had been making movies abroad, this was a return to U.S. filmmaking. On the other hand, for equally established star Hayakawa, this entry was both his official talkie feature film debut and his finale as an American movie star. With unflattering reviews for his performance in this production and no likely future for a Japanese leading man in 1930s Hollywood, he went abroad to make pictures. His next English-language feature would be Humphrey Bogart's *TOKYO JOE* (1949).

As for Fu Manchu, he next appeared in MGM's *THE MASK OF FU MANCHU* (1932) with BORIS KARLOFF as the menacing lead.

***Daughter of the Tong* (1939)** Metropolitan/State Rights, b&w, 56 minutes. **Director:** Raymond K. Johnson; **Screenplay:** George H. Plympton; **Cast:** Evelyn Brent (the Illustrious One [aka: Carney, the daughter of the Tong]), Grant Withers (Ralph Dickson), Dorothy Short (Marion Morgan), Dave O'Brien (Jerry Morgan), Richard Loo (Wong), Dick Thane (Slade), Robert Frazer (Williams).

This film was one of several in the late 1930s to exploit the exotic mysteries of the Orient, a place of increasing American interest because of the rising aggressions of the Japanese empire and the subjugation of China (then considered a friendly ally to the United States). While there had been many better American films dealing with TONG wars (e.g., *THE HATCHET MAN*, 1932) this low-budget entry boasted former film star Brent and cheap sets that matched the cobbled-together plot line.

In Pacific City a reign of terror is attributed to the Carney gang, led by a Chinese woman known as "The Illustrious One." This prompts FBI agent Ralph Dickson to enter the scene and, through perseverance, round up the culprits with the help of Marion Morgan and other locals.

Death Ride to Osaka See *GIRLS OF THE WHITE ORCHID.*

***Deer Hunter, The* (1978)** Universal, color, 183 minutes. **Director:** Michael Cimino; **Screenplay:** Deric Washburn; **Cast:** Robert De Niro (Michael), John Cazale (Stan), John Savage (Steven), Christopher Walken (Nick), Meryl Streep (Linda), George Dzundza (John).

This stunning, brutal depiction of how war irrevocably changed man was, in many ways, more powerful than another Vietnam drama, *Apocalypse Now* (1979). Here, the Vietnam war scenes were only a portion of this lengthy drama. Nonetheless, the vividness of the film's torture sequences conducted by the Vietcong harkened back to World War II dramas and once more presented Asians as sadistic soldiers and enemies of America.

Three buddies—Michael, Steven, and Nick—are Pennsylvania steelworkers. Before undertaking their tour of duty in Vietnam, they relax on a hunting trek with their pals. Once in Vietnam, the trio are soon taken prisoners by the Vietcong and, like other captives, thrown into a cage that sits beneath a hut on stilts. Their cruel captors torture the prisoners, forcing them to play Russian roulette while betting on the outcome. Eventually, the three Americans escape, but, in the process, Steven is badly injured (later losing both legs). The emotionally disconnected Nick, once released from the U.S. base hospital, gravitates to the tenderloin district of Saigon where he plays Russian roulette for money. Michael, who has returned to Pennsylvania, has a romance with Linda, Nick's girlfriend. After encouraging the still-hospitalized Steven to readjust to civilian life, Michael flies to Saigon where he locates Nick. Trying to jolt the emotionally deadened man, Michael pushes Nick into another game of Russian roulette, one that proves fatal to Nick.

Made on a budget of $15 million, *The Deer Hunter* earned more than $27 million in domestic film rentals. It won Academy Awards for Best Director, Best Film Editing, Best Picture, Best Sound, and Best Supporting Actor (Walken). It also won Oscar nominations for Best Actor (De Niro), Best Cinematography, Best Original Screenplay, and Best Supporting Actress (Streep). Cimino later directed *THE YEAR OF THE DRAGON* (1985).

Dhiegh, Khigh (1910–1991) For many TV viewers, Khigh Dhiegh (pronounced "ki-dee") was associated most strongly with his role of villainous Wo Fat on the TV series

HAWAII FIVE-O (1968–80), who was always in deadly conflict with Det. Steve McGarrett. (Originally the character was intended to be killed off in the 1968 series pilot, but star Jack Lord wanted to keep the master menace alive for future outings.)

Dhiegh was born in Spring Lake, New Jersey. While employed in his mother's New York City bookstore, he agreed to be in a Broadway play. His film debut was in the Korean War drama *Time Limit* (1957), and in the thriller *THE MANCHURIAN CANDIDATE* (1962), he was cast as Dr. Yen Lo. An intriguing TV movie pilot, *JUDGE DEE AND THE MONASTERY MURDERS* (1974), had all the entertaining elements to lead to a series but sadly did not. In 1975 Dhiegh starred as a Chinatown detective in the brief-lasting *KHAN!* TV series, a rare opportunity in this era for a non-Caucasian to play a lead on American TV. His final acting credits included playing Four Finger Wu in the TV miniseries *JAMES CLAVELL'S NOBLE HOUSE* (1988) and Lu Ming in the telefeature *FORBIDDEN NIGHTS* (1990).

***Diamond Head* (1962)** Columbia, color, 107 minutes. **Director:** Guy Green; **Screenplay:** Marguerite Roberts; **Cast:** Charlton Heston (Richard "King" Howland), Yvette Mimieux (Sloan Howland), George Chakiris (Dr. Dean Kahana), France Nuyen (Mei Chen), James Darren (Paul Kahana), Aline MacMahon (Kapiolani Kahana), Philip Ahn (Emekona).

This turgid soap opera, based on the 1960 novel by Peter Gilman, was far better at revealing the lush sights of Hawaii than at exploring racial bigotry, mixed marriages, and the conflicts between the generations.

Richard "King" Howland is a hardnosed land baron on the island of Kauai. When his sister Sloan insists that she will wed Paul Kahana, a full-blooded Hawaiian, the racially intolerant King is furious, despite the fact that his mistress, Mei Chen, is a native. After Paul is killed accidentally, Sloan goes to Honolulu where, through the intervention of Paul's brother, Dean, she takes up residence with his mother (MacMahon). Meanwhile, Mei Chen dies giving birth to King's child, one he refuses to accept. Eventually, the ruthless landowner sees some of the error of his ways and finally acknowledges his son.

With its hodgepodge casting, it was difficult to take this production seriously. Even the usually proficient MacMahon, playing an Hawaiian matriarch, appeared stereotypical in her ethnic characterization. (The proficient actress had been Oscar-nominated for her portrayal of the Chinese wife in *DRAGON SEED*, 1944.)

***Dim Sum: A Little Bit of Heart* (1985)** Orion Classics, color, 88 minutes. **Director:** Wayne Wang; **Screenplay:** Terrel Seltzer; **Cast:** Laureen Chew (Geraldine Tam), Kim Chew (Mrs. Tam), Victor Wong (Uncle Tam), Ida F. O. Chung (Auntie Mary), Cora Miao (Julia), John Nishio (Richard), Joan Chen and Rita Yee (young Mah Jong players).

As his follow-up feature to *CHAN IS MISSING* (1982), WANG delved into one of the persistent problems for Asian Americans and other immigrant groups, that of whether or not to assimilate into the blended American culture and, if so, how much of the traditional values should be (or have to be) discarded in the process.

In San Francisco, aged Mrs. Tam worries about her unmarried daughter Geraldine who still lives with her. Both of her other children have wed (one of them, a daughter, has a bad marriage and is stepmother to an African-American child), but Geraldine won't make a matrimonial decision about her Los Angeles physician boyfriend.

Mrs. Tam, who has been an American resident for many years and understands the language well enough, still refuses to talk in English to anyone. She remains strictly rooted to her Chinese customs and is unyieldingly opposed to American ways. In contrast, Geraldine, very American in many ways, feels honor bound to remain with her parent. When the mother, who senses that her life is nearing its end, returns to her homeland for a last visit, Geraldine tries to make a traditional dinner with her uncle (Wong), but their experiment fails and they end up with a fast-food American meal. Upon her return to San Francisco, Mrs. Tam makes an effort to adapt to American ways, wanting to make the needed bridge to acculturation easier for her daughter. Geraldine, however, is still unsure of how to best handle her future.

A gentle and delicate movie, its dialogue was spoken in English and Chinese, with English subtitles utilized. CHEN, who had a bit here, would have a much larger role in Wang's *THE JOY LUCK CLUB* (1993). The independently produced comedy *Living on Tokyo Time* (1987), directed by Steven Okazaki (and involving a young Tokyo girl transplanted to San Francisco), dealt with similar themes to *Dim Sum* but was not handled as cogently.

***Dinty* (1920)** Associated First National, b&w, 6,587′. **Directors:** Marshall Neilan and John McDermott; **Screenplay:** Marion Fairfax; **Cast:** Wesley Barry ("Dinty" O'Sullivan), Colleen Moore (Doreen O'Sullivan), Tom Gallery (Danny O'Sullivan), J. Barney Sherry (Judge Whitely), Noah Beery (Wong Tai), Walter Chung (Sui Lung), Kate Price (Mrs. O'Toole), Young Hipp (Wong Tai's son).

In the 1920s, many screen comedies involved the clashing cultures of Jewish and Irish folk in the United States. In this silent photoplay, the Irish are contrasted with the mysteries of the Far East, represented by the San Francisco Chinese faction. True to the era, the Chinese depicted typically were (1) living in a ghetto—the local Chinatown, (2) considered to be suspicious folks with peculiar traditions, costumes, and religion, and (3) often involved in illegal activities such as opium smuggling.

Doreen O'Sullivan arrives in San Francisco with her infant son, Dinty. She learns that her husband has died, and to support the household, she becomes a scrubwoman. Twelve years pass, and Dinty takes over earning the family's income as a newsboy. Later, he proves helpful to Judge

Whitely when Wong Tai's gang steals the lawyer's daughter, a deed done in retribution for the judge having sentenced Wong Tai's offspring to jail. As a reward, the judge adopts Dinty, whose mother has recently died of tuberculosis.

Here, the cast boasted a mixture of Caucasian Americans and Asian-Americans portraying denizens of Chinatown.

directors of Asian- and Asian-American-themed motion pictures One of the most famous names in the history of Hollywood cinematography was James Wong Howe (1899–1977), a two-time Oscar winner for his camera work. Besides occasionally helping directors on the set, he helmed a few Hollywood feature films. None of them had Asian themes. *Go, Man, Go!* (1954) revolved around the formation of the Harlem Globetrotters basketball team, while *The Invisible Avenger* (1958) concerned the superhero, the Shadow. In contrast Caucasian SAMUEL FULLER made several Asian-themed pictures over his long career. He was one of the few to do so.

While the studio system of Hollywood's golden age did not permit or foster ethnic minority directors—especially Asians—the situation changed by the 1970s with the rise of independent filmmaking and the availability of new, less-expensive camera processes, which made it easier for fledgling directors to find financing. One of the earliest talents to rise on this revamped American scene was Hong Kong–born WAYNE WANG, whose first feature was the well-received *CHAN IS MISSING* (1982). It led to later Chinese-themed productions, such as *THE JOY LUCK CLUB* (1993) and *The Chinese Box* (1997).

Taiwanese ANG LEE's first American project was being on the set of Spike Lee's *Joe's Bed-Stuy Barbershop: We Cut Heads* (1983). It propelled him to *THE WEDDING BANQUET* (1993) and *Eat Drink Man Woman* (1994), both of which encompassed Taiwanese experiences dealing with American culture in the United States. But Lee proved to be quite at ease in non-Asian subjects (e.g., *Sense and Sensibility*, 1995) and only returned to themes about his heritage with the artful and popular martial-arts fantasy *CROUCHING TIGER, HIDDEN DRAGON* (2000), for which he was Oscar nominated in the Best Director category.

China-born JOHN WOO was making features in Hong Kong from the mid-1970s onward, gaining international fame in the 1980s with martial arts features starring CHOW YUN-FAT. Woo made his American film directing debut with *Hard Target* (1993), a Jean-Claude Van Damme vehicle, but it was the action-packed, inventive *Broken Arrow* (1996), starring John Travolta, that made Woo bankable as an American director. His TV movie *John Woo's Once a Thief: Brother Against Brother* had Asian characters, but his *Face/Off* (1997), boasted fewer. By the time of *Mission: Impossible II* (2007), Woo was an entrenched Hollywood superstar director.

Steven Okazaki, born in Venice, California, in 1952, was a third-generation Japanese American who studied filmmaking at San Francisco State University. After directing several educational films, he made the documentary *Survivors* (1982—his first in English), dealing with Hiroshima and Nagasaki. His next work, *Unfinished Business*, concerned the relocation camps to which Japanese Americans were shipped during World War II. It was nominated for an Academy Award in 1985. His *Days of Waiting* (1991) won the Oscar for Best Documentary Short Subject. Meanwhile he made the low-budget feature-length comedy *Living on Tokyo Time* (1987) that dealt with western-culture stereotypes of the Asian American. His next feature, *The Liza Theory* (1994), was a romantic drama and was followed by the documentary *Black Tar Heroin: The Dark End of the Street* (1999).

New York City–based Christine Choy (1954–) gained industry fame as a maker of documentaries, many of which she both directed and photographed (e.g., *Best Hotel on Skid Row, 1990; Shot Heard 'Round the World*, 1997). She won an Academy Award nomination in the category of Best Documentary, Features for *Who Killed Vincent Chin?* (1998). The film traced the murder of an automotive engineer and how his killer was freed by the courts. She won a Sundance Film Festival award in the cinematography category for *My America . . . or Honk If You Love Buddha* (1996). Choy's *Ha Ha Shanghai* (2001) was made over an eight-year period and recounted her journey to Shanghai to trace the ownership of a home her mother had maintained there in the early 1970s.

One of the even later Asia-to-America directors to emerge on the American scene was Tony Bui. Born in Saigon in 1973, he came to the United States at age two and grew up in Sunnyvale, California, where his father operated a video store. He enrolled in the film program at Loyola Marymount University in Los Angeles and, still an undergraduate, he revisited Vietnam, then wrote the short subject *Yellow Lotus* (1995), and received permission to bring a crew to Saigon to film it. It led to *THREE SEASONS* (1999), starring Harvey Keitel, the first American feature-length movie to be shot in Vietnam since the war. *Green Dragon* (2001), his next, had both New York and Hong Kong settings and featured Patrick Swayze and Forest Whitaker. This tapestry of America's experience with Vietnam was coauthored, coproduced, and second-unit directed by Tony Bui. His brother Timothy Linh Bui was director/scenarist (a reverse of capacities for the siblings from *Three Seasons*). The poignant *Green Dragon* was nominated for the Grand Jury Prize—in the dramatic film category—at the 2001 Sundance Film Festival.

Other Asians (Americans) who worked on the American scene included Hong Kong émigré Tony Chan who made *COMBINATION PLATTER* (1993), which he produced, directed, cowrote, and coedited. Also from Hong Kong, Ronny Yu, who attended high school in England and then the University of Ohio, directed sixteen features in his homeland (including *The Bride with White Hair*, 1993) before relocating to the United States. His first Hollywood feature was the fantasy/adventure entry *Warriors of Virtue* (1997), followed by *Bride of Chucky* (1998), *Chasing Dragon* (1999), and *51st Street* (2001), an action comedy with Samuel L. Jackson. Established actress JOAN CHEN, born in China, shot her first feature on the fly in mainland China. *Xiu Xiu: The Sent-Down Girl* (1998) was much acclaimed for its dramatic reflection of life in the "new" China. Her follow-up feature was the American-made *Autumn in New York* (2000) starring Richard Gere and Winona Ryder and was assessed a too-conventional tear-jerker.

San Francisco-born Montgomery Hom, who acted in *Village of the Damned* (1995), produced and directed the one-hour documentary *We Served with Pride: The Chinese American Experience in WWII* (1999). Peter Chan, born of Chaozhou parents, moved to Thailand when he was twelve, then studied in the United States, and returned to Hong Kong in 1983. He served as translator on a John Woo picture and was then production manager on three JACKIE CHAN features. The second-unit director on Chan's *THE PROTECTOR* (1985), by 1989 he was producing his own movies, some shot in China. A decade later he was in the United States, directing the romantic comedy *The Love Letter* (1999) starring Kate Capshaw and Tom Selleck, followed by *My Four Seasons* (2000). James Wong, who came to the United States from Hong Kong when he was very young and attended El Cajon High School in San Diego, wrote his first screenplay in 1986 *(The Boys Next Door)*. He gravitated to TV producing (e.g., 1991's *The Commish*, 1993's *The X Files*, 1995's *Space: Above and Beyond*, and turned director for the teen thriller *Final Destination* (2000), for which he wrote the script.

Dr. Gillespie's New Assistant* (1942)** Metro-Goldwyn-Mayer, b&w, 87 minutes. ***Director: Willis Goldbeck; **Screenplay:** Harry Ruskin, Goldbeck, and Lawrence P. Bachmann; **Cast:** Lionel Barrymore (Dr. Leonard Gillespie), Van Johnson (Dr. Randall "Red" Adams), Susan Peters (Mrs. Howard Young [Claire Merton]), Richard Quine (Dr. Dennis Lindsay), Keye Luke (Dr. Lee Wong How).

With China a World War II ally of the United States, Hollywood set out to create a more tolerant on-screen approach to Chinese Americans. This philosophy coincided with MGM's need for a replacement in its popular Dr. Kildare movie series; its star Lew Ayres had left MGM recently after receiving unfavorable publicity for being a conscientious objector in the war. (He would serve with distinction on the front lines as a medic.) It was decided that the series' costar, veteran actor Barrymore, who played experienced but crotchety wheelchair-bound Dr. Leonard Gillespie, should become the lead in what now would be known as the Dr. Gillespie series. To round out the cast of regulars, it was agreed to feature young actors as Gillespie's aspiring new helpers.

One of those assigned to enroll in the Dr. Gillespie screen offerings was MGM contract player LUKE, who had been in Hollywood films since 1934, most noticeably in the CHARLIE CHAN series as Lee Chan, the detective's #1 son. MGM made Dr. How the true American by having him be Brooklyn born. (At the time, nothing could be more American than a clichéd screen character who was born and raised in Brooklyn.)

At Blair General Hospital, the exhausted Dr. Gillespie is finally permitted to hire a new assistant from three candidates among the interns: Dr. Randall "Red" Adams from Kansas City, Australian Dr. Dennis Lindsay on temporary duty at Blair, and Dr. Lee Wong How of Brooklyn. Gillespie quizzes them, and when all three answer the same tough question correctly, he decides to give them each a try. The focus is on Red who is pursuing a case of fake amnesia.

At the end of this entry, Dr. Lindsay conveniently returned to Australia, leaving Gillespie to assign both Red Adams and Lee Wong How as his new assistants. Adams, played by the increasingly popular Johnson, did three more entries, while Luke did four additional Gillespie episodes (ending with 1947's *DARK DELUSION*), as well as playing his physician character in an entry of another series: *Andy Hardy's Blonde Trouble* (1944).

***Dragon Seed* (1944)** Metro-Goldwyn-Mayer, sepia, 148 minutes. **Directors:** Jack Conway and Harold S. Bucquet; **Screenplay:** Marguerite Roberts and Jane Murfin; **Cast:** Katharine Hepburn (Jade Tan), Walter Huston (Ling Tan), Aline MacMahon (Ling's wife), Akim Tamiroff (Wu Lien), Turhan Bey (Lao Er Tan), Hurd Hatfield (Lao San Tan), J. Carrol Naish (Japanese kitchen overseer), Lionel Barrymore (narrator).

Just as MGM had made a mammoth screen adaptation of Pearl Buck's *THE GOOD EARTH* (1937) so they now did with her best-selling 1943 novel, *Dragon Seed.* Its focus was on World War II and how China was pushed into war by the aggressions of the Japanese within China's borders.

As MGM planned its elaborate production, the studio was conscious of the need to cast the project with box-office names to ensure a solid return on its investment. From the start, it was planned that the leads would be Caucasians and *not* Asian Americans so as to appeal to the widest number of filmgoers and to avoid creating miscegenation and creative (i.e., makeup) problems of having lead actors of different races being involved in on-screen love scenes. Many of the actresses announced for the role of the idealistic Jade Tan (including Austrian-born Luise Rainer and Hedy Lamarr, Britisher Green Garson, and American-born Judy Garland) were dropped from consideration because makeup tests revealed that their bone structure—even with the use of Asian makeup masks—was too Caucasian to disguise effectively.

Other Caucasian talent who were rejected for *Dragon Seed* roles due to makeup concerns included Edward Arnold, Fay Bainter, Donald Crisp, Van Heflin, Walter Pidgeon, and Edward G. Robinson (who had played Asians in *EAST IS WEST*, 1930, and *THE HATCHET MAN*, 1932). According to a *New York Times* article (August 22, 1943), when it came time to cast the lesser roles and the walk-ons, there was a lack of available Chinese Americans to utilize because so many had joined the armed services, leading the studio to utilize Mexican, Filipino, and "other racial groups . . . that can easily be made up to appear oriental." One of the Asian Americans cast but not used in the final release print was KEYE LUKE as a Chinese student lecturer. Most of the villainous Japanese were played by Caucasians or Chinese-American actors.

The story of *Dragon Seed* opens in the spring of 1937 in a rich farming valley of China. The wealthy Ling Tan, a devout pacifist, is content with his agrarian life and unmindful of the Japanese forces that will soon bring war to his country. Jade, married to Ling's second son, Lao Er, is increasingly angered by the Japanese aggression and urges her spouse to join the resistance movement in the mountains. Before long, the Japanese grab control of the valley, eventually leading to Ling Tan having a change of heart. With his wife, relatives, and villagers, he burns everything, and they join Jade and Lao Er in the mountains. Thereafter, Ling Tan and his wife make the journey to free China, taking their grandson (who has "the seed of the dragon") with them.

Of the major names in the cast, Hepburn and Tamiroff seemed most out of step, even with their eyes taped back to help provide an Oriental cast to their faces. The five-feet, seven-inch Hepburn, with her New England accent, was anything but Chinese in her delineation, especially as she delivered an impassioned speech to the village elders near the picture's conclusion.

Dragon Seed received two Academy Award nominations: Best Black and White Cinematography and Best Supporting Actress (MacMahon).

***Dragon: The Bruce Lee Story* (1993)** Universal, color, 109 minutes. **Director:** Rob Cohen; **Screenplay:** Edward Khmara, John Raffo, and Cohen; **Cast:** Jason Scott Lee (Bruce Lee), Lauren Holly (Linda Emery Lee), Robert Wagner (Gill Krieger), Michael Learned (Vivian Emery), Nancy Kwan (Gussie Yang), Kay Tong Lim (Philip Tan), Ric Young (Bruce's father).

In his several martial-arts movies, including *ENTER THE DRAGON* (1973), Asian-American actor BRUCE LEE developed a huge following. He was the first contemporary Asian American to develop tremendous popularity not only in Hong Kong and the Far East but also in the United States. The number and the devotion of his fans far exceeded that of such past Asian Hollywood stars as Japanese-born SESSUE HAYAKAWA or more current entrants such as JAMES SHIGETA or, later, Hong Kong-born JOHN LONE. Lee opened the path for such new martial-arts stars as Hong Kong-born JACKIE CHAN and CHOW YUN-FAT.

Two decades after the death of Bruce Lee (1940–73) Hollywood filmed this passionate, if simplistic, biography of the legendary martial arts movie star. Based on the biography *The Man Only I Knew* (1974) by his widow Linda Lee Cadwell, the picture featured Hawaiian-born JASON SCOTT LEE in the title role.

The narrative opens with Lee's father (Young) enrolling his son in kung-fu classes so that he can protect himself against the vicious dragon that the parent had dreamed attacked his boy. The chronicle then jumps to the young adult Bruce Lee, arriving in San Francisco after years with his family in Hong Kong. Encountering further racial prejudice when he enrolls in college, he finds romance with Caucasian classmate Linda Emery. She urges him to open a school to teach his brand of kung fu, which he does. Despite the prejudice of her mother (Learned) and her friends, they wed and later have two children. Recalled in the account is his role on TV's *The Green Hornet* (1966–67) and his later successful martial-arts pictures. It concludes with his death from a supposed reaction to medication.

In the course of tracing the star's life—as seen through the perspective of his wife—this movie emphasizes several of the racial issues that have beset Asian Americans for decades. In the lead role, muscular Jason Scott Lee offers a charismatic performance, filled with right vocal inflections and the fiery eyes that overcome his lack of resemblance to the late star.

The film grossed more than $35 million in domestic distribution. Only a few weeks before *Dragon: The Bruce Lee Story* was released, BRANDON LEE, Bruce's actor son, was killed in a mishap on the set of *THE CROW* (1994).

dramas—feature films From the 1930s onward, a good many of Hollywood-made serious stories involving Asian characters revolved around COMBAT DRAMAS (i.e., World War II, the Korean War, and the Vietnam War). Another topic of constant interest/concern, especially in the silent era and thereafter until mores and, in turn, misce-

Jason Scott Lee starring in *Dragon: The Bruce Lee Story* (1993). (JC ARCHIVES)

genation laws were rescinded in most jurisdictions, was the subject of interracial love. The fact that American movies dared not show mixed romances on the screen for many decades led to two strategic moviemaking ploys: (1) have the Asian role played by a Caucasian actor, and/or (2) have the romance unconsummated and end (often in the suicide or disappearance of the Asian party). Such premises were developed in *The Soul of Kura-San* (1916), *The Call of the East* (1917), *CITY OF DIM FACES* (1918), *A Heart in Pawn* (1919), *BROKEN BLOSSOMS* (1919), *DINTY* (1920), *Defying the Law* (1924), and so on. It was the basis of the 1930 talkie *SON OF THE GODS* with Richard Barthelmess and Constance Bennett, and George Raft's *LIMEHOUSE BLUES* (1934). The topic lay submerged through much of the World War II years but returned to the screen in such postwar entries as *JAPANESE WAR BRIDGE* (1952), *LOVE IS A MANY-SPLENDORED THING* (1955), *BRIDGE TO THE SUN* (1961), *A GIRL NAMED TAMIKO* (1962), *The Sand Pebbles* (1966), *If Tomorrow Comes* (1971—TV movie), *CHINA GIRL* (1987), *COME SEE THE PARADISE* (1990), *Snow Falling on Cedar* (1999), and so on. At the end of the twentieth century came *ROMEO MUST DIE* (2000), in which one member of a romantic couple was Asian and the other African American and their families maintaining that the two races must never mix.

An offshoot of the interracial love stories were the entries dealing with the purveyors of the white slave trade, who in many pre-World War II films were depicted as pernicious, lustful Asians (e.g., *Broken Fetters*, 1916).

An unusual drama that dealt with discrimination and that included such other ethnic minorities as Native Americans and Hispanics was *Black Gold* (1947). Starring Anthony Quinn and his then-wife, actress Katherine DeMille, it dealt with an orphaned Chinese boy (played by Ducky Louie) who was befriended by Charley Eagle (Quinn) and became a jockey for a crucial horse race.

As Asian-American film directors began to make their own features in the United States, the subject of generation gaps and culture clashes became a recurrent theme, as seen in *DIM SUM: A LITTLE BIT OF HEART* (1985), *EAT A BOWL OF TEA* (1989), *THE JOY LUCK CLUB* (1993), *HEAVEN & EARTH* (1993), *Eat Drink Man Woman* (1994), *Blindness* (1999), *WHAT'S COOKING?* (2000), *Catfish in Black Bean Sauce* (2000), and so on.

Throughout the decades, Hollywood produced occasional historical dramas/spectacles dealing with the Far East, HAWAII, or POLYNESIA. These included: *The Adventures of Marco Polo* (1938), *ANNA AND THE KING OF SIAM* (1946), *Damien* (1950), *THE CONQUEROR* (1956), *THE BARBARIAN AND THE GEISHA* (1958), *HAWAII* (1960), *55 DAYS AT PEKING* (1963), *Genghis Khan* (1965), *THE HAWAIIANS* (1970), *TAI-PAN* (1986), *Little Buddha* (1993), *RAPA NUI* (1994), *KUNDUN* (1997), *Seven Years in Tibet* (1997), and *ANNA AND THE KING* (1999). There were also such big-budgeted TV miniseries dealing with past centuries of the Orient as *SHOGUN* (1980), *JAMES CLAVELL'S NOBLE HOUSE* (1988), and the fantasy/adventure TV movie *The Lost Empire* (2001).

drama series—television One of the first non-situation comedies to utilize an Asian-American character in a recurring role was *Mr. Broadway* (1964), about a New York City public-relations whiz played by Craig Stevens. His character had two helpers, legman Hank McClure and a girl Friday named Toki (played by Lani Miyazaki). On *Sarge* (1971–72), set at St. Aloysius Parish in San Diego, Father Samuel Cavanaugh (played by George Kennedy) had previously been a police detective. Others on the staff included the rectory cook Kenji Takichi (played by Harold Sakata).

Midnight Caller (1988–91) dealt with a San Francisco-based late-night radio call-in show. One of the hosts, Jack Killian, an ex-San Francisco police detective, was played by Gary Cole. His engineer and producer, Billy Po (played by Dennis Dun) helped Jack when Killian became involved in helping out some of his callers. Billy's talent was his large number of contacts in the city's Asian enclave. On *Island Son* (1989–90), a medical drama starring Richard Chamberlain as an adopted Hawaiian, Chamberlain's character was a doctor returning to Honolulu to practice at a local medical center. It allowed the physician to interact with his adoptive parents (played by Kwan Hi Lim and Betty Carvalho) and his stepbrother (played by Ray Bumatai). On this series, Clyde Kusatsu was seen as the medical center's Dr. Kenji Fushida.

The nighttime drama, *Twin Peaks* (1990–91), set in the Pacific Northwest, had as one of its interweaving story lines, Asian Jocelyn Packard (played by JOAN CHEN) as a murderous widow who inherited a sawmill from her late husband. *Byrds of Paradise* (1994) was a family drama set in Hawaii about the headmaster (played by Timothy Busfield) of the fancy Palmer School. The widower, who boasted three teenaged children, had the domestic help of Sonny and Manu Kaulukukui (played by Robert Kekaula and Lani Opunui-Ancheta), as well as fringe characters played by Asian-American actors. On *ALLY MCBEAL* (1997–2002), a mix of drama and comedy, one of the newer partners at the bizarre Boston law firm was Ling Woo (played by LUCY LIU), a cool beauty who brooked no nonsense from her peers or her Caucasian boyfriend—the firm's founding partner. *Mysterious Ways* (2000–2002), which examined unusual phenomena, had Rae Dawn Chong as the associate of the lead investigator (played by Adrian Pasdar).

Also see: ACTION AND ADVENTURE SERIES—TELEVISION; COMBAT SERIES—TELEVISION; CRIME, DETECTIVE, AND POLICE SERIES—TELEVISION; and MEDICAL SERIES—TELEVISION.

E

***East Is West* (1922)** Associated First National, 1922, b&w, 7,737′. **Director:** Sidney Franklin; **Screenplay:** Frances Marion; **Cast:** Constance Talmadge (Ming Toy), Edward Burns (Billy Benson), E. A. Warren (Lo Sang Kee), Warner Oland (Charley Yong), Frank Lanning (Hop Toy), Nick De Ruiz (Chang Lee), Jim Wang (proprietor of love boat).

The exotic appeal of Asian women to Caucasian men was further explored in this melodrama based on the 1918 Broadway play by Samuel Shipman and John B. Hymer. Ming Toy, the oldest of Hop Toy's progeny, is about to be auctioned off in marriage. She is saved by Billy Benson and is sent to the United States where she arouses the interest of powerful San Francisco Chinatown figure Charley Young. The latter wants to marry her, but she refuses. Once again she is helped by Benson. It is revealed that Ming Toy, as a baby, was kidnapped from her American parents. That resolved, she and Benson can wed.

With its plot twist, *East Is West* skirted the issue of interracial love. For OLAND, this was one of several times when he played an on-screen Asian beyond his outings as FU MANCHU and CHARLIE CHAN. Most of the other celluloid Orientals here were played by Caucasian actors. The film was remade in 1930.

***East Is West* (1930)** Universal, b&w, 74 minutes. **Director:** Monta Bell; **Screenplay:** Tom Reed; **Cast:** Lupe Velez (Ming Toy), Lew Ayres (Billy Benson), Edward G. Robinson (Charlie Yong), Mary Forbes (Mrs. Benson), E. Alyn Warren (Lo Sang Kee), Henry Kolker (Mr. Benson), Tetsu Komai (Hop Toy).

Dusting off the vintage 1918 Broadway play by Samuel Shipman and John B. Hymer that had been made as a 1922 silent feature, this new edition boasted sound and the presence of energetic Mexican actress Velez. The plot was similar to the earlier version, with Warren repeating his part as Lo Sang Kee. In this presentation, at least, more of the key roles were handled by non-Caucasians. In the 1930 Spanish-language edition of *East Is West*, entitled *Oriente y Occidente*, both Velez and Komai repeated their screen parts, with Manuel Arbo as Charlie Young, Daniel F. Rea as Lo Sang Ki, and Barry Norton as Billy Benson.

***Eat a Bowl of Tea* (1989)** Columbia, color, 102 minutes. **Director:** Wayne Wang; **Screenplay:** Judith Rascoe; **Cast:** Cora Miao (Mei Oi), Russell Wong (Ben Loy), Victor Wong (Wah Gay), Lee Sau Kee (Bok Fat), Eric Tsiang Chi Wai (Ah Song), Law Lan (Aunt Gim).

Produced by PBS-TV's *American Playhouse*, this comedy drama focused on the change in laws in post–World War II United States to allow Chinese women to immigrate with their husbands to the new country. Ben Loy travels to China to visit his mother and there meets a villager, Mei Oi, whom he marries and brings back to America. Their problems are just starting, as they must deal with their respective fathers who want their offspring to have a child as quickly as possible. The pressures exerted on the couple by relatives, friends, and neighbors lead to each having an extramarital affair, which brings shame on their families. The couple is shunned by their culture, and they leave the ghetto neighborhood. Eventually they reunite—thanks to the magic qualities of special oriental tea—and move to San Francisco.

In the guise of a gentle comedy, this drama, based on a story by Louis Chu, recorded the ways in which foreigners adapted to a new culture and how similar this was to the period of adjustment for newlyweds. Told from the point of view of Asian Americans, this film was by WANG, already noted for his *CHAN IS MISSING* (1982) and *DIM SUM: A LITTLE BIT OF HEART* (1985).

***Empire of the Sun* (1987)** Warner Bros., color, 152 minutes. **Director:** Steven Spielberg; **Screenplay:** Tom Stoppard and Menno Meyjes; **Cast:** Christian Bale (Jim Graham), John Malkovich (Basie), Miranda Richardson (Mrs. Victor), Nigel Havers (Dr. Rawlins), Joe Pantoliano (Frank Demerest), Masato Ibu (Sergeant Nagata), Takatoro Kataoka (Kamikaze boy pilot).

This feature was an entirely different look at World War II and the Japanese enemy than was customary for Hollywood productions, even in the let's-look-back-at-the-war period. Based on J. G. Ballard's autobiographical novel (1984), this expansive motion picture was told from the perspective of a British boy living in Shanghai at the outbreak of the war. He was a privileged youth who felt more kinship to idealized Japanese fliers than to the impoverished Chinese living in the city about him.

In the crush of Shanghai residents fleeing from the approaching Japanese as the city falls to the invaders, young Jim Graham is separated from his parents. The advantaged boy, who has been isolated from his environment by his well-to-do parents, now must scrounge on his own in this life-and-death situation. Fortuitously, he encounters street-smart merchant-seaman Basie who becomes both his protector and exploiter. The two are soon caught by the Japanese and placed in a prison camp. Now emancipated from his family's rarified regimen, Graham, under Basie's unorthodox guidance, survives the daily horrors of the overcrowded internment camp. Even in the midst of the misery, he finds childish delight in exploring his new world. Later, in 1945, with the war against Japan finally over, the much-matured Graham is shunted to a center to be reunited with his parents. The gulf of years and his unique experiences, however, have made him a stranger to them and vice versa.

An extremely visual feature film, it was followed by Spielberg's *Schindler's List* (1993), which examined the horror of war as experienced by the persecuted Jews, again with a neutral subject (i.e., the Polish entrepreneur Oskar Schindler) providing the central point of view.

Made at a cost of $35 million, *Empire of the Sun* was not the box-office success anticipated. (It grossed $22 million in domestic distribution.) The film received six Academy Award nominations: Best Art Direction/Set Decoration, Best Cinematography, Best Costume Design, Best Film Editing, Best Original Score, and Best Sound.

***Enter the Dragon* (1973)** Warner Bros, color, 98 minutes. **Director:** Robert Clouse; **Screenplay:** Michael Allin; **Cast:** Bruce Lee (Lee), John Saxon (Roper), Jim Kelly (Williams), Shih Kien (Han), Bob Wall (Oharra), Ahna Capri (Tania), Angela Mao Ying (Su-Lin), Sammo Hung and Jackie Chan (bits).

Through the decades, this film gained cult status, especially because its beloved star LEE died three weeks before the movie premiered. Filmed on a $550,000 budget, it grossed many times that amount. It also featured brief stunt bits by future action stars CHAN and HUNG.

To penetrate the island fortress of Han, a government agent recruits Lee to enter a martial-arts contest there. Once on the isle, Lee meets two former army buddies, Roper and Williams, who have come to participate. While the elimination rounds are progressing, Lee goes after Han, bent on punishing his assistant, Oharra, who was responsible for the death of Lee's sister. Eventually Lee emerges victorious, but not without the cost of lives, including that of Williams.

With Lee's dazzling display of martial arts, this movie, despite careless plotting and poor acting, became a genre classic. It did much to further legitimize action movie stars who specialized in the art of self-defense. It also further entrenched Lee as an icon and role model.

***Escapade in Japan* (1957)** Universal/RKO, color, 90 minutes. **Director:** Arthur Lubin; **Screenplay:** Winston Miller; **Cast:** Teresa Wright (Mary Saunders), Cameron Mitchell (Dick Saunders), Jon Provost (Tony Saunders), Roger Nakagawa (Hiko), Philip Ober (Lieutenant Colonel Hargrave), Kuniko Miyake (Michiko), Clint Eastwood (Dumbo).

In its own way, this was a colorful travelogue of post-World War II Japan as seen through the eyes of two youngsters. One is Tony Saunders, on his way to meet his parents in Japan. His plane makes a forced landing off the coastline. He is separated from the crew and rescued by a local fisherman whose family befriends the boy, even though they don't speak English; Tony becomes especially friendly with the fisherman's child Hiko. The two youths run off when they think the police are searching for Tony to punish him for doing something wrong. Their adventures take them through many aspects of daily Japanese life, including a stopover at a GEISHA house.

By now, for many, memories of World War II were fading, and as Japan and the United States developed strong economic ties, more Hollywood-produced films utilized the islands of the rising sun as backdrop for civilian story lines.

F

***55 Days at Peking* (1963)** Allied Artists, color, 150 minutes. **Director:** Nicholas Ray; **Screenplay:** Philip Jordan, Bernard Gordon, and Robert Hamer; **Cast:** Charlton Heston (Maj. Matt Lewis), Ava Gardner (Baroness Natalie Ivanoff), David Niven (Sir Arthur Robertson), Flora Robson (Dowager Empress Tzu-Hsi), John Ireland (Sergeant Harry), Leo Genn (General Jung-Lu).

In 1900 in the capital city of Peking (Beijing), the German ambassador is murdered by the Boxers, who want all foreigners out of their country. British ambassador Sir Arthur Robertson suggests that a stand be made at the international compound while a call for reinforcements is made to the eleven nations involved. U.S. Marine Major Lewis is placed in charge of the defense. The siege lasts for fifty-five days.

While many of the cast (e.g., Heston and Niven) were stiff lipped or, in other cases, a parody of their former vamp persona (e.g., Gardner), Robson was relatively proficient as the mad dowager empress who conspired with the Boxers to eradicate the foreigners. Like the British-born Robson, many of the cast who played Asians on camera here were of other ethnic backgrounds. Typical of this era, it never seriously occurred to producer Samuel Bronston to use Asian-American actors for the appropriate screen roles.

Despite its many flaws, *55 Days at Peking* presented an interesting chapter in China's history.

***First Yank in Tokyo* (1945)** RKO, b&w, 82 minutes. **Director:** Gordon Douglas; **Screenplay:** J. Robert Bren and Gladys Atwater; **Cast:** Tom Neal (Sergeant Takishima [Maj. Steve Ross]), Barbara Hale (Abby Drake), Marc Cramer (Louis Jardine), Richard Loo (Col. Eco Okunura), Keye Luke (Haan-Soo), Leonard Strong (Major Nogiea), Benson Fong (Captain Tanaho).

This was one of the *most* fanciful of all Hollywood-made World War II dramas, filled with contrived coincidences and stereotypes of sadistic Japanese officers, kindly Koreans, and nearly invincible Caucasian Americans. Despite its flaws and its stereotypes of the treacherous Nipponese, it was an entertaining action entry.

Major Ross, a World War II USAAF pilot, is requested by the U.S. government to undergo plastic surgery to make him look Japanese. The government's plan is to have him infiltrate a Japanese prisoner-of-war camp to contact scientist Louis Jardine, who has the formula to create an atomic bomb. The remarkable scheme succeeds, with Ross posing as Sergeant Takishima. He makes contact with Jardine, even encountering his one-time girlfriend—army nurse Abby Drake who doesn't recognize him—and is nearly successful in his scheme to spirit her, Jardine, and himself out of the country. However, Colonel Okunura suddenly realizes from the way Takishima sprints (just like he did on the football field at school) that he is Ross, his one-time college roommate.

In the climax, only Drake and Jardine make it back to Allied territory. Ross/Takishima, along with the faithful underground worker (Luke), sacrifice themselves for the cause. Their deaths, so the film says, allow for the development and use of the atomic bomb (on Hiroshima, etc.) so that "mankind can walk unafraid in peace with goodwill toward men." (It also provided a way out for the scripters who had painted themselves into a censorship corner. If Ross/Takishima had lived and if reverse plastic surgery was not a viable option—as the script suggested—how could the "interracial" characters have continued their interrupted romance?) Another reason for the film's twisted ending was that five months after shooting on the movie had wrapped, the United States dropped atom bombs on Hiroshima and Nagasaki. The script was hastily revamped and additional scenes staged to take advantage of current events.

For a change, the Japanese and Koreans were played by Asian Americans, albeit not always of the correct racial background for their given characters.

***Flash Gordon* (1936)** Universal, b&w, 13-chapter serial. **Director:** Frederick Stephani; **Screenplay:** Stephani, George Plympton, Basil Dickey, and Ella O'Neill; **Cast:** Larry "Buster" Crabbe (Flash Gordon), Jean Rogers (Dale Arden), Charles Middleton (Emperor Ming), Priscilla Lawson (Aura), John Lipson (King Vultan), Richard Alexander (Prince Barin), Frank Shannon (Dr. Zarkov); **Chapters:** (1) The Planet of Peril, (2) The Tunnel of Terror, (3) Captured by Shark Men, (4) Battling the Sea Beast, (5) Destroying Ray, (6) Flaming Torture, (7) Shattering Doom, (8) Tournament of Death, (9) Fighting the Fire Dragon, (10) The Unseen Peril, (11) In the Claws of the Tigron, (12) Trapped in the Turret, (13) Rocketing to Earth.

Based on Alex Raymond's comic strip that first appeared in 1934, this serial, made at a then high cost of $500,000, proved to be one of the most popular of the sound era chapterplays. Its energy and enthusiasm compensated for its primitive special effects. Following in the Hollywood and literary tradition of an Asian peril a la DR. FU MANCHU, *Flash Gordon* boasted an interplanetary counterpart, the sinister Emperor Ming. In his bizarre outfit, shaved head, and penciled-on eyebrows, the dastardly Ming (with mustache and goatee similar to Fu Manchu) is the ultimate serial villain—slick and cold blooded. He is Ming the Merciless, who rules the gypsy planet Mongo.

In this action-packed serial, the planet Mongo is hurtling toward Earth. This prompts Flash Gordon, joined by pretty Dale Arden and resourceful Dr. Zarkov, to race into outer space in the latter's new rocket ship. They land on Mongo, where a bizarre world is controlled by the sinister Ming. Ming captures them, makes known his rapacious desire for Dale, and schemes to utilize the brainy Zarkov to help him conquer the Earth.

Throughout the serial, the outlandish Ming is front and center. Although there are monkey-men, dinosaurs, shark-men, and Gocko (Ming's clawed dragon) to contend with, it is this Asian-style evil man who remains most memorable in the celluloid proceedings.

Like Fu Manchu and other Asian screen villains, Ming personifies the American movie stereotype of Asians as the horrendously evil "Yellow Peril." Of course, with the rising tide of Japanese imperialism in the 1930s, there were many who spotted the analogy between the grasping Ming out for world domination and the not dissimilarly looking Japanese leaders who were grabbing for global control.

The successful *Flash Gordon* spawned two further serials (each featuring Ming the Merciless): *Flash Gordon's Trip to Mars* (1938) and *Flash Gordon Conquers the Universe* (1940). The 1936 *Flash Gordon* was also reedited into three separate feature films: *Rocket Ship*, *Spaceship to the Unknown*, and *Space Soldiers*. Universal Pictures created a new Flash Gordon movie in 1980 starring Sam J. Jones (Flash Gordon), Melody Anderson (Dale Arden), Topol (Dr. Hans Zarkov), and Max von Sydow (Emperor Ming). Despite its high budget, it lacked the zip of the original 1936 serial.

***Flower Drum Song* (1961)** Universal, color, 133 minutes. **Director:** Henry Koster; **Screenplay:** Joseph Fields; **Cast:** Nancy Kwan (Linda Low), James Shigeta (Wang Ta), Juanita Hall (Auntie [Madame Liang]), Jack Soo (Sammy Fong), Miyoshi Umeki (Mei Li), Benson Fong (Wang Chi-Yang), Victor Sen Yung (Frankie Wing).

Richard Rodgers and Oscar Hammerstein II had taken C.Y. Lee's 1957 novel *The Flower Drum Song* and converted it into a precious musical (1958) that ran for 600 performances on Broadway. Part African-American HALL, Japanese-born UMEKI, and Japanese-American SOO from the New York cast were imported to Hollywood for the overdone, overly sweet screen version.

Among the film's excesses was recreating portions of San Francisco's Chinatown (including Grant Avenue) on sound stages rather than employing the real thing. SHIGETA, the Hawaiian-born Asian American, and Hong Kong-born KWAN completed the cast headliners. In using Asians to portray Chinese in its presentations of Chinese as simplistic and naïve, this condescending screen musical prompted protests from Chinese-American groups.

Unsophisticated Mei Li arrives in San Francisco's Chinatown, a "picture bride" promised in marriage to Sammy Fong, the crafty owner of a local nightclub. Fong, however, is against the traditional custom of having a bride selected for him and prefers to wed Linda Low, a performer at his hip club. Always the operator, Fong hopes to convince a well-to-do local Chinese family to have Mei Li, instead, wed their son, Wang Ta. Meanwhile, Wang Ta has been seeing Linda, not knowing that she is mostly impressed by his money. When it is announced later that Wang Ta and Linda will be united, both Mei Li and Fong are tremendously upset. Eventually, using New World creativity, the Old World is pacified, and a double wedding properly pairs the quartet.

Flower Drum Song received five Oscar nominations: Best Art Direction/Set Decoration (Color), Best Cinematography (Color), Best Costume Design (Color), Best Scoring of a Musical, and Best Sound. (In October 2001, the stage version of *Flower Drum Song* was revived in Los Angeles, but with an authorized, revised new book by David Henry Hwang, which removed some of the story's stereotypes and updated the plot.)

***Flying Tigers* (1942)** Republic, b&w, 102 minutes. **Director:** David Miller; **Screenplay:** Kenneth Gamet and Barry Trivers; **Cast:** John Wayne (Jim Gordon), John Carroll (Woody Jason), Anna Lee (Brooke Elliott), Paul Kelly (Hap Davis), Gordon Jones (Alabama Smith), Mae Clarke (Verna

Bales), Tom Neal (Reardon), Richard Loo (doctor), Willie Fung (waiter).

In the first of several combat feature films that would make him an American icon, Wayne appeared as the squadron leader within the American volunteer group that flies combat missions against the Japanese in the months before the attack on Pearl Harbor. These Flying Tigers (the nickname for the group) were serving on behalf of China's General Chiang Kai-Shek and under the command of Gen. Claire Chennault. Some of the men were patriots; others were mercenaries, wanting the $500 for each enemy plane shot down. Many of the characteristics that became standard fare for such war movies were present: the smart-aleck new recruit (Carroll), the faithful second-in-charge (Kelly), the loving nurse (Lee), the comedic team member (Jones), and so on.

As comedy relief and/or human interest in such World War II combat films, there were often friendly or humorous Chinese characters, here represented respectively by LOO as a doctor and FUNG in one of his stereotypical parts as the sing-song-talking waiter, the character who would not eat the Chinese dishes.

It was a Hollywood irony in those decades that built-in prejudices against all talent with Asian heritages led casting departments to hire the same ethnic actors sometimes as friendly, humanistic Chinese or, on other occasions, as snarling, vicious Japanese—on the assumption that all non-Caucasians looked the same to undiscerning American audiences (and insensitive filmmakers).

Fong, Benson (1916–1987) To film buffs, he was known best as CHARLIE CHAN's #3 son Tommy in that movie series. Later, he was associated with being the owner of the Ah Fong chain of Chinese restaurants in the Los Angeles area.

He was born in Sacramento, California, the son of a merchant who went bankrupt and died during the Great Depression. Growing up in northern California, Fong was cognizant of outward differences between Caucasian peers and himself. As he told the *Los Angeles Times* (May 7, 1978): "For a person of Chinese ancestry it was sheer hell to go to school alone, . . . I set my goal at winning acceptance from others. I always carried peanuts and candy with me. Whenever other kids came around, I'd give them some goodies to nibble on. It wasn't cowardice. I just wanted friendship."

After high school, Fong received his college education in China and then returned to Sacramento where he and a cousin opened a grocery store. In 1942, he was approached by a film-studio talent scout and signed to appear in Alan Ladd's starrer, *CHINA* (1943). As he further recollected for the *Los Angeles Times,* "I couldn't read lines too well, but World War II was under way and all the studios were looking for actors with Oriental features. I bicycled around town from one set to another, playing a Japanese here, a Filipino there, a Chinese on still other days."

Charlie Chan in the Secret Service (1944) was the start of Fong's two-year association with that movie series. He was Moy Ling in *THE PURPLE HEART* (1944), a devious Japanese in *Secret Agent X-9* (1945—serial), and a salesclerk in *Boston Blackie's Chinese Venture* (1949). By the time of *Submarine Command* (1952), he was a South Korean officer. His roles in the 1960s ranged from the western *WALK LIKE A DRAGON* (1960) to the musical *FLOWER DRUM SONG* (1961) and included Elvis Presley's *Girls! Girls! Girls!* (1962) and the role of Carol Channing's all-wise servant in *Thoroughly Modern Millie* (1967). By the 1970s his acting career had tapered off (he was Han Fei on the *KUNG FU* series, 1972–75). His final screen part was as "The Old One" on the telefeature *KUNG FU: THE MOVIE* (1986).

***Footlight Parade* (1933)** Warner Bros., b&w, 102 minutes. **Director:** Lloyd Bacon; **Musical** Numbers **Creator/Choreographer:** Busby Berkeley; **Screenplay:** Manuel Seff and James Seymour; **Cast:** James Cagney (Chester Kent), Joan Blondell (Nan Prescott), Ruby Keeler (Bea Thorn), Dick Powell (Scotty Blair), Frank McHugh (Francis), Guy Kibbee (Sy Gould), Ruth Donnelly (Mrs. Harriet Gould).

This third of the seven Ruby Keeler–Dick Powell Warner Bros. 1930s musicals was bolstered by the presence of Cagney and Blondell and Berkeley's great musical staging. A backstage tale, theatrical producer Kent successfully directs prologue numbers to be presented live before the cinema unspools its feature film presentation. The plot concoction allowed for a spectacular variety of kaleidoscopic song-and-dance numbers (e.g., "By a Waterfall").

The most striking musical routine was the "Shanghai Lil" number, which featured Cagney hoofing with tap-dancing Keeler. Set in a Shanghai saloon overcrowded with randy American sailors and tough broads, Cagney's character sadly sings of his search for his beloved Shanghai Lil, a bar prostitute. The hunt progresses to an opium den and then back to the saloon where a brawl erupts among sailors, marines, and civilian patrons. Outfitted in a sailor suit, Cagney's character finds his inamorata (Keeler in a dark black wig and with slant eyes). Happily reunited, the couple taps up and down the bar and she delivers some of her lyrics in a simulated Chinese accent. Thereafter, Cagney and the other gobs head back to their ship. As they depart the bar, they and their Chinese women execute precision fast steps, turning the ensemble into configurations of the Stars and Stripes and the American eagle and even President Franklin Roosevelt's face. The chief image that remains of this spectacular musical number is Keeler as the exotic Asian poseur.

***Forbidden Nights* (1990)** CBS-TV, color, 96 minutes. **Director:** Waris Hussein; **Teleplay:** Tristine Rainer; **Cast:** Melissa Gilbert (Judith Shapiro), Robin Shou (Liang Hong), Victor Wong (Ho), Tzi Ma (Li Dao), Beulah Quo (Vince Dean Yin), Khigh Dhiegh (Lu Ming).

Based on an article ("The Rocky Course of Love in China") by Judith Shapiro, this Hong Kong–filmed telefeature dealt with the opening of (Red) China to the West. In 1979, schoolteacher Judith Shapiro is invited to teach for two years at Shang Sa, Hunan, China. As the stranger in a foreign land, she must adapt to their lifestyle. Making matters more complicated, she falls in love with one of her students, Liang Hong, a radical who works diligently on behalf of his homeland. Becoming more involved with the young man, her life and principles are put on the line.

There were similar themes here to *Iron & Silk* (1990), a theatrical feature about a young American instructor (Mark Saltzman), teaching English in mainland China and learning martial arts as he seeks to find himself.

Besides Gilbert, this TV movie used an all Asian-American cast.

Fuller, Samuel (1912–1997) This veteran film director/scripter/iconoclast, born in Worcester, Massachusetts, was a frequent purveyor of Asian-themed movies, ranging from battle-set entries like *The Steel Helmet* and *Fixed Bayonets* (both 1951 and about the Korean War) to *CHINA GATE* (1957—the brewing Vietnam conflict). His *HOUSE OF BAMBOO* (1955), set in Japan, concerned criminal activity there in the postwar era, while *THE CRIMSON KIMONO* (1959) dealt with an Asian-American police detective and involved the art of karate. Sometimes his features dealt with other topics but somehow worked Asian characters into the plot.

Fu Manchu, Dr. British author Arthur Sarsfield Ward, under the pseudonym of Sax Rohmer, wrote several novels featuring the sinister Dr. Fu Manchu, including *The Return of Dr. Fu Manchu* (1916). In 1923, in England, Harry Agar Lyons appeared in a series of fifteen Fu Manchu silent shorts. Later, in 1929 Hollywood, Paramount Pictures released *THE MYSTERIOUS DR. FU MANCHU* with Swedish-born WARNER OLAND in the title part. That led to Oland portraying the Yellow Peril in a skit within the all-star variety picture *Paramount on Parade* (1930) as well as in *The Return of Dr. Fu Manchu* (1930) and *DAUGHTER OF THE DRAGON* (1931). In the latter, ANNA MAY WONG was cast as the offspring of the nefarious master criminal.

After Oland became CHARLIE CHAN on screen and was unavailable for further Fu Manchu installments, Metro-Goldwyn-Mayer took over the property. BORIS KARLOFF was featured as the fiendish villain in *THE MASK OF FU MANCHU* in which Myrna Loy essayed his corrupt offspring. Thereafter, it was not until 1940 that the sinister Oriental returned on camera, this time in a fifteen-chapter serial *(Drums of Fu Manchu)* produced by Republic Pictures. German-born Henry Brandon was showcased as the evil warlord, aided by the Si Fan secret organization. The chapterplay was condensed into a feature-length version for distribution in 1943.

Meanwhile, on radio, *The Shadow of Fu Manchu* ran on the CBS network in a thirty-minute format from 1932 to 1934 and reappeared from 1939 to 1940 as a fifteen-minute syndicated program. First John C. Daly and then Harold Huber performed as the Chinese doctor gone wrong.

In 1952, Sir Cedric Hardwicke starred in a pilot for a proposed Fu Manchu TV series that never evolved. Three years later, author Sax Rohmer negotiated the sale of the rights to his literary creation to Republic Pictures for $4 million. They produced a thirty-minute syndicated version of *THE ADVENTURES OF DR. FU MANCHU* that aired its thirty-nine episodes in 1956. Glen Gordon had the lead part, with Lester Matthews as Sir Dennis Nayland-Smith, Clark Howat as Dr. John Petrie, and Laurette Luez as Karamanch.

Afterward, the Fu Manchu property lay dormant for a decade. Then a British film company produced a series of low-budget, almost campy entries starring Christopher Lee: *The Face of Fu Manchu* (1965), *The Brides of Fu Manchu* (1966), *The Vengeance of Fu Manchu* (1967), *Blood of Fu Manchu* (1968), and, the worst of the lot, *The Castle of Fu Manchu* (1969).

By the time of the atrocious *The Fiendish Plot of Dr. Fu Manchu* (1980), political correctness argued against the disparaging stereotype of the vengeful Chinese mastermind. Nevertheless, Orion Pictures in Hollywood produced this comic turkey. Britisher Peter Sellers, in what proved to be his final new film, starred in the project, which was set in the 1930s. The star, who delighted in being a man of many faces, also played his on-camera nemesis Nayland-Smith. This unhappy release was picketed by assorted special interest groups.

Fung, Willie (1896–1945) Pudgy and usually mustached, he made close to 100 features in two decades of Hollywood screen work. Frequently assigned to playing jovial domestics (e.g., *Hop-Along Cassidy*, 1935), he could just as easily turn up as a nasty sort (e.g., *LOST HORIZON*, 1937, as the bandit leader).

Born in Canton, China, Fung was in Los Angeles by the early 1920s, appearing in such 1922 silent films as *Hurricane's Gal* and *Broken Chains.* In the changeover to talkies, he played a cook in *The Virginian* (1929) and made an impression as a cheerful houseboy in the Clark Gable-Jean Harlow jungle entry, *Red Dust* (1932). Occasionally, he switched on-screen nationalities as in Shirley Temple's India-set *Wee Willie Winkie* (1937), where he was Mohammet Dihn. His final three screen roles showed the unfortunate career rut that befell Asian actors during Hollywood's Golden Age: *A Desperate Chance for Ellery Queen* (1942—as an Oriental waiter), *The Black Swan* (1942—as a Chinese cook), and *They Got Me Covered* (1943—as a laundry man).

G

***Gallery of Mme. Lui-Tsong, The* (aka: *Mme. Lui-Tsong*) (1951)** Dumont-TV series, b&w, 30 minutes. **Cast:** Anna May Wong (Mme. Lui-Tsong).

In the early years of commercial television, the four existing networks were far more experimental in their fare, often having ethnic minority-themed shows (e.g., *The Goldbergs:* 1949–54, 1955–56) as regular programming. As viewership for TV spread from coastal urban centers to middle America, such entries were typically dropped or not initiated due to sponsorship concerns of offending or disinteresting the majority of Caucasian America.

Veteran Chinese-American film and stage star WONG starred in this modest vehicle that lasted three months in the fall of 1951. In the opening episodes, she was the proprietress of an art gallery in search of new objects to sell. In the remaining five segments, her profession was altered to exporter, and her activities continued to include combating evildoers.

***Geisha Boy, The* (1958)** Paramount, color, 95 minutes. **Director/Screenplay:** Frank Tashlin; **Cast:** Jerry Lewis (Gilbert Wooley), Marie McDonald (Lois Livingston), Sessue Hayakawa (Mr. Sikita), Barton MacLane (Major Ridgley), Suzanne Pleshette (Pvt. Betty Pearson), Nobu McCarthy (Kimi Sikita), Robert Hirano (Mitsuo Watanabe).

As a fumbling magician, comedian Lewis joins a USO show touring Japan and Korea. He gets along famously with the group's shapely headliner, Lois Livingston, but has problems with Major Ridgley. When Wooley becomes involved with the show's interpreter Kimi Sikita, her orphaned nephew (Hirano) latches onto Wooley and even follows him to the United States.

Besides the visual tour of Japan, *The Geisha Boy* offered a brief cameo by HAYAKAWA spoofing his Academy-Award nominated role in THE BRIDGE ON THE RIVER KWAI (1957). Released a year after SAYONARA in which two star-crossed lovers involved in an interracial romance committed suicide, *The Geisha Boy* permitted the developing interracial romance between Wooley and Kimi not to sidetrack the plot line: The fumbling hero returns to Japan not only to bring the stowaway boy back to his relatives but also to see his Japanese (girl)friend again. (Perhaps the filmmakers reasoned that because Lewis was playing a buffoon in a slapstick farce, the multicultural romance would not be taken seriously by filmgoers and thus would cause no offense.)

Canadian-born McCarthy would have one of her most effective screen assignments in the western *WALK LIKE A DRAGON* (1960).

geishas In the Japanese culture, a geisha refers to a Japanese woman who has been specially trained in the traditional art of being a professional singer, dancer, and companion for men. It never infers, as Westerners have long assumed and/or suspected, that such a female's activities involve being a prostitute. Playing the role of a geisha on screen—as Hollywood scriptwriters interpreted or often misrepresented them—was considered an acting challenge (or novelty opportunity) for actresses in Hollywood-made films.

Among the American-made feature films involving geishas or geisha-type, traditionally costumed females were: *MADAME BUTTERFLY* (1915 and 1932), *A Heart in Pawn* (1919), *TEAHOUSE OF THE AUGUST MOON* (1956), *Joe Butterfly* (1957), *SAYONARA* (1957), *Cry for Happy* (1961), *MY GEISHA* (1962), and *AMERICAN GEISHA* (1986—TV movie). (See MUSICALS—FEATURE FILMS for movies in which a performer sang arias from the opera *Madama Butterfly*.)

On television, one of the more famous "geisha" impersonations was by Lucille Ball in the "Lucy Goes to Japan" episode (1962) of *The Lucille Ball-Desi Arnaz Show.*

General Died at Dawn, The **(1936)** Paramount, b&w, 98 minutes. **Director:** Lewis Milestone; **Screenplay:** Clifford Odets; **Cast:** Gary Cooper (O'Hara), Madeleine Carroll (Judy Perrie), Akim Tamiroff (General Yang), Dudley Digges (Mr. Wu), Porter Hall (Peter Perrie), William Frawley (Brighton), Philip Ahn (Oxford), Lee Tung-Foo (Mr. Chen), Val Duran (Wong), Willie Fung (bartender).

Hollywood was in the midst of a relative explosion of big-budgeted Chinese-themed epics in the mid 1930s, creating, as a result, a shortage of Chinese talent available for the sound stages. Because *The General Died at Dawn*, based on Charles G. Booth's 1936 novel, required more than 700 Chinese extras, farmers from the San Joaquin Valley in northern California were employed.

This atmospheric war drama focuses on American soldier-of-fortune O'Hara who is based in China, where General Yang is maneuvering to control the country's twelve provinces and thus the lucrative markets in opium, silk, and rice. Yang's rival, Wu, hires O'Hara to acquire an armament shipment from an American gun runner (Frawley), now in Shanghai. Meanwhile, Yang commissions two Americans—Perrie and his daughter Judy—to waylay O'Hara, grab his armament money, and turn the adventurer over to Yang. The plan goes awry, leading to the death of Perrie and others, including Yang. O'Hara and Judy pursue their love.

Russian-born Tamiroff and Irish actor Digges had key roles as opposing Chinese warlords, with several familiar Asian-American actors, such as AHN, playing subordinate parts. *The General Died at Dawn* received three Oscar nominations: Best Cinematography, Best Score, and Best Supporting Actor (Tamiroff).

Girl Named Tamiko, A **(1962)** Paramount, color, 110 minutes. **Director:** John Sturges; **Screenplay:** Edward Anhalt; **Cast:** Laurence Harvey (Ivan Kalin), France Nuyen (Tamiko), Martha Hyer (Fay Wilson), Gary Merrill (Max Wilson), Michael Wilding (Nigel Costairs), Miyoshi Umeki (Eiko), Bob Okazaki (Kimitaka).

Following the lead of *SAYONARA* (1957), *THE WORLD OF SUZIE WONG* (1960), and *BRIDGE TO THE SUN* (1961), this derivative entry, based on the 1959 novel by Ronald de Levington Kirkbride, delineated an interracial relationship that had built-in roadblocks against success. Here, the antihero is Ivan Kalin, a Russo-Chinese; his lover, Tamiko, is Japanese (from a well-respected family). This potential intermingling of cultures is especially handicapped because Kalin has a burning hatred of the Japanese, who killed his parents during the war (the only new twist).

What made the interaction between the couple unimpressive was the fact that Kalin, a photographer working in Japan, was a phenomenal manipulator of anyone who could help him achieve his goals of relocating to the United States and becoming well known in his field. His craftiness led him into an affair with Fay Wilson, a receptionist at the U.S. Embassy. Along the way, he ditched his live-in mistress, Eiko, and exploited a casual friendship with a renowned Japanese painter (Okazaki) to do a photo essay. In true movie non-logic, at the finale, Kalin did not join Fay on a one-way ticket to America but remained behind with Tamiko.

The film's highlights were the location shots of the Toshogu Shrine at Nikko, the Todaiji Temple, Lake Biwa near Kyoto, and Tokyo.

Girls of the White Orchid **(aka: *Death Ride to Osaka*) (1983)** NBC-TV, color, 100 minutes. **Director:** Jonathan Kaplan; **Teleplay:** Carole Raschella and Michael Raschella; **Cast:** Jennifer Jason-Leigh (Carol Heath), Thomas Byrd (Don Potter), Mako (Mori), Carolyn Seymour (Mme. Mori), Richard Narita (Shiro), Soon-Tek Oh (Hatanaka), Ann Jillian (Marilyn).

Mixing the topics of prostitution with the allure of Japanese scenery and its Mafia, *Girls of the White Orchid* was more soap opera than solid drama. It involves a naïve young singer (Jason-Leigh) from Los Angeles who is hired to work in a seedy Tokyo nightclub. Before long, she is drawn into a white-slavery ring controlled by the Yakuza (the Japanese underworld).

This narrative was based on the true-life events of a young woman who answered an ad for American singers to entertain in Japan and found herself corralled into a prostitution–slavery ring. Any similarity between the Japanese underworld detailed here and that in Robert Mitchum's superior *THE YAKUZA* (1975) was purely coincidental. MAKO was wasted in his minimized role in this TV movie.

Go for Broke! **(1951)** Metro-Goldwyn-Mayer, b&w, 92 minutes. **Director/Screenplay:** Robert Pirosh; **Cast:** Van Johnson (Lt. Michael Grayson), Lane Naiano (Sam), George Miki (Chick), Akira Fukunaga (Frank), Ken K. Okamoto (Kaz), Henry Oyasato (Takashi), Harry Hamada (Masami).

Pirosh, the Academy Award-winning scripter of MGM's *Battleground* (1949), was researching that acclaimed combat picture when he came across information on the 442nd Regimental Combat Team, composed entirely of Japanese-American volunteers. During World War II, they and the similarly constituted 100th Infantry Battalion had a distinguished war record: seven major campaigns in Europe, 9,486 casualties, 18,143 individual decorations, and seven presidential unit citations. It was decided to make a positive motion picture saluting these little-known heroes rather than, as initially suggested by studio head Dore Schary, do a realistic film based on the American internment camps for Japanese-American civilians during World War II, a project that could only be unflattering to the United States.

Before *Go for Broke!* (a pidgin English expression meaning "shoot the works") dissolved into a standard war entry, it followed Lt. Michael Grayson, who is eager for his assignment at Camp Shelby, Mississippi, in 1943. The biased Texan is aghast when he is told that his platoon will be composed entirely of Japanese-American volunteers. His commanding officer insists that Grayson carry out the assignment. As Grayson comes to know the Nisei, he appreciates their enthusiasm and steadfastness. The unit is not sent to the Pacific Theater of War for fear that, during combat, Allied soldiers would mistake them for the Axis enemy. Instead, the Japanese-American soldiers ship out in May 1944 to Italy, where they prove themselves repeatedly in battle, despite debilitating acts of bigotry from fellow soldiers (and from captured German troops).

Having popular and wholesome Johnson in the lead role created a safety net in marketing this offbeat film, but it also distracted from the real-life members of the 442nd who performed in this retelling of their battle campaigns.

***Golden Gate* (1993)** Samuel Goldwyn, color, 90 minutes. **Director:** John Madden; **Screenplay:** David Henry Hwang; **Cast:** Matt Dillon (Kevin Walker), Joan Chen (Marilyn Song), Bruno Kirby (Ron Pirelli), Teri Polo (Cynthia), Tzi Ma (Chen Jung Song), Stan Egi (Bradley Ichiyasu).

Hwang's screenplay crammed too much activity into the film's ninety minutes, and the characters emerged as merely types. The movie, however, was important because it highlighted another section of "hidden" U.S. history dealing with Chinese Americans—the latter's persecution at the hands of the omnipresent FBI.

In 1952 young Kevin Walker, an FBI agent in their San Francisco office, is ordered to uncover, by any means possible, an increasing quota of alleged communists to please Bureau chief, J. Edgar Hoover. One of his unmaskings is that of honest laundry worker Chen Jung Song who sends money to his family in China. On the basis of that and trumped up charges, the innocent man is railroaded to prison. When released a decade later, the disheartened ex-convict commits suicide near the Golden Gate Bridge. A remorseful Walker attends the funeral, leading to his romance with the deceased's daughter, Marilyn. When she discovers his association to her past, she rebuffs him.

Six years later, Walker is investigating supposed seditious activities at a local campus. Marilyn belongs to one of the minority groups on whom the bureau is keeping a close watch. Meanwhile, she weds activist Bradley Ichiyasu, although she still loves Walker. With a belated sense of conscience, the guilt-ridden Walker helps Song by giving her the FBI's file on her dad. By the finale, Marilyn's dad has killed himself.

***Good Earth, The* (1937)** Metro-Goldwyn-Mayer, b&w [originally released in sepia tones], 138 minutes. **Director:** Sidney Franklin and uncredited Victor Fleming; **Screenplay:** Talbot Jennings, Tess Slesinger, and Claudine West; **Cast:** Paul Muni (Wang Lung), Luise Rainer (O-Lan), Walter Connolly (Uncle), Tilly Losch (Lotus), Charley Grapewin (Old Father), Jessie Ralph (Cuckoo), Soo Yong (Aunt), Keye Luke (Elder Son), Roland Lui (Younger Son), Suzanna Kim (Little Fool), Harold Huber (Cousin).

Pearl Buck's Pulitzer Prize-winning novel, *The Good Earth* (1931), and its short-lasting Broadway adaptation (1933) by Owen Davis and Donald Davis provided the basis for this elaborate drama. Because China was then an ally of the United States, MGM toned down the book's occasional unflattering references to China and/or its people. In softening the material, for example, the "Lotus" figure, a prostitute, is depicted euphemistically as an entertainer, sexual situations were removed, the romantic triangle among Lotus, Wang, and Younger Son was downplayed, and so on.

From 1933 onward, the studio tested an assortment of performers of varying nationalities and races for lead parts. Most of the choices for Wang Lung were Caucasian and included Swedish-born Nils Asther and French-born Charles Boyer. Eventually middle-European émigré Muni won the assignment. Discussed to play O-Lan were American-born Katharine Cornell and Barbara Stanwyck, but it was Austrian actress Rainer who got the prized part. Among those tested for Lotus were ANNA MAY WONG, Lotus Lui, and MAMO CLARK, but Viennese performer Losch did the role. PHILIP AHN, PHILSON AHN, RICHARD LOO, and Ray Mala were in contention to play Elder Son; American-born KEYE LUKE was hired for the part. Complicating the casting decisions were two strictures: (1) If a key part was given to a non-Caucasian, then to avoid the "taint" of miscegenation on the screen, the performer playing opposite that individual must be of the same racial heritage; (2) the Chinese government had stated publicly that no actor of Japanese descent was to be cast or the film would not receive the country's approval of the movie. Finally, of the fifteen performers listed in the on-screen credits, only seven were of Asian backgrounds.

The mammoth production—the last produced by studio executive Irving Thalberg, who died a few weeks after principal photography was completed—was shot in the Los Angeles area. When released, this well-mounted epic was regarded favorably by critics and public alike for its narrative of a simple Chinese family beleaguered by poverty and greed. A key highlight of the lengthy picture was the invasion of locusts that destroyed the Chinese farmers' crops.

The Good Earth won Academy Awards for Best Actress (Rainer) and Best Cinematography. It received Oscar nominations for Best Director, Best Film Editing, and Best Picture. Made at a cost of almost $3 million, the prestigious picture grossed almost $4 million in domestic and foreign release.

Green Hornet, the Superheroes were gaining in popularity in the 1930s as the world became engulfed in the Great Depression. *The Green Hornet* began as a radio property in 1936 telling of Britt Reid, the playboy publisher who, according to the show's opening, "hunts . . . public enemies that even the G-men cannot reach." Assisting Reid in his constant new adventures is Kato, his helpful Oriental houseboy. (As was typical in this era, Asian characters, like African Americans, were generally used in storylines featuring Caucasians only as either domestics or as dastardly villains.) Kato was played during the radio years by Raymond Hayashi, Rollon Parker, and Michael Tolan. In December 1941, when the United States declared war on Japan, the nationality of Kato was switched from Japanese to Filipino.

The radio series continued—with a few breaks in between when the program changed networks—through 1952. Meanwhile, in 1940, Universal turned out two thirteen-chapter serials: *THE GREEN HORNET* and *The Green Hornet Strikes Again.* The first featured Gordon Jones as the Green Hornet with KEYE LUKE (of CHARLIE CHAN fame and of Chinese heritage) as his faithful Kato. The second chapterplay had Luke again as Kato but now with Warren Hull as the playboy publisher.

In the mid-1960s, encouraged by the success of its campy *Batman* (1966–68) TV series, Twentieth Century-Fox produced a companion piece, *THE GREEN HORNET* (1966–67). It featured Van Williams as Britt Reid (who now also owned a TV station) and BRUCE LEE as the hero's manservant Kato.

In 2001, plans to bring *The Green Hornet* to the big screen with JET LI as Kato fizzled.

***Green Hornet, The* (1940)** Universal, b&w, 13 chapters. **Directors:** Ford Beebe and Ray Taylor; **Screenplay:** Basil Dickey, Lyonel Margolies, George H. Plympton, and Morrison Wood; **Cast:** Gordon Jones (the Green Hornet [Britt Reid]), Keye Luke (Kato), Wade Boteler (Michael Axford), Phillip Trent (Jasper Jens), Cy Kendall (Monroe), Anne Nagel (Lenore Case), Arthur Loft (Joe Ogden); **Chapters:** (1) The Tunnel of Terror, (2) The Thundering Terror, (3) Flying Coffins, (4) Pillar of Flame, (5) The Time Bomb, (6) Highways of Peril, (7) Bridge of Disaster, (8) Dead Or Alive, (9) The Hornet Trapped, (10) Bullets and Ballots, (11) Disaster Rides the Rails, (12) Panic in the Zoo, (13) Doom of the Underworld.

Based on the highly popular radio series of THE GREEN HORNET, which ran from 1936 to 1952, this hastily assembled serial featured crusading publisher and playboy Britt Reid combating, in thirteen cliffhanger installments, a variety of criminal gangs (munitions racketeers, auto theft groups, etc.). In the guise of the masked Green Hornet, Reid, accompanied by his trusty Japanese servant Kato (also masked), pursued the nefarious crooks.

For a rare change on screen, here was an Asian-American hero, albeit in the subservient role of servant/helper. Nevertheless, it was a big change from the stereotype of the sinister Yellow Peril, DR. FU MANCHU. LUKE, who had already played CHARLIE CHAN'S #1 son Lee and other (would-be) sleuths was properly adept as the accomplished assistant to his Caucasian boss. He could keep a home tidy, repair the Black Beauty car, and hold his own against rampaging hoodlums. The fact that Luke was a New York City-born Chinese American and not Nipponese did not seem to matter to the filmmakers (or for most Caucasian moviegoers).

A condensed feature version of the serial was issued by Universal who, the next year, released the thirteen-episode *The Green Hornet Strikes Again*, with Luke remaining as Kato, but this time Warren Hull was Britt Reid/The Green Hornet.

By this point, Twentieth Century-Fox had already discontinued its MR. MOTO series because it felt that Japan's growing worldwide aggression dictated against having a Japanese hero on screen. Although Universal felt no such compunction, the radio version of *The Green Hornet* switched Kato's nationality from Japanese to Filipino *after* the Japanese attack on Pearl Harbor in December 1941.

***Green Hornet, The* (1966–1967)** ABC-TV series, color, 30 minutes. **Cast:** Van Williams (the Green Hornet [Britt Reid]), Bruce Lee (Kato), Wende Wagner (Lenore "Casey" Case), Lloyd Gough (Mike Axford), Walter Brooks (D.A. F. P. Scanlon), Gary Owens (TV newscaster).

With the success of their *Batman* TV series (1966–68), the same production team rushed this adventure offering on the air. Taking up where the radio adventures (1936–52) and 1940s movie serials of THE GREEN HORNET left off, the show featured playboy Britt Reid who owned *The Daily Sentinel* newspaper (and a TV station) and in his spare time fought organized crime as the masked wonder man, the Green Hornet. His Asian manservant Kato was his helper on the home and crime-fighting front.

Kato was portrayed by handsome, athletic LEE, a master of his own brand of kung fu. His lightning-fast body-crunching blows were the highlight of the show. But since Kato was a subordinate on the series, most of the camera time was devoted to Reid, the Caucasian crime fighter. Nevertheless, Lee was the sole Asian-American icon for young America watching television in the mid-1960s.

***Gung Ho* (1986)** Paramount, color, 111 minutes. **Director:** Ron Howard; **Screenplay:** Lowell Ganz and Babaloo Mandel; **Cast:** Michael Keaton (Hunt Stevenson), Gedde Watanabe (Kazihiro), George Wendt (Buster), Mimi Rogers (Audrey), John Turturro (Willie), Soh Yamamura (Sakamoto), Sab Shimono (Saito), Rodney Kageyama (Ito).

This middling comedy about culture clashes exploits American businesses' infatuation with Japanese methods of corporate management, a craze that reached its height in the mid-1980s. The movie propounds the commonly held theory that although Japan may have lost World War II, it conquered much of the globe thereafter with its astounding economic recovery and expansion.

Set in the run-down factory town of Hadleyville, Pennsylvania, the premise focuses on the arrival of Japanese executives, under the command of determined Kazihiro, to reopen the closed auto plant that will now use Japanese methods of production-line efficiency and teamwork. Hunt Stevenson, the one who engineered the deal, now finds himself leading his American pals at the plant into fulfilling the output expectations of the new Nipponese owners (and interceding when the two sides clash).

A TV series adaptation of *Gung Ho* ran for a season (1986–87), featuring Watanabe and several others from the original cast.

H

Hall, Juanita (1901–1968) She gained her show business reputation playing Asians. (Actually she was three-quarters Scottish-Irish, one-eighth African American, and one-eighth Chinook Native American.) On screen, she was Bloody Mary, the boisterous, betel-chewing native in *SOUTH PACIFIC* (1958—a role she created on Broadway) and later cavorted as the Chinese Auntie Liang in *FLOWER DRUM SONG* (1961).

Born in Keyport, New Jersey, she was on her own at age fourteen, was on Broadway in the 1930s in *The Green Pastures* as a member of the Hall Johnson Choir, and returned to Broadway to play the Mango Woman in the tropical-set *The Pirate* (1942) with Alfred Lunt and Lynn Fontanne. In Rodgers and Hammerstein's stage musical *South Pacific* (1949), she gained acclaim singing "Bali Ha'i." She came back to the New York stage a decade later for the composer's *Flower Drum Song*. Her film debut was in *Paradise in Harlem* (1939).

***Happy Days* (1974–1984)** ABC-TV series, color, 30 minutes. **Cast:** Ron Howard (Richie Cunningham: 1974–80), Henry Winkler (Arthur "Fonzie" Fonzarelli), Tom Bosley (Howard Cunningham), Marion Ross (Marion Cunningham), Anson Williams (Warren "Potsie" Weber: 1974–83), Donny Most (Ralph Malph: 1974–80), Erin Moran (Joannie Cunningham), Pat Morita (Arnold [Matsuo Takahashi]: 1975–76, 1982–83), Scott Baio (Charles "Chachi" Arcola: 1977–84).

In this exceedingly popular nostalgia series set in 1950s and 1960s Milwaukee, Wisconsin, the scene sometimes shifted from the Cunningham household to such local spots as Arnold's Drive-In, a malt shop/hamburger joint located near the school that Ritchie and the other students attended. The proprietor was feisty, hot-tempered, but well-meaning Japanese-American Arnold (whose actual name is Matsuo Takahashi). His presence in the show's predominantly Caucasian cast was used for generating laughs, not to provide his character's development.

By the fall of 1976, Arnold disappeared from the cast of regulars as MORITA had earned his own TV series. He was replaced by the character of Alfred Delvecchio (1976–82) played by Al Molinaro. When that figure left the show, Morita's Arnold returned for recurring appearances during the 1982–83 season of *Happy Days*, by which time Fonzie had become coproprietor of the teenager hangout. Morita participated in the 1992 *Happy Days Reunion*, which aired on television.

***Hatchet Man, The* (1932)** First National/Warner Bros., b&w, 74 minutes. **Director:** William A. Wellman; **Screenplay:** J. Grubb Alexander; **Cast:** Edward G. Robinson (Wong Low Get), Loretta Young (Toya San), Dudley Digges (Nog Hong Fah), Leslie Fenton (Harry En Hai), Edmund Breese (Yu Chang), Tully Marshall (Log Sen Yat), J. Carrol Naish (Sun Yat Ming), Charles Middleton (Lip Hop Fat), E. Allyn Warren (Soo Lat, the cobbler).

Caucasian actors often had a fascination about portraying traditional Asian characters on stage or on screen. They were drawn to these roles primarily for the opportunity to shake off their established professional image and become immersed in a portrayal that depended on subtle gestures, movements, reactions, speech cadence, as well as makeup. A past master of such impersonations was LON CHANEY in *MR. WU* (1927). ROBINSON, the star of *The Hatchet Man*, had already played an Oriental in *EAST IS WEST* (1930). Others, such as Virginia-born Warren, had been Orientals many times on camera. For costar Young, who had and would play many nationalities on screen and television, this assignment was her first in an Asian mode.

Edward G. Robinson and Loretta Young in *The Hatchet Man* (1932). (JC ARCHIVES)

Based on the play (production undetermined) *The Honorable Mr. Wong* by Achmed Abdullah and David Belasco, it told of Wong Low Get, a hatchet man for the Lem Sing Tong in early twentieth-century San Francisco. When a tong war breaks out, Wong Low is ordered to kill a dear friend. The latter (Naish), before he dies, requests that Wong Low look out for his daughter Toya and marry her when she is an adult. Years pass and Wong Low, who has done a great deal to Americanize himself, is prevented from keeping his promise because Toya plans to wed Harry En Hai. Later, Toya writes from China to say how miserable she is with Harry. Wong Low, who has suffered business reversals and is now a field hand, works shoveling coal on a steamship to pay for his passage to China to rescue Toya.

Expectedly, many in the cast, including Robinson, had great difficulty with their characterizations, vainly trying to shed their American accents and mannerisms. Filmgoers and critics alike could not accept the screen's *Little Caesar* (1931) as anything but a snarling, tough gangster. One can only imagine the amusement and/or indignation that this sensationalized screen story caused for Asian-American moviegoers.

Hawaii Long before Hawaii became the United States's fiftieth state in August 1959, it had developed an association in the minds of Americans as a lush tourist destination. Thus, Hollywood frequently used the tropical destination as a plot point in feature films, playing up its quaint association with Americans as a tourist site (e.g., *Hawaii*, 1919; *South Seas Rose*, 1929; *Flirtation Walk*, 1934; *Waikiki Wedding*, 1937; *HAWAII CALLS*, 1938; *Honolulu*, 1939; *In the Navy*, 1941; *Moonlight in Hawaii*, 1941; *Mexican Spitfire at Sea*, 1942; *Ma and Pa Kettle at Waikiki*, 1955; *BLUE HAWAII*, 1961; *Gidget Goes Hawaiian*, 1961; *Ride the Wild Surf*, 1964; *Paradise, Hawaiian Style*, 1966; *North Shore*, 1987; *Aloha Summer*, 1988; and *Saved by the Bell–Hawaiian Style* (1992—TV movie). Contemporary big-screen soap operas such as *DIAMOND HEAD* (1962), as well as feature films such as *HAWAII* (1966) and its sequel, *THE HAWAIIANS* (1970), sought to present the history of the islands, focusing on how the white man corrupted the peaceful natives.

Everything changed, of course, for Hawaii with the Japanese attack on Pearl Harbor in December 1941. Thus, Hawaii was frequently also depicted on screen as the site of the tragedy that led to America's official entry into World War II. For decades after the Japanese attack, sinister contra-American activities in Hawaii and recreations of the sneak attack on Pearl Harbor were a constant theme of Hollywood-made productions, including: *Remember Pearl Harbor* (1942), *From Here to Eternity* (1953), *The Revolt of Mamie Stover* (1956), *In Love and War* (1958); *TORA! TORA TORA!* (1970), *From Here to Eternity* (1979—TV miniseries), *Pearl* (1979—TV miniseries), and *Pearl Harbor* (2001).

Another aspect of Hawaii that appealed to moviemakers was the public's association of Hawaii with the inscrutable Far East. Thus it created a perfect site for entries in big screen detective series (e.g., *THE BLACK CAMEL*, 1931), as a hotbed of communist infiltrators (e.g., *Big Jim McLain*, 1952) and other nefarious undertakings (e.g., *Blue, White and Perfect*, 1941; *Code Name: Diamond Head*, 1977—TV movie; *M Station: Hawaii*, 1980—TV movie; *Hard Ticket to Hawaii*, 1987; *Blackbelt*, 1993).

In the television media, Hawaii was a favored exotic spot for TV series of a variety of genres. It was assumed that the use of the tropical locale, a few subordinate Asian-American characters, and native music would enhance any entry, no matter how ordinary. Among the many teleseries to be set there were: *HAWAIIAN EYE* (1959–1963), *HAWAII FIVE-O* (1968–80), *BIG HAWAII* (1977), *MAGNUM P.I.* (1980–88), *Hawaiian Heat* (1984), *Island Son* (1989–90), *Byrds of Paradise* (1994), and *BAYWATCH HAWAII* (1999–2001).

***Hawaii* (1966)** United Artists, color, 186 minutes. **Director:** George Roy Hill; **Screenplay:** Dalton Trumbo and Daniel Taradash; **Cast:** Julie Andrews (Jerusha Bromley), Max Von Sydow (Abner Hale), Richard Harris (Rafer Hoxworth), Carroll O'Connor (Charles Bromley), Elizabeth Cole (Abigail Bromley), Torin Thatcher (Reverend Thorn), Gene Hackman (John Whipple), Jocelyn La Garde (Queen Malama), Manu Tupou (Keoki), Ted Nobriga (Kelolo), Bette Midler (ship's passenger).

James A. Michener's epic novel (1959) provided the basis for this sprawling study of how Americans from the mainland, in the name of godliness and/or commerce, did much to destroy the people and land of Hawaii from the nineteenth century onward. Thus, *Hawaii* presented a harrowing indictment, one that many filmgoers were not willing to accept. The inordinate length of the screen saga (which covered only a part of the novel) also put off viewers. On the plus side, the film's depiction—before the arrival of the despoilers—of the "heathen" natives and their ruler who were so content in their leisurely tropical lifestyle, was a joy to observe.

In 1820, Abner Hale, a New England farm boy, graduates from Yale Divinity School and plans to take God's words to Hawaii to convert the natives. He weds Jerusha Bromley, even though she loves the long-absent sea captain, Rafer Hoxworth. Once on the tropic isles, the convivial Jerusha makes friends with the natives and their pleasant ruler, Queen Malama. But the ultrastern, sanctimonious Hale insists on weaning the natives from their long-time rituals and rites, including their custom of incest between sister and brother. Despite this conflict, when the queen is dying, she asks to be converted to Christianity. That accomplished, her banished brother Kelolo returns to rebury her elsewhere according to pagan rites.

Over the years, as more white people come to the islands, they bring disease and cultural ruin to many of the natives. In the end, the unyielding Abner, long since a widower, is dismissed from his ministry but insists on remaining on the island to carry on God's work, while his three sons sail to England for their education.

Hawaii received six Oscar nominations: Best Cinematography (Color), Best Costume Design (Color), Best Original Score, Best Song ("My Wishing Doll"), Best Sound, and Best Supporting Actress (La Garde). The inferior *THE HAWAIIANS*, the sequel to this saga, appeared four years later with unspectacular boy office results.

***Hawaii Calls* (1938)** RKO, b&w, 72 minutes. **Director:** Edward F. Cline; **Screenplay:** Wanda Tuchock; **Cast:** Bobby Breen (Billy Coulter), Ned Sparks (Strings), Irvin S. Cobb (Captain O'Hara), Gloria Holden (Mrs. Milburn), Warren Hull (Com. Joe Millburn), Mamo Clark (Hina), Pua Lani (Pua), Philip Ahn (Julius), Birdie De Bolt (Aunty Pinau).

HAWAII, once associated mostly with lush tropical vacations, developed other connotations to American filmgoers after the attack on Pearl Harbor by the Japanese in December 1941, but three years earlier, it was still a backdrop for inconsequential musicals such as this entry. While rear projection and sound stage sets provided filmgoers a "tour" of the islands, there was a carefree quality to this low-budget offering that successfully suggested the lure of this travel destination.

Orphan Billy Coulter and his young Hawaiian pal Pua are stowaways aboard an ocean liner bound from San Francisco to Hawaii. After being caught by the ship's captain, they slip overboard and swim ashore. They first visit Pua's sister Hina and then depart for Maui, where Aunty Pinau resides. Meanwhile, foreign agents snatch secret government documents from navy Com. Joe Milburn. Billy proves to be the hero of the day and eventually returns to San Francisco, chaperoned by Milburn and his wife.

This picture was based on Don Blanding's novel *Stowaways in Paradise* (1931).

***Hawaii Five-O* (1968–1980)** CBS-TV series, color, 60 minutes. **Cast:** Jack Lord (Det. Steve McGarrett), James MacArthur (Det. Danny Williams: 1968–79), Kam Fong (Det. Chin Ho Kelly: 1968–78), Zulu (Det. Kon Kalakaua: 1968–72), Richard Denning (Gov. Philip Grey), Al Harrington (Det. Ben Kokua: 1972–74), Laura Sode (Luana: 1978–80), Moe Keale (Truck Keolooha: 1979–80), William Smith (James "Kimo" Carew: 1979–80).

An exceedingly popular police drama, this hour-long series was filmed on location in Hawaii with much of the action taking place in and around picturesque Honolulu. Hard-nosed McGarrett heads a special crime unit (the Five-O) which was part of the state police system, and he reports directly to the state's governor. With executive producer Lord in charge, there was surprisingly little turnover in the cast over the dozen years, but, to be noted in this Hawaiian jurisdiction, the squad leaders were two Caucasians, while the assistants were Hawaiian-American characters. Among the many criminals pursued, trapped, and arrested (or killed) during the long-lasting show, the most vicious and ingenious of the Hawaiian underworld proved to be Wo Fat (played by KHIGH DHIEGH). He was in the 100-minute telefeature which preceded the show's premiere on September 26, 1968, by six days, and was featured in the program's last episode entitled "Woe to Wo Fat."

***Hawaiian Eye* (1959–1963)** ABC-TV series, b&w, 60 minutes. **Cast:** Bob Conrad (Tom Lopaka), Anthony Eisley (Tracy Stele: 1959–62), Connie Stevens (Cricket Blake), Poncie Ponce (Kazuo Kim), Grant Williams (Greg MacKenzie: 1960–63), Mel Prestidge (Quon: 1960–63), Doug Mossman (Moke: 1960–63), Troy Donahue (Philip Barton: 1962–63), Clayton Naluai (Bert).

Mostly filmed on the studio back lot in Burbank, California, the series had many parallels to 77 *Sunset Strip* (1958–64) packaged by the same production team, with occasional crossovers between the two TV series. With a lobby office at the Hawaiian Village (later known as the Hilton Hawaiian Village) Hotel, young detectives Tom Lopaka and Tracy Stele operate their firm, Hawaiian Eye-Investigation-Protection. Their helper is somewhat dizzy Cricket Blake, a photographer/club singer who runs a gift shop at the hotel. Most of their indispensable backup support comes from Kazuo Kim, the cabbie who owns a one-taxi service. He has wide knowledge of the islands and has many helpful relatives and contacts.

As played by Maui, Hawaii–born Ponce, Kazuo Kim was the eccentric soul who was hardly ever without his trusty ukulele, always wore a silly straw hat, and had an inexhaustible supply of dumb jokes.

A few other actual ethnics were used on this series, including Nalusai as the hotel's parking-lot attendant and Mikio Kato as Tom Lopaka's receptionist.

***Hawaiians, The* (1970)** United Artists, color, 134 minutes. **Director:** Tom Gries; **Screenplay:** James R. Webb; **Cast:** Charlton Heston (Whip Hoxworth), Tina Chen (Nyuk Tsin), Geraldine Chaplin (Purity Hoxworth), John Phillip Law (Noel Hoxworth), Alex McCowen (Micah Hale), Mako (Mun

Ki), Miko Mayama (Fumiko), Virginia Lee (Mei Li), Naomi Stevens (Queen Liliuokalani), Khigh Dhiegh (Kai Chung).

This little-anticipated sequel to *HAWAII* (1965) took other segments of James A. Michener's sprawling historical novel (1959) and related the further disruption of the island paradise by later generations of Caucasian transplants. Whereas the earlier movie dealt with the attempted religious conversion of the natives, this follow-up depicted the commercial exploitation of the natural resources, natives, and imported Chinese "slaves" to turn the area into the Republic of Hawaii.

Whatever the casting faults in *Hawaii*, it was only compounded in this weak continuation. Between the wooden Heston, the lightweight Law, and the pouty Chaplin, there was not much life in the picture. Fortunately many of the Asian-American talents utilized in the film gave some needed verisimilitude to the vapid proceedings. But Stevens as Queen Liliuokalani (1837–1917), the last reigning queen of the Hawaiian Islands, did not compare to Oscar-nominee Jocelyn La Garde, who played Queen Malama in *Hawaii*.

Hayakawa, Sessue (1889–1973) The first Asian to become an American movie star, during Hollywood's silent era, Hayakawa was the leading man in many films, some of which he produced. In later years, as a character actor, he won an Oscar nomination as Colonel Saito in *THE BRIDGE ON THE RIVER KWAI* (1957).

Born Kintaro Hayakawa to a well-to-do family in Chiba, Japan, he intended to enter the military, but a physical impairment kept him out. Ashamed, he attempted hara-kiri. While recuperating, he studied Zen and then came to the United States in 1908 to study at the University of Chicago. Later, he came back to America with an acting company. He made his screen debut in *The Hateful God* (1913) and stood out as the villain in *THE CHEAT* (1915). His features frequently found him as an Asian who was caught in an ill-fated interracial love. Occasionally, he was seen as a Chinese as in *The Tong Man* (1919) or even as an Hispanic matador (*The Brand of Lopez*, 1920).

After an unsuccessful bid for stardom in talkies, he left Hollywood, making films primarily in France. He returned to American moviemaking with Humphrey Bogart's starrer, *TOKYO JOE* (1949) and was the humane Japanese prison camp officer in *THREE CAME HOME* (1950). In *Green Mansions* (1959) he played a South American native and was a pirate chief in *Swiss Family Robinson* (1960). During the decades, he often performed with his actress wife Tsuru Aoki.

In June 1966, Hayakawa was quoted in *Films in Review* magazine as saying, "The bias of those days [1910s and 1920s] against Orientals was a great help to me. We underscored it in our story-lines and the public never took it out on me personally."

***Heaven & Earth* (1993)** Warner Bros, color, 140 minutes. **Director/Screenplay:** Oliver Stone; **Cast:** Tommy Lee

Hiep Thi Le and Joan Chen in *Heaven & Earth* (1983). (JC ARCHIVES)

Jones (Steve Butler), Haing S. Ngor (Papa), Joan Chen (Mama), Hiep Thi Le (Le Ly Hayslip), Dustin Nguyen (Sau), Michael Paul Chan (interrogator), Vivian Wu (Madame Lien), Long Nguyen (Anh), Debbie Reynolds (Eugenia).

With *Heaven & Earth*, filmmaker Stone completed his Vietnam-themed trilogy begun with *PLATOON* (1986) and *Born on the Fourth of July* (1989). The unsubtle *Heaven & Earth* was based on the autobiographical works *When Heaven and Earth Changed Places* (1989) by Le Ly Hayslip and Jay Wurts and *Child of Wax, Women of Peace* (1993) by Le Ly and James Hayslip. The Vietnam sections of the film were shot in Thailand.

Unlike Stone's other Vietnam-focused pictures, this one is from a woman's point of view. It is narrated by the character Le Ly who, at the start, is living in a small Vietnamese farming village. When war comes, Le Ly spies for the Vietcong; later she is tortured by the South Vietnamese. Eventually, she and her mother (CHEN) relocate to Saigon, where the young woman is used and discarded by a local businessman. Tired of her daily survival struggle, Le Ly marries the American marine Steve Butler. After the fall of Saigon, he takes her to California. As the war has so totally altered her, so it has Butler. A tortured soul, he can't adjust to civilian life. Le Ly and he divorce; Butler later commits suicide. Years later, Le Ly, now successful in her own business, returns to Vietnam with her sons to revisit her family and village.

The saga of Le Ly's hellish life was unified by the woman's indomitable spirit which derived from her Buddhist faith. In some ways, her story of coming to the United States paralleled Carol Kane's Jewish immigrant character in *Hester Street* (1975) and how she created a place for herself in the new land. Both Chen and NGOR as Le Ly's parents offered sturdy performances as pawns of war caught in a changing world where their cultural traditions helped them to cope.

Heaven & Earth and the Vietnamese section of *WHAT'S COOKING?* (2000) were among the few recent mainstream U.S. films to present effectively the Vietnamese experience in the United States.

***Hell in the Pacific* (1968)** Cinerama, color, 103 minutes. **Director:** John Boorman; **Screenplay:** Alexander Jacob and Eric Bercovici; **Cast:** Lee Marvin (American soldier), Toshiro Mifune (Japanese soldier).

With a cast of only two, this unusual drama depicted the hellishness and futility of war. Because so much screen time was devoted to each participant, the film had ample opportunity to examine closely the mentality of a Japanese officer, something most American-made combat features ignored.

In 1944, somewhere in the Pacific, a Japanese naval officer and a U.S. marine pilot become separated from their own military groups and find themselves alone on the isle together. After a time, each becomes aware of the other but chooses not to kill his opponent. At one point, the Japanese soldier takes the American prisoner, but this situation is later reversed. The Japanese instigates the building of a raft, and they eventually reach a distant island, also uninhabited. They find supplies, and all is peaceful until the Asian comes across a magazine with photos of slain Japanese. Each now goes his own way. (Some release prints of the film had an alternative ending in which an explosion was detonated, suggesting that both men die.)

This was one of the several English-language film appearances by Japanese star/director Mifune (1920–97).

***Hell to Eternity* (1960)** Allied Artists, b&w, 132 minutes. **Director:** Phil Karlson; **Screenplay:** Ted Sherdeman and Walter Roeber Schmidt; **Cast:** Jeffrey Hunter (Guy Gabaldon), David Janssen (Sgt. Bill Hazen), Vic Damone (Cpl. Pete Lewis), Patricia Owens (Sheila Lincoln), Michi Kobi (Sono), George Shibata (Kaz Une), Reiko Sato (Famika), Miiko Taka (Ester), Tsuru Aoki Hayakawa (Mother Une), Sessue Hayakawa (General Matsui).

Based on a remarkable, true story, this picture depicted Mexican-American Guy Gabaldon growing up in 1930s Los Angeles. When his mother is hospitalized and he is homeless, Kaz Une, his school basketball coach, takes him to live with his parents. After the boy's mother dies, they adopt him. Years later, in late 1941, Gabaldon experiences discrimination when he is called a "Jap lover." When the United States enters World War II, Gabaldon's parents and many friends are shipped to relocation camps. Angered by this, Gabaldon refuses to join the service, but his adoptive mother convinces him it is his duty to do so. Now a marine, he is among those landed at Saipan. After experiencing fierce combat, he uses his skill at speaking Japanese to convince the locals who have hidden in caves to surrender. Later, while on a scouting mission, he overhears General Matsui ordering his weary troops to prepare for a final battle. Gabaldon persuades the enemy officer to have his men surrender, which they do. Matsui commits hara-kiri.

The United States and Hollywood were still readjusting their thinking about the Japanese, their World War II enemies, when this picture was made. Thanks to a sincere cast, there was a sturdiness about this economy production. Taka had appeared in *SAYONARA* (1957); HAYAKAWA and his actress wife Aoki had been in many Hollywood movies together during the silent era.

A much fuller study of the infamous American-based relocation camps would be provided in *COME SEE THE PARADISE* (1990).

***Hong Kong* (1960–1961)** ABC-TV series, b&w, 60 minutes. **Cast:** Rod Taylor (Glenn Evans), Lloyd Bochner (Neil Campbell), Jack Kruschen (Tully), Harold Fong (Fong: 1960), Gerald Jann (Ling: 1960–61), Mai Tai Sing (Ching Mei).

Although the network hoped to capture viewer ratings with a series set in exotic Hong Kong, most of the action was studio bound. American journalist Glenn Evans, who works for the

World Wide News Service, finds adventure, romance, and intrigue in this British crown colony. He is assisted by Neil Campbell, the chief of the local police, as well as by Tully, who operates the Golden Dragon nightclub where Evans hangs out. First Harold Fong (as Fong) and then Gerald Jann (as Ling) played Evans's houseboy. To give the nightclub set a more intriguing flavor, the character of club hostess/waitress Ching Mei was added to the line-up. Once again, the Asian characters played domestics in the proceedings.

***House of Bamboo* (1955)** Twentieth Century-Fox, color, 102 minutes. **Director:** Samuel Fuller; **Screenplay:** Harry Kleiner and Fuller; **Cast:** Robert Ryan (Sandy Dawson), Robert Stack (Eddie Kenner/Spanier), Shirley Yamaguchi (Mariko), Cameron Mitchell (Griff), Brad Dexter (Captain Hanson), Sessue Hayakawa (Inspector Kito).

Remaking the Hollywood-produced *The Street with No Name* (1948), FULLER adapted it to the Japanese idiom, which gave the crime drama new texture (bolstered by colorful scenery). American Sandy Dawson is a underworld figure in Japan who has organized the pachinko (a pinball-like game) parlors using a team of ex-American servicemen as his underlings. The U.S. Army orders one of its own (Stack) to infiltrate the gang and ferret out the killer of a GI. As part of his cover, the investigator shares living quarters with Mariko, the widow of a syndicate member. Also involved in the case is the local police inspector (HAYAKAWA), who must take a back seat to the U.S. occupiers of his country as the case unravels.

***House-Rent Party* (1946)** Toddy Pictures, b&w, 65 minutes. **Director:** Sam Newfield; **Screenplay:** Newfield and Ted Toddy; **Cast:** Pigmeat "Alamo" Markham (Pigmeat), John Rastus Murray (Shorty), Claude Demetri (Mr. Johnson), Rudolph Toombs (Slippery Jim), Bill Dillard (Officer Jack), Alfred Cortez (One Lung Lee).

An extremely low-budget effort, abounding in stereotypes, that was primarily shown in those movie theaters across America devoted to black patrons, this hastily assembled "musical" feature brought a Chinese laundry owner (Cortez) into the plot line and built him as a comedy foil to the shenanigans of star characters Shorty and Pigmeat. The latter two are African-American pals in Harlem who work in Pigmeat's barber shop but would rather gamble and chat away the day.

Hung, Sammo (1952–) Fast-kicking, hand-chopping Hung created a dent not only in the Hong Kong martial-arts film market but also on American TV as the star of the comedic action series, *MARTIAL LAW* (1998–2000). Most remarkable was that Hung was dour-faced, five feet, seven inches in height, and weighed 230 pounds. His pudgy physique and unglamorous look, however, was no obstacle in his making many more than 100 feature films.

Born Sammo Hung Kam-bo in Hong Kong, his acting career started while he was studying martial arts, dance, and acrobatics as a youngster at the Beijing Opera School, a classmate of JACKIE CHAN. Hung made his feature-film bow at the age of twelve and after that was employed on many martial-arts pictures as actor, director, choreographer, or producer. Often costarred with Chan in Hong Kong-made chopsocky entries (in *ENTER THE DRAGON*, 1973, Sammo Hung was a stuntman and matched moves with BRUCE LEE), his recent films included *Raging Silence* (2001) *Legend of the Fist Master* (2001), and *Summer Assassin* (2002).

I

impersonations—Caucasian actors playing Asian and Asian-American characters For many years, it was considered an acting challenge for Caucasian performers to showcase their talents and display the achievements in makeup, costuming, and so on by portraying Asian (or Asian-American) characters.

Some Caucasian actors excelled in such professional tests: Richard Barthelmess, looking pensive in the shadows of London's Limehouse district, proved effective as a romanticized depiction of a half-caste in D. W. Griffith's *BROKEN BLOSSOMS* (1919); LON CHANEY frequently enacted figures of Asian descent in silent films (e.g., *Bits of Life*, 1921; *MR. WU*, 1927); E. Allyn Warren, a Virginia-born actor, had a penchant for playing Chinese characters on screen (e.g., *A Tale of Two Worlds*, 1921; *THE HATCHET MAN*, 1932); and Swedish-born WARNER OLAND made a specialty of such characterizations, as in *Mandarin's Gold* (1919) and *CHINATOWN NIGHTS* (1929). Oland went on to be a master purveyor of what Western cinema audiences thought Chinese characters should be like on screen.

By the time Oland costarred with Marlene Dietrich in *SHANGHAI EXPRESS* (1932), he had already "become" the movies' CHARLIE CHAN in *CHARLIE CHAN CARRIES ON* (1931)—he excelled at his depiction for a total of sixteen entries. Two other Caucasians who played Chan on the screen proved adept in their own manner—again providing a very Westernized view of what they thought their sleuth of Asian heritage should be like. Both SIDNEY TOLER (from the Midwest) and ROLAND WINTERS (from Massachusetts), following the tradition established by Oland, utilized little makeup and great interior characterization to bring their portrayals successfully to life. Equally proficient was middle European PETER LORRE who made the role of Japanese businessman/amateur sleuth MR. MOTO his own for eight pictures in the late 1930s.

Once talkies began, it was not an easy matter for some actors to be convincing at portraying Asians and Asian-Americans on camera. Often, their performances were aimed at impressing their audiences as to what great thespians they were. Such was the case with Austrian-born Luise Rainer who won an Oscar playing O-Lan in *THE GOOD EARTH* (1937). (Other Caucasian actors who were Oscar nominated for playing Asians on camera included H. B. Warner for *LOST HORIZON*, 1937; Aline MacMahon for *DRAGON SEED*, 1944; and Gale Sondergaard for *ANNA AND THE KING OF SIAM*, 1946.) Rainer's costar in *The Good Earth* was Eastern European-born Paul Muni—a veteran of American Yiddish theater—and his grand-style interpretation of the farmer was *not* rewarded with an Oscar nomination. Minnesota-born Sondergaard was cast as the Eurasian wife in *The Letter* (1940) and did her best, in the brief scenes allotted her, to steal the limelight from her on-screen rival (Bette Davis). Englishman Robert Donat was effective as the mandarin in *THE INN OF THE SIXTH HAPPINESS* (1958).

In contrast, there were several actors who offered less than stellar impressions of Far Easterners. Neither Loretta Young nor Edward G. Robinson were especially believable in the TONG war melodrama, *THE HATCHET MAN* (1932). Helen Hayes and Mexican-born Ramon Novarro left much to be desired with their Chinese-American characterizations in *THE SON-DAUGHTER* (1932). Equally deficient was Myrna Loy in *THE MASK OF FU MANCHU* (1932). In that same film BORIS KARLOFF was barely believable as Fu Manchu himself—his body build, his facial structure, and his British diction worked against his success. (Nevertheless, he returned in a series of late 1930s low-budget detective features, all presenting him as MR. WONG, a Chinese detective in the Charlie Chan mold. He did not create much of an impression in these quickies.)

New Yorker George Raft, more comfortable tap dancing in a Broadway speakeasy than prowling Chinatown, was dramatically over his head in *LIMEHOUSE BLUES* (1934), a variation of the *Broken Blossoms* theme. Akim Tamiroff did not especially convince as a Chinese warlord in *THE GENERAL DIED AT DAWN* (1936).

Although DOROTHY LAMOUR was attractive in her Hollywood-version native garb, the trend she started with *THE JUNGLE PRINCESS* (1936) was not beneficial to the image of women from POLYNESIA. (But then she was more "native" than near-campy Maria Montez in such fare as 1944's *Cobra Woman.*) Caucasians Sigrid Gurie (as a Chinese princess) and George Barbier (as Kublai Khan) did not fool anyone with their on-camera interpretations in *The Adventures of Marco Polo* (1938).

Ona Munson hailed from Portland, Oregon, and her Eurasian "Mother" Gin Sling in *THE SHANGHAI GESTURE* (1941) was overly theatrical. Nevertheless, she was far more acceptable than Gene Tierney as her half-caste daughter. (Tierney was Eurasian again in *CHINA GIRL*, 1942). The Occidental cast members of *BEHIND THE RISING SUN* (1943) and those in *FIRST YANK IN TOKYO* (1945) were not up to par. New Yorker Sylvia Sidney had been passable as *MADAME BUTTERFLY* (1932), but she seemed less acceptable as James Cagney's Eurasian love interest in *BLOOD ON THE SUN* (1945).

The World War II era seemed to bring out the worst in actors playing Asians on screen. Katharine Hepburn, Turhan Bey, and Walter Huston were unacceptable as Chinese in *DRAGON SEED* (1944) and Fred Astaire in the "Limehouse Blues" sequence of *ZIEGFELD FOLLIES* (1946) did not particularly suggest a half-caste. Marvin Miller was almost laughable as Colonel Zorek in *The Shanghai Story* (1954). Angie Dickinson's Eurasian in *CHINA GATE* (1957) was only better by degrees than her title figure in *Charlie Chan and the Curse of the Dragon Queen* (1981).

The leading players of *THE CONQUEROR* (1956)—including John Wayne and Susan Hayward—were anything but viable in their Asian roles. Mexican-American Ricardo Montalban, was out of his depth as the Kabuki star in *SAYONARA* (1957). On several occasions, comedian Jerry Lewis did an unflattering imitation of a buck-toothed Japanese in his screen work (e.g., *Family Jewels*, 1965). Not to be overlooked was Shirley MacLaine's misguided comedic performance in *MY GEISHA* (1962). She "thought" she could fool her film director husband into believing that she was right to play an on-screen Asian character in their latest joint picture. For the shoddy *Genghis Khan* (1965), Omar Sharif (in the title role), James Mason (Kam Ling), and Robert Morley (emperor) received some of the worst reviews of their careers portraying Asians in this laughable misfire. The usually reliable Bette Davis was amiss as the deranged, evil title figure of the telefeature *Madame Sin* (1972). Perhaps most embarrassing of all was Peter Ustinov in his final new film role, playing Charlie Chan as low comedy in the aforementioned *Charlie Chan and the Curse of the Dragon Queen.* Hong Kong-born JOHN LONE gave many sensitive performances in his career (including *The Last Emperor*, 1987), but he was not especially convincing in his transgender role in *M. BUTTERFLY* (1993).

***Inn of the Sixth Happiness, The* (1958)** Twentieth Century-Fox, color, 158 minutes. **Director:** Mark Robson; **Screenplay:** Isobel Lennard; **Cast:** Ingrid Bergman (Gladys Aylward), Curt Jurgens (Capt. Lin Nan), Robert Donat (Mandarin), Ronald Squire (Sir Francis Jamison), Noel Hood (Miss Thompson), Joan Young (Cook), Athene Seyler (Mrs. Lawson), Peter Chong (Yang), Burt Kwouk (Li).

At first glance, the casting choices seemed ridiculous for this well-mounted movie that was based on the actual account of an ill-educated English domestic who made her way to China to work for/then succeed an elderly British Christian missionary woman. (The film was based on the 1957 novel, *The Small Woman*, by Alan Burgess.) For a change, the stars met the challenge of playing against ethnic type. Swedish Bergman was the British servant who found life's purpose by aiding the poor in rural China in the period just before and during the Japanese invasion of the country. German-born Jurgens played the Chinese army officer who fell in love with the self-sacrificing Gladys Aylward, while Britisher Donat, in his final screen role, portrayed the aged Mandarin who came to respect Gladys's wonderful way with his people.

Filmed in northern Wales, the set-piece of the movie occurred when Gladys led orphans over a mountain pass to safety from the advancing Japanese, during which they chanted what became a popular song, "This Old Man." If this picture had been made a few years later—after the success of *FLOWER DRUM SONG* (1961) and the furtherance of political correctness—undoubtedly the two lead Chinese characters would have been played by actual Asian Americans, but Hollywood had not yet reached that point, and it was still a catch-22 situation for Asian-American performers, as it was for, among others, African-American, Hispanic-American, and Native American minority performers.

J

***Jackie Chan Adventures* (2000–)** Warner Bros.-TV series, color, 30 minutes. **Voices:** Jackie Chan (Jackie), Stacie Chan (Jade), James Sie (Shendu/Jackie/Chow), Sab Shimono (Uncle), Julian Sands (Valmont), Clancy Brown (Captain Black/Ratso).

Each segment of this animated television series not only featured an amazing caper of fearless Jackie and his eleven-year-old niece Jade, but also had a live-action segment in which youngsters asked questions about Chan's training and experiences. The series replicated the Hong Kong action star's amazing and punishing stunt work and captured to a degree Jackie's ebullient personality. In 2001, a video game based on the teleseries was released.

***James Clavell's Noble House* (aka: *Noble House*) (1988)** NBC-TV miniseries, color, 355 minutes. **Director:** Gary Nelson; **Teleplay:** Eric Bercovici; **Cast:** Pierce Brosnan (Ian Dunross), Deborah Raffin (Casey Tcholok), Ben Masters (Linc Bartlett), David Henry (Bruce Johnjohn), John Houseman (Sir Geoffrey Allison), George Innes (Alexej Travkin), Gordon Jackson (Superintendent Armstrong), Nancy Kwan (Claudia Chen), Burt Kwouk (Philip Chen).

Another of James Clavell's massive tomes, this time his 1981 best-seller, became an intricate miniseries, as another installment of his Hong Kong saga, which included the theatrical release, *TAI-PAN* (1986). Dapper Brosnan starred as the head (tai-pan) of a powerful Hong Kong trading corporation who must cope with ruthless rivals in the high-stakes world of international commerce. Hong Kong was portrayed as the legendary capitalist city where espionage, stock market swindles/manipulation, and drug smuggling were carried on in high fashion. Providing the entry's romantic interlude was Ian Dunross's relationship with Casey Tcholok, an ambitious corporate executive.

Many veteran Asian-American performers appeared in this diluted version of Clavell's expansive novel. Clavell's 1980 miniseries *SHOGUN* had aroused America's interest in the exotic Far East, setting the stage for this production.

***Japanese War Bride* (1952)** Twentieth Century-Fox, b&w, 91 minutes. **Director:** King Vidor; **Screenplay:** Catherine Turney; **Cast:** Shirley Yamaguchi (Tae Shimizu), Don Taylor (Jim Sterling), Cameron Mitchell (Art Sterling), Marie Windsor (Fran Sterling), James Bell (Ed Sterling), Louise Lorimer (Harriet Sterling), Philip Ahn (Eitaro Shimizu), Lane Nakano (Shiro Hasagawa), May Takasugi (Emma Hasagawa), William Yokota (Mr. Hasagawa).

G. I. War Brides (1946) had dealt with American servicemen bringing their British wives back to the United States after World War II. This new, well-crafted drama, directed by veteran Vidor, concerned servicemen returning home with Korean or Japanese brides they had married while overseas serving in the Korean War. The inevitable culture clashes that occurred were overlaid—especially in the case of Japanese wives—with the tragic history of World War II, thus causing the families of each newlywed to be horrified at their offspring's marriage choice. Also, the film brought to light the problems to be faced by their mixed-blood children.

Army lieutenant Jim Sterling returns to Salinas, California, after serving in the Korean War, accompanied by his Japanese wife Tae. Sterling's family have mixed emotions about the new member of the household, none more so than Fran, Jim's sister-in-law, who is still in love with him. As time passes, she instigates problems, fanning the flames of bigotry in the household and among the Sterlings' neighbors. Acting as a counterbalance to the tribulations and new customs to which Tae must adjust are the Hasagawas, a second-generation Japanese-American family who own the neighboring land.

***Joy Luck Club, The* (1993)** Hollywood, color, 135 minutes. **Director:** Wayne Wang; **Screenplay:** Amy Tan and Ronald Bass; **Cast:** Kieu Chinh (Suyuan), Tsai Chin (Lindo), France Nuyen (Ying Ying), Lisa Lu (An Mei), Ming-Na Wen (June), Tamlyn Tomita (Waverly), Lauren Tom (Lena), Rosalind Chao (Rose), Chao-Li Chi (June's Father), Victor Wong (Old Chong), Christopher Rich (Rich), Nicholas Guest (hairdresser), Russell Wong (Lin Xiao), Michael Paul Chan (Harold), Phillip Moon (Ken), Vivian Wu (An Mei's mother), Andrew McCarthy (Ted).

It was a big step forward for Hollywood to make a major motion picture featuring Asians and Asian-Americans as the focal characters in such an intertwining contemporary drama. It told of four Chinese women's (mis)adventures in their homeland that led to their coming to America and assimilating to some degree, while still retaining homeland ties (e.g., memories, relatives, and traditions). Because Tam's 1989 novel had been a widespread best seller, one studio eventually concurred with the persistent producers that there might be a mainstream audience for this intricately structured woman's picture. The casting combined older (e.g., NUYEN and Wu) with new generations (e.g., WEN, Tom) of Asian and Asian-American talent. Directed by WANG (*CHAN IS MISSING*, 1985; *EAT A BOWL OF TEA*, 1989), the picture was more than four hours long before being trimmed to almost half that for its release. As a result, some of the novel's narrative sections were missing and others greatly condensed.

For years, four middle-aged Chinese women meet weekly for their game of mah-jongg. The winner of their joy luck club takes home money; the others are given the leftovers from dishes they prepare for their ritual get-together. Now that Suyuan has died, her daughter June takes her place. As the women play, they recall their many hardships back in China that led/forced them to relocate to the United States. June learns that her mother had had to leave behind her precious twin-girl babies by a prior marriage when she fled the invading Japanese during World War II. Not long before Suyuan passed away, she discovered that the daughters had survived, and she had been saving to visit them. Now, say the other club members, June must fulfill her mother's obligation, and they have accumulated the winnings from their weekly game to pay for her trip to meet her sisters. Interspersed with the accounts of life back in China are the interactions of the women with their daughters in America, who, in turn, are balancing the traditions of the past with the need to become acculturated, modern-thinking Chinese-American women.

Despite its "narrow" topic, this picture was modestly successful in release. Although not generating a stampede for other such Chinese-American themed Hollywood entries, it at least was not a step backward.

***Judge Dee and the Monastery Murders* (1974)** ABC-TV, color, 100 minutes. **Director:** Jeremy Paul Kagan; **Teleplay:** Nicholas Meyer; **Cast:** Khigh Dhiegh (Judge Dee), Mako (Tao Gan), Soon-Tek Oh (Kang I-Te), Miiko Taka (Jade Mirror), Irene Tsu (Celestial Image), James Hong (Prior), Keye Luke (Lord Sun Ming), Tadashi Yamashita (Motai).

Based on the 1957 novel *The Haunted Monastery*, one of the Judge Dee mysteries by Robert Van Gulick, this highly polished presentation had the distinction of using only Asian and Asian-American actors to play *all* its ethnic roles—a first for U.S. network television. In this aired, unsold pilot for a projected TV series, the action was set in seventh-century China. It finds Judge Dee—well played by the distinctive DHIEGH (famous as the master villain on *HAWAII FIVE-O*, 1968–80)—as he confronts a remarkable case that involves his three wives and such other bizarre ingredients as a revenging swordsman, a deceased monk, a one-armed woman, and a kidnapped nun. The monastery set utilized belonged to the network's then current series *KUNG FU* (1972–75).

***Jungle Princess, The* (1936)** Paramount, b&w, 85 minutes. **Director:** William Thiele; **Screenplay:** Cyril Hume, Gerald Geraghty, and Gouverneur Morris; **Cast:** Dorothy Lamour (Ulah), Ray Milland (Christopher Powell), Akim Tamiroff (Karen Neg), Lynne Overman (Frank), Molly Lamont (Ava), Mala (Melan), Hugh Buckler (Col. Neville Lane), Nick Shaid (head of tribe), Al Kikume, Inez Gomez, and Ray Roubert (natives).

LAMOUR rose to fame with her first starring movie role. She also solidified a Hollywood screen type of the comely Malaysian (or POLYNESIAN) who glided about in a sarong with her long dark tresses usually adorned with tropical flowers. It was an image that she also exploited in several *Road to . . .* screen comedies teamed with Bing Crosby and Bob Hope. But Lamour was not from the Eastern Hemisphere; rather, she was born in New Orleans.

In *The Jungle Princess*, an American hunter (Milland) is injured while on a tiger hunt in the Malaysian jungle. He is rescued by a pretty native, Ulah, whose companions as a child were a tiger and a chimp. While waiting for his fellow hunters to locate him, the American teaches Ulah English. In the process, they fall in love, and he abandons his fiancée to remain with her.

When the picture was reviewed by the industry production code office before its release, there was concern about the plot's ambiguity about the existence of an illicit relationship between the native and the Caucasian American. This led to snippets being taken out of the footage to ensure that the bond between Ulah and Christopher Powell in the early parts of the story came across as more platonic (teacher–student) than the amorous interplay of an emotionally interested man and woman.

K

***Karate Kid, The* (1984)** Columbia, color, 126 minutes. **Director:** John G. Avildsen; **Screenplay:** Robert Mark Kamen; **Cast:** Ralph Macchio (Daniel), Noriyuki "Pat" Morita (Miyagi), Elisabeth Shue (Ali), Martin Kove (Kreese), Randee Heller (Lucille), William Zabka (Johnny).

Taking advantage of the martial-arts craze that swept the United States, director Avildsen did for that sport in *The Karate Kid* what he had accomplished with boxing in *Rocky* (1976). The feel-good new movie was a tremendous success, grossing almost $91 million in domestic distribution. It led to three follow-ups featuring MORITA, a former stand-up comic best known for having played Arnold, the sandwich shop proprietor on the TV sitcom *HAPPY DAYS* (1975–76; 1982–83). This film series did much to offset the pervasive stereotypes of Japanese as warmongers, corporate aggressors, or nerdy tourists forever snapping photos. As had BRUCE LEE with his martial-arts movies and DAVID CARRADINE with his initial KUNG FU TV series (1972–75), *The Karate Kid* phenomenon expanded American interest in the Japanese art of self-defense, as well as that country's philosophy, art, and so on.

Moving from Newark, New Jersey, Daniel and his mother (Heller) settle into their Los Angeles life. Daniel has trouble adjusting to the California mentality at school. Problems accelerate when he becomes friendly with Ali, who formerly dated classmate Johnny. The latter becomes jealous of Ali's rapport with Daniel, and, with his stooges, attacks Daniel. Mr. Miyagi, the middle-aged gardener where Daniel and his mom live, comes to the rescue using martial arts to subdue Daniel's attackers. Later he teaches Daniel the martial-arts skills needed to compete against Johnny who is studying karate with the unscrupulous Kreese. In the climactic competition, Daniel is the victor, ensuring Ali's romantic interest in him.

One of the joys of this movie was the deep friendship that developed between Daniel and his handyman mentor. For his telling performance, Morita won an Academy Award nomination as Best Supporting Actor.

In the inevitable sequel, *The Karate Kid: Part II* (1986), Daniel helped his friend Miyagi settle a long-time score in Okinawa. To give *The Karate Kid: Part III* (1989) a different turn, when Daniel had to use his high kicks again to put things right, Miyagi refuses to help train him. Actor Macchio was not part of the next installment, *The Next Karate Kid* (1994). It featured future Academy Award winner Hilary Swank as the tomboy daughter of Miyagi's late pal who had saved his life fifty years earlier. During the narrative, Miyagi honed the girl's martial-arts skills and even taught her to waltz.

From 1989 to 1990, NBC-TV aired *The Karate Kid*, a half-hour, Saturday-morning cartoon series. It was based loosely on the 1984 film and featured the voices of Robert Ito (Miyagi Yakuga), Joe Dedio (Daniel), and Janice Kawaye (Taki).

Karloff, Boris (1887–1969) He was the pieced-together monster in *Frankenstein* (1931), *Bride of Frankenstein* (1935), and *Son of Frankenstein* (1939); he was also Imhotep, the cursed and embalmed ancient Egyptian, in *The Mummy* (1932); and he was an often mad scientist in many of his other pictures. In addition, this Britisher, who played many nationalities on camera, was also the purveyor of several Asian roles.

Born William Henry Pratt in Dulwich, England, he refused to follow the family's profession in the diplomatic corps. Instead, he immigrated to Canada where he joined a touring company. Later, during a stopover in Los Angeles in 1916, he made his film debut as an extra. Three years thereafter, he returned to Hollywood and began his movie career in earnest.

By the early 1930s—thanks to *Frankenstein* and *The Mummy*—Karloff had developed a niche in pictures as a master of menace. This led to his being selected to succeed WARNER OLAND as the dreaded Yellow Peril in *THE MASK OF FU MANCHU* (1932). Aided by makeup and wardrobe, he made a barely acceptable Chinese menace. A few years later, in *West of Shanghai* (1937), he was another Asian terror, this time Gen Wu Yen Fang, a northern China bandit–general. In 1938, Karloff starred as Mr. James Lee in *MR. WONG, DETECTIVE* (1938), a new (low-budget) detective series that was geared to compete with another studio's CHARLIE CHAN and MR. MOTO Asian sleuths. Karloff made five more Mr. Wong movies, the last being 1940's *Doomed to Die*.

For the remainder of his lengthy show-business career, Karloff lived up to or played down his association with horror films. He starred in the TV series *Colonel March of Scotland Yard* in 1954 and later hosted the 1960 television anthology show, *Thriller*. In his last years he made several quickie horror movies including *Curse of the Crimson Altar* (1968).

Kato See GREEN HORNET, THE.

***Keys of the Kingdom, The* (1944)** Twentieth Century-Fox, b&w, 137 minutes. **Director:** John M. Stahl; **Screenplay:** Joseph L. Mankiewicz and Nunnally Johnson; **Cast:** Gregory Peck (Father Francis Chisholm), Thomas Mitchell (Dr. Willie Tulloch), Vincent Price (Rev. Angus Mealy), Rosa Stradner (Mother Maria Veronica), Roddy McDowall (Francis—as a boy), Edmund Gwenn (Rev. Hamish MacNabb), Sir Cedric Hardwicke (Monsignor Sleeth), Anne Revere (Agnes Fiske), Benson Fong (Joseph), Leonard Strong (Mr. Chia).

In the stressful times of World War II, novels dealing with religious faith, self-sacrifice, and lost love were exceedingly popular. A. J. Cronin's *The Keys of the Kingdom* (1941) had all these prized ingredients and became a major best-seller. But this fiction about a Scottish Catholic clergyman's devoted missionary service in China from the 1890s to the 1930s came under immediate criticism. The Catholic Church was concerned about the book's unflattering depiction of certain priest characters and the questionable actions and words of some of the novel's Catholic missionaries and nuns. These worries were echoed by the film industry's self-censorship board. In addition, the Chinese consul to the United States was alarmed about the book's alleged distortions of life in a Chinese village and the qualities of its inhabitants.

Within the film—told in flashback—a young priest, Father Francis Chisholm, who has failed on previous assignments, is dispatched as a missionary to the village of Pai-tan in the Chekkow province of China. With little help, he struggles to build the mission. He is befriended by the wealthy Mr. Chia. Later, several nuns arrive, including imperious Mother Maria Veronica. Chisholm and the aristocratic Austrian Maria Veronica have a long adjustment period before she can appreciate this humble man of God. Through the years, there is political strife in the Chinese province as the Japanese encroach on China.

Such pictures as *The Keys of the Kingdom* gave moviegoers a fuller sense of the lifestyles of the simple members of the nation that the United States and the Allies were defending during World War II. At the same time, such dramas were escapist entertainment, carefully geared by Hollywood to project the point of view that the United States and China wished the public to absorb.

The Keys of the Kingdom won three Academy Award nominations: Best Actor (Peck), Best Cinematography (Black and White), and Best Original Dramatic Score.

Khan, Michelle See YEOH, MICHELLE.

***Khan!* (1975)** ABC-TV series, color, 60 minutes. **Cast:** Khigh Dhiegh (Khan), Irene Yah-Ling Sun (Anna Kahn), Evan Kim (Kim Khan), Vic Tayback (Lieutenant Gubbins).

In the more-progressive 1970s, a few American TV series actually starred Asian-American characters, played by Asian Americans. Each, however, including *MR. T AND TINA* (1976), was of short duration. DHIEGH, who had made such an impression with TV viewers with his recurring guest role of arch villain Wo Fat on *HAWAII FIVE-O* (1968–80), was given his own series here as a private detective in San Francisco's Chinatown who is sometimes assisted by his offspring (Sun and Kim).

The detective drama lasted on the network line-up for only one month (February) in 1975.

***King and I, The* (1956)** Twentieth Century-Fox, color, 133 minutes. **Director:** Walter Lang; **Screenplay:** Ernest Lehman; **Cast:** Deborah Kerr (Anna Leonowens), Yul Brynner (the King), Rita Moreno (Tuptim), Martin Benson (the Kralahome), Terry Saunders (Lady Thiang), Rex Thompson (Louis Leonowens), Carlos Rivas (Lun Tha), Patrick Adiarte (Prince Chulalongkorn), Yuriko (Eliza), Marion Jim (Simon Legree).

On Broadway, this Richard Rodgers and Oscar Hammerstein II musical (1951) ran for 1,246 performances. Twentieth Century-Fox, which had produced the earlier, successful dramatic screen version (*ANNA AND THE KING OF SIAM*, 1946) of Anna Leonowens's tenure in the 1860s as a schoolteacher in the royal household of Siam, created the screen adaptation of the hit musical. Eastern European-born BRYNNER recreated his Broadway interpretation of the Asian monarch who reaches out to learn western ways. As the proud British schoolmarm who is entranced by the king's children and by the "barbarian," English-born Kerr was chosen (with Marni Nixon providing her singing voice).

As for the film's other leading Asian characters, the studio followed Hollywood habits and Broadway convention of casting anyone who seems "right," no matter what their ethnic background. It was assumed that few American filmgoers were then aware of Siam (now Thailand), let alone the nuances of how its people of a century earlier looked or behaved. Originally, African-American Dorothy Dandridge was to play the fated Tuptim, but she refused this subordinate assignment and Puerto Rican Moreno was substituted. Texas-born Hispanic-American performer Rivas was signed to play the Siamese in love with Tuptim, one of the king's wives.

Given the prettification of the actual story, *The King and I*, made at a cost of $6.5 million, was a box-office success as it spun its fable of the two so-different central figures.

The financial returns of *The King and I* led to a short-lasting TV series, *Anna and the King* (1972), with Brynner again as the king, Samantha Eggar as Anna, and KEYE LUKE as the Kralahome. In 1999, there appeared both an animated feature-length children's version of the musical *The King and I* and the live-action remake of *Anna and the King of Siam*, now entitled *ANNA AND THE KING*.

The 1956 *The King and I* won Oscars for Best Actor (Brynner), Best Art Direction/Set Decoration (Color), Best Costume Design (Color), Best Scoring of a Musical, and Best Sound. It also won Academy Award nominations for Best Actress (Kerr), Best Cinematography (Color), Best Director, and Best Picture.

***King Rat* (1965)** Columbia, b&w, 134 minutes. **Director/Screenplay:** Bryan Forbes; **Cast:** George Segal (Corporal King), Patrick O'Neal (Max), James Fox (Flight Lieutenant Marlowe), Denholm Elliott (Lieutenant Colonel Larkin), Todd Armstrong (Tex), Sammy Reese (Kurt), Joseph Turkel (Dino), Michael Storka (Miller), Tom Courtenay (Lieutenant Gray), John Mills (Colonel Smedley-Taylor).

With the rising Hollywood interest in stories about U.S. military activities in Vietnam, the era of World War II combat dramas slowed down. (This meant that Asian-American actors were being called upon to switch from playing the cinematic stereotype of the Japanese enemy to that of the Vietcong if they expected much work in the Hollywood of this era.)

Based on James Clavell's 1963 novel, *King Rat* is set at a Japanese prisoner-of-war camp near Singapore as World War II comes to a close. In the compound are some 10,000 American, Australian, and British prisoners struggling to survive, each group sticking to its own kind. Although he is outranked by many others of the emaciated soldiers in the camp, Corporal King is a master of black-market manipulation among his fellow prisoners. He earns his nickname from breeding rodents and selling them as food to the others. He also speaks the native language and can communicate with the sadistic, corrupt Asian guards. When the war ends and the prisoners are freed, King and his arch adversary Marlowe (who now wants to be a friend of the man who saved his life in captivity) go their separate ways.

King Rat was filmed in Thousand Oaks, California. It received two Oscar nominations: Best Art Direction/Set Decoration (Black and White), Best Cinematography (Black and White).

***Kinjite: Forbidden Subjects* (1989)** Cannon, color, 97 minutes. **Director:** J. Lee Thompson; **Screenplay:** Harold Nebenzal; **Cast:** Charles Bronson (Lieutenant Crowe), Perry Lopez (Eddie Rios), Juan Fernandez (Duke), Peggy Lipton (Kathleen Crowe), James Pax (Hiroshi Hada), Sy Richardson (Lavonne), Mario Kodama Yue (Mr. Kazuko Hada), Kumiko Hayakawa (Fumiko Hada).

Taking a break from making more *Death Wish* (1974) sequels, Bronson starred here as a cynical Los Angeles vice cop. His current nemesis is sleazy pimp Duke who specializes in kidnapping young girls and turning them into kinky sex robots through abuse and drug addiction. Duke's latest victim is the daughter of a recently arrived Tokyo business executive, Hiroshi Hada. In rescuing Hada's girl (Hayakawa) from the vile pimp, bigoted Crowe has a change of heart about his dislike of the typically pushy Japanese who are grabbing up American businesses and real estate. Now, working with Hada and learning the Japanese culture and ways of business a bit, he perceives these "foreigners" through different eyes. In standard fashion, this glum police actioner ended with the expected shoot-out.

***Klondike Annie* (1936)** Paramount, b&w, 85 minutes. **Director:** Raoul Walsh; **Screenplay:** Mae West; **Cast:** Mae West (the Frisco Doll [Rose Carlton]), Victor McLaglen (Capt. Bull Brackett), Phillip Reed (Insp. Jack Forrest), Helen Jerome Eddy (Annie Alden), Harry Beresford (Brother Bowser), Harold Huber (Chan Lo), Soo Yong (Fah Wong), Philip Ahn (Wing).

The inestimable West was having increasing difficulty in bringing her risqué screen projects to actuality because the film industry self-censorship board had become far stricter by 1934. Not only did *Klondike Annie* shock the Hays Office due to West's array of smart double entendres, but also in this new release, her movie alter ego, the Frisco Doll, had extremely questionable morals, had murdered her lover (albeit in self-defense), and had impersonated a missionary (later changed to a settlement worker). Equally bothersome to the protest/PRESSURE GROUPS was the fact that the Doll was being kept openly by a Chinese man.

In the 1890s in San Francisco's tenderloin district, Rose Carlton, better known as the Frisco Doll, belongs to Chan Lo, who financed her rise from the gutter to queen of his lush gambling house where she is a vocalist. Near the film's start she sings "I'm an Occidental Woman in an Oriental Mood for Love," wearing a Chinese costume, while authentic Oriental instruments play a (jazz) accompaniment. Revealing her restlessness, the Doll asks the jealous Chan why he will not allow her to "have gentlemen friends of my own race?" Chan's response is to remind her of the dagger he carries, ready to use at the first sign of betrayal. Later, Chan tortures the Doll's servant, Ah Toy, when the latter will not reveal who her mistress's admirer is. Then, in a scene deleted from the release print, the Doll fatally stabs her paramour in self-defense. With that, she and her young servant, Fah

Wong, board a ship bound for the Klondike, with Fah Wong being dropped off in Seattle—which ends the Asian motif to this comedy-drama.

***Kundun* (1997)** Touchstone, color, 128 minutes. **Director:** Martin Scorsese; **Screenplay:** Melissa Mathison; **Cast:** Tenzin Thuthob Tsarong (adult Dalai Lama), Gyurme Tethong (Dalai Lama—age twelve), Tulku Jamyang Kunga Tenzin (Dalai Lama—age five), Tenzin Yeshi Paichang (Dalai Lama—age two), Tencho Gyalpo (Dalai Lama's mother).

Kundun means "Ocean of Wisdom," which is what the Dalai Lama is called by Tibetans. This very personal feature film by Academy Award-winning Scorsese provided in great detail and amazing splendor the life of the current Dalai Lama from 1937 when, at the age of two, he is discovered by monks in Tibet and declared to be the fourteenth reincarnation of Buddha, until 1959 when this pillar of nonviolence must flee violence-ravaged Tibet to seek refuge in India.

Utilizing a cast of adept nonprofessionals—including Gyalpo, the Dalai's niece, to play her own grandmother—*Kundun* reflected on the philosophy of nonviolence. (It was produced with the cooperation of the Dalai Lama and was filmed partially in Morocco.) Within the plot, the Dalai Lama's principle is put to a severe test as he copes with the reign of totalitarian terror waged by Communist China against the Tibetans. The Lama is witness to the slaughter of thousands, including nuns and monks, and finally must abandon his homeland in 1959 to stay alive and to remain the spiritual leader of his subjugated people.

With its visual sweep, fine score, and narrative flow, this production is far more engaging than other movies with overlapping topics such as *Little Buddha* (1993) or *Seven Years in Tibet* (1997). *Kundun* received four Academy Award nominations: Best Art Director/Set Decoration, Best Cinematography, Best Costume Design, and Best Original Score. Made on a budget of $28 million, *Kundun* grossed only about $6 million in domestic distribution.

***Kung Fu* (1972–1975)** ABC-TV series, color, 60 minutes. **Cast:** David Carradine (Kwai Chang Caine), Keye Luke (Master Po), Philip Ahn (Master Kan), Radames Pera (Caine—as a youth), Season Hubley (Margit McLean).

Ironically, it was the success of BRUCE LEE'S martial-arts movies that made *Kung Fu* a viable TV project. Yet, it was Carradine, a Caucasian, who got the lead assignment, not Hong Kong-born Lee who had thought of the basic idea for the program years back and badly wanted to portray its lead character.

The premise has Kwai Chang Caine born in China of the mid-1800s to Chinese-American parents. Orphaned early on, he was raised by monks at the Shaolin Temple at Whonon. As a youngster, Kwai Chang Caine was tutored in the spiritual philosophy of internal harmony combined with a strong code of nonviolence. The obliging monks also train him in the martial arts of kung fu, as a backup measure. Everything changes for Caine when he seeks, unsuccessfully, to save the life of the blind Master Po and ends by killing a nephew of the royal family. Caine flees China to the U.S. West of the 1870s, where he searches for his long-lost brother. Meanwhile, he is being hunted by Chinese imperial representatives as well as by U.S. bounty hunters.

This very popular series relied on viewers' interest in its unique hero. He was a man in the West who did not carry a gun, spoke very infrequently; when he did speak, it usually concerned his mystic philosophy. Another aspect of this hunted character was that he was an outsider, not only because of the killing back in China but also because he was one of a minority in a predominantly Caucasian society.

The ninety-minute pilot to *Kung Fu*, with guest stars Barry Sullivan, Albert Salmi, and Wayne Maunder, aired as a TV movie presentation on February 22, 1972. The series began that October. *Kung Fu* led to the made-for-television entry *KUNG FU: THE MOVIE* (1986) and the TV series: *KUNG FU: THE LEGEND CONTINUES* (1993–97). There were similarities between the *Kung Fu* series and the premise of the later JACKIE CHAN western spoof, SHANGHAI NOON (2000).

***Kung Fu: The Legend Continues* (1993–1997)** Syndicated TV series, color, 60 minutes. **Cast:** David Carradine (Kwai Chang Caine), Chris Potter (Det. Peter Caine), Kim Chan (Lo Si, the Ancient), Nathaniel Moreau (Peter—as a young man: 1993–95), Robert Lansing (Capt. Paul Blasdell: 1993–94), William Dunlop (Chief Frank Strenlich).

Picking up plot threads from *Kung Fu* (1972–75), this new TV offering presented Carradine as the grandson of the earlier show's Caine. As was related, Caine had taught his boy Peter at a Shaolin Temple that was later destroyed and that led father and son to think the other was dead. They are reunited fifteen years later. Peter is now a San Francisco law enforcer, having been raised by Capt. Paul Blasdell and his wife. Many of the installments include flashbacks to Peter's youth when his father was instructing him in the mystic philosophy and martial-arts skills. Kwai Chang often aids his son in solving cases and frequently relies on Lo Si, the ancient, a Chinatown friend, who is knowledgeable in mystical powers and martial arts.

On the show was a recurring emphasis on Kwai Chang, combating demons and evil spirits and having to conjure up magical forces to outwit them. With Carradine's experience from the prior series, it was a natural to have him in the lead in the new production, but again there was a jarring difference between his presence and those of the Asian-American performers.

***Kung Fu: The Movie* (1986)** CBS-TV, color, 100 minutes. **Director:** Richard Lang; **Teleplay:** Durrell Royce Crays; **Cast:** David Carradine (Kwai Chang Caine), Kerrie Keane (Sarah Perkins), Mako (the Manchu), William Lucking (Wyatt), Keye Luke (Master Po), Benson Fong (the Old One), Brandon Lee (Chung Wang), Paul Rudd (Rev. Lawrence Perkins).

Nearly eleven years after *KUNG FU* (1972–75) went off the air, Carradine returned in this made-for-television feature to reprise his role as Kwai Chang Caine. He is the Chinese-American Shaolin priest whose expertise at martial arts has kept him alive in the Old West, despite being hunted by representatives of the Chinese royal family and U.S. bounty hunters. In flashbacks, the blind, elderly Master Po reappears to instruct Caine and to give him courage. In this film, the late BRUCE LEE'S son, BRANDON, was introduced to American TV audiences as a feisty assassin hired by the sinister Manchu warlord to hunt for Caine in late 1880s northern California.

This well-received telefeature led to a one-hour TV pilot aired in June 1987 for *Kung Fu: The Next Generation* set in modern times. It did not sell but was revised as the series *KUNG FU: THE LEGEND CONTINUES* (1993–97) with Carradine playing Caine's grandson.

Kwan, Nancy (1939–) Forever associated with the title role of *THE WORLD OF SUZIE WONG* (1960), Kwan's cinema career never reached its true potential. Born in Hong Kong to a Chinese father (an architect) and a British mother, she was training at England's Royal Ballet School when she was screen tested to substitute for France Nuyen as the Hong Kong prostitute in *The World of Suzie Wong.* Then she had the colead as the scheming nightclub performer in the movie musical *FLOWER DRUM SONG* (1961), but her roles thereafter mostly relied on her extreme beauty. She alternated between Hollywood and European picture assignments, returning to Hong Kong in 1972 to tend to her ailing father. Kwan started her own production company as well as acting in pictures targeted for the Southeast Asian market. She returned to American films in the 1980s and was among the cast of the TV miniseries *JAMES CLAVELL'S NOBLE HOUSE* (1988) and participated in *DRAGON: THE BRUCE LEE STORY* (1993), having been a friend of the famed martial-arts star. In addition, she was a spokesperson for a facial cream. Her more recent films included: *Soul of the Avenger* and *Mr. P's Dancing Sushi Bar* (both 1997).

L

***Lady from Shanghai, The* (1948)** Columbia, b&w, 87 minutes. **Director/Screenplay:** Orson Welles; **Cast:** Rita Hayworth (Elsa Bannister), Orson Welles (Michael O'Hara), Everett Sloane (Arthur Bannister), Glenn Anders (George Grisby), Ted de Corsia (Sidney Broome), Wong Show Chong (Li), Doris Chan and Billy Louie (Chinese girls).

Based on *If I Die Before I Wake* (1938) by Raymond Sherwood King, *The Lady from Shanghai* completed filming a year before its April 1948 release. Although much of the plot took place aboard a yacht bound from New York to San Francisco and in the Golden Gate city itself, the mood of the Orient permeated this film-noir nightmare.

Within the plot, Elsa Bannister has an unsavory past in Shanghai; in fact it is Bannister's threat of exposing it that leads her to wed this crippled attorney. Once in San Francisco, Michael O'Hara, Elsa's duped lover, hides from the law in a Chinatown theater (actually the Chinese Mandarin Theater), which has a Chinese staff and patrons. This situation leads to a final (and much celebrated) shootout in an amusement-park fun house.

Lamour, Dorothy (1914–1996) Although born Mary Leta Dorothy Slaton in New Orleans, this Caucasian former big-band vocalist made her initial mark on camera playing Polynesian maidens: *THE JUNGLE PRINCESS* (1936), *The Hurricane* (1937), and *Her Jungle Love* (1938). Wearing variations of the sarong, speaking pidgin English, and frequently breaking into romantic ballads or sensual dances (often Westernized versions of the hula), she became implanted in the public's mind as the ultimate South Seas maiden. She good-naturedly spoofed that celluloid image in *Aloma of the South Seas* (1941) and in several of *The Road to . . .* screen comedies in which she costarred with Bob Hope and Bing Crosby. As late as John Ford's *Donovan's Reef* (1963) Lamour was still doing a variation of her POLYNESIAN movie type. (In 1939's *Disputed Passage*, Lamour played an Eurasian.)

Lee, Ang (1954–) Like other Asian-born directors who worked on and off within the American film system, Lee did not confine himself to projects dealing exclusively with his cultural heritage.

Born in Pingtung, Taiwan, he attended New York University. While there, he worked on the production of Spike Lee's *Joe's Bed-Stuy Barbershop: We Cut Heads* (1983). Later completing his course of study in the Tisch School of the Arts graduate program, Lee's first full-length feature, *Pushing Hands* (1992), was a U.S.–Taiwanese coproduction and depicted the cultural clash when a Chinese American brought her non–English-speaking dad to live in a New York suburb. These themes were furthered in *The Wedding Banquet* (1993), in which not only was there a generation gap between the parents who came from Taiwan to visit their son in New York City but also the offspring was gay. This mixture of comedy and drama was continued in *Eat Drink Man Woman* (1994)—dialogue not in English—in which a master chef grows old and distant from his three daughters. Thereafter, Lee proved his versatility and adeptness with directing: *Sense and Sensibility* (1995), a highly praised rendering of the Jane Austen novel of early nineteenth-century England; *The Ice Storm* (1997), centered in 1970s Connecticut; *Ride with the Devil* (1999), set during the American Civil War and dealing with bushwhackers. *Crouching Tiger, Hidden Dragon* (2000), shot in Chinese, took the Hong Kong-style martial-arts fantasy and raised it to a high level of art. (Lee was Oscar nominated in the Best Director category for this film.) His film *Berlin Diaries, 1940–45* (2001) dealt with World War II. After the thriller *Chosen* (2001), the filmmaker directed *The Hulk* (2003), the big-screen adaptation of the classic comic book series, *The Incredible Hulk*.

Lee, Brandon (1965–1993) Being the son of a dead movie icon whose legend still burned brightly was not easy. Brandon Lee wanted to be taken seriously as an actor, not merely be known as the son of the late martial-arts star, BRUCE LEE. He was on the way to achieving that goal when, like his parent, he died mysteriously during the making of a movie.

Brandon Lee was born in San Francisco, the son of Eurasian father and a blonde Caucasian mother of Swedish heritage. The year after his birth, his father, Bruce Lee, gained a degree of popularity by playing Kato in the TV series *THE GREEN HORNET* (1966–67). By the early 1970s, the Lees were living well in Hong Kong, where Bruce was starring in several money-making martial-arts movies. Brandon had already appeared in one of his dad's picture, *Legacy of Rage* (1970), in a clip of a TV appearance made earlier by the young Lee.

Following Bruce Lee's untimely death in 1973, Mrs. Lee brought her two children back to Los Angeles. After a traumatic childhood due to his dad's death, Brandon enrolled at Emerson College in Boston but left in 1985. He made his professional acting bow in the made-for-TV movie *KUNG FU: THE MOVIE* (1986) starring DAVID CARRADINE. His breakthrough movie was *Showdown in Little Tokyo* (1991), a rough actioner teaming Lee with Dolph Lundgren.

In 1993, athletic Lee, who was developing both as an actor and as a potential big-name star, was hired to star in *The Crow* (1994), based on the cult action comic book. He was cast as a murdered rock star who returned to Earth guided by a crow to avenge the murder of his fiancée. During the filming in North Carolina, Lee was accidentally shot in a freak accident (the dummy gun was loaded with a live bullet) and died at the hospital. On April 3, 1999, he was laid to rest next to his father at Lake View Cemetery in Seattle, Washington.

To a lesser degree than his father, Brandon Lee, in death, became something of a legend, not exactly the way this young Asian American had planned his life.

Brandon Lee in the early 1990s. (JC ARCHIVES)

Lee, Bruce (1940–1973) His fame was so great at the time of his puzzling death that Lee remained a legend for decades thereafter—not "just" as the most charismatic of all martial-arts movie stars but also as an Asian-American role model for generations of youngsters.

Born Li Yuen Kam in San Francisco's Chinatown, he was the fourth child of Eurasian parents. His dad was a veteran of the Cantonese (vaudeville) Opera, who was touring the West Coast as a singer and comedian when Bruce was born. The family moved to Hong Kong when Bruce was three, he already having made his film debut in *Golden Gate Girl* (1941). As a preteen, precocious Lee made several movies in Hong Kong.

In 1958 the muscular but slight actor returned to San Francisco, eventually enrolling at the University of Washington where he remained for three years. Later opening his own martial-arts academy, he married a former pupil in 1964, and their son BRANDON was born in 1965. (Their other child Shannon was born in 1969.)

After martial-arts competitions led to *THE GREEN HORNET* TV assignment as Kato, there should have been more acting parts offered to Bruce, but the existent bias against Asian Americans in the entertainment industry prevented that. Instead, Lee opened another kung fu school. Students who were in the film/TV business created occasional acting work for Bruce. The ambitious Lee wanted badly to play the lead in the TV series *KUNG FU* (1972–75), but it was Caucasian actor DAVID CARRADINE who eventually won the part.

Aggravated by Hollywood's rejection of him, the handsome actor went to Hong Kong where he starred in *THE BIG BOSS* (1971) and subsequent moneymakers. This prompted a Hollywood studio to finance *ENTER THE DRAGON* (1973). Later, during the making of *Game of Death*, Lee collapsed on the set. Some weeks later, while visiting an actress friend, the star died. Amid great speculation about his passing, a coroner's inquest determined that he died due to a major allergic reaction to ingredients in the headache medication he had been given on that fatal day. Eventually, footage from the unfinished *Game of Death* was edited into a 1978 release.

Even with the ascent of such later martial-arts cinema stars as JACKIE CHAN, CHOW YUN-FAT, and JET LI, Lee still remained, for many, the greatest of all such genre celebrities.

(In late 2001 it was announced that Lee's image was to be digitally enhanced and used for a new action feature to be produced by a Korean film company and with plans for an English-language version.)

Lee, Jason Scott (1966–) In the mid-1990s, this muscular (five-feet, seven-inch) Chinese-American/Pacific Islander–American seemed poised for major stardom, displaying a strong screen presence and an ability to portray a variety of Asian cultures. The career momentum, however, somehow fell apart.

Born in Oahu, Hawaii, one of five children, he attended Pearl High School where he was noted for his volleyball skills. Lee moved to the mainland to attend Fullerton College in Orange County, California, and to study acting. He quit school in 1987 to become part of the Friends and Artists Theater Ensemble in Los Angeles, where he spent a long apprenticeship.

Lee's movie debut was in a small role as a cholo in *Born in East L.A.* (1987). After appearances in *Ghoulies 3: Ghoulies Go to College* (1991) and as the Korean adoptee searching for his roots in the TV After School special *American Eyes* (1991), he made a breakthrough as the Inuit Eskimo in the lushly romantic *Map of the Human Heart* (1993). (For the part, Lee learned to speak with a stylized Eskimo accent.) That same year, he was charismatic as the fiery martial-arts star in *DRAGON: THE BRUCE LEE STORY* (1993). But the highly touted *RAPA NUI* (1994), set in the seventeenth century on Easter Island in the South Pacific—in which he was the half-naked prince of a doomed culture—was not liked. He was fittingly virile as the loincloth-garbed Mowgli in *The Jungle Book* (1994), a role once played on screen by Sabu (the actor from India). Lee was supposed to star in *Buddha* in the mid-1990s, based on the last screenplay by Robert Bolt, but that project never materialized. Thereafter, movie supporting roles did not help Lee's sagging career. In 2000, he was seen as Aladdin in the two-part, filmed-in-Turkey TV spectacle, *Arabian Nights* with Mili Avital as Scheherezade. For the animated sci-fi feature *Lilo & Stitch* (2002), the actor provided the voice of a principal character.

Lee, Jet See LI, JET.

***Left Hand of God, The* (1955)** Twentieth Century-Fox, color, 87 minutes. **Director:** Edward Dmytryk; **Screenplay:** Alfred Hayes; **Cast:** Humphrey Bogart (Jim Carmody), Gene Tierney (Ann Scott), Lee J. Cobb (Mieh Yang), Agnes Moorehead (Beryl Sigman), E. G. Marshall (Dr. Sigman), Jean Porter (Mary Yin), Victor Sen Yung (John Wong), Philip Ahn (Jan Teng), Benson Fong (Chun Tien).

This proficient if uninspired movie was based on William E. Barrett's 1951 novel. As presented, its premise bordered on the ridiculous: In post-World War II China, a former pilot turned soldier-of-fortune is working for a rapacious warlord, Mieh Yang, and is involved with a Eurasian mistress, Mary Yin. Tiring of his ignoble life, Jim Carmody escapes his friendly captor in the disguise of a recently murdered Catholic priest. The American takes refuge in a Chinese village, where missionaries Dr. and Mrs. Sigman provide hospitality and missionary nurse Ann Scott finds herself falling in love with this man of the cloth. At the crucial juncture, the warlord reappears, threatening to destroy the village. Carmody suggests that he and his former pal have a game of chance: If Carmody wins, Mieh Yang will retreat back to the hinterlands; should Mieh Yang win the dice toss, Carmody will return as the outlaw's military adviser. Carmody wins the bet and, thanks to the Sigmans, squares himself with church authorities and Ann.

This flimsy and far-fetched story line aside, it was difficult to tell who was more ridiculous—Bogart as a snarling pretend-priest or Cobb doing another of his Asian imitations. Unlike his solemn role of Siam's prime minister in *ANNA AND THE KING OF SIAM* (1946), here Cobb was performing his Oriental rogue with tongue in cheek. His demeanor was no more convincing than his makeup

Leong, James B. (1889–1967) One of Hollywood's veteran Asian performers, Leong played a variety of nationalities on screen. Born in Shanghai, China, he and his parents immigrated to the United States when he was a boy. In 1915 he graduated from Muncie Normal College in Indiana and came to Hollywood shortly thereafter. He frequently served as a technical director on pictures involving Chinese ambiance. He was in front of the camera by 1923 *(Purple Dawn)*, was both a henchman and high priest in *Welcome Danger* (1929), and played a TONG member in *THE HATCHET MAN* (1932). Other film roles included *Ace Drummond* (1936—serial) and *The Adventures of Marco Polo* (1938). He played a Japanese on camera in *Remember Pearl Harbor* (1942), *Headin' for God's Country* (1943), and *THE PURPLE HEART* (1944). Some of his later assignments included 1956's *Around the World in 80 Days* and *THE TEAHOUSE OF THE AUGUST MOON*.

***Lethal Weapon 4* (1998)** Warner Bros., color, 123 minutes. **Director:** Richard Donner; **Screenplay:** Channing Gibson; **Cast:** Mel Gibson (Det. Martin Riggs), Danny Glover (Det. Roger Murtaugh), Joe Pesci (Leo Getz), Rene Russo (Lorna Cole), Chris Rock (Lee Butters), Jet Li (Wah Sing Ku), Kim Chan (Uncle Benny), Darlene Love (Trish Murtaugh), Eddy Ko (Hong), Steven Lam (Ping), Dalvin Jung (Detective Ng).

What began as an offbeat cop/buddy series with *Lethal Weapon* (1987) deteriorated into a callous, formula-driven franchise. Maverick Los Angeles cop Martin Riggs and his exasperated cohort Det. Roger Murtaugh are back, aided by young police detective Lee Butters and a well-meaning but obnoxious civilian Leo Getz. The group happens upon a smuggling operation that brings illegal Asian immigrants into the United States. Their investigation raises the ire of Chinatown mob boss Uncle Benny, who has a deal with triad leader Wah Sing Ku to use the smuggling profits to free several leaders of the Hong Kong triad currently in unfriendly hands.

This was the major American film debut of Hong Kong martial-arts star LI. Unfortunately, in the predictable climax, he is unable to exhibit many of his karate chops because his middle-aged opponents (Gibson and Glover) are not trained in the martial arts, so the final confrontation is more a battle of firearms. But during an earlier portion of the action entry, he does get to brutalize wisecracking Riggs with a brief exhibition of his martial-arts skills. Most of the Asian figures presented here are mobsters or their underlings.

Made at a cost of $140 million, *Lethal Weapon 4* grossed only slightly more than $129 in domestic box-office distribution.

***Letter, The* (1940)** Warner Bros, b&w, 95 minutes. **Director:** William Wyler; **Screenplay:** Howard Koch; **Cast:** Bette Davis (Leslie Crosbie), Herbert Marshall (Robert Crosbie), James Stephenson (Howard Joyce), Frieda Inescort (Dorothy Joyce), Gale Sondergaard (Mrs. Hammond), Cecil Kellaway (Prescott), Victor Sen Yung (Ong Chi Seng), Willie Fung (Chung Hi).

This is one of the most impressive of Warner Bros.' Far East–set dramas that were filmed on the studio's back lot. This atmospheric drama of passion in Malaya was based on W. Somerset Maugham's controversial 1927 play that had been transformed into a Paramount film two years later. Cast as the murderess in that movie version was Jeanne Eagels, who was repeating her stage assignment. Her colead in the 1929 film was Herbert Marshall, who appeared as the lover who is murdered; in the 1940 remake, Britisher Marshall was cast as the cuckolded husband.

In the original play Leslie Crosbie's rival for Hammond's affections is his Chinese mistress. As the stage drama concludes, Leslie is alone *without* her spouse. In the 1929 film adaptation, Hammond's Chinese love is his wife, Li-Ti. As played by Lady Tsen Mei, she has an incriminating letter that Leslie wrote to Hammond. To recover the crucial correspondence, Leslie's husband—played by Reginald Owen—must put together the needed funds, which nearly bankrupts him. The narrative ends with Leslie left to an impoverished and loveless future.

By the time it was decided to convert *The Letter* into a Davis screen vehicle, the more-stringent film-industry production code/office demanded changes: (1) The Chinese wife was to be switched to an Eurasian, and (2) Davis's character, Leslie Crosbie, must be punished for her acts of adultery and, of course, the homicide. As such, the 1940 movie has Leslie confessing her guilt to her stoic husband. That done, she steps outside where the lover's widow has been lurking in the shadows. The usually inscrutable Mrs. Hammond—performed by Sondergaard—draws a knife and stabs Leslie.

While the usual run of Asian-American actors flit through the background of *The Letter*, it is Minnesota-born Sondergaard who creates an effective representation of the Eurasian Mrs. Hammond, effectively relying on interior characterization, a degree of makeup, and the film's atmospheric lighting to portray this Far Eastern woman caught up in tradition, pride, and anger.

The 1940 *The Letter* received seven Academy Award nominations: Best Actress (Davis), Best Black and White Cinematography, Best Director, Best Film Editing, Best Original Score, Best Picture, and Best Supporting Actor (Stephenson).

The Letter was remade as *The Unfaithful* (1947) with an American setting and starring Ann Sheridan and Zachary Scott. In 1982 the tale reappeared as a made-for-TV film with Lee Remick and Ronald Pickup, with the drama now back to its original tropical setting. Kieu Chinh played the "Chinese Woman" in this telefeature, which won three Emmy Awards.

Li, Jet (aka: Jet Lee; Li Lianjie) (1963–) In the increasingly crowded field of Hong Kong martial-arts stars of the 1990s, Li was in the top echelons. Like JACKIE CHAN, CHOW YUN-FAT, and SAMMO HUNG, he ventured to the United States to capitalize on his box-office prowess.

He was born Li Lianjie in Beijing, China. His mother raised five children by selling bus tickets. As the youngest, he inherited the worn-out clothing from his two brothers and two sisters. He was only eight when he began training at the Beijing amateur Sports School in wushu (i.e., performance martial art). By age eleven, he was winning medals in homeland competitions. Later a coach of repute, he made his debut film in *Shao Lin tzu* (Shaolin Temple) (1979) and became part of the 1980s Hong Kong martial-arts film boom, directing his first feature *Zhong hua ying xiong* (Born to Defence) in 1986.

A hugely popular star in the Far East (e.g., *Once Upon a Time in China*, 1991), the five-feet, six-inch Li made his Hollywood major movie debut as the triad hoodlum Wah Sing Ku in *LETHAL WEAPON 4* (1998), holding his own against stars Mel Gibson and Danny Glover. (It was the first time he had played a villain on screen.) He rejected a role in *CROUCHING TIGER, HIDDEN DRAGON* (2000) to accept the lead in *ROMEO MUST DIE* (2000), a modern-day rendition of *Romeo and Juliet* set against Asian- and African-American gangs in San Francisco. The boyish-looking actor next starred in the Paris-shot *Kiss of the Dragon* (2001), which he coproduced, and *The One* (2001) for director James Wong, which dealt with a law enforcer fighting his evil duplicate from a parallel universe. Li was also in contention to play Kato in a new big-screen version of *THE GREEN HORNET*, but that project fell apart for the star. Li returned to China to star in the historical action drama *Hero* (2002).

Li Lian-jie See LI, JET.

***Limehouse Blues* (1934)** Paramount, b&w, 66 minutes. **Director:** Alexander Hall; **Screenplay:** Cyril Hume and Arthur Phillips; **Cast:** George Raft (Harry Young), Jean

Parker (Toni Talbot), Anna May Wong (Tu Tuan), Kent Taylor (Eric Benton), Montagu Love (Pug Talbot), Billy Bevan (Herb), Robert Loraine (Inspector Sheridan), E. Allyn Warren (Ching Lee).

Limehouse Blues utilizes themes, relationship formats, and ambiance established in D. W. Griffith's well-remembered silent drama, BROKEN BLOSSOMS (1919). The picaresque new movie features Raft—the real-life New York underworld thug-turned-hoofer/movie star—as a Chinese-American who migrates from New York's Chinatown to the seamy section of London. There, in the Limehouse Causeway on the riverfront, Young becomes a powerful force in the smuggling racket. Although he has a Chinese mistress, Tu Tuan, he covets Toni, a tattered Caucasian flower of the Limehouse district. As his unrequited love for her grows, she becomes involved with a Caucasian (Taylor), much to the amusement of Tu Tuan who had warned Young this would happen. Still not satisfied, the vengeful Tu Tuan snitches to the police about her lover and then commits suicide. As for Young, he becomes remorseful about wanting to have Toni's boyfriend murdered and in the process of saving the intended victim, is fatally wounded himself. Before he expires, he puts things right with the police about Toni's innocence in the matter. She rejoins her Caucasian boyfriend.

Once again, as in *THE HATCHET MAN* (1932) and *THE SON-DAUGHTER* (1933)—or for that matter *BROKEN BLOSSOMS*—the lead role is played (none too convincingly) by a Caucasian. (The fact that Raft was a heavily accented New Yorker with a swarthy complexion did not make his acting challenge any easier.) Nevertheless, this was a rare instance at the time for an Occidental actor (albeit playing a half-caste) in a lead role to have an overtly stated long-term relationship with an Asian, even if she is his mistress, not his wife. It would be many years before Hollywood would allow, or the filmgoing public would accept, an on-camera interracial marriage.

Ling, Bai (1970–) Chosen one of *People* magazine's "50 Most Beautiful People in the World" in 1998, she had already become a presence in American-made movies. Born in China, she served three years in the People's Liberation Army there where she performed for servicemen in Tibet. Also, before age eighteen, she had a severe depression, was hospitalized for it, and became a movie star in her homeland. By 1991 she had moved to the United States. In 1993–94, she appeared in an episode each of the TV series *Homicide: Life on the Street* and *Touched by an Angel.* She was in *THE CROW* (1994) and played a Chinese interpreter in *Nixon* (1995). Ling's career jumped forward when she was cast as Richard Gere's defense attorney in *RED CORNER* (1997), Dr. Loveless's personal assistant in *Wild Wild West* (1999), and the ill-fated Tuptim in *ANNA AND THE KING* (1999). After costarring with Thomas Gibson in the poorly received telefeature *THE LOST EMPIRE* (2001), the same year she appeared with Adrian Paul in the sci-fi entry *The Breed.* Her next picture was *Face* (2002).

***Little Tokyo, U.S.A.* (1942)** Twentieth Century-Fox, b&w, 64 minutes. **Director:** Otto Brower; **Screenplay:** George Bricker; **Cast:** Preston Foster (Michael Steele), Brenda Joyce (Maris Hanover), Harold Huber (Taimua), Don Douglas (Hendricks), June Duprez (Teru), George E. Stone (Kingoro), Abner Biberman (Satsuma), Beal Wong (Shadow), Leonard Strong (Fujiama), Richard Loo (Oshiima).

Rushed into release eight months after the United States declared war on Japan, this low-budget feature set the tone for Hollywood's depiction of the Japanese during World War II and thereafter. Using mostly Caucasians (made up as Nipponese) and a complement of non-Japanese Asian Americans to perform other Japanese roles, the modest drama tells of Axis intrigue in Los Angeles prior to the attack on Pearl Harbor in December 1941. Its plot concerns an L.A. policeman (Foster) and his newspaper-reporter girlfriend (Joyce) who stumble into the espionage activities of Japanese-American Taimua and rout his confederates.

Liu, Lucy (1967–) She was only five feet, one inch tall, but on screen she demonstrated a strong presence. Whether as the calculating Ling Woo on the TV series *ALLY MCBEAL* (1997–2001, 2002) or the karate-chopping Alex Munday in the feature film *Charlie's Angels* (2000), Liu presented a new-style image of the Asian-American woman—one who was bold, resourceful, and demanding. It was a representation that served her well in carving out a screen career in the 1990s and thereafter.

Born to Chinese immigrants (her mother was a biochemist, her father a civil engineer) who were living in Queens, New York, following graduation from Stuyvesant High School in 1986, Liu enrolled at New York University but transferred after her freshman year to the University of Michigan, from which she graduated with a degree in Chinese Language and Culture. In her senior year on campus, she won the lead in a stage production of *Alice in Wonderland;* this determined her on an acting career. She relocated to Los Angeles, where one of her first TV episode assignments was as a waitress on *Beverly Hills, 90210* in 1990; the role mirrored her daytime job. Many such bits led to her being cast as a pushy co-ed on *Pearl* (1996), the Rhea Perlman sitcom.

Her feature film career began with *Jerry Maguire* (1996) as Tom Cruise's former girlfriend, and her flintiness was showcased as the dominatrix in Mel Gibson's action picture *Payback* (1999). She was Lia, a hitchhiker in the not well-liked *Play It to the Bone* (1999), after which she joined Drew Barrymore and Cameron Diaz for the mega-hit *Charlie's Angels* (2000), which did much to boost Liu's professional stock in Hollywood. Also in 2000 she appeared in the western spoof *Shanghai Noon* (2000) starring JACKIE CHAN. She joined Burt Reynolds and David Schwimmer in the comedy *Hotel* (2001) and was in the thriller *Company Man* (2002). She next appeared in *Chicago: The Musical* (2002) and reprised her crimefighter antics in *Charlie's Angels 2* (2003).

Lone, John (1952–) With his charismatic and very different performances as the Neanderthal in *Iceman* (1984) and the sinister Chinatown underworld figure in *YEAR OF THE DRAGON* (1985), the handsome Lone seemed destined for stardom. That promise seemed to be fulfilled when he played the title character in Bernardo Bertolucci's *The Last Emperor* (1987).

By the time Lone was born in Hong Kong, his parents had already separated, and he was essentially an orphan. He was given over to a guardian, but because that family was impoverished, he had to drop out of school at a very early age. When he was nine, he was apprenticed to the Hong Kong branch (the Chin Chiu Academy) of the Peking Opera, learning traditional classical Chinese theater. Concluding that the program was too restrictive, he left at the age of eighteen and went into hiding. In this period, he became entranced with movies. He was offered a contract to make films for Run Run Shaw's studio, an organization that turned out most of the martial-arts movies for the Asian market, but Lone turned it down, as not being of interest.

Later, Lone went to the United States under the sponsorship of an American family who had been doing business in Hong Kong. He graduated from the American Academy of Dramatic Arts in Pasadena, California. In Los Angeles, he appeared in stage productions of the East/West Players and did episodic television. He made his screen debut as the Chinese cook in *King Kong* (1976) and played a bit in *Americathon* (1979). In the early 1980s, he performed in several plays by David Henry Hwang, who later wrote *M. Butterfly*. One of these, *F.O.B.* (1980), was staged by MAKO, his former director at East/West, at the Public Theater in New York City. It earned Lone an Obie Award.

In 1985 he directed a one-hour drama for PBS-TV entitled *Paper Angels*, which dealt with Chinese immigrants coming to the United States in 1915. The same year as the acclaimed *The Last Emperor*, he was in the Austrian-produced *Echoes of Paradise*. This was followed by *The Moderns* (1988) and the exotic *Shadow of China* (1991). He was the sexually ambiguous Beijing opera diva in the disappointing screen version of *M. BUTTERFLY* (1993), a part he had inadvertently turned down on stage. Lone played sinister Shiwan Khan in *The Shadow* (1994), although he once stated that he would never play such inscrutable DR. FU MANCHU types of screen roles. When not acting, Lone had a separate career as a pop recording artist for the Hong Kong market. He was on camera with JACKIE CHAN in *Rush Hour 2* (2001).

Long Cheng See CHAN, JACKIE.

Loo, Richard (1903–1983) Like PHILIP AHN, Loo was frequently cast on screen as a menacing Japanese in World War II film dramas and became identified with such villainous roles. (If he had been Japanese American, he would have doubtlessly been shipped to one of the American internment camps for such ethnics during the war.) Actually he was Chinese American and was born on Maui, Hawaii, to a family of sugar planters. As a teenager, he came to the mainland and attended the University of California at Berkeley. The Great Depression sank his business career (as manager of a Chinese import house), and he switched to acting, first on the stage (playing a rickshaw boy, although he knew no Chinese and spoke gibberish instead) and then in films (*Dirigible*, 1931). Like most Asian Americans in Hollywood of that period, he was defined by his racial heritage and not by his acting acumen. Although the parts were plentiful, the assignments were small and stereotypical: a headwaiter in *After the Thin Man* (1936), a farmer in *THE GOOD EARTH* (1937), a TONG chief in *Mr. Wong in Chinatown* (1939), and a tong leader in *Doomed to Die* (1940).

With the coming of the Second World War, Loo's career turned to playing Japanese: *They Met in Bombay* (1941), *Yanks Ahoy!* (1943), *BEHIND THE RISING SUN* (1943), *God Is My Co-Pilot* (1945), *Betrayal from the East* (1945), and *TOKYO ROSE* (1946). These parts continued into the 1950s with such entries as *I Was an American Spy* (1951), and then he moved on to the Korean War: *Battle Hymn* (1957). Occasionally, he was a good guy, as when he played the American soldier in *The Steel Helmet* (1951) and the Chinese friend of Han Suyin in *LOVE IS A MANY-SPLENDORED THING* (1955). A frequent TV performer, Loo was Master Sun in the *KUNG FU* series in 1972. His last acting work included the TV movie, *Collision Course* (1975).

Lorre, Peter (1904–1964) He was born in Hungary, stage trained in Vienna, and starred in a German film classic (1931's *M*). Later, this rotund, short actor with the raspy voice and bulging eyes provided a subtle characterization of the Japanese businessman turned amateur sleuth in Hollywood's MR. MOTO movie series.

Born Laszlo Lowenstein, he abandoned his livelihood as a bank clerk to study acting and made his film debut in Germany in 1929. After going to England for a featured role in Alfred Hitchcock's *The Man Who Knew Too Much* (1934) Lorre relocated to the United States to play Raskolnikov in Hollywood's *Crime and Punishment* (1935). The distinctive character actor first played the enterprising Kentaro Moto in THINK FAST, MR. MOTO (1937) and portrayed the astute sleuth in seven additional film adventures, ending with *Mr. Moto Takes a Vacation* (1939). In the 1940s Lorre was teamed frequently on camera with oversized screen menace Sydney Greenstreet: *The Maltese Falcon* (1941), *Casablanca* (1942), and *The Mask of Dimitrios* (1944). His last film was the teenage sand-and-music entry, *Muscle Beach Party* (1964).

***Lost Horizon* (1937)** Columbia, b&w, 133 minutes. **Director:** Frank Capra; **Screenplay:** Robert Riskin; **Cast:** Ronald Colman (Robert Conway), Jane Wyatt (Sondra), Edward Everett Horton (Alexander P. Lovett), John Howard (George Conway), Thomas Mitchell (Henry (Barnard), Margo (Maria), Isabel Jewell (Gloria Stone), H. B. Warner (Chang), Sam Jaffe (High Lama), Willie Fung (bandit leader).

This beloved Hollywood romantic classic film, based on James Hilton's 1933 novel, was an early exponent of Asian mysticism as a panacea for internal peace of mind and a positive source for a well-functioning society. With so much of the world still engulfed in the Great Depression and the approaching Second World War, Hilton caught the public's fancy with his feel-good account of the wondrous Shangri-La, a utopian fantasy village high in the Tibetan Himalayan Mountains.

In casting this major production, the studio filled the primary Asian role with British-born Warner as Chang, a lama at Shangri-La, and Jewish-American New Yorker Jaffe as the 200-year-old Belgian Father Perrault, the venerated high lama. Only a few Asians actually made it into the movie cast, with FUNG seen as a Chinese bandit, and George Chan as a priest. Among the porters of Shangri-La—played mostly by Caucasian movie bit players—was Native American chief John Big Tree. The casting decisions were a reflection of a time when political correctness or sensitivity was not a priority with Hollywood film studios or mainstream filmgoers.

Lost Horizon won an Academy Award for Best Film Editing. It received Oscar nominations for Best Picture, Best Score, Best Sound, and Best Supporting Actor (Warner).

Hilton's original book and the 1937 film would be the basis for a 1956 Broadway musical entitled *Shangri-la* (and a follow-up *Hallmark Hall of Fame* TV special presentation in 1960), as well as the 1973 film musical, *Lost Horizon.* In this poorly received new screen offering, Britisher John Gielgud was Chang with Frenchman Charles Boyer as the High Lama, with Asian-American James SHIGETA wasted in a smallish role as Brother To-Lenn.

***Love Is a Many-Splendored Thing* (1955)** Twentieth Century-Fox, color, 102 minutes. **Director:** Henry King; **Screenplay:** John Patrick; **Cast:** William Holden (Mark Elliot), Jennifer Jones (Han Suyin), Torin Thatcher (Mr. Palmer-Jones), Isobel Elsom (Adeline Palmer-Jones), Murray Matheson (Dr. Tam), Virginia Gregg (Ann Richards),

Jennifer Jones, William Holden (center), and Leonard Strong in *Love Is a Many-Splendored Thing* (1955). (JC ARCHIVES)

Richard Loo (Robert Hung), Soo Yong (Nora Hung), Philip Ahn (Third Uncle).

With the widespread commercial acceptance of its widescreen process CinemaScope in the early 1950s, Twentieth Century-Fox found a successful formula of enhancing its romantic movie dramas with the beauty of on-location filming, a gimmick that definitely creates the proper romantic aura for this romantic fiction set in Hong Kong at the time of the Korean War. Another asset of this celluloid love story was its hugely popular theme song by Sammy Fain and Paul Francis Webster.

Han Suyin's best-selling novel *A Many Splendored Thing* (1952) was fiction with autobiographical elements. The tearjerker film tells of a hard-working Eurasian physician, Suyin, in postwar Hong Kong. She thinks her life is in order until she meets Mark Elliot, a married American news correspondent. Despite knowing the problems involved in their interracial, adulterous romance, they are too attracted to one another to deny their love, which they often proclaim to each other high on the hills above Hong Kong. The couple becomes the nasty talk of the city, and the physician is snubbed by the local blue bloods as well as the influential decision makers at her hospital. Meanwhile, Elliot's wife refuses to grant him a divorce. At this crucial juncture, the journalist is ordered to Korea to observe the growing conflict there. While on assignment, he is killed. A stoic Han Suyin climbs their favorite windy hill above the Hong Kong skyline, finding happiness in her memories.

Once again, Hollywood was not ready to (1) have an interracial romance—in this case between a half-caste Chinese/European and an American—end in matrimony, or (2) use an Asian or Eurasian talent for the key role opposite a Caucasian actor. Back in 1934, for example, the latter had been the guiding principle behind casting George Raft as the half-caste of *Limehouse Blues*, but at that time, there was a feeling among mainstream Hollywood performers that playing a character of another race was not only an artistic challenge but also a catchy gimmick that would appeal to their public. By the mid-1950s, this reasoning was disappearing, but the earlier-mentioned two factors were still very much intact. It would be another few years before a film such as *THE WORLD OF SUZIE WONG* (1960) could and would employ a Hong Kong-born actress (NANCY KWAN) in the lead. By then, not only were times changing concerning attitudes to ethnic minorities, but also Broadway had already proven, with the stage version of *The World of Suzie Wong*, that using an actress (FRANCE NUYEN) of Vietnamese-French heritage to play opposite a Caucasian leading man (William Shatner) would not adversely affect the box-office take.

The feature film won three Academy Awards: Best Costume Design (Color), Best Original Dramatic Score, and Best Song ("Love Is a Many-Splendored Thing"), and received five other Oscar nominations: Best Actress (Jones), Best Art Direction/Set Decoration (Color), Best Cinematography (Color), Best Picture, and Best Sound.

From 1967–71, CBS-TV aired the daytime serial drama *LOVE IS A MANY SPLENDORED THING*, a sequel to, but not a remake of, the 1955 movie original.

Luke, Keye (1904–1991) Despite a screen career that embraced well more than 100 roles, Luke will always be associated with his role as Lee, the enthusiastic if bewildered #1 son of CHARLIE CHAN in the movie detective series.

Born in either Canton, China, or New York City, he spent his childhood in Seattle, Washington. He studied art at the University of Washington and later was hired to create artwork for use at Grauman's Chinese Theater in Hollywood. Sometimes, he would act as technical adviser for movies with Chinese backdrops. Luke made his movie acting debut in Greta Garbo's romantic drama, *The Painted Veil* (1934).

Within a year of his screen bow, Luke was playing the ebullient eldest son of the Chinese sleuth in *Charlie Chan in Shanghai* (1935), a part he continued with until the late 1930s and then returned to in the late 1940s. He took over for Boris Karloff in the MR. WONG series for one entry (*PHANTOM OF CHINATOWN*, 1940). In two 1940 serials (*THE GREEN HORNET* and *The Green Hornet Strikes Back)*, he was cast as Kato. More fortunate than most Asian-American performers, Luke was placed under MGM contract and given relatively decent roles, including being a series regular as intern Dr. Lee Wong How in the Dr. Gillespie medical series.

A prolific TV performer, his parts ranged from the western *Annie Oakley* in 1954 to *M*A*S*H* in 1972 to *The Golden Girls* in 1985. A regular on the *Kentucky Jones* sitcom (1964–65) and as Master Po on *KUNG FU* (1972–75), the latter part as the blind but masterful martial-arts and Asian philosophy instructor was his favorite. On the animated children's TV series, *THE AMAZING CHAN AND THE CHAN CLAN*, Luke provided the voice of the great Charlie Chan from 1972 to 1974. He was "the Ancient One" on the daytime soap *General Hospital* in 1985 and was Sabasan on the TV series *SIDEKICKS* (1986). His final screen assignment was in Woody Allen's *Alice* (1990) as the Chinatown herbalist giving advice to Mia Farrow. On Broadway, Keye Luke played the patriarch of a Chinese-American family in the musical *Flower Drum Song* (1958).

M

***Macao* (1952)** RKO, b&w, 80 minutes. **Directors:** Josef von Sternberg and uncredited Nicholas Ray; **Screenplay:** Bernard C. Schoenfeld and Stanley Rubin; **Cast:** Robert Mitchum (Nick Cochran), Jane Russell (Julie Benson), William Bendix (Lawrence Trumble), Thomas Gomez (Lieutenant Sebastian), Gloria Grahame (Margie), Brad Dexter (Halloran), Philip Ahn (Itzumi), Vladimir Sokoloff (Kwan Sum Tang), George Chan (Chinese photographer), James B. Leong (knifer).

Von Sternberg, who had directed such Asian-set dramas as *SHANGHAI EXPRESS* (1932) and *THE SHANGHAI GESTURE* (1941), returned to the "mysterious" Far East for this snail-paced drama that occurs at the notorious Portuguese colony. To this intriguing island locale (courtesy of the studio back lot) come three Americans: Nick Cochran, an escapee convicted for a crime he didn't commit, "entertainer"/songstress Julie Benson, and wisecracking detective Lawrence Trumble. Once in Macao, Julie is hired to sing at the gambling club owned by Halloran, a crime kingpin who takes a liking to her; this upsets Halloran's current mistress, the hot-tempered croupier Margie. Meanwhile, corrupt local police-detective Sebastian is out to grab extra money in any manner necessary.

By the early 1950s, relying on the exotic Far East as a backdrop for a drama was no guarantee of boosting a trite story line into something special, and the Caucasian and Asian-American talent used to create the atmosphere seemed as unauthentic as the sets and as lethargic as the film's plot.

***Madame Butterfly* (1932)** Paramount, b&w, 86 minutes. **Director:** Marion Gering; **Screenplay:** Josephine Lovett and Joseph Moncure March; **Cast:** Sylvia Sidney (Cho-Cho San), Cary Grant (Lt. B. F. Pinkerton), Charlie Ruggles (Lieutenant Barton), Irving Pichel (Yamadori), Helen Jerome Eddy (Cho-Cho San's mother), Edmund Breese (Cho-Cho San's grandfather).

In 1915, Mary Pickford, Marshall Neilan, and Olive West had starred in a silent screen version of *Madame Butterfly*, based on the novel (1898) by John Luther Long and the David Belasco play (1900).

For this new film edition, Giacomo Puccini's music from his famed 1904 opera was used as background orchestral accompaniment. For many viewers, casting the contemporary Sidney (née Sophie Koslow) in the key assignment was a strange choice, since her métier was urban (melo)drama. The scenario follows the well-known tale of the GEISHA girl Cho-Cho San, who weds dashing American naval lieutenant Pinkerton. Thereafter, he returns to active duty and doesn't return for three years, putting Cho-Cho San in a state of shame, especially because she has sworn to wait for him. By then her child by him is nearly three years old. Because Pinkerton reveals that he has married his American sweetheart, the grief-stricken Cho-Cho San says nothing of their boy. After Pinkerton leaves, she sends her son to be with her family, and she commits hara-kiri.

As exotic distraction and for the novelty of watching Sidney playing so against type, *Madame Butterfly* found a modest audience in the United States. Yet, with its distorted view of by-then outdated Japanese customs, the film did poorly when distributed in Japan.

Mme. Lui-Tsong See *GALLERY OF MME. LUI-TSONG, THE.*

***Magnum, P.I.* (1980–1988)** CBS-TV series, color, 60 minutes. **Cast:** Tom Selleck (Thomas Sullivan Magnum), John Hillerman (Jonathan Quayle Higgins III), Roger E.

Mosley (T.C. [Theodore Calvin]), Larry Manetti (Rick [Orville Wright]), Orson Welles (Robin Masters—voice only: 1981–85), Jeff MacKay (Mac Reynolds: 1981–82, 1984–85, 1986–88), Kwan Hi Lim (Lieutenant Tanaka: 1982–88).

No sooner had *HAWAII FIVE-O* (1968–80) gone off the air than the same TV network replaced the police drama in their lineup with *Magnum, P.I.*, another show dedicated to showcasing the lush beauty of the Hawaiian island of Oahu. The new offering boasted a more ingratiating hero (Thomas Magnum) and a more relaxed lifestyle (the rambling beachfront estate of Robin Masters) than had the now-defunct cop show. The lead character, Magnum, a former navy intelligence officer, proved to be a quite casual private detective, often racing about the island in his employer's Ferrari, wearing shorts, a flowered short-sleeve shirt, and a pair of hip sunglasses. Because so much of *Magnum, P.I.* was devoted to the detective's pursuit of lovely women, not much of any episode focused on either the police force (one of whom was Hawaiian-American Lieutenant Tanaka) or ethnic criminal types, as had been the case with *Hawaii Five-O*.

***Majority of One, A* (1961)** Warner Bros., color, 156 minutes. **Director:** Mervyn LeRoy; **Screenplay:** Leonard Spigelgass; **Cast:** Rosalind Russell (Mrs. Bertha Jacoby), Alec Guinness (Koichi Asano), Ray Danton (Jerome Black), Madlyn Rhue (Alice Black), Mae Questel (Mrs. Rubin), Marc Mamo (Eddie), Yuki Shimoda (Mr. Asano's secretary), Tsuruko Kobayashi (Mr. Asano's daughter-in-law).

In 1959, Gertrude Berg (of *The Goldbergs* radio and TV fame) starred on Broadway opposite Sir Cedric Hardwicke in Spigelgass's successful comedy, which deals with a middle-aged widow from Brooklyn who finds love with a similarly aged wealthy Japanese widower. When the project was transferred to the screen, Hollywood determined that Berg was too Jewish for the role and instead cast non-Jewish Russell in the lead assignment as a Jewish widow! With far less concern, it was decided to follow the conceit of the Broadway production and utilize a Britisher to impersonate the Japanese businessman.

If Russell was badly miscast, overdoing her accent, gestures, and matronly wardrobe, then Guinness was equally amiss, burying any potential warmth of his characterization in subtle mannerisms that made his performance both too stagy and too interior. (And there certainly was no blending of acting style between Guinness and those actors of actual Asian heritage.)

As a result this comedy with a serious message about preconceived racial bias that was amplified by World War II became a drawn-out affair, salvaged occasionally by the slapstick performance of the supporting cast.

Mako (1933–) A distinguished actor who was Oscar nominated (*THE SAND PEBBLES*, 1966) and Tony Award nominated (*Pacific Overtures*, 1976), the diminutive Mako was also the founder of the influential East/West Players in Los Angeles in 1965–66, a theater group that was geared to his vision that "ethnic" theater need not be narrowly focused.

He was born Makoto Iwamatsu in Kobe, Japan, and was raised by his grandparents because his parents were studying art in America. When Japan and the United States declared war in late 1941, his parents remained in the States working for the Office of War Information. After the surrender, they were granted U.S. residency, and Mako joined them. After studying architecture at Pratt Institute in New York, he joined the U.S. Army in the early 1950s, where he performed in shows. Later, he enrolled at the Pasadena Community Playhouse in California. He had a tiny role in the World War II film *Never So Few* (1959), and his early TV work included an episode of *McHale's Navy* in 1962.

After his meaty role as the tortured and murdered coolie in *The Sand Pebbles*, Mako remained extremely active in all media, but rarely on film did he receive assignments that were as dimensional. His black-belt status in karate led him to such action entries as *The Big Brawl* (1980) and *The Perfect Weapon* (1991). On the short-surviving TV series *Hawaiian Heat* (1984), Mako was Maj. Taro Oshira, police-department boss of two ex-Chicago cops. Recent films included *Seven Years in Tibet* (1997), a voice in the animated feature *The Rugrats in Paris: The Movie* (2000), playing Adm. Isoroku Yamamoto in *Pearl Harbor* (2001), and appearing in *She Said I Love You* (2001), a romantic comedy set in Los Angeles.

For many years, he was an outspoken advocate for racial equality in the acting profession. In 1994 he received a star on the Hollywood Walk of Fame, one of the relatively few Asian performers to do so to date.

***Manchurian Candidate, The* (1962)** United Artists, b&w, 126 minutes. **Director:** John Frankenheimer; **Screenplay:** George Axelrod; **Cast:** Frank Sinatra (Bennett Marco), Laurence Harvey (Raymond Shaw), Janet Leigh (Rosie), Angela Lansbury (Raymond's mother [Mrs. Iselin]), Henry Silva (Chunjin), James Gregory (Sen. Jon Iselin), Khigh Dhiegh (Yen Lo).

As one of Hollywood's political suspense classics, this film played effectively on the U.S. paranoia about extreme possibilities during the extended cold-war period. The narrative revisited the Korean conflict of a decade prior and set up a new enemy—the Chinese Communists. The latter became the standard villains of Hollywood's espionage thrillers of the future (e.g., *The Chairman*, 1969), especially after the Soviet government decentralized in the 1990s.

During the Korean War, team members of a U.S. Army platoon are captured and flown to Manchuria, where the Chinese Communists brainwash them into believing that one of their group, Raymond Shaw, is a hero. The men are released and they return to the United States, where Shaw is awarded the Congressional Medal of Honor. The plan is to use the heroic Shaw as a programmed pawn to eliminate a U.S. presidential candidate. The chief U.S. agent for the Chinese Communists' scheme is Shaw's avaricious mother, the wife of a current U.S. senator.

With such strong, frightening characterizations by Lansbury and to a lesser degree by Gregory as her spouse, it was little wonder that Shaw, the pawn in the operation, faded into the background. On the other hand, the sinister forces (i.e., the Chinese Reds) remained firmly in mind as the villains pulling the puppet strings in their master plan.

The Manchurian Candidate won two Academy Award nominations: Best Film Editing and Best Supporting Actress (Lansbury).

martial arts—feature films and television The ancient Japanese art of self-defense and its accompanying philosophical approach to self and to others created not only a global subculture but also a genre of Hollywood screen products and stars. Given Hollywood's long-time prejudice against Asian-American actors headlining on the screen, many of the notables associated with the genre were, until recent years, Caucasians.

One of the first to incorporate martial arts into a feature film was director SAMUEL FULLER in *THE CRIMSON KIMONO* (1960). BRUCE LEE's energetic skills in the field were displayed in the TV series *THE GREEN HORNET* (1966–67). Thereafter, when Lee could not get work in Hollywood or on TV due to racial bias, he went to Hong Kong and made several successful martial arts pictures. *ENTER THE DRAGON* (1973), in an English-language version, was released in the United States in the year of his death, proving that the format could be popular with American filmgoers. Its success engendered a rash of martial-arts movies made abroad that were distributed in the West in dubbed or subtitled versions. African-American actor Jim Kelly, who had been featured in *Enter the Dragon*, made several American action movies—as part of the black exploitation cycle—that displayed his karate talents. Meanwhile, on U.S. television, DAVID CARRADINE starred in *KUNG FU* (1972–75) playing a Chinese American who is well versed in martial arts. He also made such genre movies as *Circle of Iron* (1979) and the later TV series, *KUNG FU: THE LEGEND CONTINUES* (1993–97).

A great impetus to the Hollywood martial-arts craze of the 1980s was *THE KARATE KID* (1984) featuring PAT MORITA as the old instructor of a young boy who has the urge to win in life and is willing to learn a new approach to living. The feel-good movie inspired three big-screen sequels and encouraged the careers of such martial-arts movie stars in Hollywood as Jean-Claude Van Damme (e.g., *Bloodsport*, 1988; *Kickboxer*, 1989), Chuck Norris (e.g., *Force of One*, 1979; *An Eye for an Eye*, 1981), Michael Dudikoff (e.g., *American Ninja*, 1985, and its many sequels), Steven Seagal (e.g., *Above the Law*, 1988; *Marked for Death*, 1990), Dolph Lundgren (e.g., *The Punisher*, 1990; *Cover-Up*, 1991), and BRANDON LEE (e.g., *Showdown in Little Tokyo*, 1991; *THE CROW*, 1994).

Meanwhile, the success of the animated TV series *TEENAGE MUTANT NINJA TURTLES* (1987–93) stirred up such feature films as *Teenage Mutant Ninja Turtles: The Movie* (1990) and its sequels. This tied in with the host of low-budget screen product that involved martial arts and had "ninja" in their titles (e.g., *The Last Ninja*, 1983—telefeature; *Ninja Death Squad*, 1987; *Ninja: American Warrior*, 1990; *3 Ninjas*, 1992; *Beverly Hills Ninja*, 1996), as well as such TV series as *Walker, Texas Ranger* (1993–2001), which showcased Chuck Norris using martial arts on recalcitrant criminals. (Earlier, in the TV medium, on the series *OHARA*, 1987–88, Pat Morita among others employed martial arts to subdue the bad guys.) Other television shows that featured martial arts in particular included the aforementioned *Kung Fu: The Legend Continues*. Then Chinese-American RUSSELL WONG starred in a quartet of *Vanishing Son* TV movies in 1994 that led to the *VANISHING SON* TV series the next year.

In the later 1990s, the most famous of the Hong Kong martial-arts stars began American projects: SAMMO HUNG headlined TV's *MARTIAL LAW* (1998–2000); JET LI was featured as the villain in *LETHAL WEAPON 4* (1998) and then as the star of *ROMEO MUST DIE* (2000); JACKIE CHAN tried his luck in the United States with such vehicles as *The Protector* (1985) but had not caught on with the public, but in *RUSH HOUR* (1998), teamed with Chris Tucker, Chan finally made a substantial connection with American filmgoers and followed up with *SHANGHAI NOON* (2000) and *Rush Hour 2* (2001); CHOW YUN-FAT (who in his movies used guns and stern looks much more frequently than karate chops) held his own against Mark Wahlberg in *THE CORRUPTOR* (1999), and after stealing the drama *ANNA AND THE KING* (1999) from Jodie Foster, returned to Hong Kong to make the international success, *CROUCHING TIGER HIDDEN DRAGON* (2000), which also did well in America both financially and with the critics (and the entry won Academy Awards as well).

***Martial Law* (1998–2000)** CBS-TV series, color, 60 minutes. **Cast:** Sammo Hung (Sammo Law), Tammy Lauren (Det. Dana Doyle: 1998), Louis Mandylor (Det. Louis Malone), Tom Wright (Capt. Benjamin Winship), Kelly Hu (Grace Chen [Chen Pei Pei]), Arsenio Hall (Terrell Parker).

HUNG, another of Hong Kong's action-movie stars, relocated to Hollywood to participate in the martial-arts craze in film and on TV, a cycle spearheaded by JACKIE CHAN. In past eras, Hung's portly build, his ultra serious demeanor, and his fractured English would have doomed his chances with American audiences. Now, however, thanks to viewers' fondness for watching karate-chopping Asian stars do their well-choreographed thing—no matter how inscrutable they might be—Hung's chunky presence was no deterrence to his starring in this police-themed series. The added gimmick here was that, as in many of Chan's pictures, Hung's character did not take himself seriously, and he allowed the viewer to feel part of the fun, especially in the deliberately over-the-top action sequences.

In this genre send-up, which ran for forty-four episodes, Sammo Law of the Chinese police department is on short-term assignment to the Los Angeles Police Department. Chen Pei Pei, his attractive assistant from the Shanghai Police Department, joins him in California, first as an undercover agent and then as a member of the LAPD, using her Americanized name, Grace Chen. Adding zip to the proceedings is fast-talking, cool-cat Terrell Parker, a department spokesperson who melds into Sammo's special squad.

***M*A*S*H* (1970)** Twentieth Century-Fox, color, 116 minutes. **Director:** Robert Altman; **Screenplay:** Ring Lardner Jr.; **Cast:** Donald Sutherland (Hawkeye Pierce), Elliott Gould (Trapper John McIntyre), Tom Skerritt (Duke Forrest), Sally Kellerman (Maj. Hot Lips Houlihan), Robert Duval (Maj. Frank Burns), Jo Ann Pflug (Hot Dish), Rene Auberjonois (Dago Red), Gary Burghoff (Radar O'Reilly), Fred Williamson (Spearchucker), Yoko Young (Japanese servant), Sumi Haru (Japanese nurse).

Years earlier, the turgid, very formulistic *Battle Circus* (1953)—with Humphrey Bogart and June Allyson—had dealt with the Mobile Army Surgical Hospital in Korea during the then recent war. Sufficient years had passed by 1970 to find the "humor" in the madness of that military action and to highlight the zany exploits of the idiosyncratic medical crew working frantically to save lives near the combat zone.

Based on the 1968 novel by Richard Hooker (the pseudonym for Dr. H. Richard Homberger and William Heinz), this antiwar, "dark" comedy was unheralded at the time of production but proved to be a substantial box-office winner. The hilarious screen activity focused on U.S. Army surgeons Hawkeye Pierce and Duke Forrest, along with the later-arriving "chest cutter" Trapper John McIntyre who are in daily skirmishes with pompous Major Burns. Adding distraction for the team is shapely nurse Maj. Margaret O'Houlihan, whose amorous activities suggested her nickname of "Hot Lips."

When not operating on the wounded or chasing nurses, Hawkeye and Trapper John have a respite in Japan when they are ordered to perform surgery on a congressman's son. The Asian roles here, as well as those in the Korean scenes, are purely background and often are played for salacious laughs.

This film led to the long-running M*A*S*H TV series (1972–83). The feature film won an Oscar for Best Adapted Screenplay and received Academy Award nominations for Best Director, Best Film Editing, Best Picture, and Best Supporting Actress (Kellerman).

***M*A*S*H* (1972–1983)** CBS-TV series, color, 30 minutes. **Cast:** Alan Alda (Hawkeye [Capt. Benjamin Franklin Pierce), Wayne Rogers (Trapper John [Capt. John McIntyre]: 1972–75), Loretta Swit (Hot Lips [Maj. Margaret Houlihan]), Larry Linville (Maj. Frank Burns: 1972–77), Gary Burghoff (Radar [Cpl. Walter O'Reilly]: 1972–79, McLean Stevenson (Lt. Col. Henry Blake: 1972–75), Jamie Farr (Cpl. Maxwell Klinger: 1973–83), Harry Morgan (Col. Sherman Potter: 1975–83), Mike Farrell (Capt. B.J. Hunnicut: 1975–83), Kellye Nakahara (Nurse Kellye: 1973–74), Rosalind Chao (Soon-Lee: 1983).

Two years after the release of the popular Robert Altman–directed feature *M*A*S*H*, this TV sitcom spin-off was produced. In translating the characters of the 4077th Mobile Army Surgical Hospital—still stationed behind the lines during the Korean War—to TV, the personalities of the cast member regulars were softened from the movie and made more humane for long-term home-viewing consumption. But these figures still remained iconoclastic and bizarre, as they struggled to maintain some degree of sanity in their harried lives while they worked nonstop, repairing or easing the suffering of the war victims. Although many of the show's lead male military characters had spouses or girlfriends back in the United States, in Korea they were a randy lot who half-seriously propositioned every (attractive) female who came their way.

As the movie version had featured a few black cast members, so did the sitcom edition. As for Korean characters, because of the lengthy number of seasons the show remained on the air, there were far more occasions than in the big-screen original to have the Americans interact with South Korean villagers/soldiers and the occasional wounded, captured North Korean enemy. Thus, there were some (but not many) roles for Asian-American talent on the much-beloved TV show, but these were rarely highlighted. Among the few regular series roles were Nakahara as Nurse Kellye and CHAO as Soon-Lee; the latter married Corporal Klinger and came back to the United States with him in the spin-off series *AfterMASH* (1983–84).

When the TV edition of *M*A*S*H* began, the United States was still fighting in Vietnam, and many parallels between the action in this show and in the then-current Asian war were found. By the time the show went off the air in 1983, having won many Emmys and other awards, it had been judged a true classic. The two-and-a-half-hour finale episode drew huge ratings. Characters from this sitcom were spun off into *Trapper John, M.D.* (1979–86) and the aforementioned *AfterMASH*.

***Mask of Fu Manchu, The* (1932)** Metro-Goldwyn-Mayer, b&w, 68 minutes. **Director:** Charles Brabin and uncredited Charles Vidor; **Screenplay:** Irene Kuhn, Edgar Allan Woolf, and John Willard; **Cast:** Boris Karloff (Dr. Fu Manchu), Lewis Stone (Nayland-Smith), Karen Morley (Sheila Barton), Charles Starrett (Terrence Granville), Myrna Loy (Fah Lo See), Jean Hersholt (Professor Von Berg), Lawrence Grant (Sir Lionel Barton), Willie Fung (waiter).

Sax Rohmer's masterful creation, the fiendish DR. FU MANCHU, had appeared four times on the American screen since 1929 with WARNER OLAND in the lead role, but Swedish-born Oland had gone on to become the cinema's CHARLIE CHAN, and now the Rohmer property was controlled by MGM. They utilized the screen's *Frankenstein* (1931) sensation, Britisher BORIS KARLOFF, as the fantastic Yellow Peril, who was lethal to anyone with whom he came into contact.

Based on Rohmer's 1932 novel, this film plays out like a wildly constructed serial chapterplay, only on a grander scale. In this tale, the sinister Fu Manchu is hunting for the legendary tomb of Genghis Khan. As such he is competing with Sir Lionel Barton, who has formed an expedition to locate the historic site. Nothing is sacred to Fu Manchu as he even offers his daughter Fah Lo See to Sir Lionel if he will reveal the whereabouts of the prized tomb. Meanwhile Sir Lionel's daughter, Sheila, and her team locate Khan's resting place. Her steadfast fiancé, Terrence Granville, is dispatched to Fu Manchu to offer him the priceless Khan mask and sword if he will release Sir Lionel.

It was such creations as the Asian Fu Manchu that fostered the public's negative association of evilness and unspeakable mystery with the Chinese race.

***M. Butterfly* (1993)** Warner Bros., color, 100 minutes. **Director:** David Cronenberg; **Screenplay:** David Henry Hwang; **Cast:** Jeremy Irons (René Gallimard), John Lone (Song Liling), Barbara Sukowa (Jeanne Gallimard), Ian Richardson (Ambassador Toulon), Annabel Leventon (Frau Baden), Shizuko Hoshi (Comrade Chin).

This was the account of an ultimate impersonation, based on the Tony Award–winning drama (1988) by Hwang that starred John Lithgow and B. D. WONG on the Broadway stage, which derived from a true-life incident.

In 1964 Beijing, China, René Gallimard, a married minor French diplomat, is introduced to Song Liling, an actor who performs women's roles (especially Cio-Cio San in *Madama Butterfly)* at the Beijing Opera. Self-contained, racist Gallimard is unaware that this charming female whom he comes to adore is a male or that Song Liling is spying for the Chinese government. To sustain the deception with his lover, the impersonator uses a variety of ruses, even eventually producing a baby. The Cultural Revolution splits apart the couple. Song serves time on a work farm while Gallimard returns to Paris. Later he and Song reunite but are arrested for their espionage activities. At their trial, the prosecution is amazed that Gallimard never discovered the truth about his lover. In prison, the repelled Gallimard dons the facial makeup of a Beijing Opera performer and kills himself.

Compared to the well-received play, the film adaptation was a general disappointment, diffusing the thrust of the playwright's theme that the submissive Nipponese female was really a western convention.

McCarthy, Nobu (1934–2002) Like many talented performers of Asian heritage, McCarthy found the quantity and quality of screen and TV roles extremely limiting in the United States. To broaden her opportunities, she devoted a goodly portion of her time to stage work as well as to teaching theater. In 1989, she succeeded MAKO as artistic director of the Los Angeles–based East/West Players, a post she retained through 1994.

Born in Ottawa, Canada, she was in Tokyo during World War II when the family's home was destroyed, so she spent the next two years separated from them, living in northern Japan with elementary school students. After the war, McCarthy became a ballerina and a top fashion model. Her marriage in 1956 brought her to Los Angeles, where she was discovered in Little Tokyo for a role in Jerry Lewis's *THE GEISHA BOY* (1958). This led to such films as *WALK LIKE A DRAGON* (1960) and such TV assignments as guest spots on *HAPPY DAYS*, *BARNEY MILLER*, *T.J. HOOKER*, and *China Beach*.

Starting in 1970, McCarthy devoted a good deal of time to theater work, including the lead role in David Henry Hwang's play *As the Crow Flies.* Her participation in Philip Kan Gotanda's play *The Wash* in 1987 led to her New York City stage debut, later turning to directing in the theater. In 1999 she teamed with African-American actor Danny Glover to star on the Los Angeles stage in the premiere of Gotanda's *Yohen* and that same year was on screen in her final films *Last Chance* and *After One Cigarette.*

medical series—television One of the early breakthroughs (albeit small) for Asian-American actors on TV series where they were not cast as extras, in walk-on bits, or as on-camera orderlies and the like was in doctor-themed series. There, the Asian-American character could be given a role of respect but yet still not have his character have to integrate with Caucasians in a nonwork-related situation. (Sometimes, he would be a practitioner of Eastern medicine, such as an acupuncturist.) One of the first such dramas to utilize Asian-American characters was *ST. ELSEWHERE* (1982–89). For the 1982–84 seasons, Kim Miyori functioned as Dr. Wendy Armstrong, a resident who eventually committed suicide. A more revealing characterization on the show was provided by FRANCE NUYEN as Dr. Paulette Kiem for the 1986–88 seasons. As a Vietnamese doctor, not only was her professional life displayed, but also the viewer got glimpses into her personal life (e.g., her long-distance marriage, problems with her runaway son). Within *Kay O'Brien* (1986), set at Manhattan General Hospital in New York City, one of the heroine's medical peers was Dr. Michael Kwan played by Keone Young.

Island Son (1989–90) brought Richard Chamberlain (the former star of *Dr. Kildare*, 1961–66) back to series TV. As a child, his character had been adopted by Hawaiians, and now he wanted to be near them and serve their community. At the Kamehameha Medical Center was Dr. Kenji Fushida (played by Clyde Kusatsu).

On *Medicine Ball* (1995) set in Seattle, Washington, at Bayview Medical Center, the focus was on first-year resident doctors. Among the fledgling physicians were Dr. Nia James (played by Kai Soremekum) and Dr. Max Chang (played by Darryl Fong). In contrast, on *ER* (1994–), set at Chicago's County General Hospital, there were relatively few Asian Americans—either as staff or as patients. Ming-Na [Wen] was cast as a resident in 1995 and returned to the show in 2000 with her character becoming a single parent. Another of Asian-American background was Gedde Watanabe who, since the fall of 1997, appeared recurrently as a good-natured orderly.

***Midway* (1976)** Universal, color, 132 minutes. **Director:** Jack Smight; **Screenplay:** Donald S. Sanford; **Cast:** Charlton Heston (Capt. Matt Garth), Henry Fonda (Adm.

Chester W. Nimitz), James Coburn (Capt. Vinton Maddox), Glenn Ford (Rear Adm. Raymond A. Spruance), Toshiro Mifune (Adm. Isoroku Yamamoto), Robert Mitchum (Adm. William F. Halsey), James Shigeta (Vice Adm. Chuichi Nagumo).

A big-name cast, a gimmicky sound system (creating vibrating rumbles on the floor of the theater auditorium), and a presentation of the decisive 1942 Battle of Midway from the points of view of the Americans and the Japanese did not save this cheesy combat feature from unfavorable critical and relatively mild audience reaction. (It earned only little more than $21 million in domestic film rentals.) Like the earlier *In Harm's Way* (1965), *Midway* sought to personalize its battle-heavy narrative with personal stories such as that of Capt. Matt Garth's son Tom, a lieutenant, who loves a Japanese-Hawaiian woman and how the military and his own family frown on the potential union.

Some of the Japanese talent had their dialogue dubbed, as in the case of Mifune, and it made them appear foolish on camera.

Ming-Na (aka: Ming-Na Wen) (1963–) Her versatility in playing tense drama (e.g., *THE JOY LUCK CLUB*, 1993), television situation comedy (e.g., *THE SINGLE GUY*, 1995–97), or continuing nighttime TV drama *(ER*, 1995, 2000–) made her much in demand in the 1990s as a quite-contemporary actress who happened to be Chinese.

She was born Ming-Na Wen (her first name translates as "enlightenment") on the then-Portuguese island of Macao. When she was an infant, her parents divorced; her mother, who had become a nurse, wed a Chinese-American businessman, and the family moved first to Queens, New York, and then to her stepfather's hometown of Mt. Lebanon, Pennsylvania. During high school, she made her professional stage debut in a production of *South Pacific*, and then, after graduating Carnegie Mellon University as a theater major, she joined the cast of *As the World Turns*. From 1988 to 1991 on this daytime TV drama, she played Lien Truong, a young woman with a mysterious parentage. A key assignment thereafter was the role of introspective June in *The Joy Luck Club*. After appearing opposite Jean-Claude Van Damme in *Street Fighter* (1994), she joined *ER* in 1995 as a high-achieving med student, Deborah Chen, a role where her ethnicity was a nonissue. Later, she appeared on a new sitcom, *The Single Guy* and on Broadway was in *Golden Child* (1998), a drama by David Henry Hwang.

In *MULAN* (1998), the Disney animated-feature version of an ancient Chinese legend, she had key roles as the voices of Fa Mulan and Fa Ping. In January 2000, Ming-Na (who had shortened her name in the later 1990s) returned to the cast of *ER*, again as Dr. Deborah Chen. She continued to supply her voice for animated productions: the feature *Final Fantasy: The Spirits Within* (2001), the 2001 TV series *House of Mouse*, and the direct-to-video movie *Mulan 2* (2003).

***Mr. T. and Tina* (1976)** ABC-TV series, color, 30 minutes. **Cast:** Pat Morita (Mr. T. [Taro Takahashi]), Susan Blanchard (Tina Kelly), Pat Suzuki (Michi), Ted Lange (Harvard), Miriam Byrd-Nethery (Miss Llewellyn), "Jerry" Hatsuo Fujikawa (Uncle Matsu), June Angela (Sachi), Gene Profanato (Aki).

MORITA relinquished his supporting role as Arnold on the *HAPPY DAYS* TV series for this starring vehicle. He is the supersmart Japanese inventor who is sent by his firm to establish an American-based branch of Moyati Industries in Chicago. Joining him are his two motherless children (Angela and Profanato) as well as his tradition-steeped Uncle Matsu. Hired to bring order into their new environment is giddy but well-meaning Tina Kelly, a Nebraskan who clearly doesn't appreciate the culture clash that she causes in the household.

With the clichéd premise once established, there was not much for this comedy series to explore productively. The program disappeared after five weeks on the air.

At this juncture, there was so little opportunity for any Asian-American talent to star on a mainstream U.S. TV series that it was understandable why, in retrospect, Morita made the career decision he did regarding *Happy Days*, a berth to which he would return for that show's 1982–83 season.

***Mr. Wong, Detective* (1938)** Monogram, b&w, 69 minutes. **Director:** William Nigh; **Screenplay:** Houston Branch; **Cast:** Boris Karloff (Mr. James Lee Wong), Grant Withers (Capt. Sam Street), Maxine Jennings (Myra Ross), Evelyn Brent (Countess Dubois [Olga]), George Lloyd (Devlin), Lucien Prival (the Baron [Anton Mohl]), John St. Polis (Carl Roemer), Lee Tong Foo (Tchin).

With the success of the CHARLIE CHAN and MR. MOTO film series, poverty-row studio Monogram Pictures entered the race with its own Asian detective property (MR. WONG) based on Hugh Wiley's short stories. The British-born KARLOFF had already portrayed an Asian, the infamous arch criminal in *The Mask of Fu Manchu* (1932). With minimum makeup, a slight stooping of the shoulders, and a change of cadence to his voice, the actor created his Chinese detective, the cultured and bright individual who perceived clues that the police had overlooked. The production values were threadbare, and the plot holes fairly large, but the cast galumphed through the proceedings to its inevitable solving of the triple murders involving a poisonous gas. "Helping" Wong in this whodunit were Capt. Sam Street of the San Francisco police department and the latter's girlfriend, Myra Ross.

Relatively successful given its minimal production cost, this was the first of six Mr. Wong entries in the detective series; five of them would star Karloff, and the last (*PHANTOM OF CHINATOWN*, 1940) cast KEYE LUKE as the sleuth's college student son. *Mr. Wong, Detective*, would be remade partially as the 1947 Charlie Chan entry, *Docks of New Orleans*, starring ROLAND WINTERS as the Chinese investigator.

Lon Chaney and Gertrude Olmstead in *Mr. Wu* (1927). (JC ARCHIVES)

***Mr. Wu* (1927)** Metro-Goldwyn-Mayer, b&w, 7,460′. **Director:** William Nigh; **Screenplay:** Lorna Moon; **Cast:** Lon Chaney (Mr. Wu/Mr. Wu's grandfather), Louise Dresser (Mrs. Gregory), Renée Adorée (Nang Ping), Holmes Herbert (Mr. Gregory), Ralph Forbes (Basil Gregory), Gertrude Olmstead (Hilda Gregory), Mrs. Wong Wing (Ah Wong), Claude King (Mr. Muir), Sonny Lu (Little Wu), Anna May Wong (Loo Song).

Promoted as "the Man of a Thousand Faces," CHANEY was an expert at delving into bizarre characterizations for the screen and, through extreme makeup and physical will, altering his appearance greatly from one picture to the next. On several prior occasions, he had played Asians on camera (e.g., *OUTSIDE THE LAW*, 1920; *Bits of Life*, 1921; *Shadows*, 1922). In *Mr. Wu*, he donned Oriental garb once again, this time in two roles—as Mr. Wu and Mr. Wu's grandfather—at his best as he crafted his two Asian characters with a range of small details that included subtle gestures, body movement, and, most importantly, the delicate shadings of reactions to situations and people around him. (Little wonder that screen artists were attracted to playing Far Easterners on camera—it was a great challenge to submerge their western ways into the understated movements of sophisticated men from a much different culture.)

Based on the 1914 New York play by Maurice Vernon and Harold Owen, which had been filmed in 1920 with Matheson Lang in the lead, *Mr. Wu* traces the tragedy of a Chinese man whose daughter, Nang Ping, falls in love with a Westerner, betraying her commitment to wed a mandarin. In expiation for her broken vow, Wu reluctantly takes his daughter's life. However, his act ultimately leads to his own demise.

Dramas such as this propagated racial bigotry by insisting that interracial love was wrong, that the crime of rape was more heinous when the victim was Caucasian and its perpetrator an Asian, and ultimately that an Asian's act of self-destruction was of little consequence because he was the result of an outmoded honor-bound tradition of the Far East.

A Spanish-language sound version of *Mr. Wu* was made in 1930. *Wu Li Chang* starred Ernesto Vilches as Mister Wu.

Morita, Pat (1930–) One of the veteran entertainers of the film and TV industries, this diminutive, round-faced talent capped his career with his Oscar-nominated role as Mr. Miyagi, the astute martial-arts master in the feel-good *THE KARATE KID* (1984), a dimensional dramatic assignment in a career filled with vignettes, and a part he repeated in three sequels. In addition, for many years, especially on television, he played an assortment of light comedy (e.g., Arnold in *HAPPY DAYS*, 1975–76, 1982–83) and dramatic roles (e.g., *OHARA*, 1987–88) that made him a very familiar face to viewers.

He was born Noriyuki Morita in Isleton, California. His parents, emigrants from Japan, were itinerant fruit pickers and later operated a Chinese restaurant that catered to African-American, Hispanic, and Filipino trade. From the ages of two to eleven, he was hospitalized in a sanitarium near Sacramento for tuberculosis of the spine and spent most of that period in a body cast; not long thereafter, Morita was sent to an internment camp near Arizona with his family and other Japanese Americans during World War II. After the surrender, when everyone was freed, he attended high school and then college (as a premed student) for more than two years but had to quit his education due to lack of tuition money. Instead, he became a computer programmer, who spent his days off working at the Ginza West Club, where he developed his thirst for show business.

At age thirty, he quit his regular job to become a stand-up comic, billing himself as "the hip Nip" and often performing on the Playboy Club circuit. In 1967 he acted in an episode of TV's *Gomer Pyle, U.S.M.C.* and had a role as Oriental #2 in the screen musical *Thoroughly Modern Millie.* He worked earnestly in both mediums thereafter, although, when no acting jobs were forthcoming in the later 1970s, he moved to Hawaii, where he did TV commercials and made a business out of hosting fundraisers.

During the decades, he was featured in several TV situation comedies/lighthearted shows besides *Happy Days: The Queen and I* (1969), *Sanford and Son* (1974–75), *MR. T. AND TINA* (1976—in which he starred), *THE MYSTERY FILES OF SHELBY WOO* (1998), and *The Adventures of Kanga Roddy* (1998). He participated in several dramatic films, many with World War II themes: *MIDWAY* (1976), *Captive Hearts* (1987—which he scripted), and *Hiroshima: Out of the Ashes* (1990). Recent movie have included *Talk to Taka* (2000), *The Center of the World* (2001), *Shadow Fury* (2001), and *The*

Biggest Fan (2002). In 2001, he hosted *Pioneer Living*, a nine-part TV educational series devoted to issues of interest to immigrants.

In 1987 Morita received a Lifetime Achievement Award from the Association of Asian-Pacific American Artists.

Moto, Mr. With the ongoing success of its long-running CHARLIE CHAN detective series, Twentieth Century-Fox enthusiastically launched another Asian sleuth movie series. It paid famed writer John P. Marquand $7,000 for the rights to his short story "That Girl and Mr. Moto," which had been serialized in the *Saturday Evening Post* in the fall of 1936. Austrian-born PETER LORRE was contracted to star as diminutive Mr. Kentaro Moto, the bespectacled Japanese businessman/amateur detective, in *THINK FAST, MR. MOTO* (1937). (Apparently, the Hollywood studio never considered using an actual Asian or an Asian American for the title role, although in one later episode *[Mr. Moto's Last Warning]* of the Lorre entries, the impersonator pretending to be the real sleuth was played by Teru Shimada.)

The slickly made, appreciated debut Moto entry led to *Thank You, Mr. Moto* (1937), *Mr. Moto's Gamble* (1938), *Mr. Moto Takes a Chance* (1938), *Mysterious Mr. Moto* (1938), *Mr. Moto's Last Warning* (1939), *Mr. Moto in Danger Island* (1939), and *Mr. Moto Takes a Vacation* (1939). All the installments were in black and white, none ran more than 72 minutes, and the episodes often featured Moto displaying his expertise in the art of jujitsu. *Mr. Moto's Gamble* had the oddity of the character of Charlie Chan's #1 son, Lee (KEYE LUKE), appearing within the plot. This was done to take advantage of footage shot for an uncompleted Charlie Chan entry, shelved when its star WARNER OLAND died in 1937.

By late 1939, Twentieth Century-Fox determined that, with the growing world concern over the increased military aggressions by Japan, it would be politic to drop the Japanese-themed series. Years later, in 1951 *Mr. Moto* debuted as a network radio series, featuring James Monks as the Japanese-born American citizen. The show ran from May to October of that year.

In 1957, *Stopover Tokyo*, the fifth and last of Marquand's Mr. Moto novels, was published. Twentieth Century-Fox made a wide-screen, color adaptation of it that year that was loosely based on the book but *omitted* the Moto character.

In the mid-1960s, Twentieth Century-Fox, wanting to take advantage of the current craze for James Bond espionage-style movies, resurrected Marquand's famed Asian detective for *The Return of Mr. Moto* (1965). The lackluster feature, shot economically in black and white, presented Brooklyn-born Henry Silva, who was of Puerto Rican descent, in the lead part. Wearing dark-rimmed spectacles, slicked down hair, and emphasizing a slight overbite, he looked more forbidding than mysterious. It was a sad end to a once illustrious screen property.

Peter Lorre (second from left) as the intrepid amateur sleuth Mr. Moto, along with Warren Hymer (left), Robert Lowery, and Richard Lane (right) in *Mr. Moto in Danger Island* (1939). (JC ARCHIVES)

***Mulan* (1998)** Buena Vista, color, 1998. **Directors:** Barry Cook and Tony Bancroft; **Screenplay:** Rita Hsiao, Jodi Ann Johnson, and Alan Ormsby; **Voices:** Ming-Na Wen (Mulan), Lea Salonga (Mulan—singing), Eddie Murphy (Mushu), B. D. Wong (Captain Li Shang), Donny Osmond (Captain Li Shang—singing), Harvey Fierstein (Yao), Jerry Tondo (Chien-Po), James Hong (Chi Fu), Miguel Ferrer (Shan-Yu), Soon-tek Oh (Fa Zhou), Pat Morita (Emperor), George Takei (First Ancestor), James Shigeta (General Li).

Based on a Chinese folk tale, this stylish but unexceptional animated feature was important in the progress of Asian-American integration on the American screen because it devoted its entire narrative to ethnic minority characters. It also provided work for several prominent members of the Asian-American actors community. (The same studio, Disney, had earlier focused on Native Americans in the animated feature *Pocahontas*, 1995.)

Mulan tells of the invasion of China by the Huns under the leadership of Shan-Yu. To meet the crisis, the emperor decrees that one male from each family in China must join the military. Aged Fa Zhou is prepared to volunteer, but his daughter Mulan disguises herself as a male and takes his place. Mulan passes through training camp, but during a skirmish with the Huns, her identity is discovered. Later, it is Mulan who comes to the aid of Shang and helps China stave off the invaders. The grateful emperor asks Mulan to join his council; instead she returns to her family, where Shang arrives to pay his respects and reveal his love for her.

With its strong feminist theme and outstanding visuals, *Mulan*, made on a budget of $70 million, grossed more than $120 million at the box office in domestic distribution. *Mulan* received an Oscar nomination for Best Original Musical/Comedy Score. A sequel, *Mulan 2*, was set to appear in 2003 with many of the same performers providing voices for the further adventures of their screen characters.

musicals—feature films One of the first sound features from Hollywood to utilize an extended Chinese sequence was *The Show of Shows* (1929), in which Myrna Loy was spotlighted in a "Chinese Fantasy" sequence. *FOOTLIGHT PARADE* (1933) had its "Shanghai Lil" number, staged by Busby Berkeley and danced by Ruby Keeler in the title role, made up and outfitted to look somewhat Asian. In W. C. Fields's *International House* (1933) there was the Asian-themed song performed "She's Just a China Tea-Cup." Another Caucasian talent, Mae West, performed a Chinese-motif number in *KLONDIKE ANNIE* (1936), singing "I'm an Occidental Woman in an Oriental Mood for Love."

Within the oversized production number, "I'll Sing You a Thousand Love Songs," in *Cain and Mabel* (1936), Marion Davies was costumed as a Chinese princess, complete with lute and backed by an elaborately costumed chorus. In *Anything Goes* (1936), Ethel Merman was seen in Chinese garb for the "Shang-de Ho" routine, backed by Caucasian chorus girls (in rather bad wigs). In the course of *Stowaway* (1936), Shirley Temple both conversed and sang in Chinese. In the big-budgeted drama *THE GOOD EARTH* (1937), Austrian-born Tilly Losch appeared as the exquisite Chinese dancer who came between a Chinese husband and his wife. Losch had a dancing sequence within the saga.

Nan Wynn sang "Honorable Moon" in *Princess O'Rourke* (1943), a number with an Asian theme. *Nob Hill* (1945), a musical set in the early 1900s on San Francisco's Barbary Coast, included the characters of Chinese showgirls (played by Teri Toy and Jean Wong). In the low-budget *HOUSE-RENT PARTY* (1946), a weak comedy with songs, the setting was Harlem, but members of a Chinese laundry got involved in the song-and-dance proceedings. *ZIEGFELD FOLLIES* (1946) devoted an elaborate production number to Fred Astaire (as a Limehouse half-caste) in love with an exotic Asian lady (played by Lucille Bremer), whom he notices passing by on the street.

The movie adaptation of Rodgers and Hammerstein's *FLOWER DRUM SONG* (1961) was set in San Francisco's Chinatown and featured several Asian-American performers in key singing-dance roles (although some of the stars were dubbed). In *Star!* (1968), a distorted screen biography of British stage star Gertrude Lawrence, Julie Andrews went "yellow faced" in the "Limehouse Blues" production number. *Indiana Jones and the Temple of Doom* (1984) presented leading lady Kate Capshaw performing the song "Anything Goes" in Chinese during the credits sequence. She was backed by Caucasian cuties in Chinese outfits. The Disney-made *MULAN* (1998), a full-length animated fable of ancient China, had mostly Asian Americans providing the voices of the leads, and a few of the singing voices were also Asian-Americans.

As for Japan, actresses/singers/opera stars performing arias from Giacomo Puccini's opera, *Madama Butterfly* (1904), was long a favorite on-camera selection as it allowed the actress the opportunity to wear exotic makeup and costumes. Among those who performed the Cho-Cho San role from *Madame Butterfly* on screen were: Grace Moore *(One Night of Love*, 1934; *I'll Take Romance*, 1937), Jeanette MacDonald *(Broadway Serenade*, 1939), Kathryn Grayson *(So This Is Love*, 1953), and Eleanor Parker *(Interrupted Melody*, 1955). The Puccini opera aside, Betty Grable appeared as a rather sleazy geisha in the "Japanese Girl Like American Boy" number from *Call Me Mister* (1951). Dan Dailey and a little Japanese girl sang "My Lucky Charm" in 1956's *Meet Me In Las Vegas*. The youngster, Mitsuko Sawamura, also performed a number entirely in Japanese.

HAWAII was a popular locale/motif for Hollywood musicals, especially as it provided ample opportunity for female dancers to perform in grass skirts, but generally the featured dancers were Caucasians who were either cast as Hawaiians or else playing Caucasians visiting from the mainland. *Flirtation Walk* (1934), one of the several Dick Powell–Ruby Keeler musicals, opened with a large luau and an extravagant Hawaiian production number.

Waikiki Wedding (1937) with Bing Crosby and Martha Raye was set on the islands and had several Hawaiian-themed songs and dances with several women in grass skirts, as did *HAWAII CALLS* (1938) with young singing talent Bobby Breen. Dancing star Eleanor Powell was incited to hula dancing in *Honolulu* (1939) as was Jeanette MacDonald in *I Married an Angel* (1942).

Betty Grable and Alice Faye donned hula skirts and strummed ukuleles in *Tin Pan Alley* (1940). The three Andrews Sisters sang and hula-ed through "Hula Ba Luau" during *In the Navy* (1941). *Navy Blues* (1941) with Ann Sheridan and Martha Raye featured a Polynesian dance sequence. *Moonlight in Hawaii* (1941) had a production number ("Aloha Low Down") that showcased Maria Montez and several curvaceous hula girls.

Song of the Islands (1942), highlighting Betty Grable, had her hula dancing with Asian-American talent as backdrop to her performance. Vera Hruba Ralston was seen in a hula-on-ice number in *Ice Capades Revue* (1942). For *Rhythm of the Islands* (1943), a production-line quickie, there were multiple Polynesian dance scenes featuring the Lester Horton dancers (who were largely African Americans). Two of Elvis Presley's cookie-cutter musicals were set in Hawaii—*BLUE HAWAII* (1962) and *Paradise, Hawaiian Style* (1966)—and featured Hawaiian-style songs and authentic ethnic-culture dances.

Many Hollywood movies set in POLYNESIA and other parts of the South Pacific focused on native dancing, singing, and chanting—but rarely in Hollywood's golden age was Asian-American talent utilized. In *Down to Their Last Yacht* (1934), largely set on a South Seas island, there were several native-style songs and dances performed, including a big native-dance production number. Child star Shirley Temple danced the hula in *Curly Top* (1935)—and topless at that. DOROTHY LAMOUR created a vogue with *The Jungle Princess* (1936), playing beautiful native women who sang and danced in Hollywood's approximation of what such music should be like. Bud Abbott and Lou Costello arrived on an uncharted South Pacific isle in *Pardon My Sarong* (1941), and the premise allowed for some tropical musical interludes (e.g., "Vingo Jingo" and "Lovely Luana").

Danny Kaye and Vera-Ellen performed "Bali Boogie" in *Wonder Man* (1945). Although the Esther Williams–Howard

Keel starrer *Pagan Love Song* (1950) included Hispanic Rita Moreno as a Tahitian lovely, it boasted authentic Polynesian dancing and dancers. *My Blue Heaven* (1950), another Betty Grable–Dan Dailey vehicle, featured the number "Friendly Island." Virginia Mayo executed a Polynesian musical number in *Starlift* (1951), and that same year, *Bird of Paradise* boasted a dance number ("Sacrifice the Virgin to the Volcano"). *The Road to Bali* (1953), one of the Lamour–Bob Hope–Bing Crosby series entries, offered a temple dance sequence. Mitzi Gaynor was cast as a native woman and did Polynesian-style movements in *Down Among the Sheltering Palms* (1953). Peggy Lee wrote and sang "We Are Siamese If You Please," a number performed by Si and Am, the Siamese felines (voiced by Lee) in Disney's animated feature *Lady and the Tramp* (1955). The title song of *Les Girls* (1957) had a Balinese dance in it.

Rodgers and Hammerstein's Broadway success *THE KING AND I* (1951) reached the screen in 1956. Set in 1860s Siam, it starred Russian-born Yul Brynner as the chauvinistic monarch and a cast of generally non-Asian Americans in the key support roles, such as Hispanic Rita Moreno as Tuptim. There were several intricately staged "native" song-and-dance numbers including "The Small House of Uncle Thomas." (The 1999 animated-feature version of the musical also utilized mostly non-Asian Americans for its major speaking and singing voices.)

The height of such representation came in the screen adaptation of Rodgers and Hammerstein's *SOUTH PACIFIC* (1958). The narrative had two leading native characters, one the irrepressible Bloody Mary (played by African-American JUANITA HALL), and the other daughter (performed by Vietnamese-French FRANCE NUYEN)—both of their singing voices were dubbed. (This classic musical was restaged as an elaborate TV film in 2001 with Glenn Close and Rade Serbedzija. Harry Connick Jr. was Lieutenant Cable, while Hong Kong-born Natalie Jackson Mendoza was his love interest, Liat, and Lori Tan Chinn played her zesty mother, Bloody Mary.)

***My Geisha* (1962)** Paramount, color, 119 minutes. **Director:** Jack Cardiff; **Screenplay:** Norman Krasna; **Cast:** Shirley MacLaine (Lucy Dell/Yoko Mori), Yves Montand (Paul Robaix), Edward G. Robinson (Sam Lewis), Bob Cummings (Bob Moore), Yoko Tani (Kazumi Ito), Tatsuo Saito (Kenichi Takata), Tamae Kyokawa (Amatsu Hisako).

In the annals of one-joke movies, *My Geisha* might win an award, but as for impersonations of a Japanese by a Westerner, the film earned no prize. MacLaine treated the cinematic excursion—produced by her then real-life husband Steve Parker, who was residing in Japan—as a grade-school production. Her mincing gait and fluttering eyelids and fan did no one any credit. Tani, as the real GEISHA, made MacLaine look even more foolish.

The premise had Paul Robaix, the movie-director husband of cinema star Lucy Dell, determined to break out of her shadow by directing a new version of *Madame Butterfly*, one to star a Japanese actress. Dell learns of the plan and masquerades as Yoko Mori, a geisha. She wins the lead in the movie and even restores her husband's crumbling self-confidence.

Two pluses in this flat comedy were the on-location filming in Japan and the use of selections from the score to Puccini's 1904 opera, *Madama Butterfly*. At least, in the 1932 dramatic version of *MADAME BUTTERFLY*, Sylvia Sidney had made a professional effort to be convincing in her Asian guise.

My Geisha was Oscar nominated for Best Costume Design (Color).

***Mysterious Dr. Fu Manchu, The* (1929)** Paramount, b&w, 80 minutes. **Director:** Rowland V. Lee; **Screenplay:** Florence Ryerson and Lloyd Corrigan; **Cast:** Warner Oland (Dr. Fu Manchu), Jean Arthur (Lia Eltham), Neil Hamilton (Dr. Jack Petrie), O. P. Heggie (Nayland-Smith), William Austin (Sylvester Wadsworth), Claude King (Sir John Petrie), Noble Johnson (Li Po), Evelyn Selbie (Fai Lu), Laska Winter (Fu Mela).

This was Hollywood's first foray into the sinister world of Asian arch-fiend DR. FU MANCHU, based on Sax Rohmer's novel. Contrary to later excursions, here the Chinese scientist was presented initially as a compassionate soul. However, during the Boxer Rebellion, his wife and child die at the hands of the advancing allied troops. Meanwhile, during the chaos, Fu Manchu saves the life of little Lia Eltham. Years pass, and the embittered Fu Manchu is still determined to punish those who brought death to his loved ones. He hypnotizes the adult Lia and has her romance Jack Petrie, the grandson of the British army officer whom he vows to kill. First the grandfather and then the father of Jack are murdered. Fortunately, Lia's Chinese servant helps Scotland Yard prevent Fu Manchu from eliminating Jack, who then pursues his romance with Lia.

With its mix of an exotic locale, a menacing and inscrutable Chinese master criminal, and overtones of the thriller and chapterplay genres, *The Mysterious Dr. Fu Manchu* found a ready market with moviegoers willing to accept this latest Hollywood example of "the Yellow Peril."

***Mystery Files of Shelby Woo* (1996–1999)** Nickelodeon cable series, color, 30 minutes. **Cast:** Irene Ng (Shelby Woo), Pat Morita (Grandpa Mike Woo), Preslaysa Edwards (Cindi Ornette: 1996–99), Adam Busch (Noah Allen: 1996–99), Steve Purnick (Det. Whit Hineline: 1996–99), Eleanor Noble (Angie Burns: 1999), Noah Klar (Vince Rosania: 1999), Ellen David (Det. Sharon Delancey: 1999).

Geared for the young-teen market, this adventure cable-TV series had many parallels to the Nancy Drew character of American literature. It presented a young leading lady who was bright and inventive and had the tenacity to follow through on clues to solve capers. She was a 1990s role model who just happened to be Chinese. As such, this was a big advancement for such ethnic-minority characters being presented on TV.

Seventeen-year-old Shelby Woo arrives in America to live with her grandfather, Mike Woo, a former criminologist who now owns an inn in Cocoa Beach, Florida. When not in school, Shelby has an intern post at the local police department where she is better than Det. Whit Hineline in solving crimes. In early 1999, the series switched its locale to Wilton, Massachusetts, following much the same format.

The show benefited from the presence of veteran talent MORITA as the heroine's helpful grandfather.

N

***New Adventures of Charlie Chan, The* (1957)** Syndicated TV series, b&w, 30 minutes. **Cast:** J. Carrol Naish (Charlie Chan), James Hong (Barry Chan), Rupert Davies (Inspector Duff), Hugh Williams (Insp. Carl Marlowe).

The enduringly popular Earl Derr Biggers's creation CHARLIE CHAN received an uninspired translation to the small-screen in this British-produced TV series. It starred New York-born Irishman Naish, who in the 1940s had played several dastardly Asian villains on screen (e.g., *THE BATMAN* serial, 1943; *BEHIND THE RISING SUN*, 1943). During the course of thirty-nine episodes, the ever-courteous, astute Chinese sleuth, now based in London, solved mysteries and was assisted by his enthusiastic son, Barry.

Ngor, Dr. Haing S. (1940–1996) Along with MIYOSHI UMEKI (*SAYONARA*, 1957), Ngor was one of the few Asians to win an Academy Award, earning his prize for *The Killing Fields* (1984). (PAT MORITA was nominated for an Oscar for *THE KARATE KID*, 1984.) Ngor was the only Oscar-winning actor to have ever been murdered. It was ironic that the physician, having immigrated to the United States as a refugee seeking asylum from the troubles of his homeland, should be murdered outside his Los Angeles apartment.

He was born in 1940 in Samrong Yung, a small farming village near the capital of Cambodia. His father was Chinese and his mother was Khmer. His country was war torn during his youth and his family was frequently impoverished. Nevertheless, they found ways to send him to school. He later attended medical school and, having graduated, operated his own clinic in Phnom Penh. When the city was overrun by Cambodian guerrilla fighters in 1975, he went into hiding doing odd jobs to survive. Later, he was captured, tortured, and sentenced to forced labor. His whole family died in the takeover. In 1979, he escaped to a refugee camp in Thailand and the next year came to the United States, eventually settling in Los Angeles. He became a caseworker with the Chinatown Service Center, helping Southeast Asian refugees find employment.

Ngor was asked to test for *The Killing Fields*, a brutally graphic drama of the Pol Pot regime and their genocide of the Cambodians. For his portrayal of Dith Pran, the first-time screen actor won an Oscar. It led to his appearing on episodes of such TV series as *Miami Vice*, *China Beach*, *The Commish*, and *VANISHING SON* and making such feature films as *The Iron Triangle* (1989), *HEAVEN & EARTH* (1993), and *The Dragon Gate* (1999). In 1987, his autobiography, *A Cambodian Odyssey*, was published.

When the trio of culprits who had killed Ngor were caught, it was determined at their trial that the tragedy had resulted from a robbery gone bad.

Nguyen, Dustin (1962–) It was playing (1987–90) the hip undercover cop Ioki on the popular TV series *21 JUMP STREET* that made Nguyen a much-recognized entertainment personality, especially to adoring teenage girls. Then he had the parts of Chief Sahn on the TV series *seaQuest DSV* (1993–94) and Hung in the telefeatures *Vanishing Son II* and *IV*, both 1994 and both starring RUSSELL WONG.

Nguyen was born in Saigon, South Vietnam. His father was a well-known entertainer who frequently performed on television and occasionally dragged his shy son along for bit roles. After the fall of Saigon in 1975, the family escaped to the United States, settling in St. Louis. After mastering English, the teenager learned the art of tae kwon do, which gave him a sense of self. In 1980, he enrolled at Orange Coast College in southern California, where he gravitated to theater work. He became so entranced with creative expression that he dropped out of school.

Nguyen made his TV debut on episodes of *MAGNUM, P.I.*, in 1985, followed by roles in 1986–87 on TV's *The A-Team* and *Shell Game*. He played Suki for a year on the daytime TV drama *General Hospital*. His feature film bow was in *Sunset Strip* (1985), a low-budget murder mystery. More-recent assignments included playing a blond-wigged member of a bad-guy trio in *3 Ninjas Kick Back* (1994), a clerk in *The Doom Generation* (1995), and a part in the German-made TV series *Gang, Die* (aka: *Waterfront*) (1997). In 1998, Dustin joined the Pamela Anderson Lee TV series *V.I.P.*

ninjas The growing interest in MARTIAL ARTS movies, spurred on by BRUCE LEE's box-office hits in the 1960s and 1970s, escalated thereafter, thanks to the *KUNG-FU* (1972–75) TV series with DAVID CARRADINE and the several action films of Chuck Norris, Michael Dudikoff, Steven Seagal, and others. Amid this rash of movies involving martial arts came the *KARATE KID* series in the 1980s and the later *TEENAGE MUTANT NINJA TURTLES* movies of the 1990s, the latter property based on a cartoon-book franchise that began in 1983.

Capitalizing on the martial-arts trend, moviemakers around the world added ninjas into their mix, characters who were based on the tradition of the feudal Japanese society of mercenaries, men highly trained in combat and stealth. These nimble soldier types were translated into the contemporary modern world, and thus was started a rash of pictures involving some aspect of ninjas (e.g., *The Last Ninja*, 1983—TV movie; *Ninja III: The Domination*, 1984; *Ninja Death Squad*, 1987; *American Ninja 3: Blood Hunt*, 1989; *Ninja Brothers of Blood*, 1989; *Ninja: American Warrior*, 1990; *3 Ninjas*, 1992; *The Hunted*, 1995; *Beverly Hills Ninja*, 1997; *Shadow Fury*, 2002.

During the same period, occasional American TV series creatively incorporated ninja themes, such as *The Master* (1984) with Lee Van Cleef, Timothy Van Patten, and Sho Kosugi, as well as *Nasty Boys* (1990) with Jeff Kaake, Benjamin Bratt, Don Franklin, and Craig Hurley. American-made children's TV series on the same topic included the animated *Teenage Mutant Ninja Turtles* (1987–97) and the live-action *Mighty Morphin Power Rangers* (1993–96).

Noble House See *JAMES CLAVELL'S NOBLE HOUSE*.

Nuyen, France (1939–) On Broadway, she was the title figure in *The World of Suzie Wong* (1958) and that same year was on screen as Liat involved in an interracial romance with Lieutenant Cable in *SOUTH PACIFIC*. This musical proved to be the peak of her lengthy show-business career.

She was born France Nguyen Vannga in Marseille, France, of Vietnamese-French ancestry. She turned to modeling, which led to stage work. After leaving the film cast of *THE WORLD OF SUZIE WONG* (1960—replaced by NANCY KWAN), she was in two war-themed dramas: *In Love and War* (1958) and *Satan Never Sleeps* (1962)

Nuyen's ethnic background defined her screen roles, leading to narrow casting in the likes of *A GIRL NAMED TAMIKO* and *DIAMOND HEAD*, both 1962. Like many performers of Asian extraction, she turned up on episodes of such American TV series as *HAWAII FIVE-O*, *KUNG FU*, and *MAGNUM P.I.* and was a frequent featured player in TV movies of the 1970s and 1980s, often assigned to be a mysterious exotic, such as the businesswoman with supernatural powers in the telefeature *Deathmoon* (1978). From 1986 to 1988, Nuyen was a Vietnamese doctor on the staff of *ST. ELSEWHERE*. She played the wife of JAMES SHIGETA in the British-made *China Cry: A True Story* (1991), dealing with the cultural/political changes in 1950s China, and in *THE JOY LUCK CLUB* (1993) portrayed Ying Ying. Subsequent movies included *Angry Café* (1995) and *A Smile Like Yours* (1997).

O

***Objective, Burma!* (1945)** Warner Bros., b&w, 142 minutes. **Director:** Raoul Walsh; **Screenplay:** Ranald MacDougall and Lester Cole; **Cast:** Errol Flynn (Capt. Chuck Nelson), James Brown (Sergeant Treacy), William Prince (Lt. Sidney Jacobs), George Tobias ("Gabby" Gordon), Henry Hull (Mark Williams), Warner Anderson (Colonel Carter), Dick Erdman ("Nebraska" Hooper), Asit Koomar (Gurkha), Liparit (Burmese man), Abdul Hjassan and Raul Singh (Burmese priests).

This was one of the most rousing World War II combat movies ever made by Hollywood. As the Allies organize efforts to recapture Burma and regain a foothold in Southeast Asia, the military determines that a Japanese radar station secreted in the Burmese jungle must first be destroyed. Heading the dangerous operation is Capt. Chuck Nelson, assisted by Lieutenant Jacobs and two Gurkha guides from Nepal. Nelson and his paratroopers are to land in the jungle, take out the station, and then get to an abandoned airstrip where they are to be airlifted out of the area. The radio station is destroyed, but the Axis troops now know of the paratroopers' presence. Later, one of the splinter groups led by Jacobs is ambushed by the Japanese, with the Allied survivors tortured and mutilated. Eventually, the remainder of Nelson's men reach a new pick-up site. Having completed their mission of distracting the Japanese while the Burmese invasion begins, the troops are returned to base.

The movie concludes with the postscript: "This story has a conclusion but not an end—It will end only when the evil forces of Japan are totally destroyed. This film is gratefully dedicated to the men of the American, British, Chinese and Indian Armies, without whose heroic efforts Burma would still be in the hands of the Japanese." With such high-charged words and the earlier illustrations of the barbaric acts of the Japanese soldiers, it was no wonder that filmgoers had difficulty burying their inflamed hatred of the Japanese even when World War II concluded.

This superior war movie utilized Chinese and Filipino extras to play the Japanese soldiers. More than 100 Burmese farm laborers were brought in from the central valley of California to portray villagers in the film. *Objective, Burma!* was nominated for three Academy Awards: Best Film Editing, Best Original Dramatic Score, and Best Story. The film was remade by director Walsh as *Distant Drums* (1951) with the narrative now focused on the Seminole tribe in Florida and Gary Cooper in the lead role.

To be noted, at the time of its original release, *Objective, Burma!* was heavily criticized by the British press for making it seem on camera that without the United States, the Allied campaign in Burma would have failed.

Oh, Soon-teck See OH, SOON-TEK.

Oh, Soon-tek (aka: Soon-teck Oh) (1933–) With a balance between acting and civic work, Soon-tek Oh participated in film, television, and stage work, often teaching his craft both in the United States and in his homeland of Korea. He was brought up during the difficult years of World War II and the Korean War. After the peace, he developed an interest in show business from watching American movies. He won a scholarship to the University of Southern California where he majored in cinema. Later, he studied at the Neighborhood Playhouse in New York City and eventually became a graduate instructor in the theater arts department at USC.

Soon-tek Oh began his TV acting with parts on *The Invaders* and *The Wild, Wild West* in 1967. His first screen role of note was in the western, *One More Train to Rob* (1971). That same year, he played a Korean officer in the TV movie,

The Reluctant Heroes. He appeared on segments of such TV series as *HAWAII FIVE-O*, *M*A*S*H*, and *MAGNUM P.I.* and was in a three-part installment (1980–81) of *Charlie's Angels* that was set in Hawaii. For the telefeature *The Return of Charlie Chan* (1979), he was one of the Chan clan; Caucasian actor Ross Martin played the Chinese sleuth.

Along with MAKO and others, he was one of the founding members of Los Angeles's East/West Players. He taught theater at Sogang University in Seoul and at the Seoul Institute of the Arts in 1972–73. Back in Los Angeles, he helped to organize theater teaching curriculum in conjunction with the Korean-American Theater Ensemble, in 1993 established his own company, and also became artistic director for the Society of Heritage Performers. Meanwhile, he and Mako had lead roles in the Broadway musical *Pacific Overtures* (1976), and later he was the featured performer in the 1995 bicoastal tour of *Woman Warrior*. His more recent films included *YELLOW* (1998), *MULAN* (1998—voice), *Last Mountain* (2000), and *Special Weapons and Tactics* (2002).

***Ohara* (1987–1988)** ABC-TV series, color, 60 minutes. **Cast:** Pat Morita (Lieutenant Ohara), Kevin Conroy (Capt. Lloyd Hamilton: 1987), Jon Polito (Captain Ross: 1987), Madge Sinclair (Gussie Lemmons: 1987), Richard Yniguez (Lt. Jessie Guerrera: 1987), Catherine Keener (Lt. Cricket Sideris: 1987), Jack Wallace (Sgt. Phil O'Brien: 1987), Robert Clohessy (Lt. George Shaver), Rachel Ticotin (Asst. U.S. Atty. Teresa Storm).

With the success of *THE KARATE KID* (1984) and its sequels, MORITA had a high popularity quotient with viewers in the mid-1980s. ABC-TV, for whom he had played Arnold in *HAPPY DAYS* (1975–76; 1982–83) and starred in *MR. T. AND TINA* (1976), concocted this police series as a fresh showcase for the veteran entertainer. It was a cop show with a tremendous difference. Lieutenant Ohara (pronounced Oh-HAR-Ra) is a widower who believes in daily meditation, does not drive a car, never carries a gun, and prefers to utilize fortitude and persuasion to resolve his case load. As a last choice, he resorts to his martial-arts skills. Although Ohara is a twenty-year veteran of the Los Angeles Police Department, some of his peers remain skeptical of his Far Eastern ways.

When the initial format did not draw viewership, the network altered the show's premise. Now Ohara became part of a federal task force supervised by hard-working Tessa Storm. His partner was the Asian American's physical opposite: the tall, young, and hunky Lt. George Shaver. The "new" Ohara packs a gun and drives a car. In February 1988, the show's premise was reshaped yet again, with Ohara and Shaver resigning from the LAPD and opening a private detective agency. When that restructuring did not impress the public, everyone admitted defeat, and the show was canceled at the end of the 1987–88 season.

***Oil for the Lamps of China* (1935)** Warner Bros., b&w, 97 minutes. **Director:** Mervyn LeRoy; **Screenplay:** Laird Doyle; **Cast:** Pat O'Brien (Stephen Chase), Josephine Hutchinson (Hester Adams), Jean Muir (Alice), Lyle Talbot (Jim), Arthur Byron (the boss), Willie Fung (Kin), Tetsu Komai (Ho), Keye Luke (young Chinese man).

Alice Tisdale Hobart's sweeping 1933 novel was a sharp indictment of the oil industry, in particular how badly oil companies (who proclaimed that they took care of their own) actually treated their hard-working, loyal employees. For her tapestry, Hobart's primary backdrop was strife-torn China of the 1930s. Relying on rear-projection special effects, the film version never left the studio lot in Burbank, California, in this sanitized adaptation. As such, the narrative moved from Manchuria to Yokohama, to the Siberian border, on to Shanghai, and, finally, back to southern China.

Before the pending production was finalized, the studio showed a treatment of the project to the Los Angeles-based motion-picture representative of the Chinese government. According to reports in the trade paper *Daily Variety* in early 1935, objections to the working script included such items as "civil war sequences, the bound feet of women, the wearing of queues, concubinage, opium smoking, superstitious belief and the use of the words 'Chinaman' and 'Chink.'" In short, the movie was shaping up to be a very Westernized view of China and its people, who were there only to be of use to the Caucasian focal characters. (As it resulted, few "compromises" were made by the studio to the wishes of the representatives of China in the actual shooting of the film.)

The emphasis in this saga was on the turmoil of earnest Stephen Chase, who devotes all his energy to the global oil company for whom he works. While based in Manchuria, he invents a kerosene lamp that burns fuel inexpensively. He is thanked, but the credit for the invention goes to another company man. At the mercy of his bosses for every move in life that he undertakes, he marries Hester Adams to save face when his fiancée jilts him. They grow to love one another, but just when she is to give birth to her baby, he leaves her alone to handle an oil-well emergency. Their infant dies, but still Chase won't abandon his faith in the firm. At the finale, it is his courageous spouse who blackmails the oil corporation into giving her husband the position that he so well deserves.

For local flavor, beyond the background footage shot on the sly in China, there were such staples of 1930s Hollywood as the constantly working FUNG, here as another jovial celluloid domestic. *Oil for the Lamps of China* was remade by the studio as the low-budget *Law of the Tropics* (1941), with the setting switched to South America and the industry altered to the rubber business.

Oland, Warner (1880–1938) Intriguingly, this Swedish-born, five-feet, eleven-inch actor gained his greatest professional acclaim playing the inestimable Chinese sleuth CHARLIE CHAN in several feature films. Earlier, he had made noteworthy appearances in pictures as the "Yellow Peril," the loathsome DR. FU MANCHU.

Born Johan Verner Ölund in Nyby, Vaserbotten, Sweden, he moved to the United States with his parents in 1892 and gravitated to the theater, where he became a respected stage performer and was noted for his translations/productions of August Strindberg's plays. Oland began to appear in American films in 1915, including a serial that year entitled *The Romance of Elaine.* His somewhat Slavic looks made him a natural to play Russians in such films as *The Yellow Ticket* (1918) and he was called upon to play Asians, including *Mandarin's Gold* (1919), *Wu Fang* (1919), *EAST IS WEST* (1922), and *Tell It to the Marines* (1926). Oland continued that specialty in talkies and made a strong impression as the sinister master nemesis in *THE MYSTERIOUS DR. FU MANCHU* (1929) but abandoned that ongoing villainous part in 1931 to star in *CHARLIE CHAN CARRIES ON*. So successful were these detective capers that he made fifteen others, through *Charlie Chan at Monte Carlo* (1937). During the 1930s, he also turned up on screen in non-Chan characterizations but was usually forced to don his Asian persona as in *SHANGHAI EXPRESS* (1932), *The Painted Veil* (1934), and *SHANGHAI* (1935).

***Old San Francisco* (1927)** Warner Bros., b&w, 7,961′. **Director:** Alan Crosland; **Screenplay:** Anthony Coldeway; **Cast:** Dolores Costello (Dolores Vasquez), Warner Oland (Chris Buckwell), Charles Emmett Mack (Terrence O'Shaugnessy), Josef Swickard (Don Hernandez Vasquez), John Miljan (Don Luis), Anders Randolf (Michael Brandon), Sojin (Lu Fong), Angelo Rossitto (dwarf), Anna May Wong (Chinese girl).

At the turn of the twentieth century in San Francisco, cruel Chris Buckwell is the kingpin of the unsavory part of town, especially exploitive of the Chinese in the neighborhood, but what is not generally known is that he is a half-caste. Meanwhile, he schemes to grab the estate of Don Hernandez Vasquez and, in the process, kills the grandee. Vasquez's daughter, Dolores, vows revenge. When she discovers that Buckwell is half-Chinese, she encourages his dwarf sibling (Rossitto) to denounce him. Buckwell kidnaps Dolores but is thwarted when he is killed by the earthquake of 1906 that rumbles through San Francisco.

Bolstered by special effects of the great quake, this silent feature with a music score once again equated unscrupulous and rapacious activities bordering on the barbaric with Asian men, in this instance a sinister half-Chinese villain. Such movies as *Old San Francisco* reinforced negative stereotypes of Asian Americans in the minds of filmgoers.

***Outside the Law* (1920)** Universal, b&w, 7,754′. **Director:** Tod Browning; **Screenplay:** Lucien Hubbard and Browning; **Cast:** Priscilla Dean (Silky Moll [Molly Madden]), Wheeler Oakman (Dapper Dan Ballard), Lon Chaney (Black Mike Sylva/Ah Wing), Ralph Lewis (Silent Madden), E.A. Warren (Chang Low), Wilton Taylor (inspector).

In one of the several film associations of Browning and CHANEY, the latter played a corrupt criminal leader living in Chinatown, where he organizes his illegal activities. Thanks to the prompting of Confucian Chang Low, Molly and her dad, Silent Madden, drop out of the gang. In retaliation, Black Mike Sylva, has the father framed and sent to jail. Molly seeks revenge by means of a new robbery in which she and Dapper Dan Ballard will grab the jewels from Sylva's men and hide out in an apartment building. In a final shootout, Sylva is killed by Ah Wing (also played by Chaney), but through Chang Low's intervention, Molly and Ballard, who have been implicated in the homicide, are set free by the police.

It had become standard practice for Hollywood filmmakers to set illegal activities in the mysterious streets of Chinatown where any activity—from opium dens to the white slave trade—supposedly flourished.

P

***Paradise Road* (1997)** Twentieth Century Fox, color, 122 minutes. **Director:** Bruce Beresford; **Screenplay:** David Giles, Martin Meader, Alfred Uhry, and Beresford; **Cast:** Glenn Close (Adrienne Pargiter), Pauline Collins (Margaret "Daisy" Drummond), Julianne Margulies (Topsy Merritt), Frances McDormand (Dr. Verstak), Cate Blanchett (Susan Macarthy), Clyde Kusatsu (the Snake), Sab Shimono (Colonel Hiroyo), Stan Egi (Captain Tanaka), David Chung (interpreter), Yoshi Adachi (Mr. Moto), Mitsu Sato (Rags), Taka Nagano (Boris).

Based on an actual World War II account, this drama followed a group of women of disparate types/nationalities who flee aboard a ship from 1942 Singapore as the Japanese forces advance. The vessel is bombed, and the survivors land in Sumatra where they are imprisoned in an arduous work camp run by the Japanese. Because of their cultural differences, Adrienne Pargiter, who attended the Royal Academy of Music, decides to form an a capella "vocal" orchestra to bring the women closer together. Initially, their captors oppose the project but eventually come to appreciate it. Finally, at the war's end, the prisoners remaining in the camp are freed.

This intriguing concept for a film floundered due to its cast filled with diverse acting styles and the failure of the dread mood of the prison camp and the uplifting musical interludes to mesh properly. In addition, the Japanese compound staff was presented as more one-dimensional than should have been allowed. The movie suffered in comparison to the well-crafted *THREE CAME HOME* (1950) or to the riveting *Playing for Time* (1980), the latter, a TV movie about the women's orchestra in a World War II Nazi concentration camp.

***Phantom of Chinatown* (1940)** Monogram, b&w, 62 minutes. **Director:** Phil Rosen; **Screenplay:** Joseph West; **Cast:** Keye Luke (Jimmy Lee Wong) Grant Withers (Captain Street), Lotus Long (Win Len), Charles Miller (Dr. John Benton), Huntley Gordon (Wilkes), Dick Terry (Toreno), Lee Tung Foo (Charley One [Victor Wong]).

With BORIS KARLOFF busy elsewhere, Monogram Pictures continued their low-budget *MR. WONG, DETECTIVE* series for one last entry. This time LUKE, who had played the enterprising Lee Chan, the son of CHARLIE CHAN, in that successful Asian detective movie series, was on hand as Mr. Wong's college student son. He stepped in to assist Captain Street of San Francisco's Chinatown homicide squad to solve several puzzling murders.

The caper opens with the strange death of archaeologist Dr. John Benton who has come to San Francisco after discovering the ancient tomb of a Ming emperor. The burial site contains the long-sought secret of the Temple of Eternal Fire, information of great use to China in locating a much-needed reserve of untapped oil. Jimmy Lee Wong, a student of the late Benton, is spurred on to find his teacher's killer, aided by Win Len, Benton's secretary.

With his usual enthusiastic demeanor, Luke, then age thirty-six, gave the whodunit some needed bounce. Lending additional flavor was Long as his sleuthing assistant. She appeared in a few earlier Mr. Wong entries (in different roles), as well as participating in the unconnected entry, *THE MYSTERIOUS MR. WONG* (1935) and even in an entry of the rival MR. MOTO series, *THINK FAST, MR. MOTO* (1937).

***Pink Lady* (1980)** NBC-TV series, color, 60 minutes. **Cast:** Pink Lady [Mei Nemoto and Kei Masuda] and Jeff Altman (hosts), Cheri Eichen, Anna Mathias, Jim Varney, Ed Nakamoto, and the Peacock Dancers (regulars).

At the time, Nemoto and Masuda—two shapely Japanese talents who comprised a rock duo—were a big hit in their native

Mei Nemoto (left), Jeff Altman, and Kei Masuda (right) on the TV variety show *Pink Lady* (1980). (VINCENT TERRACE)

land and had a crossover hit ("Kiss in the Dark") in the United States. Hoping that U.S. audiences would be amused and titillated (a regular part of each episode spotlighted the bikini-clad Pink Lady duo soaking in a hot tub), this variety/comedy series debuted. Comedian Altman was the host, and beyond the regulars and the guest stars, there were skits that played up the difficulty of the two Nipponese headliners in their attempt to master English and to adjust to American ways. At the time, and especially in retrospect, the culture clash gimmick was overtly condescending. The show vanished after little more than a month on the air.

***Platoon* (1986)** Orion, color, 111 minutes. **Director/Screenplay:** Oliver Stone; **Cast:** Tom Berenger (Sergeant Barnes), Willem Dafoe (Sergeant Elias), Charlie Sheen (Chris), Forest Whitaker (Big Harold), Francesco Quinn (Rhah), John C. McGinley (Sergeant O'Neal), Richard Edson (Sal), Kevin Dillon (Bunny), Johnny Depp (Lerner).

If any U.S.-made combat drama reflected the intense hell of the Vietnam War, it was *Platoon.* Based on filmmaker Stone's own horrific wartime experiences, it depicted in horrendously graphic terms the brutality of combat and how it transforms civilized individuals into beasts who struggle for survival and revenge on the enemy.

As a backdrop to the warfare, the Vietnamese civilians were fodder for the mass destruction perpetrated by both sides, and just as in 1940s Hollywood films about World War II China, the Vietnamese villagers in Vietnam War movies were used to point out the atrocities, rapes, starvation, and other sufferings heaped on civilians by both sides. Thus, such films provided roles of only a limited dimension for Asian performers, particularly in the Philippines where many of these celluloid dramas (e.g., *Apocalypse Now*, 1979) were shot. Typically, it was in the Vietnam War movies dealing with the hunt for missing soldiers (e.g., *Missing in Action*, 1984; *Rambo: First Blood Part II*, 1985) that the Vietcong captors had more sizable, if one-dimensional, villainous, roles. *Platoon* was part of a rash of late 1980s Vietnam War pictures that included the explicit and harrowing *Hamburger Hill* (1987).

Set in 1967 Vietnam, the narrative of *Platoon* is presented through the eyes of eighteen-year-old Chris, a college dropout who volunteered for duty. He is now part of a seasoned interracial platoon that is split by two widely diverse leaders: battle-scarred Sergeant Barnes who has become a one-man war machine without humanity, and his opposite number, Sergeant Elias, who is equally adept in the ways of war but who has maintained a sense of compassion for his struggling troops. This definitive war film ends with Chris, a Vietnam veteran, being evacuated out of the chaos and a plea for tolerance and optimism among all races.

Platoon won Academy Awards for Best Director, Best Film Editing, Best Picture, and Best Sound. It received Oscar nominations for Best Cinematography, Best Original Screenplay, and Best Supporting Actor (Berenger and Dafoe). Made on a $6 million budget, *Platoon* grossed $138 million in domestic distribution.

Polynesia Geographically, Polynesia is located in the part of the central Pacific Ocean to the east of Micronesia and Melanesia, encompassing all the islands from the Hawaiian group in the north to the Marquesas Islands, Tonga, Samoa, and the Cook Islands to the south, and also French Polynesia. In Hollywood terms, it was any tropical isle that seemed to be a delightful escape from the madness of the civilized United States, Europe, and so on. Rarely in the pre-1980s did U.S. moviemakers cast leading players who were of that ethnic background to play Polynesians.

One of the most picturesque early examples of this genre was *Aloma of the South Seas* (1926), a silent feature that starred Caucasian shimmy dancer Gilda Gray as Aloma and was filmed partly on location in Puerto Rico. *White Shadows in the South Seas* (1929), which boasted talking sequences, starred Mexican-born Raquel Torres and was shot in the Marquesas Islands.

In the early sound period, *Bird of Paradise* (1932; remade in 1951) had Mexican-born Dolores Del Rio as Luana, the daughter of a South Seas island chief, who fell in love with a Caucasian sailor (Joel McCrea). The seafaring epic that set the standard for escapist movies was *Mutiny on the Bounty* (1935) in which English sailors rebelled against stern shipboard life and found peace of sorts with native women in Pitcairn Island. This classic was remade in 1962 and 1984 (as *The Bounty*). There were also such movie serials as *Robinson Crusoe of Clipper Island* (1936) that used a tropical paradise as a backdrop.

In the 1930s, Louisiana-born DOROTHY LAMOUR created a fashion trend and awoke travel desire among moviegoers with her series of romantic/musical exotica such as *THE JUNGLE PRINCESS* (1936), *Her Jungle Love* (1938), *Aloma of the South Seas* (1941), and *Rainbow Island* (1944). She was followed in the 1940s by Maria Montez (from the Dominican Republic) in such tropical fantasies as *South of Tahiti* (1941), *White Savage* (1943), and *Cobra Woman* (1944). Meanwhile, *The Moon and Sixpence* (1942), based on W. Somerset Maugham's 1919 novel, was a thinly veiled account of French painter Paul Gauguin and his escape from marital and career dissatisfaction to a life of painting in Tahiti. (The novel was readapted for a 1959 American TV special starring England's Laurence Olivier in the title role.)

Also in the tropical arena were such action entries as *Port of Hate* (1939), the horror entry *The Island of Lost Souls* (1933; remade in 1977 and 1996), romantic dramas such as *Seven Sinners* (1940) with Marlene Dietrich (remade as *South Seas Sinner*, 1950, with Shelley Winters), pirate adventures such as *South of Pago Pago* (1940), and such "native" comedies as *The Tuttles of Tahiti* (1942) and *Tahiti Nights* (1945).

Other later films dealing with escapism to Polynesia—and still using (mostly) Caucasians to fill the roles—were *South Seas Woman* (1953), *Return to Paradise* (1953), *His Majesty O'Keefe* (1953), *Drums of Tahiti* (1954), *Enchanted Island* (1958), *Donovan's Reef* (1963), *The Blue Lagoon* (1980), *Return to the Blue Lagoon* (1991), and *RAPA NUI* (1994). Along the way full-blown musicals included *Pagan Love Song* (1950) with Esther Williams, and Rodgers and Hammerstein's *SOUTH PACIFIC* (1958 and 2001—TV movie) and the occasional comedy/romance/war picture such as *Father Goose* (1964) with Cary Grant and Leslie Caron on a South Seas island, coping with the Japanese enemy.

pressure groups Organizations (beyond such broad-based groups as the American Civil Liberties Union and Common Cause) that were involved in specifically protecting the rights of Asian-American talent and helping to further integrate the entertainment media have included the Association of Asian-Pacific American Artists (AAPAA), the Japanese Association of Southern California, the National Asian-American Telecommunications Association (NAATA), and the National Association of Asian American Professionals (NAAAP).

***Protector, The* (1985)** Golden Harvest, color, 95 minutes. **Director/Screenplay:** James Glickenhaus; **Cast:** Jackie Chan (Insp. Billy Wang), Danny Aiello (Danny Garoni), Roy Chiao (Harold Kol), Victor Arnold (police captain), Kim Bass (Stan Jones), Richard Clarke (Superintendent Whitehead), Saun Ellis (Laura Shapiro).

This Hong Kong/U.S. English-language coproduction introduced CHAN for a second time to American film audiences. (He had tried to break into the western-movie marketplace a few years earlier with such rickety vehicles as 1981's *The Cannonball Run* starring Burt Reynolds, in which Chan was lost in the crowd as a Subaru driver.) *The Protector* begins with a speedboat chase and a shootout in New York harbor and then transfers to Hong Kong—shown as a hotbed of corruption, vice, and nude women. There, New York cops Billy Wang and Danny Garoni are on the trail of a drug czar who has kidnapped the daughter (Ellis) of a suspected drug trafficker.

With its bursts of action sequences, the showcasing of Chan's charisma, and a sense of fun about the blending of genres (i.e., the American cop picture with James Bond–like adventures) and using a Hong Kong Chinese action star, *The Protector* should have made Chan an American box-office favorite long before *RUSH HOUR* (1998) and *SHANGHAI NOON* (2000).

***Purple Heart, The* (1944)** Twentieth Century-Fox, b&w, 99 minutes. **Director:** Lewis Milestone: **Screenplay:** Jerome Cady; **Cast:** Dana Andrews (Capt. Harvey Ross), Richard Conte (Lt. Angelo Canelli), Farley Granger (Sgt. Howard Clinton), Kevin O'Shea (Sgt. Jan Skvoznik), Donald Barry (Lt. Peter Vincent), Sam Levene (Lt. Wayne Greenbaum), Richard Loo (Gen. Ito Mitsubi), Peter Chong (Mitsuru Toyama), H.T. Tsiang (Yuen Chiu Ling), Benson Fong (Moy Ling), Key Chang (Adm. Kentara Yamaghichi).

This was one of the most effective propaganda dramas produced by Hollywood during World War II. The graphic offering was inspired by the actual April 1942 bombing raid on Japan, which was launched from the aircraft carrier USS *Hornet* and led by Lt. Col. James H. Doolittle. (The event would also prompt another studio to produce *THIRTY SECONDS OVER TOKYO*, 1944.)

The Purple Heart told of eight captured fliers (of assorted ethnic backgrounds) from that daring raid who are brought to trial in a Tokyo civilian court. The mockery is conducted by General Mitsubi, Admiral Yamaghichi, and three judges, one of whom, Mitsuru Toyama, is head of the Black Dragon Society. Refusing to heed the defendants' claim that the proceedings are illegal for a nonmilitary tribunal, the Japanese bring in witnesses who insist that the fliers intentionally bombed civilian and nonmilitary sites. Later, when the prisoners refuse to confirm that their flights originated on an aircraft carrier, they are individually tortured and mutilated, leaving one of their number, Skvoznik, crazed. Knowing that they will be put to death if they don't reveal information about the *Hornet*, the men agree to meet their fate. After their leader Ross delivers a patriotic speech to the courtroom, a chastised Mitsubi commits suicide. Toyama sentences the Americans to be executed. The prisoners walk proudly from the room.

Only after the end of World War II was it learned that, in actuality, three of the eight fliers from the Doolittle raid had been executed, one died in captivity, and the four others were released from a Japanese prison in August 1945 by U.S. troops.

With its account of great bravery under horrific torture, *The Purple Heart* was and is unforgettable film fare. There was concern at the time of production that its shocking account of Japan's inhumane treatment of prisoners would lead to reprisals. The screenplay was careful to delineate that the bulk of Chinese characters involved in the drama were loyal to the Allies. This prompted the sequence in *The Purple Heart* in which the traitorous Chinese witness Yuen Chiu Ling was shot in court by his son, who felt compelled to atone for his father's betrayal.

Q

***Quincy, M. E.* (1976–1983)** NBC-TV series, color, 60 minutes. **Cast:** Jack Klugman (R. Quincy, M.E.), Garry Walberg (Lt. Frank Monahan), Robert Ito (Dr. Sam Fujiyama), Lynette Mettey (Lee Potter: 1976–77), Val Bisoglio (Danny Tovo), John S. Ragin (Dr. Robert Astin), Joseph Roman (Sergeant Brill), Diane Markoff (Diane, the waitress: 1980–83), Anita Gillette (Dr. Emily Hanover: 1982–83).

One of television's most popular weekly offerings boasted a premise that potentially might have dissuaded viewers from tuning in. The show's hero, a former well-established physician, was now a medical examiner for the Los Angeles County Coroner's Office (LACCO). As the program's opening credits montage repeatedly indicated with its batch of squeamish newcomers passing out while viewing an autopsy, dealing with corpses was definitely not for everyone. But Klugman proved so engaging as the hyperenergetic, determined coroner who acted more like a police detective than a M. E. that the series won a steady following. If self-important Dr. Robert Astin, Quincy's superior at the LACCO, was often a royal pain, then Quincy's young assistant, Dr. Sam Fujiyama, was a joy. Proficient, responsible, and loyal to his boss's unorthodox methodology for concluding a case, Fujiyama seemed as tireless as the older Quincy. Sam was always available to assist his mentor, be cheerful, and never demand to share the limelight, not that gruff but idealistic Quincy would have minded.

The Canadian-born Ito, who was actually only nine years younger than Klugman, brought a quiet dignity to his portrayal of the good-natured assistant physician. It was the type of role too infrequently given at that time to an Asian-American performer. Although, in the broader sense, this Asian American was in essence the same type of helper to his Caucasian boss as, for example, SAMMEE TONG had been on the TV sitcom, *BACHELOR FATHER* (1957–62), at least the character was now not stuck being a houseman but was a professional person.

R

***Rapa Nui* (1994)** Warner Bros., color, 107 minutes. **Director:** Kevin Reynolds; **Screenplay:** Tim Rose Price and Reynolds; **Cast:** Jason Scott Lee (Noro), Esai Morales (Make), Sandrine Holt (Ramana), Emilio Tuki Hito (Messenger), Gordon Hatfield (Rino), Faenza Reuben (Heke), Hori Ahipene (overseer).

Rapa Nui is POLYNESIAN for "Easter Island," the isle in the Southeast Pacific, west of Chile. It was first settled by Polynesians about A.D. 400, and its famous gigantic statues of human heads date from the period 1000–1600. That said, this expensively mounted, gorgeously photographed feature was a travesty. Coproduced by actor Kevin Costner in the American moviemaking tradition of casting against ethnic types, the leads were played by a Hawaiian (Lee), a Native American (Holt), and a Hispanic (Morales); many of the supporting cast were Maori and not Polynesians.

In simplistic terms reminiscent of the primitive *One Million B.C.* (1940), *Rapa Nui* was set in the seventeenth century and dealt with the conflict between Noro of the elitist Long Ears tribe on Easter Island, who covets Ramana, a dark-skinned Short Ears (the island drones), and his rival for Ramana's love, Make of the Short Ears. To determine who will have this woman, the two compete in the annual race to claim the first egg from the sacred birds' offshore hatchery.

Made on a budget of $20 million, the well-intentioned *Rapa Nui* reclaimed only a fraction of its cost in its U.S. distribution. Its themes of class struggle and a government ruled by a supreme god became lost in its too modernistic dialogue and the cast's incongruous accents.

***Real Glory, The* (1939)** United Artists, b&w, 96 minutes. **Director:** Henry Hathaway; **Screenplay:** Jo Swerling and Robert R. Presnell; **Cast:** Gary Cooper (Dr. Bill Canavan), David Niven (Lt. Terrence McCool), Andrea Leeds (Linda Hartley), Reginald Owen (Capt. Steve Hartley), Broderick Crawford (Lieutenant Larsen), Kay Johnson (Mrs. Manning), Vladimir Sokoloff (the Datu), Benny Inocencio (Miguel), Rudy Robles (Lieutenant Yabo), Tetsu Komai (Alipang).

This grand-scale military drama was set in 1906 as American troops were being withdrawn from Fort Mysang on Mindanao, the second-largest island in the Philippines. Despite concerns that Moro bandits led by Alipang will grab control from the natives, the decision to leave remains in place. Colonel Hatch gathers a team to train the locals to defend themselves. As feared, Alipang, aided by the Datu, a Moro chieftain, does his best to kill the U.S. officers and native Lieutenant Yabo so that the Filipinos will flounder and be easy for the Moros to subdue. In the final showdown, Yabo and his followers outmaneuver the Moros, and peace reigns again. The surviving American officers depart the island.

In the late 1890s and early 1900s, the Philippines had been a favorite site for brief travelogues and newsreels by U.S. cinematographers searching for exotic locales. Thereafter, it had been used infrequently as a backdrop for Hollywood-made features. But in the late 1930s, as the imperialistic grasp of Japan reached closer to the Philippines, there was renewed interest in that part of the world.

When *The Real Glory* was completed, Manuel Quezon, the then-president of the Philippines, asked for a screening of the film for his representatives. Afterward, it was requested that certain sequences of the movie be trimmed or removed—any that showed the Filipinos as lesser individuals, as fearful of the Moros, or depicting the Commonwealth's people as not being courageous. The desired changes were made. When the movie was reissued in 1942, the Motion Picture Division of the Office of War Information asked that it be withdrawn because of its plot point showing dissension between Americans and Filipinos (because, by then, the

Moros of the Philippines had become associated with U.S. war forces).

***Red Corner* (1997)** Metro-Goldwyn-Mayer, color 119 minutes. **Director:** Jon Avnet; **Screenplay:** Robert King; **Cast:** Richard Gere (Jack Moore), Bai Ling (Shen Yuelin), Bradley Whitford (Bob Ghery), Byron Mann (Lin Dan), Tsai Chin (Chairman Xu), James Hong (Lin Shou), Roger Yuan (Huan Minglu), Jessey Meng (Hong Ling), Tzi Ma (Li Cheng), Li Jia Yao (Director Liu).

This courtroom thriller utilized Gere's well-publicized dislike of the current Chinese government to promulgate a narrative about an innocent U.S. defendant coping with the culture shock of being bound by a far different jurisprudence system. As Gere's lead character discovered to his horror, he was guilty—period.

Yuppie media attorney Jack Moore arrives in Beijing to negotiate a deal for his international conglomerate employer, competing in the bid with a West German corporation. At dinner with an esteemed Chinese official, Lin Shou, and the man's son, Lin Dan, Moore encounters a chic model (Meng), whom he takes back to his hotel room. The next morning, she is found dead there, and he is arrested for homicide. In court, he learns that she was the daughter of influential General Hong and that his only hope—because the U.S. Embassy chooses not to intervene—is his attractive court-appointed attorney, Shen Yuelin. A romance blossoms between the two that causes Moore, after escaping an assassination attempt, to return to custody so as not to put his lawyer in jeopardy.

Filmed in Los Angeles on a Beijing set that was created on a sound stage, the movie utilized special process camerawork to take advantage of photos and footage taken on the fly in the actual Chinese capital. BAI, from the People's Republic of China, had appeared already in a few Hollywood films (e.g., *THE CROW*, 1994) and would play Tuptim in *ANNA AND THE KING* (1999).

Had this project been made decades earlier, the Asian characters would certainly have been played by Caucasians.

***Red Dust* (1932)** Metro-Goldwyn-Mayer, b&w, 83 minutes. **Director:** Victor Fleming; **Screenplay:** John Mahin; **Cast:** Clark Gable (Dennis "Fred" Carson), Jean Harlow (Vantine), Gene Raymond (Gary Willis), Mary Astor (Barbara Willis), Donald Crisp (Guidon), Tully Marshall (McQuarg), Forrester Harvey (Limey), Willie Fung (Hoy).

One of the most ribald, delightful romantic dramas made before the Hollywood production code was strictly enforced as of 1934, *Red Dust* was a gem of tropical atmosphere, although it was shot in Hollywood and bolstered by the use of stock footage.

Dennis Carson operates a rubber plantation in the wilds of Indochina, rarely leaving his domain. His prostitute friend Vantine has been hiding from the authorities at Carson's. The arrival of Carson's new surveyor (Raymond) and his aristocratic wife Barbara causes Vantine, who loves Dennis, to become jealous, but she leaves as planned. Carson and Barbara start an affair, but it ends when he realizes it will destroy her husband. After the couple depart for America, Vantine, who returned earlier, remains to start a new future of sorts with Dennis.

One of the joys of this snappy entry was the presence of FUNG as the amusing and amused house servant Hoy. It was a type of role the Canton, China-born performer played frequently.

Red Dust was based on the 1928 Broadway play by Wilson Collison. The movie would be remade with Gable as *Mogambo* (1953), but the setting was switched to Africa. A distillation of *Red Dust*, blended with another Collison work (*Congo Landing*, 1934) led to the movie *Congo Maisie* (1940) with Ann Sothern.

Reeves, Keanu (1964–) Several times in his acting career, which is full of twists and turns, Hollywood seemed to write off this often inscrutable actor who preferred to perform with his punk-folk band, Dog Star. Yet, on several occasions he enjoyed surprise movie hits (e.g., *Bill & Ted's Excellent Adventure* 1989; *Speed*, 1994; *The Matrix*, 1999) that reestablished him professionally. His ancestry was a mixture of Asian/Hawaiian/British; his lifestyle ranged from grunge to nonconformist. In his career, this Amerasian tried most screen genres, ranging from sports comedy to Shakespeare to high-tech action flicks. Only once did he play a character explicitly of Asian heritage—in *Little Buddha* (1993), where he was cast as Siddhartha. In that Bernardo Bertolucci feature about Tibetan holy men, past and present, Reeves was Prince Siddhartha who lived 2,000 years ago.

Born in Beirut, Lebanon, his geologist father (of Hawaiian-Chinese descent) and his British mother (showgirl turned theatrical costume designer) split apart when Keanu (which meant "Cool breeze over the mountain") was young. Reeves and his two sisters grew up in Toronto, Canada, to which their mother had relocated. He dropped out of high school in the early 1980s to try stage work and later made several telefeatures including *Act of Vengeance* (1986). Reeves had a part in the Canadian-lensed ice-hockey movie *Youngblood* (1986) and displayed versatility with *Permanent Record* (1988)—a tale of teenage suicide—and *Dangerous Liaisons* (1988), the latter set in eighteenth-century France.

The dopey *Bill & Ted's Excellent Adventure* cleaned up at the box-office and allowed the twentysomething actor a wide choice of upcoming movie projects. He teamed with friend River Phoenix as gay street hustlers in *My Own Private Idaho* (1991) and thereafter jumped from being Jonathan Harker in *Dracula* (1992) to posturing as Don John in *Much Ado About Nothing* (1993). Reeves experienced the romantic genre with *A Walk in the Clouds* (1995) and participated in the action entry, *Chain Reaction* (1996). Having played in a football comedy (*The Replacements*, 2000), he moved on to a serial-killer caper (*The Watcher*, 2000) and returned with two sequels to his last big hit: *The Matrix Reloaded* and *The Matrix 3* (both 2003).

***Rising Sun* (1993)** Twentieth Century-Fox, color, 129 minutes. **Director/Screenplay:** Peter Kaufman; **Cast:** Sean Connery (John Connor), Wesley Snipes (Web "Spider" Smith), Harvey Keitel (Tom Graham), Cary-Hiroyuki Tagawa (Eddie Sakamura), Kevin Anderson (Bob Richmond), Mako (Yoshida-San), Ray Wise (Sen. John Morton), Stan Egi (Ishihara).

Michael Crichton's popular 1992 novel, which highlighted the differences between U.S. and Japanese business and culture, was charged with Japan bashing. In adapting the novel of East versus West to the screen, filmmaker Kaufman softened the story's "attack" on Japanese corporate practices in the United States. In transforming the thriller into more of a police procedural narrative, one of the two Los Angeles investigator leads was given to African-American Snipes, which allowed for an added dimension of racial comparisons and airing of ethnic prejudices. What emerged was, for many viewers, an overly complex story where everything was sacrificed to visual style.

When a call girl is murdered in a Century City high-rise building belonging to Nakamoto, an aggressive Japanese conglomerate, bigoted law enforcer Tom Graham is upset when the higher-ups insist that both liaison officer Web Smith and semiretired police detective John Connors (a specialist in Japanese matters) be brought into the case. At first it seems "clear" from videotape evidence that the dead woman's spoiled boyfriend, Eddie Sakamura, the son of a major competitor to the building's owner, is the culprit; then it is learned that the video evidence has been doctored and that the trail points to a U.S. senator who is involved in the buyout of an American computer company by the Nakamoto leadership.

The genre conventions aside, *Rising Sun* presented an intriguing comparison of contrasting cultural lifestyles as the scene shifted from affluent white residential areas to grungy African-American neighborhoods and also examined the mentality of the Japanese business community.

***Romeo Must Die* (2000)** Warner Bros., color, 114 minutes. **Director:** Andrzej Bartkowiak; **Screenplay:** Eric Bernt and John Jarrel; **Cast:** Jet Li (Han Sing), Aaliyah (Trish O'Day), Isaiah Washington (Mac), Russell Wong (Kai), DMX (Silk), Delroy Lindo (Isaak O'Day), D. B. Woodside (Colin), Henry O (Ch'u Sing), Jonkit Lee (Po Sing).

A wild mix of hip hop, MTV, ghetto drama, and martial arts were combined in this variation on the *Romeo and Juliet* theme. LI, following (but not rising above) JACKIE CHAN'S footsteps as the screen's martial-arts king, had a paucity of dialogue to speak, preferring to let his looks or his trusty fist/feet talk for him. (The action scenes were designed by Hong Kong genre master Corey Yuen, who had worked with Li in seven prior features.)

Han Sing is a good guy/former cop from Hong Kong who arrives in Oakland, California, to exact revenge for his younger brother's murder. He learns that Po died during a turf war between African-American and Chinese gangs over control of waterfront properties. Not dealing well with his own father, Ch'u Sing, the Asian crime lord in some sort of truce with the African-American gangs, Han Sing goes after the killers himself. Meanwhile, he meets Trish O'Day, whose dad Isaak heads the rival faction. As the body count accelerates, Han Sing and Trish, now in love, are amazed by the duplicity of relatives and others whom they once trusted.

If the screenplay had plot gaps, the characterizations (especially of the Asians) were underdeveloped, the romancing between the two leads was minimal, and the stylized martial-arts sequences (which creatively used any object at hand) had a hypnotic spell all their own. Two of the supporting characters—as played by WONG and Lindo—came off best in this action entry. Made on a $25 million budget, this picture grossed $56 million in domestic distribution.

***Rush Hour* (1998)** New Line, color, 94 minutes. **Director:** Brett Ratner; **Screenplay:** Ross LaManna and Jim Kouf; **Cast:** Jackie Chan (Detective Inspector Lee), Chris Tucker (Det. James Carter), Tom Wilkinson (Griffin/Juntao), Elizabeth Peña (Officer Johnson), Tzi Ma (Consul Han Solon), Julia Hsu (Soo Yung), Ken Leung (Sang), Michael Chow (dinner guest).

Back in 1982, African-American comedian Eddie Murphy had ridden to screen fame as one half of a buddy/cop movie (*48 HRS*), which teamed him as a wisecracking crook with a tough Caucasian lawman (Nick Nolte). Similarly, sixteen years later, CHAN, making another bid for U.S. film stardom, was paired with fast-talking comic Tucker. This action entry combined Chan's joyous martial-arts gifts with the motormouth comedic antics of a racist African-American cop (Tucker). Made at a cost of $35 million, the feature grossed more than $141 million at the domestic box office.

In this formulistic police-action exercise, Hong Kong Detective Inspector Lee comes to Los Angeles to help his friend (Tzi Ma) recover his kidnapped daughter (Hsu). The FBI are in charge of the case, with LAPD Detective Carter assigned as a liaison to keep Lee out of the way. Annoyed at having to nursemaid this foreigner, Carter is determined to solve the case before the federal agents do, which, in turn, puts him into competition with Lee. How these two contrasting lawmen utilize their natural talents and contacts to ferret out the guilty parties forms the plot device.

Chan's Lee had comparatively little dialogue while Tucker's cop had too much, but it was the display of Chan's martial-arts skills and his fearless stunt work that gave the picture its zest. Like the later *ROMEO MUST DIE* (2000), which also contrasted Chinese-American and African-American cultures in the context of an action entry, not enough was made of the differences in their traditions and lifestyles. (As if to cover all bases, the film had Hispanic-American actress Peña as an LAPD officer who helped Carter.)

Rush Hour ended with big talker Carter turning down a FBI post to join his new pal Lee in Hong Kong. That set the stage for a sequel, *Rush Hour 2* (2001).

S

Sand Pebbles, The (1966) Twentieth Century-Fox, color, 193 minutes. **Director:** Robert Wise; **Screenplay:** Robert W. Anderson; **Cast:** Steve McQueen (Jake Holman), Richard Attenborough (Frenchy Burgoyne), Richard Crenna (Captain Collins), Candice Bergen (Shirley Eckert), Marayat Andriane (Maily), Mako (Po-han), Larry Gates (Jameson), Richard Loo (Major Chin), Paul Chinpae (Cho-jen).

In 1926, as nationalism sweeps China, the U.S. gunboat *San Pablo* patrols the Yangtze River. One of the new crew members is mechanic Jake Holman. A veteran aboard is Frenchy Burgoyne, a sailor in love with Maily, a Chinese woman ashore who has been forced into prostitution. Meanwhile, as hostilities increase, Captain Collins is ordered to use his gunboat to protect local American civilians—including the missionary Jameson and the school teacher Shirley Eckert. As the unrest escalates and marines land in Shanghai, the *San Pablo* is blockaded by the Chinese. In the upheaval to reach the cut-off mission, several die, including Jake and the captain.

In some ways, the relationship of Frenchy with his English-speaking common-law wife Maily paralleled that of the ill-fated interracial lovers (Red Buttons and MIYOSHI UMEKI) in *SAYONARA* (1957). Then too, commentators at the time noted the similarity between McQueen's character becoming increasingly upset by his superior officers (and their policies of American imperialism) with the rising discontent by many citizens over the United States's then escalating involvement in Vietnam.

The Sand Pebbles was nominated for eight Academy Awards: Best Actor (McQueen), Best Art Direction/Set Decoration (Color), Best Cinematography (Color), Best Film Editing, Best Original Score, Best Picture, Best Sound, and Best Supporting Actor (MAKO).

Sands of Iwo Jima (1950) Republic, b&w, 110 minutes. **Director:** Allan Dwan; **Screenplay:** Harry Brown and James Edward Grant; **Cast:** John Wayne (Sergeant Strykker), John Agar (Pfc. Peter Conway), Adele Mara (Allison Bromley), Forrest Tucker (Cpl. Al Thomas), Wally Cassell (Pfc. Benny Ragazzi), James Brown (Pfc. Charlie Bass), Richard Jaeckel (Pfc. F. Flynn).

Along with such entries as *FLYING TIGERS* (1942), *BACK TO BATAAN* (1945), and *They Were Expendable* (1945), *Sands of Iwo Jima* was another in the canon of Wayne World War II dramas. The star received his first Oscar nomination for playing tough Sergeant Strykker, and the film also received Academy Award bids for Best Film Editing, Best Sound, and Best Story.

With side excursions into personal accounts of several of Strykker's marines, *Sands of Iwo Jima* focuses on the bloody assault against the Japanese on the atoll of Tarawa, one of the Gilbert Islands in the South Pacific. After leave in Honolulu, the marines return to war, part of the force landing at Iwo Jima, the heavily fortified, rocky-cliffed island where the Japanese had an airbase. Following three weeks of concentrated fighting, the men reach the top of Mount Suribachi, and the American flag is hoisted. Later, while Strykker rests for a minute, he is struck dead by a Japanese bullet.

One of the film's gripping moments occurs on Tarawa where Japanese soldiers overrun a foxhole holding two marines. In the melee, the Americans are bayoneted and because the others cannot reach them, the latter spend the night listening to the agonized pleas for help from one of the badly wounded. Such scenes, made five years after the end of World War II, reinforced negative attitudes by Americans about the Japanese everywhere.

Saturday Night with Connie Chung (1989–1990) CBS-TV series, color, 60 minutes. **Cast:** Connie Chung (anchorperson).

Today, it is not quite so unusual, especially with the proliferation of Asian-American personalities (e.g., Tricia Toyota) on network and major local markets, but in 1984 it was a major achievement in minority integration in network television, to have hard-working newscaster CHUNG starring in her own prime-time news-magazine-format series.

In mid-1990, the program changed its name to *Face to Face with Connie Chung* and switched its focus to celebrity and noncelebrity interviews.

***Sayonara* (1957)** Warner Bros., color, 147 minutes. **Director:** Joshua Logan; **Screenplay:** Paul Osborn; **Cast:** Marlon Brando (Maj. Lloyd Gruver), Ricardo Montalban (Nakamura), Red Buttons (Joe Kelly), Patricia Owens (Eileen Webster), Martha Scott (Mrs. Webster), James Garner (Capt. Mike Bailey), Miiko Taka (Hana-ogi), Miyoshi Umeki (Katsumi), Kent Smith (General Webster), Reiko Kuba (Fumiko-san).

At the time of its release, some labeled *Sayonara* an updated *MADAME BUTTERFLY* because of its motif of interracial love. The picture actually followed in the tradition of *JAPANESE WAR BRIDE* (1952), also set at the time of the Korean War and involving an American serviceman who fell in love with a Japanese woman. (It was reported that in the mid-1950s more than 10,000 American servicemen had defied military regulations and wed Japanese women.)

Within *Sayonara*, there are two parallel stories. There is the happy-go-lucky enlisted man Joe Kelly in love with a Japanese woman named Katsumi but unable—due to army regulations—officially to have an interracial marriage. Meanwhile, his buddy from Korea, Major Gruver, now assigned to an air base in Japan, becomes entranced with Hana-ogi, a member of the Matsubayashi dance troupe (a dedicated group that discourages contact with outsiders). Kelly becomes distraught when he is informed that all servicemen "married" to Japanese women will be sent home without their spouses. Unwilling to leave his pregnant love, Kelly commits suicide with Katsumi. This double tragedy gives Gruver the impetus to break down Hana-ogi's resistance to their budding relationship. He proposes marriage, she accepts, and he plans to quit his military post.

With its gorgeous photography, a lush Franz Waxman score, and the use of Irving Berlin's memorable song, "Sayonara," this production proved a huge success and alerted many uninformed or bigoted moviegoers to a different point of view about (1) the Japanese and (2) the topic of interracial romance/marriage. This production provided the film debut of Seattle, Washington-born TAKA (née Betty Ishimoto) and for Otaru, Japan-born UMEKI.

On the strange side in *Sayonara* was the bizarre southern accent of Brando and the casting of Mexican-American star Montalban as a Kabuki theater actor. On the plus side, *Sayonara*, based on the 1954 novel by James A. Michener, won four Academy Awards: Best Art Direction/Set Decoration, Best Sound, Best Supporting Actor (Buttons), and Best Supporting Actress (Umeki). It also received Oscar nominations for Best Actor (Brando), Best Adapted Screenplay, Best Cinematography, Best Director, Best Film Editing, and Best Picture. In 1994 a pre-Broadway musical stage version of *Sayonara* was mounted unsuccessfully.

science fiction—feature films One of the early Hollywood genre features to present an Asian character was *Twelve to the Moon* (1960) in which Michi Kobi played Dr. Hideko Murata. Following in the wake of the *STAR TREK* TV series, several of the *Star Trek* feature films utilized Asian characters (in a minimal manner) from the television programs to fill out the multicultural crews of the movie spin-offs.

Star Trek: The Motion Picture (1980), *Star Trek II: The Wrath of Khan* (1982), *Star Trek III: The Search for Spock* (1984), *Star Trek IV: The Voyage Home* (1986), *Star Trek V: The Final Frontier* (1989), and *Star Trek VI: The Undiscovered Country* (1991) all included GEORGE TAKEI's Mr. Sulu, the chief navigator of the USS *Enterprise*. *Star Trek Generations* (1994) was the first of the big-screen series to feature the cast of TV's *Star Trek: The Next Generation* (1987–94). Part of the crew in the film version was Nurse Ogawa, played by Patti Yasutake. Also aboard for this big-screen installment was Jacqueline Kim as Demora. For *Star Trek: First Contact* (1996), Yasutake's Nurse Ogawa was again part (in a small way) of the proceedings. *Star Trek: Insurrection* (1998), the third feature film to be derived from the *Star Trek: The Next Generation* series had, in a tiny assignment, Jennifer Tung as an ensign.

Other Asian characters in science-fiction movies included the role of Emperor Wang (played by William Hunt) in *Flesh Gordon* (1973), a softcore pornography parody of the 1930s FLASH GORDON serials in which Wang was a takeoff on the sinister Asian-like Emperor Ming.

More recently the remake of *Planet of the Apes* (2001) included actors Cary-Hiroyuki Tagawa and Freda Foh Shen. (In the earlier *Conquest of the Planet of the Apes*, 1970, David Chow played Alda, and in *Battle for the Planet of the Apes*, 1973, FRANCE NUYEN was seen as Alma.) BAI LING was teamed with Adrian Paul in the genre entry *The Breed* (2001).

science fiction series—television If Asian-American characters were hardly represented on contemporary-set American TV series, at least a few of this ethnic minority made it into outer space. On *STAR TREK* (1966–69), a pioneer in racial equality themes and characterizations, the chief navigator was Lieutenant Sulu, played by GEORGE TAKEI. That show was later translated into a Saturday-morning cartoon series, *Star Trek* (1973–75), which featured the original cast providing voices for their animated likenesses on the small screen. Takei's Sulu was among the participants.

On the successor to *Star Trek*, *Star Trek: The Next Generation* (1987–94), Transporter Chief Miles O'Brein married Keiko Ishikawa (played by ROSALIND CHAO from 1991–93) who appeared on the series occasionally. The Keiko character also showed up (1992–97) on *Star Trek: Deep Space Nine* (1993–99), which involved a space station orbiting the planet Bajor. Now, her husband Miles O'Brien was a Chief Operation Officer. Also participating on *Star Trek: The Next Gener-*

ation was Patti Yasutake (as Dr. Elissa Ogawa). On *Star Trek: Voyager* (1995–2001) the Federation ship had aboard Ensign Harry Kim (played by Garrett Wang), who was just out of Starfleet Academy. His great love of the clarinet led to his using all his "replicator" rations for a week to duplicate a clarinet so that he could continue playing after *Voyager* became lost in the Delta Quadrant.

The teleseries *The Planet of the Apes* (1974), which lasted four months on the air, had Asian figures. On *Battlestar Galactica* (1978–80), set thousands of years into the future, a character on the show's first season was Colonel Tigh, played by Terry Carter. On *Space Rangers* (1993), a short-lasting, satirical series set in the year 2014 on the planet Avalon, Cary-Hiroyuki Tagawa played Zylyn, a strange and powerful figure from the planet Grakka. *Earth: Final Conflict* (1997–2002) featured a race of Taeolons who came to Earth under the pretext of friendliness but aroused the angst of a group of human disbelievers. There were Asian characters in the plot line in the fifth STAR TREK TV series, *Enterprise* (2001–); Linda Park played Japanese communications officer Ensign Hoshi Sato.

***Secret of the Wastelands* (1941)** Paramount, b&w, 66 minutes. **Director:** Derwin Abrahams; **Screenplay:** Gerald Geraghty; **Cast:** William Boyd (Hopalong Cassidy), Andy Clyde (California Carlson), Brad King (Johnny Nelson), Soo Yong (Moy Soong) Barbara Britton (Jennifer Kendall), Douglas Fowley (Slade Salters), Richard Loo (Quan), Lee Tung Foo (Doy Kee), Roland Got (Ying).

One of the more unusual of the Hopalong Cassidy western series was *Secret of the Wastelands*, which derived both from characters created by Clarence E. Mulford and the 1940 novel by Bliss Lomax. With Asians so much on everyone's mind as World War II was accelerating, the introduction of Chinese characters into this installment was timely.

Hoppy and his pals (Clyde and King) hire out to escort an expedition to the desert ruins of Pueblo Grande where archaeologist Dr. Birdsall is seeking ancient artifacts. Jennifer Kendall, niece of Birdsall, brings along Doy Kee, a Chinese cook. Clay Elliott, representing the U.S. Mint as part of the team, hopes to gain information on the source of strange gold nuggets that are similar to ones tracked to local Chinese merchants Eventually, it becomes known that the Chinese community is maintaining a secret valley, cultivated for years using that gold they mine in the vicinity to support their efforts.

With its secret valley a "borrowing" from Shangri-La of *LOST HORIZON* (1937), the narrative makes a point of describing the Chinese group as feeling that they are second-class citizens and unaware (according to the plot) that, as native Californians, they could purchase the hidden valley, which is in public domain, and that they could stake a claim to their valuable mine. At one point, Moy Soong sends Cassidy to file the claim for her, suggesting that she believes that as a Caucasian he will be treated better by the government official.

***Secret Sin, The* (1915)** Paramount, b&w, 5 reels. **Director:** Frank Reicher; **Screenplay:** Margaret Turnball; **Cast:** Blanche Sweet (Edith Martin/Grace Martin), Hal Clements (Dan Martin), Alice Knowland (Mrs. Martin), Sessue Hayakawa (Lin Foo), Thomas Meighan (Jack Herron).

One of many silent features to spotlight the vices supposedly to be found in any Chinatown area of a city, this film deals superficially with opium dens. Sweet plays dual roles as sisters, both in love with Dan Martin. One of them, Grace, becomes addicted to opium and morphine to ease the pain of an ailment. HAYAKAWA, in an early film appearance adds flavor to the Chinese ghetto sequences, even though he is actually Japanese born.

Secrets of a Soul See *CONFESSIONS OF AN OPIUM EATER*.

Sen Young, Victor See SEN YUNG, VICTOR.

Sen Yung, Victor (aka: Victor Sen Young) (1915–1980) Broad-featured Sen Yung, like the equally prolific KEYE LUKE, remained best known for playing one of the eager would-be detective sons of CHARLIE CHAN in that Chinese sleuth series. Sen Yung also had a long-run as cook Hop Sing on the TV western series, *Bonanza* (1959–73).

Born in San Francisco, he worked his way through the University of California at Berkeley. By then he was interested in acting. He had an unbilled role in *THE GOOD EARTH* (1937) and by the next year was signed to play Jimmy Chan, Charlie's #2 son, in the long-running Charlie Chan series when WARNER OLAND had died and Luke bowed out of the property. Sen Yung worked with two different on-camera Chans: SIDNEY TOLER and then ROLAND WINTERS. His nonseries roles during the 1940s included *THE LETTER* (1940) and *Betrayal from the East* (1945).

Although continuing with screen assignments in the 1950s, he gravitated to television, appearing on installments of such diverse fare as *Adventures of Superman* in 1953 and *The Lone Ranger* in 1956. He was SAMMEE TONG's cousin Charlie on the TV comedy *BACHELOR FATHER* from 1961 to 1962. During his *Bonanza* years, he made occasional forays into feature films. In 1972, Sen Yung was much in the news as being a gunshot victim during a shootout between two hijackers and federal agents aboard a flight on the runway at San Francisco International Airport. He authored a Chinese cookbook in 1974 and was writing a second at the time of his death from accidental asphyxiation from gas fumes in his small dilapidated bungalow in North Hollywood, California.

In his obituary, the *Los Angeles Times* (November 11, 1980) quoted Sen Yung as having said three years earlier: "I've been all over the country selling a [cook] book and everyone thinks I worked on every show (in *Bonanza*) and that I am a millionaire. . . . The truth is that I appeared (as Hop Sing) in about 20% of the shows over 14 years, and that was not enough to sustain myself. You do all kinds of things When someone needs me to drive a truck I can drive a truck. When someone needs a cook I can cook."

serials—motion pictures For a variety of reasons the chapterplay format—which disappeared from American moviemaking in the mid-1950s—seemed to thrive on expanding existing movie stereotypes, often making them broader and more vivid in the wild serial plots. By so doing, they enlarged on the negative images of those stereotypes, even when applied to the more solid ethnic types being depicted.

One of the more outlandish examples of this type of exaggeration was provided by New York-born J. Carrol Naish in *THE BATMAN* (1943), where he was the sinister Dr. Daka, the Japanese spy leader who combatted the Caped Crusader. Naish's performance was definitely over the top—full of hissed accented words and exaggerated dramatics. At the time of its release, however, it was considered a viable depiction as part of the World War II patriotic push against the nasty Axis.

Years before the Japanese became one of the perils of the free world in the 1930s and thereafter, racial slurs were generally reserved by U.S.-made serials for the Chinese. As in feature films, the implicit reference was that anything could and did happen in Chinatown, ranging from opium dens to white-slave trading. This was suggested in such serials as *The Yellow Menace* (1916), which cast Caucasian actor Edwin Stevens as the vicious Al Singh, a fanatic Oriental bent on destroying America. By its mere title, *The Chinatown Mystery* (1928) indicated that the hero (Joe Bonomo) and the heroine (Ruth Hiatt) would have their hands full in the unchartered backwaters of the Chinese ghetto. The same held true from another silent chapterplay, *Chinatown After Dark* (1928), released by Trinity.

With the coming of sound serials in the late 1920s (and the rise of Japan as a world military power), the emphasis switched from the mysterious Chinese to the sinister Japanese. For example, *The Jade Box* (1930), starring Jack Perrin, dealt with members of a mysterious Eastern cult. Universal's thirteen-chapter entry *Ace Drummond* (1936) pitted the titular hero (played by John King) against the baffling Dragon, who would do anything to ensure that Mongolia was not part of a planned global air service. A mixture of Caucasians (e.g., Guy Bates Post and Arthur Loft) and Asian Americans (e.g., JAMES B. LEONG) portrayed the good and bad Orientals.

The classic *FLASH GORDON* (1936) serial introduced the vile Emperor Ming (Charles Middleton) to moviegoers. He was portrayed as a cross between a rapacious DR. FU MANCHU and a vicious Japanese warlord. (The treacherous Ming returned for 1938's *Flash Gordon's Trip to Mars* and 1940's *Flash Gordon Conquers the Universe.* The chapter play *Shadow of Chinatown* (1936) featured Bela Lugosi as an insane Eurasian inventor—who hated everyone of whatever race—aided by the duplicitous Eurasian Sonya (played by Luana Walters). The twelve-chapter *Jungle Jim* (1937) boasted in its cast of characters the potentially shady Shanghai Lil. As part of the thirteen-episode *Red Barry* (1938) starring Larry "Buster" Crabbe, there was the nefarious Quong Lee (played by Frank Lackteen), an Eurasian underworld kingpin determined to grab $2 million in bonds stolen from an Asian nation that is friendly to the United States.

Bringing Dr. Fu Manchu back to the screen, Republic Pictures cast Henry Brandon as the menacing Oriental involved with the deadly secret group known as Si Fan. In the fifteen-chapter *Drums of Fu Manchu* (1940), Si Fan's master plan was to foment war in Central Asia. Fu Manchu was aided by his evil daughter, Fah Lo See. *Terry and the Pirates* (1940) offered the comic-strip character caught in chaos in Asia as the half-caste warlord Fang (played by Caucasian Dick Curtis) masterminded treachery from episode to episode.

A splinter group of the movies' Dead End Kids team starred in *Junior G-Men of the Air* (1942), fighting against Axis agents, including Araka (played by Austrian-born Turhan Bey), who was part of the deadly Order of the Black Dragonfly. *King of the Mounties* (1942), set in Canada, had well-meaning Native Americans working with the Royal Mounted Police, but they all were up against the combined forces of the Germans, the Italians, and Admiral Yamata (performed by Milwaukee, Wisconsin-born Abner Biberman, who specialized in vicious Nipponese characters during World War II).

Just as *THE GREEN HORNET* (1940) and *The Green Hornet Strikes Again* (1940) showcased a positive Asian-American character in the form of Kato, the hero's trusty helper, *G-Men vs. the Black Dragon* (1943) had Chang (played by Roland Got), who assisted the hero (played by Rod Cameron) in his fight against the nefarious Black Dragon Society. The latter was led by Haruchi (performed by Nino Pipitone), who had been smuggled into the United States from Japan. In *The Masked Marvel* (1943), the supercharacter was on the hunt for Sakima (played by Johnny Arthur) who was on a rampage of sabotaging vital war industries. KEYE LUKE, who had been #1 son of CHARLIE CHAN in many of those movies, played a good guy posing as a nefarious enemy agent in *Secret Agent X-9* (1945). Lloyd Bridges was the champion. In that cliffhanger, the Black Dragon Intelligence Service was the chief culprit, and its regiment of rogues included the duplicitous Eurasian named Nabura (handled by Victoria Horne).

7 *Faces of Dr. Lao* (1964) Metro-Goldwyn-Mayer, b&w, 100 minutes. **Director:** George Pal; **Screenplay:** Charles Beaumont; **Cast:** Tony Randall (Dr. Lao/Merlin the Magician/Pan/the Abominable Snowman/Medusa/the Giant Serpent/Apollonius of Tyana), Barbara Eden (Angela Benedict), Arthur O'Connell (Clint Stark), John Ericson (Ed Cunningham), Eddie Little Sky (George G. George).

This fantasy parable was based on Charles G. Finney's novel *The Circus of Dr. Lao* (1935), which told of the venerable circus showman, Dr. Lao, a Chinese entertainer who arrives in the desert town of Abalone where his tent show will be performed. Before the magical big-top entertainment has concluded, the enigmatic Lao has altered the lives of many in this western town, including newspaper publisher Ed Cunningham, his widowed girlfriend (Eden), and town tormentor Clint Stark. To prompt the changes, Lao performs feats of true magic.

On one level, this movie was an enjoyable fantasy geared for family viewing; on a deeper level, it was a telling tale of bigotry in which Lao literally held a mirror up to the townsfolk so that they could witness their frailties and become better human beings. Randall, with a penchant for overacting, was more restrained than usual, but the central role would have been more poignant had it been played by a true Asian American. Makeup artist William Tuttle won a special Academy Award for his creative efforts on this project.

***Shanghai* (1935)** Paramount, b&w, 76 minutes. **Director:** James Flood; **Screenplay:** Gene Towne, Graham Baker, and Lynn Starling; **Cast:** Loretta Young (Barbara Howard), Charles Boyer (Dmitri Koslov) Warner Oland (His Excellency, Lun Sing) Alison Skipworth (Aunt J.B.), Fred Keating (Tommy Sherwood), Keye Luke (Chinese ambassador's son), Willie Fung (Wang).

For many moviegoers in the mid-1930s—as later—the issue of interracial romance was an enticing but frightening subject because so many cultures and countries, including many states in the United States, had laws outlawing mixed-blood marriages. How to present this taboo topic on the screen and then work the plot around the subject so as not to offend film censorship boards and/or moviegoers was a recurrent challenge to film scripters. In the well-mounted *Shanghai*, the screenwriters enticed the viewer with the potential of the unallowable and then, at the crucial moment, split the lovers apart.

American socialite Barbara Howard arrives in Shanghai to visit her Aunt J.B. Almost immediately, she encounters rickshaw driver Dmitri Koslov, who, unknown to Barbara, is part Russian and part Chinese (his late mother was a mandarin princess). Through a chain of circumstances, Dmitri become wealthy and soon owns an investment firm. He is already in love with Barbara, but his friend Lun Sing, the Chinese ambassador, warns him of the folly of jeopardizing Miss Howard's social standing and future. When she learns the truth of Koslov's ancestry, she is devastated, prompting Dmitri to exit the city. She follows him. Later, the couple return to Shanghai where Lun Sing reveals that Dmitri's mother, years ago, had killed herself to allow her husband and their child (Dmitri) to be free of the bigotry that had left them penniless and disgraced. This revelation, in turn, causes Dmitri and Barbara to agree that their love is *not* stronger than racism. They part, hoping that one day intermarriage won't be a damning situation.

***Shanghai Express* (1932)** Paramount, b&w, 84 minutes. **Director:** Josef von Sternberg; **Screenplay:** Jules Furthman; **Cast:** Marlene Dietrich (Shanghai Lily [Magdalen]), Clive Brook (Captain Donald "Doc" Harvey), Anna May Wong (Hui Fei), Warner Oland (Henry Chang), Eugene Pallette (Sam Salt), Lawrence Grant (Mr. Carmichael), Louise Closser Hale (Mrs. Haggerty), Madame Sojin (bit).

High kitsch or exotic melodrama, *Shanghai Express* was one of the outstanding motion pictures produced in 1930s Hollywood. It was captivating both for its striking atmospheric recreation of 1931 China and for its parade of intriguing characters, each caught in a whirlwind of prejudices. It was also the American movie that made Dietrich, the alluring German import, a legend.

Boarding the Shanghai Express train at Peking is Shanghai Lily, whom the British Medical Corps' Dr. Harvey recognizes as his one-time lover Magdalen. The stiff-upper-lip Englishman is aghast to learn that his ex-lover has become "The White Flower of the Chinese Coast"—in short, a high-priced prostitute. Also aboard the slow-moving train is American-educated Hui Fei, another coaster who is embarrassed by the shame that her profession has brought on her ancestors. Portly Henry Chang, a vicious warlord, is a half-caste who is ashamed of his Caucasian blood.

Before long, Chang has waylaid the crowded train, taken Harvey hostage, and demands that Shanghai Lily submit to him. When she refuses, he ravishes Hui Fei who, later, stabs him to death. Thereafter, as the remaining passengers disembark at Shanghai, Harvey recognizes how much Lily means to him.

Above and beyond the film's memorable ambiance, the picture revealed much about contemporary thoughts on class and caste based on racial background. Perhaps the most honest passenger aboard the train is Hui Fei. Yet, it was Hui Fei who, in the course of the cinema train trip, was raped and who (convenient for the story line) sacrificed herself by killing the evil warlord. The latter, a half-caste, was caught between two worlds: wanted by neither and "forced" to create his own power base, which in the end was not sufficient to save him.

At the time of original release, China was so incensed by the depiction of its country and its people within *Shanghai Express* that it threatened to ban within China not only that release but all future Paramount movies. Eventually, a settlement released the sanction on condition that the studio avoid such celluloid topics in the future.

Garmes won an Academy Award for Best Cinematography for *Shanghai Express*. The film received two other Oscar nominations: Best Director and Best Picture. Harry Hervey's original story for *Shanghai Express* also formed the basis for the undistinguished budget entry *Night Plane from Chungking* (1942) starring Robert Preston, Ellen Drew, Tamara Geva, VICTOR SEN YUNG, and Soo Yong. *Shanghai Express* was remade in 1951 as *Peking Express*. In that retread excursion, Joseph Cotten and Corinne Calvet were the leads, with Marvin Miller as the Chinese bandit leader and Soo Yong as Li Eiu, the role paralleling that of WONG's in the 1932 classic.

***Shanghai Gesture, The* (1941)** United Artists, b&w, 98 minutes. **Director:** Josef von Sternberg; **Screenplay:** von Sternberg, Gez Herczeg, Jules Furthman, and Kurt Vollmoeller; **Cast:** Gene Tierney (Poppy Smith [Victoria Charteris]), Walter Huston (Sir Guy Charteris), Victor Mature (Dr. Omar), Ona Munson ("Mother" Gin Sling), Phyllis Brooks (Dixie Pomeroy, the chorus girl), Albert Bassermann (the commissioner), Maria Ouspenskaya (the amah), Eric Blore (Caesar Hawkins, the bookkeeper).

Back in 1926, John Colton's play *The Shanghai Gesture* had seemed daring and exotic with its tale of Mother Goddam, the wealthy owner of a Chinese whorehouse in Shanghai, who demanded revenge against the white man (Sir Guy Charteris) who wronged her so grievously two decades earlier. At a dinner that Sir Guy attends at Mother Goddam's—not knowing who she really is (i.e., his lover and the mother of their child, Poppy)—she makes him watch as their illegitimate daughter is sold into prostitution. Later, when Poppy has degenerated into a drug-addicted nymphomaniac, the Oriental woman strangles her half-caste offspring. The Broadway play starring Florence Reed ran for 331 performances.

Hollywood tried for years to bring this shocking vehicle to the screen but could never work around the demands of the industry's censorship board. Finally, with much watering down (i.e., changing the villainess's name, switching the whorehouse to a gambling casino, etc.), the movie adaptation was produced. Unfortunately, in the process it lost most of its initial zest and appeal, and Tierney, in one of her early exotic roles, was not up to the complexities of the demanding part.

The mural seen in Mother Gin Sling's apartment was created especially for the film by actor KEYE LUKE.

***Shanghai Noon* (2000)** Touchstone, color, 110 minutes. **Director:** Tom Dey; **Screenplay:** Alfred Gough and Miles Millar; **Cast:** Jackie Chan (Chon Wang, the Shanghai Kid), Owen Wilson (Roy O'Bannon), Lucy Liu (Princess Pei Pei), Roger Yuan (Lo Fong), Walter Goggins (Wallace), Xander Berkeley (Marshal Nathan Van Cleef), Jason Connery (Calvin Andrews, tutor to the Princess).

Having demonstrated his prowess at the U.S. box office with the cop comedy *RUSH HOUR* (1998), acrobatic CHAN returned in a far better American-made movie showcase, *Shanghai Noon.* Despite the lack of solid plot continuity, this comic sagebrush tale provided set pieces for the star to demonstrate his impressive agility, whether combating Caucasian outlaws or helping one tribe of Native Americans against another. More important, the production allowed Chan to emphasize his character's sense of joy and humor, ingredients that were so much a part of his persona in his Hong Kong action movies. Made on a budget of $55 million, this Hollywood-produced western spoof—filled with communication and cultural-barrier jokes—grossed $57 million in domestic distribution.

In 1881, when Princess Pei Pei is sold to Lo Fong, a rogue ex-imperial guard who now heads mining operations near Carson City, Nevada, Chon Wang and two other guards are dispatched to deliver her ransom to the United States and return the royal person to the Forbidden City. In the wild West, fate teams the unorthodox Chon Wang with a lackadaisical outlaw, Roy O'Bannon. Along the way, Chon Wang is presented with a Native American "bride" named Falling Leaves, and by the finale he has rescued the princess.

Paying homage to the western film genre (e.g., Chan's character name was a mangled ethnic pronunciation of icon John Wayne), the script presented Chan as the outsider in a rugged U.S. setting. Unlike the comedic western *Wild Wild West* (1999)—where not much was made of costar Will Smith being African American in the context of the Old West—here Chan played up his cultural heritage, contrasting it slyly with that of Caucasians and Native Americans. Whenever this unique hero of the wide open spaces tried to fit in—adopting traditional cowboy gear—he looked goofy, and the smile on his face confirmed that he knew it. Thus, there were parallels to *The Frisco Kid* (1979) in which the Polish rabbi (played by Gene Wilder), traveling across nineteenth-century America, dealt with Native Americans and outlaws in his own special way.

In 2002, Chan and Wilson appeared in *Shanghai Nights*, the sequel to *Shanghai Noon.*

Shigeta, James (1933–) In the early 1960s, Shigeta appeared likely to be Hollywood's first major Asian-American romantic leading man since the silent era's SESSUE HAYAKAWA, but the career that seemed launched tapered off rather quickly, leaving the six-feet-tall actor to become a solid screen character performer in later years.

He was born in Honolulu, Hawaii, the Nisei son of a successful building contractor and attended New York University and the Juilliard School of Music. After winning on *Ted Mack's Original Amateur Hour* radio program, he launched a singing career using the name Guy Brion. When the Korean War broke out, Shigeta enlisted in the marines and after the war played supper clubs in the United States, a musical in Japan, and recordings there. Gaining popularity, he did a TV series and four other stage musicals in Japan, having learned Japanese from a tutor. Back in the United States, he appeared on a TV show with actress Shirley MacLaine, who had seen him perform in Japan.

James Shigeta and Carroll Baker in *Bridge to the Sun* (1961). (JC ARCHIVES)

Shigeta's screen debut was in a costarring role as a Nisei police detective in THE CRIMSON KIMONO (1959). (Earlier Shigeta had auditioned for movie roles in 1956's THE KING AND I and 1957's SAYONARA but lost those parts to Carlos Rivas and Ricardo Montalban respectively; he was told that he did not look Oriental enough.) After playing Wang Ta in FLOWER DRUM SONG (1961), he worked opposite Carroll Baker in the interracial love story BRIDGE TO THE SUN (1961). By 1966, however, he was supporting Elvis Presley in *Paradise, Hawaiian Style*. Shigeta turned to more stage and club work, sporadically appearing on such TV series as MAGNUM, P.I. in 1983, *Mission: Impossible* in 1989, and a three-part episode on *Beverly Hills, 90210* in 1999. His more recent film assignments included: *China Cry: A True Story* (1991), *Cage II* (1994), MULAN (1998—voice), and *Brother* (2000).

***Shogun* (1980)** NBC-TV miniseries, color, 12 hours. **Director:** Jerry London; **Teleplay:** Eric Bercovici, Benjamin A. Weissman, Donald R. Rode, and Jack Rucker; **Cast:** Richard Chamberlain (Pilot-Maj. John Blackthorne), Toshiro Mifune (Lord Toranaga), Yoko Shimada (Lady Toda Buntaro—Mariko), Frankie Sakai (Kasigi Yabu), Alan Badel (Father Dell'Aqua), Michael Hordern (Friar Domingo), Damien Thomas (Father Alvito), Yuki Meguro (Omi), Nobuo Kaneko (Lord Ishido), Hideo Takamatsu (Buntaro), Hiromi Senno (Fujiko), Orson Welles (narrator).

James Clavell's massive best-selling novel (1975) was turned into an extraordinary TV event. The twelve-hour epic, shown over five nights, was part of a new American interest in Asia in general and specific interest in MARTIAL ARTS films, BRUCE LEE, and Far Eastern philosophy. This multipart TV event made Americans very conscious of Japan, especially its ancient culture and traditions.

In early seventeenth-century Japan, English ship pilot John Blackthorne, who has a mostly Dutch crew in his fleet, is shipwrecked on the Japanese coast. As he is acculturated, he is forced to cope with the country's two most powerful lords—Toranaga and Ishido—who vie for the ultimate power of being shogun. Meanwhile, Blackthorne falls in love with his interpreter (Shimada) and along the way becomes a samurai, the first such from the western world.

Beyond the beautiful scenery, the elaborate costumes, the complex traditions, the occasional humor (e.g., when Blackthorne has his first Japanese-style bath), the moments of extreme violence (e.g., the beheading of a man for not showing respect, the boiling alive of a crew member), the heightened drama (e.g., characters caught in the preparation/act of committing hara-kiri), this romanticized saga comes across as a total experience in learning ancient Japanese culture. It also exposed many TV viewers to some of Japan's finest performers, including Mifune. Many sequences were spoken in Japanese with no English subtitles (until later released versions of the project).

Shogun won Emmy Awards for Costume Design, Main-title Design, and Outstanding Dramatic Series. It received Emmy nominations in the categories of acting, art direction/set decoration, cinematography, direction, editing, production design, and sound editing. *Shogun* would be reedited for further TV viewings, foreign theatrical release, and home entertainment.

JAMES CLAVELL'S NOBLE HOUSE, another TV miniseries, aired in 1988. *Shogun* was converted into a Broadway musical in 1990 but did not do well.

***Sidekicks* (1986–1987)** ABC-TV series, color, 30 minutes. **Cast:** Gil Gerard (Sgt. Jake Rizzo), Ernie Reyes Jr. (Ernie Lee), Nancy Stafford (Patricia Blake), Frank Bonner (Det. R. T. Mooney), Keye Luke (Sabasan), Vinny Argiro (Captain Blanks).

Stretching ever further for an attention-grabber premise to win audience interest, *Sidekicks* came up with a wild idea. Aged, dying Sabasan deposits his grandson, Ernie Lee, with Sgt. Jake Rizzo, a hard-working, bachelor law enforcer. Sabasan is convinced that Rizzo will make a suitable substitute dad for his parentless grandchild. It develops that ten-year old Ernie is a karate champ. Before long, the boy, who has too much time on his hands and misses his grandpa, is assisting Rizzo with his capers. It helps the boy's chances for success that Sabasan blessed the child with magical powers.

The real-life Reyes, who had already performed in martial-arts bouts and was a junior-division black belt, was instructed in his karate routines by his dad, Ernest Reyes, Sr.

***Single Guy, The* (1995–1997)** NBC-TV series, color, 30 minutes. **Cast:** Jonathan Silverman (Johnny Eliot), Joey Slotnick (Sam Sloane), Ming-Na Wen (Trudy Sloane), Mark Moses (Matt Parker: 1995–96), Jessica Hecht (Janeane Percy-Parker: 1995–96), Ernest Borgnine (Manny), Olivia d'Abo (Marie: 1996–97), Shawn Michael Howard (Russell: 1996–97).

This well-meaning but quite derivative situation comedy hoped to be a younger version of *Seinfeld* (1990–98) but had no distinctive personality of its own. Wanting to appeal to a wide viewership, the cast consisted of single Jewish Johnny Eliot, a struggling Manhattan novelist in tandem with his married friends: Sam Sloane, a wacky studio engineer, and his very-together art gallery owner wife, Trudy; and financial adviser Matt Parker and his homemaker wife/new mother, Janeane. Rounding out the ensemble as the voice of experience was Manny, the veteran building doorman.

Perhaps Trudy was the sanest member of the ensemble. A bright, attractive, sensible but fun-loving woman, the most unique point of her characterization, as played by WEN, was that no one made anything special out of her being Chinese American or that she and Sam have an interracial marriage This set-up reflected just how far U.S. mainstream television—echoing American culture—had come in its acceptance of integrated minority talent. (In contrast, on a story arc on the situation comedy *Friends*—May 1995 to January 1996—Ross Geller returned from a paleontology field trip to

Top row: Ernest Borgnine and Shawn Michael Howard; bottom row: Olivia d'Abo, Jonathan Silverman, Joey Slotnick, and Ming-Na Wen in the TV comedy *The Single Guy* (1995–97).

China with a Chinese-American woman friend he had encountered there. For many reasons, this girlfriend would never be accepted by the "group" at the Central Perk coffeehouse. Unstated but felt was the fact that this "foreigner" did not fit in with the Caucasian pack of pals.)

Sing Lung See CHAN, JACKIE.

situation comedy series—television As with African-American characters used in the early decades of American commercial TV, Asian-American figures were typically present in the plot line as domestic help, there to serve the Caucasian characters as houseboys, cooks, and so on, and to feed straight lines to the lead players.

A pioneer Asian-American character on TV sitcoms was SAMMEE TONG on BACHELOR FATHER (1957–62). Houseman and jack-of-all-trades to a wealthy Hollywood lawyer and his orphaned niece, Tong's alter ego sometimes functioned as a confidant to both his employer and the teenaged girl. On *McHale's Navy* (1962–66), involving the commander and the bizarre crew of a PT boat in World War II, Yoshio Yoda (as Fuji Kobiaji) was on hand as a Japanese prisoner-of-war who functioned as the squadron's cook. For VALENTINE'S DAY (1964–65), JACK SOO's Rockwell "Rocky" Sin was valet to a snappy New York publishing executive; they had been army buddies and now Rocky was his man-of-all-tasks *plus* confidant. On *Hey Landlord* (1966–67) set in a New York City brownstone, one of the diverse tenants was played by Miko Mayama. *The Queen and I* (1969) had PAT MORITA among the crew of a beached ocean liner. On *The Courtship of Eddie's Father* (1969–72) dealing with single parent (Bill Bixby) and young son (Brandon Cruz), the housekeeper was performed by MIYOSHI UMEKI. (In the 1963 feature film on which this sitcom was based, the parallel role had been portrayed by Caucasian Roberta Sherwood.)

ANNA AND THE KING OF SIAM (1946) had been a romantic drama on the screen, leading to *THE KING AND I*, a hugely popular Broadway song-and-dance musical adaptation and feature-film version (1956). The TV series adaptation of the property, *Anna and the King* (1972), billed as a (romantic) comedy, featured KEYE LUKE (the Kralahome), Brian Tochi (Crown Prince Chulalongkorn), and Lisa Lu (Lady Thiang). For one season (1974–75) of *Sanford and Son*, Pat Morita was aboard as the feisty Ah Chew, feeding straight lines to series lead Redd Foxx as Fred Sanford. Set during the Korean War, *M*A*S*H* (1972–83) had several local villager characters played by Asian-American performers. On the medical staff was Kellye Nakahara as Nurse Kellye from 1974 to 1983. The nostalgic *HAPPY DAYS* had part of its action set at Arnold's Drive-In, with its proprietor played by Pat Morita from 1974–75. The character returned during the 1982–83 season. *BARNEY MILLER* (1975–82) took place at a Greenwich Village police precinct, and one of its police detectives was performed by Jack Soo, who died during the 1978–79 season. Within the brief-running *MR. T. AND TINA* (1976), Pat Morita starred—a rarity of the era—as a Japanese inventor who was brought to the United States to run a branch of his firm. He brought his sister-in-law (Pat Suzuki) and his uncle (Hatsuo Fujikawa) with him, as well as his two motherless children (played by Caucasian actors).

The Six O'Clock Follies (1980) was set in 1967 Vietnam and featured the staff of the Armed Forces Vietnam Network (AFVN) news program that was tagged "The Follies." Among the group was George Kee Cheung as Ho. *AfterMASH* (1983–84), set in middle America, had ROSALIND CHAO as Soon-Lee Klinger, the Korean war bride of the Max Klinger character. *Gung Ho* (1986–87) dealt with the culture clash in a Pennsylvania auto plant that was taken over by Japanese management. Among the new executive team was Gedde Watanabe (as Kaz Kazuhiro), Sab Shimono (Mr. Saito), and assorted other employees, as well as Patti Yasutake (as Mrs. Kazuhiro) and Emily K. Kuroda (as Mrs. Saito). It was based on the 1986 movie in which Watanabe had first played Kaz. *Together We Stand* (aka: *Nothing Is Easy*) (1986–87) dealt with a couple who have an ethnically mixed group of adopted/natural children, one of whom was an Asian-American played by Ke Huy Quan. *Rags to Riches* (1987–88), a comedy drama revolving around a playboy millionaire (Joseph Bologna) who adopted five orphans, had the sixteen-year-old of the group, Rose, played by Kimiko Gelman.

In the 1990s, *Down Home* (1990–91) was set in the Gulf Coast fishing village of Hadley Cove. One of the locals was Tran played by Gedde Watanabe and another by Kodama Yue. *Teech* (1991) was the only African-American instructor at the exclusive Winthrop Academy in suburban Philadelphia; its attractive assistant headmaster was played by Maggie Han. *Big Wave Dave* (1993) was a quick-departing series about a trio of Chicagoans who relocate to Hawaii and open a surf shop. Their competitor was cynical Danny Kinimaka (played by Ray Bumatai). *Black Tie Affair* (1993), a serialized satire of film-noir detective movies, featured Maggie Han as Cookie. Perhaps the most-hyped of any U.S. TV sitcom involving Asian Americans was *ALL-AMERICAN GIRL* (1994–95) featuring stand-up comedian MARGARET CHO. It concerned the culture clash between generations of Korean Americans. A comedy that tried to be very politically correct was *THE SINGLE GUY* (1995–97), which dealt with a struggling New York City writer and his married circle of friends. One of the couples was interracial: a Jewish sound studio maven (Joey Slotnick) and his smart wife (played by MING-NA WEN), who operates an art gallery. Nothing was said on the series about the culture clash between the couple. The unfunny *Pearl* (1996–97) featured Rhea Perlman as a widow who was taking night classes at college. One of her peers was Ami Li (played by LUCY LIU), a compulsive perfectionist. Liu was later a regular (1998–2002) on *ALLY MCBEAL*, a comedy/drama about a quirky Boston law firm. Liu was cast as Ling Woo, the sleek attorney girlfriend of Caucasian Richard Fish (played by Greg Germann), the firm's founding partner. *One World*, a Saturday-morning TV series that began in 1998, featured a multiethnic cast of characters (living under one roof), including an Asian-American teenager. *DAG* (2000–2001) featured Lauren Tom as a White House secretary. *The Gilmore Girls* (2000–) concerned the bonding/need for space between a contemporary mother and daughter. One of the supporting cast included Keiko Agenda as Korean-American Lane Kim, with Emily Kuroda as her mom. On another Mr. Mom-type series, *Daddio* (2000), starring Michael Chiklis, one of the neighborhood women, Holly Martin, was performed by Suzy Nakamura. The sitcoms *Off Centre* (2000–), *Some of My Best Friends* (2001), and *That 80s Show* (2002–) each featured Asian-American actors: respectively, John Cho, Alec Mapa, and Eddie Chin.

soap opera series—television The first daytime drama to feature an Asian-American character was *Love Is a Many Splendored Thing* (1967–73) created by Irna Phillips. This CBS-TV daytime drama was a sequel of sorts to the 1955 feature film *LOVE IS A MANY-SPLENDORED THING* (1955) and paired Mia Elliott (played by Nancy Hsueh), the daughter of an American (killed in the Korean War) with an Eurasian doctor, come to San Francisco from Hong Kong to study medicine. The Amer-Asian Mia fell in love first with Paul Bradley (played by Nicholas Pryor) and then with Dr. John Abbott (played by Robert Milli).

Considered quite daring at the time, there was concern at the network that the interracial romance was too much for daytime audience. Rather than just have the relationship break apart, the powers that be had Mia's character leave town (and the show), upset over the illegal abortion performed by Dr. Abbott that resulted in the woman's death. Thus the first Asian-American character on network soap operas came and went within a matter of months.

In the mid-1980s on the long-lasting *General Hospital* (1963–), the villainous Mr. Wu (played by Ali Keong) controlled the crime activity in the Asian quarter of Port Charles. His niece in this story arc was played from 1985–87 by Tia Carrere, with Patrick Bishop appearing as Dr. Yank Se Chung. Also in 1985, veteran performer KEYE LUKE made guest appearances on this daytime drama, cast as the Ancient One. In 1986, DUSTIN NGUYEN, in his pre-*21 Jump Street* (1987–90) days, played Suki on *General Hospital*.

During the course of *As the World Turns* (1956–), detailing the intertwining lives of the locals of Oakdale, Illinois, MING-NA WEN—from 1988 to 1991—played Lien Hughes, the Amerasian daughter of focal character Tom. Her character was involved in several interracial romances on the show. More recently, Lea Salonga, who won a Tony Award for playing in *Miss Saigon* on Broadway, took over the Lien Hughes role. (Also, before he became well known for *VANISHING SON* [1994], RUSSELL WONG appeared on this daytime series.)

On *All My Children* (1970–) in 1991, Irene Ng turned up as An-Li Chen, the daughter of a woman who worked as a domestic at Cortlandt Manor, one of Pine Valley's big mansions. Despite An-Li being romantically pursued by a young African American, she was enamored of white teen Brian Bodine, and he wed her to help An-Li gain her green card. (The role of An-Li was taken over by Lindsey Price from 1991 to 1993.)

During *One Life to Live* (1968–) from 1991 to 1993, Amerasian actress Mia Korf played Blair Daimler. When she left the program to do a stage play, her character was written off and later reintroduced with fully Caucasian Kassie Wesley in the part.

Within the ongoing narrative of *The Young and the Restless* (1973–) set in Genoa City, Wisconsin, Elizabeth Sung's Luan Volien arrived on the scene in 1994 as the Vietnam War romance Jack Abbott (played by Peter Bergman) had had, and Luan brought her daughter (not related to Jack Abbott) with her. Later, she was reunited with her son Keemo (played by Philip Moon), who had resulted from her relationship with Abbott. Luan and Jack's emotional roller-coaster relationship was observed by the locals, ending suddenly in a 1996 plot twist that had Luan succumb to a rare, unspecified disease. But at least before she expired, she had her longed-for-wedding (on Valentine's Day) to Jack.

During the course of the relatively short-lived *Sunset Beach* (1997–99), which was set on the California shorelines, one of the figures during the show's first half-year was the doctor Rae Chang, played by Kelly Hu

On nighttime continuing drama, Chau-Li Chi had the role of Chau-Li on *Falcon Crest* (1981–90), a soap opera set in the wine country of Napa Valley, California. In the plush household of matriarch Angela Channing (played by Jane Wyman),

Chau-Li was the head butler. A recurring figure in nearly every episode, it was not until the seventh season that his status in the credits switched from guest star to cast regular. On *Beverly Hills 90210* (1990–2000), Lindsey Price, who has played Asians on both *All My Children* and later *The Bold and the Beautiful*, was introduced as Janet Sosna in 1998 on *90210*. Her character wed the Caucasian Steve Sander (played by Ian Ziering).

Sojin (1884–1954) In Hollywood's silent era, Sojin was a prolific performer, including his Mongol Prince in *The Thief of Bagdad* (1924) and his interpretation of CHARLIE CHAN in *THE CHINESE PARROT* (1927). With his thin bony face, squinted eyes, and razor-thin eyebrows (and often shaved head), he was frequently cast as villainous Asians, often the proprietor of infamous opium dens and sometimes the tormentor—per the Hollywood stereotype—of innocent young white women.

He was born Kamiyama Sojin in Sendai, Japan. Once he completed his studies as an actor, he began to tour Japan with a stock company, often playing such classical roles from western theater as Hamlet, Othello, and Mephistopheles. Arriving in the United States in the early 1920s, Sojin was discovered by film director/actor Raoul Walsh and was given the flashy part of the Mongol Prince in Douglas Fairbanks's *The Thief of Bagdad.* Two years later, in 1926, he was in *The Road to Mandalay* with LON CHANEY; then, in Cecil B. DeMille's *The King of Kings* (1927), he was seen as the Prince of Persia. In *The Crimson City* (1928), as Sing Yoy he shared screen time with Myrna Loy (in another of her Asian roles) and ANNA MAY WONG. In *China Slaver* (1929) he was supreme ruler of an island that was the headquarters for white slavery and narcotic trafficking.

With the coming of sound, Sojin's career in Hollywood greatly diminished. He had bits in the all-star variety entry *The Show of Shows* (1929), John Gilbert's *Way for a Sailor* (1930), and the operetta *Golden Dawn* (1930). In 1931, he departed California (leaving a wife and a child behind) and returned to Japan. He worked with the Shochiku Studio in Tokyo, even making films during the height of the bombing raids during World War II. In *Shichinin no samurai* (Seven Samurai), released the year he died, he played the Minstrel.

***Son-Daughter, The* (1933)** Metro-Goldwyn-Mayer, b&w, 80 minutes. **Directors:** Clarence Brown and uncredited Robert Z. Leonard; **Screenplay:** John Goodrich and Claudine West; **Cast:** Helen Hayes (Lien Wha), Ramon Novarro (Tom Lee [Prince Chun]), Lewis Stone (Dr. Dong Tong), Warner Oland (Fen Sha [the Sea Crab]), Ralph Morgan (Fang Fou Hy), Louise Closser Hale (Toy Yah), H. B. Warner (Sin Kai).

Adapted from the 1919 play by George M. Scarborough and David Belasco, *The Son-Daughter* was a far more theatrical and much less satisfying piece than the prior year's *THE HATCHET MAN.* Each relied on the novelty of well-known Caucasian actors impersonating Chinese characters, a task not well handled by either Hayes or Mexican-born Novarro, each of whom acted in a respectively coy and clumsy manner. In contrast, OLAND, well experienced at playing dastardly Asians on screen, proved effectively sneaky as the wealthy San Francisco merchant who was actually the Sea Crab. It is Oland's Fen Sha who works against the local Chinese Americans in their efforts to help their homeland oppose their oppressors, and it is Fen Sha who bids the most to marry the sacrificial Lien Wha. The drama ends with both Tommy Lee (actually Prince Chun) and Fen Sha dead. Lien Wha, whose father has also been murdered, sails to China with the arms shipment for her people. She is happy in the knowledge that, having killed Fen Sha and shepherding the weapons to her homeland, she has avenged her loved ones and is helping her people.

At one point in preproduction, Chinese-American actress ANNA MAY WONG was considered for the lead, but, as repeatedly would occur when Hollywood was making Asian-themed films, it was felt that audiences would be too shocked (and the censorship boards) if the two romantic leads were of different races.

Nearly thirty years later, another tale of star-crossed lovers in San Francisco trying to defy cultural traditions would be much better received. By the time of the musical SOUTH PACIFIC (1958) and the drama THE WORLD OF SUZIE WONG (1960), Hollywood—and moviegoers—had passed the point where pretend-ethnics were acceptable in such major screen assignments.

***Son of the Gods* (1930)** First National, b&w with color sequences, 92 minutes. **Director:** Frank Lloyd; **Screenplay:** Bradley King; **Cast:** Richard Barthelmess (Sam Lee), Constance Bennett (Allana), Dorothy Mathews (Alice Hart), Barbara Leonard (Mabel), James Eagle (Spud), Mildred Van Dorn (Eileen), King Hoo Chuang (Moy), E. Allyn Warren (Lee Ying).

Based on a Rex Beach novel that was serialized in *Hearst's International Cosmopolitan* magazine in 1928 and 1929, *Son of the Gods* played fast and loose with the audience's expectations of a supposedly racy tale of interracial love. Instead, the movie provided a cop-out ending.

Brought up in San Francisco's Chinatown by an affluent merchant, Sam Lee attends college where this half-caste is tolerated only because of his wealthy pedigree. Eager to prove that life has more to offer, he makes his way to the Riviera where he meets Allana, a rich, young American woman. She falls in love with him, insistent that nothing in his background could possibly upset her, but learning that he is Chinese, the shocked Caucasian woman lashes at him with her riding crop. The heartbroken Lee returns to San Francisco to pay his respects to his dying father. It is then that he learns that actually he is the orphan of Caucasian parents. When Allana returns to America, the couple are happily reunited.

Barthelmess had fared far better as the Chinaman in London's Limehouse in *BROKEN BLOSSOMS* (1919).

Soo, Jack (1916–1979) Before World War II, Soo was a popular comedian on the West Coast. When the war broke out—because he was Japanese American—he was confined to the Topaz relocation center in Utah for two years. Later, he adopted a Chinese stage name to work because there was still a prevalent anti-Japanese bias in the United States.

He was born Goro Suzuki in Oakland, California, and attended the University of California at Berkeley for three years, where he was an English major; on campus, Soo was drawn to dramatics, but there were few available parts for Asians. As an outlet, he sang at small underground San Francisco clubs on the weekends and developed his comedy patter from such engagements. He quit college to take a stage role. After World War II, he worked as a comedian, first at a Chinese nightclub in Cleveland, Ohio, and later as an emcee for a stripper troupe. Thereafter, he teamed for a time as straight man for Caucasian performer Joey Bishop. Soo's big break came when he was cast as the San Francisco nightclub owner in the stage musical *FLOWER DRUM SONG* (1958), a part he repeated in the 1961 film version and in later stage tours.

On television, flip-talking Soo was the poker-playing valet of Tony Franciosa on the situation comedy *VALENTINE'S DAY* (1964–65). He returned to comedy club work frequently because he hated the meager screen/TV roles he was then being offered. He did play Colonel Cai in John Wayne's *The Green Berets* (1968) and a doctor in the TV movie, *She Lives* (1973). Everything turned around when Soo was cast as deadpan Det. Nick Yemana, who was celebrated for his dry wit and lousy coffee, on *BARNEY MILLER*. The TV situation comedy, which was set in a Greenwich Village police precinct, debuted in 1975, and Soo played the part until 1978. By then, he was suffering from terminal cancer of the esophagus and had to miss the last three months of filming.

***So Proudly We Hail* (1943)** Paramount, b&w, 126 minutes. **Director:** Mark Sandrich; **Screenplay:** Allan Scott; **Cast:** Claudette Colbert (Lt. Janet "Davey" Davidson), Paulette Goddard (Lt. Joan O'Doul), Veronica Lake (Lt. Olivia D'Arcy), George Reeves (Lt. John Sumners), Barbara Britton (Lt. Rosemary Larson), Sonny Tufts (Kansas), Mary Servos (Capt. "Ma" McGregor), Dr. Hugh Ho Chang (Ling Chee), Isabel Cooper, Amparo Antenercruz, and Linda Brent (Filipino nurses).

Even more than MGM's *CRY HAVOC* (1943), starring Ann Sothern and Margaret Sullavan. So *Proudly We Hail* was a striking documentary to the bravery of female nurses on front-line combat duty during World War II. Taking its title from a line within "The Star-Spangled Banner," this drama traced the hellish lives of several army nurses under the command of Lt. Janet "Davey" Davidson from the time of the Japanese attack on Pearl Harbor, to their stationing at the U.S. Army hospital on the Bataan peninsula, until the May 1942 evacuation of the eight surviving nurses from the devastated base. Although this well-crafted feature made concessions to its star cast, it was graphic in its depiction of the nightmare of war as seen through the eyes of these courageous nurses.

As now had become typical with Hollywood's World War II combat dramas set in the Pacific, care was taken to include in the narrative the depiction of helpful adult Filipinos (here nurses, volunteers, and soldiers) and a few bewildered Filipino children (to add pathos to the situation). To personalize the enemy (i.e., the Japanese), focus was directed in the narrative to Lt. Olivia d'Arcy who, in a dramatic moment, recounts seeing her fiancé die in the Pearl Harbor attack and how it makes her hate the Japs. In the course of the film, d'Arcy volunteers to look after the wounded Japanese prisoners at Bataan and plans to impair their care, but she finds that she cannot kill them. Later, however, when Japanese soldiers surround the nurses' camp, Olivia defiantly walks into the midst of their captors, pulling the pin of a secreted grenade at the last moment. The explosion, causing her death, allows the others to escape. To many moviegoers this sequence created, as intended, an indelible image of the Japanese as the vicious, despicable enemy.

Giving this powerful film additional credence were the hard facts: When the Japanese took control of Bataan in April 1942, some 75,000 Allied soldiers and Filipinos were imprisoned by their captors, many of whom died in captivity; a few weeks later at the battle of Corregidor more than 800 soldiers died, and the navy was able to evacuate only about seventy-five personnel (mostly women, many of them nurses); of those who surrendered to the Japanese, more than one-third died while imprisoned.

So Proudly We Hail received three Academy Award nominations: Best Cinematography (black and white), Best Original Screenplay, and Best Supporting Actress (Goddard).

Souls for Sale See *CONFESSIONS OF AN OPIUM EATER*.

***South Pacific* (1958)** Twentieth Century-Fox, color, 171 minutes. **Director:** Joshua Logan; **Screenplay:** Paul Osborn; **Cast:** Rossano Brazzi (Emile De Becque), Mitzi Gaynor (Nellie Forbush), John Kerr (Lieutenant Cable), Ray Walston (Luther Billis), Juanita Hall (Bloody Mary), France Nuyen (Liat), Candace Lee (Ngana—Emile's daughter), Warren Hsieh (Jerome—Emile's son).

Most people, when they recall the 1949 Broadway megahit *South Pacific*, based on James A. Michener's fictional *Tales of the South Pacific* (1947), think of such classic musical-comedy songs by Richard Rodgers and Oscar Hammerstein II as "Some Enchanted Evening," "I'm Gonna Wash That Man Right Out of My Hair," "There Is Nothing Like a Dame," and so on. Few recall the number—in both the play and the overbloated film version—"Carefully Taught," an ironic song performed by Lieutenant Cable (in the movie the voice of Bill Lee substitutes for on-screen actor Kerr) that reflects the play's secondary theme of racial discrimination.

In *South Pacific*, Cable, a young marine on World War II duty in the South Pacific, falls deeply in love with the beautiful daughter (NUYEN) of the avaricious, mirthful native, Bloody Mary (HALL). Knowing the rules of the military—and especially of conservative, prejudiced Philadelphians back home—Cable realizes that he and Liat can never anticipate a happy future together as man and wife. This being a musical comedy (and the era in which it was created), their romance ends with his death in combat, thus avoiding the plot-line need to resolve the mixed-blood issue.

South Pacific, adored by the public but not by the critics, won a token Academy Award: Best Sound. It was also nominated for Best Cinematography (Color) and Best Scoring of a Musical. This was the screen debut of French-born Nuyen, an actress of Vietnamese-French background. As had been true in the stage original, the presentation of the natives was more comedic than factual, and most of these extremely subordinate roles were played by Caucasians.

In 2001, a lush new edition of *South Pacific* was mounted as a TV movie special, with Glenn Close and Rade Serbedzija in the leads, pop/jazz vocalist Harry Connick Jr. as Lieutenant Cable, Hong Kong-born Natalie Jackson Mendoza as his love interest, Liat, and character actress Lori Tan Chinn as Bloody Mary. In the musical's newly revamped book, the interracial theme was given more prominence.

***Star Trek* (1966–1969)** NBC-TV series, color, 60 minutes. **Cast:** William Shatner (Capt. James T. Kirk), Leonard Nimoy (Mr. Spock), DeForest Kelley (Dr. Leonard McCoy), Grace Lee Whitney (Yeoman Janice Rand: 1966–67), George Takei (Mr. Hikaru Sulu), Nichelle Nichols (Lt. Nyota Uhura), James Doohan (Eng. Montgomery Scott), Majel Barrett (Nurse Christine Chapel), Walter Koenig (Ens. Pavel Chekov: 1967–69).

In its initial incarnation, the *Star Trek* series was not that popular with home viewers, and it was only after the TV program had been canceled that this science fiction entry slowly developed its huge cult status through reruns, the subsequent feature films, and the enormous number of books (and merchandising) dealing with the television program.

As with all sci-fi entries, special effects—or what passed for them at the time—were considered an important ingredient, but given the low-budget production values on this project, it was the unusual set of characters and the thin-veiled moralizing scripts that made *Star Trek* such an enduring classic series.

The narrative was set in the twenty-third century. Aboard the starship USS *Enterprise,* which represents the United Federation of Planets, are heroic Captain Kirk, the half-breed Vulcan, Mr. Spock, and surgeon Dr. Leonard McCoy. Of equal interest—especially to ethnic-minority viewers—were the presence of African-American Nichols as Lieutenant Uhura, the communications officer, and Asian-American TAKEI as Mr. Sulu, who was first a physicist assigned to the *Enterprise,* before being transferred to his helmsman duties. He had a daughter and later became a captain of starships himself.

Although Uhura and Sulu's roles were relatively small on *Star Trek* compared to the size of the parts allocated to Kirk and Spock, their presence was still a giant leap forward in racial integration on American TV, doing a great deal to instill hope in (young) viewers that there would be racial equality in the (distant) future. Thus, the show established role models for African Americans and Asian Americans who previously, and typically, had characterizations of their races shown as domestics or as objects of ridicule or, sometimes, as the enemy.

What made such racial integration feasible at a time when most other TV series were not doing so was that (1) this was a show set in the future, so the actions of its characters were distanced from home viewers who would not feel "threatened" by integrated crews at some distant time centuries later, and (2) Sulu's character, in particular, was not involved in any on-camera romances, especially of the interracial kind.

In 1973–75, NBC-TV aired *Star Trek,* a thirty-minute cartoon series, which detailed the later explorations of the starship USS *Enterprise.* The same crew, including Takei as Mr. Sulu, were aboard. Takei was also on board the celebrated spacecraft for the first six *Star Trek* feature films from 1980's *Star Trek: The Motion Picture* to 1991's *Star Trek VI: The Undiscovered Country.*

In 2001, a new *Star Trek* TV series, *Enterprise,* was started. This syndicated show served as a prequel to the original *Star Trek* series, in that this new one depicts the beginning years of human space exploration and interstellar travel (in the mid-22nd century). On board the starfleet ship *Enterprise,* is the Japanese Comm officer, Ensign Hoshi Sato. She is in her late twenties and is a language expert. Sato is in charge of the craft's communications, and also serves as the ship's translator in encounters with other life forms (humanoid and otherwise). She is played by actress Linda Park. For a complete listing of major cast characters of the new series, see the *Star Trek* essay and listings within the African-American chapter of this book.

T

***Tai-Pan* (1986)** DeLaurentiis Entertainment Group, color, 127 minutes. **Director:** Daryl Duke; **Screenplay:** John Briley and Stanley Mann; **Cast:** Bryan Brown (Dirk Struan—the Tai-Pan), Joan Chen (May-May), John Stanton (Tyler Brock), Tim Guinee (Culum), Bill Leadbitter (Gorth), Russell Wong (Gordon), Katy Behean (Mary), Kyra Sedgwick (Tess), Janine Turner (Shevaun), Chang Cheng (Jim Qua), Lisa Lu (Ah Gip), Zhang Jie (Lin).

Veering from the pattern of making epic TV miniseries out of Clavell's massive novels of the Far East (e.g., *SHOGUN*, 1980; *JAMES CLAVELL'S NOBLE HOUSE*, 1988), the author's 1966 tome became a feature film, one too short to translate the complex narrative of the history of Hong Kong into a cohesive product. This confused chronicle attempted to relate the blossoming of Hong Kong as a free port and the question of who would become its Tai-Pan (i.e., British merchant leader). The fight for supremacy narrows down to a battle between Scottish buccaneer Dirk Struan and the corrupt Tyler Brock. Others involved in the intricate account include the prostitute May-May, the sashaying Shevaun, Struan's son Culum, and Brock's brutal offspring Gorth.

The actual Asian-American actors in this compressed saga received short shrift on camera, and the viewer was left baffled by the haphazard presentation of Hong Kong's rich history. This was the first Hollywood film to gain permission to shoot in the new China. Made at a cost of some $25 million, it grossed only $4 million at the domestic box office.

Takei, George (1940–) As Hikaru Sulu, the physicist turned helmsman aboard the USS *Enterprise*, Takei zipped through space for three seasons (1966–69) on the *STAR TREK* TV series and costarred in six feature films based on the cult program. By the time he retired from the franchise with *Star Trek VI: The Undiscovered Country* (1991), his character's rank had risen from lieutenant to captain. As a member of that iconic TV/film series, he became a role model for generations of Japanese Americans who were pleased to see that, in the outer space of the future, at least, minority ethnics were not objects of discrimination.

Born in Los Angeles to second-generation Japanese Americans, he and his family were among thousand of Japanese Americans shipped to detention camps (their compound was in Arkansas) once the United States entered the war against Japan. His mother was among the many such imprisoned Japanese Americans who renounced their U.S. citizenship; as a result, the Takeis were relocated to a California prison camp for the duration. After the war, Takei graduated from high school in Los Angeles and attended the University of California at Berkeley, where he became involved with an importer of Japanese-language science-fiction films and dubbed voices in English on the films' soundtracks. This led him to transfer to the University of California at Los Angeles and to switch his major from architecture to acting.

At UCLA, Takei was featured in classmate Francis Ford Coppola's student film, *Christopher;* at the time, the actor was also part of the Desilu (Acting) Workshop at that TV studio. Meanwhile, he had a bit part in the Frank Sinatra combat picture *Never So Few* (1959) and was soon playing small roles on episodes of such TV series as *HAWAIIAN EYE* and *Perry Mason.* In the Cary Grant comedy *Walk, Don't Run* (1966), Takei was cast as a police captain.

After the *Star Trek* series left the air, Takei became more involved in community affairs, hosting a local talk show on PBS-TV entitled *Expressions: East/West.* In 1973, he ran for a seat on the Los Angeles City Council but lost. He joined the other original-cast members to provide voices for the animated *Star Trek* cartoon series, which ran from 1973 to 1975. After his *Star Trek* features, Takei appeared in such films as *Live by the Fist* (1993), *Chongbal* (1994), *Oblivion 2: Backlash* (1996). *Bug Buster* (1998), and *Noon Blue Apples* (2002). In

1991, he appeared on the New York stage in *The Wash*. Having already coauthored a science fiction novel, *Mirror Friend, Mirror Foe* (1980), Takei wrote his autobiography (*To the Stars*) in 1994.

***Teahouse of the August Moon, The* (1956)** Metro-Goldwyn-Mayer, color, 123 minutes. **Director:** Daniel Mann; **Screenplay:** John Patrick; **Cast:** Marlon Brando (Sakini), Glenn Ford (Captain Fisby), Machiko Kyo (Lotus Blossom), Eddie Albert (Captain McLean), Paul Ford (Col. Wainwright Purdy III), Jun Negami (Mr. Seiko), Nijiko Kiyokawa (Miss Higa Jiga), Frank Tokunaga (Mr. Omura).

By the time of John Patrick's Pulitzer Prize-winning, long-running Broadway comedy (1953) based on the 1951 original novel by Vern J. Sneider, World War II seemed long ago to many. (Already, another war, in Korea, had redrawn the United States into the global power struggle.) How to deal with the vanquished was a serious subject, one treated humorously in *The Teahouse of the August Moon* as the U.S. Army occupation forces on Okinawa directed the locals into postwar recovery.

Within the plot, bumbling Captain Fisby is sent to an out-of-way village to supervise the building of a schoolhouse and a women's club and to establish the Pentagon's version of democracy. Before long, he is manipulated by his crafty interpreter Sakini into accepting Lotus Blossom as a "gift" from the villagers, having a GEISHA house constructed, and helping the natives build a thriving business of making and selling their home-brewed brandy. Expectedly, neither blustering Colonel Purdy nor army psychiatrist Captain McLean have any better luck than Fisby in controlling the "incorrigible" Okinawans. By movie's end, the natives have rebuilt their demolished geisha house and restored the apparatus to produce their potent liquor. The conquered have conquered.

Viewers either loved or hated Brando's stylized interpretation of the astute Sakini, who narrates the action of the comedy. Kyo, who had acted in such Japanese-made classic films as *Rashomon* (1950) and *Jigokumon* (Gate of Hell) (1953) before making *The Teahouse of the August Moon* did not speak English before this movie assignment. Most of the roles of Okinawans were played by authentic Japanese performers, a big change from Hollywood productions of pre-World War II, which typically used Caucasian actors for such ethnic parts.

The Teahouse of the August Moon was filmed largely on location in Japan. Saul Chapin, who supervised the music used for this picture, relied on mostly Japanese/Okinawan works to add atmosphere to the production. *Joe Butterfly* (1957) starring Burgess Meredith (as the Asian) and Audie Murphy (in the Glenn Ford-type role) was a distillation of *The Teahouse of the August Moon* on a lesser artistic level. Ford returned to the interracial comedy premise with *Cry for Happy* (1961), which found him and pals in post-World War II Japan, using a geisha house as their headquarters.

A 1962 TV production of *The Teahouse of the August Moon* featured MIYOSHI UMEKI in the lead female role.

***Teenage Mutant Ninja Turtles* (1990)** New Line, color, 93 minutes. **Director:** Steve Barron; **Screenplay:** Todd W. Langen and Bobby Herbeck; **Cast:** Judith Hoag (April O'Neil), Elias Koteas (Casey Jones), Josh Pais (Raphael/passenger in cab), Michelan Sisti (Michelangelo/pizza man), Leif Tilden (Donatello/foot messenger), David Forman (Leonardo/gang member), Michael Turney (Danny Pennington), Jay Patterson (Charles Pennington), James Satto (The Shredder), Toshishiro Obata (Tatus), Ju Yu (Shinsho), Tac Pak (talkative foot #1), Kevin Clash (voice of Splinter).

In 1983, the *Teenage Mutant Ninja Turtles* began as a comic book by Kevin Eastman and Peter Laird and soon attained cult status, leading to a prime-time TV special, this feature-length film (and several sequels), and a Saturday-morning TV cartoon series (1987–95), involving a theme of MARTIAL ARTS. Its impetus was the ongoing craze of NINJA-themed movies, many of them U.S. produced.

In this highly successful (it grossed more than $135 million in domestic distribution) feature film, which boasted elaborate computer-generated special effects, the four New York City-based humanized turtles live in the sewers, talk, walk erect, and adore eating pizza. Their mentor is the wise, one-eared rat Splinter (from Japan), who educates them into becoming Ninja fighters. Their arch enemy is the Shredder, who wears an elaborate mask that suggests Japanese armor. He and his helper Tatus have a band of Ninja teenagers who do their bidding until they realize how badly they are being used.

Within this youngster-oriented offering—which has a dark, sinister look to it—mostly evil Asian forces are at work, reminiscent of the stereotypes of old (e.g., *DR. FU MANCHU*). This popular movie led to the sequels: *Teenage Mutant Ninja Turtles II: The Secret of the Ooze* (1991) and *Teenage Mutant Ninja Turtles III* (1993). In the latter, the quartet of talking turtles abandon New York and their sewer home to turn up in feudal era Japan where they assist rebel villagers to conquer their wicked lord.

***Think Fast, Mr. Moto* (1937)** Twentieth Century-Fox, b&w, 70 minutes. **Director:** Norman Foster; **Screenplay:** Howard Ellis Smith and Foster; **Cast:** Peter Lorre (Mr. Kentaro Moto), Virginia Field (Tanya [Gloria Danton]), Thomas Beck (Bob Hitching), Sig Rumann (Nicolas Marloff), Murray Kinnell (Joseph Wilkie), John Rogers (Carson), Lotus Long (Lela Liu), George Cooker (Muggs Blake), J. Carrol Naish (Adram), Sam[me] Tong (Chee).

Acclaimed author John P. Marquand was celebrated for his novels (e.g., the Pulitzer Prize-winning *The Late George Apley*, 1937) of Bostonians wanting to break out of their conservative New England behavior. As a change of pace, he wrote detective stories about a witty Japanese amateur detective whose powers of observation were the equal of (or some said superior to) that other Asian sleuth of literature and film, CHARLIE CHAN. The MR. MOTO movie series began with this entry, based on the serialized story "That Girl and Mr.

Moto" that had appeared in the *Saturday Evening Post* in the fall of 1936. To play the lead, Twentieth Century-Fox hired Austro-Hungarian-born LORRE, who developed his astute characterization with a minimum of makeup, conveying his alter ego's Oriental background through interior characterization and a careful utilization of an appropriate stance, walk, and mannerisms.

The fast-paced, diamond-smuggling caper opens in San Francisco's Chinatown on the Chinese New Year when a rug merchant on the lam from the police proves to be Mr. Kentaro Moto, a Japanese merchant. The action takes him aboard the *Marco Polo* ocean liner where, during the journey to Shanghai via Honolulu, he has a close encounter with a henchman (whom he throws overboard). Upon arrival in China, he is challenged by smuggler Nicolas Marloff as well as by shipping-office manager Joseph Wilkie. Then, there is the mysterious Gloria Danton who is actually Tanya, a White Russian immigrant. Before the case is closed, Moto has had to kill one of the culprits and cope with the wounding of his assistant, Lela Liu.

In contrast to the same studio's Charlie Chan, the bespectacled Moto proved to be much more of a man of action. He was not afraid to kill an assailant, nor was he shy about taking the initiative in a physical confrontation. Like the Chinese Mr. Chan, the Japanese Mr. Moto was cultured, shrewd, full of sly witticisms, and a keen observer. But in contrast to the Chinese police detective, he did not spout aphorisms, nor was he married with a slew of meddlesome offspring. Also unlike Chan, Moto was a master of disguise. Then too, professionally, the two men differ; Chan was a long-term police detective, while Moto proved to be the well-to-do owner of the Dai Nippon Trading Company who, in his spare time, was an amateur detective.

This first entry augured well for the series, which soon included seven additional installments all featuring Lorre.

***Thirty Seconds Over Tokyo* (1944)** Metro-Goldwyn-Mayer, b&w, 138 minutes. **Director:** Mervyn LeRoy; **Screenplay:** Dalton Trumbo; **Cast:** Spencer Tracy (Lt. Col. James H. Doolittle), Van Johnson (Lt. Ted Lawson), Robert Walker (David Thatcher), Tim Murdock (Dean Davenport), Don DeFore (Charles McClure), Gordon McDonald (Bob Clever), Phyllis Thaxter (Ellen Lawson), Robert Mitchum (Bob Gray), Leon Ames (Lieutenant Jurika), Dr. Hsin Kung (Dr. Chung), Benson Fong (young Dr. Chung), Ching Wah Lee ("Guerrilla Charlie").

Because of military secrecy, this account of the first bombing of Japan in World War II by U.S. fliers could not be told until 1944, the same year that another studio's picture (*THE PURPLE HEART*) released its version of what happened to some of the fliers on the crucial aerial mission who were captured by the Japanese. This film was based on Ted W. Lawson's book (1943) and an article (publication undetermined) by Lawson and Robert Considine.

Following the air raid on Tokyo, Ted Lawson and the crew of his B-25 bomber (nicknamed "The Ruptured Duck") crash-land short of their destination (i.e., the free Chinese coast). Some of them badly injured, they are rescued by Guerrilla Charlie, a local resistance fighter, who guides them to a small village where Dr. Chung and his son attend to their injuries. As the Japanese forces approach, Lawson and the other injured men are taken to Chungking to be returned to the United States.

As had become customary, such Hollywood war films of the period as this entry played up the heroics of Chinese countrymen because China was then a U.S. ally. Frequently, such dramas presented the Chinese locals bravely rescuing and/or helping the U.S. forces, unmindful (at least on camera) that such activity often would lead to their deaths when the Japanese arrived and to reprisals on their towns and villages. In a way, it resembled Hollywood's attitudes to pre-1960 film African-American servants who had no visible lives of their own but were only too willing to help/sacrifice for their white employers. Also of note, in many of these combat features, even when Axis troops/fliers were shown, they were not credited in even official, detailed cast listings of the films

The well-received *Thirty Seconds Over Tokyo* earned an Academy Award nomination for Best Cinematography (Black and White).

***Three Came Home* (1950)** Twentieth Century-Fox, b&w, 106 minutes. **Director:** Jean Negulesco; **Screenplay:** Nunnally Johnson; **Cast:** Claudette Colbert (Agnes Newton Keith), Patric Knowles (Harry Keith), Florence Desmond (Betty Sommers), Sessue Hayakawa (Col. Michio Suga), Sylvia Andrews (Henrietta Thomas), Mark Keuning (George Keith), Howard Cuman (Lieutenant Nekata), Devi Dja (Ah Yin), Taka Iwashaiki (Captain), David Matsushama (evil guard).

Agnes Newton Keith's factual account (1947) of her incarceration in a Japanese prisoner-of-war camp during World War II became a best-seller. At the time that the film adaptation was released, Keith explained in a letter (March 26, 1950) to the *New York Times* the reasons she had written the book. "For horror of war I want others to shudder with me at it. . . . The Japanese in *Three Came Home* are as war made them, not as God did, and the same is true of the rest of us."

In 1941, Agnes Newton Keith, a nonfiction writer, is the sole American residing in Sandakan in British North Borneo, is wed to a British colonial officer, and is expecting their second child. Before they can send their son George back to the United States, the Japanese attack Pearl Harbor, and soon thereafter the Japanese troops under Colonel Suga arrive. He speaks English, knows of her books, and even talks to her of his home life.

By mid-1942, Agnes has had a miscarriage. The Japanese order all European noncombatants removed from the area and sent to prison camps—men and women to separate places. First at Berhaha, then at a more brutal prison compound, Agnes and the women/children struggle to survive as they labor in the rice paddies. The "compassionate" Colonel Suga comes to oversee the new camp for a time, but when he leaves, the brutal Lieutenant Nekata is in charge. He almost has Agnes executed when she, after being tortured, refuses to deny that she was severely attacked by a Japanese guard whom she cannot identify. Suga returns in time to save her. Later, with news of war's end, Suga tells Agnes that his wife and children died at Hiroshima. Australian troops liberate the POW camp, and Suga is taken prisoner. Agnes and her boy are reunited with Harry.

This harrowing depiction of Keith's years of incarceration largely avoided theatricality and was more evenhanded than might be expected in its depiction of the Japanese captors. For former Hollywood silent-film star HAYAKAWA, his role here was a precursor to his part as the labor camp commandant in *THE BRIDGE OVER THE RIVER KWAI* (1957). Two other screen studies of women being held prisoner by the Japanese during World War II were the inept TV movie *Women of Valor* (1986) and the well-intentioned *PARADISE ROAD* (1997).

***Three Seasons* (1999)** October Films, color, 113 minutes. **Director/Screenplay:** Tony Bui; **Screenplay:** Tony Bui and Timothy Linh Bui; **Cast:** Don Duong (Hai), Ngoc Hiep Nguyen (Kien An), Manh Cuong Tran (teacher Dao), Harvey Keitel (James Hager), Diep Bui (Lan), Huu Duoc Nguyen (Woody), Phat Trieu Hoang (Huy).

This was the first independent American feature to be shot in Vietnam with a native-speaking cast since the Vietnam War. Vietnamese-born but U.S.-raised, Bui had previously directed *Yellow Lotus* (1995), a short subject that was released with Vietnamese-language dialogue.

In present-day Saigon, the lives of five characters are traced as their existences take on a greater perspective. They include cyclo driver Hai, young flower peddler Kien An, street boy Woody, prostitute Lan, and ex-marine James Hager who is on the hunt for his Amerasian daughter.

Three Seasons won the Independent Spirit Award for Best Cinematography, which it also did at the Sundance Film Festival. It received a nomination from the Independent Spirit Award in the Best First Feature category. The film was coscripted and coproduced by Bui's brother Timothy, the latter also serving as second-unit director.

***Tokyo Joe* (1949)** Columbia, b&w, 88 minutes. **Director:** Stuart Heisler; **Screenplay:** Cyril Hume and Bertram Milhauser; **Cast:** Humphrey Bogart (Joe Barrett), Alexander Knox (Mark Landis), Florence Marly (Trina), Sessue Hayakawa (Baron Kimura), Jerome Courtland (Danny), Teru Shimada (Ito), Hideo Mori (Kanda).

Not one of Bogart's better movies, *Tokyo Joe* attempted to recapture the magic of *Casablanca* (1942) and failed in creating a believable premise, a memorable love story, or a credible action feature. It did succeed in presenting post-World War II Tokyo to late 1940s filmgoers. (*Tokyo Joe* was the first feature film after the war to gain approval from the American Army of Occupation to shoot footage in Japan.) This movie also marked the return of HAYAKAWA to American filmmaking.

With the war over, Joe Barrett, ex-army hero/nightclub owner returns to Japan to reopen his night spot, Tokyo Joe's which was operated during his absence by his partner, Ito. Barrett discovers that his Russian wife, Trina, did not die during the war but that she is married to an U.S. attorney (Knox). Joe also learns that she had his baby during the war and that to protect the child, she worked for the Japanese government. Meanwhile, Barrett has taken over an airline franchise business and is involved with underworld figure Baron Kimura.

This downer of a film, filled with blackmail, double-crossing, pseudo-intrigue, and attempted hara-kiri, had Bogart's (sardonic but heroic, of course) character taking one too many bullets in the final shootout.

***Tokyo Rose* (1946)** Paramount, b&w, 67 minutes. **Director:** Lew Landers; **Screenplay:** Geoffrey Homes and Maxwell Shane; **Cast:** Byron Barr (Peter Sherman), Osa Massen (Greta Nordstrom), Don Douglas (Timothy O'Brien), Richard Loo (Colonel Suzuki), Keye Luke (Charlie Otani), Grace Lem (Soon Hee), Leslie Fong (Wong), H. T. Tsiang (Chung Yu), Lotus Long (Tokyo Rose).

This potboiler exploited the myth of Tokyo Rose, the supposed Japanese American who made broadcasts to the Allied (especially U.S.) troops during World War II to demoralize them. (Reportedly, actually, some twenty-seven Japanese-American women were utilized by the Japanese for such propaganda broadcasts during the war.)

In this carelessly assembled film, Peter Sherman, an American prisoner-of-war, is one of the GIs who Colonel Suzuki wants to meet with Tokyo Rose. Fearing that this is a ploy to gather anti-American propaganda, Sherman breaks free of his captives and masquerades as a Swedish foreign correspondent. He works with the underground movement and eventually snatches Tokyo Rose whom he intends to stand trial under U.S. authority for her war crimes.

Toler, Sidney (1874–1947) It was not until he was well into middle age that this six-feet-tall, bulky actor succeeded the late WARNER OLAND as the screen's new CHARLIE CHAN. Toler could have mimicked the performance of Swedish-born Oland. Instead, with a minimum of makeup and a good deal of interior characterization—as well as a monotone voice and halting walk—he took the celluloid Chinese sleuth into new creative directions. The Chan assignment gave Toler a professional prominence that he surely never anticipated.

Born in Warrensburg, Missouri, stage actor Toler entered the film industry in 1929 by playing Dr. Meriviel in *Madame X*. The jowly-faced actor with the heavy-eyed look frequently was cast in small roles as on-camera detectives: *Blonde Venus* (1932), *That Certain Woman* (1937), and so on. His first Chinese detective entry was *CHARLIE CHAN IN HONOLULU* (1938). When Twentieth Century-Fox dropped the series after *Castle in the Desert* (1942), astute Toler acquired the screen rights to the famous character from the widow of

Lotus Long, Keye Luke, and Byron Barr in *Tokyo Rose* (1945). (JC ARCHIVES)

creator Earl Derr Biggers. The series began anew at poverty-row studio Monogram Pictures with *CHARLIE CHAN IN THE SECRET SERVICE* (1944). Toler's last entry was *The Trap* (1947). After his death, the part was assumed by ROLAND WINTERS. During Toler's Chan years, he occasionally did other movie roles but was frequently type-cast as an Asian (*Adventures of Smilin' Jack*, 1943—serial) or as a sleuth: *It's in the Bag!* (1945).

Tom, Lauren (1961–) Along with MING-NA, who also appeared in *THE JOY LUCK CLUB* (1993), Tom represented the younger set of Asian-American talent in the early 1990s. Born in Highland Park, Illinois, Tom, was a third-generation Asian American who began as a dancer in the theater, playing in the national touring company of *A Chorus Line* and, in 1983, repeating her part on Broadway for more than a year. Later, she won an Obie in the New York Shakespeare Festival's production of *American Notes.* She had bit parts in some movies but made her mark as the aggressive dim sum waitress in Robin Williams's *Cadillac Man* (1990). This led to appearances on TV's *The Tonight Show Starring Johnny Carson*, which gained her industry attention and prompted roles in such movies as *Mr. Jones* (1993) and *When a Man Loves a Woman* (1994).

In *The Joy Luck Club*, Tom played Lena. Perhaps her greatest visibility occurred when she performed the recurring role of Julie, the girlfriend of Ross Geller, on the TV sitcom *Friends* from 1995 to 1996. In the mid-1990s, she wrote and performed a solo show entitled *25 Psychics* and in 1996 played a colead in *Ikebana*, for the Los Angeles-based East/West Players. In recent years, Tom did a great deal of television, including the telefeatures *Murder Live!* (1997) and *Y2K* (1999); also in 1999, she was the voice of Dana Tan on the animated series *Batman Beyond* and of Agent Lee in *The Zeta Project*, the 2001 cartoon series spin-off of *Batman Beyond.* Tom appeared as secretary Ginger Chin in the TV sitcom *DAG* (2000–2001), a comedy set in the White House. For the direct-to-video animated feature *Mulan 2* (2003), Tom provided the voice of Princess Mei.

Tong, Sam See TONG, SAMMEE.

Tong, Sammee (aka: Sam Tong) (1901–1964) On the TV sitcom *BACHELOR FATHER* (1957–62) he played Peter Tong, houseman to a wealthy Beverly Hills attorney, the man's orphaned niece, and a large dog named Jasper. It was the standard fare being offered to Asian-American and other minority performers during the era of racial inequality in show business. Tong performed his potentially demeaning situation-comedy part with joviality, a refreshing self-confidence, and a minimum of the pidgin English that he had adopted for screen/TV roles over the decades.

Born Sam Shee in San Francisco, the diminutive talent went to high school in Honolulu and planned to attend Stanford University; either because of insufficient academic credits or because of his innate attraction to the entertainment business, he instead became a comedian in vaudeville houses in the Golden Gate city. Later, he put together a variety act called the Three Celestials, who were spotted by a Hollywood talent scout; Tong was cast in the film *Happiness Ahead* (1934). He continued in movies for the next several years, playing bits (often as cooks or houseboys). Thereafter, he returned to personal appearances as a club singer, comedian, and master of ceremonies and hosted his own radio show in San Francisco.

By the mid-1950s, Tong was back in Hollywood, cast as the camp cook in the Walt Disney TV series *Spin and Marty* (1955), which was set at a boys' camp. In the Mickey Rooney sitcom *Mickey* (1964–65), Tong appeared as the star's nemesis, the hotel manager. In October 1964, for no apparent reason, he committed suicide with an overdose of sleeping pills at his West Los Angeles apartment. A suicide note read "No one is to be blamed." His final film, *Fluffy* (1965), was released posthumously.

tong, the This term referred to a fraternal or secret society of the Chinese, usually involved in criminal activity. Gang wars between tong factions often provided the basis of feature film plots, including *The Flower of Doom* (1917), *The Tong Man* (1919), *Purple Dawn* (1923), *THE HATCHET MAN* (1932), *Captured in Chinatown* (1935), *DAUGHTER OF THE TONG* (1939), *CONFESSIONS OF AN OPIUM EATER* (1962), *An Eye for an Eye* (1981), *Armed Response* (1986), *Small Faces* (1996), and *THE CORRUPTOR* (1999).

***Tora! Tora! Tora!* (1970)** Twentieth Century-Fox, color, 143 minutes. **Directors:** Richard Fleischer (U.S.) and Toshio Masuda and Kinji Fukasaku (Japan); **Screenplay:** Larry Forrester, Hideo Oguni, and Ryuzo Kikushima; **Cast:** Martin Balsam (Adm. Husband E. Kimmel), Soh Yamamura (Adm. Isoroku Yamamoto), Jason Robards, Jr. (Gen. Walter C. Short), Joseph Cotten (Henry L. Stimson), Tatsuya Mihashi (Comd. Minoru Genda), E. G. Marshall (Lt. Col. Rufus S. Bratton), Takahiro Tamura (Lieutenant Commander Fuchida), James Whitmore (Adm. William F. Halsey), Elijiro Tono (Adm. Chuichi Nagumo).

Less than thirty years after the Japanese surprise air attack at Pearl Harbor launched America into World War II, the two nations joined together for this expensive coproduction. In great detail, it retold from both sides the key government and military events (and blunders) that led up to the monumental bombing of the U.S.'s primary naval base in the Pacific. Included in the meticulous reconstruction is the Japanese fleet setting out toward Hawaii and how U.S. naval intelligence intercepts but cannot decode the enemy orders regarding that armada. Once carried out, the Japanese think that their attack is only moderately successful because the U.S. aircraft carriers—the prime targets—were not in port at the time. As the film concludes, Admiral Yamamoto, who spearheaded the attack, predicts sadly that the United States will be goaded to a severe retaliation on the Japanese.

In the years that it took to package this large-scale project, it was decided finally to make two separate features (one for the United States and the western marketplace; one for Japan and the Asian marketplace) with different technicians behind the cameras; the features were spliced together into different versions for each market. Not successful in the West, the movie was popular in Japan. Footage from this feature showed up in such war "epics" as *MIDWAY* (1976) and *MacArthur* (1977).

Tora! Tora! Tora! won an Academy Award for Best Visual Effects. It received four Oscar nominations for Best Art Direction/Set Decoration, Best Cinematography, Best Film Editing, and Best Sound.

With such feature films as this, the era of the grand-scale Hollywood World War II combat dramas was coming to a close, as were the long-enduring screen stereotypes of the sadistic Japanese warmonger that replaced the sinister Yellow Peril who conspired in opium dens to molest Caucasian women savagely and to destroy their men. Of course, with the bellicose Japanese figure vanished from the screen, there were newer negative on-camera types—the sinister Vietcong and the conniving Chinese Communists.

In 2001, the overbloated *Pearl Harbor* (made at a reputed cost of more than $153 million) tried to recreate the patriotic combat dramas of old Hollywood but succeeded only in reminding critics and viewers alike how much superior earlier genre entries were (save in the area of special effects). With the release of *Pearl Harbor*, starring Ben Affleck, Josh Hartnett, and Kate Beckinsale came renewed interest in the far more authentic *Tora! Tora! Tora!*

***Tour of Duty* (1987–1990)** CBS-TV series, color, 60 minutes. **Cast:** Terrence Knox (Sgt. Zeke Anderson), Kevin Conroy (Capt. Rusty Wallace: 1987–88), Stephen Caffrey (Lt. Myron Goldman), Joshua Maurer (Pvt. Roger Horn: 1987–88), Steve Akahoshi (Pvt. "Doc" Randy Matsuda: 1987–88), Tony Becker (Cpl. Danny Percell), Ramon Franco (Pvt. Alberto Ruiz), Kim Delaney (Alex Devlin: 1989–90), Carl Weathers (Colonel Brewster: 1989–90).

Certainly one of the most graphic of any TV series dealing with war, this time the focus was on Vietnam in 1967. Among the multicultural cast of characters of American soldiers in Company B was Asian-American Pvt. "Doc" Randy Matsuda. He, like the Captain Wallace character, was killed in action during the first season's episodes. In short, his character—and ethnic representation—was considered dispensable to the story line. The Vietcong enemy utilized in segments of the series were usually faceless opponents, firing from the jungle cover.

***21 Jump Street* (1987–1991)** Fox (and later first-run syndicated) TV series, color, 60 minutes. **Cast:** Johnny Depp (Off. Tom Hanson: 1987–90), Peter DeLuise (Off. Doug Penhall: 1987–90), Holly Robinson (Off. Judy Hoffs), Dustin Nguyen (Off. Harry Truman "H. T." Ioki [Vinh Von Tran]: 1987–90), Frederic Forrest (Capt. Richard Jenko: 1987), Richard Grieco (Off. Dennis Booker: 1988–89).

This youth-oriented series was exceedingly popular with young viewers who appreciated a police drama geared to their age group. The premise had a quartet of young officers assigned to a special squad of the Los Angeles Police Department where, because of their youthful look, they could go undercover easily at high schools in their pursuit of criminals preying on teens. (In many ways *21 Jump Street* was a variation of TV's *The Mod Squad*, 1968–73.)

The four central police officers were a diverse multicultural group: "White bread" Caucasian Tom Hanson, the son of a cop; Italian-American Doug Penhall; African-American Judy Hoffs, formerly on the vice squad; and Vietnamese refugee Harry Truman "H. T." Ioki. The ethnic diversity of the cast not only made the show more realistic but also attracted a broader range of viewers.

The series provided a good deal of background on the leading characters but in particular on the intriguing H. T., who was born Vinh Von Tran. When he was fourteen and Saigon was invaded by the Vietcong, he fled and eventually made his way to America and to St. Louis. Following high school graduation, he moved to San Francisco and changed his identity. After graduating from the police academy, he was assigned to the Jump Street unit. In the course of the series, occasional flashbacks to H. T.'s earlier life back in Vietnam were more elaborate than those of other lead characters. Some sequences showed his parents (played by Keone Young and Haunani Minn). (Much of the background of the Ioki character reflected aspects of the life of NGUYEN who portrayed this series figure.)

In this series, the Asian-American co-lead was one of the most fully developed of any such role on American TV.

U

Umeki, Miyoshi (1929–) The first and one of the few Asian Americans to have ever won an Academy Award, Umeki received her Oscar for her sensitive performance as the Japanese girl whose interracial romance in *SAYONARA* (1957) ended in suicide.

Born in Otaru, Hokkaido, Japan, the youngest of nine children in the family, Umeki survived World War II to become a nightclub and radio vocalist in the later 1940s and thereafter—billed as Nancy Umeki—made several films in her native land. Coming to the United States, the petite performer became a regular on the television variety show *Arthur Godfrey and His Friends* in 1955. This led to club engagements (where she performed in a kimono) and to her being cast in the big screen hit *Sayonara*, followed by her Broadway debut in the Rodgers and Hammerstein musical, *FLOWER DRUM SONG* (1958). Umeki repeated her role in the screen version, but thereafter her movie career declined. She had the lead part in a 1962 *Hallmark Hall of Fame* TV production of *THE TEAHOUSE OF THE AUGUST MOON*. In the mid-1960s, she performed in episodes of *The Man from U.N.C.L.E.*, *I Spy*, and *The Wild, Wild West*. Her biggest assignment on the small screen was as Mrs. Livingston, the trustworthy but sometimes befuddled housekeeper to a widower and his son on the situation comedy *The Courtship of Eddie's Father* (1969–72).

Bill Bixby, Brandon Cruz, and Miyoshi Umeki, on the TV situation comedy *The Courtship of Eddie's Father* (1969–72). (VINCENT TERRACE)

V

***Valentine's Day* (1964–1965)** ABC-TV series, b&w, 30 minutes. **Cast:** Tony Franciosa (Valentine Farrow), Jack Soo (Rockwell "Rocky" Sin), Janet Waldo (Libby Freeman), Mimi Dillard (Molly), Jerry Hausner (O. D. Dunstall), Eddie Quillan (Grover Cleveland Fipple).

This production-line sitcom hardly left a dent, except for the fact that it provided a television series role for smart-mouthed SOO and made the Asian-American character, for a change on U.S. TV, less than subservient. The former army buddy of Valentine Farrow, a Manhattan publishing executive, Rocky Sin is now Farrow's manservant at an elegant East Side townhouse. Reportedly, Soo accepted the series role only because the show's premise placed his and Franciosa's characters on an equal social footing despite the disparity of their jobs and income. With a surname of Sin, Rocky could not help but be a crafty con artist who much prefers playing poker to straightening up either the house or the love life of his frenetic charmer of a boss/friend.

***Vanishing Son* (1994)** Syndicated, color, 100 minutes. **Director:** John Nicolella; **Teleplay:** Rob Cohen; **Cast:** Russell Wong (Jian-Wa Chang), Chi Moui Lo (Wago Chang), John Cheung (Sifu Yamou), Marcus Chong (Fu Qua), Rebecca Gayheart (Clair), Rob Cohen (teacher Beaton), Brian Fong (Bones Lee Hoy), Glenn Kubota (White Powder Leong), Dr. Haing S. Ngor (the General), Vivian Wu (Lili).

Put together by Cohen who had directed and co-scripted *DRAGON: THE BRUCE LEE STORY* (1993), this made-for-television movie followed much the same concept as the earlier TV series *KUNG FU* (1972–75); in fact, it also explored a man's wandering through America, using his martial arts and religious/philosophical education to cope with adverse situations. The major difference was that the series starred a Chinese American, RUSSELL WONG, rather than a Caucasian play-acting as an Asian, as had been the case with DAVID CARRADINE on *Kung Fu.* Several of the supporting cast were of Asian heritage, including Vietnamese DR. HAING S. NGOR, who had won an Academy Award for *The Killing Fields* (1984).

In *Vanishing Son*, Jian-Wa and his younger brother Wago Chang flee political oppression in the People's Republic of China and come to America where the latter—the more headstrong of the two—joins a Vietnamese gang. The more-centered Jian-Wa balances his life by pursuing music (violin playing). Clair is the musician who helps Jian-Wa find the right direction for his life.

With its mix of martial-arts action, mystical philosophy, and touches of romance, *Vanishing Son* also took occasion to reference such topics as the smuggling of aliens (especially Chinese) into the United States and how immigrants were treated in the new country.

Thanks to the charismatic, handsome Wong in the lead assignment, *Vanishing Son* did sufficiently well in the ratings to be followed by three more telefeatures, which, in turn, led to the thirteen-episode *VANISHING SON* TV series in 1995.

***Vanishing Son* (1995)** Syndicated TV series, color, 60 minutes. **Cast:** Russell Wong (Jian-Wa Chang), Jason Adams (Agent Dan Sandler), Stephanie Niznik (Agent Judith Phillips), Chi Moui Lo (Wago Chang).

As a follow-up to the quartet of *VANISHING SON* TV movies that starred WONG and aired in 1994, this weekly series continued the (mis)adventures of Jian-Wa Chang, the student/musician with martial-arts skills who had come to America from Beijing, China, in search of freedom. He was accompanied by Wago, his impulsive, hot-headed younger brother, who had become involved with a vicious gang. When Jian-Wa tried to extricate him from their clutches,

Wago and two government agents were killed. Agent Dan Sandler, the Immigration and Naturalization Service Department superior of the two murdered government men, is convinced that Jian-Wa is the guilty party and continues to hunt him. In contrast, Agent Judith Phillips, a new team member working for Sandler, is not sure of Jian-Wa's complicity and is willing to seek the truth. (The actual villain in Wago's death was "the General," a Vietnam émigré who was engaged in profitable illegal activities while on the government's payroll as an informant.)

Much like *KUNG FU* (1972–75) and *KUNG FU: THE LEGEND CONTINUES* (1993–97), *Vanishing Son* contained a great deal of mysticism and Eastern philosophy. Frequently, the spirit of Jian-Wa's dead brother appeared to help his sibling in times of need as he traveled from place to place avoiding the law while trying to assist others. The show's concept smacked of *The Fugitive* (1963–67; 2000–2001), but like the *Vanishing Son* TV movies, it benefited greatly from the muscular and magnetic Wong. More so than BRUCE LEE in his martial-arts feature films of the 1960s and early 1970s, Wong's character in this TV offering was a leading man ready for romance and, thanks to the plot line, was much more integrated into the lives of the characters he encountered on his wanderings around the United States.

At the time, the only other Asian-American star on U.S. network television besides Wong was comedian MARGARET CHO, who had a sitcom TV series, *ALL-AMERICAN GIRL* (1994–95).

W

***Wake Island* (1942)** Paramount, b&w, 87 minutes. **Director:** John Farrow; **Screenplay:** W. R. Burnett and Frank Butler; **Cast:** Brian Donlevy (Maj. Geoffrey Caton), Macdonald Carey (Lieutenant Cameron), Robert Preston (Joe Doyle), William Bendix (Pvt. Aloysius "Smacksie" Randall), Albert Dekker (Shad McCloskey), Walter Abel (Commander Roberts), Barbara Britton (Sally Cameron), Richard Loo (Mr. Saburo Kurusu), Angelo Cruz (Rodrigo/Japanese captain), James B. Leong (secretary to the Japanese envoy).

This coral atoll in the Pacific Ocean, north of the Marshall Islands, was the scene of severe combat between the United States and Japanese forces early in World War II. *Wake Island* proved to be one of the most realistic depictions of that war and, like *Bataan* (1943), was one of the finest "last-stand" battle pictures turned out by Hollywood.

The chronicle begins in June 1941 when two marine units establish control of the island and Major Caton is placed in charge of the installation. After the Pearl Harbor assault, the same Japanese force attacks Wake Island, causing many casualties. Further poundings by the Axis lead the Japanese to demand that all Wake Island troops surrender. Caton refuses. On December 23, 1941, he and his surviving men fight to the bitter end. (In actuality, during the clash at Wake Island, 800 Japanese soldiers were killed while 120 Americans died and 1,500 were taken prisoner.)

In its documentary-style depiction of the phony last-minute negotiations between the Japanese envoy and the U.S. government supposedly to prevent war between Japan and the United States and Japan's subsequent military assault its targets, *Wake Island* ironically provided many screen roles for Asian-American actors.

Wake Island, produced with the supervision of the U.S. War Department, received Academy Award nominations for Best Director, Best Original Screenplay, Best Picture, and Best Supporting Actor (Bendix).

***Walk Like a Dragon* (1960)** Paramount, b&w, 95 minutes. **Director:** James Clavell; **Screenplay:** Clavell and Daniel Mainwaring; **Cast:** Jack Lord (Linc Bartlett), Nobu McCarthy (Kim Sung), James Shigeta (Cheng-Lu), Mel Torme (the Deacon), Josephine Hutchinson (Ma Bartlett), Benson Fong (Wu), Lilyan Chauvin (Mme. Lili Raide), Kam Tong (Sam).

This unusual western was produced, directed, and coscripted by Clavell, the author of such novels as *King Rat* (1962) and *Shogun* (1975), each of which were translated to the screen. The film's title refers to the "new" Chinese who prefer to "walk like a dragon" and not be bound by ancient traditions of servitude.

In San Francisco of the Old West, Linc Bartlett saves a beautiful Chinese girl, Kim Sung, from being sold into prostitution and brings her to the mining town of Jerico, accompanied by Cheng Lu. The latter is a well-educated recent Chinese immigrant who is joining his uncle, Wu, the owner of a laundry in Jerico. Once there, a rivalry develops between the two men for Kim Sung's affections. Realizing that by the local custom one can kill a man in self-defense and not be punished, Cheng trains to fire a gun so that he can shoot it out with Linc, but in the process kills his instructor, the Deacon. The townsfolk arrest him, but Bartlett, who has learned a great deal about fairness and justice from Kim Sung, intervenes, insisting that there must be one law for everyone. Kim Sung, now quite emancipated, prevents the two rivals from shooting it out and chooses to wed Cheng.

Because this movie used the western action format and included enough of the genre staples (i.e., beautiful women, the crowded saloon, the shootouts, etc.) to sugarcoat its message of tolerance, it found a modest market. Lord's affinity for Asian themes reemerged in his long-running TV series, *HAWAII FIVE-O* (1968–80).

Wang, Wayne (1949–) One of the earlier major Asian talents to transfer to the United States, Wang produced an impressive body of work, only some of which was Chinese themed or dealt with the Asian-American experience in America.

Born in Hong Kong and named after his father's movie icon, John Wayne, Wang came to California to study at the College of Arts and Crafts and then went back to Hong Kong to pursue those fields. Later, based in San Francisco, with grants from the American Film Institute and the National Endowment for the Arts, he directed *CHAN IS MISSING* (1982). His next, *DIM SUM: A LITTLE BIT OF HEART* (1984), also studied the new generation's changing viewpoints on their Chinese heritage. After the melodrama *Slamdance* (1987), Wayne made *EAT A BOWL OF TEA* (1989), which dealt with newlyweds in pre-1950s Chinatown. *Life Is Cheap . . . But Toilet Paper Is Expensive* (1990) was set in Hong Kong and was (at times) bloody, abstract, and experimental. *THE JOY LUCK CLUB* (1993) was Wang's most mainstream picture to that point, based on the well-appreciated Amy Tan novel. He followed that with the oblique *Smoke* (1995), a tapestry revolving around a Brooklyn smoke shop, and its companion piece, *Blue in the Face* (1995). The director refocused on Hong Kong—in the period just before its transfer back to Chinese control—in *Chinese Box* (1997). Like many Americanized Asian directors, themes of his later period were frequently directed to the broader U.S. experience: *Anywhere But Here* (1999—a battle of wills between a mother and her daughter) and *The Center of the World* (2000—set in Las Vegas). Next, he wrote and directed *Beautiful Country* (2001), followed by the romantic comedy *The Chambermaid* (2002) with Jennifer Lopez.

***Wedding Banquet, The* (1993)** Samuel Goldwyn, color, 107 minutes. **Director:** Ang Lee; **Screenplay:** Lee, Neil Peng, and James Schamus; **Cast:** Winston Chao (Wai Tung Gao), May Chin (Wei-Wei), Ah-Leh Gus (Mrs. Gao), Sihung Lung (Mr. Gao), Mitchell Lichtenstein (Simon), Neal Huff (Steve), Jeffrey Howard (street musician), Ang Lee (wedding guest).

This light-hearted and charming comedy transcended racial and sexual prejudices in its presentation/discussion of such topics as Asian Americans, homosexuality, and interracial love. In Manhattan, Caucasian Simon and Taiwanese Wai Tung have a happy live-in relationship, are in love with one another, and are successful in their careers. But naturalized American Wai Tung, still hiding his lifestyle choice from his family, feels guilty that his parents are concerned about his bachelor status. Simon devises a plan to appease them: He suggests that Wai Tung make a marriage of convenience with Wei-Wei, an artist who will earn her green card by wedding Wai Tung. The wrinkle to the plan occurs when Wai Tung's parents arrive for the wedding. Not only must the five live in close proximity, but also the three young people must remember to play-act for the sake of Wai Tung's parents. The civil wedding and the huge banquet lead to a wild night of confusion in which the newlyweds sleep together. By the time the parents return to Taiwan, each has been told or acknowledges to knowing that Wai Tung and Simon are lovers.

Dealing simultaneously with two minority situations within the American landscape, director LEE created a shrewd picture of assimilated Asian Americans versus those (i.e., Mr. and Mrs. Gao) who were clinging to the old ways to some degree. Made on a $750,000 budget, *The Wedding Banquet* was yet another example of Lee's accomplished diversity.

Wen Ming-Na See MING-NA.

westerns—feature films and television Capitalizing on the apparent incongruity of having Asian characters turn up in the Old West, during the decades, Hollywood feature films occasionally included a few such ethnic minority characters to give the standard sagebrush tale a new twist. Very often, these figures were trail camp cooks, or if the setting was a more sophisticated part of the turf, they might be the owner of a local laundry or a restaurant. Some of the screen epics depicting the building of the transcontinental railroads featured "coolie" laborers, or if the setting were old San Francisco, there were often Asian extras in street scenes or as lowly helpers at saloon casinos, hotels, restaurants, or laundries.

For the silent western comedy-drama, *Little Red Decides* (1918), Goro Kino plays the Chinese cook Duck Sing on a big ranch spread. In *The She Wolf* (1919), starring Texas Guinan, the saloon keeper (played by Ah Wing) covets the virginal Caucasian daughter—secretly engaged to a white miner—and is killed for his licentious behavior. Tom Mix's *The Cyclone* (1920) finds the cowboy star as a member of the Northwest Mounted Police, investigating the smuggling of Chinese workers across the border.

Another negative stereotype—the avaricious Nipponese—is presented in *Shadows of the West* (1921), set during World War I out West. While patriotic Caucasian males are in the front lines in France, Japanese Frank Akuri (played by Seymour Zeliff) institutes a plan to help colonize America for his homeland: He begins to buy up nearby ranches, but his plan is thwarted by American Legionnaires on horseback. *Pals of the West* (1922) has a Chinese villain in the West who foments dissension between two mining partners so that he will benefit. *Roarin' Broncs* (1927), starring Buffalo Bill Jr., is one of several sagebrush entries that has as a subplot the smuggling of Chinese across the Mexican border into the United States. (The film was remade as a talkie in 1934 as *Riding Speed*.)

The Jack Perrin western, *Hair-Trigger Casey* (1936) also features the theme of Chinese being snuck across the

Mexico-U.S. border, as well as incorporating plot points about the Chinese ghetto in a border town. A more ingenious use of an Asian theme occurs in William Boyd's *SECRET OF THE WASTELANDS* (1941) where troubleshooter Hopalong Cassidy uncovers a lush hidden valley where the Chinese began their own community. In the Randolph Scott action entry, *The Cariboo Trail* (1950), Lee Tung Foo is seen as Ling, the Chinese cook attached to Scott and his partner (played by Bill Williams); for a change, the character is not relegated just to culinary duties but also participates in a plot line that involves Native Americans. Henry Nakamura (as Ito the cook) is among the male crew helping Robert Taylor shepherd a wagon train of brides-to-be to his California community in *Westward the Women* (1951), set in the old West of 1851.

WALK LIKE A DRAGON (1960), headlining Jack Lord, has both NOBU MCCARTHY and JAMES SHIGETA coping with prejudice out West, as well as dealing with the conflict of old traditions versus new ways. In *Young Guns* (1988), starring Emilio Estevez as Billy the Kid and several Brat Pack members as other gunslingers, Alice Carter is cast as Yen Sun, the Chinese slave of Jack Palance's character and the tempting female who attracts the attention of Kiefer Sutherland's Doc Scurlock. Hong Kong martial-arts star JACKIE CHAN was successful at the box office with *SHANGHAI NOON* (2000), which has him on a sagebrush search for a kidnapped Chinese princess (interpreted by LUCY LIU). It led to Chan and costar Owen Wilson making a sequel to *Shanghai Noon* for release in 2002.

On American TV westerns Asian-American characters were ever rarer. One of the few instances was on *Bonanza* (1959–73) where VICTOR SEN YUNG was on hand as Hop Sing, the cook. However, on that long-running series, Sen Yung appeared only in scattered episodes.

***What's Cooking?* (2000)** Trimark, color, 100 minutes. **Director:** Gurinder Chadha; **Screenplay:** Chadha and Paul Mayeda Berges; **Cast:** Joan Chen (Trinh Nguyen), Julianna Margulies (Carla), Mercedes Ruehl (Elizabeth Avila), Kyra Sedgwick (Rachel Seelig), Alfre Woodard (Audrey Williams), Lainie Kazan (Ruth Seelig), Will Yung Lee (Jimmy Nguyen), Kristy Wu (Jenny Nguyen), Francois Chau (Duc Nguyen), Kieu Chinh (Grandma Nguyen), Chao Li Chi (Grandpa Nguyen).

This pleasingly solid drama traced the daily travails of four contrasting ethnic (African-American, Asian-American, Hispanic, and Jewish) families in Los Angeles at Thanksgiving. In the Nguyen household—where the family runs a neighborhood video store—there is a collision between the immigrant parents' fears of the New World and their children's acculturation. One family member has a loaded gun, and it not only precipitates problems within the household but also supplies the gimmick for the story's finale that ties together the four family units showcased in this movie.

Having the well-established CHEN in one of the focal roles of the Vietnamese household narrative gave her on-

Joan Chen, Kristy Wu, and Kieu Chinh in *What's Cooking?* (2000). (ECHO BOOK SHOP)

camera family greater interest to the filmgoers. The same casting ploy (i.e., using well-known performers) was employed with the other ethnic minority households as well. This art-house release grossed only over $1 million in domestic distribution.

***Who Is to Blame?* (1917)** Triangle, b&w, 5 reels. **Director:** Frank Borzage; **Screenplay:** E. Magnus Ingleton; **Cast:** Jack Abbe (Taro San), Jack Livingston (Grant Barton), Maude Wayne (Marion Craig), Lillian West (Tonia Marsh), Lillian Langdon (Mrs. Craig).

This sympathetic portrayal of a Japanese servant ill-used by fate has Taro San, a Japanese rickshaw boy, brought back to America as valet to Grant Barton. After Barton weds Marion Craig, he becomes involved with a vamp (West), causing a break-up with his wife. In contriving to assist his bereft employer, Taro is fired by Barton. Although Barton and his wife reunite, the well-meaning Taro returns to his homeland.

For a change, this was a compassionate depiction of a Nipponese, albeit seen as a (lowly) domestic and still an outsider.

Winters, Roland (1904–1989) A reliable film character actor often on display as the blustery executive, Winters changed his screen demeanor when he was hired to replace the late SIDNEY TOLER in a series of CHARLIE CHAN movies being churned out by low-budget studio Monogram Pictures in the late 1940s. As had his predecessor, he used a minimum of makeup to create his screen characterization; on the other hand, he performed the notable role with more physical agility, assertiveness, and acerbity than had the earlier on-camera Chinese sleuths.

Born Roland Winternitz in Boston, Massachusetts, he began in theater, frequently playing in stock productions, became active in radio in the 1930s, and made his first impression in films in James Cagney's World War II espionage thriller *13 Rue Madeline* (1946). Winters's initial Chan feature was *THE CHINESE RING* (1947); his sixth and final performance of the role was in *The Sky Dragon* (1949).

On television, he essayed series roles on *Mama* (1951–52) as the Norwegian Uncle Chris, played a lead on *Doorway to Danger* (1952), was the pompous boss Mr. Boone on *Meet Millie* (1953–56), and took a supporting part on the TV sitcom *The Smothers Brothers Show* (1965–66). His last acting was as a judge in the TV movie *You Can't Go Home Again* (1979).

Wo hu zang long See *CROUCHING TIGER, HIDDEN DRAGON.*

Wong, Anna May (1905–1961) In U.S. films of the silent era, Japanese-born SESSUE HAYAKAWA and his Nipponese actress wife Tsuru Aoki were stars in the 1910s and 1920s. Wong, however, was the first Chinese American to gain stardom in Hollywood pictures—and in later movies made in Europe. This was at a time when it was impossible for ethnic minorities to gain meaningful work in Hollywood pictures. While the U.S. movie industry has since seen subsequent Asian-American talent in leading roles (e.g., NANCY KWAN, FRANCE NUYEN, JOAN CHEN, and MING-NA), Wong was a pioneer, as well as an outspoken advocate of racial equality in motion pictures. Early on, she grew tired of being typecast in such stultifying roles as the offspring of the sinister DR. FU MANCHU in *THE DAUGHTER OF THE DRAGON* (1931). In a 1933 British magazine interview (cited in *Notable Asian Americans*, 1999), Wong complained, "When I left Hollywood I vowed I would never act for the film again! . . . I was so tired of the parts I had to play. Why is it that the screen Chinese is always the villain of the piece?"

Anna May Wong with a fellow transatlantic passenger, actor Colin Clive, arriving in New York City in 1930.
(JC ARCHIVES)

She was born Wong Liu Tsong (which means "frosted yellow willow") in Los Angeles, a third-generation Chinese American. Her parents owned a laundry, and Wong and her seven siblings grew up in the apartment above the ramshackle business. As a youngster, she became entranced with movies. One of her earliest screen assignments was an uncredited part in the silent *The Red Lantern* (1919); *The First Born* (1921) allowed her to appear with movie star Hayakawa in one of his vehicles; for *Bits of Life* (1921), she was the wife of LON CHANEY; in the Technicolor silent feature, *Toll of the Sea* (1922) she had the lead as Lotus Flower, a variation of the title character from *Madame Butterfly;* in swashbuckling Douglas Fairbanks's *The Thief of Bagdad* (1924), Wong appeared as the Mongol slave girl; that same year she was native North American Keok in *The Alaskan* (1924); in *The Crimson City* (1928), she had the humiliation of playing support to Myrna Loy who was made up to play the Asian female lead.

Leaving Hollywood, Wong made pictures in England such as *Piccadilly* (1929) and starred on the stage as well (teamed with Laurence Olivier in 1930's *Circle of Chalk*). She made foreign-language versions of her British features in France and Germany, and then returned to America to play the lead on Broadway in the thriller *On the Spot.* The apogee of her screen career was in SHANGHAI EXPRESS (1932) as the Chinese prostitute who found redemption in murder. Later, Wong was considered for the role of the villainess in MGM's *THE GOOD EARTH* (1937), but she wished only to play the female lead of O-lan. The studio worried about a Chinese-American actress performing love scenes with a Caucasian (Paul Muni) and, instead, chose Austrian actress Luise Rainer for the key assignment. Thereafter, a discouraged Wong traveled to China where she found that many of her films had been banned because of her celluloid portrayals of fallen or evil Chinese women. Back in Hollywood, she made a few programmers, including playing a sleuth in *DAUGHTER OF SHANGHAI* (1937).

In 1943, overwhelmed by the shape of her career, she retired, devoting her efforts to the United China Relief Fund and to USO tours. She returned yet again to movies with the mystery *Impact* (1949) and had the lead in the 1951 TV series *THE GALLERY OF MME. LIU-TSONG.* Later, she turned up in the Lana Turner screen drama, *Portrait in Black* (1960) as the taciturn housekeeper. While preparing for a role in the movie musical *FLOWER DRUM SONG* (1961), Wong died in her sleep.

Wong, B. D. (1962–) He was in his midtwenties in 1988 when he won the Tony Award (and several others) as best featured actor in *M. Butterfly*, which was his Broadway debut. On television, he co-starred with MARGARET CHO in the TV series *ALL-AMERICAN GIRL* (1994–95). A frequent film and TV performer, he always focused a good deal of his energies on stage work. He also was a strong advocate for improving the opportunities of Asian-American performers in show business.

Born Bradley Darryl Wong in San Francisco, he began his career in musical theater. After dropping out of college, he moved to New York City in 1981 and thereafter worked for several years in dinner theater and showcases. Then came *M. Butterfly*. His film career, at first, comprised extended tiny roles that he made count. He was a boy on the street in *The Karate Kid, Part II* (1986), a student in the TV movie *Crash Course* (1988), and a Chinese gang lord in *Mystery Date* (1991). He made an impression as the assistant to Martin Short's wedding coordinator from hell in *Father of the Bride* (1991). He replayed the humorous character of Howard Weinstein (now an interior decorator) in *Father of the Bride, Part II* (1995). On cable TV, Wong appeared in the late 1990s as Father Ray Mukada on the prison-set series *OZ*. He was the voice of Captain Li Shang in the animated feature *MULAN* (1998) and took on the role of Bubba in *The Salton Sea* (2001). For *Mulan 2* (2003), the full-length cartoon, he reprised his voice role of Li Shang. On the TV series *Law & Order: Special Victims Unit* (1999–) Wong showed up in the spring of 2001 in the recurring role of Dr. George Huang, a police psychiatrist.

Wong, Mr. Attracted by the success Twentieth Century-Fox was enjoying with its CHARLIE CHAN and MR. MOTO detective series, economy studio Monogram Pictures took advantage of the trend and began its own, utilizing short stories written by Hugh Wiley for *Collier's* magazine. To play the cultivated Chinese detective who often worked in conjunction with police Captain Sam Street, Monogram contracted BORIS KARLOFF, the veteran British actor most associated with the Monster in *Frankenstein* (1931). Physically not right for the part, the five-feet, ten-inch Karloff adopted a stoop-shouldered and squinty-eyed approach to his exceedingly polite law-enforcer character. Only in the vaguest way did the gambit suggest an individual of Asian heritage. Made on the cheap, Karloff appeared in five entries all directed by William Nigh: *MR. WONG, DETECTIVE* (1938), *Mystery of Mr. Wong* (1939), *Mr. Wong in Chinatown* (1939), *The Fatal Hour* (1940), and *Doomed to Die* (1940). When Karloff hastily left the series, Monogram quickly substituted KEYE LUKE (who had previously played Lee Chan in the Charlie Chan series) as Jimmy Lee Wong, the son of the celebrated sleuth, to star in *PHANTOM OF CHINATOWN* (1940) directed by Phil Rosen. It was the end of the programmer series, which had been produced in black and white cinematography.

Boris Karloff (second from left) as the inscrutable Mr. Wong with Guy Usher (left), Wilbur Mack, and Grant Withers (right) in *Doomed to Die* (1940). (JC ARCHIVES)

Wong, Russell (1963–) From 1972 to 1975, Caucasian DAVID CARRADINE starred in the TV series *KUNG FU*, playing a Chinese-American hero with a penchant for Far Eastern meditation and philosophy and a knack for MARTIAL ARTS. It was a role that the handsome Asian-American actor Wong was made for. Fortunately in the mid-1990s Wong had the opportunity to star in his own TV series, a variation of martial-arts-meets-*The Fugitive* (1963–67). VANISHING SON began as four TV movies in 1994 and then as a thirteen-episode series in 1995. Wong was seen as devoted human-rights activist Jian-Wa Chang who fled from Communist China to America with his younger brother. The highly promoted show was a fitting showcase for the handsome Wong. During its brief reign, it made Wong, along with MARGARET CHO and costar B. D. WONG of the sitcom *ALL-AMERICAN GIRL* (1994–95), the only Asian-American actors to then be starring on U.S. television.

He was born in Troy, New York, of a Chinese father from Shandung and a mother of Dutch, French, Canadian, and Indian ancestry. Russell was the fifth of six brothers and had an older sister. The father owned a Chinese restaurant and later a nightclub, where the children helped out in their free time. Russell was interested in singing from an early age. When his parents divorced, he stayed with his mother who remarried and attended Santa Monica College in California, where he began to take acting classes.

His first professional break came when a Hong Kong talent agent negotiated a three-picture deal for six-feet-tall Wong. He had to learn Cantonese for a part in 1985's *The Musical Singer*, which led to his becoming a well-known performer in the Hong Kong film industry. (His younger brother Michael also became a Hong Kong movie leading man.) *TAI-PAN* (1986) introduced Russell to western filmgoers. He subsequently appeared in *CHINA GIRL* (1987) and was Ben Loy, the young Chinese American who returns to China to find a bride in *EAT A BOWL OF TEA* (1989), directed by WAYNE WANG. For *China White* (1989), Wong was cast as the would-be godfather of the Amsterdam Triad who was attracted to a lady cop. Roles in *New Jack City* and *China Cry: A True Story*, both 1991, followed. In *THE JOY LUCK CLUB* (1993), Wong was seen as Lin Xiao. During the years, he appeared in music videos, made recordings, and had a stint on the daytime soap opera, *As the World Turn*. More recently he was Kai in *ROMEO MUST DIE* (2000). At one point in the mid-1990s when a new CHARLIE CHAN movie was announced, Wong was to have starred in the project, but it was later canceled. In 2001, Russell played the Monkey King in the adventure/fantasy telefeature *The Lost Empire*, but the "real" lead was, in typical fashion, given to a Caucasian (Thomas Gibson as the American journalist).

Woo, John (1946–) As a director of Hong Kong MARTIAL ARTS and gangster dramas, Woo proved to be among the very best. When he transferred to American filmmaking, he quickly adapted his smooth, inventive directing approach to western culture, imparting his trademark method onto Hollywood's brand of extravagant action thrillers. With his *Mission: Impossible II* (2000) grossing more than $215 million at the U.S. box-office (on a $125 million budget), he was installed in the hierarchy of global-action directors.

He was born Wu Yusen in Guangzhou in southern China, grew up in Hong Kong, and began his professional career as an assistant director in 1969—employed at the Shaw Brothers Studios. Following his directing debut in 1973, Woo was extremely productive in a variety of celluloid genres. His specialty proved to be highly violent underworld sagas, thrillers with intricate action sequences shot with a distinctive, gripping style: He directed several pictures with CHOW YUN-FAT including the highly-regarded *A Better Tomorrow* (1986). Another of these entries with Yun-Fat (*The Killer*, 1989) made an impact in the U.S. film marketplace and led to his American directing debut, Jean-Claude Van Damme's *Hard Target* (1993). Much more successful was *Broken Arrow* (1996), a tense thriller featuring John Travolta and Christian Slater and filled with memorable action set pieces.

If Woo's choice of film topics in his American-made entries did not usually reflect Asian-American experiences in the late twentieth century, he did demonstrate his sense of craft, which was developed in the Hong Kong cinema industry. It was this style that elevated such entries as *Face/Off* (1997) with Travolta and Nicolas Cage, *Mission: Impossible II* with Tom Cruise, and *Windtalkers* (2002) with Cage. For his next project, *Honor Among Thieves* (2002), Woo returned to his career-making idiom (Hong Kong action films).

***World of Suzie Wong, The* (1960)** Paramount, color, 129 minutes. **Director:** Richard Quine; **Screenplay:** John Patrick; **Cast:** William Holden (Robert Lomax), Nancy Kwan (Suzie Wong), Sylvia Syms (Kay O'Neill), Michael Wilding (Ben), Laurence Naismith (Mr. O'Neill), Jacqueline Chan (Gwenny Lee), Andy Ho (Ah Tong), Yvonne Shima (Minnie Ho).

On Broadway (1958), this corny tearjerker by Paul Osborn, based on the 1957 novel by Richard Mason, ran for a healthy 508 performances. On screen it became an overblown melodrama that gave an extremely distorted picture of the tough life of Hong Kong prostitutes. It so sugarcoated their existence that "Suzie Wong" became a fantasy image of the erotic, supposedly easily accessible foreigner. On the plus side, the play and, in turn, the film created a small wave of screen dramas about interracial romances, bringing the issue to the public's attention. Holden had appeared previously in *LOVE IS A MANY-SPLENDORED THING* (1955), also set in Hong Kong

Filled with sumptuous location photography, *The World of Suzie Wong* focuses on American architect Robert Lomax who comes to Hong Kong to try his skill as a painter. He meets Suzie and only belatedly discovers that she is a prostitute and that much else that she has told him of her past is fiction. With the usual double standards applied to such melodramas, he wants her but hates that other men can have her. The issue of her Chinese heritage becomes a problem as he grows more serious about this desirable woman, causing a Caucasian (Syms) who loves him deeply to give up hope. Eventually, the love-struck American asks Suzie to marry him.

The World of Suzie Wong was the film debut of KWAN, who took over the lead in the movie after France NUYEN, who had played the part on Broadway, left the movie during production.

Y

***Yakuza, The* (aka: *Brotherhood of the Yakuza*) (1975)** Warner Bros., color, 112 minutes. **Director:** Sydney Pollack; **Screenplay:** Paul Schrader and Robert Towne; **Cast:** Robert Mitchum (Harry Kilmer), Takakura Ken (Tanaka Ken), Brian Keith (George Tanner), Herb Edelman (Oliver Wheat), Richard Jordan (Dusty), Kishi Keiko (Tanaka Eiko), Okada Eiji (Tono Toshiro), James Shigeta (Goro).

At the time of release, this was an unappreciated gangster/buddy drama that mixed elements of the traditional Yakuza (a Japanese version of the Mafia) with the western world's crime-drama format and filled its complex story with the ambiance and characters of present-day Japan.

When the daughter of shipping magnate George Tanner is kidnapped to pressure him into delivering weapons he has promised to the Yakuza, Tanner turns to his old army buddy Harry Kilmer to get her back. Once in Tokyo, Kilmer, the ex-G.I. who had once been stationed in Japan, must deal with his former love, Tanaka Eiko, who refused to marry him decades back because of their differing cultures. Tanaka's "brother," Takakura Ken, is part of the Yakuza, drawing Kilmer into the grip and traditions of the Japanese underworld.

In this narrative of misstated relationships, double-crosses, and Japanese ritual, the action is often fast-paced and brutal. There are similarities between *The Yakuza* and the later, more pretentious *The Challenge* (1982), directed by John Frankenheimer and starring Scott Glenn and Toshiro Mifune. *The Yakuza* strikingly revealed the "new" Japan to American filmgoers, balancing the contemporary landscape with characters bound by ancient traditions of honor and culture. The film unveiled a mostly new generation of Japanese actors, but SHIGETA was a holdover from Hollywood's Asian-themed films of the early 1960s.

***Year of the Dragon* (1985)** Metro-Goldwyn-Mayer/United Artists, color, 134 minutes. **Director:** Michael Cimino; **Screenplay:** Cimino and Oliver Stone; **Cast:** Mickey Rourke (Cap. Stanley White), John Lone (Joey Tai), Ariane (Tracy Tzu), Leonard Termo (Angelo Rizzo), Raymond Barry (Louis Bukowski), Caroline Kava (Connie White), Joey Chin (Ronnie Chang), Victor Wong (Harry Yung), K. Dock Yip (Milton Bin).

Utilizing Robert Daly's novel (1981), this expensively produced ($18 million) police action thriller chose to recreate portions of New York's Chinatown on a studio back lot in North Carolina. This elaborate feature was directed by Cimino who had gained success with *THE DEER HUNTER* (1978). In drawn-out terms, *Year of the Dragon* fells of a rising new-breed crime lord, Joey Tai, who is anxious to control all the underworld activities of Manhattan's Chinese ghetto. Opposing his power play is ruthless Capt. Stanley White of the New York police force. White, a Vietnam vet, is bigoted and single minded: Once he fastens on bringing down Joey Tai, nothing else matters. In the process, several people fall (innocent) victim to White's obsession: The cop's wife (Kava) and a fellow detective are murdered, his partner is injured, and his Chinese-American girlfriend, Tracy Tzu, is raped by Tai's gang. The final shootout on a train trestle near the city's docks finds White severely wounding the persistent Tai. The latter, not wishing the humiliation of being captured by the approaching American police, asks his adversary for a gun—and commits suicide.

Amid the (over/under) acting of the too divergent cast, the film meticulously presented its theme of the old and new guard of the Chinese underworld operating in the overcrowded, hectic New York Chinatown. As depicted, the conservative, old underworld element was fearful of the damage that Tai's out-of-control activities would bring through increased media attention. In addition, the Italian mob was pressuring Chinese old-guard criminals not to permit Tai's recklessness to change the balance of criminal power apportioned within the city. Intertwined in the narrative were the highly prejudiced attitudes of White and many of his fellow law enforcers, which made their tasks all the more difficult in Chinatown.

***Yellow* (1998)** Phaedra, color, 101 minutes. **Director/Screenplay:** Chris Chan Lee; **Cast:** Michael Daeho Chung (Sin Lee), Burt Bulos (Alex), Angie Suh (Grace), Mia Suh (Teri), John Cho (Joey), Jason J. Tobin (Yo Yo), Mary Chen (Mina), Lela Lee (Janet), Soon-tek Oh (Woon Lee).

In the same vein as *Dazed and Confused* (1993), *Yellow* concerned a group of eight high-school seniors in Los Angeles who spend a night together, knowing that soon they will be engulfed by the adult world. Sin Lee tells the others that he lost $1,500 of his father's money when he was held up in his dad's Korean grocery. The depressed Sin Lee is convinced that his parents learning of the robbery will end his college plans and he will be forced to work in the store. His pals want to raise the replacement funds, leading to a wild night.

This was one of the first Korean-American features directed by newcomer Lee.

Yeoh, Michelle (aka: Michelle Khan; Yang Zigiong; Yeung Chi-King) (1962–) She was already a top Hong Kong martial-arts movie star when she was hired to play Col. Wai-Lin, the Chinese agent who ran neck-and-neck with Pierce Brosnan's James Bond to prevent the start of World War III in *Tomorrow Never Dies* (1997). She proved in that Bondian cinema excursion that she was as agile in her action scenes as she was attractive on camera.

Yeoh was born in Ipoh, Perak, Malaysia, attended the Royal Academy of Dance in London where she earned a B.A. in dance and drama, and the next year, 1983, was named Miss Malaysia in a beauty contest. That led to her entering the world of TV commercials and movie appearances with the likes of JACKIE CHAN and CHOW YUN-FAT. One of her early feature films was *The Owl vs. Bumbo* (1984). She followed that with several more genre entries, always as the woman asserting herself as a fighter, a novelty in the Asian marketplace. After retiring for a few years for marriage, she returned to the screen as co-star to Chan in *Super Cops* (1992) in which she did her own stunts. Yeoh came to appreciate firsthand the dangers of that athletic profession when she starred in *The Stunt Woman* (1996): The actress fell seventeen feet from a bridge and broke her back. In 1997, *People* magazine chose her as one of "The 50 Most Beautiful People in the World."

More recently, the charismatic Yeoh played a cameo as the former partner and friend of the cop (Leslie Cheung) in the romantic drama *Moonlight Express* (1999). More importantly she costarred with Chow Yun-Fat in ANG LEE's *CROUCHING TIGER, HIDDEN DRAGON* (2000) as the mystical warrior full of gravity-defying agility. She joined with Ben Chaplin and Brandon Cheng for the Peter Pau-directed *The Touch* (2002).

Yeung Chi-king See YEOH, MICHELE.

Z

***Ziegfeld Follies* (1946)** Metro-Goldwyn-Mayer, color, 110 minutes. **Director:** Vincente Minnelli and all uncredited Robert Lewis, Roy Del Ruth, Lemuel Ayres, George Sidney, and Norman Taurog; **Screenplay:** Peter Barry, David Freeman, Harry Tugend, George White, Roger Alton, Al Lewis, and Irving Brecher; **Cast:** William Powell (Florenz Ziegfeld); *Limehouse Blues* number: Fred Astaire (Tai Long), Lucille Bremer (Moy Ling), Robert Lewis (Moy Ling's escort), George Hill and Jack Deery (men), Harriet Lee (singer in dive).

In this potpourri of elaborate production and specialty numbers featuring many of MGM's roster of stars, the "Limehouse Blues" segment was certainly one of the most stylized. Billed as a Dramatic Pantomime, it had Astaire in yellow face and body makeup as a timid Chinese coolie captivated by a glamorous Chinese woman (Bremer), whom he noticed in the Limehouse district. Seeing her admire a fan in a shop window, he schemes as to how he might purchase the expensive gift for her. Later, after being shot during a burglary, he dreams that they are united in a magnificent Chinese-style setting and then, with the fantasy completed, he dies.

Requiring eighteen days of rehearsal, ten days to film, and two days to record the sound tracks, the sophisticated interlude cost more than $228,000 to prepare. The segment benefited greatly from Astaire's gracefulness, which offset the sequence's heavy-handed artiness. The imagery presented of the introverted Chinaman was reminiscent of the stereotype of such earlier Hollywood films as *BROKEN BLOSSOMS* (1919) and *LIMEHOUSE BLUES* (1934), but in those past movies, one party was half-caste and the other white.

Zigiong Yang See YEOH, MICHELLE.

Hispanic Americans

A

Acosta, Rodolfo "Rudy" (1920–1974) This prolific character actor, because of his burly build and sharp, ethnic features, often played bandits or Native Americans in Hollywood features. Born in Chihuahua, Mexico, his family moved to Los Angeles when he was three. He studied dramatics in college and at the Pasadena Playhouse and earned a scholarship to the Palacio de Bellas Artes in Mexico City. After serving in the U.S. Navy, he returned to stage work. John Ford hired him for a small role in *THE FUGITIVE* (1947), which led to his working in Mexican movies such as *Salón México* (1949) for director Emilio Fernández. He returned to American pictures with *ONE WAY STREET* (1950) and earned a studio contract. Acosta acted in such varied productions as *Yankee Buccaneer* (1952), *City of Bad Men* (1953), *THE LITTLEST OUTLAW* (1955), *BANDIDO* (1956), and *The Sons of Katie Elder* (1965) with John Wayne. Acosta's last films included *FLAP* (1970) starring ANTHONY QUINN and *The Great White Hope* (1970) with James Earl Jones.

***Addams Family, The* (1964–1966)** ABC-TV series, b&w, 30 minutes. **Cast:** Carolyn Jones (Morticia Frump Addams), John Astin (Gomez Addams), Jackie Coogan (Uncle Fester Frump), Ted Cassidy (Lurch), Blossom Rock (Grandmama Addams), Ken Weatherwax (Pugsley Addams), Lisa Loring (Wednesday Friday Addams).

Inspired by Charles Addams's *The New Yorker* magazine cartoons of the 1930s, this competition to TV's *The Munsters* (1964–66) provided viewers with another bizarre small-screen family. Somber Morticia was the mother, and devilish, destructive Gomez Addams was her comically dashing spouse. The couple shared their castlelike home with other human (?) oddities, including the seven-feet-tall butler Lurch.

If Anglo Astin gave his character (with the Hispanic first name) a bit of a Latin American flavor, that characteristic was less emphasized in the first of two subsequent TV cartoon versions of *The Addams Family*. For 1973–75 Lennie Weinrib was the voice of Gomez Addams, while Astin returned to his sitcom role in new TV cartoon adventures of the family from 1992 to 1995. Puerto Rican–born RAUL JULIA played Gomez Addams with a dashing Hispanic bent in two popular big screen adaptations: *THE ADDAMS FAMILY* (1991) and *Addams Family Values* (1993).

***Addams Family, The* (1991)** Orion/Paramount, color, 99 minutes. **Director:** Barry Sonnenfeld; **Screenplay:** Caroline Thompson and Larry Wilson; **Cast:** Anjelica Huston (Morticia Addams), Raul Julia (Gomez Addams), Christopher Lloyd (Uncle Fester Addams/Gordon Craven), Dan Hedaya (Tully Alford), Elizabeth Wilson (Abigail Craven), Judith Malina (Granny), Carel Struycken (Lurch), Dana Ivey (Margaret Alford), Christina Ricci (Wednesday Addams), Jimmy Workman (Pugsley Addams).

Charles Addams's *The New Yorker* cartoons that began in the 1930s led to the well-remembered TV situation comedy (1964–66) starring Carolyn Jones and John Astin as that bizarre married couple Morticia and Gomez Addams. The sitcom was transferred to the big screen with an impressive cast ensemble, including Huston as the ghoulish Morticia and JULIA as the overly debonair Gomez. With slicked-back hair and a thin moustache, Julia played his role flamboyantly akin to the oversized on-screen banditos of 1930s Hollywood movies. When not engineering train crashes with his toy trains, Gomez loved to dance, fence a la ZORRO, or display his physical agility by doing back flips out the window. He safeguarded the family fortune—which was amassed in Spanish doubloons.

The thin plot had the Addams's shyster lawyer (Hedaya) using Abigail Craven and her son Gordon to trick the Addams clan out of their fortune. At one point the family has been dispossessed from their home and a glum Gomez sits staring at the tiny TV set in their motel room. But everything ends happily for the Addamses when Gordon Craven proves to be the real long-lost Uncle Fester.

Silly as the movie was, including the antics of suave, over-the-top Gomez, it grossed more than $113 million in domestic distribution. The film was nominated for an Academy Award for Best Costume Design. It led to *Addams Family Values* (1993), with Julia again playing Gomez. In 1998, there was a direct-to-video feature *The Addams Family Reunion* with Tim Curry as Gomez, and there followed the debut of the TV sitcom *The New Addams Family* (1998–99) in which Glenn Taranto was the new Gomez.

Adventures of Kit Carson, The **(1951–1955)** Syndicated TV series, b&w, 30 minutes. **Cast:** Bill Williams (Kit Carson), Don Diamond (El Toro).

One of the many early western TV series, this entry took a swipe at the popular *THE CISCO KID* television show (1950–56) by providing the Anglo Carson with El Toro, his Mexican sidekick. Adding insult to injury, the clichéd, subservient role of the Hispanic helper was played by Brooklyn-born Diamond.

A.K.A. Pablo **(1984)** ABC-TV series, color, 30 minutes. **Cast:** Paul Rodriguez (Paul [Pablo] Rivera), Joe Santos (Domingo Rivera), Katy Jurado (Rosa Maria Rivera), Alma Cuervo (Sylvia Rivera), Martha Velez (Lucia Rivera Del Gato), Hector Elizondo (Jose Sanchez/Shapiro).

Like his on-screen alter ego (Paul Rivera) in this short-lasting TV sitcom, this property was to be the breakthrough project for comedian RODRIGUEZ who, up to then, had had only a few movie acting roles. This uninspired show was cocreated by comedy meister Norman Lear, who had discovered Rodriguez. At the time, this was a relatively rare example of a sitcom featuring a Hispanic lead character, but the producers dissipated its effect by populating the proceedings with ethnic clichés (e.g., the large, noisy Rivera family all living in one cramped household).

The plot premise gives comedian Paul Rivera his own TV series. This is exciting news to his huge family, but his father Domingo, in particular, wants his son (whom he still calls Pablo) to be deferential to his heritage and never use embarrassing material from his home life in his stand-up act.

Alambrista! **(1977)** Filmhaus, color, 110 minutes. **Director/Screenplay:** Robert M. Young; **Cast:** Domingo Ambriz (Roberto), Trinidad Silva (Joe), Linda Gillin (Sharon), Paul Berrones (Berto), Edward James Olmos and Julius Harris (drunks).

This absorbing drama concerned Roberto, a young Mexican who sneaks across the border into the United States. Thereafter, he suffers the plight of the illegal alien—exploited by employers and scorned by documented Americans. Throughout the traumatic relocation, he tries desperately to adapt to the new country, which obviously does not want him.

This picture first played on PBS-TV in 1977 and then had minor theatrical distribution. At the Cannes Film Festival, the picture was nominated as Best First Feature.

Alamo, the Several Hollywood projects dealt with the defeat of the American defenders at the Alamo in 1836 Texas at the hands of Mexican troops under the command of General Santa Anna. The films included: *The Immortal Alamo* (1911), *Martyrs of the Alamo* (1915), *Davy Crockett* (1916), *Davy Crockett at the Fall of the Alamo* (1926), *Heroes of the Alamo* (1937), *Man of Conquest* (1939), *The Man from The Alamo* (1953), *Davy Crockett, King of the Wild Frontier* (1955), *THE LAST COMMAND* (1955), *The First Texan* (1956), *THE ALAMO* (1960), *The Alamo: Thirteen Days to Glory* (1987—TV movie), *TEXAS* (1994—TV movie), *Two for Texas* (1998—TV movie), and the contemporary spoof *VIVA MAX!* (1969).

Alamo, The **(1960)** United Artists, color, 192 minutes. **Directors:** John Wayne and John Ford (uncredited); **Screenplay:** James Edward Grant; **Cast:** John Wayne (Col. David Crockett), Richard Widmark (Col. James Bowie), Laurence Harvey (Col. William Travis), Frankie Avalon (Smitty), Richard Boone (Gen. Sam Houston), Patrick Wayne (Capt. James Butler Bonham), Linda Cristal (Flaca), Chill Wills (Beekeeper), Joseph Calleia (Juan Seguin), Carlos Arruza (Lieutenant Reyes), Ruben Padilla (General Santa Anna).

During the decades, Hollywood released many productions dealing with the ALAMO and the Americans' defeat in 1836 by Mexico's General Santa Anna and his troops. But, perhaps, no one in the American film industry ever wanted to make a story on the subject more than Wayne. For almost a dozen years, he worked to develop, finance, and make this personal project. The resultant feature was big, sprawling, and at times extremely slow-paced. In typical Wayne fashion, there were no gradations in the film's point of view: The Americans in Texas were patriotic saints; the Mexicans were dirty dogs who, although they greatly outnumbered their adversaries by a tremendous ratio, could barely overcome the valiant defenders of the stronghold. Even Wayne's characterization of legendary Davy Crockett (coonskin cap and all) had a paternalistic (almost patronizing) attitude toward the Mexican Flaca, with whom he had an on-camera romance. (The only qualification the Hollywood film industry's censorship board had with the planned film was that the Mexican soldiers should not be depicted brutalizing too much the corpses of the Alamo's staunch defenders.)

Much of the film concerned the build-up to the climactic fight at the Alamo, as Col. James Bowie and Col. William Travis compete to be in charge of the fortress where the 187 men intend to stand off Santa Anna's army of 7,000 troops. For thirteen days they hold out, but eventually they all fall victim to the Mexicans.

Shot at Brackettsville, Texas, at a cost of $12 million and with a rousing score by Dmitri Tiomkin, the epic was authentically detailed in its look, if not in its characterizations that gave short shrift to depicting Santa Anna or, for example, his emissary, Juan Sequin. In directing the feature, Wayne called in favors from several of his industry friends such as John Ford who directed (uncredited) some of the battle scenes at the finale. For box-office appeal, singing heartthrob Avalon was added to the cast and allowed to vocalize on camera. *The Alamo* grossed only slightly less than $8 million in its domestic distribution. It received an Academy Award for Best Sound and nominations for Best Cinematography (Color), Best Film Editing, Best Original Dramatic Score, Best Picture, Best Song ("The Green Leaves of Summer"), and Best Supporting Actor (Wills).

The Alamo was banned from distribution in Mexico at the time of its original release. On post-road-show engagements, the film was often chopped down to 140 minutes.

***All in the Family* (1971–1983)** CBS-TV series, color, 30 minutes. **Cast:** Carroll O'Connor (Archie Bunker), Jean Stapleton (Edith "Dingbat" Bunker: 1971–80), Sally Struthers (Gloria Bunker Stivic: 1971–78), Rob Reiner (Mike "Meathead" Stivic: 1971–78), Liz Torres (Teresa Betancourt: 1976–77), Abraham Alvarez (José: 1979–83).

In this groundbreaking situation-comedy series, acerbic remarks by bigoted Archie Bunker about ethnic minorities were always the first order of the day. In the 1976–77 season Puerto Rican Teresa Betancourt became a boarder at the Bunkers' after Archie was laid off at work and the family needed extra income. As played by bombastic TORRES, Archie almost met his match with this emotional soul. In a later format of the series when Archie bought the neighborhood bar, the show became known as *Archie Bunker's Place* (1979–83). Among the new regulars at the tavern was José, the busboy, played by Alvarez.

Alonso, Maria Conchita (1957–) This attractive talent found that Hollywood roles for ethnic actresses in the 1980s and thereafter were still few in quantity and lesser in quality. Born in Cienfuegos, Cuba, she grew up in Caracas, Venezuela. There, as a past beauty-contest winner (e.g., Miss Teenage World, 1971; Miss Venezuela, 1975), Alonso acted in TV soap operas, made a few features, and became a recording star. She relocated to the United States in 1982 and in 1984 appeared opposite Robin Williams in *Moscow on the Hudson*. Her other films included *The Running Man* (1987), *COLORS* (1988), the TV miniseries *TEXAS* (1994), the KATY JURADO role in the middling TV remake (2000) of *HIGH NOON* (1952), and a recreation of the late Mexican star LUPE VÉLEZ in *Babylon Revisited* (2001).

***American Family* (2002–)** PBS-TV, color, 60 minutes. **Cast:** Edward James Olmos (Jess Gonzalez), Sonia Braga (Berta Gonzalez), Constance Marie (Nina Gonzalez), Esai Morales (Esteban Gonzalez), Raquel Welch (Aunt Dora), A. J. Lamas (Cisco Gonzalez), Rachel Ticotin (Vangie Gonzalez).

Coming in the wake of two cable TV dramatic series dealing with Latino families—*THE BROTHERS GARCIA* (2001–) and *RESURRECTION BLVD.* (2001–)—this much-heralded project was two years in development by filmmaker GREGORY NAVA (who utilized here several actors from his 1995 feature *MY FAMILY: MI FAMILIA*). Judging the new entry, the *New York Times* (January 23, 2002) described, "Unabashedly emotional and determinedly ethnic, *American Family* can be quite touching, as well as a little exhausting. . . . The show feels unwieldy and melodramatic at times, but also warm and lively."

Set in the barrio of East Los Angeles, the series focuses on the Gonzalez household where the American-born patriarch (soon a widower within the story line) rules his middle-class Latino family with firmness and a good deal of heart, but accompanied by a large number of prejudices. (OLMOS played the role with great authority and obvious relish.) The dialogue is largely English-language, although at times, the Mexican-American characters launch into Spanish, especially when they become highly emotional. In the Gonzalez clan Jess has five offspring, including Nina, an attorney; Vangie, a fashion designer wed to a wealthy Anglo; Esteban, a former gang member and ex-con now a firefighter and desperate to keep custody of his young son and to avoid the boy's mother, a drug addict whom the family refuses to let in the house. Unlike stereotypical presentations of the barrio, which focus on poverty and gang activity, *American Family* spotlighted the domestic scene, one filled with sufficient intricate and overlapping problems to propel the series forward. One of the more flavorful characters in the proceedings was WELCH's as the striking Aunt Dora, an optimistic romantic who has bad luck in choosing her men.

Daily Variety (January 22, 2002) pointed out that while the show hyped itself as the first Latino-cast drama show on broadcast TV, "it certainly doesn't come across as groundbreaking. In many ways, its thematic explorations feel rote, as characters embody different aspects of being both Mexican and American." *Hollywood Reporter* (January 23, 2002) noted that the show "is more interested in the ties that bind [the family] than the pressures that divide" and that "Nava is a consummate storyteller who clearly relishes the chance to mix traditional material with unconventional perspective." The trade paper judged of *American Family:* "For the most part, it is the type of drama that went out with *The Waltons* [1972–81]."

***American Me* (1992)** Universal, color, 119 minutes. **Director:** Edward James Olmos; **Screenplay:** Floyd Mutrux and Desmond Nakano; **Cast:** Edward James Olmos (Santana Montoya), William Forsythe (JD), Pepe Serna (Mundo), Danny De La Paz (Puppet), Evelina Fernández (Julie), Cary-Hiroyuki Tagawa (El Jupo).

This project had been in development for eighteen years and, when finally made, it proved to be a who's who of Hispanic-American talent in front of and behind the camera. As directed by star OLMOS, it emerged an unrelenting study of gang life in the Los Angeles barrio from the early 1940s onward. One (unintentional) result of this grim feature was to entrench further in filmgoers' minds the association of Hispanics with gang membership.

During the Los Angeles Zoot Suit Riots of 1943, Santana Montoya's father is savagely beaten and his mother raped. Thereafter, Montoya and his pals rumble with a rival gang, leading to murder and a trip to Juvenile Hall. It is the start of their life in and out of jail. In prison Montoya learns the art of controlling gang activity (fostering a Mexican Mafia); outside he has great difficulty adjusting to the freedom of civilian life. He meets a single mother (Fernández) whom he discovers he cares for deeply. Having tenderness for her—which continues when he is incarcerated again—leads ironically to his death in prison at the hand of rival gang members.

With its dour mood of crushed dreams and lives, its mostly unsympathetic characters, and its unrelenting focus on the tough worlds of the barrio and prison, this Chicano-themed picture was *not* for everyone. Made on a $16 million budget, it grossed slightly more than $13 million in domestic distribution.

Americano, The **(1955)** RKO, color, 85 minutes. **Director:** William Castle; **Screenplay:** Guy Trosper; **Cast:** Glenn Ford (Sam Dent), Frank Lovejoy (Bento Hermanny), Cesar Romero (Manuel), Ursula Thiess (Marianna Figuerido), Abbe Lane (Teresa), Rudolfo Hoyos Jr. (Cristino).

American Sam Dent, shepherding Brahma bulls to a Brazilian rancher whom he finds has been murdered, becomes embroiled in a range war on the pampas in South America. Sinister cattle baron Bento Hermanny is fighting newcomers who want to farm on grazing land. Dent joins forces with benevolent bandito Manuel to assist the underdog agrarians.

Had this been set in the old West of the United States it could have been a standard western. Cuban-American ROMERO, who once played the lead in the CISCO KID movie series, was again portraying the munificent soul helping the downtrodden. As for Ford's hero, he could easily be considered a symbol of the U.S.'s self-granted role as the gringo solver of other countries' problems. This created the negative inference that these countries were incapable of fixing their own troubles without American know-how and power.

. . . And Now Miguel **(1966)** Universal, color, 95 minutes. **Director:** James B. Clark; **Screenplay:** Ted Sherdeman and Jane Klove; **Cast:** Pat Cardi (Miguel), Michael Ansara (Blas), Guy Stockwell (Perez), Clu Gulager (Johnny), Joe De Santis (Padre de Chavez), Pilar del Rey (Tomasita), Ted Butterfield (Native American chief).

Considering the rarity with which topics dealing with Mexican characters were being produced by Hollywood in this era, this well-photographed family movie was all the more important. Shot on location in Abequin, Santa Fe, and San Ildefonso Pueblo, New Mexico, the narrative was based on Joseph Krumgold's well-regarded 1953 book. It told of Miguel, a ten-year-old Mexican who dreams of the day he will be allowed to accompany his father, Blas, on the treks to the mountains to graze their sheep. Each year, Blas tells his offspring that he is not yet old enough for the climb. Frustrated, Miguel prays to San Ysidro, the farmers' patron saint. Later, the sheep run off during a storm. While Blas is searching for them, industrious Miguel locates and shepherds them home, despite the threat of stalking wolves. As a reward, Blas promises to take his son on the next trip to the mountains.

Albeit leisurely-told, *. . . And Now Miguel* shows that the American film industry was willing to reach out—on a low-budget project like this—to focus on an ethnic minority. Ansara, of Lebanese-American descent, had already made a specialty of playing Native Americans on camera (e.g., *Broken Arrow*, 1950).

. . . and the Earth Did Not Swallow Him **(1995)** Kino International, color, 99 minutes. **Director/Screenplay:** Severo Pérez; **Cast:** José Alcala (Marcos), Art Bonilla (Lalo), Evelyn Guerro (Lupita), Sal Lopez (El Mohado), Lupe Ontiveros (Dõna Rosa), Rose Portillo (Florentina), Marco Rodriguez (Joaquin), Miguel Rodriguez (narrator), Daniel Valdez (Bartolo), Sam Vlahos (Doon Cleto).

Produced by PBS-TV's *American Playhouse* series, this drama was also released on the art-house theater circuit. It was adapted from Tomas Rivera's well-reviewed 1971 semiautobiographical novel *. . . Y no se lo tragó la tierra.* Set in 1952, it concerned the difficulties faced by migrant farmworkers—and the strength of their family ties—as they move from farm to farm during the harvest season. The point of view is from twelve-year-old Marcos as his family makes their annual shift from Texas to Minnesota (where the movie was filmed), while they cope with worrying about a son stationed with the army in Korea and deal with the prejudice they encounter in America.

Despite its slow pace, this well-photographed film emerged a moving entry.

animation—feature films In the arena of theatrical release short subjects, Columbia Pictures offered a trio of entries between 1942 and 1947 about *Tito*, a pudgy Mexican youth who had adventures accompanied by his burro Burrito. Then there was the character of a trouble-prone Mexican mouse who was a fast runner with an active mind. The property began in 1953 as an unnamed animal within the entry

Cat-Tails for Two. This cartoon short prompted the development of a new series character who made his first official appearance in 1955's *Speedy Gonzales* and won an Academy Award as Best Cartoon. Three other later entries were Oscar nominated. The series ran through 1968 with Mel Blanc providing voices. Later in the series, Speedy was joined by a comical pal Slowpoke Rodriguez. Often, Daffy Duck appeared in these animated proceedings.

DePatie-Freleng/Mirisch Films, which made the popular *Pink Panther* cartoons, debuted a Spanish-accented toad named Poncho and his young trainee toad Toro in the animated short *Tijuana Toads* (1969), which became the name of the series. Several entries were released through mid-1972. When these items were screened on TV, it was considered more politically correct to call the lead characters Fatso and Banjo and refer to them as "the Texas Toads."

The Walt Disney studio, which turned out many cartoons with South American flavor during the 1940s, had great success with *Saludos Amigos* (1943), which was part live-action travelogue blended with animation sequences all dealing with south-of-the-border characters. The studio next turned out *THE THREE CABALLEROS* (1945), a full-length feature that was more of the same, using footage of Donald Duck and other characters (live and animated) to bridge both old and new material. It was part of the studio's salute to the South American "Good Neighbor Policy" and was well received.

Five decades later Dream Works Studio used a Hispanic theme in the full-length animated feature *The Road to El Dorado* (2000). It followed the adventures of two small-time criminals (the voices of Kevin Kline and Kenneth Branagh) who left Spain in 1519 and traveled to Mexico seeking the legendary city of gold in the Americas. Once at El Dorado, they were mistaken by the natives as Gods, but one of their number, Chel (voice of ROSIE PEREZ), knew better. Made on a $95 million budget, the movie was not that well received and grossed only about $51 million in domestic distribution. *The Emperor's New Groove* (2000) was a full-length animated feature dealing with the Incas of Peru. It featured David Spade, John Goodman, and Eartha Kitt in the lead voiceover roles.

animation series—television It was a long time before Hispanic characters were a recurring part of any animated series on American TV. In 1980 an international coproduction, *Amigo and Friends* premiered as a syndicated half-hour series, with the voices dubbed into English and featuring educational tours around the world and discussions of noteworthy topics for youngsters. The program ran for two years. *Where On Earth Is Carmen Sandiego?* (1994–96) was a half-hour animated series based on a PBS-TV game show that traced the whereabouts of a missing agent by giving viewers educational clues. RITA MORENO provided the voice of the title character. *Santa Bugito* (1995–96) was a Saturday morning program promoted as the "world's first Tex-Mex cartoon." With Hispanic music driving the show, it used insects for its characters and was set in a Texas/Mexican town. Among the performers providing voices was Cheech Marin. *Freakazoid!* (1995–97) took place in Washington, D.C., where the title character (voice of Paul Rugg) was a weird superhero protecting the country against dangers. Veteran actor RICARDO MONTALBAN provided the voice of Armondo Gutierrez. *The PJs* (1999–2001), created by Eddie Murphy and starring his voice, dealt with families in a housing project. One of the regulars was Pepe Serna as Mr. Sanchez. *Dora the Explorer,* which debuted in summer 2000, concerned the adventures of the seven-year-old Latina heroine and her monkey pal Boots. *Teamo Supremo* (2001–) dealt with a trio of eight-year-old superheroes, two of whom were Latino.

***Appaloosa, The* (1966)** Universal, color, 98 minutes. **Director:** Sidney J. Furie; **Screenplay:** James Bridges and Roland Kibbee; **Cast:** Marlon Brando (Matt Fletcher), Anjanette Comer (Trini), John Saxon (Chuy Medina), Emilio Fernández (Lazero), Alex Montoya (Squint-Eye), Rafael Campos (Paco), Frank Silvera (Ramos).

Having starred in and directed the western *One-Eyed Jacks* (1961), Brando returned to the genre with this beautifully lensed drama. American Matt Fletcher, a former buffalo hunter, is now partnered with Paco to breed frisky Appaloosa horses. While visiting a church in the Mexican border town of Ojo Prieto, he is outsmarted by Trini, a pretty young woman, who steals his horse and rides off. Her jealous lover, bandito Lazero, punishes Fletcher for her disappearance. While pursuing his valuable steed, Matt falls in love with Trini, and together they combat the wicked Lazero. By the finale, the couple, along with the Appaloosa, are returning across the border to Texas.

Despite the efficiency of director Furie, *The Appaloosa* abounded with trite representations of Mexicans, from the fiery "heroine" to the cunning bandit and his swarthy, lecherous band, as well as a full spectrum of "types" seen south-of-the-border. Because of his swarthy looks, Brooklyn-born Saxon (né Carmen Orrico) sometimes was cast as a Hispanic in films. Here he sported the typical Mexican villain's trademarks a la Hollywood: bushy mustache and greasy hair (i.e., a throwback to the old "greaser" stereotype of early American films).

Based on Robert MacLeod's 1963 novel, *The Appaloosa,* featuring a stocky Brando, did mediocre business at the box office. It was considered too lethargic and arty for popular consumption—despite the menacing activities of the film's key villain.

***Argentine Nights* (1940)** Universal, b&w, 72 minutes. **Director:** Albert S. Rogell; **Screenplay:** Arthur Horman, Ray Golden, and Sid Kuller; **Cast:** Al, Harry, and Jimmy Ritz (themselves), Maxene, Patty, and LaVerne Andrews (themselves), Constance Moore (Bonnie Brooks), George Reeves (Eduardo Estaban), Peggy Moran (Peggy), Ferike Boros (Mama Viejos), Paul Porcasi (Papa Viejos).

As the U.S.'s involvement in World War II grew imminent, the country became increasingly friendly with its South American neighbors. This, in turn, led Hollywood to increasingly feature south-of-the-border locales on camera as part of the U.S. government's "Good Neighbor Policy." This trifle, noteworthy as the screen debut of the highly popular Andrews Sisters, teamed them with a trio of Jewish brothers in a musical nonsense set on studio back lot Argentina. Portraying the South American playboy was Reeves, later famous as TV's *Superman* in the 1950s series. Here, he depicted Hollywood's stock conception of the dashing Argentinean caballero, but neither his outfits nor his accent were credible.

Within the light-hearted proceedings, the nearly broke Ritz Brothers stow away on an Argentina-bound ship that contains their clients—including Bonnie Brooks, the leader of an all-girl band—headed for a resort hotel engagement. Also aboard is well-to-do Eduardo Estaban who intrigues Brooks. Upon docking, Brooks mistakes Estaban for "El Tigre," a notorious bandit. But all ends well, with the Andrews Sisters having sung, among others, "Rhumboogie" and "Hit the Road."

This was but one of many 1940s features to highlight a Latin American backdrop and to be packed with types supposedly inhabiting those tropical countries. Unfortunately, when the seemingly harmless *Argentine Nights* debuted in South America—especially in Buenos Aires, Argentina—it upset local filmgoers who felt that the featherweight and erroneous depiction of their country's people was a major insult. The repercussions helped to bring about the formation of a special Hollywood movie-industry branch of the U.S. Department of State's Coordinator of Inter-American Affairs (CIAA) to prevent such tactical errors in the future.

***Arise, My Love* (1940)** Paramount, b&w, 113 minutes. **Director:** Mitchell Leisen; **Screenplay:** Charles Brackett and Billy Wilder; **Cast:** Claudette Colbert (Augusta "Gusto" Nash), Ray Milland (Tom Martin), Dennis O'Keefe (Shep), Walter Abel (Phillips), Dick Purcell (Pink), George Zucco (prison governor), Frank Puglia (Father Jacinto).

As World War II spread through the world, the late 1930s Spanish Civil War faded into history. *Arise, My Love* was one of the last American movie fabrications about the conflict, made while the topic was still fresh in moviegoers' minds. (A belated major entry on the topic came with 1943's *FOR WHOM THE BELL TOLLS*, which stemmed from Ernest Hemingway's novel.) In retrospect, *Arise, My Love* was a transition from the public's infatuation with the "glamorous" fight on behalf of the peasant Spanish people—demonstrated by American volunteers who fought in Spain against General Franco's Nationalist forces—to the U.S.'s overt involvement in World War II at the end of 1941.

The film's two leads—chic news reporter Augusta "Gusto" Nash and pilot/volunteer Tom Martin—view the Iberian peninsula struggle through their American eyes. The narrative is launched when Gusto's clever ruse springs Martin from a jail cell in 1939 Spain where he awaits execution for his activities on behalf of the country's partisans. Later, the couple witness the growing Nazi menace (i.e., the torpedoing of the ship on which they are returning to New York). In the finale, following the fall of Paris, the duo set out for home to alert Americans to the growing German menace.

***Arizona Kid, The* (1930)** Fox, b&w, 88 minutes. **Director:** Alfred Santell; **Screenplay:** Ralph Block; **Cast:** Warner Baxter (the Arizona Kid), Mona Maris (Lorita), Carol[e] Lombard (Virginia Hoyt), Soledad Jiménez (Pulga), Theodore Von Eltz (Nick Hoyt), Arthur Stone (Snakebite Pete).

Having won an Academy Award for his *IN OLD ARIZONA* (1929) portrayal of the CISCO KID, BAXTER returned to "greaser" type in this lazy follow-up, shot largely in Utah's Zion National Park. Again Baxter was the romantic bandit in the old West who seemingly never committed a really bad deed. This time the Arizona Kid poses as the Mexican owner of a lucrative gold mine that he has kept secret from others. Currently, the love of his life is Lorita, a local dance hall worker. Everything changes when attractive blonde Virginia Holt and her (supposed) brother Nick arrive in town. As the inevitable showdown evolves, the scoundrel Nick proves to be Virginia's husband. At the finale, the Kid kills Hoyt and, then, casually rides out of town with Lorita.

Thus once again the myth of the glamorized Mexican bandito was enlarged upon in this feature.

Armendáriz, Pedro (1912–1963) Not only a popular star in his native Mexico, Armendáriz became a Hollywood fixture, as well as a talent with a strong personality on the international movie scene. He was born in Churubusco, Mexico, of a Mexican father and an American mother. Part of his youth was spent in Laredo, Texas, but after his parents died in 1921, he was raised by his uncle and attended Polytechnic Institute of San Luis Obispo, California. Returning to Mexico, he eventually was discovered by director Miguel Zacarias. His film debut came in 1936 with three releases, including *Maria Elena*. Along with DOLORES DEL RÍO and

Pedro Armendáriz, Harry Carey Jr., and John Wayne in *The Three Godfathers* (1948). (JC ARCHIVES)

actor/director Emilio Fernández, Armendáriz became one of Mexico's best-known film personalities.

Armendáriz's Hollywood debut occurred in John Ford's *THE FUGITIVE* (1947), leading to roles in *Fort Apache* (1948), *Border River* (1954), and *THE LITTLEST OUTLAW* (1955). (Meanwhile he had starred in 1948's *THE PEARL*, the first English-language movie to have been filmed in Mexico.) Armendáriz was featured in *The Conqueror* (1956) with his good friend John Wayne and made such later films as *Francis of Assisi* (1961), *From Russia With Love* (1963), and *Captain Sinbad* (1963). Like many others involved in making *The Conqueror*, Armendáriz developed cancer. When faced with the prognosis that his condition was terminal, he shot himself. His son, Pedro Armendáriz Jr. (b. 1941), had a prolific career in both the Mexican and American cinema.

Arnaz, Desi (1912–1986) In the 1940s, this noted club performer in the United States was famous for playing the bongos, leading conga lines, and singing such numbers as "Cuban Pete" and "Babalu." But Arnaz gained immortality thereafter playing opposite his then-wife Lucille Ball as the costar of TV's *I LOVE LUCY* (1951–57). He was one of the first Latin crossover artists to gain major success in the United States.

Born Desiderio Alberto Arnaz y de Acha III in Santiago, Cuba, he and his family immigrated to Miami, Florida, to escape the 1933 Cuban revolution. Besides odd jobs, Arnaz found work as a band guitarist and eventually joined music-maker XAVIER CUGAT's group in New York City. Desi's good looks and talent led to his being featured in the Broadway musical *TOO MANY GIRLS* (1940). While repeating his role on film, he met and married movie star Ball. His best screen role was as a doomed soldier in *BATAAN* (1943). There were not many viable screen parts available to Hispanics—even notables—in late 1940s Hollywood, and such foolishness as *Holiday in Havana* (1949) did not advance his career, so Desi focused on club work. As the result of the enormous success of *I Love Lucy*, Arnaz became a TV mogul (and director), owning Desilu Studios with his wife. His final film was *The Escape Artist* (1982), a Francis Ford Coppola production. Both his children (Lucie and Desi Jr.) with Ball became performers.

In *THE MAMBO KINGS* (1992) Desi Jr. portrayed his father on camera. The year before, in the telefeature *LUCY AND DESI: BEFORE THE LAUGHTER* (1991), Maurice Benard had played singer/actor Arnaz.

***At Play in the Fields of the Lord* (1991)** Universal, color, 180 minutes. **Director:** Hector Babenco; **Screenplay:** Jean-Claude Carriere and Babenco; **Cast:** Tom Berenger (Lewis Moon), John Lithgow (Leslie Huben), Daryl Hannah (Andy Huben), Aidan Quinn (Martin Quarrier), Tom Waits (Wolf), Kathy Bates (Hazel Quarrier), Stenio Garcia (Boronai), Nelson Xavier (Father Xantes), José Dumant (Commandante Guzman), Niilo Kivirinta (Billy Quarrier)

Peter Matthiessen's best-selling 1965 novel on which this R-rated feature was based had been a National Book Award winner. The movie's director, Argentinean Babenco, created an epic of visual beauty (if tinged with too much heavy-handed self-importance) that underscored the dire results as American missionaries and Brazilian soldiers clashed in their efforts to harness a simple but fearsome native culture in the rain forest. The irony of the piece was that the "uncivilized" natives altered the "civilized" Americans.

At Mae de Deus in Brazil, Leslie Huben, in charge of an American evangelical missionary group, and his wife Andy await the arrival of Martin Quarrier and his wife Hazel, who are to be dispatched into the rain forest to convert the Niaruna Indians to Christianity. Meanwhile, local police chief Boronai offers a pair of down-on-their-luck pilots—Cherokee half-breed Lewis Moon and mercenary Wolf—a way to leave the territory: They are to bomb the Niaruna village (as the turf is wanted for its prized natural resources). After flying over the village and returning to base, Moon decides to join the tribe, who eventually come to think of him as a god. Meanwhile the Quarriers, along with their young son, take over their proselytizing post. While Martin develops compassion for the natives' way of life, his wife, after their son dies of a fever, goes mad, adding to Martin's disillusionment with his faith. Later, after a romantic encounter with Andy Huben, Martin unknowingly brings a flu virus back to the simple villagers and the epidemic decimates their numbers.

At Play in the Fields of the Lord grossed a paltry $1.34 million in domestic distribution.

***Avenger, The* (1931)** Columbia, b&w, 72 minutes. **Director:** Roy William Neill; **Screenplay:** George Morgan; **Cast:** Buck Jones (Joaquin Murrieta), Dorothy Revier (Helen Lake), Edward Peil Sr. (Ike Mason), Otto Hoffman (Black Kelly), Sidney Bracey (Windy), Edward Hearn (Captain Lake), Walter Percival (Al Goss).

One of several movies featuring the legendary nineteenth-century Mexican bandito JOAQUÍN MURRIETA, who carried out daring raids in the California mining country after being discriminated against by white men, this low-budget offering starred well-liked cowboy hero Jones.

Murrieta quarrels with a trio of prospectors (Peil Sr., Hoffman, and Percival) that leads to his father and brother being killed by the three men who steal ownership to a gold mine. In retaliation, Murrieta dons the disguise of "The Black Shadow" and robs stagecoaches that carry ore from the mine. Eventually, the enterprising Murrieta tricks the three villains into dying, and he wins the love of Helen Lake.

Acknowledging the historical reality of bigotry toward Mexicans in this quickie western, *The Avenger* took advantage of the popularity of the CISCO KID persona in developing its lead character. The feature was remade in 1942 as *Vengeance of the West*, starring Bill Elliott and Tex Ritter.

B

***Bad Man, The* (1930)** First National/Warner Bros., b&w, 80 minutes. **Director:** Clarence Badger; **Screenplay:** Howard Estabrook; **Cast:** Walter Huston (Pancho López), Dorothy Revier (Ruth Pell), James Rennie (Gilbert Jones), O. P. Heggie (Henry Taylor), Sidney Blackmer (Morgan Pell), Marion Byron (Angela Hardy), Arthur Stone (Pedro).

Thanks to *IN OLD ARIZONA* (1929) and its tale of the CISCO KID, Hollywood underwent a cycle of westerns featuring swaggering Mexican bandits who were portrayed as heroes rather than dastardly villains. In this case, as played by Huston, he was less romantic and glamorous than WARNER BAXTER's interpretation of the roguish but charming Cisco Kid. (And again it was an Anglo playing the Latino good bad guy.)

Based on the 1920 Broadway play by William Harris Jr., *The Bad Man* had been made as a silent picture in 1923, featuring Holbrook Blinn and Enid Bennett. The talkie version retold the story of López, an infamous Mexican outlaw, who repays a favor to Gilbert Jones by eliminating the scheming Morgan Pell. Thus, Jones's ranch and its rich mineral deposits are saved, and the way is now open for Jones and the widowed Ruth Pell to pursue a romance. As for the hard-living López, he meets his fate bravely at the hands of pursuing Texas Rangers.

With his broken English delivered in an unconvincing Mexican accent, Huston was not at his best in this sagebrush vehicle. The picture was revamped—with a more flattering presentation of its Mexican characters—for the Spanish-language version of the movie entitled *El hombre malo.* Condensed to sixty-nine minutes, it teamed Antonio Moreno and Rosita Ballesteros, was adapted with special dialogue by Baltasar Fernández Cué, and was directed by William McGann. (There was also a French-language edition made that year entitled *Lopéz, le bandit.*) In 1940 *The Bad Man* was remade yet again, this time with boisterous Wallace Beery as the Mexican culprit.

***Ballad of Gregorio Cortez, The* (1982)** Embassy, color, 104 minutes. **Director:** Robert M. Young; **Screenplay:** Victor Villaseñor; **Cast:** Edward James Olmos (Cortez), Tom Bower (Boone Choote), Bruce McGill (Bill Blakely), James Gammon (Sheriff Fly), Alan Vint (Sheriff Trimmell), Pepe Serna (Romaldo Cortez), Rosana DeSoto (Carlota Munoz).

Filmed as part of the PBS-TV *American Playhouse* series, this stark, sympathetic drama was later released theatrically on a limited basis. It derived from the 1965 novel *With His Pistol in His Hands* by Américo Paredes.

This narrative deals graphically with the real-life events in 1901 Texas of a Mexican who cannot understand the local sheriff's explanation in English (nor can the lawman comprehend the San Antonio cowhand's Spanish) as to why he is being arrested. (His arrest is actually due to mistaken identity.) This leads to the Mexican shooting the Anglo sheriff in what, ordinarily, would be termed self-defense. Thereafter, a posse of Texas Rangers and others chase the fleeing man for eleven days as he darts about Mexico. He surrenders only when he learns that his wife and children are being held hostage. At his trial, the defendant, who is almost lynched, is sentenced to fifty years in prison. (In actuality, he was released after twelve years behind bars.) The unfortunate incident prompted a ballad that gained currency and made a folk hero of this Mexican American

The movie, a pet project of OLMOS, was shot in the actual Texas courthouse where the trial had taken place.

Banderas, Antonio (1960–) This appealing Spanish-born leading-man actor became a global movie star playing a variety of nationalities on camera. He was born José Antonio Domínguez Banderas in Málaga, Spain, to a policeman father and a schoolteacher mother. His hopes of becoming a soccer star ended at age fourteen when he suffered a foot injury. Turning to acting, the handsome talent made his initial reputation in several movies directed by Pedro Almodóvar (e.g., *Labyrinth of Passion*, 1982; *Tie Me Up! Tie Me Down*, 1990). Banderas appeared in Madonna's documentary *Truth or Dare* (1991), followed by a lead part as a young Cuban musician in the American-made *THE MAMBO KINGS* (1992). His next productions included *Philadelphia* (1993) and the part of El Mariachi in *Desperado* (1995). He was revolutionary Che Guevara to Madonna's title role in the musical *EVITA* (1996). Banderas displayed charm and energy in the swashbuckling *The Mask of Zorro* (1998). For *Crazy in Alabama* (1999) featuring his actress-wife Melanie Griffith, he directed the vehicle. Later acting assignments included *Play It to the Bone* (1999), *Spy Kids* (2001), *Femme Fatale* (2002), *Spy Kids 2: The Island of Lost Dreams* (2002), and *Once Upon a Time in Mexico* (2003—again playing El Mariachi).

***Bandido* (1956)** United Artists, color, 92 minutes. **Director:** Richard Fleischer; **Screenplay:** Earl Felton; **Cast:** Robert Mitchum (Wilson), Ursula Thiess (Lisa), Gilbert Roland (Escobar), Zachary Scott (Kennedy), Rudolfo Acosta (Sebastian), Henry Brandon (Gunther), José I. Torvay (Gonzalez).

With Hollywood gradually moving away from the traditional cowboys-and Indians westerns, there was an increased usage of Mexican landscapes as an alternative setting and theme. It provided not only new scenery but also a fresh ambiance, especially as American moviemakers switched from traditional Hollywood back-lot filming to location shoots. *Bandido* was lensed in Mexico and gave veteran Mexican-born actor ROLAND, one of the screen's former CISCO KIDS, a colorful role as the enterprising bandit.

With his sardonic look in place and tongue firmly planted in cheek, Mitchum (who also contributed to the script) is the American mercenary Wilson who heads south-of-the-border in 1916, hoping to profit from the rumored brewing revolution. Charming rogue Escobar hires Wilson to intercept an arms shipment being dispatched to government forces by Kennedy. By the time the guns are in the hands of Escobar, Wilson has acquired a more valuable property for himself—Kennedy's sultry wife (Thiess).

***Bandolero!* (1968)** Twentieth Century-Fox, color, 107 minutes. **Director:** Andrew V. McLaglen; **Screenplay:** James Lee Barrett; **Cast:** James Stewart (Mace Bishop), Dean Martin (Dee Bishop), Raquel Welch (Maria Stoner), George Kennedy (Sheriff Johnson), Andrew Prine (Roscoe Bookbinder), Rudy Diaz (Angel Muñoz), Perry Lopez (Frisco).

This big-budgeted western, filmed in Brackettsville, Texas, and Glen Canyon, Utah, was far too lethargic for its own good. It relied on Mexico and Mexicans to provide stale plot points for its tale of lust and greed. The title referred to the word for Mexican bandit.

Having rescued his younger brother Dee and his gang from being hung for committing a murder during a bank holdup, Mace Bishop finishes the robbery before joining Dee and the others south-of-the-border. They hole up in a deserted town, using the murdered man's widow, Maria Stoner, as hostage. Pursuing the lawbreakers are Sheriff Johnson and his posse. Though the lawman and his group capture the robbers, bandoleros, headed by Angel Muñoz, lay siege to the town. In the gunplay, both Bishop brothers are murdered, while Maria, a woman with an unsavory past, kills Muñoz who has ravished her. Matters settled, the sheriff and Maria ride back to Texas.

By now, unsavory Mexican bandits had again become standard fare in Hollywood westerns. Typically, as here, their trite characterizations were haphazard, with little dimension.

***Baron of Arizona, The* (1950)** Lippert, b&w, 96 minutes. **Director/Screenplay:** Samuel Fuller; **Cast:** Vincent Price (James Addison Reavis), Ellen Drew (Sofia de Peralta-Reavis), Vladimir Sokoloff (Pepito Alvarez), Beulah Bondi (Loma Morales), Reed Hadley (John Griff), Margia Dean (Marquesa de Santella), Angelo Rossitto (Angie).

A spirited performance by Price elevated this ambitious drama from a nonmajor studio. It was based on the article "The Baron of Arizona" by Homer Croy that appeared in *American Weekly* magazine (January 1949). Filmmaker Fuller weaved an engaging narrative of the real-life James Addison Reavis who, in the late nineteenth century, undertook a crafty plan to gain ownership to much of what became the state of Arizona in 1912. Relying on a Mexican acquaintance (Sokoloff) and the training provided by a governess (Bondi), Reavis grooms Sofia (who is actually of Native American background) to pretend to be a baroness as he begins his complex plan to swindle the U.S. government. The scheme requires Reavis to sail to Spain so that he can alter land grant records in a monastery and, later, at the Spanish castle of Marquesa de Santella. Once back in the United States, the plot eventually falls apart, and Reavis is jailed for several years.

Besides being a well-engineered study of a master schemer, *The Baron of Arizona* was a pocket history of the thirty-eighth state of the United States. As was true with other ethnic minorities portrayed on the Hollywood screen at this time, very few used in this film were actually Mexican or Spanish.

***Bataan* (1943)** Metro-Goldwyn-Mayer, b&w, 114 minutes. **Director:** Tay Garnett; **Screenplay:** Robert D. Andrews; **Cast:** Robert Taylor (Sgt. Bill Dane), George Murphy (Lt. Steve Bentley), Thomas Mitchell (Cpl. Jake Feingold), Lloyd Nolan (Cpl. Barney Todd [Danny Burns]), Lee Bowman (Capt. Henry Lassiter), Robert Walker (Leonard Purchett), Desi Arnaz (Pvt. Felix Ramirez), Barry Nelson (Pvt. Frances Xavier Matowski), Roque Espiritu (Cpl. Juan Katigbak).

One of the most affecting of Hollywood's World War II combat features turned out during the 1940s, this rousing entry delivered a patriotic message about America's fighting force, bravely combating the enemy, as in this case, to the bitter end. Of equal importance, *Bataan* was a milestone in presenting the U.S. military as a diverse mixture of races—and integrated at that. In structure, the film followed the format of John Ford's *The Lost Patrol* (1934) in which the complement of soldiers dwindled down to one and then to none.

Sgt. Bill Dane and Cpl. Jake Feingold of the U.S. Army are ordered to assist Capt. Henry Lassiter wipe out a bridge along the Bataan Peninsula in the Philippines that is crucial to the onrushing Japanese forces. The task will help the American and Filipino armed forces as they retreat from Manila. Among the several diverse types who form Dane's group is Pvt. Felix Ramirez, formerly of the California National Guard. (Although his precise ethnic origin was not stated, his role was played by Cuban-born ARNAZ.) As the onslaught of Axis troops advance, Dane's squad steadily diminishes in number. Ramirez, who has contracted malaria, deliriously recites a prayer in Latin and then passes away

Bataan was a step forward for Hollywood by depicting Hispanic characters as equal to whites, in this case on the battlefield fighting America's enemies. During the course of preproduction, the film's script was doctored to make the American characters' attitudes to the Filipinos less patronizing.

Bauer, Rocky See BAUER, STEVEN.

Bauer, Steven (aka: Rocky Bauer; Rocky Echevarría (1956–) When this strikingly good-looking Hispanic talent appeared as Al Pacino's gangster buddy in *SCARFACE* (1983) and drew attention away from the star, it seemed his standing in American films was assured, but, instead, Bauer had a roller-coaster career thereafter. He was born Steven Rocky Echevarría in Havana, Cuba. By age three he was living in Miami, Florida. As Rocky Echevarría he was featured in the Miami-based PBS-TV series, *Qué Pasa, U.S.A.?* (1977). This led to roles on TV shows ranging from *The Rockford Files* to *HILL STREET BLUES*. On the teleseries *From Here to Eternity* (1979–80), he was Pvt. Ignacio Carmona. He had a lead in *Thief of Hearts* (1984) and was featured in such TV movies as *Sword of Gideon* (1986), where he played an Israeli commando. Bauer took over as the key undercover agent in the short-lasting, revamped *WISEGUY* (1990). His later credits included *Navajo Blues* (1996), *The Versace Murder* (1998), *Traffic* (2000), *Speed Limit* (2001), *Forever Lulu* (2000—with ex-wife Melanie Griffith), and *King of Texas* (2001—TV movie).

***Believers, The* (1987)** Orion, color, 114 minutes. **Director:** John Schlesinger; **Screenplay:** Mark Frost; **Cast:** Martin Sheen (Dr. Cal Jamison), Helen Shaver (Jessica Halliday), Harley Cross (Chris Jamison), Robert Loggia (Lt. Sean McTaggert), Elizabeth Wilson (Kate Maslow), Harris Yulin (Donald Calder), Carla Pinza (Mrs. Ruiz), Jimmy Smits (Tom Lopez), Raúl Dávila (Sezine).

This well-crafted and graphic horror thriller utilized a plot involving the voodoo cult of Santeria, allowing an on-screen gore fest of blood splattering. According to the screenplay, based on Nicholas Conde's 1982 novel *(The Religion)*, the cult is of African-Caribbean origin, involves sacrifices and a hierarchy of saints, and has enthusiastic practitioners, especially in Spanish Harlem. (Like the earlier *THE POSSESSION OF JOEL DELANEY*, 1972, this new entry associated mystic, voodoolike, often sinister behavior with the Hispanic culture.)

Dr. Cal Jamison, whose wife recently died in a mysterious household accident, moves from Minneapolis to New York with his young son, Chris. Jamison soon becomes involved with the police and, in particular, with a young Hispanic cop (SMITS). The latter becomes hysterical over a young boy's death and later commits suicide (with a snake found in his stomach). As police Lt. Sean McTaggert investigates what he thinks is the product of a serial killer, Jamison becomes prey to the cult's mentality. Their strange beliefs include the sacrifice of one's firstborn to ensure worldly success and a long life.

For prolific actor SHEEN, this R-rated feature proved to be a box-office success, grossing almost $19 million in domestic distribution.

Beltran, Robert (1953–) His best-known role was as Commander Chakotay, the brave Maquis captain, on *STAR TREK: VOYAGER* (1995–2001). Of Mexican–Native American ancestry, he was born and grew up in Bakersfield, California. He graduated from Fresno State University where he majored in theater arts. His screen debut came with a tiny role in *ZOOT SUIT* (1981). The next year he had a key assignment in *EATING RAOUL*, followed by playing the Native American Ahbleza in the TV production of *The Mystic Warrior* (1984). He was Luis in *Gaby: A True Story* (1987) and Juan in *Scenes from the Class Struggle in Beverly Hills* (1989). Before his *Star Trek* sojourn, he had roles in such TV movies as *Shadowhunter* (1993) and *Runway One* (1994). He appeared more recently in such features as *Managua* (1996), *Trekkies* (1997—as himself), and in *LUMINARIAS* (1999).

In *STAR TREK: VOYAGER* (in a two-part episode, "Future's End," in the series' third year), Beltran's character Chakotay explored his mixed Native American background. His wilderness skills, taught him by his Native American father, frequently came in handy during *Voyager*'s journey.

***Ben-Hur* (1925)** Metro-Goldwyn-Mayer, b&w and color, 141 minutes. **Directors:** Fred Niblo and Ferdinand P. Earle; **Screenplay:** Bess Meredyth, Carey Wilson, and June Mathis; **Cast:** Ramón Novarro (Ben-Hur), Francis X. Bushman (Messala), May McAvoy (Esther), Betty Bronson (Mary), Claire McDowell (Princess of Hur), Kathleen Key (Tirzah), Carmel Myers (Iras), Nigel De Brulier (Simonides).

This silent epic made Mexican-born NOVARRO a major player in the Hollywood hierarchy. (As such he was among Hollywood's LATIN LOVER stars in the 1920s, a group that included Rudolph Valentino.) Based on Lew Wallace's *Ben-Hur, a Tale of the Christ* (1880), this saga told of the Jewish Ben-Hur, a wealthy man in ancient Jerusalem, who earns the enmity of Roman officer Messala. This conflict sets off a chain of events that forever change the life of Ben-Hur as he moves from galley slave to adopted Roman to famed charioteer. The film was remade spectacularly in 1959 with Charlton Heston taking over the lead role.

***Bill Dana Show, The* (1963–1965)** NBC-TV series, b&w, 30 minutes. **Cast:** Bill Dana (José Jimenez), Jonathan Harris (Mr. Phillips), Gary Crosby (Eddie: 1963–64), Don Adams (Byron Glick), Maggie Peterson (Susie).

During his run as a writer on TV's *The Steve Allen Show* in the 1950s, comedian Dana created and played the character of José Jimenez, a Latin-American bumbler. The characterization proved a hit with audiences and led to popular comedy recordings and a nightclub act. A more realistic version of José Jimenez was a recurring guest on *The Danny Thomas Show* (1957–64) in the role of the clumsy doorman and elevator operator. This success led to the character having his own series.

On this show Jimenez, a Latin American (of no particular country), is a bellhop at the Park Central Hotel, which is his world. As the naïve soul, he looks for the best in everyone—except his fellow bellhop Eddie. Mr. Phillips is the stern hotel manager while Byron Glick is the none-too-swift hotel detective.

As the civil rights movement of the 1960s intensified, the bumbling José Jimenez character became a sore point with activists, who regarded the presentation as an embarrassing and offensive stereotype. Eventually, Dana moved on to other show-business projects.

***Blackboard Jungle, The* (1955)** Metro-Goldwyn-Mayer, b&w, 100 minutes. **Director/Screenplay:** Richard Brooks; **Cast:** Glenn Ford (Richard Dadier), Anne Francis (Anne Dadier), Louis Calhern (Jim Murdock), Margaret Hayes (Lois Judby Hammond), John Hoyt (Mr. Warneke), Richard Kiley (Joshua Y. Edwards), Sidney Poitier (Gregory W. Miller), Vic Morrow (Artie West), Dan Terranova (Belazi), Rafael Campos (Peter V. Morales), Paul Mazursky (Emmanuel Stoker).

When released this was a highly controversial film because it depicted juvenile delinquency in public high schools. It also reflected the bigotry that guided many students—and teachers—in urban classrooms. (In the course of this trend-setting drama, the dialogue included the usage of such slur words as *spic*, *mick*, and *nigger*.) Tame by today's standards, *The Blackboard Jungle* was considered strong fare in the mid-1950s.

Ex-serviceman Richard Dadier begins his assignment as an English teacher at North Manual High, an inner-city school with an all-male student body. The idealistic Dadier meets resistance from his pupils, especially punk Artie West and his cronies. Efforts to rally such students as African-American Gregory W. Miller or Hispanic Peter V. Morales prove fruitless initially. Before long, a teacher (Hayes) is almost raped, and Dadier, along with the new math instructor, Joshua Y. Edwards, is severely beaten by West and his stooges. In addition, Dadier's pregnant wife (Francis) receives threatening calls at home. Refusing to yield, Dadier wins out over West and his chief thug (Terranova) and determines to be an even more dedicated teacher.

The classroom depicted in *The Blackboard Jungle* was far different from that shown in the same year's *Good Morning, Miss Dove*, the latter being particularly saccharine. *The Blackboard Jungle* reflected the problems of inner-city turbulence that had reached from street gangs to the classrooms. It presented a diversity of ethnic minorities as pupils, including those played by Poitier, CAMPOS, and Mazursky, and allowed these characters to emerge as more than silent stick figures as had been the case in past decades in Hollywood product.

Based on Evan Hunter's 1954 novel, *The Blackboard Jungle* was filmed in El Segundo, California. The song "Rock Around the Clock" sung by Bill Haley and His Comets over the film's credits became a top-ten selection of the year. *The Blackboard Jungle* was nominated for Academy Awards for Best Art Direction, Best Cinematography (Black and White), Best Film Editing, and Best Screenplay (Adapted).

Blades, Rubén (1948–) Musician, actor, politician—he has been all of them. Born and raised in Panama City, Panama, Blades studied law at the University of Panama and then resided in New York City; afterward, he returned home to obtain his law degree. A musician since childhood, Blades performed with several salsa bands in New York City. Besides playing instruments, he also wrote music, which made him a natural to star in the movie *CROSSOVER DREAMS* (1985) as the Hispanic seeking success in the Anglo music world. In *THE MILAGRO BEANFIELD WAR* (1988), he was the sheriff. By the time of the made-for-cable *Dead Man Out* (1989), Blades was a proficient talent, and his performance won him the CableAce Award as Best Actor. He was in Spike Lee's *Mo' Better Blues* (1990), played an Italian count in the elaborate TV production of *The Josephine Baker Story* (1991), and was Emmy Award nominated for his sensitive role opposite Christine Lahti in *Crazy from the Heart* (1991—TV movie). Later assignments included *Color of Night* (1994), *The Devil's Own* (1997), *All the Pretty Horses* (2000), *Empire* (2001), *Assassination Tango* (2002), and *Once Upon a Time in Mexico* (2002). In the TV series *Gideon's Crossing* (2000–01) he was cast as the hospital's psychiatrist/administrator.

In the political arena, Blades was founder of the Papa Egaro Party in his native Panama. In 1994 he ran for president of his country, and, even though he lost, his party won several seats in the country's legislature.

***Blondie Goes Latin* (1941)** Columbia, b&w, 70 minutes. **Director:** Frank R. Strayer; **Screenplay:** Richard Flournoy and Karen De Wolf; **Cast:** Penny Singleton (Blondie Bumstead), Arthur Lake (Dagwood Bumstead), Larry Simms (Baby Dumpling Bumstead), Daisy (the dog), Ruth Terry (Lovely Nelson), Tito Guízar (Manuel Rodriguez), Jonathan Hale (J. C. Dithers).

Joining the escalating Hollywood fad for all things Latin American, the Blondie film series—based on Chic Young's comic strip that began in 1930—made its ninth screen entry a South American-flavored fiesta. It featured singer GUÍZAR (born in Guadalajara, Mexico), who had already established himself in Hollywood pictures and on U.S. radio.

Addled Dagwood Bumstead takes his wife Blondie, their baby son (Simms), and their dog (Daisy) on a South American cruise, courtesy of his boss (Hale). As usual, Bumstead messes up, this time failing to get ashore in time to close a business deal with his employer. Back aboard ship, Bumstead receives advice and assistance from the vocalist (Terry) of the ship's orchestra, which leads a confused Blondie to think he is having an affair. Before everything is resolved, Dagwood has been forced to become the band drummer in drag, while Dithers discovers that passenger Manuel Rodriguez wants to make a much more lucrative offer than the one Dagwood was supposed to resolve.

To give the proceedings its Latin ambiance, there are song renditions of "Brazilian Cotillion," "Querida," and "Solteiro e melhor."

***Blood and Sand* (1922)** Paramount, b&w, 8,110′. **Director:** Fred Niblo; **Screenplay:** June Mathis; **Cast:** Rudolph Valentino (Juan Gallardo), Lila Lee (Carmen), Nita Naldi (Dõna Sol), George Field (El Nacional), Walter Long (Plumitas), Rosa Rosanova (Señora Augustias), Leo White (Antonio).

Although set in Spain and starring Italian-born VALENTINO—like the actor's earlier *THE FOUR HORSEMEN OF THE APOCALYPSE* and *The Sheik*, both 1921—this feature helped to establish the Hollywood concept of the LATIN LOVER. The drama, based on the novel *Sangre y arena* (1908) by Vicente Blasco-Ibáñez, focused on the rise of Juan Gallardo, a young matador in Spain, who weds Carmen but later falls prey to the charms of Dõna Sol. Distracted by the unfaithful Dõna Sol, Gallardo meets his death in the bull ring. As he lays dying in Carmen's arms, the crowd is cheering a new matador.

Blood and Sand was remade by Hollywood in grand style in 1941 starring Tyrone Power, Linda Darnell, Rita Hayworth, and ANTHONY QUINN (as the rival bullfighter). A 1989 Spanish-made version of the drama featured Chris Rydell, Sharon Stone, Ann Torrent, and Guillermo Montesinus.

***Bold Caballero, The* (aka: *The Bold Cavalier*) (1936)** Republic, color, 60 minutes. **Director/Screenplay:** Wells Root; **Cast:** Robert Livingston (Zorro [Don Diego Vega]), Heather Angel (Isabella Palma), Sig Rumann (Commandante Sebastian Golle), Ian Wolfe (priest), Robert Warwick (General Palma), Emily Fitzroy (duenna), Charles Stevens (Vargas).

In 1920, Douglas Fairbanks Sr. starred as ZORRO in a rousing version of Johnston McCulley's 1919 story, "The Curse of Capistrano." This piecemeal new adaptation, using facets of McCulley's story and his character of the fop who was actually the resourceful ZORRO, failed to do justice to the material, despite its then still-novel use of color cinematography.

Western star Livingston was not particularly suited to playing the dual role of the swaggering Don Diego Vega and the bold Zorro. In his disguise as the prissy Vega, he pretends to be on the side of the cruel Comandante Sebastian Golle, the official exploiting the peasants under Spanish rule in nineteenth-century California. It is Golle who kills the new governor (Warwick), lays the blame on Zorro, and places Palma's daughter Isabella in charge. Eventually truth is revealed, and the locals rebel against the comandante, leaving Zorro and Isabella to romance.

Undaunted by this lackluster entry filled with non-Hispanic performers playing the key roles, Republic Pictures continued the Zorro characterization in several movie serials.

Bold Cavalier, The See *BOLD CABALLERO, THE.*

Bonanova, Fortunio (1895–1969) The multitalented Bonanova was an opera singer and actor abroad before he migrated to Hollywood, where he became a most recognizable character actor in scores of movie roles. Born in palma de Mallorca, Spain, he followed his father's profession by studying law. He also studied voice in Madrid, Milan, and in Paris. The baritone settled on an opera career, leading to roles with opera companies around the world. He was in the Spanish-made silent film *Don Juan Tenorio* (1922). His American movie debut was in Gloria Swanson's *The Love of Sunya* (1927). In the early 1930s, he was featured in several Spanish-language films made in Europe, Mexico, and South America. By the late 1930s he was ensconced in Hollywood, playing character parts in such items as *Tropic Holiday* (1938). In the next several decades, Bonanova appeared in such entries as *Two Latins from Manhattan* (1941), *FOR WHOM THE BELL TOLLS* (1943), *The Falcon in Mexico* (1944), *Thunder in the Sun* (1959), and *The Running Man* (1963).

***Border Incident* (1949)** Metro-Goldwyn-Mayer, b&w, 96 minutes. **Director:** Anthony Mann; **Screenplay:** John C. Higgins; **Cast:** Ricardo Montalban (Pablo Rodriguez), George Murphy (Jack Bearnes), Howard da Silva (Owen Parkson), James Mitchell (Juan Garcia), Arnold Moss (Zopilote), Alfonso Bedoya (Cuchillo), Teresa Celli (Maria), Charles McGraw (Jeff Amboy), José Torvay (Pocoloco).

In the post–World War II era of increased enlightenment on matters of race, several ethnic minorities were gradually being featured—albeit in small doses—on the Hollywood screen. No longer was the movie industry (or the public) agog over the novelty of Latin American scenery, topics, or personalities as they had been before. Now the Mexican Americans on camera were far grittier. A prime example was *Border Incident*, featuring MGM contractee MONTALBAN in one of his first dramatic roles at the studio. The movie was shot as a semidocumentary in an uncompromising manner by director Mann.

In the late 1940s, a growing problem along the Mexico–California border are the braceros—workers who cross over daily into the United States as (often illegal) day laborers. Compounding the problem, these exploited individuals are frequently targeted (and sometimes killed) by robbers on their way home. The U.S. and Mexican governments launch a joint venture, with Pablo Rodriguez (for Mexico) and Jack Bearnes (for the United States) investigating the escalating border difficulties. Before long, Rodriguez has targeted as chief culprit Owen Parkson, an American handler of illegal workers. In the process Bearnes is caught by Parkson, tortured, and killed. Meanwhile, Rodriguez incites the braceros to riot against Parkson, which leads to the death of the racketeer and several of his henchmen.

Despite solid reviews, MGM was unsure of how to best handle such a strong drama and, as a result, the film received neither the promotion nor public attention it merited.

***Bordertown* (1935)** Warner Bros., b&w, 89 minutes. **Director:** Archie Mayo; **Screenplay:** Laird Doyle and Wallace Smith; **Cast:** Paul Muni (Johnny [Juanito] Ramirez]), Bette Davis (Marie Roark), Margaret Lindsay (Dale Elwell), Eugene Pallette (Charlie Roark), Robert Barrat (Padre), Soledad Jiménez (Mrs. Ramirez), Arthur Stone (Manuel Diego).

At the time *Bordertown* was released, Hollywood's most typical use of Hispanic characters was as Mexican figures in tales of the Old West (especially California) or old Mexico, where they were presented as banditos or peasants. If a 1930s Hollywood movie was set in contemporary times and utilized Mexican characters, they were typically background types in urban montages. But the socially relevant *Bordertown* was singularly different. It presented a full-blown chronicle of a modern-day Mexican. Rather than being a wealthy playboy from South America (a plot type acceptable to Hollywood story conventions of the 1930s), Muni's Juanito Ramirez was a day laborer who worked his way through law school, only to find real and imagined discrimination—abetted by his hot temper—halting the advancement of his career and social life.

Johnny Ramirez, a poor Mexican living in the Los Angeles barrio, works his way through night law school. He dreams of being financially successful. When he has his first big court case, however, he loses because of ill preparation. Exploding at a supposed snub by the opposing counsel, Ramirez hits him and is disbarred. The disillusioned man moves to a bordertown where he eventually becomes the coowner, with Charlie Roark, of a thriving nightclub. Marie Roark, who has an obsessive love for Ramirez, kills her husband, only to find that her marital freedom does not induce Ramirez to love her. He, instead, adores socialite Dale Elwell, but Dale insists that their very different lifestyles make a serious romance impossible. In fleeing from him one night, she is killed by an onrushing car. A remorseful Ramirez sells his nightclub, donates heavily to a law school, and returns to his old Los Angeles neighborhood to be with his own people.

Herein, Hollywood seemed to be reinforcing the general belief by the white majority of the time that, on the whole, the culture and social background of a Mexican was not compatible to have a romance with a white person. As Richard Watts Jr. (*New York Herald Examiner*) noted in his review (November 24, 1935): "Upon occasion it seems to hint that Americans of Mexican parentage should keep their place and not try to mingle with their superiors."

Bordertown, based on Carroll Graham's novel *Border Town* (1934), provided the source for an unofficial screen remake, *They Drive By Night* (1941).

***Born in East L.A.* (1987)** Universal, color, 84 minutes. **Director/Screenplay:** Richard (Cheech) Marin; **Cast:** Cheech Marin (Rudy Robies), Paul Rodriguez (Javier), Daniel Stern (Jimmy), Kamala Lopez (Dolores), Jan-Michael Vincent (McCalister), Neith Hunter (Marcie), Alma Martinez (Gloria), Tony Plana (Feo), Lupe Ontiveros (Rudy's mother).

After a fifteen-year partnership with Tommy Chong, MARIN struck out on his own, creating a new screen image that no longer relied on his playing a drugged-out Chicano eager to outsmart the gringos. The movie was prompted by a newspaper account of a Mexican American illegally deported to Mexico and by Bruce Springsteen's song, "Born in the USA." Marin was prompted to create a new song, "Born in East L.A.," which led to a music video and then an offer for him to write/direct/star in the feature. Marin proved himself quite accomplished in all capacities in this film.

When Rudy Robies, a resident of East L.A., visits his cousin Javier at a local toy factory, he is caught in a sweep by Immigration and Naturalization Service. Because he has forgotten his wallet that day and his relatives are away on a trip, he can't prove his identity. Along with the others, he is sent back across the border. Without funds and only the most rudimentary knowledge of Spanish, he scrambles to survive. He works for the American Jimmy, who runs a sleazy club. He also sells fruit on the street, touts phony passports, becomes a tattoo artist, and so on—all so he can earn enough money to get back across the border. Meanwhile he meets Dolores, an El Salvadorian who is also broke and knows no English. Eventually, leading a large group of illegals, Robies and the others make it into the United States.

This touching, effective comedy grossed more than $17 million in domestic distribution, doing so well in its initial distribution that the studio quickly released Spanish-titled and/or dubbed prints of the film to capture the growing Hispanic market in the United States.

***Boulevard Nights* (1979)** Warner Bros., color, 102 minutes. **Director:** Michael Pressman; **Screenplay:** Desmond Nakano; **Cast:** Richard Yniguez (Raymond Avila),

Danny De La Paz (Chuco Avila), Marta Du Bois ("Shady" Landeros), James Victor (Gil Moreno), Betty Carvalho (Mrs. Avila), Victor Millan (Mr. Landeros).

Not that far removed emotionally from the movie musical *WEST SIDE STORY* (1961), *Boulevard Nights* was a documentary-style drama of life in Los Angeles, in particular, the barrio of East Los Angeles. It depicted the work, social, and gang habits of several young people in the Mexican section of town. Although its cast of general unknowns gave the film a sense of bleak reality, the movie's predictable thesis—something good lies ahead if one is honest and patient—diluted the grittiness of the ambiance in which most of the neighborhood people were caught up in their environment.

Raymond Avila has dropped out of his local gang (the VGVs), has a steady job, and plans to wed Shady Landeros. In contrast, his younger brother, Chuco, an active VGV member, is caught up in the drama of besting their rivals, the 11th Street gang. Raymond gets his brother a job, but Chuco prefers the drug-heavy life of the gang. At Raymond's wedding, his mother is accidentally shot by a 11th Street member. Raymond plans his revenge, but Chuco beats him to a deadly confrontation with the killer to spare his older brother from being dragged into the gang life again.

Executive produced by actor Tony Bill, *Boulevard Nights* was written by newcomer Japanese-American scripter Nakano. At the time of release, segments of Mexican-American communities in various American cities protested the film's violent depiction of Chicano life.

Braga, Sonia (1950–) This exotic, intense actress gained initial fame in her homeland of Brazil in several steamy TV soap operas (e.g., *Selva de Pedra*, 1972; *Fogo Sobre Tera*, 1974). Although she had made earlier feature films, her presence first became really known in the United States with her 1977 Brazilian picture *Dona Flor and Her Two Husbands*. After other TV serial drama roles, she was in *I Love You* (1981) and *Gabriela* (1983), the latter with Marcello Mastroianni. She had the title role in the picture *KISS OF THE SPIDER WOMAN* (1985), which was made when she had not yet perfected her English and often was unaware what her dialogue meant. In the Robert Redford-directed *THE MILAGRO BEANFIELD WAR* (1988), Braga had the key role of Ruby Archuleta. She was Loah in *The Last Prostitute* (1991—TV movie), played Maria Garza in *Larry McMurtry's Streets of Laredo* (1995—TV miniseries), and was Carlota Alvarez in the brief-lasting *Four Corners* (1998) TV series. Later roles included *From Dusk Till Dawn 3: The Hangman's Daughter* (2000), *Angel Eyes* (2001), *Empire* (2002), and she participated in the PBS-TV series *AMERICAN FAMILY* (2002–). Often, to keep working in the industry, she played characters of many different nationalities.

Bratt, Benjamin (1963–) For a span of four years (1995–99), he was Det. Reynaldo Curtis on TV's *Law & Order*, giving him professional popularity as did his live-in relationship with movie star Julia Roberts, which ended in mid-2001. Born Benjamin Bratt Banda in San Francisco, the middle of five children, his Peruvian Indian mother came from Lima to the United States at age fourteen. (She later became a Native American activist.) His professional training included studies at the American Conservatory Theater in San Francisco. One of his earliest roles was on TV's *Police Story: Gladiator School* (1988), which led to the TV series *Knightwatch* (1988–89) and *Nasty Boys* (1990). In the TV movie *Shadowhunter* (1993), he was Nakai Twobear and played Captain Ramirez in *Clear and Present Danger* (1994). Following his *Law & Order* stint—one of whose episodes featured his then girlfriend, movie star Julia Roberts—he was in such pictures as *The Last Producer* (2000), *Miss Congeniality* (2000), *After the Storm* (2001), and *Abandon* (2002). One of his most acclaimed performances was in *PIÑERO* (2001) as the famed Latino poet, playwright, and actor.

***Brave Bulls, The* (1951)** Columbia, b&w, 106 minutes. **Director/Screenplay:** John Bright; **Cast:** Mel Ferrer (Luis Bello), Miroslava (Linda de Calderon), Anthony Quinn (Raul Fuentes), Eugene Iglesias (Pepo Bello), José Torvay (Eladio Gomez), Charlita (Raquelita).

Based on Tom Lea's 1949 book, *The Brave Bulls* was an uncompromising look at the special world of bullfighting, both the complex emotions that brought matadors to such a dangerous profession and the mentality of the fickle crowds who were always quick to boo or to cheer the matadors in the ring. This was a far more realistic study of the "sport" than such movies as *BLOOD AND SAND* (1922, 1941, and 1989).

Luis Bello, a leading matador in Mexico, loses his confidence after a near-fatality in the ring. His greedy manager, Raul Fuentes, craftily manipulates Bello back to seeming fearlessness, using Linda de Calderon as the tempting bait. Later, when Bello returns to face his next bull, his awkward performance earns the crowd's disfavor. His world falls apart when Linda dies in an auto crash. Branded a coward in the press, the frightened matador makes a wavering return to the sport in an engagement in a small town. On the same program, his younger brother Pepe makes his debut in the ring and is gored by the charging bull. Luis springs to action, his anger overcoming his fear as he deals with his four-legged opponent. Cheered by the crowd, Luis is again the confident master of the game.

With its many observations on the topic of machismo, *The Brave Bulls* was a multilayered depiction of the south-of-the-border sport with on-location filming in Mexico City. At the time of its delayed release a year after it had been made, the picture's director was in public disfavor because of the House Un-American Activities Committee probe of supposed Communists. As a result, the well-crafted movie, with its excellent cinematography, got good reviews but little distribution. Later print versions of the movie restored the bloodier bullfighting footage deleted from the initial release edition.

***Brave One, The* (1956)** RKO, b&w, 100 minutes. **Director:** Irving Rapper; **Screenplay:** Robert Rick [Dalton

Trumbo], Harry Franklin, and Merrill G. White; **Cast:** Michel Ray (Leonardo), Rodolfo Hoyos (Rafael Rosillo), Elsa Cardenas (Maria), Carlos Navarro (Don Alejandro), Joi Lansing (Marion Randall), George Trevino (Salvador).

A minor classic, this picture examined the art of bullfighting, not from the matador's point of view, but from that of the little owner of a bull who did not want his beloved pet to die in the ring.

Leonardo, the son of a Mexican farmer, is dedicated to Gitano, a superb bull whom he has tended since its birth. (The magnificent animal was given to him by a rich rancher.) Later, when the rancher dies and his bulls are sold at auction, Michel cannot produce proper papers of ownership. He follows his bull to Mexico City where the animal is to be used in a contest with a famed matador. Desperate to save his pet, Michel sneaks in to see the president of Mexico at his palace. The leader is so touched by the boy's affection for Gitano that he provides a letter to the bullring owner asking that the bull he spared. Leonardo arrives just as Gitano charges into the ring. During the fierce battle with the matador, the bull is unvanquished. The crowd demands that the bull be spared, and Michel rushes into the ring in a joyous reunion with his beloved pet.

Using a mostly Mexican cast, *The Brave One* rightly received solid reviews. It won an Academy Award for Best Story. (It was not until two years thereafter that blacklisted writer Trumbo acknowledged that under the pseudonym of Robert Rick he had written the story. In 1975 he was officially given his Oscar by the Academy of Motion Picture Arts & Sciences.) *The Brave One* was also Oscar nominated for Best Film Editing and Best Sound.

***Bridge of San Luis Rey, The* (1929)** Metro-Goldwyn-Mayer, b&w, 86 minutes. **Director:** Charles Brabin; **Screenplay:** Alice D. G. Miller, Ruth Cummings, and Marian Ainslee; **Cast:** Lily Damita (Camila), Ernest Torrence (Uncle Pio), Raquel Torres (Pepita), Don Alvarado (Manuel), Duncan Renaldo (Esteban), Henry B. Walthall (Father Juniper), Michael Vavitch (viceroy), Emily Fitzroy (Marquesa), Gordon Thorpe (Jaime), Mitchell Lewis (Captain Alvardo).

Relying on Thornton Wilder's well-regarded novel (1927), the first American screen version of this property was a prestige production relying more on visuals than dialogue. (Made in the early talkie era, it was also released in a silent version.) Although lensed on studio sound stages, it is a frequently atmospheric handling of the drama set in 1714 Peru. Only at the beginning and end of the film is there any spoken dialogue.

A well-worn bridge built long ago on a high mountain road leading to the chapel at San Luis Rey near Lima in Peru collapses, killing five. The villagers are convinced that it is a bad omen and that St. Louis, who blessed the bridge, is angered with them. They ask guidance from Father Juniper. To explain why these people died, he explores their lives. All of them were troubled souls of some sort.

Father Juniper concludes that the deceased had suffered for their love and grown stronger through their pain. He tells the villagers that "There is a land of the living and the land of the dead—and the bridge is Love—the only survival, the only meaning."

***Bridge of San Luis Rey, The* (1944)** United Artists, b&w, 107 minutes. **Director:** Rowland V. Lee; **Screenplay:** Herman Weissman and Howard Estabrook; **Cast:** Lynn Bari (Michaela), Akim Tamiroff (Uncle Pio), Francis Lederer (Manuel and Esteban), Alla Nazimova (the Marquesa), Louis Calhern (the Viceroy), Blanche Yurka (the Abbess), Donald Woods (Brother Juniper), Emma Dunn (Dona Mercedes), Joan Lorring (Pepita).

This second screen version of Thornton Wilder's Pulitzer Prize-winning novel (1927) was more complex in plot structure than the 1929 production and was more faithful to the original book in its account of five individuals killed on the rickety old bridge at San Luis Rey. It had Czechoslovakian-born actor Lederer take on both roles of the twin brothers, Manuel and Esteban. The other lead players were a mixture of nationalities with Tamiroff and Nazimova from Eastern Europe and the others from the United States, or, in the case of Lorring, from Hong Kong. Despite Peruvian artist Reynaldo Luza being the technical adviser and costume designer for this picture, there was too little flavor in this production of Peruvian life from the high-born Marquesa to the humble Uncle Pio or the inquisitive man of God, Brother Juniper.

The 1944 edition of *The Bridge of San Luis Rey* was nominated for an Academy Award for Best Original Score by Dmitri Tiomkin. In January 1958 *The Bridge of San Luis Rey* was produced as an episode of CBS-TV's *Dupont Show of the Month* starring Hume Cronyn and Viveca Lindfors.

***Brothers Garcia, The* (2000–)** Nickelodeon cable series, color, 30 minutes. **Cast:** John Leguizamo (narrator), Alvin Alvarez (Larry Garcia), Vaneza Leza Pitynski (Lorena Garcia), Bobby Gonzalez (George Garcia), Jeffrey Licon (Carlos Garcia), Carlos Lacamara (Ray Garcia), Ada Maris (Sonia Garcia).

As part of its schedule of airing shows of ethnic diversity for children, *The Brothers Garcia* was produced. It featured LEGUIZAMO as the storyteller of this program about three young boys—Larry, George, and Carlos—growing up with their sister Lorena in a quirky, fun Latino household in San Antonio, Texas.

***Buddy Holly Story, The* (1978)** Columbia, color, 113 minutes. **Director:** Steve Rash; **Screenplay:** Robert Gittler; **Cast:** Gary Busey (Buddy Holly), Don Stroud (Jesse), Charles Martin Smith (Ray Bob), Bill Jordan (Riley Randolph), Maria Richwine (Maria Elena Holly), Conrad Janis (Ross Turner), Albert Popwell (Eddie Foster), Gailard Sartain (the Big Bopper), Gilbert Melgar (Richie Valens).

This was a surprisingly effective depiction of the brief life of the rock 'n' roll great Buddy Holly (e.g., "That'll Be the

Day," "Peggy Sue," "Chantilly Lace") who died in his early twenties in a plane crash in 1959. This popular and acclaimed movie detailed the history of the boy from Lubbock, Texas, who loved to make music and who courted/wedded a New York Puerto Rican (Richwine), leading to multicultural concerns. Portrayed briefly in this screen biography was Chicano musician Richie Valens, who also died in the crash. His life story was told later in *LA BAMBA* (1987).

The Buddy Holly Story received Oscar nominations for Best Actor (Busey) and Best Sound.

***Bullfighter and the Lady* (1951)** Republic, b&w, 87 minutes. **Director:** Budd Boetticher; **Screenplay:** James Edward Grant; **Cast:** Robert Stack (Chuck Regan), Joy Page (Anita de la Vega), Gilbert Roland (Manolo Estrada), Virginia Grey (Lisbeth Flood), John Hubbard (Barney Flood), Katy Jurado (Chelo Estrada), Antonio Gomez (himself).

In an uncompromising fashion, this gripping fiction of the bullring was also an illustration of how American cockiness abroad could have tragic results for locals. Along with *THE BRAVE BULLS*—released the same year—it was one of the finest Hollywood-made studies of the world of bullfighting, a sport so associated with Hispanics. It also presented both ROLAND and JURADO at their best. To make the narrative more authentic there was a mixture of English and Spanish spoken in the film. However, it proved to be a distraction to non–Spanish speaking viewers.

Brash American Chuck Regan, a Broadway producer, is vacationing in Mexico. Wanting to impress the young and attractive Anita de la Vega, he convinces famous, aging bullfighter Manolo Estrada to teach him the art of bullfighting. Overconfident of his skills in the ring, Regan makes a near fatal error. Estrada comes to his rescue and dies in the process. Later, despite the hatred of Mexicans for this interloper, Regan insists upon appearing at a benefit for Estrada's widow. The crowd, who had come to cheer his probable death in the ring, are amazed at his agility in the ring. Spurred on by the spirit of the late matador, Regan performs nobly in his contest with the bull, thus earning Anita's respect.

Filmmaker Boetticher had studied bullfighting in his younger days, and his passion for the subject was evident in this film. (His story for the film received an Oscar nomination for Best Original Screenplay.) Shot in Mexico City, the picture featured several famous bullfighters either as themselves (e.g., Gomez) or as stunt doubles for Stack and Roland. This entry's initial release was truncated to eighty-seven minutes (by director John Ford, a friend of the movie's producer, John Wayne). In the late 1980s the movie was restored to its 124-minute original length. Boetticher also directed two other genre pieces: *THE MAGNIFICENT MATADOR* (1955) and the documentary *Arruza* (1972).

***Burning Hills, The* (1956)** Warner Bros., color, 93 minutes. **Director:** Stuart Heisler; **Screenplay:** Irving Wallace; **Cast:** Tab Hunter (Trace Jordan), Natalie Wood (Maria Cristina Colton), Skip Homeier (Jack Sutton), Eduard Franz (Jacob Lantz), Earl Holliman (Mort Bayliss), Claude Akins (Ben Hinderman), Ray Teal (Joe Sutton), Frank Puglia (Tio Perico), Tony Terry (Vicente Colton), Julian Rivero (Miguel).

In *The Searchers* (1955), Wood played a white girl brought up by Comanches. In *The Burning Hills* she was an Anglo Mexican, a role that she handled none too convincingly. Based on Louis L'Amour's 1955 novel, the film used broad strokes to paint its tale of brutality and revenge in the Old West. Potential problems of the mixed-blood romance between heroine and hero (Hunter) were deemphasized in this by-the-numbers tale of retribution.

Trace Jordan tracks the murderers of his brother to the ranch of Joe Sutton. Wounded in a showdown with Sutton, Jordan is later rescued by a young half-breed Mexican named Maria. With her brother Vicente and their uncle Perico, Maria tends a small flock of sheep. Sutton's vicious son Jack leads his men in search of Jordan. In the showdown, Jordan emerges victorious, aided in the end by the half-breed tracker Jacob Lantz.

***The Burning Season: The Chico Mendes Story* (1994)** HBO cable, color, 100 minutes. **Director:** John Frankenheimer; **Teleplay:** William Mastrosimone, Michael Tolkin, and Ron Hutchinson; **Cast:** Raul Julia (Chico Mendes), Edward James Olmos (Wilson Pinheiro), Carmen Argenziano (Sezero), Sonia Braga (Regina), Esai Morales (Jair), Tony Plana (Galvao).

Based on Andrew Revkin's *The Burning Season: The Murder of Chico Mendes and the Fight for the Amazon River* (1990), this was the true story of impassioned Chico Mendes who gave his life fighting to save his home and the inhabitants of the Brazilian rain forest. (The picture was actually filmed in Mexico.) Not only did this well-acted TV movie earn solid critical response, but JULIA, who died in 1994, received a posthumous Emmy Award as Outstanding Lead Actor in a Miniseries or a Special. Frankenheimer won an Emmy for his directing, while the movie itself and the teleplay were Emmy nominated, as were OLMOS (Outstanding Supporting Actor) and BRAGA (Outstanding Supporting Actress).

***Bye Bye Birdie* (1963)** Columbia, color, 120 minutes. **Director:** George Sidney; **Screenplay:** Irving Brecher; **Cast:** Janet Leigh (Rosie DeLeon), Dick Van Dyke (Albert Peterson), Ann-Margret (Kim McAfee), Maureen Stapleton (Mama), Bobby Rydell (Hugo Peabody), Jesse Pearson (Conrad Birdie), Paul Lynde (Mr. McAfee).

When this hit musical debuted on Broadway in 1960, Hispanic-American Chita Rivera played Hispanic-American Rosie DeLeon, the patient secretary/helper to struggling songwriter Albert Peterson. In the restructured screen adaptation, blond Leigh donned a black wig to portray the singing and dancing Rosie, who arranged for rock 'n' roll idol Conrad Birdie, about to be drafted into the army, to sing one of Peterson's songs on national TV. In addition, Rosie, who loves Peterson, helps him escape from his ultrapossessive mother (Stapleton). In keeping with the diminished Hispanic flavor of the screen adaptation, one of the show's original numbers, "Spanish Rose" (sung by Rivera on Broadway), was deleted from the picture.

Bye Bye Birdie received two Oscar nominations: Best Adapted Score and Best Sound. In the 1995 TV adaptation of *Bye Bye Birdie,* Jason Alexander was Albert Peterson with Vanessa L. Williams as his secretary, here called Rose Alvaraz. The number "Spanish Rose" was reinstated for this version.

C

***Cade's County* (1971–1972)** CBS-TV series, color, 60 minutes. **Cast:** Glenn Ford (Sheriff Sam Cade), Edgar Buchanan (J. J. Jackson), Taylor Lacher (Arlo Pritchard), Victor Campos (Rudy Davillo), Peter Ford (Pete).

In trying to make this police drama "different," the setting was rambling Madrid County in the U.S. Southwest, where Sheriff Sam Cade was in charge of maintaining law and order. His helpers included Mexican-American Rudy Davillo, as well as Arlo and Pete, two other deputies. None of the characters exerted much personality in this formula outing.

***California Conquest* (1952)** Columbia, color, 80 minutes. **Director:** Lew Landers; **Screenplay:** Robert E. Kent; **Cast:** Cornel Wilde (Don Arturo Bordega), Teresa Wright (Julia Lawrence), Alfonso Bedoya (José Martinez), Lisa Ferraday (Princess Helena de Gagarine), Eugene Iglesias (Don Ernesto Brios), John Dehner (Don Fredo Brios), George Eldredge (Capt. John C. Fremont).

Spirited but modest, this production traced the turbulent history of California during the years 1825 to 1841 when the area, then a province of Mexico, was targeted by the French and Russians, each seeking control of the rich land. Meanwhile, many Californians were hopeful of being annexed to the United States (which finally occurred in 1850).

Don Arturo Bordega is among the California caballeros who want the area to become part of the United States. On the other hand, bandit José Martinez and his men are in the employ of the unscrupulous Brios brothers (who are working for the Russians) and are raiding ranches of Californians to foment trouble. Bordega infiltrates Martinez's gang aided by American Julia Lawrence whose gunsmith father was murdered by Martinez. By the finale, the Russians have been routed, while Bordega and Julia look to a future together.

With the focus on swashbuckling action and dollops of pseudo history, *California Conquest* was educational and entertaining but hardly sterling drama. Several sources at the time of the film's release noted parallels between the movie's story of the Russian threat to California and the then-current situation of the much feared Red Menace imperiling the safety of America.

Campos, Rafael (1936–1985) Ironically, his first screen role, as an inner-city school student in *THE BLACKBOARD JUNGLE* (1955), remained his most famous movie part. Born in the Dominican Republic, he arrived in the United States with his family in 1949 and attended the famed High School for the Performing Arts in Manhattan, which, in turn, led to his being cast as a Puerto Rican youth in *The Blackboard Jungle* starring Glenn Ford. Campos appeared again with Ford as the Mexican-American defendant in *TRIAL* (1955). His other screen parts included *The Light in the Forest* (1958—as a Native American), *Lady in a Cage* (1964), *THE APPALOOSA* (1966), and *Hangup* (1974). For the 1977–78 season of the TV sitcom *Rhoda* he was Ramon Diaz Jr., a Puerto Rican helper in the shop where Rhoda worked. Rafael's final acting was in *Fever Pitch* (1985), directed by Richard Brooks who had helmed *The Blackboard Jungle.*

***Can You Hear the Laughter? The Story of Freddie Prinze* (1979)** CBS-TV, color, 100 minutes. **Director:** Burt Brinckerhoff; **Teleplay:** Dalen Young; **Cast:** Ira Angustain (Freddie Prinze), Kevin Hooks (Nat Blake), Randee Heller (Carol), Julie Carmen (Rose), Ken Sylk (David Brenner).

Puerto Rican–American stand-up comedian FREDDIE PRINZE (1954–77) committed suicide at age twenty-two. At the time, he was in the midst of the successful run of his TV sitcom

CHICO AND THE MAN (1974–78) in which he played a Chicano. The tragedy robbed audiences of a talented young man and ethnic minorities of a positive role model. This telefeature, using two young actors (Angustain and Hooks) from the TV series *THE WHITE SHADOW* (1978–81), recreated the chronicle of the New Yorker who hungered for success but ended it all in January 1977 when he shot himself. One of Prinze's legacies was his actor son, FREDDIE PRINZE JR., born in March 1976.

***Captain Courtesy* (1915)** Paramount, b&w, 5 reels. **Directors:** Lois Weber and Phillips Smalley; **Cast:** Dustin Farnum (Captain Courtesy [Leonardo Davis]), Courtney Foote (George Granville), Winifred Kingston (Eleanor), Herbert Standing (Father Reinaldo), Jack Hoxie (Martinez), Carl Von Schiller (Jocosa).

This silent feature was another excursion into California's tumultuous history during the 1840s when it was controlled by Mexico and when American settlers were in constant danger from Mexican marauders. Its hero in disguise was a precursor of the ZORRO format.

After his parents are killed by turncoat George Granville and Mexican soldiers, Leonardo Davis becomes the masked highwayman Captain Courtesy, whose mission is to terrify Mexican wrongdoers and create justice. At a stopover at the San Fernando Mission, Davis becomes entranced with the orphaned Eleanor who is in the care of Father Reinaldo. Later, it is she who persuades him not to kill Granville and to focus on their future.

The later *CALIFORNIA CONQUEST* (1952) had a similar plot premise.

***Captain from Castile* (1947)** Twentieth Century-Fox, color, 140 minutes. **Director:** Henry King; **Screenplay:** Lamar Trotti; **Cast:** Tyrone Power (Pedro de Vargas), Jean Peters (Catana Pérez), Cesar Romero (Hernán Cortéz), Lee J. Cobb (Juan Garcia), John Sutton (Diego de Silva), Antonio Moreno (Don Francisco), Thomas Gomez (Father Bartolome Romero), Alan Mowbray (Professor Botello), Barbara Lawrence (Luisa de Caravajal), George Zucco (Marquis de Carvajal), Jay Silverheels (Coatl), Reed Hadley (Juan Escudero).

A splendiferous $4.5 million adaptation of Samuel Shellabarger's 1945 novel, this extravagant historical epic depicted sixteenth-century Spain when the Inquisition was in full throttle and then transferred its narrative to Mexico and the conquest of the Aztecs by Hernán Cortéz and his Spanish troops. The expansive saga was shot in Mexico at Morelia (about 350 miles southeast of the capital), at Uruapan, and at a location near Acapulco. Using primarily a Hollywood cast for the leading players, including Cuban-American ROMERO and Spanish-born MORENO, the film employed many thousands of Mexican and Indian (especially Tarascan) extras. (The movie was made with the cooperation of the Mexican government.) To be noted among the featured performers was Silverheels, here as the Aztec Coatl. Silverheels gained later fame in *The Lone Ranger* TV series (1949–56) and two Lone Ranger feature films (1956 and 1958) playing Tonto, the faithful friend of the masked rider.

Opening in 1518 Spain, young nobleman Pedro de Vargas flees the Inquisition and eventually joins the expedition of Hernán Cortéz. The latter has raised an armada to explore the Indies, which leads to the invasion of Mexico against the Aztecs. In the midst of this sweeping drama is de Varga's ongoing battle with the sinister Diego de Silva, one of the chief powers of the Inquisition; the adventurer's idealized love for the aristocratic Luisa de Carvajal; and his romance with tavern girl Catana Pérez, who bears his child.

Within this far-reaching, massive spectacle, full of pageantry (especially in the presentation of the Aztecs) and grandiose conflicts, the Spanish imperial power in the New World was well depicted, as they grabbed the lands from Montezuma and his Aztec followers, all in the name of their God.

This feature, full of entertainment values but distorted historical facts about sixteenth-century Spain (especially regarding the horrors of the Inquisition) and the early days of the North American continent, was extremely popular in its release. Alfred Newman's lush music score was nominated for an Academy Award. Romero, most famous as one of the cinema's CISCO KID portrayers, received favorable reviews for his interpretation of Cortéz.

Carrillo, Leo (1881–1961) As jovial Pancho, the heavily accented sidekick to the hero on TV's *THE CISCO KID* (1950–56), veteran actor Carrillo gained a whole new generation of fans (and also perpetuated a stereotype that upset others). But this versatile entertainer had years of show-business performances before that, as well as his distinguished pedigree as a true Californian. He was born in Los Angeles, the fifth of eight children in a family whose lineage traced back to the first Spanish settlers in California. His grandfather was a Los Angeles judge, and his father was once Santa Monica's mayor. After college he planned to be an artist but instead became a cartoonist for the *San Francisco Examiner*. He drifted into vaudeville, where he developed his knack as a dialectician. He had a role in the Broadway edition of *Twin Beds* (1914) and was the star of *Lombardi, LTD* (1917). His screen debut came in 1929's *Mister Antonio*. In the 1930s he was frequently cast as a bandito (e.g., *The Broken Wing*, 1932, *THE GAY DESPERADO*, 1936), playing a more refined version of the "greaser" outlaw from silent movies. He made many westerns in the 1940s (e.g., *The Kid from Kansas*, 1941; *Frontier Badmen*, 1943) but occasionally had a dramatic part (e.g., *THE FUGITIVE*, 1947). When Duncan Renaldo took over the role in the Cisco Kid movie series in 1948 with *The Valiant Hombre*, Carrillo was hired to be his jovial, heavily accented cohort Pancho. After four more features, he joined Renaldo for the successful TV show.

***Che!* (1963)** Twentieth Century-Fox, color, 96 minutes. **Director:** Richard Fleischer; **Screenplay:** Michael Wilson;

Cast: Omar Sharif (Che Guevara), Jack Palance (Fidel Castro), Cesare Danova (Ramon Valdez), Robert Loggia (Faustino Morales), Woody Strode (Guillermo), Barbara Luna (Anita Marquez), Frank Silvera (goat herder).

This specious production starred Egyptian-born Sharif as Dr. Ernesto Guevara de la Serna (1928–67), the Argentinean revolutionary and legendary guerrilla leader. Che had a large role in the Cuban revolution of 1956–59 and, under Fidel Castro's regime, became a government minister. Later, while training guerrillas for an hoped-for uprising in Bolivia, Ernesto was caught and executed by the Bolivian army. If in this dramatization Sharif was a bit vague as the charismatic Guevara, Palance was over-the-top as the Cuban dictator Castro. Luna played the nurse who tended to the wounded guerrillas.

Using a flashback format, the unfocused movie that presented no real political point of view, told of Guevara's arrival on Cuba in 1956 with Castro and the band of rebel freedom fighters. This led to Castro's overthrow of the Batista regime, the visionary's disenchantment with Castro, and Guevara's later work/death in Bolivia. The movie utilized Puerto Rico as a substitute for Cuba (with local actors taking supporting parts), and the Bolivian sequences were shot in California.

In the screen musical *EVITA* (1995), ANTONIO BANDERAS played Guevara, while in the two-part made-for-cable feature *FIDEL* (2002), Gael García Bernal was Che.

***Chicago Hope* (1994–2000)** CBS-TV series, color, 60 minutes. **Cast:** Mandy Patinkin (Dr. Jeffrey Geiger: 1994–95, 1999–2000), Adam Arkin (Dr. Aaron Shutt), Hector Elizondo (Dr. Phillip Watters), Peter Berg (Dr. Billy Krunk: 1995–99), Christine Lahti (Dr. Kathryn Justin: 1995–99).

Never in the same league as *ER* (1994–), this Illinois-set medical drama kept changing its underlying format and cast in its search of a winning formula. Part of the glue holding together the scattered series was ELIZONDO's Dr. Phillip Watters, the self-contained, veteran chief of staff. Played as a sophisticated soul, Watters enjoyed good wine and a fine cigar and could be charming on the rare occasions when he dated. He also lost his temper as the egos of his staff physicians became overbearing and could be grief-stricken, as when his hard-to-control son committed suicide. One of his four *Chicago Hope* Emmy Award nominations for Outstanding Supporting Actor in a Drama led to a victory. His Hispanic background was not emphasized in this show, which presented an urban mixture of ethnic types.

***Chico and the Man* (1974–1978)** NBC-TV series, color, 30 minutes. **Cast:** Jack Albertson (Ed Brown), Freddie Prinze (Chico Rodriguez: 1974–77), Scatman Crothers (Louie), Della Reese (Della Rogers: 1976–78), Gabriel Melgar (Raul Garcia: 1977–78), Charo (Aunt Charo: 1977–78).

Much like *ALL IN THE FAMILY* (1971–83), *Chico and the Man* was aimed at exposing and airing racial biases and differences by using comedy to point out the absurdities of these ethnic prejudices. The format had grouchy old Anglo Ed Brown ("the Man"), who owned a run-down garage in the Los Angeles barrio, becoming involved in the life of Chicano Chico Rodriguez. The young Mexican-American exhorts Brown to acknowledge that Rodriguez wants to work at Ed's garage and is responsible enough to become his business partner. Eventually, Brown appreciates the newcomer's effort, but the duo remain miles apart in lifestyles and understanding of the other's cultural heritage.

After PRINZE's suicide in early 1977, he was replaced for the show's last season (1977–78) by Raul Garcia, a Mexican boy who had stowed away in Brown's car trunk while the old man was visiting Tijuana, Mexico.

Although *Chico and the Man* was a commercial success, a segment of the public (Chicanos and Mexicans) at the time of original airing was vocal in complaining that Prinze (a part–Puerto Rican from New York City) was not properly characterizing a Chicano and thus was (inadvertently) misrepresenting the Mexican-American ethnic group.

***CHiPS* (1977–1983)** NBC-TV series, color, 60 minutes. **Cast:** Larry Wilcox (Off. Jon Baker: 1977–82), Erik Estrada (Off. Frank "Ponch" Poncherello), Robert Pine (Sgt. Joe Getraer), Lew Saunders (Off. Gene Fritz: 1977–81), Randi Oakes (Off. Bonnie Clark: 1979–82).

Following the episodic format established by a prior police series, *Adam 12* (1968–75), this show focused on the on- and off-duty activities of two young bachelor members of the California Highway Patrol. Whether riding their motorcycles on the maze of California freeways, dating attractive young women, or doing good deeds in their spare time, Baker and Ponch were a fantasy duo that appealed to viewers. Although little was made of his Hispanic background on the series beyond that he was born in the barrio, Estrada became a major sex symbol during this period and thus a role model for this ethnic minority. During the fall of 1981 when the star had a salary dispute with the show's producers, he was temporarily replaced by former Olympic athlete, Bruce Jenner.

***Choices of the Heart* (1983)** NBC-TV, color, 100 minutes. **Director:** Joseph Sargent; **Teleplay:** John Pielmeier; **Cast:** Melissa Gilbert (Jean Donovan), Peter Horton (Doug), Helen Hunt (Kathy), Mike Farrell (Ambassador Robert White), René Enríquez (Archbishop Oscar Romero), Martin Sheen (Rev. Matt Phelan).

Jean Donovan was the lay missionary in El Salvador who, in late 1980, along with three Maryknoll nuns, was raped and murdered by troops of that country's national guard. Sheen portrays the Irish clergyman who inspired Donovan in her mission, while Enriquez is the church official assassinated for speaking out against the tyranny. This well-handled made-for-television drama covered events also presented in the theatrical feature *ROMERO* (1989).

Cisco Kid, the O. Henry's short story "Caballeros' Way" in *Everybody's Magazine* (July 1907) was the basis for a long succession of presentations of the Mexican bandito, the Cisco Kid, in a variety of media. As the character developed a fully depicted persona, the figure became more romantic and less crude and vicious than the stereotypical "greaser" Mexican outlaw portrayed in early twentieth-century fiction and on the screen. As time wore on, the Cisco Kid became synonymous with the glamorized screen outlaw—a Mexican Robin Hood helping the poor against tyrants. Typically, he was dressed immaculately in an all-black outfit.

One of the first representations of the Cisco Kid on screen was in the 1914 three-reel silent film, released by Eclair, entitled *The Caballero's Way*. This was followed by the 1919 two-reeler silent entry from Universal, *The Border Terror*. In 1929, Fox Films released *IN OLD ARIZONA*, which starred Anglo Warner Baxter with an unconvincing accent. (The veteran star was noted as a ladies' man, which fit in with his devil-may-care screen role.) Not only was this talkie—one of the first filmed outdoors—extremely popular, but it also won Baxter an Academy Award for his unsubtle portrayal. He returned to the role twice more: *THE CISCO KID* (1931) and *The Return of the Cisco Kid* (1939). Then, Baxter, who was now in his late forties and looking his age, relinquished the celluloid part. Deciding to make the property into a B-picture series, the lead was taken over by suave Cuban-American CESAR ROMERO, who, ironically, disliked horseback riding. In the last two of Baxter's series entries, the do-gooder had had as a steady sidekick, Gordito, played by the swarthy, pudgy Chris-Pin Martin, who would remain in the series until the end of Romero's reign in the role in 1941.

Romero's entries as the Cisco Kid were: 1939: *The Cisco Kid and the Lady;* 1940: *Viva Cisco Kid*, *Lucky Cisco Kid*, *The Gay Caballero;* 1941: *Romance of the Rio Grande*, *Ride On, Vaquero*. At this juncture, Twentieth Century-Fox was receiving a lot of pressure to discontinue the series that was felt by Mexicans and Mexican Americans as denigrating to their countrymen and perpetuating stereotypes best forgotten. Because the United States was heavily involved in fostering good relationships with Latin American countries during World War II, the studio agreed to drop the property for the time being.

Meanwhile, on radio, *The Cisco Kid* began on the Mutual network in October 1942 with Jackson Beck in the lead. Louis Sorin was heard as Pancho, the Kid's fat, humorous sidekick. After the series left the air in 1945, it returned in 1946 on the Mutual network, this time with Jack Mather heard as Cisco and Harry Lang as Pancho. A year later, the show moved into transcribed syndication where it was heard weekly until 1956.

With World War II coming to an end, Hollywood again decided to pick up the Cisco Kid property. In 1945, Spanish-born DUNCAN RENALDO made a trio of the Cisco Kid adventures (*The Cisco Kid Returns*, *The Cisco Kid in Old New Mexico*, and *South of the Rio Grande*) for low-budget Monogram Pictures. Martin Garralaga was his on-screen cohort, Pancho. Then the lead was handed over to Mexican-born GILBERT ROLAND who made six economy installments at Monogram (1946: *The Gay Cavalier*, *South of Montery*, *Beauty and the Bandit;* 1947: *Riding the California Trail*, *Robin Hood of Monterey*, *King of the Bandits*) with Garralaga continuing as Pancho. Many fans consider that Roland was the most effective and authentic of all the Cisco Kids, giving the right authenticity to the Kid's adventures and amours. With him in the lead assignment, the Cisco Kid became much more of a dashing lover, a daring rogue who recited poetry to the señoritas he encountered and could be a brutal killer when the occasion demanded.

Duncan Renaldo as TV's *The Cisco Kid* (1950–56). (JC ARCHIVES)

At this juncture, Roland dropped out of the series and Renaldo returned to the role two years later, this time with LEO CARRILLO cast as Pancho and with the films (1949: *The Valiant Hombre*, *The Gay Amigo*, *The Daring Caballero*, *Satan's Cradle;* 1950: *The Girl from San Lorenzo*) being released by United Artists.

In 1950 Renaldo, who controlled the rights to the Cisco Kid property, brought the show to the relatively new medium of TV and during the next six years, he and Carrillo (as Pancho) turned out 156 half-hour popular adventures as the duo roamed the old Southwest.

From 1956 until 1994, the property remained dormant in the United States and then suddenly there appeared a made-for-cable movie of *The Cisco Kid*, with Puerto Rican–American Jimmy Smits in the lead role and Mexican-American CHEECH MARIN as Pancho (and he also sang the title tune).

While the two amigos were pleasant in their camaraderie, the entry itself was forgettable.

***Cisco Kid, The* (1931)** Fox, b&w, 61 minutes. **Director:** Irving Cummings; **Screenplay:** Al Cohn; **Cast:** Warner Baxter (the Cisco Kid), Edmund Lowe (Sgt. Michael Patrick "Mickey" Dunn), Conchita Montenegro (Carmencita), Nora Lane (Sally Benton), Frederick Burt (Sheriff Tex Ransom), Willard Robertson (Enos Hankins), Chris-Pin Martin (Gordito), Charles Stevens (Lopez), Douglas Haig (Billy), Marilyn Knowlden (Annie), Consuelo Castillo de Bonzo (Maria).

After the huge box-office success of *IN OLD ARIZONA* (1929), which won Baxter an Academy Award, the actor was starred in another similar venture, *THE ARIZONA KID* (1930), which dealt with the same lead character without using the name "Cisco Kid." In this third entry, Baxter and costar Lowe repeated their roles from the 1929 feature, with Baxter again portraying the accented, swashbuckling figure created by O. Henry.

This somewhat slapdash affair, with a brief sixty-one-minute running time, had the happy-go-lucky Cisco Kid carousing near the Mexican border in the 1890s. His adversary, New Yorker Sergeant Mickey Dunn, is in the vicinity and does his best to capture the Kid, who has been rustling cattle with the help of his pals Gordito and Lopez. Meanwhile, the Kid and Sheriff Tex Ransom vie for the affections of Carmencita, a dance hall singer at a café in Carrizo. But the Kid's affections for her are slight compared to his interest in the widow Sally Benton, who is fighting to keep her ranch from being foreclosed by banker Enos Hankins. In a grand gesture, the bandito robs Hankins's bank for money to give Sally to keep her land. When Dunn learns of this gallantry, he allows the Kid to escape across the border.

Beyond its Robin Hood theme of robbing from the rich to help underdogs, *The Cisco Kid* depicted acts of discrimination, especially in the different ways that the Kid treated the Mexican entertainer Carmencita and from the more respectful way in which he interacts with the white woman Sally and her two children. Hollywood and much of the white majority in the United States at the time (i.e., the 1930s) were blind to the inherent offensiveness of the stereotypical bandito so often used by U.S. moviemakers, The CISCO KID screen character increasingly came under criticism in the 1940s from Mexico and other Mexican-American PRESSURE GROUPS who decried the negative image being projected on the Hollywood screen. Then too, the cartoonlike manner in which actors such as Baxter portrayed the benevolent desperado only added to the enmity created by the characterization.

Baxter played his Oscar-winning character one more time in *THE RETURN OF THE CISCO KID* (1938).

***Cisco Kid, The* (1950–1956)** Syndicated TV series, color, 30 minutes. **Cast:** Duncan Renaldo (the Cisco Kid), Leo Carrillo (Pancho).

Having starred in several feature films in the later 1940s about the CISCO KID, RENALDO (who held the film rights) and CARRILLO repeated their roles in this early TV western series, one of the first shows to be filmed for posterity. It was wisely lensed in color, which enhanced its value over the coming years when color TVs became feasible for everyone. What made the series so pleasurable was not the presence—actually fairly minimal—of gunplay and fistfights, but the rapport between Cisco and Pancho as they roamed the Southwest helping those in need. Smartly dressed in black, the Cisco Kid rode his beloved horse Diablo, while heavy-set Pancho rode Loco.

At the time regarded as humorous, Pancho's heavy accent ("Ceesco") and overly fractured English were later considered derogatory toward an ethnic minority.

***City Across the River* (1949)** Universal, b&w, 90 minutes. **Director:** Maxwell Shane; **Screenplay:** Shane, Dennis Cooper, and Irving Shulman; **Cast:** Stephen McNally (Stan Albert), Thelma Ritter (Katie Cusack), Luis Van Rooten (Joe Cusack), Jeff Corey (Lieutenant Macon), Sharon McManus (Alice Cusack), Sue England (Betty), Barbara Whiting (Annie Kane), Richard Benedict (Gaggsy Steens), Peter Fernandez (Frankie Cusack), Al Ramsen (Benny Wilkes), Joshua Shelley (Theodore "Crazy" Perrin), Anthony [Tony] Curtis (Mitch), Drew Pearson (himself), Mickey Knox (Larry).

Adapted from Shulman's sexy, tough novel *The Amboy Dukes* (1947), *City Across the River* was an early Hollywood example of juvenile delinquents of various ethnicity joined in a street gang not for casual mischief, like the slum youths of *Dead End* (1937), but bent for serious trouble. A great deal of the rawness, sexuality, and violence of the original novel was toned down severely for this screen presentation filmed in the Canarsie, Prospect Park, and Williamsburg sections of Brooklyn, as well as at Burbank High School in California. As to the cast, as a youngster Fernandez (of Cuban-Irish background) had been a John Robert Powers Agency model who then became a radio and Broadway actor. This was the first speaking screen role for Curtis, who gained movie fame as Tony Curtis.

Stuck in the slum neighborhood of Brooklyn, Frankie Cusack finds relief with his pals, "the Dukes." Their leader, Larry, constantly gets his friends into trouble. If they are not stealing or roughing up people, they are having fights among themselves. Frankie and his pal Benny Wilkes get involved in an altercation with one of their teachers, and Benny accidentally shoots and kills the man. Lieutenant Macon investigates the case, which leads him to Larry. Eventually Larry and Benny get into a dangerous tussle, with the survivor facing a grim future.

***Code of Silence* (1985)** Orion, color, 101 minutes. **Director:** Andrew Davis; **Screenplay:** Michael Butler, Denis Shryack, and Mike Gray; **Cast:** Chuck Norris (Eddie Cusack), Henry Silva (Luis Comacho), Bert Remsen (Commander Kates), Mike Genovese (Tony Luna), Nathan Davis (Felix Scalese), Ralph Foody (Cragie), Ron Henriquez (Victor Comacho).

One of Norris's better action features, this entry was set in Chicago where vice cop Eddie Cusack bucks his fellow cops when they refuse to break the code of silence and snitch on an old-line law enforcer (Foody) who killed an innocent Latino youth during a major drug bust. While this interdepartmental battle is raging, the law must deal with the gang rivalry between Italian mobsters led by Tony Luna and the newcomers to the turf, the vicious Latin-American contingent headed by Luis Comacho.

Code of Silence grossed more than $8 million in domestic distribution.

***Colors* (1988)** Orion, color, 120 minutes. **Director:** Dennis Hopper; **Screenplay:** Michael Schiffer; **Cast:** Sean Penn (Danny McGavin), Robert Duvall (Bob Hodges), Maria Conchita Alonso (Louisa Gomez), Randy Brooks (Ron Delaney), Grand Bush (Larry Sylvester), Don Cheadle (Rocket), Trinidad Silva (Frog), Damon Wayans (T-Bone).

At the time of release, this movie caused tremendous controversy because of its highly violent, nihilistic point of view as engineered by actor/director Hopper. There was so much concern that showings of the film would incite riots that many cities banned the movie or, when screened, ensured that there was a heavy contingent of security guards on hand at each theater. Several reviewers saw this artistically unremarkable entry as a new generation version of *West Side Story* (1961) with the turf now East L.A. and the violence quotient magnified a great deal. Once again the assorted ethnic groups were stereotyped as dangerous figures.

Within the contrived (and clichéd) plot line, Los Angeles policeman Bob Hodges, shortly to retire, is reassigned to a gang-related police unit and has a new partner, Danny McGavin. The latter, young and violent, has his own methods for handling the job, all of which clash with his veteran coworker. A drive-by shooting leads to an all-out war between the Bloods and the rival Crips. Another of the multiracial gangs is the Chicano 21st Street Gang, of which Frog is a member. To protect his brother, Frog agrees to do undercover work for Hodges, but in the ongoing gang war Hodges is killed. Meanwhile, McGavin has a romance with Louisa Gomez, who operates a taco stand and who has grown up in the dangerous barrio.

Colors grossed slightly more than $46 million in domestic distribution.

combat dramas—feature films By the late nineteenth century, newsreel photographers of the silent era were already filming the arrival of U.S. troop ships in the Philippines during the Spanish-American War as well as military maneuvers there, travelogues, and montages of the Filipinos. The same was true of Cuba, with Teddy Roosevelt and the Rough Riders allied with Cuban natives against the Spanish. (Among later sound feature films dealing with Americans fighting in the Spanish-American War were *A Message to Garcia* (1936) and the 1997 TV movie *Rough Riders*.

Hollywood's World War War I-based dramas did not present Hispanic-American characters as part of the American Expeditionary Forces in Europe, but by the time of the Spanish Civil War in the mid-1930s, a linkage was shown between U.S. volunteers and partisans in Spain during that conflict. This alliance between the United States and portions of Spain was represented in such movies as *LAST TRAIN FROM MADRID* (1939), *ARISE, MY LOVE* (1940), *FOR WHOM THE BELL TOLLS* (1943), and the espionage drama, *Confidential Agent* (1945), set in England.

By the time of World War II, combat-themed features such as *The Navy Comes Through* (1942) were occasionally including Hispanic figures as part of America's multiethnic fighting forces. *BATAAN* (1943), a well-constructed genre piece, featured a memorable performance by DESI ARNAZ as a Hispanic American who died (of malaria) while part of the American forces fighting the Japanese. Other World War II-themed films that had Hispanic representation in the proceedings included *Bombardier* and *Guadalcanal Diary* (both 1943), *Tampico* (1944), *Battleground* (1949), *Battle Cry* (1955), *Hell to Eternity* (1960), *The Dirty Dozen* (1967), and *Victory* (1981).

By the early 1950s, the Korean War combat dramas generally had, as a matter of course, brief (and sometimes subtle) Hispanic representation among the diverse cultures of the U.S. troops (e.g., *One Minute to Zero*, 1952; *Men in War*, 1957; *All the Young Men*, 1960). Jumping ahead to the Vietnam War, as in real life, the U.S. troop forces were "fully" integrated and depicted Hispanic members of the U.S. fighting men, albeit not represented nearly to the degree of African-American soldiers (e.g., *Platoon*, 1986; *Full Metal Jacket*, 1987; *Hamburger Hill*, 1987; *We Were Soldiers*, 2002).

combat series—television The few World War II–theme TV series did not feature Hispanic-American characters as program regulars. However, by the time of the Vietnam War, a small degree of integration had occurred in series. *TOUR OF DUTY* (1987–90) had Pvt. Alberto Ruiz (played by Ramon Franco) and Pvt. Marcus Taylor (played by Miguel A. Nunez Jr.); *China Beach* (1988–91) included Maj. Lila Garreau (played by Concetta Tomei).

comedies—feature films As with so many minority ethnic groups, U.S.-made comedy films laughed at these "outsiders" before they laughed with them. For example, Charlie Chaplin made his *Burlesque on Carmen* (1916), utilizing the famed 1847 novel by Prosper Mérimée and the subsequent Georges Bizet opera (1874) as the basis for his spoof of the Spanish officer falling in love with the gypsy girl. The various versions of *Charley's Aunt* (1925, 1930, and 1941) had, as part of their premise, the hero impersonating his Spanish aunt, Donna Lucia. *A Divorce of Convenience* (1921) had Nita Naldi as a fiery Spanish vamp stuck with two spouses. The silent comedy *A California Romance* (1922) featured John Gilbert as a Spaniard in California in love with a Mexican young woman.

A favored target for comedy (slapstick and satire) was the world of bullfighting and lofty matadors. Eddie Cantor pretended to be a Mexican star of the ring in *THE KID FROM SPAIN* (1932). This gambit was broadened further by Stan Laurel and Oliver Hardy in *The Bullfighters* (1945) and even more so by Bud Abbott and Lou Costello in *MEXICAN HAYRIDE* (1948). Perhaps the chief purveyor of caricaturing the south-of-the-border spitfire was LUPE VÉLEZ. She had begun as an ingénue playing in serious dramas, romances, and action films of 1920s Hollywood, but by the 1930s she was lampooning her screen image (e.g., *Hollywood Party*, 1934). In the late 1930s, beginning with *THE GIRL FROM MEXICO* (1939), she commenced a several-year run in the *MEXICAN SPITFIRE* movie comedies. Even LATIN LOVERS, such a viable commodity in the 1920s U.S. silent cinema, came in for a ribbing in *The Sheik Steps Out* (1937) featuring a former Latin Lover, RAMÓN NOVARRO. (Many decades later Billy Crystal would parody the newer breed of vain Latin Lover in his spoofs on TV.)

As America approached its official entry into World War II in late 1941, South Americans and Hispanics became a diplomatic concern, and there were many Hollywood features, especially musical comedies, fostering the "Good Neighbor Policy." (Nevertheless, the Caucasian scriptwriters in Hollywood stuck to stereotypes, whether it be the hot-blooded romantic leading character, the lazy, jovial peasants, or the spoof of the culture's intricate rituals.) Surpassing Velez (who died in 1944) as the leading purveyor of South American caricature was CARMEN MIRANDA, always cast as the colorful but highly jealous individual who talked in fast "jibberish," wore eye-blinding colorful outfits, and had great rhythm. Other films of the 1940s and early 1950s featuring stereotypes of Hispanics included *Shut My Big Mouth* (1942), *The Gay Senorita* (1946), *Cuban Pete* (1946), *The Road to Rio* (1947), *Cuban Fireball* (1951), and *The Fabulous Senorita* (1952).

Even by the time of DESI ARNAZ's *FOREVER DARLING* (1956), the star's Cuban persona was being exploited for hackneyed, exaggerated character traits, as was that of the "simplistic" Mexican played by Mexican-born Cantinflas in *Pepe* (1960), a big-budgeted Hollywood production. The silly *VIVA MAX!* (1969) lampooned South American traits, as did such later variations on "silly" south-of-the-border governments, social figures, and peasants in *Blame It on Rio* (1984), *Bad Medicine* (1985), *Three Amigos!* (1986), and *Moon over Parador* (1988).

A new trend arrived with *Up in Smoke* (1978), the first of several screen teamings of Mexican-American CHEECH MARIN and Asian-Canadian Tommy Chong that continued until the mid-1980s. Here, if Hispanic-American characters were being satirized, at least the Hispanic American was in charge of the spoof's conception and execution.

The 1990s had a split image of Hispanics in Hollywood comedies. There were farces such as *THE ADDAMS FAMILY* (1991) and *Cosmic Slop* (1994), but, on the other hand, romantic comedies, such as *Miami Rhapsody* (1995) with ANTONIO BANDERAS, *Fools Rush In* (1997) with SALMA HAYEK, *What's Cooking?* (2000), and *TORTILLA SOUP* (2001) treated Latino characters as normal figures involved in non-negative comedic actions.

comedy series—television See SITUATION COMEDY SERIES—TELEVISION.

***Condo* (1983)** ABC-TV series, color, 30 minutes. **Cast:** McLean Stevenson (James Kirkridge), Brooke Alderson (Kiki Kirkridge), Luis Avalos (Jesse Rodriguez), Yvonne Wilder (Maria Rodriguez), Julie Carmen (Linda Rodriguez), James Victor (José Montoya).

The premise of this TV comedy—a distillation of the old Cohens and the Kellys/Abie's Irish Rose concept of two ethnically opposed families coming into frequent contact—found upwardly mobile landscaper Jesse Rodriguez leaving the barrio and moving his family into a condo. In contrast, WASP insurance salesman James Kirkridge is having a shaky career. He has sold his house and moved his family into a condo next door to the Rodriguez clan. The two groups clash except for Kirkridge's son and Rodriguez's daughter who plan to wed. Victor was cast as the grandfather in the Rodriguez household.

***Covenant with Death, A* (1966)** Warner Bros., color, 98 minutes. **Director:** William Conrad; **Screenplay:** Larry B. Marcus and Saul Levitt; **Cast:** George Maharis (Ben Morealis Lewis), Laura Devon (Rosemary Berquist), Katy Jurado (Eulalia Lewis), Earl Holliman (Bryan Talbot), Arthur O'Connell (Judge Hochstadter), Sidney Blackmer (Colonel Ates), Gene Hackman (Harnsworth), Wende Wagner (Rafaela), Emilio Fernandez (Ignacio).

What should have been a biting drama was diminished in its presentation. Based on Stephen Becker's novel (1964), the narrative takes place in an unspecified city (actually it was filmed in Santa Fe and Santa Fe County, New Mexico) in the Southwest of the 1920s, thus distancing the viewer from the story. Its lead character is a young Mexican-American judge. Because the part was played by New York-born Greek-American Maharis, the ethnicity of the hero was badly softened. Only JURADO as the hero's cigar-smoking mother and FERNANDEZ as the lively uncle added authentic flavor to the melodramatic proceedings.

When a young woman is murdered, her husband, Bryan Talbot, is found guilty of the homicide on circumstantial evidence. After the senior judge (O'Connell) goes on vacation, his young associate, Ben Lewis, is placed in charge of supervising the hanging. At the execution, the frantic Talbot accidentally kills the hangman. Soon thereafter, it is learned that another man has confessed to the death of Talbot's wife. At the second trial, Lewis must decide if the accused is guilty of murder in the hangman's death, considering that he was an innocent man wrongly charged with homicide.

***Cowboy and the Señorita, The* (1944)** Republic, b&w, 77 minutes. **Director:** Joseph Kane; **Screenplay:** Gordon Kahn; **Cast:** Roy Rogers (Roy), Mary Lee (Chip Williams), Dale Evans (Ysobel Martinez), John Hubbard (Craig Allen), Guinn "Big Boy" Williams (Teddy Bear), Fuzzy Knight (Fuzzy), Dorothy Christie (Lulubelle), Luis Monte (Rodriquez).

This first screen teaming of Rogers and Evans led to many more joint films, TV series, and their off-screen marriage. With its several song-and-dance interludes, this western was another of the many 1940s Hollywood pictures influenced by the then current "Good Neighbor Policy" toward Latin America. Here the U.S.'s fascination with Hispanic themes was reflected in the presence of the character Ysobel Martinez and by the choice of ethnic songs (i.e., "Besame mucho," "The Enchilada Man," "The Cowboy and the Señorita") performed in the movie.

Down-on-their-luck prospectors Roy Rogers and his pal Teddy Bear ride to Bonanza, hoping to find work in town. En route, they come across a gold bracelet, which happens to belong to young Chip Williams, who is now missing. Chip's stepsister Ysobel and the others conclude that Rogers and Teddy Bear kidnapped the teenager. It is discovered later that she ran away from home to find the buried treasure her late father said was in the seemingly worthless mine the family owns. Still later, Chip's charm bracelet is revealed to hold clues to the whereabouts of a rich vein of gold ore in the mine. It is this treasure that local citizen Craig Allen has been trying to wangle from Ysobel's control.

***Crazy/Beautiful* (2001)** Touchstone, color, 95 minutes. **Director:** John Stockwell; **Screenplay:** Phil Hay and Matt Manfredi; **Cast:** Kirsten Dunst (Nicole), Jay Hernandez (Carlos), Bruce Davison (Tom Oakley), Herman Osorio (Luis), Miguel Castro (Eddie), Tommy De La Cruz (Victor).

One of the more affecting and realistic teen dramas of interracial love and the inevitable culture clash that occurs in such "forbidden" romances, this film is set at Pacific Palisades High in southern California where Carlos, a Latino from a poor family, has maneuvered to be enrolled. He is a high achiever in academics, sports, and so on and has fallen in love with a problem-filled blonde Anglo girl, Nicole (who is from an affluent family). In one of the picture's ironies that broke from the clichés of most of Hollywood's mixed-culture romance tales, the girl's congressman father (Davison) does not warn Carlos to stay away from his daughter because she is too good for him, but just the reverse! (The girl, whose mother committed suicide and whose father remarried and remains distant, has substance-abuse problems and is sexually promiscuous.)

Budgeted at $14 million, this film grossed more than $16 million in domestic distribution.

***Crazy from the Heart* (1991)** TNT cable, color, 100 minutes. **Director:** Thomas Schlamme; **Teleplay:** Linda Voorhees; **Cast:** Christine Lahti (Charlotte Bain), Rubén Blades (Ernesto Ontiveros), William Russ (Dewey Whitcomb), Louise Latham (Mae Esther), Tommy Muñiz (Tomas Ontiveros), Kamala Lopez-Dawson (Alcira Ontiveros).

This charming, well-received telefeature portrayed the unlikely romance between a conventional high-school principal in a Texas town and a Mexican-American farmer (who also worked as the school's janitor) whose business was going bust. Charlotte Bain has just broken off her relationship with sports coach Dewey Whitcomb. Realizing that life is passing her by, she seeks new options. Also involved in the situation is tough Alcira, Ontiveros's daughter and a lawyer.

BLADES received an Emmy nomination for his performance in this romantic comedy that realistically treated a multicultural romantic relationship and its repercussions.

***Crime & Punishment* (1993)** NBC-TV series, 60 minutes. **Cast:** Jon Tenney (Det. Ken O'Donnell), Rachel Ticotin (Det. Annette Rey), Carmen Argenziano (Lt. Anthony Bartoli), Lisa Darr (Jan Sorenson), Maris Celedonio (Tanya), James Sloyan ("Interrogator").

Although this police drama promoted its gimmick of having a character named the "Interrogator" interview the police, the criminals, and the victims regarding the case at hand, the more interesting idea was presenting a male and a female cop as equal partners in the Los Angeles Police Department. Det. Annette Rey is a single parent coping with her formerly estranged daughter (Celedonio); Det. Ken O'Donnell has a steady girlfriend, medical intern Jan Sorenson. To make the mix more politically correct, O'Donnell is Anglo and Rey is Hispanic.

Unfortunately, this series lasted only for six installments.

crime, detective, and police dramas—feature films Since the time of *THE BLACKBOARD JUNGLE* (1955), urban crime stories frequently featured Hispanic-American characters as lawbreaking gang members or participants in criminal organizations (e.g., *SCARFACE*, 1983; *CODE OF SILENCE*, 1985; *Running Scared*, 1986; *Extreme Prejudice*, 1987; *COLORS*, 1988; *Drug War: The Cocaine Cartel*, 1992—TV movie; *El Mariachi*, 1992; *Assassins*, 1995; *Desperado*, 1995; *Traffic*, 2000).

In contrast, ethnic minority lead characters in detective series have featured Asians (e.g., the Charlie Chan and Mr. Moto series), African Americans (e.g., the Shaft series), Jews (e.g., Moses Wine of *The Big Fix*, 1979), and so on but not a noteworthy Hispanic main character to date.

Mexican-born RICARDO MONTALBAN played law enforcers in *BORDER INCIDENT* (1949) and *MYSTERY STREET* (1950), as did Cuban-American CESAR ROMERO in *FBI Girl* (1951) and other programmers. One of the first important American feature films to provide an ethnic minority police investigator was Orson Welles's *Touch of Evil* (1958) with the Mexican-American law enforcer portrayed by Charlton Heston. This led to more cop entries with Hispanic-American characters on the police force but mostly *not* in lead roles (e.g., *Badge 383*, 1973; *Fort Apache, The Bronx*, 1981, *Renegades*, 1989). An exception was *Freebie and the Bean* (1974) with Alan Arkin as Benito "Bean" Vasquez, a San Francisco plainclothes cop partnered with James Caan's Freebie Waters.

In 1990's *Internal Affairs* (1990), Andy Garcia was on hand as a dedicated Los Angeles Police Department investigator ferreting out bad cops, including Richard Gere's corrupt character. The same year's *Q & A* offered the fine character actor Luis Guzman as a Hispanic-American police detective in New York (with Armand Assante as a slimey criminal named Bobby Texador). Lorenzo Lamas was a FBI special agent in *The Rage* (1997), and STEVEN BAUER was another governmental law representative in the action quickie *Naked Lies* (1998). EDWARD JAMES OLMOS took on the role of Det. Anthony Piscotti in the remake of the subway hijacking drama, *The Taking of Pelham One Two Three* (1998—TV movie).

crime, detective, and police series—television As TV fare became less constricted regarding the use of ethnic minorities in its programming, several of the police dramas began to use Hispanic-American characters more frequently as criminal gang perpetrators or barrio victims (e.g., *HILL STREET BLUES*, 1981–87; *MIAMI VICE*, 1984–89; *Law & Order*, 1990– ; *NYPD BLUE*, 1993– ; *NEW YORK UNDERCOVER*, 1995–2000; *The Division*, 2001–).

In the category of detective dramas, *Harry-O* (1974–76) starred David Janssen as a California private eye, often working in conjunction with Det. Lt. Manuel "Manny" Quinlan when the show was set in San Diego during its first season. The daytime soap opera *Santa Barbara* (1984–93) had A MARTINEZ playing a serious police detective from 1984 to 1992. On *B. L. Stryker* (1989–90), in which Burt Reynolds was a Palm Beach, Florida, private detective, his ex-wife Kimberly (played by RITA MORENO) was sometimes part of the plot line. On *Sweating Bullets* (1991–95), which featured a Caribbean island backdrop, a former DEA agent was a private investigator who tangled with Lieutenant Carillo (played by Pedro Armendáriz Jr.) during the show's first season. On *Total Security* (1997), a misfire created by Steven Bochco about a Los Angeles-based private investigation/security company, Tony Plana enacted Luis Escobar, the manager of a hotel that was one of the firm's clients.

In the realm of police-themed series, *Dan August* (1970–71) had Ned Romero as Sgt. Joe Rivera. *The Strike Force* (1970–71) concerned government agents combating organized crime; Percy Rodriguez played one of their number. On *CADE'S COUNTY* (1971–72), Victor Campos was a deputy. A major show to showcase a Hispanic-American character was *CHIPS* (1977–83) with ERIK ESTRADA as Off. Frank "Ponch" Poncherello. The highly regarded *Hill Street Blues* offered René Enríquez as Lt. Ray Calletano. Another high-profile cop show was *Miami Vice* in which EDWARD JAMES OLMOS was Lt. Martin Castillo and Saundra Santiago was Det. Gina Navarro Calabrese. Other genre shows of the 1980s featuring ethnic minority characters included *Tough Cookies* (1986), *Houston Knights* (1987–88), *Ohara* (1987–88), and *Wiseguy* (1987–90).

In the 1990s, *Law & Order* featured Benjamin Bratt as Det. Reynaldo "Rey" Curtis from 1995 to 1999. Jimmy Smits was Det. Bobby Simone on *NYPD Blue* from 1994 to 1998; on the other side of the country, in Santa Monica, California, Mario Lopez was Off. Bobby Cruz on the bike squad for the last two years of *Pacific Blue* (1996–2000). Up in San Francisco, *Nash Bridges* (1996–2002) featured the combination of an Anglo cop (played by Don Johnson) and his Hispanic-American partner (performed by CHEECH MARIN). Also set in San Francisco, but dealing with female law enforcers, *The Division* offered Lisa Vidal as Insp. Magdalena "Magda" Ramirez. ESAI MORALES joined *NYPD Blue* as Lt. Tony Rodriguez in 2001. Other police series of the decade and therefore with ethnic minority representation included the *Hat Squad* (1992), *New York Undercover*, *Profiler* (1996–2000), *High Incident* (1996–98), *Ryan Caulfield: Year One* (1999), *The Job* (2001–2), *UC Undercover* (2001–2), and *The Shield* (2002–).

***Crisis* (1950)** Metro-Goldwyn-Mayer, b&w, 96 minutes. **Director/Screenplay:** Richard Brooks; **Cast:** Cary Grant (Dr. Eugene Ferguson), José Ferrer (Raoul Farrago), Paula Raymond (Helen Ferguson), Signe Hasso (Señora Isabel Farrago), Leon Ames (Sam Proctor), Ramón Novarro (Colonel Adragon), Gilbert Roland (Emilio Nierra), Teresa Celli (Rosa Aldana), Mario Siletti (General Valdini), Vicente Gomez (Cariago), Martin Garalaga (Señor Magano), Pedro de Cordoba (Father Del Puento).

One of Grant's less successful feature films, this entry focused on a doctor's moral dilemma when he was forced to make life-or-death decisions regarding a tyrant (well played by FERRER) under his medical care. The action was set in an unspecified South American country very similar to Argentina under Juan Perón's dictatorship.

Noted brain surgeon Dr. Eugene Ferguson is honeymooning in South America with his bride Helen. They are arrested by Colonel Adragon and hurried off to the palace of President Raoul Farrago. They learn from the dictator's wife (Hasso) that her husband is suffering from a severe brain tumor that requires Ferguson's surgical skills. The doctor agrees to operate, but when he observes the leader's tyranny of his people, he has second thoughts. As a revolution brews, Ferguson sends his wife back to America. Unknown to him, she is kidnapped by revolutionary Emilio Nierra who intends to use her to force Ferguson to kill the dictator during surgery. The physician never learns this fact and operates successfully on his patient. Later, Farrago dies of a brain hemorrhage, leading Nierra to believe that the American killed the dictator, and Helen is returned. In the ensuing revolution, Nierra takes over the country and immediately proves to be no less an oppressor than his predecessor. In a volley of gunfire, the new ruler is injured, and now Ferguson must decide whether to help him.

Crisis was filmed on studio sound stages, lessening its verisimilitude. On the plus side, three silent film LATIN LOVERS, ROLAND, NOVARRO, and MORENO, were employed on the project. Adding further ambiance to the picture, a good deal of the conversation between South American characters was presented in Spanish. First-time director Brooks had heavily researched this project on a South American trek he had made in 1949 to bring greater realism to the drama. The movie was based on George Tabori's 1950 short story "The Doubters."

During the making of *Crisis*, the industry's Production Code Administration suggested script changes so that it would not present a doctor deliberately killing a patient. The feature was banned in Mexico and Peru as being "derogatory" to Latin America and was proscribed in Colombia on political grounds. Made at a cost of $1.6 million, *Crisis* lost $713,000 in its initial distribution.

Cristal, Linda (1935–) This earthy, beautiful actress had a rush of popularity in the United States in the late 1950s and early 1960s, highlighted by her role in John Wayne's *THE ALAMO*.

Born Marta Luisa Moya Burges in Buenos Aires, Argentina, she was an orphan by age thirteen. Four years later while in Mexico, film director/producer Raúl de Anda spotted her and cast her in his film *Genio y figura*. After more pictures, she came to Hollywood for *Comanche* (1956) and got a big build-up for romantic comedy *The Perfect Furlough* (1958). She worked for John Ford in *Two Rode Together* (1961) and on TV was one of the costars of the western series, *THE HIGH CHAPARRAL* (1967–71). Later she was in *Love and the Midnight Auto Supply* (1978), the TV movie *Condominium* (1980), and the Argentinean-made TV series *Rossé* (1985).

***Crossover Dreams* (1985)** Miramax, color, 86 minutes. **Director:** Leon Ichaso; **Screenplay:** Manuel Arce and Ichaso; **Cast:** Rubén Blades (Rudy Veloz), Shawn Elliott (Orlando), Elizabeth Peña (Liza Garcia), Virgilio Marti (Chico Rabala), Tom Signorelli (Lou Rose), Frank Robles (Ray Soto), Joel Diamond (Neil Silver).

Although not a new premise, this one was told effectively with Latin sensibilities felt throughout the production. Salsa artist Rudy Veloz, who lives in East Harlem, is tired of working (with his group) in the rundown nightclub operated by Ray Soto. Veloz dreams of moving downtown and being a success in the Anglo world. Fate and luck bring him into contact with record producer Neil Silver, who signs him to a contract. Flush with apparent success, the musician begins to change his lifestyle, which leads him to drop his girlfriend Liza Garcia and to remove Orlando, a long time friend/fellow musician, from his recording group. When the album is released, it fails to click, and before long, Veloz is back where he started. By now Liza has married (an Anglo dentist). Veloz makes amends with Orlando, and the two plan to start up their old band again.

This was one of the earliest feature film appearances of Panamanian-born BLADES.

***Crowded Paradise* (1956)** Tudor, b&w, 94 minutes. **Director:** Fred Pressburger; **Screenplay:** Arthur Forrest and Marc Connelly; **Cast:** Hume Cronyn (George Heath), Nancy Kelly (Louise Heath), Mario Alcalde (Juan Negron Figueroa), Frank Silvera (Papa Diaz), Enid Rudd (Felicia Diaz) Ralph Dunn (Detective Green), Carlos Montalban (Uncle Felipe).

A strong indictment (for its time) of racial bigotry, *Crowded Paradise* prompted the *New York Times* (June 22, 1956) to report, "Although it fails to solve the many problems besetting Manhattan's burgeoning Puerto Rican population, *Crowded Paradise* . . . dramatizes a few of these ills with restraint and compassion."

Puerto Rican Juan Figueroa arrives in New York to wed Puerto Rican–American Felicia, although her self-made immigrant father disapproves of the union. Figueroa's confidence in finding work in Manhattan as a mechanic ends when he discovers that he needs special training for the job and that many employers won't hire a Puerto Rican. Meanwhile, the discouraged young man encounters George Heath, the bigoted alcoholic superintendent of the building where Felicia lives. After difficult periods in their relationship, the young couple wed, only to have the celebration ruined by the drunken, vicious Heath, who is then carted off to jail. Trying to salvage the situation and to learn from others, Figueroa invites Jewish police detective Green, whom he had met earlier, to partake of the festivities.

Displaying a relatively powerful social consciousness, *Crowded Paradise* lost some of its impact through overly dramatic situations that seemed too stagy. Likewise, its "happy" ending did not match the film's earlier focus on class struggle and racial bigotry, both from without and within the Puerto Rican community in New York City.

***Cuba* (1979)** United Artists, color, 122 minutes. **Director:** Richard Lester; **Screenplay:** Charles Wood; **Cast:** Brooke Adams (Alexandra Pulido), Sean Connery (Robert Dapes), Jack Weston (Gutman), Hector Elizondo (Ramirez), Denholm Elliott (Skinner), Martin Balsam (General Bello), Chris Sarandon (Juan Pulido), Danny De La Paz (Julio Mederos).

With its serious drama punctuated by satirical moments, critics and filmgoers alike were uncertain how to take this study of the overthrow of the Fulgencio Batista regime in Cuba by Fidel Castro and his forces.

In late 1959, retired British army major Robert Dapes arrives in Havana to assist General Belo shore up the collapsing Batista regime. Dapes soon encounters Alexandra Pulido, with whom he had a romance fifteen years ago in North Africa. She is now married to the dissolute Juan Pulido, who operates a cigar and rum business that is faltering. As he assesses the situation, Dapes begins to question his acceptance of the post of security adviser to the corrupt and brutal Batista faction. Once the revolution is underway, both Dapes and Alexandra are taken prisoners but later escape. Dapes departs, but Alexandra eventually decides to remain in Cuba. Meanwhile, Pulido is murdered by the avenging brother (De La Paz) of the girl with whom he had an affair.

Laced into the drama is the comparison between the earlier upheaval that brought Batista to power and the new revolution under Castro's control.

Filmed in Spain, the downbeat *Cuba* met with general indifference at the box office, as did the later and lesser *Havana* (1990) with Robert Redford and Lena Olin, which also was set in Cuba during the last stand of Batista's government in 1959 and that received a critical drubbing from critics.

***Cuban Love Song, The* (1931)** Metro-Goldwyn-Mayer, b&w, 86 minutes. **Director:** W. S. Van Dyke; **Screenplay:** C. Gardner Sullivan and Bess Meredyth; **Cast:** Lawrence Tibbett (Terry), Lupe Velez (Nenita Lopez), Ernest Torrence (Romance), Jimmy Durante (O. O. Jones), Karen Morley (Crystal), Louise Fazenda (Elvira), Hale Hamilton (John), Mathilda Comont (Aunt Rosa), Ernesto Lecuona and the Palau Brothers' Cuban Orchestra (themselves).

Metropolitan opera star Tibbett and fiery Mexican-born VELEZ made a strange combination in this goofy, sometimes clumsy musical. The picture reflected the filmgoing public's then-attraction to Latin American screen characters (as long as they were as unrealistically peppery and sultry as this picture's Nenita Lopez). Two of the movie's numbers ("The Cuban Love Song" and "The Peanut Vendor's Song") became huge hits with the public.

In 1917, Terry says farewell to his girlfriend Crystal as he and his marine pals (Torrence and Durante) leave San Francisco for Cuba. Once there, Terry encounters sizzling peanut vendor Nenita Lopez. They have a passionate but stormy romance, which ends when he is reassigned to duty in World War I France. After he is injured in combat he returns home to America and he and Crystal eventually wed. Years later, on his tenth anniversary, he gets drunk in a New York City club and later finds himself on a ship bound for Cuba. Once there, he finds that Nenita has died but that she had given birth to

Xavier Cugat and orchestra with Lina Romay in *The Heat's On* (1943). (JC ARCHIVES)

their son Terry Jr. Father and son return to New York where they are greeted by an understanding Crystal.

***Cuban Pete* (1946)** Universal, b&w, 61 minutes. **Director:** Jean Yarbrough; **Screenplay:** Robert Presnell Sr. and M. Coates Webster; **Cast:** Desi Arnaz and His Orchestra (themselves), Joan Fulton (Ann Williams), Beverly Simmons (Brownie), Don Porter (George Roberts), Jacqueline de Wit (Theresa Lindsay), Pedro de Cordoba (Manuel Perez), Rico De Montez (Cuban driver).

This quickly assembled programmer demonstrated ARNAZ's performance charm in the years before TV's weekly sitcom *I LOVE LUCY* (1951–57) made him famous. It also proved that he was capable of carrying a picture, even a low-caliber offering such as this.

Ann Williams is dispatched to Cuba to sign up the unknown Desi Arnaz and his Cuban Rhythm Band to appear on a radio show sponsored by impulsive perfume manufacturer Theresa Lindsay. Once in Havana, she has trouble convincing bongo-playing Arnaz to relocate to Manhattan because his sister and brother-in-law died in that city and he has been caring for his niece Brownie ever since. Eventually, the troupe makes the trek north, only to be confronted by Lindsay who insists on performing with them on air. Fate and connivance force Lindsay to the sideline, the radio show is a hit, and Arnaz and Ann confirm their love.

Among the musical numbers in this assembly-line quickie were "Cuban Pete" (which became a favorite performance number for Arnaz), "El Cumbanchero," and "Rhumba Matumba."

Cugat, Xavier (1900–1990) As America's "Rumba King" in the 1930s and 1940s, he was noted for his smart ethnic dance orchestra, his string of band vocalists/curvaceous wives, and his popularization of Latin American music in the United States. He was born Francisco de Asís Javier Cugat Mingall in Barcelona, Spain, but was brought up in Cuba before coming to the United States. By late 1928, Cugat was leading a successful dance group at the famed Cocoanut Grove nightclub in Los Angeles. He made his feature film debut in Mae West's *Go West, Young Man* (1936) and played himself (with his violin and his orchestra always on hand) in several MGM musicals (e.g., *Two Girls and a Sailor,* 1944, *On an Island with You,* 1948). He had a TV variety series in 1957 that featured his then-wife Abbe Lane.

D

***D.A., The* (1971–1972)** NBC-TV series, color, 60 minutes. **Cast:** Robert Conrad (Dep. D.A. Paul Ryan), Harry Morgan (Chief Dep. D.A. "Staff" Stafford), Ned Romero (D. A. Investigator Bob Ramirez), Julie Cobb (Public Defender Katherine Benson).

On *Dan August* (1970–71), the Burt Reynolds police series, Romero played the star's partner. Here, he fulfilled a similar function as support for the star (Conrad). It was such casting as this that helped slowly to break down the barrier of having Hispanics as coregulars on Anglo-oriented TV series.

***Danny Thomas Show, The* (1957–1964)** ABC-TV series, b&w, 30 minutes. **Cast:** Danny Thomas (Danny Williams), Marjorie Lord (Mrs. Kathy Williams), Rusty Hamer (Rusty Williams), Sherry Jackson (Terry Williams: 1957–58), Bill Dana (José Jimenez).

One of the most popular TV series in its era, this domestic comedy program had begun as *Make Room for Daddy* (1953–57). Under the new format that began in the fall of 1957, club entertainer and widower Danny Williams had remarried. One of the recurrent characters to crop up on the new premise was building doorman and elevator operator José Jiminez. This well-meaning but fumbling Latin American spoke little English but, nevertheless, managed to get laughs from his on-camera moments. DANA went on to star in his own series, *THE BILL DANA SHOW* (1963–65), in which he had greater freedom to showcase his fractured English character. (At a later time, the exaggerated Jiminez figure became politically incorrect enough to force Dana to drop the characterization.)

***Daughter of the Don, The* (1916)** State Rights, b&w, 10 reels. **Director:** Henry Kabierske; **Screenplay:** Winfield Hogaboom; **Cast:** Hallam Cooley (Lieutenant Nelson), Marie McKeen (Ysabel Hernandez), V. O. Whitehead (Don Hernandez), William Ehfe, and Grant Churchill.

Like the earlier *CAPTAIN COURTESY* (1915) and the much later *CALIFORNIA CONQUEST* (1952), this silent feature dealt with the decade before California became the thirty-first of the United States in 1850. It depicted the conflict between cultures inflamed by patriotism. Once again, the tug-of-war is between upper-class members of each opposing side.

In 1846, Lieutenant Nelson, a member of the U.S. Army, loves Ysabel Hernandez, whose father is a California don. When fighting breaks out between the United States and the Californians, Ysabel, a partisan wearing a man's uniform, joins the Californian cause, successfully using her equestrian skills. At the decisive battle at Los Angeles, Nelson nearly kills soldier Ysabel. Later, when she is captured by an Englishman (who helped to foment the hostilities), Nelson comes to her rescue.

***D.E.A.* (aka: *DEA—Special Task Force*) (1990–1991)** Fox-TV series, color, 60 minutes. **Cast:** Chris Stanley (Nick Biaggi), Tom Mason (Bill Stadler), Jenny Gago (Teresa Robles), David Wohl (Phil Jacobs), Byron Keith Minns (Jimmy Sanders).

The most unusual aspect of this typical police drama was its effort to blend realistic TV news footage into its stories. The focus in this short-lasting program was on the difficult and frequently dangerous work of Drug Enforcement Agency field workers as they battled the flow of narcotics into the United States. The three younger staff members were Nick, Jimmy, and Hispanic-American Teresa. One of the first cases showcased on the series involved an Ecuadorian crime family, with Miguel Sandoval portraying the head of the group, John Vargas as a lieutenant, Roya Megnot as the daughter of a rival

South American crime family, and Pepe Serna seen as her bodyguard.

At least, in this TV series, some of the Hispanic characters were good guys, a change of pace from most entries of the time that stereotyped south-of-the-border figures as negative members of society.

DEA—Special Task Force See D.E.A.

***Death of a Gunfighter* (1969)** Universal, color, 97 minutes. **Director:** Alan Smithee (Robert Totten and Don Siegel); **Screenplay:** Joseph Calvelli; **Cast:** Richard Widmark (Marshal Frank Patch), Lena Horne (Claire Quintana), John Saxon (Lou Trinidad), Carroll O'Connor (Lester Locke), David Opatoshu (Edward Rosenbloom), Kent Smith (Andrew Oxley).

At the time of production, much was made of the fact that famed African-American singer/actress Horne was playing the on-camera lover (and later the wife) of the Caucasian leading man (Widmark). But in the final release print, her role was severely diminished, and her character's ethnicity was suggested as Mexican, not African American. This movie, begun by Totten and completed by Siegel—thus, the use of the pseudonym—was based on Lewis B. Patten's 1968 novel.

Middle-aged marshal Frank Patch has been the law enforcer of Cottonwood Springs for more than twenty years. The progressive townsfolk let it be known that they now want a new breed of law enforcer. One of the few to remain loyal to the lawman is his Mexican mistress Claire Quintana, who owns the local saloon/brothel. When Patch shoots a citizen in self-defense, the town leaders request his resignation, but he refuses. Later, a townsman blames Patch for the suicide of his newspaper-publisher father and vows revenge. Meanwhile, Mexican Lou Trinidad, the county sheriff and an old friend who is indebted to Patch, is brought to Cottonwood to persuade/force Patch to quit. He is unsuccessful and leaves. After Patch and Claire wed, Oxley forces the marshal into a gun battle, which leads to both of their deaths.

As seen on screen, the town of Cottonwood was full of bigotry, with the good citizens disliking Mexican saloon-owner Quintana because of her racial heritage and her profession as a madam. They also had little use for Trinidad, whom they referred to as a "greaseball." As for Patch, not only had he outlived his usefulness to them, but he also consorted with a Mexican woman and had another Mexican—Trinidad—for a friend.

Had *Death of a Gunfighter* been more successfully executed, it might have presented its depiction of racial intolerance more effectively.

De Córdova, Arturo (1908–1973) In the mid-1940s when many Hollywood leading men were away serving in the World War II military, Mexican movie star De Córdova had the lead in several high profile movies but still never became a truly popular figure with American moviegoers.

He was born Arturo García Rodríguez in the city of Merida in southeast Mexico. After a career as a sports writer and announcer, he began to work in Mexican movies: *Cielito lindo* (1936), *El milagro de Cristo* (1940), and *El conde de Montecristo* (1942). Brought to Hollywood by Paramount Pictures, he played Agustin in the big-budgeted *FOR WHOM THE BELL TOLLS* (1943) and was the swashbuckling pirate in *Frenchman's Creek* (1944) with Joan Fontaine. He played opposite Dorothy Lamour (*MASQUERADE IN MEXICO* and *A MEDAL FOR BENNY*, both 1945) and Betty Hutton (*INCENDIARY BLONDE*, 1945). After *Adventures of Casanova* (1948), De Córdova returned to the Mexican cinema where he remained active until 1970 (e.g., *Despedida de soltera*, 1965).

Arturo de Córdova with Joan Fontaine in *Frenchman's Creek* (1944). (ECHO BOOK SHOP)

Del Río, Dolores (1905–1983) Most famous movie beauties enjoy a relatively short screen career. In contrast, Del Río maintained a lengthy stay in both American and Mexican cinema, as well as on the stage in her homeland. She was the first Mexican screen actress to have an international appeal.

Born Dolores Martínez Asúnsolo y López Negrete in Durango, Mexico, this daughter of a banker wed when she was fifteen. She took her husband's surname of Del Río, which she used professionally when American film director Edwin Carewe brought her to Hollywood for a role in the silent photoplay *Joanna* (1925). She had great success in the war story *What Price Glory?* (1926) and the interracial love tale *Ramona* (1928). She made a successful transition to talkies, switching from exotic to more glamorous roles: *FLYING DOWN TO RIO* (1933), *Madame DuBarry* (1934). By the late 1930s her Hollywood movie career had faded, but it was resurrected when her boyfriend Orson Welles featured her in his production of *Journey into Fear* (1942).

By the mid-1940s Del Río had returned to Mexico and had become the premier artiste of the country's cinema (e.g., *Maria Candelaria*, 1944; *Bugambilia*, 1945; *La malquerida*, 1949). She worked for John Ford in *THE FUGITIVE* (1947), and thirteen years later played the half-breed mother of Elvis Presley in *Flaming Star* (1960). She was another Native American in *Cheyenne Autumn* (1964) and remained active in pictures till nearly the end (e.g., *The Children of Sanchez*, 1978).

Del Toro, Benicio (1967–) As the Tijuana policeman coping with the international world of drug trafficking, he won

Dolores Del Río in the 1940s. (JC ARCHIVES)

a Best Supporting Actor Oscar for *Traffic* (2000). By then, this actor with the expressive eyes (and the perpetual dark circles under them) had been acting for thirteen years and had become a favorite in the world of independent cinema.

He was born in San Germán, Puerto Rico. Both his parents were lawyers, and his mother died when he was nine. When Benicio was thirteen, he was sent to a boarding school in Pennsylvania, where he was a basketball star and artist. By the time he attended the University of California at San Diego, he knew he wanted to be an actor. His family urged him to pick a more stable profession—such as law. Nevertheless, Del Toro chose to study at the Stella Adler Conservatory of Acting on a scholarship. He began to appear on episodes of TV series (e.g., *MIAMI VICE* and *Ohara*) in 1987. His movie debut came the next year in *Big Top Pee-wee*. Thereafter, he was in such films as *The Indian Runner* (1991), *Fearless* (1993), *The Usual Suspects* (1994), and *The Fan* (1996), generally playing Hispanic characters.

In the critically slammed *Fear and Loathing in Las Vegas* (1998), starring Johnny Depp, method actor Benicio gained forty pounds for his role and, for further realism, insisted on burning himself with cigarettes to replicate the character he was portraying. Later films included *The Way of the Gun* (2000), *The Pledge* (2001), and *The Hunted* (2002).

***Desperado* (1995)** Columbia, color, 106 minutes. **Director/Screenplay:** Robert Rodriguez; **Cast:** Antonio Banderas (El Mariachi), Salma Hayek (Carolina), Joaquin de Almeida (Bucho), Cheech Marin (short bartender), Steve Buscemi (Buscemi), Carlos Gómez (Right Hand), Quentin Tarantino (pick-up guy), Carlos Gallardo (Campa), Albert Michel Jr. (Quino).

As a follow-up to 1991's *El Mariachi,* which was made for $7,000 and was quite popular with critics and the public, wunderkind RODRIGUEZ made *Desperado,* which some saw as a sequel to the earlier work or as a remake on a grand scale.

The nameless musician, known as El Mariachi, is still on his quest for revenge against the drug lords who caused the death of his girlfriend and injured his left hand (ending his career as a musician). Having avenged himself against several drug dealers along the Texas/Mexico border, his one remaining target is notorious Bucho. The musician travels with his friend, an unnamed person (Buscemi) to find this opponent. In the small, sleepy town where Bucho lives, El Mariachi prepares for the inevitable battle with his sworn enemy. Two of his musician friends (Gallardo and Michel) show up to help even the odds, and there is much gunplay in the streets of town. Meanwhile, El Mariachi has taken up with Carolina, who runs the town's bookstore. In the final showdown with Bucho, El Mariachi discovers that the man is his brother—but that doesn't stop the battle. Later, El Mariachi leaves town with Carolina and his trusty guitar case in tow.

Made for $7 million, *Desperado* grossed almost $26 million in domestic distribution. It led to Rodriguez's *Once Upon a Time in Mexico* (2003), which recounted the further adventures of El Mariachi (Banderas) during an uprising against the Mexican government.

***Dime with a Halo* (1963)** Metro-Goldwyn-Mayer, b&w, 94 minutes. **Director:** Boris Sagal; **Screenplay:** Laslo Vadnay and Hans Wilheim; **Cast:** Barbara Luna (Juanita), Rafael Lopez (Chuy Perez), Roger Mobley (José), Paul Langton (Mr. Jones), Robert Carricart (cashier), Manuel Padilla Jr. (Rafael), Larry Domasin (Cesar).

This unpretentious, low-budget, feel-good drama took place among the impoverished people of Tijuana, Mexico. Each week, a quintet of street waifs scrape together enough coins to purchase a $2 ticket at the Caliente racetrack. Their intermediary is a congenial American named Jones. For many weeks, their race choices fail to win. To change their luck, they make God part of the equation. They take a dime from the church poor box, blend it with their weekly pooling of funds, and have Jones place another bet. They win $81,513. When they look for Jones, he can't be found, and they are fearful of letting anyone else collect the money for them. Finally, Jones is reached in Los Angeles, but when, the next day, he is about to present the winning ticket at the pay window, he dies from a heart attack. The ticket blows away and eventually ends in a garbage pile. Unable to find their ticket, the boys, nevertheless, go back to the church and place a dime in the poor box.

Mexican-American Padilla, who was born in Los Angeles in 1956, stole the movie as the urchin Rafael. He gained his greatest show business attention as Joi in the *TARZAN* TV series (1966–69) starring Ron Ely.

directors of Hispanic-American-themed motion pictures As Hollywood became less parochial after World War II, it began to experiment in making films away from the studio back lot and sound stages, as well as filming more outside of the United States. One of the first coproductions with Mexico was *THE FUGITIVE* (1947), directed by John Ford and costarring DOLORES DEL RÍO. Mexican filmmaker Emilio Fernández had been associate producer on that production and provided creative ideas. Fernández was the director of *THE PEARL* (1949), another coproduction of the United States and Mexico that was shot in Mexico and released in both a Spanish- and an English-language version.

A U.S. director with a penchant for Hispanic subjects was Indiana-born Norman Foster (1900–76). His Latino-themed movies included such Hollywood products as *Viva Cisco Kid* (1940), *Charlie Chan in Panama* (1940), *SOMBRERO* (1953), and ZORRO TV episodes in 1957–58. He also helmed several Mexican-made movies (e.g., *La fuga*, 1944; *El ahijado de la muerte*, 1946). Another U.S. director, Illinois-born Budd Boetticher (b. 1916), had a penchant for the art of bullfighting and its stories, and he translated this interest to the screen. Among his Hispanic-themed pictures were *BULLFIGHTER AND THE LADY* (1951), *THE MAN FROM THE ALAMO* (1953), *THE MAGNIFICENT MATADOR* (1955), and the documentary *Arruza* (1972) narrated by ANTHONY QUINN. California-born GREGORY NAVA made several films dealing with Hispanic Americans including the well-liked *EL NORTE* (1983), *My Family* (aka: *My Family: Mi Familia* [1995]), *SELENA* (1997), and *Killing Pablo* (2002). He also directed the TV series *AMERICAN FAMILY* (2002–).

The bright ray of 1990s independent filmmaking was ROBERT RODRIGUEZ with his impressive first feature *El Mariachi* (1992). This led to *DESPERADO* (1995), *Spy Kids* (2001), and *Once Upon a Time in Mexico* (2003).

During the years, a few Hispanic-American film personalities also have directed feature films (e.g., Anthony Quinn: *The Buccaneer*, 1958; CHEECH MARIN: *BORN IN EAST L.A.*, 1987; PAUL RODRIGUEZ: *A Million to Juan*, 1994).

***Dr. Quinn, Medicine Woman* (1993–1998)** CBS-TV series, color, 60 minutes. **Cast:** Jane Seymour (Dr. Michaela "Mike" Quinn), Joe Lando (Byron Sully), Chad Allen (Matthew Cooper), Erika Flores (Colleen Cooper: 1993–95), Shawn Toovey (Brian Cooper), Michelle Bonilla (Teresa Morales: 1996–97), Alex Meneses (Teresa Morales: 1997–98).

For many viewers, this was an exceedingly popular drama not only for its wholesome family values but also for its feminist point of view. The program traces the life of Bostonian Dr. Michaela Quinn who moves to Colorado Springs, Colorado, in 1860 after her father dies. Reminiscent of *Little House on the Prairie* (1974–83), its episodes provided a full spectrum of drama during its years on the air. Recurrent are segments dealing with the white settlers' reaction to the local Native Americans. Then, in the 1996–97 season, Mexican-American Teresa Morales—whose husband was killed by a mountain lion—arrives in town to replace Rev. Timothy Johnson as the schoolteacher. This causes dissension with the more bigoted souls in Colorado Springs, a situation that accelerates when Teresa chooses to marry the town's barber, an Anglo.

With the interaction of the assorted ethnic types on this series, viewers are given a sense of perspective about the long history of clashing cultures in America and how they eventually learn (to a degree) to deal with one another.

***Don Q, Son of Zorro* (1925)** United Artists, b&w, 10,264′. **Director:** Donald Crisp; **Screenplay:** Jack Woods; **Cast:** Douglas Fairbanks (Don César de Vega/Zorro), Mary Astor (Dolores de Muro), Jack McDonald (General de Muro), Donald Crisp (Don Sebastian), Stella De Lanti (the Queen), Warner Oland (the Austrian Archduke), Jean Hersholt (Don Fabrique).

In the silent film era with no telltale accent to betray the actor, it was relatively simple—with good makeup and costuming—to have nearly anyone assume a screen role of most any nationality. Such was the case with *Don Q, Son of Zorro*, in which the Hispanic characters were largely played by Caucasians, including Danish-born Hersholt as Don Fabrique. This movie was the sequel to Fairbanks's highly-successful *THE MARK OF ZORRO* (1920). It was based on the 1925 novel *Don Q's Love Story* by Hesketh Prichard and Kate Prichard.

In the first half of the nineteenth century, Californian Don César de Vega is dispatched by his father, ZORRO, to Spain to complete his education in the ways of the world and the traditions of his forebears. While on the continent, he becomes enamored of pretty Dolores de Muro and, at the Spanish court, makes all the proper contacts. After the visiting Austrian archduke is assassinated, de Vega is falsely accused of the crime. He pretends to commit suicide, which allows him—and his recently arrived father—to locate the real culprit. With his reputation restored, de Vega pursues his interest in Dolores.

***Drug Wars: The Camarena Story* (1989)** NBC-TV miniseries, color, 300 minutes. **Director:** Brian Gibson; **Teleplay:** Rose Schacht, Ann Powell, Mel Frohman, and Christopher Canaan; **Cast:** Steven Bauer (Enrique "Kiki" Camarena), Elizabeth Peña (Mika Camarena), Miguel Ferrer (Tony Riva), Benicio Del Toro (Carol Quintero), Guy Boyd (George Gilliard).

This riveting television miniseries was based both on fact and the 1988 book *Desperados* by Elaine Shannon. In 1985, U.S. Drug Enforcement Administration agent Enrique "Kiki" Camarena, who had uncovered a huge marijuana operation, is captured, tortured, and killed in Mexico by drug lords suspected of being tied to important local government officials. Both Camarena's widow and other DEA officers join together to solve the case. They cope with seeming apathy from American officials and a trail of greed, corruption, and violence. The made-for-television project was filmed in Los Angeles and Spain (filling in for Mexico because that government refused permission to shoot there).

Drug Wars: The Camarena Story won an Emmy Award for Outstanding Miniseries and led to a sequel *Drug War 2: The Cocaine Cartel* (1992), which concerned DEA agents aiding the collapse of Colombia's Medellin drug lords.

E

***Eating Raoul* (1982)** Twentieth Century-Fox, color, 90 minutes. **Director:** Paul Bartel; **Screenplay:** Bartel and Richard Blackburn; **Cast:** Mary Woronov (Mary Bland), Paul Bartel (Paul Bland), Robert Beltran (Raoul), Buck Henry (Mr. Leech), Richard Paul (Mr. Kray), Susan Saiger (Doris, the Dominatrix).

This very black comedy (made on a $350,000 budget) offended some reviewers, amused others, but left still others bored. Nevertheless, it became a cult favorite. On closer examination, some commentators found interwoven within this picture satirical jabs at societal class structure, particularly corrupted middle-class values and how they can greatly affect others. BELTRAN shines as Raoul, the leather-dressing Hispanic burglar who is full of machismo and startling quirks.

Mary and Paul Bland fantasize about owning a restaurant in the country and getting away from the crime-infested city. By accident, they kill a perverted neighbor and find that he has a wad of cash in his wallet. This leads the couple to embark on a murder spree, killing swinging couples and, after taking their cash and jewelry, stuffing the corpses into trash bags. Burglar Raoul happens on their scheme, becomes their middle man in getting rid of the bodies (he sells the corpses to a dog-food manufacturer), and fences the jewelry. But when Raoul becomes too annoying, the self-righteous couple kill him and serve the nonconformist for their dinner.

Echevarría, Rocky See BAUER, STEVEN.

***Electric Company, The* (1971–1977)** PBS-TV series, color, 30 minutes. **Cast:** Bill Cosby, Rita Moreno, Lee Chamberlain, Morgan Freeman, Luis Avalos, Danny Seagren, and Irene Cara (regulars).

Following much the same format as *Sesame Street*, which began on TV in 1969, *The Electric Company* was produced by the Children's Television Workshop. It was aimed primarily at seven to ten year olds to help them with their reading skills.

With its multicultural audience, this frequent Emmy-winning series used a multicultural mix of talent to entertain/teach its young viewers. Included in the line-up were such Hispanic Americans as MORENO and Cara, as well as such African Americans as Cosby and Freeman.

Elizondo, Hector (1936–) In his screen and TV roles, Elizondo made a strong reputation as a dependable actor who brought a special warmth to his characterizations, often playing an avuncular figure. A good example was his Emmy Award-winning role as Dr. Phillip Watters on the TV series *CHICAGO HOPE* (1994–2000).

Born and raised in New York City, his father was half-Puerto Rican and half-Basque, and his mother was born in Puerto Rico. He began his acting career on the stage. He won an Obie for playing "God" in the off-Broadway production of *Steambath* (1970) and was on Broadway in *The Prisoner of Second Avenue* (1973) and *Sly Fox* (1976). Early screen roles include *The Landlord* (1970) and *Pocket Money* (1972). By the end of the decade, his parts had grown (e.g., *CUBA*, 1979), and in the next decade, he was in several short-lasting TV series (e.g., *Freebie and the Bean*, 1980–81; *A.K.A. PABLO*, 1984; *Foley Square*, 1985–86). Elizondo was among the cast of such big hits as *Pretty Woman* (1990) and *Runaway Bride* (1999)—both for director/producer Garry Marshall with whom he worked frequently—and such lesser vehicles as *Getting Even with Dad* (1994) and *Picking Up the Pieces* (2000). He returned to

Hector Elizondo and Sophia Loren in *Courage* (1986—TV movie). (JC ARCHIVES)

series TV with the unsuccessful feel-good drama, *Kate Brasher* (2001). Later credits included *The Princess Diaries* (2001), *TORTILLA SOUP* (2001—a remake of Ang Lee's 1994 movie *Eat Drink Man Woman*), *Fidel* (2002—made-for-cable movie), and *How High* (2002).

***El Norte* (1984)** Island Alive, color, 139 minutes. **Director:** Gregory Nava; **Screenplay:** Anna Thomas and Nava; **Cast:** Zaide Silvia Gutiérrez (Rosa Xuncax), David Villalpando (Enrique Xuncax), Ernest Gómez Cruz (Arturo Xuncax), Alicia Del Lago (Lupe Xuncax), Eraclio Zepeda (Pedro).

Another of the sobering cinematic projects made in conjunction with PBS-TV's *American Playhouse*, this film admirably told the harrowing account of two young Guatemalans—a brother and a sister—who lose their parents (the political activist father is murdered; the mother is carted away by the authorities). The simple youngsters leave their village with one goal in mind—to go north and somehow enter the United States. Once they accomplish their arduous goal, life is no easier for these undocumented souls. They are exploited by employers, hounded by the Immigration and Naturalization Service, and live hand to mouth. Through their ordeal, they miraculously retain their pride, even when one of them dies from an ailment contracted during their harrowing trek northward to the United States.

El Norte, which was presented in the Spanish language with English subtitles, received an Oscar nomination for Best Original Screenplay.

***El Súper* (1979)** New Yorker, color, 90 minutes. **Directors:** Leon Ichaso and Orlando Jiménez-Leal; **Screenplay:** Ichaso and Manuel Arce; **Cast:** Raymundo Hidalgo-Gato (El Súper), Zully Montero (Aurelia), Reynaldo Medina (Pancho), Elizabeth Peña (Aurelia), Juan Grande (Cuco).

As one of the first American-made movies to deal with the plight of Cuban refugees in the United States, it was based on a play first produced at New York City's Cuban Cultural Center. It took a long time for the filmmakers to finance this $250,000 project.

Using both Spanish and English dialogue and subtitles, *El Súper* tells of a superintendent of a Manhattan tenement building who had fled Cuba and is trying to make a new life for himself and his wife (Montero) and daughter (PEÑA). Although he has trouble adjusting to the new environment, his family does it with relative ease, leading to conflict at home. Although he wishes he could return to Cuba one day, it is not a viable option; rather, he dreams of somehow relocating to Miami, Florida.

What could have been a grim political treatise on discrimination against aliens is a balanced mix of pathos, humor, and astute observation.

Estevez, Emilio (1962–) The oldest son of Hispanic-American actor MARTIN SHEEN, Estevez chose to take his father's actual surname for his acting career. Emilio's fame in the 1980s was often related to his membership in Hollywood's Brat Pack along with Rob Lowe, Emilio's actor brother Charlie Sheen, and others. Born in New York City, but reared mostly in Los Angeles, the baby-faced performer made his TV acting debut in telefeatures, often cast as the troubled teen (e.g., *In the Custody of Strangers*, 1982—opposite his father). He was one of many future stars in *The Outsiders* (1983) and was in the cult entry *Repo Man* (1984); directed and starred in *Wisdom* (1986) but fared much better playing Billy the Kid in the Brat Pack westerns: *Young Guns* (1988) and *Young Guns II* (1990); and headlined the Disney live-action comedy *The Mighty Ducks* (1992) and its two sequels (1994 and 1996). By the end of the decade, Estevez was out of the mainstream but still acting/directing (e.g., *Rated X*, 2000).

Estrada, Erik (1949–) As California motorcycle highway patrolman Frank "Ponch" Poncherello on CHIPS (1978–83), Estrada forged a screen image for himself as the new generation's Hispanic hunk. Born of Puerto Rican parents in New York City, he made his film debut in *The Cross and the Switchblade* (1972) as an ethnic gang leader. Also that year he was the Mexican-American policeman in *The New Centurions*. Later he played Lieutenant "Chili Bean" Ramos in the war drama *Midway* (1976). After *CHiPS* Estrada's career went downhill. He was featured in the Mexican telenovela (TV soap opera) *Dos mujeres, un camino*, which gave him more prominence than such movies as *The Divine Enforcer* (1991), *The Final Goal* (1995), *Oliver Twisted* (2000), or *UP, Michigan!* (2001). On TV guest appearances and commercials, he often spoofed his *CHiPS* character.

***Evita* (1996)** Buena Vista, color, 135 minutes. **Director:** Alan Parker; **Screenplay:** Alan Parker and Oliver Stone; **Cast:** Madonna (Eva "Evita" Perón), Antonio Banderas (Che

Guevara), Jonathan Pryce (Gen. Juan Domingo Perón), Jimmy Nail (Agustin Magaldi).

For years after the rock opera *Evita*, with music by Andrew Lloyd Webber and lyrics by Tim Rice, opened on Broadway in 1979, the project was announced as a film project for a string of actresses and directors. When finally produced, familiarity and time had erased a good deal of the magic from the original. Nevertheless, it was still the tale of Maria Eva Duarte (1919–52), the illegitimate daughter of an Argentinean midlevel businessman; her goal of overcoming the poverty of her youth leads her on a journey from man to man as each helps to elevate her station in life. Eventually, she meets politician Juan Perón (1895–74) and they soon marry. With her help, Perón is eventually elected president of his country. Unaccepted by the governing class, Eva creates her own sphere of important friends. She constantly proclaims her love and support of the country's lower class while her husband's dictatorial regime exploits and tyrannizes them. Later, the woman, who has become a legend to the Argentinean working class, dies of cancer.

While history was served to a degree within this musical, the recitative dialogue focused on the fantasy vision of Evita's ambition along with the ongoing observations of the passionate revolutionary Che Guevara. Madonna, a better song stylist than actress, lacked charisma here as the lead figure who performed the show's signature song, "Don't Cry for Me, Argentina," as well as such lesser numbers as "Rainbow High." Banderas, as the one-man Greek chorus, stole the proceedings, especially with such renditions as "And the Money Kept Rolling In (and Out)."

Evita received an Academy Award for Best Song ("You Must Love Me"). It received Oscar nominations for Best Art Direction/Set Decoration, Best Cinematography, Best Film Editing, and Best Sound. Made at a cost of $55 million, *Evita* grossed only about $50 million in domestic distribution. (Back in 1981, Faye Dunaway gave a galvanic performance in a sturdy TV movie biography entitled *Evita Perón.*)

***Extreme Prejudice* (1987)** TriStar, color, 104 minutes. **Director:** Walter Hill; **Screenplay:** Deric Washburn and Harry Kleiner; **Cast:** Nick Nolte (Texas Ranger Jack Benteen), Powers Boothe (Cash Bailey), Michael Ironside (Maj. Paul Hackett), Maria Conchita Alonso (Sarita Cisneros), Rip Torn (Sheriff Hank Pearson).

A stylized and violent exercise in the battle between good and evil, this film abounded in stereotypes: sinister Mexican thugs, an enticing señorita, and the ambiance of Mexicans living in unsavory conditions.

Two childhood friends are now enemies. Jack Benteen of the Texas Rangers resides in El Paso, Texas, and is devoted to battling drug dealers. Across the border in a little Mexican town, Cash Bailey has risen to be a powerful drug lord, controlling the locals population with his gang of thugs. Both men are involved with Sarita Cisneros, a cantina singer. She used to be Bailey's girlfriend; now she is with Benteen but is weary of being ignored because of his demanding work. Later, Bailey grabs her back. Meanwhile, Maj. Paul Hackett and his men, supported by the CIA, are set to rob an El Paso bank where Bailey's loot and, perhaps, evidence of his underhanded dealings are stored. The scheme fails, but Hackett asks Benteen to join him in a south-of-the-border raid to eliminate Bailey. However, Hackett plans to kill Benteen, thereby double-crossing Bailey with whom he has a secret deal. A bloody showdown occurs between Hackett and Bailey's men, leaving Sarita to return to the victor, Benteen.

Noteworthy for its excessive brutality, exaggerated performances, and ethnic clichés, *Extreme Violence* grossed about a mild $11 million in domestic distribution.

F

***Family Martinez, The* (1986)** CBS-TV series pilot, color, 30 minutes. **Cast:** Robert Beltran (Hector Martinez), Anne Betancourt (Anita Martinez), Karla Montana (Rainbow Martinez), Daniel Faraldo (Romeo Ortega), James Shigeta (Judge Yamamoto).

Produced by Tommy Chong and Howard Brown, this series pilot set in contemporary times aired on August 2, 1986, but the show never made it to the official season line-up. Directed by Oz Scott, the potential comedy series revolves around Hispanic Hector Martinez, a one-time gang member turned trial lawyer who returns home to his family. Even at this relatively late date in the history of American television, it was a rare example of a series (pilot) in which the major characters were not Caucasian figures.

***Fantasy Island* (1977–1984)** ABC-TV series, color, 60 minutes. **Cast:** Ricardo Montalban (Mr. Roarke), Hervé Villechaize (Tattoo: 1978–83), Wendy Schaal (Julie: 1981–82), Christopher Hewett (Lawrence: 1983–84).

The casting of two heavily accented actors—tall debonair Mexican MONTALBAN and short, rambunctious Frenchman Villechaize—created an unlikely duo, but they worked well together on camera. This anthology series (which sprang from two popular TV movies aired in 1977 and 1978) was a highly successful variation of *The Love Boat* (1977–86), also produced by Aaron Spelling.

Very little is revealed about Mr. Roarke's past. We learn in one episode that an evil spirit 300 years earlier loved Mr. Roarke and returns to the present day to revenge herself on him because he had refused to marry her. There is also the recurring appearance of the Devil (played by Roddy McDowall) who wants to even a score with Mr. Roarke, who might be God's messenger. What the viewer does know is that Roarke is philosophical, patient, charming, all-knowing, and impeccably groomed (always garbed in white suit). As such, he is a complex but positive image of a Hispanic character.

In the unsuccessful 1998–99 new edition of *Fantasy Island*, Britisher Malcolm McDowell was cast as Mr. Roarke, the host of the unusual resort, supported by a trio of assistants (played by Mädchen Amick, Edward Hibbert, and Louis Lombardi).

Ferrer, José (1912–1992) Most famous as the Oscar-winning (the first Hispanic) star of *Cyrano de Bergerac* (1950), a part he played on stage, TV, and in another film, the multitalented Ferrer was the first actor to receive the U.S. National Medal of Arts in 1985. (He also earned three other Oscar nominations.)

He was born Vicente Ferrer de Otero y Cintrón in Santurce, Puerto Rico. It was at Princeton University, where he majored in architecture, that he gravitated to the theater. With his distinctive, crisp voice and authoritarian manner he soon found work on Broadway and kept busy for years. He made his screen debut playing the Dauphin in Ingrid Bergman's *Joan of Arc* (1948). In the thriller *CRISIS* (1950), starring Cary Grant, Ferrer who played a variety of nationalities on camera had one of his relatively few opportunities to portray a Hispanic—here as a cruel South American dictator. One of Ferrer's great screen characterizations was as the deformed French painter Toulouse-Lautrec in *Moulin Rouge* (1952). He directed himself in *The Cockleshell Heroes* and *The Shrike* (both 1955) and *I Accuse!* (1958—as Captain Alfred Dreyfus). He continued unabated with a wide range of movies like *Laurence of Arabia* (1962), *Enter Laughing* (1967), *The Big Bus* (1976), and *A Midsummer Night's Sex Comedy* (1982) and was also quite active in TV movies (e.g., *An*

Evening in Byzantium, 1978; *Evita Perón*, 1981; *Strange Interlude*, 1987). His son, Miguel, by his singer/actress wife Rosemary Clooney, became an actor.

***Fidel* (2002)** Showtime cable, color, 200 minutes. **Director:** David Attwood; **Teleplay:** Stephen Tolkin; **Cast:** Víctor Huggo Martín (Fidel Castro), Gael García Bernal (Che Guevara), Mirta (Patricia Velasquez), Celia Sánchez (Cecilia Suarez), Tony Plana (General Batista).

Based on the books *Guerrilla Prince* (1991) by Georgie Anne Geyer and *Fidel Castro* (1993) by Robert E. Quirk, this two-part made-for-cable feature was one of several recent small-screen movies dealing with past and present political dictatorships operated by America's southern neighbors. These included: *Noriega: God's Favorite* (2000—set in Panama) and *In the Time of the Butterflies* (2001—the Dominican Republic). *Fidel* was certainly an improvement over the glossy and vapid *CHE!* (1963), which had covered some of the same biographical and geographical turf.

LA Weekly (January 25, 2002) reported, "Everything here is streamlined and simplified, of course . . . but certainly it is not the easiest subject to compress. . . . [T]here is, notably, a fine cast, all of them—for a change in a Hollywood film about Latinos—actually Latino." Weighing the value of this production, the *Hollywood Reporter* (January 24, 2002) concluded, "Things get a bit muddled the longer we focus on Fidel and try to figure out whether he's the hero of a . . . [cable movie] or a real-life political activist and yes, visionary. The two are never quite the same." While championing the merits of this production, *Daily Variety* (January 24, 2002) pointed out, "pic isn't especially insightful or sophisticated about Castro's political evolution, preferring a blunt turn from good guy to dictator once he and his guerrilla warriors take power." For the *New York Times* (January 26, 2002), one of the picture's flaws was the performance of Mexican actor Martín who was making his English-language debut here: "He sounds as if he had learned his lines phonetically. He delivers every speech, no matter how intimate, at full oratorical lilt."

***Fighter, The* (aka: *The First Time*) (1952)** United Artists, b&w, 78 minutes. **Director:** Herbert Kline; **Screenplay:** Aben Kandel; **Cast:** Richard Conte (Felipe Rivera), Vanessa Brown (Kathy), Lee J. Cobb (Durango), Frank Silvera (Paulino), Roberta Haynes (Nevis), Hugh Sanders (Roberts), Claire Carleton (Stella), Martin Garralaga (Luis), Rodolfo Hoyos Jr. (Alvarado).

Conte's intense performance elevated this entry based on Jack London's 1911 short story. Although the Italian-American actor was born in Jersey City, New Jersey, he gave a creditable interpretation of the Mexican freedom fighter.

In 1910, after fleeing Mexico, Felipe Rivera arrives in El Paso, Texas, intent on joining fellow exiled countrymen in overthrowing the regime of Mexican president Porfirio Diaz. The group is wary of him, all except the American Kathy whose husband was killed by the Federales. As the two become close, he tell her of his past when he had helped to hide Durango, a guerrilla leader, in the mountains above his village and Lake Pátzcuaro. However, while he was doing this, his village was burned and his parents and fiancée died. The man responsible for the massacre was named Alvarado.

Eventually, Rivera is dispatched to Mexico to contact Durango. He finds the man imprisoned but rescues him and takes his captor, Alvarado, prisoner. Durango holds a "trial" of the tyrant, and the man is sentenced to death based on Rivera's testimony of the bloodbath at his village. Returning to Texas, Rivera delivers Durango's request for more firearms. He finds a way to finance the weapons purchase and takes them to Mexico, hoping they will help to bring an end to Diaz's oppression.

The fight sequences were shot at Lake Pátzcuaro and at the village of Janitzio on Pátzcuaro Island. Stock footage was utilized from filmmaker Kline's *The Forgotten Village* (1941). London's "The Fighter" had already been the basis for the Mexican-made *El mexicano* (1944) starring David Silva and Lupita Gallardo. That picture was remade in Mexico in 1977 under the same title and starred Jorge Luke and Pilar Pellicer.

***Finding the Way Home* (1991)** ABC-TV, color, 100 minutes. **Director:** Rod Holacomb; **Teleplay:** Scott Swanton; **Cast:** George C. Scott (Max Mittelmann), Hector Elizondo (Ruben), Beverly Garland (Arleen), Julie Carmen (Elena), Raul V. Carrera (older Trujillo brother). George Garza (younger Trujillo brother).

In Texas, life is not going well for Max Mittelmann. His marriage has soured over the years and his business is near bankruptcy. After he is involved in a car accident, he develops amnesia and later wanders into a camp for Mexican migrant laborers. The place is unofficially run by Ruben. While there, Mittelmann, a whiz with repairing equipment, encounters a variety of people, including Elena and the Trujillo brothers.

Based on a novel (publication undetermined) by George Raphael Small, this unpretentious TV movie presented positive images of Hispanics in contrast to many then-current theatrical features.

***Fires Within* (1991)** Metro-Goldwyn-Mayer/United Artists, color, 86 minutes. **Director:** Gillian Armstrong; **Screenplay:** Cynthia Cidre and Peter Barsocchini; **Cast:** Jimmy Smits (Nestor), Greta Scacchi (Isabel), Vincent D'Onofrio (Sam), Luis Avalos (Victor Hernandez), Bertila Damas (Estella Sanchez).

This well-meaning but rather uninvolving drama received scant theatrical release before being shunted to home-video distribution. The production was not helped by having Italian actress Scacchi in the key female assignment, as her Cuban accent and mannerisms rang false throughout. In contrast, SMITS as the Cuban martyr did his best to bring intensity to the curiously flat proceedings.

While her husband languishes in a Cuban prison for his anti-Castro newspaper reporting, Isabel and her daughter escape the island as boat people. They are rescued by Anglo fishing-boat captain Sam. Later, Sam falls in love with her, while Isabel, a teacher, finds a livelihood from an illegal numbers operation. Now, eight years later, Nestor is released and arrives in Miami. He is declared a hero by the population of Little Havana, and there are factions that want him to return to political causes. Meanwhile, he burns with jealousy at his wife's attachment to the fisherman. Isabel can't make up her mind between the two men. But Nestor does it for her by announcing to the political group that he must put wife and family first.

Fires Within was filmed in Miami, Florida, where Cuban-born coscripter Cidre resided. It was yet another entry that utilized the tyranny of rulers to explicate Hispanic sensibilities.

First Time, The See FIGHTER, THE.

***Flying Down to Rio* (1933)** RKO, b&w, 89 minutes. **Director:** Thornton Freeland; **Screenplay:** Cyril Hume, H. W. Hanemann, and Erwin Gelsey; **Cast:** Dolores Del Río (Belinha De Rezende), Gene Raymond (Roger Bond), Raul Roulien (Julio Rubeiro) Ginger Rogers (Honey Hale), Fred Astaire (Fred Ayers), Blanche Friderici (Dõna Elena), Walter Walker (Carlos De Rezende), Etta Moten (carioca singer).

Flying Down to Rio could not have come at a better time for RKO. The surprise hit musical kept the studio solvent and launched the enormously popular screen dance team of Astaire and Rogers. Not to be overlooked were the facts that the nominal stars of this chic landmark film included an exceedingly beautiful DEL RÍO and that the on-camera art deco/fantasy representation of Rio de Janeiro—all created on the studio sound stages—focused the attention of Depression-weary moviegoers on the exotic allure of South America. (The film used then-common stereotypes of Latin Americans, enhancing them with the studio's conception of Brazilian café society, most of whose denizens were presented on screen as oversized comedic figures.) Then too, one of the picture's most impressive numbers, "The Carioca," launched a dance craze that aided Hollywood's desire to use South American musical themes on camera—a fad that reached a peak in the 1940s.

The loopy plot had playboy band leader Roger Bond falling in love with upper-crust Belinha De Rezende in Miami, Florida, not knowing that the Brazilian beauty is already engaged to Julio Rubeiro. Bond and Belinha meet again in Rio de Janeiro where her father Carlos De Rezende is the beleaguered owner of a financially troubled hotel. Bond conceives a spectacular entertainment (chorus girls strapped to the wings of planes flying over the hotel) to pull De Rezende back from bankruptcy. Meanwhile, Bond's friend (and the band's choreographer/accordion player) Fred Ayers and the band's singer, Honey Hale, have not only discovered a new dance ("The Carioca") but also are pleased that Bond and Belinha have chosen to marry.

Left unnoticed by most critics at the time of release was the movie's assumption (reflecting America's then general belief) that the Brazilian heroine would, of course, choose the blond Anglo as her mate over her fellow countryman. Thus, Rubeiro, as the plot's other man, has to parachute out of the plane that carries the love-happy Bond and Belinha northward.

Flying Down to Rio received an Academy Award nomination for Best Song ("The Carioca").

***Flying Nun, The* (1967–1970)** ABC-TV series, color, 30 minutes. **Cast:** Sally Field (Sister Bertrille), Marge Redmond (Sister Jacqueline), Madeleine Sherwood (Mother Superior), Alejandro Rey (Carlos Ramirez), Shelley Morrison (Sister Sixto), Vito Scotti (Police Capt. Gaspar Formento: 1968–69), Manuel Padilla Jr. (Marcello, the orphan boy: 1969–70).

Based on the book *The Fifteenth Pelican* (1965) by Tere Rios, this offbeat situation comedy centered on the (mis)adventures of energetic, optimistic, and fulsome Sister Bertrille, a young novice at the Convent San Tanco, located on a hilltop not far from San Juan, Puerto Rico. (This was one of the few American teleseries of that era to be set in such a locale.) One of the more unusual things about the ninety-pound Sister Bertrille was that she could fly! Among her compatriots were Sister Sixto, a Puerto Rican nun who "amusingly" stumbled over her English. Locals in the area included handsome playboy Carlos Ramirez, who operated a club in town, and police official Formento.

For a time, Argentinean-born Rey developed a status as a (minor) sex symbol because of his role on *The Flying Nun.* On the series, Frank Silvera and Henry Corden occasionally played the uncles of the swinging Ramirez. Morrison, as the Puerto Rican nun, was actually a New Yorker of Sephardic Jewish background. She gained later fame as the Hispanic maid on the hit TV sitcom *WILL & GRACE* (1998–).

***Forever Darling* (1956)** Metro-Goldwyn-Mayer, color, 96 minutes. **Director:** Alexander Hall; **Screenplay:** Helen Deutsch; **Cast:** Lucille Ball (Susan Vega), Desi Arnaz (Lorenzo Xavier Vega), James Mason (the guardian angel), Louis Calhern (Charles Y. Bewell), John Emery (Dr. Edward R. Winter), John Hoyt (Bill Finlay).

With the success of their weekly TV series, *I Love Lucy* (1951–57), married co-stars Ball and ARNAZ made the hit big screen comedy *The Long, Long Trailer* (1954) where they played a newly married couple with Arnaz's character apparently of Italian heritage. Two years later they starred in the romantic fantasy *Forever Darling.* Here Arnaz was cast as a Hispanic American, a dedicated research chemist who is so busy perfecting a new insecticide that he ignores his increasingly irritated wife (Ball). As their marriage falls apart, her guardian angel (Mason) materializes to help her resolve her domestic dilemma.

Unlike *The Long, Long Trailer*, the Vegas were upper-class and their marital woes transpired in plush settings. Thus the average filmgoer became disinterested, especially when Ball did not display her patented brand of pratfalls and slapstick comedy until near the end of the lackluster film. Arnaz's heavily accented alter ego here was much like his Ricky Ricardo of *I Love Lucy*—hard working, excitable, charming, and chauvinistic.

***Forged Passport* (1939)** Republic, b&w, 64 minutes. **Director:** John H. Auer; **Screenplay:** Franklin Coen and Lee Loeb; **Cast:** Paul Kelly (Dan Frazer), June Lang (Helen), Lyle Talbot (Jack Scott), Billy Gilbert (Nick Mendoza), Cliff Nazarro (Shakespeare), Maurice Murphy (Kansas Nelson), Frank Puglia (Chief Miguel).

Years before the shipment of illegal aliens across the Mexican border became such a major financial and social concern to the United States, this low-caliber action entry dealt with the topic—but only as an excuse for its action and to reflect that the hero was sufficiently daring to merit the heroine's love.

U.S. immigration officer Dan Frazer has a hot temper but an eagle eye and stops several truckloads of Mexicans being shipped illegally into the United States. His activities lead the smuggling gang to target Frazer for execution. Unfortunately, Frazer's pal walks into the trap. As a result, Frazer is dismissed from the agency. He goes undercover by opening a gas station near Tijuana, Mexico, and, eventually, with the help of his club singer girlfriend (Lang) learns the identity of gang leader "Lefty" and shuts down his operation.

Sicilian-born Puglia was Miguel, the Mexican police chief, while Kentucky-born Gilbert was seen as ethnic and quite loquacious nightclub owner Nick Mendoza.

***For the Soul of Rafael* (1920)** Equity, b&w, 7,090′. **Director:** Harry Garson; **Screenplay:** Dorothy Yost; **Cast:** Clara Kimball Young (Marta Raquel Estevan), Bertram Grassby (Rafael Artega), Eugenie Besserer (Doña Luisa), Juan De La Cruz (El Capitan), J. Frank Glendon (Keith Bryton).

Moviemakers continued to tap the rich history of old California, as in this silent photoplay.

Marta Raquel Estevan heeds the request of her demanding guardian, Doña Luisa, that she wed the woman's wild son, Rafael Artega. But fate intervenes when she rescues Keith Bryton from his Native American captors and falls in love with him. Not admitting defeat, Doña Luisa maneuvers so that the marriage still takes place. Later, the reckless Artega runs off with another woman and, in the process, is killed by the bandit El Capitan. Marta and Bryton are reunited.

Based on Marah Ellis Ryan's 1906 novel, this picture was shot on locations around California and utilized tribal members from the Cocopah, Pima, and Soboba reservations in the Los Angeles vicinity. The movie's Hispanic characters were mostly played by non-Hispanics.

***For Whom the Bell Tolls* (1943)** Paramount, color, 170 minutes. **Director:** Sam Wood; **Screenplay:** Dudley Nichols; **Cast:** Gary Cooper (Robert Jordan), Ingrid Bergman (Maria), Katina Paxinou (Pilar), Akim Tamiroff (Pablo), Arturo De Córdova (Agustin), Vladimir Sokoloff (Anselmo), Mikhail Rasumny (Rafael), Fortunio Bonanova (Fernando), Eric Feldary (Andres), Victor Varconi (Primitivo), Joseph Calleia (El Sordo).

Ernest Hemingway's best-selling novel (1940) became a $3 million screen production that was released to great acclaim in 1943 during the height of World War II. Its gorgeously photographed, highly romanticized tale of the idealistic American college professor Robert Jordan, who in 1937 joined the Republican cause during the Spanish Civil War (1936–39), fit in with the patriotic mood of U.S. filmgoers. The fact that most of the peasant guerrilla/gypsy force of Spanish patriots were actors from other countries (e.g., Sweden's Bergman, Greece's Paxinou, Russia's Sokoloff, Hungary's Varconi) didn't bother most critics or moviegoers of the time. (To be noted, Bonanova was from Spain and DE CÓRDOVA was from Mexico.)

Its sweeping story told of teacher-turned-demolition-specialist Jordan who works with the Republicans in the mountains as they fight the Nationalists. He falls in love with Maria, a Spanish refugee who had been raped by the Nationalists after they killed her parents. In the guerrillas' effort to destroy a key bridge that will hinder a Nationalist attack, Robert is injured. Unable to escape with the others, he remains to hold off the approaching enemy while the group flees. Maria must be content with remembering her lover's bravery.

As this blockbuster movie moved into general distribution in 1944 after its initial road show release, many of the sequences showing the cruelty of the Spanish peasants/guerrillas to disloyal fellow Spaniards were deleted from the prints. This saga earned a sizable $7.1 million in film rentals during its domestic distribution. *For Whom the Bell Tolls* won an Academy Award for Best Supporting Actress (Paxinou) and received Oscar nominations for Best Actor (Cooper), Best Actress (Bergman), Best Cinematography (Color), Best Film Editing, Best Original Dramatic Score, and Best Picture. *For Whom the Bell Tolls* was unofficially remade as the modest *Fighter Attack* (1953) with Sterling Hayden and Joy Page and the action transferred to World War II Italy.

***Four Faces West* (1948)** United Artists, b&w, 90 minutes. **Director:** Alfred E. Green; **Screenplay:** Graham Baker and Teddi Sherman; **Cast:** Joel McCrea (Ross McEwen), Frances Dee (Fay Hollister), Charles Bickford (Pat Garrett), Joseph Calleia (Monte Marquez), William Conrad (Sheriff Egan), Martin Garralaga (Florencio).

This low-key western benefited from its ambiance of nineteenth-century New Mexico and its inclusion of such Mexican characters as the gambler Monte Marquez (played by

Malta-born CALLEIA) and the farmer Florencio (played by Spanish-born GARRALAGA).

Needing money to save the family ranch, Ross McEwen robs a bank in Santa Maria, New Mexico. U.S. Marshal Pat Garrett pursues McEwen, who has become romantically involved with railroad nurse Fay Hollister. At one point, McEwen stops at a ranch for a new mount. There he discovers that the owner Florencio, his wife, and their two sons are suffering from diphtheria. After trying to nurse them himself, he signals for help, which brings Garrett, Fay, and others to the ranch. Garrett persuades the robber to give himself up, promising to speak on his behalf. Fay plans for them to be together once he is released.

Made at a cost of approximately $1 million, *Four Faces West* was not a financial success. Location work for the feature was done at El Morro National Monument, San Rafael, and the White Sands National Monument, all in New Mexico. The western was based on the novelette "Pasó Por Aqui" by Eugene Manlove Rhodes published in the *Saturday Evening Post* in February 1926.

***Four Horsemen of the Apocalypse, The* (1921)** Metro, b&w, 11 reels. **Director:** Rex Ingram; **Screenplay:** June Mathis; **Cast:** Rudolph Valentino (Julio Desnoyers), Alice Terry (Marguerite Laurier), Pomeroy Cannon (Madariaga, the Centaur), Josef Swickard (Marcelo Desnoyers), Brinsley Shaw (Celendonio), Alan Hale (Karl von Hartrott), Bridgetta Clark (Doña Luisa), Beatrice Dominguez (dancer).

Spanish writer Vicente Blasco-Ibáñez's popular antiwar novel of 1916 was published in an English translation in 1918 and three years later became an elaborate American silent photoplay. It quickly established Italian-born VALENTINO as a major American movie star and was the beginning of his reign as the king of the LATIN LOVERS. The sequence in which his character, outfitted as a gaucho, stalks onto the dance floor, interrupts a couple, and performs a dramatic tango with Dominguez, remains a sensual highlight of the silent cinema.

Spanish immigrant Madariaga becomes a wealthy cattle baron in Argentina. One of his two daughters weds a Frenchman, the other a German. After the old man dies, the two sons-in-law dispose of their estates and take their families to Europe. The Frenchman takes his son and daughter to Paris, while the German with his three sons goes to Berlin. In France, Julio purchases a castle on the Marne and opens a studio, painting pictures and entertaining. Soon he falls deeply in love with Marguerite Laurier, the young wife of a well-known lawyer. When World War I breaks out, Marguerite joins the Red Cross, while her husband enlists. Finding her spouse blinded, she resists Julio's further attentions. Meanwhile, encouraged by the words of a mystic, who invokes the Four Horseman (War, Conquest, Famine, and Death), Julio enlists. After proving himself a hero on the battlefield, he is killed in action by his cousin, an officer in the German army.

The popular film was remade in 1962 with the story line updated and the results far less appealing.

***Four Horsemen of the Apocalypse, The* (1962)** Metro-Goldwyn-Mayer, color, 153 minutes. **Director:** Vincente Minnelli; **Screenplay:** Robert Ardrey and John Gay; **Cast:** Glenn Ford (Julio Desnoyers), Ingrid Thulin (Marguerite Laurier), Charles Boyer (Marcelo Desnoyers), Lee J. Cobb (Julio Madariaga), Paul Henreid (Etienne Laurier), Paul Lukas (Karl von Hartrott), Yvette Mimieux (Chi-Chi Desnoyers), Karlheinz Böhm (Heinrich von Hartrott), Angela Lansbury (voice of Marguerite Laurier).

Forty-one years after Vicente Blasco-Ibáñez's grim antiwar novel was translated into a hugely successful Hollywood silent film starring RUDOLPH VALENTINO, it was remade as a splashy, wide-screen, colorful entry. Ford, then the King of Remakes, assumed the Valentino role with little distinction. The action of the drama in the remake was moved up twenty years to the 1930s. While the two adaptations are based on the same original work, they move in quite different directions.

To cattle baron Madariaga's horror, he discovers that his German-reared grandson, Heinrich von Hartrott, just returned to the old homestead, has become an avid Nazi. The elderly patriarch becomes so agitated that he foretells that the Four Horsemen of the Apocalypse (Conquest, War, Pestilence, and Death) will soon scour the earth. With that, he dies in the arms of his beloved grandson Julio, a careless playboy.

As the decade ends, Julio leaves the pampas and goes to Paris with his French father, Marcelo. Drawn into the social circle of idealistic Etienne Laurier, Julio quickly falls in love with the man's wife, Marguerite. Laurier is later sent to a concentration camp. When he is eventually released, he is a broken man, which prompts Marguerite to break with Julio. After the death of Julio's sister Chi-Chi—who was active in the Resistance—Julio, who had also joined the underground, participates in the destruction of the Nazi headquarters in Normandy. Once at the key building, Julio is confronted by Heinrich. Realizing they are fated to die, the cousins drink a last toast to the joy their families once shared.

The costly, overbloated new edition of *The Four Horsemen of the Apocalypse* in color and widescreen process was both a critical and commercial flop (it lost $6 million). Despite the on-location filming in France of many key scenes, everything about this project was synthetic and dull.

***Fugitive, The* (1947)** RKO, b&w, 104 minutes. **Directors:** John Ford and (uncredited) Emilio Fernández; **Screenplay:** Dudley Nichols; **Cast:** Henry Fonda (the fugitive), Dolores Del Río (Maria Dolores), Pedro Armendáriz (police lieutenant), Ward Bond (El Gringo), Leo Carrillo (chief of police), J. Carrol Naish (police spy), Robert Armstrong (police sergeant), John Qualen (doctor), Fortunio Bonanova (the governor's cousin).

This remarkably austere, atmospheric production was based on Graham Greene's novel *The Power and the Glory* (1940). It signified the first major joint filmmaking venture between the United States and Mexico with much of the lensing accomplished at RKO's Churubusco Studios outside Mexico City. Besides Mexican cinematographer Gabriel Figueroa, the production boasted Mexican filmmaker Emilio Fernández as associate producer and directorial associate, with Richard Hageman's music score performed by the Mexico City Symphony Orchestra. (Most of the remaining crew was Mexican as well.)

In a nameless South American dictatorship, religion has been banned, and the government has eliminated all priests but one. This lone survivor arrives in a little village dressed in tattered peasant clothes. In an abandoned church, the frightened man encounters Maria Dolores, an Indian. He confesses his background to her, while she begs him to baptize her illegitimate baby. He does so at great danger to himself. Already the police, led by the lieutenant, are closing in on him. While the police shoot hostages in the surrounding villages to encourage the locals to give up the secreted priest, the man of God hides in terror. Meanwhile, an American fugitive, El Gringo, arrives in town with a large cache of stolen money. Later, the priest is captured by the persistent lieutenant (the same man who had cast off his one-time mistress, Maria Dolores). The prisoner is offered his freedom if he will recant his religion. But, now renewed in his faith, the priest regains his courage and marches to his death in front of the firing squad. While this is happening, another man of God arrives at the church to pray.

This stark, powerful passion play caused a furor in some Mexican quarters (and among left-wing groups in the United States) who felt that *The Fugitive* depicted the Mexican government and its people in an unflattering manner. Despite several complimentary reviews—many of which noted the parallels between *The Fugitive* and Ford's earlier Irish-set *The Informer* (1935)—the highly stylized movie, which cost more than $1 million, lost more than $500,000 in its initial distribution. Greene's book was later adapted for television in 1959 (with James Donald) and in 1961 (with a cast featuring Laurence Olivier, George C. Scott, and Patty Duke).

***Fun in Acapulco* (1963)** Paramount, color, 100 minutes. **Director:** Richard Thorpe; **Screenplay:** Allan Weiss; **Cast:** Elvis Presley (Mike Windgren), Ursula Andress (Margarita Dauphine), Elsa Cardenas (Dolores Gomez), Paul Lukas (Maxmillian Dauphine), Larry Domasin (Raoul Almeida) Alejandro Rey (Moreno), Robert Carricart (José).

This candy-colored romp set in Acapulco was mostly filmed on a studio sound stage with the second-unit camera crew capturing landmarks of the Mexican vacation Mecca to insert into the film. Although this was just another production-line entry in the prolific film career of Presley, it boasted a better-than-usual cast, gorgeous scenery, and an infectious ambiance. (Its utilization of a south-of-the-border fun locale was reminiscent of the 1940s when such exotic foreign settings were employed to provide the story with an intriguing flavor.)

Former circus trapeze artist Mike Windgren is still emotionally crippled due to his guilt over an accident years ago that killed his work partner. As such, he accepts a job as lifeguard and part-time singer at the Acapulco Hilton Hotel. There he meets the assistant social director Margarita Dauphine, and the couple soon fall in love, despite the competition for her attention from exhibition high-diver Moreno, and Windgren's flickering interest in Dolores Gomez, a bullfighter. Eventually, to prove his worth to himself and to Margarita, Windgren substitutes for an injured Moreno in his nightly 136-foot dive from La Quebrada. With this success, he now plans to return to his circus work, and Margarita intends to go with him.

Among the numbers sung by Presley were his vocalizing in Spanish "Vino, Dinero y Amor" and "Guadalajara."

G

Gang's All Here, The **(1943)** Twentieth Century-Fox, color, 103 minutes. **Director:** Busby Berkeley; **Screenplay:** Walter Bullock; **Cast:** Alice Faye (Eadie Allen), Carmen Miranda (Dorita), Phil Baker (himself), Benny Goodman and His Orchestra (themselves), Eugene Pallette (Andrew J. "A. J." Mason Sr.), Charlotte Greenwood (Blossom Potter), Edward Everett Horton (Peyton Potter), Tony De Marco (himself), James Ellison (Sgt. Phil Casey [Sgt. Andrew J. Mason Jr.]), Sheila Ryan (Vivian Potter).

Brazilian bombshell MIRANDA was at the peak of her popularity when she made this Technicolor musical that set new standards for the juxtaposition of eye-catching hues on screen. The highlight of this extremely popular feature was the elaborate sex-laden number "The Lady in the Tutti Frutti Hat" led by exotic, one-of-a-kind Miranda in a thirty-two-feet-high headdress, decked with bananas, flowers, and fruit. She was accompanied in the routine by a chorus of sixty attractive chorines (dressed as native girls on a South Sea island) who maneuvered to dance steps while carrying overtly phallic huge bananas.

Wrapped around the extravagant musical numbers, which included the climactic "The Polka Dot Polka" filled with exceptional kaleidoscopic visions, was the simple screwball account of upper-class serviceman Sgt. Andrew J. Mason Jr. who has two girlfriends—the wealthy Vivian Potter and the club entertainer Eadie Allen—and how he (and the scripters) resolve his romantic dilemma.

It was long rumored that "The Lady in the Tutti Frutti Hat" number led Brazil to ban the movie from distribution in that country, but there was no evidence this occurred.

Garcia, Andy (1956–) Earnest, intense, and charming, Garcia proved to be one of the more endurable younger stars of the 1990s. He was nominated for an Academy Award for *The Godfather: Part III* (1990) and a decade later received a Golden Globe nomination for his work in the telefeature *For Love or Country: The Arturo Sandoval Story* (2000).

He was born Andrés Arturo García Menéndez in Havana, Cuba. His family moved to Florida in 1961, and as a teenager he began his acting career in regional theater. While still in the Miami area, he was in the PBS-TV series *Qué pasa, U.S.A.* in 1977. After moving to Los Angeles, he appeared in the pilot episode of *HILL STREET BLUES* (1981–87). With memorable screen roles in *8 Million Ways to Die* (1986), *The Untouchables* (1987), and *Black Rain* (1989) Garcia's career ascended. He alternated stark dramas (e.g., *Things to Do in Denver When You're Dead,* 1994) with goofy comedies (e.g., *Just the Ticket,* 1999) or arty entries (e.g., *The Disappearance of Garcia Lorca,* 1997). More recent pictures included *Ocean's Eleven* and *The Man from Elysian Fields* (both 2001), and *Basic* (2002).

Garcia received his star on the Hollywood Walk of Fame in 1995.

Gaucho, The **(1927)** United Artists, b&w and color sequences, 9,358′. **Director:** F. Richard Jones; **Screenplay:** Lotta Woods; **Cast:** Douglas Fairbanks (the Gaucho), Lupe Vélez (the mountain girl), Eve Southern (girl of the shrine), Joan Barclay (girl of the shrine as a child), Gustav von Seyffertitz (Ruiz, the usurper), Nigel de Brulier (the padre), Mary Pickford (Our Lady of the Shrine).

In Argentina, a reckless gaucho leader, on the wrong side of the law, is the sworn enemy of the rebel Ruiz. The cowboy is adored by a mountain girl. The sizzling young woman is overcome with jealousy when her beloved shows an interest in the young lady of the shrine, known as the miracle girl. To spite her love, she tells the authorities where to find him. He, however, escapes and reunites with his followers in time to save the lives of the miracle girl and the helpful padre.

For his gimmick in this swashbuckling feature, nimble Fairbanks made use of the *boleadoras* (or bolas). This whiplike device, made of three leather thongs, is tied together in the form of a Y, with the ends fastened to stone or metal balls about the size of apples. Fairbanks utilized this device with the same agility as he had the whip in *DON Q, SON OF ZORRO* (1925). Fairbanks's wife, movie star Pickford, appeared in the feature briefly as Our Lady of the Shrine.

Filled with escapist entertainment values, *The Gaucho* made no attempt to duplicate the real Argentina of any era but created—at Fairbanks's insistence—a fictionalized representation that meshed with moviegoers' expectations of Argentinean life. As the wild, passionate mountain girl, Mexican-born VÉLEZ made a strong impression on audiences.

***Gay Defender, The* (1927)** Paramount, b&w, 6,376′. **Director:** Gregory La Cava; **Screenplay:** Ray Harris, Sam Mintz, and Kenneth Raisbeck; **Cast:** Richard Dix (Joaquin Murrieta), Thelma Todd (Ruth Ainsworth), Fred Kohler (Jake Hamby), Jerry Mandy (Chombo), Robert Brower (Ferdinand Murrieta), Harry Holden (Padre Sebastian), Fred Esmelton (Commissioner Ainsworth).

In nineteenth-century California, JOAQUÍN MURRIETA, the son of a Spanish land baron, is enamored of Ruth Ainsworth, the offspring of the U.S. Land Commissioner. Meanwhile, Murrieta's servant catches Bart Hamby stealing gold from the Murrietas. Later, Hamby's brother Jake forces Joaquin into dueling with him, but it ends in a dead heat. Now more determined than ever to grab the Murrietas' wealth, Jake murders Commissioner Ainsworth (when he refuses to help defraud Joaquin) and frames Murrieta for the crime. Caught by the law, Joaquin escapes and vows revenge on Hamby, who has burned his hacienda and bled the territory with heavy taxes. Eventually, Murrieta has his showdown with Hamby, whom it is learned, had killed Joaquin's father.

This silent photoplay was one of many features to fictionalize the legendary Murrieta. The trade paper *Variety* (December 28, 1927) was not impressed by Dix's impersonation of the Hispanic Robin Hood: "Dix has sideburns and a mustache, but it's still a tough job for him to look Spanish. He ought to remain on this side of the border."

***Gay Desperado, The* (1936)** United Artists, b&w, 86 minutes. **Director:** Rouben Mamoulian; **Screenplay:** Wallace Smith; **Cast:** Nino Martini (Chivo), Ida Lupino (Jane), Leo Carrillo (Pablo Braganza), Harold Huber (Campo), James Blakeley (Bill), Stanley Fields (Butch), Mischa Auer (Diego), Alan Garcia (police captain), Frank Puglia (Lopez), Chris-Pin Martin (Pancho).

Despite the talents involved, this lighthearted musical comedy, mostly set in Mexico, was hard to accept, even with Metropolitan Opera star Martini's vocalizing and CARRILLO's jovial spoofing of American movie gangsters.

Mexican bandito Pablo Braganza is extremely impressed by Hollywood-made underworld capers. One day while watching a new gangster movie, he insists that his henchmen should act as tough as their screen counterparts. A brawl breaks out in the theater that is quelled by Chivo, a singing employee. The impressed Braganza hires him as a full-time helper. Before long, Braganza has kidnapped a young American couple (Lupino and Blakeley), the man being heir to a fortune. During their captivity, she falls in love with Chivo. She and her boyfriend later escape but are captured by American hoodlum Butch, who returns them to Braganza's stronghold. Eventually, Chivo and his lady love are reunited, while Braganza, having had enough posturing as an American punk, returns to his own underworld style south-of-the-border.

The main attraction of this confection was Carrillo enacting his patented Mexican-bandit routine, this time enhanced by his mimicry of American movie ruffians (e.g., James Cagney and George Raft).

***Gay Señorita, The* (1945)** Columbia, b&w, 69 minutes. **Director:** Arthur Dreifuss; **Screenplay:** Edward Eliscu; **Cast:** Jinx Falkenburg (Elena Sandoval), Jim Bannon (Phil Dolan [Phil Prentiss]), Steve Cochran (Tomas Obrion [Tim O'Brien]), Corinna Mura (herself), Isabelita (Chiquita), Thurston Hall (J. J. Prentiss), Isabel Withers (Kitty), Marguerita Sylva (Dõna Maria Sandoval), Luisita Triana (Loreto), Lola Montes (herself).

Born in Barcelona, Spain, and raised in Chile, this film's star, Falkenburg, became a top U.S. model and an occasional movie personality. Here she was cast as Elena Sandoval, who is spearheading a movement in the Mexican-American section of a West Coast city to save its cultural heritage by having a street devoted to exhibiting its culture and crafts. Her plans are sidetracked by greedy businessman J. J. Prentiss who intends to construct a huge warehouse on the same land. The entrepreneur assigns his nephew Phil to somehow convince Elena to sell the desired property. Eventually, the capitalist capitulates, and Phil and Elena fall in love.

Within this hastily assembled trifle, there was a wealth of Mexican-American talent, a host of ethnic songs (e.g., "Buenas Noches," "Tico-Tico no fuba," and "Cielito lindo"), and an early example on the Hollywood screen of Chicano pride as the neighborhood comes together to preserve their ethnic roots. Although neither Los Angeles nor its Olvera Street was mentioned in the film, the movie reflected an actual movement at the time to preserve that colorful street as a display of Mexican-American culture.

***Giant* (1956)** Warner Bros., color, 201 minutes. **Director:** George Stevens; **Screenplay:** Fred Guiol and Ivan Moffat; **Cast:** Elizabeth Taylor (Leslie Benedict), Rock Hudson (Bick Benedict), James Dean (Jett Rink), Carroll Baker (Luz Benedict II), Jane Withers (Vashti Snythe), Chill Wills

(Uncle Bawley), Mercedes McCambridge (Luz Benedict), Sal Mineo (Angel Obregon III), Dennis Hopper (Jordan Benedict III), Elsa Cardenas (Juana), Victor Millan (Angel Obregon I), Pilar del Rey (Mrs. Obregon).

Edna Ferber's 1952 best-selling novel *Giant* seemed a natural selection for a big-budgeted screen adaptation, but it met with initial resistance within the Hollywood film industry. There was great concern about its commercial possibilities because of its strong take on racial discrimination in its presentation of Mexican-American characters interacting with wealthy Texan bluebloods. The movie was, of course, finally made. Within the course of its hefty running time, *Giant* emerged the first of Hollywood's major motion pictures to address racial bigotry against Mexican Americans, much as a few years earlier, such films as *Pinky* and *Lost Boundaries*—both 1949 releases—depicted the plight of segregated black America.

In the 1920s, millionaire Texas rancher Bick Benedict weds well-bred Leslie Lynnton of Maryland and brings her to live at his sprawling ranch, Reata. Not only must Leslie deal with Bick's possessive older sister Luz, but also she quickly learns that her husband is a chauvinist and is prejudiced against his Mexican-American workers whom he refers to as "those people." Later, Jett Rink, a hot-tempered, crude cowboy at Reata is left a piece of property when Luz dies in a horse-riding accident. The land proves to be oil-rich and is the start of his huge fortune.

As the years pass, the Benedicts' son Jordan III becomes a doctor but upsets his father by wedding a Mexican-American nurse named Juana. The Obregons, one of the families in the Mexican section of town whom Leslie has befriended, lose their son Angel III in World War II. Thereafter, Rink, who has always coveted Leslie, asks her daughter Luz II to marry him, but she declines. At a big celebration to honor the successful Rink as Mr. Texas, the embittered man is drunk and Luz II sees him for the person he really is. Driving home from the banquet where Rink has disgraced himself in a fight with Jordan, Bick and Leslie, along with Luz II, Juana, and the latter's baby stop at a roadside diner. While there, the bigoted owner, who only allowed Juana into the premises because of Benedict, refuses service to an elderly Mexican couple. The angered Benedict brawls with the oversized owner. Although Bick loses the fight, he gains tremendous respect from his family.

In reviewing this saga, *Variety* (October 10, 1956) reported that the film does "not flinch the discrimination angle. *Giant* isn't preachy—although in the end it comes close to it—but instead a powerful indictment of the Texas superiority complex." The trade paper observed, "Not since Darryl F. Zanuck found the courage to make *Pinky* [1949] and *Gentlemen's Agreement* [1947] has the screen spoken out with such a clear voice against group snobbery."

The wildly popular *Giant* grossed more than $12 million in domestic distribution. It received an Academy Award for Best Director. The film was also Oscar nominated for Best Actor (Dean and Hudson), Best Adapted Screenplay, Best Art Direction/Set Decoration (Color), Best Costume Design (Color), Best Film Editing, Best Original Dramatic Score, Best Picture, and Best Supporting Actress (McCambridge).

***Gilda* (1946)** Columbia, b&w, 110 minutes. **Director:** Charles Vidor; **Screenplay:** Marion Parsonnet; **Cast:** Rita Hayworth (Gilda Mundson), Glenn Ford (Johnny Farrell), George Macready (Ballin Mundson), Joseph Calleia (Obregon), Steven Geray (Uncle Pio), Joe Sawyer (Casey), Gerald Mohr (Captain Delgado).

With World War II finished and the U.S. government's hype over the "Good Neighbor Policy" diminishing, Hollywood's on-screen depiction of South America was changing from the continent of lush scenery, exotic women, and captivating music to that mysterious territory where international intrigue and ex-Nazis often lurked. One such example was Alfred Hitchcock's *Notorious* (1946); another that same year was *Gilda*. The latter encapsulated everything that Hollywood scriptwriters felt now should be present in a movie about mystifying Argentina: an exceedingly alluring woman, pulsating and passionate music, deceptions big and small, and men totally twisted by love. If it all sounded like the ingredients of a classic film noir/American gangster tale, it was. Actually, the reason that the story was set in South America was that Hollywood's Production Code Administration deemed the story too lurid to be set in the United States and "requested" that the film's locale be changed to a foreign site.

In Buenos Aires, Argentina, newly arrived gambler Johnny Farrell saves the life of well-to-do Ballin Mundson. The grateful man places Johnny in charge of the casino he owns. Later Mundson weds Gilda, a sultry, immoral woman who, unknown to Mundson, had once broken Farrell's heart. It develops that Mundson is tied to a group of ex-Nazis who demand he return control of a tungsten cartel they allowed him to front when World War II was ending. Several murders ensue. In escaping the authorities, Mundson apparently dies in a plane crash while Farrell and Gilda later wed. To the couple's surprise, Mundson reappears. It remains for Gilda's faithful friend, washroom attendant Uncle Pio to resolve the deadly love–hate triangle.

This was the profitable feature, with its sensual number "Put the Blame on Mame," that made Hayworth an international movie star/sex goddess. Her singing of "Amado Mio" was dubbed by Anita Ellis. When *Gilda* was released in Buenos Aires, the distributor raised the admission price to cinemas, causing riots in that city.

***Girlfight* (2000)** Screen Gems, color, 90 minutes. **Director/Screenplay:** Karyn Kusama; **Cast:** Michelle Rodriguez (Diana), Jaime Tirelli (Hector), Paul Calderon (Sandro), Santiago Douglas (Adrian).

Trading on a new phenomenon—women boxers—this much-discussed but little-seen (it grossed only $1.5 million in domestic distribution) film concerned an eighteen-year-old Brooklyn high-school student at the end of her rope who soon channels her many life's frustrations into the boxing ring, where she is trained by Hector. Before long, she is attracted to another boxer (Douglas) and is forced to balance her detachment in life and her toughness (heightened by her sports workout) with her growing affection for this featherweight fighter.

Both the star and the director of this gritty, thoughtful film were nominated and/or won festival prizes around the world. At the 2001 ALMA Awards, the movie received two nominations: Outstanding Feature Film and Outstanding Latino Cast in a Feature Film. With its depiction of ethnic minority life as well as the added complexity of a woman involved in a man's sport, this entry makes an intriguing companion piece to *PRICE OF GLORY* (2000), about a Latino boxing family in Los Angeles.

***Girl from Mexico, The* (1939)** RKO, b&w, 71 minutes. **Director:** Leslie Goodwins; **Screenplay:** Lionel Houser and Joseph A. Fields; **Cast:** Lupe Vélez (Carmelita Fuentes), Donald Woods (Dennis Lindsey), Leon Errol (Uncle Matt), Linda Hayes (Elizabeth Price), Donald MacBride (Renner), Edward Raquello (Tony Romano), Elisabeth Risdon (Aunt Delia).

This zany entry that launched the profitable MEXICAN SPITFIRE film series was intended originally as a one-shot, modest production. It was aimed at returning peppery movie star VÉLEZ to the Hollywood screen after many months away from the industry. It was a celluloid role tailor made for the volatile Vélez, a petite bundle of hyperenergy with a broad comedy talent and an appealing dose of exotica (especially her heavy foreign accent).

Advertising executive Dennis Lindsey hastens to Mexico to hire a vocalist for a client's radio program. He encounters spicy Carmelita, and after several skirmishes, she signs a contract with Lindsey to please her family. Having posted a $10,000 bond guaranteeing her employment and proper moral behavior while in the United States, she comes north-of-the-border. Once in New York, Carmelita stays with Lindsey and his Aunt Delia and Uncle Matt. She soon decides that she wants Lindsey as her boyfriend and does her best to sabotage his relationship with his fiancée, Elizabeth Price. She uses a Mexican wrestler to make Lindsey jealous, and after many misunderstandings and clarifications, Carmelita and Lindsey marry.

Both moviegoers and critics approved of Vélez and rubber-legged comedian Errol in this mindless entertainment. Its box-office success prompted RKO to feature the Mexican firecracker and veteran Errol in seven additional screen adventures of the zany Carmelita and Uncle Matt. This series revitalized Vélez's sagging movie career.

***Girl of the Rio* (1932)** RKO, b&w, 70 minutes. **Director:** Herbert Brenon; **Screenplay:** Elizabeth Meehan and uncredited Louis Stevens; **Cast:** Dolores Del Rio (Dolores), Leo Carrillo (Don José Maria Lopez Y Tostado), Norman Foster (Johnny Powell), Stanley Fields (Mike Marovich), Frank Campeau (Bill).

Once again CARRILLO, stuck in a formulaic assignment, performed on cue as the best (and most heavily accented) caballero in all of Mexico—a boast that took his character the entire picture to prove—and allowed the production to showcase the beautiful DEL RIO.

In Mexicana, Mexico, Don José Maria Lopez Y Tostado is attracted to comely café singer Dolores. She rebuffs him, claiming to have a gun-toting boyfriend. Unfazed, Don José hosts a party in her honor at the café. Meanwhile she meets and instantly falls in love with Johnny Powell, a croupier at a nearby gambling club. They choose to marry, but Don José, learning of the plan has the man jailed on a phony charge. To save his life, Dolores agrees to spend the night with Don José at his hacienda. En route, Dolores attempts suicide but is unsuccessful. Having escaped custody, Powell pleads his love of Dolores to Don José. In a turnabout, the latter sends them on their way, insisting that his good deed proves what a great caballero he really is.

Based on Willard Mack's Broadway play *The Dove* (1925), the property had been filmed as *The Dove* (1927), a silent photoplay starring Norma Talmadge and Noah Beery, using a European setting. The property was remade again in 1939 as the low-budget *The Girl and the Gambler*, with Carrillo repeating his role, opposite Steffi Duna.

***Gloria* (1980)** Columbia, color, 123 minutes. **Director/Screenplay:** John Cassavetes; **Cast:** Gena Rowlands (Gloria Swenson), Juan Adames (Philip Dawn), Buck Henry (Jack Dawn), Julie Carmen (Jeri Dawn), Lupe Guarnica (Margarita Vargas), Jessica Castillo (Joan Dawn).

One of filmmaker Cassavetes's best productions, this was a fine showcase for his actress-wife Rowlands and for screen newcomer Adames, the New York-born offspring of parents from the Dominican Republic.

Gloria Swenson is a forty year old who has earned a tidy income being a prostitute for Mafia bigwigs. Her next-door neighbor, Jack Dawn, an accountant for mobsters, is planning to turn over his diary (detailing illegal transactions he processed over the years) to federal authorities. He fears mob reprisals and asks his neighbor, Gloria, to take care of his and his Puerto Rican wife's (Carmen) children, Philip and Joan. The older child insists on remaining with her parents, while Philip is taken to Gloria's apartment. Soon thereafter, the mob slaughters the Dawns, putting Gloria (with the diary and a gun) and the boy on the lam. Between her tough-as-nails demeanor and his street-smart, wise-mouth behavior, they make an odd couple. At one point, Gloria shoots it out with a car full of hit men and successfully dispatches them. Later, she visits an old customer/friend, but the don refuses to help her. Gloria and the boy, who have developed a rapport, continue on the run.

Rowlands received an Oscar nomination as Best Actress for her performance. The movie was remade by director Sidney Lumet in 1999 with Sharon Stone starred. The new edition was both an artistic and commercial failure.

***Golden Stallion, The* (1949)** Republic, color, 67 minutes. **Director:** William Witney; **Screenplay:** Sloan Nibley; **Cast:** Roy Rogers and Trigger (themselves), Dale Evans

(Stormy Billings), Estelita Rodriguez (Pepita "Pepi" Valdez), Pat Brady (Sparrow Biffle), Douglas Evans (Jeff Middleton), Foy Willing and the Riders of the Purple Sage (specialty performers).

A favorite setting for westerns of Rogers (e.g., *Sunset in the West*, 1950), Gene Autry (e.g., *Mexicali Rose*, 1939), and William "Hopalong Cassidy" Boyd (e.g., *In Old Mexico*, 1938) was the border region between Mexico and America. It allowed for plot lines involving smuggling, banditos from across the border, pretty señoritas, quaint haciendas, and the chance for someone to croon a Spanish tune or two. Republic Pictures, a prime maker of westerns, was especially fond of the format/setting and had under contract Cuban-born Rodriguez to add a pleasant note of "authenticity" for these south-of-the-border entries. In *The Golden Stallion* she provided the Hispanic flavoring.

Jeff Middleton heads a gang in Oro City on the Mexican-American border. They smuggle diamonds into the United States from Mexico by secreting the gems in the fake hoof of a wild horse. Rancher Rogers becomes innocently involved in their criminal activities, and when Trigger is blamed for the fatal hoof blow to one of Middleton's henchmen, Rogers goes to jail. He is eventually released, proves his innocence, and recaptures the "smartest horse in the movies," who has gone wild and sired a colt with a bell mare. Rogers calls the offspring Trigger Jr.

In *The Golden Stallion*, Rodriguez played Pepi, the spirited friend of Stormy Billings who owns the Circle B Ranch and who is a pal of Rogers. The musical interludes in this compact feature included "Down Mexico Way."

Gomez, Thomas (1905–1971) The rotund character with hunched shoulders and big, expressive eyes proved himself the epitome of versatility during Hollywood's Golden Age and for several years thereafter. (One of his specialties was playing the crafty villain.) His paternal grandfather was from Santander, Spain. His paternal grandmother came from Gibraltar. He was born Sabina Thomas Gomez in New York City. Following high school, he worked, for several years, for the husband/wife acting team of Alfred Lunt and Lynn Fontanne and gained a reputation as a reliable performer on Broadway. He signed a contract with Universal Pictures in 1942 where he became a utility featured player (e.g., *Who Done It?* 1942; *Phantom Lady*, 1944; *A Night in Paradise*, 1946). He earned an Academy Award nomination for his performance in *RIDE THE PINK HORSE* (1947) as the drunk Mexican peasant. Once Gomez became a freelance film actor, his roles grew even meatier: *Key Largo* (1948), *The Furies* (1950), *The Magnificent Matador* (1955). He continued acting in film and TV until near his death: *STAY AWAY, JOE* (1968) and *Beneath the Planet of the Apes* (1970).

***Green Mansions* (1959)** Metro-Goldwyn-Mayer, color, 104 minutes. **Director:** Mel Ferrer; **Screenplay:** Dorothy Kingsley; **Cast:** Audrey Hepburn (Rima), Anthony Perkins (Abel), Lee J. Cobb (Nuflo), Sessue Hayakawa (Runi), Henry Silva (Kua-Ko), Nehemiah Persoff, (Don Panta), Michael Pate (priest).

William Henry Hudson's well-known novel *Green Mansions* (1904), a fantasy about a mystical and delicate girl-child of the South American forest, had long appealed to Hollywood. In 1932, RKO purchased the screen rights as a potential vehicle for Mexican-born DOLORES DEL RIO, but the film was never made. Years later, in 1953, MGM acquired the rights to the book, thinking to star Italian Pier Angeli in the property with Vincente Minnelli directing. Finally, with Ferrer directing his Belgian-born wife, Hepburn, the project got underway in 1958 with the filmmaker and his crew scouting through Venezuela, British Guiana (renamed now as Belize), and Colombia shooting outdoor background footage. In Brazil, famed composer Heitor Villa-Lobos was contracted to write special music for *Green Mansions*, his debut as a film composer.

Within the plot, Abel, a Venezuelan flees a revolution by escaping into the wilds in search of gold. Instead he comes across Rima, the bird girl who communes with nature. He is entranced with her but loses her when superstitious local Indians destroy her in a fire because they believe that she possesses an evil spirit. Later, the distraught Abel sees, so he thinks, the image of Rima through the mist, beckoning to him.

With its rarified premise, awkward casting, and slow plot development, *Green Mansions* was a box-office failure.

***Guadalcanal Diary* (1943)** Twentieth Century-Fox, 1943, b&w, 90 minutes. **Director:** Lewis Seiller; **Screenplay:** Lamar Trotti; **Cast:** Preston Foster (Father Donnelly), Lloyd Nolan (Sgt. Hook Malone), William Bendix (Cpl. Aloysius "Taxi" Potts), Richard Conte (Captain Davis), Anthony Quinn (Jesus "Soose" Alvarez), Richard Jaeckel (Pvt. Johnny "Chicken" Anderson), Roy Roberts (Capt. Jim Cross), Minor Watson (Colonel Grayson).

The well-received *Guadalcanal Diary* (1943) was Richard Tregaskis's firsthand account of the hell endured by U.S. Marines during World War II, in particular, their daily struggle against Japanese forces on Guadalcanal in the Solomon Islands in the South Pacific. As production began for this screen adaptation, it was suggested to Twentieth Century-Fox, according to an August 1943 studio press release, "that it would help the popularity of the United States in Latin American countries if Hollywood would curtail the practices of putting Latins in 'heavy' roles. Furthermore, [Anthony] Quinn greatly resembles Sgt. Frank Few, an Arizona Indian who was one of the great Guadalcanal heroes." Thus, Mexican-born QUINN, already a veteran of many movies and including several Native American roles, was cast as the fictional Jesus "Soose" Alvarez. It was an important step in the slow integration of Hispanic characters into the mainstream of Hollywood-made movies.

In mid-1942, a large contingent of U.S. Marines are transported to Guadalcanal where they land on August 7. Among them are Colonel Grayson, Capt. Jim Cross, Captain Davis, Sgt. Hook Malone, Cpl. "Taxi" Potts, Alvarez, Father Donnelly, and the very young Pvt. Johnny Anderson (named "Chicken" because of his inexperience). During one of the patrols on the island, the men are attacked by Japanese snipers. Only Soose survives the ordeal, returning to the base and joining with the others as they attack the enemy at a nearby village. By November 1942, as more reinforcements and supplies arrive, a major offensive is launched against the Japanese. During the assault, Soose is killed, while Chicken kills several of the attackers. By December 10, 1942, as the weary marines depart camp, their army replacements take over.

***Guns for San Sebastian* (1968)** Metro-Goldwyn-Mayer, color, 111 minutes. **Director:** Henri Verneuil; **Screenplay:** James R. Webb; **Cast:** Anthony Quinn (León Alastray), Anjanette Comer (Kinita), Charles Bronson (Teclo), Sam Jaffe (Father Joseph), Silvia Pinal (Felicia), Jorge Martinez de Hoyos (Cayetano), Jamie Fernández (Golden Lance).

An international coproduction between the United States, France, Italy, and Mexico, the film had separate scripts written for the English-, French-, Italian-, and Spanish-language versions, which were dubbed accordingly into the completed prints. Based on William Barby Faherty's book, *A Wall for San Sebastian* (1962), it was shot in Mexico (Durango and Mexico City) in 1967.

QUINN provided the project's energy in his portrayal of the mid-eighteenth-century Mexican bandit/patriot León Alastray who takes refuge with an old Franciscan priest, Father Joseph. Disguised in a friar's robes, he accompanies the old man to the remote village of San Sebastian, which they find deserted following an attack by Yaqui warriors. After Father Joseph dies and the villagers return, they mistake Alastray for a priest. While Teclo, a Yaqui half-breed, pressures the locals to abandon their faith or die, Kinita, who knows Alastray's background, convinces her fellow villagers not to hang their new man of God. Alastray guides the peasants in building a dam and wangles guns and ammunition from the wife of the governor whom he once knew. The Yaqui eventually attack. Alastray kills Teclo, and the villagers help Alastray and Kinita escape when government troops arrive with a new priest for San Sebastian.

H

***Hangin' with the Homeboys* (1991)** New Line Cinema, color, 88 minutes. **Director/Screenplay:** Joseph P. Vasquez; **Cast:** Doug E. Doug (Willie), Mario Joyner (Tom), John Leguizamo (Johnny), Nestor Serrano (Vinny), Kimberly Russell (Vanessa), Mary B. Ward (Luna), Reggie Montgomery (Rasta).

Unlike so many American ethnic minority films of the period, *Hangin' with the Homeboys* avoids the stereotypes of depicting only drug dealers and gang members. Rather, it is an astute, honest character study of four young South Bronx friends—African-American Willie and Tom and Puerto Ricans Johnny and Nestor—who spend a night out on the town (mostly in the ghetto above 125th Street). Written and directed by resourceful filmmaker Vasquez (1962–95), the film gains stature in retrospect, especially LEGUIZAMO's resourceful performance.

The quartet consists of would-be actor Tom who sells magazine subscriptions for a living, Willie who won't work and who blames everything bad on supposed prejudice against his racial heritage, goof-off Vinny who pretends to be both Italian and a stud with the ladies, and supermarket worker Johnny who wants to attend college but is scared to fill out the application. On their Friday out, the four reveal their differing points of view on life and each other as they crash a party, smash up Tom's car, visit a porno peep show, encounter Tom's girl who is cheating on him, play pool with a bunch of yuppies, and end up at a hip downtown club. In the midst of the night they encounter racist cops and also have a spontaneous moment on a subway where they pretend to be battling one another to get a reaction from other passengers.

By the end of their excursion, Johnny plans to risk filling out his college application, and there is an indication that Willie has glimpsed his dead-end future and may change his priorities.

Made for almost $2 million, the resourceful but nonviolent *Hangin' with the Homeboys* grossed only $532,933 in domestic distribution, a victim of its uniqueness in a genre typically filled with explicit, violent gang action.

***Harry-O* (1974–1976)** ABC-TV series, color, 60 minutes. **Cast:** David Janssen (Harry Orwell), Henry Darrow (Det. Lt. Manuel "Manny" Quinlan: 1974–75), Anthony Zerbe (Lt. K. C. Trench: 1975–76), Paul Tulley (Sgt. Don Roberts: 1975–76), Keye Luke (Dr. Fong: 1976).

One of several TV series outings for Janssen, this time he was on hand as an unorthodox private detective who lived near San Diego in a beachfront abode. He often took the bus because his car was frequently broken. In solving his capers, Orwell sometimes worked with or against Det. Lt. Manuel Quinlan of the San Diego Police Department. This Hispanic-American character died in a February 1975 episode, which led to Orwell relocating to Santa Monica, California, permitting a change in the show's format.

This was a fairly early example of a Hispanic character having a major role on an American TV series. The part was played by New York City-born Darrow (né Henry Thomas Delgado).

Hayek, Salma (1966–) The petite (five-feet, two inch) Hayek became one of Hollywood's more intriguing imports of the 1990s, playing a variety of parts that frequently did not stress her ethnic background.

Born Salma Hayek-Jiménez in Coatzacoalcos, Veracruz, Mexico, her father was Lebanese and her mother Mexican. She began her acting career in children's theater and moved to series work on Mexican TV, including the soap opera *Un nuevo amanecer* (1988). By the early 1990s, she had relocated to Los Angeles where she had a featured role in 1993 on the TV sitcom *The Sinbad Show*. She played Gata in the feature *MI VIDA LOCA* (1994), followed by parts in several works by director ROBERT RODRIGUEZ (e.g., *Roadracers*, 1994—TV movie; *Desperado*, 1995). She went from the romantic comedy *Fools Rush In* (1997) to playing Esmeralda in a TV production that year of *The Hunchback* (of Notre Dame). She was Rita Escobar in *Wild Wild West* (1999) and played Rose in the experimental *Timecode* (2000). Later came *In the Time of the Butterflies* (2001) and *Death to Smoochy* (2001). In Rodriguez's *Once Upon a Time in Mexico* (2003), she repeated her characterization of Carolina.

***Head of the Class* (1986–1991)** ABC-TV series, color, 30 minutes. **Cast:** Howard Hesseman (Charlie Moore: 1986–90), Billy Connolly (Billy MacGregor: 1990–91), William G. Schilling (Dr. Harold Samuels), Leslie Bega (Maria Borges: 1986–89), Michael DeLorenzo (Alex Torres: 1989–91).

For a change, a school-set TV sitcom was dealing with bright students, albeit ones wise in academics, but not in the ways of life. In New York City, substitute teacher Charlie Moore does his best for his academically sharp pupils at Manhattan High School (later Fillmore High). Among the ethnically diverse students he instructs are Hispanic-Americans Maria Borges and Alex Torres. High-achieving Maria abhors the thought of receiving any grade below an A, but she is also blessed with great compassion for others. After three years at the school, she leaves to attend the local High School for the Performing Arts to pursue her singing career.

***High Chaparral, The* (1967–1971)** NBC-TV series, color, 60 minutes. **Cast:** Leif Erickson (Big John Cannon), Cameron Mitchell (Buck Cannon), Henry Darrow (Manolito Montoya), Linda Cristal (Victoria Cannon), Frank Silvera (Don Sebastian Montoya: 1967–70), Roberto Contreras (Pedro: 1967–70), Rudy Ramos (Wind: 1970–71).

Frequently in the history of TV series, ethnic integration occurred first in westerns and science-fiction genre entries because, being set in noncontemporary eras, they were *not* "threatening" to viewers who were racially sensitive. One of the prime examples of Hispanic-Anglo integration occurred on this sagebrush series set in Tucson, in the Arizona Territory of the 1870s.

Rancher Big John Cannon weds Victoria Montoya, the daughter of Don Sebastian who, like Cannon, has huge cattle holdings. The merging of the two clans leads to expected culture clashes, but it also exposed TV watchers to two contrasting families coping with the other's different ethnic roots. (However, all was not totally ethnically harmonious, for the common enemy here—besides rustlers—is the marauding Native Americans, one of whom had killed Big John's first wife.)

When program regular Silvera died (accidentally electrocuted) in 1970, GILBERT ROLAND was introduced on *High Chaparral* as Don Sebastian's brother. Other Hispanic characters on the show included Contreras as ranch hand Pedro and Ramos as a half-breed who was made a member of the Cannon household for his many accomplishments.

***High Noon* (1952)** United Artists, b&w, 84 minutes. **Director:** Fred Zinnemann; **Screenplay:** Carl Foreman; **Cast:** Gary Cooper (Will Kane), Thomas Mitchell (Jonas Henderson), Lloyd Bridges (Harvey Pell), Katy Jurado (Helen Ramirez), Grace Kelly (Amy Fowler Kane), Otto Kruger (Judge Percy Mettrick), Lon Chaney (Martin Howe), Henry Morgan (Sam Fuller), Ian MacDonald (Frank Miller), Lee Van Cleef (Jack Colby).

Reportedly based on scenarist Foreman's disgust with being blacklisted during the Communist witch-hunt period in the late 1940s and early 1950s, *High Noon* emerged as one of Hollywood's most memorable westerns. This landmark production, based on John W. Cunningham's short story "The Tin Star" (1947), gained fame for its gripping real-time drama, its gunslinging showdown, and the picture's exceedingly popular title tune sung on the soundtrack by cowboy star Tex Ritter. This was also the first Hollywood-made feature for Mexican screen actress JURADO, who had appeared the year before in the Mexican-shot *BULLFIGHTER AND THE LADY* (1951). For her role as the smoldering Helen Ramirez, Jurado, who had to learn her English-language lines phonetically for the picture, received the Golden Globe and New York Film Critics' Award for Best Supporting Actress.

In the western town of Hadleyville in 1870, veteran marshal Will Kane marries attractive young Quaker, Amy Fowler, and, to please her, resigns his dangerous post. News spreads through town that outlaw Frank Miller has just been released from prison and is due on the noon train. Already three of his confederates (Van Cleef, Wilke, and Wooley) have arrived in Hadleyville. To his amazement, Kane, who is apprehensive about having to face down the man he arrested for murder years ago, finds that everyone in town has an excuse for not coming to his assistance. Even Miller's former girlfriend, Helen Ramirez, a local businesswoman, who had once been involved with Kane, is leaving on the noon train. In the long run, it is only the marshal's pacifist bride who comes to his aid. With matters resolved, the disillusioned Kane tosses his lawman's badge in the street dust and resolutely leaves town with his wife.

One of the film's most effective sequences occurred when the patrician blonde bride Amy visits the earthy, smoldering dark-haired Helen and they size up one another. In short order, Ramirez convinces the younger woman that she has nothing to fear from her, and the two develop an immediate bond—both concerned for Kane's safety.

High Noon won Academy Awards for Best Actor (Cooper), Best Film Editing, Best Original Dramatic Score, and Best Song ("Do Not Forsake Me, Oh My Darlin'"). It also received Oscar nominations for Best Director, Best Picture, and Best Screenplay. A TV movie sequel (*High Noon: Part 2: The Return of Will Kane*, 1980) starring Lee Majors, did not include the Helen Ramirez character. A 2000 made-for-cable remake of *High Noon* featuring Tom Skerritt as Will Kane and Suzanna Thompson as his bride, presented MARIA CONCHITA ALONSO as Helen Ramirez. The new version suffered greatly in comparison to the Cooper original.

Hill Street Blues **(1981–1987)** NBC-TV series, color, 60 minutes. **Cast:** Daniel J. Travanti (Capt. Frank Furillo), Michael Conrad (Sgt. Phil Esterhaus: 1981–84), Michael Warren (Off. Bobby Hill), Charles Haid (Off. Andy Renko), Veronica Hamel (Joyce Davenport), Bruce Weitz (Det. Mike Belker), René Enríquez (Lt. Ray Calletano), Trinidad Silva (Jesus Martinez).

Set in a major, unnamed Eastern city, this acclaimed, Emmy Award-winning drama revolved around the daily routine, dangers, and human interest aspects of a police officer's life. In the large lineup of characters there was Lt. Ray Calletano, of Colombian heritage. In a remarkably strong episode in 1982, Calletano was named Hispanic of the Year by the department. At the awards banquet, he is identified as a Puerto Rican and then asked to dine on Mexican food; the usually reserved man berates the guests with the observation that the only Hispanics in the room besides himself are waiters and busboys.

Another Hispanic character on the show was Jesus Martinez who started out as a ghetto gang member but by the end of the series had turned his life around and become a social worker and a lawyer.

Just like the TV police comedy BARNEY MILLER (1975–82), *Hill Street Blues* presented, to a degree, a diverse ethnic mix, which helped to give racial minorities some visibility on the screen. On the down side, *Hill Street Blues* often characterized Hispanic characters in the weekly installments as gang members or powerless victims of crime.

Hold Back the Dawn **(1941)** Paramount, b&w, 116 minutes. **Director:** Mitchell Leisen; **Screenplay:** Charles Brackett and Billy Wilder; **Cast:** Charles Boyer (George Iscovescu), Olivia de Havilland (Emmy Brown), Paulette Goddard (Anita Dixon), Victor Francen (Van Den Luecken), Walter Abel (Inspector Hammock), Curt Bois (Bonbois), Rosemary DeCamp (Berta Kurz), Eric Feldary (Josef Kurz), Nestor Paiva (Flores), Eva Puig (Lupita), Mitchell Leisen (Mr. Saxon).

This highly romanticized drama concerned the quickie marriages that often occurred in border towns between Mexico and the United States as individuals who had fled Europe during World War II hoped to bypass a potentially long quota/waiting period to enter America. With few exceptions, most of the scenes for this popular picture were shot on the studio home lot, including the street used to resemble a Mexican border town.

Romanian émigré George Iscovescu slips onto the Paramount Studio lot in Hollywood where he tells filmmaker Mr. Saxon the bizarre account of his previous year, hoping to get a much-needed $500 for the rights to his unusual story. He recalls how he first arrived in Mexico and at a cheap local hotel encountered his former girlfriend/dance partner Anita Dixon. She tells him that it could take years to gain legal entrance into the United States. She suggests that he follow her alternative—marry and then divorce an American. The charming Iscovescu promptly meets naïve young schoolteacher Emmy Brown. They wed and only belatedly does she learn of his con game. Driving away in disgust, she is involved in an auto accident and is in critical condition at a California hospital. Iscovescu who has come to love her, sneaks across the border and visits her. Having given her the will to live, he makes his way to the movie studio where he wheedles time with film director Saxon.

Hold Back the Dawn was nominated for several Academy Awards: Best Actress (de Havilland), Best Art Direction/Set Decoration (Black and White), Best Cinematography (Black and White), Best Picture, Best Scoring of a Dramatic Picture, and Best Screenplay.

Holiday in Mexico **(1946)** Metro-Goldwyn-Mayer, color, 127 minutes. **Director:** George Sidney; **Screenplay:** Isobel Lennart; **Cast:** Walter Pidgeon (Jeffrey Evans), José Iturbi (himself), Roddy McDowall (Stanley Owen), Ilona Massey (Toni Karpathy), Xavier Cugat (himself), Jane Powell (Christine Evans), Hugo Haas (Angus), Mikhail Rasumny (Baranga), Helen Stanley (Yvette Baranga), Amparo Iturbi (herself).

This lavish Technicolor confection was as full of diverse musical talent as it was of global accents: Canada (Pidgeon), Spain/Cuba (Cugat), Czechoslovakia (Haas), England (McDowall), Hungary (Massey), Spain (Iturbi), and the United States (Powell). It was all filmed on the studio's sound stages and led the Production Code Administration to alert its producer Joe Pasternak that the production failed to present Mexicans as more than "underlings and servants," requesting that MGM find a way to "get into your picture some nice Mexicans." Reportedly, this led Pasternak to revamp a sequence so that ingénue Powell danced (briefly) with a Mexican youth rather than the originally planned French teenager.

Fifteen-year-old Christine Evans believes herself now an adult and wants to help her widowed father, the U.S. ambassador to Mexico. As the meddlesome miss takes charge of a forthcoming garden party, she tries to persuade classical pianist Iturbi, orchestra leader Cugat, and the latter's singer, Toni Karpathy, to appear at the diplomatic function. However, she causes turmoil as several people come to confuse their romantic relationships to others. All's well that ends well, and the party is a success.

Among the diverse numbers sung, played by Iturbi and his concert pianist sister or conducted by orchestra leader Iturbi, was "Yo Te Amo Much—And That's That."

Hombres armadas See *MEN WITH GUNS*.

***Honeyboy* (1982)** NBC-TV, color, 100 minutes. **Director:** John Berry; **Teleplay:** Berry and Lee Gold; **Cast:** Erik Estrada (Rico "Honeyboy" Ramirez), Morgan Fairchild (Judy Wellman), James McEachin (Nate Walker), Robert Costanzo (Tiger's trainer), Yvonne Wilder (Hortensia Ramirez), Jem Echollas (Tiger Maddox).

Following the example of *Golden Boy* (1939), this lightweight drama featured Estrada in his *CHIPS* (1977–83) heyday as the handsome sex symbol. Here he is the tough product of Spanish Harlem who allows fame and the attraction for his Anglo publicist (Fairchild) to go to his head. His conceit is deflated when he learns that one of his biggest fights in the ring had been fixed.

Even though the lead character suffered from an overinflated ego, it was refreshing to have the focal figure of a Hollywood production be a non–Anglo-Saxon ethnic type.

***House of Buggin'* (1995)** Fox-TV series, color, 30 minutes. **Cast:** John Leguizamo, Jorge Luis Abreu, Tammi Cubilette, Yelba Osorio, David Herman, and Luis Guzman (regulars).

This madcap comedy variety series showcased Hispanic sensibilities and revolved around the humorous antics of Colombian-born, New York-raised LEGUIZAMO. With his ensemble of regulars, he created a four-month forum for zany humor from the Latino perspective. Interestingly, he often portrayed other ethnic types including an Asian talk-show host; he also appeared in drag. The show received an Emmy Award nomination for Outstanding Individual Achievement in Choreography. One of those who performed on the show was ROSIE PEREZ.

***House of the Spirits, The* (1993)** Miramax, color, 132 minutes. **Director/Screenplay:** Bille August; **Cast:** Jeremy Irons (Esteban Trueba), Meryl Streep (Clara Del Valle Trueba), Glenn Close (Ferula), Winona Ryder (Blanca), Antonio Banderas (Pedro), Vincent Gallo (Esteban Garcia), Vanessa Redgrave (Nivea), Maria Conchita Alonso (Transito), Teri Polo (Rosa), Miriam Colon (nun).

Isabel Allende's best-selling novel *La casa de los espíritus* was translated into English in 1985 and became a success again. From the time that casting was announced for this international film coproduction, there was a large outcry about the choosing of so many Anglos to play the key roles of the Chileans, while Latin-American talent was shunted, at best, to small parts. When the resultant movie was released, it received extremely poor notices, not only for the directorial vision presented (i.e., a serious approach to romantic soap opera in which women were the key driving force) but also for the way in which (in particular) Irons, Streep, and Close mangled their characterizations in accents and mannerisms that were anything but Chilean. Filmed in Copenhagen, the feature earned slightly more than a paltry $6 million in American distribution. Originally released in Europe at 145 minutes, it was cut down to 132 minutes for U.S. theatrical release and then to 109 minutes for home-video distribution.

The House of the Spirits follows the Trueba family in Chile from 1926 to 1971. Esteban weds Clara after her older sibling dies. The union causes problems with the dour Ferula, Esteban's possessive spinster sister, who has a physical yen for Clara, a woman with mystical powers. Later, Clara has a child, Blanca, while Esteban is contending with an illegitimate son, Esteban Garcia, whose peasant mother had been raped by Trueba. When Blanca grows up, she has a romantic relationship with Pedro, who works on her father's ranch and is fomenting a revolt among the migrant workers. When thrown out of the family estate for sleeping with Clara, Ferula dies, and her spirit comes back to haunt the house. As for Pedro, when Trueba exiles him from the estate, he still finds a way to carry on his affair with Blanca. The power-hungry Trueba has, by now, risen to political power, but in the right-wing military coup of 1971, Blanca is nearly a victim of the regime's crackdown. In the chaos of his life, Trueba turns to his mistress (now a bordello madam) Transito for help. At the finale, Trueba realizes how empty so much of his life has been, and he dies not long after seeing the late Clara in a vision.

***Human Cargo* (1936)** Twentieth Century-Fox, b&w, 66 minutes. **Director:** Allan Dwan; **Screenplay:** Jefferson Parker and Doris Malloy; **Cast:** Claire Trevor (Bonnie Brewster), Brian Donlevy (Patrick "Packy" Campbell), Alan Dinehart (Lionel "Bulldog" Crocker), Ralph Morgan (D.A. Joe Carey), Helen Troy (Susie), Rita Cansino [Hayworth] (Carmen Zoro), Ralf Harolde (Tony Sculla).

This efficient programmer details the smuggling of illegal aliens into the United States and the subsequent blackmailing of such trespassers. Structured as a newspaper/crime caper, it features veteran reporter Patrick "Packy" Campbell (Donlevy) who investigates the smuggling racket and is forced to work with—and then be in competition with—the daughter (Trevor) of one of the paper's principal advertisers. One of their prime witnesses, Latin dancer Carmen Zoro, works at the 500 Club; unfortunately, before she can tell tales on the operation, she is shot by gangster Tony Sculla. (Cansino, on the verge of becoming Rita Hayworth, was featured in a dancing sequence and then has dramatic moments as the Mexican performer being blackmailed.)

With its compactness, *Human Cargo* told its tale far more effectively than such protracted later entries about smuggling foreigners into the United States as *Illegal Entry* (1949) featuring Howard Duff, Marta Toren, and George Brent.

I

***I Like It Like That* (1994)** Columbia, color, 101 minutes. **Director/Screenplay:** Darnell Martin; **Cast:** Lauren Vélez (Lisette Linares), Jon Seda (Chino Linares), Tomas Melly (L'il Chino Linares), Desiree Cassado (Minnie Linares), Isaiah Garcia (Pee Wee Linares), Jesse Borrega (Alexis), Lisa Vidal (Magdalena Soto), Griffin Dunne (Stephen Price), Rita Moreno (Rosaria Linares).

This refreshing and vibrant study of inner-city life among young Puerto Ricans was smoothly directed by Martin. With her ethnic minority background, she provided a picture of ghetto life with a woman's perspective, an overriding tone of humor, and, best of all, a sense of naturalness.

When Chino Linares is sent to jail for looting a store, his wife Lisette, who wants to make something of her life on 167th Street in the Bronx, travels to midtown Manhattan and find works with smug record producer Stephen Price. Their work relationship makes her uptown neighbors think she is having an affair with him (which she later does). The same assumption leads Chino, once released from jail, to take up with Magdalena Soto. Eventually, Lisette breaks off with Price but is not so quick to forgive her husband.

Shot in the Bronx, Manhattan, Brooklyn, and Coney Island, *I Like It Like That* grossed almost $2 million in domestic distribution.

***I Love Lucy* (1951–1957)** CBS-TV series, b&w, 30 minutes **Cast:** Lucille Ball (Lucy Ricardo), Desi Arnaz (Ricky Ricardo), Vivian Vance (Ethel Mertz), William Frawley (Fred Mertz), Richard Keith (Little Ricky Ricardo: 1956–57).

I Love Lucy was the classic of all classic TV sitcoms. This pioneering comedy did a great deal not only to expose American television viewers to Cuban-born ARNAZ (both as a comedic and musical performer) but also to demonstrate to audiences that a mixed-culture marriage was much like any other marital union. As depicted humorously over the show's run, the Ricardos—one Cuban, one Anglo—had their share of joys, disappointments, compromises, and sentimentality.

While the character of Ricky Ricardo was a humorous exaggeration (that sometimes bordered on pure stereotype) of a hot-blooded Hispanic character—complete with the heavy accent that others sometimes had difficulty understanding—Arnaz's alter ego brought Cuban/Hispanic culture to the attention of mainstream America. Sometimes, it was reflected in the music at the Tropicana Club where Ricardo worked, by the Cuban relatives and friends who showed up on the series over the years, or in Ricky's efforts to adjust to and become a success in America. As such, *I Love Lucy* did much to accelerate the trend of integrating ethnics within the American media.

Although most TV viewers tended initially to think of *I Love Lucy* as a purely Ball vehicle, Arnaz made tremendous contributions to the show's success both in front of and behind the cameras.

impersonations—non-Hispanic actors playing Hispanic roles In silent films, it was relatively easy for non-Latin performers to use makeup and costuming to transform themselves into Hispanic characters (e.g., Douglas Fairbanks Sr. in *THE MARK OF ZORRO*, 1920; Richard Dix, *The Gay Defender*, 1927). However, when talkie pictures started, performers had to adopt a proper accent to go along with their Latino characterizations. In the Hollywood sound cinema, for every solid performance of a Caucasian as a Hispanic (e.g., Paul Muni in *BORDERTOWN*, 1935, and *JUAREZ*, 1939; Jennifer Jones in *WE WERE STRANGERS*, 1949; Marlon

Brando in *VIVA ZAPATA!*, 1952), there were a multitude of failed performances in this category. Sometimes, the misguided actor was done in by vocal inflection, other times, it was too American a manner or a mix of everything about his/her presentation of a figure of another culture. These flawed interpretations included Warner Baxter (*IN OLD ARIZONA*, 1929, and his other CISCO KID portrayals), Walter Huston (*THE BAD MAN*, 1930), Wallace Beery (*VIVA VILLA!*, 1934, and *The Bad Man*, 1940), Fay Wray (*Viva Villa!*), John Garfield (*Juarez*, 1939), Humphrey Bogart (*Virginia City*, 1940), George Reeves (*Argentine Nights*, 1940), George Tobias (*Torrid Zone*, 1940), Katina Paxinou (*FOR WHOM THE BELL TOLLS*, 1943), Bette Davis (*Beyond the Forest*, 1949), Gene Tierney (*WAY OF A GAUCHO*, 1952), Charlton Heston (*Touch of Evil*, 1958), Yul Brynner (*Villa Rides!*, 1968), Martin Balsam (*Cuba*, 1979), Robby Benson (*WALK PROUD*, 1979), Meryl Streep et al. in *THE HOUSE OF THE SPIRITS* (1993), and Anjelica Huston (*THE PEREZ FAMILY*, 1995).

***In Caliente* (1935)** First National/Warner Bros., b&w, 90 minutes. **Director:** Lloyd Bacon; **Screenplay:** Jerry Wald and Julius Epstein; **Cast:** Dolores Del Río (La Espanita [Rita Gomez]), Pat O'Brien (Larry MacArthur), Leo Carrillo (José Gomez), Edward Everett Horton (Harold Brandon), Glenda Farrell (Clara), the DeMarcos (specialty number), Phil Regan (Peter), Winifred Shaw (Lois), Soledad Jiménez (maid), Judy Canova and the Canova Family (specialty number).

With its musical numbers created and staged by Busby Berkeley, *In Caliente* was a featherweight offering that allowed Hollywood to showcase the Mexican-flavored resort of Agua Caliente, a favorite gambling center for the movie crowd in the 1930s. It starred DEL RÍO—looking her most glamorous—as fiery club dancer La Espanita, who has a score to settle with Larry MacArthur, the publisher of a New York magazine, who once gave her act a scathing review. When MacArthur is dragged to Agua Caliente by his partner Harold Brandon to escape gold-digging Clara, he is entranced with beautiful Rita. He doesn't realize who she is, which leads to a romance in which she plans her revenge. But by the end, the couple are totally in love.

***Incendiary Blonde* (1945)** Paramount, color, 113 minutes. **Director:** George Marshall; **Screenplay:** Claude Binyon and Frank Butler; **Cast:** Betty Hutton (Texas Guinan), Arturo De Córdova (Bill Romero Kilgannon), Charles Ruggles (Cherokee Jim), Albert Dekker (Joel Cadden), Barry Fitzgerald (Mike Guinan), Mary Phillips (Bessie Guinan), Bill Goodwin (Tim Callahan).

Put into production in late 1943, this feature sat on the shelf for more than a year as part of the glut of Hollywood feature films that were mass produced during World War II. When finally released, there were registered protests in the South and from other parts of the United States because the real-life Irishman Bill Kilgannon had been transformed into an Irish Mexican American on camera to accommodate Paramount contract leading man, Mexican-born DE CÓRDOVA, and because of his shared romantic scenes with the character played by Caucasian Hutton. (The previous year, De Córdova had played a French pirate in the studio's big-budgeted *Frenchman's Creek*.) Originally, Alan Ladd had been cast as Hutton's leading man here, but he was drafted into military service. When the studio failed in its efforts to borrow Humphrey Bogart from Warner Bros and Paramount contract player Brian Donlevy refused the Kilgannon role, the studio turned to De Córdova.

The musical biography was loosely based on the life of Texas Guinan (1884–1933), who began her career in Wild West shows, then transferred to Broadway, and then became hostess of speakeasy nightclubs during Prohibition. The narrative was told in flashback at a New York parade celebrating her memory. The film proceeded to trace her event-filled life, including her romance with Kilgannon (a rodeo owner turned movie actor) and her compromise marriage to good-natured Tim Callahan, a reporter, press agent, and manager. *Incendiary Blonde* was nominated for an Academy Award for Best Music (Scoring of a Musical Picture).

***In Old Arizona* (1929)** Fox, b&w, 97 minutes. **Directors:** Raoul Walsh and Irving Cummings; **Screenplay:** Tom Barry; **Cast:** Edmund Lowe (Sgt. Mickey Dunn), Dorothy Burgess (Tonia Maria), Warner Baxter (the Cisco Kid), J. Farrell MacDonald (Tad), Fred Warren (piano player), Henry Armetta (barber), Roy Stewart (commandant), Alphonse Ethier (sheriff), Soledad Jiménez (cook).

In actuality, Lowe, as the Brooklyn Irishman and member of the U.S. 17th Cavalry, was the hero of this screen piece, rather than the charming rogue, the CISCO KID, who he was pursuing. Sergeant Dunn had been after the outlaw for a long time, and the latter's daring robberies and dangerous liaisons had almost resulted in his capture on several past occasions.

Back from cattle rustling in Guadalupe, the Kid arrives in Wolf's Crossing to visit his half-breed Mexican girlfriend, Tonia Maria. He is amazed to discover that she is involved with Sergeant Dunn and his scheme to kill the Kid. To gain revenge, the outlaw intercepts a note from Tonia Maria telling Dunn to meet at her place. The outlaw adds a few lines to the message saying that the Kid will be disguised as a woman. Dunn shows up and shoots what he thinks is the Kid but instead kills Tonia Maria. The Cisco Kid's retribution achieved, he rides off laughing into the sunset.

Using several Cisco Kid stories by O. Henry, it was decided to soften the presentation of the Mexican rogue, removing a good deal of his vicious traits. The resultant feature was extremely popular when released because it was the first outdoor western to be shot in full sound. Director Walsh had originally planned to star in the production, but an accident during production forced him to bow out as the star and to have Cummings direct scenes while he recuperated. Shot in Utah (at Zion and Bryce Canyon National Parks) and in California (Mojave Desert and the San Fernando Mission), the highly popular feature won an Academy Award for Baxter. The film received Oscar nominations for Best Cinematography, Best Director, Best Picture, and Best Writing.

Baxter returned unofficially to his Cisco Kid role in *THE ARIZONA KID* (1930) and was joined by Lowe for the official sequel, *THE CISCO KID* (1931).

***Internal Affairs* (1990)** Paramount, color, 115 minutes. **Director:** Michael Figgis; **Screenplay:** Henry Bean; **Cast:** Richard Gere (Dennis Peck), Andy Garcia (Sgt. Raymond Avila), Nancy Travis (Kathleen Avila), Laurie Metcalf (Sgt. Amy Wallace), Richard Bradford (Lieutenant Sergeant Grieb), William Baldwin (Van Stretch).

High-profile police officer Dennis Peck, based in Los Angeles' San Fernando Valley, has four ex-wives and several children. The crooked cop spends most of his time organizing illegal activities and collecting the profits. In addition, he is romancing an assortment of women, some for pleasure, others to put them and their husbands in his power. In contrast, hard-working Sgt. Raymond Avila of Internal Affairs is totally devoted to duty, in fact, so much so that his wife Kathleen feels totally neglected. As Avila and his lesbian police partner, Sgt. Amy Wallace, close in on the corrupt Peck who has already committed murder to cover his tracks, Peck pursues Kathleen, hoping to use her as bait to divert Avila from his pursuit. In the end, Peck's schemes lead him to a fateful end.

By now, positive image Hispanic-American characters were beginning to receive attention in Hollywood films. With Cuban-American GARCIA in the colead role, this was one of the first fully developed characterizations in which the Hispanic figure was not loaded down with negative traits. However, Avila's character was so filled with clichéd machismo that Peck found it easy to arouse the man's jealousy and ego.

The R-rated *Internal Affairs* grossed almost $28 million in domestic distribution.

Iturbi, José (1895–1980) A world-renowned pianist and conductor, this personable foreign-born celebrity made several MGM musicals in the 1940s, including *Holiday in Mexico* (1946). He always played himself and sometimes performed piano pieces in tandem with his concert pianist sister, Amparo. Iturbi had the knack of being able to translate classical music into an idiom that an untutored audience would accept and enjoy. He was very much a part of the upsurge in Hispanic-flavored entertainment provided by Hollywood during the World War II era (and thereafter).

He was born José De Iturbi in Valencia, Spain. A child prodigy, he was teaching piano (and supporting his family) by age seven. Later, after spending four years at the Zurich Conservatory, he became a world-famous virtuoso, performing in concert around the globe. Lured to Hollywood, he was featured in such pictures as *Thousands Cheer* (1943), *Anchors Aweigh* (1945), and *That Midnight Kiss* (1949). He dubbed Cornel Wilde's piano playing for the screen biography of Chopin entitled *A Song to Remember* (1945). Iturbi's disc of the Polonaise in A-flat sold more than a million copies. Almost to his death, he continued to give concerts to enthusiastic audiences.

J

***Jacobo Timerman: Prisoner Without a Name, Cell Without a Number* (1983)** NBC-TV, color, 100 minutes. **Director:** Linda Yellen; **Teleplay:** Yellen, Jonathan Platnick, and Oliver P. Drexell Jr.; **Cast:** Roy Scheider (Jacobo Timerman), Liv Ullmann (Risha Timerman), Terrance O'Quinn (Col. Thomas Rhodes), Sam Robards (Daniel Timerman), Zach Galligan (Hector Timerman), Trini Alvarado (Lisa Castello).

Based on the book by Timerman that was published in English in 1981, the somewhat timid TV movie depicted the arrest and torture in a secret prison of Argentinean newspaper publisher Jacobo Timerman who had the courage to print the list of more than 10,000 Argentineans who were tortured and killed by government army officers during the purge of dissidents.

It seemed strange casting to have Anglo Scheider and Swedish Ullmann in the lead roles, but then the movie utilized New York City and New Jersey to stand in for Argentina in the filming.

James A. Michener's Texas See *TEXAS.*

***Jesse* (1998–2000)** NBC-TV series, color, 30 minutes. **Cast:** Christina Applegate (Jesse Warner), George Dzundza (John Warner Sr.: 1998–99), David DeLuise (Darren Warner: 1998–99), Eric Lloyd (Little John), Bruno Campos (Diego Vasquez), Liza Snyder (Linda Vasquez).

This floundering sitcom was set in Buffalo, New York, as harried single mother Jesse copes with family, work, dating, and her appealing next-door neighbor Diego Vasquez, a handsome South American artist. As played by Brazilian-born Campos, the role was a good showcase for his accented charm, which was reminiscent of FERNANDO LAMAS—with sensitivity thrown into the mix. Even in the late 1990s, it was still rare to have a non-Anglo as a TV series lead, especially when the part called for a positive characterization.

***Jivaro* (1954)** Paramount, color, 93 minutes. **Director:** Edward Ludwig; **Screenplay:** Winston Miller; **Cast:** Fernando Lamas (Rio), Rhonda Fleming (Alice Parker), Brian Keith (Tony), Lon Chaney Jr. (Pedro), Richard Denning (Jerry Russell), Rita Moreno (Maroa), Marvin Miller (Chief Kovanti), Kay Johnson (Umari), Rosa Turich (native woman).

Despite being an economy production, this entry boasted beautiful color cinematography of the Amazon jungle and displayed virile Argentinean-born LAMAS at his prime.

Gorgeous Alice Parker arrives in South America from California to wed her fiancé Jerry Russell whom she hasn't seen in two years and who she thinks owns a rubber plantation. Unwilling to tell the American the truth about the dissolute Russell who has gone off in search of gold, Rio, who operates the jungle trading post at Pedrone, escorts her through the jungle. Before long, they have fallen in love, a situation resolved when it is learned that Russell has been killed by the Jivaro headhunters who, later, attack them.

Puerto Rican-born MORENO was stuck with the thankless role of the native woman who once held Rio's romantic interest.

***Joe Kidd* (1972)** Universal, color, 87 minutes. **Director:** John Sturges; **Screenplay:** Elmore Leonard; **Cast:** Clint Eastwood (Joe Kidd), Robert Duvall (Frank Harlan), John Saxon (Luis Chama), Don Stroud (Lamarr), Stella Garcia

(Helen Sanchez), James Wainwright (Mingo), Pepe Hern (priest).

One of Eastwood's lesser westerns, it presented the gringo as a righteous guardian of the downtrodden ethnic minorities (here Mexican Americans).

The action was set in 1900 Sinola, New Mexico, where sinister Frank Harlan is pushing the Mexican Americans off their land, utilizing fake Spanish land grants to keep the law on his side. As the Mexican who willingly sacrifices others to save himself, Saxon's Luis Chama is hardly an admirable character, especially as he has others fight his battles for him. Garcia, one of Chama's group, is the señorita who draws Joe Kidd's romantic attention when he is not serving as protector.

***John Larroquette Show, The* (1993–1996)** NBC-TV series, color, 30 minutes. **Cast:** John Larroquette (John Hemingway), Liz Torres (Mahalia Sanchez), Gigi Rice (Carly Watkins), Daryl "Chill" Mitchell (Dexter Wilson), Lenny Clarke (Officer Hampton).

A decidedly dark sitcom, the series was set at the Crossroads, a seedy St. Louis, Missouri, bus terminal where intelligent John Hemingway, having lost his career and family to alcoholism, is now the unhappy night shift manager. At times dour and sarcastic, his chief assistant is Mahalia Sanchez. She knows more about the operation of the squalid depot than her boss and lets everyone know it. This heavily accented, outspoken, and dependable soul whose husband left her for a younger woman is raising four children on her own. TORRES, by now well into her zaftig period, gave the show much needed punch and pathos.

***Juarez* (1939)** Warner Bros., b&w, 125 minutes. **Director:** William Dieterle; **Screenplay:** John Huston, Wolfgang Reinhardt, and Aeneas MacKenzie; **Cast:** Bette Davis (Empress Carlotta), Paul Muni (Benito Pablo Juarez), Brian Aherne (Maximilian von Hapsburg), Claude Rains (Napoleon III), John Garfield (Porfirio Diaz), Donald Crisp (Marechal Bazaine), Joseph Calleia (Alejandro Uradi), Gale Sondergaard (Empress Eugenie), Gilbert Roland (Col. Miguel Lopez), Henry O'Neill (Miguel Miramon), Pedro de Cordoba (Riva Palacio).

This lavish screen biography focused on the life (1806–72) of the beloved Mexican statesman who was president of Mexico from 1858 to 1872, except for 1864–67 when the French-endorsed Emperor Maximilian ruled the country. (The movie was based on Franz Werfel's 1925 play *Juarez and Maximilian* and Bertita Harding's 1934 novel, *The Phantom Crown.*) For many, Juarez was the Mexican equivalent of Abraham Lincoln, the latter a politician whom Juarez much admired. Made at a then huge cost of almost $2 million, the heavily researched drama boasted, among others, an eleven-acre set on the studio ranch at Calabasas, California, where a full Mexican village was recreated.

In France, in 1863, crafty Emperor Louis Napoleon fears losing control of Mexico. He connivingly places the naïve Maximilian von Hapsburg of Austria on the throne of Mexico. Accompanied by his emotionally frail wife Carlotta, Maximilian arrives in Mexico, only to discover the fraud that the French ruler has engineered. Determined not to undo all the reforms instituted by Juarez, Maximilian earns the enmity of Louis Napoleon and cannot win the trust of the suspicious Juarez. With his power-hungry wife pushing him onward, Maximilian is caught between opposing forces. As Juarez and the revolutionaries—led by Porfirio Diaz—gain adherents with the aid of the United States, Louis Napoleon withdraws the protecting French troops. Juarez recovers control of the country and takes Maximilian and his trusty followers prisoner. Rather than desert his men, Maximilian goes to his death with them in front of a firing squad.

Praise was given Ukrainian-born Jewish actor Muni for his impersonation of the complex Mexican-Indian Juarez, even though his overly stoic look (partially caused by his heavy makeup to recreate the famed man's profile) made him more a frozen image than a human being. There were the usual hosannas for Davis as the mad Empress Carlotta and compliments for Aherne's delicate shadings of the duped nobleman. On the other hand, there was much scorn for the casting of New York Jewish actor Garfield in the inaccurately presented part of the patriot Diaz (1830–1915). Between Garfield's contemporary ethnic look and his overt New York accent, he lessened the picture's credibility.

The epic *Juarez* received Academy Award nominations for Best Black and White Cinematography and for Best Supporting Actor (Aherne). Decades later, in the 1970s, an active Chicano minority in California pressured television stations *not* to air *Juarez* because so many of the Mexican roles in the picture were performed by non-Mexicans.

In 1940, Warner Bros. briefly released *The Mad Empress*, a U.S.–Mexican production dealing with the same topic as *Juarez*. It featured Medea de Novara (Empress Carlotta of Mexico), Lionel Atwill (Marechal Bazaine), Conrad Nagel (Maximilian von Hapsburg), Earl Gunn (Porfirio Diaz), Jason Robards Sr. (Benito Pablo Juarez).

Julia, Raul (1940–1994) For much of his acting career this suave performer with the droopy eyes was best known for his heavily dramatic and romantic roles. That altered when he demonstrated a flair for wacky comedy in the big-screen version of *THE ADDAMS FAMILY* (1991) and its sequel *Addams Family Values* (1993).

Born Raúl Rafael Carlos Julia y Arcelay in San Juan, Puerto Rico, he was the son of a successful restaurant owner. A pre-law student, he graduated from the University of Puerto Rico and chose acting, relocating to New York City where he soon became associated with the New York Shakespeare Festival. Julia made his Broadway debut in *The Cuban Thing* (1968), a drama about Castro's revolution, and his movie bow in the Mafia drama, *Stilleto* (1969). On PBS-TV's *Sesame Street*, he played Rafael from 1971 to 1973. Movie roles ranged from the goofy *The Gumball Rally* (1976) to the thriller *Eyes of Laura Mars* (1978). His sturdy playing of Valentin Arregui in *Kiss of the Spider Woman* (1985) should have made him a major star. He was General Santa Anna in

Raul Julia in *Trading Hearts* (1988). (JC ARCHIVES)

the TV movie *The Alamo: Thirteen Days to Glory* (1987) and had the title role in the TV production of *Onassis: The Richest Man in the World* (1988). Julia received acclaim for his *Macbeth* (1990) for the New York Shakespeare Festival. His intensity was impressive in *ROMERO* (1989) and flashy as the defense attorney in *Presumed Innocent* (1990). He won an Emmy Award for playing the slain environmentalist in *THE BURNING SEASON: THE CHICO MENDES STORY* (1994).

Jurado, Katy (1927–2002) One of the early new-generation Hispanic stars to migrate to Hollywood, Jurado generally was cast as the smoldering south-of-the-border beauty, later as the long-suffering mother, or sometimes as a Native American woman.

Born María Cristina Estela Marcela Jurado García in Mexico City, her mother was an opera singer and her father a rancher. She began in films in the early 1940s, one of her most popular entries being *La vida inútil de Pito Pérez* (1943). She inaugurated her Hollywood phase as the wife of aging bullfighter GILBERT ROLAND in *BULLFIGHTER AND THE LADY* (1951). One of Jurado's best movie roles was as Gary Cooper's former love in *HIGH NOON* (1952). She was a half-breed in *Arrowhead* (1953) and the Native American spouse of Spencer Tracy in *Broken Lance* (1954). For the latter, she was Oscar-nominated as Best Supporting Actress. Her other screen assignments included *ONE-EYED JACKS* (1961), *STAY AWAY, JOE* (1968), *The Children of Sanchez* (1978), *Evita Peron* (1981—as Evita's mother in this TV movie), *Under the Volcano* (1984), and *The Hi-Lo Country* (1998). She was a cast regular on the TV sitcom *A.K.A. PABLO* (1984), seen as the mother of PAUL RODRIGUEZ.

Katy Jurado in *Smoky* (1966). (JC ARCHIVES)

K

***Key Witness* (1960)** MGM, b&w, 82 minutes. **Director:** Phil Karlson; **Screenplay::** Alfred Brenner and Sidney Michaels; **Cast:** Jeffrey Hunter (Fred Morrow), Pat Crowley (Ann Morrow), Dennis Hopper ("Cowboy" William L. Tompkins), Joby Baker ("Muggles"), Susan Harrison (Ruby), Johnny Nash ("Apple"), Corey Allen ("Magician"), Frank Silvera (Det. Rafael Torno), Eugene Iglesias (Emelio Sanchez).

A graphic depiction of a prowling teenage gang, this picture portrayed this multiethnic group realistically, with members referring to one of their number as "nigger." Law enforcement was represented by a dedicated Mexican-American police detective (Silvera).

Los Angeles real-estate agent Fred Morrow turns off the freeway and stops in a café in East Los Angeles to make a phone call. He witnesses William L. Tompkins—the leader of the pack and known as Cowboy—knife Emelio Sanchez. Although there are other onlookers to the homicide, no one but Morrow reports the matter to the law. Police detective Rafael Torno who is handling the case is aware of the pressure the gang will put on the witness and his family not to testify.

During succeeding days, Cowboy and his followers torment Morrow and his family, hoping to scare him from testifying. The reign of terror eventually works on Morrow, who admits in court that he must have been mistaken when he identified Cowboy as the culprit. Later, as the gang turns on Apple, the African-American member of the group (and the only one of them with a conscience), Morrow finds himself coming to the youth's aid as the cops arrive to haul away the gang. Morrow is once again ready to testify.

***Kid from Spain, The* (1932)** United Artists, b&w, 96 minutes. **Director:** Leo McCarey; **Screenplay:** William Anthony McGuire, Bert Kalmar, and Harry Ruby; **Cast:** Eddie Cantor (Don Sebastian II [Eddie Williams]), Lyda Roberti (Rosalie), Robert Young (Ricardo), Ruth Hall (Anita Gomez), John Miljan (Pancho), Noah Beery (Alonzo Gomez), J. Carrol Naish (Pedro), Robert Emmet O'Connor (Crawford), Paul Porcasi (Gonzales), Stanley Fields (José).

Despite its goofy, dated premise, *The Kid from Spain* was prime Cantor as the pop-eyed stage/film musical-comedy star pranced through another nonsensical plot. Although actual Mexican bullfighters were imported to Hollywood to double for the star in the bullring sequences, there was little that was authentically south-of-the-border in this filmed-in-Los Angeles production, which cost more than $1 million. Most of the movie's Hispanic characters, as was customary at the time, were played by non-Mexicans.

Thanks to a practical joke by his classmate Ricardo, Eddie Williams is also expelled from college just before graduation. The duo decide to visit Ricardo's home in Mexico, but before Williams can depart, he becomes an innocent pawn in a bank robbery. Eventually, he reaches his south-of-the-border destination but is convinced that American detective Crawford is there to arrest him. Williams disguises himself as Don Sebastian II, a great bullfighter, but as such he is forced into the arena. His initial plan to fight a trained bull goes awry, and he is confronted with Diablo, a killer bull. Miraculously, nimble-footed Williams survives the ordeal, and all ends well.

The musical numbers—among them "The College Song," "Look What You've Done," "In the Moonlight," and "What a Perfect Combination"—were staged by Busby Berkeley and featured the Goldwyn Girls, who included Betty Grable.

***Kissing Bandit, The* (1948)** Metro-Goldwyn-Mayer, color, 102 minutes. **Director:** Laslo Benedek; **Screenplay:** Isobel Lennart and John Briard; **Cast:** Frank Sinatra

(Ricardo), Kathryn Grayson (Teresa), J. Carrol Naish (Chico), Mildred Natwick (Isabella), Mikhail Rasumny (Don José), Billy Gilbert (General Torro), Sono Osato (Bianca), Clinton Sundberg (Colonel Gomez), Henry Mirelez (Pepito), Ricardo Montalban, Ann Miller, and Cyd Charisse (fiesta dancers).

Sinatra inherited the role originally planned for John Carroll, John Hodiak, or Tony Martin. With his quite contemporary demeanor and New Jersey accent, the crooner was an extremely poor choice to play a Spaniard in 1830 California who was the timid, college-educated son of the legendary Kissing Bandit. The movie proved to be the low point of Sinatra and Grayson's screen careers. To "salvage" the fiasco, a postproduction fiesta dance sequence was added to the picture. Robert Alton choreographed the "Dance of Fury" by Nacio Herb Brown. This burst of on-screen energy from MONTALBAN, Miller, and Charisse was the movie's sole highlight. The project was another instance of Hollywood blithely trading on a rich historical period in America's past without utilizing appropriate casting for the ethnic minority characters.

Ricardo, who has been away at college, returns to California and is horrified to discover that his father has become a celebrated bandito. Chico, who had been his parent's chief accomplice, determines to make a "respectable" highwayman out of Ricardo. While fumbling his new career, Ricardo falls in love with Teresa, the governor's daughter. Posing as tax collectors from Spain, Ricardo and Chico invade the governor's hacienda so the romance can be furthered.

***Kiss of the Spider Woman* (1985)** Island Alive, color, 119 minutes. **Director:** Hector Babenco; **Screenplay:** Leonard Schrader; **Cast:** William Hurt (Luis Molina), Raul Julia (Valentin Arregui), Sonia Braga (Leni Lamison/Marta/Spider woman), José Lewgoy (warden), Milton Goncalves (Pedro).

Set in an unnamed South American country, effeminate Luis Molina is jailed for having had sexual relations with a minor. His cellmate, Valentin Arregui, is a political prisoner—a leftist journalist—who is tortured for information. He clings to memories of his girlfriend (BRAGA) to help him through the torment. Unknown to Arregui, Molina has agreed to wheedle information from the radical in exchange for special treatment. At first, Arregui is repulsed by the swishy newcomer, but as boredom, pain, and loneliness overwhelm him, he becomes more emotionally open to the man. Meanwhile, to kill time, Molina reenacts a variation of one of his favorite movies (which features Braga). Soon, the two men develop an emotional bond that leads to lovemaking. Later, Molina convinces the warden to free him, claiming it will push the lonely Arregui into telling the authorities what they want to know. Arregui asks Molina to contact an associate on the outside. When Molina does, he is shot for fear he will lead the police to them. The police, who have been trailing Molina, allow him to die because he refuses to tell them the contact's phone number.

The highly praised *Kiss of the Spider Woman* grossed more than $6 million in domestic distribution. It earned an Academy Award for Best Actor (Hurt). It received Oscar nominations for Best Adapted Screenplay, Best Director, and Best Picture. In mid-1992, the book was adapted to the musical stage, premiering in Toronto, Ontario, Canada, starring Chita Rivera (Spider Woman), Brent Carver (Molina), and Anthony Crivello (Valentin). The show later played in London, England, and on Broadway.

L

***La Bamba* (1987)** Columbia, color, 108 minutes. **Director/Screenplay:** Luis Valdez; **Cast:** Lou Diamond Phillips (Ritchie Valens), Esai Morales (Bob Morales), Rosana DeSoto (Connie Valenzuela), Elizabeth Peña (Rosie Morales), Danielle von Zerneck (Donna Ludwig), Joe Pantoliano (Bob Keene).

In many ways foreshadowing the later screen biography *SELENA* (1997), *La Bamba* was the narrative of rock 'n' roll star Ritchie Valens (1941–59), who grew up in an impoverished barrio in the San Fernando Valley of Los Angeles. Rather than being purely a movie musical with a recitation of Valens's greatest hits (e.g., "La Bamba," "Donna"), this romantic feature was far more encompassing. It was a strongly dramatic narrative of the young Chicano (born Ricardo Valenzuela) who wants to make something of life—especially to please his single parent (DeSoto), to be accepted by the family of his Anglo girlfriend (von Zerneck), and to see his rowdy, jealous older half-brother, Bob, settle into a happier life mode. The movie covered Ritchie's rapid rise to fame and reached its dramatic climax with the death of seventeen-year-old Valens in February 1959 in a plane crash.

La Bamba grossed more than $54 million in domestic distribution. It boosted the screen careers of Morales and especially PHILLIPS, both still relative newcomers to filmgoing audiences. It also demonstrated to Hollywood that there was a ready-made large Hispanic audience interested in being gratified by relevant films dealing with their culture.

Joe Pantoliano and Lou Diamond Phillips in *La Bamba* (1987). (ECHO BOOK SHOP)

Lamas, Fernando (1915–1982) At the height of his acting career in the early 1950s, he was MGM's resident LATIN LOVER, a stereotype that limited his professional options. Later, thanks to comedian Billy Crystal's satire of Lamas on *TV's Saturday Night Live* and a revealing commentary on him by his last wife, swimming star Esther Williams, the public belatedly developed a new sense of the "real" Lamas.

He was born in Buenos Aires, Argentina, and began to act with a local small theater while a teenager. He was in movies by the early 1940s (e.g., *En el último piso*, 1942; *Villa rica del Espiritu Santo*, 1945). As of the 1950s, he was in Hollywood and was cast as the roguish playboy (e.g., *The Merry Widow*, 1952). Sometimes, he used his fine singing voice (e.g., *Rose Marie*, 1954). Later, as a freelancer, he directed and starred in such unsuccessful items as *La Fuente mágica* (1962) and *The Violent Ones* (1967). Later, he directed a great deal of TV, including episodes of *Falcon Crest*, the nighttime soap costarring his son Lorenzo by actress wife Arlene Dahl.

***Lambada* (1990)** Warner Bros, color, 98 minutes. **Director:** Joel Silberg; **Screenplay:** Sheldon Renan and Silberg; **Cast:** J. Eddie Peck (Blade [Kevin Laird]), Melora Hardin (Sandy), Shabba-Doo (Ramone), Ricky Paull Goldin (Dean), Basil Hoffman (Superintendent Leland). Dennis Burkley (Uncle Big).

Chicano Kevin Laird, an assimilated American, teaches math at a fancy Beverly Hills high school. At night, he returns to the barrio where, using the alias Blade, he spends time at the No Man's Land, an East Los Angeles disco where he is a king of the Lambada. But he has an ulterior purpose: With textbooks "borrowed" from his daytime gig, he runs an unofficial class in the club's back room to tutor local students, which eventually leads to math and dance competitions between barrio and Beverly Hills students.

Showcasing its new stereotype of the hot Latin with rhythm, *Lambada* exchanged one clichéd image of the Mexican American for another. With its ludicrous plot and constant sexual tease, this film had highly critical reviews. *Lambada* grossed more than $4 million in domestic distribution. Following in its wake, to exploit the brief-lasting Lambada dance craze, came such entries as *Lambada: The Forbidden Dance* (1990). (Earlier, there had been an attempt to profit from another Latino dance "craze" in 1988's *Salsa.*)

***Last Command, The* (1955)** Republic, color, 110 minutes. **Director:** Frank Lloyd; **Screenplay:** Warren Duff; **Cast:** Sterling Hayden (James Bowie), Anna Maria Alberghetti (Consuela), Richard Carlson (William Travis), Arthur Hunnicutt (Davy Crockett), Ernest Borgnine (Mike Radin), J. Carrol Naish (Gen. Antonio López de Santa Anna), Ben Cooper (Jeb Lacey), John Russell (Lieutenant Dickinson), Jim Davis (Evans), Eduard Franz (Lorenzo de Quesada), Otto Kruger (Stephen Austin), Hugh Sanders (Sam Houston), Argentina Brunetti (Maria), Alex Montoya (Mexican colonel).

Although not on the same grand scale as John Wayne's *THE ALAMO* (1960), this film was still a big-scale undertaking. It benefited from sound performances by Hayden, Borgnine, and especially NAISH as Antonio López de Santa Anna (1794–1876), the Mexican general who triumphed over the Americans at the battle of the ALAMO in 1836. Unlike many earlier Hollywood films that touched on troublesome relationships between the United States and Mexico in the nineteenth century, there was much less bias here in the presentation, due as much to America's preoccupation with the continued cold war as to anything else.

By the 1830s, trouble is brewing in the Mexican republic north of the Rio Grande. American settlers have been arriving in greater numbers, and there is a growing desire for independence from Mexico. Colonel Jim Bowie, who fought in battles beside General Santa Anna, now Mexico's president, has conflicting loyalties to his friend Santa Anna on the one hand and to the American settlers on the other. Meanwhile, he romances Consuela, the niece of Lorenzo de Quesada, a Mexican of Spanish heritage who lives in Texas. Eventually, there is a showdown between Santa Anna's forces and the Texans under Jim Bowie's command. The locale is a broken-down fort called the Alamo. There, the Texans hold out against the Mexican army for several days, but finally the men, including Davy Crockett, are overwhelmed and killed by the enemy. Later, Sam Houston explains to Consuela that the great sacrifice at the Alamo gave the Americans time to consolidate their forces against the Mexicans.

Many of the smaller roles in this historical feature were played by Mexican talent. The movie was shot in Brackettsville, Texas, and at the Republic studio in Los Angeles.

***Last of the Fast Guns, The* (1958)** Universal, color, 82 minutes. **Director:** George Sherman; **Screenplay:** David P. Harmon; **Cast:** Jock Mahoney (Brad Ellison), Gilbert Roland (Miles Lang), Linda Cristal (Maria O'Reilly), Eduard Franz (Padre José), Lorne Greene (Michael O'Reilly), Carl Benton Reid (John Forges), Eduardo Noreiga (Cordoba), Jorge Treviño (Manuel).

Despite its thin budget and standard plot line, *The Last of the Fast Guns*, shot in Cuernavaca, Mexico, utilized much Mexican talent and included Argentinean Cristal, who was just beginning her Hollywood filmmaking career. Yet again, Mexico was depicted as just a hotbed of unlawful activity, an entrenched cliché in Hollywood films.

Brad Ellison is anxious to retire as a gunfighter (having outlived such other quick draws as Billy the Kid and Jesse James), but he is offered $25,000 to locate John Forges's long-lost brother, who is supposedly living somewhere in Mexico. The trail south-of-the-border leads to the ranch of Michael O'Reilly, where Ellison becomes involved romantically with the rancher's daughter, Maria. Also, there is the ranch foreman Miles Lang who proves to be in the employ of Forges's unscrupulous partner. As for the missing person, Padre José, a benevolent friend to the locals, proves to have an interesting background.

As he had done so often over his more than thirty years in the cinema, Mexican-born ROLAND stole the show.

***Last Train from Madrid, The* (1937)** Paramount, b&w, 85 minutes. **Director:** James Hogan; **Screenplay:** Louis Stevens and Robert Wyler; **Cast:** Dorothy Lamour (Carmelita Castillo), Lew Ayres (Bill Dexter), Gilbert Roland (Eduardo de Soto), Karen Morley (Baroness Helen Rafitte), Lionel Atwill (Colonel Vigo), Helen Mack (Lola), Robert Cummings (Juan Ramos), Olympe Bradna (Maria Ferrer), Anthony Quinn (Capt. Ricardo Alvarez), Lee Bowman (Michael Balk).

Highly touted as Hollywood's first feature film to focus on the then raging Spanish Civil War, this movie actually dealt very little with any political point of view (which was also true of the studio's later and far more expensive *FOR WHOM THE BELL TOLLS*, 1943). What emerged were interweaving episodes of melodrama a la *Grand Hotel* (1932). Here the studio's stock company of featured players performed in an assortment of often unbelievable Spanish characterizations (e.g., Cummings and Mack). The much underrated ROLAND and the rising star QUINN came off best in this drama, which had background scenes lensed in Palencia, in northwest Spain.

As the Spanish Civil War devastates Madrid, the military gives passes to several people caught in the city, permitting them to board a train destined for Valencia at midnight. One of the passengers is Eduardo de Soto, a political prisoner who has agreed to participate in the brutal fighting at Cordoza. Capt. Ricardo Alvarez, an assistant to Colonel Vigo, is a longtime friend of de Soto and helps him to escape the military police. De Soto rushes to see his one-time girlfriend, Carmelita Castillo, who has been dating Alvarez, not knowing the two men were acquainted. Among the others caught in the rush to leave the city are American reporter Bill Dexter and a soldier, Juan Ramos, who is sentenced to fight at Cordoza for insubordination. The former has a brief romance with a female soldier (Bradna), and the latter has a short liaison with Lola, a woman from his town, before she is killed by robbers. Baroness Helene Rafitte kills her money-hungry lover (Bowman) to get his pass for de Soto, and, at the last, Ricardo sacrifices himself so that de Soto may board the train.

Latin Lovers During the early 1920s when Hollywood was still manufacturing silent movies, a new craze swept the movies—that of the so-called Latin Lover. The trend was established by Italian-born Rudolph Valentino (1895–1926), put into motion by his playing the fiery Argentinean in *THE FOUR HORSEMEN OF THE APOCALYPSE* (1921), and confirmed in such later films as his Spanish matador in *BLOOD AND SAND* (1922). Hollywood and the public became so entranced with the image of the passionate Latino that a rash of romantic dramas and adventures (often set in the past) starring Latin Lovers were created. There was Spanish-born Antonio Moreno (1886–1967), who made such vehicles as *My American Wife* (1922), *The Spanish Dancer* (1923), and *The Temptress* (1926). Mexican-born Ramón Novarro (1899–1968) reached a career apex playing the Jew in *Ben-Hur* (1925) but made several features in which he portrayed a Hispanic character: *Mr. Barnes of New York* (1922), *Thy Name Is Woman* (1924), *The Road to Romance* (1927).

On the other hand, because the movies had no spoken dialogue in the 1920s, a little makeup and the proper costuming made Latin Lovers of some very non-Hispanic personalities. There was Ricardo Cortez (1899–1977—né Jacob Krantz, born in Vienna, Austria) in *Argentine Love* (1924), *The Spaniard* (1925), *The Torrent* (1926). Another was Britisher Ronald Colman (1891–1958) who appeared in ethnic roles in such movies as *The White Sister* (1923), *Romola* (1924), *The Night of Love* (1927). Other Hollywood leading men channeled into the Hispanic mode for one or more such roles in the 1920s included John Gilbert, Rod La Rocque, and Charles Farrell.

With the coming of talkies in the late 1920s the Latin Lover fad died but was renewed in the 1940s and early 1950s by such Hispanic talent performing in Hollywood features as Mexican-born ARTURO DE CÓRDOVA and RICARDO MONTALBAN, Cuban-born DESI ARNAZ, and Argentine-born FERNANDO LAMAS. More so than ERIK ESTRADA (e.g., *CHIPS* TV series, 1977–83), Puerto Rican-American JIMMY SMITS, Cuban-born ANDY GARCIA, Spanish-born ANTONIO BANDERAS, and Cuban-born BENICIO DEL TORO in the 1990s reestablished, to a degree, the Latin Lover type image but generally in contemporary stories.

Ramón Novarro, a "Latin Lover" star of the 1920s and 1930s. (ECHO BOOK SHOP)

***Latin Lovers* (1953)** Metro-Goldwyn-Mayer, color, 104 minutes. **Director:** Mervyn LeRoy; **Screenplay:** Isobel Lennart; **Cast:** Lana Turner (Nora Taylor), Ricardo Montalban (Roberto Santos), John Lund (Paul Chevron), Louis Calhern (grandfather Santos), Jean Hagen (Anne Kellwood), Eduard Franz (Dr. Lionel Y. Newman), Beulah Bondi (woman analyst), Joaquin Garay (Zeca), Dorothy Neumann (Mrs. Newman), Rita Moreno (Christina).

Evidently, by MGM standards, one South American leading man was as good as another, especially if it was a Lana Turner vehicle. When the movie siren's off-screen romance with Argentinean LAMAS dissolved very publicly, the studio quickly substituted Mexican-born MONTALBAN as her vis-á-vis in this production. In the process, the studio discarded several song numbers that Lamas had already prerecorded.

Latin Lovers asked the traumatic question of whether an heiress (with $37 million) could be happy with a polo-loving man (Lund) whose estate was worth $48 million. When her blasé mate Paul Chervron flies to Brazil for three weeks of polo, Nora Taylor follows, hoping the tropical clime will improve their amour. Once there, Chevron is laid up with an injury, and Nora quickly finds romance with handsome Roberto Santos, who is wealthy but not in the same league with her. While grandpa Santos urges on the romance, Nora wonders if Roberto loves her for herself or for her bank accounts. Matters resolve when the heiress assigns all her funds over to Roberto so there will be no question of who is richer!

In this trivial offering, more noted for Turner's Helen Rose wardrobe, Montalban and Turner shared a dance sequence together. There was very little authentic south-of-the-border flavor to the proceedings as the film was shot on the studio sound stages, in Culver City, California.

***Latino* (1985)** Cinecom International, color, 105 minutes. **Director/Screenplay:** Haskell Wexler; **Cast:** Robert Beltran (Lt. Eddie Guerrero), Annette Cardona (Marlena), Tony Plana (Sgt. Ruben Trevino), Ricardo López (Attila), Luis Torentes (Luis), Juan Carlos Ortiz (Juan Carlos), Julio Medina (Edgar Salasar), Marta Tenorio (Luis's mother).

This highly political entry with a strong left-wing point of view translated the angst and complicity of the Vietnam War to the U.S. involvement with the Contras in their fight against the Sandinista government of Nicaragua. It also encapsulated as one of its themes opinions and reactions to the clandestine U.S. foreign policy in South America (and elsewhere). Made in 1984 on location in Honduras, *Latino* had limited distribution.

In 1983, Hispanic Green Beret veterans Lt. Eddie Guerrero and Sgt. Ruben Trevino—the "spic pair extraordinaire"—are ordered by their military superiors to Honduras to train Contras for planned raids across the border into Nicaragua. Guerrero meets Marlena, a Nicaraguan agronomist who lives in Honduras with her son Juan Carlos. Later, Guerrero is disturbed at seeing prisoners from Nicaragua—whom he comes to regard as near kin—tortured and killed if they don't "join" the anti-Sandinista movement. On a big offensive into Nicaragua at El Porvenir where Marlena has gone, Trevino is killed and Guerrero is captured before detonating explosives to destroy the grain silos at the cooperative.

As James Leahy wrote in (British) *Monthly Film Bulletin* (October 1986): "Part of the strength of *Latino* derives from its research and documentation, which provide a clear and coherent narrative framework that is able to absorb images, situations, motifs and themes from that very potent genre, the Hollywood war movie, and then reverse the genre situation and its standard political message. . . . The emotional power of *Latino* lies . . . in those moments which relate the individual to his community and its struggle for survival."

BELTRAN, of Mexican-Native American ancestry, shone in the complex lead role.

***Lawless, The* (1950)** Paramount, b&w, 83 minutes. **Director:** Joseph Losey; **Screenplay:** Geoffrey Homes [Daniel Mainwaring]; **Cast:** Macdonald Carey (Larry Wilder), Gail Russell (Sunny Garcia), John Sands (Joe Ferguson), Lee Patrick (Jan Dawson), John Hoyt (Ed Ferguson), Lalo Rios (Paul Rodriguez), Maurice Jara (Lopo Chavez), Tab Hunter (Frank O'Brien), Pedro de Cordoba (Mr. Garcia).

As scriptwriter Homes explained to the *New York Times* (March 5, 1950) about his writing of this picture (which was, according to him, "the first picture to be made about discrimination against Mexican-Americans"): "Though it is true that discrimination against guys named Garcia and Chavez is more prevalent in the Texas and California border towns and in Los Angeles, it exists wherever there is a Mexican community. This I wanted to say on film." *The Lawless* was shot in eighteen days on location in Grass Valley and Marysville, California, at a cost of under $400,000. Rios, who had previously been a housepainter, had appeared earlier in the 1950 film, *The Bandit Queen.* Low-budget producers William J. Pine and William C. Thomas chose Caucasian Russell for the female lead when they claimed they could not find a suitable Mexican-American actress for the part.

In northern California, at Santa Marta, Paul Rodriguez, a Mexican-American fruit picker, hopes someday to own a farm. In contrast, his pal Lopo Chavez, a World War II veteran, is cynical because of both the discrimination he has faced over the years and his life of poverty. Chavez is involved in a minor traffic accident with a Caucasian, which leads to a fist fight at the accident site and to a bigger brawl at a nearby dance that evening. In turn, this causes Larry Wilder, the new owner of a local newspaper, to bow to community pressure and to print an exaggerated account of the dispute, which is blown further out of proportion. Later, Rodriguez is accused falsely of assaulting a white farm girl, which escalates into a lynch mob chasing both Rodriguez and his pal Chavez. By the resolution, Wilder has gained a new perspective on objective journalism and has formed a romance with Sunny Garcia, the Mexican-American daughter of a Spanish weekly newspaper owner.

In commenting on *The Lawless* while it was in preproduction, Joseph I. Breen, Director of the Production Code Administration, informed Paramount Pictures (October 5, 1949): "The shocking manner in which the several gross injustices are heaped upon the head of the confused but innocent young American of Mexican extraction, and the willingness of so many of the people in your story to be a part of, and to endorse, these injustices, is, we think, a damning portrayal of our American social system."

Leguizamo, John (1964–) This multitalented performer, writer, and risk taker seemed too full of high energy to confine himself to only one medium, so he jumped successfully from film to TV to stage; in the process he provided impressive strength, insight, and character delineation to his varied roles.

Director Spike Lee (left) with John Leguizamo, the star of the cable TV special *John Leguizamo: Freak* (1998). (JC ARCHIVES)

Born in Bogotá, Colombia, he moved with his family to the United States when he was four and grew up in Jackson Heights, Queens, New York. Leguizamo had brief screen roles in *Casualties of War* (1989) and *Die Hard 2* (1990) but made his mark off-Broadway with his acclaimed one-man show *Mambo Mouth* (1991), which later was taped for cable TV (as were his later stage specials *Spic-O-Rama* and *Freak*). He stood out in *HANGIN' WITH THE HOMEBOYS* (1991), was impressive in drag in *To Wong Foo, Thanks for Everything, Julie Newmar* (1995), and held his own against Kurt Russell in the action entry *Executive Decision* (1996). John displayed his creative flair with the first Latin comedy/variety series on U.S. network TV— *HOUSE OF BUGGIN'* (1995). His other movies included *Spawn* (1997), *Summer of Sam* (1999), *Moulin Rouge* (2001), *Ice Age* (2001—voice), *Empire* (2002), and *Spun* (2002). In the late 1990s his book *Freak: A Semi-Demi-Quasi-Pseudo Autobiography* appeared. In spring 2002, the actor brought his hit one-man Broadway show (*Sexaholix: A Love Story*, 2001) to cable TV as a special.

Leguizamo won both an Emmy and an ALMA Award for his TV special *Freak* (1998); the next year he was nominated for an ALMA Award in the category of Outstanding Actor in a Feature Film for his performance in Spike Lee's *Summer of Sam* (1999).

***Life in the Balance, A* (1955)** Twentieth Century-Fox, b&w, 74 minutes. **Director:** Harry Horner; **Screenplay:** Robert Presnell Jr. and Leo Townsend; **Cast:** Ricardo Montalban (Antonio Gomez), Anne Bancroft (Maria Ibinia), Lee Marvin (the murderer), José Perez (Paco Gomez), Rodolfo Acosta (Lieutenant Fernando), Carlos Muzquiz (Captain Saldana).

Based on a George Simenon story, this unpretentious film was lensed in Mexico City. The economy-style murder mystery—at times too contrived in its plot logic—used the urban locale as an integral part of the plot line rather than as mere scenic background. MONTALBAN, quietly authoritative as the father who is more desperate to save his son than to prove his own innocence, was effective, but it was Perez as the ten-year-old boy who made the biggest impression on camera.

Out-of-work musician Antonio Gomez, a single parent, is accused of having murdered a woman neighbor, one of several murders that occurred in the vicinity. Meanwhile, Gomez's son, Paco, has seen a stranger (Marvin) leaving the murder scene and follows him. When the deranged killer discovers he is being trailed, he takes the youngster captive. Gomez is arrested by the police on suspicion of homicide and has a difficult time convincing them that he is innocent and that his child is in danger. The tense denouement occurs at a university complex, where Gomez jumps into action to protect his offspring. Maria Ibinia is the down-on-her-luck woman who forms a romance with musician Gomez.

***Littlest Outlaw, The* (1955)** Buena Vista, color, 73 minutes. **Director:** Roberto Gavaldón; **Screenplay:** Bill Walsh; **Cast:** Pedro Armendáriz (General Torres), Joseph Calleia (padre), Rodolfo Acosta (Chato), Andrés Velásquez (Pablito), Pepe Ortiz (matador), Laila Maley (Celita).

This charming Walt Disney narrative was filmed in Mexico by Mexican director Gavaldón in both English- and Spanish-language editions. Because it was released by the Disney organization, it was seen by far more of a mainstream U.S. audience than could have been expected otherwise and was the start of a slow trend toward exposing American filmgoers to an increasing number of Hispanic topics, characters, and locales on screen.

Ten-year-old Pablito appeals to General Torres not to destroy a rambunctious horse that has thrown the officer's daughter. He explains that the beloved animal had been trained badly by the boy's stepfather. When the general refuses, the boy steals the horse and runs away, later seeking help from a padre. Pablito is later separated from the horse but finds him as a bullring attraction about to be gored by a bull. The youngster rushes into the arena and rides his pet to safety.

***Lone Wolf McQuade* (1983)** Orion, color, 107 minutes. **Director:** Steve Carver; **Screenplay:** B. J. Nelson; **Cast:** Chuck Norris (J. J. McQuade), David Carradine (Rawley Wilkes), Barbara Carrera (Lola Richardson), Leon Isaac Kennedy (Marcus Jackson), Robert Beltran (Arcadio "Kayo" Ramos), L. Q. Jones (Dakota), Dana Kimmell (Sally McQuade).

Years before he starred on TV as *Walker, Texas Ranger* (1993–2001), martial-arts whiz Norris headlined this action entry in which BELTRAN was cast as his Chicano rookie partner. The buddy picture also featured Nicaraguan-born Carrera and African-American Kennedy.

Tough-as-nails Texas Ranger J. J. McQuade, an unorthodox law enforcer, is determined to capture Rawley Wilkes and his pals who stole U.S. Army weapons and offered them for sale to Central American terrorist factions. Assisting the "Lone Wolf" are his partner Kayo and FBI agent Jackson, as well as Native American Lola Richardson, originally tied to Wilkes but changing sides when she becomes entranced with judo-chopping McQuade.

Combining elements of the spaghetti western with the mindless mayhem thriller, this noisy entry grossed more than $12 million in domestic distribution.

Lopez, Jennifer (1970–) One of the highest-profile Hollywood stars in the early twenty-first century, Lopez forged a multifaceted career as dancer, movie star, recording artist, and tabloid favorite. Her Hispanic heritage added a spicy ingredient to her leading lady status, outshining such contemporaries as SALMA HAYEK.

The middle of three sisters, she was born in the Bronx, New York, where her father was a computer technician and her mother a kindergarten teacher. (Both parents were originally from Puerto Rico.) She began to take singing/dancing lessons at age five. After high school, determined to be a show business success, she moved to Los Angeles, where she was one of "The Fly Girls" on the African-American-oriented comedy/variety show, *In Living Color* (1991–94). Lopez appeared in such failed TV series as *South Central* and *Hotel Malibu*—both 1994—before her supporting role in the movie *MY FAMILY: MI FAMILIA* (1995). Her energetic and sincere performance as Selena Quintanilla in the movie biography *SELENA* (1997) launched Lopez's stardom. Later film roles included *Out of Sight* (1998), *The Cell* (2000), *Angel Eyes* (2001), *Enough* (2002), *The Chambermaid* (2002), and *Gigli* (2003).

Lopez won tributes from ALMA Awards for her performances in *Selena* and *Out of Sight*, and she received ALMA's Special Achievement Awards as Female Entertainer of the Year in both 2000 and 2001.

***Lotta Land* (1995)** CFP, color, 87 minutes. **Director/Screenplay:** John Rubino; **Cast:** Larry Gilliard (Hank), Wendell Holmes (Milton), Barbara Gonzalez (Joy), Suzanne Costallos (Florence), Jaime Tirelli (Papi), Luis Guzman (bit).

Following in the tradition of Spike Lee, Rubino's warmhearted film debut dissected life in a Brooklyn neighborhood full of Hispanics and African-American characters. The focus of this drama was on Hank, a high-school grad who worked in a nearby liquor store managed by Florence. The latter is parenting Hank's girlfriend, Joy, who is headed to college. Their daily lives change when news spreads that someone in the area has won $27 million in the lottery.

***Lucy and Desi: Before the Laughter* (1991)** CBS-TV, 100 minutes. Color. **Director:** Charles Jarrott; **Teleplay:** William Luce and Cynthia A. Cherbak; **Cast:** Frances Fisher (Lucille Ball), Maurice Benard (Desi Arnaz), Robin Pearson Rose (Vivian Vance), John Wheeler (William Frawley), Bette Ford (De-De).

On October 15, 1951, the half-hour sitcom *I LOVE LUCY* debuted on TV and quickly became a tremendous success. This biographical telefeature opens just as the debut show is to be filmed. The narrative then flashes back to 1940, when the couple first met, and progresses through the subsequent eleven years, detailing their roller-coaster marriage. As Lucille Ball and the Cuban-born DESI ARNAZ, both Fisher and Benard captured the essence of the two stars' contrasting personalities to a certain extent.

***Luminarias* (1999)** New Latin Pictures, color, 101 minutes. **Director:** Jose Luis Valenzuela; **Screenplay:** Evelina Fernández; **Cast:** Evelina Fernández (Andrea), Scott Bakula (Joseph), Cheech Marin (Jesus), Robert Beltran (Joe), Marta DuBois (Sofia), Angela Moya (Lilly), Dyana Ortelli (Irene).

Described as a Latina *Waiting to Exhale* (1995), this comedic drama revolved around four Hispanic professional women: divorced attorney Andrea, flamboyant clothes designer Irene, artist Lilly, and therapist Sofia. They meet frequently at Luminarias in East Los Angeles to discuss their lives. As their problems unfold, the viewer learns that Andrea, who is angered by Anglo men who want a Hispanic woman only as a love toy, is amazed to find herself becoming interested in a white Jewish lawyer (Bakula). Irene is dealing with her own biases regarding her transvestite brother. Meanwhile, Lilly is coping with the prejudice of her boyfriend's Korean-American family, and Sofia, overanxious to be acculturated, is surprised to find herself intrigued by a hot-blooded Mexican waiter.

Most important herein is the film's discussion of the changing roles of Hispanic Americans as the U.S. culture breaks down some of their racial barriers and how this process affects the traditional battle of the sexes.

M

***Machete* (1958)** United Artists, b&w, 75 minutes. **Director:** Kurt Neumann; **Screenplay:** Carroll Young and Neumann; **Cast:** Mari Blanchard (Jean Montoya), Albert Dekker (Don Luis Montoya), Juano Hernandez (Bernardo), Carlos Rivas (Carlos), Lee Van Cleef (Miguel).

This turgid drama of romantic intrigue was set on a Puerto Rican sugar plantation. Its cast—struggling to make their ethnic roles more than just types—was unable to elevate this soap opera in any meaningful way. According to this film, the machete was a symbol of honor to Puerto Ricans.

Young Jean Montoya weds wealthy, much older Don Luis and the couple return to his sugar plantation in Puerto Rico. Soon, she is ensnaring Carlos into her romantic trap, but hanger-on Miguel tells Señor Montoya the truth, leading to household chaos.

***Magnificent Matador, The* (1955)** Twentieth Century-Fox, color, 94 minutes. **Director:** Budd Boetticher; **Screenplay:** Charles Lang; **Cast:** Maureen O'Hara (Karen Harrison), Anthony Quinn (Luis Santos), Richard Denning (Mark Russell), Thomas Gomez (Don David), Lola Albright (Mona Wilton), William Ching (Jody Wilton), Eduardo Noriega (Miguel), Lorraine Chanel (Sarita Sebastian).

Filmmaker Boetticher earlier had made the atmospheric *BULLFIGHTER AND THE LADY* (1951), and QUINN had already played an on-screen matador in such features as *Blood and Sand* (1941) and *THE BRAVE BULLS* (1951). Here Quinn was cast as an aging matador who confounds the public when he becomes afraid of fighting in the ring. Due to Hollywood movie industry production-code standards of that time, many of the more graphic bullfighting sequences were cut from the final release print, thus removing much of its atmosphere.

Concerned about ill omens forecast for young bullfighter Rafael Reyes, seasoned professional Luis Santos, who has been chosen to train him, leaves the ring rather than have the newcomer face a vicious bull. Santos seeks escape in a romance with American bullfighting enthusiast Karen Harrison, much to the annoyance of her boyfriend (Denning). Eventually Luis acknowledges that Reyes is his illegitimate son, a fact the boy had already known. With renewed confidence, father and son enter the ring to face the ferocious bull, and they acquit themselves well.

The landscape was the highlight of this entry, which utilizes several real-life Mexican matadors.

***Magnificent Seven, The* (1960)** United Artists, color, 128 minutes. **Director:** John Sturges; **Screenplay:** William Roberts and (uncredited) Walter Bernstein and Walter Newman; **Cast:** Yul Brynner (Chris Adams), Eli Wallach (Calvera), Steve McQueen (Vin), Horst Buchholtz (Chico), Charles Bronson (O'Reilly), Robert Vaughn (Lee), Brad Dexter (Harry Luck), James Coburn (Britt), Rosenda Monteros (Petra).

In remaking Akira Kurosawa's Japanese classic *The Seven Samurai* (1954), director Sturges set the action in Mexico and initially had all the hired gunslingers scripted as American characters. But the Mexican government complained and, as a compromise, two of the septet (Buchholtz and Bronson) became Mexican so it could be seen that Mexicans can protect other Mexicans from banditos. There was also governmental concern about having the picture divert the tourist trade by being too violent.

The Mexican village of Ixcatlán regularly is savaged by Calvera and his bandit gang. In desperation, the villagers contract Chris Adams to bring them protection. Soon, Adams rides into Ixcatlán with his crew, drawn from gunslingers and fugitives in need of work and diversion: Vin, Lee, Harry Luck, Britt, the Mexican-Irish half-breed O'Reilly, and the Mexican-Indian Chico. The group train the townsfolk, and when Calvera returns, many of his men are killed, but Calvera escapes. Now that it is no longer a business situation for the seven gunslingers, they suddenly realize they care about the villagers. In a reencounter with Calvera, they overcome his forces, but four of the gunslingers die. While Adams and Vin ride off to their future, Chico remains in the village to wed Petra and become a farmer.

With its international cast, its sharpened visuals, and the psychological undertones (e.g., the passing of the age of the antihero gunslinger) the violent *The Magnificent Seven*—which boasted an Oscar-nominated Elmer Bernstein score—became a major box-office hit and led to *Return of the Seven* (1966), *Guns of the Magnificent Seven* (1969), and *The Magnificent Seven Ride* (1972). A 1998 ninety-minute TV movie pilot, *The Magnificent Seven,* had a Native American chief hire seven gunslingers to defend tribal lands from outlaws. It prompted the 1998–99 TV entry *The Magnificent Seven: The Series* with Vaughn from the original cast as Judge Orin Travis.

***Mambo Kings, The* (1992)** Warner Bros., color, 101 minutes. **Director:** Arne Glimcher; **Screenplay:** Cynthia Cidre; **Cast:** Armand Assante (Cesar Castillo), Antonio Banderas (Nestor Castillo), Cathy Moriarty (Lanna Lake), Maruschka Detmers (Delores Fuentes), Desi Arnaz Jr. (Desi Arnaz Sr.), Celia Cruz (Evalina Montoya), Tito Puente (himself).

This quasi-musical was based on the Pulitzer Prize-winning novel *The Mambo Kings Play Songs of Love* (1989) by Oscar Hijuelos as well as José Marti's poem "Guantanamera." The project was directed by first-timer Glimcher, an art gallery entrepreneur. With its uncertain tone and the unrealized development of many of its musical scenes, *The Mambo Kings* did not much capture the public's fancy, grossing less than $7 million in domestic distribution. On the plus side, the romantic fable delineated some of the richness of Hispanic culture in its depiction of the 1950s in Havana and then in New York City. The surprise performance of the film was that of Spanish-born BANDERAS.

Forced to flee Cuba where he has fallen in love with a club owner's woman, Nestor Castillo and his brother travel north to New York City in the early 1950s where they hope to capitalize on the mambo craze sweeping the United States. Offstage, the musician brothers are very different—Nestor is brooding and romantic; Cesar is volatile and a womanizer. In front of audiences, however, their music styles blend well. They become quite popular in the New York club circuit, and Nestor writes a tune ("Beautiful Maria of My Soul") that becomes a major hit. This eventually brings the duo to the attention of musician/actor DESI ARNAZ, who hires them for an episode of TV's *I LOVE LUCY*. Meanwhile, Nestor weds Delores Fuentes but still pines for his lost Cuban love, while Cesar barely disguises his lust for his sister-in-law. Later, Nestor dies in a car crash, leaving behind his legacy of music.

The Mambo Kings was nominated for an Academy Award for Best Song ("Beautiful Maria of My Soul").

***Man from Del Rio* (1956)** United Artists, b&w, 82 minutes. **Director:** Harry Horner; **Screenplay:** Richard Carr; **Cast:** Anthony Quinn (Dave Robles), Katy Jurado (Estella), Peter Whitney (Ed Bannister), Douglas Fowley (Doc Adams), John Larch (Bill Dawson), Whit Bissell (Breezy Morgan).

This offbeat Hollywood western had as its theme racial tolerance toward Mexican Americans, which was unusual given the era in which it was produced. It is easy to see why their screen assignments appealed to the Mexican-born QUINN and JURADO.

Saloon-owner Ed Bannister who runs Mesa, a Texas border town, asks Mexican American Dave Robles (who has just killed several gunslingers) to become the community's new sheriff. Thinking that the position will not only give him a livelihood ($100 a month plus room and board) but also some standing in the town, he accepts. Robles soon learns, however, that he is wanted only for his shooting skills and that the townsfolk are still prejudiced against him because of his heritage. Meanwhile, he attempts to romance Doc Adams's Mexican-American assistant, Estella, a widow whose daughter is living with relatives in Wichita. She does not respect Robles because her late husband, a gunfighter, left her a single parent. Eventually in a showdown with Bannister, the latter proves to be spineless, and Robles chooses to remain in town, as does Estella who now loves him.

This compact feature, with its study of moral strength and cowardice, owed a nod to *HIGH NOON* (1952), which also featured Jurado.

***Man from the Alamo, The* (1953)** Universal-International, color, 79 minutes. **Director:** Budd Boetticher; **Screenplay:** Steve Fisher and D. D. Beauchamp; **Cast:** Glenn Ford (John Stroud), Julia Adams (Beth Anders), Chill Wills (John Gage), Hugh O'Brian (Lt. Tom Lamar), Victor Jory (Jess Wade), Neville Brand (Dawes), John Day (Cavish), Mark Cavell (Carlos).

Rather than focus on the 1836 battle of the ALAMO, which had been covered in other films, this tale of revenge dealt with the one man who escaped the massacre by Mexican General Santa Anna and his troops. Also within the plot was a story gimmick sometimes used in westerns where marauding braves attacking settlers prove to be white men in disguise.

At the Alamo, the men from the town of Ox Bow draw lots to determine who will leave the stronghold to warn their women and children of the approaching Mexican army. John

Stroud "wins" and he departs for Ox Bow only to find everyone in town dead, including his wife and son. The only survivor of the ordeal, a young Mexican youth (Cavell), alerts Stroud that it was actually gringos disguised as Mexicans who did the killings. Later, when news reaches the town of Franklin about the massacre at the Alamo, Stroud is on hand there and is soon branded a coward by the locals. Coping with this disabuse, he pursues the murderers, finally tracking down the vicious Jess Wade. Having redeemed himself in his own eyes, Stroud rides off to join Sam Houston and his men at San Jacinto for a major assault on the Mexican forces.

***Manito* (2002)** 7th Floor, color, 77 minutes. **Director/Screenplay:** Eric Eason. **Cast:** Franky G. (Junior Moreno), Leo Minaya (Manny Moreno), Manuel Cabral (Oscar Moreno), Julissa Lopez (Miriam), Hector Gonzalez (Abuelo), Panchito Gómez (Rodchenko).

Making his feature film bow here, screenwriter/director Eason deals with two days in the traumatic lives of a Washington Heights (New York City) Latino household. Adding chaos to the daily routine is Manny's imminent high school graduation. The father (Cabral), who operates a local bodega, is not invited to the teenager's celebration but he shows up and is ejected from the party. (It develops that Oscar's criminal activities once caused his older son, Junior, to be jailed and that thereafter the parent had deserted his family.)

Daily Variety (January 23, 2002) rated this an "electrifying feature" and added, "Furiously paced—just shy of the sensory-overload point—pic duly merits comparison to its spiritual granddaddy *Mean Streets* [1973], not in the usual imitative sense but rather in the freshness, character acuity, and low-budget high style brought to a different New York City ethnic milieu."

***Marcus Welby, M.D.* (1969–1976)** ABC-TV series, color, 60 minutes. **Cast:** Robert Young (Dr. Marcus Welby), James Brolin (Dr. Steven Kiley), Elena Verdugo (Consuelo Lopez), Anne Baxter (Myra Sherwood: 1969–70), Sharon Gless (Kathleen Faverty: 1974–76), Pamela Hensley (Janet Blake: 1975–76).

Dr. Welby was everyone's wish fulfillment of the kindly, wise physician who always made time to go the extra step for his patients in his Santa Monica, California, practice. He was assisted by young Dr. Steven Kiley, innovative in techniques but a bit rough in diplomacy. Running their office efficiently was Mexican-American Consuelo Lopez, the warm-hearted nurse/office manager. Her off-work life was depicted, including a January 1970 episode in which her mother (DOLORES DEL RIO) was dying of cancer.

In this era, it was still rare in a U.S. network TV series to have a Hispanic character integrated into the story line in such a major, positive fashion. It was a part handled with warmth by veteran VERDUGO.

Marin, Cheech (1946–) His nickname Cheech came from the word *chicharron*, a spicy fried-pork-skin Mexican snack. Marin's talent ran deeper than his stereotype as the Hispanic doper of the Cheech and Chong comedy team that had a commercially successful fifteen-year run. Later, Marin demonstrated his acting resourcefulness as Don Johnson's police partner on the TV cop series *Nash Bridges* (1996–2002).

He was born Richard Marin in the Watts section of Los Angeles, one of four children of a Los Angeles police officer. Raised in the San Fernando Valley, he was a top high-school student and worked menial jobs to put himself through college as an English major. When he joined the improvisational group City Works in Vancouver, British Columbia, Canada, in the late 1960s, he began a long association with Asian-Canadian talent Tommy Chong. The two continued as a duo, performing in clubs and launched a wildly successful comedy-album career (including the Grammy-winning *Los Cochinos*). Their first feature, *UP IN SMOKE* (1978), was a box-office winner, and one of their last together was *Get Out of My Room* (1985), which Marin wrote and directed. After the team split, Marin wrote, directed, and starred in *BORN IN EAST L.A.* (1987). Thereafter, Marin was a support regular on the TV sitcom *The Golden Palace* (1992–93), the follow-up to *The Golden Girls* (1985–92). In 1994, Cheech played Pancho, the jovial sidekick of JIMMY SMITS, in the TV movie *The Cisco Kid* and was the voice of Banzai in the animated feature, *The Lion King*. The next year, he provided the voice of Lencho the Flea in *Santo Bugito*, a TV cartoon series. Besides his *Nash Bridges* TV chores, Marin was featured in such pictures as *DESPERADO* (1995), *Tin Cup* (1996), *LUMINARIAS* (1999), *Spy Kids* (2001), and *Once Upon a Time in Mexico* (2003). On TV's *RESURRECTION BLVD* (2000–) the actor/comedian was seen as Hector Archuletta, owner of an East L.A. auto repair shop.

***Mark of Zorro, The* (1920)** United Artists, b&w, 8 reels. **Director:** Fred Niblo; **Screenplay:** Elton Thomas [Douglas Fairbanks]; **Cast:** Douglas Fairbanks (Don Diego Vega/Señor Zorro), Noah Beery (Sergeant Pedro), Charles Hill Mailes (Don Carlos Pulido), Claire McDowell (Dõna Cataline), Marguerite De La Motte (Lolita), Robert McKim (Capt. Juan Ramon), George Periolat (Governor Alvarado).

This was the American cinema's first rendition of what would prove to be an inordinately popular character with the public over the decades. This silent, swashbuckling feature was based on *The Curse of Capistrano* by Johnston McCulley that was serialized in 1919 in *All-Story Weekly* (and published in book form in 1924). It was adapted to the screen by movie star Fairbanks using the pseudonym of Elton Thomas.

In the 1840s, Don Diego Vega completes his schooling in Spain and returns to old California. To his dismay, he finds an oppressive governor (Periolat) in charge. To right the wrongs being done, Diego adopts two roles. He pretends to be a foolish fop while, on the other hand, wearing a mask, he is the dashing ZORRO who becomes the Robin Hood of the territory. With ingenuity and fencing skills, Zorro pushes the odious governor from power and wins the love of the aristocratic Lolita, who has been engaged to the prissy Diego.

Essentially playing two characters, Fairbanks was comedic as the fop and at his athletic best as the dashing Zorro who defends the rich and poor alike. Many of the figures in this movie are no more than stereotypes, but they are balanced between positive and negative images of Hispanics in Old California. In contrast to the CISCO KID, another constantly recurring Hispanic screen character who was a bandit at heart, Zorro was an aristocratic, bright, and agile Hispanic—a hero for all the ages.

Fairbanks returned to the athletic Zorro character in *DON Q, SON OF ZORRO* (1925).

***Mark of Zorro, The* (1940)** Twentieth Century-Fox, b&w, 93 minutes. **Director:** Rouben Mamoulian; **Screenplay:** John Taintor Foote, Garrett Fort, and Bess Meredyth; **Cast:** Tyrone Power (Don Diego Vega/Zorro), Linda Darnell (Lolita Quintero), Basil Rathbone (Capt. Esteban Pasquale), Gale Sondergaard (Inez Quintero), Eugene Pallette (Fra Felipe), J. Edward Bromberg (Don Luis Quintero), Montagu Love (Don Alejandro Vega).

Since Douglas Fairbanks Sr.'s portrayal of the dashing ZORRO in two 1920s silent movies, there had been other Zorros on the screen (both in a feature and in movie serials). This new elaborate production, also based on Johnston McCulley's *The Curse of Capistrano* (1919), proved to be an exuberant, lavish production that launched Power onto a series of swashbuckling screen assignments. If he lacked the athletic agility of Fairbanks in the earlier renditions of Zorro, Power was more handsome, more charming, and more adept in the romantic scenes. Like Fairbanks he was an Anglo, and his characterization lacked the authentic Hispanic sensibility. On the other hand, minor roles were played by ethnic performers (e.g., Pedro De Cordoba, Chris-Pin Martin). The highlight of this movie—beyond its well-appointed sets and exquisite costuming—was the climactic sword fight between Zorro and the snide, cruel Captain Pasquale.

Advertisement for *The Mark of Zorro* (1940). (ECHO BOOK SHOP)

The very popular *The Mark of Zorro* generated an Oscar nomination for Best Original Score. The success of this movie adaptation led to other Zorro movies in the future, including *THE MASK OF ZORRO* (1998).

Martinez, A (1948–) An enduring Hollywood figure, he created his greatest impact as a sexy presence on TV's *Santa Barbara* (1984–92), *L.A. LAW* (1992–94), and *General Hospital* (1999–). Born Adolfo Martinez in Glendale, California, he was at UCLA when he made his film debut in *The Young Animals* (1968). He became a cast regular on the politically correct TV drama, *STOREFRONT LAWYER* (1970–71), and played a Mexican cowboy in the film (1972) and TV series (1974) of *The Cowboys*. After playing Tranquilino Marquez in the TV miniseries *Centennial* (1978–79), Martinez joined Angie Dickinson for TV's *Cassie & Co.* (1982) and then took on the roles of Low Wolf in the telefeature *Born to the Wind* (1982) and Buddy Red Bow in the Native American acculturation drama *Powwow Highway* (1989). For the police TV series *Profiler*, he was seen as agent Nick Cooper from 1996 to 1997. More recently he appeared in such movies as *Last Rites* (1998), *What's Cooking?* (2000), and *Ordinary Sinner* (2001).

***Mask of Zorro, The* (1998)** Columbia TriStar, color, 136 minutes. **Director:** Martin Campbell; **Screenplay:** Ted Elliott, Terry Rossio, and John Eskow; **Cast:** Antonio Banderas (Alejandro Murrieta/Zorro), Anthony Hopkins (Zorro/Don Diego de la Vega), Catherine Zeta-Jones (Elena Montero/Elena Murrieta), Stuart Wilson (Don Rafael Montero), Matt Letscher (Capt. Harrison Love), William Marquez (Fray Filipe), Victor Rivers (Joaquin Murrieta).

Filmed in central Mexico on a $65 million budget, this screen adventure of ZORRO was in the tradition of 1940's *THE MARK OF ZORRO*. It combined the swashbuckling exploits of Zorro with 1990s filming techniques and was bolstered by Spanish-born BANDERAS and Britisher Hopkins, both of whom displayed a wonderful chemistry working together. They created a new Zorro box-office success, with the feature grossing more than $93 million in domestic distribution.

After twenty years in prison for foiling the plans of the dastardly Don Rafael Montero, Don Diego de la Vega, who had been the masked avenger Zorro, escapes from prison in old California. He intends to revenge the murder of his wife by Montero. Meanwhile, de la Vega encounters Alejandro Murrieta, an outlaw whose brother has been killed by Montero's henchman, Capt. Harrison Love. De la Vega teaches Murrieta to be a skilled swordsman so that he can triumph over his sibling's killer. As part of his scheme to break into Love's inner circle, Murrieta disguises himself as a Spanish nobleman and at a party meets Elena, who was brought up by Montero but who is actually de la Vega's child. By the finale, the two key villains are dispatched, Murrieta and Elena are in love, and de la Vega, before he dies from exertion in dispatching his enemies, passes on the mantle of Zorro to Murrieta.

***Masquerade in Mexico* (1945)** Paramount, b&w, 96 minutes. **Director:** Mitchell Leisen; **Screenplay:** Karl Tunberg; **Cast:** Dorothy Lamour (Contessa de Costa Mora [Angel O'Reilly]), Arturo De Córdova (Manolo Segovia), Patric Knowles (Tom Grant), Ann Dvorak (Helen Grant), George Rigaud) Condé de Costa Mora [Boris Cassall]), Mikhail Rasumny (Pablo), Martin Garralaga (José).

This pleasant trifle with impressive sets was a remake of the 1939 Claudette Colbert–Don Ameche comedy *Midnight* (set in Paris), which was also directed by Leisen. Mexican-born DE CÓRDOVA was quite at home as the flirtatious Mexican bullfighter who pursues an assortment of females during the proceedings. The large supporting cast included many Mexican talents.

Set in various Mexico locales but filmed at the Hollywood studio, the musical told of an American nightclub singer named Angel O'Reilly, who flies to Mexico City, where she is coerced by banker Tom Grant into flirting with bullfighter Manolo Segovia to divert him from romancing Grant's wife Helen. Meanwhile, Angel's ex-suitor, the crooked Boris Cassall, shows up in Mexico City, and she realizes again that he is not the man for her. Flushing out this well-appointed comedy of assumed identities and marital infidelity was a ballet interlude and several songs: e.g., "Noche de ronda" (Forever Mine), "Adios Mariquita Linda" (Adios and Farewell My Lover), and "Buscandote" (That's Love).

***Medal for Benny, A* (1945)** Paramount, b&w, 77 minutes. **Director:** Irving Pichel; **Screenplay:** Frank Butler; **Cast:** Dorothy Lamour (Lolita Sierra), Arturo De Córdova (Joe Morales), J. Carrol Naish (Charley Martin), Mikhail Rasumny (Raphael Catalina), Fernando Alvarado (Chito Sierra), Charles Dingle (Zack Mibbs), Frank McHugh (Edgar Lovekin), Rosita Moreno (Toodles Castro), Nestor Paiva (Frank Alviso).

This quiet, unassuming, but effective drama focused on contemporary Mexican Americans. As such, it was the early beginning of Hollywood treating this ethnic minority with a degree of sensitivity on screen. As the foreword to the picture stated, "In the old part of town are the Paisanos—Americans of mixed Indian and Spanish blood. A simple, friendly people, they . . . are the original California settlers."

In 1942, in the California fishing town of Pantera, lackadaisical Joe Morales purchases a small fishing boat; now that he has a career he can ask Lolita Sierra to marry him, but, as she reminds him, she plans to wed Benny Martin. The latter left town in disgrace after a run-in with a local policeman and has not been heard of since. Meanwhile, Morales, who already used money from Charley—Benny's father—to buy the boat, convinces the simple man to loan him more money—this time to pay his rent.

Later, it is learned that Benny had joined the army and has become a hero, having killed 100 Japanese enemy in the Philippines. Charley's excitement is diminished when he discovers that the medal to be given his son will be posthumous. He is even more upset when the town's mayor and his cronies relocate him to a fancy house so that, when the governor and a general present the award, the town won't be embarrassed by having the festivities occur at Martin's simple abode. Martin insists that the ceremony be conducted at his real house. At the presentation, he makes a heartfelt speech about his late offspring. Morales joins the army, hoping that it will give Lolita and Charley Martin time to adjust to Benny's passing so that he can ask her again to marry him.

Based on a twenty-page story idea by John Steinbeck and Jack Wagner, the well-received *A Medal for Benny* earned Oscar nominations for Best Original Story and for Best Supporting Actor (Naish). Also in 1945, Mexican-born DE CÓRDOVA teamed with Louisiana-born Lamour in *MASQUERADE IN MEXICO*.

medical series—television An early example of a Hispanic character on a medical TV drama was that of Consuelo Lopez (played by ELENA VERDUGO) on *MARCUS WELBY, M.D.* (1969–76), set in Santa Monica, California. On *Doctors' Hospital* (1975–76), set in Los Angeles, Victor Campos played Dr. Felipe Ortega. *Kay O'Brien* (1986), located at Manhattan's General Hospital, included Priscilla Lopez as Nurse Rosa Villaneuva. On *Nurses* (1991–94), a Miami-localed sitcom, Carlos LaCamara was on hand as support staff member Paco Ortiz. Within the more-lofty medical drama *Chicago Hope* (1994–2000), HECTOR ELIZONDO was the overworked chief of staff. Meanwhile, on *ER* (1994–), one of the only Latinos on the show was Laura Cerón who played Nurse Chuny Marquez from 1995 onward. On the medical show *Crisis Center* (1997), Clifton Gonzales Gonzales was featured as a street-savvy youth counselor.

The short-lasting *Gideon's Crossing* (2000–2001) went out of its way to provide a diverse ethnic cast and included in its roster RUBÉN BLADES as a hospital administrator who happened to be a psychiatrist. Equally multicultural was *Third Watch* (1999–), which had Anthony Ruivivar as a paramedic and Lisa Vidal cast as a physician (besides offering Eddie Cibrian as a fireman). On the highly women-oriented *Strong Medicine* (2000–), Rosa Blasi costarred as Dr. Luisa Delgado, running a free women's clinic at the Rittenhouse Hospital in Philadelphia. On the sitcom *Scrubs* (2001–), Judy Reyes appeared as a bright nurse dealing with a romance with a fellow staff member at the hospital.

***Men with Guns* (aka: *Hombres armadas*) (1998)** Sony Pictures Classics, color, 128 minutes. **Director/Screenplay:** John Sayles; **Cast:** Federico Lupi (Dr. Humberto Fuentes), Damian Delgado (Domingo, the soldier), Dan Rivera González (Conejo, the boy), Damián Alcázar (Padre Portillo the priest), Tania Cruz (Graciela, the mute girl), Mandy Patinkin (Andrew).

Sayles, a leading light of independent American cinema, made this unique offering in Spanish and indigenous Latin American languages with English subtitles. Among other literary works, this movie was inspired by characters within Francisco Goldman's *The Long Night of White Chickens* (1992). It was filmed in Mexico.

In Central America, aged physician Dr. Humberto Fuentes learns that all his medical students—part of a government program to help poor villagers—are now missing and presumed dead. Reportedly, sadistic men with guns have been rampaging communities and killing the doctors (to get their drugs and other medical supplies). Fuentes sets out to determine if, perhaps, any of his former pupils survived. En route, he is joined by an orphan (González), a soldier named Domingo who is fleeing the army, and a former priest. Later, at one burned-out village, the ex-priest is detained, but the others are let go. The trio take with them Graciela, a young woman raped by a soldier. The search leads to a rain forest where Fuentes is hopeful of finding a former female student. But before they do, the elderly Fuentes dies. Meanwhile, Domingo has taken on the mantle of physician and treats an ailing Indian.

Filled with flashbacks (in black and white), this lyrical quest of the old doctor became a search for the meaning of lives. Most impressively, the characters evolved as full-bodied individuals, not Anglo stereotypes imposed upon another culture.

Men with Guns, definitely an art house release, grossed $742,032 in domestic distribution. It was nominated for a Golden Globe Award as Best Foreign Language Film.

***Mexican Hayride* (1948)** Universal-International, b&w, 77 minutes. **Director:** Charles T. Barton; **Screenplay:** Oscar Brodney and John Grant; **Cast:** Bud Abbott (Harry Lambert), Lou Costello (Humphrey Fish [Joe Bascom]), Virginia Grey ([Mary] Montana), Luba Malina (Dagmar), John Hubbard (David Winthrop), Pedro de Cordoba (Señor Martinez), Fritz Feld (Professor Ganzmeyer), Chris-Pin Martin (mariachi leader), the Flores Brothers (trio).

Based quite loosely on the Broadway musical *Mexican Hayride* (1944), book by Herbert and Dorothy Field and music by Cole Porter, the screen adaptation dropped Porter's songs and, instead, focused on Abbott and Costello's antics. The nonsensical plot allowed the duo to mine their slapstick with a Mexican backdrop, courtesy of the studio's backlot.

In Mexico during American Friendship week, Joe Bascom is hunting for con artist Harry Lambert, who got him in trouble with the police. By error, Bascom's one-time girlfriend Mary—now known as Montana—names him and not Lambert the winner of the Amigo Americana contest. The prize is a week's tour through Mexico. By the end of the trek, Bascom has undone the latest mischief (i.e., stock in a phony silver mine) in which Lambert and his fiery girlfriend Dagmar have involved the feckless Bascom. The proceedings end in a bull ring where Bascom finds himself dancing a samba with a ferocious bull, then retrieving the ill-gotten money from Lambert, and ending up with the fetching Dagmar.

In his efforts to bring a madcap quality to the uninspired proceedings, Costello's character donned several disguises, which included being a mariachi player and a tortilla-selling señorita. Many Mexican-American performers were utilized in subordinate background roles.

Mexican Spitfire Mexican-born LUPE VÉLEZ, a longtime Hollywood star, was in a film career slump when this free spirit made the quickly assembled *THE GIRL FROM MEXICO* (1939). She was the peppery señorita named Carmelita Fuentes who soon wed an advertising executive (played by Donald Woods) and became involved with his somewhat henpecked Uncle Matt (played by Leon Errol). The zany movie caught the public's fancy, partially because of Vélez's high-energy shenanigans, fractured English, and zesty look. Another noteworthy ingredient was comedian Errol's rubber-legged shtick and broad double takes. The studio promptly decided to make a series to take advantage of the public's growing interest in all things South American during this pre–World War II era when the United States was fostering a "Good Neighbor Policy" with south-of-the-border countries. As of the second entry, Errol played both Uncle Matt Lindsay and Lord Basil Epping. Entries four through six featured Charles "Buddy" Rogers as the heroine's beleaguered spouse; Walter Reed took over as Dennis Lindsay for entries seven and eight. The series was brought to a sudden halt because of Vélez's suicide in 1944. The series entries, all directed by Leslie Goodwins, were 1939: *The Girl from Mexico, Mexican Spitfire;* 1940: *Mexican Spitfire Out West, Mexican Spitfire's Baby, Mexican Spitfire at Sea;* 1942: *Mexican Spitfire Sees a Ghost, Mexican Spitfire's Elephant;* 1943: *Mexican Spitfire's Blessed Event.*

***Miami Vice* (1984–1989)** NBC-TV series, color, 60 minutes. **Cast:** Don Johnson (Det. James "Sonny" Crockett), Philip Michael Thomas (Det. Ricardo Tubbs), Edward James Olmos (Lt. Martin Castillo), Saundra Santiago (Det. Gina Navarro Calabrese), Olivia Brown (Det. Trudy Joplin).

With its MTV-style visuals and sound, flamboyant wardrobes and cars, and art deco styling, the true star of this hip police drama series was the city of Miami and its array of multiethnic characters.

The show revolved around two flashy resort-city cops. Det. James "Sonny" Crockett lives on a sailboat *(St. Vitus Dance)*, is rough-edged and boisterous, and drives a Ferrari. His partner, a former New York City street cop, the African-American Det. Ricardo Tubbs, is more sullen. The dynamic duo report to Lt. Martin Castillo, their grumpy Latino superior.

Despite its several Emmy Awards (including one to OLMOS for his characterization of the surly Castillo), high ratings, and occasional ethnic minority role models, the weekly episodes presented an array of drug lords, vicious criminals, prostitutes and their pimps, and so on—most of whom were either Hispanic or African American.

In the pilot to this series, JIMMY SMITS played Crockett's partner but was killed in the plot line and GREGORY SIERRA was the two cops' superior, Lt. Lou Rodriquez.

***Milagro Beanfield War, The* (1988)** Universal, color, 118 minutes. **Director:** Robert Redford; **Screenplay:** David Ward and John Nichols; **Cast:** Rubén Blades (Sheriff Bernabe Montoya), Richard Bradford (Ladd Devine), Sonia Braga (Ruby Archuleta), Julie Carmen (Nancy Mondragon), James Gammon (Horsethief Shorty), Melanie Griffith (Flossie Devine), Carlos Riquelme (Amarante Cordova).

Based on the first book (1976) in a trilogy by John Nichols, *The Milagro Beanfield War* took nine years of off-camera difficulties to become an on-screen reality. In condensing the 626-page book, filled with a mix of fantasy and reality, into a reasonable length picture, many characters and much detail were eliminated. In addition, Redford's softening of the class conflict within the tale flattened some of the book's sharpness.

Within this fanciful film, a sudden burst of flowing water from a sluice gate galvanizes the small New Mexico town as the locals polarize around the pros or cons of this action. The situation inspires Ruby Archuleta, who owns the town's auto-repair shop (and a plumbing service), to take a stand against the controversial recreation development under the aegis of Anglo landowner Ladd Devine. The latter asks the governor for help, and, before long, local sheriff Bernabe Montoya is caught in the middle of the situation.

Much publicized for its use of Hispanic talent in front of and behind the camera, *The Milagro Beanfield War*, which cost close to $20 million to produce, grossed only about $14 million in domestic distribution. The whimsical feature received an Oscar nomination in the Best Original Score category for David Grusin's music. The movie was shot in Espanola, Las Truchas, Los Alamos, and Santa Fe, New Mexico.

Miranda, Carmen (1909–1955) With fruit-laden turbans, high platform shoes, gyrating hands, and a devilish smile, five-feet, two-inch Miranda swayed to Latin American rhythms and insinuated herself into show business immortality with her high energy, exaggerated persona. One of Brazil's most famous exports, she became a Hollywood star of the 1940s and a camp legend thereafter. Like many others who abandoned their homelands for a lucrative American movie career, Miranda discovered that her South American fans felt deserted, which affected her deeply for the rest of her life.

The Brazilian Bombshell was born Maria do Carmo Miranda Da Cunha near Lisbon, Portugal. Soon thereafter, her family moved to Rio de Janeiro where she grew up. Always a singer, she had a recording contract in the late 1920s and became a major name in Brazil. Her screen debut was in the documentary *A Voz do Carnaval* (1933), and her Broadway debut was in the late 1930s; Miranda made her American movie debut in *Down Argentine Way* (1940) in an extended cameo. So great was public reaction to this novelty entertainer that she was soon churning out Technicolor musicals, adding her South American styling and heavy accent to *THAT NIGHT IN RIO* (1941), *Springtime in the Rockies* (1942), and *The Gang's All Here* (1943). By the end of World War II and the downplaying of the U.S. government's Good Neighbor Policy with Latin America, her career diminished: She was only a featured performer in *A Date with Judy* (1948) and *Nancy Goes to Rio* (1950). Her last movie was *Scared Stiff* (1953) with Dean Martin and Jerry Lewis. She died of a heart attack just after completing a guest appearance on Jimmy Durante's TV variety show.

In 1994, the documentary *Carmen Miranda: Bananas Is My Business* was released.

***Missing* (1982)** Universal, color, 122 minutes. **Director:** Constantin Costa-Gavras; **Screenplay:** Donald Stewart and Costa-Gavras; **Cast:** Jack Lemmon (Ed Horman), Sissy Spacek (Beth Horman), Melanie Mayron (Terry Simon), John Shea (Charles Horman), Charles Cioffi (Capt. Ray Tower), David Clennon (Consul Phil Putnam).

This stark, spellbinding drama (based on a real-life situation in Chile) dissected political ideologies of North Americans and South Americans. The gripping film depicted a range of human suffering as the father and the wife of a vanished American journalist (who is a political activist) discovered duplicity within the bureaucracy of their own government's State Department as they battered the shield of silence in the South American dictatorship where the young man disappeared. Filmed in Mexico, this was the first English-language feature by Greek-born Costa-Gavras and was based on Thomas Hauser's *The Execution of Charles Horman* (1978).

American Ed Horman, a right-winger and a Christian Scientist, and his politically liberal daughter-in-law, Beth, who have opposing thoughts on most subjects, search for her husband in an unnamed South American dictatorship. Before long they lose their naiveté as they discover the injustices and torments suffered by the locals and the callousness of American officials. In demanding to know what happened to Charles Horman, they cope with American diplomats and agents who have their own agenda and bend the truth at will.

Missing received an Academy Award for Best Adapted Screenplay. It garnered Oscar nominations for Best Actor (Lemmon), Best Actress (Spacek), and Best Picture. The highly controversial film aroused the ire of several sectors of the U.S. government. On the other hand, some critics complained that filmmaker Costa-Gavras made the story too abstract and diluted some of its potential power by not naming names. For others, this depiction of a tyrannical South American regime was just a confirmation of what past Hollywood movies (e.g., *CRISIS*, 1950) had already revealed about brutal Latin or South American dictatorships.

***Mr. Majestyk* (1974)** United Artists, color, 104 minutes. **Director:** Richard Fleischer; **Screenplay:** Elmore Leonard; **Cast:** Charles Bronson (Vince Majestyk), Al Lettieri (Frank Renda), Linda Cristal (Nancy Chavez), Lee Purcell (Wiley), Paul Koslo (Bobby Kopas), Taylor Lacher (Gene Lundy), Julio Tomaz (Bert Santos), Eddy Reyes and Larry Cortinez (Chicano prisoners).

Adapted by Leonard from his own paperback original novel (1974), *Mr. Majestyk* preceded into release by a few months Bronson's ultrasuccessful *Death Wish* (1974). But it followed the same violent revenge motif of the concerned citizen, pushed too far by brutal lawbreakers, who takes the law into his own hands. This time, the offenders were Mafioso; the good guys were itinerant Mexican-American fruit pickers. Left unstated—whether intentionally or not—was the ethnic background of the Vietnam War veteran antihero, Vince Majestyk, who might well be Mexican American himself. Latin American-born CRISTAL provided the requisite pulchritude in her poorly developed character.

On his Colorado farm, rugged Vince Majestyk employs migrant Mexican-American workers to pick his melon crop. This upsets labor racketeer Bobby Kopas, who insists that the farmer should hire Kopas's crew. When Kopas pressures Majestyk, the latter physically removes Kopas from the farm. Kopas files charges, and Majestyk is arrested. When Majestyk escapes in the prison bus on the way to court, Frank Renda, a Mafia killer, is a handcuffed prisoner aboard. Renda later flees and swears that he will kill Majestyk who almost foiled his break to freedom. The police permit Majestyk to return to his farm, hoping that Renda will fall for the bait. With most of the workers scared off by Kopas, labor organizer Nancy Chavez can round up only a few helpers to work the crop. The pickers are terrorized by Renda's men, and Majestyk turns avenger. With Nancy tagging along, Majestyk successfully takes on the killers.

***Mi Vida Loca* (aka: *My Crazy Life*) (1994)** Sony Pictures Classics, color, 92 minutes. **Director/Screenplay:** Allison Anders; **Cast:** Angel Aviles (Sad Girl), Seidy Lopez (Mousie), Jacob Vargas (Ernesto), Marlo Marro (Giggles), Jesse Borrego (El Duran), Magali Alvarado (La Blue Eyes), Salma Hayek (Gata).

Using several nonprofessionals within its cast (which led to some awkward screen moments but was better than having miscast actors pretending to be these life-tough women), Anders intelligently dissected Chicano gang life in Echo Park, a subsection of Los Angeles. Focusing on the females in the group, Anders paints a strong portrait of their bleak existence where often their men die young or end up in jail and the women are left to carry on life and tend to the children. Two of the participants are Sad Girl and Mousie, who each have a child by Ernesto (who is later killed by a disgruntled Anglo drug customer). The two women now focus on their friend Giggles, about to be released from jail. To their surprise, she no longer wishes to be a gang leader. Later, the plot centers on a stolen van whose ownership is in dispute, Sad Girl's college-attending sister (Alvarado), and the senseless shooting of an innocent girl during a rival gang's reprisal. At the finale, the members swear they want to break out of their gang rut, but there is no assurance that they can or will.

Filmed in Echo Park, *Mi Vida Loca* grossed more than $3 million in domestic distribution. This was the first American-made feature film for HAYEK.

***Mixed Blood* (1916)** Universal, b&w, 5 reels. **Director:** Charles Swickard; **Screenplay:** J. Grubb Alexander; **Cast:** Claire McDowell (Nita Valyez), George Beranger (Carlos), Roy Stewart (Big Jim), Wilbur Higby (Joe Nagle), Jessie Arnold (Lottie Nagle).

Half-Spanish and half-Irish, Nita Valyez finds herself both attracted to and repelled by bad guy Carlos. In contrast, Big Jim, the local sheriff, merits only her cursory interest. Later, after Carlos murders a man, he drags Nita with him when he flees. Big Jim pursues and reaches them in a border town. By now Carlos is dying of a disease, and the law enforcer brings Nita back to their town, hoping to wed her one day.

Had Nita's character been of another ethnic mix (e.g., African American), conventions of the era would *not* have permitted the two lead characters to unite by the fadeout.

Montalban, Ricardo (1920–) From the start of his Hollywood movie years, this handsome, serious actor was forced into the mold of LATIN LOVER, a category he found limiting to his dramatic range and his career growth. Later on, he played Asians (e.g., *Sayonara*, 1957), Native Americans (e.g., *Cheyenne Autumn*, 1964, and his Emmy Award-winning role as Chief Satangkai in the miniseries *How the West Was Won*, 1978), and galaxy villains (e.g., *Star Trek: The Wrath of Khan*, 1982). He remained most closely associated with his assignment as the mysterious, immaculate Mr. Roarke in TV's *FANTASY ISLAND* (1977–84).

Montalban was born in Mexico City, the youngest of four siblings. Later he came to Los Angeles with his older brother Carlos, and then moved to New York City, where he gained stage work. After returning to Mexico, where he made more than a dozen features in the early to mid-1940s, he was brought back to Hollywood by MGM where he debuted for the studio in *Fiesta* (1947). For every cotton-candy musical (e.g., *Neptune's Daughter*, 1949), he managed to do a few solid dramas (e.g., *Battleground*, 1949; *RIGHT CROSS*, 1950). By the mid-1950s Montalban was freelancing and became a frequent TV performer: Captain Esteban in the 1974 TV version of *The Mark of Zorro* and Manuel the fisherman in a TV rendition of *Captains Courageous* (1977), among others. Slowed down by a disabling back condition, Montalban's most recent TV series were *Heaven Help Us* (1994), playing a guardian angel, and the children's TV cartoon series *Freakazoid!* (1995–97), providing the voice of Armondo Guitierrez. Over the years, the star was quite active in Mexican-American and Hispanic PRESSURE GROUPS, trying to bring equality to ethnic minorities in show business and elsewhere. In 1994, Montalban received the Life Achievement Award from the Screen Actors Guild.

Montez, Maria (1912–1951) A shrewdly self-created legend, this extremely beautiful Hispanic dominated the Technicolor fantasy extravaganzas churned out by Universal Pictures in the 1940s. Her overstated exotic presence no longer fit the post–World War II Hollywood, and she moved to France with her actor-husband Jean-Pierre Aumont, making several lesser European coproductions before her untimely death of a heart attack.

She was born María Africa Vidal de Santo Silas in Barahona, Dominican Republic. Her Spanish consul father had her educated in the Canary Islands. After traveling with her family, she had a brief marriage and then arrived in New York to capitalize on her striking looks. A movie contract quickly followed. Despite her heavy accent, she soon became a hot commodity (billed as the Caribbean Cyclone) in Hollywood. She teamed with Jon Hall for several costumed escapist adventures, including *Arabian Nights* (1942), *Ali Baba and the Forty Thieves* (1944), and *Cobra Woman* (1944—as twins). After the failure of *Siren of Atlantis* in 1948, she departed for the Continent. Among her last films were *Revenge of the Pirates* and *City of Violence*, both 1951.

Moreno, Rita (1931–) Her career is noteworthy not only for its versatility and longevity, but also for her array of honors (winning an Oscar, a Tony, an Emmy, and a Grammy) and appearances in several screen projects that illuminated Hispanic life in America (e.g., *THE RING*, 1952; *POPI*, 1969).

She was born Rosita Dolores Alverio in Humacao, Puerto Rico. When her parents divorced, her mother took her five-year-old daughter to New York City. A born entertainer, the girl began dancing lessons early and was on Broadway in *Skydrift* (1945). After frustrating years as a club performer, she went to Hollywood, debuting in a story of juvenile delinquency (*So Young, So Bad*, 1950). MGM had her under contract for two years (e.g., *Singin' in the Rain*, 1952) but then dropped her. Typecast as a Latin spitfire, she was sometimes used on camera as a Native American (e.g., *The Yellow Tomahawk*, 1954) or as an Asian (e.g., *The King and I*, 1956). Winning an Oscar for her Anita in *WEST SIDE STORY* (1961) did not break the stereotyping or lack of viable roles, and Moreno returned to the Broadway stage, winning a Tony for *The Ritz* and repeating the role in the 1976 movie adaptation. She labored through the TV sitcom *9 TO 5* (1982–83), had a popular exercise video in 1990, and played Bill Cosby's helper in the unsuccessful *The Cosby Mysteries* (1994). In the mid-1970s, she played a prostitute character on the TV detective series *The Rockford Files*, a role she recreated effectively in the TV movie *The Rockford Files: If It Bleeds . . . It Leads* (1999). Her more recent features included *Carlo's Wake* (1999), *Blue Moon* (2000), and PIÑERO (2001).

For her recurring role as Sister Peter Marie Reimondo on the cable TV series *Oz* (1997), Moreno won an ALMA Award (as Outstanding Actress in a Drama Series) in 1999 and was nominated in the same category in subsequent years for her performance.

Murieta, Joaquín See MURRIETA, JOAQUIN.

Murrieta, Joaquín (aka: Joaquín Murieta) (1828?–1853 or ca. 1878) Unlike the fictitious CISCO KID and ZORRO, there was a real-life Joaquín Murrieta, a nineteenth-century Mexican who relocated to the California Territory and built a near-mythical reputation as a celebrated bandito. As such—according to different versions of his history—he righted wrong, helped the poor, and was a great ladies' man. One of his great passions was to revenge himself on gringos, who, according to legend, had badly discriminated against him during his stay in the California gold fields. As payback, Murrieta vowed to even the score and, supposedly, gathered together a band of men to execute his plans. Various versions of his death include his having been captured and beheaded by a California ranger, anywhere from 1853 to 1878. All of these "facts" and myths were embellished upon over the years as Murrieta appeared and reappeared in literature and assorted screen presentations in Hollywood (and Mexican) movies. Depending on the film production and its star, Murrieta was showcased as gruff or charming, fierce or compassionate, and so on.

The following are among the actors who have portrayed Murrieta in American-made movies: Richard Dix (*THE GAY DEFENDER*, 1927), Buck Jones (*THE AVENGER*, 1931), Warner Baxter (*THE ROBIN HOOD OF EL DORADO*, 1936), Shepperd Strudwick (*Joaquin Murrieta*, 1938), Bill Elliott (*Vengeance of the West*, 1942), Phillip Reed (*The Bandit Queen*, 1950), Jeffrey Hunter (*Joaquin Murrieta*, 1965), Diego Sieres and Victor Rivers (*THE MASK OF ZORRO*, 1998).

musicals—feature films When the studios converted to sound and song-and-dance films were all the rage, one of Hollywood's big musicals of the late 1920s was *Rio Rita* (1929). It was set in a Texas town on the Mexican border. Two of LATIN LOVER Ramón Novarro's 1930 operettas (*In Gay Madrid* and *Call of the Flesh*) were set in Spain. *THE CUBAN LOVE SONG* (1931) teamed MEXICAN SPITFIRE LUPE VÉLEZ with the Metropolitan Opera's Lawrence Tibbett.

The movie that really ushered in Hollywood's enthusiasm for Hispanic-flavored romps was *FLYING DOWN TO RIO* (1933), set in the capital of Brazil (courtesy of the studio's back lot). This first teaming of Fred Astaire and Ginger Rogers introduced the tropical beat of "The Carioca." That film's DOLORES DEL RIO also did duty in *In Caliente* (1935), which was full of Hispanic flavoring. Meanwhile, the short subject *La Cucaracha* (1934), set at a Mexican Café, won an Academy Award as Best Short Subject and was an early use of the three-strip Technicolor process. Another similarly ethnic-themed short was *La Fiesta de Santa Barbara* (1935), featuring a young Judy Garland and her two sisters. *Rose of the Rancho* (1936) was set in Monterey just after California became part of the United States but featured Metropolitan Opera star Gladys Swarthout as a Spanish señorita who led a vigilante band. *Tropic Holiday* (1938) was a Mexican-set musical comedy featuring Dorothy Lamour, Martha Raye, and Tito Guizar.

In 1940, the great era of Hispanic-flavored Hollywood musicals got underway with *ARGENTINE NIGHTS* starring the Andrews Sisters, while the American-set *TOO MANY GIRLS* featured the screen bow of Cuban-born DESI ARNAZ. Brazil's CARMEN MIRANDA did her first American movie with *Down Argentine Way* (1941), which led to a slew of colorful tropical-infused song-and-dance films: *THAT NIGHT IN RIO* (1941), *Weekend in Havana* (1941), *You Were Never Lovelier* (1942), *Brazil* (1944), *Mexicana* (1945), *The Thrill of Brazil* (1946), *Carnival in Costa Rica* (1947), *Fiesta* (1947), and *Nancy Goes to Rio* (1950). Also during the decade, such other ethnic talent as Spanish-born XAVIER CUGAT (and his band) and pianist JOSÉ ITURBI, as well as Mexican-born vocalist Tito Guizar lent their talents to American movies.

In the 1950s Hollywood turned away from South American themes and talent. It was a big jump from the turgid melodrama of the music-laden *Serenade* (1956), set partially in Mexico and starring Mario Lanza, to the multi-Oscar winning *WEST SIDE STORY* (1961), dealing with Puerto Rican rumbles in New York City. Elvis Presley's *FUN IN ACAPULCO* (1963) tried to recapture the magic of earlier films set south-of-the-border. The decade ended with the New York-set *Sweet Charity* (1969), which added some Hispanic tones to the tale of a wistful prostitute thanks to the inclusion of RICARDO MONTALBAN and Chita Rivera in the cast.

The relatively few Latin-flavored musicals of recent decades have been urban set and offered a multiethnic cast and multicultural music in the mix. These included such entries as *Saturday Night Fever* (1977), *Fame* (1980), and *Rooftops* (1989). Much more focused on Hispanic Americans were *LA BAMBA* (1987), *Salsa* (1988), *LAMBADA* (1990), *La Pastorela* (1991), *SELENA* (1997), and *Dance with Me* (1998). The long-delayed transfer of the stage musical *EVITA* (1979) to film (1996) featured Madonna and ANTONIO BANDERAS in a tale of the rise and fall of Eva Perón wed to Argentina's dictator. *Carmen: A Hip Hopera* (2001—made-for-cable movie) featured Beyoncé Knowles as Carmen Brown in a contemporary rendition of the classic tale.

My Crazy Life See *MI VIDA LOCA*.

***My Darling Clementine* (1946)** Twentieth Century-Fox, b&w, 97 minutes. **Director:** John Ford; **Screenplay:** Samuel G. Engel and Winston Miller; **Cast:** Henry Fonda (Wyatt Earp), Linda Darnell (Chihuahua), Victor Mature (Doc Holliday), Cathy Downs (Clementine Carter), Walter Brennan (Old Man Clanton), Tim Holt (Virgil Earp), Ward Bond (Morgan Earp), John Ireland (Billy Clanton).

One of the best accounts of the gunfight at the O.K. Corral had an excellent character delineation of (a romanticized) Wyatt Earp and Doc Holliday. Darnell was cast as the Mexican prostitute Chihuahua who loved Holliday.

In nineteenth-century Arizona in the town of Tombstone, Wyatt Earp is the new sheriff. After a bad start, he and the consumptive Doc Holliday become good friends. The latter's girlfriend, the pouty, passionate Chihuahua deeply loves Holliday and is jealous when prim Easterner Clementine Carter, Holliday's ex-fiancée, shows up in Tombstone. Earp is obsessed with revenging the deaths of his brothers at the hands of the Clanton gang. Meanwhile, Billy Clanton shoots Chihuahua for incriminating him in the killings. Doc and the Clanton boys die at the O.K. Corral, and Clanton's father is later gunned down by Morgan Earp. Wyatt and Morgan leave town, but Clementine remains in Tombstone, hoping that Earp will one day come back.

The beautiful, immoral, and possessive Chihuahua was secondary to the gunslinging action and the interrelationship between Earp and Holliday. Nevertheless, this Hispanic character who vainly hoped Doc would take her to Mexico to be married, made a strong impression—far more so than the staid Eastern woman (Downs). It was a matter of screen convention—and industry censorship codes—that an impure saloon singer such as Chihuahua should suffer her fate. Besides, according to the standard reasoning of the white majority at the time, this tragic woman was Mexican and therefore less worthy of sympathetic treatment on screen.

Shot mostly in Monument Valley, Utah, *My Darling Clementine* grossed almost $3 million in domestic distribution. Based on Stuart N. Lake's book *Wyatt Earp, Frontier Marshal* (1931), the novel served as the basis for the earlier *Frontier Marshal* (1939), in which Binnie Barnes played the Caucasian dance-hall character; in the later *Powder River* (1953), also derived from Lake's novel, Corinne Calvet was Frenchie, the counterpart to Chihuahua's character.

My Family See *MY FAMILY: MI FAMILIA*.

***My Family: Mi Familia* (aka: *My Family*) (1995)** New Line Cinema, color, 125 minutes. **Director:** Gregory Nava; **Screenplay:** Nava and Anna Thomas; **Cast:** Jimmy Smits (Jimmy Sanchez), Esai Morales (Chucho), Eduardo López Rojas (José Sanchez), Jenny Gago (Maria Sanchez), Elpidia Carrillo (Isabel Magano), Lupe Ontiveros (Irene Sanchez), Edward James Olmos (Paco, the narrator), Enrique Castillo (Memo Sanchez).

NAVA, who directed the well-regarded EL NORTE (1983), returned to similar turf in *My Family: Mi Familia.* The film's broad historical tapestry traced three generations of a Mexican-American family in Los Angeles in the 1920s, 1950s, and 1980s as the city, attitudes, prejudices, and lifestyles change.

The chronicle was narrated by the eldest son Paco, a writer. The story opens in the 1920s as Paco's father, José Sanchez, travels on foot from central Mexico, finally reaching Los Angeles after two years. As Sanchez marries and has children, his struggle to maintain the sense of family and traditions in this strange new country take their toll. One son, Chucho, grows to be a lazy ladies' man, resentful of the class struggles his people face in America. Another offspring, Jimmy, matures into an irate individual who turns burglar and ends in prison. Another son, Memo, relocates out of the barrio and becomes a lawyer and a very acculturated Mexican American with an Anglo wife, which causes rifts within the family.

Told with sympathy, humor, and a story emphasis on Hispanic culture, this picture poignantly reflects the angst of Mexican Americans who are considered foreigners in their own country.

Filmed in the greater Los Angeles area and in Mexico (Michoacán, Ocumichu, Patamba, and Pátzcuaro), *My Family: Mi Familia* grossed more than $11 million in domestic distribution.

***My Man and I* (1952)** Metro-Goldwyn-Mayer, b&w, 99 minutes. **Director:** William A. Wellman; **Screenplay:** John Fante and Jack Leonard; **Cast:** Shelley Winters (Nancy), Ricardo Montalban (Chu Chu Ramirez), Wendell Corey (Ansel Ames), Claire Trevor (Elena Ames), Robert Burton (sheriff), José Torvay (Manuel Ramirez), Jack Elam (Celestino Garcia), Pascual García Peña (Willie Chung).

This unpretentious drama was one of the politically "relevant" features produced during Dore Schary's regime as head of MGM. Despite a contrived plot line, the movie's superior acting and its message of ethnic minority assertiveness and pride gave it substance. In the presentation of Ansel and Elena Ames, *My Man and I* (the picture's title derived from a lyric in the song "Stormy Weather," which was played during the film) delineated the degree of racism that existed at the time. There was dialogue within the picture where Mrs. Ames uses such weighted words as "dirty rag head," "chink," "another foreigner," and noted that all Mexicans "can look mean." In response, Chu Chu Ramirez mockingly added another derogatory term to her lexicon: "greaser."

Ricardo Montalban and Shelley Winters in *My Man and I* (1952). (JC ARCHIVES)

Mexican-born Chu Chu Ramirez has become an American citizen and even has exchanged correspondence with the U.S. president. Ramirez is a migrant farm laborer who works in California's San Joaquin Valley near Fresno. Unlike his cousin Manuel or their friends Celestino Garcia and Willie Chung, Chu Chu saves his money and tries to better educate himself. He finds work at the Ames's farm where Elena, despite her racial biases, is sexually drawn to the young man. He rebuffs her advances. In town, Chu Chu meets Nancy, who is down on her luck and has become drink dependent from mourning her late test-pilot husband.

When Ansel Ames gives Chu Chu a salary check that bounces, it leads to an altercation, which only escalates when Ames still does not pay the laborer what is owed him. Later Ames lies about how he was shot in the shoulder (actually, an accident) and tells the police that Chu Chu is responsible. Ramirez is jailed, later breaking out to see Nancy who has attempted suicide. Eventually, Celestino and the others prevail on Mr. and Mrs. Ames to tell the truth, and Ramirez is freed. He convinces the reluctant Nancy that they should marry.

In the plot of *My Man and I*, the Nancy character repeatedly stated she was not worth Chu Chu's time and that he would do better to find another woman. Because she was alcoholic, suicidal, and of a lower social class, it was deemed—so the script suggested—okay for the Mexican Chu Chu to wed the white Nancy.

***Mystery Street* (1950)** Metro-Goldwyn-Mayer, b&w, 93 minutes. **Director:** John Sturges; **Screenplay:** Sydney Boehm and Richard Brooks; **Cast:** Ricardo Montalban (Lt. Peter Morales), Sally Forrest (Grace Shanway), Bruce Bennett (Dr. McAdoo), Elsa Lanchester (Mrs. Smerring), Marshall Thompson (Henry Shanway), Jan Sterling (Vivian Heldon), Edmon Ryan (James Joshua Harkley), Betsy Blair (Jackie Elcott).

Searching for viable roles for their Mexican-born contract leading man Montalban, the studio cast him as Portuguese-American police Lieutenant Peter Moralas who investigates the murder of a young woman on Cape Cod. In this film noir, the juxtaposition of working-class Moralas against the blue-blood old Boston society being investigated provided an added dimension to this police procedural tale. That the socially prominent killer resented an ethnic such as Moralas, also raised in Boston, rubbing shoulders with him added an edge to the caper.

In Boston pregnant prostitute Vivian Heldon tries to blackmail one of her customers, well-to-do, married James Joshua Harkley, but he, instead, murders her during their confrontation on a deserted stretch of Cape Cod. Morales investigates the case, receiving a great deal of forensic help from Dr. McAdoo at Harvard University. The trail at first leads to Henry Shanway, in whose car the victim's corpse was found. Another interested party was the dead woman's eccentric landlady Mrs. Smerring.

N

***Naked Dawn, The* (1955)** Universal, color, 82 minutes. **Director:** Edgar G. Ulmer; **Screenplay:** Nina and Herman Schneider [Julian Zimet]; **Cast:** Arthur Kennedy (Santiago), Betta St. John (Maria), Eugene Iglesias (Manuel), Charlita (Tita), Roy Engel (Guntz).

This economy production, filmed in Mexico, depicted how greed changed the lives of three individuals. The cast's strong performances and the low-key Mexican ambiance gave this strong tale added substance.

A crook named Santiago persuades simple young Mexican farmer Manuel to help him deliver the loot from a train robbery to Guntz, the man who engineered the heist. When Guntz refuses to make good the promised fee, Santiago takes the money by force. Before long, Manuel considers killing Santiago so that he and his wife Maria can have a bigger cut of the loot. Meanwhile, Maria suggests to Santiago that the two of them run away together with the money. However, the police track down Santiago, and he is fatally wounded in the shootout. Before he dies, he gives the cash to the young couple, instructing them to start a fresh life.

Nava, Gregory (1949–) In several of his screen works, Nava demonstrated a passion and directness about his ethnic heritage, which made his films that much better. Born in San Diego, California, his background was Mexican and Basque. He attended the UCLA Film School; there, his student project *The Journal of Diego Rodriguez Silva*—dealing with the life of famed Spanish poet Federico Garcia Lorca—was honored as Best Dramatic Film at the National Student Film Festival in the early 1970s. He wrote, directed, and produced *The Confessions of Amans* in 1973, which went on to win the Best Feature Award at the Chicago International Film Festival for 1976. For *EL NORTE* (1983), which he wrote and directed, he and co-writer Anna Thomas were nominated for an Oscar in the Best Original Screenplay category. After *A Time of Destiny* (1988) starring William Hurt, Nava wrote and directed *MY FAMILY: MI FAMILIA* (1995), a generational saga of a Mexican-American family in Los Angeles. Next, he scripted and directed *SELENA* (1997) starring JENNIFER LOPEZ as the famed singer. He executive produced and helmed *Why Do Fools Fall in Love* (1998), which told of the life of rock 'n' roll singer Frankie Lymon. In 1999, Nava's documentary, *20th Century: In the Melting Pot* aired. He was one of the scripters of *Frida Kahlo* (2001) starring SALMA HAYEK, ANTONIO BANDERAS, and Edward Norton. Nava's dramatic feature, *Killing Pablo* (2002), was based on Mark Bowden novel, *Killing Pablo: The Hunt for Pablo, the World's Greatest Outlaw* (2001). He created a TV series, *AMERICAN FAMILY*, about a Latino household in East Los Angeles, which aired on the PBS network in 2002.

***New York Undercover* (1994–1998)** Fox-TV series, color, 60 minutes. **Cast:** Michael DeLorenzo (Det. Eddie Torres: 1994–97), Malik Yoba (Det. James "J. C." Williams), Patti D'Arbanville-Quinn (Lt. Virginia Cooper: 1994–97), Lee Wong (M. E. Wong: 1994–97), Lauren Vélez (Det. Nina Moreno: 1995–98), Lisa Vidal (Carmen Torres: 1994–95), Mike Torres (José Pérez: 1994–95).

One of the most gritty TV police dramas, it was bolstered by a driving music beat (in its early seasons). At New York's Fourth Precinct in Harlem, optimistic black Det. James "J. C." Williams and impulsive Puerto Rican-American Det. Eddie Torres were partners, doing overtime to bust bad guys. Their off-duty lives balanced the show's focus. There was Torres's sister (Vidal) and their dad (Perez), a saxophonist and recovering drug addict. In season two, street-tough

Det. Nina Moreno joined the proceedings, leading to a romance between her and Eddie. Torres's character was killed by a car bomb at the end of the 1996–97 season, By the finale of the series, J.C. and Moreno were dating casually, reflecting yet another step in the growing ethnic integration on TV series.

***9 to 5* (1982–1983; 1986–1988)** ABC- (then Syndicated) TV series, color, 30 minutes. **Cast:** Rita Moreno (Violet Newstead), Rachel Dennison (Doralee Rhodes Brooks), Valerie Curtin (Judy Bernly), Jeffrey Tambor (Franklin Hart: 1982), Peter Bonerz (Franklin Hart: 1982–83), Jean Marsh (Roz Keith: 1982–83), Tony Latorra (Tommy: 1983).

This TV adaptation of the hit 1980 movie that starred Jane Fonda, Dolly Parton, and Lily Tomlin never had the impact of the original. It repeated the premise of a trio of secretaries who fought a constant battle against sexual harassment and gender discrimination from their incompetent boss, Franklin Hart, at the corporation where they toiled.

Within the setup, there was Hispanic Violet Newstead, a widow with a twelve-year-old son (Latorra), shapely country girl Doralee Rhodes Brooks, and college graduate Judy Bernly. For a change, little was made of Violet's ethnic background, the heavy accent of stereotyped characterization was bypassed, and Puerto Rican-American MORENO was allowed to function as a normal, modern female in the business world, *not* as a subordinate racial type.

After the series left the air in 1983, it returned in first-run syndication from 1986 to 1988, with only Dennison and Curtin returning from the original cast.

Top row: Herb Edelman, Jean Marsh, and Peter Bonerz; bottom row: Rachel Dennison, Rita Moreno, and Valerie Curtin in the TV sitcom *9 to 5* (1982–83). (VINCENT TERRACE)

***NYPD Blue* (1993–)** ABC-TV series, color, 60 minutes. **Cast:** David Caruso (Det. John Kelly: 1993–94), Dennis Franz (Det. Andy Sipowicz), James McDaniel (Lt. Arthur Fancy: 1993–2001), Sharon Lawrence (Asst. D. A. Sylvia Costas: 1994–99), Nicholas Turturro (Off./Det./Sgt. James Martinez: 1993–2000), Jimmy Smits (Det. Bobby Simone: 1994–98), Kim Delaney (Det. Diane Russell: 1995–2001), Rick Schroder (Det. Danny Sorenson: 1998–2001), Esai Morales (Lt. Tony Rodriguez: 2001–), Mark Paul Gosselaar (Det. John Clark: 2001–), Jacqueline Obradors (Det. Rita Ortiz: 2001–).

This hard-edged police series is noted as much for its constant cast changes as for its story line and occasional (tasteful) nudity. In season two of this New York-set melodrama, sensitive Det. Bobby Simone (extremely well played by SMITS) becomes partners with gruff Det. Andy Sipowicz, leading to conflicts. Still grieving for his dead wife, Simone romances and eventually weds Det. Diane Russell. For a time, he is off the force, accused of being a dirty cop. Once reinstated, he is soon diagnosed with heart disease and, in a highly rated fall 1998 episode, dies. Another Hispanic member of the squad is Officer James Martinez, who has several affairs but finally marries. He was a detective by the time his character disappeared from the narrative in 2000. Yet another was Tony Rodriguez. As played by Morales, he joined the series as the department's new lieutenant. Another new face at the precinct was Obradors as Det. Rita Ortiz.

O

***Old Man and the Sea, The* (1958)** Warner Bros., color, 86 minutes. **Directors:** John Sturges and (uncredited) Henry King and Fred Zinnemann; **Screenplay:** Peter Viertel; **Cast:** Spencer Tracy (the old man), Felipe Pazos (the boy), Harry Bellaver (Martin), Don Diamond (café proprietor), Don Blackman (hand wrestler).

Ernest Hemingway's Pulitzer Prize-winning novella, *The Old Man and the Sea* (1952), a parable about man's struggle with nature and the depth of his courage and endurance, proved daunting to picturize. It cost the Hollywood film studio $6 million during two years and involved the departure of the original director (Fred Zinnemann) and endless hours devoted to shooting Tracy (as the semiliterate, poor Cuban fisherman who talked to himself) on actual waters and in studio tanks.

The movie related elderly Manuel's contest with a giant marlin he hooks that drags his little boat for almost a day, reminding the fisherman of his times as a wrestler called El Campeón. As the veteran seaman brings his catch home, the bloody fish attracts sharks that he valiantly fights off, although by the time he reaches the shore, his prize is merely a skeleton. (With its tale of man against nature, this was a rare early occasion of Hollywood depicting a non-Anglo in a relatively positive light as the earnest soul combats nature and the meaning of life.)

The Old Man and the Sea was a box-office disappointment. However, the movie won an Academy Award for Best Scoring of a Dramatic or Comedy Picture. It received Oscar nominations for Best Actor (Tracy) and for Best Cinematography.

In 1990 ANTHONY QUINN successfully tackled the difficult title role of Santiago for a NBC-TV telefeature production of *The Old Man and the Sea.*

Olmos, Edward James (1946–) Long regarded as an articulate and dedicated spokesperson of the Latino artistic community, Olmos early in life had planned on becoming a baseball player. This ambition was put aside at age thirteen when he fell in love with rock music. By the early 1970s the hard-working performer was taking acting classes. By the time he became a multi-media success in subsequent years, he had become a strong, positive role model for Latinos.

Born in East Los Angeles of a Mexican father and a Mexican-American mother, he was raised in the Boyle Heights district. By the time he was a young teenager, he had become enthralled by the music of such performers as Little Richard and James Brown. Before long he was forming garage bands and, by the late 1960s, he was playing his music at clubs along Los Angeles' Sunset Strip. Thereafter, he expanded his performing interests to theater and took acting classes. In 1978 he had a starring role in the Los Angeles production of *Zoot Suit,* a drama that was later remounted for Broadway and led Olmos to being nominated for a Tony Award and to winning a prestigious Theatre World Award. (In 1981 he recreated his role of El Pachuco for the movie adaptation of ZOOT SUIT.) Earlier, the actor had made his feature film acting debut in *Aloha Bobby and Rose* (1975) and had appeared in episodes of mainstream TV series (*Kojak, Hawaii Five-0*). Olmos was asked to play a Native American in the movie *Wolfen* (1981), but refused the part. He insisted the filmmaker cast the part with an American Indian, but when they failed to find one for the role, he reluctantly accepted the assignment. In 1984 Olmos debuted as somber Lt. Martin Castillo on the teleseries *Miami Vice.* During the police show's five-season run he won an Emmy Award (1986).

A highlight of his career was taking on the role of Bolivian teacher Jaime A. Escalante in the inspirational movie STAND AND DELIVER (1987). For his sterling performance of the passionate teacher he was nominated for an Academy Award and a Golden Globe. The veteran talent turned to film directing with *American Me* (1992) for which he also produced and starred. His later screen performances included the comedy *A Million to Juan* (1994) and the family drama, *MY FAMILY: MI FAMILIA* (1995). In *SELENA* (1997), he played the father of the slain songstress. Meanwhile, he was nominated for an Emmy Award for his supporting role in TV's *THE BURNING SEASON: THE CHICO MENDES STORY* (1994). All through this period he was an ardent activist (and at one time an ambassador for UNICEF) who made many personal appearances each year advocating the rights and needs of (Latino) youth. In 1999 Olmos received an ALMA Award for his crossover role in the telefeature *The Taking of Pelham: One Two Three* (1998). Two years later he was sentenced to twenty days in prison in Puerto Rico for trespassing on U.S. Navy land (on the island of Vieques) during protests against navy bombing practice there.

Recent projects for Olmos included the animated feature *The Road to El Dorado* (2000), the TV movie *The Judge* (2001), the political feature *In the Time of the Butterflies* (2001), and the PBS-TV series AMERICAN FAMILY (2002–).

***One-Eyed Jacks* (1961)** Paramount, color, 141 minutes. **Director:** Marlon Brando; **Screenplay:** Guy Trosper and Calder Willingham; **Cast:** Marlon Brando (Rio), Karl Malden (Dad Longworth), Katy Jurado (Maria), Pina Pellicer (Louisa), Slim Pickens (Lon), Ben Johnson (Bob Amory), Sam Gilman (Harvey), Larry Duran (Modesto), Rodolfo Acosta (Rurales officer).

Director Stanley Kubrick began this film in late 1958 but star Brando took over direction when Kubrick left, and six months later, this project was finally completed with the budget jumping from $1.8 million to more than $6 million. The lengthy western, filled with the star's acting excesses, grossed less than $4 million in its initial domestic distribution. It featured strong Mexican atmosphere both in several of its characters (especially JURADO and Pellicer) and in its locales (especially Monterey). (Location filming was accomplished in Death Valley and Monterey, California.)

In 1880, bank robbers Rio and Dad Longworth are left with one horse and with the Mexican law pursuing them. Longworth agrees to get a fresh mount and hurry back. Instead he leaves Rio to be captured and spend the next five years imprisoned in brutal misery. After escaping prison, Rio learns that Longworth is now the sheriff of Monterey, California, and has married a Mexican woman with a grown daughter. Determined to gain revenge, Rio joins with Amory and Harvey, the latter two planning to rob the Monterey bank. Encountering Longworth, Rio pretends friendship and soon seduces the man's stepdaughter, Louisa. Later, recuperating from a beating by Longworth for killing a drunk in self-defense, Rio returns to town. By now, Louisa is pregnant, and Rio plans to call off the feud, but when Amory and Harvey rob the bank, Longworth jails Rio for the deed and intends to hang him. Rio escapes, has a final showdown with the sheriff, and then rides from town, having promised Louisa he will be back.

One-Eyed Jacks won an Oscar nomination for Best Cinematography (Color). The film was based on Charles Neider's novel, *The Authentic Death of Hendry Jones* (1956).

***100 Rifles* (1969)** Twentieth Century-Fox, color, 110 minutes. **Director:** Tom Gries; **Screenplay:** Gries and Clair Huffaker; **Cast:** Jim Brown (Lydecker), Raquel Welch (Sarita), Burt Reynolds (Yaqui Joe), Fernando Lamas (General Verdugo), Dan O'Herlihy (Grimes), Hans Gudegast (Von Klemme), Michael Forest (Humara).

Shot in Spain, this violent R-rated western gained much publicity because of the interracial romantic sparring on camera between WELCH (of Bolivian-American heritage) and Brown (an African American). Within the violent tale, Reynolds, a part Seminole, displayed the charm that made him a big box-office star of the 1970s, while Latin American-born LAMAS was the dastardly villain. The handsome, ethnically diverse cast gave the action movie great momentum at the box office.

Set in the early 1900s, *100 Rifles* has half-breed Yaqui Joe robbing an Arizona bank and then riding across the border to Nogales. He finds General Verdugo, aided by a German military adviser (Gudegast), waging a war against the Yaqui. African-American U.S. lawman Lydecker arrives in time to distract Verdugo from shooting Yaqui Joe, and the two fugitives hide in the hills. There they meet Sarita, a Yaqui revolutionary. She is responsible later for rescuing them when the two men are again caught by Verdugo's forces. In the seesawing battle against Verdugo, Sarita is later killed; Lydecker returns to the States, and Yaqui Joe is inspired to lead the Yaqui.

***One Man's War* (1991)** HBO cable, color, 91 minutes. **Director:** Sergio Toledo; **Teleplay:** Michael Carter and Toledo; **Cast:** Anthony Hopkins (Dr. Joel Filartiga), Norma Aleandro (Nidia), Rubén Blades (Perrone), Claudio Brook (Robledo), Fernanda Torres (Dolly).

In Paraguay, dedicated Dr. Joel Filartiga often treats his impoverished patients at his health clinic at his own expense. (He finances his charitable work by selling his art work in the United States.) When he vehemently opposes the repressive government's cruel treatment of its people during one of his business trips to America, the military faction retaliates by torturing and killing his son. Seeing the body of his mutilated boy leads Filartiga the crusader to join forces with a crusading lawyer (Blades) to force justice to be done in the court system that is controlled by the dictatorship.

Narratives such as this docudrama reinforced in viewers' minds, images of South Americans and their countries as frequently barbaric.

***One Way Street* (1950)** Universal, b&w, 79 minutes. **Director:** Hugo Fregonese; **Screenplay:** Lawrence Kimble; **Cast:** James Mason (Dr. Frank Matson), Marta Toren (Laura), Dan Duryea (John Wheeler), Basil Ruysdael (Father

Moreno), William Conrad (Ollie), King Donovan (Grieder), Jack Elam (Arnie), Tito Renaldo (Hank Torres), Rodolfo Acosta (Francisco Morales).

This engrossing character study contrasted good simple people (the Mexican peasants) with corrupted Anglos; however, the production was marred by a pretentious tone and a clichéd finale that diminished the story's impact. This was the first American feature for Argentine director Fregonese. Mexican vice consul Ernesto Romero was hired as the film's technical adviser, but the Mexican village featured in the plot was constructed on the studio's back lot.

In California, Dr. Frank Matson is part of a gang that has just committed a bank robbery. With a clever ruse, Matson grabs the money from gangster John Wheeler. Laura, Wheeler's lover, asks to join Matson as he flees town. Once the couple cross the Mexican border, they hire a plane to fly to Mexico City, but it breaks down near a small village. There they are given shelter by Father Moreno, and, before long, Matson is assisting the villagers with their medical problems. Their good deeds give the newcomers a fresh lease on life. Matson and Laura return to California, intending to return the money to Wheeler. Although the hoodlum is already dead, his henchman Ollie is not. This leads to a showdown between the physician and the punk, with a sudden twist of fate ending the sequence of events.

***Only Once in a Lifetime* (1979)** Movietime, color, 97 minutes. **Director/Screenplay:** Alejandro Grattan; **Cast:** Miguel Robelo (Dominguez), Estrellita López (Consuelo), Sheree North (Sally), Claudio Brook (Jimenez).

This bittersweet entry was more successful at capturing snatches of life in the Los Angeles barrio in the late 1970s than in presenting a realistic drama. It was an example of an independently made American picture that recognized (1) the growing Hispanic population in the United States and (2) that moviegoers might be interested in a story about this increasing segment of American culture.

An impoverished Mexican-American artist named Dominguez is haunted by the memory of his late wife. His only companion is his aged dog. He is stalled in life, as his artwork is not currently fashionable and he refuses to change his style. Also, he wants to grow and sell produce on his property, but zoning laws forbid it. A good-natured social worker (North) tries to help him but to no avail. Even Consuelo, an appealing Chicano schoolteacher, can't raise him from his lethargy. Then, suddenly, spurred by the need to get on with life, he reawakens to activity and to the interest of Consuelo.

***Our Man in Havana* (1960)** Columbia, b&w, 111 minutes. **Director:** Carol Reed; **Screenplay:** Graham Greene; **Cast:** Alec Guinness (Jim Wormold), Burl Ives (Dr. Haselbacher), Maureen O'Hara (Beatrice Severn), Ernie Kovacs (Captain Segura), Noël Coward (Hawthorne), Ralph Richardson ("C"), Jo Morrow (Milly Wormold), Gregoire Aslan (Cifuentes), José Prieto (Lopez).

Based on Greene's 1958 novel, this droll espionage spoof came before the 1960s James Bond movie series made the spy genre once again so appealing to moviegoers. It was set in the Cuba run by President Fulgencio Batista before Fidel Castro's 1959 revolution changed the country completely.

In Havana, Jim Wormold, who operates a vacuum-cleaner agency, is approached by British secret-service agent Hawthorne to become a spy. Wanting money to buy his daughter Jo a horse, he agrees to do so but has no idea how to proceed. He is told to spy on Captain Segura and to build a spy network to help him. Needing to feed the London office with some results, he fabricates (using vacuum-cleaner designs) giant installations in the hills. Before long, London has sent him an assistant (O'Hara); his good friend, German Dr. Haselbacher, is murdered; and his target, Segura, is spying on him. Wormold is almost poisoned at a banquet. Eventually, overwhelmed by his deceit, Wormold confesses all. He is deported back to England where he is bestowed on O.B.E.

Considered too subtle and/or too lengthy, *Our Man in Havana* was not appreciated at the time of its release. Years later came the film *The Tailor of Panama* (2001), based on the 1996 novel by John Le Carre and starring Pierce Brosnan. It bore plot and mood parallels to the earlier picture.

***Outrage, The* (1964)** Metro-Goldwyn-Mayer, b&w, 97 minutes. **Director:** Martin Ritt; **Screenplay:** Michael Kanin; **Cast:** Paul Newman (Juan Carrasco), Laurence Harvey (the husband), Claire Bloom (the wife), Edward G. Robinson (the con man), William Shatner (the preacher), Howard da Silva (the prospector), Albert Salmi (the sheriff), Thomas Chalmers (the judge), Paul Fix (the Indian).

In 1959, *Rashomon*, a play by Fay Kanin and Michael Kanin, starring Rod Steiger and Claire Bloom, ran for 159 performances on Broadway. It was based on the 1950 Japanese film of the same title by Akira Kurosawa. This MGM 1964 release relied on both the play and the film original. It offered a badly miscast (blue-eyed) Newman (wearing "greaser" makeup) as the notorious late nineteenth-century outlaw Juan Carrasco, who received a death sentence in court and was hanged for having murdered a southern gentleman and raping the man's wife. Later, at a deserted railway station—somewhere in the Southwest—a pessimistic con man, an unkempt prospector, and a disheartened preacher discuss the case. The prospector and preacher tell the con man what they heard witnesses say at the trial. Each testifier has a different version of what happened and how/why the southern colonel died, with the prospector holding the clue for what really happened.

Newman's overly melodramatic characterization of the bandito was a throwback to the unflattering ethnic stereotypes played on camera by LEO CARRILLO in so many 1930s films (e.g., THE GAY DECEPTION, 1935).

***Ox-Bow Incident, The* (1943)** Twentieth Century-Fox, b&w, 75 minutes. **Director:** William A. Wellman; **Screenplay:** Lamar Trotti; **Cast:** Henry Fonda (Gil Carter), Dana Andrews (Donald Martin), Mary Beth Hughes (Rose Mapen), Anthony Quinn (Francisco Morez), William Eythe (Gerald Tetley), Henry Morgan (Art Croft), Jane Darwell (Jenny "Ma" Grier), Matt Briggs (Judge Daniel Tyler), Harry Davenport (Arthur Davies), Frank Conroy (Major Tetley), Francis Ford (Alva "Dad" Hadwick).

One of the great Hollywood-made westerns, this grim, uncompromising study of mob violence/justice was based on Walter Van Tilburg Clark's 1940 novel.

In 1885 in Bridger's Well, Nevada, a trio of men are arrested for allegedly having rustled cattle and having killed the owner, a Mr. Kincaid. The three are young Donald Martin who protests his innocence, a dazed old man called "Dad," and a Mexican named Francisco Morez, who initially does not appear to speak English. Major Tetley, a former Confederate officer, who has taken charge of the posse in the sheriff's absence, decides that the suspects will be hung at dawn. Still pleading his innocence, Martin writes a letter to his family, while Dad sits uncomprehendingly. Morez eats a meal prepared for him and then tries to escape. He is shot in the leg and brought back. Kincaid's gun is found on him, and the suddenly articulate Mexican insists that he found the weapon on the roadside. After the accused are executed, it is discovered that Kincaid is alive and that the actual rustlers have been caught. The major commits suicide, and at the saloon one of the onlookers to the hanging, Gil Carter, reads Martin's letter aloud.

Anthony Quinn in *The Ox-Bow Incident* (1943).
(JC ARCHIVES)

With the array of western types within *The Ox-Bow Incident*, QUINN was the sullen-looking Mexican presumed guilty just because of his race—just as he was assumed ignorant by his captors because of negative ethnic stereotyping.

The Ox-Bow Incident received an Academy Award nomination as Best Picture. Despite strongly positive reviews, it was not successful when initially released because World War II era filmgoers considered it too somber.

P

***Pacific Blue* (1996–2000)** USA-cable series, color, 60 minutes. **Cast:** Rick Rossovich (Lt. Anthony Palermo: 1996–98), Jim Davidson (Off./Sgt./Lt. Terence "T. C." Callaway), Darlene Vogel (Off. Chris Kelly), Paula Trickey (Off./Sgt. Cory McNamara), Marcos Ferraez (Off. Victor Del Toro: 1996–98), Mario López (Off. Bobby Cruz: 1998–2000).

Labeled "*Baywatch* on Bikes," this police action series revolved around the Santa Monica (California) Beach Bike Patrol as it peddled its way against crime on the oceanfront turf. During its run, it added more ethnically diverse cast members including Ferraez and López, with the latter especially geared to attract a younger viewership. It was still a rare instance for a TV series to present a Hispanic-American character as (1) a program regular and (2) a positive role model.

***Pan-Americana* (1945)** RKO, b&w, 84 minutes. **Director:** John H. Auer; **Screenplay:** Lawrence Kimble; **Cast:** Phillip Terry (Dan Jordan), Audrey Long (Jo Anne Benson [Joan Parker]), Robert Benchley (Charlie Corker), Eve Arden (Helen "Hoppy" Yopkins), Bill Garvin (Sancho), Frank Marasco (Miguel), Joan Beckstead (Miss Peru), Valerie Hall (Miss El Salvador), Luz Vasquez (Miss Mexico), Betty Joy Curtis (Miss Bolivia), Goya Del Valle (Miss Panama), Carmen Lopez (Miss Paraguay), Aldonna Gauvin (Miss Uruguay), Velera Burton (Miss Dutch Guiana), Ruth Lorran (Miss Honduras), Alma Beltran (Miss Guatemala), Nina Bara (Miss Argentina).

This efficiently mounted budget musical—made when the Latin America "Good Neighbor Policy" was still being promoted by the U.S. government—was structured around the plot gimmick of Charlie Corker, the foreign editor for *Western World*, explaining the genesis of how his magazine came to sponsor a Pan-American musical revue. Numbers in this sound-stage-filmed South American musical travelogue included: "Rhumba Matumba," "Babalu," "Negra Leono," "La morena de mi copla," "No taboleiro de bahiana," and "Cuban Challenge." Among the ethnic talent utilized for this vintage feature were Rosario and Antonio, Miguelito Valdes, Harold and Lola, Chinita Marin, Chuy Castillon, the Padilla Sisters, Chuy Reyes and His Orchestra, and Nestor Amarale and His Samba Band. As such, this modest feature provided a record of South American talent of the times.

***Passport to Danger* (1954–1956)** Syndicated TV series, b&w, 30 minutes. **Cast:** Cesar Romero (Steve McQuinn)

In the early years of commercial TV, aging movie stars found a fresh career in the new medium. One of them was Cuban-American ROMERO who brought his dapper good looks, smart wardrobe, and sly charm to this international intrigue series. As a U.S. diplomatic courier, McQuinn traveled a lot, allowing viewers a peek at exotic locales, with conventional spy trickery thrown in for good measure. Thus Romero's Steve McQuinn was an early example of a positive ethnic role model on American TV.

***Pawnbroker, The* (1965)** Landau Releasing, b&w, 114 minutes. **Director:** Sidney Lumet; **Screenplay:** David Friedkin and Morton Fine; **Cast:** Rod Steiger (Sol Nazerman), Geraldine Fitzgerald (Marilyn Birchfield), Brock Peters (Rodriguez), Jaime Sanchez (Jesus Ortiz), Thelma Oliver (Ortiz's girl), Baruch Lumet (Mendel), Juano Hernandez (Mr. Smith).

Not only was this bleak drama a landmark in the on-screen depiction of post-Holocaust survival, but also it was a richly textured study of life in the mid-1960s in Spanish Harlem. (The movie, based on Edward Lewis Wallant's 1961 novel, was shot on location in New York City.)

At the dreary pawnshop run by downtrodden Jewish refugee Sol Nazerman, his assistant is Jesus Ortiz, an impetuous but perceptive young Puerto Rican. The enthusiastic young man senses that beneath the emotionally dead exterior of his boss, another (better) man lies trapped. Despite his eagerness to see the better side of life, Ortiz is emotionally beaten down by Nazerman who one day viciously tells the helper that he means nothing to him. In frustration, the young man arranges for the pawnshop to be burgled. When the robbers arrive, Nazerman refuses to hand over his money even when threatened with death. A remorseful Ortiz jumps in the way and is shot with the bullet intended for the old man. The boy dies in Nazerman's arms. Belatedly, Nazerman realizes that despite everything, he cared for this boy.

The Pawnbroker received an Academy award nomination for Best Actor (Steiger).

***Pearl, The* (1948)** RKO, b&w, 77 minutes. **Director:** Emilio Fernández; **Screenplay:** John Steinbeck, Fernández, and Jackson Wagner; **Cast:** Pedro Armendáriz (Kino), María Elena Marqués (Juana), Charles Rooner (village doctor), Alfonso Bedoya (godfather of Juanito), Gilbert González (Gachupin), Juan García (Sapo), Maria Cuadros (Juanito), Endina Diaz de Léon (medicine woman).

This remarkably austere parable was extremely well photographed by Gabriel Figueroa, bolstering this adaptation of Steinbeck's novel, which was first serialized in *Woman's Home Companion* (December 1945) with the title *Pearl of the World.* The movie, the first Mexican-made English-language picture to be released in the United States, was shot in both a Spanish and an English version during 1946 at RKO's Churubusco Studios in Mexico. Additional lensing was done on the outskirts of Mexico City, on the coast of Guerrero, and in Los Angeles at RKO and Universal studios. (By the time of this film's release, its Mexican-born star, ARMENDÁRIZ, had already begun to make movies in Hollywood.)

Pearl diver Kino, his wife Juana, and their infant Juanito live a simple existence in a Mexican west-coast village. Life has been difficult for the family and for their village. One day, while diving, Kino spots an enormous old oyster very deep down in the ocean. Eventually, he brings it to the surface; it contains a large, perfectly shaped pearl. News travels fast of Kino's extreme good fortune, but before long, the village's doctor and the local patron—both mercilessly greedy—compete to grab the pearl. Kino has to murder two of the patron's henchmen who try to steal the treasure, and later the patron kills the doctor. In the final showdown, tiny Juanito is gunned down, with Kino seeking revenge on the physician. Left alone, the bereft couple toss the cursed pearl back into the ocean.

The two different language versions of *The Pearl* were made for a combined total of $400,000. The movie grossed $2 million in the United States and received five Ariel Awards from the Mexican Motion Picture Academy: Best Character Role (Garcia), Best Director, Best Male Star (Armendáriz), Best Photography, and Best Picture. The film also won the International Prize at the San Sebastian Film Festival.

Peña, Elizabeth (1959–) This extremely versatile performer quietly used her beauty to enhance her acting rather than the reverse. She was born in Elizabeth, New Jersey, but spent her first eight years in Cuba from where her parents had come. They moved to New York City in the mid-1960s where her mother was the founder and supervisor of the Latin American Theatre ensemble and her father was a director, writer, and actor. She attended the High School of the Performing Arts and by graduation had already been in many off-Broadway productions. Her screen debut was EL SUPER (1979), but her next big film was not until *CROSSOVER DREAMS* (1985) with RUBÉN BLADES. She was the disappointed girlfriend in *LA BAMBA* (1987) and a zesty woman in *Vibes* (1988). For the John Sayles-created TV series, *SHANNON'S DEAL* (1990), she appeared as Lucy Acosta. Other movies included *The Waterdance* (1992), *Lone Star* (1996), *Rush Hour* (1998), *Seven Girlfriends* (1999), *On the Borderline* (2000), *TORTILLA SOUP* (2001), and *The Imposter* (2002). On the cable TV series *RESURRECTION BLVD.* (2000–), she appeared as Bibi and won an ALMA award in 2001 as Best Actress in a New Television Series.

Perez, Rosie (1966–) With her exuberant personality and acting credentials, it is often forgotten that dimple-cheeked Perez is a gifted choreographer. She was Emmy Award nominated for her work on TV's *In Living Color* (1990–94) and staged many music videos over the years. One of eleven children, she was born Rosa Maria Perez in Brook-

Tyra Ferrell, Wesley Snipes, Woody Harrelson, and Rosie Perez in *White Men Can't Jump* (1992). (JC ARCHIVES)

lyn, New York. Perez was a sixth-generation Puerto Rican American and followed in the wake of a fellow artist, Puerto Rican RITA MORENO.

Perez made her screen acting debut in Spike Lee's *Do the Right Thing* (1989) but really made her acting mark as Gloria Celente, the woman desperate to be a *Jeopardy* TV game show contestant in *White Men Can't Jump* (1992). In her dramatic assignment for *Fearless* (1993) as the young mother who lost her infant, she was Oscar nominated. Perez was a producer on TV's *Subway Stories: Tales from the Underground* (1997) and acted in a segment. She also coproduced *The 24-Hour Woman* (1999) in which she starred. For the animated feature *The Road to El Dorado* (2000), she supplied the voice of Chel. More recent pictures included *Riding in Cars with Boys* and *Human Nature* (both 2001), as well as the telefeature *Widows* (2002).

***Perez Family, The* (1995)** Samuel Goldwyn, color, 91 minutes. **Director:** Mira Nair; **Screenplay:** Robin Swicord; **Cast:** Marisa Tomei (Dorita "Dottie" Evita Perez), Anjelica Huston (Carmela Perez), Alfred Molina (Juan Raul Perez), Chaz Palminteri (Lt. John Pirelli), Trini Alvarado (Teresa Perez), Celia Cruz (Luz Paz), Diego Wallraff (Angel Diaz).

There were thematic parallels between this study of a Cuban-American household and that of Mexican Americans in *MY FAMILY: MI FAMILIA* of the same year. Each revealed the hardships in leaving one's homeland and the strains of adjusting to a new country and its particular lifestyle. In contrast, *My Family*, despite its tragic moments, maintained a sense of humor and perspective on its topic, while *The Perez Family* frequently took itself too seriously and became too morose. Made at a cost of $11 million, *The Perez Family* grossed less than $3 million in domestic distribution. The film was based on Christine Bell's 1990 book.

Juan Raul Perez is finally released after two decades as a political prisoner in Cuba. In the boatlift to Miami, he encounters Dottie Perez, a sugarcane worker and prostitute who is excited about the possibilities of her new life in America. Upon entering the United States, the two are confused by authorities as a married couple, and they carry on the pretense to obtain priority assistance. Meanwhile, Carmela Perez, who has waited patiently for her husband and has raised their daughter (Alvarado) as a single parent, is mistakenly told that Juan did not arrive with the others on the boatlift. Grief-stricken, she finds comfort with a flirtatious police officer (Palminteri). Later, Juan and Carmela are reunited but quickly discover that time has eroded their mutual love. Carmela returns to her policeman lover, while Juan and the aggressive Dottie pursue their romance.

Hispanic PRESSURE GROUPS were extremely unhappy with this film, primarily because it cast so many non-Hispanics in key acting assignments but also because the director and scripters were not Hispanic either.

Phillips, Lou Diamond (1962–) See entry in Native Americans chapter.

***Piñero* (2001)** Miramax, color, 103 minutes. **Director/ Screenplay:** Leon Ichaso; **Cast:** Benjamin Bratt (Miguel Piñero), Giancarlo Esposito (Miguel Algarin), Talisa Soto (Sugar), Nelson Vasquez (Tito), Michael Irby (Reinaldo Povod), Michael Wright (Edgar), Rita Moreno (mother), Jaime Sánchez (father), Mandy Patinkin (Joseph Papp).

This low-budget screen biography covers the turbulent life of Puerto Rican–born poet/playwright/actor Miguel Piñero who spent much of his later life in New York City where he died of cirrhosis of the liver in 1988 at age forty-one. As presented in this drama, Piñero's strong creativity is constantly subjugated to his craving for booze and drugs. BRATT brings intensity to the role of the passionate artist and street-smart crook whose artistic expression focused on the cultural traditions of New York's exploited Puerto Rican community. One of his most telling works was the prison drama *Short Eyes* (1974) written while he was in jail. The picture uses black-and-white photography to recreate the past, which is interposed with the present (shot in color). The project was directed with passion by Ichaso who earlier made *EL SÚPER* (1979).

***Popi* (1969)** United Artists, color, 115 minutes. **Director:** Arthur Hiller; **Screenplay:** Tina Pine and Les Poine; **Cast:** Alan Arkin (Abraham "Popi" Rodriguez), Rita Moreno (Lupe), Miguel Alejandro (Junior Rodriguez), Ruben Figueroa (Luis Rodriguez), John Harkins (Harmon), Joan Tompkins (Miss Musto), Arny Freeman (Diaz).

This was an affecting family drama of New York City Puerto Ricans, an unpretentious entry filled with comedic overtones, but beneath its surface, it had serious points to make about class structure and ethnic discrimination in the United States. It also demonstrated that Hollywood was now willing to go beyond topics involving white America for its stories.

Puerto Rican immigrant and widower Abraham Rodriguez (known affectionately as "Popi" to his sons) lives with his two young boys (Alejandro and Figueroa) in the squalor of Spanish Harlem. Despite working several jobs to make ends meet, he is concerned about his sons' welfare and how they will survive the tough ghetto life. Although he wants to marry the appealing Lupe, Popi is more concerned with devising a scheme to ensure his offspring's future.

Knowing that America treats Cuban refugees far better than it does the Puerto Rican poor living in New York City, Popi engineers an elaborate ruse whereby his boys will be set adrift in a small boat off the coast of Florida and then, once rescued, will be hailed as brave Cuban youngsters who have escaped to freedom. The plan works well, with offers of assistance and adoption pouring in for the kids. Popi dons several disguises in his effort to sneak into his sons' room at the Miami hospital. When he leaves their bedside, the children follow him, and soon their deception is uncovered. Popi and his two now-happy sons return to New York City.

The cast was superior in this poignant yet humorous picture. Seven years later, HECTOR ELIZONDO starred in a short-lasting TV series adaptation of *Popi*.

***Popi* (1976)** CBS-TV series, color, 30 minutes. **Cast:** Hector Elizondo (Abraham Rodriguez), Edith Diaz (Lupe), Anthony Perez (Junior Rodriguez), Dennis Vasquez (Luis Rodriguez), Lou Criscuolo (Maggio).

The 1969 movie *POPI* starring Alan Arkin had been a modest commercial success, but the TV adaptation lacked the dramatic focus of the original (i.e., the faked Cuban refugee/boat rescue escapade) to give it momentum with a seemingly apathetic public. It featured ELIZONDO as the Puerto Rican immigrant and widower raising two young boys in Manhattan. Diaz played Lupe, a building neighbor of Popi who was his current romantic interest.

The pilot aired in May 1975, but the series did not debut till early 1976. After the network showed five installments, the show was shelved till that summer when the remainder of the original segments were seen.

***Possession of Joel Delaney, The* (1972)** Paramount, color, 108 minutes. **Director:** Waris Hussein; **Screenplay:** Matt Robinson; **Cast:** Shirley MacLaine (Norah Benson), Perry King (Joel Delaney), Michael Hordern (Dr. Justin Lorenz), David Elliott (Peter Benson), Lisa Kohane (Carrie Benson), Barbara Trentham (Sherry), Lovelady Powell (Erika Lorenz), Edmundo Rivera Alvarez (Don Pedro), Teodorina Bello (Mrs. Perez), Miriam Colon (Veronica).

Ramona Stewart's 1970 novel received a jumbled adaptation in this bizarre feature dealing with superstition, possession, and voodoo rites. Yet, beneath the thriller aspects was a good deal of scorn displayed between the two New York City factions depicted: the sophisticated well-to-do, inflexible whites of the upper East Side (and the Long Island beachside) and the financially less fortunate Puerto Ricans who existed in the Harlem and East Village ghettos and relied on their own set of religious and day-to-day values.

Rich, controlling divorcée Norah Benson resides in Manhattan with her two children (Elliott and Kohane) and is disturbed at the behavior of her younger brother, Joel Delaney, who insists on living in the Puerto Rican part of the East Village. Before long Delaney is dressing and talking like a Puerto Rican and referring to his Puerto Rican pal Tonio Perez. Soon, Delaney's girlfriend (Trentham) and then his therapist (Powell) are found decapitated. Eventually, through her Puerto Rican maid (Colon) and by attending a séance, Norah unravels that the wild Tonio is long dead and that his spirit is possessing her brother. Just as the deranged Delaney is about to kill Norah and her children at her Hampton beach house, the police arrive and shoot him. As he lies dying in Norah's arms, Tonio's spirit passes to Norah.

This illogical claptrap did not sit well with moviegoers of any cultural heritage.

pressure groups Organizations (beyond such broad-based groups as the American Civil Liberties Union and Common Cause) involved in specifically protecting the rights of Hispanic-American talent and helping to integrate further the entertainment media have included Cuban American National Council (CNC), Grand Council of Hispanic Societies in Public Service, Mexican-American Opportunity Foundation (MAOF), Hispanic Organization of Latin Actors (HOLA), Hispanic Society of America (HAS), National Federation of Hispanics in Communications (NFHC), National Hispanic Media Coalition (NHMC), National Latino Communications Center, National Puerto Rican Forum (NPRF), and the Puerto Rican Association for Community Affairs (PRACA),

***Price of Glory* (2000)** New Line Cinema, color, 118 minutes. **Director:** Carlos Avila; **Screenplay:** Phil Berger; **Cast:** Jimmy Smits (Arturo Ortega), Jon Seda (Sonny Ortega), Clifton Collins Jr. (Jimmy Ortega), Ernesto Hernández (Johnny Ortega), Maria del Mar (Rita Ortega).

This film—part sports entry, part family drama—offered a variation on the plot theme of the obsessed stage mother who would do anything for/to her offspring to get them ahead in their careers. Herein, the Hispanic Arturo was a one-time boxer who remains bitter that his career was unduly cut short years ago due to a dishonest fight manager. He feeds his acrimony into his obsession that his three sons must and will win boxing championships. The movie focuses on the now adult sons as they deal with their parents' refusal to allow a professional manager to control their boxing careers and how it affects their relationship with their determined father, their sympathetic mother, and with one another.

Made at a cost of $10 million, the picture grossed a bit upward of $3 million in domestic distribution. On the plus side, the film detailed the dynamics of a Hispanic-American family in unvarnished detail.

Prinze, Freddie [Sr.] (1954–1977) This talented Puerto Rican American committed suicide at a young age and thus had little opportunity to fulfill his potential as a comedian and an actor. Nevertheless, in his brief life he made his mark as a Hispanic talent who won respect from both peers and TV viewers and who had the ability to make a success of himself in the mainstream world.

He was born Frederick Karl Pruetzel to an immigrant Hungarian Jewish father and an immigrant Puerto Rican mother. (The star to be liked to call himself "Hungarian.") He grew up in New York City and attended the High School for the Performing Arts (made famous in the 1980 movie *Fame*). While there, he did comedy gigs at Manhattan's Improv Club and later dropped out of school to pursue stand-up work. In 1973, Prinze was a guest on TV's *The Tonight Show Starring Johnny Carson*, and the exposure led to Freddie costarring (1974–77) with Jack Albertson on the TV sitcom *CHICO AND THE MAN*. By the mid-1970s, fame had caught up with Prinze, leading him to become drug-dependent and unusually depressed. In Los Angeles, on January 22, 1977, Prinze, who had an eight-month-old baby boy, FREDDIE JR., shot himself.

In 1979 a TV movie biography, *CAN YOU HEAR THE LAUGHTER? THE STORY OF FREDDIE PRINZE*, aired, starring Ira Angustain.

Prinze, Freddie, Jr. (1976–) The handsome son of the late comedian-actor FREDDIE PRINZE was only a few months old when his father committed suicide. One-fourth Puerto Rican, Prinze Jr. was born and grew up in Albuquerque, New Mexico. After graduating from La Cueva High School in 1994, he relocated to Los Angeles. The six-feet, one-inch newcomer found almost immediate work in TV, appearing in an episode of the sitcom *Family Matters* in 1995. His big-screen debut occurred in *To Gillian on Her 37th Birthday* (1996) in which he shared scenes with Claire Danes. His popularity leaped ahead after *I Know What You Did Last Summer* (1997). This led to a series of high-profile frothy comedies for the young set: *She's All That* (1999), *Down to You* (2000), and *Head over Heels* (2001). In *Scooby-Doo* (2002), the live-action big-screen adaptation of the cartoon series, he played Fred Jones. In the animated feature *Happily Never After* (2003) he provided the voice of Ride.

***Professionals, The* (1966)** Columbia, color, 117 minutes. **Director/Screenplay:** Richard Brooks; **Cast:** Burt Lancaster (Bill Dolworth), Lee Marvin (Henry "Rico" Fardan), Robert Ryan (Hans Ehrengard), Woody Strode (Jacob Sharp), Jack Palance (Capt. Jesús Raza), Claudia Cardinale (Maria Grant), Ralph Bellamy (J. W. Grant), Joe DeSantis (Ortega), Rafael Bertrand (Fierro), Jorge Martínez de Hoyos (Padilla).

An extremely violent western that, despite its plot twist finale, perpetuated the Hollywood screen fantasies about the voluptuous Mexican spitfire, the dirty, nasty Latino banditos, and the overall superiority of white American know-how and the power of American money.

Shortly after the Mexican revolution of 1917, J. W. Grant, a ruthless American millionaire, hires a quartet of mercenaries at $1,000 each to rescue his Mexican wife, the much younger Maria, who has been abducted by Capt. Jesús Raza, a Mexican bandit. The four rugged men are Bill Dolworth (dynamite specialist), Henry "Rico" Fardan (expert soldier), Hans Ehrengard (pack master and wrangler), and African-American Jacob Sharp (a tracker and skilled archer). The group ride south-of-the-border into the heart of the Mexican desert, where they find Raza's camp. After they abscond with Maria, she informs them that Raza is actually her lover and that she refuses to return to Grant. Nevertheless, wanting their reward, the men press onward. While ordering the others to head for the border, Dolworth has a showdown with Raza and his men, wounding Raza, and then riding to the rendezvous. Desperate to return to Raza, Maria details Grant's brutality to the others. When Raza comes into view to get Maria, the four professionals hold off Grant and his crew until the couple are well on their way back into the Mexican desert.

With Italian Cardinale and Pennsylvania-born Palance as the two lead Mexican characters, authenticity was sacrificed in this action-packed adventure. Based on Frank O'Rourke's novel *A Mule for the Marquesa* (1964), the hit movie grossed almost $9 million in domestic distribution. It received Oscar nominations for Best Adapted Screenplay, Best Cinematography (Color), and Best Director.

***Pusher, The* (1960)** United Artists, b&w, 82 minutes. **Director:** Gene Milford; **Screenplay:** Harold Robbins; **Cast:** Kathy Carlyle (Laura Byrne), Douglas F. Rodgers (Lt. Peter Byrne), Felice Orlandi (Gonzo, the pusher [Doug]), Robert Lansing (Steve Carella), Sara Aman (María Hernández), Sloan Simpson (Harriet Byrne), Beatrice Pons (Mrs. Hernández).

Prolific, best-selling novelist Robbins wrote this screenplay as the first vehicle for his production company. Oscar-winning film editor Milford, also one of the movie's producers, made his directorial debut with this movie, which was shot entirely in Manhattan.

The Pusher played more like an episode of TV's *Naked City* (1958–63) than a self-contained feature film. In retrospect, its plot line was hackneyed but, in its time, it was an early on-camera depiction of young-adult drug addicts. More importantly, it presented the New York City Puerto Rican characters as a minority who acknowledged truths that the Hollywood cinema had been avoiding thus far: that this ethnic minority was being discriminated against by the "system" and that the victims had now come to expect it. On the other hand, the movie depicted several of its Puerto Rican characters as pushers and drug users who were "typical" of the Puerto Rican ghetto.

When Lt. Peter Byrne and his partner Steve Carella investigate the death of Anibal Hernández, a teenager in Spanish Harlem, they are not convinced that the hanging of the Puerto Rican youth was suicide. (A hypodermic needle was found near the corpse.) Meanwhile Byrne's daughter, Laura, proves to be a drug addict, whose pusher (Orlandi) knows all about Anibal's suicide/murder. Later Anibal's sister, Maria, a drug addict herself, is murdered, and in trying to capture the killer, Carella is badly wounded. As for Laura, her father makes her endure drug withdrawal, and, now contrite, she hopes to make a clean start.

Q

***Q & A* (1990)** TriStar, color, 134 minutes. **Director/ Screenplay:** Sidney Lumet; **Cast:** Nick Nolte (Lt. Mike Brennan), Timothy Hutton (Al Reilly), Armand Assante (Bobby Texador), Patrick O'Neal (Kevin Quinn), Lee Richardson (Leo Bloomfield), Luis Guzman (Det. Luis Valentin).

Returning to the terrain of his *Serpico* (1973) and *Prince of the City* (1981), longtime filmmaker Lumet again delved into corruption within the New York City Police Department in this raw and violent drama based on Edwin Torres's 1977 novel.

At the film's heart was Lt. Mike Brennan who seems to be one of the city's finest cops. In actuality, however, this hard-living Irishman is not only corrupt but also an extreme bigot. He kills an unarmed Hispanic drug dealer and plants a gun on the victim. This death leads to another Irishman, young Al Reilly of the District Attorney's office, investigating the killing. Reilly is upset to discover that his ex-girlfriend is currently dating Bobby Texador, a vicious Puerto Rican drug lord who witnessed Brennan's supposed clean killing. (Intolerant Det. Luis Valentin is also involved in the troublesome case.)

Despite Nolte's impressive performance, this movie was considered too much of a rehash of Lumet's earlier screen work. *Q & A*, which pounded home the cliché of the unlawful "spic," grossed about a modest $11 million in domestic distribution.

Quinn, Anthony (1915–2001) Mexican-born Quinn, who won two Best Supporting Actor Oscars (*VIVA ZAPATA!* 1952; *Lust for Life*, 1956), was often cast to play characters of other cultural backgrounds ranging from warrior braves (e.g., *THE PLAINSMAN*, 1936) to Native Alaskans (e.g., *The Savage Innocents*, 1959). Sometimes, Hollywood actually allowed the versatile talent to portray Mexican Americans on camera.

Born in Chihuahua, Mexico, of Mexican-Irish parentage, he spent his young years in the United States and was a professional boxer before he became an actor. Quinn was an army captain in the Spanish Civil War drama, *LAST TRAIN FROM MADRID* (1937); in Bob Hope's comedic *The Ghost Breakers* (1940), he had dual roles as Hispanics; in the harrowing *THE OX-BOW INCIDENT* (1943), he was the Mexican lynched by a mob in the old West; he was. Pvt. Jesus "Soose" Alvarez in *GUADALCANAL DIARY* (1943) and a brave Filipino hero in *BACK TO BATAAN* (1945). Perhaps his best assignment was as the bullying brother of the twentieth-century Mexican hero (played by Marlon Brando) in *Viva Zapata!* for which he won his first Academy Award.

Quinn had portrayed a Spanish matador in *Blood and Sand* (1941) and was a Mexican bullfighter in *THE MAGNIFICENT MATADOR* (1955). *MAN FROM DEL RIO* (1956) allowed Quinn to shine as the uneducated Mexican gunslinger. *GUNS FOR SAN SEBASTIAN* (1968) showcased the actor as the legendary eighteenth-century Mexican patriot/bandit. One of his best latter roles was as the aging Cuban fisherman fighting the elements in the TV movie of Ernest Hemingway's *The Old Man and the Sea* (1990).

R

***Red Sky at Morning* (1971)** Universal, color, 112 minutes. **Director:** James Goldstone; **Screenplay:** Marguerite Roberts; **Cast:** Richard Thomas (Josh Arnold), Catherine Burns (Marcia Davidson), Desi Arnaz Jr. (William "Steenie" Moreno), Richard Crenna (Frank Arnold), Claire Bloom (Ann Arnold), John Colicos (Jimbob Buel), Harry Guardino (Romeo Bonino), Nehemiah Persoff (Amadeo Montoya), Pepe Serna (Chango Lopez), Mario Aniov (Lindo Velarde), Gregory Sierra (Chamaco), Victoria Racimo (Viola Lopez).

Set in 1944, this drama reversed the typical premise of an ethnic minority coping with the white majority. Here seventeen-year-old Caucasian Josh Arnold had to integrate himself into a school and a town that was largely Hispanic.

When Frank Arnold enters active military service, he moves his wife Anne and son Josh from Alabama to the family's summer home in Sagrado, New Mexico. There, Anglo Josh has a difficult adjustment because the bulk of his classmates are Hispanic and he is the outsider. One of those he must deal with at school is Steenie Moreno. It doesn't help Josh's standing with his peers when he takes an interest in Viola, the sister of Chango Lopez, who already dislikes Josh as newcomer. Meanwhile, at home, Josh is muddling through because his mother is alcoholic and spends most of her time with her peculiar, freeloading cousin, Jimbob Buel. Later, when Josh helps Viola out of a difficult situation, he is wounded by the crowd. Not too long after Josh learns his father has died in action, he and Steenie (who are now friends) enlist in the military.

Two of the toughest characters within *Red Sky at Morning* were Chango Lopez and Lindo Velarde. Although their portrayals bordered on caricature, they created a strong impression—far tougher hombres than the juvenile delinquents of the earlier *THE BLACKBOARD JUNGLE* (1955).

Renaldo, Duncan (1904–1980) Best remembered as playing the CISCO KID in films in the late 1940s and on TV in the early 1950s, this Hispanic actor had a long acting career that was interrupted by traumatic immigration problems.

He was born Renault Renaldo Duncan in Spain. (Some sources state that he was actually born Vasile Dumitree Coghleanas and that his birth country was Romania.) An orphan, he immigrated to the United States in 1921. Once in New York, he worked in silent movies as a design artist, production person, and later as assistant director. Handsome and personable, he gravitated to acting and made his debut in two silent 1928 dramas: *The Naughty Duchess* and *Clothes Make the Woman*. He made his first talkie for MGM as Esteban in *THE BRIDGE OF SAN LUIS REY* (1929), followed by the big-budgeted *Trader Horn* (1931), lensed in Africa.

At this crucial career juncture, Renaldo was prosecuted for having entered the United States illegally. After much litigation and time served in a detention center, he was granted a presidential pardon in 1936 by Franklin D. Roosevelt. Humbly, he returned to movies, playing smaller roles. He regained his industry footing when he was cast as the Mexican Rico in the Three Mesquiteers cowboy movies.

Wisely acquiring the screen rights to the Cisco Kid western series when Twentieth Century-Fox dropped the vehicle in 1941, Renaldo began in the role in *The Cisco Kid Returns* (1945). From 1950 to 1956, 156 half-hour episodes of the TV version were produced, with Renaldo as the lead and LEO CARRILLO repeating his role as the comical sidekick Pancho.

***Requiem for a Heavyweight* (1962)** Columbia, b&w, 85 minutes. **Director:** Ralph Nelson; **Screenplay:** Rod Serling; **Cast:** Anthony Quinn (Mountain Rivera), Jackie Gleason (Maish Rennick), Mickey Rooney (Army), Julie Harris (Grace Miller), Stanley Adams (Perelli), Mme. Spivey (Ma

Top row: Elizabeth Peña, Mauricio Mendoza, Tony Plana, Nicholas Gonzalez, and Daniel Zacapa; bottom row: Marisol Nichols, Michael DeLorenzo, and Ruth Livier in the TV drama *Resurrection Blvd.* (2000–). (ECHO BOOK SHOP)

Greene), Jack Dempsey (himself), Cassius Clay [Muhammad Ali] (fight opponent).

In October 1956, Jack Palance had starred on TV in the *Playhouse 90* production of "Requiem for a Heavyweight." Serling's acclaimed drama, which won an Emmy Award for its story, reached the screen six years later. QUINN inherited the key role, with Nelson again repeating his directorial chores. Whereas Palance's character was of an Irish background, in the Quinn version, the pugilist was Mexican American. Because Quinn had boxed in his own youth, the sport was not alien to him. Reportedly, he based his character somewhat on the boxer Primo Carnera (1906–67), whose life had already formed the basis of the boxing drama *The Harder They Fall* (1956) starring Humphrey Bogart.

Rivera, a Mexican American, has won 111 fights during a seventeen-year career but is now washed up. His doctor has advised that if he fights again, he could lose his eyesight. The physically and mentally battered giant is at a loss what to do next. He discovers that his longtime manager, Maish Rennick, had bet against him lasting beyond a certain round in the last match in which he got knocked out. This shocking revelation is coupled with the fact that now Rennick must come up with the money owed the mob or else. Meanwhile, employment counselor Grace Miller tries to place Rivera in a new career, but his options are limited, and Rennick sabotages one of his better opportunities. In the end, loyal to a fault, Rivera makes a buffoon of himself by stepping into the wrestling ring as a caricature of himself so that he can help Rennick pay off his urgent debt.

As the modern-day beaten-down warrior with an inner nobility, Quinn provided—in an oblique way—a positive presentation of a Mexican American.

***Resurrection Blvd.* (2000–)** Showtime cable, color, 60 minutes. **Cast:** Michael DeLorenzo (Carlo Santiago), Nicholas Gonzalez (Alex Santiago), Ruth Livier (Yolanda Santiago), Maurice Mendoza (Miguel Santiago), Marisol Nichols (Victoria Santiago), Elizabeth Peña (Bibi Corrales), Tony Plana (Roberto Santiago), Daniel Zacapa (Rubén Santiago), Cheech Marin (Hector Archuletta).

Created by Dennis E. Leoni, this well-received adult drama utilized Latino talent both in front of and behind the camera—a first on U.S. network (cable) TV. Set in East Los Angeles, it featured the Santiago household as they coped with acculturation issues that affected all aspects of their often difficult daily life.

The head of the Santiago family is Roberto, a widower, who is employed in an auto-repair shop. His hopes for the family are focused on middle son, Carlos, a boxing contender, who is guided by older son Miguel, a former boxer. The younger Santiago, Alex, is a pre-med student; another child, Yolanda, works in a Beverly Hills law firm. The "baby" of the family is Victoria, a high school student who is drawn to the wrong influences at school. Roberto's brother Daniel, who never talks, became brain-injured from too many rounds in the ring. Rounding out the household is optimistic Bibi, Roberto's sister-in law.

In 2001, *Resurrection Blvd.* won two ALMA Awards: Outstanding Actress in a New Television Series (Peña) and Outstanding Series. The previous year, it earned a Nosotros Golden Eagle Award as Outstanding New English-Language Series.

***Reward, The* (1965)** Twentieth Century-Fox, color, 92 minutes. **Director:** Serge Bourguignon; **Screenplay:** Bourguignon and Oscar Millard; **Cast:** Max von Sydow (Scott Swenson), Yvette Mimieux (Sylvia), Efrem Zimbalist Jr. (Frank Bryant), Gilbert Roland (Captain Carbajal), Emilio Fernández (Sargento Lopez), Henry Silva (Joaquin), Nino Castelnuovo (Luis), Rodolfo Acosta (patron), Julian Rivero (El Viejo).

This first English-language film by acclaimed French director Bourguignon (e.g., *Sundays and Cybele*, 1962) was based on Michael Barrett's 1955 novel. It proved to be pretentious and static in its allegorical study of greed and how it affected individuals. None of the characters emerged as believable from their paper-thin portraits. Most of the cast played Mexican characters, and sections of the movie's dialogue were delivered in Spanish with English subtitles. This box-office misfire was shot in Death Valley, California, and at Old Tucson in Nevada.

Texas crop-duster Scott Swenson accidentally crashes his plane into the water tower of a small Mexican village. While trying to settle matters with local police captain Carbajal and discovering how expensive the replacement of the tower will be, he notes that there is a $50,000 reward for Frank Bryant, an old friend, on a kidnapping/murder charge. Coincidentally, Swenson has just seen Bryant riding through town with an attractive woman named Sylvia. Swenson offers to split the reward with the police captain, and the hunt is on. The search party also includes Sargento Lopez, the Indian Joaquin, and Luis, who hopes to become a bullfighter. Soon, Lopez learns of the reward, and the drama turns brutal as the participants fight among themselves as to who will or will not share in the booty. At the end, Lopez chases after his runaway mount into the desert, Carbajal (suffering with malaria) has been left to his own devices, and the only survivors, Swenson and Sylvia, are going for help.

***Ride the Pink Horse* (1947)** Universal, b&w, 101 minutes. **Director:** Robert Montgomery; **Screenplay:** Ben Hecht and Charles Lederer; **Cast:** Robert Montgomery (Lucky Gagin), Thomas Gomez (Pancho), Rita Conde (Carla), Iris Flores (Maria), Wanda Hendrix (Pila), Grandon Rhodes (Mr. Edison), Tito Renaldo (bellboy), Andrea King (Marjorie), Art Smith (Bill Retz), Richard Gaines (Jonathan), Martin Garralaga (bar keep), Edward Earle (Locke), Maria Cortez (elevator girl), Fred Clark (Frank Hugo).

Dorothy B. Hughes's 1946 novel provided the basis for this well-executed film noir, directed by veteran actor Montgomery, who had already helmed the superior detective caper *Lady in the Lake* (1946). The New Mexican town of San Pablo featured in the crime drama was actually an amalgam of the Mexican sections of Albuquerque, Santa Fe, and Taos, New Mexico. Location filming on *Ride the Pink Horse* was accomplished in Santa Fe. Despite the use of sound stages and back lot sets for most of the narrative, a believable and memorable ethnic ambiance was created in this entry.

World War II veteran Lucky Gagin arrives in crowded San Pablo, New Mexico, only to find it crowded because of the annual fiesta. Gagin is determined to avenge the death of his buddy Shorty Thompson—a fellow blackmailer—who was murdered by one-time war profiteer/mobster Frank Hugo. Gagin plans to blackmail Hugo over bribes he had paid to get wartime military contracts. Later, Gagin is warned by government agent Bill Retz not to try anything on his own against Hugo, but Gagin is undeterred, even when he learns that Hugo's partner, Locke, has hired thugs to eliminate him.

At the local cantina, the newcomer meets Pancho, who runs the fiesta carousel concession. That evening, the duo encounter Pila, a homeless young girl who spends the night on Pancho's merry-go-round. Eventually, after being beaten up and then killing one of Locke's men, Gagin has a pang of conscience and turns his evidence against Hugo over to Retz. Before the cynical Gagin can break up with Pila, she surprises him by ending their relationship.

Ride the Pink Horse received an Oscar nomination for Best Supporting Actor (GOMEZ).

***Ride, Vaquero!* (1953)** Metro-Goldwyn-Mayer, color, 91 minutes. **Director:** John Farrow; **Screenplay:** Frank Fenton; **Cast:** Robert Taylor (Rio), Ava Gardner (Cordelia Cameron), Howard Keel (King Cameron), Anthony Quinn (José Esqueda), Kurt Kasznar (Father Antonio), Ted de Corsia (Sheriff Parker), Charlita (singer), Jack Elam (Barton).

For its first full-length wide-screen movie, MGM chose this downbeat western, one in which supporting-lead player QUINN as the bandito far outshone the trio of top-billed stars. (Several reviewers felt that Quinn's performance was excessive, but for others, it was the only sparkle to the leaden proceedings.)

After the Civil War, Anglo settlers flood into Texas. In the southern part of the state, José Esqueda and his men rule the territory, warning away newcomers. When Esqueda burns the ranch of newly arrived King and Cordelia Cameron, Cameron organizes a town meeting to fight these marauding vaqueros (cowboys). Cameron rebuilds his homestead and Esqueda orders Rio, his Caucasian friend who was raised by Esqueda's mother, to burn down the new ranch home. As the locals team up on opposite sides, Cordelia expresses her interest in Rio, but he rebuffs her. Meanwhile, Esqueda and his followers rob the bank at Brownsville, killing the sheriff in the process. Further emboldened by his invincibility, Esqueda intends to kill Rio (who is more sympathetic to the settlers these days) and the Camerons. In a final shootout between Rio and Esqueda, neither survives. The Camerons choose to repair their marriage.

***Right Cross* (1950)** Metro-Goldwyn-Mayer, b&w, 90 minutes. **Director:** John Sturges; **Screenplay:** Charles Schnee; **Cast:** June Allyson (Pat O'Malley), Dick Powell (Rick Garvey), Ricardo Montalban (Johnny Monterez), Lionel Barrymore (Sean O'Malley), Teresa Celli (Marina Monterez), Barry Kelley (Allan Goff), Mimi Aguglia (Mom Monterez), Marilyn Monroe (Dusky La Dieu).

As the middleweight boxing champion Johnny Monterez, Montalban had one of his best Hollywood screen assignments. His earnestness in and out of the boxing ring made this sports movie—which avoided genre clichés—solid entertainment. Powell, whose screen career was sagging, was brought into this project as the "other man" at the request of his then wife, studio star Allyson.

Aged fight promoter Sean O'Malley, now confined to a wheelchair, has narrowed his protégé list to primarily Johnny Monterez. Sean's daughter Pat increasingly handles most of the negotiations required for Monterez's career. Pat and Monterez are in love, but he is far too focused on his career and dealing with his cynical view of perceived discriminations due to his Mexican heritage. (Johnny also insists that his sister Marina is a fool to be dating a gringo who, he claims, is using her just to get to him.) Pat's best friend is hard living, veteran sports writer Rick Garvey, who gets drunk frequently and has an unrequited love for the feisty younger woman.

When Monterez learns that his injured hand could become permanently disabled, he keeps the medical news secret. Later, the boxer signs with Allan Goff, a rival fight promoter. The news so upsets Sean that he becomes increasingly ill and dies. Pat blames Monterez for her dad's passing, but she still loves her boyfriend. Later, after losing the big match, Monterez punches Garvey when the journalist tells him the truth of matters (i.e., that Pat loves Johnny and not Garvey). Now, Johnny's hand is permanently damaged, but he doesn't mind for he and Pat are already planning a new future together.

The fact that at the fadeout the culturally diverse couple planned to wed—and the woman was played by top movie star Allyson—made this entry an important stepping stone in the history of Hispanics on the Hollywood screen.

***Ring, The* (1952)** United Artists, b&w, 79 minutes. **Director:** Kurt Neumann; **Screenplay:** Irving Shulman; **Cast:** Gerald Mohr (Pete Genusia), Rita Moreno (Lucy Gomez), Lalo Rios (Tommy Kansas [Tomas Cantanios]), Robert Arthur (Billy Smith), Robert Osterich (Freddy Jack), Martin Garralaga (Vidal Cantanios).

Rios, who had been in the earlier *THE LAWLESS* (1950), was the lead in this boxing drama that, like *RIGHT CROSS* (1950), dealt with another Mexican-American fighter on the defensive because of the racial discrimination he suffered while growing up in Los Angeles. Based on Shulman's novel *The Square Trap* (1952), this low-budget feature, which offered a mostly unstereotypical view of Chicano life and attitudes, was generally disparaged at the time of release. For example, the trade paper *Hollywood Reporter* (August 20, 1952) decided the movie offered "such a bleak outlook for the Mexican-American that it emerges only as the type that does this country definite disservice abroad."

After suffering prejudicial treatment by whites, Mexican-American Tomas Cantanios loses his temper when two "Anglos" make lewd gestures about his girlfriend Lucy Gomez. His impromptu fisticuffs with them is observed by boxing manager Pete Genusia, an assimilated Mexican American, who wants to represent Tomas in the ring. Using the fight name of Tommy Kansas, the newcomer wins several preliminary matches. He gives his father Vidal money so that he can fulfill his dream of owning a merchandise stand on Olvera Street, where tourists flock to see Chicano products and culture. Although Kansas later loses the big match to Aragon (another Mexican American), he decides to quit the ring. Instructing his younger brother Pepe not to follow him into this dangerous profession, Tommy listens to advice from Lucy. She tells him that he should fight—not in the ring but for matters that are important. Seeing his father now a contented merchandise seller on Olvera Street, Tommy maps his future.

***Rio Rita* (1929)** RKO, b&w and color, 135 minutes. **Director:** Luther Reed; **Screenplay:** Russell Mack; **Cast:** Bert Wheeler (Chick Bean), Robert Woolsey (Lovett), Bebe Daniels (Rita Ferguson), John Boles (Capt. Jim Stewart), Dorothy Lee (Dolly), Don Alvarado (Roberto Ferguson), Georges Renavent (General Ravinoff [El Kinkajou]).

Based on the hit Broadway musical (1927) by Guy Bolton and Fred Thompson, the screen edition proved to be a major hit during the song-and-dance genre craze of the early talkies in the late 1920s. A frivolous, fictitious, and often primitive representation of Mexican bandits, señoritas, and life south and north of the border, this clumsy operetta made screen stars of the comedy team of Wheeler and Woolsey who had been in the New York original cast.

Attractive Rita Ferguson, living in a Mexican border town, is intrigued with the mysterious Jim Stewart, a dashing gringo. Predictably, the dastardly General Ravinoff has unkind things to say about his rival Stewart. Later, at a party at the general's villa, he proves to Rita that Stewart is a dreaded Texas Ranger who plans to arrest her brother (thought to be the mystifying bandito, El Kinkajou). Remaining loyal to Stewart, Rita later helps the ranger cause Ravinoff's floating gambling casino to drift to the U.S. side of the Rio Grande. Stewart unmasks Ravinoff as El Kinkajou. With everything resolved, Stewart and Rita wed, cheered on by a contingent of Texas Rangers.

Among the songs performed in this screen musical were "Rio Rita," "The Rangers' Song," "The Kinkajou," and "Long Before You Came Along."

In 1942, the warhorse stage property, *Rio Rita*, was altered into a musical comedy tailor-made for the team of Abbott and Costello and for rising actress/songstress Kathryn Grayson (cast as Rita Winslow the owner of a resort hotel). To be topical, the plot's mysterious Mexican bandito was changed to a Nazi spy, but the Texas Rangers were still on hand to provide support within the narrative.

***Robin Hood of El Dorado* (1936)** Metro-Goldwyn-Mayer, b&w, 86 minutes. **Director:** William A. Wellman; **Screenplay**: Wellman, Joseph Calleia, and Melvin Levy; **Cast:** Warner Baxter (Joaquín Murrieta), Ann Loring (Scñorita Juanita de la Cuesta), Bruce Cabot (Bill Warren), Margo (Rosita), J. Carrol Naish (Three-Fingered Jack), Soledad Jiménez (Madre Murrieta), Carlos de Valdez (José Murrieta), Eric Linden (Johnnie "Jack" Warren).

It had been five years since BAXTER had starred in *THE CISCO KID*, the sequel to *IN OLD ARIZONA* (1929) for which he had won an Academy Award. Now in his midforties, he played a similar role, this time as the legendary young JOAQUÍN MURRIETA who is reputed to have led fellow Mexicans against Anglos in 1840s California before the territory became one of the United States.

Based on the book *The Robin Hood of El Dorado* (1923) by Walter Noble Burns, this feature suffered from clichéd ethnic performances by Baxter and the others and from the inexperience of screen newcomer Loring in a lead role. Keeping to a romanticized version of the mythical Murrieta, the movie depicts the sympathetic bandito as justified in his killing and stealing.

In the 1840s, Mexican farmer Joaquín Murrieta has a good life, enjoys his work, and is married to Rosita. Then gold is discovered at Sutter's Mill in California, which draws a huge influx of white prospectors and settlers. One such group of newcomers rapes Rosita, and she dies. Murrieta avenges her death by killing each of the men responsible. Now a wanted man, tragedy comes anew when his innocent brother (de Valdez) is accused of stealing a donkey from a gringo and is hung. The disillusioned Murrieta joins forces with Mexican bandit Three-Fingered Jack and later becomes their leader. In a fierce battle that follows, Murrieta's Mexican followers—and many of their women—are killed; the wounded Murrieta reaches the grave of his wife where he dies.

In reviewing this feature, the trade publication *Harrison's Reports* (March 21, 1936) noted, "This action melodrama is too brutal for most picture-goers; its appeal will be directed mainly to men. In presenting the plight of the Mexicans in the days when California was taken over by the Americans, the producers have omitted none of the gory details, . . . One feels deep sympathy for the oppressed Mexicans . . . But the details are too harrowing for entertainment purposes."

Rodriguez, Paul (1955–) This pleasant, pudgy, stand-up comic long displayed his Mexican-American sensibilities in his club act, on TV, and in movies. He was born in Mazatlán, Mexico, in 1955, the son of migrant workers, and raised in California. As a relatively young comedian, he gained a job in TV doing audience warm-ups before tapings of the sitcom *Gloria* (1982–83). This led to producer Norman Lear starring him in the TV situation comedy *A.K.A. PABLO* (1984). Four years later, he costarred with Eddie Velez in the comedy series *Trial and Error* (1999) about two Hispanics who grew up in the East L.A. barrio. That same season, he was the comedic host of the revived *The Newlywed Game*. Next came *Grand Slam* (1990), a short-lasting series with John Schneider about San Diego bail bondsmen. He had previously appeared in feature films (e.g., *D.C. Cab*, 1983; *Quicksilver*, 1986). In 1994, he directed and starred in *A Million to Juan*, a lighthearted big-screen comedy. Since then, he has appeared in such entries as *Melting Pot* (1997), *Mambo Café* (1989), *Crocodile Dundee in Los Angeles* (2001), *Ali* (2001), and *Time Changer* (2002). During the years, Paul headlined several popular HBO cable comedy specials.

Rodriguez, Robert (1968–) He shot *El Mariachi* (1992) for $7,000 in a two-week period. After $200,000 was put into postproduction costs, Columbia Pictures released the violent picture that Rodriguez had written, directed, photographed, done the sound and special effects for, and so on, and the movie grossed more than $2 million in domestic

Gilbert Roland with Norma Talmadge in *Camille* (1927). (JC ARCHIVES)

distribution. Therefore, the young talent became a legend among low-budget, independent moviemakers and a breakthrough professional in the Hispanic-American world.

He was born and raised in San Antonio, Texas. From the age of thirteen, he made home movies. After attending St. Anthony's High School and then St. Anthony's University, he matriculated at the University of Texas at Austin. After college graduation, he made his first film, a short subject, *Bedhead* (1991), which had a children's theme and utilized his relatives as cast members. To raise the $7,000 needed to make *El Mariachi*, he subjected himself to experimental drug studies. *El Mariachi* won the Audience Award at the 1993 Sundance Film Festival. His made-for-cable movie, *Roadracers* (1994), starred David Arquette and Salma Hayek and dealt satirically with a 1950s young man confronting life, his interracial romance, and a corrupt sheriff. *DESPERADO* (1995) headlined ANTONIO BANDERAS as the nameless guitar player-gunman El Mariachi. Other pictures Robert directed included *From Dusk Till Dawn* (1996) and *The Faculty* (1998).

In a return to the children's genre, Rodriguez helmed *Spy Kids* (2001) about two youngsters who discovered that their parents were really secret agents. Made on a $35 million budget, the well-reviewed picture—which also starred Banderas—grossed more than $106 million in domestic distribution. It led to *Spy Kids 2: The Island of Lost Dreams* (2002) and *Once Upon a Time in Mexico* (2003), the latter featuring Banderas in further adventures of El Mariachi.

Roland, Gilbert (1905–1994) This handsome Mexican-born star had a long Hollywood career in which he survived several industry changes and emerged repeatedly as a popular performer. Until almost the end, he retained the virile good looks that had been his trademark, along with his moustache, ever-lit cigarette, and his suavity.

One of six siblings, he was born Luis Antonio Damasco de Alonso in Ciudad Juárez, Mexico. His parents were of Spanish ancestry and fled PANCHO VILLA and the Mexican Revolution in 1913. They moved to El Paso, Texas, where the future actor grew up in the barrio selling newspapers and so on to help the household survive. Long a movie fan, he migrated to Los Angeles at age fourteen. Odd jobs led to extra and stunt work in the movies, and by 1925, he had a real role in Clara Bow's *The Plastic Age*. (His adopted screen name came from two film favorites: John Gilbert and Ruth Roland.) Roland played Armand Duval in the silent photoplay *Camille* (1927) starring his off-camera love, the married Norma Talmadge.

When the LATIN LOVER craze dissolved during the transition to talkies, Roland's career waned but revived when Constance Bennett, whom he was dating (and whom he much later married), cast him in her movie vehicles. He also turned to making Spanish-language features in Hollywood. Periodically, he had good screen parts (e.g., *THE LAST TRAIN FROM MADRID*, 1937; *The Sea Hawk*, 1940). After World War II service, Roland effectively played the CISCO KID on screen in six low-budget entries starting with *Beauty and the Bandit* (1946). His industry standing rebounded with a striking performance in *WE WERE STRANGERS* (1949) as a Cuban revolutionary. It led to parts in *BULLFIGHTER AND THE LADY* (1951), *BANDIDO* (1956), and *Cheyenne Autumn* (1964—as Chief Dull Knife). He made spaghetti westerns in Europe (e.g., *Any Gun Can Play*, 1967), was Don Alejandro Vega in the 1974 TV production of *The Mark of Zorro*, and played a Mexican elder in *Barbarosa* (1982), his last movie. Earlier, in 1959, a TV series pilot entitled *Amigo* would have featured Roland as a police detective working the border towns of Juarez and El Paso.

***Romero* (1989)** Four Seasons, color 94 minutes. **Director:** John Duigan; **Screenplay:** John Sacret Young; **Cast:** Raul Julia (Archbishop Oscar Arnulfo Romero), Richard Jordan (Fr. Rutillo Grande), Ana Alicia (Arista Zalads), Tony Plana (Father Morantes), Harold Gould (Francisco Galedo).

Financed by the U.S. Roman Catholic Church and produced by its Paulist Pictures, this stirring documentary-style feature concerns the real-life Archbishop Oscar Arnulfo Romero of El Salvador who was assassinated in 1980 while conducting a mass in a hospital chapel. His killer was never apprehended. The movie focuses on the last three years of the martyr's life as Romero changes from a traditional and mild man of God to an outspoken advocate for human rights and the needs of his impoverished congregation, and becomes a liberal thinker (even in theological matters). In the central role, JULIA offers a riveting performance as he reacts with passion and action to the horrors of the death squads and other tyranny around him. Mexico City was used as a backdrop to stand in for San Salvador.

Despite its relatively wider release, *Romero*, made on a budget of more than $3 million, grossed only slightly more than $1 million in domestic distribution.

Romero, Cesar (1907–1994) Like GILBERT ROLAND—who also played the CISCO KID on screen—Romero was a survivor who lasted through decades of being the tall, dark, and handsome leading man. Always immaculately groomed, Romero had a continental elegance that only improved with maturity. He frequently portrayed Hispanics on camera, often as a LATIN-LOVER playboy.

Romero was born in New York City, his mother (Maria Mantilla) a concert pianist, his father an Italian-born sugar exporter, and his grandparent, José Marti y Perez, a Cuban writer and patriot. Romero's show-business career began as a ballroom dancer and then as a stage actor. He made his movie debut in *The Shadow Laughs* (1933) and was among the cast of the classic *The Thin Man* (1934). Using his dapper charms, he was opposite Carole Lombard in *Love Before Breakfast* (1936). After signing with Twentieth Century-Fox, he had a wide variety of movie roles: He was Khoda Khan in Shirley Temple's *Wee Willie Winkie* (1937) and did musicals with Sonja Henie (e.g., *Happy Landing*, 1938) and westerns (e.g., *Frontier Marshal*, 1939—as Doc Holliday). He had been Lopez in *The Return of the Cisco Kid* (1939) with Warner Baxter

Cesar Romero (right) with Milton Berle in *A Gentleman at Heart* (1942). (JC ARCHIVES)

in the lead but took on the title role for *Viva Cisco Kid* (1940) and five more entries. He danced in Alice Faye's *Weekend in Havana* (1941) and made merry with Betty Grable in *Springtime in the Rockies* (1942). After U.S. Coast Guard service in World War II, he had one of his best assignments as the Spanish conquistador Hernando Cortez in the historical saga, CAPTAIN FROM CASTILE (1947).

When the movie studio system died in the early 1950s, he turned to TV, starring in the adventure entry PASSPORT TO DANGER (1954–55) and was a panelist on the game show *Take a Good Look* (1959–61). His great success in the 1960s on the *Batman* TV series (1966–68) caused him to return repeatedly as the sinister Joker. Two decades later, he was cast as shipping magnate Peter Stavros (1985–87) on *Falcon Crest*, the nighttime TV drama. His final films included *The Third Hand* (1988) and *Simple Justice* (1990).

***Roosters* (1995)** I.R.S., color, 95 minutes. **Director:** Robert M. Young; **Screenplay:** Milcha Sánchez-Scott; **Cast:** Edward James Olmos (Gallo Morales), Sonia Braga (Juana), Maria Conchita Alonso (Chata Morales), Danny Nucci (Hector Morales), Mark Dacasco (Filipino's son), Sarah Lassez (Angela Morales).

Based on the 1987 play by Sanchez-Scott, *Roosters* aspired to be an intense drama of Hispanic family relationships.

After seven years in prison for manslaughter, Gallo Morales returns home expecting to reestablish his patriarch status. But his son Hector has inherited the prized fighting rooster that his grandfather bred for the family business. A battle of wills (and machismo) develop between the resentful Gallo and Hector. Meanwhile, Gallo's fourteen-year-old daughter (Lassez) suffers from the tensions at home, her growing womanhood, and the cruel environment to which she is exposed. Juana is Gallo's long-suffering wife, and Chata is his sensual sister.

The creatively deficient *Roosters* had limited theatrical release (where it grossed almost $200,000 in domestic distribution) before being shunted to home-video sales.

S

***Salt of the Earth* (1954)** Independent Productions, b&w, 94 minutes. **Director:** Herbert J. Biberman; **Screenplay:** Michael Wilson; **Cast:** Will Geer (sheriff), David Wolfe (Barton), David Sarvis (Hartwell), Mervin Williams (Alexander), Rosaura Revueltas (Esperanza Quintero), William Rockwell (Kimbrough), Juan Chacón (Ramón Quintero), Henrietta Williams (Teresa Vidal), Angela Sánchez (Consuela Ruiz), Clorinda Alderette (Luz Morales), Virginia Jencks (Ruth Barnes), Clinton Jencks (Frank Barnes).

The drama behind the making of this film was the subject of several books (e.g., *Salt of the Earth: The Story of a Film*, 1965, by Biberman) and documentaries (e.g., *A Crime to Fit the Punishment*, 1984). In essence, several blacklisted members of the film industry (including producer Paul Jarrico) decided to film a fictional account of an actual 1951–52 strike in the United States by the International Union of Mine, Mill and Smelter Workers against Empire Zinc. Two people (Chacón and Clinton Jencks) from that strike participated in *Salt of the Earth*, which had a mixture of professional and nonprofessional actors.

During production, the project ran into crippling difficulties, not only from the unsympathetic American film industry but also from the townsfolk in New Mexico where the movie was shot. When completed, it had only rare showings in the United States because of an industry "boycott" of the property, but it received good reviews when distributed abroad. Later, *Salt of the Earth* was acknowledged as a film classic. Integral to the project was its depiction of Mexican Americans and the many ways in which they were discriminated against.

In Zinc Town, New Mexico, Ramón Quintero works for the local mine, while his wife Esperanza—pregnant with her third child—is coping with dreadful living conditions at home. Even before an accident occurs at the mine that causes the men to strike, the womenfolk discuss picketing the company because of the unsanitary living conditions they must endure. As the strike proceeds, Ramón is beaten by the police, and Esperanza is denied proper medical help when she goes into labor. Ramón and the others criticize Barnes, the Anglo union leader, for not learning more about the Mexican-American workers—their culture and their needs.

As a way around the Taft-Hartley law regarding strikers (which only applies to miners), the wives take over the picket line. When they, in turn, are arrested Esperanza brings her children and infant with her to jail. This inspires the other women to chant for her release. While she is incarcerated, Ramón takes over the housework and suddenly realizes what his wife and the other women must withstand because of poor living conditions. Eventually released from jail, Esperanza and the other women threaten to picket again. This frightens off the sheriff and his men, leading the corporate owners of the mine to finally settle the strike. Ramón, Esperanza, and the others celebrate, knowing the legacy they have created for the next generations.

***Salvador* (1987)** Hemdale, color, 123 minutes. **Director:** Oliver Stone; **Screenplay:** Stone and Richard Boyle; **Cast:** James Woods (Richard Boyle), James Belushi (Dr. Rock), Michael Murphy (Ambassador Thomas Kelly), John Savage (John Cassady), Elpidia Carrillo (Maria), Tony Plana (Major Max), Carlos Ruiz (Archbishop Romero).

Real-life journalist Boyle coauthored this searing, violent, and forthright drama that concerns the bloody 1980 to 1981 civil war in El Salvador. The right-wing government of Roberto d'Aubuisson and his Arena Party utilize their "death squads" to silence opposition as the American government under President Ronald Reagan looked on in general silence.

(Some of the same material was covered in the 1989 entry, *ROMERO*.)

The dynamic Woods was outstanding as the sleazy veteran journalist Boyle, who traveled south from San Francisco with his unemployed disc jockey pal (Belushi). Once in El Salvador, they experience the horrors of the regime that murders dissidents, including nuns, and casually carts its victims' corpses to a dumping ground. Boyle's revulsion at what he sees and experiences—including the assassination of Archbishop Romero—leads to his regeneration as a person, and his relationship with Salvadorian Maria ends in tragedy: he is eventually allowed to flee the country, but she and her children are not permitted past the border.

Salvador received Academy Award nominations for Best Actor (Woods) and Best Original Screenplay.

***Saved by the Bell* (1989–1993)** NBC-TV series, color, 30 minutes. **Cast:** Mark-Paul Gosselaar (Zack Morris), Mario Lopez (A. C. Slater), Dustin Diamond (Samuel "Screech" Powers), Tiffani-Amber Thiessen (Kelly Kaposki), Elizabeth Berkley (Jessie Spano).

A diverse (i.e., politically correct) grouping of students populate this Saturday morning sitcom set at Bayside High School in Palisades, California. Among the frothy crowd is dark and handsome Hispanic A. C. Slater, the first of his classmates to have his own car and the athlete of the bunch—a star on the wrestling team. When the show followed the characters past graduation, it became *Saved by the Bell: The College Years* (1993–94), with much of the same personnel enrolling at California University. Slater was among them, thanks to a wrestling scholarship. Meanwhile, the Saturday-morning version of the series gained a fresh cast, and the show was retitled *Saved by the Bell: The New Class* (1993–2000). Among the enrollees were Tommy "Tommy D" DeLuca (played by Jonathan Angel), a not-so-bright Hispanic-American student. (A variation of this multicultural-youth format was the teen-oriented sitcom *One World*, which began in 1998 and presented an ethnically diverse cast of characters residing under one roof.)

***Scarface* (1983)** Universal, 170 minutes, color. **Director:** Brian De Palma; **Screenplay:** Oliver Stone; **Cast:** Al Pacino (Tony Montana), Steven Bauer (Manny Ray), Michelle Pfeiffer (Elvira), Mary Elizabeth Mastrantonio (Gina), Robert Loggia (Frank Lopez), Miriam Colon (Mama Montana), F. Murray Abraham (Omar Swarez), Ángel Salazar (Chi Chi).

Using the classic 1932 *Scarface, The Shame of a Nation* (with Paul Muni) as the merest springboard, this overinflated, hugely violent feature solidified a new mold for Hispanic stereotypes, this time as ruthless, street-smart drug lords. Although the lead role of the Cuban-born, Miami-based drug kingpin was played in excessive (almost laughable) fashion by Anglo Pacino, the film's outlandish brutality pushed his character into the forefront of screen types for the 1980s and thereafter.

In the new scenario, Tony Montana is one of the 20,000 Cuban miscreants and/or misfits shipped to Florida by Cuba's Fidel Castro. Before long, the enterprising Montana rises in Miami's drug world. Not only does he supplant his boss (Loggia) as chief of the dope racket, but he also grab's the man's blonde mistress (Pfeiffer). Later, the cocaine-crazed Montana realizes that it is his sister Gina whom he truly covets. Others trapped in this excessive brutality are Colon as Montana's mother and Bauer as Montana's best friend who is killed for romancing Gina.

Made on a $25 million budget, the *Scarface* remake grossed almost $45 million in domestic distribution. In its way, it made a star of Miami, which the film fabricated as a tropical den of iniquity that is seemingly controlled by Cubans. It set the stage for the hip TV cop series, *MIAMI VICE* (1984–89), which also used the multicultural Florida as its backdrop.

science fiction—feature films and television During the decades, Latino actors were not a favored component in the cast of characters of science fiction movies made by Hollywood. (Some of the few participants included THOMAS GOMEZ and GREGORY SIERRA in 1970's *Beneath the Planet of the Apes* as well as RICARDO MONTALBAN in 1971's *Escape from the Planet of the Apes* and in 1982's *Star Trek: The Wrath of Khan*.) In more politically correct times, a few TV series provided Hispanic representation. For example, *Something Is Out There*, the short-lasting TV series (1988)—a spin-off from a 1988 TV miniseries of the same name—had Sierra as Lt. Victor Maldonado. The show involved earthlings battling aliens in an American metropolis. *seaQuest, DSV* (1993–95), set aboard a supersubmergence vehicle at the bottom of the ocean, boasted Sensor Chief Miguel Ortiz (played by Marco Sánchez) among the craft's crew. *STAR TREK: VOYAGER* (1995–2001) included Roxann Biggs-Dawson as Chief Eng. B'Elanna Torres, a former member of the Maquis, who became chief engineer on the USS *Voyager*. On the genre series *Roswell* (1999–2002), set in the famed New Mexico town, one of the teen characters was the Latino Maria DeLuca, played by Majandra Delfino.

***Selena* (1997)** Warner Bros., color, 127 minutes. **Director/Screenplay:** Gregory Nava; **Cast:** Jennifer Lopez (Selena Quintanilla), Edward James Olmos (Abraham Quintanilla Jr.), Jon Seda (Chris Perez), Constance Marie (Marcela Quintanilla), Jacob Vargas (Abie Quintanilla), Panchito Gómez (young Abraham).

This was a very sanitized biography of Selena Quintanilla-Perez, the "Queen of Tejano pop" who was murdered in March 1995 by the president of her fan club when the successful singer was just twenty-three. Most refreshing within the drama was the dynamic performance of LOPEZ, who rose to stardom as a result of this frequently corny movie production.

The other main focus of this glossy feature was Selena's very controlling father Abraham, who tried to supervise all aspects of her life. The screen biography contained a flashback to the dad's unsuccessful attempt to breach racial bias when he had his doo-wop group Los Dinos and tried to crash the musical marketplace in the early 1960s. Jumping ahead, Abraham monitors every aspect of Selena's existence, deciding when she must learn Spanish to gain acceptance by singing Spanish-language numbers and then, later (not that long before her death), crossing over to make her show business success in the Anglo world. In the course of the screen drama, he and his daughter battle over her right to wed the lead guitarist (Seda) of her back-up group. (Selena wins that contest.)

Made at a cost of more than $11 million, *Selena* grossed more than $35 million in domestic distribution. Lopez won a 1998 ALMA Award as Outstanding Actress in a Motion Picture.

serials—motion pictures In contrast to other ethnic minority groups, Hollywood did not use Hispanic characters very often in chapterplay plots. Usually, such figures were worked into the story if the setting was the old West, where the Spanish influence was still a vital force and before the territories became part of the United States. (If it was a contemporary story, there was not a Latino in sight.) Thus, in *The Painted Stallion* (1937), a twelve-chapter western entry featuring Ray Corrigan and Hoot Gibson, the old and new Spanish governor of Santa Fe figured into the premise.

One of the more frequent times when a Spanish-flavored character was in a serial occurred when the legendary ZORRO was involved. However, these tales revolved around later generations of the famed masked swordsman or of a leading figure who took on the Zorro guise to right wrongs. These entries were: *Zorro Rides Again* (1937), *Zorro's Fighting Legion* (1939), *Zorro's Black Whip* (1944), *Son of Zorro* (1947), and *Ghost of Zorro* (1949).

Seven Cities of Gold **(1955)** Twentieth Century-Fox, color, 102 minutes. **Director:** Robert D. Webb; **Screenplay:** Richard L. Breen and John C. Higgins; **Cast:** Richard Egan (Lt. José Mendoza), Anthony Quinn (Don Gaspar de Portola), Michael Rennie (Fr. Junipero Serra), Jeffrey Hunter (Matuwir), Rita Moreno (Ula), Eduardo Noriega (sergeant), Leslie Bradley (José de Gálvez).

The Nine Days of Father Serra (1951) by Isabelle Gibson Ziegler was the basis for this somewhat shallow feature that could not decide whether it was to be an adventure spectacle or a historical study of the founding of the string of California missions in the late 1760s by the Catholic priest, Father Junipero Serra. While muddling some of the historical facts, it did provide a primer for the early history of California. With the exception of QUINN as the hardened Spanish mercenary officer Don Gaspar de Portola, the other lead players were badly miscast as Spaniards or Native Americans.

Money-hungry Portola and his more gentle fellow soldier Lt. José Mendoza arrive in Mexico City where they are ordered to occupy southern California. While planning their difficult mandate, they also dream of discovering the legendary Seven Cities of Gold there. The tough Portola is put in charge of the expedition. Once at the site of what is present-day San Diego, Portola and a detachment of soldiers march northward, leaving Mendoza in charge. Meanwhile, Father Serra, the spiritual director of the expedition, who remains at San Diego, makes friends with the Diegueño Indians, in particular their future chief, Matuwir. As for Mendoza he begins a romance with Ula, Matuwir's sister.

Eventually, Portola's party returns to San Diego from its trek northward, having failed to subdue the natives or find the cities. About to return to Mexico, Mendoza rejects Ula who commits suicide. War with the Diegueño is averted only when Mendoza surrenders to the warriors who put him to death. The discouraged expedition is excited to see the ship *San Antonio* sail into view. It contains bells meant for the potential mission at Monterey. Serra is happy to install them at San Diego, now a permanent garrison and mission for the Spaniards.

Shannon's Deal **(1990–1991)** NBC-TV series, color, 60 minutes. **Cast:** Jamey Sheridan (Jack Shannon), Elizabeth Peña (Lucy Acosta), Jenny Lewis (Neala Shannon), Richard Edson (Wilmer Slade), Miguel Ferrer (D. A. Todd Spurrier), Martin Ferraro (Lou Gondolf).

Created by famed independent filmmaker John Sayles this little seen series tried to avoid the clichés of TV legal drama. Its lead figure was a former prominent Philadelphia lawyer whose gambling addiction and disillusionment with his fancy corporate practice led to his becoming a small-time criminal lawyer handling worthy cases. His secretary was Lucy Acosta, an aggressive person who is paying off the debt her boyfriend incurred in legal fees to Shannon. PEÑA gave the role bite, making her Hispanic worker an unconventional series support figure.

Sheen, Martin (1940–) A tremendously productive actor over several decades, he earned his greatest recognition later in life playing U.S. president Josiah "Jed" Bartlet in the dramatic TV series *West Wing* (1999–). This versatile and well-respected stage, film, and TV performer also gained notability as the father of Brat Pack actors EMILIO ESTEVEZ and Charlie Sheen. In addition, Martin Sheen was long a devoted political activist, taking a strong stand on a range of topical issues. His picketing for such controversial causes sometimes led to his being arrested.

He was born Rámon Estévez in Dayton, Ohio, one of ten offspring of an Irish mother and a Spanish immigrant father. Instead of attending college, he relocated to Manhattan to study acting. There, he changed his surname to Sheen to avoid the ethnic typecasting and discrimination so prevalent during that period. He made his off-Broadway bow in *The*

Connection (1959) and had his feature film debut playing a toughie threatening subway passengers in *The Incident* (1967). The next year, he repeated his stage role in the film of *The Subject Was Roses.* He was impressive as a young killer on the loose in *Badlands* (1973), had the title role in the TV movie, *The Execution of Private Slovik* (1974), survived a near-fatal heart attack during the making of *Apocalypse Now* (1979), was noteworthy as the reporter in *Gandhi* (1982), and impersonated John F. Kennedy in the TV miniseries *Kennedy* (1983).

He made many telefeatures including *The Fourth Wise Man* (1985) and *Conspiracy: The Trial of the Chicago 8* (1987). That same year, he acted in *Wall Street* with his son Charlie. He was General Robert E. Lee in *Gettysburg* (1993), gangster John Dillinger in *Dillinger and Capone* (1995), and the U.S. president for the TV miniseries *Medusa's Child* (1997). Sheen directed the telefeature *Babies Having Babies* (1986), which featured his offspring Renée, and *Cadence* (1991) in which he again costarred with his son Charlie. Sheen's recent films included *The Time Shifters* (1999—TV movie), *O* (2001), and *The Confidence Game* (2002).

situation comedy series—television Although on the one hand, *I LOVE LUCY* (1951–57), a classic TV comedy, helped to acclimate mainstream American home viewers to the personality and culture of Cubans, on the other it also propagated preconceived notions of the heavily accented, quickly agitated Hispanic as portrayed by DESI ARNAZ. *THE DANNY THOMAS SHOW* (1957–64) featured Bill Dana as José Jiminez, the Latino building doorman. Again, this was a comedic stereotype of the well-meaning, nonambitious, bumbling South American. Programs such as *The Real McCoys* (1957–63), *THE BILL DANA SHOW* (1963–65), *THE ADDAMS FAMILY* (1964–66—with John Astin as hot-blooded Gomez), and *F Troop* (1965–67) all perpetuated Hispanic-(American) negative stereotypes. However, *The Flying Nun* (1967–70) with Sally Field had Alejandro Rey as a new-style Latin Lover in the San Juan, Puerto Rico, setting.

There were Hispanic Americans in *ALL IN THE FAMILY* during the later 1970s and on *Sanford and Son* (1972–77) and *Calucci's Department* (1973). Much more focused on ethnic minorities was *CHICO AND THE MAN* (1974–78), which, until his suicide in early 1977, featured Puerto Rican-American FREDDIE PRINZE as a Chicano. Other comedies in the 1970s having Hispanic-American characters were *Hot'l Baltimore* (1975), *On the Rocks* (1975–76), *Phyllis* (1975–77), *WELCOME BACK, KOTTER* (1975–79), *Barney Miller* (1975–82), *POPI* (1976), and *A.E.S. Hudson Street* (1978).

RITA MORENO played a Hispanic lead character in *9 TO 5* (1982–83), as did Tomas Milian in *Frannie's Turn* (1982) and Paul Rodriguez in *A.K.A. PABLO* (1984). Other sitcoms of the decade with Hispanic-American representation included *THE FAMILY MARTINEZ* (1985), *Sanchez of Bel Air* (1985), *I Married Dora* (1987–88), *Roseanne* (1988–97), *Trial and Error* (1988), *Knight & Daye* (1989), and *SAVED BY THE BELL* (1989–93).

In the 1990s, such shows as *City* (1990) with Liz Torres, *Golden Palace* (1992–93) with CHEECH MARIN, *The Sinbad Show* (1993–94) with SALMA HAYEK, *The John Larroquette Show* (1993–97) with Torres, *HOUSE OF BUGGIN'* (1994) with JOHN LEGUIZAMO, and *WILL & GRACE* (1998–) with Shelley Morrison gave much stronger representation to Hispanic-American characters, allowing for fuller characterizations and less stereotypical depictions. Other comedy TV series of the decade featuring ethnic minority characters included *Bakersfield P.D.* (1993–94), *Saved by the Bell: The College Years* (1993–94), *That '70s Show* (1998–), *Love Boat: The Next Wave* (1998–99), and *THE BROTHERS GARCIA* (2000–). Christina Vidal was presented in the title role of *Taina* (2001–), a fifteen-year-old New Yorker who dreams of becoming a star and who has just started at the Manhattan School of the Arts. Aired over the Nickelodeon cable network, *Taina* featured a predominantly Latino cast. Also aimed at a teen audience was the short-lasting *All About Us* (2001), which concerned four Chicago girls from a blue-collar background who existed in a seemingly trouble-free vacuum. *Scrubs* (2001–), an ensemble comedy set at a hospital, found Judy Reyes as the comely nurse Carla Espinosa. In *George Lopez* (2002) stand-up comic Lopez was cast as an assembly line worker who has just been promoted to a manager at the plant. Between problems at work and at home with his family, he had his hands full.

Smits, Jimmy (1955–) The lanky (six-feet, three-inch) actor with the soulful eyes proved to be one of the more resourceful actors of recent decades. Smits especially shone on television as Victor Sifuentes (1986–91) on L.A. LAW and as Det. Bobby Simone (1994–98) on *NYPD BLUE.* In both these focal roles, he was Emmy-nominated several times (and won for *L.A. Law* in 1990) and found it satisfying personally to present positive images of Hispanic-American characters.

He was born in Brooklyn, New York. His father was from Surinam, and his mother was Puerto Rican. He graduated from Brooklyn College and received his MFA from Cornell University. After appearing off-Broadway and working with the New York Shakespeare Festival, he turned to TV work. As such, he was a guest performer on the pilot of *MIAMI VICE* in 1984 as Don Johnson's partner who was killed in the plot line. He made his feature film debut in *Running Scared* (1986) as an ethnic crime boss. He was in the horror movie *THE BELIEVERS* (1987) and such TV movies as *Glitz* (1988). Smits appeared as the young Mexican General Tomas Arroyo in *Old Gringo* (1989) with Jane Fonda, played in Blake Edwards's *Switch* (1991), and was the Cuban political prisoner Nestor in *FIRES WITHIN* (1991). On television he participated in *Stephen King's The Tommyknockers* (1993), had the title part in *The Cisco Kid* (1994—TV movie), and was the biblical ruler in *Solomon & Sheba* (1995—TV movie). He was part of GREGORY NAVA's underrated *MY FAMILY: MI FAMILIA* (1995). His more recent movies included *The Million Dollar Hotel*, *Angel*, and *Star Wars: Episode II—Attack of the Clones* (all 2002).

soap opera series—television More so than with many other ethnic groups, it was decades after TV network soap operas began to air that Hispanic-American characters were added slowly to the shows' casts of regulars. One major cause was that many of the original daytime video dramas took place in the North in geographical or economic areas where, at the time, there was little or no actual Hispanic representation. Yet, even when a genre piece was set in a locale with a high concentration of Hispanics, the soap opera format ignored this ethnic minority in its recurring major roles (e.g., *Texas*, 1980–1982).

One of the first daytime soaps to present a Hispanic character was the New York-set *Ryan's Hope* (1975–89). There Alicia Nieves (played by Ana Alicia) during 1977–78 had an interracial romance with lead figure Dr. Pat Ryan (played at the time by Malcolm Groome). On *The Young and the Restless* (1973–), during 1980 to 1981, a story arc was set on a tropical isle where Katherine Chancellor (portrayed by Jeanne Cooper) was rescued from a drowning/suicide attempt by Filipe Ramirez (enacted by Victor Mohica), a rebel revolutionary from the Caribbean. In 1984, on *General Hospital* (1963–), June Lockhart showed up as Maria Ramirez in the story line, and a very blue-eyed, blonde beauty, Felicia Jones Scorpio (played by Kristina Wagner), was introduced as an Aztec princess.

Santa Barbara (1984–93), set in the California coastal community, had several Hispanic-American characters, ranging from the Andrade family (Rosa, Santana, and Danny) to Cruz Castillo, the latter played from 1984 to 1992 by A MARTINEZ. He was showcased as an earnest police detective who had a steamy, long-lasting romance with WASPy Eden Capwell (played by quite blonde, blue-eyed Marcy Walker). That relationship gathered a lot of attention for the show. By 1988 the interracial couple had married in the plot, despite all the obstacles (mostly kidnappings and murder attempts, rather than the potential "problems" of mingling two contrasting cultures). (Years later, in 1999, Martinez joined the cast of *General Hospital*, this time as a character named Roy DeLucca.)

By the 1990s there was a growing trend to add Hispanic-American characters to daytime soaps. This ranged from bringing singer Ricky Martin onto *General Hospital* in 1994 to *The Young and Restless* having ANTHONY QUINN's son Francesco playing novelist Tomas Del Cerro (as well as David Lago portraying a figure called Raul and Anthony Pena cast—without much of a story line until the mid- to late 1990s—as the butler, Miguel Rodriguez). *All My Children* (1970–) had an interracial marriage between Mateo Santos, a character with a once-prominent family, and Anglo heiress Hayley Vaughn. (Mark Consuelos and Kelly Ripa, who played Mateo and Hayley, were wed in real life.) Within *One Life to Live* (1968–), there were the Vega family, including the mother, who was a former maid now-coffee-shop-owner, and her son Antonio (portrayed by Kamar De Los Reyes), an ex-con who was cleared of all charges and became a law enforcer. Another son, Christian (played by Yorlin Madera and later by David Fumero), an artist, was divorced and was having an interracial romance with heiress Jessica Buchanan (played by Erin Torpey). *Guiding Light* (1952–) presented the Santos clan, a mob family. *Port Charles* (1997–) had its Detective Garcia as well as a minor female love interest named Gabriela Garza. *Passions* (1999–), had the Lopez-Fitzgeralds (half-Hispanic, half-Irish). *The Bold and the Beautiful* (1987–), long noted for being "lily-white," added Gladis Jiminez in late 2000 as Carmen, the girlfriend to a white club owner.

In the new millennium, *TV Guide* (July 21, 2001) reported that all the daytime soap operas, facing diminished viewership, were angling for Hispanic viewers. Explained the publication's Michael Logan: "The Hispanic population in the U.S. has surpassed 35 million, and that vast audience, already nuts for *telenovelas*, has American soap programmers drooling." (This led some of the daytime dramas to employ Spanish-language simulcast as well as to add and/or increase the number of Hispanic characters on their programs.)

Nighttime dramas were just as reluctant to present Hispanic characters as regular cast members. One of the first such genre programs to do so was the iconoclastic satire *Soap* (1977–81). During its last season, Jessica Tate (played by Katherine Helmond) had a romance with Carlos "El Puerco" Valdez (played by Gregory Sierra), who was described as a rebel leader from a war-engulfed Caribbean isle. On *Beverly Hills 90210* (1990–2000) Jewish Andrea Zuckerman (played by Gabrielle Carteris) met and married Hispanic-American law student Jesse Vasquez (played by Mark Damon Espinoza) and had his child in a story arc than ran from 1993 to 1995. In this instance, the show played up the religious/cultural differences that bedeviled Andrea and Jesse regarding the rearing of daughter Hannah.

Interestingly, on *Falcon Crest* (1981–90), set in California's Napa Valley, two lead performers (Ana Alicia and Lorenzo Lamas) on the show who were (part) Hispanic played Italian-American figures. In the series' eighth season, the program introduced a Hispanic family, the Ortegas. Ironically, its lead figure, Pilar, was portrayed by Italian actress Kristian Alfonso.

***Sombrero* (1953)** Metro-Goldwyn-Mayer, color, 103 minutes. **Director:** Norman Foster; **Screenplay:** Josefina Niggli and Foster; **Cast:** Ricardo Montalban (Pepe Gonzales), Pier Angeli (Eufemia Caldero), Vittorio Gassman (Alejandro Castillo), Cyd Charisse (Lola de Torrano), Yvonne De Carlo (Maria), Rick Jason (Ruben), Nina Foch (Elena Cantu), Kurt Kasznar (Father Zacaya), Walter Hampden (Don Carlos Castillo), Thomas Gomez (Don Homero Calderon), José Greco (Gintanillo de Torrano).

Using three of the ten tales contained in Niggli's novel *A Mexican Village* (1945), producer Jack Cummings (noted for his Esther Williams musicals) presented this fabricated representation of life south of the border in a trio of tales, each segment bolstered by musical numbers (e.g., Montalban singing "Carta a Ufemia" and Charisse performing "Gypsy Dance"). For box-office appeal, each story featured one of the costarring LATIN LOVERS. (Besides the already established, Mexican-born, MGM contract leading man MONTALBAN, the meandering *Sombrero* employed MGM's imported Italian actor Gassman, as well as New York-born screen newcomer Jason.)

In the *Romeo and Juliet*–like episode, Eufemia Caldero and Pepe Gonzales are from villages that are feuding with one another. Before the couple can wed, the townsfolk of each settlement must be appeased. In the next episode, Lola de Torrano adores street candy peddler Ruben, much to the embarrassment of her proud bullfighter brother, Gintanillo. To be spiteful, he persuades Ruben to enter the bull ring, where it is Gintanillo instead who meets his death. Later, the couple marry but cannot find happiness till she lifts the curse of her late brother from their union. In the final story, wealthy Alejandro Castillo loves impoverished Maria despite his family's objections. He learns that he is dying and suggests they wed anyway. She refuses, instead matching him up with Elena Cantu in a loveless situation. Belatedly, Alejandro's father, Don Carlos, tries to make amends to Maria, giving her a place in his home.

Sombrero was shot on location in Mexico, especially at Tepotzlán, Tetecala, and near Cuernavaca. With its contrived, episodic story lines and mostly cartoonish characterizations (which accentuated Hispanic stereotypes), the gaudy film did not fare especially well in the United States.

***Stand and Deliver* (1987)** Warner Bros., color, 1987. **Director:** Ramón Menéndez; **Screenplay:** Menéndez and Tom Musca; **Cast:** Edward James Olmos (Jaime Escalante), Lou Diamond Phillips (Angel), Rosana De Soto (Fabiola Escalante), Andy Garcia (Ramirez), Ingrid Oliu (Lupe), Mark Eliot (Tito), Bodie Olmos (Fernando Escalante), Adelaida Alvarez (sexy girl).

This was a feel-good, fact-based movie with a difference. It was about Hispanic students who, against all odds, overcame the general mediocrity of the public educational system in the barrio and went on to score high in the Advanced Placement Test in calculus.

Their guru is Bolivian-born teacher Jaime Escalante, who quits his mainstream job to become a computer teacher and suddenly finds himself in charge of math at Garfield High School. His classroom is filled with gang-influenced delinquents, girls coping with a chauvinistic lifestyle, and others downtrodden by life in the barrio. Refusing to admit defeat with his disinterested class, Escalante adopts unorthodox methods to gain his students' attention and interest, including that of Angel, a gang banger.

After converting his disinterested pupils into hardworking enthusiasts, they suffer racial prejudice when it is arbitrarily decided by the Educational Testing Service—and the investigation headed by Ramirez—that these students *must* have cheated to gain such high scores. To prove everyone wrong, the class takes a more difficult test and scores well.

The film highlights the students not only in class but also at home and on the streets. Made for $1.5 million by first-time director Menéndez, a Cuban UCLA graduate, the movie went on to gross $14 million in domestic distribution. The picture received an Academy Award nomination for Best Actor (OLMOS).

Released in the same year as *LA BAMBA*—which also costarred PHILLIPS—*Stand and Deliver* gave promise (not yet fulfilled) for an upsurge of Hispanic-themed Hollywood films that would go beyond the drug-pusher and gang-banger stereotypes already in place.

***Star Trek: Voyager* (1995–2001)** UPN-TV series, color, 60 minutes. **Cast:** Kate Mulgrew (Capt. Kathryn Janeway), Robert Beltran (First Officer Chakotay), Tim Russ (Security Chief Tuvok), Ethan Phillips (Neelix), Robert Picardo (emerging medical hologram, the "Doc"), Roxann Biggs-Dawson (Chief Engineer B'Elanna Torres), Robert Duncan McNeill (Lt. Tom Parris), Jennifer Lien (Kes: 1995–97), Garrett Wang (Ens. Harry Kim).

This was the fourth *Star Trek* series and was light years more sophisticated than the original 1966–69 TV entry. It featured Capt. Kathryn Janeway, whose difficult task was to return her ship (which also contains the crew from a destroyed Maquis terrorist craft) back to the part of the galaxy from which they were hurled by an unknown force. Among those aboard were Chakotay, a Native American, who had been captain of the Maquis ship and was now first officer of the consolidated crew. He was played by Hispanic-American BELTRAN. Another Hispanic-American performer on this science fiction series was Biggs-Dawson cast as Chief Engineer B'Elanna Torres, the attractive female who was half-human and half-Klingon. Toward the end of the series, she and Tom Parris fell in love, and she became pregnant

As was true with the first *Star Trek* TV series that used an interracial cast for the crew of the *Enterprise*, the science fiction genre was always a forum for allowing cultural changes to be presented to audiences. Because the show took place in a supposedly integrated future and there were so many technical and physical trappings to make the setting seem "alien," it did not generally upset racially sensitive viewers with its examples and messages of racial tolerance and ethnic intermingling.

***Stones for Ibarra* (1988)** NBC-TV, color, 96 minutes. **Director:** Jack Gold; **Teleplay:** Ernest Kinoy; **Cast:** Glenn Close (Sara Everton), Keith Carradine (Richard Everton), Alfonso Arau (Chuy Santos), Ray Oriel (Domingo Garcia), Trinidad Silva (Basilio Garcia), Jorge Cervera Jr. (Rose Reyes), Ron Joseph (Dr. De la Luna).

Part of the *Hallmark Hall of Fame* series, this made-for-television movie was based on Harriett Doerrs's 1984 novel and concerned an American couple, Sara and Richard Everton, who inherited a copper mine in Mexico and moved there to operate it. Their dreams fall apart when the husband contracts leukemia. What made this presentation unique was that the small village to which they have relocated was filled with real characters, not Hollywood's usual ethnic stick figures.

***Sudden Terror: The Hijacking of School Bus #17* (1996)** ABC-TV, color, 100 minutes. **Director:** Paul

Schneider; **Teleplay:** Jonathan Rintels; **Cast:** Maria Conchita Alonso (Marta Caldwell), Marcy Walker (Lt. Kathy Leone), Michael Paul Chan (Harry Kee), Dennis Boutsikaris (Frank Caldwell), Bruce Weitz (Lieutenant Caroselli), Emiliano Díez (Eduardo Sanchez), Leesa Halstead (Juanita Sanchez).

Based on a real-life incident, ALONSO was showcased as the brave school bus driver who had to deal with a hijacker who had taken control of her vehicle filled with mentally challenged children. The Cuban-born Alonso made her character an appealing role model, still a comparative novelty on American network TV.

***Sword of Justice* (1978–79)** NBC-TV, series, color, 60 minutes. **Cast:** Dack Rambo (Jack Cole), Bert Rosario (Hector Ramirez), Alex Courtney (Arthur Woods), Colby Chester (Buckner).

After New York playboy Jack Cole served a prison term on false charges, he became a crusader against white-collar criminals. He used his former blue-blood status as his job cover. His buddy in these adventures was his smart-mouthed, Puerto Rican former cellmate, Hector Ramirez.

Interestingly, on *Sword of Justice*, although the Anglo's character was innocent of any crime, his Hispanic buddy did not have that ameliorating background in his character's premise. It was another illustration of American TV playing to established racial types.

T

***Tarzan* (1966–1969)** NBC-TV series, color, 60 minutes **Cast:** Ron Ely (Tarzan), Manuel Padilla Jr. (Jai).

Although the enduring Edgar Rice Burroughs jungle character was still swinging from African vines, this TV series was shot entirely in Mexico. Adding to the Latino flavor was the casting of Hispanic-American youngster Padilla as Jai, the young orphan friend of Tarzan. In this teleseries edition of the jungle man's adventures, there was no Jane, and Tarzan's English had decidedly improved. Nonetheless, the King of the Jungle still had close ties to the chimp Cheetah.

***Texas* (aka: *James A. Michener's Texas* (1994)** ABC-TV, color, 200 minutes. **Director:** Richard Lang; **Teleplay:** Sean Meredith; **Cast:** Maria Conchita Alonso (Lucha Lopez Garza), Benjamin Bratt (Benito Garza), Frederick Coffin (Zave), Patrick Duffy (Stephen Austin), Stacy Keach (Sam Houston), David Keith (Jim Bowie), John Schneider (Davy Crockett), Miguel Sandoval (General Cos), Lloyd Battista (General Santa Anna).

Tapping into the prodigious literary output of novelist James A. Michener, his sprawling fiction *Texas* (1985) provided the basis for this expansive but quite routine two-part telefeature.

Beginning in 1821, Stephen Austin and his followers settle in the Texas Territory leading to conflicts with Mexico and Mexicans in the area, as well as Native Americans. Fiery Lucha Lopez Garza, wed to vaquero Benita Garza, provides the spark in this chronicle, which includes Sam Houston stirring the settlers toward statehood. All this leads to the battle at the ALAMO against the forces of Mexico's General Santa Anna and the later retribution by the Americans at the engagement of San Jacinto. BRATT made a dashing lead figure herein. The historical drama was promoted with the catchphrase: "In the heat of battle, in the hearts of lovers, passion has no boundaries."

***That Night in Rio* (1941)** Twentieth Century-Fox, color, 90 minutes. **Director:** Irving Cummings; **Screenplay:** George Seaton, Bess Meredyth, and Hal Long; **Cast:** Alice Faye (Baroness Cecilia Duarte), Don Ameche (Larry Martin/Baron Manuel Duarte), Carmen Miranda (Carmen), S. Z. Sakall (Arthur Penna), J. Carrol Naish (Machado), Curt Bois (Felicio Salles), Leonid Kinskey (Pierre Dufond), the Banda Da Lua (Carmen Miranda's orchestra), the Flores Brothers (specialty act).

Down Argentine Way (1940) had introduced MIRANDA to American movie audiences, but *That Night in Rio* (1941) gave her a real on-camera part to play. This musical and Miranda were part of the growing interest in Latin America by North Americans, started as a diplomatic gesture for the U.S. government's "Good Neighbor Policy" but blossoming into a cultural craze during the World War II years. With Miranda's distinctive personality, heavy accent, and exotic wardrobe (from those platform shoes to her fruit-bedecked turbans), she, more than anyone, personified the South American image for Americans. The Portuguese-born star was often cast by the studios as various nationalities (e.g., Argentinean, Mexican, or, as in *That Night in Rio*, Brazilian).

Based on the play *The Red Cat* (1934) by Rudolph Lothar and Hans Adler and a remake of the Maurice Chevalier–Merle Oberon–Ann Sothern musical film *Folies Bergère* (1935), the sophisticated *That Night in Rio* dealt with financier Baron Duarte who was having financial problems due to his airline investment. His marriage to Cecilia was also in need of refurbishing. While out on the town in Rio, they encounter entertainer Larry Martin, who has a striking resemblance to the

Baron. Martin is hired by the Baron's backers (Sakall, Bois, and Kinskey) to substitute for the entrepreneur while he is away on business. As such, he and Cecilia have a flirtation that leads to their spending the night together. As a result, in the morning, Cecilia isn't sure with whom she has slept. By the finale, the Baron's business and marriage are repaired, and Martin's relationship with fiery Carmen, who once was the Baron's girlfriend, is salvaged.

Besides the flashy costumes and sets, the film boasted such musical numbers as "I-Yi-Yi-Yi (I Like You Very Much)," "Chica Chica Boom Chick," "Boa Noite," and "They Met in Rio," with Hermes Pan providing inspired choreography for the "Chica Chica" interlude. Miranda's own group, Banda Da Lua, and the Flores Brothers dance act added to the exciting tropical flavor. *That Night in Rio* was remade as the Danny Kaye comedy vehicle *On the Riviera* (1951).

***Third Watch* (1999–)** NBC-TV series, color, 60 minutes. **Cast:** Michael Beach (Monte "Doc" Parker), Coby Bell (Tyron "Ty" Davis Jr.), Bobby Cannavale (Robert "Bobby" Caffey: 1999–2001), Eddie Cibrian (James "Jimmy" Doherty), Molly Price (Faith Yokas), Kim Raver (Kimberly "Kim" Zambrano), Anthony Ruivivar (Carlos Nieto), Amy Carlson (Alexandra "Alex" Taylor: 2000–), Lisa Vidal (Dr. Sarah Morales: 1999–2001).

The gimmick of this TV drama series was to feature the night shift activities and off-work romances of interacting police officers, firefighters, and paramedics based in the fictional 55th Precinct of New York City. Its very multicultural cast included Hispanic-American performers Cibrian, Ruivivar, and Vidal. The program won an Emmy in 2000 for Outstanding Sound, and Félix Enríquez Alcalá won an ALMA Award in 2001 as Outstanding Director of a Drama Series.

***Three Amigos!* (1986)** Orion, color, 103 minutes. **Director:** John Landis; **Screenplay:** Steve Martin, Lorne Michaels, and Randy Newman; **Cast:** Chevy Chase (Dusty Bottoms), Steve Martin (Lucky Day), Martin Short (Ned Nederlander), Patrice Martinez (Carmen), Alfonso Arau (El Guapo), Tony Plana (Jefe), Philip Gordon (Rodrigo), Michael Wren (cowboy), Fred Asparagus (bartender), Gene Hartline and William Kaplan (silent movie banditos).

This drawn-out comedy utilized the same essential premise as Richard Dreyfuss's *Moon over Parador* (1988), which, in turn, was inspired by *The Magnificent Fraud* (1939) starring Akim Tamiroff, that premise being of actors hired to impersonate protectors and rescuers of folk south of the border. Typical of such Hollywood plot contrivances, the Mexican or South American recipients always seemed to emerge as clichéd impoverished peasant types or smooth connivers who require American know-how to solve their many problems. *Three Amigos!* typified this approach, with the Mexicans presented as dim-witted, impractical, and expectant of guidance. Even Arau's notorious bandito who was going through a midlife crisis, seemed a distillation of the type of colorful outlaw character played by LEO CARRILLO in 1930s pictures.

A trio of American silent movie western stars (Chase, Martin, and Short) find themselves out of work and gladly accept an offer from villager Carmen who asks their help to end the tyranny of the infamous outlaw El Guapo, who is terrorizing her village. The three actors think the request is (1) for a personal appearance and (2) that they will be paid for their time and effort. Once in Santa Poco, they wake up to reality and do the right thing for the villagers.

Only fitfully funny, *Three Amigos!*, trading on the reputations of its three *Saturday Night Live* costars, grossed more than $39 million in domestic distribution.

***Three Caballeros, The* (1945)** RKO, color, 71 minutes. **Directors:** Norman Ferguson, Clyde Geronimi, Jack Kinney, Bill Roberts, and Harold Young; **Screenplay:** Homer Brightman, Ernest Terrazzas, Ted Sears, Bill Peet, Ralph Wright, Elmer Plymmer, Roy Williams, William Cottrell, Del Connell, and James Bodrero; **Cast:** Aurora Miranda (singer), Carmen Molina (dancer), Dora Luz (singer), Sterling Holloway (Professor Holloway/narrator), Clarence Nash (voice of Donald Duck), Joaquin Garay (voice of Panchito), José Oliveira (voice of Joe Carioca and the Aracuan bird).

As part of its World War II effort to stimulate goodwill between Latin and North America, the Walt Disney studio had turned out *Saludos Amigos* (1943), a 43-minute mixture of travelogue, animation, and songs. The follow-up to that success, was the popular *The Three Caballeros*—part of it conceived and started at the same time as the earlier work. It was a highly creative, eye-catching blend of animation, live action, and songs.

The story premise finds Donald Duck receiving a sizable package on his birthday from his Latin American pals. There are several gifts inside. One is a projector and a reel of film. This leads the viewer into the tale of a penguin named Pablo who decides life in the tropics would be more to his liking. This is followed by the tale of the "Flying Burrito." When Donald opens his next gift, a book, Joe Carioca (a character from *Saludos Amigos*) springs forth and provides Donald with a tour of Brazil. As part of this imaginative excursion, there is an extensive production number featuring Miranda (the sister of Carmen) and the famous duck. Next comes Donald's sojourn in Mexico, where he and Joe Carioca team with a rooster (named Panchito) and make the rounds of the countryside, including their participation in a bullfight and giant fireworks. Among the songs in this inventive entry were "Os Quindins de Yaya," "Mexico," "The Three Caballeros," and "You Belong to My Heart."

The Three Caballeros received Academy Award nominations for Best Scoring of a Musical and for Best Sound.

***Three Hundred Miles for Stephanie* (1981)** NBC-TV, color, 100 minutes. **Director/Teleplay:** Clyde Ware;

Cast: Tony Orlando (Alberto Rodriguez), Edward James Olmos (Art Vela), Pepe Serna (Bobby Hernandez), Julie Carmen (Rosa Sanchez), Rosana De Soto (Lydia), Gregory Sierra (Dr. Galfas), T. J. Olivares (Stephanie).

Singer Orlando made his dramatic acting bow in this made-for-television movie about a San Antonio, Texas, policeman who had a brain-damaged, very ill five-year-old daughter. To show his faith in God's help, he decides to run a grueling 300 mile race within five days, hoping that his little girl will be at the finish line to cheer him on. For a change, in this period of American TV, Mexican-American figures were presented occasionally not only in lead roles but also as positive role models with their cultural heritage undiminished by plot points.

***Tijuana Story, The* (1957)** Columbia, b&w, 72 minutes. **Director:** Leslie Kardos; **Screenplay:** Lou Morheim; **Cast:** Rodolfo Acosta (Manuel Acosta Mesa), James Darren (Mitch), Robert McQueeney (Eddie March), Jean Willes (Liz March), Joy Stoner (Linda Alvarez), Paul Newlan (Peron Diaz), George E. Stone (Pino), Robert Blake (Enrique Acosta Mesa), Ric Vallin (Ricardo), Paul Coates (narrator).

This formula crime exposé was based on a real-life episode. Narrated by Coates who reported the actual corruption, the film focused on crusading Mexican newspaper editor Manuel Acosta Mesa, who uses the press to fight the local crime syndicate headed by Peron Diaz. For his good deed, Mesa is killed. His enraged son Enrique takes over the newspaper and his late father's battle. He gains public support and ensures that the culprits are routed from the border town. (Teenage heartthrob Darren was cast as an American youth whose use of marijuana led indirectly to his death and helps stir the story into action.)

Acosta made a marked impression as the vigilant newsman, although his role was relatively small.

***Tony Orlando and Dawn* (1974–1976)** CBS-TV series, color, 60 minutes. **Cast:** Tony Orlando, Telma Hopkins, Joyce Vincent Wilson, Alice Nunn, and Lonnie Schorr (regulars).

What began as a summer TV replacement show became a popular musical variety offering, featuring the song styling of Orlando and Dawn (Hopkins and Wilson), a recording team most famous for their number "Tie a Yellow Ribbon Round the Old Oak Tree." Hispanic-American Orlando and his back-up singers also did comedy skits with visiting guest stars such as Kate Smith.

***Too Many Girls* (1940)** RKO, b&w, 85 minutes. **Director:** George Abbott; **Screenplay:** John Twist; **Cast:** Lucille Ball (Connie Casey), Richard Carlson (Clint Kelly), Ann Miller (Pepe), Eddie Bracken (Jojo Jordan), Frances Langford (Eileen Eilers), Desi Arnaz (Manuelito), Hal LeRoy (Al Terwilliger), Harry Shannon (Harvey Casey).

Beyond the fact that Ball and ARNAZ met while filming this musical, *Too Many Girls* was notable as the screen debut of Cuban-born Arnaz, who had appeared in the stage original. This song-and-dance entry was based on the hit Broadway show (1939) by George Marion, with music by Richard Rodgers and lyrics by Lorenz Hart. As the Mexican collegiate Manuelito, Arnaz made a handsome, charming impression, qualifying him as a new version of the 1920s LATIN LOVER.

Heiress Connie Casey enrolls at Pottawatomie College in Stop Gap, New Mexico, to be near her latest beau, British playwright Beverly Waverly. Hoping to keep his offspring out of trouble, her father (Shannon) hires Clint Kelly, Jojo Jordan, Manuelito, and Al Terwilliger, campus gridiron heroes, to watch over Connie. By film's end, Kelly has led his team to victory on the field and has won the heart of Connie. The boisterous proceeding—spotlighting a lively Miller as one of the tap-dancing co-eds—featured such tunes as "I Don't Know What Time It Was" and "Spic and Spanish."

***Torrid Zone* (1940)** Warner Bros., b&w, 86 minutes. **Director:** William Keighley; **Screenplay:** Richard Macaulay and Jerry Wald; **Cast:** James Cagney (Nick Butler), Pat O'Brien (Steve Case), Ann Sheridan (Lee Donley), Andy Devine (Wally Davis), Helen Vinson (Gloria Anderson), George Tobias (Rosario La Mata), George Reeves (Sancho).

On the surface, this was one of the several successful screen teamings of Cagney and Sheridan in a wise-cracking, steamy drama, this time in (supposedly) Honduras. But in the history of Hollywood cinema, this movie was notable in that it solidified the celluloid image of the so-called South American banana republic in which its chief port city—according to the scripters and set designers—was a dirty hole filled with bordellos, gaming saloons, and nasty-smelling sewage trenches. The climate there was as hot as the disenfranchised peasants who were mercilessly exploited by corrupt local officials and representatives of a U.S. fruit corporation. To keep the local bigwigs and the American overseers content, there was one or more Anglo tramps working in the clubs. This free-wheeling depiction of a South American city was accepted by Hollywood's Production Code Administration, although there reportedly were demands that the script delete such racist terms as *greaseballs* and *spigottiers*. But on the whole, the filmmakers and public accepted this fiction as the "real" thing.

In Puerto Agular in Central America, Anglo plantation supervisor Steve Case rules with an iron thumb, from ordering the execution of volatile revolutionary Rosario La Mata to demanding that American Lee Donley (a club "singer" and card cheat) be expelled from the seamy country. Before long, Case's smart-mouth foreman Nick Butler and tough-as-nails Lee show up at the plantation, while La Mata escapes from prison and begins to incite a revolution. By film's end, La Mata has eluded capture yet again, while Butler and Lee—who have fallen in love—decide to remain in the country.

In the course of *Torrid Zone*, Sheridan sang a Latino torch song, "Mi Caballero." *Blowing Wild* (1953), with Gary

Cooper and Barbara Stanwyck, was a loose remake of *Torrid Zone.*

***Tortilla Flat* (1942)** Metro-Goldwyn-Mayer, b&w, 105 minutes. **Director:** Victor Fleming; **Screenplay:** John Lee Mahin and Benjamin Glaser; **Cast:** Spencer Tracy (Pilon), Hedy Lamarr (Dolores "Sweets" Ramirez), John Garfield (Danny Alvarez), Frank Morgan (the Pirate), Akim Tamiroff (Pablo), Sheldon Leonard (Tito Ralph), John Qualen (José Maria Corcoran), Donald Meek (Paul D. Cummings), Connie Gilchrist (Mrs. Torrelli), Allen Jenkins (Portagee Joe), Henry O'Neill (Father Ramon), Mercedes Ruffino (Mrs. Marellis).

MGM gathered together a sterling cast, who, with the aid of skin-darkening makeup, played the folks of John Steinbeck's *Tortilla Flat.* Based on that author's humorous account (1935) of romance and little adventures, the fiction concerned paisanos living in the California hills outside Monterey. (According to Steinbeck, paisanos were "a mixture of Spanish, Indian, Mexican, and assorted Caucasian bloods" who have a skin color "like that of a well-browned meerschaum pipe.")

To his surprise and confusion, Danny Alvarez is bequeathed two houses in Tortilla Flat from his granddad. The crafty Pilon easily convinces Alvarez that owning property is a tremendous responsibility. Pilon maneuvers his friend into renting him one of the two houses for a low fee and then convinces another friend, Pablo, to share the abode and pay all the rent. By morning, thanks to the careless new tenants, the house is set partially ablaze. By now, Alvarez is in love with the "Portagee" woman named Dolores Ramirez whom he calls Sweets. She is looking for a responsible husband so that she and her future family can avoid a life of picking beans.

While Alvarez gets to work at the cannery, Pilon is conning the Pirate, an old vagabond with a strong love for dogs. Pilon plans to steal the money that the drifter has hoarded over the years but has a change of heart when he overhears the eccentric talking about giving a gold candlestick to the church if his ill canine recovers. Later, when Alvarez is injured at work. Pilon arranges to pay for a raffle so that Alvarez can have a fishing boat to support Sweets in marriage.

What could have been a condescending tale of uneducated, unambitious peasants turned into a strong character study, even with some of the cast (e.g., Lamarr) playing so against screen type. A few of the minor roles were played by actual Mexican-American performers. The film earned an Academy Award nomination for Best Supporting Actor (Morgan).

***Tortilla Soup* (2001)** Samuel Goldwyn, color, 102 minutes. **Director:** Maria Ripoll; **Screenplay:** Tom Musca, Ramon Menendez, and Vera Blasi. **Cast:** Hector Elizondo (Martin), Jacqueline Obradors (Carmen), Elizabeth Peña (Letitia), Tamara Mello (Maribel), Nikolai Kinski (Andy), Raquel Welch (Hortensia), Paul Rodriguez (Orlando), Constance Marie (Yolanda).

Ang Lee's Taiwan-made *Eat Drink Man Woman* (1994) was transferred to a Hispanic East Los Angeles setting in a comedy that proved to be nearly as felicitous as the charming screen original. The plot revolves around a talented chef (ELIZONDO) who must not only deal with losing his sense of taste, but also has to cope with the assorted problems of his trio of grown-up daughters. The domestic complications accelerate when the middle offspring (Obradors), a corporate consultant, accepts a high-profile position in Barcelona. As the father handles the household chaos, he finds a new romance. His love connection is not with attractive, manipulative Hortensia, but with her comely daughter, Yolanda, a single mother.

Daily Variety (July 6, 2001) decided, "Easy to swallow is the decision to completely avoid issues of ethnic and economic conflict, making this genuine crowd-pleaser an utterly gang-and-drug free look at Hispanic subculture."

***Touch of Evil* (1958)** Universal, b&w, 95 minutes. **Directors:** Orson Welles and (uncredited) Harry Keller; **Screenplay:** Welles; **Cast:** Charlton Heston (Ramon Miguel "Mike" Vargas), Janet Leigh (Susan Vargas), Orson Welles (Capt. Hank Quinlan), Joseph Calleia (Sgt. Pete Menzies), Akim Tamiroff ("Uncle Joe" Grandi), Valentin De Vargas (Pancho), Ray Collins (District Attorney Adair), Marlene Dietrich (Tanya), Victor Millan (Manelo Sanchez), Mercedes McCambridge (gang leader), Joseph Cotten (detective), Zsa Zsa Gabor (strip-joint owner).

Despite all the production problems involved, the studio politics that doomed the film's initial distribution, and the mystique that built up about this project over the decades, *Touch of Evil* was and is a cinema masterpiece. More importantly, this film noir, shot in Venice, California, and based on Whit Masterson's 1956 novel *Badge of Evil,* was full of racial tension, interracial marriage, and Mexican ambiance.

When a construction kingpin is murdered in Los Robles, a rundown border town on the U.S. side, Mexican Ramon Vargas, head of the Pan-American Narcotics Commission, volunteers to investigate even though he is on his honeymoon with his white wife, Susan. He works with Capt. Hank Quinlan, an obese, bigoted soul, who is abetted by his flunky, Sgt. Pete Menzies (who has Mexican roots), and district attorney Adair. Meanwhile, Susan is taken to meet with "Uncle Joe" Grandi, a minor crime boss, who warns her that if her husband continues to prosecute his brother on a drug charge, bad things can happen.

A suspect in the homicide case proves to be a bewildered shoe clerk (Millan). The man protests his innocence, earning the wrath of ethnically prejudiced Quinlan. The altercation leads onlooker Vargas to claim Quinlan planted evidence against the man, escalating the racial enmity between them. Then Susan is kidnapped and raped. When Quinlan finds her, he frames her for the murder of Grandi, which he himself has committed. In the denouement, a disillusioned Menzies learns the truth about his boss, and, in return, Quinlan shoots him. The latter receives his just desert and dies floating in the canal.

In this drama of ambiguity, half-truths, and abiding prejudices, the most truth is spoken by Tanya, the fortune-telling operator of a seedy brothel. It is she who said with sadness of the late Quinlan that he was "some kind of man," and then, in a moment of cynicism that seemed to counter everything the film had already delineated, she asked rhetorically, "What does it matter what you say about a man?"

Reportedly, Welles had wanted to shoot the movie in Tijuana, Mexico, but, according to some sources, the Mexican government was unhappy with the unfavorable light the film would cast on its country and countrymen. (Another source says that the Hollywood studio feared letting Welles out of their sight for such an extended location shoot.)

***Tour of Duty* (1987–1990)** CBS-TV series, color, 60 minutes. **Cast:** Terence Knox (Sgt. Zeke Anderson), Kevin Conroy (Capt, Rusty Wallace: 1987–88), Stephen Caffrey (Lt. Myron Goldman), Joshua Maurer (Pvt. Roger Horn: 1987–88), Eric Burskotter (Pvt. Scott Baker: 1987–88), Ramon Franco (Pvt. Alberto Ruiz), Miguel A. Nunez Jr. (Pvt. Marcus Taylor).

Especially for TV viewership, this is an extremely gritty, honest depiction of hellish combat life in Vietnam in 1967. The focus is on Company B, under the tutelage of battle-savvy Sgt. Zeke Anderson, who cared about his recruits. One of the newcomers to the group is street-smart Pvt. Alberto Ruiz, a tough Puerto Rican American from the Bronx. (He is in direct contrast to such other new B Company troopers as California surfer Private Baker and the glum Private Taylor.)

It had been rare to this point for any military drama on TV to give a spotlight to Hispanic-American actors/characters.

***Treasure of the Sierra Madre, The* (1948)** Warner Bros., b&w, 126 minutes. **Director/Screenplay:** John Huston; **Cast:** Humphrey Bogart (Fred C. Dobbs), Walter Huston (Howard), Tim Holt (Curtin), Bruce Bennett (Cody), Barton MacLane (McCormick), Alfonso Bedoya (Gold Hat), Arturo Soto Rangel (Presidente), Manuel Dondé (El Jefe), José Torvay (Pablo), Margarita Luna (Pancho), Bobby Blake (Mexican boy), John Huston (man in white suit).

Not only was this stark feature an uncompromising study of the venality of greed, but it also reflected a seemingly revisionist Hollywood attitude toward Mexicans. With World War II over and the "Good Neighbor Policy" toward south-of-the-border countries languishing, the Mexicans again became the greasers/banditos as they had been portrayed so often in pre-1940s American pictures.

In the port city of Tampico, Mexico, of 1925, Fred C. Dobbs takes odd jobs to scrape by. Having met fellow U.S. citizen Curtin while working in the oil fields, the two join old-time prospector Howard to look for gold. En route to the Sierra Madre, their train is attacked by bandits led by Gold Hat. Dobbs almost kills the leader, but the man gets away. Once in the mountains, the trio are successful in locating the rich gold ore, but Dobbs becomes paranoid—just as Howard foretold—of his partners. One day a stranger, Cody, shows up on the scene and insists he be made a partner. The others refuse, but it doesn't matter for they are suddenly attacked by Gold Hat and his men. In the fray, Cody is killed. Later, Dobbs turns against the other two who survive the ordeal; Dobbs is thereafter murdered by Gold Hat. As for the precious gold, the bandito and his gang think it is sand and dump the bags in the desert. Before long, the outlaws are caught and shot; Howard and Curtin return to the site where Dobbs died. By now, a windstorm has blown the gold away. Curtin plans a trip to Texas (to visit Cody's widow); Howard returns to the Indian village where he was honored recently as a medicine man for having saved a child's life.

Based on the 1935 novel by B. Traven [actually Polish-born Herman Albert Otto Maksymillian Feige], *The Treasure of the Sierra Madre* was budgeted at a cost of almost $4 million. Location filming was accomplished in Mexico and in Kernville, California. The film received Academy Awards for Best Director, Best Screenplay, and Best Supporting Actor (Walter Huston). The film was also Oscar nominated for Best Picture.

***Trial* (1955)** Metro-Goldwyn-Mayer, b&w, 105 minutes. **Director:** Mark Robson; **Screenplay:** Don M. Mankiewicz; **Cast:** Glenn Ford (David Blake), Dorothy McGuire (Abbe Nyle), Arthur Kennedy (Barney Castle), John Hodiak (John J. Armstrong), Katy Jurado (Consuela Chavez), Rafael Campos (Angel Chavez), Juano Hernandez (Judge Theodore Castillo), John Hoyt (Ralph Castillo), Paul Guilfoyle (Cap Grant).

Trial was as concerned with anticommunist propaganda as it was with delineating racism and bigotry in a small southern California town. This well-intentioned drama bogged down in its solemnity. The movie was based on Mankiewicz's 1955 novel.

David Blake, a California state university law professor, needs practical court experience to gain campus tenure. He takes a summer job in the nearby community of San Juno, working for lawyer Barney Castle. The latter is just about to defend a new client, Mexican-American Angel Chavez, accused of murdering a white female classmate. The incident enflames prejudices in the town, with racists Ralph Castillo and Cap Grant stirring up the townsfolk. Blake and Castle save Chavez from being lynched by a mob of locals.

Later, Blake flies to New York to help Castle and the defendant's mother, Consuela Chavez, raise money for the boy's defense. By now, Blake is convinced that his associate is using the case to further Communist Party aims. At the trial, which is presided over by an African-American judge, the defendant is found guilty. The next day at the sentencing hearing, Blake speaks out against Castle's devious purpose of using the teenager as a martyr for the Communist cause. Taking everything in account, the judge gives the defendant a short reform-school sentence. Castle labels the judge an "Uncle Tom" and is given a thirty-day contempt sentence.

Within the confines of their relatively small roles, both Mexican JURADO and Dominican Republic–born CAMPOS brought sincerity to their parts, but their characterizations were written as archetypes rather than dimensional people. It was an unusual move to have an African-American judge at this period in U.S. history or in Hollywood production. As played by Puerto Rican Hernandez, the role became well defined.

U

***Up in Smoke* (1978)** Paramount, color, 86 minutes. **Director:** Lou Adler; **Screenplay:** Tommy Chong and Cheech Marin; **Cast:** Cheech Marin (Pedro De Pacas), Tommy Chong (man), Stacy Keach (Sergeant Stedenko), Tom Skerritt (Strawberry), Edie Adams (Tempest Stoner), Strother Martin (Mr. Stoner), Harold Fong (chauffeur).

The cult comedy team of Mexican-American Cheech and Asian-Canadian Chong made their debut in this low-caliber feature. It went on to gross an amazing (at the time) $28 million in domestic distribution. Then, and much later, it was debatable whether this film was a satire about the drug culture and the supposed ethnic stereotypes associated with that lifestyle or it was a somewhat crass effort that emphasized such ethnic typing. Whatever the origins, this picture and its several sequels (e.g., *Cheech & Chong's Next Movie,* 1980) were extremely popular.

The simplistic plot—an excuse for drug-related and bodily function jokes—centers on Pedro De Pacas, a not-so-bright Mexican American who gives a ride to a woeful hitchhiker (Chong) who has been ejected from his family's home. De Pacas suggests that his new pal join his rock band. They head to Tijuana, Mexico, later returning in a van packed with marijuana weed. Once in Los Angeles, their music group participates in the "battle of the bands," competition. Emerging successful, the two dopers weave off in their raunchy car to their next adventure.

V

Vélez, Lupe (1909–1944) If Hollywood's most publicized Hispanic actress of the 1920s was DOLORES DEL RÍO and that of the 1940s was CARMEN MIRANDA, the 1930s belonged to Vélez, who was often termed the "MEXICAN SPITFIRE." Like Del Río and Miranda, she had an innate sense of how to merchandize her ethnic charms to maximum advantage within the film industry and for the American public. While Vélez began in American movies in the mid-1920s as a beautiful, petite performer geared as a "threat" to Del Río for Latino screen roles, Lupe developed into a broad comedienne in the 1930s. She ended the decade with a popular group of slapstick comedies in her Mexican Spitfire movie series.

She was born María Guadalupe Vélez de Villalobos in San Luis Potosí, Mexico. Supposedly, her father was an army colonel and her mother was the offspring of an opera singer. Allegedly, she was educated at a convent in San Antonio, Texas. Reportedly, Vélez began her show-business career as a dancer in Mexico City. Coming to Hollywood in the mid-1920s, she soon made a strong impression as the Mountain Girl in Douglas Fairbanks's *THE GAUCHO* (1927), a silent picture.

In talkies, her heavy accent and (deliberately) mangled English, combined with her energetic presence, made her quite popular: *Wolf Song* (1929), *THE CUBAN LOVE SONG* (1931), and *Hot Pepper* (1933). She sometimes made Spanish-language versions of her Hollywood projects (e.g., *Oriente y occidente*, 1930). By the mid-1930s, her novelty had worn thin, and she tried the stage, as well as making British films (e.g., *The Morals of Marcus*, 1935) and an occasional Mexican feature (e.g., *La Zandunga*, 1938). *THE GIRL FROM MEXICO* (1939) was made as a cheap one-shot film farce; however, it proved so entertaining to filmgoers that it was the start of Vélez's Mexican Spitfire movies, which went on for seven more entries.

In 1944, depressed about being pregnant and unwed as well as being in her mid-thirties, the highly volatile Velez committed suicide. Her last movie, which received respectable reviews, was the Mexican-made *Nana* (1944).

Lupe Vélez, the Mexican Spitfire, in a 1930s Hollywood glamour pose. (ECHO BOOK SHOP)

***Vera Cruz* (1954)** United Artists, color, 94 minutes. **Director:** Robert Aldrich; **Screenplay:** Roland Kibbee and James R. Webb; **Cast:** Gary Cooper (Benjamin Trane), Burt

Lancaster (Joe Erin), Denise Darcel (Countess Marie Duvarre), Cesar Romero (Marquis de Labordere), Sarita Montiel (Nina), George Macready (Emperor Maximilian), Ernest Borgnine (Donnegan), Morris Ankrum (General Aguilar), Charles Buchinsky [Bronson] (Pittsburgh).

This high-spirited (if overly dramatic) action feature played loose with historical facts as it wove its illogical south-of-the-border plot toward a Production Code Administration-approved finale where the bad guy paid with his life. Filming was accomplished in Mexico at Cuernavaca, Morelos, Chapultepec Castle, and so on, with interiors lensed at Mexico City's Churubusco Studios.

In 1866, soldiers-of-fortune Benjamin Trane (a former Confederate officer) and Joe Erin (an outlaw) head to Mexico to find work. Young Nina tries to convince the serious Trane that they should fight on the side of Juarez and his revolutionaries. On the other hand, the Marquis de Labordere, in the employ of Emperor Maximilian, dangles rewards if the boisterous duo will assist the French cause. Meanwhile, the wealthy Countess Marie Duvarre contracts the two to guard her journey as she transports a secret shipment of gold from Mexico City to Maximilian's forces in Vera Cruz. The countess soon suggests that she and the Americans steal the gold and share it amongst themselves. This prompts the marquis and his followers to grab the treasure and haul it to Vera Cruz, where Erin regains control over the riches. By now, Trane has been converted to the revolutionists' cause and kills his partner to hand the gold over to Nina and her people.

Made at a cost of less than $2 million, the visually appealing *Vera Cruz* had a worldwide gross of more than $11 million.

Verdugo, Elena (1927–) Best known for her role as compassionate Nurse Consuelo Lopez on MARCUS WELBY, M.D. (1969–76)—for which she was twice nominated for an Emmy Award—Verdugo had a long show-business career. Born in Paso Robles, California, she had a lineage as a true Californian, as she was a direct descendant of Don José Maria Verdugo to whom the king of Spain issued a land grant more than two hundred years earlier in what was later known as the San Fernando Valley.

Because of her dancing talent, she began lessons at a young age and was soon appearing in stage shows at Los Angeles movie theaters. She also did recordings, including a rendition of "Tico Tico" with XAVIER CUGAT and His Orchestra. Her film debut was as an unbilled dance extra in *Down Argentine Way* (1940). Verdugo's first important screen role was as Ata the Tahitian lovely in *The Moon and Sixpence* (1942). Because of her exotic looks she was mostly cast as native girls or harem girl types (e.g., *The Lost Tribe*, 1949; *The Big Sombrero*, 1949). Surprisingly, television gave her acting career a new life. She starred on the sitcom *Meet Millie* (1952–56), followed by such series as *Redigo* (1963) and *Many Happy Returns* (1964–65). After her successful stint on *Marcus Welby, M.D.*, her most recent assignment was in the telefeature *The Return of Marcus Welby, M.D.* (1984).

***Victims for Victims: The Theresa Saldana Story* (1984)** NBC-TV, 100 minutes. **Director:** Karen Arthur; **Teleplay:** Arthur Heinemann; **Cast:** Theresa Saldana (herself), Adrian Zmed (Fred Feliciano), Lelia Goldoni (Mrs. Saldana), Lawrence Pressman (Dr. Stein), Mariclare Costello (Jane Bladow).

This entry was a rare case where the actual person was playing herself, here being the part-Hispanic Saldana. Not long after completing a role in the Martin Scorsese-directed boxing movie *Raging Bull* (1980), Saldana was attacked by a deranged stalker/fan. After the traumatic ordeal, in which she was badly scarred physically and emotionally, she became a spokesperson for Victims for Victims, an organization she helped to form.

Villa, Pancho The renowned Mexican revolutionary (1878–1923), born Doroteo Arango, had a strong role in his country's revolution of 1910–11. In 1914, he joined forces with Venustiano Carranza and overthrew the dictatorial regime of Gen. Victoriano Huerta. Thereafter, Villa teamed with Emiliano Zapata and broke with Huerta. Pancho's strong personality and his many controversial exploits over the years created many legends that were translated to screen adventures, some more fictitious than others.

Among the actors who played Villa in American films were: Pancho Villa (playing himself) and Raoul Walsh (*The Life of General Villa*, 1914), George Humbert (*Why America Will Win*, 1918), Wallace Beery (*VIVA VILLA!*, 1934), Maurice Black (*Under Strange Flags*, 1937), LEO CARRILLO (*Pancho Villa Returns*, 1950), Alan Reed (*VIVA ZAPATA!*, 1952), Yul Brynner (*Villa Rides!*, 1968), HECTOR ELIZONDO (*Wanted: The Sundance Woman*, 1976–TV movie), and Pedro Armendáriz Jr. (*Old Gringo*, 1989). Villa also appeared in such silent documentaries as *Following the Flag in Mexico* (1916). Although Villa is much discussed and is a part of the plot of *The Treasure of Pancho Villa* (1955), his character did not appear in the film.

***Viva Max!* (1969)** Commonwealth United, color, 93 minutes. **Director:** Jerry Paris; **Screenplay:** Elliot Baker; **Cast:** Peter Ustinov (Gen. Maximilian Rodrigues de Santos), Pamela Tiffin (Paula Whitland), Jonathan Winters (Gen. Billy Joe Hallson), John Astin (Sergeant Valdez), Harry Morgan (Police Chief George Sylvester), Keenan Wynn (Gen. Barney Lacomber).

There was more excitement generated over the filming of this picture than its resultant release. Mexican Americans were concerned that so many key roles were being played by non-Mexicans, and Mexico banned the film from distribution in its country during the initial release. On the other hand, patriotic Lone Star State groups (e.g., the Daughters of the Republic of Texas) picketed the movie production so intensively in San Antonio that shooting had to relocate to Italy to lens sequences inside a studio-built Alamo.

Within this farce, laid in 1969, Gen. Meximilian Rodrigues de Santos—to impress his girlfriend—leads a contingent of eighty-seven Mexican troops (out of uniform) over the border to San Antonio where they occupy the Alamo. This seizure brings out the National Guard, not to mention a right-wing faction who think the Communist Chinese have taken over the historical shrine. A day after hoisting the Mexican flag atop the Alamo, de Santos and his troops slip quietly back to Mexico.

***Viva Valdez* (1976)** ABC-TV series, color, 30 minutes. **Cast:** Rodolfo Hoyos (Luis Valdez), Carmen Zapata (Sophia Valdez), James Victor (Victor Valdez), Nelson D. Cuevas (Ernesto Valdez), Lisa Mordente (Connie Valdez), Claudio Martinez (Pepe Valdez), Jorge Cervera Jr. (Jerry Ramirez).

This situation comedy was not well liked and had only a short summer run. Its chief virtue was its attempt to showcase a Mexican-American family, using several talented ethnic performers in the process. Set in East Los Angeles, it revolves around a supportive family unit, headed by Luis, who operates a plumbing business with Victor, his eldest son. Also involved is Sophia, Luis's wife; their son Ernesto, who is training with the phone company but wants to pursue an artistic career, and twelve-year-old Pepe, a sports fan. Rounding out the crowded, noisy household is Jerry Ramirez, a relative just arrived from Mexico.

***Viva Villa!* (1934)** Metro-Goldwyn-Mayer, b&w, 112 minutes. **Directors:** Jack Conway and (uncredited) Howard Hawks and William A. Wellman; **Screenplay:** Ben Hecht; **Cast:** Wallace Beery (Pancho Villa), Leo Carrillo (Sierra), Fay Wray (Teresa), Donald Cook (Don Felipe), Stuart Erwin (Johnny Sykes), Henry B. Walthall (Francisco Madero), Joseph Schildkraut (General Pascal), Katherine DeMille (Rosita).

So intent was MGM on producing this feature film that the studio undertook extensive preproduction research and delicate negotiations with Mexican officials. The film endured the workings of several different directors, and it suffered the loss of some of the Hawks-directed footage for the project in a plane crash. Most of all, the studio had to cope with the international incident caused in November 1933 by colead Lee Tracy who was playing the American reporter Johnny Sykes in this celluloid biography of Mexican revolutionary PANCHO VILLA (1878–1923). Tracy's alleged disrespectful/obscene act done on the balcony of his hotel led the MGM production to depart hastily from its Mexican location filming. Studio head Louis B. Mayer apologized to President Abelardo Rodríguez of Mexico, and cast replacements were made that went far beyond just Irwin substituting for Tracy. (In addition, there were complaints about the casting of Beery, primarily known as a comedic actor, in the heavy dramatic role of this key Mexican historical figure. As his characterization emerged on camera, Beery's well-received performance was that of a gruff, overgrown child constantly puzzled that the world so often misunderstood his actions.)

The foreword to this screen biography stated that the movie was "fiction woven out of truth." (It was also loosely suggested by the 1933 book by Edgcumb Pinchon and O. B. Stade.) As contrived, this new interpretation of the celebrated/notorious Villa presents him as a misunderstood ruffian who, as a result of childhood tragedies and class struggle, grew into a bandito. In the 1910s, thanks to patrician revolutionary Don Felipe, Villa and his men become followers of Francisco Madero in the fight to oust the dictatorial Porfirio Diaz. Eventually, Madero exiles Villa to Chihuahua for his cruel excesses. After Medero's assassination, Villa is persuaded by reporter Johnny Sykes to abandon his drunken life in E1 Paso, Texas, and return to Mexico to oust General Pascal's reign of terror. With that done, Villa temporarily becomes Mexico's leader, only to later retire from the too complex administrative office. Thereafter, now a private citizen, one day in Chihuahua, Villa is murdered by Don Felipe, whose sister Teresa (whom Villa had pursued romantically) had been killed by Villa's chief henchman, Sierra.

Viva Villa! received Oscar nominations for Best Adapted Screenplay, Best Picture, and Best Sound. Beery's effective if historically inaccurate interpretation as Villa made this the most remembered of the several Hollywood features over the decades to deal with that Mexican notable.

***Viva Zapata!* (1952)** Twentieth Century-Fox, b&w, 113 minutes. **Director:** Elia Kazan; **Screenplay:** John Steinbeck; **Cast:** Marlon Brando (Emiliano Zapata), Jean Peters (Josefa Espejo), Anthony Quinn (Eufemio Zapata), Joseph Wiseman (Fernando Aguirre), Arnold Moss (Don Nacio), Alan Reed (Pancho Villa), Margo (La Soldadera), Frank Silvera (Huerta), Fay Roope (Pres. Porfirio Diaz).

If the far more conventional *VIVA VILLA!* (1934) orbited around the audience-pleasing performance of Wallace Beery as the Mexican bandito/revolutionary PANCHO VILLA, the much more factual if episodic *Viva Zapata!* was a rousing history lesson. Based on the book *Zapata the Unconquerable* (1941) by Edgcumb Pinchon, it details the situation in Mexico in the early 1900s as the thirty-four-year reign of tyrannical president Porfirio Díaz is being brought down by Mexican patriot Emiliano Zapata in support of Francisco Madero. Further into the narrative, Zapata is betrayed by cerebral patriot Fernando Aguirre who sells out Emiliano to Huerta and the military. Also caught up in the peons' revolution against the landed upper class is Zapata's surly brother Eufemio. Once the revolution succeeds, he becomes a petty land tyrant who is more interested in chasing women and getting drunk than in helping the people.

Because of past unhappy experiences with Hollywood, the Mexican government did not cooperate with the making of *Viva Zapata!* The movie received an Academy Award for Best Supporting Actor (QUINN). It received Oscar nominations for Best Actor (Brando), Best Art Direction/Set Decoration (Black and White), Best Original Dramatic Score, and Best Story and Screenplay.

Made at the height of the House Un-American Activities Committee communist witch hunt, there was speculation at the time (and later) that *Viva Zapata!* was influenced by procommunist ideology, given the fact that director Kazan made such a high-profile appearance before HUAC several months after making this movie. It was filmmaker Kazan, who directed both Brando and Quinn in a stage production of Tennessee Williams's *A Streetcar Named Desire*, who picked Caucasian Brando over Mexican Quinn to play the Mexican patriot.

Viva Zapata! was one of the first Hollywood-made features to tell a major story from the point of view of a Mexican, not, as was usually done, from that of a gringo.

W

***Walk Proud* (1979)** Universal, color 102 minutes. **Director:** Robert Collins; **Screenplay:** Evan Hunter; **Cast:** Robby Benson (Emilio Mendez), Sarah Holcomb (Sarah Lassiter), Henry Darrow (Mike Serrano), Pepe Serna (Cesar), Trinidad Silva (Dagger), Ju-Tu Cumbuka (Sergeant Gannett), Irene DeBari (Mrs. Mendez)

This contemptuously silly attempt by Hollywood at depicting gritty Chicano gang life cast Jewish-born, blue-eyed Benson as a Los Angeles barrio gang member who must endure his rite of initiation. His heart, however, is soon diverted by wealthy white girl Sarah Lassiter, and he can't decide whether she or the gang is more important to him. Later, while in Mexico for his grandmother's funeral, he meets his long-absent father, an alcoholic drifter. The encounter changes Emilio's outlook. Returning across the border, he quits the gang, but the others nearly kill him for his action.

In 1980 this embarrassing feature was given the Golden Turkey Award for the "most ludicrous racial interpretation in Hollywood history."

***Warriors, The* (1979)** Paramount, color, 90 minutes. **Director:** Walter Hill; **Screenplay:** David Shaber; **Cast:** Michael Beck (Swan), James Remar (Ajax), Thomas Waites (Fox), Dorsey Wright (Clean), Brian Taylor (Snow), David Harris (Cochise), Tom McKitterick (Cowboy), Marcelino Sánchez (Rembrandt), Roger Hill (Cyrus), Lynn Thigpen (D.J.), Ginny Ortiz (candy-store girl).

It was hard to believe that in the same year Hollywood could release three movies about multiethnic street gangs that were so different: the soft *BOULEVARD NIGHTS*, the laughable *WALK PROUD*, and the laudable *The Warriors*. The latter was promoted with the tag lines: "These are the Armies of the night. They are 100,000 strong. They outnumber the cops five to one. They could run New York City." With such a campaign, the heavy-duty action film soon gained notoriety during distribution when rival gang members chose movie theater turfs to strut their machismo, leading to physical violence. As a result, this imaginative, high-caliber film received a bad reputation that it did not deserve. This entry was loosely based on Sol Yurick's 1965 novel, which drew parallels from Greek mythology.

At a gigantic rally in New York City, Riffs gang leader Cyrus makes a bid to combine all the local gangs into one big organization. The representatives of the various factions agreed to come unarmed, but one brings a weapon and Cyrus is killed. Blame is put on the Anglo Warriors. Its targeted members, which include Swan and Cochise, must make it back to Coney Island by passing through the turf of every rival gang now out to get them. The Warriors have only themselves and their street smarts to help them. Among the diverse gangs they run up against are the Lizzies, a tough group of Hispanic females, who use weapons and their bodies to assault the Warriors.

***Way of a Gaucho* (1952)** Twentieth Century-Fox, color, 91 minutes. **Director:** Jacques Tourneur; **Screenplay:** Philip Dunne; **Cast:** Rory Calhoun (Martin), Gene Tierney (Teresa), Richard Boone (Salinas), Hugh Marlowe (Miguel), Everett Sloane (Falcon), Enrique Chaico (Father Fernández), Jorge Villoldo (Valverde), Mario Abdah (horse dealer).

This feature, based on the 1948 novel by Herbert Childs, was shot on assorted magnificent locations in the Argentine pampas, using well-known Argentinean actors for subordinate roles, and it had the approval of the country's government. But with its melodramatic plot, it was still a western at heart, and its lead actors lacked the ability to make their characterizations as Argentineans at all believable.

In the 1870s, gaucho Martin moves to the wrong side of the law for killing a man in self-defense and is sentenced to militia duty rather than prison. Hating the strict regimentation, he escapes, and, with his band of outlaws, preys on a railroad that runs through the pampas. Giving chase to Martin is railroad lawman Salinas, who once was Martin's military commanding officer. By the bittersweet finale, Martin abandons his reckless way and plans ahead with his pregnant love, Teresa.

Welch, Raquel (1940–) A studio-fabricated sex goddess, the statuesque (five-feet, six-inch) Welch was at the peak of her box-office allure in the late 1960s and early 1970s. Dismissed by many at different stages of her career as being a mere sultry beauty with no talent, she consistently proved her detractors wrong, especially with her surprising flare for comedy.

She was born in Chicago, Illinois, of a Bolivian-born father (an engineer) and an English mother. Raised in California, she took dancing lessons from an early age and began to enter beauty contests at age fourteen. Married in her late teens and soon the mother of two, she engineered a publicity campaign that landed her in movies. Her debut was a bit in Elvis Presley's *Roustabout* (1964). The voluptuous, exotic Welch was already the country's leading sex symbol by the time she made *Fantastic Voyage* and *One Million Years B.C.* (both 1966), the latter providing a legendary poster shot. Later films included *BANDOLERO!* (1968) *100 RIFLES* (1969), and *Myra Breckinridge* (1970). She displayed an amusing sense of (slapstick) comedy in *The Three Musketeers* (1973) and *The Four Musketeers* (1974). When movie roles dried up in the 1980s, she tackled a cabaret act and took over the lead on Broadway in the musical *Woman of the Year.* She produced and starred in a much-troubled TV movie production of *The Legend of Walks Far Woman* (1982) and was a glamorous addition to the failing nighttime TV drama *Central Park West* (1996). Her more recent films included *TORTILLA SOUP* and *Legally Blonde* (both 2001). In the PBS-TV series *AMERICAN FAMILY* (2002–) she plays flashy Aunt Dora.

Welcome Back, Kotter **(1975–1979)** ABC-TV series, color, 30 minutes. **Cast:** Gabriel Kaplan (Gabe Kotter), Marcia Strassman (Julie Kotter), John Travolta (Vinnie Barbarino), Robert Hegyes (Juan Luis Pedro Phillipo de Huevos Epstein), Lawrence-Hilton Jacobs (Freddie "Boom Boom" Washington), Ron Palillo (Arnold Horshack).

Obviously not role models for budding students, the "Sweathogs" are a group of remedial students at James Buchanan High in Brooklyn. Alumnus Gabe Kotter returns to the school and is assigned to nurture these ill-equipped pupils, who need a great deal of assistance to cope with classroom activities and life itself. Juan Epstein was the half-Hispanic, half-Jewish member of the special clan, which is led by Vinnie Barbarino in this sitcom that is filled with stock characters.

West Side Story **(1961)** United Artists, color, 155 minutes. **Director:** Robert Wise; **Screenplay:** Ernest Lehman; **Cast:** Natalie Wood (Maria), Richard Beymer (Tony), Russ Tamblyn (Riff), Rita Moreno (Anita), George Chakiris (Bernardo), Simon Oakland (Lieutenant Schrank), William Bramley (Officer Krupke).

At the time, it was hard to argue with the success of the movie *West Side Story*, based on the hugely popular 1957 Broadway musical. Made at a cost of $6 million, the film grossed almost $20 million in distributors' domestic film rentals. It won ten Academy Awards for Best Art Direction/Best Set Decoration (Color), Best Cinematography (Color), Best Costume Design (Color), Best Director, Best Film Editing, Best Picture, Best Scoring of a Musical, Best Sound, Best Supporting Actor (Chakiris), and Best Supporting Actress (MORENO). (The picture also received an Oscar nomination for Best Adapted Screenplay.)

At the time, this distillation of Shakespeare's *Romeo and Juliet* set to music appeared relevant and polished. It didn't seem to matter to many admirers then that the lead cast was primarily made up of Anglos (e.g., Wood) playing Hispanics, that the main performers' singing was dubbed, and that any resemblance between the reality of life in Spanish Harlem and that depicted superficially in *West Side Story* was purely coincidental. (On the plus side, the movie presented the basic ghetto problems, and, in its presentation, the audience's sympathy was drawn to the Hispanics trying to acculturate to their new homeland.)

West Side Story tells of Puerto Rican Maria who falls in love with Polish-American Tony and the tragedy engendered by their star-crossed love, pushed to the breaking point by the rivalry of the street gangs the Jets and the Sharks. One of the score's most ironic and telling numbers was sung by Anita as she told what life was really like in "America" for Puerto Ricans.

Intentionally or not, *West Side Story* perpetuated stereotypes about Puerto Rican life from fiery tempers and passionate lovemaking to knife-wielding dudes and women of easy virtue. Later, such types took a far more cynical and brittle turn, evolving into the street gang dramas depicted in *COLORS* (1988) and the like.

westerns—feature film Frequently in sagebrush tales set in the Old West—in territories that were not yet part of the United States and still had a strong Spanish (and later Mexican) presence—a leading theme was the warring between the Spanish and the Anglos. For example, there were many westerns dealing with conflict between the Spanish/Mexicans and the Americans in California before the area was admitted to statehood in 1850: *THE DAUGHTER OF THE DON* (1916), *A California Romance* (1922), *The California Trail* (1933), *The Californian* (1937), *Pirates of Monterey* (1947),

CALIFORNIA CONQUEST (1952). Sometimes, the action was (partially) set in Mexico: *Rio Grande* (1920), *RIO RITA* (1929), *Romance of the Rio Grande* (1929), *Riders of the Rio* (1931), *The Cyclone Ranger* (1935), *In Old Mexico* (1938), *Down Mexico Way* (1941), *VERA CRUZ* (1954), *BANDIDO* (1955), *THE MAGNIFICENT SEVEN* (1960), *THE PROFESSIONALS* (1966), *BANDOLERO!* (1968), and *100 RIFLES* (1969).

In addition, several U.S. westerns featured the legendary Hispanic heroes the CISCO KID and ZORRO, as well as the real-life Mexican figures JOAQUÍN MURRIETA and PANCHO VILLA. One long-running western sidekick character was the Latino Chito Jose Gonzales Bustamante Rafferty (played by Richard Martin, born in Spokane, Washington). He first played the character in NEVADA, a 1944 western starring Robert Mitchum. From 1947 to 1952, he played the same character in a series of RKO cowboy adventures starring Tim Holt. In addition, several westerns dealing with Texas statehood often dealt with the defeat of the American defenders at the ALAMO in San Antonio.

western series—television One of commercial TV's first sagebrush series was the highly successful *THE CISCO KID* (1950–56) starring DUNCAN RENALDO and LEO CARRILLO, the latter as Cisco's jovial sidekick, Pancho. A copycat of the formula was *THE ADVENTURES OF KIT CARSON* (1951–55), which had the Caucasian lead character (played by Bill Williams) joined by a comical Mexican cohort, El Toro (played by Don Diamond). Another entry was *Zorro* (1957–59) with Guy Williams starring as the masked swordsman.

In *Wichita Town* (1959–60), starring Joel McCrea and his son Jody, Carlos Romero portrayed Rico Rodriguez, a reformed Mexican gunslinger. On another series western, *Rawhide* (1959–66), Clint Eastwood was on a cattle drive and one of his crew members was Hey Soos Patines, played by Robert Cabal from 1961 to 1964. *Empire*, set on a huge ranch in contemporary New Mexico, had lasted one season (1962–63). Charles Bronson was cast as Paul Moreno, an Hispanic subordinate character. The show, starring Richard Egan, was reformulated as *Redigo* (1963) with a new supporting cast that included ELENA VERDUGO as the Latino hotel manager, while Frank Martinez and his wife Linda (played by Rudy Solari and Mina Martinez) were part of the hero's ranch family. *THE HIGH CHAPARRAL* (1967–71) featured Leif Erickson as an 1870s rancher in the Arizona Territory who weds an Hispanic woman (played by LINDA CRISTAL), which led to greater interaction between the primary gringo rancher and his Mexican-American in-laws.

The Cowboys (1974), based on the John Wayne movie (1972), featured a narrow ethnic mix but did include A MARTINEZ as one of the young ranch hands in 1970s New Mexico Territory. In *Wildside* (1985), a series located in the Old West of California, John DiAquino was on hand as a local blacksmith. *Zorro: The Legend Continues* (1990–93) brought back the famed fixer of wrongs. On *Ned Blessing–The Story of My Life & Times* (1993), Luis Avalos played Crescencio, the Hispanic sidekick of the hero (played by Brad Johnson). On *Dr. Quinn, Medicine Woman* (1993–98), which took placed in 1860s Colorado, one of the townsfolk, played by Terera Morales, was a Latin-American widow who became the town's new schoolmarm and coped with local prejudice. She was played by Michelle Bonilla (1996–97) and by Alex Meneses (1997–98). *The Magnificent Seven: The Series* (1998–99) derived from the classic 1960 western and included Ron Perlman as Josiah Sanchez, one of the gunslinging septet.

***We Were Strangers* (1949)** Columbia, b&w, 106 minutes. **Director:** John Huston; **Screenplay:** Huston and Peter Viertel; **Cast:** Jennifer Jones (China Valdes), John Garfield (Tony Fenner), Pedro Armendáriz (Armando Ariete), Gilbert Roland (Guillermo), Ramón Novarro (Chief), Wally Cassell (Miguel), David Bond (Ramon), José Pérez (Toto).

At the time of release, this slow-moving drama was considered by some sources to be pro-communist propaganda. In reality, it was a strong indictment against the reign of terror of Cuban president Gerardo Machado in the late 1920s and early 1930s.

In 1933 Cuba, China Valdes joins the revolutionary cause to avenge her brother's murder. At a gathering of the underground, she meets Cuban-American Tony Fenner, who announces a plan to assassinate Cuban government leaders. His scheme is to dig a tunnel from China's house to a nearby cemetery. A bomb will be planted in the tunnel. After an important government figure is assassinated, the other higher-ups will be blown up when they attend the funeral. At the last minute, the dignitary is buried elsewhere and the plan fails. In a final gesture of revolt, Fenner and China attack Armando Ariete, the head of the government's police force. The enemy is driven away, but Fenner is mortally wounded. As he dies, he hears bells ringing throughout the city—they are announcing the start of the revolution.

Jones displayed a credible Cuban accent, but most effective was ARMENDÁRIZ as the cruel head of the secret police. ROLAND as a revolutionary and Novarro as a rebel chief delivered viable performances.

***White Shadow, The* (1978–1981)** CBS-TV series, color, 90 minutes **Cast**: Ken Howard (Ken Reeves), Ed Bernard (Jim Willis: 1978–80), Nathan Cook (Milton Reese: 1978–80), Timothy Van Patten (Mario "Salami" Pettrino), Ken Michelman (Abner Goldstein: 1978–80), Ira Angustain (Ricky Gomez: 1978–80).

Former pro basketball player Ken Reeves is appointed the basketball coach of Carver High in Los Angeles. At the inner city school, there is a wide spectrum of ethnic diversity in the classroom and on the ball court. One of the players (till his character graduated with several others in the spring of 1980 after winning the L.A. City Basketball Championship) is Hispanic Ricky Gomez. As with the other ball-playing students, episodes revolved around each of the key teenagers.

The White Shadow was well regarded not just as a sports show but also as a mostly intelligent, realistic drama about young people coping with life's obstacles, especially those faced by the multicultural residents of tough neighborhoods. On the negative side, some commentators noted the presence here of the typical Hollywood conceit of having a white hero coming to the rescue of the less fortunate (i.e., ethnic minority folks).

Will & Grace **(1998–)** NBC-TV series, color, 30 minutes. **Cast:** Eric McCormack (Will Truman), Debra Messing (Grace Elizabeth Adler), Megan Mullally (Karen Walker), Sean Hayes (John "Jack" Phillip McFarland), Shelley Morrison (Rosario Ynez Consuela Yolanda Salazar McFarland: 1999–), Gregory Hines (Ben Doucette: 1999–2000).

This sitcom brought gay pride to a new level on national TV. The series explored the friendship of uptight gay attorney Will Truman and his best friend, heterosexual interior designer Grace Adler, as they dealt with being singles in New York City. Also aboard the show was Truman's good pal, the loafing, outgoing, gay Jack McFarland, and Adler's alcoholic, wealthy, nonfunctioning office assistant, Karen Walker. Karen had a love-hate relationship with her outspoken, no-nonsense maid Rosario who was her friend. The latter, to stay in the United States, had a brief sham marriage to McFarland, a situation that pleased neither party.

Hard-working Rosario broke the TV stereotype of the Hispanic domestic by being extremely forthright and right on the mark with her barbs. The part was played to perfection by New York-born Morrison (née Rachel Mitrani), whose background was not Hispanic but actually Sephardic Jewish.

Among the many nominations and awards won by *Will & Grace* was Morrison's nomination for an ALMA Award in 2001 as Outstanding Supporting Actress in a Series.

Wiseguy **(1987–1990)** CBS-TV series, color, 60 minutes. **Cast:** Ken Wahl (Vinnie Terranova: 1987–90), Steven Bauer (Michael Santana: 1990), Jonathan Banks (Frank McPike), Jim Byrnes ("Lifeguard" [Daniel Benjamin Burroughs]), Maximilian Schell (Amado Guzman: 1990), Manolo Villaverde (Rafael Santana: 1990).

This highly acclaimed and popular police drama, created by Stephen J. Cannell, featured Wahl as Vinnie Terranova, an Italian-American undercover agent for the government's Organized Crime Bureau. When Wahl left the series after its third season, he was replaced by BAUER who was cast as Michael Santana, a disbarred Cuban-American federal prosecutor. (The series was cancelled in late 1990, only a few months into its fourth season.)

In the plot line, Michael Santana was the individual whom Terranova contacted not long before he vanished as a possible victim of a Salvadoran death squad. As such, Terranova's boss, Frank McPike, is forced to interact with Santana. The latter goes undercover to spy on Amado Guzman, a wealthy and corrupt businessman for whom Santana's father, Rafael, worked.

Y

***You Were Never Lovelier* (1942)** Columbia, b&w, 97 minutes. **Director:** William A. Seiter; **Screenplay:** Michael Fessier, Ernest Pagano, and Delmer Daves; **Cast:** Fred Astaire (Robert Davis), Rita Hayworth (Maria Acuna), Adolphe Menjou (Eduardo Acuna), Leslie Brooks (Cecy Acuna), Adele Mara (Lita Acuna), Isobel Elsom (Mrs. Maria Castro), Xavier Cugat and His Orchestra (themselves), Lina Romay (singer).

A remake of the 1941 Argentinean film *Novios Para Las Muchacas* (Sweethearts for the Girls), *You Were Never Lovelier* reunited Astaire and Hayworth after their winning *You'll Never Get Rich* (1941).

Out-of-work dancer Robert Davis has lost his last money at the Buenos Aires racetrack. He seeks an engagement at Eduardo Acuna's hotel but with no luck, despite the help of his friend, bandleader XAVIER CUGAT. Meanwhile, Davis becomes intrigued with Acuna's elder daughter Maria. Maria's two younger sisters (Cecy and Lita), who are not allowed to wed till Maria does, do their best to match up Davis with Maria. Finally realizing that Davis really loves Maria, Acuna gives his blessing to the courtship and the couple finally acknowledge their mutual love.

With graceful dancing by Astaire and Hayworth to the songs (e.g., "Dearly Beloved," "You Were Never Lovelier," "I'm Old Fashioned") of Jerome Kern and Johnny Mercer, this charming musical was popular with audiences of the day. If the cast was far from Hispanic in their characterizations, they were not offensive caricatures. Reportedly, it was the Motion Picture Society for the Americas who persuaded Columbia Pictures to have its cast prepare a special promotional trailer in which the players spoke in Spanish and enunciated their delight in being able to entertain their neighbors to the south.

Z

***Zoot Suit* (1981)** Universal, color, 103 minutes. **Director/Screenplay:** Luis Valdez; **Cast:** Daniel Valdez (Henry Reyna), Edward James Olmos (El Pachuco), Charles Aidman (George), Tyne Daly (Alice), Abel Franco (Enrique), John Anderson (judge), Tony Plana (Rudy).

Adapted from the Broadway play that was initially presented in Los Angeles in 1978, *Zoot Suit* was the first major Hollywood studio film to be directed and written by a Mexican-American talent. It was filmed on a theater stage in Los Angeles in a two-week period at a cost of $2.5 million and used many of the original cast.

The facts in the narrative were based on the actual 1942 Sleepy Lagoon murder case in Los Angeles, in which several Hispanics were sent to jail on a frame-up for supposedly murdering another youth at a Los Angeles party. The unfair decision led to racial tension and the so-called Zoot Suit riots of 1942 and 1943 in Los Angeles.

The story is narrated and controlled by the finger-snapping, knife-wielding OLMOS as the kinetic El Pachuco (dressed in a zoot suit), a man of power. With wit and sly charm he comments on the case being unfairly handled due to racial bigotry. In his persona there are intimations of the ethnic minority rising from repression to demand fair treatment and their share of the American dream.

The drama revolves around Henry Reyna, the chief one of the youths, as well as their girlfriends and the others they encounter during the course of their arrest and trial. As the property is a musical, there is intermingling of music and dancing, ranging from swing dancing of the big band era to ethnically inspired numbers based on the Mexican-American culture.

At the time considered "too political," too ethnic, and too contrived (because of its stage-bound limitations), *Zoot Suit* did not fare well in the general marketplace.

Zorro The celebrated fictional masked swordsman (*Zorro* in Spanish means "fox"), who masqueraded as a fop (Don Diego de la Vega) in old California, began as a five-part story by Johnston McCulley in August 1919 in *All-Story Weekly* magazine. (It was later published in book form in 1924.) This popular character first came to the American screen in 1920's *THE MARK OF ZORRO*, starring Douglas Fairbanks Sr. So successful was that silent movie that the star made a sequel, *DON Q, SON OF ZORRO* (1925). Eleven years later, the swashbuckling Zorro made his sound film debut in Hollywood in *THE BOLD CABALLERO* featuring cowboy star Robert Livingston. The next year, 1937, the same studio (Republic Pictures) turned out the first of its Zorro serials, *Zorro Rides Again*, with John Carroll headlined in a contemporary story where the hero took on the identity of Zorro. In 1939 came another twelve-chapter serial, *Zorro's Fighting Legion* with Reed Hadley in the athletic key role. (Republic would trade on Zorro's box-office draw in three more serials, with the leads following in the footsteps of the "real" masked do-gooder: *Zorro's Black Whip*, 1944; *Son of Zorro*, 1947; and *Ghost of Zorro*, 1949.)

In 1940 Tyrone Power starred in an elaborate remake of *THE MARK OF ZORRO* that did much to revive the mystique of this fascinating Robin Hood of Spanish California. Jumping ahead seventeen years, the Walt Disney Studio produced a live-action TV series, *Zorro* (1957–59) with Guy Williams showcased in the lead part. Williams was in two feature films edited from episodes of the TV series: *Zorro the Avenger* (1959) and *The Sign of Zorro* (1960).

A complete change of pace was *The Erotic Adventures of Zorro* (1972) with Douglas Frey showcased in this salacious retelling of the Zorro legend. Frank Langella was cast in the TV movie *The Mark of Zorro* (1974) and, in 1980, George Hamilton was featured in the satirical *Zorro, the Gay Blade*.

On television, a thirteen-episode animated series, *The New Adventures of Zorro*, aired in 1981. Then came a new live-action series *Zorro and Son* (1983). For this short-lived sitcom, Henry Darrow was the aged Zorro, and Paul Regina was seen as his son. A more traditional presentation of the Zorro myth was in *Zorro: The Legend Continues* (1990–93) with Duncan Regehr as the young Don Diego de la Vega and Efrem Zimbalist Jr. (later replaced by Henry Darrow) as the elder aristocrat. A 1997 Warner Bros. International animated TV series. *The New Adventures of Zorro*, featured the voice of Michael Gough as Diego/Zorro.

More recently, in the theatrical release *THE MASK OF ZORRO* (1998), Anthony Hopkins was the masked avenger with ANTONIO BANDERAS as Zorro's protégé. In the syndicated TV series *Queen of Swords* (2000–2001), Tessie Santiago played an adventurous distaff version of Zorro swashbuckling through nineteenth-century California.

Jewish Americans

A

***Abie's Irish Rose* (1928)** Paramount, b&w, 80 minutes. **Director:** Victor Fleming; **Screenplay:** Anne Nichols, Herman Mankiewicz, and Julian Johnson; **Cast:** Charles Rogers (Abie Levy), Nancy Carroll (Rosemary Murphy), Jean Hersholt (Solomon Levy), J. Farrell MacDonald (Patrick Murphy), Bernard Gorcey (Isaac Cohen), Ida Kramer (Mrs. Isaac Cohen).

Based on Anne Nichols's 1922 Broadway hit that ran for years. By the time of this part talkie, there had been several celluloid imitations of the play. In addition, there had been *THE COHENS AND KELLYS* (1926), the start of a popular movie series also relying on stereotypes of the Irish and Jews waging cultural warfare. Although broad Gaelic types were already acceptable movie fare, to play it safe at the box office, non-Jewish players portrayed the Semitic father and son.

***Abie's Irish Rose* (1946)** United Artists, b&w, 98 minutes. **Director:** A. Edward Sutherland; **Screenplay:** Anne Nichols; **Cast:** Michael Chekhov (Solomon Levy), Joanne Dru (Rosemary Murphy), Richard Norris (Abie Levy), J. M. Kerrigan (Patrick Murphy), George E. Stone (Isaac Cohen), Vera Gordon (Mrs. Cohen).

This "updated" remake is old fashioned and, given the horrors of the recent World War II, much of its coarse ethnic humor offended audiences, not to mention the Jewish Anti-Defamation League and the National Conference of Christians and Jews. Two years earlier a radio series of Nichols's property had been canceled because listeners had protested.

***Address Unknown* (1944)** Columbia, b&w, 72 minutes. **Director:** William Cameron Menzies; **Screenplay:** Herbert Dalmas; **Cast:** Paul Lukas (Martin Schultz), Carl Esmond (Baron von Friesche), Peter Van Eyck (Heinrich Schultz), Mady Christians (Elsa Schultz), Morris Carnovsky (Max Eisenstein), K. T. Stevens (Griselle Eisenstein).

Although many Hollywood movies of the World War II era—including *Hitler's Children* (1943) and *None Shall Escape* (1944)—focused on the Nazi reign of terror, few such American features dealt expressly with the persecution of Jews. An exception was *Address Unknown* based on Kressman Taylor's 1939 novel.

San Francisco art-gallery owner Martin Schultz returns to Germany on business and is indoctrinated into the Third Reich's party line. His U.S. partner's daughter, Griselle, in Berlin to act, is persecuted. He refuses to aid her, and she is killed by the police. Schultz's son engineers a scheme to bring his anti-Semitic father to justice.

Daring as *Address Unknown* was, it still had Griselle played by nonethnic, blonde Stevens. That was done to soften the presented ethnicity of the Eisenstein family, in which the father was played by the Jewish actor Carnovsky.

Adler, Luther (1903–1984) Part of a famous YIDDISH THEATER acting family, his bulky build and jowly features determined that he would play screen villains. Ironically twice on camera he was Adolf Hitler: *The Magic Face* and *The Desert Fox* (both 1951).

Born Lutha Adler in New York City, he was an offspring of Yiddish stage luminary Jacob Adler. Luther started to perform with his father's troupe at age five. He made his Broadway debut in 1923, returned to the Yiddish stage in 1930, and joined the Group Theater in 1932. His film debut was *Lancer Spy* (1937), but he was absent from films until *Cornered* (1945). Meanwhile, he was in the HOLOCAUST-themed stage pageant *We Will Never Die* (1943). His celluloid criminal kingpin in *D.O.A.* (1950) typecast him thereafter. Occasionally, he broke out of mold: the gypsy in *Hot Blood* (1956), Dr. Max Vogel in *THE LAST ANGRY MAN* (1959). Jacob Zion in *Cast a Giant Shadow* (1966), and the therapist on the 1971 TV series *The Psychiatrist.* His final work was as Uncle Santos Malderone in *Absence of Malice* (1981).

Allen, Woody (1935–) The Yiddish word *schlemiel* (shleh-MEAL) suggests a foolish or unfortunate soul; a clumsy misfit and often a naïve pipsqueak. This definition fit many screen characters played by scruffy-haired, bespectacled Allen.

In Allen's earliest features (e.g., *Take the Money and Run*, 1969), traditional Judaism was subjected to verbal/visual gags. By *ANNIE HALL* (1977—for which he won two Oscars) and *MANHATTAN* (1979), his on-screen alter egos were complex, neurotic Jewish New Yorkers. In contrast to BARBRA STREISAND, another Brooklyn-born Orthodox Jew/filmmaker, Allen's Jewish antiheroes were intellectual, obsessive fence-sitters who acted impulsively out of lust or frustration.

He was born Allan Stewart Konigsberg in the Flatbush district of Brooklyn. Fascinated with comedy early on, he began to submit jokes to columnists and comedians. By age seventeen, he was writing for professional entertainers. Thereafter, he was a TV network comedy scribe for SID CAESAR and others. Later, Allen turned to stand-up comedy.

In 1965 Allen wrote the mainstream screen hit *What's New Pussycat?* After his feature debut directing/scripting/acting in *Take the Money and Run*, he penned Broadway comedies (e.g., *Play It Again, Sam*, 1969) that became movies. His satirical *EVERYTHING YOU ALWAYS WANTED TO KNOW ABOUT SEX BUT WERE AFRAID TO ASK* (1972) was filled with deep truths. *THE FRONT* (1976) concerned the 1950s communist witch hunt.

A Midsummer Night's Sex Comedy (1982) was the first of Mia Farrow's movies with Allen, her off-camera amour. That union blew apart in 1992, just as his *Husbands and Wives* was released. The scandal/court case made Allen unpopular for a time. He was back in step with *Bullets Over Broadway* (1994) for which he won Oscar nominations for directing and coscripting. He made a surprisingly lighthearted musical (*Everyone Says I Love You* 1996) and in *Celebrity* (1998) had Kenneth Branagh appear as his alter ego. As if returning full circle, Allen was a fumbling felon in *Small Time Crooks* (2000). Later projects included *The Curse of the Jade Scorpion* (2001) and *Hollywood Ending* (2002).

A revealing study of Allen came in *Wild Man Blues* (1998), a documentary about Allen touring Europe with his New Orleans jazz band.

***American Tail, An* (1986)** Universal, color, 80 minutes. **Director:** Don Bluth; **Screenplay:** Judy Freudberg and Tony Geiss; Animation Directors: John Pomeroy, Dan Kuenster, and Linda Miller; **Voices:** Erica Yohn (Mama Mousekewitz), Nehemiah Persoff (Papa Mousekewitz), Amy Green (Tonya Mousekewitz), Phillip Glasser (Fievel Mousekewitz), Christopher Plummer (Henri), Madeline Kahn (Gussie Mausheimer).

In the 1880s, the Mousekewitz household immigrate to America to escape the Russian pogroms. En route, Fievel, the youngster, is separated from his relatives. He washes up to New York City in a bottle. There he copes with the new world and predatory felines.

Executive producer STEVEN SPIELBERG named the hero mouse after his grandfather, a Russian Jewish immigrant. Some applauded this parable for its handling of real-life Jewish problems in the new land. Others thought the Jewish characters too quickly became homogenized, American figures.

One of the film's songs, "Somewhere Out There," was Oscar-nominated. This success led to *An American Tail: Fievel Goes West* (1991) with Glasser again voicing the young mouse. *Fievel's American Tails* (1992–93) was an animated TV series with the Mousekewitz clan in the Old West. To be noted, Papa Mousekewitz had a Yiddish accent. Other direct-to-video series entries followed.

animation—feature films Several full-length American-made animated features highlighted Jewish characters and themes. A frequent purveyor of such works was Ralph Bakshi with his output of adult-oriented full-length cartoons. In the cynical adventures of street-smart *Fritz the Cat* (1972), there were several unflattering presentations of Jewish characters (i.e., a Jewish policeman, Fritz's hiding from the law at a synagogue where he disguised himself as a rabbi complete with flowing beard, etc.). The animated *Heavy Traffic* (1973), which used live actors at its finale, told of the son of a Jewish woman and an Italian father who plotted to become a cartoonist while hanging out on the mean streets of Manhattan. In the animated *American Pop* (1981), Bakshi's ode to American music and commentary on people's success compulsion, the lead figures were generations of offspring of Russian Jewish immigrants. Over the decades, they were shown involved with different musical trends in the United States.

In 1974, Warner Bros. released a full-length animated feature of Charles Dickens's *OLIVER TWIST*, written in the late 1830s. Les Tremayne provided the voice of Fagin, with Josh Albee heard in the title role of the British waif. The picture was reedited and aired as a special on NBC-TV in 1981.

The Steven Spielberg-produced animated feature *AN AMERICAN TAIL* (1986) presented the Jewish Russian immigrant mouse (Fievel Mousekewitz) who came to 1880s New York. It detailed how he survived in the big city. The follow-up, *An American Tail—Fievel Goes West* (1991), as well as a TV series, *Fievel's American Tails* (1992–93), set in the Old West. (More Fievel tales were released as direct-to-video items.) Another animated feature, *Oliver & Company* (1988), was derived from Charles Dickens's book *OLIVER TWIST*, published in the late 1830s. Dom DeLuise provided the voice of Fagan, the human who operated a pack of street-smart dogs and who allowed a stray kitten, Oliver, to join their number. Springing from the animated TV series *Rugrats*, which began in 1991, the full-length animated features *The Rugrats Movie*

(1998) and *The Rugrats in Paris: The Movie* (2000) contained Jewish characters.

In a totally different arena was the feature-length animated movie, *The Prince of Egypt* (1998), filled with spectacular animation and songs. It retold the Old Testament account of Moses leading the people of Israel out of Egypt and their journey to the promised land. Among the celebrity voices utilized were: Val Kilmer (Moses/God), Ralph Fiennes (Rameses), Michelle Pfeiffer (Tzipporah), Sandra Bullock (Miriam), Jeff Goldblum (Aaron), Danny Glover (Jethro), Patrick Stewart (Pharoah Seti I), Steve Martin (Hotep), and Brian Stokes Mitchell (as the singing voice of Jethro). Another biblical animated feature that also incorporated songs was *Joseph: King of Dreams* (2000), a direct-to-video/DVD production. Its biblical account of the Jews—drawn from the Bible's Book of Genesis—was set in a period before the above-mentioned *Prince of Egypt*. Voices were provided by Ben Affleck (Joseph), Mark Hamill (Judah), Steven Weber (Simeon), Judith Light (Zuleika), James Eckhouse (Potiphar), and David Campbell (the singing voice of Joseph).

animation series—television The cartoon series *Kid Power* (1972–74) featured a multicultural grouping of children characters including Jerry, a Jewish friend of chunky kid Oliver. The youths were part of the Rainbow Club, which tried to promote social and racial harmony. This Saturday-morning, half-hour program was based on cartoonist Morrie Turner's *Wee Pals* newspaper strip that debuted in 1965. *Rugrats*, a Saturday morning cartoon series that began in 1991 and later spawned feature-length animated movies, had Jewish characters among the regulars. There were special episodes devoted to explain the Jewish characters' heritage, including "A Rugrats Passover" (1995) and "Rugrats Chanukah" (1997).

***Annie Hall* (1977)** United Artists, color, 93 minutes. **Director/Screenplay:** Woody Allen; **Cast:** Woody Allen (Alvy Singer), Diane Keaton (Annie Hall), Tony Roberts (Rob), Carol Kane (Allison), Paul Simon (Tony Lacey)

The wistful *Annie Hall* was a landmark for ALLEN. It was an ingratiating and insightful examination of a contemporary Jewish bachelor—a comedy writer—in New York City and his attraction to a gentile woman.

Alvy Singer is intelligent and worldly but also naïve and insecure. Singer meets bubbly midwesterner Annie Hall, a would-be songster, with whom he develops a live-in romance. But once this total-opposite union blossoms, she accepts a Hollywood offer, deserting paranoid Alvy.

Annie Hall, reflecting Allen's actual romance with Keaton, won four Academy Awards: Best Actress (Keaton), Best Director, Best Original Screenplay, and Best Picture.

This film was one of several late 1970s features examining single Jewish bachelors in the Big Apple: e.g., Neil Simon's *THE GOODBYE GIRL* (1977) and *Chapter Two* (1979), the interracial romance *Love in a Taxi* (1979), ALAN ARKIN's *Simon* (1980), and Allen's MANHATTAN (1979).

anti-Semitism—feature films and television productions about The irony of this prejudice was that one of the forms in which it manifested itself during the decades in Hollywood—often at the hands of anti-Semitic Jewish studio bosses (such as Jack L. Warner and Louis B. Mayer)—was to make Jewish topics or characters or actors' heritage invisible on screen. An example of this was the popular 1937 Broadway play, *Having Wonderful Time*. It starred JOHN GARFIELD and dealt with Jewish vacationers seeking romance at a CATSKILL RESORT. When it reached the screen in 1938 with Ginger Rogers and Douglas Fairbanks Jr., the Jewish elements had been deleted and/or vastly toned down. In the same vein, actors whose names sounded too Jewish were required by the movie studios to "Americanize" them: e.g., Muni Weisenfeld became PAUL MUNI, Sophie Kossow turned into SYLVIA SIDNEY, Emanuel Goldenberg was transformed into EDWARD G. ROBINSON, and Bernard Schwartz emerged as TONY CURTIS. BARBRA STREISAND and a few others aside, Jewish performers with overgenerously sized noses were ordered by filmmakers to have "corrective" surgery. Those who refused, such as DANNY KAYE, might, at the least, have to dye their hair (as he did to red/blond) to tone down the ethnic look.

Other ways that anti-Semitism was fostered on the American screen was by depicting Jewish characters—especially in the GHETTO DRAMAS of the silent era and early talkies—as quaint foreigners who did not deserve to be treated with equality. This anti-Jewishness sometimes manifested itself by the lack of Jewish characters in stories—even urban dramas—or by relegating them to background roles. In contrast, when a character from a classic novel had an image of negative stereotyping of Jewish characteristics (such as Fagin in Charles Dickens's *OLIVER TWIST*), every time Hollywood insisted on making a screen adaptation of the literary masterpiece, there would be shouts of foul play by ethnic PRESSURE GROUPS.

On the screen, an early example of anti-Jewish bigotry was in *THE YELLOW PASSPORT* (1916) depicting hatred against the Russian-born heroine and her family. A similar theme and setting was found in *THE YELLOW TICKET* (1918), which would be remade in 1931. In *As a Man Thinks* (1919), another silent melodrama, one character was not allowed to wed his sweetheart when her father learned that he was Jewish. *Who's Your Brother* (1991) dealt with anti-Jewish massacres over the years in Europe, as well as the prejudice of one suitor against his rival for the heroine's affection.

Thereafter, American-made movies did not focus directly on anti-Semitic subjects until World War II. In the mystery-comedy *Margin for Error* (1943), based on a 1939 play, the character of the Jewish policeman played by MILTON BERLE, found himself stationed at the German consulate and forced to protect a virulent anti-Semite. Two 1944 releases dealt with the topic: *ADDRESS UNKNOWN* and *TOMORROW THE WORLD!* both involving Nazi brainwashing of malleable minds. In *PRIDE OF THE MARINES* (1945), the Jewish soldier pal (Dane Clark) of the blinded war hero (John Garfield) had a sizable speech explaining that, while he knew all about prejudice, he was sure the nastiness was the work of only a relatively few individuals and not the many.

A landmark entry touching seriously on the subject of anti-Semitism was *CROSSFIRE* (1947), which presented as a whodunit. It sparked a lot of commentary because of its daring presentation. *GENTLEMAN'S AGREEMENT* (1947)— spearheaded by non-jewish studio mogul Darryl F. Zanuck, which went on to win a Best Picture and two other Oscars—dealt directly with the subject but, like its book original, used the gimmick of a gentile pretending to be a Jew. The little-seen, low-budget *Open Secret* (1948) concerned a virulent anti-Jewish group who murdered a witness to their sinister activities. *Prejudice* (1949), coproduced by the Protestant Film Commission, preached tolerance between Jews and gentiles, and in *The Magnificent Yankee* (1950) the appointment of real-life judge Louis Brandeis to the U.S. Supreme Court was questioned because of his heritage. A segment within the saccharine *It's a Big Country* (1951) presented an initially anti-Semitic situation in which the Jewish target of abuse (a returning soldier from World War II) showed the bigot (the mother of his dead soldier buddy) that he is a decent person after all.

After a few years of silence in Hollywood films, the topic of anti-Semitism arose again in *GOOD MORNING, MISS DOVE* (1955), *HOME BEFORE DARK* (1958), *THE YOUNG LIONS* (1958), and *DARK AT THE TOP OF THE STAIRS* (1960), all of which tentatively tiptoed around the issue of how discrimination affected lives.

As the 1960s progressed, Jewish characters were given full-bodied presentations on screen, which suggested that they had finally reached "mainstream" status—by Hollywood standards. Nevertheless, the proportion of screen fare involving Jewish themes or characters had and does remain relatively small.

In the 1990s, a few big-screen dramas dealt with intolerance toward Jews. In *The Chamber* (1996), based on the John Grisham novel (1994), a young lawyer in the South defended his bigot grandfather who, thirty years earlier, had bombed the office of a Jewish civil rights attorney and had accidentally killed the man's two children. Within the international coproduction *I Love You, I Love You Not* (1996), a coming-of-age story, the young student Daisy (Claire Danes) had no real sense of what being Jewish meant. Through her grandmother (Jeanne Moreau), a Holocaust survivor, she came to appreciate her roots and to be sensitive to anti-Semitism at her school. In 1999's *Waterproof*, Burt Reynolds was seen as an elderly Jewish man who refused to stop operating his store in what had become a contentious African-American neighborhood. *The Believer* (2001), based on a true story, told of a militant anti-Semitic skinhead in the United States who had been brought up a strict Jew. Also in 2001 came *Focus*, based on an Arthur Miller novel (1945) about a couple in Brooklyn at the end of World War II being persecuted by anti-Semitic neighbors.

On network American television, displays of anti-Semitism over the years, sometimes linked with neo-Nazi movements, were plot threads on episodes of such diverse series as *Bonanza* (1959–73), *The Defenders* (1961–65), *All in the Family* (1971–79), *THE MARY TYLER MOORE SHOW* (1970–77), *Little House on the Prairie* (1974–83), *Lou Grant* (1977–82), *Archie Bunker's Place* (1979–83), *The Golden Girls* (1985–92), *L.A. Law* (1986–94), *Wiseguy* (1987–90), *Beverly Hills 90210* (1990–2000), *Law & Order* (1990–), *Reasonable Doubts* (1991–93), *Picket Fences* (1992–96), *Dr. Quinn, Medicine Woman* (1993–98), *Murder One* (1995–97), and *Promised Land* (1996–99).

In the area of TV specials/movies, sometimes the subject was handled by exploring the bias of two minority groups as in "A Storm in Summer," a 1970 *Hallmark Hall of Fame* presentation regarding an elderly Jewish man and an African-American adolescent. The two groups also might be the subject of others' prejudice as in *Summer of My German Soldier* (1978), a TV movie set in the Georgia countryside during World War II, or as in *Murder in Mississippi* (1990), a telefeature about the killing of Jewish and African-American civil rights workers in 1964.

One of the most memorable made-for-television movies dealing with anti-Semitism was *SKOKIE* (1981). It starred Danny Kaye as a concentration-camp survivor living in an Illinois town where the National Socialist Party of America planned to demonstrate. Sometimes, the plot twist of a TV production would deal with the investigation of and lawsuit about anti-Semitism spearheaded by non-Jewish concerned citizens. This was the thesis of two 1988 TV movies based on the same actual case: *Evil in Clear River* with Lindsay Wagner and *SCANDAL IN A SMALL TOWN* starring Raquel Welch.

For the Very First Time (1991) was a telefeature set back in the 1960s. Two teenagers, an Irish Catholic girl and a Jewish boy fall into lust, but their religious differences split them apart, ending their burgeoning romance. In *Not in This Town* (1997), a Jewish couple (Kathy Baker and Adam Arkin), living in Billings, Montana, observed the arrival of a white supremacist group that preached hate and committed violence against minorities. The Jewish woman almost single-handedly rallied the town against the intruders. The two-part TV movie *Haven* (2001) focused on a young Brooklyn woman, a journalist, who in the last months of World War II helped to bring 1,000 Jewish refugees to the United States despite the many roadblocks put up by anti-Semitic factions in the U.S. government and elsewhere. *Conspiracy* (2001), a made-for-cable offering, reconstructed a meeting of the German high command in the early 1940s—their purpose to resolve the "Jewish Question" with mass extermination at the concentration camps.

***Anything but Love* (1989–1992)** ABC-TV series, color, 30 minutes. **Cast:** Jamie Lee Curtis (Hannah Miller), Richard Lewis (Marty Gold), Ann Magnuson (Catherine Hughes), Richard Frank (Jules Kramer—later Jules Bennett), Holly Fulger (Robin Dulitski).

A poor man's mix of *MAD ABOUT YOU* (1992–99) and *MARY TYLER MOORE* (1970–77), *Anything But Love* featured Marty Gold, an investigative reporter at *Chicago Weekly* who is in love with the non-Jewish Hannah Miller, an on-staff researcher/writer. Using a distillation of his neurotic persona as a stand-up comic, LEWIS made Marty a close cousin to the intellectual paranoids played on screen by WOODY ALLEN.

This sitcom ignored any obstacle that such an interfaith relationship might have on Marty's widowed mother or his married sister. The same applied to Hannah's family, whose religion was unspecified.

A kindred spirit to Marty Gold was the Jewish Jack Stein, the *New York Post* columnist in *Love & War* (1992–95) whose romantic inclinations ran to gentile women. An aggressive loudmouth, Stein wore his religion like a badge of honor.

***Apprenticeship of Duddy Kravitz, The* (1974)** Paramount, color, 120 minutes. **Director:** Ted Kotcheff; **Screenplay:** Mordecai Richler; **Cast:** Richard Dreyfuss (Duddy), Micheline Lanctot (Yvette), Jack Warden (Max), Randy Quaid (Virgil), Joseph Wiseman (Uncle Benjy).

Based on Richler's well-known novel (1959), this Canadian film set in 1948 Montreal used several Hollywood players. Its spotlight is on a materialistic young Jewish go-getter (DREYFUSS), whose get-rich-quick schemes produce mixed results for him and his family. Although this touching and sometimes funny chronicle focuses on pressure-driven young people in general, many Jewish groups took the antihero's corruption personally. For a rare change in this era, Jewish characters were presented as dimensional personalities.

***Apt Pupil* (1998)** TriStar, color, 111 minutes. **Director:** Bryan Singer; **Screenplay,** Brandon Boyce; **Cast:** Ian McKellen (Kurt Dussander), Brad Renfro (Todd Bowden), Bruce Davison (Richard Bowden), Elias Koteas (Achie), Joe Morton (Dan Richler).

This richly textured study of the horrors of the HOLOCAUST, brought into sharp focus for today's youth, was based on Stephen King's novella (1982). Set in 1984, a high school senior (Renfro) who is studying the terror levied on Jews during World War II, realizes that an elderly man (McKellen) he has spotted on a bus is actually a former Nazi concentration camp commander. The boy agrees to keep quiet only if the old person tells him about his heinous past. But the unrepentant "victim" is too experienced in evil to keep to such a bargain.

This movie was aimed especially at those who thought the Holocaust may never have happened.

Arkin, Alan (1934–) A multitalented actor with a knack for accents and playing characters of different nationalities, Arkin blossomed professionally in the mid-1960s and thereafter became a character star. He first starred on Broadway as the Jewish Bronx delivery boy in *ENTER LAUGHING* (1963). Thereafter, he was Oscar nominated as the wacky Russian sailor in *The Russians Are Coming, the Russians Are Coming* (1966) and as the deaf-mute in *The Heart Is a Lonely Hunter* (1968).

Born Alan Wolf Arkin in New York City, his family moved to Los Angeles when Arkin was a teenager. He spent two years at Bennington College. Next he became a folk singer/songwriter. As part of a trio named the Tarriers, he made his film debut with them in *Calypso Heat Wave* (1957).

On screen he was the lead in Neil Simon's *Last of the Red Hot Lovers* (1972), played Sigmund Freud in *The Seven-Per-Cent Solution* (1976), and portrayed the dentist, Dr. Sheldon Kornpett, in the crime spoof *The In-Laws* (1979). That same year in *The Magician of Lublin*, Arkin was Yasha Mazur. He played the concentration camp prisoner in the TV movie *Escape from Sobibor* (1987). More recently, Arkin appeared in *The Jerky Boys* (1995), *Gattaca* (1997), *JAKOB THE LIAR* (1999), *Arigo* (2000), and *13 Conversations About One Thing* (2002). On the TV series *100 Centre Street* (2000–2002), he excelled as the iconoclastic, humanist New York City judge.

Arkin's son Adam became an actor, especially active as a TV series star.

***Ask Dr. Ruth* (1987–1988)** Syndicated TV series, color, 30 minutes. **Cast:** Dr. Ruth Westheimer (host), Larry Angelo (cohost).

Talk television in the 1980s—before the arrival of shock hosts like Howard Stern and Jerry Springer—was more dignified and low keyed. Bursting onto this scene in 1984 was diminutive WESTHEIMER, a heavily accented European-born Jewish therapist who had made an impact on viewers with her Lifetime cable TV series, *Good Sex! with Dr. Ruth Westheimer* (1984–86). With *Ask Dr. Ruth*, the grandmotherly personality transferred to a less controversial format (i.e., omitting reenactments) of answering sex-related questions from guests. This and her later talk/call-in TV programs, made the overtly ethnic Dr. Ruth a household name across America. It demonstrated that a gimmick and a good presentation could minimize the fact that such an offbeat TV host was so uniquely different from stereotypical middle America.

assimilation—feature films For all ethnic groups migrating to the United States in the later nineteenth and early twentieth century, there was tremendous conflict between blending into the great American melting pot and retaining their old-world customs and traditions. This was especially the case with Jewish immigrants coming to America, many of whom had been victims of pogroms in eastern Europe. Early American feature films such as *CHILDREN OF THE GHETTO* (1915) depicted the newcomers typically congregated on Manhattan's LOWER EAST SIDE, living in cramped quarters as they acclimated to their new environment. (Such depictions set into motion what became known as GHETTO DRAMAS.) Having experienced so much oppression in their homelands, some of these Jews became involved in socialist causes in the United States, seeking better working and living conditions, as reflected in movies such as *The Right to Happiness* (1919). Often, the more successful Jewish workers moved uptown to more spacious quarters while others, unimpressed by materialistic needs, remained in the familiar neighborhoods. This battle of the generations—of the old versus the new—led to such pictures as *HIS PEOPLE* (1925), *THE YOUNGER GENERATION* (1929), and to a lesser degree *MARJORIE MORNINGSTAR* (1958).

The need to blend in, to became acculturated to the American way, was a focus of the landmark motion picture *THE JAZZ SINGER* (1927) starring AL JOLSON, whose choice of profession—show business—separated him from his family and his heritage. (The theme would be repeated not only in two remakes of this feature but also in two very popular autobiographical films of Jolson's life, *THE JOLSON STORY*, 1946, and *JOLSON SINGS AGAIN*, 1949.) Other films, such as the popular *THE COHENS AND KELLYS* series, took a comical approach to the Americanizing of newcomers and their U.S.-born offspring.

By the 1960s, even when the subjects of such assimilation dramas/comedies were already second- or third-generation Americans, the decades-long battle of fitting in continued. *BYE BYE BRAVERMAN* (1968) concerned several New York Jewish intellectuals, the happiest of the lot being the traditionalist (Joseph Wiseman). In *GOODBYE, COLUMBUS* (1969), the self-made, affluent businessman (Jack Klugman) looked with scorn on his daughter's boyfriend who refused to be a U.S.-style go-getter. For others, true assimilation was confirmed by interfaith marriages or having a trophy gentile lover. This was the guiding force of Charles Grodin's character in *THE HEARTBREAK KID* (1972) and of RICHARD BENJAMIN's emotionally disturbed antihero in *PORTNOY'S COMPLAINT* (1972). The premise received a turnaround in *THE WAY WE WERE* (1973) where the very Jewish heroine (BARBRA STREISAND) sets her sights on the extremely WASP male lead (Robert Redford). In *A Price Above Rubies* (1998), a dissatisfied young Hasidic housewife (Renée Zellweger) in New York City wants more out of life than her religious traditions allow.

assimilation series—television While commercial TV in the United States began in the late 1940s—by which time many of the Jewish immigrants and their children had become acculturated to the new land—the small-screen medium was more reluctant to deal with this serious subject even in a casual manner. (Networks were fearful of offending sponsors and/or losing viewership.) Thus, few television drama/comedy series after the early 1950s dealt with focal Jewish characters. (One exception to this was the 1979 miniseries *Studs Lonigan*, which was based on James T. Farrell's 1930s book trilogy. Set in Chicago of the 1910s to the 1930s, it depicted a Jewish character converting to Catholicism and marrying a Catholic.)

Often, according to TV fare, the only time an assimilated Jew would be recognized as such would be at the time of death, when a traditional Jewish funeral is held and friends/associates suddenly realize the deceased's background. This occurred in the situation comedy series *All in the Family* (1971–83) where Archie Bunker's pal/coworker Stretch Cunningham proved to be Jewish. It was also the case in the 1984 miniseries *Ellis Island*. Sometimes, the character delineated might be totally amoral—a gangster—and seemingly without religious affiliation, only to prove to be Jewish at the time of death (as on segments of *The Untouchables*, 1959–63, and other such genre series).

Picking up where the movies' *ABIE'S IRISH ROSE* (1928 and 1946) left off, *BRIDGET LOVES BERNIE* (1972–73) took a comedic/romantic approach to a mixed marriage as the couple (she Irish and he Jewish) sought to create an ethnically neutral household. On a more dramatic note, the Michael Stedman character on *THIRTYSOMETHING* (1987–91) had great difficulty coping with his assimilated lifestyle once his daughter and, especially, his son were born, wondering what had become of his traditional religious values. The same doubts occurred to the lawyer character Stuart Markowitz when he was about to wed gentile Ann Kelsey on *L.A. Law* (1986–94). A more traumatic blending of cultures and religions occurred on *Beverly Hills 90210* (1990–2000) with the marriage of Andrea Zuckerman to Jesse Vasquez, which soon proved to be troubled by spiritual differences as well.

However, by the 1990s, as in the sitcom *MAD ABOUT YOU* (1992–99) or the drama *Once and Again* (1999–2002), religious disparity appeared to be a nonissue—at least as presented on the small screen. *State of Grace* (2001–) set in the South of the 1960s involved two young teens girls—one from a Jewish family, the other from a wealthy gentile clan—and how they relate with one another, their peers, and most of all with members of their eccentric households.

***Attic: The Hiding of Anne Frank, The* (1988)** CBS-TV, color, 120 minutes. **Director:** John Erdman; **Teleplay:** William Hanley; **Cast:** Mary Steenburgen (Miep Gies), Paul Scofield (Otto Frank), Eleanor Bron (Edith Frank), Lisa Jacobs (Anne Frank), Frances Cuka (Mrs. Van Daan), Jeffrey Roberts (Albert Dussell).

Long after the Broadway (1955) and Hollywood (1959) versions of *THE DIARY OF ANNE FRANK*, as well as three TV adaptations (1967, 1980, and 1987), came this new interpretation of the familiar tale of the German Jewish girl hiding with family and friends in the attic of an Amsterdam building during the Nazi occupation of World War II.

Filmed in Amsterdam and England, the production received positive reviews, especially for Steenburgen as the brave soul who protected the victims and who later rescued Anne's diary.

Eight years later, Kellie Martin starred in *Hidden In Silence*, a TV movie dealing with a seventeen-year-old Polish Catholic domestic who hides Jews in her loft during the German occupation of the early 1940s.

In 2001 appeared the lengthy telefeature *Anne Frank: The Whole Story* that extended the tragic saga of the Jewish family/friends to their fate once they were captured by the Nazis and shipped to their concentration camp destination.

***Avalon* (1990)** TriStar, color, 126 minutes. **Director/Screenplay:** Barry Levinson; **Cast:** Armin Mueller-Stahl

(Sam Krichinsky), Aidan Quinn (Jules Kaye), Elizabeth Perkins (Ann Kaye), Joan Plowright (Eva Krichinsky), Lou Jacobi (Gabriel Krichinsky).

Based on the real-life reminiscences of director LEVINSON, who received an Academy Award nomination for his Best Original Screenplay, this affectionate but hardly cohesive portrait concerns an often boisterous Russian Jewish family who settle in Baltimore, Maryland, at the end of World War II. As the inevitable assimilation process accelerates, over the years, the clan's variant goals, lifestyles, and needs sadly pull the once close-knit group into different directions.

B

Badge of Shame, The See *YELLOW PASSPORT, THE.*

Balsam, Martin (1919–1996) His everyman face belied the intense actor who made more than 100 films. Besides being a murder victim in *Psycho* (1960), he was in *12 Angry Men* (1957), *Cape Fear* (1962), *Seven Days in May* (1964), *The Stone Killer* (1973), *All the President's Men* (1976), and *The Goodbye People* (1986). He played many Jewish screen characters, ranging from *MARJORIE MORNINGSTAR* (1958), *Harlow* (1965), *RAID ON ENTEBBE* (1977—TV movie), and *THE CHILD SAVER* (1988—TV movie). On the TV sitcom *Archie Bunker's Place* (1979–81), he was the Jewish partner confronted with bigoted Archie. As Jason Robards Jr.'s unimaginative brother, he won a Best Supporting Actor Oscar for *A Thousand Clowns* (1965). He was a frequent Broadway performer who spent his final years making movies in Rome, Italy.

Born in New York City, Balsam began his professional acting by 1941 and was on Broadway that same year in *Ghost for Sale*. After World War II service, he joined the Actors Studio and was very busy on television in the 1950s and 1960s. His movie debut was *On the Waterfront* (1954). His daughter Talia became an actress.

***Ben-Hur* (1925)** Metro-Goldwyn-Mayer, b&w and color, 141 minutes. **Director:** Fred Niblo; **Screenplay:** Bess Meredyth, Carey Wilson, and June Mathis; **Cast:** Ramón Novarro (Ben-Hur), Francis X. Bushman (Messala), May McAvoy (Esther), Betty Bronson (Mary), Claire McDowell (Princess of Hur).

The novel *Ben-Hur* (1880) by General Lewis Wallace had been adapted successfully to the stage and had provided the basis for a 1907 Kalem silent movie short. Lensed partially on location in Italy, this costly epic boasted magnificent sets and a color sequence. The book original is subtitled *A Tale of the Christ*, but this sweeping saga of ancient Jerusalem focuses more on the effects his presence has on a wealthy Jewish man (Novarro) whose friendship with a Roman centurion (Francis X. Bushman) leads to obstacles that test Ben-Hur's faith. Because this silent film entry is so spectacle oriented—especially the climactic coliseum chariot race—contemporary audiences overlooked the fact that so much of the narrative is about a Jew (played by Catholic, Mexican-born Novarro).

Francis X. Bushman (left) and Ramón Novarro (center) in *Ben-Hur* (1925). (JC ARCHIVES)

***Ben-Hur* (1959)** Metro-Goldwyn-Mayer, color, 212 minutes. **Director:** William Wyler; **Screenplay:** Karl Tunberg; **Cast:** Charlton Heston (Judah Ben-Hur), Jack Hawkins (Quintus Arrius), Stephen Boyd (Messala), Haya Harareet (Esther), Hugh Griffith (Sheik Ilderim).

Among the many differences between the silent 1925 version and the 1959 screen remake of Wallace's novel was its very updated interpretation, lacing in parallels between the Roman centurions who had conquered Judea and the Nazis of the Third Reich. Made at a then staggering cost of more than $12 million, the 1959 rendition grossed more than $40 million and won eleven Academy Awards.

For a change, one of the lead roles of a Hebrew was actually played by a Jewish performer, in this case Israeli actress Harareet. Star Heston had played the Jewish biblical figure Moses in *THE TEN COMMANDMENTS* (1956).

Benjamin, Richard (1938–) Early on in his career, clean-cut Benjamin played young Jewish men coping with conflicting ethnic/moral traditions. In *GOODBYE, COLUMBUS* (1969) and *PORTNOY'S COMPLAINT* (1972), his screen portraits were accepted by many viewers as typical of the modern assimilated Semite. As a director, his features often revolved around Jewish ambiances (e.g., *MY FAVORITE YEAR*, 1982).

Born in New York City, Benjamin attended the High School of Performing Arts. As a fledgling actor he apprenticed in Shakespeare and did occasional TV episodes (*Dr. Kildare*, etc.), before his Broadway debut in *The Star-Spangled Girl* (1966). He and his actress-wife Paula Prentiss co-starred in the TV sitcom *He & She* (1967–68).

Following *Goodbye, Columbus*, he acted in *Catch-22* (1970) and then a film trio about discontented Jewish men, including *Diary of a Mad Housewife* (1970). In *The Sunshine Boys* (1975), he was Walter Matthau's well-meaning nephew and Jewish physicians in *House Calls* (1978) and *Love at First Bite* (1978).

Benjamin's film directing has included *Racing with the Moon* (1984) and *The Money Pit* (1986). His *Mermaids* (1990) had Cher and Winona Ryder improbably cast as a Jewish mother and daughter. As an actor, Benjamin was among the ensemble cast of WOODY ALLEN's *Deconstructing Harry* (1997); in *The Pentagon Wars* (1998), a comedic TV movie Benjamin also directed, he appeared as Casper Weinberger, secretary of defense.

More recently, Benjamin guided Nathan Lane through a cable-TV movie production of Neil Simon's *Laughter on the 23rd Floor* (2001—about 1950s TV comedian SID CAESAR) and directed Lisa Kudrow and Damon Wayans in *Marci X* (2003), a comedy about a Jewish-American Princess who took control of a hip-hop record label.

Benny, Jack (1894–1974) Unlike many of his peers—AL JOLSON, EDDIE CANTOR, and FANNY BRICE—Benny developed a stage persona in vaudeville that was essentially nonethnic and full of human foibles (his cheapness, his bad violin playing, his old Maxwell car). In contrast to later Jewish-born comedians such as ALAN KING or BILLY CRYSTAL, Benny's stage self was nonsectarian, unanalytical, and willing to be the butt of jokes. It endeared him to generations of fans, few of whom gave any real thought to his Jewish origins.

Born Benjamin Kubelsky in Waukegan, Illinois, he flunked out of high school. On the vaudeville circuit, he eventually introduced comedy patter to salvage his violin-playing routine. Later his wife, Mary Livingstone (née Sadie Marks), joined his stage act. By 1932 Benny had his own radio show and a repertoire company that included several cultural types, including Eddie Anderson as African-American servant Rochester and Dennis Day as an addled Irish crooner. In 1950, Benny transferred to television with a similarly formatted weekly program.

Benny made his screen bow in *The Hollywood Revue* (1929) and his finale with a cameo in *A Guide for the Married Man* (1967). In between, he starred in such items as the classic dark comedy *TO BE OR NOT TO BE* (1942). In most of his features, he played the vain, slick lothario of indeterminate religious background (e.g., *Man about Town*, 1939). No twentieth-century entertainer got more comedic mileage out of a single, expertly timed word ("w-e-e-l-l") or from an exaggerated gaiting stride.

***Benny Goodman Story, The* (1956)** Universal, color, 116 minutes. **Director/Screenplay:** Valentine Davies; **Cast:** Steve Allen (Benny Goodman), Donna Reed (Alice Hammond), Berta Gersten (Dora Goodman), Barry Truex (Benny Goodman, age fourteen), Robert F. Simon (Dave Goodman).

In 1950s Hollywood, film biographies of show-business celebrities were a cottage industry, especially when *The Glenn Miller Story* (1954) did so well at the box office. The life and times of jazz/classical clarinetist and bandleader Benny Goodman (1909–86) were rendered in a cookie-cutter fashion. Cast in the lead of the Jewish musician was non-Jewish TV talk-show host/humorist Steve Allen (with his instrument playing dubbed in).

Unlike *THE EDDIE CANTOR STORY* (1953), which greatly downplayed any suggestion of that Jewish superstar's ethnic background, *The Benny Goodman Story* defined the subject's humble beginnings on the LOWER EAST SIDE, with his parents depicted as working class Jews. One of the film's major dramatic arcs occurred when Goodman romanced a beautiful blue blood (Donna Reed). Little was made of how the society girl's parents reacted. In contrast, which was considered safer to do because Jews were still regarded as an underdog minority, Benny's mother was shown as bewildered by the love match. Eventually, for the sake of harmony (and to give the movie a happier tone), the parent came around, and the union between Jew and gentile could take place.

Berg, Gertrude (1899–1966) Her masterful creation *THE GOLDBERGS*—a popular vehicle for radio, Broadway, television, and motion pictures—created for America an image of Jewish life in the New York tenements (although Berg, from an upper-class family, didn't live there). As Molly Goldberg, she became America's favorite Jewish mama.

Born Gertrude Edelstein in the Harlem section of New York City in 1899, her father operated a CATSKILL RESORT. (She wrote the sketches performed for the guests' entertainment in the hotel's showroom.) At eighteen, she wed a Columbia University engineering student and for the next decade devoted herself to being a homemaker and mother. Her first professional work came in the late 1920s, reading a commercial in Yiddish over New York's WMCA station. During this period she wrote a series skit (*Effie and Laura*) that the CBS radio network aired in 1929 but cancelled after one episode.

Another of Berg's scripts was green-lighted by NBC radio—*The Rise of the Goldbergs*, which bowed in November 1929. By mid-1931, it was on six times a week, making it the first Jewish show on the airwaves, also credited by many as radio's first soap opera. Detailing the struggles and joys of a Bronx family, *The Goldbergs*—as it was later retitled—became a success. (Her "Yoo-hoo, I'm calling" and "Enter, whoever" became popular catchphrases.) Berg was the show's star, scripter, and owner.

In 1948, Berg brought the Goldbergs to Broadway in *Me and Molly*, and two years later, the radio series was a springboard for the movie, *MOLLY*. Meanwhile, in 1949, *The Goldbergs* premiered on television, Berg had a major success on Broadway in *A Majority of One* (1959) as a middle-aged Jewish widow who is courted by a Japanese gentleman. Later (1961–62), she starred on TV in *MRS. G. GOES TO COLLEGE* (aka: *The Gertrude Berg Show*) and returned to Broadway in *Dear Me, The Sky Is Falling* (1963), yet another tale of a warm-hearted Jewish matron.

Milton Berle—Mr. Television—performing on his variety show in the early 1950s. (JC ARCHIVES)

Berle, Milton (1908–2002) As "Mr. Television," "Uncle Miltie" became a national phenomenon in the late 1940s and early 1950s. Yet, this craftsman had already been performing (silent movies, vaudeville, Broadway, then more movies) for more than four decades. Most noted for playing the ultimate buffoon—wide grin, big cigar—who would stop at nothing (including drag routines) for laughs, he utilized his Jewish background as part of his act, employing ethnic humor and catch-phrases to punctuate old routines.

Born Milton Berlinger in New York City, he was doing Charlie Chaplin imitations at age five, and by 1914, he had bits in movies. He was on Broadway in the musical *Floradora* (1920) and then turned to vaudeville and nightclubs. He returned to movies for *New Faces of 1937* (1937) and continually worked in radio. With the debut of his TV show *The Texaco Star Theater* (aka: *The Milton Berle Show*, 1948–56), the boisterous talent hogged the camera with pratfalls, ancient jokes, and hoary burlesque routines—all heavily laden with matzo-ball humor. (One of the most noteworthy cast regulars on Berle's television outing was the ethnic Arnold Stang—he of the prominent nose, oversized eyeglasses, nasal voice, and whiney manner.)

From the 1950s onward, Berle had several TV series, usually trying to recapture his past success. Sometimes, the trouper turned in dramatic appearances on TV (1961's "Doyle Against the House" on *The Dick Powell Theater*) or in feature films (1966's *The Oscar*). Even in such straight-laced fare as the telefeatures *Seven in Darkness* (1969) or *Family Business* (1983), viewers kept looking (or hoping) for the former Uncle Miltie—the buffoon whose foolish grin revealed blacked-out teeth and who squirted unsuspecting souls with seltzer water or pitched pies in their faces. His more recent screen work included roles in *Driving Me Crazy* (1991) and the telefeature *Two Heads Are Better Than None* (2000).

***Bette* (2000–2001)** CBS-TV series, color, 30 minutes. **Cast:** Bette Midler (Bette Midler), Joanna Gleason (Connie Randolph), Kevin Dunn (Roy), James Dreyfus (Oscar), Lindsay Loban (Rose).

In *DOWN AND OUT IN BEVERLY HILLS* (1986) and several later pictures, MIDLER offered her California version of the Jewish American Princess. In the unsuccessful sitcom *Bette* she played a self-focused, affluent Beverly Hills wife/mother who is absorbed by her performing career. Her character pays as much attention to her business manager or therapist as she does to her spouse or daughter, each of whom must accept "the" Bette way.

The show did not focus on the ethnic background of Midler's character, but assumed viewers would equate the role with a mature version of her patented Jewish-American princess and also forgive the character's daffiness because it was being played by Midler. There was a revolving door of cast members, none of whom could salvage the problematic show.

biblical stories—feature films The New Testament portion of the Bible dealt with the birth of Jesus Christ and thereafter; the Old Testament focused on the genesis of humanity and the history of the Israelites during the centuries before Christ's birth. This portion of the Bible supplied the inspiration for many screen adaptations involving Jewish figures, and because such adaptations came from such a universally recognized work, it was assumed that such presentation of Jewish figures would not offend viewers, even in more politically incorrect decades.

One of the earliest was the silent short film *The Life of Moses* (1909), a part of a series. D. W. Griffith directed *Judith of Bethulia* (1914) with Blanche Sweet in the title role of the noble widow who seduced and beheaded the Assyrian general (Henry B. Walthall) whose troops were laying siege to the fortress of Bethulia in ancient Judea. Also in 1914 was the six-reel silent entry, *Joseph and His Coat of Many Colors*, based on the 1913 Broadway play and starring John Sainpolis. Much the same story was told in the four-reel *Joseph in the Land of Egypt* (1914), directed by Eugene Moore and featuring James Cruze and Marguerite Snow.

In 1923, filmmaker Cecil B. DeMille thought it would be prestigious (and a good excuse to intersperse moments of eye-catching grandeur and decadence into the story line) to make the lavish silent drama, *THE TEN COMMANDMENTS*. Its prologue dealt with the Bible's Book of Exodus and the Jews' suffering under the yoke of the ancient Egyptians. (The bulk of the narrative, however, was set in contemporary San Francisco and did not feature Jewish characters.) The movie was a big success.

Next came the spectacular *BEN-HUR* (1925), which, besides its famous chariot race, showed Jewish characters in ancient Jerusalem coping with their Roman rulers. DeMille returned to the Bible for *THE KING OF KINGS* (1927), his version of the life of Christ. At the time, Jewish groups were offended by its unfavorable presentation of Jewish moneychangers and Caiaphas, High Priest of Israel. Thus, when Nicholas Ray directed the remake (*King of Kings*, 1961), he toned down these aspects of his picture. In *Noah's Ark* (1929), which boasted talking sequences and a synchronized music score, an account of the great biblical flood and Noah and the Ark was paralleled with a modern story.

In 1949, DeMille utilized the Bible once again to create the blockbuster *SAMSON AND DELILAH*, again relying on material from the Old Testament. The movie was such a colossal hit that other filmmakers rushed to make their genre entries, bigger, more colorful, and more titillating. Filmmakers understood that, in this post–World War II era, presenting contemporary stories of Jewish life would still not appeal to some filmgoers but that setting such stories in ancient times created a distance and thus would not upset less-tolerant moviegoers.

DAVID AND BATHSHEBA (1952), about famed King David from the Bible, was followed by such entries as *The Prodigal* (1955) and *The Silver Chalice* (1956), which encompassed Israelites more as a subplot. When DeMille remade *THE TEN COMMANDMENTS* in 1956, the saga concentrated entirely on the Israelites versus their stern Egyptian masters. A sequence in the slapdash *The Story of Mankind* (1957) concerned Moses and the Ten Commandments. *Solomon and Sheba* (1958) was a silly depiction of the Jewish biblical leader, but the decade ended with the superior remake of *BEN-HUR* (1959).

By the 1960s, most biblical/costume action dramas (e.g., *Sodom and Gomorrah*, 1963) were foreign made—often lensed in Italy—and many were only later dubbed for distribution in English-speaking countries. Most of the genre entries produced by and/or in Hollywood were production-line items such as *ESTHER AND THE KING* (1960), *A Story of David* (1960), and *The Private Lives of Adam and Eve* (1961). An exception to this Hollywood economy trend was the lavish *The Bible . . . in the Beginning* (1966). It was one of the last hurrahs of big-screen biblical spectacles. Thereafter, because of still rising production costs, biblical entries became the province of television and the telefeature/miniseries format.

The rather flat comedy *Wholly Moses* (1980) presented a befuddled Dudley Moore as the ancient Israelite who believed it was his duty to lead the people out of Israel. In MEL BROOKS's satirical *History of the World—Part 1* (1981), one particularly funny segment explained how Moses ended up with "only" ten commandments. *KING DAVID* (1985) starred an incongruously cast Richard Gere as the ancient Israelite ruler who is more concerned with romance than with the field of combat. Its financial failure to find an audience ended, for the time being, Hollywood's interest in biblical topics.

The full-length, animated, musical feature *The Prince of Egypt* (1998) told in striking fashion the story of Moses who led his people to freedom from ancient Egypt. It offered the voices of Val Kilmer (Moses/God), Ralph Fiennes (Pharaoh), Michelle Pfeiffer (Tzipporah), Sandra Bullock (Miriam), and Patrick Stewart (Pharaoh Seti). The direct-to-video/DVD entry *Joseph: King of Dreams* (2000), also with songs, was adapted from the Book of Genesis. It told of Joseph who was sold into slavery but who was destined to be a king among men. Supplying voices were Ben Affleck (Joseph), Mark Hamill (Judah), Richard Herd (Jacob), Judith Light (Zuleika), James Eckhouse (Potiphar), Steven Weber (Simeon/Slave Trader), Rene Auberjonois (Butler), and Richard McGonagle (Pharaoh).

biblical stories—television One of the first nationwide programs on U.S. television to utilize the Bible as "story" material was *The Christophers* (1949–87). In its early years, this syndicated half-hour program used celebrity actors to narrate and/or star in short plays, often contemporary parables, but sometimes Bible stories from the Old and New Testaments. In 1978 through the early 1980s, a television network series, *The Greatest Heroes of the Bible*, featured condensed versions of familiar tales about David and Goliath, Abraham's Sacrifice, Moses, the story of Noah, and so on, featuring such veteran performers as Gene Barry, John Carradine, Dorothy Malone, Jeff Corey, Lew Ayres, and John Marley. Years later, Charlton Heston went on location to the Holy Land to do multipart readings from the Bible. In 1994 appeared the TV series, *Mysteries of the Bible*, including Old Testament stories narrated by Richard Kiley, Jean Simmons, and others.

In the field of full-length television filmed productions, 1960's *A Story of David* starred JEFF CHANDLER. (Made for TV, it received theatrical release instead.) It repeated in simpler terms the well-known tale of David, the king of Israel. In the 1970s, as the scope and budgets of made-for-television movies increased and the new form of TV miniseries was introduced, the number of Bible stories on television increased, using the old Cecil B. DeMille formula of combining loosely adapted biblical tales with romantic and action interludes. Often, these were filmed in Europe where production costs were less expensive. A relatively big production was the two-part television film *The Story of Jacob and Joseph* (1974), which recounted the story of the last of the patriarchs in the Book of Genesis. Directed by Michael Cacoyannis, it starred Tony Lo Bianco (Joseph) and Keith Michell (Jacob) and featured Herschel Bernardi and Colleen Dewhurst, with Alan Bates narrating.

In 1984, a new TV-made rendition of *SAMSON AND DELILAH* headlined Antony Hamilton as the strong man, Belinda Bauer as Delilah, and Victor Mature, who had starred in the 1949 Cecil B. DeMille theatrical feature, as Samson's father. (*Samson and Delilah* would receive yet another television rendition in 1996. Directed by Nicolas Roeg, Eric Thal was the muscled Jew, Elizabeth Hurley was the temptress, and Dennis Hopper was General Tariq.) The Italian-United Kingdom-produced and U.S.-television-show *Moses, the Lawgiver* (1975) was a 141-minute rendition of the life of the Israelite leader. It offered Burt Lancaster as the elder Moses and Lancaster's son William as the younger Moses.

In the 1990s, a rash of biblical retellings from the Old Testament was produced for cable television on TNT. *Abraham* (1994) had Richard Harris in the title role with Barbara Hershey as Sarah and Anthony Quayle as Terach. In *Jacob* (1994), Matthew Modine was the man who cheated his brother out of his birthright and labored for many years to win the hand of the woman (Lara Flynn Boyle) he loved. *Joseph* (1995) featured Paul Mercurio as the Israelite sold into bondage by his brothers; Ben Kingsley played Potiphar, while Alice Krige was Rachel, and Martin Landau was seen as Jacob. For *Moses* (1996), Ben Kingsley had the lead assignment of the man who could work miracles and who freed his enslaved people from the Egyptians under Ramses (Christopher Lee).

In *David* (1997), the fifth of these made-for-cable TV productions, Nathan Parker was the adult title figure; Gideon Turner played the younger Israelite shepherd. *Jeremiah* (1998) presented Patrick Dempsey in the title role, with Stuart Bunce (Baruch), Klaus Maria Brandauer (King Nebuchadnezzar), Silas Carson (Hananiah), Hicham Ibrahimi (King Josiah), and Simon Kunz as Gemariah. For *Esther* (1999), dealing with the peasant Jewess of ancient times who became queen and saved her people from the Persians, the cast included Louise Lombard (Esther), F. Murray Abraham (Mordecai), Jürgen Prochnow (Haman), and Thomas Kretschmann as King Ahasuerus.

Loosely adapted from the Book of Genesis and padded out with special effects and many subplots, *Noah's Ark* (1999) told in 178 minutes the account of the flooding of the world and how Noah (Jon Voight) rescues his family and the animals in the gigantic vessel. Others in this miniseries included Mary Steenburgen (Naamah), F. Murray Abraham (Lot), and Carol Kane (Sarah).

In 1999, a filmed version of the long-running stage musical, *Joseph and the Amazing Technicolor Dream Coat* aired, recounting in lighthearted terms the story of the Israelite sold into bondage who has a reckoning in later years with his siblings. It featured Donny Osmond (Joseph), Richard Attenborough (Jacob), and Joan Collins (Potiphar's wife).

In the Beginning (2000), made by Hallmark Productions for NBC-TV, was an elaborate, nearly four-hour production of events detailed in Genesis and Exodus, involving Abraham's (Martin Landau) devotion to God and Joseph's (Eddie Cibrian) betrayal. Others involved were Jacqueline Bisset (Sarah), Billy Campbell (Moses), Christopher Lee (Ramses I), and Alan Bates (Jethro).

Big Fix, The **(1978)** Universal, color, 108 minutes. **Director:** Jeremy Paul Kagan; **Screenplay:** Roger L. Simon; **Cast:** Richard Dreyfuss (Moses Wine), Susan Anspach (Lila), Bonnie Bedelia (Suzanne), John Lithgow (Sam Sebastian), F. Murray Abraham (Eppis).

This screen adventure derived from one (1973) of Roger L. Simon's novels about former 1960s campus radical Moses Wine, now a Los Angeles private investigator. The gimmick of having an intellectual Jewish gumshoe was ably handled by DREYFUSS, who had previously etched a Jewish young man in *THE APPRENTICESHIP OF DUDDY KRAVITZ* (1974).

As in many caper entries, it was not the plot (tracking a fugitive hippie cult leader and the smearing of a politician) that counted, but the colorful characters and settings (from Bel Air to the L.A. barrio and the Jewish section of town).

This was to be the first of a series, but the public was too indifferent to make the planned sequels feasible.

Bishop, Joey (1918–) Best known as the longest-surviving member of Frank Sinatra's Rat Pack of the 1950s and 1960s, Bishop made his mark as a deadpan stand-up comedian and later as a television sitcom and talk-show host. Unlike fellow Sinatra clan member Sammy Davis Jr. who was also Jewish (through conversion), Bishop never highlighted or deemphasized his ethnic background, but its presence was felt even when the role he played was non-specifically Jewish.

Born Joseph Abraham Gottlieb in Bronx, New York, he grew up in South Philadelphia. A high-school dropout, he formed a comedy act that played burlesque and nightclubs and at CATSKILL RESORTS. After World War II service, he worked as a lounge act in forgettable venues.

Bishop's screen debut was in the World War II actioner *The Deep Six* (1958) and then the Rat Pack's *Ocean's Eleven* (1960) and *Sergeants Three* (1963). On TV, he was a quiz-show panelist on *Keep Talking* (1956–60) and starred in the sitcom *The Joey Bishop Show* (1961–65) as well as a talk show (1967–69). Later, he was a TV panelist on *Liar's Club* (1976–78) and made occasional movies. His Broadway debut occurred in 1981 when he substituted for Mickey Rooney in *Sugar Babies.*

blacklist, the From the late 1940s to the mid-1950s, the United States was engulfed in the hysteria of the communist witch hunt spearheaded by publicity-seeking Sen. Joseph McCarthy (1908–57). He and his House Un-American Activities Committee hounded and persecuted a variety of alleged subversives, first in government employment and then especially in the entertainment industry. The careers of many performers—several of whom were Jewish—were ruined or put on temporary hold (e.g., JOHN GARFIELD, ZERO MOSTEL, EDWARD G. ROBINSON) while one committed suicide in face of the victimization (e.g., Philip Loeb of TV's *THE GOLDBERGS*). McCarthy would be censured by the Senate in 1954 for his unorthodox activities.

Two films that explored the overlap between Jewish intellectuals and socialistic/leftist causes were WOODY ALLEN's *THE FRONT* (1976) and to a lesser extent, the BARBRA STREISAND–Robert Redford romantic drama, *THE WAY WE WERE* (1973). In *Fellow Traveller* (1989), a made-for-cable political thriller movie, RON SILVER was a scriptwriter in 1950s Hollywood who fled to England when the blacklist ruined his career. *Guilty by Suspicion* (1991), starring Robert De Niro and Annette Bening, dealt with the Hollywood blacklist era, and while some of the industry characters whom it depicted were Jewish, they were incidental to the narrative's main thrust. (The British-made *One of the Hollywood Ten*, 2000, focused on the horrors of the blacklist era and its devastating effect on several Hollywood personalities of the 1940s and 1950s. Jeff Goldblum played defiant movie director Herbert Biberman while Sean Chapman portrayed Edward Dmytryk, the noted filmmaker who eventually named names in order to work again within the Hollywood establishment.)

Several actors portrayed in TV productions real-life Jewish lawyer Roy Marcus Cohn (1927–86), who served as a "henchman" assistant to Senator McCarthy in his blacklist war against alleged communists in the United States. These performers included George Wyner (*Tail Gunner Joe*, 1977), Joe Pantoliano (*Robert Kennedy & His Times* (1985—miniseries), Garrick Hagon (*Onassis: The Richest Man in the World*, 1988), and James Woods (*Citizen Cohn*, 1992).

***Blazing Saddles* (1974)** Warner Bros., color, 93 minutes. **Director:** Mel Brooks; **Screenplay:** Brooks, Norman Steinberg, Andrew Bergman, Richard Pryor, and Alan Uger; **Cast:** Cleavon Little (Bart), Harvey Korman (Hedley Lamarr), Madeline Kahn (Lili Von Shtupp), Gene Wilder (Jim), Mel Brooks (Governor Lepetomane/Indian chief).

Some regarded MEL BROOKS's *THE PRODUCERS* (1967) as his finest film, but for many *Blazing Saddles* was a close second. This wild western was full of racial outrage, bodily function jokes, and a wacky mix of Jewish and African-American humor.

A wily entrepreneur (Korman) can make a fortune when a railroad is built through a western town if he can persuade the locals to sell their land cheaply. In cahoots with the corrupt governor (Brooks), he appoints a black sheriff (Little) to scare off the bigoted citizens. They order a saloon singer (KAHN) to twist the lawman to the crooks' needs.

There are many comic villains and stooges on board: Lamarr peppers his orders with Yiddish slang, and the cross-eyed Native-American chief rattles on in Yiddish. By the finale, several minorities (Jews, African Americans, Chinese, etc.) triumph over their oppressors.

Blazing Saddles grossed more than $45 million in domestic distribution. Both Kahn and the title song were Oscar nominated.

***Boardwalk* (1979)** Atlantic Releasing, color, 98 minutes. **Director:** Stephen Verona; **Screenplay:** Verona and Leigh Chapman; **Cast:** Ruth Gordon (Becky Rosen), Lee Strasberg (David Rosen), Janet Leigh (Florence), Joe Silver (Leo), Eli Mintz (Mr. Friedman).

In New York's Coney Island, an elderly Jewish couple (Gordon and STRASBERG) cope with gangs that are vandalizing neighborhood buildings, including the synagogue. After Becky dies, David and others take a stand against the chaos around them. In an ethnic role that does not suit her, Leigh, with a very gentile persona, is the Rosens' daughter.

By this time presenting the travails of Jewish characters—young or old—had become relatively commonplace in Hollywood films.

Boosler, Elayne (1952–) A forerunner of the new class of female comedians (including Sandra Bernhard) that emerged in the late 1970s and early 1980s, Elayne evolved as a recognizable spokesperson for the foibles of the modern American woman. Although steeped in Jewish culture, much of Boosler's humor was mainstream.

Born in New York City, she studied at the Joffrey Ballet and then became a singer. Working as a waitress/hostess at Manhattan's Improv comedy club, she added emceeing, joke telling, and singing to her chores. During the mid-1970s, she had a close relationship with comedian Andy Kaufman.

Touring the comedy club and college campus circuit led Elayne to network TV talk-show exposure. This brought her guest roles on such TV sitcoms as *Night Court* in the mid-1980s and voiceovers on *Duckman* in the mid-1990s. Her observational humor about single (Jewish) women was witty and inoffensive.

***Boston Public* (2000–)** Fox-TV series, color, 60 minutes. **Cast:** Jessalyn Gilsig (Lauren Davis), Chi McBride (Principal Steven Harper), Anthony Heald (Vice-Principal Scott Guber), Nicky Katt (Harry Senate), Loretta Devine (Marla Hendricks), Fyvush Finkel (Harvey Lipschultz).

Created by TV genius David E. Kelley, *Boston Public* focused on teachers at a Beantown high school who struggle with student inertia and their own dysfunctional lives. Politically correct with its ethnic diversity among students and teachers, this TV program had a black principal (McBride).

Among the educators is crotchety, elderly history teacher Lipschultz, who has encountered anti-Semitism in the past and is forthright about voicing supposed grievances on the topic. The dedicated instructor constantly shocks colleagues and students with bizarre diatribes, full of blunt truths. Ironically, his unusual approach makes him an effective instructor.

This series' ethnic representations made *Boston Public* far removed from such earlier genre shows as the bland, nonethnic *Mr. Novak* (1963–65).

Brice, Fanny (1891–1951) BARBRA STREISAND may have "been" Fanny Brice on stage (*Funny Girl*, 1964) and on film (*FUNNY GIRL*, 1968; *FUNNY LADY*, 1975), but the real Fanny was equally unique and much beloved by her public. Brice of the big mouth and bulging eyes was no physical beauty; rather, she was a mix of chanteuse (especially singing "My Man"), broad dialectical comic who specialized in Yiddish-flavored monologues, and mimic (e.g., her Baby Snooks character). Brice's use of pathos gained audience empathy for her often heavily Jewish portraits.

Fyvush Finkel as teacher Harvey Lipschultz in *Boston Public* (2000–). (ECHO BOOK SHOP)

Born Fannie Borach to New York City saloon owners, she was a natural entertainer. By 1910, she had been in burlesque and was touring with *The College Girl*. Her success led stage entrepreneur Florenz Ziegfeld to feature her on Broadway in that year's *Ziegfeld Follies* and in several later editions. Brice was nearing forty when she made her movie debut in *My Man* (1928). (Her last film was 1946's *Ziegfeld Follies*.) But she was too mature, boisterous, and special looking to succeed in Hollywood films. On radio, she became exceedingly popular in the 1930s and 1940s. Her spouses included gambler Nicky Arnstein and Broadway composer/producer Billy Rose, the latter featuring Fanny in his shows *Sweet and Low* (1930) and *Crazy Quilt* (1931).

Throughout her career, Brice proudly claimed her Jewish heritage.

***Bridget Loves Bernie* (1972–1973)** CBS-TV series, color, 30 minutes. **Cast:** David Birney (Bernie Steinberg), Meredith Baxter (Bridget Fitzgerald Steinberg), Harold J. Stone (Sam Steinberg), Bibi Osterwald (Sophie Steinberg), Audra Lindley (Amy Fitzgerald), David Doyle (Walter Fitzgerald).

A young Jewish man falls in love with a beautiful Irish Catholic girl. This premise of *Bridget Loves Bernie* dated back at least to the 1922 Broadway hit *ABIE'S IRISH ROSE*, its screen adaptations (1928 and 1946), and the ensuing imitations, but for network television, this was a daring series twist. It featured Baxter as the offspring of a wealthy Central Park West couple who found love with the writer/taxi driver son (Birney) of delicatessen store owners on the LOWER EAST SIDE.

The series pondered: Can uptown meet downtown New York City and live happily ever after following a civil marriage repeated later with a rabbi and priest officiating? The younger generation can, but their parents have a tough time adjusting.

Bridget Loves Bernie was canceled after one season—some insisted because religious PRESSURE GROUPS were upset by the casualness of the characters' interfaith mingling. Off camera, Baxter and Birney wed in 1984 and divorced in 1989.

A similar interfaith premise provided the crux of *CHICKEN SOUP* (1989) as well as a plot device of *ANYTHING BUT LOVE* (1989–92), *Love & War* (1992–95), and *Dharma & Greg* (1997–2002).

***Brighton Beach Memoirs* (1986)** Universal, color, 108 minutes. **Director:** Gene Saks; **Screenplay:** Neil Simon; **Cast:** Blythe Danner (Kate), Bob Dishy (Jack), Brian Drillinger (Stanley), Stacey Glick (Laurie), Judith Ivey (Blanche), Jonathan Silverman (Eugene).

This first of Simon's trilogy of memory plays about his childhood in 1930s Brooklyn was a huge Broadway success in 1983 but, unfortunately, lost its sparkle in the screen transfer.

Eugene is a passionate sixteen-year-old who thinks only about baseball and naked women. His father (Dishy), the archetypical, self-sacrificing Jewish father, drags through life, supporting his wife (Danner), two sons (Silverman and Drillinger), a widowed aunt (Ivey), and her two daughters (Glick and Waltz). Unfortunately, Danner is too unethnic in her performance. What gave the plot resonance besides the comical one-liners was the viewer's knowledge that Eugene would grow up to become playwright/screenwriter Neil Simon.

Part two of the trilogy, *Biloxi Blues*, was filmed in 1988 with Matthew Broderick as Eugene, who has been drafted into World War II military service. By the time of *Neil Simon's Broadway Bound* (1992), the property was reduced to being made as a telefeature. The disappointing results featured Silverman, now anxious to start his adult life in show business. This time, Anne Bancroft was the mother and Jerry Orbach played the unfaithful father.

***Broadway Danny Rose* (1984)** Orion, b&w, 86 minutes. **Director/Screenplay:** Woody Allen; **Cast:** Woody Allen (Danny Rose), Mia Farrow (Tina Vitale), Nick Apollo Forte (Lou Canova), Howard Cosell and Milton Berle (themselves).

After several arty productions—including *Stardust Memories* (1980) and *ZELIG* (1983)—ALLEN returned to a successful format in this unpretentious entry that featured a small-time talent agent with bizarre clients. His only partially viable talent is lounge singer Lou Canova.

Faithful Danny pretends to date Canova's uncouth girlfriend (Farrow in a wig and gaudy outfits) so that her mobster boyfriend won't suspect the singer of being her lover. The irony of the tale is that once Canova's career jump-starts, he drops his faithful agent. The narrative is told by show-business types who reminisce at a Broadway delicatessen.

In his earlier screen comedies—*ANNIE HALL* (1977) and *MANHATTAN* (1979)—Allen had played an ambivalent, neurotic loser. Here, the nebbish was dumb in business but somewhat lovable for his devotion to his clients. Allen's Danny had become the exemplary Jewish (stage) mother and spiritual guide (i.e., rabbi). As such, Danny Rose was one of Allen's most Jewish, albeit not traditionally religious, onscreen alter egos.

***Brooklyn Bridge* (1991–1993)** CBS-TV series, color, 30 minutes. **Cast:** Danny Gerard (Alan Silver), Marion Ross (Sophie Berger), Louis Zorich (Jules Berger), Amy Aquino (Phyllis Berger Silver), Peter Friedman (George Silver), Mathew Louis Siegel (Nathaniel Silver), Jenny Lewis (Katie Monahan).

TV series creator Gary David Goldberg (*Family Ties*, etc.) utilized this entry to evoke his youth in 1950s Brooklyn. This rare mainstream TV program focused almost entirely on an extended Jewish family, giving them dimension as did the earlier *THE GOLDBERGS* (1949–54; 1955–56).

Postal worker George Silver is the head of his household, but his working wife (Aquino) makes some decisions. There is also her mother, Sophie Berger, who lives in the same apartment building. Sophie, the all-knowing matriarch, rules everyone. The episodes center on the clan's daily lives, with special focus on fourteen-year-old Alan. The love of the boy's life is classmate Katie Monahan.

In highlighting the interfaith romance between Jewish Alan and Irish Catholic Katie, the series recalled *BRIDGET LOVES BERNIE* (1972–73) and the film versions of *ABIE'S IRISH ROSE* (1928, 1946). An interesting aspect to this sitcom was that although Grandma Sophie accepted Alan's ethnically diverse classmate friends, it concerned her (as it does Katie's parents) that her grandson was dating outside his religion.

During the first season (1991–92), CAROL KANE, the star of *HESTER STREET* (1975), made several guest appearances as the beatnik Aunt Sylvia who dared to venture into the shocking world of bohemia by living in Greenwich Village.

Brooks, Albert (1947–) If painting one's neuroticisms on a large canvas was the key to success for WOODY ALLEN, the younger Brooks focused on a narrower tapestry. His cerebral comedy of phobias came from the same Jewish tradition as Allen's but was geared in a less-personalized reality. Not as popular or prolific as Allen, Brooks's movies have often been box-office disappointments, but they were filled with insightful comic moments and his deadpan cynical presence.

Born Albert Einstein in Los Angeles, he was the son of comedian Harry Einstein who gained fame in the 1930s on EDDIE CANTOR's radio show. A high-school classmate of RICHARD DREYFUSS and Rob Reiner, Albert developed a silly act as a clumsy ventriloquist and then as a stand-up comic. Short films he created for TV's *Saturday Night Live* in the mid-1970s led to movies both as an actor (*Taxi Driver*, 1976; *PRIVATE BENJAMIN*, 1980; *Broadcast News*, 1987) and more cogently as writer/director/actor (*Real Life*, 1979; *Modern Romance*, *Lost in America*, 1985; *Defending Your Life*, 1991).

More recently his screen projects included Debbie Reynolds as the know-it-all *Mother* (1996) and Sharon Stone as *The Muse* (1999). In the Christine Lahti-directed *My First Mister* (2001), Brooks and Leelee Sobieski were caught in a May–October romance.

Brooks, Mel (1924–) In his outrageous world, nothing was too sacred to satirize on screen, and no bodily function was too gross to be a laugh-getter. On camera, Brooks employed his extreme sense of the absurd to ridicule screen genres, always inserting Jewish humor and phrases. Whereas the movies of fellow comedian, filmmaker, and New Yorker WOODY ALLEN showcased Allen's neuroticisms, the less cerebral Brooks was often content to rely on coarse humor to prompt laughs.

Born Melvyn Kaminsky in New York City in 1924, he lost his father when he was two. The misfortune created hostility and the fear of death, which Brooks masked with comedy. After World War II military service, he became a professional drummer. While performing in the CATSKILL RESORTS, he switched to stand-up comedy. In 1949, a friend, SID CAESAR, asked Brooks to write comedy for *The Admiral Broadway Revue*, which began his long-running stint as a TV comedy writer, including *Your Show of Shows* (1950–54). In 1960, Brooks, who also acted in small roles, began to make comedy records with Carl Reiner in which Brooks played a 2,000-year-old man with a thick Yiddish accent.

He made his film debut directing *THE PRODUCERS* (1967), a ribald tale about staging a Broadway musical *(Springtime for Hitler)*. It led to such big screen genre satires as *BLAZING SADDLES* (1974), *Young Frankenstein* (1974), *High Anxiety* (1977), *Spaceballs* (1987), and *Dracula: Dead and Loving It* (1995). Besides writing, directing, and producing these comical vehicles, he frequently starred in them.

In more recent years, Brooks formed his own production company, which, among other projects, produced the drama, *The Elephant Man* (1980). He had a great success in 2001 when he adapted his *The Producers* into a Tony Award-winning Broadway musical megahit.

Burns, George (1896–1996) He was a testament to the durability of simplicity. Once having devised the "perfect" act with his wife Gracie Allen, he kept his routine fairly frozen for the next thirty-five years until she retired in 1958. Unlike most of his peers—EDDIE CANTOR, FANNY BRICE, or his pal JACK BENNY—cigar-chomping Burns worked best in tandem with another. His person of choice was Irish-American, Catholic Gracie Allen. That Gracie looked very much a colleen did much to broaden the appeal of the Jewish Burns. (Like Benny, but unlike Cantor or Brice, Burns did *not* make his stage persona ethnic specific.)

Born Nathan Birnbaum on Manhattan's LOWER EAST SIDE, his father died when he was seven and the boy—one of twelve siblings—helped to support his family. Later, he quit school to form a singing quartet, and then as a single act, he worked the vaudeville circuit. He met Gracie Allen in 1923. With he the glib question-asker and she the daffy respondent, they became a successful act.

By 1929, Burns and Allen were making movie shorts and then switched to feature films: *College Humor* (1933), *The Big*

George Burns (left) with his wife Gracie Allen, and Jack Benny (right) with his wife Mary Livingstone at New York City's Stork Club in the 1950s. (JC ARCHIVES)

Broadcast of 1936 (1935), *College Holiday* (1936). Burns and Allen were a natural for radio where they had a popular weekly program from 1932 to 1950. By the 1950s, they had transferred their show to TV. After Allen's death in 1964, Burns searched for a new teammate but finally settled on being a solo act, by which time his image had transformed into a feisty older Jewish gentleman.

Jack Benny's death in 1974 left a vacancy in the upcoming filming of Neil Simon's *The Sunshine Boys* (1975). George took over the part and won an Oscar as Best Supporting Actor. It led to such movie follow-ups as *Oh, God!* (1977), *Going in Style*, (1979), and *Oh, God! You Devil* (1984). He also wrote books, undertook nightclub tours, and recorded several comedy albums. He died a few months after his centennial birthday.

Buttons, Red (1919–) In his lengthy show-business career, compact comedian Buttons was a singing waiter and a burlesque comic, played in a hit army show, starred on TV, and earned an Academy Award (*Sayonara*, 1957). He was often cast as a wisecracker. As he aged, his performances had more of a Jewish edge.

Born Aaron Chwatt, he grew up on New York's LOWER EAST SIDE. By age twelve, he was winning amateur night contests. In 1935, he did double duty as a bellboy and a waiter at Dinty Moore's, a Bronx tavern. As legend had it, because of his red hair and his button-decorated uniform, patrons nicknamed him Red Buttons, which stuck. He worked his comedy act in the CATSKILL RESORTS and in the late 1930s tried burlesque. In 1943, he was drafted into the army and was assigned to a fund-raising effort, *Winged Victory*. When the hit play was filmed in 1944, he was part of the cast.

Demobilized in 1946, he did a movie bit *(13 Rue Madeline)* and acted on the New York stage (e.g., *Barefoot Boy with Cheek*, 1947). He gravitated to TV, eventually starring on *The Red Buttons Show* (1952–55). His sagging career revived when he played a G.I. who commits suicide with his Japanese wife in *Sayonara*. This led to more screen assignments, including 1969's *They Shoot Horses, Don't They?*

Buttons had another TV series (*The Double Life of Henry Phyfe*, 1966). Subsequently, he was in *The Poseidon Adventure* (1972), participated in television celebrity roasts, and, in 1987, had a recurring role on TV's *Knots Landing*.

More recently, the diminutive performer appeared on the sitcoms *Roseanne* (1993 and 1994) and *Cosby* (1997), the drama series *Family Law* (2000) and *Philly* (2002). Buttons was extremely touching in a four-part story arc on *ER* (1996) about an elderly Jewish man whose wife dies. He also appeared in the made-for-cable movie *Secret Time* (2002).

***Bye Bye Braverman* (1968)** Warner Bros., color, 94 minutes. **Director:** Sidney Lumet; **Screenplay:** Herbert Sargent; **Cast:** George Segal (Morroe Rieff), Jack Warden (Barnet Weiner), Jessica Walter (Inez Braverman), Phyllis Newman (Myra Mandelbaum), Godfrey Cambridge (taxicab driver), Joseph Wiseman (Felix Ottensteen), Sorrell Booke (Holly Levine), Alan King (Rabbi).

Based on Wallace Markfield's *To an Early Grave* (1964), this was a rare, early mainstream Hollywood examination of Jewish intellectuals (although this film focused more on aspects of their lonely existence).

When a writer dies, four friends (SEGAL, Warden, Booke, and WISEMAN) set out on an odyssey to Brooklyn for the funeral. The most ambivalent of the quartet of New Yorkers is self-indulgent Morroe Rieff, who is shocked into introspection by his friend's passing but is equally dismayed when the pal's widow (Walter) tries to seduce him. En route, the group—piled into a tiny Volkswagen—have a road accident with an African-American cabbie (Cambridge) who turns out to be a Yiddish-speaking Jew. They reach the cemetery just as their friend is buried and then return home sadder but no wiser.

Segal, who was Hollywood's preeminent purveyor of the assimilated American Jew, also starred that same year in the thriller *NO WAY TO TREAT A LADY*. Wiseman, best known as the villain of *Dr. No* (1963), played the prideful communist and the superintellectual. Stand-up comic King was the rabbi delivering a nonsensical eulogy; the very non-ethnic Walter was miscast as the Jewess.

C

***Cabaret* (1972)** Allied Artists, color, 124 minutes. **Director:** Bob Fosse; **Screenplay:** Jay Presson Allen; **Cast:** Liza Minnelli (Sally Bowles), Michael York (Brian Roberts), Helmut Griem (Maximilian von Heune), Joel Grey (Master of Ceremonies), Fritz Wepper (Fritz Wendel), Marisa Berenson (Natalia Landauer).

This galvanizing screen musical derived from 1930s short stories by Christopher Isherwood, a 1951 play by John Van Druten—which became a 1955 British-filmed movie—and the 1966 Broadway musical with songs by John Kander and Fred Ebb.

Set in decadent 1930s Berlin as Germany succumbs to Nazism, the focus is on American Sally Bowles, a singer at the seedy Kit-Kat Club emceed by an androgynous host (Grey). Sally falls in love with a British writer (York) who is simultaneously having an affair with a German playboy (Griem). In a subordinate plot, a department-store heiress (Berenson), who has kept her Jewish roots secret, loves a gigolo (Wepper), who also is hiding his Jewish identity.

Although the HOLOCAUST was no longer fresh screen material, the film's depictions of anti-Semitism, in juxtaposition to the story's musical numbers and romantic sequences, proved effective. Because the horror of oppression was part of a vibrant musical, it was seen by a great many viewers who might have avoided the underlying subject matter had it not been sugarcoated.

The movie grossed almost $43 million in domestic distribution and won eight Academy Awards.

Caesar, Sid (1922–) A sharp satirist who was a master at mimicking different languages, including Yiddish (and he also was expert at verbally creating odd sound effects), and was a pioneering comic genius of U.S. television, Caesar reached his prime in the early 1950s. Later in that decade, he began a creative dry period (1958–78) because of, as he revealed in his autobiography *Where Have I Been?* (1982), substance abuse.

He was born Isaac Sidney Caesar in Yonkers, New York, in 1922. At his dad's luncheonette, the boy developed a knack for mimicking the multiethnic clientele. Later, he became an expert saxophonist, playing in dance bands, and he also became a stand-up comic in the CATSKILL RESORTS. During World War II, he served in the U.S. Coast Guard and toured in a military revue, *Tars and Spars*, which was made into a 1946 movie. Later, he appeared in the Broadway revue, *Make Mine Manhattan* (1948).

Caesar starred on TV's *Your Show of Shows* (1950–54), a weekly comedy revue in which he teamed with Imogene Coca. This led to *Caesar's Hour* (1954–57) and *Sid Caesar Invites You* (1958). During his decades of substance abuse, he still played nightclubs, had another TV series (*The Sid Caesar Show*, 1963–64), starred in a Broadway musical (*Little Me*, 1962), and occasionally acted in movies.

Once getting his life back under control, he continued to perform. His stage production, *A Touch of Burlesque* (1981), was taped for cable TV in 1982. He was in both *Grease* movies (1978 and 1982), appeared with Chevy Chase in *Vegas Vacation* (1997), appeared in an episode of the TV sitcom, *MAD ABOUT YOU* (1992–99) and in such later features as *The Wonderful Ice Cream Suit* (1998). He was among the comedians interviewed on camera in the documentary *Let Me In, I Hear Laughter* (1999). *Laughter on the 23rd Floor* (2001—made-for-cable feature) was Neil Simon's revamped Broadway play (1994) in which Nathan Lane played a variation of Sid Caesar during his 1950s peak as TV's king of comedy.

***Camp Stories* (1997)** Artistic License, color, 99 minutes. **Director/Screenplay:** Herbert Beigel; **Cast:** Elliott Gould (older David Katz), Jerry Stiller (Schlomo Mendelsohn), Paul Sand (Moishe Rubinowitz), Zachary Taylor (young David Katz), Ted Marcoux (Chaim), Jason Biggs (Abraham "Abby" Fishcoff).

This small-budgeted feature was set almost entirely in 1958 at an Orthodox Jewish summer camp in Pennsylvania. (This was a big leap away from the overblown and homogenized Hollywood version of a summer retreat for Jewish youngsters depicted in 1958's *MARJORIE MORNINGSTAR*.)

Camp Stories focused on an Ohio youngster (Taylor) at the camp on scholarship and how he gained knowledge of his Jewish heritage and of self during a fateful summer. There was also infighting between counselors (Sand and Marcoux) who were anxious to be the heir apparent to the aged camp owner (Stiller). In addition, the camp youngsters explored relationships with females in a nearby town.

Beyond its intriguing cast, which included Jason Biggs (the young star of 1999's *American Pie*), the movie was autobiographical and reflected a way of life unfamiliar to most film viewers, even those Jewish.

Cantor, Eddie (1892–1964) Like his professional rival AL JOLSON, the diminutive Cantor was an enduring master of many mediums who often performed in blackface. His hyperactive, prancing persona—emphasized by hugely expressive "Banjo Eyes" (his nickname) and clapping/gyrating hands—was often effete, wisecracking, and full of Yiddish shtick. From playing brash young underdogs to avuncular older men, he was the smart-mouthed Manhattanite who verbally outmaneuvered opponents while winning girls with snappy songs ("If You Knew Susie").

Born Isidore Itzkowitz of Russian immigrants on Manhattan's LOWER EAST SIDE, Cantor began in burlesque, graduated to vaudeville, and moved on to Broadway *(Ziegfeld Follies of 1917)*. His feature film debut was the silent *Kid Boots* (1926). A major star of 1930s screen musicals (*WHOOPEE!*, 1930; *Roman Scandals*, 1933), his greatest fame was on radio (1931–49). On TV, he headlined *The Eddie Cantor Show* (1950–54).

As a blend of the old and the new world, bouncy Cantor had great appeal to Jewish audiences, an inspiration of quasi-assimilation whose occasional blackface routine didn't hide his ethnic roots. For non-Jewish fans, his appeal was as a boastful jokester, a shy, naïve soul who needed *everyone's* approval.

Although Keefe Brasselle played Banjo Eyes in *THE EDDIE CANTOR STORY* (1953), the vocals were provided by the real Cantor. Others who played the star on screen included James Quinn (*Pretty Ladies*, 1925), Buddy Doyle (*The Great Ziegfeld*, 1936), Franky Farr (*It Happened in Hollywood*, 1937—as a Cantor double), and Richard Shea (*Ziegfeld: The Man and His Women*, 1978—TV movie).

***Cast a Giant Shadow* (1966)** United Artists, color, 144 minutes. **Director/Screenplay:** Ted Berkman; **Cast:** Kirk Douglas (Colonel David "Mickey" Marcus), Senta Berger (Magda Simon), Angie Dickinson (Emma Marcus), Luther Adler (Jacob Zion), Haym (Chaim) Topol (Abou Ibn Kader).

This big-budgeted action picture depicted a real-life American Jew, West Point graduate, lawyer, and World War II hero David "Mickey" Marcus. In 1947, as the British prepare to withdraw from Palestine, he is asked by an Israeli representative to reorganize their army as that nation fights for its independence. At first, Marcus feels apart from the Israelis' struggle, but the challenge of the assignment, a love of war, and a reconnection with his Jewish roots draws him into the task.

If subtlety was missing in this production, DOUGLAS brought intensity to his portrait. The ironic ending finds both the United States recognizing Israel and a temporary cease-fire between Jews and Arabs. As Marcus is about to return to the United States, he is ordered to Jerusalem, where an Israeli sentry challenges him in Hebrew. Not knowing the language, Marcus continues walking and is shot dead.

Despite distracting cameos by Frank Sinatra, John Wayne, and Yul Brynner, this production was a far sturdier study of war-torn Palestine in the late 1940s than *Judith* (1966) starring Sophia Loren. But *Cast a Giant Shadow* lacked the emotional verve of *EXODUS* (1960), which also treated of this same time period.

Catskill resorts The Catskill Mountains (known as the Catskills) are a moderately low range of mountains located in southeast New York, west of the Hudson River. If traffic is not congested, it is less than a two-hour drive from Manhattan. Starting in the late eighteenth century, the rocky area began to sprout small resorts. By the early twentieth century, immigrant Jews from Eastern Europe, who had made their way to the area intending to become farmers, had discovered that the soil wouldn't support their needs. To bolster their income, they took in boarders; thus began the era of the Jewish resorts. The region soon became a vacation haven for Jewish residents of the overcrowded buildings of New York City's LOWER EAST SIDE. As the popularity of the Catskills grew, the number of resorts reached into the hundreds, ranging from dilapidated motor-court complexes to fancy large hotels (e.g., Grossinger's, the Concord, Brown's, the Nevele, Kutsher's) that vied with one another for guests.

One of the chief attractions of these resorts—beyond the plentiful kosher food, clean rooms, mountain air—was the free entertainment each institution provided its patrons. In the beginning, these clubs frequently used their waiters and other help to stage the shows; soon fledgling entertainers took to performing engagements in the Catskills as a training ground. Often, such talent would be booked to appear at several different resorts during a single weekend, or even on the same night (which demanded an organized schedule of staggered performances). This traipsing from resort to resort to perform led to the phrase *borscht-belt circuit* in reference to the favored beet soup that so many eastern European Jews demanded as a meal course.

Especially from the late 1920s to the 1950s, these resorts gave a variety of future show-business personalities their professional start, including DANNY KAYE, SID CAESAR, JACKIE MASON, Sam Levenson, MEL BROOKS, Jan Murray, Buddy Hackett, and JOAN RIVERS.

By the 1960s, the Catskill resorts were in decline. Most people had televisions for entertainment and air conditioners to make summers at home more bearable. Moreover, the flow of Jewish immigrants to the United States—prime candidates to visit the Catskills once they had earned some money—had greatly diminished. The older generations who had made the area a vacation habit were dying off. The new generation no longer wanted to gorge on fattening kosher meals, and the more assimilated American Jews fancied cruises or the Bahamas as a vacation option or relied on Manhattan's many singles bars to find dates. By the 1980s, the rising price of real estate forced many of these Catskill resorts to be razed for residential development. The era had ended.

Only a few Hollywood-made films drew upon the Jewish Catskill resorts for subject matter: *DIRTY DANCING* and *SWEET LORRAINE* were both 1987 releases, and *A Walk on the Moon* was released in 1999. The latter, set in a bungalow colony in 1969, starred Diane Lane as a young wife/mother who enters into a summer fling with a free-spirited hippie (Viggo Mortensen). Her puzzled husband (Liev Schreiber), a Brooklyn TV repair man, wonders how to salvage the relationship.

Chandler, Jeff (1918–1961) One of the underappreciated virile leading men of 1950s Hollywood, the rugged six-feet, four-inch Chandler with the chiseled features, resonant voice, and prematurely gray curly hair played a variety of screen types during his prolific years under studio contract.

Born Ira Grossel in Brooklyn, New York, the Jewish talent became active as a radio performer after serving in World War II. In one of his early action films, the western *Broken Arrow* (1950), he was nominated for an Academy Award for playing the Native American chief Cochise; he repeated the offbeat casting as the famed warrior in *The Battle at Apache Pass* (1952) and *Taza, Son of Cochise* (1954).

Only once early and once late in his prolific screen career did he play overtly Jewish characters on screen, such was the rarity of projects about these figures at the time. In the 1949 *SWORD IN THE DESERT* he was the rebel leader Kurta, fighting for the formation of Israel. At what proved to be near the end of his life—he died from apparent malpractice during surgery for a slipped disk—he starred in *A Story of David* (1960), a rather tedious British-made religious epic.

***Chicken Soup* (1989)** ABC-TV series, color, 30 minutes. **Cast:** Jackie Mason (Jackie Fisher), Lynn Redgrave (Maddie Peerce), Rita Karin (Bea Fisher), Katherine Erbe (Patricia Peerce), Johnny Pinto (Donnie Peerce).

There was much excitement when it was announced that former rabbi MASON would star in a sitcom in which his character romances a non-Jewish woman. The expectations for this sitcom were far more exciting than the actual show.

In this illustration of the attraction of opposites, Jackie Fisher retires from business to do volunteer duty at the Henry Street Settlement House. Living next door is Maddie Peerce, a svelte Irish Catholic divorcee who has three young children. She is the supervisor at the inner-city center where Jackie now works. While this contrasting couple fall in love, Jackie's mother constantly complains of the interfaith situation, as does Maggie's bigoted brother. The only relief from the bickering occurs when Fisher goes upstairs to the roof to complain aloud to God about his overly complex life.

Less than two months after it debuted, *Chicken Soup* was dropped from the network line-up. Among the protesters of this program was the Jewish Defense League, upset by the handling of the mixed-religion romance.

***Children of the Ghetto* (1915)** Box Office Attraction/Fox, b&w, 5 reels. **Director:** Frank Powell; **Screenplay:** Edward José; **Cast:** Wilton Lackaye (Reb Shemuel), Ruby Hoffman (Hannah), Ethel Kaufman (Esther Ansell), Frank Andrews (Moses Ansell), Luis Alberni (Pincus, the poet).

Based on Israel Zangwill's novel (1892) and play (1899) *The Children of the Ghetto: A Study of a Peculiar People*, this production featured Lackaye, who had starred in the stage edition.

The silent feature relates the rabbi's problems with his wild son, who dies after a barroom brawl, and the learned man's daughter Hannah. Because she weds a gentile in a civil ceremony, her traditionalist father disowns her. Years later, the now elderly rabbi, who has lost his wife, sits alone at the Passover seder. Suddenly, his widowed daughter and her two children arrive to share in the festivities.

At the time this film was made, its story was a familiar one to moviegoers, especially in urban centers. Its message that devoutness has its own rewards was reassuring to poor Jewish immigrants who struggled to overcome their ghetto existences in America.

children's series—television Frequently, it was the character of the host, star, or featured performer—who happened to be Jewish—that gave an ethnic tone to several television programs. One of the first Jewish hosts of a children-oriented national TV show was Pinky Lee (né Pincus Leff), a former burlesque comic who had been around in various forms of show business for years. His TV outing, *The Pinky Lee Show*, ran for several months in 1950; another variation of his show began on television in early 1954 and lasted until mid-1956.

Another of the medium's early and very popular youth-oriented shows was *Captain Midnight* (1954–56). This low-budget adventure of the crime-fighting hero featured Jewish actor Sid Melton as Ikky Mudd, Midnight's fumbling assistant. Also in the mid-1950s came the advent of that unique TV personality, Soupy Sales (né Milton Supman), who had local shows in Detroit, Los Angeles, and later New York, intermittently turning to network programs over the years. His various series offered a mix of jokes, songs, and sketches with a variety of puppets (e.g., White Fang, Black Tooth) and his trademark pie-in-the-face routine.

It was hard to categorize the talents/appeal of actor Paul Reubens, but in the persona of Pee-wee Herman, his *Pee-wee's Playhouse* (1986–91) won plaudits for its innovative, hip approach to daytime fare for young and old. *The Amazing Live Sea Monkeys* (1992–93) was hosted by Jewish comedian/actor HOWIE MANDEL who created this Saturday-morning show based on three fish-faced characters named Aquarius, Bill, and Dave. (Earlier he had created, provided voices, and appeared as himself on *Bobby's World*, a Saturday-morning cartoon that premiered in 1990.)

***Chosen, The* (1981)** Contemporary, color, 108 minutes. **Director:** Jeremy Paul Kagan; **Screenplay:** Edwin Gordon; **Cast:** Maximilian Schell (David Malter), Rod Steiger (Reb Saunders), Robby Benson (Danny Saunders), Barry Miller (Reuven Malter), Hildy Brooks (Mrs. Saunders).

Based on Chaim Potok's 1967 novel, this film was a rare American film excursion into the total ambiance of Judaism, where it was not Jews versus gentiles but rather factions within Judaism opposing each other on major issues of concern—Zionism, assimilation, the importance of religious tradition, the role of personal independence in a deeply traditional culture, and crucial family ties. It was a movie full of theological debate and an extensive depiction of Hasidic life.

In 1940s Brooklyn, Danny Saunders, the son of a Hasidic rabbi (STEIGER) injures Reuven Malter (Miller), the offspring of a Talmudic scholar (Schell), during a baseball game. The two become friends, exposing one another to their different ways and their parents' plans for each of their divergent lives. What stalls their growing friendship are the fathers, who have diametrically opposed views on Zionism and the legitimacy of the formation of the state of Israel. Once that event becomes a reality, the two young men discover they have each changed: Danny plans now to study psychology at Columbia University while Reuven intends to enter the rabbinate.

With Steiger's showy performance as the film's strength, *The Chosen* was an insightful film. It had a limited secular appeal, as did the Canadian-made *The Quarrel* (1991), but was far sturdier than SIDNEY LUMET'S *A STRANGER AMONG US* (1992), featuring a very obviously gentile Melanie Griffith.

***Civilization's Child* (1916)** Triangle, b&w, 5 reels. **Director:** Charles Giblyn; **Screenplay:** C. Gardner Sullivan; **Cast:** William H. Thompson (Boss Jim McManus), Anna Lehr (Berna), Jack Standing (Nicolay Turgenev), Dorothy Dalton (Ellen McManus), Clyde Benson (Jacob Weil).

This standard melodrama from Thomas Ince's Triangle Film Corp. was set in Russia and, later, the slums of New York City. It detailed the tumultuous life of Berna, who flees a pogrom and comes to the United States, where she is exploited in a sweatshop, made pregnant by her boss (Thompson), and later, destitute, becomes a prostitute. Even when she finds happiness with a musician (Standing), that is spoiled by her enemy's daughter (Dalton) who steals him away. The distraught Berna eventually shoots the villainous Boss McManus, who caused her so much grief.

Catering to an audience of urban-based immigrants in the United States who could relate to the heroine's sufferings, such dramas as these were a staple of Jewish-themed movies in the silent era.

***Clancy's Kosher Wedding* (1927)** Film Booking Offices of America, b&w, 5,700′. **Director:** Arvid E. Gilstrom; **Screenplay:** J. G. Hawks; **Cast:** George Sidney (Hyman Cohen), Will Armstrong (Timothy Clancy), Ann Brody (Mamma Cohen), Mary Gordon (Molly Clancy), Sharyn Lynn (Leah Cohen), Rex Lease (Tom Clancy), Ed Brady (Izzy Murphy).

This was another of the many Hollywood imitations inspired by the Broadway success of *ABIE'S IRISH ROSE* (1922), which itself did not come to the screen until 1928. Cashing in on Universal Pictures' comedy-series franchise of *THE COHENS AND KELLYS* (1926), the FBO studio utilized *The Cohens and Kellys* lead actor, SIDNEY, to play a character here also named Cohen.

Hyman Cohen and Timothy Clancy are rival clothing-store owners who are unhappy that their offspring (respectively, Lynn and Lease) are in love. Because this is a silent photoplay, the title cards and broad physical humor provide the usual clichés of ethnic humor. For the record, the Izzy Murphy character is a Jewish prizefighter.

classroom dramas—feature films Although some of the GHETTO DRAMAS of the silent movies and several urban dramas of the 1930s featured (brief) classroom sequences as the multicultural mix of students progressed through the grades, it was not until *GENTLEMAN'S AGREEMENT* (1947) that the subject of anti-Semitism in the United States came to the fore in Hollywood pictures. Thereafter, when a student in a movie story line was given a very ethnic-sounding name or look, it seldom was done by accident but to serve a story-line purpose. For example, in *GOOD MORNING, MISS DOVE* (1955), a Jewish boy who faced taunts from bigoted classmates as a youngster grew into a successful adulthood. *Getting Straight* (1970), a college-campus-unrest drama, had plain-looking Judy Kramer (played by the frequenter of such roles, Jeannie Berlin). By the time of *Fame* (1980), a greater delineation of ethnic types existed among students in films. As Hollywood became more multiethnic by the end of the twentieth century, such films as *Clueless* (1995) and *American Pie* (1999) would nonchalantly blend ethnic and racial groups without any apparent focus on differences based on their heritage.

classroom series—television In typical media fashion, most pre-late 1970s television school series did not focus on differences between ethnic types; when they did, it was usually in a very lighthearted comic fashion. For example, in *WELCOME BACK, KOTTER* (1975–79), not only was the title figure (a teacher) Jewish, but so also was his on-camera wife and also Juan Epstein, the Puerto Rican Jew. On the comedic *The Facts of Life* (1979–88), the character Natalie Green, who dreamed of becoming a journalist, was overtly Jewish, but it was her weight and her ambitions that were generally her issues. In the dramatic series *The White Shadow* (1978–81), set at Carver High in Los Angeles, among the student basketball players was Abner Goldstein. In *FAME* (1982–87), a drama/musical, a focal character from 1982 to 1985 was Doris Schwartz and her problems as she struggled with her show-business career. On *Making the Grade* (1982), set at a St. Louis high school, one of the characters was David Wasserman, a lady-chasing English teacher. The syndicated program *Buchanan High School* (1985–86) had Jewish representation among the students who were involved in putting out the school newspaper, *The Bugle*. Several of the instructors and pupils of *The Bronx Zoo* (1987–88), a drama set at the multicultural, troubled Benjamin Harrison High School, were Jewish and/or suggested to be.

Later, another "serious" entry—*Beverly Hills 90210* (1990–2000), set in high-toned Los Angeles—centered its early seasons on classroom life of such Jewish characters as Andrea Zuckerman and David Silver, each of whom had a variety of problems at home. (A few episodes featured Andrea encountering bigotry on campus and her decisive reaction to such perceived anti-Semitism. Then, when she wed a Hispanic, mixed-marriage problems arose.) The short-lasting *Class of '96* (1993) was set at a fictional Ivy League school in the northeast; one of its freshmen was Jessica Cohen, an assimilated Jewish student who discovered her roots when she has to confront bigotry on the Havenhurt campus. On *Freaks and Geeks* (1999–2000) set in the 1980s, the school roster includes such ethnic students as Neil Schweiber and Millie Kentner.

On *Boston Public* (2000–), the urban high-school setting was backdrop to a bizarre, aged, Jewish social-studies instructor (played by Fyvush Finkel), who, among many other self-created problems, believed that his students treated him differently because he was Jewish.

Close to Eden See *STRANGER AMONG US, A.*

Cobb, Lee J. (1911–1976) This burly performer, long-recognized as a great actor, was a stalwart of film, TV, and stage. He was the original Willie Lohman in the Broadway production of *Death of a Salesman* (1949).

He was born Leo Jacoby in New York City. When a wrist injury precluded a career as a concert violinist, he focused on acting. After studying at the Pasadena Playhouse in California, he made his Broadway debut in *Crime and Punishment* (1935). As a member of the renowned Group Theater, he appeared in *Golden Boy* (1937) and *The Gentle People* (1939). After World War II he returned to the industry, playing a Siamese in *Anna and the King of Siam* (1946) and a Chinese warlord in *The Left Hand of God* (1955).

After stressfully testifying in the mid-1950s to the House Un-American Activities Committee regarding his brief, earlier communist affiliation, he suffered a near-fatal heart attack. Frequently cast against type as an Italian gangster, he sometimes played a Jew on screen: *Exodus* (1960—as Paul Newman's father), *Come Blow Your Horn* (1963—as Frank Sinatra's dad), *Dr. Max* (1974—as the crotchety, benevolent doctor in a TV movie very similar to *THE LAST ANGRY MAN*).

***Cohens and Kellys, The* (1926)** Universal, b&w, 7,774′. **Director:** Harry Pollard; **Screenplay:** Alfred A. Cohn; **Cast:** Charlie Murray (Patrick Kelly), George Sidney (Jacob Cohen), Vera Gordon (Mrs. Cohen), Kate Price (Mrs. Kelly), Olive Hasbrouch (Nannie Cohen), Jason Robards (Tim Kelly), Nat Carr (Milton Katz), Mickey Bennett (Milton J. Katz).

Loosely based on the play *Two Blocks Away* (1921), this property aired a by-then hackneyed premise: the fierce but essentially friendly conflict between exaggerated Jewish and Irish New Yorkers. Although suspicious of each other, the families develop a tight bond when Cohen's daughter weds Kelly's offspring. Although the Broadway source of *The Cohens and Kellys* came before *ABIE'S IRISH ROSE* (1922), its screen adaptation was inspired by *Abie* and the profusion of *Abie* rip-offs being churned out by Broadway and Hollywood, including the *POTASH AND PERLMUTTER* series and the later *The Shamrock and the Rose* (1927).

George Sidney and Charlie Murray in *The Cohens and Kellys* (1926). (JC ARCHIVES)

In New York City, Jewish dry-goods-store owner Jacob Cohen is always in contention with Irish policeman Patrick Kelly over one thing or another. When Cohen's daughter Nannie weds Kelly's son Tim, the rivalry gets out of hand, especially after Cohen inherits a fortune and Nannie becomes pregnant. Everything ends in a (temporary) truce when Cohen and Kelly go into business partnership.

The Cohens and Kellys was sufficiently popular to become a film series, set in different locales, lasting for several years and carrying over into the talkie era: *in Paris* (1928), *in Atlantic City* (1929), *in Scotland* (1930), *in Africa* (1931), *in Hollywood* (1932), and *in Trouble* (1933). Although SIDNEY remained Mr. Cohen for all the installments, the role of Patrick Kelly was also played by J. Farrell MacDonald, Mack Swain, and Charles Murray. GORDON was replaced as Mrs. Cohen in one entry by Emma Dunn, as was Price as Mrs. Kelly in one episode by Esther Howard.

This property was one of the few and most commercially rewarding Jewish series ever made by Hollywood. A recurring theme of the entries was that Cohen, the little guy (and indeed Kelly physically towered over him) and the outsider, needed to be protected by the more assimilated Kelly. The one arena where Cohen could best his "foe" Kelly was in the area of business (which is a watered-down version of the old stereotype of the shrewd Jewish merchant).

Sidney had long played Jewish types on screen, going back to such pictures as *Busy Izzy* (1915).

***Coke Time with Eddie Fisher* (1953–1957)** NBC-TV, b&w, 15 minutes. **Cast:** Eddie Fisher (himself), Don Ameche (host: 1953), Freddy Robbins (announcer; host: 1954–57), Axel Stordahl and His Orchestra (themselves), the Echoes (themselves: 1956–57).

In 1949, entertainment star EDDIE CANTOR supposedly discovered twenty-one-year-old Fisher at Grossinger's Resort in the CATSKILLS; thereafter, Fisher was featured on Cantor's weekly radio show. Later, with such recording hits as "Any Time," Fisher became a nationwide favorite of teenagers. In 1952 this Jewish talent from South Philadelphia was drafted into the army but continued to appear on TV. He earned his own twice-weekly TV outing with the *Coke Time* show. He was at the peak of his popularity when he wed non-Jewish movie actress Debbie Reynolds in 1955 at Grossinger's.

As star of this musical interlude TV show, the handsome Fisher was to his young audience what Frank Sinatra had been to bobbysoxers in the 1940s. Although there were several Jewish comedians starring in their own shows on TV in the early 1950s, Fisher was one of the few Jewish singers to earn such a show business position.

Later, he was host of *The Eddie Fisher Show* (1957–59), by which time he had left Reynolds and married (May 1959) Elizabeth Taylor in a temple service in Las Vegas. Carrie, the daughter of Fisher and Reynolds, became an actress and writer.

combat dramas—feature films At the time of World War I, the silent films being made in the United States with war themes did not focus on the real-life mix of multicultural regiments of U.S. soldiers that included Jews. Even in the mid to late 1920s, with the renewed cycle of Hollywood films being made about World War I combat (from *The Big Parade*, 1925, to *Wings*, 1928), the servicemen depicted—especially in lead roles and featured parts—were homogenized "Americans" or, if not pure WASP, then a close proximity to such. A rare exception to this rule was *Private Izzy Murphy* (1926) starring stage/vaudeville entertainer George Jessel. In that silent film, he played a Russian Jew who came to America. Later, he enlisted in an all-Irish regiment of the U.S. Army and once on the battlefields of France inspired his comrades to victory.

The irony (or the reality?) of the plot situation within *Private Izzy Murphy* occurred when he returned as a hero to the United States: When his sweetheart's father learned he was Jewish, the man refused to permit his daughter to wed Izzy. It remained for his regimental buddies to save the day. (Jessel made a follow-up, *Sailor Izzy Murphy*, 1927, but it dealt with trouble aboard a wealthy man's yacht.) Later, in *The Fighting Sixty-Ninth* (1940), another World War I combat drama, actor Sammy Cohen played a soldier called Mike Murphy, whose surname was actually Moskowitz.

If Hollywood had intentionally avoided using explicit Jewish characters in most of their 1930s releases, they had a slight change of heart in the next decade when making combat dramas dealing with World War II. With the government urging Hollywood to emphasize democracy in their product, it became standard fare on screen to have a mixture of stereotypes representing a cross section of American types: the Midwestern farm boy, the city slicker, the Brooklynite, the Irishman, and so on. (Such groupings, however, did *not* generally include African Americans, Native Americans, or Asian Americans.) Among these "representative" celluloid soldiers would frequently be a character with a Jewish surname, which would typically be the only Semitic element about the person (e.g., Robert Rose as Sammy Klein in 1943's *Guadalcanal Diary*, Mary Treen's Lt. Sadie Schwartz in 1943's *So Proudly We Hail*, Corp. Jake Feingold as played by Thomas Mitchell in 1943's *Bataan*, George Tobias's Corporal Weinberg in *Air Force* (1943), Harry Cline's Corporal Kramer in 1945's *A Walk in the Sun*, or William Prince's Lieutenant Jacobs in 1945's *Objective, Burma!*).

An exception in the World War II-themed movies of the 1940s were the soldiers played by experienced Jewish actor SAM LEVENE (né Levine): the civilian Jewish character who was murdered within the plot of 1947's *CROSSFIRE*, Lt. Wayne Greenbaum in *The Purple Heart* (1944), and so on.

Within the well-made *PRIDE OF THE MARINES* (1945), the hero (JOHN GARFIELD) was blinded and shipped back to the United States to recuperate. Discouraged about his disability, he was given a pep talk by his serviceman buddy Lee Diamond (played by Dane Clark), who acknowledged his Jewish background by talking of the discrimination he had experienced. Another World War II-set drama, *The Caine Mutiny* (1954), based on Herman Wouk's Pulitzer Prize-winning novel (1951) and his play (1954), had defense attorney Lt. Barney Greenwald (José Ferrer) reference his Jewishness and sharpness as a lawyer. On the other hand, a good deal of the original thematic material from the novel (in which it was made clear that his religion made him an outsider even among his fellow military men) was deliberately missing in the film.

In the 1958-released World War II-themed drama *THE YOUNG LIONS* the picked-upon soldier Noah Ackerman was performed by non-Jewish Montgomery Clift. He essayed a man who experienced anti-Semitism not only from his girlfriend's father but also from his own Army "buddies." Much later in time, in Steven Spielberg's *Saving Private Ryan* (1998), also set in World War II, Adam Goldberg was cast as Private Mellish, but nothing in particular was made of his background.

The few Korean War dramas made in the 1950s did not focus on Jewish soldiers in the fighting forces, relegating them to the background of the story line, as in *Sabre Jet* (1953). When it came time for Vietnam War-themed entries to be made in the 1970s and thereafter, Jewish characters still remained submerged and were not focal characters, as in 2002's *We Were Soldiers.* (This was also almost as true on the few TV series devoted to the Vietnam War. On *Tour of Duty*, 1987–90, there was Lt. Myron Goldman, the platoon's uptight leader always in conflict with the more seasoned Sgt. Zeke Anderson, the show's lead character. At least in the program's second season, Goldman had a relationship with one of the women characters added to the roster—attractive Alex Devlin, a wire service reporter.)

On the other hand, in the peacetime army, one Jewish recruit won star treatment. In the comedy *PRIVATE BENJAMIN* (1980), Goldie Hawn headlined as a Jewish-American Princess who enlisted in the peacetime army only to be dismayed that her notion of military life and the service differed widely.

An offshoot of the combat dramas featuring U.S. military in various wars during the twentieth century was those dealing with the founding of Israel. SWORD IN THE DESERT (1949) and EXODUS (1960) both explored Israeli conflicts with the British and the Arabs to found the state of Israel. In *CAST A GIANT SHADOW* (1965) a much-decorated, Jewish U.S. officer of World War II was persuaded to help the Israelis fine-tune the organization of their military in their fight for liberty.

comedians It was Jewish lore that for centuries Jews around the world suffered so many adversities that to survive they learned to laugh at situations and especially at themselves. Whether true or not, a great many twentieth-century American humorists were Jewish. Many of them in the early 1900s, such as GEORGE BURNS and the MARX BROTHERS, rose out of the LOWER EAST SIDE ghetto of New York City to fame and fortune. A good many (e.g., MILTON BERLE, EDDIE CANTOR, George Jessel, the RITZ BROTHERS) were on the vaudeville circuit as youngsters. Others, such as JOEY BISHOP and JERRY LEWIS, started at CATSKILL RESORTS in upstate New York. Then there was MOLLY PICON who gained comedic experience in YIDDISH THEATER. For some—Pinky Lee, RED BUTTONS, and PHIL SILVERS among others—playing burlesque houses provided their special training ground. Individuals such as RODNEY DANGERFIELD and DON RICKLES made the rounds of nightclubs to gain experience. In total contrast, JACKIE MASON, an ordained rabbi and a fledgling comedian, tried out jokes on his synagogue congregations.

When commercial television blossomed in the United States in late 1948, the medium—as had radio—hired established performers to headline shows, assuming correctly that they would draw in audiences. The early 1950s saw MOREY AMSTERDAM, Berle, Burns (with Gracie Allen), JACK BENNY, Cantor, Jack Carter, and Sam Levenson (a former teacher) among the primary laugh-getters on television. One of their number, SID CAESAR, was primarily a TV-created personality. His sidekicks and writing staffs on *Your Show of Shows* (1950–54) and his later series were a breeding ground for developing comedy talent both in front of and behind the camera (e.g., WOODY ALLEN, MEL BROOKS, Neil Simon, and CARL REINER).

As television developed its own coterie of talent in the 1960s and 1970s, there emerged such divergent Jewish comedians as David Brenner, ALAN KING, Robert Klein, and JOAN RIVERS, some of whom had earlier exposure in other mediums. Such comedy-variety series as *Saturday Night Live* (1975–) showcased many rising funsters, including ALBERT BROOKS, BILLY CRYSTAL, Laraine Newman, and Gilda Radner. Meanwhile, as the comedy-club phenomenon grew around the United States in the 1970s and early 1980s, they were excellent testing venues for such upcoming TV talent as Roseanne Barr, Sandra Bernhard, ELAYNE BOOSLER, HOWIE MANDEL, PAUL REISER, and JERRY SEINFELD. The comedy-club venue still exists today, both live in cities across the country and on TV, and still remains an excellent testing ground for new talent, Jewish and otherwise. Later entrants into the field included Pauly Shore.

comedies—feature films In Hollywood's silent era, Jewish characters were frequently utilized as broad comedy foils, their ethnic traits played up primarily for good-natured, lowbrow amusement. (That making fun of people's differences from typical Americans might be construed as subtle maliciousness was not apparent or important to most people in those prepolitically correct decades.) Early examples of this included *COHEN'S LUCK* (1915), which in the best tradition of the YIDDISH THEATER mixed comedy with drama.

With this stereotype of the "funny" foreigner with gesticulating hands and old-country traditions and lifestyles, there arose in films (as it had on the stage) the image of the comic Jew, usually a person living on New York's LOWER EAST SIDE. He was depicted as overly involved in the struggle to get ahead and making certain his offspring did well in life. This combined representation led to such silent movie series as *POTASH AND PERLMUTTER* (1922). (Because motion pictures were still silent, to convey the accented, often ungrammatical speech of such characters, the title cards inserted in the film to explain the dialogue would often be written in "funny" English.)

Playing further on the stereotype of the unassimilated Jewish immigrant in the United States, a tradition developed of presenting the Jewish stereotype in stark contrast to another ethnic group, one usually considered more Americanized—often the Irish. Prodded by the example of the hit Broadway show *Abie's Irish Rose* (1922), which boasted "humorous" conflicts between Jews and the Irish, Hollywood developed its own version of the good-natured battles between the two groups, primarily *THE COHENS AND KELLYS* (1926). Its ongoing success led the film industry to create such copycat comedies involving Jews versus other ethnic groups as *Sailor Izzy Murphy* (1927), *CLANCY'S KOSHER WEDDING* (1927), and *George Washington Cohen* (1928). By the time that talkies became a reality in the late 1920s, the trend—which had long been a staple of vaudeville acts and stage comedies—was wearing thin. Once the novelty of being able to hear the ethnic speech on screen lost its freshness, Jewish characters were downplayed on the Hollywood screen. Thus, in the 1930s, with the exception of the remaining *Cohens and Kellys* movie follow-ups, Jewish characters—clearly identified as such or not—became comedy relief through their accents and mannerisms in brief bits in urban dramas. (An extension of this type would be the Louie Dumbrowsky screen character played by Bernard Gorcey as the recurring figure of the little old sweetshop owner in the Bowery Boys comedies of the 1940s and 1950s.)

With the onslaught of World War II and the HOLOCAUST, the juxtaposition of Jewish characters and screen comedies seemed tasteless to most in Hollywood. Only Charles Chaplin's occasionally slapstick *THE GREAT DICTATOR* (1940) and Ernst Lubitsch's witty *TO BE OR NOT TO BE* (1942) used satire to make jokes at the expense of the Nazis.

In the post-World War II era through the mid-1960s, with political correctness on the rise and ethnic PRESSURE GROUPS in place, the use of identified Jewish characters in motion pictures nearly disappeared, or, if they were included in the story line, their heritage would be indicated merely by indirection (e.g., the décor of the house, the way the characters dressed, or especially by an accented voice or a profession—shop owner, peddler, or, at the other extreme, banker, lawyer, or doctor). In this "invisible" period, there was scant use of Jews for comedy relief on screen, let alone having a Jewish character of dimension be involved in comical situations.

A rare exception was *MOLLY* (aka: *The Goldbergs*) (1950) featuring the well-known GERTRUDE BERG who had already made a hit of the Bronx family comedy/drama property on radio, stage, and TV. A decade later, one of Berg's big stage hits, *A MAJORITY OF ONE* (1959), a warm-hearted comedy with serious overtones about ethnic bigotry, reached the screen. It was considered safe to produce because (1) it came from an established Broadway success, (2) it cast the obviously non-Jewish Rosalind Russell in the female lead, and (3) it dealt with not just Jews but also Japanese, each learning to bypass their racial prejudices. As such, here was a serious comedy in which the film studio could get away with ethnic comedy because it was a message picture and because the humorous contrast of Jews with others was focused primarily on a non-Jewish performer (just as the Japanese businessman was played by Britisher Alec Guinness).

In the late 1960s—with the Hollywood studio system in decline—a trio (WOODY ALLEN, MEL BROOKS, and BARBRA STREISAND) of divergent Jewish talent (who both acted and directed) emerged with early screen successes (respectively, *Take the Money and Run*, 1969; *THE PRODUCERS*, 1967; FUNNY GIRL, 1968). None of them made a secret of their Jewishness, and the on-camera characters they portrayed (or featured as director) were plainly ethnic. Their first such films and their follow-ups launched the three to predominance as purveyors of Jewish-themed subjects that were often handled in a comedic mode.

The one-man writing machine, Neil Simon, had several of his stage comedies (typically filled with overt Jewish characters) reach the screen (e.g., *Come Blow Your Horn*, 1963; *THE ODD COUPLE*, 1968), leading Simon to a string of later successes, including several original screenplays (e.g., *THE GOODBYE GIRL*, 1977). In the early movie adaptations of Simon's work, such as *Come Blow Your Horn*, it was still standard Hollywood practice to have, say, the parents (e.g., Lee J. Cobb and Molly Picon) be well delineated as Jewish characters but their offspring (e.g., Frank Sinatra and Tony Bill), who had the focal roles, be obvious gentiles who apparently just happened to have Jewish relatives. This was done on the theory that it softened the Jewishness of such presentations and widened the films' potential audience base.

While Streisand turned to serious filmmaking in the 1980s with *NUTS* (1987), Brooks (e.g., *The History of the World—Part 1*, 1981; *TO BE OR NOT TO BE*, 1983) and Allen (e.g., *BROADWAY DANNY ROSE*, 1984; *RADIO DAYS*, 1987) remained rooted primarily in comedic works. They were joined by such newer talent as ALBERT BROOKS, who focused usually, in the Allen mode, on neurotic, quite assimilated Jewish characters (e.g., *Real Life*, 1979; *Lost in America*, 1984; *Mother*, 1996).

By the 1990s, the stream of Jewish-themed comedy works had diminished to an occasional feature such as *Used People* (1992) and *The Cemetery Club* (1992) that still used the old Hollywood gambit of mostly gentile talent playing Jewish types. On the other hand, Ben Stiller frequently played Semitic characters, especially in his comedies (e.g., *Meet the Parents* and *Keeping the Faith*, both 2000).

Then there was *WHAT'S COOKING?* (2000), which offered ethnic characters—including Jews—as humorous beings, often stereotypes, as enacted, for example, by LAINIE KAZAN (the successor to SHELLEY WINTERS in playing the oversized Jewish mama) in *The Big Hit* (1998) and *What's Cooking?* The Hollywood cycle, it seemed, had come full turn. In *Marci X* (2003), Lisa Kudrow was a Jewish-American Princess who took over a hip-hop record label and had to deal with a controversial black rapper (Damon Wayans). *Kissing Jessica Stein* (2002) was a romantic comedy about a Jewish New York City single who finds herself in a lesbian relationship with a smart and funny Manhattanite.

***Compulsion* (1959)** Twentieth Century-Fox, b&w, 103 minutes. **Director:** Richard Fleischer; **Screenplay:** Richard Murphy; **Cast:** Orson Welles (Jonathan Wilk), Diane Varsi (Ruth Evans), Dean Stockwell (Judd Steiner), Bradford Dillman (Artie Strauss), E. G. Marshall (Horn).

One of the more publicized murder trials of twentieth-century America involved the 1924 killing of a fourteen-year-old by two University of Chicago students, a deed committed purely for the sake of committing the perfect crime. Both defendants (Nathan Leopold and Richard Loeb) were highly intelligent young men from wealthy Chicago families, and each was Jewish. The homicide exacerbated anti-Semitic feelings in the United States.

In 1956, Meyer Levin wrote a best-selling novel of this thrill crime that was turned into a Broadway play (1957) and two years later was adapted to the screen. Just as the culprits' names were altered in the movie—as was that of their famous defense attorney Clarence Darrow changed to Jonathan Wilk—so were the killers' homosexuality and Jewish background submerged as only a subtext within the picture. This ploy was abetted by using non-Jewish looking actors in the leads. Even the name of Dillman's character, not changed from the novel or play, received an assimilated pronunciation—it became "Straws," not the more ethnic-sounding "Strauss."

The Leopold–Loeb case had already provided a basis for the Alfred Hitchcock movie, *Rope* (1948), where the thrill murderers were also played by non-Jewish types (Farley Granger and John Dall). In *Swoon* (1992), directed by Tom Kalin, the screenplay used the real-life names of its subjects and, while not disguising their Jewish backgrounds, focused more on their homosexual master–slave relationship.

concentration camps Part of the "final solution" for the Third Reich included the rounding up and extermination of undesirables, including all Jews. As the reality of this nightmare reached Hollywood in the 1930s, it was considered too touchy a subject to handle (i.e., fear of losing European marketplaces for film releases, concern by Hollywood and the U.S. government that Americans might believe that the only reason the United States was entering World War II was to fight on behalf of the beleaguered European Jews, and apprehension that depicting the German mistreatment of Jews would incite more anti-Semitism in the United States. Finally, in 1940, two features (*ESCAPE* and *THE MORTAL STORM*) from the MGM studio touched on the horrifying subject, showing/telling of detention camps in a Germany-like country and *suggesting* that the prisoners were there because they were Jewish.

Although some fictional war movies of the 1940s dealt with escapes from concentration camps (e.g., *The Seventh Cross*, 1944), the fleeing victims were not necessarily depicted as innocent Jews seeking freedom. Actually, it was graphic movie theater newsreels of the 1940s, especially after the liberation of various German prison camps, that showed Americans on the home front the reality of the HOLOCAUST. One of the early features to depict the liberation of the concentration camps and the Allied soldiers' horror of the prisoners' plight was *THE YOUNG LIONS* (1958). Three years later, the all-star courtroom drama, *JUDGMENT AT NUREMBERG*, included actual newsreels of these extermination camps and the barely alive survivors, along with the mounds of corpses stacked in open pits. Both *THE PAWNBROKER* (1965) and *SOPHIE'S CHOICE* (1982) included flashback sequences as their lead characters relived the horror of the camps and why the experiences had so scarred them. *The Grey Zone* (2002) depicted an organized uprising attempted by inmates at Auschwitz.

For many, it was the television miniseries *HOLOCAUST* (1978) that indelibly etched the horrors of the death camps, a theme revisited in a miniseries trilogy: *THE WINDS OF WAR* (1983), as well as *War and Remembrance* (1988) and *War and Remembrance: The Final Chapter* (1989). In the made-for-television movie *PLAYING FOR TIME* (1980), the focus was on a group of imprisoned female musicians forced to play concerts for their captors to avoid the fate of other camp prisoners. The telefeature *Escape from Sobibor* (1988) concerned inmates attempting to break out of the death camp at Treblinka.

Several telefeatures of the 1990s included flashback scenes to the terror of the concentration camps, but none equaled the impact of the theatrical feature, *SCHINDLER'S LIST* (1993), which showed the shocking horror of life in one of these prison camps. *Apt Pupil* (1998), based on a Stephen King novel, concerned a high-school student who discovers his neighbor is a Nazi war criminal and blackmails the man into recounting his horrendous deeds at a World War II concentration camp. The newest TV movie rendition of *Anne Frank: The Whole Story* (2001) did not use the famous teenager's diary or the stage play as the basis for its story but relied on the facts surrounding the family's torment as they went into hiding in Amsterdam during the German occupation and were later caught and sent to concentration camps to meet their fates.

In 2000 appeared the TV movie *NUREMBERG*, which detailed the trials of several high-ranking Nazi officers who had been key members of the Third Reich in plotting and executing the genocide policy. The next year, the made-for-cable feature *Conspiracy*, with a script by Loring Mandel and starring Kenneth Branagh and Stanley Tucci, dealt with the top-secret meeting held outside Berlin in the early 1940s by several top German officers (including Adolf Eichmann, Reinhard Heydrich, Dr. Erich Neumann) who calmly—during a buffet meal and recorded music—discussed a consolidated plan for the "final solution" against millions of Jews.

***Counsellor-at-Law* (1933)** Universal, b&w, 80 minutes. **Director:** William Wyler; **Screenplay:** Elmer Rice; **Cast:** John Barrymore (George Simon), Bebe Daniels (Regina "Rexy" Gordon), Doris Kenyon (Cora Simon), Isabel Jewell (Bessie Green), Melvyn Douglas (Roy Darwin).

As the wave of Jewish immigrants from Europe gave way to the new generation of American-born Jews, there were increasing numbers of self-made Jewish career success stories. Reflecting this were such comical entries as *THE HEART*

OF NEW YORK (1932) and several of the entries in the 1920s to 1930s film series, *THE COHENS AND KELLYS*. On a more serious note—and one for which Hollywood was extremely reluctant to use Jewish actors in topics involving Jews—was *Counsellor-at-Law*, based on Elmer Rice's 1931 Broadway success that had starred PAUL MUNI. Rather than use Muni or another Jewish actor for the lead, the studio selected the mainstream Barrymore, who, in an effort to be "authentically" Jewish, exaggerated his gestures and mannerisms, making him unconvincing as a Hebrew.

George Simon is a self-made criminal lawyer who rose from the LOWER EAST SIDE to an important New York City practice. He has a gentile trophy wife who is having an affair with a member (Douglas) of her social set. Simon tries to help a woman from his old neighborhood whose communist-agitator son has been arrested. When the victim dies from the injuries inflicted by the police and Simon is later blackmailed by a society attorney on other matters, the lawyer grows desperate. Upon learning that his wife has left him, he tries to commit suicide but is stopped by his secretary (Daniels). Just then the phone rings. Simon is needed to handle a new sensational case, and this revives his spirits.

Overtly theatrical in structure and overwhelmed by Barrymore's star turn, *Counsellor-at-Law* was still a positive step forward in Hollywood's presentation of Jewish themes on screen.

crime, detective, and police dramas—feature films One of the early screen tales to feature a Jewish character (innocently) involved with crooks was the silent movie, *Time Lock Number 776* (1915). More than twenty years later, the same situation occurred in *That I May Live* (1937) in which a good-natured man (played by J. Edward Bromberg) befriended an ex-convict, not knowing of the man's past or that he had been implicated in a bank robbery/murder.

COMPULSION (1959), dealing with the actual 1920s thrill killing of a youngster by two young Jewish men (Nathan Leopold and Richard Loeb), only acknowledged the characters' Jewish background by subtle indirection (the same way the two men's homosexuality was handled in this drama).

Previous to 1960, the depiction on screen of Jewish gangsters never directly mentioned their ethnic roots. By the time of *Murder, Inc.* (1960) and *King of the Roaring 20's—The Story of Arnold Rothstein* (1961) that situation changed. *The Plot Against Harry* (1969) revolved around a small-time Jewish racketeer who returned to his old neighborhood and found that it was heavily populated with Hispanics and blacks. Five years later, in Francis Ford Coppola's *THE GODFATHER, PART II*, there would be a clear portrait of a Jewish mobster (played by LEE STRASBERG), purportedly based on real-life Meyer Lansky. This led to the out-in-the-open depiction of Jewish hoodlums in the telefeature *The Virginia Hill Story* (1984), the movie *LEPKE* (1975), and such later features as *Once Upon a Time in America* (1984), *Bugsy* (1991), *Billy Bathgate* (1991—with DUSTIN HOFFMAN as Dutch Schultz), and the more recent TV movie, *Lansky* (1999), starring RICHARD DREYFUSS in the title role of the infamous hoodlum. In the independent theatrical feature, *Six Ways to Sunday* (1998), Adrien Brody appeared as a lawbreaker named Arnie Finkelstein, involved with the Jewish mob.

(Not to be overlooked were such nebbishy crooks as WOODY ALLEN's alter ego in 1969's *Take the Money and Run* and 2000's *Small Time Crooks* and JACKIE MASON's petty offender in 1972's *The Stoolie*.)

For whatever reason, Jews (at least on the screen) were rarely depicted as a private detective or police officer, and, if they were, it was typically as a background character and they became just another ethnic representation. One exception to the rule was Lieutenant Abrams of the San Francisco Homicide Squad who turned up in *After the Thin Man* (1936) and *Shadow of the Thin Man* (1941). He was played with a mixture of exasperation, amusement, and perseverance by SAM LEVENE. Another exception to the rule was *NO WAY TO TREAT A LADY* (1968) with GEORGE SEGAL as one of New York's finest, who matched wits with a serial killer but was unable to best his nagging mother (Eileen Heckart). Another trend-breaker was Richard Dreyfuss as the Jewish Moses Wine, the Los Angeles-based private eye who had as many domestic problems as he had with individuals trying to prevent him from solving the caper. He appeared in *THE BIG FIX* (1978), which was to have been the start of a new series but lasted for only one entry. In *Double Take* (1985—TV movie), the start of a series of telefeatures about relentless New York City police detective Frank Janek II (played by Richard Crenna), his partner was Aaron Greenberg (portrayed by Cliff Gorman).

Bringing the law enforcer into the 1990s was *Homicide* (1991) written and directed by David Mamet. It was a dour study of a nonreligious Jewish cop (Joseph Mantegna) who saw his focus as a solid police detective diminishing as his interest in his ethnic roots accelerated, which creates unintentional grief to others and to himself.

crime, detective, and police series—television In television's early history, period police dramas such as *The Untouchables* (1959–63) and *The Lawless Years* (1959–61), as well as the period newspaper drama, *The Roaring Twenties* (1960–62), dealt with many notorious underworld figures, but those who were Jewish in real life were not particularly identified as such on these TV series. (*The Lawless Years*, however, did feature a multipart episode about an East European Jewish immigrant who became deranged by his sister's murder and turned into an underworld big shot.)

Jumping ahead two decades, the police/crime drama *Wiseguy* (1987–90) featured several Jewish subordinate characters involved one way or another with crime. These included the characters played by JERRY LEWIS, RON SILVER, Patricia Charbonneau, and Harry Goz in the 1988–89 season. *Law & Order* (1990–) set in New York City, had its share of Jewish wrongdoers (as well as victims). JUDD HIRSCH had a short TV run as Leo Wagonman, a small-time Jewish crook on the lam from Las Vegas mobsters in *George & Leo* (1997–98).

On the right side of the law, the unsuccessful *LANIGAN'S RABBI* (1977) offered Bruce Solomon as Rabbi David Small who assisted a small-town California police chief (Art Carney) in solving cases. Judd Hirsch, who frequently played ethnic roles, did so again in *Detective in the House*, a show that lasted on the air for one month in spring 1985. He was cast as a successful engineer who had a yen to be a private detective and bumbled his way through cases.

On the police front, the often serious situation comedy *BARNEY MILLER* (1975–82) featured Hal Holbrook in the lead role of the Jewish Greenwich Village police captain, and Abe Vigoda as Det. Phil Fish. (The latter character was spun off into his own series, *Fish*, 1978–79, which focused on the domestic life of the rundown cop and his spouse Bernice.). *Hill Street Blues* (1981–87) highlighted several Jewish police officers (including Officer Leo Schnitz), while the precinct shown in the New York-set *Cagney & Lacey* (1982–88) encompassed a Jewish police lieutenant (played by Al Waxman) and such Jewish police sleuths as Det. Jonah Newman. A member of the undercover anticrime unit of the N.Y.P.D. in *Baker's Dozen* (1982) was played by Ron Silver. One of the screwball California cops in *Pacific Station* (1991–92) was Capt. Ken Epstein, who never outgrew his need for mama. The cop drama, *Leaving L.A.* (1997) offered Ron Rifkin as the Jewish and offbeat chief medical examiner. On the roster of *Law & Order: SVU* (1999–) was Det. John Munch—a carryover character from *Homicide: Life on the Street* (1993–99)—played by Jewish stand-up comic Richard Belzer. His series part was enacted with urban brittleness, and in one episode of *Homicide: Life on the Street* he reexplored his Jewish roots. *The Shield* (2002–), a hard-hitting series of the new millennium, had occasional Jewish characters in the force, but in subordinate roles.

***Crimes and Misdemeanors* (1989)** Orion, color, 104 minutes. **Director/Screenplay:** Woody Allen; **Cast:** Alan Alda (Lester), Woody Allen (Clifford Stern), Claire Bloom (Miriam Rosenthal), Mia Farrow (Hailey Reed), Joanna Gleason (Wendy Stern), Anjelica Huston (Dolores Paley), Martin Landau (Judah Rosenthal).

This morality tale with interweaving stories set in New York City was one of Woody Allen's most deeply philosophical and mature films and one that revealed much of the auteur's outlook on life. Jewish ophthalmologist Judah Rosenthal had been carrying on an affair with Dolores Paley behind the back of his wife Miriam. When the distraught Dolores threatens to expose the doctor, his hoodlum brother suggests that the woman be murdered. She is. Meanwhile, dedicated documentary filmmaker Clifford, unhappily wed to Wendy, becomes entranced with Hailey Reed, the producer of a documentary he is making on Lester, his unpleasant TV comic brother.

Many regarded this complex mix of drama and comedy as one of Allen's most Jewish projects. The film's tone was bleak, as pointed out by the characters' fates: Judah gets away with his crime, and Clifford loses Hailey to his smug brother Lester. Meanwhile, Clifford's other brother, a rabbi, goes blind but refuses to complain about his fate.

Crimes and Misdemeanors was nominated for three Academy Awards: Best Director, Best Original Screenplay, and Best Supporting Actor (Landau).

***Crossfire* (1947)** RKO, b&w, 86 minutes. **Director:** Edward Dmytryk; **Screenplay:** John Paxton; **Cast:** Robert Young (Police Captain Finlay), Robert Mitchum (Sgt. Felix Keeley), Robert Ryan (Sergeant Montgomery), Gloria Grahame (Ginny Tremaine), Paul Kelly (the Man), Sam Levene (Joseph Samuels).

Although this landmark message film never got to the heart of its controversial subject (i.e., anti-Semitism), it was, along with *GENTLEMAN'S AGREEMENT* (1947), one of the first of the new Hollywood movies in the post-World War II era to deal with the hot topic. Based on *The Brick Foxhole* (1945) by Richard Brooks, the novel concerned the killing of a homosexual and the apprehension of the bigot who did it. For the screen adaptation, the victim became a Jew, which was then considered less of a taboo subject at both the box office and the film industry's censorship office.

Set in Washington, D.C., the narrative concerns the murder of a civilian, a Jewish man named Joseph Samuels. Investigating Police Captain Finlay narrows down the suspects to two World War II veterans: Sergeant Montgomery and Sgt. Felix Keeley. Eventually the law enforcer deduces that the killer is the one who murdered his victim without having any clear understanding of the man but rather thought of him as a "draft-dodging Jew boy." The police set a trap for the murderer and get their culprit.

At the time of preproduction, the head of RKO production Dore Schary (who was very active in Jewish causes) was requested by PRESSURE GROUPS, including the American Jewish Committee, to either not make this film or, at least, to change the murder victim to an African American. Other factions of Jewish special interest organizations were concerned that the movie would stir up more anti-Semitic feelings, instead of airing/clearing this long-existing situation.

Made on a $589,000 budget, *Crossfire* grossed more than $1 million at the box-office and helped to set the tone in Hollywood for what would be acceptable subject matter on screen when dealing with Jewish themes/characters.

***Crossing Delancey* (1988)** Warner Bros., color, 97 minutes. **Director:** Joan Micklin Silver; **Screenplay:** Susan Sandler; **Cast:** Amy Irving (Isabelle Grossman), Peter Riegert (Sam Posner), Reizl Bozyk (Bubbie Kantor), Jeroen Krabbe (Anton Maes), Sylvia Miles (Hannah Mandelbaum).

Sandler adopted her 1985 off-Broadway play *Crossing Delancey* to the screen. It was directed by SILVER, responsible for the earlier *HESTER STREET* (1975), another study of Jewish assimilation in New York. Irving, the star of this movie, had been a leading player in BARBRA STREISAND's *YENTL* (1983). For PETER RIEGERT, it was yet another opportunity to play the contemporary Jewish man.

Told in the format of a love story, *Crossing Delancey* was more a study of how too much assimilation could lead a modern woman into ignoring her roots—ethnic and cultural ties that could help her cope with life.

On the surface, Isabelle Grossman is a self-sufficient, content thirty-three-year-old woman living in uptown Manhattan and working for a "real" bookstore—not a chain emporium. She mingles with the intelligentsia and carries on an affair with a self-centered author (Krabbe). Meanwhile, her elderly, outspoken grandmother, Bubbie Kantor, still living on the LOWER EAST SIDE, insists that her granddaughter needs the love of a good Jewish man. Thus, she hires a matchmaker (Miles) to find a candidate. The choice is Sam Posner, a devout but quite contemporary Orthodox Jew residing in the old neighborhood who runs the pickle business inherited from his father. It takes Isabelle a good while to appreciate this intelligent, kind man who is nobody's fool.

Irving was fine as the woman questioning the value of ethnic ties. Miles brought gusto to her role, and Bozyk, a veteran of the Yiddish stage, was extremely effective with her well-meaning interference. But Riegert was the heart of the movie. His Sam was a responsible, intelligent but romantic man who refused to be pigeonholed by his religion, work, or neighborhood. As such he became one of the American cinema's most positive Jewish role models.

Crystal, Billy (1947–) He made his initial show-business mark playing the openly gay son on the satirical TV situation comedy, *Soap* (1977–81). Years later, in the 1990s, Crystal did much to restore entertainment value to the annual Academy Awards presentation by frequently hosting the high-profile Oscar Awards show on TV. In between, he was a nonstop performer in many medias, generally playing a variation of the urban Jew.

Born William Crystal in 1947, he grew up in Long Beach, Long Island, New York. His father's father was a Yiddish actor, and his mother frequently performed in shows at the local synagogue. From an early age, Billy had a talent for mimicking in dialect and frequently performed for relatives at their annual Passover seders.

After college (New York University), he formed an improv comedy trio, later becoming a solo act. He made his feature film debut in *Rabbit Test* (1978), directed by JOAN RIVERS. If *The Billy Crystal Comedy Hour* (1982) was a TV flop, he was a big success as a regular on TV's *Saturday Night Live* in the mid-1980s. When not hosting award shows (e.g., the Grammys; later the Oscars), he was in several popular movies, including *When Harry Met Sally . . .* (1989) and *City Slickers* (1991). For both *Mr. Saturday Night* (1992) and *Forget Paris* (1995), Crystal not only costarred, but also cowrote and directed the features. He joined WOODY ALLEN's stock company for *Deconstructing Harry* (1997) and had an enormous success teaming with Robert De Niro in the 1999 comedy *Analyze This*, which led to a sequel (*Analyze That*, 2002). In 2001, he directed and produced the baseball-themed cable-TV movie *61**. Crystal served as writer, producer, and actor in the comedy *America's Sweethearts* (2001), starring Julia Roberts. He utilized his distinctive voice to play a lead character in the mega-successful animated feature *Monsters, Inc.* (2001).

More intent on providing dimensional character moments than indulging in observational comedy, Crystal built his reputation on energetic but low-keyed performances. He creates his humor from life's bittersweet moments and frequently deals with the angst of Jewish men coping with life's vagaries as they grow older.

Curtis, Tony (1925–) His lengthy screen career—more than 100 feature films—began under the studio star system where studio executives decided that newcomer Bernard Schwartz would be more successful with the public if he was rechristened Anthony (later Tony) Curtis to take advantage of his swarthy good looks and to disguise his Jewish origins. (He was the son of a Hungarian immigrant who, in his native Budapest, had been an amateur actor.) While his telltale Bronx accent and tough manner (developed during childhood years mingling with street gangs) long remained trademarks, the five-feet, nine-inch actor had an intriguing array of screen assignments as he jumped from costume adventure yarns to westerns and "dramas." He proved especially astute in the interracial entry *The Defiant Ones* (1958) and earned an Oscar nomination. The next year, he costarred with Marilyn Monroe and Jack Lemmon in the comedy classic *Some Like It Hot*. He was earnest as Native-American World War II hero Ira Hayes in *The Outsider* (1961) and riveting as serial killer Albert De Salvo in *The Boston Strangler* (1968).

Infrequently in his prolific career did he play Jewish characters. He starred with then wife Janet Leigh in *Houdini* (1953), a fictionalized account of the great magician. The Jewish background of the celebrated illusionist was, in typical Hollywood fashion, noted only by indirection. *Captain Newman, M.D.* (1963) found Curtis as the hyperactive, comedic Corp. Jackson Leibowitz. In one of the star's undervalued performances, he was notorious gangland personality Louis Buchalter in *LEPKE* (1975), which, unlike earlier features on the subject, did not disguise the hoodlum's Jewish origins.

On television, Curtis had two notable roles as ethnic characters. He was casino owner Philip Roth, on the detective series *Vega$* (1978–81). In the TV movie *The Scarlett O'Hara War* (1980), he was cast as Semitic movie mogul David O. Selznick and was particularly effective.

D

Dangerfield, Rodney (1921–) His catchphrase, "I don't get no respect," belied his years of show-business success in a variety of mediums. The bug-eyed, chunky comedian had been around for decades, coping with professional ups and down and bouts of dark depression. Best known for his neck-and-shoulders-twitching and tie-straightening neuroticisms, his self-effacing humor ran the gamut from the ribald to the puerile.

Born Jacob Cohen in Babylon, Long Island, New York, he was an infant when his father deserted the family. Growing up in Queens, Jacob felt inadequate because of his financial struggles and unwanted because of the anti-Semitic remarks of his teachers. He developed a sense of humor to disguise his hurt. Later, as Jack Roy, he was a struggling comedian at CATSKILL RESORTS. Then he abandoned show business for more than a decade to become a businessman. Still writing jokes for the likes of JOAN RIVERS and JACKIE MASON, he returned to the club circuit, now billed as Rodney Dangerfield. He opened his own Manhattan comedy club in 1969.

His first film roles included *The Projectionist* (1971) and *Caddyshack* (1983). Then he turned to writing his own screen vehicles, casting himself as the good-natured, obsessed rascal who might have a crude demeanor but had a good heart: *Easy Money* (1983), the quite popular *Back to School* (1986), *Meet Wally Sparks* (1997), *My 5 Wives* (2000), *The 4th Tenor* (2001), and so on.

***Daniel* (1983)** Paramount, color, 130 minutes. **Director:** Sidney Lumet; **Screenplay:** E. L. Doctorow; **Cast:** Timothy Hutton (Daniel Isaacson), Edward Asner (Jacob Ascher), Mandy Patinkin (Paul Isaacson), Lindsay Crouse (Rochelle), Joseph Leon (Selig Mindish), Amanda Plummer (Susan Isaacson).

When Julius and Ethel Rosenberg were executed in 1953 as American spies convicted for passing atomic secrets to the Russians, there was a huge cry from those who insisted the couple had been framed by the U.S. government. At the time, having Jews branded as American traitors stirred up a lot of anti-Semitism. Doctorow's fictional account of the Rosenberg case was published in 1971.

The film focuses on the son (Hutton) of the Isaacsons (i.e., the Rosenbergs), who in the 1960s is a graduate student with leftist leanings. He and his emotionally disturbed sister (Plummer) have buried their anger, guilt, and confusion about their parents' deaths by participating in radical causes. As the siblings investigate the case, they become aware of how much the traumatic incident has colored their entire lives.

Directed with conviction if not impartiality by LUMET, who had helmed many Jewish-themed pictures, *Daniel* was an exploration of the legacy of grief foisted on the children of the convicted couple.

***Dark at the Top of the Stairs, The* (1960)** Warner Bros., color, 123 minutes. **Director:** Delbert Mann; **Screenplay:** Harriet Frank Jr. and Irving Ravetch; **Cast:** Robert Preston (Rubin Flood), Dorothy McGuire (Cora Flood), Eve Arden (Lottie), Angela Lansbury (Mavis Pruitt), Shirley Knight (Reenie Flood), J. Lee Kinsolving (Sammy Golden).

Set in a 1920s Oklahoma town, this drama of marital discord and maturing adolescents—based on William Inge's Broadway hit (1987) that earned a Pulitzer Prize—included an anti-Semitism subplot.

Teenager Reenie Flood considers herself a wallflower. Her parents (McGuire and Preston) are too concerned with their faltering marriage and his lack of work to be of much guidance. Reenie meets Sammy Golden, the neglected son of a movie actress, who attends a nearby military academy. Unknowingly, he becomes her blind date for a birthday celebration being given at the local country club. When the party hostess learns that Sammy is Jewish, she informs Sammy that the club is restricted against Jews. The couple depart with Reenie attempting to make amends to Sammy. He rejects her offer to stay with him, and the next day he attempts suicide. Later he dies in the hospital.

Had this too-theatrical narrative been set in the present day, its discussion of anti-Semitism might have had more impact on audiences. Even the dialogue segment where Reenie's bigoted aunt (Arden) made cracks about the Jews lacked punch. Moreover, Sammy's death was handled off-camera, which distanced moviegoers from the tragedy.

Knight received an Academy Award nomination in the Best Supporting Actress category.

***David and Bathsheba* (1952)** Twentieth Century-Fox, color, 116 minutes. **Director:** Henry King; **Screenplay:** Philip Dunne; **Cast:** Gregory Peck (David), Susan Hayward (Bathsheba), Raymond Massey (Nathan), Kieron Moore (Uriah), James Robertson Justice (Abishai), Francis X. Bushman (King Saul).

With the huge success of *SAMSON AND DELILAH* (1949), Hollywood turned out more biblical epics, focusing on massive sets, casts of thousands, and gaudily clad temptresses but relied on thin plots (suggested by the Old Testament) and populated them with cardboard characters. Because many of the figures drawn from the Bible for these spectacles were Jewish, they could not be easily changed for the screen; yet, the filmmakers made little effort to enrich these characters' presence with dimension or any sense of Jewish culture.

David and Bathsheba was ostensibly based on the second book of Samuel from the Old Testament. In the Bible, David, the shepherd king, was king of Judah and Israel. He killed the Philistine giant Goliath and, after Saul's death, became king. In this movie translation, most of the emphasis is on David's

Jayne Meadows (left), Gregory Peck, Susan Hayward, and James Robertson Justice in *David and Bathsheba* (1951). (JC ARCHIVES)

lust for Bathsheba and how the duo cope with their current spouses, their adultery, and their eventual marriage.

Despite Peck's stentorian performance and the too contemporary feistiness of Hayward, the saga was stunning. The picture received five Academy Award nominations, including Best Story and Screenplay.

Among the screen performers who played the biblical King David on the American screen were Jeff Chandler (*A Story of David*, 1960), Timothy Bottoms (*The Story of David*—television movie, 1976), and Richard Gere (*KING DAVID*, 1985).

***Diary of Anne Frank, The* (1958)** Twentieth Century-Fox, b&w, 170 minutes. **Director:** George Stevens; **Screenplay:** Frances Goodrich and Albert Hackett; **Cast:** Millie Perkins (Anne Frank), Joseph Schildkraut (Otto Frank), Shelley Winters (Mrs. Van Daan), Richard Beymer (Peter Van Daan), Gusti Huber (Edith Frank), Dody Heath (Miep Gies).

While some 6 million Jews were annihilated during the HOLOCAUST of World War II, for many, the torment and tragedy of that era was symbolized by one person, young Anne Frank (1929–45). This was the German Jewess who kept a diary during the two years that she and her family hid in a cramped attic in Nazi-occupied Amsterdam. Later, shortly before the Allies liberated the city, the Gestapo ferreted out and imprisoned the group. Anne died in the Bergen-Belsen concentration camp of typhus. Only the grief- and guilt-stricken father Otto survived. The personal journal of this young victim was first published in 1947 in Holland (as *Het Achterhuis* [*Behind the House*]) and was translated into an American edition in 1952. In 1955, a Broadway adaptation of the diary was presented as *The Diary of Anne Frank*, winning the Pulitzer Prize.

By the time of this reverential adaptation, many filmgoers were well aware of the subject matter and of the drama itself. Of key importance was that, several years after the victory, this was the *first* Hollywood feature film to finally deal in a head-on major way with the persecution of Jews in Europe during World War II. The resultant motion picture was treated with great dignity by director George Stevens (who years before helmed the comedy *The Cohens and Kellys in Trouble*, 1933, which was full of stereotypical Jewish characters).

Deliberately shot in black and white to avoid a look of Hollywood glamorization, the picture depicted how the Franks and friends, cramped into an attic, sought to live a "normal" existence as they hid from the Gestapo. Each character was presented fully, with the focus on Anne as she emerged from childhood into young adulthood and experienced a range of female emotions, including her attraction to Peter Van Daan. A key emotional sequence occurred when the group celebrated the first night of Chanukah, singing traditional songs.

Perhaps the chief fault of 1959's *The Diary of Anne Frank* was entrusting such a major assignment to a newcomer (Millie Perkins) who could not encapsulate all the feelings that viewers brought to this beloved story. As happened with so many adaptations to the screen, the unique voice of the narrator (i.e., Anne) became diminished in making her a screen ingénue suffering the plight of first love. In addition, the casting of inept Beymer in such a major part was heavily criticized. Several of the cast, including SCHILDKRAUT and Huber, were repeating their Broadway assignments. Among several Oscar nominations and wins for the project, WINTERS won a Best Supporting Actress Oscar.

There were many later adaptations to the (small) screen of *The Diary of Anne Frank*.

***Diary of Anne Frank, The* (1980)** NBC-TV, color, 120 minutes. **Director:** Boris Sagal; **Teleplay:** Frances Goodrich and Albert Hackett; **Cast:** Melissa Gilbert (Anne Frank), Maximilian Schell (Otto Frank), Joan Plowright (Edith Frank), James Coco (Mr. Van Daan), Doris Roberts (Mrs. Van Daan), Scott Jacoby (Peter Van Daan), Anne Wyndham (Miep Gies).

Periodically, *The Diary of Anne Frank* was revived on stage or as a new television production. In 1967, as part of *ABC-TV Theater*, a well-received two-hour production was aired starring Max von Sydow (Otto Frank), Lilli Palmer (Edith Frank), Diana Davila (Anne Frank), Marisa Pavan (Margot), and Suzanne Grossman (Miep Gies). An unlucky thirteen years later, a new TV staging occurred, this time produced by Twentieth Century-Fox Television for NBC-TV. Melissa Gilbert (of *Little House on the Prairie* TV fame) produced the venture and the presentation was not especially liked, in particular for Gilbert's less-than-stellar performance in the focal role. There was little sense that she was a Jewish girl or that she was coping with a life-and-death situation.

In 1987, a new two-hour TV presentation, directed by Gareth Davies, debuted, featuring a cast that was generally unfamiliar to American television viewers: Emrys James (Otto Frank), Elizabeth Bell (Mrs. Frank), Katharine Schlesinger (Anne Frank), Janet Amsbury (Miep Gies), and Steven Mackintosh (Peter van Daan).

Far more relevant and enticing to viewers was 1988's *THE ATTIC: THE HIDING OF ANNE FRANK* on CBS-TV, which switched the focus to Miep Gies (Mary Steenburgen). In 1996, TV actress Kellie Martin starred in a television movie (*THE HIDDEN*), reminiscent of *The Diary of Anne Frank*. It featured Martin as a Catholic Polish girl who secreted thirteen people in her attic during the Nazi occupation.

In 2001, ABC-TV debuted a four-hour telefeature of *Anne Frank: The Whole Story*, starring Hannah Taylor-Gordon (of *JAKOB THE LIAR*) as Anne. Others in the cast, directed by Robert Dornheim, included Ben Kingsley (Otto Frank) and Lili Taylor (Miep Gies). It was based on Melissa Muller's *Anne Frank: The Biography*, first published in the United States in 1998. With a teleplay by Kirk Ellis and filmed largely in Prague, it extended the story line beyond the girl's diary entries, depicting her happy youth before the family went into hiding. It also focused on the plight of the Franks and others once they were captured by the Nazis.

***Dick Van Dyke Show, The* (1961–1966)** CBS-TV series, b&w, 30 minutes. **Cast:** Dick Van Dyke (Rob Petrie), Mary Tyler Moore (Laura Petrie), Rose Marie (Sally Rogers), Morey Amsterdam (Maurice "Buddy" Sorrell), Larry Mathews (Ritchie Petrie), Richard Deacon (Melvin Cooley), Jerry Paris (Dr. Jerry Helper), Ann Morgan Guilbert (Millie Helper).

When this classic sitcom created by CARL REINER was conceived, Reiner was to play the lead and did so in the pilot *Head of the House* (1960). When the show didn't sell, he restructured the series and, for the part, chose Dick Van Dyke. Reiner would occasionally appear on the series as egotistical TV personality Alan Brady for whom Rob Petrie is the chief writer. One of Petrie's coworkers was Maurice "Buddy" Sorrell who is married to Pickles (rarely seen on the series). Because so many movies and TV shows depicted (often by vague references and signals) Jewish people as integral members of show business, it was considered "safe" not only to have Buddy's character be Jewish (actually more New Yorker than ethnic specific) but also to have the part played by TV perennial Amsterdam.

When staff writer Buddy Sorrell is not making wisecracks about his bosses at the show, he is reciting borscht-belt jokes, ordering pastrami sandwiches, and coping with his spouse, Pickles. Thus, Sorrell is an early example of a full-bodied Jewish character on a major TV series.

Less obvious as Jewish figures were Jerry and Millie Helper. He is a dentist, and she a suburban housewife. Especially with Millie, the lilt to her voice and its pronounced cadence, plus her facial characteristics, define her as an undeclared (by the show) ethnic type.

directors of Jewish-themed motion pictures In Hollywood's history, several American motion picture directors "specialized" in making Jewish-themed feature films, including the Jewish WOODY ALLEN, MEL BROOKS, BARRY LEVINSON, SIDNEY LUMET, PAUL MAZURSKY, JOAN MICKLIN SILVER, STEVEN SPIELBERG, BARBRA STREISAND, as well as the non-Jewish filmmaker EDWARD DMYTRYK. Stanley Kramer, who produced Jewish-themed movies such as *THE JUGGLER* (1953), directed a few genre entries: *JUDGMENT AT NUREMBERG* (1961) and *SHIP OF FOOLS* (1965).

***Dirty Dancing* (1987)** Vestron, color, 97 minutes. **Director:** Emile Andolino; **Screenplay:** Eleanor Bergstein; **Cast:** Jennifer Grey (Baby Houseman), Patrick Swayze (Johnny Castle), Jerry Orbach (Jake Houseman), Cynthia Rhodes (Penny Johnson), Jack Weston (Max Kellerman).

In the late 1980s, it seemed safe—especially when the film was set in the past—to present this story where the gentile was the outsider. To minimize the impact, the antihero Johnny Castle, the resort dance instructor/entertainer, was from the wrong side of the tracks, which suggested an equally important reason for the parents of the Jewish heroine to reject him.

In 1963, Baby, a high school graduate, is spending the summer before college with her parents, largely at Kellerman's resort in New York's Catskill Mountains, a world dominated by the Jewish clientele and where gentiles are relegated to being entertainers or staff help. Unlike the Jewish college-boy waiters, the non-Jewish workers are ordered by Kellerman *not* to fraternize with the guests.

Before long, rebellious Baby becomes infatuated with the "forbidden" Johnny. This causes Baby to challenge her doctor father's moral values. At the same time, she acknowledges how much she wants his respect. By the finale, her dad modifies his intolerance of non-Jews, especially those who are not well educated. As for Johnny, thanks to Baby, he has gained a new perspective on life.

The song "(I've Had) the Time of My Life" won an Academy Award. In the fall of 1988, a short-enduring TV series *Dirty Dancing*, based on the film, aired, featuring Patrick Cassidy and Melora Hardin. Another movie—*SWEET LORRAINE* starring Trini Alvarado and Maureen Stapleton—set in the CATSKILL RESORTS was also released in 1987.

***Disraeli* (1921)** United Artists, b&w, 6,800′. **Director:** Henry Kolker; **Screenplay:** Forrest Halsey; **Cast:** George Arliss (Benjamin Disraeli), Florence Arliss (Lady Beaconsfield), Margaret Dale (Mrs. Noel Travers), Louise Huff (Clarissa), Reginald Denny (Charles, Viscount Deeford).

The British Tory Benjamin Disraeli (1804–81) of Italian-Jewish descent was England's prime minister (1868, 1874–80) and was knighted as Lord Beaconsfield. He was perhaps one of the most famous statesmen of his century and helped to remove limitations upon Jews entering British politics. His colorful life became the subject of stage plays as well as screen interpretations. One of the first made in the United States was the 1921 silent drama starring Britisher George Arliss, who was repeating his stage role. The movie adaptation was based on Louis Napoleon Parker's 1911 play and focused on England, under Queen Victoria, seeking to control the Suez Canal. It did not delve much into the politician's Jewish heritage, but audiences were familiar with the man's pedigree.

(In actual life, Disraeli was baptized in 1817 as a result of a dispute between his father and the Sephardic synagogue of Bevis Marks. It was this baptism that allowed him under British law to become a member of Parliament. He was instrumental in removing the prohibition against Jews in Great Britain who wished to hold government offices.)

***Disraeli* (1929)** Warner Bros., b&w, 89 minutes. **Director:** Alfred E. Green; **Screenplay:** Julian Josephson; **Cast:** George Arliss (Disraeli), Joan Bennett (Lady Clarissa Pevensey), Florence Arliss (Lady Beaconsfield), Anthony Bushell (Charles, Lord Deeford), David Torrence (Lord Probert), Margaret Mann (Queen Victoria).

Arliss, with his distinguished voice, could now be heard in the talkie rendition of *Disraeli*, which utilized a new screenplay, although still based on Louis Napoleon Parker's 1911 play. In the second version, there was a decided emphasis on the politician's Jewish background and his battles in Parliament against his rivals. The movie also highlighted the statesman's personal life, depicting him as a benign patriarch. This reverent interpretation of the Jewish politician was a remarkable, if temporary, advance in how politically incorrect Hollywood would treat such ethnic characters—real-life figures or not.

Disraeli was nominated for an Academy Award as Best Picture, while Arliss won the Oscar as Best Actor. Others who played Disraeli on the Hollywood screen included Miles Mander (*Suez*, 1938). In England, the Victorian politician was portrayed on screen by Dennis Eadie (*Disraeli*, 1916), Douglas Munro (*The Life Story of Lloyd George*, 1918), Derrick de Marney (*Victoria the Great*, 1938, and *Sixty Glorious Years*, 1938), John Gielgud (*The Prime Minister*, 1941), Abraham Sofaer (*The Ghosts of Berkeley Square*, 1947), Alec Guinness (*The Mudlark*, 1950), and Ian MacShane (*Disraeli*—1979 TV miniseries).

Arliss later starred in *THE HOUSE OF ROTHSCHILD* (1934), another historical chronicle about another celebrated Jew, this time from the world of international banking.

Dmytryk, Edward (1908–1991) This non-Jewish filmmaker frequently made movies dealing with Semitic themes.

Born of Ukrainian immigrants in Canada, he was raised in Los Angeles and as a teenager held a variety of film studio jobs. His movie directing debut came with the western, *Trail of the Hawk* (1935). He helmed *CROSSFIRE* (1947), a pathfinding Hollywood picture that condemned anti-Semitism. Others of his oeuvre that contained Jewish topics were *THE JUGGLER* (1953), *The Caine Mutiny* (1954), and *THE YOUNG LIONS* (1958).

Despite having directed fifty-four features, writing autobiographies, and teaching filmmaking, Dmytryk was best remembered for being one of the "Hollywood Ten" who did not initially cooperate with the House Un-American Activities Committee during its 1940s–1950s investigation of alleged communists within the film industry. He spent several months behind bars before renouncing communism and testifying again before HUAC, this time providing names.

***Dr. Katz: Professional Therapist* (1995–1999)** Comedy Central cable series, color, 30 minutes. **Voices:** Jonathan Katz (Dr. Katz), H. Jon Benjamin (Benjamin Katz), Laura Silverman (Laura Sweeney), Will Lebow (Stanley), Julianne Shapiro (Julie, the bartender).

This wry, animated TV series for adults, was created by and starred (the voice of) Jonathan Katz. The premise had the deadpan urban psychotherapist dealing rationally with his irrational patients (often the voices of professional comics) as Katz handled his idle twentysomething son and his impudent receptionist (voice of Silverman).

Just as in the early twentieth century, a stereotype of Jews shown in movies might be as an old world patriarch, a displaced scholar, or a street corner peddler; so, from the 1950s onward, Jewish characters—often as minor figures—were seen as professionals, frequently bankers, doctors, or lawyers. In this cartoon series, this New York Jewish therapist fit the newer image of the Jew on screen.

Douglas, Kirk (1916–) It used to be standard show-business procedure that a newcomer with a too-foreign/ethnic-sounding name had to Anglicize it to be considered more appealing to potential fans. That happened to, among others, JACK BENNY, EDWARD G. ROBINSON, PAUL MUNI, SYLVIA SIDNEY, RED BUTTONS, Gene Barry, DANNY KAYE, JUDY HOLLIDAY, SHELLEY WINTERS, JEFF CHANDLER, TONY CURTIS, and KIRK DOUGLAS. More so than most of his peers, Douglas—he of the jutting dimpled chin, edgy voice, and strong opinions—chose to play Jewish characters. They included his roles in *THE JUGGLER* (1953), *CAST A GIANT SHADOW* (1966), *VICTORY AT ENTEBBE* 1976—TV movie), and *REMEMBRANCE OF LOVE* (1982—TV movie)

Born Issur Danielovitch Demsky in Amsterdam, New York, to Russian immigrant parents, his childhood was a struggle against poverty and anti-Semitism. He fastened on an acting career as a way out of his ghetto existence. He attended college in Canton, New York, and then, in 1939, entered the American Academy of Dramatic Arts. While there, he made his Broadway debut in *Spring Again* (1941). Douglas enlisted in the navy during World War II, but he was demobilized in 1944 due to an injury and returned to stage acting. Through former acting classmate Lauren Bacall (née Betty Persky and already a Hollywood star), Douglas was hired for the movie *The Strange Love of Martha Ivers* (1947). *I Walk Alone* (1948) was the first of many costarring vehicles with Burt Lancaster. As the self-centered boxer in *Champion* (1949), Douglas became a star.

With his bulging physique, he was at home in westerns (e.g., *Along the Great Divide*, 1954), costume epics (e.g., *Ulysses*, 1954), and action pictures (e.g., *The Racers*, 1955). He was Oscar nominated for *The Bad and the Beautiful* (1952) and *Lust for Life* (1956). His moral principles led him to make the antiwar drama *Paths of Glory* (1957) and the intellectual epic *Spartacus* (1960). While contemporaries fell by the wayside professionally, he continued moviemaking, even directing a few. In 1986 he and Lancaster made *Tough Guys*, their last joint film.

In 1988, the still active actor wrote his autobiography *(The Ragman's Son)*, the first of several books that would also include other autobiographical works in 1997 and 2001. By then, he had survived a helicopter crash (1991) and a stroke (1996), received an honorary Oscar (1996), and would go on to be bar mitzvahed and make *Diamonds* (1999) with Bacall. One of his four sons, Michael, became a movie superstar.

In 1991, Douglas received a Life Achievement Award from the American Film Institute. In 1996, he was given a honorary Oscar for his fifty years in the movie industry, and in 2001 the Producers Guild of America bestowed their Milestone Award on him.

***Down and Out in Beverly Hills* (1986)** Touchstone, color, 97 minutes. **Director:** Paul Mazursky; **Screenplay:** Mazursky and Leon Capetanos; **Cast:** Nick Nolte (Jerry Baskin), Richard Dreyfuss (Dave Whiteman), Bette Midler (Barbara Whiteman), Little Richard (Orvis Goodnight), Tracy Nelson (Jenny Whiteman), Elizabeth Peña (Carmen).

This comedy was filled with insightful observations about the woes of materialism in modern Jewish culture and how often family, faith, and cultural roots suffered in the process. As his source for this project, director Mazursky relied on the French film classic, *Boudu Saved from Drowning* (1932), which, in turn, was based on the earlier play *Boudu Sauve Des Eaux* by Rene Fauchios.

Within the narrative, a bum, Jerry Baskin, attempts to drown himself in the swimming pool of the Whitemans, Beverly Hills nouveau riche. Dave Whiteman, a self-made millionaire, saves him. Once cleaned up, the surprisingly astute Baskin—who beds many of the women in the household including the maid (Peña)—provides a catalyst for restoring the sanity of family members: the Jewish-American Princess wife (Midler), the anorexic daughter (Nelson), and the son (Evan Richards) who can't communicate with his dad. Throughout, a panorama of oddball and often absurd characters, themselves a panoply of ethnic types, are depicted.

This box-office success was converted into a short-lasting TV series (1987) under the same title with Hector Elizondo as the spoiled rich man, Anita Morris as his wife, and Tim Thomerson as the philosophical bum.

dramas—feature films In the continuum of American-made motion pictures with Jewish themes and/or characters, dramas formed a major category and, in turn, fell into topical groupings.

In the silent-film era which extended from the early 1900s to the late 1920s, a good many of the U.S.-made features with Jewish themes were GHETTO DRAMAS, highly melodramatic stories set in Manhattan's LOWER EAST SIDE. They often dealt with the generation gap between immigrants born in the old country and their offspring who were American born and educated. Typical of these excursions were *HUMORESQUE* (1920) and *A Harp in Hock* (1927). Sometimes the presentations had a partial or full comic overtone and became, essentially, comedies as was the *COHENS AND KELLYS* series. (Occasionally the ghetto drama was transported to a different American turf, such as in 1921's *No Woman Knows* set in Winnebago, Wisconsin, and Chicago, as well as Dresden, Germany.) Not long after the coming of talkies in the late 1920s, both the ghetto dramas and their comedic offshoots faded out of popularity.

In the pretalkie period, American-made silent features also dealt with Jewish immigrants' homelands, typically in eastern Europe. Dramas such as *CIVILIZATION'S CHILD* (1916) and *THE YELLOW TICKET* (1918) were examples of this format.

Not part of the ghetto dramas/comedies were the adaptations of classic literature featuring Jewish characters. Most prominent were the many versions of *OLIVER TWIST*, based on Charles Dickens's nineteenth-century novel that featured the greasy Fagin, the arch thief who had a group of young boys to steal for him. This unfavorable Jewish prototype endured through many decades of screen adaptations, placing Fagin on a par as a negative image with Shylock the Moneylender from William Shakespeare's sixteenth-century play *The Merchant of Venice*.

Other times, a Jewish character was drawn into a plot line for "exotic" novelty as in *Pagan Love* (1920). In this silent drama with a miscegenation theme, a young man (Togo Yamamoto) from China came to the United States where he fell in love with a blind woman (Mabel Ballin), she being part Jewish and part Irish.

From the 1930s until the late 1950s, Hollywood made few dramas dealing with Jewish characters and themes for an assortment of reasons, including the fear of upsetting Jewish PRESSURE GROUPS who resented the use of conventional stereotypes on screen, a rising tide of anti-Semitism among even the Jewish studio moguls, a fear of fanning the flames of anti-Semitism already stirred up by the Third Reich, and a wish not to lose distribution in those European countries that were anti-Jewish.

The stalemate on airing Jewish topics on screen began to crack with the release of *CROSSFIRE* and *GENTLEMAN'S AGREEMENT*, two 1947 dramas that dealt with anti-Semitism. The next year, *Big City* concerned a little girl (Margaret O'Brien) who was adopted by an Irish policeman, a Protestant clergyman, and a Jewish cantor. The latter had a sizable role but was played by the non-Jewish Danny Thomas. In the historical drama, *The Prairie* (1949), set in the early eighteenth century in the Louisiana Purchase territory, several of the lead characters were Jewish.

In the guise of drama, *Prejudice* (1949) was a sermon on overcoming bigotry between Jews and gentiles, as was one of the eight segments of *It's a Big Country* (1951) that concerned a returning Jewish soldier from World War II visiting the intolerant mother of his dead battlefield buddy. Most of the other dramas of the late 1950s and early 1960s that featured Jewish characters (in small roles) dealt with anti-Semitism, including *GOOD MORNING, MISS DOVE* (1955) and *DARK AT THE TOP OF THE STAIRS* (1960).

Many of the more serious of the few films that focused on Jewish figures in the 1960s through the early 1980s revolved around the characters' further assimilation into the American culture. These ranged from the contemporary *PORTNOY'S COMPLAINT* (1972) and *Girlfriends* (1978) to *HESTER STREET* (1975), the latter set at the turn of the twentieth century, and such other entries as Neil Diamond's remake of *THE JAZZ SINGER* (1980) and Woody Allen's *STARDUST MEMORIES* (1980).

Several of the Jewish-flavored dramas of the mid-1980s through the end of the twentieth century had period settings. They included *TORCH SONG TRILOGY* (1988), covering several years in the life of a Jewish gay man who worked for a time as a drag queen; *ENEMIES: A LOVE STORY* (1989), which took place in late 1940s Brooklyn; *AVALON* (1990), tracing the history of a European Jewish immigrant family in Baltimore; *Never Forget* (1991), a TV movie starring Leonard Nimoy as a Holocaust survivor who confronts a neo-Nazi organization in court; *Alan* and *Naomi* (1992) set in 1940s Brooklyn where a young man helps a girl cope with her memories of Nazi terror; *SCHOOL TIES* (1992), which dealt with anti-Semitism at a 1950s New England prep school; *LIBERTY HEIGHTS* (1999), highlighting the life of a Jewish family in 1950s Baltimore; *A Walk on the Moon* (1999), a bittersweet romance set at a Catskills bungalow court in 1969; *Focus* (2001), concerning a Brooklyn couple during World War II who were mistakenly identified as Jewish by their anti-Semitic neighbors. Other such entries included *Just Looking* (2000), directed by Jason Alexander and dealing with a Jewish youth in the 1950s Bronx and Queens who wants to learn more about sex.

Features released in the 1990s and thereafter that dealt with contemporary Jewish families included *The Twilight of the Golds* (1997—made-for-cable movie) in which relatives had to come to terms with the son's homosexuality; *You Can Thank Me Later* (1998), in which a controlling mother and her highly neurotic offspring awaited the outcome of the father's surgery; and *Requiem for a Dream* (2000) in which a Jewish parent, her adult son, and his girlfriend were all addicted to drugs for variant reasons. *Brooklyn Babylon* (2000) focused on interracial interaction between a black rapper and a young Jewish woman and her friends and relatives. *All Over* (2001) and *Kissing Jessica Stein* (2000) both focused on New York Jewish lead characters and their love relationships.

drama series—television As the small-screen medium "bravely" began to expand its scope by presenting more ethnic diversity in its programming, TV drama series began to add Jewish characters as regulars. Although the medical drama *City Hospital* (1952–53) was not specific about the ethnic background of its lead character, Dr. Barton Crane, there was no doubt about the religion of Dr. Bernard Altman (played by LUTHER ADLER) on Los Angeles-set *The Psychiatrist* (1971). The short-lasting *Sons and Daughters* (1974) told of teenage love in the mid-1950s in the town of Stockton, California. One of the lead characters was Anita Cramer, and the soap opera plot also concerned her family, including her recently separated parents. Also of short duration was the series *Number 96* (1980–81) set at an apartment complex in southern California. Among the tenants were the Sugarmans. *ST. ELSEWHERE* (1982–88), the classic medical show set in Boston, had several Jewish characters, ranging from residents Dr. Wayne Fiscus and Dr. Elliott Axelrod, to nurse Helen Rosenthal, and senior physician/administrator Dr. Daniel Auschlander.

Among the Beverly Hills law firm members on *L.A. Law* (1986–94) were such Jewish attorneys as tax expert Stuart Markowitz, partner Douglas Brackman Jr., and New York transplant Eli Levinson, a latecomer to the show. The latter was played by Alan Rosenberg, who had interpreted the same character on *Civil Wars* (1991–93) in which the Eli Levinson figure had suffered a nervous breakdown.

On *Our House* (1986–88), a family-oriented offering, the ethnic character of Joe Kaplan (played by Gerald S. O'Loughlin) was a long-time friend of patriarch Gus Witherspoon. The baby boomer show *thirtysomething* (1987–91) featured the Jewish Michael Steadman (played by Ken Olin), the co-owner of a small Philadelphia ad agency who was married to a Presbyterian. Michael's single cousin, Melissa (played by Melanie Mayron), a photographer, was another of the yuppies seen regularly on that show. *The Trials of Rosie O'Neill* (1990–92) cast Ron Rifkin as Ben Meyer, a Los Angeles public defender.

The quirky drama *Picket Fences* (1992–96), set in Rome, Wisconsin, counted among its eccentric characters, the bizarre Douglas Wambaugh (played by Fyvush Finkel), a medical examiner. During the run of *Chicago Hope* (1994–2000), Dr. Aaron Shutt went through a divorce, a near-fatal medical emergency, and a change of specialties within his profession. *Byrds of Paradise* (1994) was laid in Hawaii to which a widowed professor and his three children relocate. Dr. Murray Rubenstein (played by Bruce Weitz) was the psychiatrist who counseled the newcomer family. On *Felicity* (1998–2002), Sean Blumberg (portrayed by Greg Grunberg), the roommate of one of the main characters, was a budding entrepreneur, who, when faced with a potentially fatal illness, began to explore his Jewish roots. On *Bull* (2000), dealing with Wall Street movers and shakers, one smarmy stock broker was the married Marty Decker (played by Ian Kahn). Among the participants on *Gideon's Crossing* (2000–01), a medical show with Andre Braugher cast as the focal physician, resident Dr. Bruce Cherry (enacted by Hamish Linklater) found that his Jewishness helped his romantic life. *City of Angels* (2000) and *Strong Medicine* (2000–) also highlighted Semitic physicians among their cast of characters. *100 Centre Street* (2001–2002), an old-fashioned drama created by SIDNEY LUMET, featured Alan Arkin as an eccentric Manhattan night court judge, with Phyllis Newman as his patient wife.

See also: CLASSROOM SERIES—TELEVISION; CRIME, DETECTIVE, AND POLICE SERIES—TELEVISION.

Drescher, Fran (1957–) Years ago, it was the radio/TV character of Molly Goldberg (on *THE GOLDBERGS*) who typified the American Jewish mother. Then, media personality VIRGINIA GRAHAM entered the picture with her version of the Semitic New York matron. In later decades, JOAN RIVERS and BARBRA STREISAND represented the Jewish-American Princess, and then came svelte, nasal-toned, Queens-accented Drescher as *THE NANNY* (1993–99). Her Fran Fine was a caricature of a middle-class Jewish girl, but her image and sound stuck in viewers' minds.

She was born Francine Drescher in Flushing, Queens, New York. At Hillcrest High School in Jamaica, New York, she was a classmate of future comedian/TV sitcom star Ray Romano. Another classmate was her husband-to-be, Peter Marc Jacobson, whom she wed in 1978.

From an early age, she knew she wanted to be an actress but tried higher education (Queens College) for a year. She then attended cosmetology school as something to fall back on financially—which she did. Her first movie roles were *Saturday Night Fever* (1977) and *American Hot Wax* (1978). It was not until the mockumentary *This Is Spinal Tap* (1984) that she clicked with critics and the public. Later, she was in such features as *The Big Picture* (1989) and *Cadillac Man* (1990). Her first costarring TV series, *Princesses*, playing a pampered Jewess, lasted for a few weeks in 1991.

It was Drescher and her husband who created *The Nanny*, which debuted on TV in November 1993. She was the loud-mouthed, loud-dressing young woman from Queens who stumbles into a nanny's post in Manhattan with a conservative British theatrical producer and his three children. Her unique presence made a strong impression with viewers

In down time from the series, she starred in such feature films as *Jack* (1996) and *The Beautician and the Beast* (1997). She also wrote her autobiography, *Enter Whining*. After *The Nanny* ended in mid-1999, she appeared in, among others, WOODY ALLEN's *Picking Up the Pieces* (2000) as Sister Frida. In 2000 she underwent successful surgery for uterine cancer and later wrote a book, *Cancer Schmancer* (2002), about her travails.

Dreyfuss, Richard (1947–) Like the older DUSTIN HOFFMAN, Dreyfuss was never typical Hollywood movie-star material. He was on the short side, pudgy, and radiated high energy neuroticism. Nevertheless, Dreyfuss won an Academy Award (*THE GOODBYE GIRL*, 1977) and an Oscar nomination (*Mr. Holland's Opus*, 1995). Frequently he played overanxious, phobic Jewish characters.

Born Richard Stephan Dreyfuss in New York City, he moved with his family to Los Angeles in 1956. By the time he was in high school, he was already doing professional acting jobs. In college he was drafted for the army but as a conscientious objector spent two years as a file clerk at a Los Angeles hospital.

His first TV work was as a regular in the sitcom *Karen* (1964–65). He had a substantial movie role in *The Young Runaways* (1968) and made his Broadway debut in *But Seriously . . .* (1969). Still baby faced, Dreyfuss played a teen in *American Graffiti* (1973), which led to *THE APPRENTICESHIP OF DUDDY KRAVITS* (1974) as an aggressive young Jew. Following the megahit *Jaws* (1975), he did the TV movie *VICTORY AT ENTEBBE* (1976), cast as an Israeli colonel. Then came the science fiction entry *Close Encounters of the Third Kind* (1977) and *THE BIG FIX* (1978).

During the early 1980s, his movie career atrophied, and Dreyfuss coped with a much-publicized substance abuse problem. He made a comeback in *DOWN AND OUT IN BEVERLY HILLS* (1986) as the affluent Jewish father and then was the attorney representing a jailed prostitute (BARBRA STREISAND) in *NUTS* (1987). Later, Dreyfuss was seen as the frustrated therapist in *What About Bob?* (1991) and Uncle Louie in Neil Simon's *Lost in Yonkers* (1993). Throughout this period, he remained active on the stage (*Death and the Maiden*, 1992) and on TV (Fagin in *OLIVER TWIST*, 1997; the Jewish gangster in *LANSKY*, 1999; the president in the live TV production of *Fail Safe*, 2000). More recently, Dreyfuss filmed *The Old Man Who Read Love Stories* (2001) in French Guiana, teamed with Tim Allen for the comedy *Who Is Cletis Tout?* (2001), and for one season (2001–2) played a crusty, widowed history professor at a women's college in the TV series *The Education of Max Bickford.*

E

***Eddie Cantor Story, The* (1953)** Warner Bros., color, 115 minutes. **Director:** Alfred E. Green; **Screenplay:** Jerome Weidman, Ted Sherdeman, and Sidney Skolsky; **Cast:** Keefe Brasselle (Eddie Cantor), Marilyn Erskine (Ida Tobias Cantor), Aline MacMahon (Grandma Esther), Arthur Franz (Harry Harris), Alex Gerry (David Tobias), Eddie and Ida Cantor (Themselves).

EDDIE CANTOR (1892–1964), one of the great twentieth-century entertainers, deserved better than this picture. Producer Sidney Skolsky and director Green, who had conceived *THE JOLSON STORY* (1946), failed to make this a viable study of the diminutive showman who went from vaudeville success to Broadway, Hollywood, radio, and television fame. At the heart of the problem was Brasselle as Cantor. Too tall, too good-looking, and insufficiently dynamic, he failed to convey the subject's uniqueness. (At least, the real Cantor supplied the singing voice of the star, and he and his real-life wife were included in a few framing moments at the start and finish of the screen biography.)

Equally at fault in this bland fare was the lack of authentic Jewish flavor. MacMahon was given little to work with as his maternal grandmother, Esther Kantrowitz, who raised the orphan after his parents died when he was two. As for Erskine as Ida Tobias who wed Cantor and bore him several daughters, she was insipid.

It remained for later screen biographies such as *FUNNY GIRL* (1968), the story of FANNY BRICE, to utilize, not bury, a Jewish star's ethnic origins when picturizing his or her life story.

***Enemies: A Love Story* (1989)** Twentieth Century-Fox, color, 119 minutes. **Director:** Paul Mazursky; **Screenplay:** Roger L. Simon and Mazursky; **Cast:** Ron Silver (Herman Broder), Anjelica Huston (Tamara), Lena Olin (Masha), Margaret Sophie Stein (Yadwiga), Alan King (Rabbi Lembeck), Judith Malina (Masha's mother), Paul Mazursky (Yasha Kotik).

If so much tragedy did not permeate this mainstream movie, a sound screen adaptation of Isaac Bashevis Singer's story originally written in Yiddish (1966) and published in English in 1972, it could have been considered a sex farce concerning a man with three disparate wives. But Broder was a HOLOCAUST survivor, whose faith in Judaism had been sorely tested.

Back during World War II, while his wife Tamara and their two children vanished to the CONCENTRATION CAMPS, he remained hidden by his non-Jewish, Polish servant, Yadwiga. Later, he married her, and now (1949) they are living in Coney Island, New York. Unhappy with this well-meaning gentile, he is having an affair with Masha, another Nazi victim. When Masha tells him that she is pregnant, he marries her. Meanwhile, his first wife, Tamara, thought to have died in the war camps, turns up. Eventually, Masha commits suicide. Broder disappears but periodically sends money to Yadwiga who has had his child, which she and Tamara raise.

MAZURSKY infused his narrative with insights into the traumatic postwar life of Holocaust survivors. Ironically, all three women who had suffered so much pain were tied to a tormented man who was only half-alive.

Unlike *THE PAWNBROKER* (1965), which dealt so grimly with a Holocaust survivor, *Enemies: A Love Story* was subtler in its juxtaposition of clashing personalities tied to their past.

This film received Academy Award nominations for Best Adapted Screenplay and for Best Supporting Actress (both Huston and Olin).

***Enter Laughing* (1967)** Columbia, color, 112 minutes. **Director:** Carl Reiner; **Screenplay:** Joseph Stein and

Reiner; **Cast:** José Ferrer (Mr. Marlowe), Shelley Winters (Mrs. Kolowitz), Elaine May (Angela), Jack Gilford (Mr. Foreman), David Opatoshu (Mr. Kolowitz), Reni Santoni (David Kolowitz).

REINER'S autobiographical novel, *Enter Laughing* (1958), was adapted successfully to Broadway in 1963 with ALAN ARKIN as the young hero; four years later, the property became a film. Set in the 1930s, Bronx teenager David Kolowitz is bored working at Mr. Foreman's machine shop. While David's blue-collar parents imagine him becoming a pharmacist, the boy dreams of an acting career. Following his ambition, he works nights with a rundown theater troupe headed by alcoholic Marlowe and his flirtatious daughter Angela. Meanwhile, the Kolowitzes borrow money so that their offspring can enter pharmacy school. Undaunted, David remains with the players. Despite the misadventures of opening a new production, David is thrilled to make his acting debut. His reconciled family rush backstage to congratulate their offspring.

The film dealt with the conflicts of the new-generation (in the 1930s) American Jew who puts creative aspirations above practical career choices and the diminishing priorities of old country traditions. Unfortunately, the film's cast overacted in conflicting comedy traditions that diminished the play's original ethnic flavor.

Even with its watered-down ethnicity, *Enter Laughing* was one of the few Hollywood films of the early to mid-1960s to deal with the Jewish lifestyle. Other screen comedies that also sanitized the leading role of a Jewish character were *A MAJORITY OF ONE* (1961) and Neil Simon's *Come Blow Your Horn* (1963).

***Escape* (1940)** Metro-Goldwyn-Mayer, b&w, 104 minutes. **Director:** Mervyn LeRoy; **Screenplay:** Arch Oboler and Margaret Roberts; **Cast:** Norma Shearer (Countess von Treck), Robert Taylor (Mark Preysing), Conrad Veidt (Gen. Kurt von Kolb), Alla Nazimova (Emmy Ritter), Felix Bressart (Fritz Keller).

Based on the 1939 novel by Ethel Vance, *Escape* suffered from the same problem as MGM's *THE MORTAL STORM* (1940). Here, the offending country was referred to as Germany, but nowhere in the war drama was it mentioned that the imprisoned Emmy Ritter, a once great stage actress, was Jewish. One had to infer her ethnic background by how she was regarded and treated in the CONCENTRATION CAMP as her American son (Taylor) worked to rescue her.

What started in *Escape* as a brave woman's stand against oppression ended as a conventional love story featuring Taylor and Shearer. Nevertheless, thanks to Nazimova's magnetic characterization, her battle of wills against her captors was memorable.

***Esther and the King* (1960)** Twentieth Century-Fox, color, 109 minutes. **Director:** Raoul Walsh; **Screenplay:** Walsh and Michael Elkins; **Cast:** Joan Collins (Esther), Richard Egan (King Ahasuerus), Denis O'Dea (Mordecai), Sergio Fantoni (Haman), Rick Battalgia (Simon).

This was one of the weakest in the series of Hollywood-produced (in this case a coproduction with Italian moviemakers) biblical epics, supposedly inspired by portions of the Old Testament. A very wooden Collins starred as the Jewess Esther who wed the Persian ruler (Egan) so that he would spare her people who long had been exiled in his country.

Several commentators regarded this and other such biblical entries as implicit statements on the HOLOCAUST and a story parallel of the Jewish race avoiding extinction during World War II.

***Everything You Always Wanted to Know About Sex* (*But Were Afraid to Ask)* (1972)** United Artists, color, 87 minutes. **Director/Screenplay:** Woody Allen; **Cast:** Woody Allen (Victor/Fabrizio/Fool/Sperm), John Carradine (Dr. Bernardo), Lou Jacobi (Sam), Louise Lasser (Gina), Tony Randall (Operator), Burt Reynolds (Switchboard), Gene Wilder (Dr. Ross).

In 1969, Dr. David Reuben authored a book on sexual fears and eccentric behavior. ALLEN paid to utilize its title and concept as a springboard for his new picture, creating several episodes (seven remained in the film) that were shot in directorial styles satirizing the European-made arty movies. Many found this excursion—filled with the theme of Jewish guilt—to be Allen's most ethnic project to that date.

Of particular note were three of the movie's segments. In a quiz-show parody, *What's My Perversion?*, an elderly rabbi challenges the celebrity panel. He acts out his secret: observing his wife eating pork. In *What Is Sodomy?* a starry-eyed Jewish doctor (Wilder) is cornered by his spouse as he makes love to a sheep. In *Are Transvestites Homosexuals?* a Jewish businessman is dining at the home of his daughter's fiancé. He feels compelled to browse through his hostess's wardrobe closet. Soon he is dressed in drag—his compulsion—and then finds it necessary to flee the premises. He encounters his surprised dinner companions outside on the street. For some, this episode is a parable dealing with people closeted about their Jewish heritage.

***Exodus* (1960)** United Artists, color, 212 minutes. **Director:** Otto Preminger; **Screenplay:** Dalton Trumbo; **Cast:** Paul Newman (Ari Ben Canaan), Eva Marie Saint (Kitty Fremont), Ralph Richardson (General Sutherland), Peter Lawford (Major Caldwell), Lee J. Cobb (Barak Ben Canaan), Sal Mineo (Dov Landau).

The backstory of this epic had its own ironies. Proactive Jewish film executive Dore Schary was head of Metro-Goldwyn-Mayer and wanted to film the story of the emergence of the state of Israel. He commissioned Leon Uris to write the saga, which was published to great acclaim in 1958 and was then to be a studio project. But MGM fretted that such a release would alienate the British (shown in an unfavorable light in the book) and would obviously upset pro-Arab interests. MGM sold (for $75,000) the screen rights to *Exodus* to independent filmmaker Preminger. The Jewish director hired once blacklisted screenwriter Trumbo to adapt the 626-page book to the screen.

The narrative opens at a displaced persons camp on Cyprus in 1947 and moves on to Palestine, where there is a clash of power between two groups—the proterrorist Irgun and the antiterrorist Haganah—who dream of Israel becoming a nation. After the British withdraw from Palestine, there are many setbacks, much killing, and enormous negotiation before the United States recognizes Israel.

Mixed into this sweeping chronicle of fact and fiction is a conventional romance between a gentile American war widow (Saint) and a Palestinian (Newman). A side issue involves the HOLOCAUST survivors who reach Palestine to fulfill the long-cherished dream of returning to the promised land.

Exodus was extraordinary for its time. It was a blockbuster action tale in which Jews and Judaism dominated the screen. In addition, *Exodus* did not rely on the usual commercial safety net of having the Jewish leaders be biblical characters, which would have made the film story less threatening to non-Jewish filmgoers. Then too, the focal figure, Ari Ben Caanan, was not Hollywood's stereotypical meek or avaricious Jew but a man of action and bravery. (On the other hand, his character was not a traditionally devout Jew.)

Exodus was a box-office bonanza, but in some quarters the picture was labeled a "Jewish Western" because there were many story parallels to settlers claiming America from Native Americans. There were pro-Israeli factions who insisted that the film was historically inaccurate. Other Jewish groups feared that the movie would stir up anti-Semitism.

With fine support from veteran Jewish actors (including COBB, DAVID OPATOSHU, and GREGORY RATOFF), much was made of Italian-American Mineo playing the focal character of a concentration camp survivor turned daring anti-Arab terrorist. Yet, he created a memorable characterization and was Oscar nominated as Best Supporting Actor.

Exodus won an Academy Award for Ernest Gold's Best Original Dramatic Score. In 1971, a Broadway musical version of *Exodus* starring David Cryer, Constance Towers, and John Savage lasted nineteen performances.

F

***Fatherland* (1994)** HBO cable, color, 106 minutes. **Director:** Christopher Menaul; **Teleplay:** Ron Hutchinson and Stanley Weiser; **Cast:** Rutger Hauer (Xavier March), Miranda Richardson (Charlie Maguire), Peter Vaughan (Gen. Arthur Nebe), Michael Kitchen (Jaeger), John Woodvine (Luther).

Using the "what-if" gimmick, *Fatherland* was set in 1964, by which time the Third Reich had won World War II. Hoping to overwhelm Russia, Hitler concludes a peace treaty with the United States. When several high-ranking German officers are killed, SS detective Hauer and American journalist Richardson investigate, leading to the Nazi cover-up of the HOLOCAUST, which could end America's negotiations with Hitler.

An intriguing premise, based on Robert Harris's 1992 novel, this entry reinforced the ugly genocide chapter in history that some insist never happened. *Fatherland* was nominated for an Emmy Award for Outstanding Visual Effects.

***Fiddler on the Roof* (1971)** United Artists, color, 180 minutes. **Director:** Norman Jewison; **Screenplay:** Joseph Stein; **Cast:** Chaim Topol (Tevye), Norma Crane (Golde), Leonard Frey (Motel), Molly Picon (Yente), Paul Mann (Lazar Wolf), Rosalind Harris (Tzeitel), Paul Michael Glaser (Perchik).

It was hard to argue with such a sensational venture as *Fiddler on the Roof.* Based on the writings of Sholom Aleichem, the Broadway musical (1964), starring ZERO MOSTEL and a host of succeeding actors, ran for 3,242 performances. As a $9 million feature film, it grossed more than $28 million in domestic distribution. (It won three Oscars, including one for Best Cinematography, and five Academy Award nominations, including Best Director and Best Picture.) This success proved that a nostalgic, semifaithful look—with uplifting music—at the tough peasant Jews struggling in early twentieth-century Russia could have major box-office appeal.

What gave the picture its bounce (beyond songs like "Tradition," "Matchmaker, Matchmaker," and "If I Were a Rich Man") was its buoyant optimism. The movie depicted the poor villagers of Anatevka—including Tevye the milkman who has five unwed daughters without dowries—coping with the harsh climate and the Russian pogroms. Despite such adversities they remain philosophical, joke, and keep to their traditions. They always hope for a better future, meanwhile maintaining a close relationship with God.

Norma Crane and Molly Picon in *Fiddler on the Roof* (1971). (JC ARCHIVES)

If Mostel was passed over to star in the movie, at least YIDDISH THEATER veteran PICON was brought in to make the proceedings more zesty.

In 1939, Yiddish theater star Maurice Schwarz had directed and starred in a dramatic version of *Tevye*. It was based on his own screen adaptation of Aleichem's Yiddish play *Tevye der Milkhiker*, which in turn was derived from the short story "Khavah" from Aleichem's series (1896–1914) of tales about the milkman.

Fierstein, Harvey (1954–) As the flamboyant drag queen in his self-authored TORCH SONG TRILOGY, Fierstein won two Tony Awards—as playwright and as actor. It established the raspy-voiced, up-front personality as a dominant force in delineating on-screen variations of the contemporary gay Jew.

Born in Brooklyn, New York, to a Russian immigrant family, he studied art after high school and then entered show business as a drag queen performer in the East Village. His club work led to his off-off-Broadway acting for the La Mama Experimental Theatre and other stage groups in the 1970s and thereafter. After his *Torch Song Trilogy* success, he wrote the book for the musical stage version of *La Cage aux Folles* (1983). That same year, he made his TV movie debut as a voice in *The Demon Murder Case*. He played a lonesome Jewish homosexual in *GARBO TALKS* (1984), repeated his role of Arnold Beckoff in the screen version of *Torch Song Trilogy* (1988), and had a part in WOODY ALLEN's *Bullets Over Broadway* (1994). His recent acting assignments have included *Kull the Conqueror* (1997), the animated feature *Mulan* (1998), the gay-themed made-for-cable movie *Common Ground* (2000), and the Robin Williams comedy, *Death to Smoochy* (2002). His children's book, *The Sissy*, was published in 2002.

***For Pete's Sake* (aka: *July Pork Bellies*) (1974)** Columbia, color, 90 minutes. **Director:** Peter Yates; **Screenplay:** Stanley Shapiro and Maurice Richlin; **Cast:** Barbra Streisand (Henry), Michael Sarrazin (Pete), Estelle Parsons (Helen), William Redfield (Fred), Molly Picon (Mrs. Cherry), Heywood Hale Broun (Judge Hiller).

Having already starred in the successful screwball comedy *WHAT'S UP, DOC?* (1972), Streisand hoped to renew the magic here. The results, however, were feeble, and the illogical slapstick was almost embarrassing. The plot's premise was an extended illustration of the theory that there was nothing a good Jewish woman would not do for her husband.

"Henry" is the loud-mouthed wife of cabbie Pete. He wants to go back to school, but can't afford to quit his job. He'd like to gamble in the stock market with futures on pork bellies but doesn't have the necessary $3,000 for the risky venture. She borrows the money from a loan shark, who in turn sells the IOU to Mrs. Cherry, a motherly madam. The latter enlists Henry in her enterprise with disastrous results.

The only real juice here was provided by YIDDISH THEATER veteran PICON, as an enterprising, folksy, madam.

***Freud* (aka: *Freud: The Secret Passion*) (1962)** Universal-International, b&w, 139 minutes. **Director:** John Huston; **Screenplay:** Charles Kaufman and Wolfgang Reinhardt; **Cast:** Montgomery Clift (Sigmund Freud), Susannah York (Cecily Koertner), Larry Parks (Joseph Breuer), Susan Kohner (Martha Freud), Eric Portman (Dr. Theodore Meynert).

Like so many other Hollywood-financed screen biographies of Jewish notables (e.g., *THE EDDIE CANTOR STORY*, 1953; *I'll Cry Tomorrow*, 1955), little was made here of the Jewish background of Sigmund Freud (1856–1939), the pioneer/founder of psychoanalysis. Casting the lead assignment with Clift only further disguised the Jewishness of the celebrated Austrian.

A few scenes within the picture tacitly acknowledged that Freud was a Hebrew, for example, his traditional marriage service, complete with guests saying "mazel tov" as he wed Martha. In a later sequence, the therapist wondered why he cannot grieve and pray at his father's grave. He then recalled an incident years before when, as a child, his dad had been branded a "dirty Jew" by an aggressive anti-Semite, but the parent had not fought back. The boy's embarrassment and anger, Freud now understood, had colored their relationship thereafter. (The movie also showed the doctor's extreme closeness to his mother, a situation both typical and stereotypical of early twentieth-century Jewish European, and later American, families.)

Freud was not a financial success. The character of the great doctor was interpreted on screen by, among others, ALAN ARKIN (*The Seven-Per-Cent Solution*, 1976), Alec Guinness (*Lovesick*, 1983), Bud Cort (*The Secret Diary of Sigmund Freud*, 1984), the voice of Frank Finlay (*Nineteen, Nineteen*, 1985), Tim McKew (*Young Einstein*, 1988), Rod Loomis (*Bill & Ted's Excellent Adventure*, 1989), Peter Michael Goetz (*The Empty Mirror*, 1997), and on television by David Suchet in a six-part 1984 TV series and by John Bennett in the TV movie, *Sherlock Holmes and the Leading Lady*, 1990.

Freud: The Secret Passion See *FREUD*.

***Friends* (1994–)** NBC-TV series, color, 30 minutes. **Cast:** Courteney Cox [Arquette] (Monica Geller), Jennifer Aniston (Rachel Green), David Schwimmer (Ross Geller), Matthew Perry (Chandler Bing), Matt LeBlanc (Joey Tribbiani), Lisa Kudrow (Phoebe Buffay).

One of the major TV successes of the 1990s, this amiable sitcom is set in Manhattan and features six (post-) twentysomething characters whose favorite occupation is hanging out at the Central Perk coffee shop complaining about their (little) woes and unsatisfying relationships. Three of the bonded group are Jewish, including two Jewish-American Princesses from the suburbs. Monica is a formerly chubby girl, now a chef, who is obsessive about neatness and having her way. Beautiful Rachel, who never thought about life's serious side until recently, is self-absorbed, loves to shop, and expects the world to wait on her. In contrast is love's perpetual victim, Ross, the paleontologist brother of Monica, a bright schnook who is constantly rebuffed by the women he loves/marries. Most ethnic of the trio's parents are Ross and Monica's parents (Elliott Gould and Christina Pickles). The acerbic wife rules their affluent suburbanite roost, while the well-meaning spouse constantly makes peace in the family.

Despite their pedigree, the assimilated trio of Jewish characters never deals directly with religious issues nor lets interfaith relationships concern them.

***Frisco Kid, The* (1979)** Warner Bros., color, 122 minutes. **Director:** Robert Aldrich; **Screenplay:** Michael Elias and Frank Shaw; **Cast:** Gene Wilder (Avram Belinsky), Harrison Ford (Tommy), Ramon Bieri (Mr. Jones), Val Bisoglio (Chief Gray Cloud), George DiCenzo (Darryl Diggs).

Had this movie come before the superior *BLAZING SADDLES* (1974), it might have made far more of an impact. Then too, there was a lack of subtlety to this venture that coasted on the incongruity of an Orthodox Jew floundering in the Old West.

On the plus side, this film allowed Wilder to utilize his sad-sack/schlemiel persona. It was also one of the few mainstream Hollywood movies to employ extended conversations in Yiddish to set the atmosphere.

In 1850s Poland, the rabbis conclude that freshly graduated rabbinical student Belinsky should take over a synagogue in San Francisco. (That sets the point of view for the picture: Old World Jewish tradition versus New World, secular America.) After misadventures in Philadelphia with a trio of con men, he meets cowpoke Tommy. The mismatched pair become partners crossing the country. As they near San Francisco, the greenhorn encounters his opponents from back east. In a showdown, he murders one of the swindlers. Reaching San Francisco, Avram must take charge of a congregation despite having violated the commandment "Thou shall not kill."

Beyond Wilder's usual shtick and Ford's charm, a highlight of the film occurred when the cowboy robbed a bank and the rabbi refused to ride to safety because it was the Sabbath.

Earlier examples of the Jewish characters caught in the American Old West included *The Yiddisher Cowboy* (1911) and *Tough Guy Levi* (1912). A more recent one was *The Duchess and the Dirtwater Fox* (1976).

***Front, The* (1976)** Columbia, color, 94 minutes. **Director:** Martin Ritt; **Screenplay:** Walter Bernstein; **Cast:** Woody Allen (Howard Prince), Zero Mostel (Hecky Brown), Herschel Bernardi (Phil Sussman), Michael Murphy (Alfred Miller), Andrea Marcovicci (Florence Barrett).

In this serious study—with comic overtones—of the communist witch hunt of the 1950s, several of its participants (including director Ritt, scenarist Bernstein, and costar Mostel) had actually been BLACKLISTed. The narrative was a fictional account of real-life actor Philip Loeb, the costar of TV's *THE GOLDBERGS* who, when forced out of industry work because of alleged leftist affiliations and no longer able to maintain his ill son in a private institution, committed suicide in 1955. *The Front* dealt with such grave matters. On the down side, it did not always successfully blend old newsreel material with the new (comic) footage, nor did ALLEN's persona mesh well in the story line.

As the Jewish cashier/bookie who fronts for blacklisted writers in the 1950s by signing his name to their scripts, the nebbishy Howard Prince becomes a celebrity. The schnook enjoys his status change until he realizes that it is built on the misery of others. Meanwhile, Prince is under government surveillance because of his suspect associates. This leads to comedian Hecky Brown, one of these suspicious characters, telling the committee about Prince. Ashamed of his actions, Hecky commits suicide. Later, when Prince is subpoenaed, he refuses to betray his pals.

More so than *THE WAY WE WERE* (1973) with its sequences portraying the Unfriendly Ten and the March on Washington by Hollywood celebrities, *The Front* presented both the world of Jewish intellectuals and that of leftist sympathizers during the time of Red-baiting. A later movie, the inept *Guilty by Suspicion* (1991), starring Robert De Niro, covered the blighted period in Hollywood but without pointing to any strong links between Jews and liberal or communist causes. (Another entry dealing with Jewish talent affected by the 1950s blacklist was the 1989 cable movie *Fellow Traveller* starring RON SILVER.)

***Funny Girl* (1968)** Columbia, color, 151 minutes. **Director:** William Wyler; **Screenplay:** Arnold Schulman and Jay Presson Allen; **Cast:** Barbra Streisand (Fanny Brice), Omar Sharif (Nick Arnstein), Kay Medford (Rose Brice), Anne Francis (Georgia Jones), Walter Pidgeon (Florenz Ziegfeld).

Making her screen debut, STREISAND repeated her Broadway musical success (1964) and tied for a Best Actress Academy Award (with Katharine Hepburn) for her imaginative interpretation of legendary comedian/singer FANNY BRICE (1891–1951) and for singing "People," "I'm the Greatest Star," and Brice's signature number, "My Man." The opening scenes set in Manhattan's LOWER EAST SIDE were replete with a depiction of turn-of-the-century Jewish ghetto life. Streisand was so oversized in her portrayal that most filmgoers lost track of the story's real-life original (Brice) or of Fanny's charming no-good man, Nick Arnstein.

Nevertheless, Streisand established a positive screen image of an unconventional-looking Jewish woman who refused to be a wallflower but who often made poor choices in her men. Had *Funny Girl* been made even a few years before, Hollywood would have disguised the subject's ethnic background, but by the late 1960s the Jewish flavor of Brice's life and Streisand's performance became key selling points.

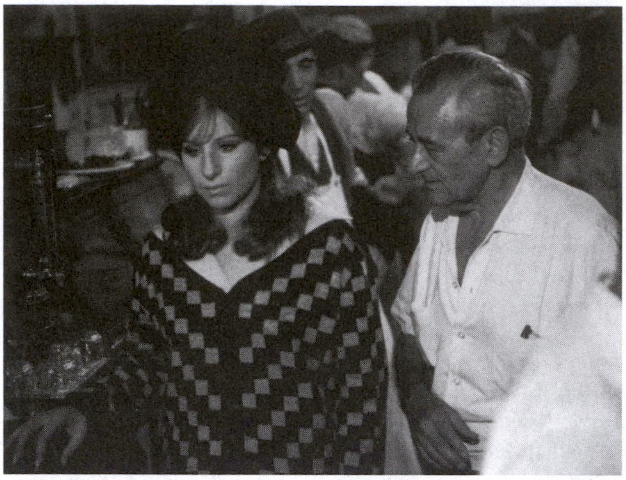

Barbra Streisand and director William Wyler on the set of *Funny Girl* (1968). (JC ARCHIVES)

This musical set the way for *ME, NATALIE* (1968), *THE HEARTBREAK KID* (1972), *SHEILA LEVINE IS DEAD AND LIVING IN NEW YORK* (1975), *Girlfriends* (1978), and all of Streisand's future movies, including *FUNNY LADY* (1975), the sequel to this box-office hit. *Funny Girl* earned more than $26 million in domestic film rentals and several Oscar nominations.

***Funny Lady* (1975)** Columbia, color, 136 minutes. **Director:** Herbert Ross; **Screenplay:** Arnold Schulman and Jay Presson Allen; **Cast:** Barbra Streisand (Fanny Brice), James Caan (Billy Rose), Omar Sharif (Nick Arnstein), Roddy McDowall (Bobby), Ben Vereen (Bert Robbins).

The follow-up to *FUNNY GIRL* (1968), beginning in 1930, found beloved comedian FANNY BRICE rejecting husband Nick Arnstein in favor of songwriter/Broadway producer/womanizer Billy Rose. The best of STREISAND's numbers was the Oscar nominated "How Lucky Can You Get?" Trying hard to duplicate/parallel its predecessor, *Funny Lady* featured Streisand as a refined star, not much like the subject. Brice's memory was further distorted by the weak story.

With both lead figures in the plot Jewish (as were Streisand and Caan in real life), the musical incorporated their Jewish backgrounds into their characterizations, peppering the script with Yiddishisms. *Funny Lady* earned five Oscar nominations, including Best Picture, and accumulated more than $19 million in domestic rentals.

G

game and quiz show series—television With the primary exception of Monty Hall *(Let's Make a Deal)* and Pee-wee Herman *(You Don't Know Jack!)*, TV game-show hosting was not the province of Jewish personalities. On the other hand, as celebrities, they were often featured as panelists on quiz shows. An early such program to showcase a wide ethnic mix was *The Quiz Kids* (1949–53), a carryover from a successful radio series.

One of the most noteworthy hosts of a quiz program was Groucho Marx, the most loquacious of the MARX BROTHERS comedy team. Having begun *You Bet Your Life* as a radio series (1947–49), wisecracking Groucho transferred the vehicle to the small screen in 1950 and continued through 1961. (The series returned briefly in 1981–82 with another Jewish comedian, Buddy Hackett, in charge. A decade later, African-American comedy star Bill Cosby headlined yet another version of the program that ran in 1992–93.)

Among the many Jewish personalities to have been long-term panelists on TV quiz shows were Sam Levenson (*Two for the Money*, 1955–57; *Masquerade Party*, 1958–60; etc.), Henry Morgan (*I've Got a Secret*, 1952–67), Bess Myerson (*The Big Payoff*, 1953–53; *The Name's the Same*, 1954–55; *I've Got a Secret*, 1956–67), and Soupy Sales (the syndicated *What's My Line*, 1968–75).

***Garbo Talks* (1984)** Metro-Goldwyn-Mayer/United Artists, color, 103 minutes. **Director:** Sidney Lumet; **Screenplay:** Larry Grusin; **Cast:** Anne Bancroft (Estelle Rolfe), Ron Silver (Gilbert Rolfe), Carrie Fisher (Lisa Rolfe), Catherine Hicks (Jane Mortimer), Steven Hill (Walter Rolfe), Harvey Fierstein (Bernie Whitlock).

If there was supposedly nothing a good Jewish mother would not do for her offspring, then the reverse should be true. When eccentric, left-wing advocate Estelle Rolfe, a New Yorker, learns that she is dying, she begs her son to do her one last favor—arrange a meeting with her life-long movie idol Greta Garbo. Gilbert becomes obsessed with locating the reclusive ex-movie star who also lives in Manhattan. Scouring the city for any lead to the legendary lady, Gilbert sacrifices work and his marriage (Fisher) to accomplish the mission before his parent succumbs. He not only succeeds but finds a new romance (Hicks) as well.

Filled with New York and Jewish atmosphere, *Garbo Talks* depicted a typical contemporary on-screen Semitic household, with an overbearing mother, a weak father, and a mother-dominated son.

Garfield, John (1913–1952) Renowned as a great celluloid tough guy, he made his mark playing the angry loner. He became typecast in such underdog roles.

He was born Jacob (but known as Julie) Garfinkle in New York City, the son of Russian immigrants. His father was a part-time cantor. Growing up in tough sections of the city, he almost drifted into a gangster's life until his junior-high-school principal suggested that he try boxing and, later, dramatics. After dropping out of high school, he studied at the American Laboratory Theater and was on Broadway in *Red Rust* (1929). He turned to Golden Gloves boxing tournaments in 1930 and, the next year, hitchhiked to California. Back on the East Coast, he worked in the CATSKILL RESORTS and appeared on Broadway in *Counsellor-at-Law* (1932). As part of the radical leftist Group Theater, he was in, among others, *Awake and Sing!* (1935). Promised the lead but given only a supporting part in the Group's *Golden Boy* (1937), he tried films again.

Garfield had already made his screen debut in a bit in the Warner Bros. musical *Footlight Parade* (1933). That studio signed him in 1938 and, as the young loser in *Four Daughters* (1938), he established a new mold of screen leading man—imperfect and inwardly sensitive. Kept out of World War II duty by a bad heart, he entertained troops overseas and helped form the Hollywood Canteen.

His screen roles improved with *PRIDE OF THE MARINES* (1945) and *The Postman Always Rings Twice* (1946). In *GENTLEMAN'S AGREEMENT* (1947), he was the Jewish pal of the gentile writer investigating anti-Semitism. He played a boxer who was disillusioned by fame in *Body and Soul* (1947), in which his character was only vaguely suggested to be Jewish, and then alternated between screen and stage roles. In 1951, he was called before the House Un-American Activities Committee. Never proved to be a communist, his film career was, nevertheless, stymied. Returning to stage work in New York, he succumbed to a heart attack at age thirty-nine.

gays and lesbians—feature films If from the mid-1930s until the early 1960s Hollywood movies treated Jewish characters like invisible citizens of the United States, the same applied to the depiction of overt Jewish homosexual figures. What was presented in either category was largely by indirection and inference. That changed with the raunchy black action entry, *Cleopatra Jones* (1973), in which Jewish-born SHELLEY WINTERS was seen as a very ethnic underworld drug trafficker, hoodlum, and butch lesbian. (Winters had already portrayed a lesbian in the arty release, *The Balcony*, 1962, and would play another variation of one in *S.O.B.*, 1981.) In both *SHEILA LEVINE IS DEAD AND LIVING IN NEW YORK* (1975) and *Girlfriends* (1978), the lead characters were single young Jewish women coping with life in the Big Apple; each was approached by lesbians who thought they were "that way," which the surprised heroines insisted was not the case.

On the male side of the fence, two of the crew in *Boys in the Band* (1970) were Jewish homosexuals, each depicted as prancing nellies. That same year, in the satirical *WHERE'S POPPA?* Ron Leibman was Sidney Hocheiser, the married brother *not* stuck caring for their senile mother. On one mad night that found him forced to race across Central Park twice (!), he was attacked by muggers who forced him to rape an undercover vice cop in drag. The next day, the Jewish man was surprised to receive long-stemmed roses from the law enforcer. Yet another 1970 release, the crime caper *The Anderson Tapes*, presented Martin Balsam as an effete gay antique dealer whose actions indicated that his character was Jewish. Then there was HARVEY FIERSTEIN's character, Arnold, the drag-queen performer in his self-written *TORCH SONG TRILOGY* (1988), based on his earlier stage play. (Among many other such screen roles, Fierstein had already played a Jewish gay in 1984's *GARBO TALKS*, as he would in the later TV movie *Common Ground*, 2000, and the theatrical release, *Playing Mona Lisa*, 2000.)

The character of lawyer Roy Marcus Cohn—who had been chief counsel to Wisconsin senator Joseph McCarthy during the politician's communist witch hunt—appeared in several movies (especially those focusing on John and Robert Kennedy in political office). Yet, it was in a made-for-cable feature, *Citizen Cohn* (1992), that the sinister attorney was fully depicted as a Jew who loathed Jews and a gay who hated gays.

In great contrast, in *The Wedding Banquet* (1993), which crossed racial and sexual barriers, two male New Yorkers (a Taiwanese and a Manhattan Jew) had a live-in relationship that got amusingly out of hand when the Asian, now an American citizen, was involved in a marriage of convenience to please his traditionalist parents.

The Delta (1996) focused on an eighteen-year-old Jewish youth who kept his homosexuality hidden from family and friends but found a sexual connection with a twentysomething Vietnamese whom he took to his father's cruiser on the Mississippi River. In the delightful comedy/drama, *WHAT'S COOKING?* (2000), an independent-minded Jewish woman, a lesbian in her thirties, brought her lover to her parents' home for the Thanksgiving holiday, much to the confusion and sometimes anger of her mother and father. Within *Kissing Jessica Stein* (2002), a young woman working in the publishing industry found herself attracted to a female art gallery manager, a free spirit she met through the personal ads.

gays and lesbians—television One of the more controversial made-for-television offerings in the early 1980s was *Sidney Shorr: A Girl's Best Friend* (1981). Created in the pre-AIDS epidemic era, the overtly cute plot gimmick had the lead character, a fussy Jewish man, grieving over the death of his lover. The role was given to Tony Randall, a Jewish-born performer, who had played the ultimate fussbudget—but heterosexual—in *THE ODD COUPLE* (1970–75). The TV movie did decently in the ratings; Oliver Hailey received an Emmy Award nomination for his teleplay. Then this property was developed into a TV series, *Love, Sidney* (1981–83) with Randall still in the focal role. By now, however, his character had been so neutered that only from vague inferences on the show could astute viewers assume he was living a gay lifestyle.

On *MAD ABOUT YOU* (1992–99), centering on a Jewish clan (the Buckmans), Debbie, the on-screen sister of the series lead (played by PAUL REISER), had previously been married to a man and was now divorced. Later, she picked a female obstetrician as her new life partner. Amazingly, it was all handled tastefully and nonchalantly on the series, even when used as a running gag. On the TV series *The Crew* (1995–96), a sitcom about young adults working for a small airline based in Miami, Florida, one lead character (played by David Burke) was gay and was the constant target of wisecracking by his supervisor (Christine Estabrook). *Relativity* (1996–97), set in Los Angeles, had Rhonda Roth (played by Lisa Edelstein) as the lesbian sister of a Jewish house painter (the series lead played by David Conrad), who, having been dumped by her girlfriend, was left vulnerable, insecure, and uncertain about finding a new mate.

The made-for-cable movie *The Twilight of the Golds* (1997) was based on a play by Jonathan Tolins. It had the futuristic premise that a new genetic analysis test could determine if a child would be born gay, as was the story's lead character, the Jewish David Gold (played by Brendan Fraser). This test precipitated a further rift between David and his parents (Faye Dunaway and Garry Marshall), with David wondering whether they would have chosen to abort him if the test had been available before he was born. *Queer as Folk* (2000–) set in Pittsburgh has five key male gay characters, all focused on their sex lives and careers. One of them is an accountant whose Jewishness is not a major theme, to date, of his characterization.

***Gentleman's Agreement* (1947)** Twentieth Century-Fox, b&w, 118 minutes. **Director:** Elia Kazan; **Screenplay:** Moss Hart; **Cast:** Gregory Peck (Phil Green), Dorothy McGuire (Kathy Lacy), John Garfield (Dave Goldman), Celeste Holm (Anne Detrey), Anne Revere (Mrs. Green), June Havoc (Ethel Wales [Estelle Walofsky]).

Based on Laura Z. Hobson's novel (1947), *Gentleman's Agreement* was the next giant step after the earlier *CROSSFIRE* (1947) in tackling anti-Semitism within the United States. Its thesis was that such bigotry was not isolated to a few cases.

Gentile reporter Phil Green pretends to be Jewish as he researches/writes a magazine series on anti-Semitism. Before long, many in his life think he is Jewish. Among the discriminatory acts he encounters are a hotel management that won't accept Jews, a Jewish worker (Havoc) who is herself anti-Semitic, a wealthy New England town that has a "gentleman's agreement" not to sell property to Jews, and name-calling against Jews.

A tremendously important film in the history of modern Judaism, this movie paved the way for future exploration of Jewish themes and characters on screen. It benefits greatly from the performance of GARFIELD as a returning GI who explains to Green that, over the centuries, Jews had learned to become insulated to anti-Semitism. What marred the impact of Green's experiences was that his character was only pretending to be Jewish and could return to mainstream America at any time. (It was felt that this plot device was needed, as in the book, so that audiences of the day would relate better to the questioning hero who was one of them, *not* a Jewish outsider.)

The heads of many other Hollywood movie studios tried to convince Twentieth Century-Fox, and its head, non-Jewish Darryl F. Zanuck, either not to make this picture or to soften its message greatly. Zanuck refused to yield. *Gentleman's Agreement* won Oscars for Best Picture, Best Director, and Best Supporting Actress (Holm).

Decades after its release, *Gentleman's Agreement* still remains the best-known Hollywood film dealing with anti-Semitism.

***George Jessel Show, The* (1953–1954)** ABC-TV series, b&w, 30 minutes. **Host:** George Jessel.

Veteran Jewish entertainer Jessel had been the Broadway star of *THE JAZZ SINGER* (1925) and had turned down doing the movie version (1927), which was Hollywood's first big part-talkie. (The assignment went to AL JOLSON and made his screen career.) Besides stage, club, and radio work, as well as movie producing, Jessel became famous as the "Toastmaster General," always ready to host a tribute, funeral, or fundraiser. Using that guise in this TV series, he emceed special testimonials to celebrities, often from the field of show business. His demeanor and jokes had ethnic tinges.

Gertrude Berg Show, The See *MRS. G. GOES TO COLLEGE.*

ghetto dramas This form of American screen fare centered on Jewish immigrants living in New York's LOWER EAST SIDE in the late nineteenth and early twentieth century. Reflecting reality, it dealt with newcomers to Manhattan, usually from the pogroms of eastern Europe. Typically, such dramas concerned the conflict between the older generation of new arrivals, who clung to their traditions, religion, and manners (including talking in Yiddish), and their children, who were often born in the new country and wanted to assimilate. Frequently in the process of acculturating, the offspring, who had been schooled in the new country to speak English, moved from the old neighborhood to uptown, to the suburbs, or out of the area altogether. Often embarrassed or ashamed of their parents' old-fashioned ways, the young folk usually would be prompted by some traumatic event to seek a new perspective. Shaken by their epiphany, they—as the formula required—would move back to the Lower East Side to be close to their relatives and their traditional (religious) values.

Another aspect of such entries was that, often, the patriarch was a rabbi or scholar who had been respected back home; now in the new world of commerce, where his talents had few material rewards, it was the money-earning children or the more adaptable spouse who had people's respect. Sometimes mixed in the brew was a clash between opposing cultures, most especially the Irish and the Jew—taking their cue from the long-lasting Broadway hit, *ABIE'S IRISH ROSE* (1922).

An early screen example of this idiom was *CHILDREN OF THE GHETTO* (1915), based on an 1892 novel and a 1899 Broadway play. In 1920, one of Fannie Hurst's 1919 magazine stories would be adapted into the silent photoplay *HUMORESQUE*, receive great acclaim, and become the prototype of ghetto dramas. (The movie, with its contents restructured and the Jewish ethnic slant neutralized, would be remade in 1946 with Joan Crawford and JOHN GARFIELD.)

Other silent film entries in this genre included *Barricade* (1921), *Breaking Home Ties* (1922), *Second Hand Rose* (1922), *None So Blind* (1923), *His People* (1925), *SALOME OF THE TENEMENTS* (1925), *Rose of the Tenement* (1926), *Sally in Our Alley* (1927), and *George Washington Cohen* (1928). There were also Yiddish-language movies of the period that fell into the ghetto drama category.

The genre, which had often become an aspect of comedies such as *THE COHENS AND KELLYS* (1926), revived in the late 1920s, helped along by the success of Al Jolson's *THE JAZZ*

SINGER (1927). In the part-talkie *East Side Sadie* (1929), the tried-and-true formula was used yet again. Fannie Hurst was the creator of THE YOUNGER GENERATION (1929)—released in sound and silent versions—based on her 1927 play.

The last blossoming of such ghetto pieces in American-made films was in 1932. Besides *No Greater Love*, which was geared for pathos, there was the humorous THE HEART OF NEW YORK (featuring the famous vaudeville team of Smith and Dale) and the dramatic HEARTS OF HUMANITY. The most noteworthy entry was again based on a Fannie Hurst screen story. In SYMPHONY OF SIX MILLION, Hurst returned to her sentimental, highly cheerful view of the pluses (!) of tenement life and the belief that they could restore a person's dignity and emphasize their best virtues.

By the mid-1930s, the ghetto dramas seemed out of date. By then a great many first- and second-generation American Jews had forgotten their roots and had moved away from the Lower East Side. Most of the original immigrants from the 1880–1920 period were dead or too ill or too preoccupied with surviving the Depression to attend movies. Most audiences wanted something more American. Besides, Hollywood was beginning to listen to the objections of Jewish PRESSURE GROUPS to these Semitic stereotypes. Then, too, the intensifying anti-Semitism in Europe led American film producers to focus on a more broad-based, less specifically ethnic type of urban drama (e.g., STREET SCENE, 1931; *Dead End*, 1937; *Angels Wash Their Faces*, 1938). Thereafter, when the camera panned in on the multicultural mix of a neighborhood scene in films, there might be Jewish representations in the mix, but they were not emphasized.

Later, in the 1940s when the Hollywood movie studios were making screen musicals based on the lives of great Jewish musicians and composers, in such films as RHAPSODY IN BLUE (1945)—dealing with the lives of George and Ira Gershwin—the Lower East Side would be pictured as quaint and the depiction of family life would be generalized.

Scenes in the opening segments of FUNNY GIRL (1968), the musical about comedian/singer FANNY BRICE, concerned themselves with life below 14th Street at the turn of the twentieth century. Likewise, HESTER STREET (1975), directed by JOAN MICKLIN SILVER, dealt with Manhattan's Lower East Side at the turn of the century. However, this well-wrought drama of Jewish immigrants coping with the new environment was too idiosyncratic to be labeled as part of the earlier ghetto-drama cycle.

In the STEVEN SPIELBERG-produced AN AMERICAN TAIL (1986), an animated feature, a family of Jewish Russian mice immigrated to the United States. The film encapsulated in detail the (Jewish) immigrant experience in New York of the 1880s.

***Godfather, Part II, The* (1974)** Paramount, color, 200 minutes. **Director:** Francis Ford Coppola; **Screenplay:** Coppola and Mario Puzo; **Cast:** Al Pacino (Michael Corleone), Robert Duvall (Tom Hagen), Diane Keaton (Kay), Robert De Niro (Vito Corleone), Talia Shire (Connie), John Cazale (Fredo), Lee Strasberg (Hyman Roth).

In this excellent sequel to the 1971 underworld epic, which also interweaved the history of Vito Corleone coming to New York many years before, Michael Corleone is in charge of the crime empire that his father created. He rules his domain from Lake Tahoe, Nevada. One of his business associates is Hyman Roth, with whom he opens a plush casino in Havana. Never trusting the wily elder man, Michael suspects that Roth was behind a failed assassination attempt on Corleone and his family. Later, after Fidel Castro takes over Cuba, Roth flees but is murdered by Michael's hit men.

Although Jewish criminals had been depicted on camera before (e.g., *The French Connection*, 1971; *The Hot Rock*, 1972; *Hit!*, 1973), never had one been presented in such venal terms as in *The Godfather, Part II*. Loosely suggested by the infamous Meyer Lansky (1902–83), STRASBERG's arch criminal was presented as a frail but cunning old man who could not be trusted. He was revealed as a man without redeeming virtues. His betrayal of his Italian benefactors, the Corleones, left him exposed—again the Jew on the outside—and a man who had to be exterminated.

Made at a cost of $12 million, this feature won several Academy Awards and other nominations, and grossed more than $30 million in domestic distribution.

***Goldbergs, The* (1949–1954; 1955–1956)** CBS-TV series (then NBC-TV, DuMont-TV, and Syndicated TV), b&w, 30 minutes. **Cast:** Gertrude Berg (Molly Goldberg), Philip Loeb (Jake Goldberg: 1949–51), Harold J. Stone (Jake Goldberg: 1952), Robert H. Harris (Jake Goldberg: 1952–56), Larry Robinson (Sammy Goldberg: 1949–52), Tom Taylor (Sammy Goldberg: 1954–56), Arlene McQuade (Rosalie Goldberg), Eli Mintz (Uncle David).

THE GOLDBERGS, written by and starring BERG, had begun on radio in 1929. Twenty years later, it jumped to early commercial TV and became a favorite with viewers. As in the other medium, it traced the everyday life of the Goldbergs on Tremont Avenue in the Bronx. Jake runs a dress business while Molly is queen of the roost at home and in her apartment building, always calling "Yoo-hoo!" to her neighbors through her open window.

The household contains Molly, Jake, and their children—Rosalie and Sammy—as well as the retired Uncle David. The series depicts an average, working-class Jewish family; their religion frequently comes into play, with annual episodes devoted to Seder feasts at home and Yom Kippur high holydays services at the synagogue. From the start, there was no disguising (or any intention to cover over) the characters' Jewishness. For many American TV viewers, this show was their first encounter with Jewish people.

In 1952, Berg was pressured by the TV network to replace Loeb, who had been blacklisted for being a supposed communist. Reluctantly, and to save the program, Berg did so, first with Stone and then with Harris. (Loeb would commit suicide in 1955). For 1955–56 *The Goldbergs* became a syndicated TV series with all new episodes, and the family in the plot line had relocated to Haverville, a fictional town in upstate New York.

Had *The Goldbergs* never been such an enormous hit on radio, or had it not been broadcast in the infancy of TV networks before executives and sponsors were fearful of what they presented to viewers, it is unlikely that such a minority ethnic series would have made it to the air. The spiritual descendant of *The Goldbergs* was *BROOKLYN BRIDGE* (1991–93) and to a lesser extent *State of Grace* (2001–).

The Goldbergs also appeared in other mediums. In 1948, Berg brought her property to Broadway in *Me and Molly* and a few years thereafter a tepid film adaptation of the radio series was released, entitled *MOLLY* (1950).

***Goldbergs, The* (1950)** See *MOLLY*.

***Golden West, The* (1932)** Fox, b&w, 70 minutes. **Director:** David Howard; **Screenplay:** Gordon Rigby; **Cast:** George O'Brien (David Lynch/Motano), Janet Chandler (Betty Summers/Betty Summers Brown), Marion Burns (Helen Sheppard), Arthur Pierson (Robert Summers), Bert Hanlon (Dennis Epstein).

In the early 1930s, Hollywood utilized Jewish characters as comedy relief (*THE COHENS AND KELLYS* series) or as inner-city flavor for dramas (*SYMPHONY OF SIX MILLION*, 1932). Occasionally, they showed up in westerns, as in *Cimarron* (1931), as peddlers or merchants but were always subordinate and perpetually the outsider.

The Golden West, based on a 1909 Zane Grey novel, was a different matter. Here, Dennis Epstein the Jewish character (actually a Jew from Ireland!), popped up *throughout* the narrative. While the story gave him no family, no homestead, no community ties, he was not a disregarded outsider but rather a man who frequently helped the lead characters solve their problems. Despite his carrying firearms, he was a moralizing peacemaker, one who broke up squabbles between two feuding African Americans. Interestingly, he was not shown as a traditional religious Jew but in a more flexible and modernized presentation of a Jew.

Nevertheless, the filmmakers also hedged their bets here. To soften his Jewishness, the movie had Epstein talk with an Irish inflection and sing Shamrock-laced ditties.

***Goodbye, Columbus* (1969)** Paramount, color, 105 minutes. **Director:** Larry Peerce; **Screenplay:** Arnold Schulman; **Cast:** Richard Benjamin (Neil Klugman), Ali MacGraw (Brenda Patimkin), Jack Klugman (Mr. Patimkin), Nan Martin (Mrs. Patimkin), Michael Meyers (Ron Patimkin).

Utilizing Philip Roth's 1959 novella *Goodbye, Columbus* brought the angst of modern American Jews into focus. Idealistic Neil Klugman served in the military. Now discharged, the college dropout lives with his aunt in the Bronx and is a library worker. He meets attractive Brenda Patimkin, a Radcliffe student and the daughter of a newly rich businessman (Klugman) and his wife (Martin) who live in Westchester County. Mr. Patimkin makes it clear that he doesn't find Neil suitable for his offspring. As for Neil, although he is increasingly annoyed by pampered Brenda and the Patimkins' materialism, he wants to bed her. Later, when he discovers that she (sub)consciously ensured that her parents would discover the fact that the couple was sleeping together, the affair ends.

In several ways, *Goodbye, Columbus*, which had parallels to *The Graduate* (1967), set the tone for future films dealing with Jewish topics. The portrait of the Patimkins was unflattering. Unlike celluloid Jewish fathers of old, Patimkin was crude and without much cultural knowledge, and his daughter had been refined (nose surgery, braces, etc.) and molded to be just like her parents.

Also evident in *Goodbye, Columbus* was the outsider theme. But ironically in this movie Neil was an outcast among fellow Jews—here the rich suburban set.

***Goodbye Girl, The* (1977)** Warner Bros., color, 110 minutes. **Director:** Herbert Ross; **Screenplay:** Neil Simon; **Cast:** Richard Dreyfuss (Elliott Garfield), Marsha Mason (Paula McFadden), Quinn Cummings (Lucy McFadden), Paul Benedict (Mark), Barbara Rhoades (Donna).

This was one of SIMON's more dimensional comedies in which his characters had priority over plot and one-liner jokes. Originally conceived for Robert De Niro, the part was assumed by DREYFUSS. His on-screen persona essentially turned the movie into the romantic encounters of a Jewish single man who was looking for love in Manhattan and who found it with a sexually satisfying, emotionally suspicious gentile woman.

Through a subleasing mix-up, a former stage dancer, the divorced Paula McFadden, must share her New York apartment with quirky Elliott Garfield, an aspiring actor. Also part of the household is Paula's precocious young daughter, who eventually brings the couple together.

For a change, in contrast to WOODY ALLEN's film alter ego, here was a single Jewish male who demonstrated that he was caring and not an intellectual who just wanted to mold a mind and then hastily depart.

Dreyfuss won a Best Actor Oscar for *The Goodbye Girl*. The movie was later turned into a short-lasting Broadway musical with Martin Short.

***Good Morning, Miss Dove* (1955)** Twentieth Century-Fox, color, 107 minutes. **Director:** Henry Koster; **Screenplay:** Eleanore Griffin; **Cast:** Jennifer Jones (Miss Dove), Robert Stack (Tom Baker), Kipp Hamilton (Jincey Baker), Robert Douglas (John Porter), Peggy Knudsen (Billy Jean), Jerry Paris (Maurice Levine).

As she awaits surgery, spinster schoolmarm Miss Dove recalls how she assisted many students over the years. During the narrative, her former pupils appear—some having stayed in

Liberty Hills, and others, such as Maurice Levine, who have left. Now a famed playwright, Levine was once a picked-upon pupil. He was then an eleven-year-old Polish refugee; when the others made fun of him, Miss Dove lectured her charges about how Levine's family was no different essentially from any other household.

At times overly saccharine, *Good Morning, Miss Dove* nevertheless was one of the few 1950s mainstream films not only to deal openly with a Jewish character but also to present him sympathetically and on equal terms with others. Not heralded at the time, this leap forward on behalf of the Jewish minority seemed more striking in retrospect.

Good Morning, Miss Dove, based on the 1954 novel by Frances Gray Patton, was produced by the studio that had released the ground-breaking *GENTLEMAN'S AGREEMENT* (1947). Paris, who portrays the adult Levine here, went on to play the Jewish Dr. Jerry Helper on TV's *THE DICK VAN DYKE SHOW* (1961–66).

Gordon, Vera (1886–1948) For many years—especially in the silent era—Gordon was the penultimate embodiment on screen of the typical Jewish mother.

Born Vera Nemirov in Russia, she came to the United States with her family at age seven. As a youngster she was involved in New York's YIDDISH THEATER and also played the vaudeville circuit. Her screen debut was as the matriarch in *HUMORESQUE* (1920), the GHETTO DRAMA that set the tone for her movie career. She played Rosie Potash in *POTASH AND PERLMUTTER* (1923) and was George Sidney's spouse in five of *THE COHENS AND THE KELLYS* comedic features. Her screen career faded in the late 1930s but was revived briefly when she appeared as one of the parents in the 1946 remake of *ABIE'S IRISH ROSE*.

Gould, Elliott (1938–) For a time, he was known as Mr. BARBRA STREISAND, but there was far more to this multitalented performer.

Born Elliott Goldstein, he grew up in Brooklyn and then West Orange, New Jersey, and began acting classes when he was eight. By high school, he was involved in summer theater and working in the CATSKILL RESORTS. After years of struggle as an actor, he won the lead in the Broadway musical *I Can Get It for You Wholesale* (1962), which featured Streisand in a small role. They wed and had a child. As her career rose, his faltered in the later 1960s. They divorced and he reshaped himself as a screen comedy lead in *Bob & Carol & Ted & Alice* (1969). He became one of the busiest performers in early 1970s movies, including *M*A*S*H* (1970) and *The Long Goodbye* (1973). By decade's end, however, he was in another acting slump.

Gould reemerged as a character lead, playing the Jewish restaurauteur in *OVER THE BROOKLYN BRIDGE* (1985). Thereafter, he turned up frequently in small roles in bigger films and larger parts in small pictures. On TV's *FRIENDS* (1994–), he was the father of Ross and Monica Geller, playing the stereotypical Jewish suburban dad. More recent films included *Playing Mona Lisa* (2000—again as the good-natured schnook), *Ocean's Eleven* (2001), *The Experience Box* (2002), and *Voltage* (2002).

Graham, Virginia (1912–1998) This self-assertive Jewish housewife, with her full figure and wide smile, already had much media experience when she gave American TV viewers *Girl Talk* (1962–69), a forerunner of the intimate talk-show format. Friendly aggressiveness, a gravelly voice, and colorful caftans were her trademarks.

Born Virginia Komiss in Chicago, she married a New Yorker in 1936 and soon became a mother. For fun, she wrote for radio, first commercials and then doing a Manhattan-based local cooking show. Hostessing a beauty trade show got her a guest appearance on TV's *Today Show*. This led to her daytime TV show *Virginia Graham and Food for Thought* (1952–57). By 1953, Graham was also a panelist on the TV quiz show *Where Was I* and, in 1956, became a cohost on NBC radio's *Weekday*. She made a pilot for *Girl Talk* in 1961, and the innovative TV series lasted for much of the 1960s.

Never one to be idle, Graham returned with the syndicated television program *The Virginia Graham Show* (aka: *Virginia Graham Talks*) from 1970 to 1973 and later in the decade was a correspondent on the TV magazine show,

TV talk-show maven Virginia Graham in the 1980s. (ECHO BOOK SHOP)

America Alive! She played a matron on the soap opera *Texas* in 1982 and was in the movie *Slapstick of Another Kind* (1984) with JERRY LEWIS. In 1988, she guested on the sitcom. *Roseanne;* in 1995, she appeared as herself on an episode of TV's *THE NANNY*.

***Great Dictator, The* (1940)** United Artists, b&w, 127 minutes. **Director/Screenplay:** Charles Chaplin; **Cast:** Charles Chaplin (Adenoid Hynkel, Dictator of Tomania/a Jewish barber), Paulette Goddard (Hannah), Jack Oakie (Napaloni, Dictator of Bacteria), Reginald Gardiner (Schultz), Henry Daniell (Garbitsch).

It was paradoxical that, at the time, the one power in Hollywood to speak out against the anti-Semitic policies of the Third Reich was non-Jew Charles Chaplin. (Interestingly, over the decades, film historians often commented that Chaplin's trademark Little Tramp character was reminiscent of the traditional outcast Jewish figure.)

With his industry status, Chaplin had the resources to make this major film, which he had first conceived of three years earlier. From the time he announced the project, he was warned by his studio and industry figures that he would incur the wrath not only of Adolf Hitler's Germany but also of German sympathizers around the world—including those in the United States, but Chaplin did not care because he felt that in this—essentially his first all-talking picture—he needed an important message for his character(s) to articulate. By the time the movie went into production, World War II had begun, although America was officially still neutral.

The Great Dictator opens in World War I where a fighting Jewish soldier (Chaplin) contracts amnesia as the result of a plane crash. After hospital treatment, he flees back to Tomania, not knowing that his homeland is controlled by dictatorial Hynkel and his troops. As the ex-soldier regains his life as a barber and find happiness with Hannah, a Jewess, the narrative cuts back and forth between the barber's love story and the absurd activities of power-crazed Hynkel who is competing with Napaloni, ruler of Bacteria. At the finale, the barber impersonates Hynkel and delivers a live radio broadcast denouncing totalitarianism.

As in the later *TO BE OR NOT TO BE* (1942), *The Great Dictator* was so deadly serious that some viewers were uncomfortable at laughing at the satirical moments. (The filmmaker included many moments of fun—to break the tension of the film's message—as, for example, when the mad dictator did a ballet-style dance while involved with a balloon globe, with the soundtrack blaring Wagnerian music.) The physical resemblance between Chaplin's dictator and the real thing was frighteningly close.

The Great Dictator was a success when released and earned several Oscar nominations. In 2002 there appeared the British-German coproduced TV documentary *The Tramp and the Dictator*.

H

***Hannah and Her Sisters* (1986)** Orion, color, 106 minutes. **Director/Screenplay:** Woody Allen; **Cast:** Woody Allen (Mickey), Michael Caine (Elliot), Mia Farrow (Hannah), Carrie Fisher (April), Barbara Hershey (Lee), Maureen O'Sullivan (Hannah's mother), Max Von Sydow (Frederick), Dianne Wiest (Holly).

There was much that was different in this ALLEN excursion: He plays a subordinate character; there is a depiction of Jewish family life (in contrast to most of his films that focus on Jewish singles); the mix of sweetness and sentimentality is greater; and the conclusions about religion are more definite.

This was one of Allen's longer features, and its three distinct stories create an intricate plot as TV producer Mickey ponders the existence of God, the meaning of life, and his obsession with death. Meanwhile, his actress ex-wife (Farrow) is betrayed by her husband (Caine), who is having an affair with his sister-in-law (Hershey). The latter has been living with a pompous, controlling painter (Von Sydow).

Hannah and Her Sisters won three Academy Awards: Best Screenplay, Best Supporting Actor (Caine), and Best Supporting Actress (Wiest). The movie grossed an impressive $40 million in domestic distribution.

***Heartbreak Kid, The* (1972)** Twentieth Century-Fox, color, 104 minutes. **Director:** Elaine May; **Screenplay:** Neil Simon; **Cast:** Charles Grodin (Lenny Cantrow), Jeannie Berlin (Lila Kolodny), Cybill Shepherd (Kelly Corcoran), Eddie Albert (Mr. Corcoran), Audra Lindley (Mrs. Corcoran).

Relying on Simon's dimensional script, director May explored the Jewish male fantasy of being with a shiksa and the thinking that life and sex would be better with a non-Jewish woman. Additionally, (sub)consciously, it was a way to break further away from tradition and family.

Smug Lenny Cantrow, with aspirations of joining the WASP world, weds plain, Jewish Lila. On their Florida honeymoon, he encounters icy blonde Kelly with whom he flirts. Ditching his conventional wife, Lenny pursues Kelly to Minnesota where he copes with her father who is convinced that Lenny—because of his personality and his ethnic background—isn't right for his daughter. Nevertheless, the couple wed in a Christian ceremony, and Lenny ponders his future.

This comedic gem had much to say about the contemporary Jewish male and the contrast (albeit exaggerated here) between Jewish and gentile women. Berlin, the daughter of May, excelled as the epitome of what most men did *not* want in a spouse. Berlin would play a less klutzy version of the Jewish wallflower in *SHEILA LEVINE IS DEAD AND LIVING IN NEW YORK* (1975).

***Heart of New York, The* (1932)** Warner Bros., b&w, 74 minutes. **Director:** Mervyn LeRoy; **Screenplay:** Arthur Caesar and Houston Branch; **Cast:** Joe Smith (Sam Shtrudel), Charles Dale (Bernard Schnaps), George Sidney (Mendel), Ruth Hall (Lillian Mendel), Aline MacMahon (Bessie), Anna Appel (Mrs. Zelda Mendel).

Replete with ethnic types who converse in heavy accents and gesticulate enthusiastically, this entry features the veteran comedy team of Smith and Dale. SIDNEY of *THE COHENS AND THE KELLYS* fame plays the nonworking plumber who hopes his inventions will earn a fortune. When his family faces financial ruin, his wife Zelda offers to become the breadwinner. As Mrs. Mendel, Appel provides a progressive version of the Jewish mother, no longer kitchen-bound and limited to kvelling (bragging) over her brood.

Based on David Freedman's 1929 play (*Mendel, Inc.*), *The Heart of New York* was not another depiction just of Jewish life on the LOWER EAST SIDE but of the typical Jewish family moving uptown, only to become nostalgic for the old neighborhood.

***Hearts of Humanity* (1932)** Majestic, b&w, 65 minutes. **Director:** Christy Cabanne; **Screenplay:** Edward T. Lowe; **Cast:** Jean Hersholt (Sol Bloom), Jackie Searl (Shandy), J. Farrell MacDonald (Tom O'Hara), Claudia Dell (Ruth Sneider), Charles Delaney (Tom Varney), Lucille LaVerne (Mrs. Sneider); Richard Wallace (Joey Bloom).

Like the same year's *SYMPHONY OF SIX MILLION*, this was one of the last Hollywood entries to treat the Jewish ghetto of Manhattan with schmaltz. *Hearts of Humanity* was shot in six days at a cost of $30,000 and painted the LOWER EAST SIDE as a bastion of sentimentality and virtue.

Hersholt is the owner of a neighborhood antique shop. He adopts the son (Searl) of a dying widowed cop. Later, the boy straightens out the store owner's mischievous son (Wallace).

***Hester Street* (1975)** Midwest, b&w, 90 minutes. **Director/Screenplay:** Joan Micklin Silver; **Cast:** Steven Keats (Jake [Yankel Podkovnik]), Carol Kane (Gitl), Mel Howard (Mr. Bernstein), Dorrie Kavanaugh (Mamie Fein), Doris Roberts (Kavarsky), Stephen Strimpell (Joe Peltner).

Harking back to the screen GHETTO DRAMAS of the silent era, and taking advantage of the nostalgia for old world Jewish culture promulgated in *FIDDLER ON THE ROOF* (1971), *Hester Street* highlighted life on the LOWER EAST SIDE in 1900s New York. There, Jake, a Jewish Russian refugee, is desperate to become a "Yenkee" and to carry on with his girlfriend Mamie Fein. But Jake is already married and finally sends to the old country for his wife Gitl and their son. When they arrive, he is embarrassed by their old-fashioned ways. As for the greenhorn Gitl, she outgrows her insensitive spouse and divorces him. She turns for solace to her tenement roommate, Mr. Bernstein, a not-so-appealing scholar who has turned his back on everything in the new country.

Filmed economically in black and white, this well-engineered movie reflected on the contrasting paths immigrants took upon coming to America. Kane received a Best Actress Oscar nomination. SILVER would return to the Lower East Side for her contemporary comedy, *CROSSING DELANCEY* (1988).

Hirsch, Judd (1935–) With his heavily ethnic features, broad shoulders, and unruly, dark hair, Hirsch was an unlikely choice to become a major name is show business, but he succeeded in starring on Broadway, TV series, and films, winning Tonys and Emmys along the way.

Born in New York City, he obtained his college degree in physics and also studied architecture. Preferring an acting career, he struggled, not winning a professional acting part until he was twenty-seven. He spent the next years mostly with stock companies. He had a bit part in the cop movie *Serpico* (1973) and played the dedicated Jewish public defender in *The Law* (1974). On the police TV series, *Delvecchio* (1976–77) he had the title assignment as the noble sergeant.

Judd Hirsch on a TV sound stage in the late 1980s. (JC ARCHIVES)

Hirsch was appearing on Broadway in Neil Simon's *Chapter Two* in 1978 when he left to be Alex Rieger, the Jewish cabbie in TV's *TAXI* (1978–83). For his sympathetic role, he won two Emmys. Meanwhile, in *Ordinary People* (1980), as the understanding Semitic psychiatrist, he was Oscar nominated, and he later turned in a well-modulated performance as the 1960s radical in *Running on Empty* (1988). He was the immigrant Jewish accountant in *Talley's Folly* both off-Broadway (1979) and on Broadway (1980). Judd earned Tony Awards for *I'm Not Rappaport* (1986—played in the screen version by Jewish actor WALTER MATTHAU) and *Conversations with My Father* (1992), both very ethnic works by Herb Gardiner.

Hirsch's other TV series included *Dear John* (1988–91) and *George & Leo* (1997–98). In *Man on the Moon* (1999), starring Jim Carrey as comedian Andy Kaufman who was a *Taxi* cast member, Hirsch played himself. Judd appeared as a professor in Russell Crowe's *A Beautiful Mind* (2001).

***His People* (1925)** Universal, b&w, 8,983′. **Director:** Edward Sloman; **Screenplay:** Charles E. Whittaker; **Cast:** Rudolph Schildkraut (Rabbi David Cominsky), Rosa Rosanova (Rosie Cominsky), George Lewis (Sammy Cominsky), Bobby Gordon (Sammy Cominsky—as a boy), Arthur Lubin (Morris Cominsky), Blanche Mehaffey (Mamie Shannon).

This superior study of assimilation by the newer generation of Jews was a morality tale where inflexible traditional standards and the desire to fit in clashed. Rabbi Cominsky, who had been respected back in Russia, is forced to be a street peddler to support his family on Manhattan's LOWER EAST SIDE. His older son, the ungrateful Morris whom Cominsky favors for his intellectual abilities, becomes a lawyer. Mingling with the blue bloods and his boss's daughter, he ignores his family, especially his father whom he rebuffs as being old-fashioned. Eventually, however, thanks to his underappreciated younger brother (Sammy) who has become a prizefighter, Morris comes to his senses. Nevertheless—in the tradition of such Hollywood formula—he weds the Irish lass (Mehaffey) whom he has known for years.

The film starred the eminent YIDDISH THEATER actor Schildkraut and featured as his hard-working wife, Rosanova, who had appeared to advantage in *HUNGRY HEARTS* (1922).

historical dramas—feature films In contrast to the several biblical-themed films that prominently featured Jewish characters (but were considered "safe" movie fare because they were in the Bible), there were far fewer historical dramas (about the pre-twentieth century) dealing with Jewish figures. Part of this was due to prejudice by Hollywood filmmakers and/or their fear that audiences wouldn't respond favorably to such subjects. Another reason was that for great portions of postbiblical times, the Jewish race was so downtrodden in many countries that they were unable to rise to positions of prominence or if they somehow did, their Jewishness was often disguised at the time.

One of the early examples of an American screen work focusing on a Jewish character was *DISRAELI* (1921), a silent photoplay starring George Arliss, the British stage star who had first come to the United States to do stage plays. This prestige production focused on the life of England's famous Jewish statesman Benjamin Disraeli (1804–81) who became the first Earl of Beaconsfield. The movie was sufficiently popular that Arliss would remake the vehicle in 1929 as a talkie and win an Academy Award for his efforts. There would be other American-made movies that featured the Disraeli character but in more subordinate roles, such as *Suez* (1938) and *The Mudlark* (1950).

Again, it was Arliss who was called on to star in a dual role in *THE HOUSE OF ROTHSCHILD* (1934), another high-caliber production. It dealt with two generations of the Rothschild family, German Jews who first operated a banking house in Frankfurt in the eighteenth century and then spread their branch offices to other countries on the Continent and in England

Alfred Dreyfus (1859–1935), the French army officer of Jewish descent who had been falsely accused of selling secrets to the Germans in the late 1890s, had been the subject of movies made abroad, such as the British *The Dreyfus Case* (1931) starring Cedric Hardwicke. In 1937, the Dreyfus case was interwoven into *THE LIFE OF EMILE ZOLA*, the Hollywood screen biography of the great French writer who championed the cause of his imprisoned countryman. (The subject matter would again be adapted to the screen in the British-made *I Accuse!* of 1958 starring José Ferrer.)

historical dramas—television Even more than in the arena of theatrical releases, there was a paucity of TV dramas centered on non-biblical Jewish characters in pretwentieth century eras. One of the few such productions was *The Invincible Mr. Disraeli*, originally presented as part of the *Hallmark Hall of Fame* series in 1963. Its selling point was having movie stars in the cast, with Trevor Howard as Benjamin Disraeli and Kate Reid as Queen Victoria.

In 1991, Richard Dreyfuss starred in *Prisoner of Honor*, an HBO cable movie dealing with the French captain sent to Devil's Island on trumped-up espionage charges. Dreyfuss had the role of Colonel Picquart who was ordered to rationalize for the record the scandalous affair. Kenneth Colley was seen as Captain Dreyfus.

Hoffman, Dustin (1937–) Before Dustin Hoffman, it was rare in 1960s Hollywood for a leading man to be short (five feet, five and one half inches), *not* conventionally handsome, and overtly ethnic. But with *The Graduate* (1966), for which he was Oscar nominated, Hoffman demonstrated that it was talent, not traditional screen looks, that counted in a performer.

Born in Los Angeles, California, he majored in music at a local junior college and studied jazz and classical piano at the Los Angeles Conservatory of Music. But then the acting bug hit him. He matriculated at the Pasadena Playhouse and was eventually accepted at the Actors Studio in New York. He spent a few years with the Theater Company of Boston in the early 1960s. By 1966, he was being acclaimed for his work in the off-Broadway production *Eh?*

Hoffman's career breakthrough was being cast as *The Graduate* who is seduced by his girlfriend's mother. On a professional roll, he was also Oscar nominated for playing the deformed street hustler in *Midnight Cowboy* (1969). One of his more cerebral parts was portraying controversial Jewish comedian Lenny Bruce in *Lenny* (1974), for which he was again nominated for an Academy Award. It was for the domestic drama *Kramer vs. Kramer* (1979) that he won his first Oscar. Perhaps his biggest hit was the comedy *Tootsie* (1982) in which he masqueraded as a woman. *Rain Man* (1988) found him cast as an autistic savant, and it brought the actor his second Oscar. Earlier in the decade Hoffman had starred in the Broadway revival of *Death of a Salesman*, and in 1989, he made his Shakespearean debut as Shylock in *The Merchant of Venice.*

Ever the Method actor and always seeking new challenges, Hoffman's screen appearances in the 1990s included the criminal Mumbles in *Dick Tracy* (1990), the dastardly pirate in *Hook* (1991), the self-impressed movie director in *Wag the Dog* (1997), and the more conventional movie hero in *Sphere* (1998). Later screen work included *Goodbye Hello* (2002).

Holliday, Judy (1921–1965) Best known for playing sassy dumb blondes, she actually had an extremely high I.Q. With a high whiney stage voice and expressive eyes, she developed a special rapport with audiences.

Born Judith Tuvim in New York City, her father was a fundraiser for socialist and Jewish organizations, and her mother was a piano teacher. After graduating high school in 1938, she worked briefly as a switchboard operator for Orson Welles's Mercury Theater and had an extra role that year in his unreleased 40-minute movie *Too Much Johnson.* Next, she joined with friends—including the songwriting duo of Betty Comden and Adolph Green—to form the Revuers, a topical cabaret act that also performed on radio. In 1943, the group worked in Los Angeles. By now Judy had adopted the surname Holliday (a derivation of her Hebrew surname which meant holiday) and had small parts in two movies, including *Something for the Boys* (1944).

Back in New York as a solo act, Holliday received good notices for a small assignment on Broadway in *Kiss Them for Me* (1945) and then took over the lead in the pre-New York tryout production of *Born Yesterday*, the 1946 comedy that was a sensation, as was Judy. She had a similar role in the screen frolic *Adam's Rib* (1949). For recreating her role in the movie version of *Born Yesterday* (1950), Holliday won an Academy Award.

Judy Holliday in the mid-1950s. (JC ARCHIVES)

A downturn in her life occurred when Holliday was called before the House Un-American Activities Committee. She maneuvered out of the situation, but it slowed down her career. Eventually, she played more dumb blondes in *It Should Happen to You* (1954), *The Solid Gold Cadillac* (1956), and so on. Back on Broadway, she had a big success in the musical *Bells Are Ringing* (1956), a part she would recreate on screen (1960).

While preparing a heavily dramatic role for *Laurette* in 1960, it was discovered she had cancer. After a long recovery, she tried another musical, *Hot Spot* (1963), but the show did not mesh and Holliday was not well. She died of cancer at age forty-three in mid-1965.

Holocaust, the The term referred to the methodical mass slaughter of European Jews in the Nazi CONCENTRATION CAMPS during World War II. For Adolf Hitler's Third Reich, part of the "final solution" regarding undesirables was the arrest and extermination of all Jews.

As the reality of this much-rumored nightmare reached Hollywood, it was considered too touchy a subject to handle (i.e., fear of losing European marketplaces for movie releases, concern by the film community and the U.S. government that some Americans would believe that the United States was entering World War II only to fight on behalf of European Jews, and apprehension that any depiction of the German treatment of Jews would only bring out anti-Semitism in the United States). In 1940, two feature films (*ESCAPE* and *THE MORTAL STORM*) from MGM touch on the subject, showing detention camps and suggesting that the prisoners were there because they were Jewish.

Although some fictional war movies of the 1940s dealt with escapes from concentration camps (e.g., *The Seventh Cross*, 1944), the fleeing victims were not necessarily depicted as innocent Jews seeking freedom. Actually, it was graphic movie theater newsreels of the 1940s, especially after the liberation of various German camps, that showed Americans the true reality of the Holocaust. One of the early Hollywood feature films to depict the liberation of the concentration camps and the Allied soldiers' horror of the prisoners' plight was *THE YOUNG LIONS* (1958). Three years later, the all-star courtroom drama *JUDGMENT AT NUREMBERG* included actual newsreels of these extermination camps and the barely alive survivors, along with the mounds of corpses stacked in open pits. (This procedure would be utilized in the later two-part cable movie, *NUREMBERG*, 2000.) Both *THE PAWNBROKER* (1965) and *SOPHIE'S CHOICE* (1982) utilize flashback sequences in which their lead characters relive the horror of the camps and how it scars them for life. In the Academy Award-winning musical, *CABARET* (1972), the growing tide of virulent Nazi anti-Semitism in 1930s Germany is forcefully shown.

In the true-story telefilm *A Woman at War* (1991), the effects of the Holocaust are told from the point of view of a nineteen-year-old Belgian Jew (Martha Plimpton) whose parents are taken away by the Gestapo. Later she joins the Resistance and infiltrates Nazi headquarters to help save lives, which is complicated by her relationship with an opportunistic German businessman (Eric Stolz). The made-for-cable movie *Never Forget* (1991) tells of a Holocaust survivor (Leonard Nimoy) who confronts a neo-Nazi group in court when the latter claims that the mass extermination of Jews during World War II never happened. *In the Presence of Mine Enemies* (1996), directed by JOAN MICKLIN SILVER, has a rabbi (Armin Mueller-Stahl) in the Jewish ghetto of 1942 Warsaw, Poland, who is forced to deal with the horror around him as the Nazis persecute the Jews.

A trio of made-for-cable movies, produced by BARBRA STREISAND's production company in the later 1990s, have the common theme of brave souls (usually not Jews) coming to the aid of persecuted Jews during the Holocaust by hiding them from the Nazi pursuers. (The entries were: *Rescuers: Stories of Courage: Two Women* [1997], *Rescuers: Stories of Courage: Two Couples* [1998], *and Rescuers: Stories of Courage: Two Families* [1998].)

The Devil's Arithmetic (1999), a made-for-cable movie, featured an Alice-in-Wonderland-like premise of a contemporary young Jewish woman (Kirsten Dunst) who does not appreciate her heritage. Suddenly, she finds herself transported back to the 1940s as a prisoner in one of the German death camps. NUREMBERG, the oversize cable TV movie in 2000, involves the trial of key Nazi figures, and much of the testimony in the courtroom hearing concerns the prisoners' genocide policy against the Jews. *Anne Frank: The Whole Story*, the four-hour 2001 telefeature, shows how the anti-Jew policy affects a Jewish family and friends who hide from the Nazis in occupied Amsterdam and who are later sent to concentration camps. In the HBO cable film, *Conspiracy* (2001), Kenneth Branagh is featured as Adolf Eichmann, who joins with other high-ranking German officers in 1942 to establish the "final solution" for eradicating all Jews in Nazi-occupied Europe. The telefeature *Haven* (2001) details the real-life story of a young Jewish newspaperwoman from Brooklyn who helps to rescue 1,000 Jewish war victims in the mid-1940s and escorts them to safety in the United States. The well-mounted TV miniseries *Uprising* (2001) reenacts how a group of brave Polish Jews stave off—for several months—Nazi troops in their Warsaw ghetto during World War II. The heroic Jewish leader is played by Hank Azaria. The feature film *The Grey Zone* (2002) concerns a prisoner uprising against their World War II German captors at Auschwitz death camp.

The end of World War II and the liberation of surviving prisoners from the Nazi death camps was not the end of the Holocaust for its victims. Several feature films and made-for-television/cable productions (as well as scattered episodes of TV series) focused on the shocked status of Holocaust survivors. *THE JUGGLER* (1953) details a numbed survivor's (KIRK DOUGLAS) emotional revival by going to Palestine where he helps to build the new nation. The theatrical release, *The Man in the Glass Booth* (1975), based on a 1969 stage play, features Maximilian Schell as a glib Jewish businessman who survived the concentration camps but later, out of guilt, insists on confessing that he was a Nazi officer in them.

The telefeature *REMEMBRANCE OF LOVE* (1982) has a Polish refugee (Kirk Douglas again) living in the United States who flies to Israel to consult its data bank of Holocaust survivors to locate a lost love from the ghettos. *MAX AND HELEN* (1990), a cable television movie, presents a camp survivor (Treat Williams) who copes with his guilt for having survived the horror while his fiancée (Alice Krige) had not.

The television miniseries *HOLOCAUST* (1978) indelibly etches the horrors of the death camps, a theme revisited in a miniseries trilogy: *THE WINDS OF WAR* (1983), *War and Remembrance* (1988), and *War and Remembrance: The Final Chapter* (1989). The made-for-television movie *PLAYING FOR TIME* (1980) focuses on a group of imprisoned musicians who are forced to play concerts for their captors to avoid the fate of other camp prisoners. The made-for-TV picture *The Execution* (1985) concerns five Holocaust victims living in San Diego who draw lots to see who will kill a former concentration camp doctor who tortured them, during World War II, and who has since been acquitted in court of war crimes. The telefeature *Escape from Sobibor* (1987), starring ALAN ARKIN, is set toward the end of World War II at a death camp in eastern Poland. It concerns a small group of prisoners who are kept alive to work under the control of the Nazi guards. Unable to deal further with the horror of watching their countrymen and families be exterminated, they plan a daring escape.

In *A Call to Remember* (1997), another made-for-cable movie, two camp survivors (Blythe Danner and Joe Mantegna) who each had lost their families to the Nazis, have since married one another, moved to America, and created a new family unit. Suddenly, the wife is told that one of her original sons survived World War II. In APT PUPIL (1998), based on a Stephen King novella, a high-school student encounters a former Nazi officer, who was responsible for prison camp atrocities. The latter is still a sadistic man who has not softened with the years.

Another aspect of post-Holocaust dramas was the search for Nazi officers who perpetrated the reign of terror. The theatrical release *OPERATION EICHMANN* (1961) presents the Israelis' search for the former SS-Lieutenant Colonel. (Other productions to focus on the hunt for Eichmann hiding out in Argentina include the telefeatures *The House on Garibaldi Street* [1979] and *The Man Who Captured Eichmann* [1996]. In *Mother Night* [1996], based on the 1962 Kurt Vonnegut novel, the captured Eichmann is incarcerated in the cell next to a recently collared American double agent [Nick Nolte] of World War II who endured hell for his valiant efforts during the Holocaust.)

The expansive TV miniseries *QB VII* (1974) concerns an American writer (Ben Gazzara) who uncovers the horrific past at the Jadwiga concentration camp of a physician (Anthony Hopkins), who conducted horrific experiments on prisoners there. The telefeature *NAZI HUNTER: THE BEATE KLARSFELD STORY* (1986) tells of a German Protestant (Farrah Fawcett) who marries a Jew and devotes herself to Jewish causes, including tracking down Nazi criminals.

One of the more engrossing studies of Nazi chasers is the made-for-television movie, *Murderers Among Us: The Simon*

Wiesenthal Story (1989). The famous Nazi hunter Wiesenthal, an Austrian Jew, spends three years in concentration camps. After being liberated, he personally begins a campaign to bring Nazi war criminals to trial and over the years traces some 1,000 unprosecuted criminals, including the infamous Adolf Eichmann.

The unusual angle of the television movie *Twist of Fate* (1989) is that its lead character, Helmut von Schrader (Bruce Greenwood), undergoes plastic surgery and pretends to be a Jew to avoid capture as World War II comes to an end. Later, he finds himself in Israel where, as an army general, he grows to love his new homeland. Then one day, members of ODESSA, the underground SS organization, locate him and demand that he serve their sinister cause.

Among the many documentaries produced on the Holocaust were such Academy Award-winning entries as the 39-minute short subject, *One Survivor Remembers* (1995) and the 87-minute feature-length *The Last Days* (1998). Others dealing with the topic included: *The Eighty-First Blow* (1974—a nominee for a Best Documentary Oscar), *Who Shall Live and Who Shall Die?* (1982), *Witness to the Holocaust: The Trial of Adolf Eichmann* (1987), *Survivors of the Holocaust* (1996—with a discussion segment featuring Steven Spielberg), and *Kovno Ghetto: A Buried History* (1998).

***Holocaust* (1978)** NBC-TV miniseries, color, 450 minutes. **Director:** Marvin J. Chomsky; **Teleplay:** Gerald Green; **Cast:** Tom Bell (Adolf Eichmann), Joseph Bottoms (Rudi Weiss), Tovah Feldshuh (Helena Somova), Rosemary Harris (Berta Weiss), Michael Moriarty (Erik Dorf), Ian Holm (Heinrich Himmler), Meryl Streep (Inga Helms Weiss).

Winner of eight Emmy Awards, including Outstanding Limited Series, this landmark drama was to Judaism what *Roots* (1977) had been for African Americans. Spanning the years 1935 to 1945, the epic drama dealt with two contrasting German families who cope with the rise and fall of the Third Reich. On the one side is young attorney Erik Dorf and his household. Paralleling the Dorfs' experiences are those of the Jewish Rudi Weiss, his Catholic wife (Streep), and their relatives.

For many TV watchers, this controversial miniseries was their first real encounter with the causes and effects of the HOLOCAUST. It made a more powerful statement because of its high drama than had, for example, the earlier feature film, *JUDGMENT AT NUREMBERG* (1961). *Holocaust*, seen by an estimated 120 million home viewers, paved the way for such later World War II/Jewish issue dramas as the miniseries *THE WINDS OF WAR* (1983) and *SCHINDLER'S LIST* (1993).

***Home Before Dark* (1958)** Warner Bros., color, 136 minutes. **Director:** Mervyn LeRoy; **Screenplay:** Eileen Bassing and Robert Bassing; **Cast:** Jean Simmons (Charlotte Bronn), Dan O'Herlihy (Arnold Bronn), Rhonda Fleming (Joan Carlisle), Efrem Zimbalist Jr. (Jake Diamond), Mabel Albertson (Inez Winthrop).

Considered conventional in its day, *Home Before Dark* was more than just another big-budgeted soap opera. On the surface, it tells of Charlotte Bronn who is just released from a sanitarium after recovering from a nervous breakdown. In her absence, her New England college professor husband takes in a colleague, the Jewish Jake Diamond, as a boarder. Once home, Charlotte realizes that her demanding spouse much prefers to be with her stepsister Joan Carlisle. As matters worsen, only Jake, also an outsider in the community, gives her emotional support. Eventually, encouraged by Diamond, Charlotte leaves her husband and starts life anew—perhaps with Jake.

In the relatively few 1950s Hollywood feature films to deal overtly with Jewish characters, Zimbalist's Jake Diamond was presented sympathetically. Based on a 1957 novel by Eileen Bassing, *Home Before Dark* was ahead of its time.

***Homicide* (1991)** Triumph Releasing, color, 102 minutes. **Director/Screenplay:** David Mamet; **Cast:** Joe Mantegna (Bobby Gold), William H. Macy (Tim Sullivan), Natalija Nogulich (Chava), Ving Rhames (Randolph), Rebecca Pidgeon (Miss Klein).

It was an unexpected aspect of this police procedural movie that it should also be a vehicle for one of its characters' self-examination of his Jewish roots. But in this talky drama, the antihero found his submerged Jewish identity surfacing.

When an elderly Jewish woman is murdered, her family insists that an anti-Semitic gang is the culprit. Police detective Gold and his partner Sullivan are ordered to investigate. Gold comes to the realization—after learning that the dead woman once sold guns to Jewish activists—that the victim's wealthy family is correct in its hypothesis. During the course of the case, he analyzes his past refusal to acknowledge his Jewishness. With his new-found religious fervor, he helps a Jewish terrorist (Nogulich) and her crew destroy the headquarters of the anti-Jewish culprits.

Ironically, in finding his new identify, Gold creates problems: His partner is killed because of the lawman's distraction, and an African-American felon (Rhames) whom he is protecting is gunned down. As for Gold, wounded in the shootout, he eventually returns to police duty, only to learn that he has been demoted. Regarding the initial homicide, the old lady's death is officially labeled (wrongly on purpose) as the work of two black youths seeking easy money.

Homicide painted a bleak picture of contemporary urban life, exuding illustrations of racial bigotry between Jews, African Americans, Irish, and Italians.

***House of Rothschild, The* (1934)** United Artists, b&w and color, 88 minutes. **Director:** Alfred Werker; **Screenplay:** Nunnally Johnson; **Cast:** George Arliss (Mayer Rothschild/Nathan Rothschild), Boris Karloff (Count Ledrantz), Loretta Young (Julie Rothschild), Robert Young (Captain Fitzroy), C. Aubrey Smith (Duke of Wellington), Florence Arliss (Hanna Rothschild).

George Arliss in *The House of Rothschild* (1934). (JC ARCHIVES)

This was one of several prestigious Hollywood historical dramas starring the mannered Britisher, George Arliss. It harkened back to the mood and episodic format of *DISRAELI* (1921 and 1929), which had also showcased Arliss.

In Frankfurt, in the last decades of the eighteenth century, the Prussian Jews are ghettoized. As money changer Mayer Rothschild dies, he urges each of his five sons to move to a different country and create an international banking power. He cautions them of their religious duty to bring peace to their people. The story leaps forward to 1812 England where Nathan Rothschild is asked to help Wellington's battle against Napoleon Bonaparte financially. Meanwhile, the anti-Semitic Count Ledrantz marshals opinion against Nathan. Ledrantz later triggers anti-Jewish riots throughout Prussia but is then forced, after Bonaparte escapes from exile, to beg Nathan for help. Eventually, Wellington and the British defeat Napoleon's forces at Waterloo and England, grateful for Nathan's support, makes him a baron. A main theme is the romance between Nathan's daughter Julie and Captain Fitzroy, one of the duke of Wellington's envoys.

In the guise of a historical drama, this film seemed to be a metaphor for the persecution Jews were experiencing in twentieth-century Germany. But the picture left viewers perplexed. Was this a screen narrative in support of persecuted Jews over the centuries, or was it, in its account of money lenders (shades of Shylock from *The Merchant of Venice*) who took advantage of historical situations, pandering to anti-Semitic sentiment about supposed grasping Jewish money merchants?

The House of Rothschild received an Oscar nomination for Best Picture, and the trade paper *Film Daily* ranked it second in its list of Ten Best Pictures of 1934. In 1940, the Third Reich produced the anti-Semitic *Die Rothschilds*.

***Humoresque* (1920)** Paramount-Artcraft, b&w, 5,987′. **Director:** Frank Borzage; **Screenplay:** Frances Marion; **Cast:** Gaston Glass (Leon Kantor), Vera Gordon (Mama Kantor), Alma Rubens (Gina Berg [Minnie Ginsberg]), Dore Davidson (Abraham Kantor), Bobby Connelly (Leon Kantor, as a boy).

Popular pulp novelist Fannie Hurst had authored "Humoresque" as a short story for *Cosmopolitan* magazine in 1919. As adapted to the screen, it became the prototype of the New York Jewish GHETTO DRAMA set on the LOWER EAST SIDE and it established the image of the self-sacrificing Jewish mother. In this instance, her nobility was directed to her offspring, a violinist of great promise. He becomes successful and moves uptown. During World War I, he nearly loses the ability to play the instrument. A key theme within *Humoresque* was that of the new generation of Jews becoming more Americanized both in name and lifestyle.

Cast as the self-sacrificing mama was GORDON, a veteran of the YIDDISH THEATER who later starred in *THE COHENS AND KELLYS* movie series. Great detail went into the presentation of Jewish family life, mixing—as became the formula—drama and comedy relief. When *Humoresque* was released to general acclaim, there were complaints in some quarters that the movie's pathos reached bathos and that Gordon gave an overly schmaltzy performance.

Twenty-six years later, Warner Bros. remade the property with Joan Crawford and JOHN GARFIELD costarred. Hurst's original story was merely a springboard for the new screenplay, much of it conceived by Clifford Odets for another film, *RHAPSODY IN BLUE* (1945), the life story of Jewish musician/composer George Gershwin. In the new *Humoresque*, with additional material by Zachary Gold and others, the ethnic background of the violinist—now called Paul Boray—was ambiguous, as was that of his doting mother, played by Ruth Nelson in a much smaller part than in the 1920 original. Character actor J. Carrol Naish, frequently associated with Italian characterizations, was hired to be the violinist's father. On the other hand, casting the Jewish Garfield in the lead role of the 1946 entry led many viewers to assume that the character was Jewish.

***Hungry Hearts* (1922)** Goldwyn, b&w, 6,540′. **Director:** E. Mason Hopper; **Screenplay:** Julien Josephson; **Cast:** Bryant Washburn (David Kaplan), Helen Ferguson (Sara Levin), E. A. Warren (Abraham Levin), Rosa Rosanova (Hannah Levin), George Siegmann (Rosenblatt).

The 1920 novel by Anzia Yezierska supplied the basis for this refreshingly realistic drama of Manhattan ghetto life. For Hannah Levin, white is a symbol of purity, and it is worth the sacrifice to find the money to paint her apartment kitchen white. Once accomplished, the landlord raises the rent, and, in anger, she destroys the prized room. She is defended by a kindly young lawyer (Washburn) who later moves the family to his suburban home. As a result—in this fantasy—the Levins escape their dreary life in the ghetto.

Yezierska also authored the 1925 novel that formed the basis of that year's *SALOME OF THE TENEMENTS*, another drama set in New York City's LOWER EAST SIDE.

I

impersonations—non-Jewish actors playing Jewish and Jewish-American characters on camera Just as Caucasian actors in the early decades of American cinema in the twentieth century played on-camera African Americans, Asian Americans, and Native Americans, so over the years non-Jewish performers took on Semitic roles. Some were small parts that went unnoticed or larger roles well handled by the actor (e.g., Sal Mineo in *EXODUS*, 1960; Ruth Gordon in *WHERE'S POPPA*? 1970; Ingrid Bergman in the TV presentation *A WOMAN CALLED GOLDA*, 1982; Meryl Streep in *SOPHIE'S CHOICE*, 1982). But it was the performers who failed to offer a believable ethnic characterization that stood out over the decades. These interpretations of screen roles were especially evident when the players adopted overexaggerated accents and/or gestures or, in the opposite extreme, made their portrayal seem as WASP as could be. Some of the miscreants included: Ricardo Cortez in *Symphony of Six Million* (1932), John Barrymore in *COUNSELLOR-AT-LAW* (1933), Gregory Peck in DAVID AND BATHSHEBA (1952), Elizabeth Taylor (then not yet converted to Judaism) in IVANHOE (1952), Keefe Brasselle in *THE EDDIE CANTOR STORY* (1953), Steve Allen in *THE BENNY GOODMAN STORY* (1955), Montgomery Clift in *THE YOUNG LIONS* (1958), Natalie Wood and Claire Trevor in *MARJORIE MORNINGSTAR* (1958), Kim Novak in *MIDDLE OF THE NIGHT* (1959), Rosalind Russell in *A MAJORITY OF ONE* (1961), Frank Sinatra in *Come Blow Your Horn* (1963), Ava Gardner in *The Bible . . . In the Beginning* (1966), Sophia Loren in *Judith* (1966), Eileen Heckart in *NO WAY TO TREAT A LADY* (1968), Omar Sharif in *FUNNY GIRL* (1968) and *FUNNY LADY* (1975), Laurence Olivier in *THE JAZZ SINGER* (1980) and *The Boys from Brazil* (1978), Richard Gere in *KING DAVID* (1984), Blythe Danner and Judith Ivey in BRIGHTON BEACH MEMOIRS (1986), Anne Bancroft in *TORCH SONG TRILOGY* (1988) and *Neil Simon's Broadway Bound* (1992—TV movie), and Eddie Cibrian in the TV movie *In the Beginning* (2000).

***Infiltrator, The* (1995)** HBO cable, color, 102 minutes. **Director:** John Mackenzie; **Teleplay:** Guy Andrews; **Cast:** Oliver Platt (Yaron Svoray), Arliss Howard (Eaton), Peter Riegert (Rabbi Cooper), Alan King (Rabbi Hier). Tony Haygarth (Gunther).

The unyielding fascination/abhorrence of (neo) Nazism established a new genre of literature, several examples of which were adapted to the screen. *In Hitler's Shadow* (1994) by Yaron Svoray and Nick Taylor was one such novel.

Freelance reporter Yaron Svoray, the son of HOLOCAUST survivors, arrives in Berlin to research an article about the neo-Nazi movement. During his visit to a Turkish refugee camp, a ruckus that is instigated by skinheads breaks out. The police believe that Svoray is one of the troublemakers and arrest him. He uses this opportunity to infiltrate the group and is amazed at what he learns: that even after all these years, Nazism is not a dead cause in its homeland.

KING, who had earlier played rabbis in *BYE BYE BRAVERMAN* (1968) and *ENEMIES: A LOVE STORY* (1989), again was seen as a man of God in this production, which was based on a true story.

***In Hollywood with Potash and Perlmutter* (1924)** Associated First National, b&w, 6,685′. **Director:** Alfred E. Green; **Screenplay:** Frances Marion; **Cast:** Alexander Carr (Morris Perlmutter), George Sidney (Abe Potash), Vera Gordon (Rosie Potash), Betty Blythe (Rita Sismondi), Belle Bennett (Mrs. Perlmutter), Peggy Shaw (Irma Potash).

After the success of *POTASH AND PERLMUTTER* in 1923, producer Samuel Goldwyn turned out the next installment of this silent-movie series. Because Barney Bernard had passed away, his role was inherited by SIDNEY for the remaining

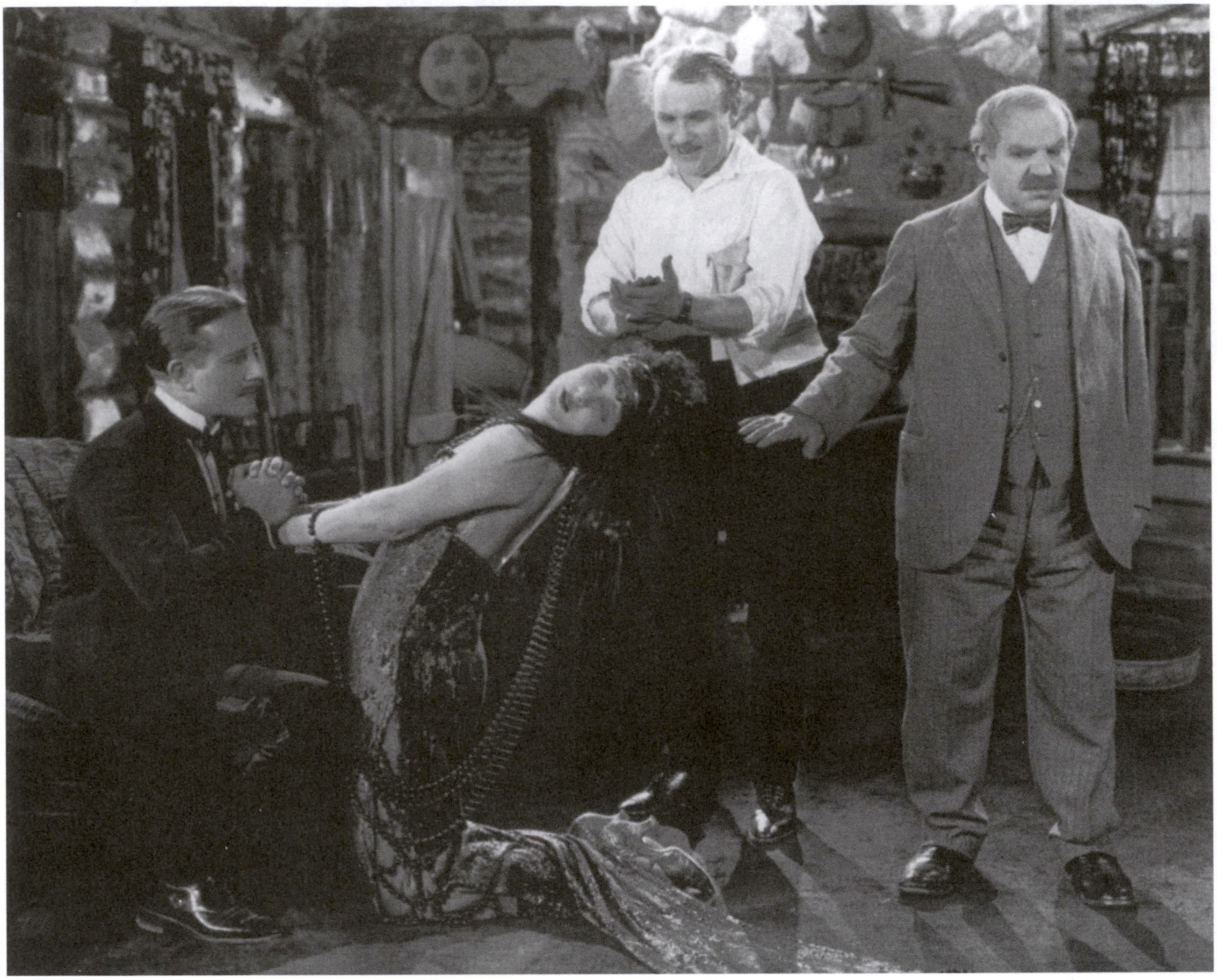

Cyril Ring, Betty Blythe, Alexander Carr, and George Sidney, costars of *In Hollywood with Potash and Perlmutter* (1924). (JC ARCHIVES)

entries. For Sidney, this property was a warm-up for him and GORDON; they played the similarly constructed Mr. And Mrs. Cohen characters in a rival studio's movie series, which debuted with *THE COHENS AND KELLYS* (1926).

Here, the feudin' and fussin' Perlmutter and Potash abandoned their textile operation to produce motion pictures. (The plot line smacked of Goldwyn's own life, a man who had previously been a glove salesman.) As would be true in the Cohen/Kelly adventures, the clash/contrast of cultures (here, Jews from the LOWER EAST SIDE versus "sophisticated" movie industry folk) was a continuing source of the film's comedy. (There would be a later parallel entry in the competing Cohens and Kellys series.)

Marion based her script on the 1917 Broadway comedy *Business Before Pleasure* by Montague Glass and Jules Eckert Goodman. Part of the "inside joke" of this film and other similar movies was that almost all of the American movie industry's founders were once greenhorn Jewish immigrants like Sidney's character.

***Inside the Third Reich* (1982)** ABC-TV miniseries, color, 300 minutes. **Director:** Marvin J. Chomsky; **Teleplay:** E. Jack Neuman; **Cast:** Rutger Hauer (Albert Speer), John Gielgud (Albert Speer Sr.), Maria Schell (Mother Speer), Blythe Danner (Margaret Speer), Derek Jacobi (Adolf Hitler), Randy Quaid (Putzi Hanfstaengl), Ian Holm (Dr. Joseph Goebbels), Renee Soutendijk (Eva Braun).

One of the many TV productions dealing with the infamy of Nazi Germany, this one was based on the 1970 English-language translation of Albert Speer's memoirs. Speer (1905–81), the German who designed the Nuremberg stadium for the Nazi Party congress of 1934, becomes Adolf

Hitler's personal architect; as a Nazi government official, he is minister of armaments and munitions. After the war and the Nuremberg trials, Speer spends twenty years in Spandau prison.

While this masterful entry centers on the inner working of the Nazi Party and its führer, running throughout the drama is a depiction of the Third Reich's policy of Aryan supremacy that lead to the extermination of millions of Jews. Chomsky, who helmed *HOLOCAUST*, the acclaimed 1978 TV miniseries, won another Emmy for *Inside the Third Reich*. The program earned six other Emmy nominations.

Entries such as this prestigious production were part of the constant (re)educating of the public to the horrors of World War II atrocities away from the battle fronts. This urgent need to remind audiences of what transpired in Europe to the Jews during the Holocaust became a recurrent theme of serious film and television fare of the second half of the twentieth century.

Israel—feature films and television productions about Israel, a 8,022-square-mile country located in the Middle East on the Mediterranean Sea was formed in 1948 from a part of the British-controlled Palestine. Within a year after it became an independent Jewish homeland, Hollywood featured the country in the action drama *Sword in the Desert* (1949) starring JEFF CHANDLER. That film deals with the furtive entry of HOLOCAUST victims into British-occupied Palestine and their battle to gain independence. Four years later, KIRK DOUGLAS starred as *THE JUGGLER*, a German Jewish survivor who arrives in Palestine after World War II and finds new meaning to life there.

The landmark *EXODUS* (1960) is a big-budget epic on the founding of Israel. It set the path for *CAST A GIANT SHADOW* (1965), in which Kirk Douglas appears as a Jewish-American military officer who helps to shape the Israeli military as they prepare to fight for statehood. The unfortunately inept *Judith* (1966) casts Sophia Loren as an Austrian Jew who comes to Palestine after World War II to track down her duplistic Nazi husband. A few years later, *The Jerusalem File* (1972) presented Bruce Davison as an American student caught in Arab-Israeli counterterrorism after the Six Day War

On television, the miniseries *QB VII* (1974) devoted part of its mammoth teleplay to three generations of an alienated Jewish family who find their way to Israel and how this changes their lives. Two competing telefilms, *VICTORY AT ENTEBBE* (1976) and *RAID ON ENTEBBE* (1977) focus on the 1976 raid of a Tel Aviv-to-Paris flight that is hijacked by Arab terrorists and how the Israelis rescue the hostages.

A television miniseries dealing with ancient Palestine and the Israelis' fight for independence is *MASADA* (1981), with Peter Strauss as the determined head of 900 inventive Jewish Zealots who combat a horde of Roman soldiers, led by Peter O'Toole.

In *REMEMBRANCE OF LOVE* (1982), Kirk Douglas is a former Polish refugee living in America who flies to Israel to track down a lost love from World War II. The unusual *TWIST OF FATE* (1989), a made-for-television feature, follows a former Nazi SS officer who disguises himself as a Jew to avoid capture, immigrates to Palestine, and becomes a general in the Israeli army.

In contrast to most Hollywood-produced movies and telefeatures dealing with Israel that have presented a favorable viewpoint, at least two took an opposite position. In the Peter Yates-directed thriller, *Eyewitness* (1981), a well-bred Jewish TV news reporter (Sigourney Weaver) is involved romantically with an Irish janitor (William Hurt). The villain of the piece is the Israeli diplomat (Christopher Plummer) who turns out to be a murderer. Later came *The Little Drummer Girl* (1984), based on the John Le Carré bestseller (1983). The main figure is Charlie (Diane Keaton), a credulous actress with a fondness for lying. She is forcibly recruited by Mossad, the Israeli intelligence agency, to trap a Palestinian bomber by pretending to be the girlfriend of his dead brother. This film caused consternation among Jewish PRESSURE GROUPS who felt that the picture was too pro-Arab and that Israeli agents were depicted as quite ruthless.

In addition, there were cable/TV movies that dealt with leading political figures of the state of Israel, in particular, those productions that involved Israeli prime ministers: Golda Meir (*21 Hours at Munich*, 1976; *A WOMAN CALLED GOLDA*, 1982; *Sword of Gideon*, 1986), David Ben-Gurion (*The House on Garibaldi Street*, 1979; *A Woman Called Golda*, 1982), Menachem Begin (*RAID ON ENTEBBE*, 1976; *Sadat*, 1983), and Yitzhak Rabin (*Raid on Entebbe*, 1976; *VICTORY AT ENTEBBE*, 1976).

***Ivanhoe* (1952)** Metro-Goldwyn-Mayer, color, 106 minutes. **Director:** Richard Thorpe; **Screenplay:** Noel Langley; **Cast:** Robert Taylor (Ivanhoe), Elizabeth Taylor (Rebecca), Joan Fontaine (Rowena), George Sanders (DeBois-Guilbert), Emlyn Williams (Wamba), Robert Douglas (Hugh De Bracy), Finlay Currie (Cedric), Felix Aylmer (Isaac).

Many classics of literature (*OLIVER TWIST*) and drama (*The Merchant of Venice*) featured Jews, reflecting the attitudes of the times in which they were created and as such often embraced anti-Semitic themes. A case in point was *Ivanhoe*, based on Sir Walter Scott's 1828 novel. In the adventure novel of twelfth-century England, the money lender and financial benefactor was presented as a kindly but nevertheless avaricious Jew.

Ivanhoe had been picturized in the 1910s in both England and the United States. Because they were such short, silent films, there was little character delineation beyond references to Isaac of York being a Jew. By the time of the sound, color, big-budget MGM screen version, Isaac and his daughter, Rebecca, had key if not main roles in the lavish proceedings. Since World War II, Hollywood, on its own and through the impact of PRESSURE GROUPS, was far more politically correct in handling Jewish characters on screen (that is when it dared or cared to present any). Dore Schary, head of MGM production, was a pro-active Jew, which ensured that, on the surface, the handling of the Semitic characters in the 1952 *Ivanhoe* was "fair."

Being fair meant being true, to a degree, to the original novel. Thus, Isaac was displayed as a wandering Jew with no home and no allegiance to any monarchy. He was, in short, a man of whom to be suspicious. In the course of this narrative, he explained how he and his people had been exiled from country after country and that hoarding money was their only means of self-protection. However, as played here by Aylmer, Isaac was presented as a noble and benevolent outsider.

In casting the beautiful Elizabeth Taylor (who in a few years would convert to Judaism to please the new love of her life) as Rebecca, Isaac's daughter, the movie created an unusual contradiction. Her rival for the love of Ivanhoe was the gentile, Lady Rowena. Certainly, while both were stunning, it was Rebecca/Taylor who was more visually fetching than Rowena/Fontaine. Yet, the plot setup demanded that the kindly Rebecca step aside in the competition for Ivanhoe's love because of her outsider's position as a Jewess. The subtext, a carryover from Scott's novel, was that Jews did not deserve to and/or should not be allowed to win, even when they had better qualifications.

Among other adaptations of *Ivanhoe* was the 1982 TV movie starring Anthony Andrews as Ivanhoe, with James Mason as Isaac of York and Olivia Hussey as Rebecca. There were also two British TV series (1956 and 1971) that were loosely based on *Ivanhoe*.

J

***Jack Benny Program, The* (1950–1965)** CBS-TV (then NBC-TV) series, b&w (then color), 30 minutes. **Cast:** Jack Benny (himself), Mary Livingstone (herself), Eddie Anderson (Rochester), Dennis Day (himself), Don Wilson (the announcer), Mel Blanc (Professor LeBlanc/Si), Artie Auerbach (Mr. Kitzel).

After decades as a radio favorite, BENNY transferred to television in 1950 (although he kept his radio show going until 1955). Much of the format of the radio show applied to the TV series, offering a representation of Benny's daily life at home and at the (rehearsal) studio for his show. Although Benny's radio alter ego was never stated to be Jewish, his high-profile support off camera of Jewish charities gave that inference. By the time Jack moved to television, there was such a blur between the real and on-stage Benny that the two melded together.

On radio, Benny, like many other stars of weekly comedy series, had a cast of regulars as well as character actors who played recurring supporting roles. One of Benny's regulars was African-American actor Anderson playing Rochester, the houseman, who is beset by his cranky, cheap boss. At the time, political correctness did not extend to finding this cast stereotypical. Rochester's character made the transition to Benny's TV series. Other ethnic characters from Benny's radio days made appearances in the visual medium. They included Day as a slightly dim-witted Irishman with a beautiful singing talent, as well as recurring spots by Si, the Mexican (Blanc), and Mr. Kitzel (Auerbach), the Jewish foil. (On Benny's radio series there had also been another Jewish character, Schlepperman, enacted by Sam Hearn.)

***Jakob the Liar* (1999)** Columbia, color, 119 minutes. **Director:** Peter Kassovitz; **Screenplay:** Kassovitz and Didier Decoin; **Cast:** Robin Williams (Jakob Heym), Alan Arkin (Frankfurter), Bob Balaban (Kowalsky), Hannah Taylor-Gordon (Lina), Michael Jeter (Avron), Armin Mueller-Stahl (Professor Kirschbaum).

A surprisingly restrained Williams stars as a Jewish café proprietor in Nazi-occupied Poland in 1944. By accident, he overhears a radio report about the defeat of the Russian army in a nearby town, and he anticipates that Allied forces are nearby. When he shares the news with others in the ghetto, it is assumed that he has access to a radio, and soon everyone wants more news. Jakob fabricates further reports to bolster his neighbors' spirits. Eventually, he is captured, tortured, and executed by the Nazis because he refuses to tell his friends that there is no radio.

Jakob the Liar might have had a better reception had there been no *Life Is Beautiful* (1997). That Italian-made, Oscar-winning movie dealt with a Jewish man who, during World War II, makes a game out of concentration camp life to help his young son survive the horrors there.

Based on Jurek Becker's 1969 novel *(Jakob der Lügner)*, this property had been previously filmed in West Germany in 1974. Mueller-Stahl was also in the earlier picture in the same role of the local physician forced to minister to a Nazi SS officer and who later committed suicide.

***Jazz Singer, The* (1927)** Warner Bros., b&w, 90 minutes. **Director:** Alan Crosland; **Screenplay:** Al Cohn; **Cast:** Al Jolson (Jack Robin [Jake Rabinowitz]), May McAvoy (Mary Dale), Warner Oland (the Cantor [Papa Rabinowitz)], Eugenie Besserer (Sara Rabinowitz), Bobby Gordon (Jake, at age eleven), Myrna Loy (chorus girl).

Much was written about the monumental affect that 1927's *The Jazz Singer* had on Hollywood. With its musical and spoken dialogue interludes, it sealed the fate of silent films and helped to usher in the talkie era. That this pivotal screen vehicle was a Jewish-themed drama was more a happenstance than calculation by the studio that it was an ideal product for the big talkie test. Originally, the screen project was to have starred George Jessel, who had headlined the Samson Raphaelson-authored Broadway play (1925) on which the movie was based. (The play, in turn, was derived from Raphaelson's 1922 short story "The Day of Atonement.") Jessel dropped out, and JOLSON signed on. The rest was cinema history, including the later controversy about Jolson's repeated use of blackface in this and other films while performing many of his musical numbers.

Harking back to *HUMORESQUE* (1920), *The Jazz Singer*—as the stage drama was redesigned for the moviegoing masses—relied on the conflict of the Old versus the New World, and the then still-current problem of first-generation Jewish Americans assimilating into the mainstream culture. Should Jack Robin (né Jake Rabinowitz) be true to his Orthodox Jewish heritage and follow in his father's footsteps as a cantor, or might he not become a Broadway performer? Unlike the play original, the calculated photoplay allows him to do both—that is, he returns home in time to substitute for his dying father and performs the Kol Nidre at the synagogue during the high holy days. After his parent's death, he is back on the Great White Way with his beaming mama sitting in the front row of the audience watching her beloved son perform.

Although *The Jazz Singer* was directed to all types of moviegoers, its natural audience was Jewish people who would appreciate the care given to reproducing ethnic traditions on camera. For those non-Jewish viewers, especially in small town America, some of the movie's ingredients must have seemed alien, including the on-screen use of such descriptive Yiddish words as *kibitzer* (i.e., a big talker, an idle gossiper) and *shiksa* (i.e., a non-Jewish woman). To help the unknowledgeable audience, a booklet was distributed to explain the meaning of these "strange" words within the screen musical.

***Jazz Singer, The* (1953)** Warner Bros., color, 110 minutes. **Director:** Michael Curtiz; **Screenplay:** Frank Davis; **Cast:** Danny Thomas (Jerry Golding), Peggy Lee (Judy Lane), Mildred Dunnock (Mrs. Ruth Golding), Eduard Franz (Cantor David Golding), Tom Tully (Dan McGurney), Allyn Joslyn (George Miller).

By the time of the second version of *The Jazz Singer*, a great deal had changed in American life—including the impact of World War II and the Korean War—and within the Jewish religion as practiced by the much more assimilated new generations of American-born practitioners. Much of the new lifestyle was reflected in this remake, which starred Thomas, a non-Jew of Lebanese roots. No longer was the cantor/father such a traditionalist with beard and other accoutrements reflecting the old country. He was more modern, more reserved, more assimilated himself. Thus the conflict between him and his son—now called Jerry Golding and a freshly returned Korean War veteran—made less sense and had much less dramatic impact than in the original. In fact, so diminished had the subject matter become over the decades that audience interest focused a great deal more on Jerry's gentile love interest (Lee).

In this version of *The Jazz Singer*, set largely in Philadelphia, the cantor comes to accept his son's new point of view, and both he and his wife attend Jerry's opening night performance.

To be noted, the editor of this film (Alan Crosland Jr.) was the son of the director of 1927's *THE JAZZ SINGER*. The movie was Oscar nominated for Best Scoring of a Musical Picture.

***Jazz Singer, The* (1980)** Associated Film Distribution, color, 115 minutes. **Director:** Richard Fleischer; **Screenplay:** Herbert Baker; **Cast:** Neil Diamond (Jess Robin [Jess Rabinovitch]), Laurence Olivier (Cantor Rabinovitch), Lucie Arnaz (Molly Bell), Catlin Adams (Rivka Rabinovitch), Franklyn Ajaye (Bubba), Paul Nicholas (Keith Lennox).

If the 1953 edition of *The Jazz Singer* was outmoded fare, then the 1980 edition was an embarrassment of arcane theatrics. Casting Diamond made sense for the musical scenes and in the producers' hope of appealing to contemporary audiences, but hiring Britisher Olivier as the cantor was an unfortunate decision. In the new adaptation, the old religious man was no longer up-to-date and clean shaven (as in the 1953 edition) but had old-fashioned customs and boasted a bushy mustache and spectacles and was usually wearing a yarmulke. He looked like the outsider within this picture. To make matters worse, Olivier's hammy performance outdid the theatrical chest-thumping performance of Warner Oland from the 1927 original.

Many changes were made to the plot line of the 1980 *The Jazz Singer*. Now, the father was a widower, a HOLOCAUST survivor who had come to the United States and had become the cantor of a small synagogue. The son is married and works at the house of worship before he is tempted to try "real" show business in Hollywood, where he finds love and career management in one person (Arnaz), marking the eventual end of his marriage.

By 1980, the conflict of old country values versus new ones had lost much of its relevance for filmgoers, and the movie, made at a cost of more than $15 million, fared poorly with audiences and critics alike.

Jolson, Al (c. 1886–1950) For later generations, his acting style and schmaltz was hopelessly dated, but in his era, he was the "world's greatest entertainer." He seemed most relaxed hiding behind blackface, down on one knee, arms spread wide, and belting out "Swanee" or his favorite "Rock-a-bye Your Baby with a Dixie Melody." Front and center, on or off stage, he was the benevolent egotist, full of quips and *always* with an eye for pretty women. His stage and film characters gained audience acceptance through huge doses of sentimentality. His occasional use of Yiddish slang in his performances came across not as heritage but as a hip guy on the inside adopting quaint old country dialect.

Born Asa Yoelson in Srednike, Lithuania, in the mid-1880s, he came to America when his cantor father brought his family to Washington, D.C., in the early 1890s. Following his older brother Harry into show business and away from ultratraditional Judaism, Al was a solo stage act (usually in blackface) by the middle of the first decade of the 1900s. On Broadway, using a runway to play directly to audiences, he was a big hit (*Robinson Crusoe, Jr.*, 1916; *Sinbad*, 1918; *Big Boy*, 1925). Later, his waning popularity was boosted by the part-talkie *THE JAZZ SINGER* (1927) in which his spoken "You ain't heard nothin' yet" thrilled moviegoers. If his films *The Singing Fool* (1928) and *Say It with Songs* (1929) were box-office successes, he was devastated that, by the time of *Go Into Your Dance* (1935), Ruby Keeler, his costar/wife, was the prime attraction.

A perennial recording artist and radio star of the 1930s, Jolson's career sagged again by the early 1940s. He rose anew (especially on radio and in recordings) with two autobiographic movies—1946's *THE JOLSON STORY* and 1949's *JOLSON SINGS AGAIN*—in which Larry Parks had the lead while Al dubbed the singing. Jolson died of a heart attack, having just returned to San Francisco from a successful USO tour in South Korea.

Jolson's on-camera blackface routines made his dated movies anathema to many viewers in later decades and caused politically incorrect numbers (e.g., "Goin' to Heaven on a Mule" from 1934's *Wonder Bar*) from his movies often to be excised from TV airings. Then and later, many viewers confused the maudlin fiction of *The Jazz Singer* with Al's real life. But that movie (remade twice) forever identified Jolson with the pull between ultraconservative Judaism and assimilated Americanism.

***Jolson Sings Again* (1949)** Columbia, color, 95 minutes. **Director:** Henry Levin; **Screenplay:** Sidney Buchman; **Cast:** Larry Parks (Al Jolson), Barbara Hale (Ellen Clark), William Demarest (Steve Martin), Ludwig Donath (Cantor Yoelson), Bill Goodwin (Tom Baron), Tamara Shayne (Mama Yoelson), Al Jolson (the singing voice of Al Jolson).

With the highly popular reception to *THE JOLSON STORY* (1946), a follow-up appeared three years later using many of the same talents and with JOLSON again providing the singing voice for Parks to mouth. It depicted the breakup of his marriage, his show-business comeback, the death of his mother, his marriage to Ellen Clark, and the making of *The Jolson Story*. It boasted an array of songs (e.g., "California, Here I Come") long associated with Jolson.

As in his first movie biography, most of the Jewish elements within the picture were connected to Jolson's home life. As in real life, the star's wives were indicated as non-Jewish, just as in actuality, except for *The Jazz Singer*, Jolson never played overt Jewish characters on camera.

***The Jolson Story* (1946)** Columbia, color, 128 minutes. **Director:** Alfred E. Green; **Screenplay:** Stephen Longstreet; **Cast:** Larry Parks (Al Jolson [Asa Yoelson]), Evelyn Keyes (Julie Benson), William Demarest (Steve Martin), Bill Goodwin (Tom Baron), Ludwig Donath (Cantor Yoelson), Tamara Shayne (Mrs. Yoelson), Al Jolson (the singing voice of Al Jolson).

Because the Broadway play (1925) and the movie (1927) of *THE JAZZ SINGER* had been based on facets of the life of legendary singer/actor JOLSON (ca. 1886–1950), when the screen biography of this Jewish talent was produced, the script became a fabricated blend of Jolson's actual chronicle and key motifs from *The Jazz Singer*. Besides recounting milestones in the career of the great entertainer—who had a penchant for doing songs in blackface—*The Jolson Story* was not shy about (1) saying that Jolson was Jewish and (2) depicting his parents' home life with all the trappings of religious ethnics. To do this in a big-budgeted, mainstream studio picture in the mid-1940s was unusual, for at the time most such screen biographies of Jewish entertainment stars either ignored or glossed over the celebrity's heritage. Jewish actor Larry Parks [né Sam Kleusman Lawrence Parks), a studio contract player in mostly B films, was given the lead, with Jolson himself dubbing the singing voice for the movie.

Made at a cost of almost $3 million, *The Jolson Story* grossed more than $8 million in domestic distribution, won two Academy Awards and several Oscar nominations, and led to *JOLSON SINGS AGAIN* (1949).

Judaism—sects Although many of the Hollywood films dealing with Judaism—particularly those produced in the silent era—were concerned with members of the faith clinging to their traditional, orthodox religions from the old country, relatively few talkies focused extensively on the practice of Judaism in the old land (especially Eastern Europe) or on maintaining strict religious practices in the present-day world.

Two musicals were particular exceptions. *FIDDLER ON THE ROOF* (1971), set in Czarist Russia, saw the oppressed Jews of their ghetto village holding onto their traditional beliefs in the face of all obstacles, including leaving their beloved Anatevka. Although nostalgic and full of song-and-dance, it had a grip on bitter reality. In contrast was *YENTL* (1983), which was also set in the Russia of the same period. In that BARBRA STREISAND vehicle, there was attention to details about the activities of yeshiva students of the period, but much of the movie's ambiance smacked of present-day Hollywood, including the finale that took place aboard the New York–bound ship.

In the nonmusical arena, *Romance of a Horsethief* (1971), directed by Abraham Polansky, showcased a turn-of-the-twentieth-century Polish village where the oppressive Cossacks (led by Yul Brynner) demanded that Jewish villagers turn over their horses to the army. Stirred on by a young revolutionary (Jane Birkin) and the help of a local brothel keeper (LAINIE KAZAN), the townsfolk stood up to their foe. Though full of atmosphere, the movie was unfortunately slow moving.

HESTER STREET (1975) starring Carol Kane was a contemporary reflection on the traditions and lifestyles in late 1890s of immigrant European Jews who resided on New York's LOWER EAST SIDE. For an updating of life in Manhattan's Jewish ghetto of the late twentieth century, there was much resonance within *CROSSING DELANCEY* (1988), in which a quite modern Jew fell in love with an up-to-date but still traditional Jew living in the old neighborhood.

In contrast, three American features of recent decades focused on the Hasidic Jews who in customs, garb, and attitudes remained closed off from Americanization. *The Chosen* (1981), directed by Jeremy Paul Kagan and set in the 1940s, highlighted the Hasidic Jewish community in Brooklyn and contrasted it with the way of life of a modern-thinking American Jew. Later, in *A STRANGER AMONG US* (1992), director SIDNEY LUMET used the culture of the Hasidic Jews as ambiance for a police procedural story as a non-Jewish (Melanie Griffith) law officer went undercover in the Brooklyn community to track the murderer of a diamond merchant. (In 1976's *Marathon Man*, a thriller starring DUSTIN HOFFMAN and Laurence Olivier, the Hasidic Jews of Manhattan's midtown diamond row were a backdrop to part of the narrative.) *A Price Above Rubies* (1998), directed by Boaz Yakin, concentrated on a dissatisfied New York City Hasidic housewife (played by Renée Zellweger) who felt that religious traditions and rules were keeping her from finding happiness. In *The Believer* (2001), a Jewish student in New York City examines his heritage in order to discover the place of (very traditional) Judaism in his life. The made-for-cable feature *Snow in August* (2001) was based on the 1997 best-selling novel by Pete Hamill. The narrative was set in 1947 Brooklyn and involved Hasidic Jews caught up in a neighborhood drama. The movie interweaves Jewish mysticism and morality into the plot line.

AN AMERICAN TAIL (1986), the animated feature produced by STEVEN SPIELBERG, boasted Russian immigrant mice who came to New York of the 1880s, bringing their long-established Jewish ways with them to the new world. It led to *An American Tail: Fievel Goes West* (1991), as well as an off-shoot TV series, the animated *Fievel's American Tails* (1992–93), and later direct-to-video follow-up films.

***Judgment at Nuremberg* (1961)** United Artists, b&w, 190 minutes. **Director:** Stanley Kramer; **Screenplay:** Abby Mann; **Cast:** Spencer Tracy (Judge Dan Haywood), Burt Lancaster (Ernst Janning), Richard Widmark (Col. Tad Lawson), Marlene Dietrich (Mme. Bertholt), Maximilian Schell (Hans Rolfe), Judy Garland (Irene Hoffman), Montgomery Clift (Rudolph Petersen).

With the old Hollywood studio system dying, independent filmmakers such as the well-established Kramer had a far easier time making projects that appealed to their visions, regardless of their suspect commerciality or whether the concepts were too daring for their time. For this major production, Mann adapted his own teleplay ("Judgment at Nuremberg") from television's *Playhouse 90*, which had aired on April 16, 1959. From that TV cast, which included Claude Rains as Haywood and Paul Lukas as Janning, only Schell (as Rolfe, the German defense attorney) repeated his assignment on screen.

Because the film version of *Judgment at Nuremberg* was so star-filled and so highly promoted, it drew huge audiences, many of whom either had (partially) forgotten or were not especially aware of the HOLOCAUST. As such, this picture had a tremendous impact on moviegoers. Like *EXODUS* (1960), it stimulated public interest in Judaism and Jewish causes.

In 1948, New England judge Dan Haywood arrives in Nuremberg to preside over a major court case: the trial of high-level German judges accused of ignoring law and justice during World War II in their support of Hitler's genocide policy against the Jews and others. Col. Ted Lawson is the outraged prosecuting attorney, and old-guard German Hans Rolfe defends his countrymen. Among the witnesses who testify are Irene Hoffman and Rudolf Petersen, two of the Nazis' many victims. Janning eventually speaks up in court, admitting that he was wrong to have defended the German wartime policies on the grounds that they were good ultimately for the country. (During courtroom recesses, Haywood comes to know the elitist Madame Bertholt, the widow of an executed German officer.) When the trial concludes the defendants are given jail sentences. Rolfe scoffs that in a few years, all of the convicted will be freed. An on-camera postscript states that of the men sentenced, not one was still incarcerated.

Judgment at Nuremberg won Academy Awards for Best Actor (Schell) and Best Adapted Screenplay, as well as nine other Oscar nominations. This box-office champion, like *EXODUS*, paved the way for such later studies of the Holocaust and its victims as *THE PAWNBROKER* (1965). In 2000, TNT cable produced the movie *NUREMBERG*, based on the book *Nuremberg: Infamy on Trial* (1994). In 2001, Schell starred in a short-lasting Broadway musical of *Judgment at Nuremberg*.

***Juggler, The* (1953)** Columbia Pictures, b&w, 84 minutes. **Director:** Edward Dmytryk; **Screenplay:** Michael Blankfort; **Cast:** Kirk Douglas (Hans Muller), Milly Vitale (Ya'El), Paul Stewart (Detective Karni), Joey Walsh (Yehoshua Bresler), Alf Kjellin (Daniel).

The late 1940s founding of the state of Israel and the need of 1950s Hollywood to go on location to exotic locales to compete with the TV medium paved the way for *The Juggler*. Its subject matter also resonated heavily with star DOUGLAS, who was Jewish, and with director EDWARD DMYTRYK, who was not. Besides *SWORD IN THE DESERT* (1949), this was the first Hollywood-produced feature to deal with contemporary Israel, and it set the tone for such entries as *EXODUS* (1960), *CAST A GIANT SHADOW* (1965—which also starred Douglas), and *Judith* (1966). Had it not been that the Zionist cause was considered a popular uprising by many in the United States, *The Juggler* and similar movies would have had a much harder time being made.

Once again, the picture's focal figure is an outsider, a HOLOCAUST survivor from Germany who had lost his whole family in World War II. The former magician/juggler comes to the new "homeland" as a final choice, not knowing where else to go—the fate of many Jews over the centuries. He meets Ya'el, a vibrant sabra (i.e., native of the country) who not only imparts her passion for life and the excitement of the Jewish cause to him but also her blonde beauty (a change from the old stereotype of the dark-haired, sometimes swarthy-skinned Jewish woman) helps to restore his zest for life.

***Julia* (1977)** Twentieth Century-Fox, color, 116 minutes. **Director:** Fred Zinnemann; **Screenplay:** Alvin Sargent; **Cast:** Jane Fonda (Lillian Hellman), Vanessa Redgrave (Julia), Jason Robards (Dashiell Hammett), Maximilian Schell (Johann), Hal Holbrook (Alan Campbell).

A short sketch within *Pentimento* (1973), a memoir by Lillian Hellman (1905–84), provided the basis for one of the most dramatic sections of this film. In the 1930s, the well-bred Hellman puts aside her playwriting to visit a childhood friend, Julia, who has been hospitalized in Vienna for injuries suffered while protesting the Hitler Youth movement. Later, when traveling to Russia, Julia's friend Johann begs Lillian to smuggle funds out of the country and into Germany where it will support anti-Nazi causes. Idealistic Hellman, who we now learn is Jewish, undertakes the dangerous mission. Only later does she learn that the Fascists killed the non-Jewish Julia not long after their last visit together in the hospital.

The compacted segment devoted to Julia within this movie resonated with suspense. Here, instead of the Jewish person being the knowing one and already a victim of Nazi oppression, it was her non-Jewish friend who had sacrificed so much already. It made Hellman's daring mission to Russia all the more poignant because she was repaying a debt on behalf of her brave friend. (It also helped to make the movie's story more viable for non-Jewish audiences.)

Julia won three Academy Awards including a Best Supporting Actress trophy for Redgrave. There was a mild uproar when Redgrave was cast in this picture because of her frequently voiced pro-Palestinian political views. When she accepted her Oscar for *Julia*, Redgrave spoke out on behalf of the Palestine Liberation Organization, prompting many in the audience to boo her.

July Pork Bellies See *FOR PETE'S SAKE*.

***Just Tell Me What You Want* (1980)** Warner Bros., color, 112 minutes. **Director:** Sidney Lumet; **Screenplay:** Jay Presson Allen; **Cast:** Ali MacGraw (Bones Burton), Alan King (Max Herschel), Myrna Loy (Stella Liberti), Keenan Wynn (Seymour Berger), Tony Roberts (Mike Berger), Peter Weller (Steven Routledge).

This much-discussed, self-indulgent motion picture remained little seen over the years. One of its points of interest was that it presented a full-bodied characterization of a Jewish entertainment industry mogul—this time as a focal character of the drama.

Max Herschel, a self-made millionaire whose conglomerate holdings encompass film and TV interests, has an unhappy marriage to an alcoholic. He has had a long string of mistresses. His current girlfriend is the non-Jewish Bones Burton who, unlike Max's faithful, long-time secretary (Loy), is too independent to be controlled. Max and Bones break apart, she turning to a young playwright (Weller), and then Herschel, the perpetual adult/child, does his best to woo her back.

In the film, much was made of Max's cultural roots and his character's spouting of show-business Yiddishisms. Some attention was focused on ailing, elderly film mogul Seymour Berger, an old-guard European Jew saddled with an ultra-contemporary grandson (Roberts). The latter was a failure at the entertainment business and was a homosexual, which meant that the family line would not be perpetuated.

This was another of the several Jewish-themed dramas helmed by LUMET.

K

Kahn, Madeline (1942–1999) Probably not since JUDY HOLLIDAY cavorted on camera in the late 1940s and throughout the 1950s had Hollywood seen a more unique screen presence than Kahn. With *BLAZING SADDLES* (1974), she became a prime member of MEL BROOKS's screen stock company.

Born Madeline Gail Wolfson in Boston, Massachusetts, she relocated to Queens, New York, with her mother when her parents divorced. Her mother, unsuccessful in her own show-business ambitions and now remarried to a Mr. Kahn, transferred her hopes to her offspring, and had her take dance, voice, and piano lessons. After earning a degree in speech therapy, she turned to show business, initially hoping to become an opera singer. She was among the *New Faces of 1968* (1968) on Broadway, as was her friend Robert Klein, with whom she also did the summer 1970 comedy/variety TV series, *Comedy Tonight*.

Kahn's screen breakthrough was in BARBRA STREISAND's screwball comedy *What's Up, Doc?* (1972). For playing the floozy in Ryan O'Neal's *Paper Moon* (1973), Kahn was Oscar nominated as Best Supporting Actress. She received a similar nomination for her hilarious performance as Lili von Shtupp in *Blazing Saddles*. Thereafter, she appeared in such screen satires as *Young Frankenstein* (1974) and *The Cheap Detective* (1978).

She didn't fare well with her TV series: *Oh Madeline* (1983–84) and *Mr. President* (1987–88). In contrast, she did far better in Broadway revivals of *Blithe Spirit* (1983) and *Born Yesterday* (1989). In the early 1990s, Kahn won a Tony Award for *The Sisters Rosensweig*.

The mid-1990s saw another professional upturn for Kahn. She was co-starring in Bill Cosby's new TV sitcom, *Cosby* (1996–2000) and was in a long-term dating relationship with a New York attorney. In September 1998, she was diagnosed with ovarian cancer, and fourteen months later, she passed away.

Kaye, Danny (1913–1987) With his frenetic movements, his ability to sing tongue-twisting songs, and a knack for pantomime and mugging, he was the crown prince of clowns. Rejected for a contract at one major Hollywood studio because he would not have his nose shortened, he nevertheless succeeded on the big screen, as well as on television and the Broadway stage.

Born David Daniel Kaminski in New York City, he dropped out of high school to enter show business. He found employment in the CATSKILL RESORTS where he was a combination waiter–entertainer–prankster. With friends he formed the Three Terpsichoreans, entertained in Asia in 1934, and toured the United States thereafter.

In 1939, while auditioning on Broadway, he reencountered pianist/songwriter Sylvia Fine, the daughter of a dentist for whom he had worked years ago. They worked together on a new revue that summer at a Jewish resort camp in Pennsylvania and brought the show *(The Straw Hat Revue)* to Broadway that fall. The couple married in 1940 and had a daughter. A Manhattan nightclub engagement led Kaye to the Broadway musical *Lady in the Dark* (1941) and then to another stage success, *Let's Face It* (1941).

Rejected for military service in World War II because of a bad back, he sold war bonds and entertained the troops. Having already made short subjects in the late 1930s, he launched a movie career under the aegis of producer Samuel Goldwyn. Danny's big screen musical comedies included *Up in Arms* (1944), *The Kid from Brooklyn* (1946), and the very popular *The Secret Life of Walter Mitty* (1947). One of his most endearing roles was as *Hans Christian Anderson* (1952). He teamed with Bing Crosby for the extremely successful *White Christmas* (1954) and went heavily dramatic for *Me and the Colonel* (1958) as a Jewish man fleeing France and the Nazis.

In 1945 Kaye had introduced *The Danny Kaye Show* on radio and it lasted for more than a decade. In 1963, he began his weekly TV variety series *(The Danny Kaye Show)* which ran for four seasons. Back in 1953, he became involved with the United Nations International Children's Emergency Fund (UNICEF). As its official ambassador-at-large, he devoted much of the next thirty years to its cause. He returned to Broadway as the biblical Noah in the 1970 musical *Two by Two* (1970). In the TV movie *SKOKIE* (1981), he was a HOLOCAUST survivor, coping with neo-Nazis in contemporary America.

Despite heart bypass surgery in 1983, Kaye did not slow down for the last four years of his life. He continued his gambit of guest-conducting symphony orchestras to mirthful results as well as his UNICEF chores.

Kazan, Lainie (1942–) Like BARBRA STREISAND, the striking Kazan was born in Brooklyn and was associated with the stage musical, *Funny Girl* (1964). Streisand was the star of that hit vehicle, while Kazan was her talented understudy.

Born Lainie Levine, she attended Hofstra University (where she was a classmate of future filmmaker Francis Ford Coppola) and later studied at the Actors Studio with LEE STRASBERG. She was a regular on TV's *Dean Martin Summer Show* (1966) and made her film debut in *Lady in Cement* (1968), playing an Italian woman, which became one of her stock-in-trade roles over the years. When not acting on Broadway or on tour or recording albums, she played in two TV series: a mother figure to Robby Benson on *Tough Cookies* (1986) and best friend to Patty Duke on *Karen's Song* (1987). Her finest TV work was as HOWIE MANDEL's widowed mother on *ST. ELSEWHERE* (1987–88), as Gabriel Carteris's grandmother on *Beverly Hills 90210* (1990–92), and as Fran Drescher's aunt on *THE NANNY* (1995–96). Starting with *MY FAVORITE YEAR* (1982), but especially in later years with her imposing presence, she became typed as the ultimate Jewish mama: *The Big Hit* (1998), *WHAT'S COOKING?* (2000), *The Crew* (2000), and *My Big Fat Greek Wedding* (2002).

***Kibitzer, The* (1930)** Paramount, b&w, 77 minutes. **Director:** Edward Sloman; **Screenplay:** Marion Dix; **Cast:** Harry Green (Ike Lazarus), Mary Brian (Josie Lazarus), Neil Hamilton (Eddie Brown), Albert Gran (James Livingston), David Newell (Bert Livingston).

THE JAZZ SINGER (1927) referred to the pal of AL JOLSON's character as a "kibitzer." Here, this type came front and center. Based on the 1929 novel by Joseph Swerling and EDWARD G. ROBINSON, the film focuses on Ike Lazarus, a tobacconist on the LOWER EAST SIDE, whose friends play pinochle nightly at his store. The sessions give Ike ample opportunity to kibitz (i.e., to comment, to joke). Through good fortune, he not only salvages his stock market holdings but also reunites his daughter (Brian) with her mechanic boyfriend (Hamilton).

Besides *THE COHENS AND KELLYS* movie series, this was one of the few movies of the early 1930s to examine so richly and fully—in a comedic manner—New York Jewish ghetto life.

King, Alan (1927–) He came a generation after the pantheon of great Jewish entertainers (e.g., JACK BENNY, FANNY BRICE, EDDIE CANTOR, and AL JOLSON) who dominated much of American show business in the first half of the twentieth century. Yet, unlike some of the Semitic comedians (e.g., David Brenner, Robert Klein, and David Steinberg) who followed King chronologically, Alan remained a vital presence over the decades. His aggressive brand of New York humor was usually softened by a wide smile and an all-encompassing desire to be liked.

Born Irwin Alan Kniberg in Brooklyn, New York, repeated absenteeism ended his high school years. Instead he played drums with a group for bar mitzvahs, weddings, and so on. Before he was sixteen, he was a performing in the CATSKILL and at New York burlesque houses. By the early 1950s, he was a seasoned performer. King was hired in 1956 to open for Judy Garland at Manhattan's Palace Theater and then to tour with her (and later with Lena Horne), giving him wide exposure, more so than bit film roles in *Hit the Deck* (1955) and *The Girl He Left Behind* (1957). In the underappreciated *BYE BYE BRAVERMAN* (1968), he was the rabbi delivering a strange funeral oratory.

By the 1970s, King was also serving as executive producers of TV series (e.g., *The Corner Bar*, 1972–73; *Ivan the Terrible*, 1976) and in 1981 did similar chores for films. When not doing his stand-up act or hosting celebrity roasts, King appeared in a stage revival of the musical *Guys and Dolls*, displayed dramatic soundness in *JUST TELL ME WHAT YOU WANT* (1980) as a business tycoon, and was BILLY CRYSTAL's self-focused father in *Memories of Me* (1988). King played a rabbi in ENEMIES: A LOVE STORY (1989), was a mobster in *Night and the City* (1992), and in the 1995 TV movie *THE INFILTRATOR* provided yet another of his on-camera rabbi interpretations. He was seen as a casino owner in Jackie Chan and Chris Rock's *Rush Hour 2* (2001) and was part of the ensemble of *Sunshine State* (2002). Also in 2002, King performed in the one-man show *Mr. Goldwyn*. It dealt with the iconoclastic Jewish film producer Samuel Goldwyn (1882–1974).

***King of Kings, The* (1927)** Producers Distributing Corp., b&w with color sequences, 115 minutes. **Director:** Cecil B. DeMille; **Screenplay:** Jeanie MacPherson; **Cast:** H. B. Warner (Jesus, the Christ), Dorothy Cumming (Mary, the mother), Ernest Torrence (Peter), Joseph Schildkraut (Judas), James Neill (James), Jacqueline Logan (Mary Magdalene).

One of the most spectacular of the silent era's biblical spectacles, this film was typical of the lavish visual display so associated with director DeMille. More concerned with depicting splendor than factuality, little effort was made to depict the Jewish characters with any dimension. Production of this 1927 feature film aroused the ire of the Anti-Defamation League of the B'nai B'rith, which encouraged its members to avoid this movie, because it presented Jewish religious authorities of ancient times in such an unflattering light. By the time of the more benign remake (1961), director Nicholas Ray was much more careful in this regard.

L

Lanigan's Rabbi **(1977)** NBC-TV series, color, 90 minutes. **Cast:** Art Carney (Chief Paul Lanigan), Bruce Solomon (Rabbi David Small), Janis Paige (Kate Lanigan), Janet Margolin (Miriam Small), Barbara Carney (Bobbie Whittaker).

In many ways, this series owed much to both the 1920s ABIE'S IRISH ROSE and *THE COHENS AND KELLYS* film series. For once again, here were two distinct cultures (the Irish and the Jewish) coming in contact with one another and working in harmony. The TV outing was based on characters created by author Harry Kellerman in a detective-book series that included *Friday the Rabbi Slept Late* (1964). That entry was transformed into *Lanigan's Rabbi*, a 1976 TV movie featuring Art Carney as Police Chief Paul Lanigan, an Irish law enforcer who, with his friend Rabbi David Small (Stuart Margolin), solved a caper in their township of Cameron, California. This pilot led to the 1977 series that aired as part of the revolving anthology entry, *The NBC Sunday Mystery Movie.*

In the TV show, Bruce Solomon assumed the role of rabbi at Temple Beth Halell Synagogue. Otherwise, the pilot's cast of regulars remained the same in the ongoing program: Carney as Lanigan the cop of twenty-two years, Paige as his wife Kate, and Margolin as Miriam Small, David's understanding spouse. By now, the rabbi, an amateur but methodical criminologist, is so proficient at figuring out crimes that his good friend Lanigan has become dependent on his help.

As the title indicated, Carney had the more dominant role, with the rabbi slightly demoted in the proceedings. This allowed Carney to capture the spotlight and to downplay the Jewish flavor within the series.

Larry Sanders Show, The **(1992–1998)** HBO cable series, color, 30 minutes. **Cast:** Garry Shandling (Larry Sanders), Jeffrey Tambor (Hank Kingsley), Wallace Langham (Phil), Rip Torn (Arthur), Linda Doucett (Darlene: 1992–94), Jeremy Piven (Jerry Capen: 1992–93).

Having made a strong impact with his innovative sitcom *It's Garry Shandling's Show* (1988–90), the Arizona-born Jewish comedian—he of the deadpan face and facile smile—was even more successful with this cable TV offering. As before, the Jewishness of Shandling's alter ego was not a stated premise but an assumption made from the star's real-life persona as frequently seen by the public on television and in clubs. The same could generally apply to the character of Hank Kingsley, Sanders' sidekick. Yet, one episode had the overly enthusiastic Hank suddenly enamored of a woman rabbi, and wanting to express his Jewishness. As the plot line developed, the network and the public disliked this overt display, and they pressured Kingsley to return to his nondenominational behavior. One could interpret this plot line in many different ways, but it did suggest that even in the late 1990s, there was concern in some quarters about being "too Jewish" on the air.

Last Angry Man, The **(1959)** Columbia, b&w, 100 minutes. **Director:** Daniel Mann; **Screenplay:** Gerald Green; **Cast:** Paul Muni (Dr. Sam Abelman), David Wayne (Woodrow Wilson Thrasher), Betsy Palmer (Anne Thrasher), Luther Adler (Dr. Max Vogel), Claudia McNeil (Mrs. Quincy), Nancy R. Pollack (Sarah Abelman), Billy Dee Williams (Josh Quincy).

In the changing traditions of Hollywood filmmaking of the 1950s, the Jew was still depicted generally as an outsider on camera, but he had now come frequently to represent a teacher of moral values to others around him. Such idealized but one-dimensional Jewish good Samaritans had turned up earlier in *Good Morning, Miss Dove* (1955), *Home Before Dark* (1958), and so on.

Based on Gerald Green's 1956 novel, this film removed most direct references to the lead characters' Jewish heritage. Nevertheless, the casting (MUNI and ADLER) and their characters' names made clear their Jewish background. The movie treated of two opposing types of Jewish doctor: the dedicated one who remained in the tenement district to help those who needed him the most, and the Park Avenue type (Dr. Max Vogel) more concerned with a hefty income. It was a theme covered in the earlier *SYMPHONY OF SIX MILLION* (1932).

In the drama, outspoken Dr. Sam Abelman, residing in Brooklyn, is chosen by a TV producer (Wayne) to be the subject of a good-Samaritan documentary. The elderly doctor finally agrees, but the needs of his patients intervene, and in trying to help a delinquent (Williams) get a grip on life, he has a heart attack and dies.

Muni was Oscar nominated for this, his last movie performance. A small but significant amount of the focus in this entry was devoted to a new trend in Hollywood, the treating of African Americans on camera. The movie featured several black performers in early screen appearances (e.g., Williams, McNeil, Cicely Tyson, and Godfrey Cambridge).

A TV movie remake of *The Last Angry Man* aired in 1974. Adapted by the original author as a series pilot, it featured Pat Hingle as Dr. Sam Abelman and Sorrell Booke as Dr. Max Vogel. A few weeks before this production aired, there appeared the telefeature *Dr. Max* starring LEE J. COBB. It was a similar tale of a curmudgeonly but benevolent doctor, this time set in Baltimore, Maryland.

***Late Show Starring Joan Rivers, The* (1986–1987)** Fox-TV series, color, 60 minutes. **Cast:** Joan Rivers (hostess), Clint Holmes (announcer), Mark Hudson and the Party Boys Plus the Tramp (music).

After years as a stand-up comedian, hosting her own TV variety/talk show in 1969 (*That Show with Joan Rivers*), being a persistent TV talk-show guest, and then serving as the permanent guest host of *The Tonight Show Starring Johnny Carson*, the self-proclaimed Jewish American Princess from Westchester, New York, hosted her own late-night gab fest. Noted for her diatribes aimed at celebrities with physical flaws, RIVERS was expected to garner huge ratings for the Fox Network. The series was targeted to gain a younger audience than the competing Johnny Carson program, but in her efforts to be Miss Nice and woo a variety of guests to her forum, Rivers became saccharine. After floundering for eight months, she left the show. She returned to the airwaves with, among others, *The Joan Rivers Show* (1989–93) and *Can We Talk?* (1994).

In many respects, Rivers was a descendant of 1960s TV talk show host VIRGINIA GRAHAM.

***Law & Order* (1990–)** NBC-TV series, color, 60 minutes. **Cast:** Christopher Noth (Det. Mike Logan: 1990–95), George Dzundza (Det. Sgt. Max Greevey: 1990–91), Paul Sorvino (Det. Phil Gerreta: 1991–92), Jerry Orbach (Det. Lennie Briscoe (1992–), Michael Moriarity (Asst. D. A. Ben Stone: 1990–94), Sam Waterston (Asst. D. A. Jack McCoy (1994–), Benjamin Bratt (Det. Reynaldo "Rey" Curtis: 1995–99), Jesse L. Martin (Det. Ed Green: 1999–), Carrie Lowell (Asst. D. A. Jamie Ross: 1996–98), Angie Harmon (Asst. D. A. Abbie Carmichael: 1998–2001), Richard Brooks (Asst. D. A. Paul Robinette: 1990–93), Jill Hennessy (Asst. D. A. Claire Kincaid: 1993–96), Steven Hill (D. A. Adam Schiff: 1990–2000), Dianne Wiest (D. A. Nora Lewin: 2000–), Elizabeth Rohm (Asst. D. A. Serena Southerlyn: 2001–).

Set in New York City where there was a heavy concentration of Jewish people, it was likely from the start that episodes and themes of this acclaimed television drama (which often draws its story lines from local news) would etch portraits of Semitic characters—good and bad—caught up in protecting or breaking the law. Sometimes, the issue of a given segment would delve into Jewish and African-American interaction, HOLOCAUST survivors, anti-Semitism, and so on.

With its revolving door of cast regulars coming/leaving the series, one constant thread on the series was having a Jewish district attorney. For a decade the role was handled by Hill, playing the observant, low-key department head who balances diplomacy and expediency with his staff's vigilant pursuit of justice. When the Adam Schiff figure departed the show in 2000, he was replaced by another Jewish character, Nora Lewin, a younger and more hands-on administrator.

A more overtly public Jewish attorney figure was that of Ben Meyer (played by Ron Rifkin) on *The Trials of Rosie O'Neill* (1990–92).

***Lepke* (1975)** Warner Bros., color, 109 minutes. **Director:** Menahem Golan; **Screenplay:** Lesley Lau and Tamar Hoffs; **Cast:** Tony Curtis (Louis "Lepke" Buchalter), Anjanette Comer (Bernice Meyer), Michael Callan (Robert Kane), Warren Berlinger (Gurrah Shapiro), Milton Berle (Mr. Meyer).

In 1974's *THE GODFATHER, PART II*, actor LEE STRASBERG offered a telling delineation of a major Jewish gangster. It was a screen type usually not depicted by Hollywood, although there had been *FOUR WALLS* (1928) with John Gilbert as a Jewish lawbreaker, Franchot Tone starring in the 1934 remake (*Straight Is the Way*), and San Jaffe as the crooked Doc Riedenschneider in *The Asphalt Jungle* (1950). Although the American screen was full of Irish and Italian gangsters in the 1920s–60s, if the mobs depicted contained Jewish members, they were always subordinate characters. Interestingly, this was in contradiction to the real-life Jewish criminals who rose to notoriety in the first half of the twentieth century, including Dutch Schultz, Arnold Rothstein, Moe Annenberg, Bugsy Siegel, and Meyer Lansky. When films were made on these notorious underworld people, their ethnic heritage was omitted to appease Jewish film executives and Jewish-interest PRESSURE GROUPS, as well as to maintain wide audience appeal for these hoodlum chronicles. This included features such as *The Rise and Fall of Legs Diamond* (1960), *Murder, Inc.* (1960—which dealt with Lepke), and *King of the Roaring 20's—The Story of Arnold Rothstein*.

In *Lepke*, CURTIS played one of his few Jewish screen characters. There was no doubt about the criminal's religion nor that of his bride-to-be (Comer) because her father (a well-handled dramatic role by comedian BERLE) insisted they have an orthodox marriage ceremony. Most of the gangster's pals were Jewish, and the film developed into a rags-to-riches story as mobster Lepke rose in the underworld.

Whatever faults one had with the film's production values, Curtis gave a solid performance. Although the picture made little impact, it added to the precedent set by Strasberg in *The Godfather, Part II* and led to other more tempered depictions of Jewish gangsters (e.g., *Bugsy*, 1991; *Mobsters*, 1991; *Billy Bathgate*, 1991).

Levant, Oscar (1906–1972) A very talented pianist and a brilliant wit, this highly neurotic individual (who eventually developed severe facial twitches) stormed through several mediums, leaving his telltale mark.

Born in Pittsburgh, Pennsylvania, he left high school to study music in New York City. While preparing to be a concert pianist, he worked with several small dance bands. On Broadway, he was in *Burlesque* (1928) and made his film debut in *The Dance of Life* (1929). He stayed in Hollywood to compose film music and became good friends with, and a devotee of, composer George Gershwin. Levant made his reputation as a wit on radio's *Information, Please!* (1938–42). In films, he was frequently seen as the wisecracking pal of the lead player—*RHAPSODY IN BLUE* (1945), *An American in Paris* (1951), and *The Band Wagon* (1953). On TV, he hosted the quiz show *G.E. Guest House* (1951) and throughout the decade became a favorite on talk shows and was a quiz-show panelist. His autobiographical books were: *A Smattering of Ignorance* (1940), *The Memoirs of an Amnesiac* (1965), and *The Unimportance of Being Oscar* (1968).

Levene, Sam (1905–1980) For a half-century this Damon Runyonesque actor with his characteristic mustache performed on stage, film, and occasionally on television. He was often cast as a mild-mannered gangster or as a hard-nosed cop and many times as a Jewish character. Infrequently, he had a serious dramatic role on screen, as in a trio of 1947 releases: *Boomerang*, *Brute Force*, and *CROSSFIRE*. Perhaps his most famous acting assignment was as gambler Nathan Detroit in the original Broadway production of the musical *Guys and Dolls* (1950).

Born Samuel Levine in Russia, he came to the United States when he was two. He grew up in New York City, and after graduating from high school, Levene worked as a salesman for his older brother in the dressmaking business. Wanting to improve his English diction for the job, he took classes at the Academy of Dramatic Arts and quickly became a full-time student. He made his Broadway debut in *Wall Street* (1927), rose to fame playing the racing addict, Patsy, in *Three Men on a Horse* (1935), and repeated the role on film. When not on Broadway he was busy working in Hollywood. During World War II, he played several screen parts as a Jewish soldier—a rarity at that time in films—including Lt. Wayne Greenbaum in *The Purple Heart* (1944).

On the stage, he was frequently cast as a Jewish figure, one of the best known being Al Lewis in *The Sunshine Boys* in 1972. His final acting assignment was opposite Esther Rolle in *Horowitz and Mrs. Washington* (1980), which he played on Broadway and in Toronto, Canada.

Levinson, Barry (1942–) Two of this filmmaker's favorite topics in his film directing and TV producing work were his hometown of Baltimore, Maryland, and his religious faith, Judaism.

A former stand-up comic and TV writer, he made his feature-film directing debut with *Diner* (1982), which he also scripted, a nostalgic look at Baltimore of the 1950s that included a Jewish character. His other motion pictures to focus on Jewish families and changing traditions included *Tin Men* (1987), *AVALON* (1990), *Bugsy* (1991), and *LIBERTY HEIGHTS* (1999). On one of the TV series Levinson produced, *Homicide: Life on the Street* (1993–99), the character of Detective John Munch reexplored his Jewish roots, while a few of the show's episodes concerned Jewish themes.

Lewis, Jerry (1926–) People either love him or hate him; there seems to be no middle ground regarding Lewis. For many years (1946–56), he was joined at the hip professionally with Dean Martin. When the team split apart, Martin surprised everyone by being an adept solo performer. As for Jerry, everyone already knew that beneath his hang-dog look and the close-cropped hair lay a comic genius.

He was born Joseph Levitch in Newark, New Jersey, the son of a vaudevillian father and a pianist mother. Mostly raised by a grandmother, supposedly at the age of fifteen, he slugged his high-school principal for making anti-Semitic remarks. The next year, on his sixteenth birthday, he quit school forever. He became a professional performer, but the work was not steady.

In 1946, he was introduced to Dean Martin in New York City, and they formed a club act: Martin (né Paul Dino Crocetti) crooned, and Jerry mugged with physical comedy. By 1948, they were playing New York City's top nightclubs and appearing on TV variety shows; the next year, the madcap duo inaugurated their own radio show and then became one of the revolving set of hosts for television's *The Colgate Comedy Hour* (1950–55)

Martin and Lewis debuted in movies with *My Friend Irma* (1949) and, before calling it quits as a pair, made fourteen other profitable comedies. Thereafter, on his own, Lewis starred in *The Delicate Delinquent* (1957) and went on to make other movies, often as producer–director–screenwriter–star.

On television, he had a short run in 1963 as a talk-show host and little success with a comedy/variety series (1967–69). His greatest small-screen success was hosting (from 1966 onward) his annual Labor Day Telethon on behalf of the Muscular Dystrophy Association.

In 1972, Lewis starred in *The Day the Clown Cried* as an alcoholic jokester locked in a Nazi CONCENTRATION CAMP and ordered to entertain the Jewish children as they are being led to the death ovens. Litigations over missed payments caused the movie to be shelved. Lewis did not make another film until *Hardly Working* (1981). One of his best screen assignments was as the talk-show host, kidnapped by deranged Robert De Niro, in *The King of Comedy* (1983).

In the mid-1990s the comedian played the devil in a Broadway revival and tour of the musical *Damn Yankees.* One of Lewis's most telling recent performances was on TV's *MAD ABOUT YOU* (1992–99). He played a demanding billionaire, and his mix of loud-mouthed shtick, expert timing, and pathos demonstrated the incredible range of talent within him.

Lewis, Richard (1947–) At the same time that WOODY ALLEN was establishing himself as filmdom's most neurotic, contemporary, intellectual Jew in the early to mid-1970s, Lewis was honing his stand-up club routine as a raconteur of repressed family life. His trademarks were his all-black clothing and his habit of pacing the stage like a cornered animal and running his hands nervously through his long, thick dark hair.

Born in Brooklyn, New York, and raised in Englewood, New Jersey, he was a graduate (1969) of Ohio State University with majors in marketing and communications. Tiring of being a copywriter, he turned to writing comedy jokes for others. In 1971, he began to perform in Manhattan comedy clubs. Appearances on TV's *The Tonight Show Starring Johnny Carson* in 1974 made him nationally known as a talented, self-deprecating comic. The star of four TV series, including the short-lasting *Daddy Dearest* (1993) in which he teamed with DON RICKLES, Lewis was most successful with *ANYTHING BUT LOVE* (1989–92) as the anxious Jewish bachelor working with and dating Jamie Lee Curtis. His film roles ranged from MEL BROOKS's *Robin Hood: Men in Tights* (1993) to *Game Day* (1999), in which he played a college basketball coach who had seen better days. In 2002, he appeared in five episodes of the TV drama *7th Heaven*, cast as a rabbi.

His amusing takes on his personal woes have been the subject of several cable specials, and his autobiography, *The Other Great Depression* (2000), told of his recovery from a severe alcohol addiction.

***Liberty Heights* (1999)** Warner Bros., color, 127 minutes. **Director/Screenplay:** Barry Levinson; **Cast:** Adrien Brody (Van Kurtzman), Bebe Neuwirth (Ada Kurtzman), Joe Mantegna (Nate Kurtzman), Ben Foster (Ben Kurtzman), Rebekah Johnson (Sylvia), Justin Chambers (Trey), Carolyn Murphy (Dubbie).

This—another loving, if often bland, tribute to a bygone era in Baltimore, Maryland—was created by LEVINSON, one of the city's greatest proponents. Levinson's earlier *Diner* (1982), *Tin Men* (1986), and *AVALON* (1990) were portraits of life in the metropolis where he grew up. In contrast, the ambitious *Liberty Heights* attempted an all-encompassing view of the city. The filmmaker stressed in the movie that racial stereotypes did not always hold true in Baltimore; for example, there were African-American physicians and Jewish hoodlums.

The chronicle was set in 1954 Baltimore where Jewish Nate Kurtzman was struggling to support his family. Because his burlesque theater is failing, he now runs a numbers operation that binds him to the underworld. His younger boy Ben is drawn emotionally to Sylvia, an African American from school. Her physician father forbids the interracial romance. Nate's older son, Van, falls in love with the beautiful gentile Dubbie, who is already the girlfriend of the wealthy Trey, a WASP whom Van has befriended. As time passes, Ben leaves for college and says goodbye to Sylvia, Nate is jailed for his criminal activities, and Van and Dubbie consummate their love.

Counterpointing the depiction of the Kurtzmans' Jewish household was the intermingling of "the other kind" (i.e., gentiles and African Americans) who either lived in or interacted with the once predominantly Jewish suburb of Liberty Heights.

***Life of Emile Zola, The* (1937)** Warner Bros., b&w, 123 minutes. **Director:** William Dieterle; **Screenplay:** Norman Reilly Raine, Heinz Herald, and Geza Herczeg; **Cast:** Paul Muni (Emile Zola), Joseph Schildkraut (Capt. Alfred Dreyfus), Gale Sondergaard (Lucie Dreyfus), Donald Crisp (Maître Labori), Gloria Holden (Alexandrine Zola), Erin O'Brien-Moore (Nana).

Several Oscars went to this distinguished film biography—including one to Joseph Schildkraut as the nineteenth-century Jewish French soldier framed for espionage because of anti-Semitism. But the well-crafted drama avoids discussion and references to the fact that (1) Dreyfus, sent to Devil's Island for a crime he did not commit, was Jewish, and (2) that he was singled out for the injustice because he was Jewish. This occurred because it was still 1930s Hollywood and the Jewish executives at Warner Bros. were still cautious about offending moviegoers with blatantly Jewish topics (even when historically true).

As the film's title implied, much of this well-mounted feature was devoted to earlier events in the life of French novelist and critic Emile Zola (1840–1902). But as in several films of the 1950s (including 1959's *THE LAST ANGRY MAN*, which also starred Muni), it was the Jewish character (Dreyfus) who made the greatest impact on gentiles Zola and France, causing each to reevaluate career paths and life choices.

A much more cogent and balanced presentation of the Dreyfus affair was offered in the British-made *I Accuse!* (1958), starring (and directed by) José Ferrer. Focusing on the spectrum of reasons—including anti-Semitism—that led to the cover-up and the trial verdicts against Dreyfus, the movie centered on the courtroom hearings, the inhumane imprisonment of the man once on Devil's Island, and the victim's eventual pardon by the French president.

A less intriguing presentation of the Dreyfus uproar was 1991's *Prisoner of Honor*, an HBO cable movie. RICHARD DREYFUSS had the lead role of Colonel Picquart who must justify for the record the scandalous affair. Kenneth Colley played Captain Dreyfus.

Lower East Side In the late nineteenth and the early twentieth century when the (Eastern) European Jewish immigrants arrived by ship in New York harbor, their next stop after being processed at Ellis Island was typically to some address on Manhattan's increasingly congested Lower East Side where friends or relatives already lived. This area became known as the Jewish ghetto, and its mass of overcrowded (tenement) buildings and peddler-crowded streets was frequently the setting for GHETTO DRAMAS—those movie melodramas dealing with New York City's immigrant Jewish population. Geographically the area was bounded on the south by Canal Street, on the north by Houston Street, on the east by the East River, and on the west by Broadway.

Lumet, Sidney (1924–) The son of Yiddish stage actor Baruch Lumet, Lumet's film acting bow occurred in *One Third of a Nation* (1939). He directed many TV works during the 1950s and made his feature-film directing debut with *12 Angry Men* (1957). In his screen productions, he frequently examined the contemporary Jewish condition in such features as *THE PAWNBROKER* (1965), *BYE BYE BRAVERMAN* (1968), *JUST TELL ME WHAT YOU WANT* (1980), *DANIEL* (1983), *GARBO TALKS* (1984), and *A STRANGER AMONG US* (1992). Most of these motion pictures, as well as such other of his entries as *Serpico* (1973), *Dog Day Afternoon* (1975), and *Night Falls on Manhattan* (1996), were shot in New York City. He returned to series TV with *100 Centre Street* (2000–2002) whose ensemble cast featured ALAN ARKIN as an eccentric, but highly ethnic New York City judge who was Jewish.

M

***Mad About You* (1992–1999)** NBC-TV series, color, 30 minutes. **Cast:** Paul Reiser (Paul Buchman), Helen Hunt (Jamie Buchman), Anne Elizabeth Ramsay (Lisa Stemple), Leila Kenzle (Fran Devanow: 1992–98), Richard Kind (Dr. Mark David Devanow: 1992–93), John Pankow (Ira Buchman: 1993–99), Cynthia Harris (Sylvia Buchman), Louis Zorich (Burt Buchman), Robin Bartlett (Debbie Buchman).

For those who found *SEINFELD* (1990–99) too self-indulgent, the flip side of the coin from that series' lead character (stand-up comedian JERRY SEINFELD as "himself") was Paul Buchman of *Mad About You.* Like the Seinfeld character, Buchman was a bright New York Jew pursuing a show-business career (as a documentary filmmaker). Both figures were parent dominated, neurotic, and well meaning, but there the similarities ended. If the Seinfeld character was always running away from commitment, his roots, and seeing the big picture, Paul was the opposite: He was (generally) happily married, doted on his annoying parents, and embraced his Jewish heritage. He was close to his cousin Ira, a frequent putz (i.e., jerk), and had a friendly rivalry with his sister Debbie who was a lesbian.

On this smartly written series, nothing was made of the fact that Paul had an interfaith marriage because his wife (Helen Hunt) was attractive, bright, and feisty, which both annoyed and impressed Paul's dominating mother, Sylvia. More refined than Nancy Walker's Ida on *RHODA* (1974–78), Sylvia was equally pushy, expert at creating guilt in her adult son (and to a lesser extent her daughter), and ruled her meek spouse; in short, she was the quintessential Jewish mother—at least by the standards of contemporary TV sitcoms.

Rounding out the ethnic ambiance of *Mad About You* were the Buchmans' close friends—the very Jewish Fran and Mark and their spoiled brat of a son. She dabbled at a career, and he was a gynecologist who underwent a midlife crisis and divorced his wife.

Helen Hunt and Paul Reiser, the coleads of TV's *Mad About You* (1992–99). (ECHO BOOK SHOP)

Stand-up comedian/actor REISER, star and cocreator of this award-winning series, frequently used veteran Jewish talent on the show to play relatives or business associates, including MEL BROOKS, SID CAESAR, JERRY LEWIS, and CARL REINER.

***Majority of One, A* (1961)** Warner Bros., color, 156 minutes. **Director:** Mervyn LeRoy; **Screenplay:** Leonard Spigelgass; **Cast:** Rosalind Russell (Mrs. Bertha Jacoby), Alec Guinness (Koichi Asano), Ray Danton (Jerome Black), Madlyn Rhue (Alice Black), Mae Questel (Mrs. Rubin).

In 1959, GERTRUDE BERG (of *THE GOLDBERGS* radio and TV fame) starred in the very successful Broadway comedy *A Majority of One*, which appealed to New York theater groups. As with so many stage vehicles transferred to the screen, the original lead performer was not chosen for the movie adaptation. In Berg's case, it was because the decision makers felt that she was "too" Jewish—and too associated with the character of Molly Goldberg—to play the Brooklyn matron who, en route to Tokyo, falls in love with a wealthy Japanese widower. He, like she, has lost loved ones in World War II.

Instead, Russell was badly miscast in the pivotal assignment, a situation that Britisher Guinness as the Japanese gentleman could not quite compensate for on camera, especially in close-ups, which revealed his Caucasian features. The comedy's charming plot gimmick of love winning out over prejudice in the case of the middle-aged American and the proud Japanese man lost its momentum frequently because Russell's Jewish persona was so blatantly artificial.

Mandel, Howie (1955–) Over the years, curly-haired, smiley-faced Mandel was a stand-up comedian and creator and starred on TV in children's programming and as a talk-show host. He also played Dr. Wayne Fiscus on *ST. ELSEWHERE* (1982–88) and was featured in movies.

Born Howie Michael Mandel II in Toronto, Ontario, Canada, he dropped out of high school and went into the carpeting business. While on a business trip to Los Angeles, friends urged the prankster with a witty take on life to perform on amateur night at the Comedy Store; that was the start of his stand-up comedy career. One of his early TV appearances was on the Canadian sketch series, *Bizarre* (1980–95). His motion picture debut was the unremarkable *Gas* (1981). In *St. Elsewhere* he was the light-hearted Jewish physician who, beneath his glibness, was a dedicated doctor, and in the movie *Walk Like a Man* (1987), he was Bobo, who was raised by wolves and was now dealing with civilization. His 1992 summer TV series, *Howie*, in which he did stand-up routines and sketches, was not successful. That same year he also had a children's TV show, *The Amazing Live Sea Monkeys*. After several forgettable movies, he returned to television with *The Howie Mandel Show* (1998–99), a daytime talk program, and in mid-2000, he promoted a new children's show he had created—*Howie Mandel's Sunny Skies*. His recent films included: *Tangerine Bear* (2000—an animated feature), *Spin Cycle* (2000), and *Spinning Out of Control* (2001—a TV movie).

***Manhattan* (1979)** United Artists, b&w, 96 minutes. **Director/Screenplay:** Woody Allen; **Cast:** Woody Allen (Isaac Davis), Diane Keaton (Mary Wilke), Michael Murphy (Yale), Mariel Hemingway (Tracy), Meryl Streep (Jill).

As a counterpoint to *ANNIE HALL* (1977), *Manhattan* was a more fully developed movie, complete with rich characterizations and serious observations on relationship issues confronting contemporary urban dwellers. Its focal figure, the self-absorbed, hung-up Jew, another typical ALLEN on-camera personification, was drawn to a series of gentile women as he bumbled his way through life in the Big Apple.

Allen's alter ego Isaac Davis is a phobic New York Jewish intellectual, an anxiety-filled weakling who is bursting with doubts about God, life, and every woman he covets. The perpetually unfulfilled man is a successful TV writer who is convinced that his talents are being wasted and whose every romance is ill matched. He remains insecure about his ex-wife (Streep) who has left him for a lesbian relationship and who is writing a book on their unsuccessful marriage. Meanwhile, Davis is dating high schooler Tracy but becomes attracted to annoying but quite nice Mary Wilke. The rest of this typical Allen film is concerned with resolving the complex relationships surrounding and involving Davis.

Manhattan earned two Oscar nominations: Best Original Screenplay and Best Supporting Actress (Hemingway).

***Marjorie Morningstar* (1958)** Warner Bros., color, 123 minutes. **Director:** Irving Rapper; **Screenplay:** Everett Freeman; **Cast:** Gene Kelly (Noel Airman [Noel Ehrman]), Natalie Wood (Marjorie Morningstar [Marjorie Morgenstern]), Claire Trevor (Rose Morgenstern), Everett Sloane (Arnold Morgenstern), Ed Wynn (Uncle Samson Morgenstern).

Herman Wouk's extremely popular novel *Marjorie Morningstar* (1955) delineated the post-World War II Jewish-American Princess, a type who would appear frequently in literature thereafter. The film was in preproduction for two years, with much speculation as to who would play the key roles of the Jewish Morgensterns. (DANNY KAYE was offered the part of Noel Airman but thought it "too" Jewish to tackle. GERTRUDE BERG tested but was found "too" Jewish to play the mother. At one point, Bette Davis and EDWARD G. ROBINSON were considered to play the heroine's parents.)

In typical fashion, the filmmakers gave in to concerns that this story would emerge too ethnic on screen and as such cast the central roles with non-Semitic types: Kelly, Wood, and Trevor. Of the ensemble, only Wynn and Sloane in less important roles offered any verisimilitude of old- and new-generation New York Jews coping with tradition and assimilation. A few scenes dealing with a bar mitzvah and a holiday dinner encompass the bulk of Jewish tradition shown on screen.

If Wood's Marjorie was hardly Jewish, then Kelly's Noel Airman, a floundering composer, was even less so, and South Wind, the Adirondacks resort of which he was social director, lost any of its intended CATSKILL flavor. Relying on a relatively few (but still more than most at the time) trappings of

Judaism, much of the dramatic tension revolved around Marjorie's indecision about whether to bed Noel without benefit of marriage or to find contentment with a more conventional catch. She ends with a hang-doggish but successful Broadway writer who loved her for years. Because Wood was overmatched by the demands of the project, her performance left much to be desired.

Noted by contemporary critics and later historians was that, here, the traditionally strong Jewish father (as seen in, for example, *THE JAZZ SINGER*, 1927, etc.) had morphed into a meek man who held his own counsel, while the Jewish wife, once so typically warm and loving, had become the controlling, ego-driven person who runs the household.

"A Very Precious Love," the theme song to *Marjorie Morningstar*, was nominated for an Academy Award.

Marx Brothers, the: Chico (1886–1961), Harpo (1888–1964), Groucho (1890–1977), Zeppo (1901–1979) They were undoubtedly one of the—if not *the*—most famous sibling groups in American show-business history. Despite the passing of decades, their celluloid antics remained fresh. Each of the three leading brothers (Chico, Harpo, and Groucho) brought a delightful air of insanity to their films, reflecting their rebellion against the establishment.

More successful than their contemporaries, the RITZ BROTHERS, the irreverent brothers Marx took a far different tack to screen comedy than the also Jewish-born Three Stooges who (1) devoted themselves to heavy-duty physical slapstick and (2) avoided being typed ethnically. As for the performing Marx Bros., if Zeppo was the normal one (i.e., bland member), and Harpo the silent, skirt-chasing harpist, Chico posed on camera as an Italian type with Italian character names. It remained for Groucho—the most verbal of the on-screen siblings—to crack jokes filled with Jewish idioms and, in his characters' rapaciousness for money and curvaceous damsels, to so exaggerate Jewish stereotypes that he made his satires deliciously foolish, not bitter.

The brothers were born in New York City. Their father, Sam (né Simon Marrix), a struggling tailor, was from the Alsace-Lorraine region of France. Their mother, Minnie (née Minna Schoenberg), originated from Germany where her parents operated a roving theater troupe. There was a fifth Marx brother, Gummo (born Milton [1893–1977]), who left the family act after being drafted into the World War I army. It remained for the four other boys: Chico (born Leonard), Harpo (born Adolph), Groucho (born Julius), and Zeppo (born Herbert) to carry on the family's show-business tradition.

The boys left school early to pursue Minnie's ambitions for them as entertainers. After much refinement of their act, they played New York's Palace Theater in 1919 and soon were vaudeville headliners. In the 1920s, they made a silent short film, *Humorisk*, but because they were dissatisfied with it, it was not released. (Harpo alone of the Marxes would be in the 1925 silent movie *Too Many Kisses*.)

With the coming of sound, the Marx Brothers quartet made their talkie movie debut at Paramount with *The Cocoanuts* (1929) and *Animal Crackers* (1930), each based on their prior Broadway hits. They moved to the West Coast to shoot *Monkey Business* (1931), *Horse Feathers* (1932), and *Duck Soup* (1933) for the studio. In these five films, as later, it was cigar-flicking Groucho—with the painted-on mustache and eyebrows and the loping gait—who was front and center, with the pompous Margaret Dumont as his frequent target. Chico provided the comical piano interludes, and Harpo—with fright wig and honking horn—communicated in pantomime, pursued women, and played the harp. Zeppo, left to being the comedy straight man, would quit the act after this string of pictures to become a talent agent.

After a two-year absence, the three Marx Brothers returned to pictures in the mid-1930s, this time at MGM. Their first, *A Night at the Opera* (1935), was a big hit and led to *A Day at the Races* (1937). Less popular was *Room Service* (1938), but they bounced back with *At the Circus* (1939) and *Go West* (1940). Their remaining joint screen outings were much less successful. The trio appeared in *The Story of Mankind* (1957) but not as a team. Meanwhile, of the brothers, Groucho continued to make movies and then enjoyed success as host of a quiz show, *You Bet Your Life*, both on radio (1947–51) and on television (1950–61). He also authored humor books and several autobiographies.

***Mary Tyler Moore Show, The* (1970–1977)** CBS-TV series, color, 30 minutes. **Cast:** Mary Tyler Moore (Mary Richards), Edward Asner (Lou Grant), Ted Knight (Ted Baxter), Gavin MacLeod (Murray Slaughter), Valerie Harper (Rhoda Morgenstern: 1970–74), Cloris Leachman (Phyllis Lindstrom: 1970–75), Nancy Walker (Ida Morgenstern).

If any television series ever captured the hearts of viewers it was—and for many, still is—*The Mary Tyler Moore Show*. Smartly conceived, this sitcom was one of the first instances in American television where its leading character (Mary Richards) was neither married nor divorced. Instead, she was a single woman over thirty who was actively pursuing her career. As such, Mary quickly became a role model for many viewers. The show won several Emmys during its run.

In contrast to idealistic, generally low-key Mary, a Presbyterian, was her Minneapolis apartment-building friend, Rhoda Morgenstern. Rhoda was from the Bronx, Jewish, aggressive, and determined to snare a husband as an alternative to being a working woman. While Mary remained optimistic about life, Rhoda was the cynical one. Their friendship grew very tight. In presenting these contrasting characters with affection rather than sarcasm, the show did much to avoid stereotyping either figure.

If Harper's Rhoda was one of the first fully developed, nondisguised Jewish leads on a network TV sitcom, she was even better etched in the episodes featuring her irrepressible mother Ida. (The latter occasionally visited Minneapolis to check on her daughter's well being.) As played by Walker, the diminutive, loud-mouthed, gesticulating Ida became a giant, equal to any challenge, but in contrast to other examples seen on the big screen (e.g., *NO WAY TO TREAT A LADY*, 1968; *PORTNOY'S COMPLAINT*, 1972), Ida was not a one-note domineering Jewish tyrant. There were times when she admitted defeat (reluctantly). More importantly, even when she demanded her own way (because a mother knew best), her heart was generally in the right place.

Both Rhoda and Ida were fleshed out at even greater length when the spin-off series *RHODA* (1974–78) aired. As for the two good friends, they would be reunited in *Mary and Rhoda* (2000), a made-for-television reunion movie, set in New York City.

***Masada* (1981)** ABC-TV miniseries, color, 400 minutes. **Director:** Boris Sagal; **Teleplay:** Joel Oliansky; **Cast:** Peter O'Toole (Cornelius Flavius Silva), Peter Strauss (Eleazar Ben Yair), Barbara Carrera (Sheva), Nigel Davenport (Mucianus), Alan Feinstein (Aaron), Giulia Pagano (Miriam).

This highly praised, four-part miniseries was based on Ernest K. Gann's novel *The Antagonists* (1970). Set in the first century B.C., it retells the saga of 900 zealous Israelites who, guided by Eleazar Ben Yair, revolt against the Roman occupiers of Palestine. They hole up in the ruins of a fortified palace in the mountains near the southwest shore of the Dead Sea. After a two-year siege, Silva and his imperial army of 5,000 Romans storm the fortifications. They discover that the remaining defenders have committed mass suicide.

Most biblical-era screen stories used the Israelites—and even their leaders—as backdrops (e.g., *Solomon and Sheba*, 1958) to tell a love and/or adventure tale, but here the characters were real fighting soldiers who were protecting their homeland. Coming in the wake of the acclaimed *HOLOCAUST* (1978), this award-winning miniseries focused on its Hebrew figures up front and close up.

Mason, Jackie (1931–) He was among the many Jewish performers to find several doors in Hollywood closed to him because of his "too" Semitic looks and, especially, his "too" Jewish diction, but Mason was certainly one of the few rabbis to be so rejected by the entertainment industry—whose membership, ironically, was often heavily composed of Jews.

He was born Yacov (Jacob) Moshe Maza in 1931 (some sources list 1930 or 1934) in Sheboygan, Wisconsin, and grew up on Manhattan's LOWER EAST SIDE. His three older brothers followed the family tradition of becoming rabbis: Mason himself became a cantor at eighteen and was ordained a rabbi after completing the seminary program at Yeshiva University. He questioned his calling but towed the line to please his father.

To keep life interesting, Mason began to inject humor into his sermons; later, he took breathers from his religious duties by performing stand-up comedy at resorts in the CATSKILLS. Once his father passed away in 1957, Mason became a full-time comedian. His strong accent and nonsmutty material hindered him in nonborscht-belt-circuit venues.

Mason's rise to fame in the 1960s in clubs and on national TV was halted in the fall of 1964 when he had a misunderstanding on air with Ed Sullivan, host of a popular weekly variety show. The angered Sullivan dropped the comedian's contract, and work was hard for Mason to come by until 1966 when the two made up. That same year, Mason's contretemps with singer Frank Sinatra "coincidentally" led the comedian to being shot at and assaulted in the coming months. The bad period continued when he produced and starred in a Broadway play (*A Teaspoon Every Four Hours*, 1969) and a film (*The Stoolie*, 1972), and both failed miserably. Also during this period, Jackie supplied the voice of the aardvark for a series of cartoon shorts (e.g., *Odd Ant Out*, 1970).

Mason's professional reputation was restored by the success of his one-man show (*The World According to Me!*), which opened on Broadway in late 1968. Now a success, he made comedy albums, wrote books, was in the screen comedy *Caddyshack II* (1988), and did a cable TV version of his stage showcase. This led to Mason's network TV series, *CHICKEN SOUP* (1989). This highly controversial situation comedy cast him as a Jewish man who fell in love with an Irish Catholic woman (Lynn Redgrave). It aroused the ire of the Jewish Defense League and other PRESSURE GROUPS, and the series was canceled in less than two months.

In the 1990s, Mason largely devoted himself to his one-man Broadway shows: *Brand New* (1990), *Politically Incorrect* (1994), and *Love Thy Neighbor* (1996).

Matthau, Walter (1920–2000) Transitioning from screen villain to cinema leading man was never an easy step, especially if the actor was (1) not young and (2) not traditionally handsome by Hollywood standards.

The future actor's father, Melas Matuschanskayasky (some sources disputed the existence of this surname), had been an Eastern Rite Catholic priest during the czarist reign in Russia. He left the priesthood and, while in Lithuania, wed a Jew, Rose Berolsky. (Some sources list the father as merely a peddler from Kiev, Russia.) The couple immigrated to America where their surname supposedly was shortened to Matthow. When his son was three, Mr. Matthow departed, leaving the mother, a garment worker, to raise her two sons on Manhattan's LOWER EAST SIDE.

As a youngster, Matthau worked at the refreshment counters of local theaters. He made his acting debut at eleven in a Yiddish-language production. After serving in the U.S. Army Air Force during World War II, he studied acting in Manhattan. His first Broadway assignment was as an understudy in *Anne of a Thousand Days* (1948), and his first lead was *Twilight Walk* (1951). Meanwhile, he became active in television but never quite registered with the viewing public (even when he had the lead in the 1961 police detective series, *Tallahassee 7000*.) In 1955, he made his movie debut, playing a villain in Burt Lancaster's *The Kentuckian*.

Jowly Matthau with the hangdog, crinkled look continued to be cast mostly as heavies on screen (e.g., *Charade*,

1963). It was playing slovenly Oscar Madison on Broadway in Neil Simon's *The Odd Couple* (1965) that convinced Hollywood to rethink its use of his talents. Mathau's role as the conniving lawyer in *The Fortune Cookie* (1966) marked the first of many movies he made with actor Jack Lemmon; it also set the mode for the Matthau screen type: the sardonic, irascible manipulator of a generally undefined ethnic background. He became the cinema's favorite grouch, as in *The Odd Couple* (1968), *Hello, Dolly!* (1969), and *The Bad News Bears* (1976). By the 1990s, he was still conforming to movie type, frequently cast with pal Jack Lemmon: *Grumpy Old Men* (1993), *Out to Sea* (1997), *The Odd Couple II* (1998). Occasionally his cranky ethnic persona had a more defined Jewishness to it, such as his Nat Moyer in *I'm Not Rappaport* (1996).

An inveterate gambler who had a long history of heart problems, Matthau's one film directorial effort was *Gangster Story* (1960) in which he also starred. He served as executive producer of *Little Miss Marker* (1980), besides playing the lead opposite Julie Andrews.

***Max and Helen* (1990)** TNT cable, color, 94 minutes. **Director:** Philip Saville; **Teleplay:** Corey Bleckman; **Cast:** Treat Williams (Max Rosenberg), Alice Krige (Helen Weiss), Martin Landau (Simon Wiesenthal), Jonathan Phillips (Werner Schultze/Mark Weiss), Adam Kotz (Peter).

In the international coproduction *Murderers Among Us: The Simon Wiesenthal Story* (1989), Ben Kingsley had played Simon Wiesenthal, the famed Nazi hunter who tracked down Adolf Eichmann. In this true-life entry based on Wiesenthal's 1982 novel, the made-for-cable feature deals with the 1962 prosecution of the head (Phillips) of a Polish factory who was a labor camp commandant during World War II. Needing witnesses to testify in the trial, Wiesenthal encounters Max Rosenberg, who lost his wife (Krige) in the concentration camps and now, years later, is still guilt ridden that he survived. Although initially Max won't help Wiesenthal, as his dramatic history is unraveled, some strange truths are revealed.

With the recurring number of television movies and miniseries devoted to the HOLOCAUST and its victims, it was evident that there was still an audience for these sobering historic dramas on the horrific topic.

Mazursky, Paul (1930–) Starting out as an actor in *Fear and Desire* (1953) and *The Blackboard Jungle* (1955), the often underrated Jewish-born film director Mazursky often dissected on screen the lifestyles of Semite characters whether set in the past (e.g., *NEXT STOP, GREENWICH VILLAGE*, 1976), over the years (e.g., *Willie and Phil*, 1980), or in the present day (e.g., *DOWN AND OUT IN BEVERLY HILLS*, 1986; *Scenes from a Mall*, 1991). One of his most cogent works on Jewish themes was *ENEMIES: A LOVE STORY* (1989). He frequently acted in other directors' productions (e.g., *Punchline*, 1988; *Man Trouble*, 1992; and *2 Days in the Valley*, 1996), typically playing a Jewish figure. On the TV series *Once and Again* (1999–2002), he made recurring appearances as Sela Ward's Jewish dad, a restaurateur, even materializing as a helpful spirit occasionally after his character had died.

***Menasha the Magnificent* (1950)** NBC-TV series, b&w, 30 minutes. **Cast:** Menasha Skulnik (Menasha), Jean Cleveland (Mrs. Davis: episode one), Zamah Cunningham (Mrs. Davis: remaining episodes).

Born in Warsaw, Poland, Skulnik had performed in the European Yiddish theater and after immigrating to the United States became a focal member (1930–50) of the Yiddish Art Theater. On radio he was heard as Uncle David on *THE GOLDBERGS* and in 1950 was the star of his own short-lived small screen series, playing a very Uncle David-type of role as manager of a LOWER EAST SIDE New York restaurant owned by the physically imposing Mrs. Davis. Ever the optimist, he would start each day singing "Oh, Vhat a Beautiful Mornin'"—but before long this sad sack was enmeshed in a new difficulty.

At the time of *Menasha the Magnificent*, another Jewish show (*THE GOLDBERGS*) was already a TV hit. Considering the paucity of Jewish-themed programming in later years of network television, this was a relative deluge of ethnic fare.

***Me, Natalie* (1969)** National General, color, 110 minutes. **Director:** Fred Coe; **Screenplay:** Martin Zweiback; **Cast:** Patty Duke (Natalie Miller), James Farentino (David Harris), Martin Balsam (Uncle Harold), Elsa Lanchester (Miss Dennison), Salome Jens (Shirley Norton), Nancy Marchand (Mrs. Miller), Phil Sterling (Mr. Miller).

A decade after *MARJORIE MORNINGSTAR* (1958), this modestly budgeted feature was still one of the few Hollywood products dealing with a Jewish girl seeking her identity in the contemporary world. (Although Natalie was clearly Jewish, she was not referred to as such, and it can be inferred as such only from the casting/performance of her parents and beloved Uncle Harold.) Duke's Natalie Miller was no physical beauty, and life was difficult for this Brooklyn high-school student.

Tired of being told that inner beauty was its own reward, after graduation she moves to Greenwich Village where her life expands. She eventually dates a handsome (non-Jewish) guy (Farentino), but he turns out to be already married. Discouraged but undefeated, the motorcycle-riding Natalie returns to her parents' domain, now more sure of her emerging self and her future place in the world, knowing that marriage at any cost is not the way for her to go.

This effective minor entry, which was told from the heroine's point of view, presented a Jewish character far different from the Jewish-American Princess of the same year's *GOODBYE, COLUMBUS*. Similar themes to *Me, Natalie* would be presented with a more contemporary twist in the later *SHEILA LEVINE IS DEAD AND LIVING IN NEW YORK* (1975) and *Girlfriends* (1978).

***Miami Rhapsody* (1995)** Hollywood Pictures, color, 95 minutes. **Director/Screenplay:** David Frankel; **Cast:** Sarah Jessica Parker (Gwyn), Gil Bellows (Matt), Antonio Banderas (Antonio), Mia Farrow (Nina), Paul Mazursky (Vic), Kevin Pollack (Jordan), Kelly Bishop (Zelda).

With the South Beach area of Florida's Miami and Coral Gables as backdrops, this comedy of an affluent Jewish family was filled with interlocking relationships and adultery. In the Marcus clan, Vic is cheating on his wife Nina with travel agent Zelda. This leads ditsy Nina to take up with a sexy Cuban male nurse (Banderas). The latter also has a fling with Nina's daughter Gwyn, a copywriter who can't make up her mind about wedding her fiancé, a zoologist (Bellows). Meanwhile, other members of the family are involved extramaritally, and the family's grandmother is coping with a serious ailment.

With its supply of one-liner jokes and an overly loquacious heroine (Parker), this picture had structural similarities to WOODY ALLEN screen comedies, with the self-focused, whiney aspects of the characters and the dysfunctional nature of this family.

Miami Rhapsody grossed more than $5 million in domestic distribution. A Miami, Florida, setting was also the backdrop for the earlier TV movie, *The Sunset Gang* (1991), which encompassed three stories about the Jewish elderly.

***Middle of the Night* (1959)** Columbia, b&w, 118 minutes. **Director:** Delbert Mann; **Screenplay:** Paddy Chayefsky; **Cast:** Kim Novak (Betty Preisser), Fredric March (Jerry Kingsley), Glenda Farrell (Mrs. Mueller), Jan Norris (Alice Mueller), Lee Grant (Marilyn), Lee Philips (George Preisser), Martin Balsam (Jack).

As a 1954 TV offering, this Jewish-oriented drama of a September-May romance featured E. G. Marshall and Eva Marie Saint. As a 1956 Broadway play, it starred EDWARD G. ROBINSON and Gena Rowlands. By the time it reached the screen, it was cast with two non-Jewish lead players who struggled to bring conviction to their offbeat love story. Although the ambiance of *Middle of the Night* was totally Jewish, like *MARJORIE MORNINGSTAR* (1958), the non-Jewish key performers distracted from the supposed ethnic background of the characters, which, in turn, made the narrative ring false, but at this time Hollywood dealmakers were still unwilling to have a major production about Jewish people be played by appropriately cast performers. (In contrast, the supporting cast was full of ethnic talent.)

In *Middle of the Night*, middle-aged widower Jerry Kingsley, a well-to-do, lonely New York garment manufacturer, is considering remarriage to a woman near his age, but he fears being trapped into a conventional lifestyle. Meanwhile, the firm's receptionist (Novak) is getting over a divorce from her irresponsible musician husband (Philips). She sees in the much older Kingsley a man of kindness and falls in love with him, as he does with her. Their families are against the match, but they throw caution to the wind and wed.

Midler, Bette (1945–) For a five-feet, one-inch, zaftig Jewish girl from Hawaii, Midler overcame many odds to make a strong impact in show business. Whether spewing forth profanities in her hip stage act, winning a Grammy for her 1988 song "Wind Beneath My Wings," or scampering through *DOWN AND OUT IN BEVERLY HILLS* (1986), she proved to be a powerhouse entertainer. On the down side, her strong personality often overwhelmed her vehicles. At her best, she was the definitive Jewish-American Princess who was ready to take on the world.

She was born in Honolulu, Hawaii, where her parents had moved from New Jersey. As a child, she pretended to be Portuguese because her family were the only Caucasians in the mostly Asian community and, according to her, Portuguese people were better accepted in the neighborhood than Jews. Insecure about her looks, she found comfort in performing. When the movie *Hawaii* (1966) was filming on the island, Bette won a bit role and went to the mainland to complete her part. She relocated to New York City, where she became a chorus member of *Fiddler on the Roof* and was eventually elevated to a key role in the Broadway musical.

Later, as a club singer and outrageous raconteur, she made news performing at Manhattan's Continental Baths, which catered to a gay clientele. It led to national TV appearances and, in 1973, starring at New York City's Palace Theater. She was on Broadway (and tour) with her bawdy revues, *Clams on the Half Shell* (1975) and *Divine Madness* (1979), and recorded albums, such as *The Divine Miss M* (1972). She made a dramatic impact on camera playing a Janis Joplinlike rock singer in *The Rose* (1979).

After 1986's *Down and Out in Beverly Hills*, Bette had a run of screen comedies, interrupted by the successful, sentimental *Beaches* (1988)—as the Jewish girl from the Bronx who made good in show business—but spoiled by the misfire *Stella* (1990) and the uninspired musical *For the Boys* (1991). Things did not improve when she teamed with WOODY ALLEN for *Scenes from a Mall* (1991). She regained her footing with a TV production of the musical *Gypsy* (1993) and especially with the hilarious screen comedy *The First Wives Club* (1996).

The year 2000 proved a mixed bag professionally for Midler. On the big screen, she was in the unfunny *Drowning Mona*, *Isn't She Great* (as a shrill version of tacky novelist Jacqueline Susann) and took a secondary role to Mel Gibson and Helen Hunt in *What Women Want*. On TV, she starred in an unsuccessful sitcom *BETTE* that collapsed in its first season (2000–01). Midler was executive producer of the feature *Divine Secrets of the Ya-Ya Sisterhood* (2002) starring Sandra Bullock and Ellyn Burstyn.

Milton Berle Show, The See *TEXACO STAR THEATER, THE*.

***Mrs. G. Goes to College* (aka: *The Gertrude Berg Show*) (1961–1962)** CBS-TV series, b&w, 30 minutes. **Cast:** Gertrude Berg (Sarah Green), Sir Cedric Hardwicke

(Professor Crayton), Mary Wickes (Maxfield), Skip Ward (Joe Caldwell), Marion Ross (Susan Green: 1961).

Back in 1959, BERG and Hardwicke costarred on Broadway in the long-running comedy, *A MAJORITY OF ONE*. They were reunited for this TV series in which Berg was the matronly woman who decides to further her education at college; the distinguished British actor played an exchange teacher from Cambridge University in England. Part way through the season, in January 1962, the show altered its name to *The Gertrude Berg Show*, hoping to entice more of her devotees to watch the program.

In this series, Berg was asked to play a variation of her radio-TV creation, Molly Goldberg, the featured character of *THE GOLDBERGS*. As such, all the mannerisms and inflections that she had developed over the many years of playing the portly Molly crept into her new characterization.

In the early 1960s, an era where most (obvious) Jewish talent were comedians featured on variety shows, this rare instance of a comedy series starring a Jewish performer playing a Jewish character was viable only because of Berg's wide fan base.

***Mr. Skeffington* (1944)** Warner Bros., b&w, 146 minutes. **Director:** Vincent Sherman; **Screenplay:** Julius J. Epstein and Philip G. Epstein; **Cast:** Bette Davis (Fanny Trellis Skeffington), Claude Rains (Job Skeffington), Walter Abel (George Trellis), George Coulouris (Dr. Byles), Richard Waring (Trippy Trellis), Marjorie Riordan (Fanny Junior).

Utilizing a 1940 novel by Mary Annette Beauchamp, Countess Russell, this was one of Davis's most elaborate screen vehicles of the decade. The chronicle opened in 1914 New York as vain Fanny finds herself marrying an older Jewish financier (Rains) to save her miscreant brother (Waring) from going to jail. As with the biblical Job, Mr. Skeffington exhibits amazing patience with his selfish spouse who becomes the mother of their daughter. Years pass. Through the ravages of age and illness, Fanny loses her beauty and now exists in isolation. Suddenly, Job reappears. He had been living in Germany and was stripped of his money, and subjected to torture in a CONCENTRATION CAMP. Now he is blind and alone. He still loves Fanny and she, in turn, knows that he will always remember her as she was. Together, they find happiness.

Although this movie toned down some of the book's conventionalization of Skeffington as an avaricious Jewish businessman, the undercurrent of negative stereotyping remained. At the start of the chronicle, the others treated Job with forced conviviality because he was powerful. By the end of the piece, he was regarded with condescending sympathy because he was a broken man. Thus, his Jewishness and how people react to Jews (from Fanny to the Germans) was a constant subtheme of this drama. Regardless, *Mr. Skeffington* was one of the few 1940s Hollywood movies to feature a Jewish character (albeit played by a non-Jewish performer).

For their work in *Mr. Skeffington*, the coleads were nominated for Academy Awards: Davis (Best Actress) and Rains (Best Supporting Actor).

***Molly* (aka: *The Goldbergs*) (1950)** Paramount, b&w, 83 minutes. **Director:** Walter Hart; **Screenplay:** Gertrude Berg and N. Richard Nash; **Cast:** Gertrude Berg (Molly Goldberg), Philip Loeb (Jake Goldberg), Eli Mintz (Uncle David), Eduard Franz (Alexander Abel), Larry Robinson (Sammy Goldberg), Arlene McQuade (Rosalie Goldberg), Betty Walker (Mrs. Kramer), David Opatoshu (Mr. Dutton), Barbara Rush (Debby), Peter Hanson (Ted Gordon).

As so often happened, what was delightful in one medium lost a lot in the translation to another art format. This occurred when Hollywood, noting the recent success of GERTRUDE BERG's *THE GOLDBERGS* on television, radio, and Broadway, made *Molly*. Although the TV cast was utilized for the film version, the studio—fearful that a too-Jewish movie could limit its box-office prospects—opened up not only the settings but also the cast of characters. In the other media, most of *The Goldbergs* had taken place in the family's Bronx apartment; to get away from the building's ethnic tenants, scenes now were set at the local high school where Molly was taking an art appreciation class. To further broaden the story, a subplot was introduced dealing with Molly's former love interest (Franz), who was now dating a much younger woman, Debby. (The latter role was played by screen newcomer Rush who had no touch of ethnicity about her.) Adding to the dilution of the story line's focus, Molly nego-

Eduard Franz and Gertrude Berg in *Molly* (1950). (JC ARCHIVES)

tiated a romance between Debby and the art history instructor, Ted Gordon. Much time was spent on the budding relationship between Debby and Gordon, both of whom appeared as non-Jewish as possible, which was the filmmakers' intent.

When initially released, the studio promoted the film as *The Goldbergs.* Then suddenly the title was changed to *Molly* to soften the ethnicity of the title. Many reviewers of the time, in describing *Molly,* made no mention of its Jewish emphasis, merely describing the family as from the Bronx.

For those who had never seen *The Goldbergs* on television, the film was a poor substitute. For Hollywood, this inexpensive experiment—to help woo home viewers back to movie theaters—would be Hollywood's last Jewish-themed movie until *MARJORIE MORNINGSTAR* (1958).

***Mortal Storm, The* (1940)** Metro-Goldwyn-Mayer, b&w, 100 minutes. **Director:** Frank Borzage; **Screenplay:** Claudine West, Anderson Ellis, and George Froeschel; **Cast:** Margaret Sullavan (Freya Roth), James Stewart (Martin Brietner), Robert Young (Fritz Marlberg), Frank Morgan (Prof. Viktor Roth), Robert Stack (Otto von Rohn), Bonita Granville (Elsa).

As the rising tide of Nazism led to World War II in Europe in the late 1930s, the United States maintained its official neutrality. Fearful of losing bookings in several European countries, Hollywood product mostly avoided overt references to the Third Reich, Hitlerism, and the mounting anti-Semitism. By 1939, however, Warner Bros. released—with trepidation—*Confessions of a Nazi Spy,* a thriller of fifth-columnist activity in the United States. It made a great impact with filmgoers and convinced other studios to be more courageous (or commercial). It caused MGM to put into production *The Mortal Storm,* based on Phyllis Bottome's 1937 novel, despite threats from the Nazi regime, which were delivered to the studio through an intermediary, a Swiss diplomat.

In packaging *The Mortal Storm,* MGM relied on the same director (Borzage) and several of the same cast (e.g., Sullavan and Young) as *Three Comrades* (1938), which dealt with rising fascism in Germany after World War I. For all the daring of *The Mortal Storm* as one of Hollywood's first features to focus on Adolf Hitler's reign of terror, it still was not a completely honest depiction. For one thing, the country where the action was set was never stated as being Germany. For another, the film's key victim, Professor Viktor Roth who was persecuted and eventually killed in a CONCENTRATION CAMP, was never referenced as being a Jew but rather was called a non-Aryan (there was a telltale "J" sewn on his shirt). Also the film was set in 1933, distancing it from the current events within Germany. Regardless, the movie so angered the Nazi regime that it banned all MGM pictures from distribution in Germany.

Also in 1940, MGM released *ESCAPE,* which dealt with some of the same issues as *The Mortal Storm* and employed the same playing-it-safe methodology. It remained for Charles Chaplin's *THE GREAT DICTATOR* (1940) to speak out about fascist anti-Semitism.

Mostel, Zero (1915–1977) Physically unique, Mostel was a talented oddity: Despite his rotund build, he was graceful on his feet; in addition to his acting acumen, he was a respected painter; although he excelled at low comedy (especially when doing stand-up or spontaneous improvisation), he could be a sensitive actor; above all, this unpredictable, flamboyant individual was a champion of the underdog, whether it be fellow victims of the 1950s communist witch hunt, targets of recurrent anti-Semitism, or victims of other social inequities.

Born Simcha Yoel Mostel in Brooklyn, New York, Samuel Joel Mostel graduated high school in 1931 and received a B.A. degree in art from City College four years later. At the height of the Depression, he took what manual-labor employment he could find. Later hired by the Work Projects Administration to lecture on art at local museums, he added humor to his "seminars" and developed a reputation as a comic.

By 1942, he had made his Manhattan club debut. (It was his agent who gave him the nickname "Zero" as a ploy to gain his client publicity.) This led to his Broadway bow in *Keep 'Em Laughing* (1942) and his movie debut in *Du Barry Was a Lady* (1943). The rest of the 1940s was a patchwork of stage and club work.

Brought back to Hollywood for *Panic in the Streets* (1950), Zero developed a penchant for playing sinister screen roles. However, his contract at Twentieth Century-Fox ended when he was blacklisted for alleged past affiliation with the Communist Party. Back in New York, he struggled to survive with stage work. His off-Broadway success in *Ulysses in Nighttown* (1958) was topped by his riveting dramatics in *Rhinoceros* (1961). The next year, he had major success in the hit Broadway musical *A Funny Thing Happened on the Way to the Forum,* which paved the way for his penultimate role as Tevye in *Fiddler on the Roof* (1964). For MEL BROOKS, Mostel was one of *THE PRODUCERS* (1967), a cult comedy masterpiece. He was the Jewish tailor in *The Angel Levine* (1970) and in WOODY ALLEN'S *THE FRONT* (1976), he played a comedian who was blacklisted, as he himself had been. It was his last live-action film assignment. The next year, after touring with *Fiddler on the Roof,* he was in Philadelphia for the pre-Broadway tryout of *The Merchant* when he died of a heart attack.

Muni, Paul (1895–1967) Like EDWARD G. ROBINSON, Muni was a Jewish refugee from abroad whom Hollywood turned into a celluloid tough guy. But unlike Robinson, the tall and good-looking Muni didn't remain confined to type after his screen success as the ruthless mob leader in *Scarface* (1932); rather, he was a "Man of Many Faces." Importantly, Muni represented a key bridge between the YIDDISH THEATER in North America and mainstream Broadway and Hollywood.

He was born Mehilem Meier Ben Nachum Favel Weisenfreund in Lemberg, Austria, which would become

Lvov, Ukraine. (He was soon nicknamed Muni or called by its variation, Munya.) He was the eldest of three sons whose parents went about the European ghettos presenting the most basic form of YIDDISH THEATER. Later, the family traveled to New York where they settled on the LOWER EAST SIDE. Muni left school in the fourth grade to help support the family.

Meanwhile, his parents encouraged their boys to learn the violin so that they might have a less precarious future than as actors, but fate intervened when Muni was cast one day in Cleveland, Ohio, as a last-minute replacement in *Two Corpses for Breakfast* (1907). It was the beginning of his career in Yiddish theater, an apprenticeship that lasted several years as he traveled about the United States. After years in Boston with a repertory group that included for a time MOLLY PICON, Muni relocated to New York in the late 1910s to be part of the Yiddish Art Theater.

For 1926's *We Americans*, Muni starred on Broadway in his first English-language assignment, playing an elderly Jewish father. This success led to other theater work and then to Hollywood to make *The Valiant* (1929—for which he was Oscar nominated) and *Seven Faces* (1929). His studio pressured him to Americanize his name, and he chose Paul Muni. Back on Broadway, he was the Jewish attorney in the well-received drama, *COUNSELLOR-AT-LAW* (1931).

With *Scarface* and *I Am a Fugitive from a Chain Gang* (1932—for which he was Oscar nominated), Muni was a major film star. He insisted upon a variety of roles, often relying on heavy makeup to alter his looks, as in *The Story of Louis Pasteur* (1936—for which he won an Academy Award) and in *The Good Earth* (1937) in which he was a Chinese farmer. In *THE LIFE OF EMILE ZOLA* (1937), he appeared as the French writer fighting to free the Jewish Alfred Dreyfus. For *Juarez* (1939) he was the renowned Mexican leader. Thereafter, Muni divided his time between stage and film work.

Muni's last Broadway hurrah was *Inherit the Wind* (1955), which earned him a Tony Award. His final screen performance—for which he received his fifth Oscar nomination—was in *THE LAST ANGRY MAN* (1959) as the elderly Jewish doctor. Thereafter, poor health forced him into retirement. With his death in 1967 from a heart attack, an era ended.

***My Favorite Year* (1982)** Metro-Goldwyn-Mayer/United Artists, color, 92 minutes. **Director:** Richard Benjamin; **Screenplay:** Norman Steinberg and Dennis Palumbo; **Cast:** Peter O'Toole (Alan Swann), Mark-Linn Baker (Benjy Stone), Jessica Harper (K. C. Downing), Joseph Bologna (King Kaiser), Bill Macy (Sy Benson), Lainie Kazan (Belle Carroca).

Produced by MEL BROOKS's film company, this superior comedy was set in the mid-1950s. Benjy Stone, a young television gag writer, is asked to watch over a fading Hollywood swashbuckling star (O' Toole) who is marking his media debut on a comedy/variety TV show. The constantly drunk, womanizing Swann leads Stone on a wild chase through Manhattan before the actual telecast.

In this joyful mixture of slapstick and nostalgia, director BENJAMIN created an effective tribute to the era of TV comedian kings like MILTON BERLE and SID CAESAR whose writing staffs were largely Jewish. One of the movie's highlights occurred when Stone takes Swann to meet his family in Brooklyn. Once there, Benjy must cope with his dominating mother—played to the hilt by KAZAN who would make a career out of playing such assignments—and assorted embarrassing relatives and friends.

A short-lasting Broadway adaptation of *My Favorite Year* opened in late 1992 with Tim Curry, Andrea Martin, and Evan Pappas co-starred.

N

***Nanny, The* (1993–1999)** CBS-TV series, color, 30 minutes. **Cast:** Fran Drescher (Fran Fine), Charles Shaughnessy (Maxwell Sheffield), Lauren Lane (Chastity Claire "C. C." Babcock), Daniel Davis (Niles), Nicholle Tom (Maggie Sheffield), Benjamin Salisbury (Brighton Sheffield), Madeline Zima (Grace Sheffield), Renee Taylor (Sylvia Fine), Ann Morgan Guilbert (Yetta), Rachel Chagall (Val).

If it weren't that the real-life DRESCHER talked and acted so much like her on-TV character (shrill and whiney), the series role would have been thought of as a pure caricature. But Drescher, a die-hard New York Jewish woman, played the role with affection, making the character ultimately lovable. On the other hand, some of the episode difficulties she and her Italian girlfriend Val got into went beyond the bounds of reality. But even then, many of the concepts came from Drescher and were springboards from situations in which she had (almost) been involved.

Fran's Jewishness was contrasted to her Broadway-producer employer (later husband) Maxwell Sheffield and, to an even greater degree, to C. C. Babcock, Sheffield's WASPish partner. Furthermore, there was Fran's zaftig mother (Taylor) and the absent-minded grandmother Yetta. Thus, in one show there were three generations of broadly outlined Jewish types.

In comparing Fran of *The Nanny* to the title figure of *RHODA* (1974–78), Fran was a much more fully realized Jewish representation; in particular her eventual marriage to Maxwell was presented as a traditional Jewish ceremony (unlike Rhoda's nearly nondenominational service).

***Nazi Hunter: The Beate Klarsfeld Story* (1986)** ABC-TV, color, 100 minutes. **Director:** Michael Lindsay-Hogg; **Teleplay:** Frederic Hunter; **Cast:** Farrah Fawcett (Beate Klarsfeld), Tom Conti (Serge Klarsfeld), Geraldine Page (Itta Halaunbrenner), Catherine Allegret (Madame Simone Lagrange), Feodor Atkine (Luc Pleyel).

Filmed entirely in France, this made-for-television feature spotlights the real-life Beate Klarsfeld, a German Protestant who is wed to a Jewish law student (Conti) whose father died at Auschwitz. It traces her involvement in helping Jewish causes, in particular tracking down Nazi war criminals. One of her chief targets is the notorious Klaus Barbie ("the butcher of Lyons") who has been in hiding in Bolivia. The suffering that this non-Jewish woman endures over the years in her pursuit of these villains provides a harrowing narrative unto itself.

This TV-movie was part of a 1980s cycle focusing on the HOLOCAUST, its survivors, and those who carried out the policy of genocide.

***Next Stop, Greenwich Village* (1976)** Twentieth Century-Fox, color, 111 minutes. **Director/Screenplay:** Paul Mazursky; **Cast:** Lenny Baker (Larry Lapinsky), Shelley Winters (Mrs. Lapinsky), Ellen Greene (Sarah), Lois Smith (Anita), Christopher Walken (Robert), Dori Brenner (Connie), Antonio Fargas (Bernstein).

This superior comedy blend of nostalgia and discovery was set in 1953 New York. Larry Lapinsky, a Brooklyn College graduate, moves away from his domineering mother (Winters) and meek father (Kellin) to Greenwich Village to explore life and to become an actor. He meets a group of local eccentrics with whom he bonds and falls in love with Sarah, only to discover that she prefers pretentious, WASPy poet Robert. As Larry confronts life—including the suicide of pal Anita and getting a film acting job in Hollywood—he cuts the physical ties with his parents. Yet, he knows that he will be always bound to them emotionally.

If anyone overshadowed the proceedings, it was WINTERS as the very overbearing (almost to the point of caricature), zaftig Jewish mother whose love and wisdom was buried beneath her whining demands, constant guilt trips, and care packages of food. Obviously, by the time of this film's release, Hollywood was no longer concerned with disguising or watering down the Jewish image on screen.

This was one of many Jewish-themed pictures by director MAZURSKY.

***Northern Exposure* (1990–1995)** CBS-TV series, color, 60 minutes. **Cast:** Rob Morrow (Dr. Joel Fleischman), Janine Turner (Maggie O'Connell), Barry Corbin (Maurice Minifield), John Corbett (Chris Stevens), Darren E. Burrow (Ed Chigliak), John Cullum (Holling Vincouer), Cynthia Geary (Shelly Tambo), Elaine Miles (Marilyn Whirlwind), Peg Phillips (Ruth Anne Miller).

Much about this quirky drama series was endearingly eccentric. This included its lead character, a pampered young Jewish doctor from Flushing, New York, who found himself stuck in a small Alaskan town to repay the state for having financed his medical-school tuition. Having left his fiancée Elaine back home, Joel Fleischman begins a tug-of-war romantic relationship with spirited Maggie O'Connell, a gentile from Michigan, who operates a local air-taxi service and is his landlord.

As Joel warms to the idiosyncratic townsfolk, he sheds much of his stereotypical Jewish-doctor persona and becomes a warm, if still romantically indecisive, human being. During the show's run, Morrow's Joel Fleischman built a new image for the "typical" Jewish doctor, no longer depicted as a money-and prestige-fixated egotist but as a sensitive individual.

***No Way to Treat a Lady* (1968)** Paramount, color, 108 minutes. **Director:** Jack Smight; **Screenplay:** John Gay; **Cast:** Rod Steiger (Christopher Gill), Lee Remick (Kate Palmer), George Segal (Morris Brummel), Eileen Heckart (Mrs. Brummel), Murray Hamilton (Inspector Haines).

Interwoven into this superior detective thriller was an intriguing study of two men and their obsessions with their mothers. Broadway producer Christopher Gill has a fixation on his late actress mother who had no time for him. He is now a serial killer, acting out his fantasies by putting on disguises to stalk his female victims. He develops a phone rapport with Manhattan police detective Morris Brummel, who still lives with his mother and is an acquiescing pawn to his parent. Rather than seek a girlfriend different from his nagging mama, he is drawn to Kate Palmer, an almost-victim of the killer. Although Kate is gentile and much younger than Mrs. Brummel, in many respects, they are the same dominating sort.

As the film's ostensible star, SEGAL delivered another of his patented good-natured Jewish schlep performances, similar to that in *BYE BYE BRAVERMAN* (1968) and *Blume in Love* (1973). For many, this movie was swallowed whole by STEIGER's scenery-chewing presence. But the picture really belonged more to Heckart, who did an enthusiastic if not entirely accurate imitation of the new-breed Jewish mother and left an indelible impression with viewers.

***Nuremberg* (2000)** TNT cable, color, 200 minutes. **Director:** Yves Simoneau; **Teleplay:** David W. Rintels; **Cast:** Alec Baldwin (Justice Robert H. Jackson), Brian Cox (Hermann Goering), Jill Hennessy (Elsie Douglas), Michael Ironside (Col. Burton C. Andrus), Christopher Plummer (Sir David Maxwell-Fyfe), Max von Sydow (Samuel Rosenman), Matt Craven (Capt. Gustav Gilbert), Colm Feore (Rudolf Hoess).

Based on Joseph E. Persico's book *Nuremberg: Infamy on Trial* (1994), this made-for-cable two-parter attempted to revisit the basic topic of *JUDGMENT AT NUREMBERG* (1961), which accomplished its purpose much more effectively. (In *Judgment at Nuremberg*, those on trial were high-level members of the Third Reich's court system; in *Nuremberg*, it was a mixture of top-echelon military and civilian personnel.) Coexecutive produced by and starring Baldwin as a U.S. Supreme Court judge, the film concerns the post-World War II trial of more than twenty Nazis accused of crimes against humanity. The prime defendant is Hermann Goering, second in command to Hitler during the Nazis' reign of oppression.

Unlike *Judgment at Nuremberg*, this television production sought to provide answers for why these German leaders undertook the horrendous things they did. The psychological investigation was accomplished by an army psychologist (Craven) who analyzed the prisoners—especially the deadly, fascinating Goering. Others involved included the vengeful Colonel Andrus, in charge of the prisoners; Sir David Maxwell-Fyfe, the chief British prosecutor; and the sinister Rudolf Hoess, the former commandant of the Auschwitz concentration camp.

As did *Judgment at Nuremberg*, the new production devoted screen time to actual newsreel footage of the horrors of the death camps.

***Nuts* (1987)** Warner Bros., color, 116 minutes. **Director:** Martin Ritt; **Screenplay:** Tom Topor, Darryl Ponicsan, and Alvin Sargent; **Cast:** Barbra Streisand (Claudia Draper), Richard Dreyfuss (Aaron Levinsky), Maureen Stapleton (Rose Kirk), Karl Malden (Arthur Kirk), Eli Wallach (Dr. Herbert A. Morrison), Robert Webber (Francis MacMillan).

In 1970, STREISAND starred as a prostitute in the comedic *THE OWL AND THE PUSSYCAT*; she returned to this on-screen trade in *Nuts*, based on a 1980 Broadway play. Again, her character was Jewish, offbeat, and a New Yorker, but there the similarities ended. In this stark drama, her Claudia Draper is an intelligent, high-priced call girl who is arrested on a manslaughter charge. Her mother (Stapleton) and stepfather (Malden) want her committed as mentally unfit to stand trial. The belligerent defendant demands a sanity hearing, and her public defender (Dreyfuss) rises to the occasion. He elicits the reasons for her long rebellious behavior—as a teenager she had been molested repeatedly by her stepfather, and her mother had not stopped the situation.

Claudia was too unique to qualify as a Jewish-American Princess; instead, she certainly fits—her profession aside—into the realm of Manhattan intelligentsia with her love of fine art, music, the written word. This only child had been betrayed by everyone: her mother's nonaction, her father's departure, and her stepfather's abuse. She was a complex modern woman with no family to provide comfort and with a career choice that alienated her from polite society. She was far removed from the sheltered *MARJORIE MORNINGSTAR* (1958) or the ingénue of *GOODBYE, COLUMBUS* (1969).

O

***Odd Couple, The* (1970–1975)** ABC-TV series, color, 30 minutes. **Cast:** Tony Randall (Felix Unger), Jack Klugman (Oscar Madison), Al Molinaro (Murray Greshner), Monica Evans (Cecily Pigeon: 1970–71), Carol Shelley (Gwendolyn Pigeon: 1970–71), Janis Hansen (Gloria Unger: 1971–75).

After being a Broadway mega-hit in 1965 and a successful movie in 1968, Neil Simon's *THE ODD COUPLE* was transferred to television. Again, the comedy was based on the premise that in the heterosexual world, male roommate opposites do *not* attract but can lead to a great deal of (good-natured) frustration and misspent energy.

The play starred the Jewish WALTER MATTHAU (as Oscar) and the non-Jewish Art Carney (as Felix); the film had cast Matthau (again as Oscar) and the non-Jewish Jack Lemmon (as Felix). When the TV adaptation was packaged, the leads were played by two Jewish performers. Ironically of the two, Klugman had more frequently played ethnic characters on screen; yet in the TV sitcom his character—the beer-swilling, sloppy sports writer—displayed less-"typical" Jewish characteristics. In contrast, Randall's screen career had been built on second-banana roles, with his movie alter egos often one-dimensional eccentrics or comedy relief. In *The Odd Couple* he manifested a great many qualities assumed to be associated with mother-dominated Jewish men: fussy, a neatnik, good cook, learned, and not adept in social or sexual situations.

Although there was only a suggestion of Felix's character being Jewish on this TV series, it was an assumption that many viewers made (both then and in the reruns), especially because the property's creator, Simon, was Jewish. This was yet again another illustration of the frequent closeted depiction of Jewish characters in 1970s television.

In the 1982–83 season, *The New Odd Couple* aired with the lead characters played by African-American performers. (An animated daytime series, *The Oddball Couple* [1975–77] featured a finicky cat and a slovenly dog.)

Oliver Twist This novel by British writer Charles Dickens was published in serialized format between 1837 and 1839. Set in early nineteenth-century England, it followed the unlucky life of workhouse foundling Oliver Twist, an innocent victim of the social class system. One of the memorable personalities whom he encounters after arriving in London is the menacing Fagin, whose occupation is to train boys to steal. Within the plot, the old Jew has been paid to bring Twist up as a thief, but after a bungled burglary, he fails to retake charge of the waif. Later, Fagin is executed by the law for his complicity in a murder case.

This popular work with its anti-Semitic stereotype of the Jewish fence was picturized several times. Fagin was played in American silent films by Nat C. Goodwin (1912), Tully Marshall (1916), and Lon Chaney (1922). (There was also the short film *A Modern Oliver Twist*, 1909, as well as the contemporary-set *Oliver Twist Jr.*, 1921, with Wilson Hummell as the Fagin figure.) In Hollywood's talkie era, Fagin was portrayed by Irving Pichel (1933). On U.S. television, George C. Scott was Fagin in a 1982 rendition, and more recently, in 1997, RICHARD DREYFUSS interpreted Fagin.

Among the several British screen versions of *Oliver Twist*, David Lean's 1948 film was considered the most striking, but within that production, Alec Guinness's portrayal of the notorious Fagin was so well handled that it caused an uproar among Jewish PRESSURE GROUPS, who protested that his performance did nothing but fan the flames of anti-Semitism.

In contrast, the Lionel Bart 1960 musical *Oliver!* as filmed in 1968, had a twinkly eyed Ron Moody as the scoundrel Fagin. The Walt Disney cartoon feature, *Oliver & Company* (1988), a takeoff on Dickens's novel, featured Oliver (a homeless kitten) who became involved with a pack of hip dogs, the latter supervised by a human, Fagin (the voice of Dom DeLuise). (There had been earlier TV cartoon specials devoted to *Oliver Twist*, including: *Oliver and the Artful Dodger*, 1975; *Oliver Twist*, 1981 [originally released as a feature in 1974]; and *Oliver Twist*, 1984.)

Opatoshu, David (1918–1996) There was something always Old World about this stately, thin actor who was born in New York City to a novelist father and a teacher mother. He studied acting at the Benno Schneider Studio and was involved with the YIDDISH THEATER in the 1930s. Debuting on film in the Yiddish-language movie *The Light Ahead* (1939), he had a bit a decade later as a Jewish police sergeant in the feature film *The Naked City*. His TV debut was on *THE GOLDBERGS* series in 1949, and he was also in *MOLLY* (1950), the movie based on that show. Opatoshu became an active participant in 1950s–1960s television, working on many major drama offerings. He was among those in *EXODUS* (1960), played the Jewish peddler in *Cimarron* (1960), and was the hero's father in *ENTER LAUGHING* (1967). For the telefeature, *RAID ON ENTEBBE* (1977), he was Israeli prime minister Menachem Begin. He appeared as the great producer's father in the made-for-television *Ziegfeld: The Man and His Women* (1978).

***Operation Eichmann* (1961)** Allied Artists, b&w, 92 minutes. **Director:** R. G. Springsteen; **Screenplay:** Lewis Copley; **Cast:** Werner Klemperer (Adolf Eichmann), Ruta Lee (Anna Kemp), Donald Buka (David), Barbara Turner (Sara), John Banner (Rudolf Hoess), Steve Gravers (Jacob).

One of the most hated Nazis of World War II was Adolf Eichmann, who was responsible for administering the Third Reich's extermination camps. That he escaped capture at the end of the war led to continual speculation as to his whereabouts. A portion of this feature was devoted to Eichmann's participation in creating the HOLOCAUST; the remainder dealt with Israeli agents (Buka and Gravers) tracking the madman to South America. They catch the former SS lieutenant colonel in Argentina and take him back to Israel to stand trial.

This film, made on the eve of the highly publicized trial, was unable to show the real-life finale to Eichmann's courtroom hearing. In actuality, he was found guilty and executed in Israel in 1962.

Despite its low budget and overt dramatics, Klemperer provided a strong characterization of the sinister Nazi. Thanks to the box-office receipts generated by *EXODUS* (1960), there was now more interest in Hollywood in dealing with Jewish topics—especially those related to Israel.

A later TV movie dealing with the same topic was *The Man Who Captured Eichmann* (1996), starring Robert Duvall as Eichmann and based on the book *Eichmann in My Hands* (1990), which was coauthored by Israeli Mossad agent Peter Malkin (played by Arliss Howard). Malkin was the principal force in capturing the Nazis' chief executioner in Buenos Aires. Largely told from Malkin's perceptions, the picture, nevertheless, sought to balance the presentation with Eichmann's viewpoint.

In the feature film *Mother Night* (1996), an American double agent (Nick Nolte) during World War II is captured after the war by the Israelis and finds himself in the cell next to the notorious Eichmann. Henry Gibson provided the voice of Eichmann, which was heard in the adjacent cell. For the HBO cable movie, *Conspiracy* (2001), Stanley Tucci portrayed Eichmann.

A variation on the Eichmann screen stories was *The Man in the Glass Booth* (1975), based on the 1969 play by actor Robert Shaw. Maximilian Schell was featured as a Jewish industrialist, a survivor of the concentration camps who insisted on "confessing" to having been an Adolf Eichmann–like officer in the prisoner compound.

***Over the Brooklyn Bridge* (1984)** Metro-Goldwyn-Mayer/United Artists, color, 106 minutes. **Director:** Menahem Golan; **Screenplay:** Arnold Somkin; **Cast:** Elliott Gould (Alby Sherman), Margaux Hemingway (Elizabeth Anderson), Sid Caesar (Uncle Benjamin), Burt Young (Phil Romano), Shelley Winters (Becky Sherman), Carol Kane (Cheryl Goodman).

This extremely New York type of story explored the hold that family, loved ones, and Jewish religious traditions and biases have on people. The presentation was not bolstered by the dated script but was abetted by a cast whose presence carried familiar associations from their past work. There was GOULD as the perpetual schlep who aspired to move from operating a Brooklyn coffee shop to owning a fine East Side Manhattan restaurant. WINTERS was yet again the overzealous Jewish mother, a loudmouth who was aghast that her son might wed a gentile (Hemingway). Kane did another of her strange-people turns as the seemingly pristine woman who was actually sexually wild. CAESAR shone as Gould's uncle, a successful businessman who would loan his nephew (Gould) money for the eatery only if he wed the Jewish Kane.

***Owl and the Pussycat, The* (1970)** Columbia, color, 98 minutes. **Director:** Herbert Ross; **Screenplay:** Buck Henry; **Cast:** Barbra Streisand (Doris), George Segal (Felix), Robert Klein (Barney), Allen Garfield (dress shop proprietor), Roz Kelly (Eleanor).

In the 1964 Broadway stage original, the role of the wacky prostitute had been played by African-American actress Diana Sands. The part was reshaped to fit STREISAND. Her Doris, a loudmouthed, emotional hooker finds herself involved with meek author/bookstore clerk Felix. During their contentious mating dance, a good many wisecracks are exchanged, and several loony plot situations occur.

It was relatively rare in Hollywood films to depict a prostitute—let alone a Jewish one—as a main character in a comedy, but Streisand's charisma led to this being a box-office success. (She was nominated for a Golden Globe for her performance.) SEGAL brought his patented Jewish schnook routine to the proceedings, making the intellectual but foolish antihero appealing. *The Owl and the Pussycat* was part of the growing Hollywood trend that brought openly Jewish lead characters to mainstream cinema.

P

***Partners Again* (1926)** United Artists, b&w, 5,562′. **Director:** Henry King; **Screenplay:** Frances Marion; **Cast:** George Sidney (Abe Potash), Alexander Carr (Mawruss Perlmutter), Betty Jewel (Hattie Potash), Allan Forrest (Dan), Robert Schable (Schenckmann), Lillian Elliott (Rosie Potash).

The third and final installment of the POTASH AND PERLMUTTER series derived from a 1922 play of the same title that had starred Carr and the late Barney Bernard.

This time, the conflicting but loyal businessmen become embroiled in the automobile business, leading to the predictable disagreements between the two. This go-around found Lillian Elliott playing the role of Potash's wife, a part previously handled by VERA GORDON.

Because producer Samuel Goldwyn abandoned the series, a rival studio (Universal) picked up the concept that same year with their *THE COHENS AND KELLYS* series, which would carry on the same formula (using both Gordon and SIDNEY) and use an Irish element as the additional butt of ethnic jokes.

***Pawnbroker, The* (1965)** Landau Releasing, b&w, 114 minutes. **Director:** Sidney Lumet; **Screenplay:** David Friedkin and Morton Fine; **Cast:** Rod Steiger (Sol Nazerman), Geraldine Fitzgerald (Marilyn Birchfield), Brock Peters (Rodriguez), Jaime Sanchez (Jesus Ortiz), Baruch Lumet (Mendel).

This bleak drama, based on Edward Lewis Wallant's 1961 novel, was a graphic example of the human wreckage left by the HOLOCAUST. A landmark genre entry, it featured flashback scenes of concentration camp brutality, especially staged for this production.

Sol Nazerman, a Jew, was once a professor in Germany. His children and wife (who was raped) died in a World War II prisoner camp. Nazerman survived the ordeal (in body only), eventually coming to New York City where he operates a Harlem pawnshop, financed by a pimp named Rodriguez. Numbed by past horrors, Nazerman remains emotionally rigid whether dealing with his ambitious helper, Jesus Ortiz, or with the compassionate neighborhood social worker, Marilyn Birchfield. Nazerman's dire approach to life eventually so upsets Ortiz that the latter has the shop robbed. In the course of the break-in, Sol almost begs the thieves to kill him; instead it is Ortiz who dies in the shooting. Suddenly coming to life, Nazerman impales his hand on the receipt spindle in the shop and then wanders outside.

With its powerful statement of human inhumanity to one another, and filled with religious symbolism/overtones, *The Pawnbroker* makes a commanding statement. The film's grim ending suggested that Nazerman must now cope with his nightmares of the past.

Directed astutely by LUMET, the film featured his father (Baruch Lumet), the Yiddish stage actor, in a prison-camp flashback. Steiger, nominated here for a Best Actor Oscar, would return in another Jewish drama in *THE CHOSEN* (1981).

***Peddler, The* (1917)** Art Dramas, b&w, 5 reels. **Director:** Herbert Blaché; **Screenplay:** Frederic Chapin; **Cast:** Joe Welch (Abraham Jacobs), Sidney Mason (Sammy), Catherine Calvert (Sarah), Kittens Reichert (Mary), Sally Crute (Mrs. Morgan).

Back in 1902, Yiddish comedian Welch had starred in this vehicle on the New York stage. Again, he was the hard-working, wandering seller of wares who opens a used-clothing store only to have his son (Mason) rob the safe to provide his mistress (Crute) with cash. Later, the repentant son returns home to beg forgiveness, marry his father's housekeeper (Calvert), and allow the old man to live his remaining years happily with his family.

As was so frequent with such highly ethnic pieces as this, the title cards for the silent movie had the appropriate dialogue in dialect, approximating some of the flavor audiences would have heard if it had been a talkie.

***Phil Silvers Show, The* (aka: *You'll Never Get Rich*) (1955–1959)** CBS-TV series, b&w, 30 minutes. **Cast:** Phil Silvers (M/Sgt. Ernest Bilko), Harvey Lembeck (Cpl. Rocco Barbella), Herbie Faye (Pvt. Sam Fender), Paul Ford (Col. John Hall), Maurice Gosfield (Pvt. Duane Doberman), Joe E. Ross (Sgt. Rupert Ritzik).

In military history, there were few craftier con artists than the fictional Ernest Bilko. As created by Nat Hiken and played by SILVERS, he emerged as one of the great creations in the annals of TV. In charge of the army-camp motor pool, no scheme was too daunting nor any commanding officer too intimidating for quick-witted Bilko. With his crew of misfits doing his bidding, he bamboozled his way through army life—the Bilko way.

Initially titled *You'll Never Get Rich*, the series was renamed *The Phil Silvers Show* because its star was so well known to home viewers. By now, bespectacled, balding Silvers had been playing the fast-talking, eye-blinking, conniving character for decades. Part of his image was the ethnicity that the Jewish Silvers brought to the part. It was understood, without being flaunted, that his TV alter ego was a Jew in the military, one who had gotten past any anti-Semitism that may have existed and had turned the tables.

Picon, Molly (1898–1992) Known as the Yiddish Helen Hayes, she was a five-feet bundle of energy who worked for years in YIDDISH THEATER and films before going mainstream with movies, Broadway, TV, and nightclubs. She was a versatile talent and was extremely agile in doing physical stunts. On stage, this irrepressible and zestful comedian might break out in a tap dance or make an appearance on horseback, or—her specialty until she was well into her sixties—somersault in front of the footlights.

Born Margaret Pyekoon in New York City, she moved with her family to Philadelphia when she was three. As of 1904, she was part of Michael Thomashefsky's Yiddish repertory troupe in Philadelphia and later worked in cabaret shows. Quitting high school to become a full-time performer, she was in Boston in 1919 as part of Jacob Kalich's Yiddish repertory company. She married Kalich, and together they toured Europe with their troupe. By the 1920s, she was starring in the New York Yiddish theater and had appeared in silent films, including *Ost und West* (aka: *East and West*) (1923). During the early 1930s, Picon and her husband performed abroad (Europe, South Africa, Argentina, etc.): In Poland, for example, she made two Yiddish-language musical comedy movies, *Yidl Mitn Fidl* (aka: *Yiddle with His Fiddle*) (1935) and *Mamele* (aka: *Little Mother*) (1938). Back in the United States, she made her Broadway debut in *Morning Star* (1940).

It was in 1949 that Molly Picon came to television, hosting a half-hour variety show. In the next decade, Picon alternated between Yiddish (e.g., *Mazel Tov Molly*, 1950) and English-language (e.g., *Make Momma Happy*, 1953) theater.

In the 1960s, Picon performed in such plays as *A Majority of One* and *Dear Me, The Sky Is Falling*, starred in the Broadway musical, *Milk and Honey* (1961), on film played Frank Sinatra's mother in *Come Blow Your Horn* (1963), and headlined the stage revue *How to Be a Jewish Mother* (1967). In the screen version of *FIDDLER ON THE ROOF* (1971), Picon was Yente the Matchmaker and was the Jewish madam in *FOR PETE'S SAKE* (1974). In her early eighties, Picon did a one-woman show, *Hello, Molly!* (1979), performed in Yiddish, and had guest roles in movies and on TV. In 1985, she received one of the first Goldie Awards for her many contributions to the Jewish performing arts.

***Playing for Time* (1980)** CBS-TV, color, 150 minutes. **Director:** Daniel Mann; **Teleplay:** Arthur Miller; **Cast:** Vanessa Redgrave (Fania Fenelon), Jane Alexander (Alma Rose), Maud Adams (Mala), Christine Baranski (Olga), Robin Bartlett (Etalina), Marisa Berenson (Elzvieta), Viveca Lindfors (Frau Schmidt), Melanie Mayron (Marianne).

This heartfelt drama of Nazi concentration camp life at Auschwitz was based on the memoirs of half-Jewish French songstress Fania Fenelon as translated into English in 1977. The teleplay by acclaimed playwright Miller gave the production prestige; the highly controversial casting of Redgrave (an outspoken advocate of the Palestine Liberation Organization [PLO]) provided the project with a divisive tone. Fenelon was publicly against Redgrave being in the TV movie and was supported in her veto by the Jewish Defense League. Nevertheless, Redgrave, who had won an Oscar playing the Jewess in *JULIA* (1977), remained aboard and acted magnificently.

Production problems aside, *Playing for Time* was a grim testament to those women prisoners during World War II who were forced to form an orchestra to play both for their Nazi captors and for the other inmates being marched to their death.

***Portnoy's Complaint* (1982)** Warner Bros., color, 101 minutes. **Director/Screenplay:** Ernest Lehman; **Cast:** Richard Benjamin (Alexander Portnoy), Karen Black (the Monkey [Mary Jane Reid]), Lee Grant (Sophie Portnoy), Jack Somack (Jack Portnoy), Jeannie Berlin (Bubbles Girardi), Jill Clayburgh (Naomi).

Philip Roth's popular novel *Portnoy's Complaint* (1969) dealt with the complexity of modern Jewish-American life, but much of the ironic humor was lost in its leaden adaptation to the screen.

Alexander Portnoy, a New York City administrator with a troubled private life, visits a psychiatrist because he is often impotent with a woman and thus frequently masturbates.

Through flashbacks, it develops that Portnoy's problems are his castrating Jewish mother (Grant) and his henpecked father (Somack). Alexander has come to equate his controlled life with Judaism at large. As such, he seeks release with an uninhibited gentile woman (Black). Knowing that his mother will disapprove of Mary Jane makes her all the more appealing, but he discovers that she is a bit too kooky, and so he drops her. Later, while visiting Israel to rediscover his roots, he is rebuffed when he attempts to seduce an Israeli (Clayburgh). Portnoy now understands that he must reevaluate his life, including his family and his religious ties.

A few years earlier, Hollywood would not have dared to make such a picture because of the overt Jewishness of the story. When released, several Jewish groups complained about the unfavorable light in which *Portnoy's Complaint* depicted Jewish mothers; others were disturbed by the narrative's interfaith relationship that they thought suggested that eligible Jewish women were not desirable.

BENJAMIN, who specialized in whining, upwardly mobile Jewish men with chaotic personal lives (e.g., *GOODBYE, COLUMBUS*, 1969), reached his peak in such roles in *Portnoy's Complaint*. Unfortunately, the miscasting of Grant (too young and attractive; too assimilated) marred the picture's impact. Although a box-office disappointment, the now little-seen movie is a major reference point in the broadening range of Hollywood films that displayed major Jewish characters. This picture also furthered the mold of the new-era Jewish mother as an oppressive, self-centered soul.

***Potash and Perlmutter* (1923)** Associated First National Pictures, b&w, 7,636′. **Director:** Clarence Badger; **Screenplay:** Frances Marion; **Cast:** Alexander Carr (Morris Perlmutter), Barney Bernard (Abe Potash), Vera Gordon (Rosie Potash), Martha Mansfield (head model), Ben Lyon (Boris Andrieff), Hope Sutherland (Irma Potash).

In 1913 the stage comedy *Potash and Perlmutter* by Montague Glass and Charles Klein had been a Broadway hit, with Barney Bernard and Alexander Carr costarring. It dealt with feuding business partners who employed a Russian refugee bookkeeper. Film producer Samuel Goldwyn (né Goldfish) hired the esteemed Frances Marion to script what would become a three-film series.

Both Bernard and Carr repeated their stage assignments as the bickering Potash and Perlmutter, with Bernard also trying to best his dominating wife Rosie (played by GORDON, the definitive Jewish mother in *HUMORESQUE*, 1920, who would play a similar role to Rosie Potash in *THE COHENS AND KELLYS* series). Gordon's performance in this property further entrenched Hollywood's depiction of the all-knowing Jewish mama. It was a screen type that would transform into the all-smothering and demanding characters of the post-World War II decades.

pressure groups Organizations (beyond such broad-based groups as the American Civil Liberties Union and Common Cause) that were involved in specifically protecting the rights of Jewish-American talent and helping to further integrate the entertainment media have included the American Jewish Committee, the American Jewish Congress (AJC), the Anti-Defamation League of B'nai B'rith, the Morningstar Commission, and the National Conference for Community and Justice (previously known as the National Conference of Christians and Jews).

***Pride of the Marines* (1945)** Warner Bros., b&w, 119 minutes. **Director:** Delmer Daves; **Screenplay:** Albert Maltz; **Cast:** John Garfield (Al Schmid), Eleanor Parker (Ruth Hartley), Dane Clark (Lee Diamond), John Ridgley (Jim Merchant), Rosemary DeCamp (Virginia Pfeiffer).

Part of the broadening effect of Hollywood movies during World War II was their depiction of a variety of ethnic types—including Jews, African Americans, and Hispanics. (There was a clear pecking order of how these stereotypes were represented, with the Christian Caucasian the center of focus and the minorities clearly secondary or walk-on-by figures.)

Pride of the Marines is a superior biography of the real-life Philadelphia welder Al Schmid who is among the marines at Guadalcanal, fighting the Japanese. Schmid is blinded in battle and is sent to recuperate at a naval hospital in California. Bitter that surgery hasn't restored his sight and fearful of the future, Schmid is comforted by his marine pal, Lee Diamond. In one pep talk, Diamond begs his blinded friend not to be a coward and points out that he, as a Jew, has faced discrimination because of anti-Semitism. Nevertheless, he has had the strength not to let it get him down; after all, he says, that is why the war is being fought—so that everyone can live at peace in a democracy.

Pride of the Marines was one of the few World War II era films to give a Jewish character such a defined focal point and to bring up the issue of anti-Semitism in the dialogue.

***Private Benjamin* (1980)** Warner Bros., color, 109 minutes. **Director:** Howard Zieff; **Screenplay:** Nancy Meyers and Charles Shyer; **Cast:** Goldie Hawn (Judy Benjamin), Eileen Brennan (Capt. Doreen Lewis), Armand Assante (Henri Tremont), Robert Webber (Col. Clay Thornbush), Albert Brooks (Yale Goodman).

This comedy, which seemed much funnier at the time of its release, is the saga of the definitive Jewish American Princess, Judy Benjamin, who is overly pampered by her wealthy parents. On Judy's wedding night, the adolescent-acting, selfish groom (BROOKS) dies while making love to her. At loose ends, twenty-eight-year-old Judy enlists in the Women's Army Corps. where she survives the abuse of the nightmarish, overbearing army officer, Captain Lewis. In the process of becoming self-sufficient, Judy begins a relationship with a Jewish gynecologist (Assante) but later abandons him. Forced to fend for herself, she is now a self-reliant woman, having shed much of her Jewish-American Princess mode characteristics.

Filled with extended slapstick, *Private Benjamin* presented an unflattering picture of Jewish life, from Judy's manipulative parents, to Judy's childish groom, and the unfaithful French doctor. Poking fun at every Jewish mother's supposed dream that her daughter marry a lawyer or doctor, the Jewish characters (except for the reformed Judy) did not emerge with positive images. This presentation might have been unthinkable in past decades, but by the 1980s, anything seemed possible to do on screen. It helped that Hawn, who produced the film, made her character appealing at heart.

Private Benjamin received three Oscar nominations, including one for Best Actress (Hawn). The box-office hit was the basis for the weak TV series (1981–83) featuring Lorna Patterson as Judy Benjamin and Brennan again as Captain Lewis.

***Producers, The* (1967)** Embassy, color, 88 minutes. **Director/Screenplay:** Mel Brooks; **Cast:** Zero Mostel (Max Bialystock), Gene Wilder (Leo Bloom), Dick Shawn (Lorenzo St. Du Bois), Kenneth Mars (Franz Liebkind), Christopher Hewett (Roger De Bris), Renee Taylor (Eva Braun).

For his filmmaking debut, multitalented BROOKS created a madcap comedy as outrageous proportioned as MOSTEL was in the lead role of a vulgar (but still lovable) Jewish shyster who cavorted as unscrupulous Broadway producer Max Bialystock. Abetting the con artist is meek Jewish accountant Leo Bloom—played with sad-eyed abandon by WILDER—who guides Max through the intricacies of illegal oversubscribed financing for a new stage musical. Their needs lead the duo to mounting a tasteless stage vehicle (*Springtime for Hitler*), conceived by a nutsy Nazi (Mars). Max and Leo end in jail, where they engineer their invest-in-a-show scam on fellow prisoners and the warden.

With its gleeful premise, the presentation of two such roguish Jewish figures in *The Producers* took on minimal negative connotations as they proved to be more sympathetic than the other zany characters. What remained foremost in mind after seeing *The Producers* was the chutzpah of Brooks to take such a horrific real-life figure as Adolf Hitler and turn him into the star of a song-and-dance show. It was this wild conceit that made *The Producers* unforgettable.

The Producers won an Academy Award for Best Story/Screenplay and an Oscar nomination for Best Supporting Actor (Wilder). The *Springtime for Hitler* "play" later became an actual stage production, while the movie was transformed into a 2001 Broadway musical hit and Tony Award-winner costarring Nathan Lane and Matthew Broderick.

Q

***QB VII* (1974)** ABC-TV miniseries, color, 375 minutes. **Director:** Tom Gries; **Teleplay:** Edward Anhalt; **Cast:** Ben Gazzara (Abe Cady), Anthony Hopkins (Dr. Adam Kelno), Leslie Caron (Angela Kelno), Lee Remick (Lady Margaret Alexander Weidman), Juliet Mills (Samantha Cady), Dan O'Herlihy (David Shawcross), Joseph Wiseman (Morris Cady), Kristoffer Tabori (Ben Cady).

An epic miniseries, this mammoth production was based on the 1970 novel by Leon Uris. The narrative is set into motion when an American journalist (Gazzara) in his book accuses a Polish physician (Hopkins), now a British citizen, of having performed inhumane operations on CONCENTRATION CAMP prisoners during World War II. When the doctor sues the writer for libel, the trial in a British court reveals unsavory chapters from the past. Part of the drama, set in Israel, follows the three generations of the Cady family who were affected by the Jewish homeland. This prestigious production was nominated for thirteen Emmy Awards and won five.

R

Radio Days **(1987)** Orion, color, 85 minutes. **Director/Screenplay:** Woody Allen; **Cast:** Woody Allen (narrator), Seth Green (Little Joe), Julie Kavner (mother), Michael Tucker (father), Dianne Wiest (Aunt Bea), Josh Mostel (Uncle Abe), Renee Lippin (Aunt Ceil), Joy Newman (Ruthie), Mia Farrow (Sally White), Jeff Daniels (Biff Baxter).

With its loving recreation of boyhood memories of the pretelevision era, *Radio Days* was one of ALLEN's most affectionate screen studies of the Jewish culture. This very episodic film, blending together real-life personalities and fictional icons from the world of radio, along with Allen's own gallery of characters to flesh out his "plot," was nostalgia at its most effective. Serving as the narrator but not appearing in the movie, Allen's alter ego, Little Joe, was played on screen by Green, who bore a striking resemblance to Allen when he was very young.

In 1940s Brooklyn, Little Joe lives with his bickering parents (Kavner and Tucker), his lovelorn maiden aunt (Wiest), his old country grandparents, and his fish-loving uncle (Mostel) and aunt (Lippin) and their daughter (Newman). The daily minicrises and minor joys of this extended family are alternated with scenes of New York City where Sally White, hoping to become a radio star, is affected by her accidental witnessing of a gangland murder.

Unlike Allen's early screen work, there were no real slams at Jewish tradition here but rather a parade of mostly Jewish characters passing through life and ruled more by luck than actions on their part.

Radio Days was nominated for two Oscars: Best Art Direction/Best Set Direction and Best Original Screenplay.

Raid on Entebbe **(1977)** NBC-TV, color, 150 minutes. **Director:** Irvin Kershner; **Teleplay:** Barry Beckerman; **Cast:** Peter Finch (Yitzhak Rabin), Martin Balsam (Daniel Cooper), Horst Buchholz (Wilfrid Boese), John Saxon (Maj. Gen. Benny Peled), Sylvia Sidney (Dora Bloch), Jack Warden (Lt. Gen. Mordechai Gur), Yaphet Kotto (President Idi Amin Dada), Charles Bronson (Brig. Gen. Dan Shamron), David Opatoshu (Menachem Begin).

This was but one of several motion pictures rushed into release that dealt with the July 4, 1976, hijacking of a plane full of hostages and their daring rescue by Israeli forces. Other productions included the one-month-earlier telefeature *VICTORY AT ENTEBBE* (1976)—which had the more star-filled cast—and the Israeli-made (in both English and Hebrew language versions) *Mivtsa Yonatan* (aka: *Operation Thunderbolt*) (1977)—which featured an international cast including Sybil Danning, Klaus Kinski, and Yehuda Efoni.

Raid on Entebbe won an Emmy Award for its cinematography and had several other Emmy nominations.

Reiner, Carl (1922–) Through the decades, he was a very creative part of the television medium as actor, writer, director, and producer, later becoming a recognized feature-film director. His associations with *Your Show of Shows* (1950–54) and *THE DICK VAN DYKE SHOW* (1961–66) ensured his place in show-business history.

Born in New York City, he originally intended to become a serious actor, but when he was drafted into World War II service, he realized that if he wanted to be assigned to entertaining the troops, he had to develop a comedy act instead of giving dramatic presentations. Later, once a civilian again, he appeared in Broadway revues that led to his joining comedian SID CAESAR'S *Your Show of Shows*. Playing second banana to Caesar—for which he won two Emmys—was excellent training for Reiner, who used his "spare" time to frequent TV panel and variety shows, sometimes as the host. With MEL BROOKS, another alumnus from Caesar's world, Reiner developed the *2,000 Year Old Man* routine that became a successful set of albums.

Reiner conceived *The Dick Van Dyke Show* (originally with himself to be the lead) and was the series' head writer, director, and occasional guest star as egomaniacal Alan Brady. His debut movie-directing assignment was *ENTER LAUGHING* (1967), based on his autobiographical novel and, in turn, the Broadway play. Later, he guided vehicles that included the cult favorite *WHERE'S POPPA?* (1970) and several Steve Martin movies such as *The Jerk* (1979) and *The Man with Two Brains* (1983); he also helmed the spoof *Fatal Instinct* (1993) and the romantic comedy *That Old Feeling* (1997) with Bette MIDLER. Through the years, Reiner continued to act in both his own properties and those of others (e.g., *Ocean's Eleven*, 2001). Reiner's son, Rob, became an actor (e.g., TV's *All in the Family*) and later a film director.

Reiser, Paul (1956–) In the contemporary world of observational (i.e., "did you ever notice") stand-up comedy, two of the masters in the "younger" set in the later twentieth century were Reiser and JERRY SEINFELD. The latter may have been more famous, but, for many, Reiser was the more versatile, both at comedy and in his acting range (not to mention his fluent knowledge of Yiddish and a flare for playing classical piano).

He was born in New York City and, after graduating (as a music major) in 1977 from the State University of New York at Binghamton, he worked in his dad's wholesale health-food firm. He quit to become a full-time comedian. As he paid his dues on the club circuit, his low-keyed comedy style was noticed.

He came to the attention of first-time director BARRY LEVINSON, who was preparing *Diner* (1982), a nostalgic study of 1950s Baltimore. Reiser was cast as Modell, the Jewish moocher who eats off everyone else's plate at the restaurant. His noteworthy performance led to late-night TV talk-show appearances. Thereafter, he won supporting roles in such film hits as *Beverly Hills Cop* (1984) and *Aliens* (1986)—all the while pursuing stand-up work.

Reiser costarred on the sitcom *My Two Dads* (1987–90) but really found his TV milieu with *MAD ABOUT YOU* (1992–99), which he cocreated. The comedy focused on a young couple who explore the meaning of being married. Reiser's somewhat neurotic documentary-filmmaker character had sufficient charm and chemistry with colead Helen Hunt so that the show became a huge hit. By the time the series left the air, Reiser was earning $1 million per episode. All the while, Reiser also did TV movies (e.g., *The Tower*, 1993) as well as theatrical features (e.g., *Bye Bye, Love*, 1995). With the series over, he returned to feature filmmaking: *The Story of Us* (1999), *One Night at McCool's* (2001), *Purpo$e* (2002), and the TV movie *Women vs. Men* (2002). Reiser also enjoyed great success authoring two nonfiction works: *Couplehood* (1994) and *Babyhood* (1997).

***Remembrance of Love* (1982)** NBC-TV, color, 100 minutes. **Director:** Jack Smight; **Teleplay:** Harold Jack Boom; **Cast:** Kirk Douglas (Joe Rabin), Pam Dawber (Marcy Rabin), Chana Eden (Leah Koenig), Yoram Gal (David Berkman), Robert Clary (himself), Eric Douglas (young Joe Rabin).

Filmed entirely on location in Israel, this emotional, made-for-television feature focused on the actual World Gathering of Holocaust Survivors. It tells of American Joe Rabin, a survivor of the Auschwitz concentration camp during World War II, who comes to Israel with his reporter daughter Marcy. There, Joe plans to use the Israeli computer data bank of Holocaust survivors to track Leah, the girl he loved in Poland during the war. Meanwhile, Marcy, whose non-Jewish mother is now deceased, falls in love with David Berkman, an Israeli security agent. He asks her to marry him and remain in the country.

This was one of several Israel-themed movies made by DOUGLAS; they included *THE JUGGLER* (1953) and *CAST A GIANT SHADOW* (1965).

***Rhapsody in Blue* (1945)** Warner Bros., b&w, 139 minutes. **Director:** Irving Rapper; **Screenplay:** Howard Koch and Elliott Paul; **Cast:** Robert Alda (George Gershwin), Joan Leslie (Julie Adams), Alexis Smith (Christine Gilbert), Charles Coburn (Max Dreyfus), Julie Bishop (Lee Gershwin), Morris Carnovsky (Pappa Gershwin), Rosemary DeCamp (Momma Gershwin), Herbert Rudley (Ira Gershwin).

Several big-budgeted musicals of the 1940s were built around the lives and times of famed contemporary composers: Cole Porter (*Night and Day*, 1946), Jerome Kern (*Till the Clouds Roll By*, 1946), Richard Rodgers and Lorenz Hart (*Words and Music*, 1948). Each of them fictionalized many different aspects of their subject's life for better story flow, to protect the privacies of the subject's family and friends, and so on, most of them choosing to make no mention of the subjects being Jewish. But in Warner Bros.' *Rhapsody in Blue*, there was clear indication of the Russian-Jewish background of George Gershwin (1898–1937), even if the lengthy narrative passed over the fact that he was born Jacob Gershowitz. The viewer still had to assume much about Gershwin's heritage by closely observing the lifestyle of George and his older brother Ira as they grew up on Manhattan's LOWER EAST SIDE, supervised by their Old World-type parents.

When *Rhapsody in Blue* was first shown on television in the 1950s, the opening section of the picture with the Gershwin brothers as boys in the Lower East Side frequently was deleted, supposedly to trim the running time to a more manageable length.

***Rhoda* (1974–1978)** CBS-TV series, color, 30 minutes. **Cast:** Valerie Harper (Rhoda Morgenstern Gerard), Julie Kavner (Brenda Morgenstern), David Groh (Joe Gerard: 1974–77), Nancy Walker (Ida Morgenstern: 1974–76, 1977–78), Harold Gould (Martin Morgenstern: 1974–76, 1977–78), Ron Silver (Gary Levy: 1976–78).

Julie Kavner and Nancy Walker in the TV sitcom *Rhoda* (1974–78). (JC ARCHIVES)

By the time Harper's Rhoda Morgenstern ended her tenure (1970–74) on *THE MARY TYLER MOORE SHOW*, she had undergone a transformation. She had originally left New York City somewhat overweight, insecure about men and career, and wanting to avoid parental control. Yet, when she returned to Manhattan, she was a more confident woman, able to deal better with her parents (especially domineering Ida) in the Bronx, and enough of a role model to become the mentor for her younger sister, Brenda. (In many ways, Brenda resembles the pre-Minneapolis Rhoda.) What really boosts Rhoda's ego—for a time—is her marriage to Joe Gerard.

If there was little doubt that Harper's Rhoda was Jewish, it was intriguing that not only was the man she wed apparently *not* Jewish (although this fact was left unstated) but also Rhoda and Joe's wedding ceremony should be civil and completely nonsectarian. Moreover, during the course of the couple's faltering marriage and separation after two seasons, no reference was made to their apparent interfaith union nor that a difference in religious background may have played a part in their eventual split up.

A subordinate character who joined the cast for its last two seasons is Gary Levy, single and Jewish, who lives in the same apartment building as Rhoda and Brenda. Gary and Brenda become platonic friends, but the playboy strikes out when he attempts to date Rhoda. In his presentation, SILVER gave a definite but soft (to suit the era) presentation of a confident Jewish single.

Lastly, but not to be overlooked, was Rhoda and Brenda's father, the mild-mannered Martin Morgenstern. A passive subordinate to his aggressive wife, he was also the peacemaker in the family and the friendly host to guests. In its presentation of Martin Morgenstern, *Rhoda* reflected the increasingly firm stereotype of Jewish men who were the breadwinners but at home always deferred to their spouses and for whose children no task was too big.

In 2000, Rhoda Morgenstern and Mary Richards were reunited in the unimaginative TV movie, *Mary and Rhoda*.

Rickles, Don (1926–) The raging stand-up comic, famous as "the Merchant of Venom," Rickles long insisted that his high-voltage put-downs were meant in fun *not* anger. That aside, what ensured his show business success was his bravado.

Born Donald Jay Rickles in Queens, New York, he served in the navy during World War II. Thereafter, he studied at the American Academy of Dramatic Arts. When no stage acting work was forthcoming, he survived in such jobs as a stand-up comic in strip joints, learning to joust verbally with hecklers. He made his film debut in the submarine drama, *Run Silent, Run Deep* (1958). Rickles made more of an impression when one night in a club he heckled patron Frank Sinatra—whom he did not know; the temperamental crooner found it funny and became a booster of the comic's career.

In the mid-1960s the acidic Jewish comedian was active on TV talk shows, guesting on sitcoms (including *THE DICK VAN DYKE SHOW*) and appearing in youth-oriented sand-and-music pictures (e.g., *Beach Blanket Bingo*, 1965). He revealed his dramatic training when he played the devious sergeant nicknamed Crapgame in *Kelly's Heroes* (1970). His TV series debut was the short-lived *The Don Rickles Show* (1968), a mix of comedy and variety, and it was followed by another quick-failing sitcom in 1972. Rickles was more on target with *C.P.O. Sharkey* (1976–78) as a navy drill instructor. He was host of *Foul-Ups, Bleeps & Blunders* (1984–85) and tried the sitcom route yet again with *Daddy Dearest* (1993), this time paired with neurotic RICHARD LEWIS. In the 1990s, Rickles, with his distinctive sound and delivery, provided voices in several nonlive-action features, including Mr. Potato Head in *Toy Story* (1996) and *Toy Story 2* (1999), as well as many TV commercials. In 1998's *Dennis the Menace Strikes Again*, Rickles was the harassed neighbor, Mr. Wilson.

Riegert, Peter (1947–) As he matured, this versatile character actor took on different guises of the contemporary Jewish man in films and television, but he also played other ethnic types.

Born in New York City and a graduate of State University of New York at Buffalo, he taught English and was a social worker before settling on an acting career. Riegert appeared with the improvisational comedy group War Babies, and made his movie debut as Donald "Boon" Schoenstein, one of the frat house crazies in *National Lampoon's Animal House* (1978). He worked for director JOAN MICKLIN SILVER in first *Chilly Scenes of Winter* (aka: *Head Over Heels*) (1979) and then as the pickle seller who captured Amy Irving's heart in *CROSSING DELANCEY* (1988). He also played roles in *Local Hero* (1983) and *Oscar* (1991). Having appeared in the miniseries *Ellis Island* (1984), he starred as a Chicagoan who was having a midlife crisis in the brief TV series, *Middle Ages* (1992). The following year, also on television, he was BETTE MIDLER's patient boyfriend in the musical *Gypsy* and portrayed a compulsive dealmaker in James Garner's *Barbarians at the Gate*. In *Traffic* (2000), Riegert played a Jewish attorney and in the TV movie *Bojangles*

(2001) was cast as the longtime manager/friend of black dancing star Bill "Bojangles" Robinson.

Ritz Brothers, the: Al (1901–1965), Jimmy (1903–1985), Harry (1906–1986) Not well remembered today, the team were in-your-face personalities, possessing high-energy, and were full of unexpected gags as they sang and danced their way through several movies. With their sharp features and type of routines, the Ritz Brothers were far more ethnic than another sibling team, the MARX BROTHERS. Their nonsensical skits often included one or more of them dressed in comical drag. With their zaniness, they—especially Harry, the team's leader—were an inspiration to many later comedians, including MILTON BERLE, SID CAESAR, DANNY KAYE, and JERRY LEWIS.

Al (born Alfred), Jimmy (born Samuel), and Harry came from Newark, New Jersey. (There was a fourth brother, George, who would act as the team's agent, and there was a sister, Gertrude.) Their father, Max Joachin, was an emigrant from Austria who eventually did well as a haberdasher and moved the family to Brooklyn. Although Al was the first to break into the entertainment field (as an extra in a 1918 movie), by 1925, the trio had made its professional bow in Coney Island, leading to vaudeville turns and Broadway revues (including *Continental Varieties*, 1934). In the process of becoming established, they changed their surname to Ritz. (Legend has it that "Ritz" was inspired by an ad on a passing laundry truck.)

A movie short subject, *Hotel Anchovy* (1934), led to a specialty contract at Twentieth Century-Fox, where, in such big-budgeted movies as *Sing, Baby, Sing* (1936) and *On the Avenue* (1936), the trio provided outrageous, nonsensical interludes in support of the films' actual stars. One of their best vehicles was their wacky spoof of *The Three Musketeers* (1939).

In the 1940s, the Ritz Brothers made a quartet of lesser features at Universal. The results lacked the production values, energy, or madcap humor of their earlier work. Afterwards, they returned to club work and later to TV guest appearances. After Al's death in the mid-1960s, Harry and Jimmy semiretired but reteamed for cameos in two 1976

The Ritz Brothers, Jimmy (left), Harry (center), and Al (right) with Joan Marsh in *Life Begins at College* (1937). (JC ARCHIVES)

releases; that same year, Harry did a solo bit in *Silent Movie* (1976) for MEL BROOKS.

Rivers, Joan (1933–) Three little words, "Can we talk?" set into motion one of the most phenomenally successful careers of any comedic woman entertainer in the United States. With her knack for insult humor that mixed gossipy patter with stringent barbs, Rivers pushed the boundaries of good taste, but because her act often demeaned herself as well as her celebrity target, audiences laughed. Here was a suburban New York Jewish American Princess who made no bones about her origins or her ground rules for navigating through life.

Joan Alexandra Molinsky was born in Brooklyn, New York, the daughter of Russian Jewish refugees. In high school, she entered a movie fan-magazine contest, winning a tiny role in the film *Mr. Universe* (1951). She attended Barnard College and then became a fashion coordinator for a clothing-store chain. On her own, she struggled as an actress and then turned to comedy, working in seamy clubs, strip joints, and CATSKILL RESORTS.

Her big breakthrough occurred on TV's *The Tonight Show* in 1965, winning the endorsement of host Johnny Carson. This led to gilt-edged comedy-club bookings, record albums, TV guest spots, and a Broadway role in *Fun City* (1972). Following in the footsteps of VIRGINIA GRAHAM, she hosted her own TV talk show (1969–71) and was a frequent substitute host for Carson on *The Tonight Show*. She directed her first movie, *Rabbit Test* (1978), which starred BILLY CRYSTAL, and from 1983–86 was the permanent guest host for *The Tonight Show*.

There was a big brouhaha when Rivers abandoned Carson to headline her own late-night forum on a rival network. That flop, *THE LATE SHOW STARRING JOAN RIVERS* (1986–87), was exacerbated by the suicide of her second husband (producer Edgar Roseberg). The answer for Rivers was nonstop work, which ranged from acting on stage (e.g., *Broadway Bound*, 1987) and in TV movies (e.g., *How to Murder a Millionaire*, 1990), writing her second autobiography (*Still Talking*, 1991), to, most importantly, starring in a syndicated talk program, *The Joan Rivers Show* (1989–93). (She soon added *Joan Rivers' Gossip, Gossip, Gossip*, 1992–93, and *Can We Shop?* 1994, to her TV repertoire.)

Never idle, she penned *Bouncing Back: I've Survived Everything . . . and I Mean Everything . . . and You Can Too!* (1997) and the later *Don't Count the Candles: Just Keep the Fire Lit!* (1999), as well as handling preshow and fashion-commentator chores for nationally televised award shows. Already a grandmother, she continued to act on camera—whether in a daytime soap opera (*Another World*, 1997), feature films (e.g., *The Intern*, 2000), or wherever the spotlights are focused on her.

Robinson, Edward G. (1893–1973) The Hollywood casting irony was that such a cultured, Jewish gentleman as Robinson should be so typecast as a crude gangland figure, typically of non-Semitic nationalities, and when he wasn't playing a celluloid hoodlum, he might be Chinese (e.g., *The Hatchet Man*, 1932), German (e.g., *A Dispatch from Reuters*, 1940), Norwegian (e.g., *Our Vines Have Tender Grapes*, 1945), or Italian (e.g., *House of Strangers*, 1949). Occasionally, he was allowed to play Jews—but such assignments (e.g., *The Ten Commandments*, 1956; *Two Weeks in Another Town*, 1962) were a rarity. As with another cinema tough guy, PAUL MUNI, Hollywood generally insisted that Robinson be anything on camera but what he actually was.

Emanuel Goldenberg was born in Bucharest. The family immigrated to the United States in 1902. In New York City, the future actor reached his second year of college before dropping out to attend the American Academy of Dramatic Arts. It was in this period that he was advised to Americanize his name, which he did reluctantly.

After years in stock and on Broadway, he made his mark playing a gangster on stage in *The Racket* (1927). He had already made his screen debut in the silent entry *The Bright Shawl* (1923) and returned to pictures halfheartedly when the Great Depression affected Broadway theatergoing. His astute playing of *Little Caesar* (1930) made the five-feet, five-inch actor a movie star. His studio wouldn't let him escape playing gangster roles often; occasionally, he did (e.g., *I Am the Law*, 1938, *Confessions of a Nazi Spy*, 1939), but it was always back to type (e.g., *Key Largo*, 1948).

Through the years, the socially conscious Robinson was attached to many liberal causes: During the communist witch hunt in Hollywood of the late 1940s and early 1950s, he testified on his own behalf repeatedly to demonstrate his loyalty to the United States. Nevertheless, he was branded a communist sympathizer, which kept him away from major filmmaking for years. His reinstatement came with *The Ten Commandments*.

Too energetic to retire in his seventies, he continued onward, often outshining younger cast members (e.g., *The Cincinnati Kid*, 1965, *Never a Dull Moment*, 1968). He was a frequent guest star on TV series and talk shows. His final screen part was in the science-fiction entry, *Soylent Green* (1973). He died of cancer before receiving the honorary Oscar that he had already been awarded.

S

***St. Elsewhere* (1982–1988)** NBC-TV series, color, 60 minutes. **Cast:** Ed Flanders (Dr. Donald Westphall), William Daniels (Dr. Mark Craig), David Birney (Dr. Ben Samuels: 1982–83), Ed Begley Jr. (Dr. Victor Ehrlich), David Morse (Dr. Jack Morrison), Howie Mandel (Dr. Wayne Fiscus), Denzel Washington (Dr. Phillip Chandler), Norman Lloyd (Dr. Daniel Auschlander), Christina Pickles (Nurse Helen Rosenthal), Stephen Furst (Dr. Elliott Axelrod: 1983–88).

Boston's St. Eligius Hospital was decrepit and understaffed, earning it the nickname of St. Elsewhere. Among its multicultural staff were several Jewish physicians, which should not have been a surprise, but most earlier TV medical series (e.g., *Dr. Christian, Ben Casey, Dr. Kildare; Marcus Welby, M.D.*) were devoid of any such ethnic representation. At the Beantown institution was veteran physician Dr. Auschlander and the new generation's Dr. Ben Samuels. Of more enduring interest was young, feisty Dr. Wayne Fiscus, played by stand-up comedian/actor MANDEL.

Following the fantasy of the Jewish man coveting a gentile woman, the series had Fiscus dating Dr. Cathy Martin (played by Barbara Whinnery), a non-Jewish resident at the sprawling facility. Their on-again off-again romance continued for many episodes. Meanwhile, Wayne's background was explicated when his parents were shown. LAINIE KAZAN was meddling, loud mouthed, and perceptive as the mother. Mr. Fiscus (performed by Jewish-born actor Bill Dana) had several touching sequences on the series as he tried to understand his offspring who had advanced so far professionally. Later, Wayne had to deal with his dad's stroke and death, and he helped his mother rebuild her life. There was the much-married Nurse Helen Rosenthal coping with extramarital romance, a mastectomy, and drug addiction. During the 1984–85 season, a recurrent patient at the facility was the irritating, lonely Mrs. Hufnagel (played by Florence Halop).

An even more full-bodied presentation of a Jewish doctor was offered by Dr. Joel Fleischman on *NORTHERN EXPOSURE* (1990–95).

***Salome of the Tenements* (1925)** Paramount, b&w, 7,017′. **Director:** Sidney Olcott; **Screenplay:** Sonya Levien; **Cast:** Jetta Goudal (Sonya Mendel), Godfrey Tearle (John Manning), José Ruben (Jakey Solomon), Lazar Freed (Jacob Lipkin), Elithu Tenenholtz (Banker Ben).

Anzia Yezierska, the author of *HUNGRY HEARTS* (which was picturized in 1922), wrote *Salome of the Tenements* in 1923. Again, she returned to the territory she knew best, New York City's LOWER EAST SIDE. In this account of a self-sufficient, bright woman (Goudal), the heroine is a clever reporter for a Jewish newspaper who interviews a gentile philanthropist (Tearle) and becomes entranced with him. To finance her courtship, in which she disguises her lower-class background, she borrows a large sum from a usurer (Tenenholtz). Later, after she weds her blue-blood boyfriend, Banker Ben attempts to blackmail her, but eventually love triumphs.

Stocked with an extremely ethnic cast, this was the reversal of the usual fantasy of the Jewish young man wishing to assimilate by marrying a beautiful gentile. Despite its melodramatic overtones, this was one of the grittier Jewish GHETTOS DRAMAS.

***Sam Levenson Show, The* (1951–1952)** CBS-TV series, b&w, 30 minutes. **Cast:** Sam Levenson (host).

In the early 1950s when television broadcast signals were available mainly in urban centers such as New York City and many shows were aired live, the ethnic humor of *THE GOLDBERGS* (1949–54, 1955–56), *THE MOREY AMSTERDAM SHOW*

(1951–52), and the like was considered appropriate audience fare. As television reception spread to small-town America, the networks and sponsors pulled back, and defined minority ethnic types nearly disappeared on television for the next several decades.

The jovial, roly-poly Levenson, very much the image of a contented family man, could be said to be the 1950s answer to the much later and a less effective Drew Carey—with Judaism thrown into the mix. The bespectacled Sam, a former teacher, had a low-key way of communicating his humor, based on folksy tales about life and relatives from his low-income youth and from his teaching career. Besides creating and serving as panelist on several quiz shows (including *This Is Show Business* (1951–54), he hosted this comedy outing in which he performed monologues commenting on social mores.

Samson and Delilah **(1949)** Paramount, color, 131 minutes. **Director:** Cecil B. DeMille; **Screenplay:** Vladimir Jabotinsky, Harold Lamb, Jesse L. Lasky Jr., and Frederic M. Frank; **Cast:** Hedy Lamarr (Delilah), Victor Mature (Samson), George Sanders (Saran of Gaza), Angela Lansbury (Semadar), Henry Wilcoxon (Ahtur), Olive Deering (Miriam).

For several decades, moviemaker Cecil B. DeMille and the Bible went hand in hand, especially because of his extravaganzas that were huge box-office successes: *THE TEN COMMANDMENTS* (1923 and 1956), *THE KING OF KINGS* (1927), and *Samson and Delilah*. According to DeMille, the story for this last epic derived from three chapters in the Book of Judges from the Old Testament. Before it reached the screen, many hands had transmuted the narrative into something more Hollywoodlike than biblical—complete with massive sets, gaudy costumes, rich Technicolor, and posturing leading players.

As would become a Jewish tradition, the Hebrew Samson—here a member of the Danite tribe—was enamored of a gentile, Semadar, the daughter of a wealthy Philistine merchant. As for Samson's betrothed (Deering), she remains passively on the sidelines. Meanwhile, Semadar's reckless younger sister, Delilah, connives to ensure the muscular Samson for herself. Before the spectacle ends, Semadar has been killed, and Samson falls prey to vindictive Delilah's wiles and is imprisoned and blinded by his enemies. Eventually, he uses his great strength to destroy the Philistines' huge temple, killing Delilah, thousands of Philistines, and himself.

As with later such spectacles, *Samson and Delilah* used the Bible as a commercial springboard for its drama. That the Jewish race was integral to the Old Testament made their inclusion in the narrative a necessity, and after World War II, when the horrors of the HOLOCAUST became evident to the world, tales of the Hebrews suffering in ancient times made a timely parallel.

Produced at a cost of $3 million, *Samson and Delilah* grossed more than $12 million at the domestic box office. It won two Oscars and two other Academy Award nominations. In the silent cinema, there had been a few short versions of the Samson–Delilah legend. Later screen adaptations include a 1984 TV movie rendition starring Antony Hamilton and Belinda Bauer, with Mature cast as Samson's father, and a 1996 telefeature teaming Eric Thal with Elizabeth Hurley.

Sandler, Adam (1966–) In the early to mid-1990s, Sandler was one of the bright lights on television's *Saturday Night Live* with his goofy characterizations, satirical skits, and loony songs. Thereafter, he became a major motion picture star with several hugely successful comedies (including *The Wedding Singer*, 1998, and *Big Daddy* 1999) that usually cast him as a good-hearted but dimwitted soul. Although on *Saturday Night Live* he occasionally played characters of Jewish origin, he rarely did so on screen. One of his few such excursions was in *Going Overboard* (1989), an amateurish low-budget comedy involving a ship's waiter who dreamed of becoming a well-known comedian. Sandler was cast as Shecky Moskowitz.

Born in Brooklyn into a traditional Jewish household, Sandler grew up in Manchester, New Hampshire, before matriculating at New York University. By then, he was testing stand-up comedy routines and soon found himself hired as a staff writer for *Saturday Night Live*. Through the years, he released several popular comedy albums. Later films included *Little Nicky* (1999), *8 Crazy Nights* (2002—animated feature), *Mr. Deeds* (2002—a remake of Gary Cooper's *Mr. Deeds Goes to Town*, 1936), and *Anger Management* (2003—with Marisa Tomei).

Scandal in a Small Town **(1988)** NBC-TV movie, color, 97 minutes. **Director:** Anthony Page; **Teleplay:** Robert J. Avrech; **Cast:** Raquel Welch (Beth Vincent), Ronny Cox (George Baker), Christa Denton (Julie), Holly Fields (Dawn), Laurence Haddon (Judge Larson).

Trading on the physical assets of aging, statuesque sex-goddess Welch, this TV movie focuses on a small town where cocktail waitress Beth Vincent, a single mother with limited education, becomes concerned at the strange interpretation of World War II and HOLOCAUST history that an anti-Semitic history teacher (Cox) is handing out to his students (which includes her daughter). Naïve but concerned, Beth pursues the matter into a courtroom hearing.

The most interesting aspect of this choppy study of anti-Semitism was the fact that *none* of the characters involved were Jewish. Three months earlier, essentially the same story was told in an ABC-TV movie, *Evil in Clear River*, starring Lindsay Wagner as the mother, with Randy Quaid as the seemingly benign high-school instructor. It too involved all non-Jewish characters.

Schindler's List **(1993)** Universal, color and b&w, 185 minutes. **Director:** Steven Spielberg; **Screenplay:** Steve Zaillian; **Cast:** Liam Neeson (Oskar Schindler), Ben Kingsley (Itzhak Stern), Ralph Fiennes (Amon Goeth), Caroline Goodall (Emilie Schindler), Jonathan Sagalle (Poldek Pfefferberg).

Not since *JUDGMENT AT NUREMBERG* (1961) and the TV miniseries *HOLOCAUST* (1978) had an "entertainment" so powerfully evoked the full horror and legacy of the Nazis' World War II policy of genocide against the Jews. Based on the novel *Schindler's Ark* (1982) by Thomas Keneally, SPIELBERG's film graphically depicted the plight of a people who were tormented and exterminated by their oppressors.

Like the movie's central figure, Oskar Schindler, who remained inexplicable, *Schindler's List* did not attempt to answer what made Germans agree to the "final solution" regarding Jews, nor did it use clichés to depict the genocide policy being carried out. Rather, Spielberg, who had the clout to make such a potentially unviable motion picture, saw the movie as a testament to his own revived sense of Judaism and to the inexplicable courage and/or craftiness of a non-Jew who rescued hundreds of Jews at his own peril.

In 1941, in Krakow, Poland, the Nazi occupiers force the Jews into a squalid ghetto. Observing this, gentile businessman Oskar Schindler has the notion of using inexpensive ghetto labor to operate an enamelware plant and then to sell to the Third Reich an ongoing supply of pots and pans. He uses seemingly meek accountant Itzhak Stern to carry out his plan. Stern realizes the operation could save Jewish lives, for those working in the factory are exempt from resettlement into the CONCENTRATION CAMPS. Stern soon adds nonessential laborers (including scholars, cripples, and musicians) to the factory employee list, while Schindler pretends not to notice.

Later, under the direction of brutal Nazi commandant, Amon Goeth, the ghetto is razed and the survivors shipped to a labor camp. By now, Schindler has developed compassion for the victims, and he bribes Goeth to allow a new factory to be created within camp confines. As the war draws to a close, Schindler uses his ingenuity and his newly gained wealth to protect as many Jews as possible from the Germans. Years later, in Jerusalem, several of the Jews Schindler protected pay tribute to their savior, placing memorial stones on his grave.

Made at a cost of $25 million, *Schindler's List* grossed more than $317 million in worldwide film rentals. Besides winning seven Academy Awards (including Best Director and Best Picture), it received five other Oscar nominations.

***School Ties* (1992)** Paramount, color, 107 minutes. **Director:** Robert Mandel; **Screenplay:** Dick Wolf and Dar-

Cole Hauser, Andrew Lowery, Brendan Fraser, Anthony Rapp, Randall Batinkoff, and Matt Damon in *School Ties* (1992). (JC ARCHIVES)

ryl Ponicsan; **Cast:** Brendan Fraser (David Greene), Matt Damon (Charlie Dillon), Chris O'Donnell (Chris Reece), Randall Batinkoff (Rip Van Kelt), Cole Hauser (Jack Connors), Ben Affleck (Chesty Smith).

Distilling themes first presented directly in American cinema in *GENTLEMAN'S AGREEMENT* (1947), *School Ties* explored anti-Semitism at a fancy New England boys' prep school in the 1950s.

Ace high-school football player David Greene is recruited to spend his senior year at St. Matthew's Prep where his gridiron abilities are sure to impress the alumni. Having experienced racial discrimination before, the blue-collar worker's son conceals his Jewish heritage. Eventually, his rival, Charlie Dillon, who has lost his girlfriend and his star status on the football field to Greene, learns the truth. Dillon incites the others to make life tough for the Jewish youth and even sets up the outsider to be blamed for cheating on a final exam. Nonetheless, the truth comes out, and Dillon is expelled.

Because this film was intended more as a showcase for rising young talent than for the airing of racial discrimination, the contrived movie became too simplistic and obvious in its execution. Nevertheless, Fraser offered a pleasing performance as the Jewish outsider, and handsome Damon was a believable villain.

science fiction—feature films and television WOODY ALLEN, the screen's perfect schlemiel, turned his satiric attention to the state of the current world by using a science-fiction motif in *Sleeper* (1973), one of the vehicles in which he scripted, directed, and starred. He was Miles Monroe, the Greenwich Village health-food-store owner who underwent ulcer surgery with complications developing. The doctors put him in a deep freeze, hoping that a future cure would come along. Monroe awakens two centuries later in a brave new world controlled by "Big Brother." Disguised as a domestic robot, Monroe escapes to the home of a wealthy woman (Diane Keaton), and together they join the revolutionaries.

As per Allen's custom, *Sleeper* was filled with ethnic jokes and witticisms, many of them pertaining to Jews. In an intervention staged to help Monroe break free from a drug-induced lethargy (caused by government agents), his friends reenacted scenes from his past. In the process, these non-Jews confused the meanings of assorted Yiddish words, causing hilarious dialogue. (There was another juncture in *Sleeper* where characters speak in heavy Jewish accents.)

Thus, the science-fiction-genre trappings of *Sleeper* provided Allen with yet another venue for promulgating his thesis of the Jew as the ultimate outsider.

In MEL BROOKS's fitfully funny *Spaceballs* (1987)—a sometimes crude, juvenile send-up of the *Star Wars* science-fiction movie series—outer space was replete with Jewish characters and dialectal speaking characters. There was Yogurt (one of two roles played by Brooks), a wizened old adviser who instructed Lone Starr, the dashing space bum, in the secret power of "the Schwartz." Passing through the story line was Dr. Schlotkin, and not to be overlooked was JOAN RIVERS's very New York accent as she supplied the off-camera voice of the Dot Matrix robot.

On television, the expensively mounted miniseries *V* (1983), about the invasion of Earth by devious aliens, featured several Jewish characters (e.g., the Bernstein clan, and especially Daniel Bernstein played by David Packer). In the 1984 miniseries follow-up, *V—The Final Battle*, the lead Bernstein character was back, again played by David Packer. (However, in the 1984–85 TV series version of *V*, the Bernsteins were not part of the action.) In the fantasy teleseries *Beauty and the Beast* (1987–90), Armin Shimerman was cast as Pascal, the Jewish sewer dweller, while in *Star Trek: Deep Space Nine* (1992–99), Shimerman was cast as Quark, a scheming Ferengi who ran a gambling operation at the station.

Segal, George (1934–) In an earlier era, this good-looking and charming ethnic actor would not have been given many of the opportunities he enjoyed on camera, nor would his film studio employers have allowed him to retain his Semitic surname. But then again, only in the poststudio Hollywood system could Segal have starred in *WHERE'S POPPA?* (1970), a twisted comedy in which he was the ultimate put-upon Jewish son.

He grew up in Great Neck, Long Island, New York. After attending a private Quaker school in Pennsylvania, he studied at Columbia University. As a child he loved to perform magic tricks; later, he took up the banjo (a lifelong vocation), and by adulthood he wanted to be an actor. An early acting assignment was in the New York revival of *The Iceman Cometh* (1956). After military duty, he pursued his career with unspectacular results. It wasn't until *SHIP OF FOOLS* (1965) that he made a cinematic mark, followed by his sturdy supporting performance in *Who's Afraid of Virginia Woolf?* (1966).

Starring in *BYE BYE BRAVERMAN* (1968) established Segal as *the* portrayer of the new breed of intellectual Manhattan Jew. Next, he was the Jewish police detective harassed by a serial killer and his own nagging mother in *NO WAY TO TREAT A LADY* (1968). Two years later, along with *Where's Poppa?* he was the stuffy Jewish intellectual brought down to earth by an eccentric prostitute (BARBRA STREISAND) in *THE OWL AND THE PUSSYCAT*.

Just when his career should have zoomed forward, years of substance abuse caught up with him (as he publicly admitted), and much of the 1970s and early 1980s was lost in a drug fog. By 1983, however, he was back in harness and soon starring in TV series: *Take Five* (1987), *Murphy's Law* (1988–89), and *High Five* (1994–95). In 1996, he reunited with Streisand for her misfire, *The Mirror Has Two Faces*. Then came his long-running TV sitcom *Just Shoot Me* (1997–) in which Segal, once again the harried New Yorker, was the randy publisher of a woman's magazine. More recent feature film appearances included *To Die For* (1995) as well as the telefeatures *The Good Doctor: The Paul*

Fleiss Story (1996), *Houdini* (1998), and *The Linda McCartney Story* (2000).

***Seinfeld* (1990–1998)** NBC-TV series, color, 30 minutes. **Cast:** Jerry Seinfeld (himself), Julia Louis-Dreyfus (Elaine Benes), Jason Alexander (George Costanza), Michael Richards (Cosmo Kramer), Liz Sheridan (Helen Seinfeld), Barney Martin (Morty Seinfeld—after first episodes), Wayne Knight (Newman: 1991–98).

In this prime TV sitcom, stand-up comedian SEINFELD played himself as a slightly neurotic, self-focused entertainer, living a bachelor's life in New York City. Like others of his peers who were Jewish and starring in TV situation comedies in the late twentieth century, his on-air alter ego used his Jewishness more to reflect/explain the colorfulness of on-camera relatives than to help define the craziness of his own adult life.

Within the series, aided or stymied by eccentric friends (Alexander, Richards, and Louis-Dreyfus), Seinfeld might be dealing with a Jewish girlfriend who observes dietary laws (i.e., not eating shellfish), coping with kosher meals on a plane, planning a circumcision rite for an acquaintance, and so on—all events on the periphery of his daily existence. Throughout the show's lengthy run, one of his character's worst transgressions occurred when his parents learn that he had been seen smooching at a movie theater while watching, of all things, *SCHINDLER'S LIST* (1993).

Julia Louis-Dreyfus, Michael Richards, Jerry Seinfeld, and Jason Alexander in the TV comedy *Seinfeld* (1990–98). (ECHO BOOK SHOP)

As far as *Seinfeld* and other such 1990s shows were concerned, the ethnic heritage of the lead character was something to be assumed by the general awareness of the real-life Jewishness of the actor playing the part. In this regard, American TV sitcoms had not changed from the vintage days of JACK BENNY and GEORGE BURNS. On the other hand, in the more closeted 1950–70s era of television, such veteran stars as Benny and Burns avoided *any* overtly Jewish plot lines.

Seinfeld, Jerry (1954–) One of the phenomena of 1990s television was the hugely popular sitcom *SEINFELD* (1990–98). For a "show about nothing," it soon captured viewers' fancy; rarely had any TV series left the airwaves with such tremendous fanfare. The program was a supposed mirror of a real-life, stand-up comic. That this self-absorbed, sometimes juvenile, and neurotic TV character often failed to be a real mensch (i.e., a man of responsibility) made his stinging commentaries on life and people easier to accept—after all, he was obviously not perfect himself.

He was born Jerome Seinfeld in Brooklyn, New York, and grew up in Massapequa, Long Island, New York. Observing his father—who made and sold commercial signs—make customers laugh deeply impressed the boy and steered the youngster to a career in comedy. After graduating from Queens College, he began his apprenticeship in New York's comedy clubs and in the declining CATSKILL RESORTS. From the start, Seinfeld kept his act clean, relying on insightful humor to gain audience approval. After appearing successfully on a RODNEY DANGERFIELD cable TV comedy special in 1976, he moved to Los Angeles and eventually landed a brief (1980–81) role as Frankie on the *Benson* TV sitcom.

Throughout the 1980s, Seinfeld was a frequent guest on TV's *The Tonight Show Starring Johnny Carson*, as well as *Late Night with David Letterman*, and made frequent guest/starring appearances on TV comedy specials and roasts. In 1988, he won an American Comedy Award for his stand-up comedy. By the end of the decade, the increasingly successful Seinfeld was still working nearly 300 club appearances a year.

In 1989, he and friend Larry David developed a TV pilot, *The Seinfeld Chronicles*. It aired in July 1989, and the series debuted in May 1990. By the time it returned in January 1991, it had built its audience and soon was a national hit. Despite his huge weekly salary and many perks, Seinfeld called it quits with the program in May 1998.

Later that year, he was on stage with his one-man show, which was also taped as a cable TV special. Demonstrating that one of America's most persistent bachelors could finally settle down, he finally wed (Jessica Sklar), and in November 2000, the couple's daughter Sascha was born.

***Seventh Avenue* (1977)** NBC-TV miniseries, color, 360 minutes. **Directors:** Richard Irving (parts one and two) and Russ Mayberry (part three); **Teleplay:** Laurence Heath; **Cast:** Steven Keats (Jay Blackman), Dori Brenner (Rhoda Gold Blackman), Jane Seymour (Eva Meyers), Anne Archer (Myrna Gold), Herschel Bernardi (Joe Vitelli), Jack Gilford (Finklestein), Alan King (Harry Lee).

Through the decades, certain facets of American life became associated with Jewish people: delicatessens, CATSKILL RESORTS, and the garment industry on New York City's Seventh Avenue. Based on the 1967 novel by Norman Bogner, this production traced the ruthless rise of Jay Blackman, a clever young man who went from tenement kid to king of Manhattan's exciting garment industry. With its plot contrivances and dramatic clichés, and boasting a colorful cast, it furthered the stereotype of the grasping Jew. Brenner and Keats were Emmy nominated for their lead roles in this three-part drama.

Seventh Avenue bore similarities to Jerome Weidman's classic *I Can Get It for You Wholesale* (1937), which had been turned into a nonethnic Susan Hayward movie (1951) and then reverted to its Jewish flavor for the Broadway musical *I Can Get It for You Wholesale* (1962), starring ELLIOTT GOULD and featuring BARBRA STREISAND.

***Sheila Levine Is Dead and Living in New York* (1975)** Paramount, color, 113 minutes. **Director:** Sidney J. Furie; **Screenplay:** Kenny Solms and Gail Parent; **Cast:** Jeannie Berlin (Sheila Levine), Roy Scheider (Sam Stoneman), Rebecca Diana Smith (Kate), Janet Brandt (Bernice), Sid Melton (Manny).

For many, the catchy title was the best ingredient of this misfire based on a 1975 Gail Parent novel. It traces the transformation of clumsy Jewish Sheila Levine, who moves into Greenwich Village where she become a liberated, feminist career woman working at a children's recording company. In the process, she falls in love with a doctor (Scheider) whom she temporarily loses to her self-centered, flashy, gentile roommate (Smith).

With its efforts at hip humor and sophistication, this lumbering movie often fell flat. Berlin had played much the same role in *THE HEARTBREAK KID* (1972); in this new entry, her character—equally klutzy, plain looking, and parentally (Brandt and Melton) dominated—managed to survive in Manhattan. (The finale in which she won back the doctor detracted from the film's message. It gave the narrative a Hollywood happy ending, based on the cliché that a respectable, young Jewish lady wanted nothing more than to marry a physician and become a housewife.)

In many ways, *Sheila Levine Is Dead and Living in New York* was an extension of the cultural themes presented earlier in Patty Duke's *ME, NATALIE* (1969), which also dealt with an unattractive Jewish miss from New York. However, there was an added twist and dimension here: *Sheila Levine* suggested that the heroine was so much a mother's girl, was so overwhelmed by her intrusive if well-meaning parent that she tried to adopt (sub)consciously her mother's warped set of values as her own.

***Ship of Fools* (1965)** Columbia, b&w, 148 minutes. **Director:** Stanley Kramer; **Screenplay:** Abby Mann; **Cast:** Vivien Leigh (Mary Treadwell), Simone Signoret (La Condesa), José Ferrer (Rieber), Lee Marvin (Bill Tenny), Oskar Werner (Dr. Schumann), Elizabeth Ashley (Jenny), George Segal (David), José Greco (Pepe), Michael Dunn (Glocken), Heinz Rühmann (Lowenthal), Charles Korvin (the Captain).

Filmmaker KRAMER had been involved earlier with several other Jewish-themed message pictures: the Israeli-set *THE JUGGLER* (1953), which he produced, and the Germany-set *JUDGMENT AT NUREMBERG* (1961), which he produced/directed. This new prestigious entry was filled with an international cast of big names and was based on the 1962 Katharine Anne Porter best-selling novel. Dubbed "Grand Hotel on the Sea," it smoothly interwove its subplots revolving around the several characters and retained the book's reflection of Nazi hatred fermenting in 1930s Germany while much of the world remained passively on the sidelines. With the character of the sinister Rieber as the film's spokesperson for anti-Semitic propaganda, the movie made a strong impact on viewers old enough to remember the pre-World War II period. It was the type of strong screen statement on the prewar Fascist racism mentality that Hollywood in the early 1940s (e.g., *THE MORTAL STORM*, 1940) had been too timid to espouse.

On a ship bound from Vera Cruz, Mexico, to Bremerhaven, Germany, are an assortment of ill-fated passengers. They include the German anti-Semite Rieber; La Condesa, the drug-addicted Spanish noblewoman who faces prison in Spain for her political activities; Mrs. Treadwell, a lonely middle-aged widow drawn to overdrinking and flirting; Bill Tenny, an ex-baseball player who has professional regrets; a young, unmarried, and unhappy couple (Ashley and Segal); and below deck, a group of Spanish laborers who had been working in Cuba and are now returning home. There is also the ship's doctor, Dr. Schumann, as well as other passengers and crew. At mealtimes, the captain invites the German contingent to sit at his table but insists that the Jew Lowenthal (who is overly optimistic about the future) and the cynical dwarf Glocken be seated elsewhere.

Ship of Fools received Academy Awards for its art/set decoration and black and white cinematography, with four Academy Award nominations, including those for Best Actor (Werner) and Best Actress (Signoret).

The British-made *Voyage of the Damned* (1976) has similar plot themes to *Ship of Fools*, even to two of the same cast members: Werner and Ferrer. Other talent included Faye Dunaway, Max Von Sydow, Orson Welles, Lee Grant, and James Mason. *Voyage of the Damned* involved a 1939 Nazi scheme of sending a boatload of Jewish refugees to Cuba, knowing that they will be refused entry there and that no other country will accept them. Thus, the vessel will be forced to return to Germany, bringing certain death for its Jewish passengers.

Sidney, George (1876–1945) For several years on Broadway, in vaudeville, and in films, this five-feet, three-inch performer was well regarded as a top dialectal star, playing the typical Old World Jew who had risen to success in business but had problems with the new generation and/or with other cultures.

Born Sammy Greenfield in Hungary in 1876, his family immigrated to the United States where he pursued a career in vaudeville and on the stage. By 1914, he was appearing on Broadway in such plays as *The Show Shop* with Douglas Fairbanks and later with FANNY BRICE in the short-lived *Why, Worry?* (1918), a comedy about a LOWER EAST SIDE restaurant waitress foiling German spies. He had a huge success with *Welcome Stranger* (1920) as the Jewish merchant who battled anti-Semitism in a New England town, eventually winning over the locals.

From his first feature film, *POTASH AND PERLMUTTER* (1923), Sidney was a hit with moviegoers, as, also, when he starred later as Cohen in *THE COHENS AND KELLYS* (1926). The latter series lasted through 1934, a total of six popular entries. Sidney had another comedic role in *THE HEART OF NEW YORK* (1932) as Mendel and continued in films through 1937. He was the uncle of moviemaker George Sidney, who directed such Hollywood pictures as *Annie Get Your Gun* (1950), *The Eddy Duchin Story* (1956), and *Bye Bye Birdie* (1963).

Sidney, Sylvia (1910–1999) In the early twentieth century, few Jewish young ladies chose (or were chosen) to have a career—let alone to star—in motion pictures. Throughout its infancy, this medium was considered by many to be a scandalous profession. A relative exception was Theodosia Goodman (1885–1955) who, as Theda Bara, made a name for herself in silent cinema as the American movies' first vamp. But to be a stage actress was different. Some such as MOLLY PICON decided upon the YIDDISH THEATER as their venue; others like Sidney had their hearts set on Broadway, and from the New York stage to Hollywood filmmaking was a small leap in the late 1920s when movies converted to sound and well-spoken actors were in much demand.

Born Sophia Kosow in Bronx, New York, her father was Russian-born and her mother was from Rumania. After her parents divorced and her mother remarried, the girl was adopted by her stepfather, Sigmund Sidney. Because she was shy, her parents encouraged any activity that made her more gregarious. She enrolled at Manhattan's American Theater Guild school and made her professional bow in *The Challenge of Youth* (1926) in Washington, D.C. Early the next year, she took over a leading role on Broadway and made her screen debut in the silent picture *Broadway Nights* (1927), playing herself in a cameo.

In 1929, Sidney made her first talkie *(Thru Different Eyes)*, but it was two years before she made another *(City Streets)*. By then, she was under contract at Paramount Pictures where she became close to B. P. Schulberg, a top studio executive. Soon—in movies like *Ladies of the Big House* (1931), *STREET SCENE* (1931), and *Jennie Gerhardt* (1933)—Sidney developed a screen type: the poor (often slum) girl beset by the Depression and men. It seemed to suit, so it was felt, her Semitic looks. Only occasionally was she allowed out of this typecasting, as in *Madame Butterfly* (1932), *Thirty-Day Princess* (1934), and *Behold My Wife* (1935).

Tired of the typecasting, she returned in 1937 to the stage and only occasionally (e.g., *Blood on the Sun*, 1945, *Les Miserables*, 1952) made movies. In New York, she was in the Jewish stage pageant *We Will Never Die* (1943) and thereafter toured with many plays. In the 1950s, besides theater, she frequently guest-starred on television. After a seventeen-year gap, she was back in pictures with *Summer Wishes, Winter Dreams* (1973) to impressive notices. Always acting—when not writing books (1968 and 1975) on her needlepoint hobby—Sylvia continued performing right up to her death. She was a favorite of director Tim Burton, who cast her in *Bettlejuice* (1988) and *Mars Attacks!* (1996). Her final appearance was in 1998 on the revived TV series, *Fantasy Island.*

Silver, Joan Micklin (1935–) Born in Omaha, Nebraska, Silver entered show business when she began to write scripts for educational film companies. Later she cowrote the screenplay for *Limbo* (1972—about Vietnam War wives). She made her feature-film directing debut with *HESTER STREET* (1975), an evocative study of Jewish immigrants on New York's LOWER EAST SIDE at the start of the twentieth century. She turned to contemporary Jews—some still living in Manhattan's Jewish ghetto—in *CROSSING DELANCEY* (1988). One of the TV movies that she directed, *In the Presence of Mine Enemies* (1996), concerned a rabbi in 1942 Poland in the Jewish ghetto of Warsaw, who attempts to keep his humanity amid all the Nazi atrocities. Another of her television projects, the made-for-cable *A Private Matter* (1992), told of the real-life Sherri Finkbine, a victim of thalidomide.

Silver, Ron (1946–) Best remembered as the flirtatious and fatuous neighbor Gary Levy on *RHODA* in the late 1970s, Silver progressed from sitcoms to heavy dramatic roles—the characters often bearded, serious, and introverted—such as the lead in *ENEMIES: A LOVE STORY* (1989) and the role of attorney Alan Dershowitz in *Reversal of Fortune* (1990).

Born in New York City, after college, he taught Spanish at a Jewish boarding school in New England and in the early 1970s, thanks to his fluency in Chinese, worked for the U.S. government in Taiwan. His debut film was *Tunnelvision* (1976), but it was as a yuppie studio executive in *Best Friends* (1982) that he clicked. After four years on Broadway, he won a Tony Award for David Mamet's *Speed-the Plow*. In the made-for-cable movie *Fellow Traveller* (1989), he was the Hollywood screenwriter who was about to testify about his past communist affiliations; in *Black & White* (1999), he played the police internal investigator. During 1996–97 he appeared on *Chicago Hope* and from 1998–99 was smug Alec Bilson, the new owner of Kirstie Alley's lingerie company, on the sitcom *Veronica's Closet.* Very active in liberal causes, he held senior offices in several of the actors' unions. Later movie credits included: *Ratz* (2000—made-for-cable feature), *When Billie*

Beat Bobby (2001—TV movie), and *Ali* (2002). In the 2001–02 season of TV's *West Wing,* Silver had a recurring role as a campaign strategist.

Silvers, Phil (1911–1985) Like Abbott and Costello, comedian Silvers started out in burlesque with such a high-energy presence that he generally stole any acting scene he was in. He was in top form playing a glib, bespectacled con artist (always ready with the snappy "Glad to meet ya" and the quick smile)—which made him the perfect choice as M/Sgt. Ernest T. Bilko on the TV sitcom *THE PHIL SILVERS SHOW* (aka: *You'll Never Get Rich*) (1955–59).

He was born Philip Silver (the "s" was added later to provide a more distinctive surname) in the Brownsville section of Brooklyn, New York. He was performing at bar mitzvahs and parties by age five but also, a few years later, was involved in petty crimes in his violent neighborhood. By 1923, he was in vaudeville and then migrated to burlesque, where he worked in semiobscurity from 1932 to 1939. His big break occurred in Broadway's *Yokel Boy* (1939), where he was cast as a devious Hollywood press agent.

Once in the movies—1940's *Hit Parade of 1941*—he was in demand as comedy relief in espionage thrillers (e.g., *All Through the Night,* 1942), musicals (e.g., *Footlight Serenade,* 1942), and comedies (e.g., *A Lady Takes a Chance,* 1943). He displayed dancing and singing acumen in *Cover Girl* (1944) and many other screen musicals. Tiring of being a cinema second fiddle, he returned to Broadway for the musical *High Button Shoes* (1947). From 1948 to 1949 he hosted *The Arrow Show* in the new medium of television and was back in another Broadway success with *Top Banana* (1950), a song-and-dance entry about a career-driven burlesque comic. He repeated the latter role for the movies (1953).

The true apex of Silvers's lengthy career was his TV sitcom, *The Phil Silvers Show.* As the beloved army shyster conning military buddies and bosses, he was superb. He reappeared on Broadway in 1960 and did a follow-up TV series *The New Phil Silvers Show* (1963–64), which wasn't successful. He had good exposure in two comedic pictures: *It's a Mad Mad Mad Mad World* (1963) and *A Funny Thing Happened on the Way to the Forum* (1966—he had turned down the lead on Broadway and now had the secondary role of Lycus). From 1969 to 1971, he was Shifty Shafer on TV's *The Beverly Hillbillies.*

Silvers finally got to star in *A Funny Thing Happened on the Way to the Forum* in the 1972 Broadway revival. In his 1973 autobiography *(This Laugh Is on Me)*, he acknowledged that gambling and paranoia deeply affected his career, his bank accounts, and his marriages.

***Single Guy, The* (1995–1997)** NBC-TV series, color, 30 minutes. **Cast:** Jonathan Silverman (Johnny Eliot), Joey Slotnick (Sam Sloane), Ming-Na Wen (Trudy Sloane), Mark Moses (Matt Parker: 1995–96), Jessica Hecht (Janeane Percy-Parker: 1995–96), Ernest Borgnine (Manny), Olivia d'Abo (Marie: 1996–97), Shawn Michael Howard (Russell: 1996–97).

Silverman, who made his professional reputation performing in Neil Simon stage comedies and screen adaptations, starred in this situation comedy. The derivative series attempted to be all things to everyone and ended by being bland. Johnny Eliot is a Jewish, single, struggling novelist living in New York City. His eccentric, ethnic pal Sam Sloane is married to an Asian American (Wen); there are also the WASPy Parkers (Moses and Hecht). Not to be overlooked is the building's congenial Italian doorman (Borgnine) who spouts domestic advice based on fifty years of marriage. In the show's second and final season, more types were added: a British divorcee (d'Abo) and an African-American law student (Howard).

The show continuously avoided dealing with ethnic questions, customs, or differences.

situation comedy series—television One of the earliest TV sitcoms to feature Jewish characters was *THE GOLDBERGS* (1949–54; 1955–56) with GERTRUDE BERG and many of the cast from the long-running radio version. Among the veteran Jewish entertainers who transferred from radio to TV in 1950 was JACK BENNY with his half-hour program that would last through 1964. GEORGE BURNS with *The George Burns and Gracie Allen Show* also began in 1950 and would remain on the airwaves through 1958.

In a few comedy series of the early 1950s, ethnic-named characters were usually played by Jewish talent. Not much if anything was made on-screen of their heritage, but it was a subtle way to introduce such characters as part of the plot mix. Examples of this included Horwitz on *Life with Luigi* (1952–53) and Alfred Prinzmetal on *Meet Millie* (1952–56).

One of the only new sitcoms in the mid-1950s to utilize a Jewish personality in a major way was *THE PHIL SILVERS SHOW* (aka: *You'll Never Get Rich*) (1955–59), starring the razor-sharp comedy styling of SILVERS as the staccato-voiced con artist who was always ready to match wits with the next chump he encountered. Silvers would return to series television with *The New Phil Silvers Show* (1963–64) playing a variation of his special prototype

The early 1960s saw a small increase of visible Jewish figures on TV comedy series. In *MRS. G. GOES TO COLLEGE* (aka: *The Gertrude Berg Show*) (1961–62), Berg played a variation of her familiar persona. Buddy Sorrel (performed by Morey Amsterdam) was the TV gag writer on *THE DICK VAN DYKE SHOW* (1961–66), and Arch Fenster was played by Marty Ingels on *I'm Dickens—He's Fenster* (1962–63). In the middle of the decade, veteran trouper RED BUTTONS came back to the medium as a meek accountant-turned-undercover-agent in *The Double Life of Henry Phyfe* (1966). Quiz-show maven Henry Morgan played a variation of his caustic self as the cynical writer friend of the lead character in *My World and Welcome to It* (1969–72).

By the 1970s, the small screen medium was offering a greater variety of ethnic types as series regulars. *THE MARY TYLER MOORE SHOW* (1970–77) presented Rhoda Morgenstern and, sometimes, her mother Ida, two very Jewish New Yorkers. Later in the decade, Valerie Harper's character was spun off into her own series, *RHODA* [1974–78], allowing for other members of her on-camera clan to make appearances. *BRIDGET LOVES BERNIE* (1972–73) showcased an Irish girl (Meredith Baxter) who wed a Jewish man (David Birney). Motor-mouthed comedian DON RICKLES had two shots at series in these years, first his own *The Don Rickles Show* (1972) and then the more successful service comedy *C.P.O. Sharkey* (1976–78).

The second half of the 1970s burst with Jewish-flavored sitcoms. In *WELCOME BACK, KOTTER* (1975–79), the title figure and his wife were Jewish, and Juan Epstein was the Puerto Rican Jewish "sweathog." Hal Linden starred as *Barney Miller* (1975–82), a Jewish police captain. Young Lenny Markowitz (played by Adam Arkin) was the focal figure on *Busting Loose* (1977), while, that same year, actor Marvin Kaplan joined the long-enduring *Alice* (1976–85) as another of his whiney alter egos. On *TAXI* (1978–83), JUDD HIRSCH was the serious Alex Rieger, the Jewish taxi driver. MARTIN BALSAM had the role of Jewish Murray Klein who became Archie Bunker's business partner for two seasons (1979–81) of *Archie Bunker's Place*. That same year, *The Facts of Life* (1979–88) debuted, with Mindy Cohn as Natalie Green, one of the quartet of student characters.

Moving into the 1980s, RON SILVER was seen as a Jewish NYPD undercover cop on *Baker's Dozen* (1982), and Philip Charles MacKenzie chased a high-school English instructor on *Making the Grade* (1982). Todd Susman played firefighters Feldman on *Star of the Family* (1982), and actor Corey Feldman was part of *Madame's Place* (1982–83). Jami Gertz played a Jewish-American Princess at Weemawee High in *Square Pegs* (1982–83). *E/R*—no relation to the later dramatic series—was a one-season (1984–85) entry, with ELLIOTT GOULD as an emergency-room doctor. Among those at *Night Court* (1984–92) was Selma Hacker the matron, played by Selma Diamond during the 1984–85 season. Jewish actor Ed Asner, who usually interpreted non-Semitic roles, was the grouchy co-owner of a Los Angeles garment factory in *Off the Rack* (1985). *Leo & Liz in Beverly Hills* (1986), similar to the theatrical feature *DOWN AND OUT IN BEVERLY HILLS* (1986), dealt with the Greens (Harvey Korman and Valerie Perrine) from New Jersey who had moved to California. Masterful stand-up comic Garry Shandling debuted his *It's Garry Shandling's Show* (1988–90) and later starred in the more successful *THE LARRY SANDERS SHOW* (1992–98), which also featured Jewish characters. A longtime (1988–96) cast member of *Murphy Brown* was the Miles Silverberg character played by Grant Shaud. As the snobbish and hyper young producer of *F.Y.I.*, a TV news-magazine program based in Washington, D.C., he was full of neuroses and was depicted as a Jewish-American Prince.

ANYTHING BUT LOVE (1989–92), a forerunner to several sitcoms that featured comedic, neurotic Jewish men, spotlighted stand-up comic RICHARD LEWIS. Ending the decade was the much-heralded but ill-conceived *CHICKEN SOUP* (1989) in which former rabbi JACKIE MASON was on tap as a middle-aged man in love with a Catholic woman.

Starting off the 1990s, *City* (1990) presented Todd Susman as the right-hand helper to the city manager (Valerie Harper). The odd *Good Grief!* (1990–91) had stand-up comic HOWIE MANDEL as a ex-con artist manipulating his in-laws who operated a mortuary. The briefly aired *The Marshall Chronicles* (1990) featured a Woody Allenlike teenager dealing with puppy love, and the overtly Jewish themed *Singer & Sons* (1990) followed a New York deli owner named Nathan Singer. Another Manhattan-set sitcom—which proved to be the hit of the decade—was *SEINFELD* (1990–98), featuring astute stand-up comic JERRY SEINFELD as the uneasy bachelor with lots of quirks and several nutsy friends.

As the decade built momentum, eccentric Capt. Ken Epstein (played by Joel Murray) was seen on *Pacific Station* (1991–92), and Rob Reiner played himself on *Morton & Hayes* (1991). Among the multiethnic summer-camp contingent in *Salute Your Shorts* (1991–93) were such characters as Michael Stein and Ronald Foster Pinksy. Richard Lewis and Don Rickles teamed for the unsuccessful *Daddy Dearest* (1993). From 1992 to 1999, stand-up comic/actor PAUL REISER costarred in *MAD ABOUT YOU* as the anxious documentary filmmaker and husband, whose parents, relatives, and sister constantly impinged on his domestic life. Another bright spot was the arrival of FRAN DRESCHER in *THE NANNY* (1993–99), playing the ultimate screechy-voiced Jewish New Yorker. In contrast, *FRIENDS* (1994–) offered more-refined suburban New York Jewish-American Princesses, parents, and so on. In *The 5 Mrs. Buchanans* (1994–95), Judith Ivey's ethnic character ran a thrift shop and talked a mile a minute.

GENE WILDER performed variations of his breaking-out-of-a-rut man in *Something Wilder* (1994–95). Adam Goldberg was one of the Manhattan bicycle messengers on *Double Rush* (1995), and Jeremy Piven was on hand as a Jewish Mr. Mom in *Pride & Joy* (1995). *Home Court* (1995–96) offered Pamela Reed as a Jewish judge in Chicago, and Jonathan Silverman was cast as the fledgling Manhattan-based writer in *THE SINGLE GUY* (1995–97). Alan Rosenberg played Ira Woodbine, the sweet but neurotic novelist and ex-husband of *Cybill* (1995–98). *NewsRadio* (1995–99) began without Jon Lovitz's Max Lewis character, but he arrived to replace the late Phil Hartman in the ensemble. On *Suddenly Susan* (1996–2000), Kathy Griffin was star Brooke Shields's Jewish coworker at the San Francisco magazine and had a solid relationship with her on-camera rabbi husband. Goofy comedian Pauly Shore was seen as a pampered Los Angeles young guy on *The Pauly Shore Show* (1997).

Within *Dharma & Greg* (1997–2002), Jenna Elfman portrayed Dharma Finkelstein, the San Franciscan with an overripe hippie father (Alan Rachins). While not emphasized, GEORGE SEGAL's Jack Gallo, publisher of *Blush* magazine, came across as one of the actor's patented Jewish intellectuals/businessmen in the sitcom *Just Shoot Me* (1997–). Stand-up comic Carol Leifer was the star of her own series, as Miami optometrist Carol Lerner on *Alright Already* (1997–98). Judd Hirsch returned to series TV with *George & Leo* (1997–98), as a small-time Jewish hoodlum who harasses the Martha's Vineyard bookstore owner (Bob Newhart) who is wed to his daughter. In the workplace comedy, *Conrad Bloom* (1998), Mark Feuerstein was on hand in the title role of a Manhattan copywriter.

As Sara Lipschitz Campbell, Judith Light played a Martha Stewartlike Jewish character on *The Simple Life* (1998). A very brief-run comedy, *You're the One* (1998), featured a genteel WASPy southerner named Lindsay Metcalf who wed a consummate New Yorker of Rumanian extraction. For two seasons (1998–2000), Ron Silver essayed shrewd entrepreneur Alec Bilson on *Veronica's Closet*, and Joshua Malina was cast as the nerdy but lovable Jewish statistician Jeremy Goodwin on *Sports Night* (1998–2000), who exhibited a surfeit of nervous energy, a lack of social graces, and an amazing encyclopedic knowledge. *Zoe, Duncan, Jack & Jane* (1999) had a very ethnic New York flavor to the show's lead character Duncan Milch, a series that returned as *Zoe* during 2000.

Essaying the high-energy, pampered BETTE (2000–1), BETTE MIDLER encapsulated the mature Jewish-American Princess, a performer, wife, and mother who never ran out of steam or things to complain about as she rushed through her hectic California-based life. On the sitcom *Will & Grace* (1998–) dealing with a gay attorney (played by Eric McCormack), Debra Messing was cast as his best friend, Grace, a Jewish single still looking for the ultra-perfect man. *State of Grace* (2001–2), set in mid-1960s North Carolina, featured two young girls, one Jewish and one gentile, who were best pals and who each had eccentric families. *3 Sisters* (2001–2) featured a trio of sisters whose father (Peter Bonerz) is Jewish but whose mother (Dyan Cannon) is not. The lead sibling weds a Jewish suitor. *Leap of Faith* (2002), a *Friends* clone, presented an ethnically diverse cast of New York city lead characters. These include one of the heroine's pals (played by Lisa Edelstein).

***Skokie* (1981)** CBS-TV, color, 150 minutes. **Director:** Herbert Wise; **Teleplay:** Ernest Kinoy; **Cast:** Danny Kaye (Max Feldman), John Rubinstein (Herb Lewisohn), Carl Reiner (Abbot Rosen), Kim Hunter (Bertha Feldman), Eli Wallach (Bert Silverman), Lee Strasberg (Morton Wiseman).

In his television acting debut, KAYE starred in this made-for-television feature based on the actual 1977 march by neo-Nazis in the primarily Jewish community of Skokie, Illinois. The narrative dealt with the affect of the pending demonstration on the citizens, many of whom were World War II concentration camp survivors.

This was the first time that Jewish-born Kaye played such an ethnic character on screen (although he did play the biblical Noah in the 1970 Broadway musical, *Two by Two*). Also featured in the cast was renowned acting coach STRASBERG, who died before the project aired.

The well-received *Skokie* received three Emmy nominations.

soap opera series—television An early representation of Jewish characters in this genre occurred on *Search for Tomorrow* (1951–86), which was among the first soap operas to debut on American television. Within the continuing drama, the comedic characters of Marge and Stu Bergman were introduced as neighbors to heroine Joanne Gardner Barron Tate Vincente Tourneur. The couple was so popular that they became permanent fixtures on the daytime show. The Bergmans' daughter Janet—played by six actresses over the period 1951–82—was frequently involved romantically with gentile characters.

On *Another World* (1964–), the character of Sylvie Kosloff was introduced in 1978 when Iris Carrington went in search of her long-lost mother. Iris discovered her in New York City where she was a clothing designer. The background of Sylvie—played by Leora Dana—involved her Polish grandfather who came to America and was employed in the garment district of Manhattan. Although Dana performed the part with ethnic mannerisms and voice inflections, the character was *not* stated as Jewish. (Reportedly, this was done so that when villainess Iris rejected her mother, it would not seem to be an act of anti-Semitism.)

On *One Life to Live* (1968–) the role of Dave Siegel (1968–72) was Jewish as was his son Tim (played first by William Cox and then by Tom Berenger). No sooner did Tim wed a nun than he died in the plot line of 1976. A decade later, the Judith Russell Sanders figure (played by Louise Sorel) was rejected by her aristocratic WASP mother-in-law for being Jewish. In this period, Judith's daughter Kate (played by Marcia Cross) was also on the scene, as was Judith's brother Jon Russell (played by John Martin). In 1992, Nora Gannon (played by Hillary Bailey Smith) turned up as another Jewish figure on the program. In the plot, Nora had a biracial daughter named Rachel and a son Matthew. In the course of their appearances on the series, their religion was mentioned and various Jewish holidays were celebrated in Nora's home.

Within *General Hospital* (1963–), attorney Jake Meyer (played by Sam Behren) was brought onto the show in 1983 as a minor figure. As the lawyer defending the program's key villainess, he was defined as quirky, a man who typically dressed in athletic clothes. As his character was expanded in the story line, he began to date an Irish Catholic widow, Rose Kelly (played by Loanne Bishop), which gave the plot an *ABIE'S IRISH ROSE* (1922) flavor.

In 1984, on *Ryan's Hope* (1975–89), a daytime drama that focused on many Irish Catholic characters, Jewish delicatessen owner Dave Greenberg (played by Scott Holmes) was introduced into the plot. He first dated Ryan family in-law Maggie Shelby (played by Cali Timmons), an aspiring model. Later Greenberg wed an actual Ryan, a granddaughter, before his character was phased out during 1985.

***Sophie's Choice* (1982)** Universal, color, 157 minutes. **Director/Screenplay:** Alan J. Pakula; **Cast:** Meryl Streep (Sophie Zawistowoska), Kevin Kline (Nathan Landau), Peter MacNicol (Stingo), Josef Sommer (narrator), Rita Karin (Yetta Zimmerman), Josh Mostel (Morris Fink), Eugene Lipinski (Polish professor).

William Styron's acclaimed (autobiographical) novel (1979) was brought to the screen in this controversial production, which received mixed reactions from Jewish groups in the United States. Criticism centered on its abstract handling of the HOLOCAUST and for having the chief villain of the piece be not the Nazis but a Jew. Beyond Streep's well-crafted performance, complete with accent, this entry was essentially a think piece on the ultimate shape of evil.

Set in a Brooklyn boarding house in 1947, the story concerns a fledgling southern writer, Stingo, who becomes entranced with Polish refugee Sophie Zawistowoska and forms a platonic friendship with her and another roomer, the Jewish Nathan Landau. The latter is a research chemist who is suffering from schizophrenia. As the three become better acquainted, the Catholic Sophie relates stories of her life in Europe during World War II. Piecing them together, it develops (as told in flashbacks shot in sepia) that she was a prisoner in the Auschwitz death camp and that the Nazis made her choose between her two children—which one to live, which one to die. Thereafter, somewhat unhinged, she was sexually abused by her captors. Back in the present, the young writer brings out the best qualities in wistful Sophie, while the deranged Nathan, full of guilt and shame, becomes her chief tormenter, leading her to tragedy.

A very leisurely told, artfully handled film, this production earned an Academy Award for Streep as Best Actress, as well as accruing four other Oscar nominations.

Spielberg, Steven (1946–) This imaginative, Oscar-winning filmmaker, producer, and studio executive achieved megasuccess by helming such genre classics as *Jaws* (1975), *Close Encounters of the Third Kind* (1976), *Raiders of the Lost Ark* (1981), and *E.T: The Extra-Terrestrial* (1982). Also in that period, he attained personal validation as the director of *The Color Purple* (1985), a rendition of the Alice Walker book classic (1982) about struggling African Americans in the Deep South.

As he reached middle age, the Cincinnati, Ohio-born Spielberg began to explore anew his Jewish roots; thus, he served as coexecutive producer of the animated feature *AN AMERICAN TAIL* (1986). In that entry, its sequel *An American Tail: Fievel Goes West* (1991), and the animated TV series for children *Fievel's American Tails* (1992–93), the adventures of the Mousekewitz family, Russian Jewish immigrant mice, coming to the United States in the 1880s were unfolded. From this project, Spielberg turned to the long-in-the-works *SCHINDLER'S LIST* (1993), a multi-Oscar winner. This was the overwhelming account of the HOLOCAUST told from the perspective of the conniving businessman/war profiteer who came to care for the Jewish camp prisoners in Poland he exploited (and later helped). In 2000, DreamWorks, the film studio of which Spielberg was cofounder, was coproducer of the full-length animated feature *Joseph: King of Dreams* dealing with the biblical story of the Israelite sold into bondage in Egypt who later became a leader of his people.

From the 1980s, Spielberg was involved with the preservation and dissemination of data about the Holocaust. He became involved with an archive on the subject begun in 1967 at the Hebrew University of Jerusalem that became known as the Steven Spielberg Jewish Film Archive. He has also participated at different levels with several documentaries dealing with the Holocaust.

In 2001 Spielberg received an honorary knighthood from Great Britain's Queen Elizabeth II in recognition of his contribution to that country's film industry. Later features that he directed included *A.I. Artificial Intelligence* (2001) and *Minority Report* and *Catch Me If You Can* (both 2002).

***Stardust Memories* (1980)** United Artists, b&w, 90 minutes. **Director/Screenplay:** Woody Allen; **Cast:** Woody Allen (Sandy Bates), Charlotte Rampling (Dorrie), Jessica Harper (Daisy), Marie-Christine Barrault (Isabel), Tony Roberts (Tony), Daniel Stern (actor), Eli Mintz (old man).

Stardust Memories was an ode to Italian film director Federico Fellini and his autobiographical movie *8½* (1963). In ALLEN's entry, the Jewish Sandy Bates copes sarcastically and sometimes aggressively with fawning critics and fans. Also presented is an assortment of Sandy's unsatisfying relationships with gentile women.

This entry differed from the director's past pictures in that, here, his on-camera alter ego is *not* a career bumbler but a successful ex-comic turned filmmaker—albeit still in need of deep therapy, and, perhaps in a salute to his own real-life quandary, Woody has Sandy ponder how best to interact with his obsequious boosters.

This production was replete with Jewish performers, ranging from Mintz (the Uncle David of TV's *THE GOLDBERGS*) to ethnic talent Stern, all of whom provided a cross section of the public involved in Sandy's life. In his depiction of Sandy Bates, the self-absorbed Jewish intellectual, Allen provided a dimensional study of a man grown cynical from success but unable to change his situation.

Steiger, Rod (1925–2002) In the early twentieth century, the YIDDISH THEATER provided a training ground for future film actors such as PAUL MUNI and MOLLY PICON. In the 1930s, New York's Group Theater was a springboard for such as JOHN GARFIELD and Morris Carnovsky into the movies. By the mid-1940s, the venue of choice was the Actors Studio operated by LEE STRASBERG. Among its graduates were Steiger, the beefy, tight-coiled actor who in the 1950s and 1960s rivaled his classmate Marlon Brando as the American screen's preeminent dramatic actor.

He was born Rodney Steiger in Westhampton, New York, to parents who had been a song-and-dance team. They divorced, his mother remarried, and Steiger was brought up as a Lutheran. Later, to escape his oppressive home life (his mother had become alcoholic), he lied about his age to enlist in the World War II navy. After the victory, Rod studied acting at the New School and the Actors Studio and made his Broadway debut in *Night Music* (1951); he was also active in live television drama in New York in the early 1950s. Steiger had had a bit in the movie *Teresa* (1951), but it was in *On the Waterfront* (1954) as the corrupt teamster and older brother of ex-boxer Brando that he made an impact and was Oscar nominated.

In the 1950s, Steiger was much in demand, jumping from musicals (e.g., *Oklahoma!* 1955) to westerns (e.g., *Jubal*, 1956) to heavy drama (e.g., *The Big Knife*, 1995) to gangster yarns (*Al Capone*, 1959). Because of his burly look, Steiger was not the usual Hollywood leading-man material, but he made his dynamic presence count, relying on Method acting. In 1965 alone, he was the opportunist Russian in *Doctor Zhivago*, played an effeminate mortician in *The Loved One*, and had his most memorable screen role, the HOLOCAUST survivor in *THE PAWNBROKER* (for which he was Oscar nominated). Two years later, he won an Academy Award as the bigoted southern sheriff of *In the Heat of the Night*.

Steiger's career momentum fell apart in the 1970s when he suffered severe bouts of depression and underwent heart surgery. He returned to the screen with *W. C. Fields and Me* (1976) but thereafter was mostly a character second lead. He portrayed Benito Mussolini in *Lion of the Desert* (1981), was a Hasidic Jewish father in *THE CHOSEN* (1981), and in the TV movie *Sword of Gideon* (1985) played a member of Israel's intelligence agency. In the 1990s he seemed to take any role offered and appeared in *The Hollywood Sign* (2001), which involved a once-famous film star hoping for a comeback.

stereotypes In the early twentieth-century United States, a well-rooted tradition in stage plays and vaudeville of presenting comic ethnic types—the thrifty Scots, the overly sentimental and/or liquor-loving Irish, and the avaricious, meddling, and overly dramatic Jews—already existed. Each came with recognizable accents, mannerisms, and traditional outfits that would immediately label them to audiences as comic figures. At the time, this was seen as good-natured ribbing of fellow participants (albeit of "strange" backgrounds) in the great American melting pot; the fact that such satirizing was usually done by more assimilated groups to less acculturated ones didn't seem to concern anyone much. Also, that such ethnic typing could turn in nasty directions apparently did not bother many of the contemporary perpetrators of this exaggerated categorization.

The early short (and silent) films—sometimes made abroad and shown in the United States—about Jews often pictured them initially as exotic foreigners (e.g., *Arabian Jewish Dance*, 1903; *Jewish Types in Russia*, 1910) or had an unfavorable connotation within their titles (e.g., *Legend of the Erring Jew*, 1909).

Paralleling this, by the 1910s, the stock Jewish character of the good-natured foreigner who mangled the language, had odd customs, and was a shrewd businessman was in place on screen with such films as *Cohen's Luck* (1915). (Often these humorous characters or aspects of their personalities were comedy relief within more serious narratives, usually set in the Jewish ghetto of New York City. They became known as GHETTO DRAMAS.)

As potentially negative as the stock funny Jew representation was, it paled next to the image of the grasping old Jew, Fagin. The latter was the well-etched, unpleasant character from Charles Dickens's novel *OLIVER TWIST* (1839), a snarling scoundrel who trained young boys to be his crew of thieves. There would be several versions of this drama as film and television productions through the years in America. In the same vein of classic negative stereotypes was Shylock, the rich Jewish moneylender from William Shakespeare's play, *The Merchant of Venice* (1596). This much-staged drama was the subject of a 1908 Vitagraph short film (featuring Julia Swayne Gordon) and also was adapted for several television productions. Similarly, the character of Isaac of York in Sir Walter Scott's novel *IVANHOE* (1820), another Jew in literature, was pictured as the wandering outsider and a controller of money. (By the time Hollywood made a full-fledged version of *IVANHOE* in 1952, political correctness was on the upswing and the characterization of this elder man was softened.)

By the early 1920s, the stock Jewish character took on oversized dimensions in two American film series, *POTASH AND PERLMUTTER* (1922) and *THE COHENS AND KELLYS* (1926). Each led to several installments, as well as to many imitations on screen.

With the advent of talkies in the late 1920s, the era of the comic Jew on screen began to fade. Both overuse of the stereotype and awakened sensitivity to the injustice of the depictions contributed to this change. Equally important, it was also the start of the era where, by decision of the mostly Jewish film studio moguls in Hollywood (who did not want to call attention to their background as discriminated against non-mainstream individuals whose forebears were pushed out of Europe and elsewhere), Jewish characters were no longer being shown overtly on screen. This situation increased as anti-Semitism intensified in Europe in the preamble to World War II.

Later, as the truth about the horrors of the HOLOCAUST became known and/or was accepted, U.S. filmmakers felt compelled, out of guilt or admiration or both toward this persecuted race, to start to think of dealing again with Jewish characters on screen. After the breakthrough of *CROSSFIRE* and *GENTLEMAN'S AGREEMENT* (both 1947), each of which concerned facets of anti-Semitism in the United States, a new stereotype of Jews began to emerge slowly on the screen. It followed the old traditional one of the Jew as outsider, the wanderer with no home. In carefully muted studies of Jewish characters in films such as *GOOD MORNING, MISS DOVE* (1955), *HOME BEFORE DARK* (1958), and *THE YOUNG LIONS* (1958), this portrait of the Jew was perpetuated.

By the time of *JUDGMENT AT NUREMBERG* (1961) and *THE PAWNBROKER* (1965), the Jew as Holocaust victim was becoming an increasingly employed topical theme for films and episodes of TV series. This and stories illustrating ANTI-SEMITISM would become frequent subjects in coming years for dramas—those that dealt with them at all—with Jewish characters. It offered Hollywood, still concerned about the commercial viability of presenting Semitic figures in major story lines, an opportunity to explore such characters in a setting that was tragic and/or noble and therefore might overcome objections by film financiers and distributors.

In the late 1960s, with the new freedom found in the poststudio-system Hollywood, there was an expansion, to a degree, of presenting Jewish topics and characters on the big and the small screen. Although most frequently it encompassed post-Holocaust themes or acts of anti-Semitism, when other story lines were used, new stereotypes became wedged into place; for example, instead of the noble, hardworking mother of the old ghetto dramas such as *Humoresque* (1920), there was now the dominating mother type of *NO WAY TO TREAT A LADY* (1968) or *PORTNOY'S COMPLAINT* (1972). As years wore on, SHELLEY WINTERS (e.g., *NEXT STOP, GREENWICH VILLAGE*, 1974) and LAINIE KAZAN (e.g., *MY FAVORITE YEAR*, 1982) transformed the at-times frightening image of the overly possessive mother into one of oversized humor.

Because of WOODY ALLEN, the neurotic, self-deprecating schlemiel became an increasingly familiar figure in films of the 1970s and thereafter. Likewise, a more refined format presented the neurotic Yuppie Jew as personified in much of the screen work of RICHARD BENJAMIN, which, in turn, became muted into a more kindly type for the later TV series of JERRY SEINFELD in *SEINFELD* (1990–98) and PAUL REISER in *MAD ABOUT YOU* (1992–99). Contrasting this amusing, phobic type was the angst-ridden Jewish male, typified by the Michael Steadman character in TV's *thirtysomething* (1987–91).

Corresponding to the new images of Jewish men in film and television was the rise of the Jewish American Princess as the pampered, self-centered rich girl. Reflected in the title character of *MARJORIE MORNINGSTAR* (1958) in a romantic, soft-focus version, this representation grew sharper with the "heroine" of *GOODBYE, COLUMBUS* (1969). Developmentally, in the several 1970s comedies of BARBRA STREISAND, this type became more earthy and less pretentious if no less manipulative; at least, as presented by Streisand she was more entertaining and less threatening. By the late 1980s, young intellectual female Jewish New Yorkers were represented in *CROSSING DELANCEY* (1988). Reevaluating life and seeking ethnic roots became the new ideal of this generalized screen/TV heroine.

On the other hand, the humorous presentation of the once intimidating Jewish American Princess had been converted—at least in screen fiction—to the caricatures provided on television by FRAN DRESCHER in *THE NANNY* (1993–99) and by BETTE MIDLER in *BETTE* (2000–2001).

Through the decades of American filmmaking, one of the most recurring stereotypes—usually more sharply and fully etched than the clichéd representation of conniving Jewish lawyers and materialistic Jewish doctors—had been that of the Hollywood film mogul (or producer or director). One of the chief purveyors of the image—certainly not generally flattering to the real-life models—was Russian-born Gregory Ratoff (1897–1960). Beginning with *What Price Hollywood?* (1932), he was often cast as the heavily accented, manipulative studio chief or conniving producer whose acts of kindness generally had a crass, ulterior motive. He replayed the part in such entries from *Once in a Lifetime* (1932) to *The Great Profile* (1940). In *All About Eve* (1950), he was the financially adept Broadway producer, Max Fabian. Another source of sharply etched Jewish film executives was ROD STEIGER: In *The Big Knife* (1955), based on Clifford Odets's 1949 Broadway play, he was Stanley Hoff, the tyrannical film studio boss. His portrayal was a reputed take-off of Harry Cohn, the Jewish head of Columbia Pictures. Steiger played another such Cohn impersonation in the telefeature, *The Movie Maker* (1967).

Stranger Among Us, A **(aka: *Close to Eden*) (1992)** Hollywood Pictures, color, 111 minutes. **Director:** Sidney Lumet; **Screenplay:** Robert J. Avrech; **Cast:** Melanie Griffith (Emily Eden), Eric Thal (Ariel), John Pankow (Levine), Tracy Pollan (Mara), Lee Richardson (Rebbe), Mia Sara (Leah).

By the time of this production, SIDNEY LUMET had long been one of the most cogent delineators of the Jewish scene on film (including *THE PAWNBROKER*, 1965; *BYE BYE BRAVERMAN*, 1968; *GARBO TALKS*, 1984). Here, his police detection story was set in Brooklyn's Hasidic Jewish community, and his offbeat ambiance paralleled Peter Weir's *Witness* (1985), which used the Amish of Pennsylvania to provide a fresh twist to its own cops-and-culprits story.

Tough New York cop Emily Eden is burned out and is assigned to a lower-profile case, tracking the disappearance (and later murder) of a Hasidic jewelry dealer whose $720,000 in diamonds is missing. Emily goes undercover, moving in with the Jewish group's rebbe (spiritual teacher, rabbi) and his adopted children: Ariel (the future next rebbe) and Leah. As Ariel helps the Christian Emily smooth out her cover, the two experience a growing attraction (although each is involved with another). As the investigation proceeds, it centers on Mara, who knew the dead man.

Putting aside the poor casting choice of Griffith in the lead, *A Stranger Among Us* was too much of an educational seminar on the ways of Hasidic Jews, one that had been presented on screen earlier in *THE CHOSEN* (1981). The elucidation of this little-known (to most filmgoers) religious group occurred as question-and-answer sessions between Emily and Ariel and thus became a plot-stopping device that hampered the movie's pacing. Whenever the movie allowed the customs and interactions of the Hasidics to be natural background material, it became intriguing local color.

Strasberg, Lee (1901–1982) Famous as the founder of the Actors Studio and the proponent of Method Acting, a style that greatly influenced American theater in the mid-twentieth century, Strasberg was also a Broadway actor and director and, late in life, a film actor.

He was born Israel Strassberg in Budzanów, Austria–Hungary (now Buzdanov, Ukraine). Eight years later his family came to New York. By age fifteen he was acting in and directing shows at a settlement house in the LOWER EAST SIDE. While working in a theatrical wig factory, he took acting lessons at the American Laboratory Theater, later becoming involved with the Theatre Guild. He helped to found the Group Theater in the early 1930s and directed for them such vehicles as *Men in White* (1933) and *Johnny Johnson* (1937). After leaving the group, he helmed *All the Living* (1938) and *Clash by Night* (1941). After some unproductive Hollywood years, in 1948 he staged *Skipper Next to God* on Broadway with JOHN GARFIELD, and the next year's *The Big Knife*, also starred Garfield. By then, Strasberg had joined the Actors Studio as its artistic director and later founded the Lee Strasberg Institute for actors and directors.

At age seventy-three, he made his feature-film debut as the sinister Jewish gangster Hyman Roth in *THE GODFATHER, PART II* (1974). He and Ruth Gordon were an aged Jewish couple living in Coney Island and dealing with encroaching gang violence in *BOARDWALK* (1979), the same year that he and GEORGE BURNS were part of *Going in Style*, about elderly men robbing a bank. In the TV movie, *SKOKIE* (1981), starring DANNY KAYE, Strasberg was among the Jewish townsfolk shocked by the arrival of neo-Nazi demonstrators.

Strasberg's first wife Paula was Marilyn Monroe's acting coach, and their daughter, Susan, was a film, stage, and TV actress.

***Street Scene* (1931)** United Artists, b&w, 80 minutes. **Director:** King Vidor; **Screenplay:** Elmer Rice; **Cast:** Sylvia Sidney (Rose Maurrant), William Collier Jr. (Sam Kaplan), Estelle Taylor (Anna Maurrant), Beulah Bondi (Emma Jones), Russell Hopton (Steve Sankey), Max Montor (Abe Kaplan), Anna Konstant (Shirley Kaplan).

Derived from Elmer Rice's Pulitzer Prize-winning Broadway play of 1928, this gritty street drama was set in the steaming Manhattan tenement where a variety of ethnics, including the Jewish left-wing radical Sam Kaplan, live. He is in love with the Irish girl, Rose Maurrant, but her goals are to leave the slums and not be encumbered by marriage. One hot night, a tenant and her lover are killed by an irate husband, another family is evicted, and still others from the building gossip about their neighbors. Kaplan is visited by his sister (Konstant), who urges him to forget about the non-Jewish Rose and to pursue a legal career. Meanwhile, Rose, disgusted by her mean surroundings, moves away.

With its unvarnished cross section of a multiethnic neighborhood, *Street Scene* was powerful fare. If many of the types, in retrospect, seemed caricatures, they were fresh then. When this movie was made, a few years before the revised production code went into effect in Hollywood, mainstream films like this could and did use such epithets as *little Yid* or *kike*. Interestingly, the Jewish-born Sidney was cast as a gentile, while the reverse situation was true of colead Collier Jr.

Streisand, Barbra (1944–) The Streisand persona became a major force of global pop culture for decades. There was no denying her powerful singing voice, but some found her personality (and screen alter ego) too aggressive, her shtick too intrusive, and her need to control situations too intimidating. But then, she was America's leading Jewish-American Princess (later turned matron).

For some, Streisand's professional affectations began when she altered her name from "Barbara" to "Barbra" and insisted on wearing bizarre outfits in her early performance years; yet in other ways, she remained true to her Brooklyn Orthodox Jewish roots: refusing to have her prominent profile reshaped, and demanding that her screen characters generally be openly Jewish women who are committed to their traditions. Then, too, who else but a Streisand would have had the stamina to fight the industry odds and get *YENTL* (1983) made. In this musical and several others of her movies, she explicated the (modern) Jewish woman, long ignored by Hollywood, at various ages, circumstances, and mindsets.

The second child of Emanuel and Diana Streisand, Barbara Joan was born in Brooklyn, New York. While still an infant, her teacher father died; when she was seven her mother remarried, and there would be a stepsister—the future singer Rosalyn Kind.

It was seeing *THE DIARY OF ANNE FRANK* on Broadway that determined the fourteen-year-old Streisand on a show-business career. Club work prompted TV talk-show appearances and an off-Broadway revue (*Another Evening with Harry Stones*, 1961). This led to her being in 1962's *I Can Get It for You Wholesale*, whose leading man (ELLIOTT GOULD) she married in 1963 and by whom she had a son, Jason (who became an actor/filmmaker). Next came *Funny Girl* (1964)—about comedienne/singer FANNY BRICE—and Streisand was now a star on Broadway and in her several album recordings. After making TV specials, she starred in the screen version of *FUNNY GIRL* (1968) and won an Oscar. Following two more Broadway-to-film musicals, she played a zany prostitute opposite GEORGE SEGAL in the comedic *THE OWL AND THE PUSSYCAT* (1970). One of her biggest screen successes was *THE WAY WE WERE* (1973) in which she played the ultimate Jewish girl lusting after the ultimate WASP (Robert Redford).

After years of effort, Streisand's *Yentl* became a reality. She not only produced, directed, and starred in this period vehicle but she also cowrote its screenplay, etc. Such chutzpah upset the boys' club in Hollywood and began the on-going friction between Streisand and the film industry. Thereafter, she directed her own projects: *NUTS* (1987—as an intellectual prostitute), *The Prince of Tides* (1991—as a psychiatrist with the longest fingernails in history), and *The Mirror Has Two Faces* (1996—in which Lauren Bacall played her mother).

In 2000, Streisand, long divorced from Gould and since wed to actor James Brolin, made her farewell concert tour. She had been one of the few entertainers to have won an Oscar, a Tony, an Emmy, and a Grammy. In 2001, she received the American Film Institute's Lifetime Achievement Award.

***Surrender* (1927)** Universal, b&w, 8,249′. **Director:** Edward Sloman; **Screenplay:** Charles Kenyon and Edward J. Montagne; **Cast:** Mary Philbin (Lea Lyon), Ivan Mosjukine (Constantine), Otto Matieson (Joshua), Nigel De Brulier (Rabbi Mendel), Otto Fries (Tarras).

This rare excursion into traditional Jewish life was not set on New York's LOWER EAST SIDE, the usual Hollywood province for such narratives; rather, it took place in Galicia (then a province of Austria, but later a part of southeast Poland and west Ukraine; and the seat of the development of Hasidic Judaism).

Based on Alexander Brody's play *Lea Lyon* (1915), this romantic drama opens in 1914 in a small town near the Russian border. As such, the Jewish inhabitants are victims of raids by both the Austrians and Russians. Rabbi Mendel's daughter meets and is intrigued by Constantine, a Russian Cossack, not knowing his true occupation. When war is declared, the Russians, under Constantine, occupy the town. He demands that Lea submit to him or he will destroy everything. To save her neighbors, she agrees, which greatly impresses the Cossack. He relents on his threats and acknowledges his love of her. Later, the townfolk stone Lea for her attraction to the enemy. By war's end, the rabbi has died in the conflict, while Constantine returns for his sweetheart, Lea.

As in many of the screen GHETTO DRAMAS of the 1910s and 1920s, the narrative ended with a mixed marriage, providing a happy if not always consistent finale. (But such blending of the religions made such film fare more palatable to the general public.)

***Sweet Lorraine* (1987)** Angelika, color, 91 minutes. **Director:** Steve Gomer; **Screenplay:** Michael Zettler and Shelly Altman; **Cast:** Maureen Stapleton (Lillian Garber), Trini Alvarado (Molly), Lee Richardson (Sam, the cook), John Bedford Lloyd (Jack, the handyman), Freddie Roman (Phil Allen), Giancarlo Esposito (Howie).

As New York-area Jews became more affluent in the 1960s and began to vacation on cruises or in the Caribbean, the CATSKILL RESORTS became passé. By the 1980s, many of the once familiar summer hotels had been razed. *Sweet Lorraine* was a tribute to one such dying hostelry. This small, meandering, independent release appeared in the same year as the blockbuster, *DIRTY DANCING*. The latter was set in the 1960s; the former was a contemporary account of a borscht-belt landmark on its last legs.

It is the summer of decisions for middle-aged Lillian Garber, the owner of the Lorraine Hotel in the Catskills. Business is down, costs are up, the establishment needs major repairs and renovations, and she is contemplating an offer made to buy the premises for its valuable property. The season opens with the usual round of daily problems in servicing the guests and with keeping control over the multicultural staff, which includes a Chinese cook. As Lillian pursues her annual romance with the resort's handyman (Lloyd), she watches over her teenaged granddaughter Molly (whose parents have just divorced), who is now working at the resort and discovering the meaning of hard effort.

***Sword in the Desert* (1949)** Universal, b&w, 100 minutes. **Director:** George Sherman; **Screenplay:** Robert Buckner; **Cast:** Dana Andrews (Mike Dillon), Marta Toren (Sabra), Stephen McNally (David Vogel), Jeff Chandler (Kurta), Philip Friend (Lieutenant Ellerton).

Predating the epic *EXODUS* (1960), this well-crafted minor picture had the topical advantage of release when Israel had recently become a state and had been recognized as such by the United Nations. It was the first Hollywood movie to deal with the fight between Jewish Zionist factions and the British in the establishment of the state of Israel. Geared as an action entry—the studio's specialty—this black-and-white picture boasted strong performances, especially by Jewish-American actor CHANDLER.

After World War II, Mike Dillon, the U.S. captain of a freighter, find himself involved with the illegal smuggling of European Jews into Palestine. Kurta is among the Jewish rebel leaders who are prepared to oust the British from their country; Sabra broadcasts propaganda via an underground radio station. Later, the British capture several rebels, but they are freed by fellow resisters.

Very pro-Israeli, this picture was considered "safe" to be made by Hollywood because it was set in a foreign land and, especially, because it was not dealing with the far touchier domestic subject of anti-Semitism in the United States.

***Symphony of Six Million* (1932)** RKO, b&w, 94 minutes. **Director:** Gregory La Cava; **Screenplay:** Bernard Schubert and J. Walter Ruben; **Cast:** Ricardo Cortez (Dr. Felix Klauber), Irene Dunne (Jessica), Anna Appel (Hannah Klauber), Gregory Ratoff (Meyer "Lansman" Klauber), Noel Madison (Magnus Klauber), Lita Chevret (Birdie Klauber).

Fannie Hurst (1889–1968), the purveyor of many melodramatic novels and short stories, had her fingers on the pulse of the New York ghetto when she wrote this screen story. Earlier, her popular writings had provided the basis for such Jewish-themed GHETTO DRAMAS as *HUMORESQUE* (1920) and *THE YOUNGER GENERATION* (1929). Although this domestic drama claimed to reproduce life on the LOWER EAST SIDE authentically, both Cortez and especially Dunne were too acculturated to provide realistic ethnic-flavored performances—which is just what the studio intended by casting them in the parts. (For RKO and filmgoers, it was sufficient that some of the picture's subordinate characters—the parents [Appel and Ratoff] in particular—fit the public's stereotype image of immigrant/working class Jews.)

Within the chronicle, Felix Klauber, through hard study, rises from the Manhattan slums to become a talented physician, happily tending the poor. His brother Magnus manages to convince Felix to become a fancy Park Avenue doctor. Later, thanks to a confrontation with Jessica, his childhood sweetheart, Felix gains a fresh perspective on his roots. He returns to the ghetto with Jessica.

T

***Taxi* (1978–1983)** ABC-TV series, color, 30 minutes. **Cast:** Judd Hirsch (Alex Rieger), Jeff Conaway (Bobby Wheeler: 1978–81), Danny DeVito (Louie De Palma), Marilu Henner (Elaine Nardo), Tony Danza (Tony Banta), Andy Kaufman (Latka Gravas), Christopher Lloyd ("Reverend Jim" Ignatowski: (1979–83), Carol Kane (Simka Gravas: 1981–83).

With the dedication often reserved for other livelihoods, Alex Rieger is extremely serious about his profession; in fact, of all the taxi drivers depicted at the little Sunshine Cab Company in Manhattan, he is the only full-time cabbie. Not much is said or done to reflect Alex's ethnic background, leaving Hirsch's persona to provide the flavor. But when his relatives appear in *Taxi* episodes, they are immediately defined as Jewish types by their demeanor or names or from the viewers' association with the performer portraying the roles: the father, Joe Rieger (Jack Gilford), sister Charlotte (Joan Hackett), ex-wife Phyllis (Louise Lasser), daughter Cathy (Talia Balsam).

Jewish-born Kaufman appeared as garage mechanic Latka Gravas. He was an emigrant from an unidentified Eastern European country, often speaking a strange dialect that confounded others, except his betrothed, Simka, another refugee from their homeland. With her past associations to *HESTER STREET* (1975), *ANNIE HALL* (1977), and similar roles, Kane could easily be assumed to be playing a Jewish woman here.

***Ten Commandments, The* (1923)** Paramount, b&w, with color prologue, 146 minutes. **Director:** Cecil B. DeMille; **Screenplay:** Jeanie MacPherson; **Cast:** *Prologue (Part I):* Theodore Roberts (Moses), Charles de Roche (Ramses), Estelle Taylor (Miriam), Julia Faye (Pharaoh's wife); *Part II:* Richard Dix (John McTavish), Rod La Rocque (Dan McTavish), Leatrice Joy (Mary Leigh), Nita Naldi (Sally Lung), Agnes Ayres (the outcast).

Many biblical-themed movies were devoted to the New Testament and to tales of the Christ, but *The Ten Commandments* was a full-fledged study of Moses, the Hebrew lawgiver who led the people of Israel out of Egypt and eventually into the promised land. Because it was set in such a distant past, focusing on Jewish characters in such a major way was considered a nonthreatening excursion for moviegoers who might be disinterested or worse regarding Jewish-oriented film fare. Making the project even more box-office proof was the use of a contemporary—and far more conventional—love triangle set in present-day San Francisco as the main story.

In this lavish, silent photoplay, DeMille devoted the extended prologue to stories derived from the book of Exodus in the Bible. It followed the cruel treatment of the captive Jews at the hands of the ancient Egyptians, their fleeing the country across the parted waters of the Red Sea, Moses receiving the Ten Commandments on Mount Sinai, and Moses later berating his followers for paying homage to the golden calf. The movie then switched to a modern story/parable set in San Francisco, where two brothers (Dix and La Rocque) competed for the love of Mary Leigh and the repercussions that followed.

So successful was this gargantuan spectacle (especially Part I) that three decades later, DeMille would devote an entire screen saga to the life and times of Moses in *THE TEN COMMANDMENTS* (1956).

***Ten Commandments, The* (1956)** Paramount, color, 219 minutes. **Director:** Cecil B. DeMille; **Screenplay:** Aeneas MacKenzie, Jesse L. Lasky Jr., Jack Gariss, and Fredric M. Frank; **Cast:** Charlton Heston (Moses), Yul Brynner (Ramses), Anne Baxter (Nefretiri), Edward G.

Robinson (Dathan), Yvonne de Carlo (Sephora), Debra Paget (Lilia), John Derek (Joshua), Martha Scott (Yoshabel), Vincent Price (Baka).

Thirty-three years after his triumphant *THE TEN COMMANDMENTS* (1923), DeMille returned to the topic of Moses and the Israelites leaving Egypt many centuries before. This time around, the saga was in sound, color, and wide-screen process. More importantly and unlike his 1923 film, the director devoted the entire narrative to the ancient Hebrews. DeMille learned from *SAMSON AND DELILAH* (1949) that given sufficient big-named actors, pomp, and color, moviegoers would sit through a lengthy excursion about the Jews of a far earlier era.

For many, the new *The Ten Commandments* was much more than a satisfying epic full of exciting special effects (e.g., the parting of the Red Sea) because it continued, reaffirmed, and extended the traditional ethnic saga of the wandering Jew who suffered, proved his worth, and then was rewarded by his God for his piety and endurance. The 1956 *The Ten Commandments* won an Oscar for Best Special Effects and received six Academy Award nominations, including one for Best Picture.

Moses would also be a focal figure in the European coproduced TV movie special *Moses: The Lawgiver* (1975) starring Burt Lancaster. Earlier, the lawgiver (played by Francis X. Bushman) was featured in the historical potpourri *The Story of Mankind* (1957), and later MEL BROOKS would play in his farcical *History of the World—Part I* (1981), while in 1996's *Moses*, Ben Kingsley was the biblical leader.

***thirtysomething* (1987–1991)** ABC-TV series, color, 60 minutes. **Cast:** Ken Olin (Michael Steadman), Mel Harris (Hope Murdoch Steadman), Timothy Busfield (Elliot Weston), Patricia Wettig (Nancy Weston), Melanie Mayron (Melissa Steadman), Polly Draper (Ellyn), Peter Horton (Prof. Gary Shepherd), David Clennon (Miles Drentell: 1989–91).

The angst of the yuppie generation was encapsulated expertly in this series, which was geared to the thirty-plus generation. (On the other hand, some found this show filled with overly pampered, whimpering characters and hardly entertainment.) Part of the ongoing, Philadelphia-set saga focused on the increasingly rocky interfaith marriage between Michael and Hope Steadman (he was Jewish; she was Christian). As in past series (e.g., *BRIDGET LOVES BERNIE*, 1972–73) that dealt with interfaith marriages, a likely time of potential contention was always the year-end holidays and whether to celebrate it as Jews or Christians or as both. If Steadman, the assimilated American, was compliant in early episodes of the show, then he became increasingly perplexed about his role as a Jew following the birth of his two children. Another time of renewed faith for Michael occurred when his father died, prompting Steadman to attend synagogue—for the first time in years—to recite the kaddish on the anniversary of his parent's death.

Contrasting with the anxiety-ridden Steadman was his far more relaxed cousin Melissa, a freelance photographer. She had found a balance between her faith and everyday life as a single modern woman, and when dating a non-Jewish man, religion never became a major issue.

In contrast to past TV series that either ignored the substance of Jewish life or treated it in a comic manner (e.g., *CHICKEN SOUP*, 1989), *thirtysomething* dealt with the sensitive issues in a dramatic vein. It was an indication that, by the late 1980s, Jewish topics on television were no longer a plot-flavoring gimmick but a substantive aspect of the ever-broadening U.S. way of life. (On the other hand, a decade later, in *Once and Again* [1999–2002], by the creators of *thirtysomething*, the Jewishness of the leading female character [played by Sela Ward], a divorced single parent, did not, at least in the show's early seasons, become even a point of discussion for her boyfriend [played by Billy Campbell]—for whatever reason.)

***To Be or Not to Be* (1942)** United Artists, b&w, 99 minutes. **Director:** Ernest Lubitsch; **Screenplay:** Edwin Justus Mayer; **Cast:** Carole Lombard (Maria Tura), Jack Benny (Joseph Tura), Robert Stack (Lt. Stanislav Sobinski), Felix Bressart (Greenberg), Lionel Atwill (Rawitch), Stanley Ridges (Prof. Alexander Siletsky), Sig Rumann (Colonel Ehrhardt).

Released a few months after Pearl Harbor (and not long after the tragic air crash that killed Lombard), this darkly serious comedy was helmed by the German-born Jewish director Lubitsch. It was a heartfelt statement against the persecution of the Jews, geared to raise social and political awareness among moviegoers on this extremely topical matter. Like Charles Chaplin's earlier *THE GREAT DICTATOR* (1940), itself a brilliant parody of Hitler's Third Reich and the first major American movie to tackle the Nazi question full on, the more sophisticated *To Be or Not to Be* also walked a fine line, trying to be satirically funny on a deadly serious subject. For some, the often savage jokes of Lubitsch's fast-paced production were based on such painful reality that many—including non-Jews—were offended by the director's tour de force.

The film is set in 1939 Poland and focuses on a Warsaw theater company headed by Joseph and Maria Tura (BENNY and Lombard). They soon become embroiled in espionage against the invading Nazis and eventually flee the country. Meanwhile, Maria is being pursued by a love-struck young Polish flyer (Stack)—part of the Polish squadron in the British RAF—and this leads everyone into contact with the duplistic Professor Siletsky, a German agent, and the buffoonish but terrorizing Colonel Ehrhardt.

Even with the war raging in Europe, Hollywood, motivated by box-office sales, was still extremely cautious about directly labeling any film characters—especially major ones—as Jewish. Thus, in *To Be or Not to Be*, there was never any clear reference to Benny's Joseph Tura being Jewish; it could only be inferred from Benny's persona (both on- and off-camera). On the other hand, Greenberg, a supporting actor in the troupe was more clearly suggested to be Jewish, that is, by his ethnic surname and features. Then too Greenberg, who would eat no ham, hoped one day to play Shylock in *The Merchant of Venice*, a very Jewish role in the canon of Shakespeare, and it was Greenberg who three times uttered the famous lines ("If you prick us, do we not bleed") from *The Merchant of Venice*, on each occasion adding more of the bard's words from that speech by Shylock as his agitation about the Nazis grew bolder. Interestingly, as would be true in other Hollywood features, the Jewish character was extremely patriotic about his country (not just about the welfare of fellow Jews) and did much to assist non-Jews.

To Be or Not to Be received one Oscar nomination: Best Original Dramatic Score. It would be remade forty-one years later.

***To Be or Not to Be* (1983)** Twentieth Century-Fox, color, 108 minutes. **Director:** Alan Johnson; **Screenplay:** Thomas Meehan and Ronny Graham; **Cast:** Mel Brooks (Frederick Bronski), Anne Bancroft (Anna Bronski), Tim Matheson (Lt. Andre Sobinski), Charles Durning (Colonel Erhardt), José Ferrer (Professor Siletski), Christopher Lloyd (Captain Schultz), James Haake and Scamp (Sasha and Muthi).

Sixteen years after *THE PRODUCERS* (1967) and its wild *Springtime for Hitler* musical within the movie, BROOKS did a more full-bodied satire based on the Führer and his campaign of anti-Semitism. In his remake of 1942's *TO BE OR NOT TO BE*, costarring his real-life wife, Anne Bancroft, the references to Jews were more direct, including the stage worker who wore a yellow star on her clothing, a labeling demanded by the Third Reich.

Although Brooks's Bronski (the new character name for Tura) was not Jewish, in the revised plot, he became the benefactor and savior of a group of fleeing victims and a supporter of the Polish Resistance. Brooks also chose to include gays (another group, like the gypsies, persecuted by the Nazis) in the plot of his remake: Bronski's helper Sasha (Haake) was an overt homosexual. More so than in the Lubitsch classic, a good deal of slapstick in the 1983 edition verged on the overstated.

Charles Durning received an Oscar nomination in the Best Supporting Actor category for his role in the revamped *To Be or Not to Be.*

***Tomorrow the World!* (1944)** United Artists, b&w, 86 minutes. **Director:** Leslie Fenton; **Screenplay:** Ring Lardner Jr. and Leopold Atlas; **Cast:** Fredric March (Mike Frame), Betty Field (Leona Richards), Agnes Moorehead (Jessie Frame), Joan Carroll (Pat Frame), Edit Angold (Frieda), Skippy Homeier (Emil Bruckner).

A year after James Gow and Arnaud D'Usseau's play *Tomorrow the World!* opened on Broadway (for a 500-performance run), it was translated to the screen. Unlike earlier Hollywood features (e.g., *THE GREAT DICTATOR*, 1940; *ESCAPE*, 1940; *TO BE OR NOT TO BE*, 1942), which were among the few to address (in)directly Nazi persecution of Jews in Europe, *Tomorrow the World!* set its drama of anti-Semitism in the U.S. Midwest. It delineated the repercussions that occur when Mike Frame, a college professor who is conducting secret research for the U.S. War Department, agrees to take in his orphaned nephew Emil, whose parents died in a CONCENTRATION CAMP.

When the young boy arrives at Frame's, he proves to be a brainwashed member of the Hitler Youth movement who insists that his dad deserved to die for being an enemy of the Third Reich. Nevertheless, everyone tries to help the cold-hearted boy adapt. These include Frame's young daughter, Pat, and Frame's fiancée, Leona Richards, a Jewish school teacher. Later, Emil has a change of mind about Nazism. He indicates that as a little boy, he was brutalized by the Nazis into conforming to their ways and that he does admire his father.

Although many commentators had trouble accepting Emil's abrupt about-face, the film created an impact and garnered much media attention. It would be a few more years, however, before Hollywood would tackle anti-Semitism on the home front again—this time exhibited not by a foreigner but by American-born characters.

***Torch Song Trilogy* (1988)** New Line, color, 120 minutes. **Director:** Paul Bogart; **Screenplay:** Harvey Fierstein; **Cast:** Anne Bancroft (Ma), Matthew Broderick (Alan), Harvey Fierstein (Arnold Beckoff), Brian Kerwin (Ed), Karen Young (Laurel), Eddie Castrodad (David), Charles Pierce (Bertha Venation).

Just as there had been a very slow transformation within mainstream American films in the direct and full-bodied presentation of Jewish topics—especially in dramas—so the depiction of subjects relating to homosexuality had been sluggish in coming out of the Hollywood closet. But the gay/lesbian field had an "advantage" over Jewish-themed films: Stories dealing with homosexuality had a built-in titillation value because they dealt with nontraditional sexual lifestyles. Then along came FIERSTEIN who in his life style, performance roles, and writings covered both categories.

Torch Song Trilogy was first mounted in its final form off-Broadway in 1982. Much had changed in the years it took for the project to reach the screen, including such gay-themed films as *Silkwood* (1983) and *An Early Frost* (1985—television movie). Thus, by the time *Torch Song Trilogy* was released, it had lost some of its punch, especially as the AIDS epidemic had negated the titillation factor for most of the public.

The narrative runs from 1971 to 1980 (so that the repercussions of AIDS did not have to become part of the drama) as the Jewish, gay Arnold, who performs a drag act in a New York City club, dates a bisexual school teacher named Ed. But Ed is still seeing a woman, so Arnold breaks off the relationship. In 1973, Arnold meets Alan, a model, and they soon are living together. Not long before they are to become foster parents to a troubled teenager (Castrodad), Alan is killed by gay bashers. Later, in 1980, Arnold reencounters Ed, the latter asking for a reconciliation.

The film also explored Arnold's complex relationship with his domineering mother who, although knowing that her son was gay, had never been told of the three men in Arnold's life. Mother's and son's frustrations with each other came to the fore, but eventually the two reach a truce.

Unfortunately, Bancroft—who had played a demanding Jewish mama in *GARBO TALKS* (1984) in which Fierstein had a small role—was too shrill in her one-note performance. That aside, she was a cinema sister to the highly controlling Jewish mama as found in films from *MARJORIE MORNINGSTAR* (1958) to *NEXT STOP, GREENWICH VILLAGE* (1974).

***21 Hours at Munich* (1976)** ABC-TV, color, 100 minutes. **Director:** William A. Graham; **Teleplay:** Edward Hume and Howard Fast; **Cast:** William Holden (Chief of Police Manfred Schreiber), Shirley Knight (Annaliese Graes), Franco Nero (Issa), Richard Basehart (Chancellor Willy Brandt), Anthony Quayle (Gen. Zvi Samir), Else Quecke (Golda Meir).

Based on Serge Groussard's *The Blood of Israel: The Massacre of the Israeli Athletes—The Olympics, 1972* (1975), this telefeature focused on the slaughter of eleven Israeli athletes by Palestinian Arab terrorists who broke into the Olympics compound at Munich. This well-handled drama broached once again the theme of ongoing German guilt over the HOLOCAUST, here emphasized because the action took place in Germany; also, the assassins were seeking retribution against Israel, a state partially founded and populated by victims of the Third Reich. This drama received two Emmy nominations.

A similar premise underlies the 1988 telefeature *The Taking of Flight 847: The Uli Derickson Story*, based on the actual 1985 hijacking. There, the German stewardess (Lindsay Wagner) refuses the captors' demand that she study each passenger's passport to pick out Jewish names and to separate them from the others aboard. Knowing her country's past history, she cannot make such deadly choices in the present.

A decade later, *Sword of Gideon* aired on HBO cable. The docudrama focuses on the efforts by the Mossad, the Israeli intelligence organization, to destroy the terrorists responsible for the 1972 Munich massacre. ROD STEIGER plays the Israeli army officer who recruits a team headed by an Israeli army officer (Steven Bauer). Colleen Dewhurst appears as Israel's prime minister, Golda Meir.

Still later came the Oscar-winning documentary *One Day in September* (1999), a perusal of that tragic 1972 event. Narrated by Michael Douglas, the film included an interview with Jamal al Gashey, the only member of the Palestinian Black September terrorist group then still living.

***Twist of Fate* (1989)** NBC-TV, color, 120 minutes. **Director:** Ian Sharp; **Teleplay:** William Bast and Paul Huson; **Cast:** Ben Cross (Ben Grossman), John Glover (Max Brodsky), Bruce Greenwood (Daniel Grossman [Helmut von Schraeder]), Sarah Jessica Parker (Miriam), Ian Richardson (Dr. Franz Schlossberg), Veronica Hamel (Deborah).

This ironic story concerned an ex-Nazi posing as a Jew to escape detection after World War II. (The topic had been dealt with earlier, and would again later, in episodes of TV series.) Here, von Schraeder has changed his look with plastic surgery and through happenstance becomes a high-ranking Israeli officer. Only later when his son (Cross) is researching Nazi war criminals does he discover his father's duplicity. Meanwhile, neo-Nazis based in South America blackmail von Schraeder, leading the man, who had grown to love his adopted country, into a dangerous plan.

A variation of this disguised ex-Nazi theme appeared the same year in the theatrical release *The Music Box*. In that disappointing entry, directed by Constantin Costa-Gavras, criminal lawyer Jessica Lange defended in court her Hungarian immigrant father (Armin Mueller-Stahl) who was accused of World War II atrocities and was facing deportation.

V

***Victory at Entebbe* (1976)** ABC-TV, color, 150 minutes. **Director:** Marvin J. Chomsky; **Teleplay:** Ernest Kinoy; **Cast:** Helmut Berger (German terrorist), Theodore Bikel (Yakov Shlomo), Linda Blair (Chana Vilnofsky), Kirk Douglas (Hershel Vilnofsky), Richard Dreyfuss (Col. Yonatan Netanyahu), Julius Harris (President Idi Amin), Helen Hayes (Mrs. Wise), Anthony Hopkins (Yitzhak Rabin), Burt Lancaster (Shimon Peres), Elizabeth Taylor (Edra Vilnofsky),

On July 4, 1976, a Tel Aviv-to-Paris flight was hijacked and forced to land in Uganda at Entebbe. The Jewish passengers were kept hostage in demand for the release of Israeli-held terrorists. The Israeli government dispatched a commando unit to save the captured.

Despite its noble intention, this telefilm smacked of the celluloid thriller formula, with dramatic cameos by a parade of high-profile actors.

Rushed into release to beat the competition, this was the first of three films at the time that dealt with the historic event. The others were the telefeature *RAID ON ENTEBBE* (1977) and the Israel-made feature film *Mivtsa Yonatan* (1977).

Kinoy was Emmy nominated for his teleplay.

W

***Wall, The* (1982)** CBS-TV, color, 180 minutes. **Director:** Robert Markowitz; **Teleplay:** Millard Lampell; **Cast:** Tom Conti (Dolek Berso), Lisa Eichhorn (Rachel Apt), Gerald Hiken (Fischel Shpunt), Rachel Roberts (Regina Kowalska), Philip Sterling (Reb Mazur), Eli Wallach (Mauritz Apt), Rosanna Arquette (Halinka Apt).

Continuing the momentum generated by such TV miniseries as *HOLOCAUST* (1978) and *MASADA* (1982), *The Wall* recounted the horrors inflicted on Warsaw's Jewish community by the Nazi regime. It narrowed in on the 1943 uprising in the Warsaw ghetto as its inhabitants valiantly fought off extermination. Based on the 1950 John Hersey novel and the 1960 Broadway adaptation, this made-for-television movie won the George Foster Peabody Award for distinguished TV fare.

***Wallenberg: A Hero's Story* (1985)** NBC-TV, color, 200 minutes. **Director:** Lamont Johnson; **Teleplay:** Gerald Green; **Cast:** Richard Chamberlain (Raoul Wallenberg), Alice Krige (Baroness Lisl Kemenyu), Kenneth Colley (Col. Adolf Eichmann), Melanie Mayron (Sonja Kahn), Stuart Wilson (Baron Gabor Kemeny).

In 1944 Budapest, the Swedish diplomat Raoul Wallenberg (1912–?) helped thousands of Jews to escape death by issuing them Swedish passports, thus bamboozling the Nazi regime. In 1945, he was imprisoned by the Soviets. Later, Russian officials insisted that Wallenberg died in prison in 1947, but his fate remained a mystery. The well-received production received five Emmys and five other Emmy nominations, as well as the Christopher Award as one of 1985's Outstanding Television Movies.

What gave this production broad appeal—as would the later *SCHINDLER'S LIST* (1993)—was having the lead character *not* be a member of the minority group being persecuted. It allowed a great number of viewers to relate to the horrific situation being detailed. Then, too, having the well-liked Chamberlain (TV's *Dr. Kildare* [1961–66]) in the key assignment also helped.

***Way We Were, The* (1973)** Columbia, color, 118 minutes. **Director:** Sydney Pollack; **Screenplay:** Arthur Laurents; **Cast:** Barbra Streisand (Katie Morosky), Robert Redford (Hubbell Gardiner), Bradford Dillman (J. J.), Lois Chiles (Carol Ann), Patrick O'Neal (George Bissinger), Viveca Lindfors (Paula Reisner).

STREISAND shone in one of her more restrained performances. Here, she was Katie Morosky, the outspoken Jewish political activist who weds and divorces the man of her dreams—the ultimate WASP, Hubbell Gardiner, a handsome aristocrat who writes a good book but then sells out his integrity to Hollywood and television. The couple first meet in college in the late 1930s, and the narrative follows them up until their accidental brief reunion years later.

Several mainstream films had already dealt with Jewish men seeking the ultimate gentile woman (e.g., *THE HEARTBREAK KID*, 1972; PORTNOY'S COMPLAINT, 1972); the fantasy is reversed in this lushly romantic drama. It presents Katie as a hard-working, bright Jewish woman who is strongly attracted to socialist causes. Individualistic, perceptive, and aggressive, she has a near-fatal flaw in her attraction to Gardiner, a self-content playboy: The two are such opposites that they are drawn to one another, and just as the antiheroes of WOODY ALLEN's movies discover, such matches do not last.

With its political overtones, *The Way We Were* devoted a narrative section to Katie's involvement in combating the communist witch hunt of late 1940s Hollywood. This segment suggested once again that many Jewish intellectuals were victims of that purge.

The Way We Were earned more than $30 million in domestic distribution and won two Academy Awards, including one for Best Song ("The Way We Were").

***Welcome Back, Kotter* (1975–1979)** ABC-TV series, color, 30 minutes. **Cast:** Gabriel Kaplan (Gabe Kotter), Marcia Strassman (Julie Kotter), John Travolta (Vinnie Barbarino), Robert Hegyes (Juan Luis Pedro Phillipo de Huevos Epstein), Lawrence-Hilton Jacobs (Freddie "Boom Boom" Washington), Ron Palillo (Arnold Horshack), John Sylvester White (Mr. Michael Woodman).

Now remembered mostly as the springboard for Travolta's first burst of fame, the comedy series was conceived as a showcase for nightclub comedian Kaplan who plays the Brooklyn-born teacher who returns to his inner-city high school to mold a group of remedial students. These problem pupils include the Puerto Rican-Jewish student, Juan Epstein.

As the battle of wills begins between Kotter and his "sweathogs," his tactic is to utilize hipness to win over the troublesome, if humorous, misfits and to prod them with practical advice to prepare for adulthood. Unlike the ethnically mixed Epstein, Kotter and his wife Julie are only nominal Jews. On another level, Kotter is a stereotype carryover of the traditional Jewish scholar who helps others find their way in life and has a patient gentile wife waiting for him at home.

westerns—feature films Although one does not immediately associate Jewish individuals with the Old West, Hollywood occasionally employed ethnic types, generally for the incongruity of the situation, often pointing up ethnic discrimination in the bargain.

One of the first recorded examples of the Jew and the cowpoke blending together occurs in *The Yiddisher Cowboy*, a Bison Films silent movie short of 1909; another was *Tough Guy Levi* (1912). In Hoot Gibson's *The Rawhide Kid* (1928), a silent western, the hero comes to the rescue of a newly arrived clothes peddler and his daughter. He not only protects them from the intolerant townsfolk, but he soon is romancing the young woman. *Cimarron* (1931), based on the Edna Ferber novel (1930), features a Jewish peddler-turned-store-owner who remains loyal to the heroine through the decades. (This characterization would be repeated in the 1960 remake of *Cimarron*.) In *THE GOLDEN WEST* (1932), the Jewish figure is no longer a minor character but proves to be of great help to the hero in the Old West.

Throughout the 1930s and early 1940s, character actor Max Davidson (1875–1950), who specialized in playing little old Jewish men, appeared in several westerns, including *Law Beyond the Range* (1935), *Rogue of the Range* (1936), and *Renfrew of the Royal Mounted* (1937). Sometimes, he was cast as a wandering peddler, and frequently he was treated benevolently by the heroic cowboy lead. (In the 1951 *Gold Raiders*, a western starring George O'Brien, the Three Stooges were along for the plot ride as ethnic peddlers who helped the hero save the day.)

A far more comical approach to the Old West is MEL BROOKS's satirical *BLAZING SADDLES* (1974), which features a Native-American chief who spouts Yiddish and looks kindly on the arriving African-American settlers. More serious but still amusing is *THE FRISCO KID* (1979), set in the 1850s and dealing with a new-to-America Polish rabbi (Gene Wilder) who heads for San Francisco accompanied by a cowpoke (Harrison Ford). In the animated feature, *An American Tail: Fievel Goes West* (1991), a sequel to *AN AMERICAN TAIL* (1986), the Jewish Russian immigrant mice (the Mousekewitzes) head across country in the 1880s where Fievel seeks to become a famous lawman and instead becomes involved with a dance-hall hostess. (The theme of the Mousekwitz clan in the Old West was continued in the 1992–93 animated TV children's series *Fievel's Animated Tails*.)

Martial arts/action hero Jackie Chan gave the nineteenth-century West a new spin in his successful *Shanghai Noon* (2000). As a member of the Imperial Guard to the emperor of China, he travels to Nevada to rescue a kidnapped princess (Lucy Liu). In the ensuing comical misadventures, he teams with a minor bank robber (Owen Wilson). Amid the Chan gymnastics, he becomes involved with several onlookers, including Jewish folk. (The movie was so popular it led to a sequel: 2002's *Shanghai Knights*.)

***What's Cooking?* (2000)** Trimark, color, 100 minutes. **Director:** Gurinder Chadha; **Screenplay:** Chadha and Paul Mayeda Berges; **Cast:** Joan Chen (Trinh Nguyen), Julianna Margulies (Carla), Mercedes Ruehl (Elizabeth Avila), Kyra Sedgwick (Rachel Seelig), Alfre Woodard (Audrey Williams), Maury Chaykin (Herb Seelig), Lainie Kazan (Ruth Seelig), Estelle Harris (Aunt Bea).

This gem of an independent feature traced the lives of four ethnic (African-American, Asian-American, Hispanic, and Jewish) families in Los Angeles at Thanksgiving time. In the Jewish household, Herb and Ruth Seelig put on a brave face as their independent daughter (Sedgwick) brings home her lover (Margulies). The dominating Ruth is heartbroken about her offspring's lifestyle choice. Her husband Herb's reaction ranges from anger to perplexity to denial as he helps his wife prepare the holiday feast and deals with their assorted dinner guests.

Although the stereotypes of the all-knowing, all-controlling Jewish mother (KAZAN) and of the lesbian couple added nothing new to such images, the ambiance of this middle-class household rang true.

***Where's Poppa?* (1970)** United Artists, color, 85 minutes. **Director:** Carl Reiner; **Screenplay:** Robert Klane; **Cast:** George Segal (Gordon Hocheiser), Ruth Gordon (Mrs. Hocheiser), Trish Van Devere (Louisa Callan), Ron Leibman (Sidney Hocheiser), Rae Allen (Gladys Hocheiser).

Perhaps Mrs. Hocheiser of *Where's Poppa?* was the ultimate Jewish mother as portrayed on the screen. But her power

Julianna Margulies, Lainie Kazan, and Kyra Sedgwick in a domestic moment from *What's Cooking?* (2000). (ECHO BOOK SHOP)

over, and ruination of, her two adult sons was so mind boggling that it could only be presented (1) as a comedy and (2) by having the parent be so senile that viewers would be more forgiving of this meddler. As directed by REINER, *Where's Poppa?* converted Klane's 1970 novel into a nonstop exercise into weird humor and outrageously tasteless jokes.

In Manhattan, Gordon Hocheiser, a Jewish lawyer with a modest practice, cares for his aged, widowed mom. Now in his thirties, he remains a bachelor because she chases away his girlfriends. When the parent nearly ruins Gordon's romance with a nurse (Van Devere), he does the unthinkable—the distraught man puts her in a nursing home and speeds away.

Whether exaggeration or heightened reality, *Where's Poppa?* presented a celluloid monster, one who thought nothing of pulling down her son's pants in front of company to kiss his tush or to discuss her boy's private parts over dinner with his visiting girlfriend. As played by Gordon, she was a mixture of seeming senility, pseudo-sweetness, and bursts of domination through guilt.

Wilder, Gene (1933–) At his peak, there were few funnier men on screen than curly haired, sad-eyed Wilder. Whenever this stone-faced, uptight individual dissolved into hysterics on camera, the results were hilarious. Sometimes, his characters were quite ethnic, as, for example, his skittish accountant in *THE PRODUCERS* (1967) or his Polish rabbi in the 1850 West in *THE FRISCO KID* (1979).

Born Jerome Silberman in Milwaukee, Wisconsin, his parents sent him to a Los Angeles military academy for a time, where he was subjected to anti-Semitism. After college graduation in 1955 and then studying at England's Old Vic Theater School, he spent his military service working in the neuropsychiatry ward at a Pennsylvania hospital.

He made his off-Broadway debut (*Roots*) in 1961 and bowed that same year on Broadway (*The Complaisant Lover*). By now, he was called Gene Wilder. He appeared occasionally in episode TV (e.g., *The Defenders*) and made his first film (*Bonnie and Clyde*) in 1967.

When Wilder was on Broadway in *Mother Courage and Her Children* (1963), its star, Anne Bancroft, introduced him to her husband, MEL BROOKS, who promised to use Gene in a film one day, which happened with *The Producers*. After less successful fare such as *Willy Wonka and the Chocolate Factory* (1971), Wilder reteamed with Brooks for the popular *BLAZING SADDLES* (1974). For Brooks's *Young Frankenstein* (1974), Wilder cowrote the parody. He then turned to writing/directing his own satires, including *The Adventures of Sherlock Holmes' Smarter Brother* (1975).

Wilder began an inspired screen partnership with hip African-American screen comedian Richard Pryor; the first of four (*SILVER STREAK*, 1976) was their best. Another movie teaming had different results: In 1982 he and former *Saturday Night Live* TV star Gilda Radner made the comedy *Hanky Panky*. They wed in 1984 and paired in two other pictures before she died of cancer in 1989.

In the 1990s, Wilder starred in a mild TV sitcom, *SOMETHING WILDER* (1994–95), acted in Neil Simon's *Laughter on the 23rd Floor* (1996) on the London stage, and later wrote and starred in a TV movie (*Murder in a Small Town*, 1999), which led to a sequel. Meanwhile, that year he was diagnosed with non-Hodgkin's lymphoma and underwent cancer treatment. In mid-2001, Wilder returned to the American stage for the first time in thirty-five years to costar with Bob Dishy and Carol Kane in *Don't Make Me Laugh* in summer theater in Connecticut.

***Winds of War, The* (1983)** ABC-TV miniseries, color, 15 hours and 43 minutes. **Director:** Dan Curtis; **Teleplay:** Herman Wouk; **Cast:** Robert Mitchum (Victor "Pug" Henry), Ali MacGraw (Natalie Jastrow), Jan-Michael Vincent (Byron Henry), John Houseman (Aaron Jastrow), Polly Bergen (Rhoda Henry), Lisa Eilbacher (Madeline Henry), David Dukes (Leslie Stole), Ralph Bellamy (President Franklin D. Roosevelt), Victoria Tennant (Pamela Tudsbury).

In the years (1939–41) preceding the U.S. entry into World War II, naval captain Victor "Pug" Henry advises President Roosevelt and other world leaders on military issues and potential repercussions of the expansion by Nazi Germany and imperial Japan. Meanwhile, Pug's son, Byron, weds Natalie Jastrow, a Jewish graduate student, while Pug, married unhappily to Rhoda, has a liaison with a British journalist, Pamela Tudsbury.

Based on Wouk's 1971 sprawling novel and made at a cost of $40 million, *The Winds of Wars* was television's most watched event up to that time, seen by 140 million viewers. This overlong drama was nominated for 13 Emmy Awards and won two.

Because *The Winds of Wars* was such a commercial gamble, the soap-opera elements within the already bloated drama were expanded to offset some of the grimness of the history-drenched plot. As the narrative whirled through history, familiar figures passed by, while the focus remained on

Mitchum and Vincent's characters, even at the expense of the drama involving the plight of the Jewish victims of the Third Reich. Tying together the elements of the narrative involving the Jewish characters was the Jastrow family, headed by Aaron, a famed scholar. He was an expatriate American based in Sienna, Italy, who only belatedly realized that the plight of Eastern European Jews would be visited on those in the West as well.

Although not having the impact of *HOLOCAUST* (1978), *The Winds of War* was so successful that it led to the eighteen-hour *War and Remembrance* (1988) and the twelve-hour *War and Remembrance: The Final Chapter* (1989), both TV miniseries based on further writings by Wouk. In these two gargantuan follow-ups, the HOLOCAUST was depicted in even bleaker terms both as to its victims and to those world leaders who looked the other way as Hitler carried out his genocide policy. By the chronicle's conclusion, the viewer had witnessed many examples of the horrors of the Holocaust. (To draw U.S. TV viewers into this essentially depressing chronicle, there was a reflection in the chronicles of the danger during World War II to U.S. citizens, whose passports did not protect them from the Nazi onslaught.)

Overwhelming in scope and length, this miniseries trilogy still lacked the overall power of the later *SCHINDLER'S LIST* (1993).

Winters, Shelley (1922–) From svelte ingénue to blowsy grandmothers, this Academy Award-winning actress played a wide variety of parts on stage, film, and TV during her lengthy career. It was not until her postleading-lady days that she began to portray dowdy, sometimes loud-mouthed Jewish types in *THE DIARY OF ANNE FRANK* (1959), *The Poseidon Adventure* (1972), *OVER THE BROOKLYN BRIDGE* (1984), and the like. On Broadway, she was the mother of the MARX BROTHERS in the unsuccessful musical *Minnie's Boys* (1970).

She was born Shirley Schrift in St. Louis, Missouri, and the family moved to Brooklyn a few years thereafter, but she quit high school to become a garment industry model. After studying acting at the New Theater School, she was on Broadway in the operetta *Rosalinda* (1942). Brought to Hollywood, she had many tiny parts before she made her mark in *A Double Life* (1947). Thereafter, Winters played on-screen victims (e.g., *A Place in the Sun* [1951], for which she was Oscar nominated), sexpots (e.g., *Frenchie*, 1951), and very dramatic roles in 1955's *The Big Knife* and *The Night of the Hunter*. When not doing Broadway shows (e.g., *A Hatful of Rain*, 1955) or TV, she returned to movies, winning Best Supporting Actress Academy Awards for 1959's *The Diary of Anne Frank* and *A Patch of Blue* (1965).

As the decades passed, Shelley grew physically larger but remained inordinately active professionally. She wrote a trio of short plays (*One-Night Stands of a Noisy Passenger*, 1970) and two autobiographies (1980 and 1989), taught at the Actors Studio in Los Angeles, and continued filmmaking. On TV, she played the recurring role of Roseanne's grandmother on *Roseanne* from 1991–97. Later film roles included *Raging Angels* (1995), *Portrait of a Lady* (1996), and *Gideon* (1999).

Wiseman, Joseph (1918–) Perhaps best known for playing the title role of the sinister mastermind villain confronting James Bond in *Dr. No* (1963), Wiseman played many other on-camera villains, using his natural severe look to advantage, including the drug-hyped bad guy in *Detective Story* (1951), a prisoner in *Les Miserables* (1952), a vengeful pioneer in *The Unforgiven* (1960), and Mafia leaders in both *Stiletto* (1969) and *The Valachi Papers* (1972). He was also frequently on screen as a Jewish character: *BYE BYE BRAVERMAN* (1968—as Felix Ottensteen), *THE APPRENTICESHIP OF DUDDY KRAVITZ* (1974—as Uncle Benjy), *QB VII* (1974—the TV miniseries as Morris Cady), *The Betsy* (1978—as Jake Weinstein), and *MASADA* (1981—the TV miniseries, as Jereahmeel). In the TV series *Crime Story* (1986–88), he was crime lord Manny Weisbord.

Born in Montreal, Canada, Wiseman moved to New York City when he was a child. He made his Manhattan stage debut in *Abe Lincoln in Illinois* (1938) and after appearing to note on Broadway in *Detective Story* (1949), made his movie bow in *With These Hands* (1950) as an Italian union enthusiast. After a long career in films and TV, he was back on the New York stage in *Red Scared* (1994) playing an aged Bolshevik.

***Woman Called Golda, A* (1982)** Syndicated TV, color, 200 minutes. **Director:** Alan Gibson; **Teleplay:** Harold Gast and Steven Gethers; **Cast:** Ingrid Bergman (Golda Meir), Ned Beatty (Sen. John Durward), Franklin Cover (Hubert Humphrey), Judy Davis (Golda Meir—as a young woman), Anne Jackson (Lou Kaddar/narrator), Robert Loggia (Anwar Sadat), Leonard Nimoy (Morris Meyerson).

With a rising interest in Zionism and the history of Israel, this well-crafted TV movie focused on the extraordinary life of Golda Meir (1898–1978) who was born in the Ukraine, immigrated to the United States in 1907, and relocated to Palestine in 1921. After Israel's independence in the late 1940s, this patriot served in cabinet posts before being elected as the nation's prime minister. (She resigned from her position in 1974 as a result of criticism for her country's losses in Israel's war with Arab nations in 1973.) The chronicle ends with Meir's historic meeting with Egypt's president Anwar Sadat in 1977.

This two-part made-for-television feature was shot entirely in Israel and was the final screen work of Bergman who was then dying of cancer. The actress received an Emmy posthumously for her performance, and the production received six additional Emmy nominations.

As a human interest story and because of the subject's ties to the United States. *A Woman Called Golda* had greater interest for general TV viewers than might have been anticipated. The biography's appeal was enhanced by featuring Swedish-born Bergman in the lead.

Other actresses who played Golda Meir on screen included Else Quecke in the 1976 TV movie *21 HOURS AT MUNICH* and Colleen Dewhurst in the international coproduction *Sword of Gideon* (1986), both dealing with the murder of Israeli athletes at the 1972 Olympics in Germany.

Y

Yellow Passport, The **(aka: *The Badge of Shame*) (1916)** World Film, b&w, 5 reels. **Director:** Edwin August; **Screenplay:** Frances Marion and Edwin August; **Cast:** Clara Kimball Young (Sonia Sokoloff), Edwin August (Adolph Rosenheimer), John Sainpolis (Fedia), Alec B. Francis (Myron Abram), John Boyle (Carl Rosenheimer).

In retrospect, this melodrama was a reminder that anti-Semitism did not originate in Nazi Germany but had occurred through many centuries and around the world. As this silent photoplay depicted, in early twentieth-century czarist Russia, the periodic pogroms terrorized and/or exterminated countless Jews. At the time of its release, this movie with its Russian locale had an exotic appeal to some filmgoers. For others (i.e., immigrant audiences), it was a reminder of why they had abandoned their homeland.

In Russia, Sonia Sokoloff, the daughter of a well-to-do Jewish family, is studying to become a concert singer. A police spy (Sainpolis) nearly rapes the young woman and later incites an anti-Semitic raid on the household. Her parents are killed, and Sonia can continue her studies only if she agrees to a yellow passport, a document reserved for prostitutes. Later, she relocates to America and becomes engaged to the son (August) of an opera impresario (Boyle). The romance is nearly ruined when it is thought that Sonia had actually warranted a yellow passport for being a fallen woman.

Although not officially derived from the 1914 Broadway play, *THE YELLOW TICKET*, there were great similarities between the two. The stage drama would be officially translated into a film in 1918.

Yellow Ticket, The **(1918)** Pathé, b&w, 55 minutes. **Director:** William Park; **Screenplay:** Tom Cushing; **Cast:** Fannie Ward (Anna Mirrel), Milton Sills (Julian Rolfe), Warner Oland (Baron Andrey), Armand Kaliz (Count Rostov), J. H. Gilmour (U.S. Consul Seaton).

In Michael Morton's shocking Broadway drama, *The Yellow Ticket* (1914), the heroine had to purchase a "yellow ticket"—the only passport allowed to Jewish women in Russia—so that she could visit her imprisoned father in St. Petersburg. Once there, she found him dead and assumed another identity to avoid having to renew her special passport monthly with the brutal police. Thereafter, she is subjected to the persistent advances of the lecherous baron, a member of the elite secret police. To avoid submitting to him, she kills him. Thankfully, an American comes to her rescue.

As a silent photoplay, *The Yellow Ticket* was released in 1918 starring Ward who enjoyed appearing in controversial vehicles. Although the movie attacked anti-Semitism, the setting, as in the play, was abroad, which distanced audiences from its subject matter with the hope of making it more palatable for those who were not pro-Jewish.

Before *The Yellow Ticket* was directly adapted to the screen, there was an "unofficial" variation of the Broadway play in *THE YELLOW PASSPORT* (1916). In 1928, a Russian-made silent version of *The Yellow Ticket*, featuring Anna Sten, reached New York. Three years thereafter, Fox Films remade the property.

Yellow Ticket, The **(1931)** Fox, b&w, 78 minutes. **Director:** Raoul Walsh; **Screenplay:** Jules Furthman; **Cast:** Elissa Landi (Marya Kalish), Lionel Barrymore (Baron Igor Andreef), Laurence Olivier (Julian Rolfe), Walter Byron (Count Nikolai), Sarah Padden (Mother Kalish), Boris Karloff (orderly).

Seventeen years after the Broadway original, the second American adaptation of *The Yellow Ticket* was released. The already creaky vehicle had the benefit of sound, as well as a cast that included Landi as the young Russian Jewess who, in 1913, obtains the dreaded special passport that will allow her to visit her incarcerated father. Once tainted by the "yellow ticket" it will, as she is told, follow her to the grave. Handling the role of the lusting baron was Lionel Barrymore, whose brother John starred in the Broadway original.

Ironically, the new screen version was made at Fox Films, the only non-Jewish-run major studio in Hollywood. It vividly depicted the persecution of Jews in Russia and how, within the confines of their squalid ghettos, they retained their pride and love of learning, no matter the obstacles. Also to be noted, in contrast to so many movies that pictured passive Jews, the heroine of *The Yellow Ticket* was a woman of action who did not blithely accept her fate as the baron's pawn.

***Yentl* (1983)** Metro-Goldwyn-Mayer/United Artists, color, 134 minutes. **Director:** Barbra Streisand; **Screenplay:** Streisand and Jack Rosenthal; **Cast:** Barbra Streisand (Yentl), Mandy Patinkin (Avigdor), Amy Irving (Hadass), Nehemiah Persoff (Papa), Steven Hill (Reb Alter Viskower), Allan Corduner (Shimmele).

More than a decade after the release of *FIDDLER ON THE ROOF* (1971), STREISAND's *Yentl* reached the screen. Like *Fiddler*, *Yentl* was a musical and dealt with a bygone era of Jewish life—that of the shtetl in early twentieth-century Russia where segregated communities of Jewish peasants, always the potential target of a pogrom, eked out their living. Unlike *Fiddler*, *Yentl* was not a hugely popular release beyond the coterie of Streisand fans and enthusiasts of Jewish culture. Many found fault with Streisand's expanded adaptation of Isaac Bashevis Singer's (1904–91) short story "Yentl the Yeshiva Boy." Not only, it was argued, had she altered the time period of the story, but she had also diverted the simplicity of the tale, which revolved around questions and contradictions of the human soul. Then too, Streisand's ending for the story (i.e., coming to America) was not in Singer's original.

Yentl, as redefined by feminist Streisand, concerns the conflict of a young woman who defies tradition to become a Talmudic scholar (by pretending to be a man named Anshel). In addition, she rejects the one (Patinkin) she loves because he expects her, once married, to become a conventional wife. He returns to his first love (Irving), and the independent-minded Yentl sails for America, singing of her dreams for life in the new land.

Yentl grossed more than $30 million in domestic distribution. It won an Academy Award for Best Original Score. It was Oscar nominated for Best Song ("Papa Can You Hear Me" and "The Way He Makes Me Feel") and for Best Art Direction–Set Decoration, as well as for Best Supporting Actress (Irving).

Yiddish films Most of the early Yiddish movies were produced in Eastern Europe. Yet, one of the first, *Joseph in Egypt* (1913), was produced in Italy and—that being the silent era of moviemaking where title cards were used to convey story line—then translated into Yiddish for consumption in the United States. Later, several Yiddish movies were made in Poland—especially by Joseph Green—where it was less expensive to produce such ventures.

With the advent of talkies, a procession of Yiddish-language films was most inexpensively (and often rather crudely) mounted. (Sometimes the film was a resplicing of an older picture or the joining together of specialty act segments from earlier screen works.) These productions included *Yiddishe Mama* (1930), *Mazel Tov* (1932), *The Wandering Jew* (1933), *What a Mother in Law!* (1934), *Yidl Mitn Fidl (Yiddle with His Fiddle!)* (1936), *Tevye* (1939), and *Mazel Tov Yidden* (1941).

World War II and the HOLOCAUST almost put an end to the production of Yiddish-language movies. Thereafter, in the late 1940s, when Israel became an independent nation and adopted Hebrew as its official language, interest in Yiddish movies declined still further. Among the few released in 1950 were *Catskill Honeymoon; God, Man and Devil;* and *Monticello, Here We Come!* (the last being a compilation made up largely of 1930s short subjects).

Yiddish theater In the latter part of the nineteenth century in eastern Europe, a Yiddish-theater culture flourished, supported by the entertainment-culture-starved Jewish population of the various countries. The plays were spoken in Yiddish (i.e., a combination of Middle High German, Hebrew, and other languages including Slavic) and, if written down, utilized the Hebrew alphabet.

As the anti-Jew pogroms within czarist Russia accelerated during the late nineteenth and early twentieth centuries, the flow of immigrants to America increased. By the early 1900s noted Yiddish actors were visiting the United States to tour the larger urban centers (especially New York City) with their repertoire of dramas and comedies.

By the 1920s, a flourishing concentration of Yiddish theaters existed on New York's LOWER EAST SIDE, especially on Second Avenue. Among the stars closely associated with the Yiddish theater were Jacob Adler, Joseph Buloff, Joseph Kessler, Maurice Schwartz, Rudolph Schildkraut, Menashe Skulnik, and Boris Thomashefsky. They often served as actor/managers of their own stock companies. Stars in this specialized field often toured with their tailor-made Yiddish-language productions to other parts of the United States, South America, and Europe. Many of the field's more noteworthy names also appeared in YIDDISH FILMS, several of which were produced in Europe. (After the advent of talkies and, later, especially during World War II, some were produced in the United States.)

Several of the new-generation performers in Yiddish theater—many of whom who had been born in the United States or had come to America as children—moved to mainstream theater and Hollywood films. They included PAUL MUNI, MOLLY PICON, EDWARD G. ROBINSON, and Joseph Schildkraut. Picon in particular, would always devote much of her creative output to Yiddish theater.

By the 1930s, the flow of emigrants from eastern Europe had greatly diminished. Older generations of Jews in the United States were moving increasingly from the urban ghettos, and those who remained were dying off. These factors led to the fading of Yiddish theaters in the United States. This situation was accelerated by the acculturated new generations who neither spoke nor could read Yiddish and wanted their entertainment performed in English.

You'll Never Get Rich See *PHIL SILVERS SHOW, THE.*

***Younger Generation, The* (1929)** Columbia, b&w, 75 minutes. **Director:** Frank Capra; **Screenplay:** Sonya Levien; **Cast:** Jean Hersholt (Julius Goldfish), Lina Basquette (Birdie Goldfish), Ricardo Cortez (Morris Goldfish), Rosa Rosanova (Tilda Goldfish), Rex Lease (Eddie Lesser).

Novelist, short-story writer, and playwright Fannie Hurst had created many GHETTO DRAMAS, inspiring such films as *HUMORESQUE* (1920) and *SYMPHONY OF SIX MILLION* (1932). In 1927, she wrote the Broadway play *It Is to Laugh*. Two years later, it became a part-talkie feature. With its overwrought plot, it melodramatically tried to prove the thesis that Old World values were better than those of assimilation. Hurst's argument also reasoned that it was better to live in the old neighborhood (regardless of whether or not it was a wretched slum on New York's LOWER EAST SIDE) than to progress uptown where values, traditions, and morality would likely be lost. In Hurst's mind, there was obviously no middle ground.

Julius Goldfish, a Jewish emigrant from Europe, lives on Delancey Street with his family and is a pushcart pot peddler. Although he is not overly ambitious, his wife Tilda hopes the best for their children, especially Morris. Years pass, and the son becomes a successful antique dealer and moves his family uptown to his chic apartment. They are ill at ease there, and Morris is embarrassed by their Old World ways that conflict with his desire to be a fully acculturated American. Eventually, Morris rejects his sister Birdie, and Julius, disgusted with his too-refined son, dies. His widow, accompanied by Birdie, returns to the old neighborhood, while the contrite Morris is left to his uptown friends.

As the Depression and the approaching World War II gave Americans new concerns and new lifestyles, such ghetto dramas as *The Younger Generation* would be relegated to the dust heap.

***Young Lions, The* (1958)** Twentieth Century-Fox, b&w, 167 minutes. **Director:** Edward Dmytryk; **Screenplay:** Edward Anhalt; **Cast:** Marlon Brando (Christian Diestl), Montgomery Clift (Noah Ackerman), Dean Martin (Michael Whiteacre), Hope Lange (Hope Plowman), Barbara Rush (Margaret Freemantle), May Britt (Gretchen Hardenburg), Maximilian Schell (Captain Hardenburg), Vaughn Taylor (Mr. Plowman).

In 1948, Irwin Shaw's novel *The Young Lions* was a big bestseller. It took a decade to reach the screen, where, given big production values and a name cast, it emerged a box-office success. In its study of three contrasting young men (two Americans, one German), the picture traced World War II from their contrasting points of views. Of key importance was that one of the trio, the GI Noah Ackerman, was Jewish. Even though played by the non-Jewish Clift, who did a variation of his *From Here to Eternity* (1953) little-guy-serviceman characterization, he was the figure being attacked because of his religion.

In the lengthy narrative, Ackerman, a draftee from California who is now in New York, meets timid Hope Plowman. They fall in love and want to marry before he is shipped out to action. She takes him back home to Vermont to meet her father (Taylor) who has never known a Jew before. The older man guides Ackerman around town to indicate the long Yankee traditions that his family has established, but Ackerman loves his daughter, so he cautiously consents to the union.

Things are less pleasant when Noah reports for basic training and encounters anti-Semitism. His chief persecutor, a bigoted captain, does his best to make life miserable for Ackerman. Eventually, after fights with four of the biggest bullies in the platoon, Noah emerges the winner. Later, in Germany, Ackerman heroically saves one of his regiment and is now more accepted by the others.

Although this film, directed by DMYTRYK who had helmed the anti–Semitism-themed *CROSSFIRE* (1947) and the pro-Israeli *THE JUGGLER* (1953), was much criticized for its conversion of the novel's Christian Diest Nazi character into a far more sympathetic, misguided German, less was said about the minimizing of the anti-Semitism experienced by Ackerman in the army. Much of the animosity was depicted more as personal grudges against an underdog soldier rather than blatant bigotry.

The Young Lions received three Academy Award nominations: Best Cinematography, Best Scoring, and Best Sound.

Z

***Zelig* (1983)** Orion, b&w and color, 80 minutes. **Director/Screenplay:** Woody Allen; **Cast:** Woody Allen (Leonard Zelig), Mia Farrow (Dr. Eudora Fletcher), John Buckwalter (Dr. Sindell), Marvin Chatinover (glandular diagnosis doctor), Stanley Swerdlow (Mexican food doctor).

After such more conventionally structured movies as *ANNIE HALL* (1977) and *MANHATTAN* (1979), ALLEN experimented with a pseudo-documentary format (using special effects to insert his focal character into old film footage, photos, etc.) to relate the bizarre life of Leonard Zelig, the human chameleon.

Zelig, the son of a Yiddish actor, who spent part of his youth with Hasidic scholars, is a man who morphs through assorted historical moments, is able to blend in with the scene, and can take on characteristics of the person(s) he is with. After medical consultations and time with a psychiatrist (Farrow) whom he finally weds, the crux of Zelig's problem is said to be a matter of assimilation. Like the definitive Jew, Zelig wants badly to fit in with contemporary life.

Zelig grossed more than $11 million in domestic distribution. It received two Oscar nominations: Best Cinematography and Best Costume Design.

Native Americans

A

***Across the Wide Missouri* (1951)** Metro-Goldwyn-Mayer, b&w, 78 minutes. **Director:** William Wellman; **Screenplay:** Talbot Jennings; **Cast:** Clark Gable (Flint Mitchell), Ricardo Montalban (Ironshirt), John Hodiak (Brecan), Adolphe Menjou (Pierre), J. Carrol Naish (Looking Glass), Maria Elena Marqués (Kamiah), Jack Holt (Bear Ghost), Howard Keel (narrator).

Its pompous voiceover narration aside, this was a well-mounted historical production, with extensive location work accomplished in the Rocky Mountains.

In the 1830s, fur trapper Flint Mitchell weds the granddaughter (Marqués) of Bear Ghost, chief of the Blackfoot tribes, hoping that this will ensure the safety of his fur-trapping expedition into Blackfoot territory. By the finale, Flint's wife has been murdered, and he takes their son—now six years old—to live with him among the Blackfoot tribes in the high Rockies.

Based on the 1947 novel by American historian Bernard DeVoto, this entry was a bit ludicrous with some of its casting of Native American roles; nevertheless, it allowed for a depiction of a "squaw man" (a Caucasian who weds a Native American). On the other hand, Hollywood—and supposedly the public—was not ready yet to have an interracial couple live "happily ever after," and this rationale occasioned the Native American maiden's death in the plot.

Within its stereotyping of Native Americans, there was a range of such characters depicted, with attention given to the tribe's traditions and lifestyle.

***Adventures of Tom Sawyer, The* (1938)** United Artists, color, 93 minutes. **Director:** Norman Taurog; **Screenplay:** John V. A. Weaver; **Cast:** Tommy Kelly (Tom Sawyer), Jackie Moran (Huckleberry Finn), Ann Gillis (Becky Thatcher), May Robson (Aunt Polly), Walter Brennan (Muff Potter), Victor Jory (Injun Joe), David Holt (Sid Sawyer), Nana Bryant (Mrs. Thatcher).

Mark Twain's classic *The Adventures of Tom Sawyer*, first published in 1876, has been adapted to film many times, including the silent American entry, *Tom Sawyer* (1917), starring Jack Pickford. Perhaps the most famous Hollywood version was the elaborate 1938 David O. Selznick production in Technicolor. All the versions on film and television featured the character of the infamous INJUN JOE, the murdering HALF-BREED. Injun Joe is the unsavory individual who says "Injun blood ain't in me for nothing." His characterization has perpetuated the negative image of the brutal half-breed Native American into modern culture.

Set in the 1840s in Hannibal, Missouri, a small town on the banks of the Mississippi River, *The Adventures of Tom Sawyer* details the pranks of Tom Sawyer, who lives with his Aunt Polly, and his misadventures with his good pal Huckleberry Finn, the social outcast. One night, the two boys are adventuring in the local cemetery when they spy Injun Joe murdering Doctor Robinson, one of his grave-robbing cohorts. The killer plants the knife on the person of his drunken crony, Muff Potter. At Potter's trial for murder, Tom clears the man's name, leading Injun Joe to throw a knife at the young testifier in the courtroom. Thereafter, when Tom and Becky explore the labyrinths of a cavern, they are confronted by the killer. In a struggle, Injun Joe falls to his death, and the youngsters find their way out of the cave and are proclaimed heroes.

As portrayed by Jory in the 1938 version, Injun Joe emerged a truly frightening man. This memorable bad character was another instance of the Native American being stereotyped as a villain on the screen. It was a harmful representation that became embedded in the minds of generations of youngsters who viewed this version (or the others) of *The Adventures of Tom Sawyer*, as well as those who had read Twain's classic novel.

***Alaskan, The* (1924)** Paramount, b&w, 6,736'. **Director:** Herbert Brenon; **Screenplay:** Willis Goldbeck; **Cast:** Thomas Meighan (Alan Holt), Estelle Taylor (Mary Standish), John Sainpolis (Rossland), Frank Campeau (Stampede Smith), Anna May Wong (Keok), Maurice Cannon (Tautuk).

Based on the 1923 novel by James Oliver Curwood, this silent photoplay was a rugged drama of the northern tundra where Alan Holt fights the machinations of a big-business syndicate run by John Graham who, in turn, controls the life of Mary Standish. Adding atmospheric flavor were Chinese-American Wong and Caucasian Cannon cast as NATIVE ALASKANS.

Alaskans See NATIVE ALASKANS.

***Allegheny Uprising* (1939)** RKO, b&w, 81 minutes. **Director:** William A. Seiter; **Screenplay:** P. J. Wolfson; **Cast:** Claire Trevor (Janie MacDougall), John Wayne (Jim Smith), George Sanders (Captain Swanson), Brian Donlevy (Callendar), Wilfred Lawson (MacDougall), Robert Barrat (Magistrate Duncan), Olaf Hytten (General Gage).

On one level, this was a traditional western, based on Neil Harmon Swanson's historical novel *The First Rebel* (1937). It concerned the rugged Indian fighter Jim Smith, his pal MacDougall, and the latter's spunky daughter Janie. Added into the mix—set in 1759 Pennsylvania—was haughty British captain Swanson as well as his obstinate commanding officer, General Gage.

On another plane, the film provided a bizarre twist, as on repeated occasions the fiercely patriotic Smith and his men slathered on war paint and the like to infiltrate and overwhelm marauding savages. Yet, their disguises (in actuality) would fool no one, let alone the Native Americans. Present in this popular movie were two recurrent racist themes: (1) Because Caucasian settlers had cultivated the land, it perforce belonged to them and not to the Native Americans who had controlled the territory *earlier*, and (2) Caucasian ingenuity was always superior to that of Native Americans. (The script had the "savages" do strategically stupid things, such as allowing the "good" settlers to overwhelm them easily.)

WAYNE, who became a star in 1939 with the release of *STAGECOACH*, often returned to his screen part as the foe of-Native Americans (e.g., *THE SEARCHERS*, 1956).

***Ambush* (1949)** Metro-Goldwyn-Mayer, b&w, 89 minutes. **Director:** Sam Wood; **Screenplay:** Marguerite Roberts; **Cast:** Robert Taylor (Ward Kinsman), John Hodiak (Capt. Ben Lorrison), Arlene Dahl (Ann Duverall), Don Taylor (Lt. Linus Delaney), Jean Hagen (Martha Conovan), Charles Stevens (Diablito), Chief Thundercloud (Tana), Flora Nez (Native American maiden).

Slowly, after World War II, Hollywood was turning away from its stereotypical depiction of Native Americans as one-dimensional killers who deserved the dire fate they received at the hands of Caucasians. Although many of the army officers were depicted as petty, duplistic, and/or amoral, the Native Americans, on the other hand, had committed what white America considered the worst offense possible—kidnapping Caucasian women and dragging them off to their tepees. (Also, warrior leader Tana was shown as not living up to his word with the army.) With such wrongs, the script justified the whites' treatment of the "savages." Taylor, who made several films (e.g., *DEVIL'S DOORWAY*, 1950; *JOHNNY TIGER*, 1966) dealing with Native Americans, had moments of sensitivity in *Ambush* as the wilderness guide in the Arizona Territory of the 1870s.

animation—feature films Although live-action westerns had frequently utilized Native American characters, it was a rarity in the arena of animation. One of the few was Walt Disney's *POCAHONTAS* (1995), a musical that retold the legend of Captain John Smith (speaking voice of Mel Gibson) in the New World encountering Native American maiden Pocahontas (speaking voice of IRENE BEDARD). This was followed three years later by *Pocahontas: Journey to a New World*, which also featured the speaking voice of Bedard in the title role; Judy Kuhn again provided the character's singing.

Among the cartoon shorts that dealt with Native Americans were *Little Hiawatha* (1937), a Walt Disney entry relating the legend of the young warrior. Also from Disney was *Hiawatha's Rabbit Hunt* (1941) in which Hiawatha, played by the character Elmer Fudd, stalks his prey—Bugs Bunny. (On more than one occasion over the years, there was a negative stereotype of a Native American found in a Bugs Bunny cartoon.) The twelve-minute cartoon *Arrow to the Sun* (1973) concerned a folk tale about the Acoma Pueblo tribe in the Southwest and a puzzling youngster on a quest to find his father, the God of the Sun.

animation series—television *THE LONE RANGER*, which had been a long-running radio and TV series as well as the source for movie features and serials, became a cartoon program in the fall of 1966 and ran for three seasons. Michael Rye provided the voice of the masked man, while Shepard Menken was heard as his faithful Native American pal, TONTO.

As part of the syndicated TV series *Festival of Family Classics*, the show aired *Hiawatha*, based on the poem ("The Song of Hiawatha," 1855) by Henry Wadsworth Longfellow, in September 1972 as a half-hour entry. The story involves a dastardly medicine man, Pearl Feather, who attempts to starve Hiawatha and his tribe. Another rendition of the Hiawatha legend was aired on CBS-TV in November 1983.

In this one-hour special, *The Legend of Hiawatha*, the mythical Native American helps his villagers deal with the problems of everyday life.

***Annie Get Your Gun* (1950)** Metro-Goldwyn-Mayer, color, 107 minutes. **Director:** George Sidney; **Screenplay:** Sidney Sheldon; **Cast:** Betty Hutton (Annie Oakley), Howard Keel (Frank Butler), Louis Calhern (Buffalo Bill), J. Carrol Naish (Chief Sitting Bull), Edward Arnold (Pawnee Bill), Chief Yowlachie (Little Horse), W. P. Wilkerson, Shooting Star, Charles Mauu, Riley Sunrise, Tom Humphreys, and John War Eagle (Native American braves).

As a Broadway musical in 1946 starring Ethel Merman—with book by Herbert Fields and Dorothy Fields and music by Irving Berlin—*Annie Get Your Gun* was a smash hit. Its transition to the screen was full of production problems that saw star Judy Garland replaced by Hutton and director Busby Berkeley traded first for Charles Walters and then Sidney. When released, the lush screen musical grossed more than $8 million.

In the movie, tomboyish Annie Oakley is a bedraggled sharpshooter who finds love (with marksman Frank Butler) and fame (as an ace shot) in the touring shows of BUFFALO BILL CODY in the late nineteenth century. A major subordinate character is Chief SITTING BULL who takes a shine to Annie, makes her an honorary member of his tribe, and then finances Buffalo Bill's Wild West show in which he and Oakley perform. Later, he becomes the matchmaker who reunites Annie and Butler. The other Native American characters in the cast are merely background set dressing.

If in real life this SIOUX leader was the fierce warrior who beat GEORGE ARMSTRONG CUSTER at the battle of Little Big-horn in 1876 and who died while trying to escape imprisonment in 1890, in the movie musical he is reduced to acting like a cigar-store wooden "Indian." Although he is depicted as self-contained and entrepreneurial, he remains one-dimensional, more a source of benign amusement than fear or respect. In the hokey interlude where Oakley is made a member of his tribe, the boisterous Annie sings "I'm an Indian Too," which did nothing to lend dignity to her, let alone to the Native American chief or his people. At the time of production, the industry's Production Code Administration advised the filmmakers that the U.S. secretary of interior wished a favorable presentation of Native Americans in the picture.

Annie Get Your Gun was turned into a TV special in 1957 starring Mary Martin and John Raitt and again in 1967 with Ethel Merman and Bruce Yarnell. The musical was frequently revived on the stage. The movie received an Academy Award for Best Musical Direction. It was also Oscar nominated for Best Art Direction/Set Direction (Color), Best Cinematography (Color), and Best Editing.

New York-born Naish also played the Sioux leader in 1954's *SITTING BULL*. In the nonmusical *ANNIE OAKLEY* (1935) starring Barbara Stanwyck and Preston Foster, CHIEF THUNDERCLOUD was Sitting Bull.

Ansara, Michael (1922–) Born in a small village in Syria, he was brought to Lowell, Massachusetts, at the age of two by his American parents of Lebanese heritage. But Ansara would gain his greatest fame playing Native Americans on camera, especially as APACHE chief COCHISE on the TV series *BROKEN ARROW* (1956–58). Initially, Ansara planned to pursue a premed course of study at Los Angeles City College but was drawn instead to the theater department. This led to studying at the Pasadena Playhouse.

One of Ansara's earliest screen roles was Hamid in the movie *Action in Arabia* (1944). It was the start of his being typecast by his swarthy, burly looks. One of his first Native American movie parts was in the low-budget *Brave Warrior* (1952). Ansara was Apache Joe in *Three Young Texans* (1954), and in the theatrical feature, *THE LONE RANGER* (1956), he was cast as Angry Horse. That same year he debuted as a costar of TV's *Broken Arrow*, playing (with a long gray wig) the noble Apache leader Cochise for two seasons. It made an indelible impression, and thereafter, no matter how many other diverse assignments he undertook, he was best recalled for his Native American portrayals. In the TV series *LAW OF THE PLAINSMAN* (1959–60), he was again a western warrior, this time one who had a Harvard education.

By the late 1970s Ansara, still playing heavies on camera, was Lame Beaver, the head of the Arapaho in Colorado, in the TV miniseries *CENTENNIAL* (1978–79). For the thriller *THE MANITOU* (1978), he was John Singing Rock, a modern-day medicine man. In the 1990s, the actor was the voice of Dr. Victor Fries/Mr. Freeze on TV's *Batman: The Animated Series*.

Apache, the The Apache (pronounced uh-PATCH-ee) lived in the southwestern area of the United States (especially New Mexico, Arizona, and western Texas) and northern Mexico. Because of their warlike history of raiding other tribes—and especially because of their famous renegade leader GERONIMO—*Apache* became synonymous with *savagery* and they were often (but not always) used in Hollywood westerns as the enemies of the white settlers and the U.S. cavalry. American movies featuring the Apache included: *Apache Gold* (1910), *Tonio, Son of the Sierras* (1925), *Riders of the Desert* (1932), *GERONIMO* (1939), *STAGECOACH* (1939), *Apache Trail* (1942), *FORT APACHE* (1948), *Apache Chief* (1950), *BROKEN ARROW* (1950), *I KILLED GERONIMO!* (1950), *RIO GRANDE* (1950), *The Last Outpost* (1951), *ARROWHEAD* (1952), *Son of Geronimo* (1952—movie serial), *THE BATTLE AT APACHE PASS* (1952), *CONQUEST OF COCHISE* (1953), *HONDO* (1953), *APACHE* (1954), *Arrow in the Dust* (1954), *Four Guns to the Border* (1954), *TAZA, SON OF COCHISE* (1954), *FOXFIRE* (1955), *Apache Woman* (1955), *The Man from Laramie* (1955), *THE LAST WAGON* (1956), *WALK THE PROUD LAND* (1956), *TROOPER HOOK* (1957), *Apache Warrior* (1957), *Fort Bowie* (1958), *Law of the Plainsman* (1959), *The Wonderful Country* (1959), *Sergeant Rutledge* (1960), *GERONIMO* (1962), *Rio Conchos* (1964), *Apache Gold* (1965), *Apache Uprising* (1966), *Duel at Diablo* (1966), *THE STALKING MOON* (1969), *The Gatling Gun* (1972), *Ulzana's Raid* (1972), *Apache Blood* (1975), *Mission to*

Glory (1980), *GERONIMO* (1993—TV movie), *GERONIMO: AN AMERICAN LEGEND* (1993), and *BUFFALO SOLDIERS* (1997—TV movie).

***Apache* (1954)** United Artists, color, 89 minutes. **Director:** Robert Aldrich; **Screenplay:** James R. Webb; **Cast:** Burt Lancaster (Massai), Jean Peters (Nalinle), John McIntire (Al Sieber), Charles Buchinsky [Bronson] (Hondo), John Dehner (Weddle), Paul Guilfoyle (Santos), Ian MacDonald (Clagg), Monte Blue (Geronimo).

DEVIL'S DOORWAY and *BROKEN ARROW* (both 1950) set the path for *Apache*, another early example of a Hollywood feature film presenting the Native American as brave and honorable. More importantly, the Native Americans were represented from their point of view, gaining the movie watcher's sympathy as they were subjected to cruel racism.

In 1886 when renegade APACHE leader GERONIMO surrenders to the U.S. cavalry, an angered subchief Massai fires on the soldiers, refusing to be a "whipped Injun." After he is arrested, he breaks free. From talking with a Cherokee who has adopted the white man's ways regarding farming, Massai gains inspiration for a new direction for his own tribe. Reaching the mountains of New Mexico, he discusses his "warrior's peace" plan with Santos, the new chief, and the latter's daughter, Nalinle. Santos betrays Massai to Indian fighter Al Sieber, but Massai escapes and launches a one-man war against the whites. Later, he is reunited with Nalinle whom he weds. Thereafter, as she is about to give birth to their child, Sieber and Massai have a showdown. Now wanting peace, Massai walks away, while the white men are amazed to see that a warlike Apache has turned to farming (corn).

Despite its flaws (e.g., director Aldrich lost his battle with the studio to have the film end more realistically with Massai being killed, and much of the movie's pro-Native American philosophizing was deleted by the film company), *Apache* was strong fare. Once the viewer adapted to Lancaster's Caucasian interpretation of a warrior brave, the Hollywoodlike version of his maiden love (played by Peters), or the snarling traitorous Hondo (enacted in sullen fashion by Bronson), the film was an intriguing retelling of the legend of Massai. Despite its factual and artistic distortions, *Apache* was a forerunner among Hollywood films in imbuing its Native American figures with pride.

***Apache Drums* (1951)** Universal-International, color, 85 minutes. **Director:** Hugo Fregonese; **Screenplay:** David Chandler; **Cast:** Stephen McNally (Sam Leeds), Coleen Gray (Sally Barr), Willard Parker (Joe Madden), Arthur Shields (Reverend Griffen), Clarence Muse (Jebu), John War Eagle (Apache guard), Maurice Jara (Native American).

This sagebrush entry referenced the historical figure Chief Victorio of the Chirichua. The latter were a key division of the APACHE people and considered the most bellicose of the Arizona-based Native Americans. The movie utilized Dr. Chris Willowbird, an authority on Native American lore, to supervise the use of Apache music for the soundtrack, including a religious chant. Besides its relatively authentic sets, music, and display of Apache customs, the *Los Angeles Daily News* (June 21, 1951) reported, "The picture is also notable for portraying an Indian as an honorable person—not just as a man who says 'Ugh!' to your face and then scalps you from the rear."

The action is set in 1880 at Spanish Boot, a desert mining town. There, gambler Sam Leeds rises to the occasion as the Apache, rebelling against their treatment by the U.S. government, go on a rampage, intending to grab the mined silver ore.

***Arrowhead* (1953)** Paramount, color, 105 minutes. **Director/Screenplay:** Charles Marquis Warren; **Cast:** Charlton Heston (Ed Bannon), Jack Palance (Toriano), Katy Jurado (Nita), Brian Keith (Captain North), Frank de Kova (Chief Chattez), Pat Hogan (Jim Eagle).

Based on W. R. Burnett's *Adobe Walls* (1953), this modestly budgeted feature was another of the several entries (e.g., *APACHE*, 1954; the TV movie *Mr. Horn*, 1979; *GERONIMO, AN AMERICAN LEGEND*, 1993) dealing with Al Sieber (1844–1907), the legendary chief of scouts of the U.S. Army of the Southwest. Here given the fictional name of Ed Bannon, he was played in stentorian fashion by Heston as the man who, having been raised by the APACHE, insisted he knew how they thought. He becomes convinced that Chief Chattez of the Chiracahua Apache does not intend to live up to his promise to move his tribe peacefully to a Florida reservation, and he is proven correct.

This was one of those Hollywood pictures that believed that the only good Native American was a dead one. That precept also applied to the half-Mexican, half-Apache woman Nita who was Bannon's devious woman. As played intensely by Jurado, she was another HALF-BREED not to be trusted.

B

Barrier, The **(1937)** Paramount, b&w, 93 minutes. **Director:** Lesley Selander; **Screenplay:** Bernard Schubert; **Cast:** Leo Carrillo (Poleon Doret), Jean Parker (Necia), James Ellison (Lieutenant Burrell), Otto Kruger (Gen. Stark), Robert Barrat (John Gale), Andy Clyde ("No Creek" Lee), Sara Haden (Alluna).

Rex Beach's novel *The Barrier* (1907) dealt with the intolerance faced by a HALF-BREED NATIVE ALASKAN in her local village. The tale was first filmed in 1917 (with Mabel Julienne Scott and Russell Simpson) and then remade in 1926 (with Marceline Day and Norman Kerry). In 1937, it had its first sound film version. In more subtle terms than its predecessors, it related the intertwining relationship between a French fur trapper (Carrillo), his Native-Alaskan woman (Haden), and the half-breed (Parker) whom he has raised as his own daughter. In the new edition, the heroine does not resolve her problem of loving a Caucasian by suddenly learning that she is white—per the usual Hollywood format. Instead, she discovers that she is indeed part Native Alaskan but the offspring of another couple. It was a small step forward for screen stories "allowing" mixed marriages.

Battle at Apache Pass, The **(1952)** Universal-International, color, 85 minutes. **Director:** George Sherman; **Screenplay:** Gerald Drayson Adams; **Cast:** John Lund (Maj. Jim Colton), Jeff Chandler (Cochise), Susan Cabot (Nona), Bruce Cowling (Neil Baylor), Beverly Tyler (Mary Kearny), Jay Silverheels (Geronimo), Jack Elam (Mescal Jack), Tommy Cook (Little Elk).

This film was part of the trilogy (including BROKEN ARROW, 1950, and *TAZA, SON OF COCHISE*, 1954) in which CHANDLER played COCHISE (ca. 1812–74). On each occasion, the Brooklyn-born actor interpreted the role of the famed APACHE leader with greater dignity than might have been expected. Here, he was matched against Canadian-born Mohawk SILVERHEELS (as GERONIMO), who had already gained recognition for playing TONTO on TV's *THE LONE RANGER* (1949–57). The movie was based on an actual incident in 1861 in which escalating mistrust between soldiers/settlers and the Apache led to twenty-five years of problems between the two groups.

As soldiers are withdrawn from the army forts in the New Mexico Territory to fight in the Civil War, the uneasy truce between the Caucasians and the Apache turns into armed hostility, thanks to a manipulative INDIAN AGENT (Cowling). As hostage taking and murders mount on each side, Cochise, the chief of the Chiricahua, must cope with Geronimo of the Mogollon Apache to control the local tribes. The situation climaxes in a battle at Apache Pass.

Historically, Geronimo was not actually implicated in the Apache Pass conflict.

Beach, Adam (1972–) Part of the new generation of Native American talent, Beach came into his own as the costar of *SMOKE SIGNALS* (1998). A member of the Ojibway tribe, he was born in Ashern, Manitoba, Canada. When he was eight, his mother was killed by a drunk driver; two months later his dad drowned. The orphan was sent to live with relatives in Winnipeg. Feeling an outsider since his parents' deaths, he found a sense of belonging in acting. When he was discovered by a casting agent at age sixteen, he dropped out of high school to take a two-month run in a stage play. This, in turn, led to a small part on the *Lonesome Dove* (1989) TV miniseries, and then he played GRAHAM GREENE's canoe partner in *Lost in the Barrens* (1990). Active in small theater in Manitoba and in Canadian TV (e.g., *North of 60*), Beach won the lead role of *SQUANTO: A WARRIOR'S TALE* (1994). That same year, he played Frank Fencepost,

Adam Beach, the star of *Squanto: A Warrior's Tale* (1994). (ECHO BOOK SHOP)

who lived on the Kidabanessee Reservation in Northern Ontario, Canada, in *DANCE ME OUTSIDE* (1994). Beach worked on the Canadian TV series *The Rez* (1996) and *Madison* (1997) and was Chibiabos in the theatrical release, *Song of Hiawatha*. After the acclaimed *Smoke Signals*, he was part of the cast of *Mystery, Alaska* (1999) with Russell Crowe, played in the Canadian-made *Little Boy Blues* (2000), and supported David Spade in the comedy *Joe Dirt* (2001). Next, the five-feet, eleven-inch Beach was in the Canadian-made comedy, *The Art of Woo* (2001). This was followed by the John Woo-directed *Windtalkers* (2002), an action drama of World War II involving NAVAJO marines. Later pictures included *Posers* and *The Big Empty* (both 2002).

***Bears and I, The* (1974)** Buena Vista, color, 89 minutes. **Director:** Bernard McEveety; **Screenplay:** John Whedon; **Cast:** Patrick Wayne (Bob Leslie), Chief Dan George (Chief A-Tas-Ka-Nay), Andrew Duggan (Commissioner Gaines), Michael Ansara (Oliver Red Fern), Robert Pine (John McCarten), Val DeVargas (Sam Eagle).

This modest but charming Walt Disney studio excursion cast Wayne as a young Vietnam veteran who hoped that living in the wilds of the Pacific Northwest would bring peace to his life. He finds himself not only parenting three bear cubs but also becomes involved in the efforts of local Native Americans to regain their land.

Notable in the cast were Canadian-born GEORGE and Lebanese-American ANSARA, both providing dimensional Native American characterizations. Coming three years after *BILLY JACK*, *The Bears and I* was part of a growing (and fashionable) trend of Hollywood films toward acting as unofficial spokespersons for this minority group. As the decade progressed, such benign on-camera battles of will (usually by Vietnam veteran characters combating anti–Native American forces) became more violent in nature.

Bedard, Irene (1967–) Heard as the speaking voice of the Native American maiden in Walt Disney's *POCAHONTAS* (1995), the already seasoned actress gained further prominence when she starred the next year in two made-for-cable movies: as Reyna in the drama *GRAND AVENUE* and as Black Buffalo Woman in *CRAZY HORSE*.

Of French Canadian/Cree and Inupiat ESKIMO heritage, she grew up in a small village in Alaska. Her first acting role of prominence was in the cable-TV movie *LAKOTA WOMAN: SIEGE AT WOUNDED KNEE* (1994) in which she was Mary Crow Dog. (She earned a Golden Globe nomination for the part and a Best Actress Award from the American Indian Film Festival.) For *SQUANTO: A WARRIOR'S TALE* (1994) featuring ADAM BEACH, she was his bride Nakooma. In 1995, *People* magazine named her one of the 50 Most Beautiful People in the World. She was in *True Women* (1997), a Texas historical TV drama, and appeared as Minnehaha in *Song of Hiawatha* (1997). In the well-regarded *SMOKE SIGNALS* (1998), Bedard was the neighbor who told Adam Beach's character about his late father. She was again heard as the famed Native American maiden in the direct-to-video animated feature *Pocahontas II: Journey to a New World* (1998).

More recently, she was in *Wildflowers* (1999), a mystery with Daryl Hannah and Eric Roberts, and the comedy *Tortilla Heaven* (2000). She was Mercedes Ruehl's long unseen blood sister in the TV movie *The Lost Child* (2000) and was featured in the comedy *Greasewood Flat* (2002).

Big Tree, John (Chief) (1865–1967) One of the most enduring Native American performers, his acting credits in silent films extended back to the Art Acord western *Author! Author!* (1915) and to the American Revolutionary War drama, *The Spirit of '76* (1917). Born Isaac Johnny John, this the Native American posed for artist James Fraser for the profile used on the well-known Indian-head nickel (issued between 1913 and 1938).

He played an assortment of warriors on camera, often as Indian chief (e.g., *The Red Rider*, 1925). He was a medicine man in both *The Overland Telegraph* (1929) and the movie serials *Custer's Last Stand* (1936) and *Hawk of the Wilderness* (1938). He changed nationalities to be an Asian porter in the classic *Lost Horizon* (1937). For Cecil B. DeMille's *North West Mounted Police* (1940), Big Tree was Blue Owl and appeared in the same director's *UNCONQUERED* (1947). For JOHN FORD, he was Pony That Walks in the noteworthy *SHE WORE A YELLOW RIBBON* (1949). Fittingly, his final movie was a featured appearance in the pro–Native American western, *DEVIL'S DOORWAY* (1950). Big Tree died on the Onondaga Indian Reservation south of Syracuse, New York.

Billy Jack This rebellious, antiestablishment HALF-BREED Vietnam veteran who was a devotee of pro–Native American causes and believed in peace through violence, was a character conceived and played on screen by actor/screenwriter/director TOM LAUGHLIN. Billy Jack first appeared in the biker movie *BORN LOSERS* (1967). Its success led to three sequels: *BILLY JACK* (1971), *The Trial of Billy Jack* (1974), and *Billy Jack Goes to Washington* (1977). The Billy Jack saga helped to popularize Native American themes in Hollywood films and TV shows. In 2002 it was touted that the Billy Jack property might be remade, perhaps with Keanu Reeves in the title role.

***Billy Jack* (1971)** Warner Bros., color, 112 minutes. **Director:** T. C. Frank [Tom Laughlin]; **Screenplay:** Frank and Teresa Christina [Delores Taylor]; **Cast:** Tom Laughlin (Billy Jack), Delores Taylor (Jean Roberts), Clark Howat (Sheriff Cole), Bert Freed (Posner), Julie Webb (Barbara), Ken Tobey (deputy), Victor Iza (doctor), Debbie Schock (Kit), Susan Sosa (Sunshine).

Iconoclastic actor LAUGHLIN had already played the HALF-BREED martial-arts expert BILLY JACK in the violent biker movie, *BORN LOSERS* (1967), which he had directed under an alias. Four years later, the character returned in this bizarre mixture of peace-versus-violence philosophizing that grossed an astounding $32 million. Its combination of vanity, excess, and baffling logic of nonviolence through violence melded together into a two-hour sermon that preached tolerance to minorities, especially aimed at Native Americans. Laughlin shrewdly cast his screen alter ego as a Vietnam vet and half-breed Native American, recognizing the growing tide of pro-underdog feeling in the United States. To appeal to other segments of moviegoers, his character was a martial-arts maven who used strong-arm methods to achieve serene goals.

In his journey through the American Southwest, righteous Billy Jack stops in a town that is seething with racial hatred, led by bigot Posner and his son Bernard. The latter two rednecks target the free school of Jean Roberts for their venom because she has gathered a student body of unwanted pupils of all races. When not scheming to eradicate the institution and its leader, Posner operates a business that captures and sells wild mustangs for dog food. When the school's pupils are refused service in an ice cream store and Bernard beats up one of their number, the young Native American Martin, Billy Jack trounces Bernard. A free-for-all between the newcomer and the townsfolk follows, which the sheriff breaks up. Before long, Martin has been murdered by Bernard. Billy Jack kills Bernard and seeks refuge in a nearby church where the media turns him into a hero. Schoolteacher Roberts persuades Billy Jack to surrender and to stand trial.

Despite the frequently awkward performances (including that of Laughlin's wife, Taylor), the cagey feature created tremendous momentum from the displays of violence and bigotry that led to a crescendo of affirmation for Billy Jack.

Two sequels followed: the labored, 175-minute-long *The Trial of Billy Jack* (1974) and the 155-minute *Billy Jack Goes to Washington* (1977—a remake of 1939's *Mr. Smith Goes to Washington*). Both follow-ups starred Laughlin who directed and cowrote them and featured Taylor. Neither picture attained the success of its predecessor. The *Billy Jack* fever had a great influence on encouraging other filmmakers to include Native American themes and characters in their projects. Moreover, *Billy Jack* was a landmark in presenting Native American activism on screen. In 2002 it was announced that the Billy Jack legend might be revived in a new screen vehicle.

Tom Laughlin in the title role of *Billy Jack* (1971). (JC ARCHIVES)

***Black Fox, The* (1995)** CBS-TV, color, 92 minutes. **Director:** Steven Hilliard Stern; **Teleplay:** John Binder; **Cast:** Christopher Reeve (Alan Johnson), Raoul Trujillo (Running Dog), Tony Todd (Britt Johnson), Nancy Sorel (Sarah Johnson), Chris Wiggins (Ralph Holtz), Leon Goodstriker (Little Buffalo), Byron Chief-Moon (Standing Bear), Denis Lacroix (Lone Wolf).

Relying on Matt Braun's 1972 novel, this telefeature was set in the mid-nineteenth century. It was a rip-roaring tale of former southern plantation owner Alan Johnson and his "blood brother" Britt, an ex-slave, who trek to Texas with their families to start anew. There, they encounter war-happy Kiowa braves. When the latter kidnap settlers, Alan and Britt ride to the rescue. Reflecting his bravery in action, Britt is named Black Fox by an impressed tribal chief.

As part of Hollywood's new consciousness regarding ethnic minorities, the Native Americans here were human beings, with individuality apportioned to each lead figure. This was the first of a trilogy of made-for-TV movies shot in 1993 and all aired in 1995: *Black Fox: The Price of Peace* portrayed the harmony between the settlers and tribes in 1860s Texas as being at risk when a racist sought to regain his wife from the Kiowa warrior with whom she had gone; *Black Fox: Good Men and Bad* focused on Alan Johnson as he tracked the killer of his wife from Texas to Kansas. Trujillo as Running Fox was a major part of the first two installments.

***Black Gold* (1947)** Allied Artists, color, 92 minutes. **Director:** Phil Karlson; **Screenplay:** Agnes Christine Johnson; **Cast:** Anthony Quinn (Charley Eagle), Katherine DeMille (Sarah Eagle), Ducky Louie (Davey), Raymond Hatton (Buckey), Kane Richmond (Stanley Lowell).

This was the first starring role for Mexican-born QUINN after forty-six movies and the only picture in which he costarred with his then-actress-wife (DeMille). He had already played a Native American in such entries as *THE PLAINSMAN* (1936) and *THEY DIED WITH THEIR BOOTS ON* (1941), but here he played a far different type of characterization—a gentle if illiterate Native American who took compassion on an orphaned Chinese boy (Louie) whom he and his well-educated wife have adopted. Much of the film was devoted to Charley Eagle's determination to enter his prize horse, Black Gold, in the Kentucky Derby. During the touching finale, the now-widowed Sarah accepts the winning trophy on behalf of all Native Americans.

Although its production values were sparse, this movie was a rarity for its time, a sympathetic study of a Native American couple in a contemporary scene. The movie also emphasized the difficulty that the Asian youth had in attending school in Oklahoma where his classmates poked fun at him because of his skin color.

***Blazing Saddles* (1974)** Warner Bros., color, 93 minutes. **Director:** Mel Brooks; **Screenplay:** Brooks, Norman Steinberg, Andrew Bergman, Richard Pryor, and Alan Uger; **Cast:** Cleavon Little (Black Bart), Gene Wilder (Jim), Slim Pickens (Taggart), David Huddleston (Olson Johnson), Mel Brooks (Governor Lepetomaine/Native American chief), Harvey Korman (Hedley Lamarr), Madeline Kahn (Lili Von Shtupp).

In the annals of screen satire, *Blazing Saddles* was a landmark of funny, foolish, and crude jokes, all geared to poke fun at both the dying western film genre and the long-established stereotypes of ethnic minorities.

The movers/shakers of a western town conspire to buy up the local land cheaply because they know a railroad will soon be going through the area. To expedite the needed sell-out by citizens, they hire an African-American sheriff (Little) to upset the town bigots. Caught up in the fracas is Marlene Dietrichlike Lili Von Shtupp, a pawn of the crooked Hedley Lamarr. In the wild melee that follows, Black Bart and his family are welcomed to the area by a cross-eyed, Yiddish-speaking Native American chief (Brooks). The latter finds the newcomers peculiar because they have darker-colored skin than he. Thus, by his logic, the chief has moved up one notch on the social totem pole.

Blazing Saddles grossed more than $119 million in domestic distribution and received three Oscar nominations: Best Film Editing, Best Song ("Blazing Saddles"), and Best Supporting Actress (Kahn).

Blood Crowd, The See *MCMASTERS, THE.*

Boone, Daniel (ca. 1734–1820) This celebrated frontiersman journeyed westward into the unsettled areas of Kentucky, helping to organize settlements and protecting the settlers against hostile warriors. As the advance guard of the whites, Boone frequently came into contact with Native Americans, some friendly and others hostile. This oversized historical figure reached the zenith of popularity in the Walt Disney TV series *DANIEL BOONE* (1964–70) starring Fess Parker. Boone figured as a central character in several American movies as played by: John Miljan (*The Great Meadow*, 1931), Jay Wilsey (*The Miracle Rider*, 1935—movie serial), George O'Brien (*Daniel Boone*, 1936), David Bruce (*Young Daniel Boone*, 1950), and Bruce Bennett (*Daniel Boone, Trail Blazer*, 1956). Besides the Walt Disney 1960s TV series, there was also *YOUNG DAN'L BOONE* (1977) featuring Rick Moses in the title assignment.

***Brave Eagle: Chief of the Cheyenne* (1955–1956)** CBS-TV series, b&w, 30 minutes. **Cast:** Keith Larsen (Brave Eagle), Keena Nonkeena (Keena), Kim Winona (Morning Star), Bert Wheeler (Smokey Joe).

A rare early example of a pro-Native American program, this TV series was a western constructed from a warrior's point of view.

Brave Eagle is a young tribal leader in Wyoming's Black Mountain region in the 1860s who has made peace with the white man, especially those at nearby Fort Wilson. The enemy of his people is the Peagan tribe. Other members of Brave Eagle's group featured on the show are Keena (his adopted son from the Lota tribe), Morning Star (who is Brave Eagle's love interest), and the HALF-BREED Smokey Joe. The latter had been in the U.S. cavalry before choosing to be with his mother's people, the CHEYENNE. Rather than using firearms, Brave Eagle and his braves carry bows and arrows as they hunt for food and deal with their adversaries.

***Braveheart* (1925)** Producers Distributing, b&w, 7,256′. **Director:** Alan Hale; **Adaptor:** Mary O'Hara; **Cast:** Rod La Rocque (Braveheart), Lillian Rich (Dorothy Nelson), Robert Edeson (Hobart Nelson), Arthur Houseman (Frank Nelson), Frank Hagney (Ki-Yote), Jean Acker (Sky-Arrow), Tyrone Power (Standing Rock), Sally Rand (Sally Vernon).

This silent photoplay, directed by character actor Hale, was an early Hollywood example of dramas detailing the rights of Native Americans that would become an established American movie subgenre after *BILLY JACK* (1971). (*Braveheart* was based on a story by William Churchill de Mille.) Unfortunately, in executing its plot line, this western emphasized the majority viewpoint of its era that, because of miscegenation statutes (and their underlying rationale of supposed Caucasian supremacy), a Native American was *not* entitled to marry a white woman. Instead, he must "settle" and wed a female of his own race.

Braveheart, a young Native American, travels East to study law so that he can be equipped to help his tribe's fishing rights (which are being jeopardized by unscrupulous canning magnate Hobart Nelson). On campus, he becomes a high achiever in the classroom and on the gridiron, but his college life ends when, to help a friend (Houseman), he takes the blame for a football scandal. Now expelled, he is also a pariah to his tribe for letting them down. Nevertheless, he pleads their fishing rights cause in court—and wins. Meanwhile, a jealous opponent (Hagney) of Braveheart has Nelson and his daughter (Rich) kidnapped. Braveheart comes to the rescue. Although he loves the white woman, he knows their interracial love can never be. Instead, he proposes to Sky-Arrow.

The leading Native American roles in *Braveheart* were entrusted to white actors, including the key assignment, handled by Chicago-born La Rocque.

***Britton of the Seventh* (1916)** Vitagraph, b&w, 4 reels. **Director:** Lionel Belmore; **Screenplay:** Jasper Ewing Brady; **Cast:** Darwin Karr (Lt. Tony Britton, age thirty), Charles Kent (Lt. Tony Britton, age seventy), Bobby Connelly (Bobby), Eleanor Woodruff (Barbara Manning), Ned Finley (George Armstrong Custer), Logan Paul (Rain-in-the-Face), Marion Henry (Otanowab).

This was an unusual handling of the oft-filmed account of GEORGE ARMSTRONG CUSTER and the Battle at Little Bighorn (1876). Much like *LITTLE BIG MAN* (1980), it subordinated that massacre to the account of its hero. Here, the focal character was Lt. Tony Britton, and the silent film concerned his tangled love/professional life. It also was told within a flashback as the elder Britton explained his past and how battles had been fought in pre-World War I days.

Back in 1876, Britton was stationed with the Seventh Cavalry led by Custer. Britton is involved innocently with the wife of an army officer, which leads to his leaving the military and becoming an Indian scout. Discovering the pending bloodbath at Little Big-horn, he tries unsuccessfully to warn Custer of the disaster. After the general's demise, a letter clearing Britton of any complicity in adultery is found in the dead officer's effects. Britton returns to the military and weds his sweetheart (Woodruff).

The "savages" here were depicted as bloodthirsty. Although prominent Native American roles were handled by Caucasians, subordinate parts/extras were assigned to Native Americans from Oklahoma reservations.

***Broken Arrow* (1950)** Twentieth Century-Fox, color, 93 minutes. **Director:** Delmer Daves; **Screenplay:** Michael Blankfort substituting for the uncredited blacklisted writer Albert Maltz; **Cast:** James Stewart (Tom Jeffords), Jeff Chandler (Cochise), Debra Paget (Sonseeahray), Basil Ruysdael (General Howard), Will Geer (Ben Slade), Jay Silverheels (Geronimo [Goklia]), Argentina Brunetti (Nalikadeya), Chris Willow Bird (Nochale), John War Eagle (Nahilzay), Iron Eyes Cody (Teese).

If *THE VANISHING AMERICAN* (1925) had presented an early positive portrayal of the Native American in the U.S. cinema, it was *DEVIL'S DOORWAY* and especially *Broken Arrow*, both 1950 Hollywood studio releases, that provided the Native American with dignity on camera. In many ways, *Broken Arrow* broke with Hollywood moviemaking traditions: It sought to be factual in its presentation (except in the manufactured romance between Jeffords and Sonseeahray), and it adhered closely to the screenplay that was based on Elliott Arnold's factual novel, *Blood Brother* (1947). *Broken Arrow* was shot on locations where the narrative reportedly occurred (i.e., the Coconino National Forest and the nearby APACHE White River Reservation in Arizona). Finally, this film tried to equalize, or even favor, the presentation of Native Americans by giving their viewpoints and characterizations equal time to that of the plot's white figures. That alone was a novelty in 1950 Hollywood.

(One concession within *Broken Arrow* was not having the Apache characters speak in their native language, which would have required using English subtitles. Another compromise was employing a largely Caucasian cast to play the Native Americans.)

Passing through the Chiricahua Apache lands in the Arizona Territory in 1870, gold prospector Tom Jeffords aids an injured Chiricahua teenager. This earns the respect of the boy's father Pionsenay and other warriors. Later, tired of the endless battles between the Apache and the whites, Jeffords gains permission from Colonel Bernall to negotiate peace with COCHISE, chief of the tribe. During the parley, the former Union army soldier becomes infatuated with the maiden Sonseeahray, not realizing that she is promised to Nahilzay. Thereafter, Jeffords persists successfully in his efforts to wed Sonseeahray even though Cochise feels that it will create racial problems for the newlyweds. Meanwhile, as the peace treaty is further developed, one of Cochise's subleaders, GERONIMO, breaks away with his renegade band of marauders. Still later, Sonseeahray is killed in an ambush by settlers. Cochise prevents the enraged Jeffords from seeking revenge, insisting that peace must reign in the territory. Jeffords leaves, keeping the memory of Sonseeahray alive in his heart.

Broken Arrow was well received by most reviewers. The *Hollywood Reporter* (July 21, 1950) praised the film for having "accomplished the miracle of portraying the American Indian as a person much more than the stereotyped rug peddler or vicious savage. Instead he is presented as a member of an ancient and honorable race whose primitive intelligence is the match of any civilized culture, . . ." In contrast Bosley Crowther of the *New York Times* (July 21, 1950) carped, "The misfortune here is that a purpose and an idea have been submerged in a typical rush of prettification and over-emphasis. Sure, the American Indian has been most cruelly maligned and his plight as a minorities' person has not yet been fully clarified. But in trying to disabuse the public of a traditional stereotype, the producers have here portrayed the Indian in an equally false, romantic white ideal." Other critics, however, complimented the dignity with which CHANDLER encased his characterization.

Broken Arrow received Oscar nominations for Best Cinematography (Color), Best Screenplay, and Best Supporting Actor (Chandler). For a 1956 episode of the *20th Century-Fox Hour* TV series, a condensed version of *Broken Arrow* was performed, starring Ricardo Montalban (as Cochise), John Lupton, and Rita Moreno. This led to the *BROKEN ARROW* TV series (1956–58), featuring Lupton and MICHAEL ANSARA.

Chandler played Cochise again in *THE BATTLE AT APACHE PASS* (1952) and *TAZA, SON OF COCHISE*; SILVERHEELS returned to his Geronimo persona in *The Battle at Apache Pass*, *WALK THE PROUD LAND* (1956), and a 1958 episode of "Texas John Slaughter," a multipart story on the *Disneyland* TV series.

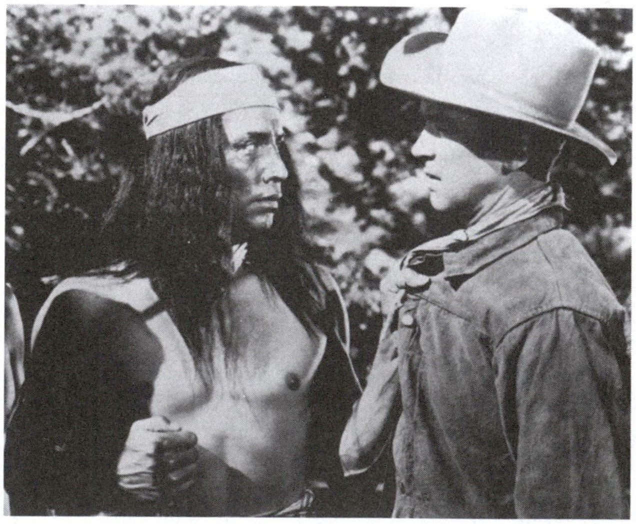

Jay Silverheels and James Stewart in *Broken Arrow* (1950). (JC ARCHIVES)

***Broken Arrow* (1956–1960)** ABC-TV series, b&w, 30 minutes. **Cast:** John Lupton (Tom Jeffords), Michael Ansara (Cochise), Tom Fadden (Duffield), Steve Ritch (Nukaya).

An offshoot of the 1950 feature film starring James Stewart as Tom Jeffords and Jeff Chandler as COCHISE, this TV western series has Lupton as the INDIAN AGENT and former U.S. cavalry officer and ANSARA as the Chiricahua APACHE leader. With Jeffords now a blood brother of Cochise, they combat evil white men and renegade warriors. Although Ansara was of Lebanese heritage, his Hollywood specialty was playing Native Americans on screen. Like the earlier *BRAVE EAGLE: CHIEF OF THE CHEYENNE* (1955–56), this was one of the few network programs to focus on Native Americans, even if largely from a white man's point of view.

***Broken Chain, The* (1993)** TNT cable, color, 93 minutes. **Director:** Lamont Johnson; **Teleplay:** Earl W. Wallace; **Cast:** Pierce Brosnan (Sir William Johnson), Graham Greene (the Peace Maker), Eric Schweig (Joseph Brant), Wes Studi (Seth/Chief/speaker for the tribes), Floyd "Red Crow" Westerman (tribal elder), J.C. White Shirt (Lohaheo), Buffy Sainte-Marie (Seth's wife).

Set during the French and Indian Wars, as the American colonies were preparing to break free from England, this true-life saga centers on two Iroquois brothers who strive to prevent their territory from being grabbed by white settlers. The drama deals with the fracturing of the Iroquois Confederacy of six tribes in the Northeast and highlights Joseph Brant (Schweig), a warrior educated in English-speaking schools. He convinced his tribe to aid the British during the revolution and then became a scourge to colonial settlers.

This exciting entry about little-known American historical facts was part of the TNT Native American TV movie series. As such, its sensibilities and point of view were clearly focused on the tribal warriors and far less concerned with the white pioneer figures. At times, the acting was a bit stiff, but the exploration of this previously little-known era more than compensated for any preachiness (at least to most TV viewers).

***Broken Lance* (1954)** Twentieth Century-Fox, color, 96 minutes. **Director:** Edward Dmytryk; **Screenplay:** Richard Murphy; **Cast:** Spencer Tracy (Matt Devereaux), Robert Wagner (Joe Devereaux), Jean Peters (Barbara), Richard Widmark (Ben Devereaux), Katy Jurado (Señora Devereaux), Hugh O'Brian (Mike Devereaux), Eduard Franz (Two Moons), Earl Holliman (Denny Devereaux), Chief Geronimo Kuthlee (miner).

This well-turned narrative told in flashback was set in the post-Civil War years in the Southwest. Joe, the HALF-BREED son of cattle baron Matt Devereaux, is made to take the blame for the destruction of a mining-company refinery, a deed actually committed by his parent. Once released from prison, he and his three Caucasian half-brothers (Widmark, O'Brian, and Holliman) feud over their late dad's estate. In a skirmish between Joe and Ben, the latter is killed by ranch foreman Two Moons. Later, Joe and his wife, Barbara, the daughter of the governor, visit Ben's grave. There, Joe finds a lance (symbolizing a blood feud). Before leaving, he breaks the lance in two, signaling that the family dispute is over.

Some commentators found parallels between *Broken Lance* and Shakespeare's *King Lear.* Other sources perceived this drama as a cautionary tale about mixed blood and the difficulty half-breeds had living in a white world, here in Joe's problems with his half-brothers. Jurado as Joe's mother made her relatively brief scenes count, while Franz as the Native American ranch foreman was an agent of good or evil, depending on how one viewed his shooting of Ben. Director DMYTRYK was noted for his films focusing on ethnic minority circumstances (e.g., *Crossfire,* 1947; *The Young Lions,* 1958). Chief Geronimo Kuthlee, who played a bit in this feature, was the grandson of GERONIMO.

Broken Lance was based on the 1949 crime movie, *House of Strangers,* itself derived from a segment of Jerome Weidman's 1941 novel *I'll Never Go There Any More.* The narrative also formed the basis for the circus movie *The Big Show* (1961). *Broken Lance* received an Academy Award nomination for Best Supporting Actress (Jurado).

Buffalo Bill See CODY, BUFFALO BILL.

***Buffalo Bill* (1944)** Twentieth Century-Fox, color, 90 minutes. **Director:** William A. Wellman; **Screenplay:** Aeneas MacKenzie, Clements Ripley, and Cecile Kramer; **Cast:** Joel McCrea (Buffalo Bill [William Frederick Cody]), Maureen O'Hara (Louisa Frederici Cody), Linda Darnell (Dawn Starlight), Thomas Mitchell (Ned Buntline), Anthony Quinn (Yellow Hand), Chief Many Treaties (Tall Bull), Chief Thundercloud (Crazy Horse).

Anxious to stress brotherhood during the height of World War II, this fictionalized and revisionist screen biography of BUFFALO BILL CODY adopted a relatively lighthearted approach to the legends surrounding the famed self-promoter. Nevertheless, a highlight of the narrative was Cody's growing realization that when he was an army scout, he had thoughtlessly caused the death of, and brought suffering to, many Native Americans. Within the chronicle, he vows to make amends through his pro–Native American activities before he can be at peace with himself. (A more realistic, if less entertaining account of Cody was presented in Robert Altman's *Buffalo Bill and the Indians, or Sitting Bull's History Lesson,* 1976.)

Buffalo Bill covered a broad base of white–versus–Native American confrontations, including the negotiations between Yellow Hand and government/business officials over railroad rights, various skirmishes and battles, the unfulfilled love Dawn Starlight (Darnell) had for Cody who chose to wed a white woman (O'Hara), and Cody's employment of Native Americans as supporting stars of his Wild West Show (which ironically glamorized Cody's past battles against the "savages").

As in so many Hollywood westerns, the authenticity of the tribal scenes, marauding war parties, costuming, and use of makeup (for warpaint) emerged as mostly Caucasian notions of what the "redskins" were really like. Also, the interracial romance of the Native American maiden was resolved, in standard Hollywood fashion, by her death. Hispanic actor QUINN gave a strong interpretation as the vicious Native American, here the son of CHEYENNE chief Tall Bull.

***Buffalo Soldiers, The* (1997)** TNT cable, color, 95 minutes. **Director:** Charles Haid; **Teleplay:** Frank Military and Susan Rhinehart; **Cast:** Danny Glover (Sergeant Wyatt), Mykelti Williamson (Corp. Wilson Christy), Carl Lumbly (Horse), Glynn Turman (Sgt. Joshua "Joyu" Judges Ruth), Michael Warren (Corp. Eddie Tockes), Timothy Busfield (Maj. Robert Carr).

Picking up the plot premise of the film *Soul Soldier* (1970), this made-for-television feature produced by Glover focused on U.S. Cavalry Troop H in the 1860s. Composed of African Americans, the group was given its name by the Plains tribes because the troops' hair reminded them of the wool of a buffalo. These minority troopers fought CRAZY HORSE, helped to capture GERONIMO, and served at Wounded Knee. Reportedly, at the time, there was a catchphrase, "No one could catch an APACHE except a Buffalo Soldier."

Shot on location in Benson, Arizona, this telefeature—like the same year's CHILDREN OF THE DUST—deals with two key ethnic minorities in the one story line: black soldiers fighting with Apache warriors who were slaughtering settlers in New Mexico. For a change, the perspective of the film was from another minority (albeit one trying harder than its white counterparts to subdue the savages) who were having trouble living harmoniously with Caucasians. As such, it created an intriguing juxtaposition of cultures, both revolving around the white world. *Buffalo Soldiers* was nominated for three Emmy Awards: Outstanding Art Direction, Outstanding Cinematography, and Outstanding Sound Mixing.

C

Cactus Jack See *VILLAIN, THE.*

***Call Her Savage* (1932)** Fox, b&w, 87 minutes. **Director:** John Francis Dillon; **Screenplay:** Edwin Burke; **Cast:** Clara Bow (Nasa Springer), Gilbert Roland (Moonglow), Thelma Todd (Sunny De Lane), Monroe Owsley (Laurence Crosby), Estelle Taylor (Ruth Springer).

One of the racial assumptions of the Caucasian world was that a HALF-BREED (i.e., mixed-blood person) was not fit to wed a white person; on the other hand, the same logic thought it was a step up for a (half-breed) Native American to marry another half-breed. This "rule" played a role in many American novels and films of the early to mid-twentieth century, One such fiction was Tiffany Thayer's 1931 novel, which was translated into a comeback screen vehicle for Bow, the "It" Girl of bygone years.

This erotic narrative concerns willful Nasa Springer who abandons the West for private schooling in Chicago. Later, her (mis)adventures with men take her to New Orleans and then on to New York. Along the way, she undergoes a regeneration that is jump-started by the death of her infant. Near the end of this (im)morality tale, Nasa learns that her real father is not Pete Springer but a Native American who had a love affair with her mother (Taylor). Understanding the roots of her wild nature, she responds to her long-time admirer, the half-breed Moonglow.

This film generated a great deal of concern among censors both within the film industry's self-governing production-code organization and on the state level regarding the sexual issues, mores, and depicted social diseases, *not* the mixed marriage Nasa had with a white playboy (Owsley) nor her sordid sexual experiences as a streetwalker. According to the script, the man-about-town character was a cad and thus not entitled to a pure-blood marriage. The same held true for the sexual experiences Nasa had while degrading herself as a prostitute. As for the two half-breed lovers left at the finale, they could be married, according to the same Hollywood racial logic (i.e., they deserved each other).

***Call of the Navajo* (1952)** New Life, color, 42 minutes. **Director:** Stan Taylor; **Screenplay:** Marian Taylor; **Cast:** Harris Arthur (Ashkee), Jack Drake (missionary), Karl Ashcroft (trader), John Arthur (father), Eva Arthur (mother), David Hemstreet (blind man), Thomas Aticitty (Ashkee, grown up), Harry Elders (narrator).

This short drama produced in 16 mm was a proselytizing tale of a young NAVAJO boy Ashkee, who coveted a silver belt that he noticed at the trading post. As bad things happen to him and his family, the child is convinced that his desire of the expensive material item—which is later stolen by another—is the source of God's anger against the missionary (Drake). When all matters are resolved, the youngster plans to finish his schooling and become a missionary himself so that he can enlighten those on the local reservation.

***Captain John Smith and Pocahontas* (1953)** United Artists, color, 75 minutes. **Director:** Lew Landers; **Screenplay:** Aubrey Wisberg and Jack Pollexfen; **Cast:** Anthony Dexter (Captain John Smith), Jody Lawrence (Pocahontas), Alan Hale Jr. (Fleming), Robert Clarke (John Rolfe), Stuart Randall (Opechanco), Shepard Menken (Nantaquas), Douglass Dumbrille (Powhatan).

This was but one of the several cinema retellings of the love between English-born Smith (ca. 1580–1631) and POCAHONTAS (ca. 1595–1617), the beautiful daughter of Powhatan, an Algonquian chief. In this low-budget rendition, Smith colonizes Jamestown, Virginia, in the early seventeenth century on behalf of the British. Thanks to Pocahontas, his life is spared when her father captures him. Eventually he returns to England, leaving his Native American wife behind to wed another (Clarke).

The legend of the adoring, pretty Native American maiden and her brave Englishman was also the subject of the full-length animated feature POCAHONTAS and the live-action movie of the same title, both 1995.

Cardinal, Tantoo (1950–) One of the most active and recognizable Native-North American actresses, she appeared in a variety of films from Hollywood's *DANCES WITH WOLVES* (1990) and *LEGENDS OF THE FALL* (1994) to Canada's *Black Robe* (1991) and the more recent *SMOKE SIGNALS* (1998). Born in Anzac, Alberta, near Fort McMurray, she was the youngest offspring of a Cree woman and a Caucasian man (making her a Métis, a French term for one of mixed blood). She was raised by her grandmother who taught her the Cree way of life. After high school and an early marriage, she made her professional acting debut in 1971 in a small role in the Canadian Broadcasting Company's TV production of *Father Lacombe*, a dramatized documentary. Later, in the Canadian-made feature *Marie Ann* (1978), she had a leading role as a tribal princess. In the early 1980s, she performed the title role in the stage production of *Jessica*, a drama about a woman of mixed blood.

In the Hollywood arena, Cardinal was in the TV movie *Gunsmoke: Return to Dodge* (1987) and was Billy Wirth's mother in the action drama *WAR PARTY* (1989). After appearing as Black Shawl in *Dances with Wolves*, she was Snow Bird from 1993 to 1995 on the TV series *DR. QUINN, MEDICINE WOMAN*. Cardinal was part of the mid-1990s upsurge in Native American-themed movies made for American television, ranging from the historical *TECUMSEH: THE LAST WARRIOR* (1995) to the documentary miniseries *500 Nations* (1995) and the contemporary drama *GRAND AVENUE* (1996). For the Canadian-produced miniseries *Big Bear* (1998), she was Running Second. More recently, she was seen as Aunt Mary in the made-for-TV drama *THE LOST CHILD* (2000) and performed in *Disappearances* (2001) with Kris Kristofferson.

***Centennial* (1978–1979)** NBC-TV miniseries, color, 21 hours. **Cast:** David Janssen (Paul Garrett/narrator), Richard Chamberlain (Alexander McKeag), Raymond Burr (Herman Bockweiss), Gregory Harrison (Levi Zendt), Barbara Carrera (Clay Basket), Michael Ansara (Lame Beaver), Chief Dan George (old Sioux), Ivan Naranjo (Gray Wolf), Nick Ramus (Lost Eagle), Robert Tessier (Rude Water), Maria Potts (Blue Leaf).

Based on James Michener's epic novel (1974) that covered a time span between the late 1700s up to the present day, this mammoth miniseries boasted a roster of name performers, a nearly $30 million budget, and twelve segments (adding up to twenty-six hours when commercials were inserted) and telecast through several months. The extensive saga traced U.S. history as seen through the experiences of Native Americans, fur trappers, pioneers, and the townsfolk of (the fictional) Rocky Mountain town of Centennial, Colorado. The early chapters, in particular, dealt with the Native Americans as they came into increasing contact with the white people (from greedy trappers and settlers to, later, the sadistic U.S. cavalry and avaricious cattlemen) who invaded their territory and forever changed their way of life.

A prime figure in the early segments of *Centennial* was ANSARA's Lame Beaver, head of the Arapaho in Colorado. He was depicted in the drama from age nine until his death at fifty-three during a confrontation with the Shawnee enemy. Carrera played his daughter Clay Basket, and her character was shown spanning the ages from fifteen to eighty-four.

The focus in *Centennial* was definitely on the Caucasians and the stories involving generations of people in Centennial Nevertheless, this massive TV undertaking reflected the growing interest, among both the Hollywood industry and movie viewers, on a more balanced perspective of the impact of the pioneers' westward movement and its effect on the land's earlier inhabitants—the North American tribes.

Chandler, Jeff (1918–1961) Born in Brooklyn, New York, as Ira Grossel, this underrated Jewish-American, Caucasian screen star played the role of COCHISE, the noble Apache warrior, in three features (*BROKEN ARROW*, 1950, *THE BATTLE AT APACHE PASS*, 1952, and *TAZA, SON OF COCHISE*, 1954). In the contemporary romantic drama, *Foxfire* (1955), Chandler was a HALF-BREED mining engineer. The muscular actor with chiseled cheekbones also frequently played a member of the Native Americans' sworn enemy—the U.S. cavalry (e.g., *Two Flags West*, 1950; *War Arrow*, 1953; *PILLARS OF THE SKY*, 1956).

***Charge at Feather River, The* (1953)** Warner Bros., color, 99 minutes. **Director:** Gordon Douglas; **Screenplay:** James R. Webb; **Cast:** Guy Madison (Miles Archer), Frank Lovejoy (Sergeant Baker), Helen Westcott (Anne McKeever), Vera Miles (Jennie McKeever), Dick Wesson (Cullen), Fred Carson (Chief Thunder Hawk), Ray Behram (old Native American).

Because this western was shot in the then-popular 3-D process, the gimmick encouraged such effects as tomahawks, lances, and knives being thrown "directly" at the audience. To incorporate such attention grabbers into the action, there had to be many skirmishes between the U.S. cavalry and the Native Americans—and there were.

Tossed into this mix were the kidnapped young McKeever women, Anne and Jennie. The latter is attracted to her captor, Thunder Hawk, and agrees to become his wife, but she and her sister are rescued by the soldiers, led by Miles Archer. By the finale, many Native Americans have been killed, including Thunder Hawk and Jennie (her corpse shot through with arrows).

***Chato's Land* (1972)** United Artists, color, 110 minutes. **Director:** Michael Winner; **Screenplay:** Gerald Wilson; **Cast:** Charles Bronson (Pardon Chato), Jack Palance (Quincey Whitmore), Richard Basehart (Nye Buell), James Whitmore (Joshua Everette), Simon Oakland (Jubal Hooker), Sonia Rangan (Chato's woman).

In one of his most taciturn movie roles, Bronson was the APACHE HALF-BREED who kills the sheriff of a New Mexico town in self-defense and then is hunted by a vengeful posse. They pursue Chato into Apache territory where they become the prey not only of the Native Americans but also of each other.

With fifteen lines of spoken dialogue (thirteen of which were in Apache dialect), Bronson's squinty-eyed hero was another illustration of Hollywood's then new attitude toward Native Americans on screen. No longer merely the menacing savage, here Chato's every murderous act was justified by the script (i.e., the rape of his woman by the posse). Made in the post-*BILLY JACK* (1971) era, *Chato's Land* presented the silent half-breed as the victim *not* the victimizer.

***Cherokee Uprising* (1950)** Monogram, b&w, 57 minutes. **Director:** Lewis Collins; **Screenplay:** Dan Ullman; **Cast:** Whip Wilson (Bob Foster), Andy Clyde (Jake Jones), Lois Hall (Mary Lou Harrison), Sam Flint (Judge Harrison), Iron Eyes Cody (Longknife), Chief Yowlachie (Gray Eagles).

This programmer was designed for fans of cowboy actor Wilson and was but one of many Hollywood features that depicted white men masquerading as leaders of Native Americans who, in turn, are cowed by the promise of whiskey into helping with holdups, and so on. This theme of Native Americans as pawns of the Caucasians perpetuated the myths of Native Americans being susceptible to liquor and, when stimulated by "firewater," being likely to behave badly toward innocent settlers.

Cheyenne, the The Cheyenne (pronounced shy-ANN) were originally based in what became Minnesota. By the early eighteenth century, they had migrated to what became North and South Dakota and later split into two groups, one faction moving south to Colorado and Kansas. White settlers referred to them as Northern Cheyenne and the Southern Cheyenne. The Northern Cheyenne became allied with their former enemy, the SIOUX, and were caught up in the 1876 battle of the Little Big-horn against GEORGE ARMSTRONG CUSTER and his Seventh Cavalry troopers. The Southern Cheyenne made peace with their once enemies, the Kiowa and the COMANCHE, and together they fought their foes—the APACHE, the Crow, the Pawnee, the Shoshone, and the Ute.

The Cheyenne figured into such American-made movies as *A Cheyenne Brave* (1910), *THE IRON HORSE* (1924), *Custer's Last Fight* (1925), *General Custer at Little Big Horn* (1926), *Treachery Rides the Range* (1936), *Custer's Last Stand* (1936—movie serial), *THE PLAINSMAN* (1936), *THEY DIED WITH THEIR BOOTS ON* (1941), *BUFFALO BILL* (1944), *The Dalton Gang* (1949), *SHE WORE A YELLOW RIBBON* (1949), *Tomahawk* (1951), *Wagons West* (1953), *THE CHARGE AT FEATHER RIVER* (1953), *Last of the Comanches* (1953), *The Yellow Tomahawk* (1954), *WHITE FEATHER* (1955), *The Gun That Won the West* (1956), *Dakota Incident* (1956), *The Guns of Fort Petticoat* (1957), *Ride Out for Revenge* (1957), *CHEYENNE AUTUMN* (1964), *The Plainsman* (1966), *SOLDIER BLUE* (1970), *POWWOW HIGHWAY* (1989), *Cheyenne Warrior* (1994—TV movie), and *CHILDREN OF THE DUST* (1995—TV movie)

***Cheyenne Autumn* (1964)** Warner Bros., color, 159 minutes. **Director:** John Ford; **Screenplay:** James R. Webb; **Cast:** Richard Widmark (Capt. Thomas Archer), Carroll Baker (Deborah Wright), Karl Malden (Capt. Oscar Wessels), James Stewart (Wyatt Earp), Edward G. Robinson (Carl Schurz), Sal Mineo (Red Shirt), Dolores Del Rio (Spanish Woman), Ricardo Montalban (Little Wolf), Gilbert Roland (Dull Knife), Arthur Kennedy (Doc Holliday), Victor Jory (Tall Tree).

This well-intentioned rambling drama was director FORD's belated apology to Native Americans for their treatment at the hands of white Americans (as well as for Ford's portrayals of vicious tribal warriors in his past movies). Hampered by its length, polemics, and some embarrassing casting (e.g., Montalban, Roland, and Mineo), *Cheyenne Autumn* never found its proper audience, even in the 1960s when public sentiment was turning in favor of Native American causes.

Based on Mari Sandoz's 1953 book, *Cheyenne Autumn* is set in the 1870s as the CHEYENNE are ordered from their Wyoming homelands and are relocated to a bleak Oklahoma reservation. For more than a year, they await the promised government assistance, with many of their number dying. The less than 300 survivors, under Dull Knife and Little Wolf, choose to make a 1,500-mile walk back to their original lands and are joined on this trip by Quaker schoolteacher Deborah Wright. Capt. Thomas Archer, who is pro-Native American, half-heartedly pursues them with his troops. Because of hot-tempered Red Shirt, several encounters with the military lead to the death of a few troopers. An unenthusiastic Wyatt Earp and Doc Holliday are pressed into organizing a posse to track down the enemy, but Earp deliberately leads the volunteers astray.

As winter approaches, half of the Cheyenne band surrenders to sadistic Captain Wessels at Fort Robinson, where he mistreats them. As a result, they retaliate and Wessels and many troopers are killed. The cavalry finally corners the Cheyenne, who are saved from annihilation by the arrival of Carl Schurz, U.S. secretary of the interior. He arranges a treaty that allows the tribe to return to its homeland. Hotheaded Red Shirt dies in a duel over Little Wolf's wife, and the disheartened Little Wolf departs into exile; Archer and his fiancée Wright join the brave Cheyenne.

Filmed in Arches National Park, Utah, Monument Valley, Utah, and Arizona, *Cheyenne Autumn* received an Oscar nomination for Best Cinematography (Color). Made at a negative cost of more than $7 million, the western earned mild reviews. It grossed only slightly more than $3 million in the domestic marketplace (and more than $6 million globally), ending with a net loss of almost $6 million.

***Chief Crazy Horse* (1955)** Universal, color, 86 minutes. **Director:** George Sherman; **Screenplay:** Franklin Coen and Gerald Drayson Adams; **Cast:** Victor Mature (Crazy Horse), Suzan Ball (Black Shawl), John Lund (Major Twist), Ray Danton (Little Big Man), Keith Larsen (Flying Hawk), Robert Warwick (Spotted Tail), Morris Ankrum (Red Cloud/Conquering Bear).

The trade publication *Harrison's Report* (February 26, 1955) observed of this feature: "It is somewhat different from most stories that deal with a conflict between Indians and whites, This time the Indians are given sympathetic treatment and are depicted as being persecuted by the whites."

One of many Hollywood movies that exploited the life of Chief Crazy Horse, the great SIOUX chief, this entry suffered from the miscasting of Mature (best known as the muscular star of the biblical spectacle *Samson and Delilah*, 1949) in the pivotal lead assignment, as well as the use of stock footage blown up to fill the CinemaScope screen. On the other hand, this was an essentially positive representation of the Native American legend.

Told within a flashback, the overly talkative film depicts how a gold rush in the Black Hills of South Dakota leads prospectors into the Sioux territory. This necessitates the construction of Fort Phil Kearny to protect the miners against the warring Native Americans. Despite the efforts of Major Twist to bring about peace between the Sioux and the military, the former decide on war rather than being herded onto a reservation. Uniting the Lakota tribes, Crazy Horse plots the ambush at Little Big-horn at which General Custer and his troops are massacred. Later, having surrendered, Crazy Horse is killed by one of his duplistic braves (Danton).

This rendition of the exploits of the famed Native American warrior was far more stereotypical in its portrayal of Native Americans than the later TV movie, *CRAZY HORSE* (1996).

***Children of the Dust* (aka: *A Good Day to Die*) (1995)** CBS-TV miniseries, color, 175 minutes. **Director:** David Greene; **Teleplay:** Joyce Eliason; **Cast:** Sidney Poitier (Gypsy Smith), Michael Moriarty (John Maxwell), Joanna Going (Rachel), Hart Bochner (Shelby Hornbeck), Regina Taylor (Drusilla), Billy Wirth (Corby/White Wolf), Shirley Knight (Aunt Bertha), Robert Guillaume (Mossberger), Farrah Fawcett (Nora Maxwell), Byron Chief-Moon (Chief Walks-the-Clouds).

Adapted from Clancy Carlile's 1995 novel, *Children of the Dust* was extensively plotted as it unfolded its busy tale set in the 1880s Oklahoma Territory. Gypsy Smith is the grizzled gunslinger and famous bounty hunter (half-black and half-Cherokee) who becomes enmeshed with two star-crossed lovers—Rachel (a Caucasian) and Corby (a CHEYENNE youth)—as he shepherds a group of freed slaves westward to establish an all–African-American town (Freedom). During the narrative, Smith is offered the chance to claim land for himself during the land rush, but he refuses, not wanting to grab more land away from his Native American people.

The miniseries delved into two racial issues as the HALF-BREED Corby encountered bigotry while romancing the Caucasian Rachel and as he interacted with the virulent Ku Klux Klan. Like the same year's TV movie, *THE BUFFALO SOLDIERS*, *Children of the Dust* melded together the discrimination faced by both minority races. Filmed in Alberta, Canada, this miniseries received Emmy nominations for Outstanding Music Composition and Outstanding Sound Editing.

Chingachgook This brave and loyal Mohican chief is a character in James Fenimore Cooper's novel *The Last of the Mohicans* (1826) and other of *The Leatherstocking Tales*, including *The Deerslayer* (1841). His friend is Natty Bumppo, known as Hawkeye, the Deerslayer, or the Pathfinder. Chingachgook (whose name meant "The Great Serpent") has a son, Uncas, who is the last of the Mohicans.

In his many representations on screen—usually played by a Caucasian actor until recent times—Chingachgook emerges as a courageous warrior and as a positive image of the Native American that is rare in literature and even rarer in prepolitically correct Hollywood.

On screen, Chingachgook was played by Wallace Reid (*THE DEERSLAYER*, 1913), Theodore Lorch (*THE LAST OF THE MOHICANS*, 1920), Hobart Bosworth (*THE LAST OF THE MOHICANS*, 1932—movie serial), Robert Barrat (*THE LAST OF THE MOHICANS*, 1936), JAY SILVERHEELS (*The Pathfinder*, 1953), Carlos Rivas (*The Deerslayer*, 1957), voice of John Doucette (*The Last of the Mohicans*, 1975—animated TV special), Ned Romero (*The Last of the Mohicans*, 1977—TV movie), Ned Romero (*The Deerslayer*, 1978—TV movie), RUSSELL MEANS (*THE LAST OF THE MOHICANS*, 1992), and GRAHAM GREENE (*The Pathfinder*, 1996—TV movie). In the TV series *HAWKEYE AND THE LAST OF THE MOHICANS* (1957), Lon Chaney Jr. played the wise warrior, Chingachgook, and on another small-screen program, *HAWKEYE* (1994–95), RODNEY A. GRANT interpreted the famed Native American fictional figure.

Christina, Frank See LAUGHLIN, TOM.

***Christopher Columbus: The Discovery* (1992)** Warner Bros., color, 120 minutes. **Director:** John Glen; **Screenplay:** John Briley, Cary Bates, and Mario Puzo; **Cast:** Marlon Brando (Tomas de Torquemada), Tom Selleck (King Ferdinand), George Corraface (Christopher Columbus), Rachel Ward (Queen Isabella), Robert Davi (Martin Pinzon), Catherine Zeta-Jones (Beatriz), Branscombe Richmond (Native American chieftain), Tailinh Forest Flower (Native American girl).

In the year celebrating the 500th anniversary of Columbus having discovered America, two overblown "epics" appeared (the other being *1492: The Conquest of Paradise* starring Gerard Depardieu). Less deadly by degrees than the other, this pompous entry was filled with the lunacy of self-conscious spectacle. Near the finale, having failed in his mission to find the great trade route to the East, Columbus sails home to parade his heathen converts and goods in front of Spain's Queen Isabella. Meanwhile, his officers and crew who are left behind are massacred by the Native Americans who have had enough of their "benefactors." Such was the start of the colonizing of America and the beginning of the problems for Native Americans.

The expensively mounted *Christopher Columbus: The Discovery* grossed only a bit more than $8 million at the box-office in domestic distribution.

***Cimarron* (1931)** RKO, b&w, 124 minutes. **Director:** Wesley Ruggles; **Screenplay:** Howard Estabrook; **Cast:** Richard Dix (Yancey Cravat), Irene Dunne (Sabra Cravat), Estelle Taylor (Dixie Lee), Nance O'Neil (Felice Venable), William Collier Jr. (The Kid), Roscoe Ates (Jesse Rickey), George E. Stone (Sol Levy), Stanley Fields (Lon Yountis), Dolores Brown (Ruby Elk, as an adult), Gloria Vonic (Ruby Big Elk, as a child).

Edna Ferber's 1930 best-seller became a mammoth screen epic that focused on the event-filled lives of adventurous Yancey Cravat and his much more conservative wife Sabra as they settled a town in the Oklahoma Territory of the 1890s. Just as the film depicted a Jewish character (played by Stone) as the loyal friend of Sabra over the years, so *Cimarron* reflected on the treatment of the Osage tribe before and after the oil boom brought them prosperity. Representing the voice *against* reason, Sabra has long scorned the Native Americans and is aghast when her son has a romance with the daughter of an Indian chief. As the saga jumps ahead decades, Sabra, a newly elected congresswoman, speaks now with respect of her Native American daughter-in-law.

Made at a time when the United States was staunchly rooted in blatant racial biases, *Cimarron*, despite the advocacy of Yancey on behalf of the Native Americans, never gave a sense that the Osage characters (and Ruby Big Elk, in particular) were anything more than second-class citizens.

Produced at a cost $1.43 million, *Cimarron* lost $565,000 in its original release, despite winning Oscars for Best Adapted Screenplay and Best Picture and garnering four other Academy Award nominations: Best Actor (Dix), Best Actress (Dunne), Best Cinematography, and Best Director (Ruggles). The epic was remade in 1960.

***Cimarron* (1960)** Metro-Goldwyn-Mayer, color, 140 minutes. **Director:** Anthony Mann; **Screenplay:** Arnold Schulman; **Cast:** Glenn Ford (Yancey Cravat), Maria Schell (Sabra Cravat), Anne Baxter (Dixie Lee), Arthur O'Connell (Tom Wyatt), Russ Tamblyn (William "The Kid" Hardy), Mercedes McCambridge (Sarah Wyatt), Vic Morrow (Wes Jennings), David Opatoshu (Sol Levy), Aline MacMahon (Mavis Pegler), Dawn Little Sky (Arita Red Feather), Eddie Little Sky (Ben Red Feather), Mickie Chouteau (Ruby Red Feather).

If the 1931 version of *Cimarron* suffered from a too-extensive plot line, this overblown remake was damaged by bad casting (e.g., accented, Austrian-born Schell as the American heroine) and by overemphasizing every element of the original. Although the celebrated land-rush sequence of the original may have been more expansively represented in this color, wide-screen edition of Ferber's novel, there was no passion to the remake. Even the moments of bigotry (e.g., the lynching of Ben Red Feather by the "good" citizens of Osage and Sabra's banishing of her son from the household for taking up with a Native American) were played without much conviction, as was the reunion/reconciliation scene between Sabra and her son (and his family). It was as if the film, and Hollywood in general, could not make up its mind in 1960 whether the Native Americans in the story, who were badly mistreated by so many, were meant to be objects of pity or only got what they "deserved."

Cochise (ca. 1812–1874) This noted APACHE leader's name meant "hardwood." His father had been a Chiricahua Apache chief. In 1861, this military strategist led his tribesmen in a decade-long battle against the U.S. cavalry for their having violated a flag of truce and having hung several tribal chiefs. He was defeated finally in 1871. His son, Taza, succeeded him. In Arizona, his homeland, Cochise County was named after the great warrior.

On screen, especially in *BROKEN ARROW* (1950), he was depicted as a wise, noble, and essentially peace-loving individual who retaliated against the whites for breaking treaty promises. He was typically portrayed on film by Caucasian actors, among whom were Antonio Moreno (*VALLEY OF THE SUN*, 1942), Miguel Inclan (*FORT APACHE*, 1948), JEFF CHANDLER (*Broken Arrow*, 1950), CHIEF YOWLACHIE (*The Last Outpost*, 1951), Chandler (*THE BATTLE AT APACHE PASS*, 1952), John Hodiak (*CONQUEST OF COCHISE*, 1953), Chandler (*TAZA, SON OF COCHISE*, 1954), Michael Keep (*40 Guns to Apache Pass*, 1966), and August Schellenberg (*GERONIMO*, 1993—TV movie). In the TV series, *BROKEN ARROW* (1956–60) MICHAEL ANSARA was seen as the famed warrior leader.

Cody, Bill See CODY, BUFFALO BILL.

Cody, Buffalo Bill (aka: Buffalo Bill; Bill Cody) (1846–1917) Born William Frederick Cody, this famed westerner gained his nickname after killing nearly 4,300 buffalo in an eight-month period (to supply food for Union Pacific Railroad laborers). Early in life, he had been a Pony Express rider and, in 1872, he was awarded the Congressional Medal of Honor for his role in pushing back the Native American forces. Later, he operated a popular Wild

West show that toured both the United States and abroad and featured such famous Native Americans as Chief SITTING BULL. Sometimes, Cody was depicted on camera as a kind-hearted man, other times not. His legendary character was often dragged into movies purely for its name value.

He was played on the American screen by such performers as George Waggner (*THE IRON HORSE*, 1924), Jack Hoxie (*The Last Frontier*, 1926), William Fairbanks (*Wyoming*, 1928), Tom Tyler (*Battling with Buffalo Bill*, 1931—movie serial), Douglass Dumbrille (*The World Changes*, 1933), Earl Dwire (*The Miracle Rider*, 1935—movie serial), Ted Adams (*Custer's Last Stand*, 1936—movie serial), James Ellison (*THE PLAINSMAN*, 1936), John Rutherford (*Flaming Frontiers*, 1938—movie serial), Joel McCrea (*BUFFALO BILL*, 1944), Richard Arlen (*Buffalo Bill Rides Again*, 1947), Monte Hale (*Law of the Golden West*, 1949), Louis Calhern (*ANNIE GET YOUR GUN*, 1950), Tex Cooper (*King of the Bullwhip*, 1951), Clayton Moore (*Buffalo Bill in Tomahawk Territory*, 1952), Charlton Heston (*Pony Express*, 1953), Malcolm Atterbury (*Badman's Country*, (1958), Jim McMullan (*The Raiders*, 1963), Guy Stockwell (*THE PLAINSMAN*, 1966), Matt Clark (*This Is the West That Was*, 1974—TV movie), Paul Newman (*Buffalo Bill and the Indians, or Sitting Bull's History Lesson*, 1976), Ted Flicker (*THE LEGEND OF THE LONE RANGER*, 1981), Ken Kercheval (*Calamity Jane*, 1984—TV movie), Jeffrey Jones (*Kenny Rogers as The Gambler, Part II,: The Legend Continues*, 1987—TV movie), and Keith Carradine (*Wild Bill*, 1995). The TV series *Buffalo Bill Jr.* (1955) had Dickie Jones in the lead; Stephen Baldwin played William "Billy" Cody on *The Young Riders* (1989–92), and in the 1994 TV program, *Lonesome Dove: The Series*, Dennis Weaver was Cody.

Cody, Iron Eyes (1907–1999) For many years, this long-active performer of Native American screen roles and the author of three books about himself and his cultural heritage had another pop-culture association. From 1971 until the 1980s, he was well known as the tribesman with the imposing profile shedding a dramatic tear for environmentally blighted America in promotional ads for "Keep America Beautiful."

Until the mid-1990s, most people took for granted Cody's story that his father was an Oklahoma Cherokee named Thomas Long Plume and that his mother was a Cree from northern Canada. It was also generally accepted that, as he detailed in his autobiography (*Iron Eyes, My Life as a Hollywood Indian*, 1982), he grew up in Oklahoma as Little Eagle and then began his career in silent films with directors such as James Cruze and JOHN FORD.

Then in 1996 the *New Orleans Times-Picayune* published an article questioning Cody's heritage and suggesting that he was actually of Italian descent. The elderly Cody denied it, although, as reported later, several Native American organizations were well aware of the masquerade. As it further developed, Cody was actually born Espera DeCorti on April 3, 1904, in Kaplan, Louisiana. He was one of four children of two emigrants from southern Italy who arrived in New Orleans at the start of the twentieth century. By 1909, the father had departed for Texas, and the mother soon remarried—this time to a native Louisianan—and had five additional children. As a child, it was reported that the boy—called Oscar by his family—liked everything Indian.

When Cody was a teenager, the household moved to Texas, but a year later, everyone but Oscar and two of his brothers (Joe and Frank) returned to Louisiana. The three brothers remained behind, staying with their biological father, whose surname was now Corti. Before the three siblings later set out for California, they adopted the last name of Cody. Once in Hollywood, the Cody brothers set about breaking into films. (Cody's two siblings had a few bit parts in westerns and then left the profession. Frank died in 1949 and Joe in 1978.)

In retrospect, it was revealed that many Native Americans, including actor JAY SILVERHEELS who knew Cody in the early 1930s in Hollywood, had been aware that the performer was not who he claimed. For assorted reasons, the truth never was made known to the general public, especially in later years after Cody had become such a symbol of Native American pride and had worked so actively for Native American causes.

In addition, Cody's movie career actually began in the early 1930s when he played a series of small roles as warriors in westerns, including *Texas Pioneers* (1932), *The Farmer Takes a Wife* (1935), and *Wild West Days* (1937). By the 1940s, his parts grew bigger (e.g., *UNCONQUERED*, 1947; *THE PALEFACE*, 1948; *Mrs. Mike*, 1949). By the 1950s, besides more westerns, Cody was in episodes of such TV series as *Adventures of Wild Bill Hickok*, *Sergeant Preston of the Yukon*, and *The Adventures of Rin Tin Tin*. Among his last screen roles were *Grayeagle* (1978) and *Ernest Goes to Camp* (1987)

Through the years, besides his "autobiography," Cody wrote *How: Indian Sign Talk in Pictures* (1950) and *Indian Talk: Hand Signals of the American Indians* (1970).

***Colorado Territory* (1949)** Warner Bros., b&w, 94 minutes. **Director:** Raoul Walsh; **Screenplay:** John Twist and Edmund H. North; **Cast:** Joel McCrea (Wes McQueen), Virginia Mayo (Colorado Carson), Dorothy Malone (Julie Ann Winslow), Henry Hull (Fred Winslow), John Archer (Reno Blake), James Mitchell (Duke Harris), Gray Eyes (old Native American).

Walsh, who had directed the classic gangster melodrama *High Sierra* (1941) starring Humphrey Bogart and Ida Lupino, remade the vehicle as a western. Besides switching genres, the tale of a good-hearted outlaw making one last haul before he retired (but failing in the process) remained the same. One of the film's new twists was having the lawbreaker's girlfriend Colorado (Mayo) be a HALF-BREED Native American. Early in the film, there is a portent of trouble when Wes McQueen first meets Colorado, a friend of Reno Blake and Duke Harris, and foresees problems ahead because of her. Again, the theme of the dangerous mixed-blood person being a troublemaker is brought forth to move the western forward. In the finale, which is more adept than a similar finale involving a half-breed in *Duel in the Sun* (1946), Wes and Colorado die in a hail of bullets from the marshal and his men.

The excellently received *Colorado Territory* was banned in West Germany—the first U.S.-made movie to have that happen—because of its alleged veneration of anti-social activities. *High Sierra* was remade yet again—as a straightforward gangster yarn—in *I Died a Thousand Times* (1955).

Comanche, the The Comanche (pronounced cuh-MANH-chee) were a people much known for their fierce skill in battle, for being rugged individualists, and for their prowess on horseback. In the seventeenth century, the Comanche apparently splintered off from the Shoshone in Wyoming and moved south. When they gained the use of horses by the start of the next century, they became far ranging, roaming from Kansas to what later became parts of Texas, New Mexico, Oklahoma, Colorado, and northern Mexico.

American movies that featured Comanche included *The Daughter of Dawn* (1920), *North of 36* (1924), *The Texans* (1938), *Young Buffalo Bill* (1940), *The Scarlet Horseman* (1946—movie serial), *Red River* (1948), *Comanche Territory* (1950), *Rose of Cimarron* (1952), *CONQUEST OF COCHISE* (1953), *Last of the Comanches* (1953), *Overland Pacific* (1954), *THEY RODE WEST* (1954), *Thunder Pass* (1954), *Kentucky Rifle* (1955), *Comanche* (1956), *THE LAST WAGON* (1956), *THE SEARCHERS* (1956), *Raiders of Old California* (1957), *The Rawhide Trail* (1958), *Comanche Station* (1960), *The Comancheros* (1961), *TWO RODE TOGETHER* (1961), *Gunfight at Comanche Creek* (1964), *Texas Across the River* (1966), *The Cowboys* (1974), *THE LEGEND OF THE LONE RANGER* (1981), *The Cellar* (1990).

combat dramas—feature films and television Most of Hollywood's depiction of Native Americans involved in warfare focused on their struggles in the eighteenth century (sometimes allied with the French or British against the colonists) and then in the nineteenth and very early twentieth centuries against the encroaching settlers and troopers within the United States. (A popular subject was the Battle at Little Big-horn in 1876 and the defeat of GEORGE ARMSTRONG CUSTER and his cavalry.) Occasionally, a film dealt with the Native Americans uniting with Mexicans against the gringos.

The all-too-few Hollywood movies depicting Native Americans fighting overseas in the twentieth century against America's enemies reflected both reality and the ongoing bias against depicting such characters in U.S. films. Their general omission from World War I-themed sagas was only alleviated slightly in Hollywood movies focused on World War II. One such dealt with the real-life Ira Hayes, the Pima tribesman, who was a marine and part of the invasion force at Iwo Jima. Hayes played himself in a recreation of the raising of the American flag at the famed battle site in *SANDS OF IWO JIMA* (1949). Later, Tony Curtis portrayed Ira in *THE OUTSIDER* (1961), a biography of the troubled man, and the narrative included World War II combat scenes. In *Battle Cry* (1955), Felix Noriego played an ethnic marine known as Crazy Horse. Much more recently, John Woo's expensively mounted *Windtalkers* (2002) dealt with the U.S. military's use of the NAVAJO and their native language in World War II for communicating coded messages. The plot concerned the danger to these Native American marines (including one played by ADAM BEACH) of being captured by the enemy.

Based on James Jones's novel (1951), which had been a feature film (1953) and a TV miniseries (1979), the teleseries *From Here to Eternity* (1979–80) centered on life in Honolulu in 1942 after war had been declared against japan. WILL SAMPSON was seen as Sergeant Cheney.

By the time of the Vietnam War, there was some recognition that Native Americans were serving in the U.S. forces in Southeast Asia. Some of the pictures depicted the aftereffects of such veterans back in America coping with civilian life. One of the most famous such movies was *BILLY JACK* (1971), starring TOM LAUGHLIN as the HALF-BREED, a part he had played earlier in *BORN LOSERS* (1967) and would again interpret in *The Trial of Billy Jack* (1974) and *Billy Jack Goes to Washington* (1977).

comedies—feature films For a good many years of the twentieth century, thanks to Hollywood, the stereotype of the bloodthirsty savage on the warpath was the primary image of Native Americans held by most moviegoers. Slowly, this began to change in the 1930s with the occasional film that depicted this ethnic minority not only as dimensional human beings but also as more often victims rather than victimizers—even in the Old West. Another film genre that helped to balance the image of the Native American gradually was screen comedies, which presented this ethnic minority as sometimes comedic figures. (Ironically, this got carried to extremes, which generated other types of incorrect, negative images about Native Americans.)

In the 1922 short silent comedy, *The Paleface*, directed and written by Buster Keaton, he played a butterfly-chasing white man who was captured by angry braves. The musical comedy *Whoopee!* (1930) had a hypochondriac (played by Eddie Cantor) at a dude ranch out west where he became involved as matchmaker of sorts in a seemingly interracial romance by a white heroine and a warrior (who proved to be Caucasian in the denouement). One of the dances staged by Busby Berkeley dealt with fetching native maidens. The lighthearted approach here to native tribesmen was the start of a trend. In the Bert Wheeler–Robert Woolsey comedy *Diplomaniacs* (1933), the farcical duo opened a barbershop at an Oklahoma reservation where they became involved in a ploy hatched by the college-educated chief of the Adoop tribe. As expected, slapstick complications ensued.

In 1940, the Marx Brothers' *Go West*, and Mae West and W. C. Fields's *My Little Chickadee* were set in the somewhat civilized later Old West, where rampaging warriors definitely could not be taken seriously. The same was true of Bud Abbott and Lou Costello's *Ride 'Em Cowboy* (1942) in which roly-poly Costello became involved with a marriage-minded village maiden. Other similar-type comedies that included jokey Native Americans were Judy Canova's *Singin' in the*

Corn (1946), the Bowery Boys entry, *Bowery Buckaroos* (1947), and Cornel Wilde as a figment of Ginger Rogers's imagination in *It Had to Be You* (1947).

The Egg and I (1947), the Claudette Colbert–Fred MacMurray tale of city folks coping with rural life, introduced moviegoers to Ma and Pa Kettle and their hick kin, which, in turn, started a long-lasting film series. Two of the subordinate characters in these joke-fests were Crowbar and Goeduck, local monosyllabic characters who were more akin to animated cigar-store Indians than to real human beings. (Crowbar was variously hammed up over the years by Vic Potel, CHIEF YOWLACHIE, Teddy Hart, Zachary Charles, and Stan Ross; John Berkes and then Oliver Blake mishandled the role of foolish Goeduck.) But the major movie to demystify the "rampaging redskins" was the Bob Hope–Jane Russell comedy, *THE PALEFACE* (1948), in which the warriors were more amusing than fearsome. (This movie was remade with Don Kotts as 1968's *The Shakiest Gun in the West.*)

The further debunking of Native Americans as merely vicious killers came in such later movies as the musical *A TICKET TO TOMAHAWK* (1950), the Pat Boone entry *All Hands on Deck* (1961) with Buddy Hackett as a wacky modern-day brave, the Three Stooges comedy *The Outlaws Is Coming!* (1965), Elvis Presley's *STAY AWAY, JOE* (1968), Bob Hope's *Cancel My Reservation* (1972), Mel Brooks's *BLAZING SADDLES* (1974—with his Yiddish-speaking chief), Kirk Douglas's *THE VILLAIN* (1979), Charlie Sheen's *Hot Shots!* (1991) and its sequel *Hot Shots—Part Deux* (1993), and Jackie Chan's *Shanghai Noon* (2000). On a quasi-comedic note were the presentations of native braves in Burt Lancaster's *THE SCALPHUNTERS* (1968), ANTHONY QUINN in *FLAP* (1970), Dustin Hoffman's *LITTLE BIG MAN* (1970), and Gene Wilder's *THE FRISCO KID* (1979). (However, many of these on-camera portrayals that kidded the fearsome, bloodthirsty warriors caused justifiable concern among Native Americans that they were now becoming on screen the butt of jokes, thereby demeaning their character.)

comedy series—television See SITUATION COMEDY SERIES—TELEVISION.

***Conqueror, The* (1917)** Fox, b&w, 8 reels. **Director/ Screenplay:** Raoul Walsh; **Cast:** William Farnum (Sam Houston), Jewel Carmen (Eliza Allen), Charles Clary (Sidney Stokes), J. A. Marcus (Jumbo), William Eagle Shirt, Chief Birdhead, and Little Bear (warrior chiefs).

This film was another drama chronicling colorful soldier/politician Samuel Houston (1793–1863). Here, Houston, the future first president of the Republic of Texas, was depicted as living comfortably among the Cherokee Indians until he encountered aristocratic Eliza Allen. She encourages him to enter the political arena and maneuvers him into a position of power. After their marriage disintegrates, he heads to Texas with a remorseful Eliza in pursuit. When she is captured by lustful Mexicans, Houston—with his trusty Cherokee comrades—rides to the rescue.

For a change, the Native Americans were presented as the equal of the Caucasians—at least in the eyes of robust Houston—and were demeaned only by the haughty Eliza.

Members of the SIOUX tribe at Pine Ridge, South Dakota appeared in this silent photoplay.

***Conquest of Cochise* (1953)** Columbia, color, 70 minutes. **Director:** William Castle; **Screenplay:** Arthur Lewis and De Vallon Scott; **Cast:** John Hodiak (Cochise), Robert Stack (Major Burke), Joy Page (Consuelo de Cordova), Rico Alaniz (Felipe), Steve Ritch (Tukiwab), Carol Thurston (Terua), Rodd Redwing (Red Knife).

Following in the wake of JEFF CHANDLER, who had played COCHISE in *BROKEN ARROW* (1950) and other movies, Pennsylvania-born Polish-American Hodiak took on the role of the APACHE leader in this budget-conscious feature that distorted history. The film proved to be as interested in demeaning its Mexican characters as it was in pigeonholing the Native Americans as "savages."

After the conflict between the United States and Mexico ends in the early 1850s, hostilities of the Apache and COMANCHE tribes against Mexican settlers increase in the Arizona Territory, leading to the intervention of the U.S. cavalry under Major Burke. Meanwhile, Cochise and Red Knife vie for control of the Apache and to determine whether or not they will join the Comanche in combat against the whites.

An interesting aspect of this programmer was the plot premise that found the Mexican Consuelo in love with Cochise but his Cochise rejecting her on the grounds that she should not be part of his life on the run.

Robert Stack and John Hodiak in *Conquest of Cochise* (1953). (JC ARCHIVES)

***Covered Wagon, The* (1923)** Paramount, b&w, 10 reels. **Director:** James Cruze; **Screenplay:** Jack Cunningham; **Cast:** Lois Wilson (Molly Wingate), J. Warren Kerrigan (Will Banion), Ernest Torrence (Bill Jackson), Charles Ogle (Mr. Wingate), Ethel Wales (Mrs. Wingate), Alan Hale (Sam Woodhull), Tully Marshall (Jim Bridger), Guy Oliver (Kit Carson).

A classic of the silent movie era, *The Covered Wagon* traces the 1848 convoy of pioneers—one group led by Will Banion, the other by Wingate—as they trek from Kansas City on the Oregon Trail to California and Oregon. Amid the panorama of the American landscape, the settlers experience a prairie fire, an attack by rampaging Native Americans, and the hurdle of crossing the Platte River. To personalize the hazardous journey, there is the romance between Banion and Molly, with the envious Sam Woodhull interfering.

Under the coordination of Col. Tim McCoy, who acted as the epic's technical adviser, many hundreds of Native Americans were hired for the film's attack scenes and other glimpses of tribal life as the whites passed through on their journey westward. Images from this well-photographed vehicle became milestones of the American cinema, including the sight of marauding "savages." It solidified American screen stereotypes that lasted for decades.

The Covered Wagon was based on Emerson Hough's 1922 book. Made on a then hefty budget of $782,000, the picture grossed nearly $4 million.

Crazy Horse (Chief) (ca. 1842–1877) His SIOUX name was Ta-Sunko-Witko, but supposedly, he gained his well-known name because a wild horse galloped through his village on the day he was born. In 1876, Crazy Horse, a man who saw visions, was passionate about stopping the whites from settling on Native American lands. He led a band of SIOUX and CHEYENNE against the U.S. cavalry in Montana and was a guiding force in the tribal confederation that defeated Lt. Colonel GEORGE ARMSTRONG CUSTER at the Battle at Little Big-horn in June 1876. The next year, Crazy Horse surrendered and was killed while in custody, allegedly while attempting to escape.

This dynamic legendary leader was frequently depicted on screen, especially in regard to his defeat of Custer, portrayed by such players as High Eagle (*Custer's Last Stand*, 1936—movie serial), ANTHONY QUINN (*THEY DIED WITH THEIR BOOTS ON*, 1941), CHIEF THUNDERCLOUD (*BUFFALO BILL*, 1944), IRON EYES CODY (*SITTING BULL*, 1954), Victor Mature (*Chief Crazy Horse*, 1955), Cody (*The Great Sioux Massacre*, 1965), WILL SAMPSON (*The White Buffalo*, 1977), Mike Mazurki (*The Incredible Rocky Mountain Race*, 1977—TV movie), RODNEY A. GRANT (*SON OF THE MORNING STAR*, 1991—TV movie), and MICHAEL GREYEYES (*CRAZY HORSE*, 1996—TV movie). On the TV series *CUSTER* (1967), Michael Dante performed as Crazy Horse and episodes of the show were later pasted together as ersatz telefeatures (e.g., *Crazy Horse and Custer, the Untold Story*, 1990).

***Crazy Horse* (1996)** TNT cable, color, 96 minutes. **Director:** John Irwin; **Teleplay:** Robert Schenkkan; **Cast:** Michael Greyeyes (Crazy Horse), Wes Studi (Red Cloud), Irene Bedard (Black Buffalo Woman), Lorne Cardinal (Young Man Afraid), John Finn (General Crook), Jimmy Herman (Conquering Bear), Peter Horton (George Armstrong Custer), Gordon Tootoosis (Akicita).

Using an entirely different approach and set of perceptions than had the action entry *CHIEF CRAZY HORSE* (1955), this well-crafted production provided a telling account of the Native American warrior who made a stand for his people and was willing to risk everything in the process. To help his people survive the white onslaught, CRAZY HORSE (GREYEYES) willingly challenged the mighty U.S. cavalry.

With its general attention to detail, great visual beauty, and use of actual Native Americans for the key roles, the telefilm recreated a true feel of the times. It was also told from the perspective of an Oglala SIOUX legend of a young man who had a vision of freedom for his people, a dream that he pursued to his untimely death in captivity—betrayed by some of his own tribesmen and stabbed by a guard while under military confinement. The film stressed the duality of his nature: his spiritual obsession and his warrior mentality.

For a change, it was not military leader GEORGE ARMSTRONG CUSTER who was the centerpiece of the drama in the battle of the Little Big-horn in 1876 but Crazy Horse and his followers. Filmed in the Black Hills of South Dakota, this well-received, made-for-television feature earned an Emmy Award nomination for Outstanding Achievement in Hairstyling.

Custer, George Armstrong (Lt. Col.) (1839–1876) This flamboyant and controversial U.S. cavalry officer had an up-and-down military career fighting for the North in the Civil War and thereafter at postings in the West, because of his unorthodox approach to following military protocol. His name became part of U.S. history after the massacre at Little Big-horn in 1876 when he and more than 260 troops were killed by warrior braves. He claimed to be very pro-Native American but fought many battles against them. Because of his extravagant nature and his controversial military career, he became a popular character for screen interpretation. A highly romanticized version of this officer was provided by swashbuckling Errol Flynn in *THEY DIED WITH THEIR BOOTS ON* (1941). At the opposite end of the spectrum, Custer was revealed to be a vainglorious buffoon in *LITTLE BIG MAN* (1970) with Richard Mulligan as Custer.

Others who played Custer on the American screen included Francis Ford (*Custer's Last Fight*, 1912), Ned Finley (*BRITTON OF THE SEVENTH*, 1916), T. D. Crittenden (*Bob Hampton of Placer*, 1921), unknown actor (*Custer's Last Fight*, 1925), Dustin Farnum (*The Flaming Frontier*, 1926), John Beck (*General Custer at Little Big Horn*, 1926), Clay Clement (*The World Changes*, 1933), Frank McGlynn Jr. (*Custer's Last Stand*, 1936—movie serial), John Miljan (*THE PLAINSMAN*,

1936), Ronald Reagan (*Santa Fe Trail*, 1940), James Millican (*Warpath*, 1951), Sheb Wooley (*Bugles in the Afternoon*, 1952), Britt Lomond (*TONKA*, 1958), Philip Carey (*The Great Sioux Massacre*, 1965), Leslie Nielsen (*The Plainsman*, 1966), Robert Shaw (*CUSTER OF THE WEST*, 1967), Richard Mulligan (*Little Big Man*, 1970), Ken Howard and James Olson (*The Court-Martial of George Armstrong Custer*, 1977—TV movie), Gary Cole (*SON OF THE MORNING STAR*, 1991—TV movie), Peter Horton (*CRAZY HORSE*, 1996—TV movie), and William Shockley (*STOLEN WOMEN, CAPTURED HEARTS*, 1997—TV movie). In the TV series *CUSTER*, 1967, Wayne Maunder played the military figure.

***Custer of the West* (1967)** Cinerama, color, 143 minutes. **Director:** Robert Siodmak; **Screenplay:** Bernard Gordon and Julian Halevy; **Cast:** Robert Shaw (George Armstrong Custer), Mary Ure (Elizabeth Custer), Jeffrey Hunter (Lieutenant Benteen), Ty Hardin (Maj. Marcus Reno), Charles Stalnaker (Lieutenant Howell), Lawrence Tierney (Gen. Philip Sheridan), Kieron Moore (Chief Dull Knife).

Like *HOW THE WEST WAS WON* (1962), *Custer of the West* was created as a cinema spectacle to utilize the Cinerama wide-screen process. Filmed as a U.S.–Spanish coproduction, the spectacle was shot in Spain and utilized an international cast, including Britishers Shaw and Moore and Scottish-born Ure to play three quite American characters. In the haphazard retelling of the saga of CUSTER who went down to defeat at the Battle of Little Big-horn in 1876, historical fact was constantly sacrificed for spectacle. The primary Native Americans involved, according to this rendition, were CHEYENNE, under the strong leadership of Dull Knife. Despite the movie's earlier showing of the massacre of Cheyenne women and children when the cavalry attacked their village, the film's point of view was that the vicious Native Americans were bloodthirsty culprits. Even the introduction into the story of the sympathetic-to-Native Americans Lieutenant Benteen did not counterbalance that perspective.

***Custer* (1967)** ABC-TV series, color, 60 minutes. **Cast:** Wayne Maunder (Lt. Col. George A. Custer), Slim Pickens (California Joe Milner), Peter Palmer (Sgt. James Bustard), Michael Dante (Chief Crazy Horse), Robert F. Simon (Brig. Gen. Alfred Terry), Grant Woods (Capt. Miles Keogh).

Striving for a less flamboyant CUSTER than provided by Errol Flynn in *THEY DIED WITH THEIR BOOTS ON* (1941), Maunder was the demoted former Civil War general who came westward in 1868 to take over the disorganized Seventh Cavalry Regiment at Fort Hays, Kansas. He is helped by his tough old army-scout pal California Joe Milner, but he finds Brig. Gen. Alfred Terry a rough opponent at the fort. The short-lasting teleseries did not reach the narrative point in time when Custer met his destiny at the battle of Little Big-horn.

Connecticut-born Dante (real name: Ralph Vitti) had played a Native American in the 1964 movie *Apache Rifles*.

D

Dakota, the See SIOUX, THE.

***Dance Me Outside* (1995)** A-Pix Entertainment, color, 87 minutes. **Director:** Bruce McDonald; **Screenplay:** McDonald, Don McKellar, and John Frizell; **Cast:** Ryan Rajendra Black (Silas Crow), Adam Beach (Frank Fencepost), Jennifer Podemski (Sadie Maracle), Michael Greyeyes (Gooch), Lisa LaCroix (Illiana), Kevin Hicks (Robert McVay), Rose Marie Trudeau (Ma Crow).

Based on the 1977 novel by W. P. Kinsella, this U.S.–Canadian production presented a coming-of-age theme involving Native Americans on the Kidabanessee Reservation in northern Ontario, Canada. In the drama-drenched entry, Silas Crow and Frank Fencepost hope to enter mechanics' school as a way out of their impoverished existence. Silas's girlfriend, Sadie Maracle, plans a career in activism and does not want to be tied down by marriage. Meanwhile, Sadie's sister, Illiana, arrives with her Caucasian husband (Hicks), which leads to confrontations when Illiana's former boyfriend (GREYEYES), just released from jail, tries to reconcile with her. Complicating everything is the senseless murder of a local girl by a hopped-up white racist. When the latter receives only a light manslaughter sentence, the tribe plots revenge.

Despite the soap-opera aspects of this biased melodrama, it reflected the emerging Native American cinema in which contemporary problems were fully addressed.

***Dances with Wolves* (1990)** Orion, color, 183 minutes. **Director:** Kevin Costner; **Screenplay:** Michael Blake; **Cast:** Kevin Costner ("Dances with Wolves" [Lt. John J. Dunbar]), Mary McDonnell (Stands With a Fist), Graham Greene (Kicking Bird), Rodney A. Grant (Wind in His Hair), Floyd "Red Crow" Westerman (Ten Bears), Tantoo Cardinal (Black Shawl), Robert Pastorelli (Timmons), Jimmy Herman (Stone Calf), Nathan Lee Chasing His Horse (Smiles a Lot), Michael Spears (Otter), Wes Studi (Toughest Pawnee).

If *LITTLE BIG MAN* (1970) and *BILLY JACK* (1971) helped to jump-start a new, more encompassing awareness in the United States about Native Americans, the multi-Oscar winning, big-grossing *Dances with Wolves* took that consciousness to yet another level. Based on the 1988 book by Michael Blake, Costner created a mammoth (in length) western, a genre that nearly had become extinct on the big screen. At the time (especially after the huge box-office take and the Oscar Award groundswell for this picture), many commentators found the offering to be sympathetic in its depiction of the Lakota SIOUX in the 1860s as westward expansion in America doomed their way of life. However, even then and more so later, some sources were critical of the movie's sprawling formlessness and that its feel-good attitude was too paternalistic and self-serving. As with, for example, *Lawrence of Arabia* (1962), they felt that this film treated the "natives" in the story line as unfortunates whom the great white man was graciously helping. In both films, the end results in the plot situations proved to be good for the whites but unfortunate for the natives. Other critics pointed out that, because *Dances with Wolves* was set so conveniently in the past, viewers could feel noble at having democratic thoughts about an ethnic minority without having to deal with the transgressions committed by white America in that century, let alone the offenses that were still occurring at the time of the movie's release (i.e., the deplorable conditions at many Native American reservations, the continued bigotry against Native Americans, etc.).

On the plus side, the PG-13-rated *Dances with Wolves* utilized a great many Native American talents, presented the

Lakota Sioux's dialogue in their native language (with English subtitles used), and paid close attention to details of daily life in the Sioux encampment as well as showing a graphic buffalo hunt. On the down side, the lengthy narrative actually had the white "hero" at the finale (albeit reluctantly) riding off into the sunset, taking with him the white woman, Stands With a Fist, who had lived among the Sioux for years. The leading figure and his companion leave behind the Sioux, who realize that their future is doomed because of the greedy white men who are decimating the area's natural resources and killing anyone or anything in their path.

Within *Dances with Wolves*, Yankee Lt. John J. Dunbar accidentally becomes a Civil War hero. However, disillusioned and adventurous, he requests a posting to the western frontier. Sent to Fort Sedgwick, a remote, rundown farmhouse in the South Dakota territory, and now on his own, he becomes acquainted with a wolf—whom he calls Two Socks—and later encounters Kicking Bird, a curious Sioux. Thereafter, he deals with the horse thief, Wind in His Hair, and Stands With a Fist. The latter is a white woman who was rescued years ago by the Sioux when her family was killed by Pawnee. She is mourning for her recently deceased husband. As Dunbar increasingly associates himself with the tribe and turns away from the white world, he finds love with Stands With a Fist, respect from the warriors, and a growing sense of life as seen through the Native American perspective. When Dunbar is caught and placed under custody by the U.S. cavalry, his Sioux friends rescue him by massacring the troopers, but fearful that the army will retaliate against the Sioux, he reluctantly leaves them, takes Stands With a Fist with him, and heads to new lands.

Made at a cost of less than $18 million, *Dances with Wolves* grossed more than $184 million in domestic distribution. It won seven Academy Awards: Best Adapted Screenplay, Best Cinematography, Best Director, Best Film Editing, Best Original Score, Best Picture, and Best Sound. It also received Oscar nominations for Best Actor (Costner), Best Art Director/Set Decoration, Best Costume Design, Best Supporting Actor (Greene), and Best Supporting Actress (McDonnell). A later version of *Dances with Wolves* used for foreign distribution and U.S. television showing was even longer, restoring deleted footage.

***Daniel Boone* (1936)** RKO, b&w, 77 minutes. **Director:** David Howard; **Screenplay:** Daniel Jarrett; **Cast:** George O'Brien (Daniel Boone), Heather Angel (Virginia Randolph), John Carradine (Simon Girty), Ralph Forbes (Stephen Marlowe), George Regas (Black "Blackie" Eagle), Dickie Jones (Master Jerry), Clarence Muse (Pompey).

This was one of the earlier Hollywood features to deal with legendary frontiersman Daniel Boone (ca. 1734–1820), whose many exploits—both real and mythic—formed the basis of several movies and a TV series through the decades. This version benefited from the robust performance by O'Brien in another of his he-man screen roles.

In 1775, rugged frontiersman Boone leads settlers from North Carolina to Kain-tu-kee across the Cumberland Mountains. Among the party is Virginia Randolph and her suitor, aristocratic fop Stephen Marlowe. Hardy outdoorsman Boone is joined by his friend of the forest, Black Eagle. Their sworn adversary is sinister Simon Girty who is in league with a contingent of unfriendly Native Americans. In the showdown, Boone and the settlers emerge victorious, with the frontiersman killing the vicious Girty.

Mingling fact and fiction this cinema biography followed along the lines of *THE LAST OF THE MOHICANS* in pairing settlers with good Native Americans against bad warriors. It was part of the slow progression on screen toward presenting Native Americans as dimensional individuals, not stock types.

***Daniel Boone* (1964–1970)** NBC-TV series, color, 60 minutes. **Cast:** Fess Parker (Daniel Boone), Albert Salmi (Yadkin: 1964–65), Ed Ames (Mingo: 1964–68), Patricia Blair (Rebecca Boone), Veronica Cartwright (Jemima Boone: 1964–68), Darby Hinton (Israel Boone), Dal McKennon (Cincinnatus), Don Pedro Colley (Gideon: 1968–69).

Having become extremely popular playing Davy Crockett for the Walt Disney Studio in the mid-1950s, Parker returned to TV as another legendary folk hero. As Daniel Boone, in the 1770s, he moves around the Kentucky–Tennessee–North Carolina territory doing surveying, helping to settle new lands, and encountering a variety of friendly and unfriendly Native Americans. His good warrior friend is Mingo; later Gideon, a black Native American, becomes his friend. More intent on detailing personal relationships than intense action, this family-oriented series at least differentiated between tribes of Native Americans as well as showing the quality of Native American warriors as either good or bad.

In 1977, a short-lived teleseries entitled *YOUNG DAN'L BOONE* featured the adventures of the Kentucky woodsman when he was in his twenties. It starred Rick Moses.

***Dark Wind, The* (1991)** Carolco, color, 111 minutes. **Director:** Errol Morris; **Screenplay:** Neal Jiminez, Eric Bergren, and Mark Horowitz; **Cast:** Lou Diamond Phillips (Officer Jim Chee), Gary Farmer (Cowboy Albert Dashee), Fred Ward (Lt. Joe Leaphorn), Guy Boyd (FBI Agent Johnson), John Karlen (Jake West), Jane Loranger (Gail Pauling).

Projected as the first in a series of screen adaptations of Tony Hillerman's popular mysteries featuring a NAVAJO tribal policeman, *The Dark Wind*—based on a 1977 novel—received bad press during casting when the producers (including Robert Redford) insisted that after a year of testing, they could not find a suitable Native American actor to play the lead and finally chose part-Native American actor PHILLIPS for the key assignment. Directed by documentary filmmaker Morris, the movie included subtitles for the Navajo and Hopi dialogue heard on screen.

Officer Jim Chee, investigating vandalism at a windmill in the Arizona desert, comes across a drug caper that escalates into several homicides. Combating the arrogant FBI agents, Chee's allies are Lieutenant Leaphorn at the reservation station and Leaphorn's pal and Hopi colleague, Cowboy Albert Dashee. With the intuition of his culture and the aid of a Hopi shaman, Chee is able to confront the dark wind—the negative force blowing through the wrongdoer(s).

For too simplistic in its genre presentation, the R-rated *The Dark Wind* was not a critical or box-office success, and the planned series did not materialize. It did, however, set the path for *THUNDERHEART* (1992), which featured an Oglala SIOUX (played by Val Kilmer) in the lead.

Davy Crockett, King of the Wild Frontier **(1955)** Buena Vista, color, 95 minutes. **Director:** Norman Foster; **Screenplay:** Tom Blackburn; **Cast:** Fess Parker (Davy Crockett), Buddy Ebsen (George Russel), Basil Ruysdael (Andrew Jackson), Hans Conried (Thimblerig), Ken Tobey (Col. Jim Bowie), Helen Stanley (Polly Crockett), Pat Hogan (Chief Red Stick), Nick Cravat (Busted Luck).

Stitched together from three *Disneyland* TV program episodes ("Davy Crockett, Indian Fighter," December 15, 1954; "Davy Crockett Goes to Congress," January 26, 1955; and "Davy Crockett at the Alamo," February 23, 1955) about the legendary frontiersman (1786–1836), this film's Davy Crockett, Fess Parker, began a pop phenomenon of the time (e.g., the hit song "Ballad of Davy Crockett," the merchandizing of coonskin caps, etc.). The TV installments and the pieced-together feature created renewed interest in America's frontier times. With a nod to history, this movie portrayed Crockett as very much pro–Native American, which in real life was not actually the case. The three-part adventure was produced with the cooperation of the Cherokee Indian Nation of North Carolina.

This biography, with songs, follows Crockett's battles with the Creek warriors, aided by his pal George Russel; his later election to Congress; and his final exploit at the battle of the Alamo in 1836 where he, Col. Jim Bowie, and others are overwhelmed by the Mexican troops.

Despite the seeming pro–Native American stance of the assembled footage (e.g., Crockett's plea to Congress on behalf of the minority), the Disney-produced chronicle treats the deaths of the "savages" in the battles cavalierly, as if their lives are less meaningful than those of the Caucasians. Hogan as Red Stick, the Creek instigator, is not especially convincing in his Native American role.

The success of this feature led to a further movie compilation about Crockett culled from the *Disneyland* TV series and to later episodes about the coonskin-capped frontiersman in 1988 on *The Magical World of Disney* TV series. With the American public, Crockett rated neck-to-neck with DANIEL BOONE, whom Crockett star Parker portrayed in a 1964–70 TV series.

Dead Man **(1996)** Miramax, b&w, 121 minutes. **Director/Screenplay:** Jim Jarmusch; **Cast:** Johnny Depp (William Blake), Gary Farmer (Nobody), Lance Henriksen (Cole Wilson), Gabriel Bryne (Charlie Dickinson), Robert Mitchum (John Dickinson), John Hurt (John Schofield), Mili Avital (Thel Russell), Billy Bob Thornton (Big George Drakoulious).

Offbeat in the strongest sense of the word, this lugubrious allegorical narrative was a convoluted homage to the western screen genre filled with surprising and often pointless cameo performances. Sometimes funny, at other times violent, and often just strange, the movie traced the odyssey of Cleveland accountant William Blake who travels westward in 1875 to the town of Machine for a promised job. When that doesn't materialize, the despairing man gets drunk. He has a liaison with Thel Russell, whose ex-boyfriend (Bryne) kills her and wounds Blake before he is killed by the easterner.

Hiding in the wilderness, Blake is rescued by Native American Nobody who, a great lover of British poetry, thinks that the stranger must be the rekindled spirit of the late English poet William Blake. After temporarily going their separate paths—during which time Blake kills two marshals who chased after him—Blake and Nobody rejoin forces and head to the village of Makah. By the time they reach their destination, Blake is dying. Nobody places his friend in a canoe and launches it out to sea. In a final shootout, Nobody and hired killer/bounty hunter Cole Wilson kill one another.

This arty feature, which long sat on the shelf, earned only slightly more than $1 million in domestic distribution, although it won several prizes and award nominations on the independent film circuit. One of the best performances in this oddity was delivered by FARMER as Nobody, the displaced, intellectual Native American.

de Kova, Frank (1910–1981) Born in New York City, he taught languages in New York City before becoming a performer. This long-working character actor played a variety of ethnics on camera (e.g., the Mexican colonel in *Viva Zapata!* 1952), but one of his specialties was that of a Native American. He became a familiar face in warrior roles of the Old West: Chief Chattez in *ARROWHEAD* (1953), Isatai in *THEY RODE WEST* (1954), Yellow Elk in *The White Squaw* (1956), and Red Cloud in *RUN OF THE ARROW* (1957). After a cycle of gangster roles (e.g., *Portrait of a Mobster*, 1961; *Follow that Dream*, 1962), he returned to form as Chief Wild Eagle on the *F TROOP* (1965–67) TV sitcom. A decade later, he was White Eagle in the contemporary drama *Johnny Firecloud* (1975).

Devil's Doorway **(1950)** Metro-Goldwyn-Mayer, b&w, 84 minutes. **Director:** Anthony Mann; **Screenplay:** Guy Trosper; **Cast:** Robert Taylor (Lance Poole), Louis Calhern (Verne Coolan), Paula Raymond (Orrie Masters), Marshall Thompson (Rod MacDougall), James Mitchell (Red Rock), Fritz Leiber (Mr. Poole), Chief John Big Tree (Thundercloud), George Sky Eagle (Lone Bear).

As part of MGM executive Dore Schary's program to make pro-American features, this rare excursion—for its time—into sympathetic portraiture of the Native American's plight was marred by several factors, among which was the casting of Caucasian box-office magnet Taylor (with heavy makeup) in the key role of the Shoshone tribe member returning home to Medicine Bow, Wyoming, after winning the Congressional Medal of Honor for service in the Civil War. The picture set the narrative in the past to keep potentially bigoted white moviegoers from feeling threatened by its compassionate attitude toward the story's hero. Moreover, the movie did not delve much into tribal lore/culture in its presentation, and it left the average viewer unable to appreciate the nuances of the lead character's viewpoint.

In this unusual western, the enemy was personified by the scoundrel Verne Coolan, an attorney who wants to grab the Poole family's rich land using a new homesteader's law as his means. The Civil War veteran discovers that his battlefield heroics mean nothing to the townsfolk who put their greed and prejudices above everything else. Poole hires comely Orrie Masters to represent him, but her efforts fail. Coolan organizes the local sheepherders to take Poole's land by force, leading to Poole and many of his men being killed.

directors of Native American-themed feature films

For much of the twentieth century, most American-made motion pictures that featured Native Americans were directed by Caucasians. Mostly, the narratives fell into the western or historical format and focused on white settlers and troops combating antagonistic warrior braves. Most action directors of the silent and sound era merely tried their hand at the format at one time or another; a few filmmakers made *frequent* forays into the genre. JOHN FORD (1895–1973) made many entries dealing with Native Americans, usually presenting them as the aggressor against the "innocent" white folk. In contrast to such of his films as *THE IRON HORSE* (1924), *STAGECOACH* (1939), *SHE WORE A YELLOW RIBBON* (1949), and *THE SEARCHERS* (1956), his last western, *CHEYENNE AUTUMN* (1964), did an about face in depicting Native Americans as the noble victims of the white settlers pushing westward.

Like Ford, spectacle-maker Cecil B. DeMille (1881–1959) used Native Americans as backdrops to his western sagas such as *THE PLAINSMAN* (1936), *UNION PACIFIC* (1939), and *UNCONQUERED* (1947). Occasionally, he presented the "savage" in a melodrama—dealing with interracial love—as in his *The Squaw Man* (1914), which he remade in 1918 and then again as a talkie in 1931.

In contrast Delmer Daves (1904–77), who began his career as an actor (e.g., *The Night Flyer*, 1928) and then a scriptwriter (e.g., *Dames*, 1934), became a feature film director by helming his screenplay for *Destination Tokyo* (1943). One of his later movies, *BROKEN ARROW* (1950), was a major Hollywood step forward in presenting the Native American sympathetically on screen. Several of his subsequent productions also featured a study of this ethnic minority (e.g., *Drum Beat*, 1954; *WHITE FEATHER*, 1955; *THE LAST WAGON*, 1956).

As the old-style western fell out of favor with moviegoers and political correctness militated against many such excursions after the 1970s, there was a slow growth in feature films being directed by Native Americans themselves. One such filmmaker was Victor Masayesva Jr., a member of the Hopi Nation. Besides being involved in the Native American Film and Video Festival at the Scottsdale Center for the Arts in Scottsdale, Arizona, and an active member of the Native American Producers Association, he both produced and directed *Imagining Indians* in the early 1990s, dealing with the images that emerge when native material is adapted to the commercial cinema. Phil Lucas (1942–), a Choctaw film director, served as writer, codirector, and coproducer of a five-part series *(Images of Indians)* that aired on PBS-TV between 1979 and 1981. Besides such later educational shorts (e.g., *Nez Perce: Portrait of a People*, 1982; *I'm Not Afraid of Me*, 1990) he produced a fifteen-part series, *Native Indians: Images of Reality* (1989) for the Canadian Knowledge Network, and an eleven-part sequel the following year. He was coproducer of the made-for-cable feature *BROKEN CHAIN* (1993) starring Pierce Brosnan, GRAHAM GREENE, and WES STUDI.

Chris Eyre (ca. 1969–) of Cheyenne-Arapaho Native American descent gained recognition with his feature film *SMOKE SIGNALS* (1998) for which he won two awards at the Sundance Film Festival. Since then, he has directed and produced the short subject *Things We Do* (1998), produced *Doe Boy* (2001—directed by Randy Redroad), and directed *SKINS* (2002) with Eric Schweig and Graham Greene. Actor GARY FARMER (1953–), who appeared on the first season of *Forever Knight* (1992–96, the police/supernatural drama), also was a segment director on this TV program. Since then, he directed the feature film *The Gift* (1999).

***Distant Drums* (1951)** Warner Bros., color, 103 minutes. **Director:** Raoul Walsh; **Screenplay:** Niven Busch and Martin Rackin; **Cast:** Gary Cooper (Capt. Quincy Wyatt), Mari Aldon (Judy Beckett), Richard Webb (Lt. Richard Tufts), Ray Teal (Private Mohair), Arthur Hunnicutt (Monk), Robert Barrat (Gen. Zachary Taylor), Larry Carper (Chief Ocala).

This lushly revamped offering of director Walsh's World War II 1945 epic *Objective, Burma!* (which had starred Errol Flynn) was filmed in the Florida Everglades at Silver Springs and at Castillo de San Marcos. Thanks to the film industry's Production Code Administration, the inflammatory tone of the movie's opening narration referring to SEMINOLE savagery was toned down. Nevertheless, not much care was devoted to having the Seminole characters dress in accurate attire because Hollywood assumed that the public was used to the stock costumes that had been employed on camera for decades in movies dealing with Native Americans.

In 1840, under orders from Gen. Zachary Taylor, naval Lt. Richard Tufts joins swamp fighter Capt. Quincy Wyatt in

Florida to undertake a campaign to defeat the Seminole who have been waging war in the swamps. After several battles in the Everglades, Wyatt has a face-off with Chief Ocala as they fight to the finish underwater. As a result, the remainder of the Seminole war party hastily leave.

As part of the slowly emerging consciousness of Hollywood about ethnic minorities, the plot presented Wyatt as the widower of a Creek princess and the father of a five-year-old son.

***Dr. Quinn, Medicine Woman* (1993–1998)** CBS-TV series, color, 60 minutes **Cast:** Jane Seymour (Dr. Michaela "Mike" Quinn), Joe Lando (Byron Sully), Orson Bean (Loren Bray), Chad Allen (Matthew Cooper), Erika Flores (Colleen Cooper: 1993–95), Jessica Bowman (Colleen Cooper: 1995–98), Shawn Tonvey (Brian Cooper), Larry Sellers (Cloud Dancing), Nick Ramus (Chief Black Kettle: 1993–95).

Set in the 1860s, this family-oriented western drama reflected a strong feminist slant in its episodes as Dr. Michaela "Mike" Quinn, a Boston doctor, moved to Colorado Springs, Colorado, to be the town's doctor. She suddenly finds herself in charge of three orphaned youngsters. Not only must she cope with the town's prejudice against women in medicine, but also she is pro–Native American—a novel idea at the time, displaying friendliness toward the CHEYENNE and to Cloud Dancing, their medicine man. Quinn develops a relationship—which leads to marriage—with Byron Sully, a mountain man who is more at home with the tribal warriors than he is with whites. In the course of the series' several seasons, the U.S. cavalry massacres many of the Cheyenne villagers, and Sully, who has become a government INDIAN AGENT, has to cope with conflicting loyalties and deal with renegade tribesmen who have left the reservation.

There was a reunion telefeature for this series—1999's *Dr. Quinn, Medicine Woman: The Movie.*

***Drums Along the Mohawk* (1939)** Twentieth Century-Fox, color, 103 minutes. **Director:** John Ford; **Screenplay:** Lamar Trotti and Sonya Levien; **Cast:** Claudette Colbert (Magdelana "Lana" Borst), Henry Fonda (Gilbert Martin), Edna May Oliver (Mrs. McKlennar), Eddie Collins (Christian Reall), John Carradine (Caldwell), Dorris Bowdon (Mary Reall), Jessie Ralph (Mrs. Weaver), Arthur Shields (Reverend Rosenkrantz), Chief John Big Tree (Blue Black), Noble Johnson (Native American brave).

The Iroquois predominated in upstate New York and parts of Canada around Lake Ontario. One of the six nations of the Iroquois were the Mohawk, who were presented as the "enemy" in this screen adaptation of Walter D. Edmonds's 1936 best-seller. Many of the skirmishes between the Mohawk and the settlers that occurred during a period of several years were consolidated within the script, a screenplay that put a far greater emphasis on the romantic interaction between Colbert and Fonda's characters. As in most of FORD'S westerns before *CHEYENNE AUTUMN* (1964), there was little sympathy displayed for the Native American characters, who emerged largely as cardboard-type "savages."

As the picture's action wa set at the start of the Revolutionary War in 1776, one might have anticipated that the British forces would have played some part in the drama. However, because Great Britain was in 1939 an ally of the United States as nations were being drawn into World War II, the bad guys were more diplomatically incorporated into the snarly Caldwell, a Tory, and his confederates. An Iroquois, BIG TREE, played one of his tribe in this feature, and the bulk of Native American extras were cast from the NAVAJO living near Monument Valley in southern Utah.

Lana Borst weds Gilbert Martin in 1776, and they set out for his farm in Deerfield in the frontier area of the Mohawk Valley in upstate New York. Having a pampered background, Lana has difficulty in coping with the rugged environment, whether it be her husband's friend Blue Back, working the fields, or living in constant fear of attacks from the Mohawk. The couple is befriended by eccentric widow, Mrs. McKlennar, who invites the Martins to stay with her after their farm is burned by Native American warriors abetted by Caldwell. In a climactic encounter, Martin and the American soldiers save the survivors (including Lana) at the besieged nearby fort.

Drums Along the Mohawk received Academy Award nominations for Best Cinematography (Color) and Best Supporting Actress (Oliver).

***Drums of the Desert* (1927)** Paramount, b&w, 5,907′. **Director:** John Waters; **Screenplay:** John Stone; **Cast:** Warner Baxter (John Curry), Marietta Millner (Mary Manton), Ford Sterling (Perkins), Wallace MacDonald (Will Newton), Heinie Conklin (Hi-Lo), Bernard Siegel (Chief Brave Bear), George Irving (Prof. Elias Manton), Guy Oliver (Indian agent).

Based on the Zane Grey story "Desert Bound" published in *McCall's* magazine (publication date undetermined), this production-line feature was shot on a NAVAJO reservation in Arizona. It offered a sympathetic portrayal of the Navajo as John Curry helped them prevent unscrupulous businessman Will Newton from stealing the oil rights on their land. But since this was a product geared for Caucasian picturegoers, the focus of this silent photoplay was switched to the budding romance between Curry and Mary Manton, the daughter of a professor who is heading an expedition into the desert region. There was also attention paid to the hijinks of two desert rats (Sterling and Conklin) who attached themselves to Manton's party.

E

***Education of Little Tree, The* (1997)** Paramount, color, 115 minutes. **Director/Screenplay:** Richard Friedenberg; **Cast:** James Cromwell (Grandpa), Tantoo Cardinal (Grandma), Joseph Ashton (Little Tree), Graham Greene (Willow John), Mika Boorman (little girl), Leni Parker (Martha), Michael Perron (Headmaster), Victoria Barkoff (teacher), Jeff Jeffcoat (voice of adult Little Tree).

This charming coming-of-age narrative dealing with Native American life was overlooked during its brief American theatrical distribution. It derived from a 1976 book (first published as a memoir) by Forrest Carter. (Later, it was revealed that Carter, who died in 1979, had been a Ku Klux Klan member and had been involved in writing speeches for Alabama governor George Wallace.)

In 1935 Tennessee during the height of the Depression, orphaned eight-year-old Little Tree is sent to live with his grandparents in the Smoky Mountains. His good-natured Scottish/Irish granddad teaches the boy to make moonshine, and his gentle Cherokee grandma instructs him in "The Way" of her people. The child's idyllic life is interrupted when an interfering relative alerts state authorities to the boy's illegal activities. As a result, he is dispatched to a state institution for Native Americans where the prime aim is to rob the children of their heritage. Chafing under the regime, Little Tree begs the Dog Star in the sky to help him. Soon thereafter, his grandfather arrives to help the boy escape the school. They return to their old life, but things again change. The old man dies and, soon thereafter, so does his philosophical wife. Little Tree becomes the ward of his grandparents' good friend Willow John.

Rarely had a screen newcomer given such a natural performance as Ashton did in the lead assignment here.

***Eskimo* (1933)** Metro-Goldwyn-Mayer, b&w, 120 minutes. **Director:** W. S. Van Dyke; **Screenplay:** John Lee Mahin; **Cast:** Mala (Kripik [Mala]), Lotus [Long] (Iva), Joseph Sauers [Sawyers] (Sergeant Hunt), W. S. Van Dyke (Inspector White), Peter Freuchen (Captain), Edgar Dearing (Constable Balk), Edward Hearn (Captain's mate).

In the tradition of *NANOOK OF THE NORTH* (1922), this documentary-style drama was an atypical depiction of NATIVE ALASKANS and their unique lifestyle and traditions. Filmed throughout a year in the Arctic by the movie crew that was based in Teller, Alaska, its star was a genuine Native Alaskan who had come to Hollywood months before to become a cameraman. The narrative was based on Peter Freuchen's books *Storfanger* (1927) and *Die Flucht ins weisse Land* (1929). Subtitles were employed to translate the native language and to explicate the complex moral code of the Eskimos, so alien to most moviegoers.

When renowned hunter Mala learns about a white man's ship anchored many miles away, he takes his wife and family on the long trek. Upon reaching the vessel, Mala trades valuable animal skins to the ship's captain in exchange for a rifle. While Mala and others are dispatched on a whale hunt, the captain rapes Mala's wife. The next day, she escapes from the ship but is shot by a sailor who mistakes her for an animal. When Mala learns the news, he kills the captain, and returns north with his children. After a period of grieving and taking on a new name (Kripik) to rid himself of his past identity, he accepts a new wife, Iva, who was given to him by a hunter. Later, Royal Canadian Mounted Police trick Kripik into returning to their outpost. He escapes with the law enforcers in pursuit. Admiring his bravery and tenacity, the Mounted Police let him go his way.

Made at a cost of $1.5 million and originally 160 minutes long, *Eskimo* won an Academy Award for Best Editing.

Eskimos See NATIVE ALASKANS.

F

Far Horizons, The **(aka: *Untamed West*) (1955)** Paramount, color, 108 minutes. **Director:** Rudolph Maté; **Screenplay:** Winston Miller and Edmund H. North; **Cast:** Fred MacMurray (Capt. Meriwether Lewis), Charlton Heston (Lt. William Clark), Donna Reed (Sacajawea), Barbara Hale (Julia Hancock), William Demarest (Sergeant Cass), Alan Reed (Charboneau), Eduardo Noriega (Cameahwait), Larry Pennell (Wild Eagle), Julia Montoya (Crow woman).

This fanciful recreation of the vital Lewis and Clark expedition (1803–06) was aimed at providing moviegoers with the excitement of skirmishes between white men and "the redskins" and clichéd situations. The depiction of the famous Sacajawea (ca. 1786–1812), the young Shoshone guide and interpreter, was pure Hollywood as interpreted by Caucasian Reed. As the film traced the trip to map the Louisiana Territory (just acquired from France) and to claim territory farther westward on behalf of the United States, the scene moves from North Dakota to the group's perilous crossing of the Rockies and their eventual reaching of the Pacific Ocean.

The movie introduces the viewer to several tribes (e.g., Minitari, Shoshone, Nez Percé), skirmishes between the whites and the Native Americans, and, of course, a protracted love story as snobbish Clark relinquishes some of his prejudice against Sacajawea's heritage and falls in love with her. When the mission is completed, she joins the others when they return to Washington, D.C., where she is introduced to the president of the United States. For the sake of the moral conventions of the 1950s, the plot has Sacajawea abandon Clark to his civilized love (Hale) and return to her own people.

The Far Horizons was based on the novel *Sacajawea of the Shoshones* (1943) by Della Gould Emmons.

Farmer, Gary (1953–) Heavy-set, round-faced, and soft-spoken, he lent his presence to such diverse features as Jim Jarmusch's anti-western, *DEAD MAN* (1995), as the guardian angel, and to *SMOKE SIGNALS* (1998) where he was the errant father of ADAM BEACH's character. In 1999, as part of the third annual Footsteps to the Future (sponsored by media unions to honor Native American performers and the Native American community) held at the Gene Autry Museum of western Heritage in Los Angeles, he was honored with the Acting Achievement Award.

A Cayuga of the Wolf clan, one of the six tribes that comprised the Iroquois Nation, he was born in Oshwekan, Ontario, Canada, on the Six Nations Reserve and grew up in Buffalo, New York. He spent three years studying photography and communications at Syracuse University and Ryerson Polytechnical Institute. By the mid-1980s, he was acting on stage and television. One of his early screen roles was a bit in the comedy *Police Academy* (1984); other early screen parts included *Big Town* (1987), *Blue City Slammers* (1988—a role he did on stage as well), and *RENEGADES* (1989). His movie breakthrough came in the buddy film *POWWOW HIGHWAY* (1989), in which he played the dreamer Philbert Bono, a Northern CHEYENNE, teamed with A Martinez. That same year Farmer was on stage playing a Cree in *Dry Lips Oughta Move to Kapuskasing*, a comic take on ethnic contemporary life.

In the 1990s, Farmer was seen in *SIOUX CITY* (1994), *Lilies* (1996), and the TV movie *Moonshine Highway* (1996). On the first season (1992–93) of the police/supernatural series *Forever Knight*, he was police captain Joe Stonetree. In the Canadian-made heist drama *Stolen Heart* (1998), he was Agent Whitaker, and in *Ghost Dog: The Way of the Samurai* (1999), Farmer was on hand playing Nobody. More recently, he appeared in *Angels Don't Sleep Here* (2000) and *The Score* (2001); in the horror thriller *ROUTE 666* (2001), Farmer was the shaman. Later movies included *SKINS*, *Adaptations*, and *A Thousand Guns* (all 2002).

In addition, he edited *Aboriginal Voices*, a publication devoted to North American indigenous cultures, directed short subjects, occasionally was a performing clown, and was always a cultural activist. As he told the *Los Angeles Times* (May 11, 1996): "I . . . mostly grew up in the white world, but for me the white world and the native world have always been like two rivers that run side by side, but will never meet. Because I feel it's my role to serve as a go-between. I have a foot in a canoe on each of these rivers, but that's a precarious position to maintain."

***Fighting Caravans* (1931)** Paramount, b&w, 92 minutes. **Directors:** Otto Brower and David Burton; **Screenplay:** Edward E. Paramore Jr., Keene Thompson, and Agnes Brand Leahy; **Cast:** Gary Cooper (Clint Belmet), Lily Damita (Felice), Ernest Torrence (Bill Jackson), Tully Marshall (Jim Bridger), Fred Kohler (Lee Murdock), Eugene Pallette (Seth Higgins), Charles Winninger (Marshall), Frank Hagney (renegade), Iron Eyes Cody (Native American Seeking Firewater).

Using Zane Grey's 1929 novel as its springboard, this expensively mounted western boasted a solid cast, a large production crew, and a story line that recalled Paramount's silent classic, *THE COVERED WAGON* (1923). (Actually, Torrence and Marshall recreated their frontiersmen's roles from that epic in this new picture.)

In the 1860s, Clint Belmet is a freewheeling young frontier scout hired to shepherd the wagon train from Missouri to California. His comrades-in-arms are older, weather-beaten Bill Jackson and Jim Bridger. The woman of the saga is the orphaned young French girl Felice who pretends to be Belmet's wife to get him out of a scrape with the law. The villain of the piece is Lee Murdock, who is in cahoots with Native American warriors and is out to betray the wagon train to them. In the climactic battle with the warriors, Belmet sets a kerosene wagon on fire, which scares off their attackers. Eventually, the caravan reaches California, and Belmet and Felice can wed.

This genre entry had all the needed (standard) components to tell its brutal tale. In the shootouts with the attacking Native Americans, as the settlers—including the women—load their rifles and keep shooting at the approaching enemy, one had the feeling of being in a shooting gallery where the outcome was assured. So much film was shot for this deluxe project that leftover footage was used for the studio's 1934 entry *Wagon Wheels*, starring Randolph Scott.

Fighting 7th, The See *LITTLE BIG HORN*.

***Flaming Star* (1960)** Twentieth Century-Fox, color, 92 minutes. **Director:** Don Siegel; **Screenplay:** Clair Huffaker and Nunnally Johnson; **Cast:** Elvis Presley (Pacer Burton), Steve Forrest (Clint Burton), Barbara Eden (Roslyn Pierce), Dolores Del Rio (Neddy Burton), John McIntire (Sam Burton), Rudolph Acosta (Chief Buffalo Horn), Marian Goldina (Ph'sha Knay), Perry Lopez (Two Moons), Rodd Redwing (Native American warrior).

Not only was this perhaps Presley's best screen performance, but it was also a superior western and a graphic study of the outcome of racial prejudice. In 1878 Texas, the Burton household consists of rancher Sam, his Kiowa wife Neddy, and two sons: Clint by Sam's first marriage, and Pacer, the HALF-BREED offspring of Sam and Neddy. When the Kiowa under Chief Buffalo Horn make one last push against the encroaching white settlers, their raid leads to retaliations by the ranchers. Among those who die are Neddy, Sam, and, in the final moments of the narrative—Pacer.

It was the dying Pacer who said as he headed to the hills to chase the flaming star of death, "Maybe someday . . . somewhere . . . people will understand folks like us." It summed up the story's characters who, on each side (Kiowa and white), had a tradition of enmity against the other that they could not shed, especially when each wanted the same lands.

Presley also played a mixed-blood character in the unsatisfactory comedy *STAY AWAY, JOE* (1968).

***Flap* (aka: *Nobody Loves a Drunken Indian*) (1970)** Warner Bros., color, 107 minutes. **Director.** Carol Reed; **Screenplay:** Clair Huffaker; **Cast:** Anthony Quinn (Flapping Eagle), Claude Akins (Lobo Jackson), Tony Bill (Eleven Snowflake), Victor Jory (Wounded Bear Mr. Smith), Don Collier (Mike Lyons), Shelley Winters (Dorothy Bluebell), Susan Miranda (Ann Looking Deer), Victor French (Sergeant Rafferty), Anthony Caruso (Silver Dollar), John War Eagle (Luke Wolf).

Aimed at making a serious statement about the plight of present-day Native Americans, this $6 million misfire instead emerged as a blundering comedy. QUINN, who had played many warriors on screen (e.g., *THEY DIED WITH THEIR BOOTS ON*, 1941; *BUFFALO BILL*, 1944) as well as a gentle Native American soul (e.g., *BLACK GOLD*, 1947), struggled with his interpretation of Flapping Eagle who spent his days drinking heavily with his cronies or cavorting with brothel madam Dorothy Bluebell, his sometimes girlfriend. Yet, beneath the rambunctious surface, Flapping Eagle had serious concerns about his impoverished reservation community in the American Southwest.

Constantly at odds with the half-breed police officer Sergeant Rafferty, who abuses his authority over the Native Americans, Flapping Eagle is counseled by the wise old lawyer, Wounded Bear Mr. Smith. As a form of protest, Flap commits "pranks" that often fall within the protection of some old treaty, until he goes too far: He steals a train, which he rolls onto the reservation, causing wide media attention. At first, he hides out in the hills but finally leads a protest parade through town where he is shot dead by Rafferty.

Had this heavy-handed production been released after *BILLY JACK* (1971), which defined a new American sensibility toward Native Americans, *Flap* might have been positioned to do better at the box office.

Ford, John (1895–1973) One of Hollywood's best-remembered and still revered directors, this prolific Irish-American filmmaker made dozens of movies in assorted genres and won several Academy Awards. Some of his westerns delineated Native Americans who were usually on the warpath, generally from a biased white point of view in which the tribesmen were mostly one-dimensional warriors: *THE IRON HORSE* (1924), *DRUMS ALONG THE MOHAWK* (1939), *FORT APACHE* (1948), *SHE WORE A YELLOW RIBBON* (1949), *WAGON MASTER* (1950), *RIO GRANDE* (1950), *THE SEARCHERS* (1956), and *TWO RODE TOGETHER* (1962). His *CHEYENNE AUTUMN* (1964) was a pro–Native American exception.

***Fort Apache* (1948)** RKO, b&w, 128 minutes. **Director:** John Ford; **Screenplay:** Frank S. Nugent; **Cast:** John Wayne (Capt. Kirby York), Henry Fonda (Lt. Col. Owen Thursday), Shirley Temple (Philadelphia Thursday), John Agar (Lt. Michael Shannon O'Rourke), Pedro Armendariz (Sgt. "Johnny Reb" Beaufort), Ward Bond (Sgt. Maj. Michael O'Rourke), George O'Brien (Capt. Sam Collingwood), Victor McLaglen (Sgt. Festus Mulcahy), Movita (Guadalupe), Miguel Inclan (Cochise), Grant Withers (Silas Meacham).

This was one of the most vital productions in FORD's extensive screen canon and the first of his three impressive cavalry pictures (the others being *SHE WORE A YELLOW RIBBON*, 1949, and *RIO GRANDE*, 1950). Suggested by James Warner Bellah's racist short story "Massacre" (1947), *Fort Apache*'s martinet fort commander was said to be a representation of the vainglorious Lt. Col. GEORGE ARMSTRONG CUSTER, who was defeated at the 1876 Battle of Little Big-horn. Eliminating much of the anti-Native American sentiment of Bellah's writing, Ford's movie treated the APACHE as victims of government-approved crooks.

In the post-Civil War era, Lt. Col. Owen Thursday is assigned to take over Fort Apache in Arizona. He is accompanied by his pretty daughter Philadelphia. Once at his new command, Thursday proves to be a strict disciplinarian who is still smarting from his military demotion when back East. Snobbish about military status, Thursday does his best to discourage the fast-growing relationship between Philadelphia and Lt. Michael Shannon O'Rourke, a recent West Point graduate and the son of a noncommissioned officer (McLaglen).

At the fort, Thursday conflicts with seasoned Plains fighter, Capt. Kirby York. The latter insists that the threat of Apache uprisings must be taken seriously, but Thursday refuses to heed his warnings. Matters between the whites and the Apache are not helped by the grasping Silas Meacham, the reservation agent. Later, while COCHISE, the proud Apache leader whose subordinates include GERONIMO, is heading for peace talks with government officials, Thursday attempts to overwhelm the warriors. Outmaneuvered, Thursday is forced to have York negotiate a temporary peace with Cochise. In a later showdown with Cochise and his braves, Thursday and many of his troops are killed. York and his group are the regiment's sole survivors and they surrender to Cochise. Some years later, York, as the head of Fort Apache, refuses to have the late commander's reputation tarnished.

Using the conventional trappings of a cavalry-versus-Indians formula, *Fort Apache* efficiently demystified the legend surrounding so-called superior white commanders. They were shown as more than matched in battle strategy by tribal leaders. In a plot parallel, just as Thursday was the flip, bad side of York, so Geronimo was the savage alter ego of the peace-desiring Cochise.

Because in usual Hollywood fashion, this film's point of view was largely from the perspective of the white fighters, the on-screen Native Americans emerged as savage and cruel but also occasionally surprisingly civilized, even when retaliating against the white man's broken promises. Although *Fort Apache* was a prestigious stepping stone in the evolution of presenting Native Americans on American film, it was no more than that. It remained for *BROKEN ARROW* (1950) to emphasize the Native American point of view and engender full-bodied sympathy for their approach to the encroaching, usually double-dealing white settlers and soldiers.

Fort Apache netted a $445,000 profit beyond its $2.1 million cost.

***Foxfire* (1955)** Universal, color, 93 minutes. **Director:** Joseph Pevney; **Screenplay:** Ketti Frings; **Cast:** Jane Russell (Amanda Lawrence Dartland), Jeff Chandler (Jonathan "Dart" Dartland), Dan Duryea (Dr.Hugh Slater), Mara Corday (Maria Conchera), Barton MacLane (Jim Mablett), Celia Lovsky (Sava Dartland), Billy Wilkerson (Apache chief).

On the surface, this may have seemed just another straightforward vehicle for buxom Russell and rugged CHANDLER but within its conventional soap-opera structure, it conscientiously delved into some of the problems of a Native American adapting his traditions to the modern world and of a Caucasian woman coping with a mixed marriage. As the *Saturday Review* (July 30, 1955) noted, the film "probes unusually deep in analyzing the position of women in an APACHE tribe and their relation to their men, with one beautifully handled sequence in which the withered Indian mother [Lovsky] explains by indirection the ways of her people to the bewildered young wife [Russell]."

Staying at a guest ranch in the Arizona desert, wealthy New Yorker Amanda Lawrence falls in love with and marries mining engineer Jonathan Dartland, a HALF-BREED Apache. Amanda soon discovers that her husband is as obsessed with his work as he is afraid of romantic commitment. On his part, he is sensitive about her initial negative attitude to Native Americans, and he misconstrues gossip by his friend's (Duryea) half-breed nurse (Corday) that Amanda is carrying on with the doctor friend. It is only after Amanda talks with her mother-in-law, Princess Aba, at the Apache reservation that the socialite begins to appreciate her husband's heritage and the complex emotional tradition of Apache men.

Chandler, who had played the Apache leader COCHISE in several films (e.g., *BROKEN ARROW*, 1950), not only wrote the lyrics to the *Foxfire* title song but also sang it on the soundtrack.

Frank, T. C. See LAUGHLIN, TOM.

***Frozen Justice* (1929)** Fox, b&w, 73 minutes. **Director:** Allan Dwan; **Screenplay:** Sonya Levien; **Cast:** Lenore Ulric (Talu), Robert Frazer (Lanak), Louis Wolheim (Duke), Ullrich Haupt (Captain Jones), Laska Winter (Douglamana), El Brendel (Swede), Alice Lake (Little Casino), James Spencer (medicine man).

Occasionally, Hollywood traveled to the far north in its story lines to deal with NATIVE ALASKANS, usually treating the on-camera excursion as a novelty act. This entry, based on Ejnar Mikkelsen's novel *Norden for lov og ret; en Alaska-Historie* (1920), was pure melodrama, and because it was made in the early sound period when musicals were in vogue, it boasted several songs as well.

Talu, who had an American father and a Native Alaskan mother, is torn between the two cultures. She loves her tribal-chief husband Lanak but craves the excitement of "nearby" Nome. When Captain Jones's ship crashes near Talu's village, he persuades her to come to Nome with him. Once in the city, Jones forces Talu to sing for her living at a local saloon. Her protector is Jones's first mate Duke, a lug who has fallen in love with her. Later, the jealous Jones kills Duke and then escapes in a sled, with Talu taken as a hostage. Lanak follows in pursuit. Jones misjudges the icy trail, and the sled crashes into the canyon below. As Lanak reaches Talu, she dies in his arms.

A similar but far-better/more-accurate account of the tundra was *ESKIMO* (1933).

***F Troop* (1965–1967)** ABC-TV series, b&w, then color, 30 minutes. **Cast:** Ken Berry (Capt. Wilton Parmenter), Forrest Tucker (Sgt. Morgan O'Rourke), Larry Storch (Cpl. Randolph Agarn), Melody Patterson (Wrangler Jane [Jane Angelica Thrift]), Frank de Kova (Chief Wild Eagle), Don Diamond (Crazy Cat).

Farcical lowjinks abound in the Old West as Capt. Wilton Parmenter bungles about as commander of Fort Courage (somewhere in the West) in 1866. He has a staff (the F Troop) of misfits, including the scheming Sgt. Morgan O'Rourke, who has gained the rights to sell tourist souvenirs for the Hekawai tribe and distribute bootleg whiskey. (O'Rourke is supplied with merchandise by Wild Eagle, chief of the Hekawai.)

Among the weekly visitors to this comical vision of the severe frontier were several eccentric Native American characters: a tribal detective named Wise Owl (Milton Berle), a 147-year-old brave called Flaming Arrow (Phil Harris), a rather addled and not-so-macho Roaring Chicken (Edward Everett Horton), and sarcastic Bald Eagle (Don Rickles) who was the son of Wild Eagle.

With everyone acting so frantically foolish on this situation comedy, it was hard to say whether the Native American characters or their white brethren were being disgraced more.

***Fury at Furnace Creek* (1948)** Twentieth Century-Fox, b&w, 88 minutes. **Director:** Bruce Humberstone; **Screenplay:** Charles G. Booth; **Cast:** Victor Mature (Tex Cameron [Cash Blackwell]), Coleen Gray (Molly Baxter), Glenn Langan (Sam Gilmore [Rufe Blackwell]), Reginald Gardiner (Captain Walsh), Albert Dekker (Leverett), Fred Clark (Bird), Robert Warwick (Gen. Fletcher Blackwell), Jay Silverheels (Chief Little Dog).

This western was a remake of John Ford's *Four Men and a Prayer* (1938), which had been set in India. It was again a tale of determination to clear the name of a man charged with dishonoring himself while under military duty. In this instance, the deceased Gen. Fletcher Blackwell was accused of diverting a cavalry unit from protecting supply wagons headed to Fort Furnace Creek. As a result, the APACHE, who had massacred the wagon train, hid in the convoy until it entered the fort and then killed the soldiers and burned the stockade. Later, Blackwell died on the witness stand during his court-martial. Thereafter, his sons, Cash, a gambler, and Rufe, a West Point graduate, go undercover independently to find the truth. In the end, Little Dog, the Apache chief who had been paid by mining syndicate head Leverett to raid the supply wagons and stage the fort massacre, is used by Cash to eliminate the villain.

Whether as rampaging warriors or pawns in the white man's power games, the Native Americans here were tools of vengeance. The sequence of the warriors decimating the troops at the fort was staged memorably.

G

George, Dan (Chief) (1899–1981) During the 1970s, when he was in his seventies, he became the best-known Native-North American performer. He was Oscar nominated in the Best Supporting Actor category for his sterling performance as Old Lodge Skins, the wise old Cheyenne in *LITTLE BIG MAN* (1970). It was only his second motion picture.

Born in North Vancouver, British Columbia, Canada, a member of the Coast-Salish tribe, Dan George was by trade a stevedore until, in 1947, an accident physically disabled him. After a time, in 1961, his oldest son, an actor on Canadian television in the series *Cariboo Country*, suggested his father as replacement for a Caucasian actor playing the role of the chief. That was the start of George's acting career. By the late 1960s, he had come to Hollywood for an episode of the western TV series *High Chaparral* and remained for the family drama *SMITH!* (1969). When not acting in film or television, he performed a ninety-minute stage show, using his entire family to showcase authentic native songs and dances.

His success in *Little Big Man* led him to the Canadian TV series *The Beachcombers* (1972) and to such diverse films as the Bob Hope comedy *Cancel My Reservation* (1972) and the well-appreciated *Harry and Tonto* (1974), where he was Sam Two Feathers. He was in the short documentary *Chief Dan George Speaks* (1974) and played in the comedy *THE BEARS AND I* (1974). In *Shadow of the Hawk* (1976), he was a medicine man coping with a grandson (Jan Michael Vincent) coming to terms with his culture. One of his best parts was as the philosophical soul in Clint Eastwood's *THE OUTLAW JOSEY WALES* (1976). For the miniseries *CENTENNIAL* (1978–79), Dan George enacted an old SIOUX.

In 1970, while promoting *Little Big Man*, Dan George said in a studio press release, "I intend to stay with acting until I cannot do it any more. I like the effect it is having on the Indian people on both sides of the border. I have received a lot of mail telling me that my work has made a difference." His last film was *Nothing Personal* (1980), a mild comedy with Donald Sutherland and Suzanne Somers. He passed away the next year in Vancouver, British Columbia, where until his final illness, he lived at the Burrard Reserve with his family.

During his lengthy life, Dan George served as elected chief of the Tse-lal-watt band, part of the Coast-Salish tribe, and later was honorary chief of both the Squamish and Sushwap bands, two of the largest such in British Columbia. On stage in the early 1970s he appeared in *The Ecstasy of Rita Joe* as the father of a girl forced into prostitution. He also authored the book *My Heart Soars* (1974), a collection of his philosophies, which was a plea to young tribespeople to retain the beliefs of their forefathers. Never part of the radical causes promoted by the American Indian Movement, he was a long-time activist for native rights and for preserving the environment.

Geronimo (ca. 1829–1909) Of any Native American warrior, the general public most associated the term *bloodthirsty savage* with Geronimo, the Chiricahua APACHE medicine man. Born Goyathlay (i.e., the Yawner; One Who Yawns), he became infamous—in white America—as the renegade Apache whose band fled the reservation, marauded the countryside, and later fought General George H. Crook and his troops in the mid-1880s in the Sierra Madre. Eventually Geronimo made peace with the U.S. government and was relocated to Fort Sill in Oklahoma where he died still a prisoner of war. Through the decades, the facts of his adventurous life were (mis)represented in many contradictory ways.

Among the actors who played Geronimo on the American screen were Tony Urchel (*Hawk of the Wilderness*, 1938—

movie serial), CHIEF THUNDERCLOUD (*GERONIMO*, 1939), Tom Tyler (*VALLEY OF THE SUN*, 1942), Chief Thundercloud (*I KILLED GERONIMO!* 1950), JAY SILVERHEELS (*BROKEN ARROW*, 1950), John War Eagle (*The Last Outpost*, 1951), Silverheels (*THE BATTLE AT APACHE PASS*, 1952), Miguel Inclan (*Indian Uprising*, 1952), CHIEF YOWLACHIE (*Son of Geronimo*, 1952—movie serial), Monte Blue (*APACHE*, 1954), Ian MacDonald (*TAZA, SON OF COCHISE*, 1954), Silverheels (*WALK THE PROUD LAND*, 1956), Chuck Connors (*GERONIMO*, 1962), Enrique Locero (*Mr. Horn*, 1979—TV movie), Joaquin Martinez (*Gunsmoke: The Last Apache*, 1990—TV movie), JOSEPH RUNNINGFOX, Jimmy Herman (*Geronimo*, 1993—TV movie), and WES STUDI (*GERONIMO: AN AMERICAN LEGEND*, 1993). Pat Hogan and then Silverheels were Geronimo in episodes of the "Texas John Slaughter" segments on the Disneyland TV series in the late 1950s.

***Geronimo* (1939)** Paramount, b&w, 89 minutes. **Director/Screenplay:** Paul H. Sloane; **Cast:** Preston Foster (Capt. Bill Starrett), Ellen Drew (Alice Hamilton), Andy Devine (Sneezer), William Henry (Lt. John Steele Jr.), Ralph Morgan (General Steele), Gene Lockhart (Gillespie), Marjorie Gateson (Mrs. Steele), Chief Thundercloud (Geronimo), Monte Blue (interpreter), Chief Thunderbird (Chief Eskiminzu).

Because GERONIMO is the title character of this western, an effort was made to rationalize his "bad Indian" behavior (i.e., white men have savagely massacred his family). From then on, the film was a tale of bloody revenge as the renegade APACHE led his band in raids against settlers and soldiers. His chief opponent is General Steele, a martinet who is commander of the fort in Grant, Arizona. The cavalry commander is drawn out from the safety of the stockade when his son (Henry) is captured by the warring Apache. At the finale, Lieutenant Steele battles Geronimo face-to-face to save his imperiled father.

Economy was the keynote of this production. Borrowing plot premises from the studio's earlier *Lives of a Bengal Lancer* (1935) and using stock footage from *THE PLAINSMAN* (1936), *The Texas Rangers* (1936), *Wells Fargo* (1937), and other Paramount movies, *Geronimo* strove to make its key character as fearsome as possible, especially in the makeup used for Geronimo. The Apache's misadventures, however, were constantly interrupted by the narrative's focus on plot points that involved white characters (e.g., the ongoing contention between General Steele and his West Point graduate son, young Steele's romance with Alice Hamilton, and new soldier Steele's desire to prove himself to his dad).

Then too, although a Native American was this picture's main figure, Geronimo's portrayer (the Native American THUNDERCLOUD) was *not* even listed by the studio among the top-clustered primary cast names. It indicated both on- and off-camera practices in 1930s Hollywood that relegated Native Americans to the bottom of the cast list, no matter what size part they were playing on screen.

***Geronimo* (1962)** United Artists, color, 101 minutes. **Director:** Arnold Laven; **Screenplay:** Pat Fiedler; **Cast:** Chuck Connors (Geronimo), Kamala Devi (Teela), Ross Martin (Mangus), Pat Conway (Maynard), Adam West (Delahay), Enid Jaynes (Huera), Lawrence Dobkin (General Crook), Denver Pyle (Senator Conrad), Mario Navarro (Giantah).

Twenty-three years after Paramount's *Geronimo*, this low-budget feature—shot in Mexico—was released. New York-born and ex-baseball player Connors starred in the key role and, despite wig and makeup, was not convincing as the war-hungry APACHE. (The female lead was given to Bombay, India-born Devi.) That aside, the chronicle was far more sympathetic to the Apache plight than its screen predecessor. In this edition, GERONIMO and his surviving followers capitulate to the U.S. cavalry. Despite promises from the U.S. government, they are forced to live on the San Carlos Indian Reservation (in southeast Arizona) and work as farmers.

On the reservation, Geronimo attracts the interest of schoolteacher Teela, who encourages him to learn to read and write so that he can better understand the Caucasian world. When duplistic government agents attempt to sell part of the reservation, the angered Geronimo and his braves rebel and escape to Mexico. Eventually, Geronimo's exploits attract sympathizers in the U.S. Congress and in the media: Senator Conrad investigates and prevents Geronimo and his men from being annihilated. Because there is now the promise of a new and better treaty, Geronimo orders his followers to surrender yet again.

Working with a simplistic script, the budget-minded 1962 *Geronimo* managed some exciting action scenes as the Apache underdogs battle untrustworthy whites. This pro–Native-American approach was now becoming more commonplace in Hollywood productions about the savage West.

***Geronimo* (1993)** TNT cable, color, 100 minutes. **Director:** Roger Young; **Teleplay:** J. T. Allen; **Cast:** Joseph Runningfox (Geronimo), Nick Ramus (Mangas Coloradas), Michelle St. John (Ishton), Michael Greyeyes (Juh), Tailinh Forest Flower (Alope), Kimberly Norris (Chelchaye), Jimmy Herman (Old Geronimo), August Schellenberg (Cochise), Ryan Black (young Geronimo).

In reviewing the TV movie *Geronimo*, which launched TNT cable's series *(Behind the Legends, Beyond the Myths)* of Native-American-themed projects, Ray Lloyd of *Daily Variety* (December 3, 1993) reported, "Geronimo, the fierce Apache war chief, finally gets a human and fair portrait after a filmic history of Hollywood distortion. . . . Although this isn't the first positive depiction of American Indians, it stands as perhaps the most multidimensional character study of Native American culture, and one more indictment of the white man's horrific final solution."

Using three different actors to play the APACHE warrior at different stages of life, this revisionist film opened with the elder and sadder GERONIMO (Herman) thinking back on his years, now that he has become a stock figure used by the U.S. government for parades and the like. Rather than just recreating the period when he was the notorious leader of renegade braves, this production traces as well his formative years and details his relationship with his three wives. It develops the treachery of Mexican soldiers against the Apache that leads Geronimo to take reprisals, putting him on his defiant path against the U.S. government.

In contrast to the earlier Hollywood theatrical releases (1939 and 1962), this TV adaptation, filmed in Arizona, resonated with authentic details and ambiance. It benefited from the striking performance of RUNNINGFOX as the full-bodied Apache terror.

***Geronimo: An American Legend* (1993)** Columbia, color, 115 minutes. **Director:** Walter Hill; **Screenplay:** John Milius and Larry Gross; **Cast:** Jason Patric (Lt. Charles Gatewood), Gene Hackman (Brig. Gen. George Crook), Robert Duvall (Chief of Scouts Al Sieber), Wes Studi (Geronimo), Matt Damon (Lt. Britton Davis), Rodney A. Grant (Mangas), Kevin Tighe (Brig. Gen. Nelson Miles), Steve Reevis (Chato), Victor Aaron (Ulzana), Stuart Proud Eagle Grant (Sergeant Dutchy), Pato Hoffman (the Dreamer).

Wes Studi as Geronimo in *Geronimo: An American Legend* (1993). (JC ARCHIVES)

A much more serious effort than past features dealing with the legendary GERONIMO, this account stressed the ambiguities in the lives of all the principle figures, with none of the characters purely good or evil. Because the picture sought to be more historically accurate than its predecessors, the APACHE warrior's campaigns against the whites were shown as a series of raids and skirmishes that did not lead to a fictional (and audience-pleasing) crescendo as in most such genre pieces.

Told from the point of view of Lt. Britton Davis, newly graduated from West Point, the narrative traces the events as Lt. Charles Gatewood, a former Confederate officer, is ordered to make Geronimo—whom he knows and admires—surrender to the white man. The Chiricahua Apache are removed to a reservation in Arizona where they take up farming. The peace is shattered when Chief of Scouts Al Sieber erroneously kills the Dreamer, a revered Apache medicine man who had predicted trouble ahead. The event leads to bloodshed. First General Crook and then his replacement combat Geronimo. Finally Gatewood, with Davis part of his small group, corrals Geronimo and his small band of starving warriors. Geronimo surrenders, and he and his men are sent to a Florida prison. Upset by the outcome, Davis resigns from the army; Gatewood's "reward" is to be reassigned to an insignificant outpost.

Shot in Moab, Utah, *Geronimo: An American Legend* grossed less than $14 million in domestic distribution. (The fact that a competing cable TV movie, *GERONIMO*, was released the same year hardly helped this theatrical release at the box office.) *Geronimo: An American Legend* received an Academy Award nomination for Best Sound. This version suffered commercially because it tried to be a thoughtful, accurate, and at times arty (e.g., the camera work and the flashes forward in black-and-white as Geronimo envisioned the future), depiction of Geronimo's life and actions—which went counter to established Hollywood screen traditions. Yet, it also did not have the courage to make Geronimo the narrative's true center; instead, the point of view was that of the green army officer Davis and/or the cynical Gatewood. This was a shame because Studi was charismatic enough as the ambiguously motivated Geronimo to have carried the film.

The real-life, resolute, and vengeful chief of scouts Al Sieber had also been a character in *APACHE* (1954—played by John McIntire) and the TV movie *Mr. Horn* (1978—played by Richard Widmark) and was the basis for the Ed Bannon figure in *ARROWHEAD* (1953—played by Charlton Heston). The actual Lt. Britton Davis, portrayed by newcomer Damon, wrote the 1929 tome *The Truth About Geronimo*, a sympathetic retelling of his military encounter with the famed Apache warrior.

God's Army See *PROPHECY, THE.*

Good Day to Die, A See CHILDREN OF THE DUST.

***Grand Avenue* (1996)** HBO cable, color, 167 minutes. **Director:** Daniel Sackheim; **Teleplay:** Greg Sarris; **Cast:** Irene Bedard (Reyna), Tantoo Cardinal (Nellie), Eloy Casados (Albert), Deeny Dakota (Justine), Alexis Cruz (Raymond), Diane Debassige (Alice), Jenny Gago (Anna), Cody Lightning (Sheldon), A Martinez (Steven).

Set in Santa Rosa, California, and using Sarris's 1994 collection of stories as its source, *Grand Avenue* is an urban drama dealing with contemporary problems facing Native Americans. It explores the dimension of their lives in the same realistic manner as *Laurel Avenue* (1993), which dissects the contemporary African-American lifestyle.

After her husband's death, Reyna leaves the reservation with her three children to start a fresh life in the city with relatives in an ethnic neighborhood of a northern California city. While she deals with her former boyfriend (Martinez) who has his own burden to carry, she and her family cope with the pressures of their new life and balance their cultural traditions with new American ways.

Grand Avenue received an Emmy nomination for Outstanding Achievement in Casting for a Miniseries or a Special. One of the project's executive producers was actor/filmmaker Robert Redford.

Grant, Rodney A. (1959–) From 1989, when he had tiny roles in his first two feature films (*WAR PARTY* and *POWWOW HIGHWAY*), Grant quickly moved to a key assignment in *DANCES WITH WOLVES* (1990) as the fierce warrior Wind in His Hair. The part earned him fantastic notices, and *People* magazine chose him in 1991 as one of the 50 Most Beautiful People in the World.

He was born a member of the Omaha tribe on a reservation near Winnebago, Nebraska, was brought up by his grandmother, and was a high-school dropout. One of his first show-business acting tasks was a documentary for Nebraska public television about Native Americans; in his first feature, *War Party*, he played a traitorous Indian scout. Once established in films, he was hired to be in the two-part telefeature *SON OF THE MORNING STAR* (1991) as Crazy Horse, the SIOUX chief who helped defeat GEORGE ARMSTRONG CUSTER at the battle of the Little Big-horn. He was at the side of the renegade APACHE in *GERONIMO: AN AMERICAN LEGEND* (1993) and was one of those caught in the unfunny western satire *Wagons East* (1994) starring John Candy.

For the 1994–95 syndicated TV series, *HAWKEYE*, based on James Fenimore Cooper's *The Leatherstocking Tales*, Grant was the noble "savage" CHINGACHGOOK. His role was subordinated to MICHAEL GREYEYES in the romantic/historical drama *STOLEN WOMEN, CAPTURED HEARTS*, a 1997 TV movie starring Janine Turner, and he supported Anthony Michael Hall in the direct-to-video action thriller *The Killing Grounds* (1997). Grant and IRENE BEDARD were among the featured cast in the made-for-cable western, *Two for Texas* (1998). Rodney's later assignments included the made-for-cable *The Jack Bull* (1999), a western with John Cusack, and *Wild, Wild West* (1999), a poor big-screen version of the classic TV series. Thereafter he appeared in *Ghost of Mars* and *Just A Dream* (both 2001).

Greene, Graham (1952–) As Kicking Bird, a Lakota SIOUX holy man who befriended the title character (played by Kevin Costner) in *DANCES WITH WOLVES* (1990), Greene was Oscar nominated as Best Supporting Actor. Since then, this Oneida actor fulfilled his acting potential in such parts as Walter Crow Horse, who helped the HALF-BREED FBI agent in *THUNDERHEART* (1992), and as Arlen Bitterbuck, in *Stephen King's The Green Mile* (1999).

He was born on the Six Nations Reserve near Brantford, Ontario, Canada, the second of six children. At sixteen, he quit school and moved to Rochester, New York, where he found employment in a carpet warehouse. He later studied welding in Toronto, Ontario, and then built railway cars in a local factory. For much of the 1970s, besides odd jobs, he was first a sound man and roadie for Toronto-area rock bands and then operated a recording studio in Lancaster, Ontario.

Greene's first acting part was as a Native American in a 1974 stage play at a Toronto little theater. He was active in theater throughout the 1980s, appearing in the dramas *The Crackwalker* as an alcoholic and in *Jessica* as the Crow. He also worked with the Theatre Passe Muraille, and for a time, he was doing collective theater in Britain. He made his movie debut in *RUNNING BRAVE* (1983) as a pal of track star Billy Mills (played by Robby Benson). After a bit as a Huron brave in the Colonial American saga *Revolution* (1985), four years passed before he was cast as a Lakota Vietnam veteran in *POWWOW HIGHWAY* (1989). Also in 1989, he won recognition for his stage work in *Dry Lips Oughta Move to Kapuskasing*.

The same year as *Dances with Wolves*, Greene played Native American roles on episodes of TV's *L.A. Law* (as a Navajo attorney) and *NORTHERN EXPOSURE* (as a shaman). In 1991, he was a mystical activist in the Canadian-made movie *Clearcut*. For the American-produced TV film, *THE LAST OF HIS TRIBE* (1992), he was the lone Yahi tribesman who linked up with white culture.

In the mid-1990s Greene was part of the TV movie upsurge on Native American themes, appearing in such entries as *Cooperstown* (1993), *THE BROKEN CHAIN* (1993), and *The Pathfinder* (1996—as CHINGACHGOOK). He was among the cast of the family movie *THE EDUCATION OF LITTLE TREE* (1997) and was in *Song of Hiawatha* (1997). He joined Pierce Brosnan for the Canadian-made *Grey Owl* (1999) and participated in the black comedy *Bad Money*. More recently, he appeared in such Canadian-produced screen dramas as *Desire* (2000), *Lost and Delirious* (2001), *Red Green: Duct Tape Forever* (2002), and *Snow Dogs* (2002). In the 2001 TV series *Wolf Lake*, set in the Pacific Northwest, Greene played Sherman Blackstone, a science teacher. He was very affective as the alcoholic tribesman in SKINS (2002).

Greyeyes, Michael (1967–) Although several Caucasian actors (e.g., Paul Mercurio) switched from ballet to acting in films, few Native American actors have taken that creative path. One of those exceptions was handsome, six-feet, two-inch Greyeyes, a full-blooded Cree, noted for his lead roles in the TV movies CRAZY HORSE (1996) and STOLEN WOMEN, CAPTURED HEARTS (1997).

He was born in Qu'Appelle Valley, Saskatchewan, Canada. At the age of ten he was the first Native Canadian to be accepted to the National Ballet School in Toronto. From 1987 to 1990, the six-feet, two-inch talent was a member of the Corps de Ballet of the National Ballet of Canada. From 1990 to 1993, he was part of the New York City-based Felds Ballets as a solo dancer. In 1992, during down time while recovering from an injury, he choreographed a stage play that was his introduction to acting.

In 1993, Greyeyes won the role of Juh in the cable TV movie GERONIMO. Since then, he has alternated between his acting career and the world of dance. He had roles in the screen dramas DANCE ME OUTSIDE (1994—as an ex-convict) and *Rude* (1995—as Spirit Dancer) and played an APACHE in *Rough Riders* (1997), a TV movie about Teddy Roosevelt. He received Best Actor Awards from First Americans in the Arts (a group that cites native achievements in the arts) for his lead assignments in *Crazy Horse* and *Stolen Women, Captured Hearts.* During this period, he was also awarded a grant by the Canada Council to study "First Nations Traditional Dance" (and in particular, powwow). In mid-1999, his children's play *How a Promise Made the Buffalo Dance* (which he wrote, directed, and choreographed) was presented in Norway.

Among Greyeyes's later screen work was playing Junior Polatkin in SMOKE SIGNALS (1998), teaming with Dolph Lundgren in *The Minion* (1998), and portraying Wandering Spirit in the Canadian miniseries *Big Bear* (1998). Along with IRENE BEDARD and TANTOO CARDINAL, he was in the TV movie THE LOST CHILD (2000). In *Skipped Parts* (2001), he was the rodeo rider involved with Jennifer Jason Leigh. Next came the R-rated drama *Zigzag* (2002) with Wesley Snipes and John Leguizamo.

***Guestward Ho!* (1960–1961)** ABC-TV series, b&w, 30 minutes. **Cast:** Joanne Dru (Babs Hooten), J. Carrol Naish (Hawkeye), Mark Miller (Bill Hooten) Flip Mark (Brook Hooten), Earle Hodgins (Lonesome), Jolene Brand (Pink Cloud), Tony Montenaro Jr. (Rocky).

Based on a 1956 book by Barbara Hooten, this back-to-nature TV situation comedy featured New York City advertising executive Bill Hooten, who, with his very unoutdoorsy wife Babs and son Brook, move to New Mexico. They have purchased a dude ranch—which turns out to be rundown—from Hawkeye, a natural-born schemer who operates the local trading post and a souvenir stand within the Guestward Ho vacation ranch. Hawkeye proves to be an extremely savvy Native American, the type who reads the *Wall Street Journal* and orders his trinkets from Hong Kong. In his own jovial way, he is getting his revenge for white settlers taking his tribe's land in the prior century. It was a rarity in the 1960s, and even today, to have a Native American character on screen frequently outmaneuvering his Caucasian associates.

Mark Miller, J. Carrol Naish, Joanne Dru, and Earl Hodgins (l to r) in the TV comedy series *Guestward Ho!* (1960–61). (VINCENT TERRACE)

New York–born Naish had played CHIEF SITTING BULL in both ANNIE GET YOUR GUN (1950) and SITTING BULL (1954).

***Gunman's Walk* (1958)** Columbia, color, 97 minutes. **Director:** Phil Karlson; **Screenplay:** Frank Nugent; **Cast:** Van Heflin (Lee Hackett), Tab Hunter (Ed Hackett), Kathryn Grant (Cecily "Clee" Chouard), James Darren (Davy Hackett), Mickey Shaughnessy (Will Motley), Robert F. Simon (Sheriff Harry Brill), Ray Teal (Jensen Sieverts), Chief Blue Eagle (Black Horse), Bert Convy (Paul Chouard).

Within the guise of a western action entry, this sturdy film examined the amount of prejudice that Caucasians in the Old West harbored against Native Americans, even those who were HALF-BREEDS.

At an Indian agency, Ed Hackett and his younger brother Davy hire extra hands to help with their horse drive to Jackson City, Wyoming. Davy finds himself in love with the beautiful half-breed SIOUX named Cecily "Clee" Chouard, whose father was a Frenchman, and defends her against Ed's crude advances. Later, in a horse-chasing competition with

Clee's half-breed brother Paul, hot-tempered Ed pushes him over a cliff. He claims it was an accident, but two Native American witnesses know differently. Thanks to a duplistic horse trader (Teal) who blackmails Ed's rancher father Lee, a former gunslinger, Ed is freed. Later, the unrepentant Ed guns down the trader and, thereafter, a deputy who has rearrested him. In the climax Lee must choose between letting ruthless Ed continue his murderous ways or taking action on his own.

Neither Grant nor Convy were particularly convincing as the mixed-blood characters. Director Karlson, had previously helmed *THEY RODE WEST* (1954), about a compassionate doctor in the Old West who treats Native Americans with respect.

***Gunsmoke* (1955–1975)** CBS-TV series, b&w and color, 30 (later 60) minutes. **Cast:** James Arness (Marshal Matt Dillon), Milburn Stone (Dr. Galen "Doc" Adams), Amanda Blake (Kitty Russell: 1955–74), Dennis Weaver (Chester Goode: 1955–64), Ken Curtis (Festus Haggen: 1964–75), Burt Reynolds (Quint Asper: 1962–65), Roger Ewing (Clayton Thaddeus "Thad" Greenwood: 1965–67).

One of the pioneering adult westerns on TV, this long-running show was based on the radio series (1952–61) of the same name, which had starred William Conrad as U.S. marshal Matt Dillon. The tough law enforcer of Dodge City, Kansas, in the 1860s has such cohorts as his deputy Chester, Miss Kitty who operates the Longbranch Saloon (and is romantically involved with the sheriff), and the town's sole physician Dr. Galen Adams. One of the other townsfolk is HALF-BREED Native American Quint Asper, the blacksmith. As played by part-Cherokee REYNOLDS, Asper is one of the several unusual characters who have settled in this tough western town. Having such a figure on *Gunsmoke* was making no more of a political statement than having Chester Goode walk with a limp. Such nontypical figures were merely employed to provide the TV series with an offbeat flavor.

H

half-breed A pejorative term once used to refer to an individual of mixed blood from different races, here, usually Caucasian and Native American. Very often—especially in U.S. films of the first half of the twentieth century—such a screen character was projected as evil and untrustworthy merely because he or she was a half-breed (e.g., INJUN JOE of the various adaptations of Mark Twain's *The Adventures of Tom Sawyer*). Another screenplay premise was that a half-breed character belonged to neither world and was thus torn between cultural roots and identity. This created problems when he or she sought to have a relationship with a member of another race (especially Caucasian). This provided the dramatic grist for all the versions of *RAMONA* (1916, 1928, and 1936). Another frequent premise, especially in the 1930s through 1950s, was that being of mixed blood made a female character wild, sensual, and unpredictable. This was the theme of, for example, *CALL HER SAVAGE* (1932) and *Duel in the Sun* (1946).

Among the many American films dealing with Native American half-breeds were *Where the Trail Divides* (1914), *THE HALF-BREED* (1916), *The Spirit of '76* (1917), *The Heart of Wetona* (1919), *Across the Divide* (1921), *Red Love* (1925), *Hawk of the Hills* (1927—movie serial and the 1929 condensed feature version), *Red Ryder* (1934—movie serial), *'Neath the Arizona Skies* (1934), *Behold My Wife* (1935), *The Miracle Rider* (1935—movie serial), *Winners of the West* (1940—movie serial), *Saddlemates* (1941), *The Scarlet Horseman* (1946—movie serial), *COLORADO TERRITORY* (1949), *The Cowboys and the Indians* (1949), *TULSA* (1949), *THE HALF-BREED* (1952), *ARROWHEAD* (1953), *HONDO* (1953), *BROKEN LANCE* (1954), *Seminole Uprising* (1955), *THE LAST WAGON* (1956), *TROOPER HOOK* (1957), *GUNMAN'S WALK* (1958), *FLAMING STAR* (1960), *ICE PALACE* (1960), *THE UNFORGIVEN* (1960), *STAY AWAY, JOE* (1968), *BORN LOSERS* (1967), *THE STALKING MOON* (1968), *100 Rifles* (1969), *BILLY JACK* (1971), *The Trial of Billy Jack* (1974), and *Billy Jack Goes to Washington* (1977).

***Half-Breed, The* (1916)** Triangle, b&w, 5 reels. **Director:** Allan Dwan; **Screenplay:** Anita Loos; **Cast:** Douglas Fairbanks (Lo Dorman), Alma Reubens (Teresa), Sam De Grasse (Sheriff Dunn), Tom Wilson (Curson), Frank Brownlee (Winslow Wynn), Jewel Carmen (Nellie).

Athletic Fairbanks brought his swashbuckling skills to the Old West in this silent picture that cast him as a HALF-BREED Indian banished from town by its white citizens. By its inferences, the film had a lot to say about what Americans thought of nonpure-blooded Caucasians.

Lo Dorman lives on the outskirts of the settlement with his adopted Native American father. In the primitive setting, he encounters another pariah, Teresa, who has escaped the law after stabbing her two-timing lover. Meanwhile, Sheriff Dunn observes the two of them together and mistakenly thinks that the woman is actually his own girlfriend Nellie; as such, the lawmaker vows to kill the outcast. Before Teresa can explain the truth to the sheriff—she having learned that he is Dorman's real father—a fire breaks out in the forest. Unable to save both Teresa and the sheriff, Dorman rescues her. Later, the couple wed.

When *The Half-Breed* was released, there was much audience and reviewer comment about physically fit Fairbanks cavorting among the redwood trees (the film was lensed in Calaveras County in a California national park), clad only in a breech-cloth. The drama was based on Bret Harte's short story "In the Carquinez Woods," which appeared in his book *In the Carquinez Woods and Other Tales* (1883). The same writing was used for the basis of *Tongues of Flame* (1918), a lesser and far differently plotted screen vehicle for Thomas Meighan and Bessie Love.

***Half Breed, The* (1922)** Associated First National Pictures, b&w. **Director/Screenplay:** Charles A. Taylor; **Cast:**

Wheeler Oakman (Delmar Spavinaw), Ann May (Doll Pardeau), Mary Anderson (Evelyn Huntington), Hugh Thompson (Ross Kennion), King Evers (Dick Kenton), Joseph Dowling (Judge Huntington).

This film provided another illustration of the continuing belief by moviemakers (and, apparently, by the U.S. moviegoing public) in the 1920s that HALF-BREEDS were tainted by nature and could never exist peacefully in the white world. This entry was based on the play *Half-Breed: a Tale of Indian Territory* by H. D. Cottrell and Oliver Morosco (ca. 1906).

Although Delmar Spavinaw, a half-breed Native American, is well educated, the bigoted Judge Huntington refuses to consider him as a prospective suitor for his daughter Evelyn. The rebuffed Spavinaw is jealous of his rival, Ross Kennion, a widower who owns a large spread that Spavinaw is convinced belongs to his Native American mother. The intolerant judge sides with Kennion and orders the "squaw" evicted from Kennion's property. This leads Spavinaw to action, including a gun battle with Kennion. Chased by the posse, he teams up with Doll Pardeau, one of Evelyn's friends. Together, they escape via train to a new future together.

***Half-Breed, The* (1952)** RKO, color, 81 minutes. **Directors:** Stuart Gilmore and uncredited Edward Ludwig; **Screenplay:** Harold Shumate and Richard Wormser; **Cast:** Robert Young (Dan Craig), Janis Carter (Helen Dowling), Jack Buetel (Charlie Wolf), Barton MacLane (Marshal Cassidy), Reed Hadley (Crawford), Porter Hall (Kraemer), Judy Walsh (Nab-Lin), Chief Thundercloud (subchief), Chief Yowlachi (Indian chief), Stuart Randall (Hawkfeather).

If *DEVIL'S DOORWAY* (1950) seemed a promising step forward in race relations by promoting better understanding and fairer treatment of Native Americans, the pedestrian *The Half-Breed* took a moral step backward. Here the HALF-BREED (Buetel) was caught between opposing forces. The APACHE were rebelling against the corrupt practices of the local INDIAN AGENT (Hall) who was in connivance with San Remo hotel owner Crawford. (Crawford was secretly aiming to take the reservation land from the Apache to gain the gold buried there.) Meanwhile, gambler Dan Craig has arrived in town, becomes friendly with the half-breed, and is pursuing saloon singer Helen Dowling.

As time passes, Craig acts as intermediary between the Apache and the U.S. Army (who have been stirred up against the warriors by Crawford and his henchmen). Eventually, Craig becomes the new Indian agent. He must deal with Crawford when the crook's men steal a supply shipment meant for the reservation. In the showdown, Craig kills Crawford, and war with the Apache is averted. As for the half-breed, his sister (Walsh) is killed, and he loses Helen's affection to Craig. Despite all this, he nobly rides off to the reservation with a resolve to teach his brethren the white man's ways!

Besides using Caucasian Buetel to play the half-breed Native American, the script gave his character typically dumb dialogue, mostly of the grunts and "ugh" variety.

***Halliday Brand, The* (1957)** United Artists, b&w, 79 minutes. **Director:** Joseph H. Lewis; **Screenplay:** George W. George and George F. Slavin; **Cast:** Joseph Cotten (Daniel Halliday), Viveca Lindfors (Aleta Burris), Betsy Blair (Martha Halliday), Ward Bond (Big Dan Halliday), Bill Williams (Clay Halliday), Jay C. Flippen (Chad Burris), Christopher Dark (Jiuaro Burris).

Bigotry against mixed-blood Native Americans permeated this brooding drama set in a close-minded town of the Old West.

Told in flashback, Sheriff Dan Halliday, who owns a large ranch and rules his family with an iron thumb, is aghast to discover that his daughter (Blair) is romancing the spread's HALF-BREED head wrangler, Jivaro Burris. Big Dan orders him off the ranch and, later, when Burris is accused of cattle rustling and murdering a landowner—crimes he did not commit—intolerant Halliday is only too happy to arrest him. Later, the supposed law enforcer leaves the jailhouse unguarded and Burris is lynched. The deceased's sister, Aleta, also a half-breed, is loved by Clay Halliday (the weak-willed son whom Big Dan later shoots down) and by the responsible older offspring Daniel. In the finale, set in the present, Big Dan dies trying to shoot unshakable Daniel.

***Hawk* (1966)** ABC-TV series, color, 60 minutes. **Cast:** Burt Reynolds (Lt. John Hawk), Wayne Grice (Det. Dan Carter), Bruce Glover (Asst. D.A. Murray Slaken), John Marley (Sam Crown), Leon Janney (Asst. D.A. Ed Gorton).

In the mid-1960s, this TV series was considered unique as a police drama because its lead character, Lt. John Hawk (played by part-Cherokee REYNOLDS), was a Native American.

Hawk, a full-blooded Iroquois, is assigned to the night shift of the New York district attorney's office. He is partnered with Det. Dan Carter and his caseload finds him dealing with the full spectrum of the city's inhabitants.

Beyond the gimmick of his cultural roots, this show was standard fare, and it left the air after only four months. A decade later, in 1976, it was brought back as a summer fill-in, trading on the star's then big-screen fame. Another police drama to utilize a Native American law enforcer was *NAKIA* (1974).

***Hawkeye* (1994–1995)** Syndicated TV series, color, 60 minutes. **Cast:** Lee Horsley (Hawkeye [Nathaniel Bumppo], Lynda Carter (Elizabeth Shields), Rodney A. Grant (Chingachgook), Lochlyn Munro (McKinney), Jed Rees (Peevey), Garwin Sanford (Capt. Taylor Shields).

Quite loosely based on James Fenimore Cooper's book series *The Leatherstocking Tales*, first published in the nineteenth century, this unimpressive syndicated program was no great addition to the television line-up. It was set in 1755 during the French and Indian War and found woodsman Hawkeye and his Delaware warrior friend CHINGACHGOOK helping to right wrongs in New York's Hudson Valley. They undertake small missions occasionally for the British, deal with the warlike Huron tribe, and help the locals. Much was made of Hawkeye's budding romance with Elizabeth Shields who operated the local trading post. Her husband had been captured by the Huron, and his fate was unknown.

This one-season entry did little for the reputations of either Cooper's classic tales or for Native Americans—everything centered around the noble hunter/sharpshooter Hawkeye. At least, this adaptation of the classic utilized a Native American to play Chingachgook (as had the 1992 feature version of *THE LAST OF THE MOHICANS*, which hired RUSSELL MEANS for the same part).

***Hawkeye and the Last of the Mohicans* (1957)** Syndicated TV series, b&w, 30 minutes. **Cast:** John Hart (Hawkeye [Nat Cutler]), Lon Chaney Jr. (Chingachgook).

In this low-budget program drawn from James Fenimore Cooper's nineteenth-century novels, *The Leatherstocking Tales*, Hawkeye was the pioneer and fur trader who, with his blood brother CHINGACHGOOK, helped newcomers in the 1750s as they settled New York's Hudson Valley.

Safely set in historical times and based on a classic of literature, the show caused no comment for teaming a Caucasian with a Native American character. As played by veteran actor Chaney Jr., the series paid scant attention to the cultural heritage of the warrior figure, nor did it bother much with authenticity. Rather, it relied on the perception of what the entertainment industry felt viewers had of "redskins."

Chaney had previously played a warrior chief in the low-budget *Battles of Chief Pontiac* (1952) and was Black Fish in the Mexican-shot *Daniel Boone, Trailblazer* (1956). Four decades later, another adaptation—more expensive but equally inaccurate and formulistic—of Cooper's literary characters appeared in *HAWKEYE* (1994–95). Several 1957 feature film releases were pasted together from episodes of this TV series, including: *The Pathfinder and the Mohican*, *The Redmen and the Renegades*, and *Along the Mohawk Trail.*

Henderson, Don See LAUGHLIN, TOM.

***Heritage of the Desert, The* (1924)** Paramount, b&w and color, 5,785′. **Director:** Irvin Willat; **Screenplay:** Shelby Le Vino; **Cast:** Bebe Daniels (Mescal), Ernest Torrence (August Naab), Noah Beery (Mal Holderness), Lloyd Hughes (Jack Hare), Ann Schaeffer (Mrs. Naab), James Mason (Snap Naab).

A silent western that boasted Technicolor sequences, this feature was based on Zane Grey's 1910 novel. This tale of a mixed-blood individual and of compliant Native Americans was given Hollywood's usual presentation of savage warriors.

Mescal, the spirited HALF-BREED ward of veteran rancher August Naab, is engaged to wed Naab's shiftless son Snap, but the spunky woman falls in love with an Easterner, Jack Hare; he became ill in the desert, was found by Naab, and was taken back to the ranch to recuperate. Later, villainous Mal Holderness, anxious to grab the water rights to this parched territory, kidnaps both Mescal and Snap. Although Snap is killed by Holderness, Mescal is rescued by Naab and friendly Native Americans.

Hickok, Wild Bill (1837–1876) The renowned frontiersman and lawman was born James Butler Hickok, and his life as a woman-chasing gambler was far from the pure version shown in many romanticized screen versions. His reputation as a fast draw led many gunmen to challenge his skills; eventually, he was killed at Deadwood, South Dakota. His many legendary adventures on the western plains often involved (warring) Native Americans. Because most of the films were told from, and for, a white perspective, Hickok always was the victor. Sometimes, Hickok was linked in narratives dealing with BUFFALO BILL CODY.

Among the actors who played this near mythical figure on the American screen were William S. Hart (*Wild Bill Hickok*, 1923), Jack Padjan (*The Iron Horse*, 1924), Yakima Canutt (*The Last Frontier*, 1932—movie serial), Charles Middleton (*The World Changes*, 1933), Gary Cooper (*THE PLAINSMAN*, 1936), Allen Greer (*Custer's Last Stand*, 1936—movie serial), William "Wild Bill" Elliott (*Wild Bill Hickok*, 1938, and a series of later western pictures), George Houston (*FRONTIER SCOUT*, 1938), *The Great Adventures of Wild Bill Hickok* (1938—movie serial), Roy Rogers (*Young Bill Hickok*, 1940), Bruce Cabot (*Wild Bill Hickok Rides*, 1941), Richard Dix (*Badlands of Dakota*, 1941), Reed Hadley (*Dallas*, 1950), Robert Anderson (*The Lawless Breed*, 1953), Forrest Tucker (*Pony Express*, 1953), Douglas Kennedy (*Jack McCall, Desperado*, 1953), Howard Keel (*Calamity Jane*, 1953), Tom Brown (*I Killed Wild Bill Hickok*, 1956), Robert Culp (*The Raiders*, 1963), Robert Dix (*Deadwood '76*, 1965), Paul Shannon (*THE OUTLAWS IS COMING!*, 1965), Don Murray (*The Plainsman*, 1966), Jeff Corey (*LITTLE BIG MAN*, 1970), Ben Murphy (*This Is the West That Was*, 1974—TV movie), Charles Bronson (*The White Buffalo*, 1977), Richard Farnsworth (*THE LEGEND OF THE LONE RANGER*, 1981), Jeff Bridges (*Wild Bill*, 1995), Sam Elliott (*Buffalo Girls*, 1995—TV movie), and Sam Shepard (*Purgatory*, 1999—TV movie). In the TV series, *Adventures of Wild Bill Hickok* (1951–58), Guy Madison played the lead; in the 1997 animated TV series, *The Legend of Calamity Jane*, Clancy Brown was the voice of Hickok.

***Hombre* (1967)** Twentieth Century-Fox, color, 111 minutes. **Director:** Martin Ritt; **Screenplay:** Irving Ravetch and Harriet Frank Jr.; **Cast:** Paul Newman (Hombre [John Russell]), Fredric March (Alexander Favor), Richard Boone (Cicero Grimes), Diane Cilento (Jessie Brown), Cameron

Mitchell (Sheriff Frank Braden), Barbara Rush (Audra Favor), Peter Lazer (Billy Lee Blake), Margaret Blye (Doris Lee Blake), Martin Balsam (Henry Mendez), Frank Silvera (Mexican bandit), Pete Hernandez and Merrill C. Isbell (Apaches).

Derived from Elmore Leonard's 1961 novel, *Hombre* was an adult, gruesome western that was well photographed by veteran James Wong Howe. It was also a shrewd study of bigotry against Native Americans.

As a child, John Russell was abducted by the APACHE and raised as one of them. Now in the 1880s, Russell, known as Hombre, holes up in the hills of eastern Arizona, making a meager livelihood as do many of his fellow Apache who are not living in squalor on the rundown reservation. Having just inherited a boarding house, he sells it in exchange for a herd of horses and leaves town on the stage.

Aboard is his friend Henry Mendez (the driver), middle-age, pompous INDIAN AGENT Alexander Favor and his much younger wife Audra, Jessie Brown (the former manager of the boarding house), a nasty stranger (Cicero Grimes), and a bickering couple (the Blakes). Because of bigoted Favor, Hombre must ride on top with the driver. The stagecoach is held up by four gunmen who work secretly for Grimes. They take the $12,000 Favor stole from government funds and carry off his wife as hostage. Russell kills two of them, including the one who had Favor's money. By the finale, the robbers are dead, but Hombre, despite his anger at the corrupt Favor and his wife who mistreated the Apache on the reservation, gives his life to save the others.

Similar to a true HALF-BREED, Newman's Hombre was a man without cultural roots or true identity. Yet, he followed the precepts of his Apache upbringing: He was a man of few words who was blunt when he did speak. He took decisive action and followed a code of honor. In contrast, the whites presented in this variation of *STAGECOACH* (1939) were either corrupt, immoral, bickering, or treacherous. As a sharply etched character study, *Hombre* made a strong antiwhite, pro–Native American statement. Its chief industry concession was having handsome, Caucasian box-office star Newman as Hombre.

***Hondo* (1953)** Warner Bros., color, 84 minutes. **Director:** John Farrow; **Screenplay:** James Edward Grant; **Cast:** John Wayne (Hondo Lane), Geraldine Page (Angie Lowe), Ward Bond (Buffalo), Michael Pate (Chief Vittorio), James Arness (Lennie), Rodolfo Acosta (Silva), Leo Gordon (Ed Lowe), Lee Aaker (Johnny Lowe).

WAYNE offered one of his best performances in this feature that was filmed in the 3-D process and was based on Louis L'Amour's short story, "The Gift of Cochise" (1952).

In the harsh Southwest of 1874, the APACHE are stirred up against the settlers and the U.S. Army. U.S. cavalry dispatch rider Hondo Lane (along with his dog Sam) takes refuge at Angie Lowe's ranch when he loses his horse in a skirmish with warring Apache. Strong-willed Angie, with the help of her young son Johnny, has run the ranch since her husband Gordon deserted the spread. Angie refuses to be cowered by the threats of Apache raids. Later, when Vittorio and his Apache band show up at the ranch, Johnny attempts to shoot them; this impresses Vittorio who makes the boy a blood brother. At the same time, Vittorio demands that the apparently husbandless Angie wed one of his followers; she refuses. Thereafter, Lane is captured by the Apache. They torture him and, in hand-to-hand combat, he kills Silva, the brother of a warrior whom Lane shot at an earlier time. Thereafter, the cavalry handles Vittorio and his men, and Lane, Angie, and Johnny start a new life together.

Hondo received an Academy Award nomination for Best Screen Story. The popular film was the basis for the 1967 TV series *Hondo* starring Ralph Taeger and Kathie Browne. On that show, Australian-born Pate repeated his role of Chief Vittorio.

horror and supernatural—feature films and television series As political correctness became more evident in the United States and was reflected in entertainment products, some theatrical releases chose to use Native American lore, superstition, and the powers of shamans and medicine men to provide plot threads for horror/supernatural tales. An early example was *THE MANITOU* (1978) about a four-century-old medicine man who became a human parasite on human victims. Another example was *NIGHTWINGS* (1979), which takes place on a *NAVAJO* reservation and involves vampire bats. The underrated *WOLFEN* (1980) concerns Native American construction workers in New York City and a pack of supertough wolves.

In *POLTERGEIST II* (1986), a Native American mystic is the "only" one who can stave off the nasty spirits prowling after the Freeling family and others. Other genre pieces included *The Cellar* (1990), which deals with a COMANCHE monster spirit, *SHADOWHUNTER* (1993), *SUNCHASER* (1996), and *Route 666* (2001). On television, the short-lived TV series *Wolf Lake* (2001), a supernatural drama, featured Native American characters. LOU DIAMOND PHILLIPS played a Seattle police detective while GRAHAM GREENE was a science teacher.

On the TV series *Forever Knight* (1992–96), the lead character was a homicide police detective who happened to be a centuries-old vampire. During the first season of this supernatural/police drama, Capt. Joe Stonetree at the precinct was played by Native-Canadian actor GARY FARMER. An unusual entry was the supernatural western TV series, *Ned Blessing: The Story of My Life and Times* (1993) (see WESTERN SERIES—TELEVISION).

***Howdy Doody* (1947–1960)** NBC-TV series, b&w and color, 30 minutes. **Cast:** Bob Smith ("Buffalo" Bob Smith), Bob Keeshan (Clarabell Hornblow: 1948–52—later by Henry McLaughlin, Bob Nicholson, and Lew Anderson), Bill LeCornec (Chief Thundercloud: 1949–60), Dayten Allen (Ugly Sam: 1949–52), Judy Tyler (Princess Summerfall Winterspring: 1951–53).

The granddaddy of children's TV fare, this pioneering program was immensely popular during the late 1940s and the early 1950s. Its cast of memorable characters ranged from the congenial host "Buffalo" Bob Smith and the clown Clarabell (with his honking horn) to the marionettes Howdy Doody and Phineas T. Bluster to the audience of kids sitting in the set's peanut gallery.

Interestingly, there were several Native Americans populating Doodyville. At first, Princess Summerfall Winterspring was a marionette on the program and then became a live-action role played by Tyler in the manner of an attractive ingénue who had just been promoted from children's theater. Chief Thundercloud came across as a mix between a cigar-store brave and the "ugh-um" benign stereotype of movies—especially comedies like *THE PALEFACE* (1948). He was a member of the Ooraognak tribe and his favorite expression was "Kowa bonga." His adversary was Chief Featherman (played by Keeshan).

***How the West Was Won* (1962)** Metro-Goldwyn-Mayer/Cinerama, color, 165 minutes. **Directors:** Henry Hathaway, John Ford, George Marshall, and (uncredited) Richard Thorpe; **Screenplay:** James R. Webb; **Cast:** Spencer Tracy (narrator), Carroll Baker (Eve Prescott), Lee J. Cobb (Lou Ramsey), Henry Fonda (Jethro Stuart), Karl Malden (Zebulon Prescott), Gregory Peck (Cleve Van Valen), George Peppard (Zeb Rawlings), Robert Preston (Roger Morgan), Debbie Reynolds (Lilith Prescott), James Stewart (Linus Rawlings), Eli Wallach (Charlie Gant), John Wayne (Gen. William T. Sherman), Richard Widmark (Mike King), Chief Weasel, Red Cloud, and Ben Black Elk (Native Americans).

Made as a showcase for the Cinerama wide-screen process, this five-part panorama of the settling of the American West was derived from a seven-part 1959 *Life* magazine series. It traced the Prescott family as they headed westward in 1829 and the events that transpired to three generations of the clan as the century came to an end. Both "The Plains" and "The Railroad" contained sections of the white settlers versus the Native Americans. Especially evident in "The Plains" was the warrior-staged attack on the California-bound wagon train carrying Lilith Prescott and Cleve Van Valen, which is invading their sacred territory.

Never more than set pieces of colorful decoration to this chronicle, the Native Americans fade from the story line as "civilization" pushes them onto reservations; by the epic's final section, "The Outlaws," the good versus evil is no longer the white settlers against the "redskins" but a white law enforcer (Peppard) in opposition to Caucasian outlaws headed by Charlie Gant.

Made at a cost of $14 million, the feature—later edited down for non–road-show engagements—grossed more than $50 million in worldwide release. It won Academy Awards for Best Film Editing, Best Sound, and Best Adapted Story/Screenplay. It received Oscar nominations for Best Art Direction/Set Decoration (Color), Best Cinematography (Color), Best Costume Design (Color), Best Original Score, and Best Picture. The feature film led to the 1976 miniseries *The Macahans*, starring James Arness and Eva Marie Saint, and the 1978–79 TV series *How the West Was Won*, headlined by Arness, Bruce Boxleitner, Fionnula Flanagan, and Kathryn Holcomb.

I

***Ice Palace* (1960)** Warner Bros., color, 145 minutes. **Director:** Vincent Sherman; **Screenplay:** Harry Kleiner; **Cast:** Richard Burton (Zeb Kennedy), Robert Ryan (Thor Storm), Carolyn Jones (Bridie Ballantyne), Martha Hyer (Dorothy Wendt Kennedy), Diane McBain (Christine Storm), George Takei (Wang), Chester Seveck (old Eskimo), Helen Seveck (old Eskimo Woman).

Edna Ferber's sweeping novel *Alaska* (1958) was published shortly before the vast northern territory became the forty-ninth state of the United States on January 3, 1959. Her narrative was truncated and trivialized in this silly movie adaptation, which did offer gorgeous cinematography and a lush Max Steiner score. The absurd plot interweaved the lives of racially bigoted Zeb Kennedy (salmon canner turned major industrialist) and Thor Stor (salmon fisherman turned politician) over several decades as their friendship turned to bitter rivalry. The soap opera involved generations of the two men, including Thor's half–NATIVE-ALASKAN son Christopher and the latter's daughter Christine.

In this bogus drama, Native Alaskans were much discussed but little seen, except for Thor's mixed-blood descendants.

***I Heard the Owl Call My Name* (1973)** CBS-TV, color, 90 minutes. **Director:** Daryl Duke; **Teleplay:** Gerald Di Pego; **Cast:** Tom Courtenay (Father Mark Brian), Dean Jagger (Bishop), Paul Stanley (Jim Wallace), Marianne Jones (Keetah), George Clutesi (George P. Hudson).

Responding to the growing interest in Native American culture, this poignant drama, based on the 1967 book by Margaret Craven, traces the growth of a young Anglican priest who is sent to a remote church in a fishing village in the Canadian Northwest to help an aged bishop (Jagger). While there, his point of view and knowledge are expanded by dealing with Native Canadians and their contrasting lifestyle.

***I Killed Geronimo* (1950)** Eagle Lion, b&w, 63 minutes. **Director:** John Hoffman; **Screenplay:** Sam Neuman and Nat Tanchuck; **Cast:** James Ellison (Jeff Smith [Capt. Jeff Packard]), Virginia Herrick (Julie Scott), Chief Thundercloud (Geronimo), Smith Ballew (Lieutenant Furness), Luther Crockett (Major Clem French).

CHIEF THUNDERCLOUD, who had played the much-dreaded Chiricahua APACHE chief in GERONIMO (1939), reprised his role in this budget feature, based more on fancy than fact.

In 1882, Capt. Jeff Packard, whose own parents were killed by Apache, is assigned to eliminate Geronimo. The much-feared Apache warrior is still on the warpath and is buying weapons from some unknown, treacherous white Americans. Using the name Jeff Smith, Packard goes undercover in the town of Larksberg, hoping to pinpoint Geronimo's contact.

By now, the name Geronimo had become—thanks to the movies—synonymous with a vicious "redskin" who showed no mercy to whites. This economy production exploited that lore.

impersonations—Caucasians playing Native American characters As with ethnic minority groups such as African Americans and Asian Americans, U.S. moviemakers (as on the stage) felt through much of the twentieth century that Caucasians not only could portray Native Americans better than actual Native Americans but also that (1) it would help the project's box office if a mainstream talent was featured in such a role, (2) it would avoid possible conflicts about having—even as actors—a Caucasian and an actual Native American having an on-camera romance and sharing kisses (if the story so required), which would violate the majority's distaste of mixed romance, and (3) there were supposedly no trained Native American performers to handle major roles. As a result, through much of the twentieth century, Hollywood utilized mostly Caucasians to be Native Americans on camera.

Occasionally, the white actor acquitted himself well in the role, usually because he was playing a noble character and he invested the part with virtuous behavior, rather than interpreting the role as a true Native American might. Examples of this included Richard Dix (*THE VANISHING AMERICAN*, 1925; and *REDSKIN*, 1929) and JEFF CHANDLER (*Broken Arrow*, 1950; *THE BATTLE AT APACHE PASS*, 1952; and *Foxfire*, 1955). On the other hand, there were an array of badly handled performances where neither makeup, costumes, or script salvaged the embarrassing interpretation by the non-Native American: Dolores Del Rio (*RAMONA*, 1928), Don Ameche (*RAMONA*, 1936), Phillip Reed (*THE LAST OF THE MOHICANS*, 1936), Yvonne De Carlo (*The Deerslayer*, 1943), Jennifer Jones (*Duel in the Sun*, 1946), Boris Karloff (*UNCONQUERED*, 1947), Vic Potel and John Berkes (*The Egg and I*, 1947), Debra Paget (*BROKEN ARROW*, 1950), Vince Edwards (*Hiawatha*, 1952), May Wynn (*THEY RODE WEST*, 1954), Rock Hudson (*TAZA, SON OF COCHISE*, 1954), Donna Reed (*THE FAR HORIZONS*, 1955), Victor Mature (*CHIEF CRAZY HORSE*, 1955), Jeffrey Hunter (*WHITE FEATHER*, 1955), Sal Mineo (*TONKA*, 1958), Chuck Connors (*GERONIMO*, 1962), Ricardo Montalban (*CHEYENNE AUTUMN*, 1964), Gilbert Roland (*CHEYENNE AUTUMN*, 1964), Julie Newmar (*McKenna's Gold*, 1969), Robert Blake (*TELL THEM WILLIE BOY IS HERE*, 1969), Charles Bronson (*CHATO'S LAND*, 1972), and Robby Benson (*RUNNING BRAVE*, 1983).

Indian agent This Caucasian government official was appointed to negotiate with Native American tribes, and, later, they acted as appointees to and for Native Americans on a given reservation. Reflecting reality and/or plot-line device, most Hollywood representations of this bureaucrat reflected the administrator as anti-Native American and usually corrupt. A rare exception was the depiction provided in *WALK THE PROUD LAND* (1956). Indian agents were characters in such American-made pictures as *THE SQUAW MAN* (1914), *The Squaw Man's Son* (1917), *THE SQUAW MAN* (1918), *THE VANISHING AMERICAN* (1925), *DRUMS OF THE DESERT* (1927), *Hawk of the Hills* (1929), *THE SQUAW MAN*, (1931), *MASSACRE* (1934), *'Neath the Arizona Skies* (1934), *Hills of Old Wyoming* (1937), *VALLEY OF THE SUN* (1942), *Frontier Fury* (1943), *Black Arrow* (1944—movie serial), *Romance of the West* (1946), *Oregon Trail Scouts* (1947), *FORT APACHE* (1948), *Indian Agent* (1948), *Daughter of the West* (1949), *SHE WORE A YELLOW RIBBON* (1949), *Cherokee Uprising* (1950), *North of the Great Divide* (1950), *New Mexico* (1951), *Apache Country* (1952), *THE HALF-BREED* (1952), *SITTING BULL* (1954), *Apache Woman* (1955), *The Broken Star* (1955), *The White Squaw* (1956), *The Lawless Eighties* (1957), *Oklahoma Territory* (1960), *HOMBRE* (1967), and *JOURNEY THROUGH ROSEBUD* (1972).

Bill Williams and Ted de Corsia in *Oklahoma Territory* (1960), one of many westerns to focus on Indian agents. (JC ARCHIVES)

Two TV shows that featured Indian agents as series regulars were *BROKEN ARROW* (1956–60) and *DR. QUINN, MEDICINE WOMAN* (1990–95).

Indian Fighter, The **(1955)** United Artists, color, 88 minutes. **Director:** Andre de Toth; **Screenplay:** Frank Davis and Ben Hecht; **Cast:** Kirk Douglas (Johnny Hawks), Elsa Martinelli (Onahti), Walter Matthau (Wes Todd), Diana Douglas (Susan Rogers), Lon Chaney [Jr.] (Chivington), Eduard Franz (Chief Red Cloud), Harry Landers (Grey Wolf), Hank Worden (Crazy Bear).

This robust adventure yarn took place in the post-Civil War era on the lands of the Teton SIOUX through which miners and settlers traveled to reach the mining territory of the West.

Rugged Johnny Hawks, having fought for the Confederacy, returns to the West and renews his friendship with Chief Red Cloud. He becomes enamored of Red Cloud's daughter Onahti. Meanwhile trouble is generated by Wes Todd and Chivington, two scoundrels attached to the wagon train that Hawks is maneuvering through the dangerous Sioux lands. The two crooks are searching for hidden gold ore on the Sioux lands. Their avariciousness and murdering of a tribal member lead to an onslaught by Red Cloud's warriors. The local fort is nearly destroyed by the Sioux braves, but Hawks, who has chosen to remain in the area with Onahti, helps to reestablish peace.

One could not fault the fast pacing of this western, but its credibility was not bolstered by having Italian actress Martinelli in a lead role as a Sioux or three Caucasian actors acting as Chief Red Cloud, Grey Wolf, and Crazy Bear. Emphasized in this drama were the Native Americans' supposed penchant for liquor and their inability to deal with "firewater." Again, the warrior chiefs were presented as cruel and vindictive.

***Indian in the Cupboard, The* (1993)** Paramount, color, 96 minutes. **Director:** Frank Oz; **Screenplay:** Melissa Mathison; **Cast:** Hal Scardino (Omri), Litefoot (Little Bear), Lindsay Crouse (Jane), Richard Jenkins (Victor), Rishi Bhat (Patrick), Steve Coogan (Tommy Atkins), David Keith (Boone), Vincent Kartheiser (Gillon).

This charming fantasy and ethnic minority morality lesson was based on the acclaimed 1981 children's book by Lynne Reid Banks. The script was by Mathison, who did similar chores on *E. T.: The Extra-Terrestrial* (1982). Its star was LITEFOOT (aka: G. Paul Davis), the Native American rapper. (To be noted, some critics found Little Bear's character perpetuating too much of the Caucasian belief that all Native Americans were warriors. Others pointed to the miniaturization of Little Bear in the narrative as a demeaning revelation of how the white world truly regarded Native Americans.)

On New York City's Lower East Side, Omri celebrates his ninth birthday. His older brother (Kartheiser) has found an old wooden cupboard as a gift for his sibling; pal Patrick gives Omri a tiny plastic figure of a Native American brave; Omri's mom, Jane, provides her youngster with a "special" key to the cupboard. After he places the three-inch-high figure in the cupboard, locks the door, and goes to sleep, strange things occur. Little Bear, an Iroquois warrior, springs to life. As the latter teaches the youngster about his people's culture and ways, Omri comes to appreciate his English-speaking visitor. Before long, Omri has also brought magically to life a vintage World War I medic (Coogan) and a boisterous cowboy (Keith) from the prior century. At the end, realizing that he must help these figures go back to their "real" lives, Omri reluctantly returns them to the magic cupboard.

In its gentle way, the well-done *The Indian in the Cupboard* creatively instructed viewers about Native Americans at the same time as it entertained. The film grossed more than $35 million in domestic release.

***Indian Wars, The* (aka: *The Wars of Civilization*) (1914)** Essanay/State Rights, b&w, 5 reels. **Directors:** Theodore Wharton and Vernon Day; **Cast:** William F. Cody, Nelson Appleton Miles, Jesse M. Lee, Frank D. Baldwin, Marion P. Maus, Charles King, H. G. Sickles, Short Bull, and Dewey Beard.

Using a documentary format, this silent film restaged four pivotal encounters between the U.S. cavalry and assorted tribes of the SIOUX nation: the Battle of Summit Springs (1869), the Battle of Warbonnet Creek (1876), the Battle of the Mission (1890), the Battle of Wounded Knee (1890), as well as the Messiah Craze War (1890–91) and the capturing of Chief Big Foot. Concluding footage depicted contemporary Native American children attending modern schools, as well as Native American farmers at work. This project was engineered by WILLIAM F. CODY (aka: Buffalo Bill) with the U.S. government, which when the project was completed was dissatisfied reportedly because it was too favorable to Native Americans. Revamped, the project was later reissued in 1917 (the year Cody died) as *THE ADVENTURES OF BUFFALO BILL*.

Injun Joe This murderous HALF-BREED character appeared in Mark Twain's novel *The Adventures of Tom Sawyer* (1876). In that classic tale set in Hannibal, Missouri, in the 1840s, Injun Joe was a mixed-blood Native American with a savage streak. He killed young Dr. Robinson, and in court he was accused of the crime by Tom Sawyer. That prompted Injun Joe to jump out of a courthouse window. Later, in a cave outside of town, Tom was almost done in by the vicious killer. This was one of the most virulent depictions of an evil half-breed in American literature and as adapted to other media. Most often, the role was played on camera by a Caucasian actor.

Among the several actors who portrayed Injun Joe on the U.S. screen were Frank Lanning (*Huck and Tom*, 1918), Charles Stevens (*Tom Sawyer*, 1930), Victor Jory (*THE ADVENTURES OF TOM SAWYER*, 1938), Kunu Hank (*Tom Sawyer*, 1973), Vic Morrow (*Tom Sawyer*, 1973—TV movie), Eric Schweig (*Tom and Huck*, 1995), Hank Williams Jr. (*Tom Sawyer*, 2001), and the voice of Hank Williams Jr. (*Tom Sawyer*, 2000—direct-to-video movie). In the 1968–69 TV series *Tom Sawyer*, Ted Cassidy portrayed Injun Joe.

***Iron Horse, The* (1924)** Fox, b&w, 10,424′. **Director:** John Ford; **Screenplay:** Charles Kenyon; **Cast:** George O'Brien (Davy Brandon), Madge Bellamy (Miriam Marsh), Cyril Chadwick (Peter Jesson), Fred Kohler (Deroux), Gladys Hulette (Ruby), James Marcus (Judge Haller), J. Farrell MacDonald (Corporal Casey), Jack Padjan (Wild Bill Hickok), George Waggner (Buffalo Bill [Colonel Cody]), Chief Big Tree (Cheyenne chief), Chief White Spear (Sioux chief).

President Abraham Lincoln signed the Pacific Railroad Act of July 1, 1862, authorizing the building of a transcontinental railroad that, when accomplished, would effectively close the American frontier. This epic feature, made to compete with the hugely successful *THE COVERED WAGON* (1923), recreated this staggering construction that began after the Civil War.

Surveyor Davy Brandon joins the Union Pacific as it starts its chore of meeting the Central Pacific at the center of the continent with laid track. He finds that the construction boss is Thomas Marsh, the father of his childhood sweetheart, Miriam, who now has a suitor, Peter Jesson, a civil engineer. As the track proceeds, SIOUX warriors attack the construction train. Brandon recognizes their white renegade leader, Deroux, as the man who years ago killed his father. The enraged Brandon kills Deroux and then leaves his job. He joins up with the Central Pacific and is present when the two railroads meet and the symbolic gold spike is pounded into the track. On a personal level, he and Miriam are reunited.

Utilizing some 800 CHEYENNE, Pawnee, and Sioux, as well as 1,000 Chinese laborers, the panoramic *The Iron Horse* well conveyed the magnitude of the actual project; on the other hand, the saga was filled with hackneyed representations of minorities from the Chinese laborers to the rampaging Native American warriors.

Many of the plot contrivances used in *The Iron Horse* were adopted by later filmmakers, and the epic itself was the inspiration for Cecil B. DeMille's *UNION PACIFIC* (1939).

***It Had to Be You* (1947)** Columbia, b&w, 98 minutes. **Directors:** Don Hartman and Rudolph Maté; **Screenplay:** Norman Panama and Melvin Frank; **Cast:** Ginger Rogers (Victoria Stafford), Cornel Wilde (George McKesson/Johnny Blaine), Percy Waram (Ned Stafford), Spring Byington (Mrs. Stafford), Ron Randell (Oliver H. P. Harrington).

Overstuffed with primitive psychobabble, *It Had to Be You* was one of the few mainstream Hollywood farces to utilize a Native American as a comedic hero. On the other hand, at the finale, the whooping warrior was *not* united with the Caucasian leading lady—thanks to a plot gimmick.

Manhattan socialite Victoria Stafford has a reputation of being fickle about marriage, having already jilted three suitors. Now engaged to stuffy Oliver H. P. Harrington, she hibernates at her Cape Cod retreat. On the train back to New York City, she dreams that a handsome warrior brave is really the man she should now wed. She awakens to find him sitting on the berth above hers, and he remains a part of her madcap life as her unpromising wedding day to Harrington approaches. Almost belatedly, she discovers that the warrior of her dreams was her childhood sweetheart, Johnny Blaine, who once wore a Native American costume. This leads her to choose Blaine as her new mate.

***I Will Fight No More Forever* (1975)** ABC-TV, color, 100 minutes. **Director:** Richard T. Heffron; **Teleplay:** Jeb Rosebrook and Theodore Strauss; **Cast:** James Whitmore (Gen. Oliver O. Howard), Ned Romero (Chief Joseph), Sam Elliott (Captain Wood), John Kauffman (Wahlitits), Emilio Delgado (Ollokot), Nick Ramus (Rainbow), Linda Redfearn (Toma), Frank Sotonoma Salsedo (White Bird), W. Vincent St. Cyr (Chief Looking Glass).

Nez Percé is French for "pierced noses," a name given by French fur traders to the Nimipu tribes (also known as the Sahaptin, Shahaptin, or Chopunish). These Native Americans lived in the territory that became central Idaho, southeastern Washington, and northeastern Oregon. In 1877, because the land was coveted by white settlers, U.S. government officials demanded that the Wallowa band of Nez Percé remove to the Nez Percé Reservation at Lapwai in the Idaho Territory. This led to the Nez Percé War and to Chief Joseph taking his people on an incredible 1,600 mile trek through (what is now) Idaho, Wyoming, and Montana, their destination being Canada.

On their amazing journey, the Nez Percé were chased by three U.S. Army groups, one led by Gen. Oliver O. Howard. After nearly accomplishing their goal, the indomitable wayfarers were overtaken by U.S. troops some thirty miles from their final destination. After days of fighting, Chief Joseph surrendered with the famous words: "My heart is sick and sad. From where the sun now stands, I will fight no more forever."

This tragic episode in U.S. history was well presented in this drama, which was produced by documentary filmmaker David L. Wolper. Romero offered a well-modulated performance in his key role. The production received Emmy Award nominations for its teleplay and editing.

J

James, Lloyd E. See LAUGHLIN, TOM.

***Jeremiah Johnson* (1972)** Warner Bros., color, 108 minutes. **Director:** Sydney Pollack; **Screenplay:** John Milius and Edward Anhalt; **Cast:** Robert Redford (Jeremiah Johnson), Will Geer (Bear Claw), Stefan Gierasch (Del Gue), Allyn Ann McLerie (crazy woman), Delle Bolton (Swan), Charles Tyner (Robidoux), Josh Albee (Caleb), Joaquín Martinez (Paints His Shirt Red).

Harkening back to the works of James Fenimore Cooper, *Jeremiah Johnson* was a picaresque saga of a man heeding the call of the wild in the 1850s. In his years as a mountain man, he encountered a wide variety of Native Americans: Some were simply enemies to be slaughtered as occasion allowed; others were prime examples of the noble savage to be respected.

Sickened by civilization, Jeremiah Johnson, a former soldier, becomes a trapper in the Rocky Mountains. He is nearly done in by the elements his first year but is saved by Bear Claw, an old trapper, who instructs him in the ways of survival. Thereafter, once again alone, he encounters a crazed woman whose family—except one child, Caleb—has been massacred by marauding warriors. She convinces him to take the boy so that she can tend the graves. Later, Johnson and Caleb meet eccentric trapper Del Gue who scalps several Flathead braves and sneaks their scalps into Johnson's possession. When they encounter a group of Blackfeet, Johnson is mistakenly hailed as a hero for having murdered so many of their Flathead enemies. Later, because Johnson inadvertently tracks through the Crow burial ground, they slaughter Caleb and the trapper's Blackfoot wife, Swan. This drives Johnson to the brink of madness and to killing Crow. Eventually tiring of his murderous life, Johnson departs for Canada. Along the way, he turns around and sees the Crow leader with his arm raised in a salute, a gesture that Johnson returns.

Based on the novel *Mountain Man* (1965) by Vardis Fisher and the story "Crow Killer" by Raymond W. Thorp and Robert Bunker, *Jeremiah Johnson* was shot in Utah. It earned an impressive $33 million in rentals during its domestic distribution.

***Jim Thorpe—All American* (1951)** Warner Bros., b&w, 107 minutes. **Director:** Michael Curtiz; **Screenplay:** Douglas Morrow and Everett Freeman; **Cast:** Burt Lancaster (Jim Thorpe), Charles Bickford (Glenn S. "Pop" Warner), Steve Cochran (Peter Allendine), Phyllis Thaxter (Margaret Miller), Dick Wesson (Ed Guyac), Jack Bighead (little boy), Suni Warcloud (Wally Denny), Al Mejia (Louis Tewanema), Nestor Paiva (Hiram Thorpe), Billy Gray (Jim Thorpe—as a child), Jimmy Moss (Jim Thorpe Jr.).

Based on the unpublished biography (*Red Sons of Carlisle*), which was written in the early 1930s by THORPE and movie publicist Russell J. Birdwell, this movie project had been in consideration since that time by the Hollywood film studios. It emerged primarily a sports biography where the obstacles to overcome included bigotry because the subject was a Native American. As such, the focus was more on Thorpe's growth as a young man of purpose and his later realization of what sports truly meant to him. Thus, this was less a precedent-breaking Hollywood study of a contemporary Native American than a history of a great athlete who just happened to be a member of the Sac and Fox tribe.

Born on the Sac and Fox Indian reservation in Oklahoma in 1888, Thorpe is a free spirit who hates the confines of school. His father (Paiva) finally sends him to the Carlisle Indian School in Pennsylvania. There, he comes under the tutelage of Glenn S. "Pop" Warner, the athletic coach who perceives the youth's great potential in track. But Thorpe has fallen in love with Margaret Miller, and to compete with her suitor on the football team, he joins that squad. Later, despite learning that Margaret is white, he remains in love with her, and they eventually wed. When he is not given the hoped-for coaching position at Carlisle, he enters the 1912 Olympics in Sweden where he wins two gold medals. When it is discovered that he was paid to play baseball on a minor league team during a summer recess, he loses his medals and his Olympic standing. To earn a living, he plays professional football and baseball. After his young son dies unexpectedly, Thorpe becomes alcoholic, moves from team to team, and eventually loses his wife. Attending the 1932 Olympics in Los Angeles inspires the athlete, and he returns to coaching neighborhood boys in sports. Several years later Thorpe is hailed by the U.S. media as the best athlete of the first half of the twentieth century.

Unmentioned in the movie were the facts that Thorpe was actually wed three times and had several children. He also had bits in Hollywood movies beginning with 1931's *Battling with Buffalo Bill* and ending with 1950's *WAGON MASTER*. Thorpe served as technical adviser on his own screen biography. The athletic Lancaster, an admirable choice to portray Thorpe, also played a Native American in *APACHE* (1954).

***Joe Panther* (1976)** Artists Creation, color, 110 minutes. **Director:** Paul Krasny; **Screenplay:** Dale Eunson; **Cast:** Brian Keith (Captain Harper), Ricardo Montalban (Turtle George), Alan Feinstein (Rocky), Cliff Osmond (Rance), A Martinez (Billy Tiger), Ray Trace (Joe Panther), Robert W. Hoffman (George Harper), Gem Thorpe Osceola (Tommy Panther), Lois Red Elk (Joe's mother).

This coming-of-age family film is set in present-day Florida—near the Everglades—with Trace in the title role as a young SEMINOLE coping in the Caucasian world. He earns his mark as a professional alligator wrestler. For advice in dealing with the alien white culture, he turns to Turtle George (a Native American elder played in near caricature by Montalban). While working as a crew member on Captain Harper's boat, Trace deals with wrongdoers who attempt to bring illegal aliens into Florida on fishing boats.

***Johnny Tiger* (1966)** Universal, color, 102 minutes. **Director:** Paul Wendkos; **Screenplay:** Paul Crabtree and R. John Hugh; **Cast:** Robert Taylor (George Dean), Geraldine Brooks (Doc Leslie Frost), Chad Everett (Johnny Tiger), Brenda Scott (Barbara Dean), Marc Lawrence (William Billie), Ford Rainey (Sam Tiger), Carol Seflinger (Wendy Dean), Steven Wheeler (Randy Dean), Pamela Melendez (Shalonee).

In this overlooked, earnest, proactive feature, Taylor, who had starred in AMBUSH (1949) and *DEVIL'S DOORWAY* (1950), returned to the subject of those films with a heartfelt performance. He was the middle-aged college professor with three children (Scott, Seflinger, and Wheeler) who accepts a post teaching youngsters of the SEMINOLE tribe living in the Florida Everglades. He is aghast at the state of the local schoolhouse and the backward conditions prevalent on the reservation. At first, the overworked resident health official (Brooks) is not of much help.

Needing assistance in getting the Native American youths to attend his school, Dean turns to Johnny Tiger, the grandson of the tribal chief. But the young man is bitter about being a HALF-BREED and being caught between two opposing worlds. Nevertheless, Tiger's attraction to Barbara, Dean's daughter, leads him to attending the school, and in turn the Seminole children follow suit. Johnny's grandfather, Sam, is upset that he is now following the ways of the white world and orders him off the reservation. Regardless, Barbara and Tiger marry. It takes a brush fire on the reservation that puts Randy Dean in jeopardy to make peace between Sam and Dean. As for Johnny, he promises Sam that he will help their people adapt to the new lifestyle.

***Journey Through Rosebud* (1972)** GSF, color, 93 minutes. **Director:** Tom Gries; **Screenplay:** Albert Ruben; **Cast:** Robert Forster (Frank), Kristoffer Tabori (Danny), Victoria Racimo (Shirley), Eddie Little Sky (Stanley Pike), Roy Jenson (park ranger), Wright King (Indian agent), Larry Pennell (Sheriff), Beau Little Sky (Stu), Dianne Running (Mrs. Blackwing).

This unsuccessful but well-intentioned character study benefited from its filming on the Rosebud SIOUX Reservation and the use of its members. Draft-dodging Danny comes to the reservation where he encounters the tribe's unofficial leader, Frank, a Vietnam veteran who is filled with bitterness. Also prominently involved with Danny is Shirley, Frank's ex-wife. Before the drama concludes, Frank dies in a car crash.

This was part of a growing number of films that equated anti-Vietnam feelings with pro–Native American activism. Such movies, often unsuccessful as "entertainment," served to bring the ways and problems of this ethnic minority to the attention of the generally oblivious Caucasian majority.

***Journey to Spirit Island* (1988)** Pal/Seven Wonders, color, 93 minutes. **Director**: Laszlo Pal; **Screenplay:** Crane Webster; **Cast:** Bettina (Maria), Marie Antoinette Rodgers (Jimmy Jim), Brand Douglas (Michael), Gabriel Damon (Willie), Tarek McCarthy (Klim), Tony Acierto (Hawk).

This family-oriented drama, set in the Pacific Northwest, explored universal truths about young teenagers as well as the mysticism inherent in the Native American culture.

Michael and Willie, two Caucasian youths from Chicago, go out West to explore the area around the Olympic peninsula and the San Juan Islands, guided by Native American Maria and her younger brother Klim. The quartet take a three-day kayak trek to the local islands. In the process, the midwestern visitors lose their preconceived notions about "Indians" and see the commonality between them all. A parallel plot involves college-educated Hawk who is excited about his tribe selling the land rights to a sacred island so that it can be exploited as a lush resort. The elders are against such a move, but the younger generation, caught up in greed rather than tradition, seemingly win out. At the last moment, Hawk's bad dealings cause the Caucasian developer to pull out of the deal.

Although considered naïve in its presentation, this beautifully photographed study still had much to offer, especially in its portrayal of the similarities between races and the need for environmental protection of cultural landmarks.

***Justice of the Far North* (1925)** Columbia, b&w, 6 reels. **Director/Screenplay:** Norman Dawn; **Cast:** Arthur Jasmine (Umluk), Marcia Manon (Wamba), Laska Winter (Nootka), Chuck Reisner (Mike Burke), Max Davidson (Izzy Hawkin), George Fisher (Dr. Wells).

Transferring a standard soap-opera plot to the great north country, this low-budget outing proved that virtue and shame in any society are the same.

Native-Alaskan chief Umluk expects to marry Wamba, a Russian HALF-BREED. But Mike Burke, co-owner of the local trading post, wins her favor by treating her like a "white woman," so she goes with him. They make her sister Nootka join them as their slave. Umluk pursues the trio, eventually catching up with them. Finally Umluk returns to his igloo with Nootka, leaving the debased Wamba behind.

Adding further stereotypes to this Arctic tale was the presence of a mercenary Jewish character, Izzy Hawkin, Burke's partner at the trading post.

K

Kilian's Chronicle **(aka: *The Magic Stone*) (1994)** Capstone, color, 112 minutes. **Director/Screenplay:** Pamela Berger; **Cast:** Christopher Johnson (Kilian), Robert McDonough (Ivar), Eva Kim (Turtle), Jonah Ming Lee (Kitchi), Gino Montesinos (Contacook), Robert Mason Ham (White Eagle), R. Michael Wresinski (Ragnar), Robert Bradford Shelton (Ole), Arthur Acusa (Dream Speaker).

This low-profile and not always professional minor family feature had the intriguing premise of a tenth-century Irish man and some Vikings coming into contact with Native Americans on the latter's territory. When Kilian, an Irish slave, escapes his Viking masters as their vessel anchors off the American shores, he is befriended by members of a local tribe, including young Kitchi. Before long, Kilian falls in love with Turtle. Meanwhile, he helps the tribe fight off other Vikings who are out to steal the village's fur cache. Eventually, Kilian remains in the New World with Turtle.

L

***Lakota Woman: Siege at Wounded Knee* (1994)** TNT cable, color, 113 minutes. **Director:** Frank Pierson; **Teleplay:** Bill Kerby; **Cast:** Irene Bedard (Mary Crow Dog), August Schellenberg (Dick Wilson), Joseph Runningfox (Leonard Crow Dog), Floyd "Red Crow" Westerman (Mary's grandfather), Tantoo Cardinal (Mary's mother), Michael Horse (Dennis Banks), Russell Means (Lawrence Bayne), Melanie Two Eagle (Charlene).

Filmed on location in South Dakota, this was part of TNT cable's Native American telefeature series of the mid-1990s and marked the debut of Native American actress BEDARD. It was based on the 1990 autobiography by Mary Crow Dog and Richard Erdoes. The cast was primarily Native American.

The narrative traces the real-life experience of Mary Crow Dog, a Lakota SIOUX woman. The offspring of an extremely poor family that lives on a reservation in South Dakota where she attends the local school, her childhood is filled with abuse. As part of the political consciousness of the 1960s, she gradually becomes aware of the injustices heaped on her people and finds her own voice to speak out and is soon enmeshed in tribal politics. She becomes part of the Native American movement and is involved personally in the 1973 armed standoff with U.S. forces at Wounded Knee (the site of an 1890 massacre of several hundred Native Americans by U.S. cavalry troops). The bloody new confrontation against federal officers lasts for seventy days, during which time she gives birth to a baby.

Bayne had the role of real-life Native American actor and activist RUSSELL MEANS.

***The Last Hunt* (1956)** MGM, color, 108 minutes. **Director/Screenplay:** Richard Brooks; **Cast:** Robert Taylor (Charles Gilson), Stewart Granger (Sandy McKenzie), Lloyd Nolan (Woodfoot), Debra Paget (young woman), Russ Tamblyn (Jimmy O'Brien), Constance Ford (Peg), Ralph Moody (Indian agent), Ed Lonehill (Spotted Hand).

An extremely gritty performance by the usually wooden Taylor enhanced this rough drama of a man driven by a thirst to kill, whether it be in war or in hunting and destroying buffalo. Both the villainous (Taylor) and the "good" Caucasian (Granger) figures treat the Native American characters within the picture in a demeaning manner, the former on purpose, the latter out of ingrained prejudices.

In graphic terms, this drama, which is set in the 1880s, recreates the slaughter of buffalo by hunters who are more concerned with the kill than with the profits to be made from the hides. (A subtext of this assertion of masculine Caucasian power is the adverse effect the vanishing of buffalo herds has on Native American life as it once was.)

Vicious Charles Gilson pressures ex-buffalo hunter Sandy McKenzie to join him on a buffalo hunt. They take along Jimmy O'Brien, a young HALF-BREED, and Woodfoot, a peg-legged drunkard. An unexpected addition to the group is the SIOUX woman (and her baby) whom Gilson drags on the trek to tend to his needs. Before long the compassionate McKenzie falls in love with the stoic squaw. By the finale, there is a settling of the score with the cruel Gilson, who has led a life of senseless killings.

The Last Hunt, based on the 1954 novel by Milton Loss, was lensed in South Dakota at Custer State Park and at the U.S. National Monument at Badlands. Paget had previously portrayed Native American characters in *BROKEN ARROW* (1950) and *WHITE FEATHER* (1955).

***Last of His People, The* (1919)** Select, b&w, 5,195′. **Director:** Robert North Bradbury; **Screenplay:** Bradbury and Frank Howard Clark; **Cast:** Mitchell Lewis (Wolf Briggs [Lone Wolf]), Harry Lonsdale (Anthony Briggs), Yvette

Mitchell (Na-ta-le), Catherine Van Buren (Yvonne Lacombe), J. J. Bryson (Robert Lacey), Eddie Hearn (Reynard Lacey).

Especially in the silent film era, a screenplay sometimes went to complex lengths to titillate the moviegoer with a romance between a "savage" and a Caucasian city woman, while not overstepping "moral" guidelines regarding the separation of the two races.

In the Pacific Northwest, Lone Wolf and his sister Na-ta-le, whose family and village died of "spotted fever," are adopted by woodsman Anthony Briggs. (His wife had abandoned him and gone to the city with lumber-camp foreman Robert Lacey.) Several years thereafter, Briggs's offspring, Yvonne Lacombe, visits the area with friends and her fiancé Reynard, the son of Lacey. As a wager, Yvonne flirts with Wolf, a situation that turns into love. After the death of Na-ta-le and Reynard, Yvonne discovers that she is part Native American and chooses to be with Wolf.

***Last of His Tribe, The* (1992)** HBO cable, color, 90 minutes. **Director:** Harry Hook; **Teleplay:** Stephen Harrigan; **Cast:** Jon Voight (Prof. Albert Kroeber), Graham Greene (Ishi), David Ogden Stiers (Dr. Saxton Pope), Jack Blessing (Tom Waterman), Anne Archer (Henriette Kroeber), Daniel Benzali (Mr. Whitney), Christianne Hauber (Miss Edna Block), Loryn Barlese (Ishi's young sister), Gilbert Bear (Ishi's father).

In the late summer of 1911, a gaunt stranger comes into the town of Oroville in northern California. This Native American speaks a dialect that no one can decipher. News of this individual reaches anthropologists Alfred Kroeber and Thomas Waterman in San Francisco. By trial and error, they discover that he is a Yahi and the last of a tribe (from that region) thought to be already extinct. He lives with whites for the rest of his life, helping people interested in native ways and customs. Born in approximately 1862, he dies in 1916, having contracted tuberculosis.

In 1978 there appeared the TV movie *Ishi: The Last of His Tribe* starring Eloy Casados in the title role and Dennis Weaver as the anthropologist Prof. Benjamin Fuller. The touching drama was based on the 1961 book *Ishi in Two Worlds* by Theodora Krober Quinn. The story, with a new teleplay, was redone in 1992 to mediocre results. Starring Voight as the austere clinician, the narrative focused on the white point of view. The far more astounding (real life) situation of Ishi (well handled by GREENE) as an anthropological curiosity was unfortunately buried in this static presentation.

Last of the Mohicans, The See CHINGACHGOOK.

***Last of the Mohicans, The* (1920)** Associated Producer, b&w, 6 reels. **Directors:** Maurice Tourneur and Clarence L. Brown; **Screenplay:** Robert A. Dillon; **Cast:** Wallace Beery (Magua), Barbara Bedford (Cora Munro), Albert Roscoe (Uncas), Lillian Hall (Alice Munro), Henry Woodward (Maj. Duncan Heyward), James Gordon (Colonel Munro), Harry Lorraine (Hawkeye), Theodore Lerch (Chingachgook), Jack F. McDonald (Tamenund), Boris Karloff (marauding brave).

Although there had been several earlier short American versions of James Fenimore Cooper's classic novel (1826), this was the first major U.S. production of *THE LAST OF THE MOHICANS*. Directed by Frenchman Tourneur and his American assistant (Brown), who took over when the former was injured during production, this silent rendition was set during the French and Indian War.

Within the plot, Cora and Alice Munro are traveling to Fort William Henry where their father Colonel Munro is in charge. The fort is being attacked by the French in collaboration with warring tribes. The two women and their party are guided by the treacherous Magua, an outcast Huron. Along the way, the group encounters frontier scout Hawkeye and his two Native American companions: CHINGACHGOOK and his son Uncas—the latter being the last of the Mohicans. In the tug-of-war over the two white women, Magua eventually kills Cora and Uncas, while Hawkeye shoots Magua.

This not very faithful version of Cooper's book highlighted Caucasian Beery as the villainous Native American Magua. The picture set the stage for later movies in which the good warriors were portrayed as "noble savages." Here, however, they were merely set dressing for this frontier tale about the white folk.

***Last of the Mohicans, The* (1932)** Mascot, b&w, 12-chapter serial. **Directors:** Ford Beebe and B. Reeves Eason; **Screenplay:** Beebe, Colbert Clark, Wyndham Gittens, and John Francis Natteford; **Cast:** Harry Carey (Hawkeye [Natty Bumppo]), Hobart Bosworth (Chingachgook, the Sagamore), Frank Coghlan Jr. (Uncas), Edwina Booth (Cora Munro), Lucille Browne (Alice Munro), Walter Miller (Maj. Duncan Heyward), Yakima Canutt (Black Fox), Edward Hearn (General Munro), Bob Kortman (Magua); **Chapters:** (1) Wild Waters, (2) Flaming Arrows, (3) Rifle Or Tomahawk, (4) Riding With Death, (5) Red Shadows, (6) Lure of Gold, (7) Crimson Trial, (8) Tide of Battle, (9) Redskins' Honor, (10) The Enemy's Stronghold, (11) Paleface Magic, (12) End of the Trail.

Cooper's 1826 literary saga, *THE LAST OF THE MOHICANS*, was converted by low-budget Mascot Pictures to the requirements of a chapterplay with cliffhanger climaxes to conclude each episode. The sets were skimpy, the actors (especially Carey) lethargic, and there was little sense of the majesty and/or cruelty of the Native Americans presented. Here, Uncas, the last of the Mohicans, was played by fifteen-year-old Coghlan, which sabotaged the original book's plot line of Uncas being in love with independent Alice Munro.

***Last of the Mohicans, The* (1936)** United Artists, b&w, 91 minutes **Director:** George B. Seitz; **Screenplay:**

Philip Dunne; **Cast:** Randolph Scott (Hawkeye), Binnie Barnes (Alice Munro), Henry Wilcoxon (Maj. Duncan Heyward), Bruce Cabot (Magua), Heather Angel (Cora Munro), Phillip Reed (Uncas), Robert Barrat (Chingachgook), Hugh Buckler (Colonel Munroe).

Although it also played fast and loose with James Fenimore Cooper's classic book, this 1936 rendition of *THE LAST OF THE MOHICANS* captured a great deal of the spirit of the original while adding standard 1930s soldiers-versus-"redskins" aspects to the drama. As in the 1932 Mascot serial, Hawkeye was the focal figure with Uncas, CHINGACHGOOK, and Magua reduced to subordinate roles. Unlike the serial, there was a growing romance here between Uncas and Cora. In fact, after Uncas fell from a cliff, the smitten Cora jumped to her death. Unlike Cooper's fiction, in which Alice pursued and eventually married Major Heywood, in this movie adaptation Hawkeye—portrayed by a handsome leading man—displayed a strong affection for the British woman. While Reed as Uncas had the physique and profile to play the last of the Mohicans, his all too obvious wig, ethnic makeup, and modern demeanor detracted from any credibility in his performance.

Until the 1992 feature film version, which relied in part on Dunne's script from this adaptation, the 1936 version of *The Last of the Mohicans* remained the most famous Hollywood production of Cooper's fiction.

***Last of the Mohicans, The* (1992)** Twentieth Century Fox, color, 122 minutes. **Director:** Michael Mann; **Screenplay:** Mann, Christopher Crowe, and Philip Dunne; **Cast:** Daniel Day-Lewis (Hawkeye [Nathaniel Poe]), Madeleine Stowe (Cora Munro), Russell Means (Chingachgook), Eric Schweig (Uncas), Jodhi May (Alice Munro), Steven Waddington (Maj. Duncan Heyward), Wes Studi (Magua), Maurice Roeves (Colonel Monroe).

Since the rousing 1936 version of *THE LAST OF THE MOHICANS*, there had been several minor adaptations of Cooper's work, including a 1977 TV movie. This expansive 1992 rendition was filmed in North Carolina and was filled with fancy camera angles and depths to exploit the scenery in wide screen. It came after *DANCES WITH WOLVES* (1990) and was part of the upsurge of Hollywood movies dealing with Native American topics. Yet, Hawkeye was still the major focal point of this account, a frontiersman who had no use for either the French or the British but preferred to be in the wilds with his adopted father, the wise CHINGACHGOOK. Then too, here it was younger, naïve Alice and *not* self-reliant Cora who had a rapport with Uncas—a relationship left surprisingly unclear in this adaptation—with Alice jumping to her death after Uncas died.

In this presentation, it was Hawkeye who, after putting the Huron-tortured Major Heywood out of his misery, expressed his love for the sexually mature Cora. As played by Day-Lewis, this Hawkeye was far more self-contained and smug compared to the robust Randolph Scott characterization in the 1936 movie production. While Schweig and MEANS (in his screen debut) were fitting as the last of the Mohicans, it was fellow Native American actor STUDI as Magua who provided the most dimension. He came across as a complex character, one who felt both hatred and frustration in his clashes with Colonel Munro and his two attractive daughters. The battle scenes and acts of barbarism in this screen rendition were far more graphic than ever before.

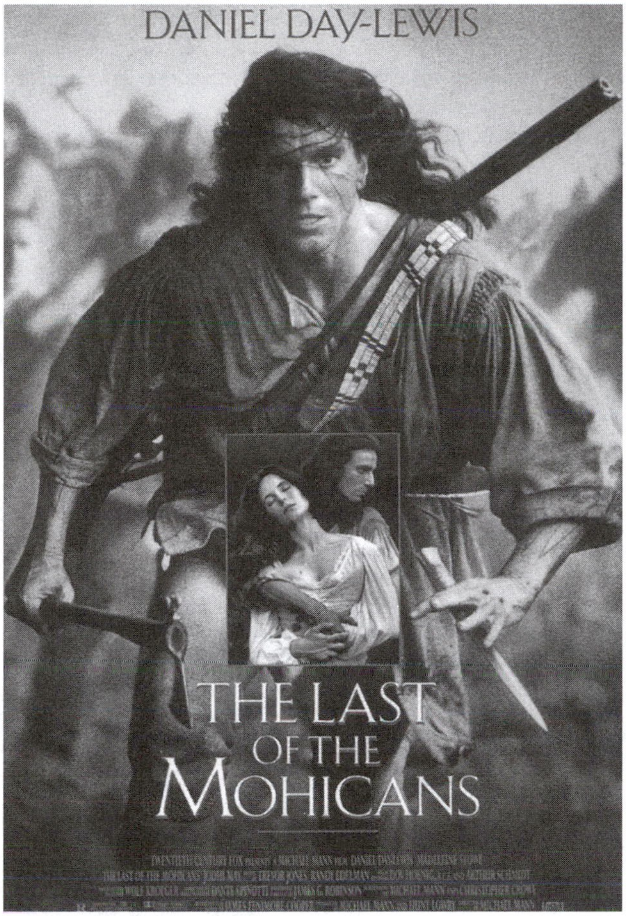

Advertisement for the 1992 version of *The Last of the Mohicans.* (AUTHOR'S COLLECTION)

This R-rated version of *The Last of the Mohicans* grossed more than $72 million in domestic distribution. During production, there were on-set problems regarding the nominal daily fee being paid to the Native American extras.

***Last Train from Gun Hill* (1959)** Paramount, color, 94 minutes. **Director:** John Sturges; **Screenplay:** James Poe; **Cast:** Kirk Douglas (Marshal Matt Morgan), Anthony Quinn (Craig Belden), Carolyn Jones (Linda), Earl Holliman (Rick Belden), Brad Dexter (Beero), Brian Hutton (Lee Smithers), Ziva Rodann (Catherine Morgan).

There were many parallels to *High Noon* (1952) and *Gunfight at the O.K. Corral* (1957) in this complex psychological western. Although the action became a tale of justice and revenge, the narrative was permeated by the townsfolk's prejudice against Native Americans. It is this canker that set into play the movie's climactic shoot-out.

Marshal Matt Morgan's Native American wife is raped and murdered by two young white men. While his Cherokee father-in-law wants to find and torture the perpetrators "the Indian way," Morgan insists on handling the situation in his own manner. He recognizes the saddle of one of the rapists' horses as belonging to his former friend Craig Belden, now a cattle baron. Morgan takes the train to Gun Hill and discovers that Belden's weakling son Rick and the latter's braggart friend Lee Smithers are the culprits. Before he leaves town on the nine o'clock train, the determined law enforcer settles the score with both wrongdoers and with amoral Belden, a man who has a paid mistress (Jones) but no one who really loves him.

***Last Wagon, The* (1956)** Twentieth Century-Fox, color, 99 minutes. **Director:** Delmer Daves; **Screenplay:** James Edward Grant, Daves, and Gwen Bagni Gielgud; **Cast:** Richard Widmark (Comanche Todd), Felicia Farr (Jenny), Susan Kohner (Jolie Normand), Tommy Rettig (Billy), Stephanie Griffin (Valinda), Ray Stricklyn (Clint), Nick Adams (Ridge), Carl Benton Reid (General Howard), Abel Fernandez (Apache medicine man).

Daves, who had directed *BROKEN ARROW* (1950), returned to the genre with this thoughtful entry that mixed action with surprisingly deep emotional relationships. Moreover, because of the HALF-BREED status of one of the characters and the rearing of another by native warriors, a wide range of reactions to Native Americans were present within the story line.

In the 1860s, Todd, who had been brought up by the Comanche, is in custody of Sheriff Bull Harper on murder charges. The two join a wagon train of youngsters heading to Tucson. Later, Todd kills the vicious Harper. As the group proceeds through dangerous territory, Todd develops a bond with the youngsters. Eventually, thanks to the intervention of cavalry scouts, the survivors of the trek reach Redrock Bluff. There, Todd is tried for the earlier homicides and is eventually released into the custody of Billy and Jenny.

As so often happened, even in the best of these "cowboys versus Indians" westerns, no matter how cogent the characters' responses to (full-blooded or half-breed) Native Americans were, as soon as the script demanded excitement, the life-and-death encounter between Caucasians and Native Americans became the good white man versus the vicious Native American warrior, with little to no remorse at the bloodshed involved.

***Laughing Bill Hyde* (1918)** Goldwyn, b&w, 5,790′. **Director:** Hobart Henley; **Screenplay:** Willard Mack; **Cast:** Will Rogers (Laughing Bill Hyde), Anna Lehr (Ponotah), John M. Sainpolis (Black Jack Burg), Mabel Ballin (Alice), Clarence Oliver (Dr. Evan Thomas), Joseph Herbert (Joseph Wesley Slayforth).

This was the first feature film for stage comedian Rogers, who was himself part Native American. The silent photoplay was based on a Rex Beach short story that appeared in *Laughing Bill Hyde and Other Stories* (1917).

After escaping from prison, Bill Hyde heads to Alaska, where he again encounters Dr. Evan Thomas who had once saved his life. The doctor has just sold a mine that he thinks worthless to a scoundrel named Slayforth. Hyde discovers that Slayforth is cheating a HALF-BREED woman named Ponotah, who is part-owner of a mine. Hyde steals back the gold from Slayforth and his henchmen, giving much of it to Ponotah and some to the physician so he can return home and be married. Hyde and Ponotah agree to wed.

***Laughing Boy* (1934)** Metro-Goldwyn-Mayer, b&w, 79 minutes. **Director:** W. S. Van Dyke; **Screenplay:** John Colton and John Lee Mahin; **Cast:** Ramon Novarro (Laughing Boy), Lupe Velez (Lily [Slim Girl]), William Davidson (George Hartshone), Chief Thunderbird (Laughing Boy's father), Catalina Rambula (Laughing Boy's mother), Tall Man's Boy (Wounded Face).

One would have thought that this movie, based on Oliver La Farge's Pulitzer Prize-winning novel (1929), might have fared better at the box office, given the growing romanticism about Native Americans as exotic "noble savages." However, it was scorned, censored, and mocked. Casting Mexican-born Novarro and Velez in the lead roles as NAVAJO certainly did not bolster the picture's credibility. Then too the clichéd plot contained the all too familiar movieland formula of a morally loose woman who found true love but resorted to prostitution to help her boyfriend financially.

What really riled (consciously or subconsciously) many critics about *Laughing Boy* was its miscegenation theme that had Lily sleeping with a white man, albeit for money. This led the trade paper *Harrison's Report* (May 19, 1934) to decry: "Putrid! . . . [I]t is indecent, immoral, and entirely distasteful. Added to all this is the fact that the leading characters are Indians, a fact which makes it of very little unappeal [sic] to American audiences."

At the Great Sing Dance on the Navajo reservation, Laughing Boy, a silversmith new to the area, encounters the beautiful orphan, Slim Girl. He is unaware that she, having been raised by Caucasians and having led a morally loose lifestyle, is regarded as a tramp by the other Navajo. After proving his manliness in a wrestling match at the festival, Laughing Boy admits his love for her. Despite his father's disapproval, he spends the night with Slim Girl but leaves the next morning, ashamed of his conduct. The downcast Slim Girl (known in town as Lily) returns to her life as mistress to white rancher George Hartshone. Later, she is drawn back to Laughing Boy, and they wed. Rejected by his people and hard pressed for money, Slim Girl falls back into her old ways. A jealous Laughing Boy tracks her down, and in trying to murder Hartshone with his bow and arrow, he kills Slim Girl. As she dies, she begs his forgiveness.

Laughlin, Frank See LAUGHLIN, TOM.

Laughlin, Tom (aka: Frank Christina, T. C. Frank, Don Henderson. Lloyd E. James, Frank Laughlin, E. James Lloyd, Mary Rose Solti) (1931–) Within the film industry, this actor, director, screenwriter, and producer was noted for his innovative distribution arrangement that made some of his feature films extremely profitable in release. He earned his pop-culture-icon status by creating and playing on camera BILLY JACK, the HALF-BREED ex-Vietnam veteran who fought for Native American rights using a philosophy of peace through violence. His timing was perfect, given the 1960s and 1970s public interest in such topics.

Born in Minneapolis, Minnesota, Laughlin came to California in 1954 and began to win supporting roles in such movies as *Tea and Sympathy* (1956), *Lafayette Escadrille* (1958), and *Tall Story* (1960). His breakthrough came with *BORN LOSERS* (1967), a biker film that he scripted and directed and in which he first essayed his antiestablishment, righteous Billy Jack characterization. That successful feature led to *BILLY JACK* (1971), which also showcased Laughlin's actress/scripter/producer wife, Delores Taylor. Made at a cost of $800,000 *Billy Jack* earned many millions of dollars and inaugurated a new Hollywood moviemaking trend of using Native American subjects and characters in positive lights.

The Trial of Billy Jack (1974) grossed more than $22 million, but the next follow-up, *Billy Jack Goes to Washington* (1977), was so heavy-handed that it had only scant release. Laughlin was the filmmaker/star of the unsuccessful western *The Master Gunfighter* (1975). Thereafter, he made a few more acting appearances (e.g., *Murder Elite*, 1985; *No Escape*, 1994) but was mostly out of public notice, except for a recurrent interest in running for national public office.

***Law of the Plainsman* (1959–1960)** NBC-TV series, b&w, 30 minutes. **Cast:** Michael Ansara (Deputy U.S. Marshal Sam Buckhart [Buck Heart]), Dayton Lummis (Marshal Andy Morrison), Gina Gillespie (Tess Logan), Nora Marlowe (Martha Commager).

Preceding such TV series as *HAWK* (1966) and *NAKIA* (1974), which utilized Native American law enforcers in a contemporary setting, *Law of the Plainsman* focused on a deputy U.S. marshal in the New Mexico Territory of the 1880s. It starred ANSARA, the American performer of Lebanese heritage who had played COCHISE on the TV series *BROKEN ARROW* (1956–58) and had been cast as Native American warriors repeatedly in feature films.

Within this western, Sam Buckhart has an intriguing back story: He is a full-blooded APACHE known as Buck Heart. In his past, during a skirmish with the U.S. cavalry, he rescues a wounded officer. A few years later, when the rescued man dies he leaves funds for the Apache to be educated at private schools and at Harvard. Now, Buckhart returns to his home land and works under Marshal Andy Morrison. His education taught him to appreciate the white man's law, and he hopes to impart its fairness to everyone, including his people. His greatest dream is to see a lasting peace between the two races.

***Legend of the Lone Ranger, The* (1981)** Universal/Associated Film Distribution, color, 98 minutes. **Director:** William A. Fraker; **Screenplay:** Ivan Goff, Ben Roberts, Michael Kane, William Roberts, and Jerry Berloshan; **Cast:** Klinton Spilsbury (the Lone Ranger), Michael Horse (Tonto), Christopher Lloyd (Cavendish), Matt Clark (Sheriff Wiatt), Juanin Clay (Amy Striker), Jason Robards (Pres. Ulysses S. Grant), John Bennett Perry (Dan Reid), John Hart (Lucas Striker), Richard Farnsworth (Wild Bill Hickok), Lincoln Tate (George Armstrong Custer), Ted Flicker (Buffalo Bill Cody), Tom Laughlin (Neeley), Merle Haggard (narrator).

Twenty-three years after *The Lone Ranger and the Lost City of Gold* came this expensively staged drama that failed miserably to revive the Masked Man franchise. Photographed beautifully in wide screen and color, this patchwork drama explored how the Lone Ranger and the COMANCHE TONTO first met before the ranger donned his mask and became involved in saving President Grant from a kidnapper (Lloyd). For some reason, the many scripters on this failed project felt it necessary to drag in such legendary heroes as WILD BILL HICKOK, BUFFALO BILL CODY, and even GEORGE ARMSTRONG CUSTER.

This problematic production went through many reedits and ended by incorporating a narration by country singer Haggard. The voice of screen newcomer Spilsbury was dubbed throughout the picture. Shot in New Mexico at a cost of $18 million, the poorly received feature grossed only $8 million in domestic distribution.

Despite growing efforts for better representation of Native Americans on screen, Tonto, as played by Horse, was not given much to do in this misadventure.

***Legend of Walks Far Woman, The* (1982)** NBC-TV, color, 145 minutes. **Director:** Mel Damski; **Teleplay:** Evan Hunter; **Cast:** Raquel Welch (Walks Far Woman), Bradford Dillman (Singer), George Clutesi (Old Grandfather), Nick Mancuso (Horses Ghost), Eloy Phil Casados (Feather Earrings), Frank Sotonoma Salsedo (Many Scalps), Hortensia Colorado (Red Hoop Woman), Nick Ramus (Left Hand Bull), Alex Hubik (Elk Hollering), Branscombe Richmond (Big Lake).

The book *Walks Far Woman* (1976) by Colin Stuart deals with the true account of an elderly Blackfoot woman who recalls her many life stories for her grandson and a white girl,

Raquel Welch in the telefeature *The Legend of Walks Far Woman* (1982). (JC ARCHIVES)

the latter's grandfather once having saved Walks Far's life. In her young years, this Native American witnessed the Battle of Little Big-horn.

Welch chose this vehicle to make her TV acting debut, starring in the production that was shot in Montana in 1979. It was not aired until 1982, by which time the three-hour telefeature had been first chopped to 160 minutes and then to the broadcast version of 145 minutes. In excising so much footage, a great deal of the last section of the narrative was deleted, creating a jumpy continuity.

Despite its production problems, this cobbled feature still gave some flavor of Native American culture as it used Walks Far Woman to trace the genesis/plight of her people while the West was being settled by greedy whites. Unusual for movies of this period, a good number of the cast were Native Americans, adding a much-needed ethnic ambiance, especially in the scene of Walks Far Woman coping with the natives of her new tribal association. As for the pivotal battle at Little Big-horn, it was witnessed by the lead character from a distant hill and lost much of its potential impact.

There was much dissatisfaction among Native American groups with former sexpot star Welch portraying this legendary figure in Native American lore.

***Legends of the Fall* (1994)** TriStar, color, 133 minutes. **Director:** Edward Zwick; **Screenplay:** Susan Shilliday and Bill Wittliff; **Cast:** Brad Pitt (Tristan Ludlow), Anthony Hopkins (Col. William Ludlow), Aidan Quinn (Alfred Ludlow), Julia Ormond (Susannah Finnacannon), Henry Thomas (Samuel Ludlow), Karina Lombard (Isabel Two), Tantoo Cardinal (Pet), Gordon Tootoosis (One Stab).

Based on Jim Harrison's 1978 novella, this romantic but too often meandering epic covers many years in the lives of the Ludlow clan. As the Old West dies and the twentieth century progresses into the Prohibition era, there is a merging of two races as one of the story's Caucasian characters weds a Native American and they have children.

As the 1900s commence, Col. William Ludlow retires from the U.S. cavalry and begins to ranch in the Montana Rockies. His wife leaves him, and he must bring up his three sons: stable, conservative Alfred; untamed and hotheaded Tristan; and idealistic Samuel, the youngest. It is Tristan, the hunter, who has a close rapport with One Stab, Ludlow's former Cree tribe scout.

Later, when Samuel returns from college, he is joined by his fiancée, Susannah. But then he rushes off to participate in World War I, with Tristan and Alfred joining up to look after him overseas. Samuel is killed in France, and the bereft Tristan removes his heart—in Native American fashion—to bring home for a traditional burial. Meanwhile, Tristan goes on a rampage against the Germans, scalping his victims. When Tristan and the wounded Alfred return from the war, both men are still attracted to Susannah. She refuses Alfred's marriage offer, and he departs to Helena to enter business and politics. Soon, Susannah becomes Tristan's lover, but his restless spirit drives him to wander around the globe, and Susannah eventually weds Alfred. Later, the wild Tristan returns home and weds Isabel Two, the HALF-BREED daughter of One Stab. They build a family, and Tristan becomes involved with the O'Banion clan. In one of his clashes with the O'Banions, Isabel Two is killed, leading to Tristan's reprisals on the murderer's family. Now on the run from the law, Tristan lives in the wild where he meets his fate with a rampaging bear.

The two major Native American characters in this entry were given modest screen time, while the Caucasian—with the spirit of a savage—had the central role. Heavily playing up the romantic nature of this drama, the movie had Tristan absorb instincts for survival from the teachings of One Stab, but his character had acquired little or none of the Native American's oneness with nature and the cycle of life.

Made on a $30 million budget in Alberta, Canada, *Legends of the Fall* grossed more than $66 million in domestic distribution. The film received an Academy Award for Best Cinematography. It received Oscar nominations for Best Art Direction/Set Decoration and Best Sound.

***Light in the Forest, The* (1958)** Buena Vista, color, 93 minutes. **Director:** Herschel Daugherty; **Screenplay:** Lawrence Edward Watkin; **Cast:** Fess Parker (Del Hardy), Wendell Corey (Wilse Owens), Joanne Dru (Milly Elder), James MacArthur (Johnny Butler [True Son]), Carol Lynley (Shenandoe Hastings), Jessica Tandy (Myra Butler), Joseph Calleia (Chief Cuyloga), Rafael Campos (Half Arrow), Iron Eyes Cody (Blackfish).

Conrad Richter's 1953 novel received a carefully researched production by the Walt Disney Studio. Unlike many 1950s feature films that were still basically cavalry-versus-"redskins" brawls, this narrative presented a more balanced picture of the two opposing cultures, but being made by a white majority, the movie's finale had the young hero happy to be accepted by the civilized whites and thrilled to be with his Caucasian girlfriend, even though one of his friends among the Delaware was not as "lucky" in his romance with a white hostage girl.

In 1764, Chief Cuyloga of the Delaware agrees to return all white prisoners to the American militia, one of whom is young Johnny Butler who had spent many years among the tribe and had become known as True Son. Back in Pennsylvania, he is reunited with his real parents, but the adjustment is difficult on both sides. He is drawn to young Shenandoe Hastings, whose family was massacred by warriors. She overcomes her reluctance to anything "Indian," and they develop a bond. In contrast, there is contention between Butler and his uncle Wilse Owens, who hates the savage "devils." Acting as referee in the situation is frontier scout Del Hardy, who was also raised among the Delaware.

Besides acting in this film, CODY also served as technical adviser and with his wife (Yewas Parker) made several costumes for the picture.

Litefoot (19??–) He gained attention as one of the first Native American rap artists. A member of the Cherokee nation, he grew up in Oklahoma. One of his role models was WES STUDI, a member of the same tribe. After schooling, this physically imposing young adult turned to rap music and toured for the next several years. His first album *(The Money)* was released on his own record label (Red Vinyl) in 1992.

In early 1994, Litefoot was in Rome, Italy, participating at a festival entitled "The Feather, the Flute, The Drum" coordinated by the American Indian College Fund. It was they who directed the makers of the forthcoming *INDIAN IN THE CUPBOARD* (1995) to Litefoot. That screen debut led to his winning the first of his several Best Actor awards from First Americans in the Arts. Next on screen, he played Ascalante in *Kull the Conqueror* (1997), and, in that same year, he was Nightwolf in *Mortal Kombat: Annihilation* and the lead performer in *Song of Hiawatha*. Thereafter, he returned to his music with his label releasing more of his own CDs and those of other Native American artists. In 1999, Litefoot received the second Rap Artist of the Year from the Native American Music Awards. In 2001, under the name G. Paul Davis, he was featured in *The Pearl*, a film adaptation of John Steinbeck's short story. He also had a role in *The Adaptation* (2002) directed by Spike Jonze starring Nicolas Cage and Meryl Streep.

Little Beaver Next to TONTO's loyal companion to THE LONE RANGER, one of the most enduring Native American characters in various media was Little Beaver, a young NAVAJO who was friends with cattle rancher/unofficial lawman Red Ryder. (As so often happened, the role was always played by a non-Native American performer.) Together they shared many adventures as they battled wrongdoers.

The property began as a comic strip by Fred Harman that ran in newspapers from 1938 to 1964. In 1940, it was transferred to the screen as a twelve-chapter serial starring Don "Red" Barry as Red Ryder with Tommy Cook as Little Beaver. In 1942, the property came to radio, where it ran until 1949. During its lengthy tenure, Red Ryder was played by Reed Hadley, Carlton KaDell, and Brooke Temple, while Little Beaver was portrayed by first Tommy Cook and then Henry Blair. Red's horse was named Thunder; Little Beaver's was Papoose.

In 1944, Republic Pictures began a Red Ryder series with Wild Bill Elliott cast as Red Ryder and Bobby Blake as Little Beaver, the young Navajo ward of Ryder. During the next four years, the team made nineteen entries: 1944: *Cheyenne Wildcat, Marshal of Reno, The San Antonio Kid, Sheriff of Las Vegas, Vigilantes of Dodge City;* 1945: *Colorado Pioneers, The Lone Texas Ranger, Marshal of Laredo, Phantom of the Plains, Wagon Wheels Westward;* 1946: *Conquest of Cheyenne, Santa Fe Uprising, The Sheriff of Redwood Valley, Stagecoach to Denver, Sun Valley Cyclone;* and 1947: *Marshal of Cripple Creek, Oregon Trail Scouts, Rustlers of Devil's Canyon, Vigilantes of Boomtown.*

The film series then went on hiatus until 1949, when it returned with Jim Bannon cast as Red Ryder and Don Kay Reynolds appearing as Little Beaver. They made four entries: 1949: *Cowboy and the Prizefighter; Ride, Ryder, Ride!; Roll Thunder Roll!;* and 1950: *The Fighting Redhead.*

In 1956, there was a thirty-nine episode syndicated TV series of *Red Ryder*. Starring in the half-hour weekly show was Allan "Rocky" Lane as Red Ryder and Louis Lettieri as Little Beaver.

Little Big-horn See CUSTER, GEORGE ARMSTRONG (LT. COL.).

***Little Big Horn* (aka: *The Fighting 7th*) (1951)** Lippert Pictures, b&w, 86 minutes. **Director/Screenplay:** Charles Marquis Warren; **Cast:** John Ireland (Lt. John Haywood), Lloyd Bridges (Capt. Phillip Donlin), Marie Windsor (Celie Donlin), Reed Hadley (Sgt. Maj. Peter Grierson), Jim Davis (Cpl. Doan Moylan), Hugh O'Brian (Pvt. Al De Walt), Rodd Redwing (Corporal Arika).

One of the biggest challenges to a budget production such as this was how to deal best with a major event—the massacre of LT. COL. GEORGE ARMSTRONG CUSTER and his troops at Little Big-horn—and still avoid the costs of recreating a huge battle set piece (such as used in *THEY DIED WITH THEIR BOOTS ON*, 1941). (At that time, the location was generally spelled *Little Big Horn.*) This efficient economy feature skirted the issue by focusing on the little-known, real-life event that occurred a few miles from where Custer met his defeat. There, nine unmarked graves were found, and this burial site was believed to be of the U.S. cavalry patrol that tried to warn Custer of the pending ambush.

In June 1876, in the Montana Territory at Fort Abraham Lincoln, Celie Donlin is having an affair with Lt. John Haywood, which her workaholic husband discovers. Soon thereafter, Captain Donlin leaves on patrol hoping to reach General Custer in time to warn him of the buildup of SIOUX near the Little Big-horn River. Weeks later, another patrol led by Haywood reconnoiters with Donlin's. Donlin orders Haywood to join his patrol, and the group go on a forced trek through hostile country hoping to reach Custer in time. However, their number is decimated by hostile Sioux, and no one survives to warn Custer of his imminent doom.

Astute moviegoers noted that, while one of the cavalry patrol (Corporal Arika) was played by a Native American, he was of a different tribe from the Sioux. He was a Crow. At the time of the movie's release, the National Film Committee for the Association of American Indian Affairs, Inc., registered their dissatisfaction about "the distortion and callousness evident in the story-line and advertising of *Little Big Horn*."

***Little Big Man* (1970)** National General Pictures, color, 147 minutes. **Director:** Arthur Penn; **Screenplay:** Thomas Berger; **Cast:** Dustin Hoffman (Jack Crabb), Faye Dunaway (Mrs. Pendrake), Martin Balsam (Allardyce T. Merriweather), Richard Mulligan (George Armstrong Custer), Chief Dan George (Old Lodge Skins), Jeff Corey (Wild Bill Hickok), Amy Eccles (Sunshine), Kelly Jean Peters (Olga), Robert Little Star (Little Horse), Cal Bellini (Younger Bear), Ruben Moreno (Shadow That Comes at Night).

Little Big Man, based on Thomas Berger's 1964 novel, came after and was a reaction to America's disillusionment over the Vietnam War, several high-profile assassinations (e.g., John F. Kennedy, Robert Kennedy, and Martin Luther King), and the counterculture response to establishment materialism. It also came at a time when the American Indian Movement (AIM) was making its presence felt in the United States with several notable demonstrations.

This highly successful feature provided a popular treatise demystifying such gun-happy nineteenth-century legends as GEORGE ARMSTRONG CUSTER and WILD BILL HICKOK. Simultaneously, it elevated Native Americans (equated by many reviewers at the time with the back-to-the-earth and the hippie movements) to a position of near equality in U.S. history. In the guise of comedy, *Little Big Man* took the next big leap from such earlier features as the trend-setting *BROKEN ARROW* (1950) and the then recent *Born Losers* (1967) and *TELL THEM WILLIE BOY IS HERE* (1969). It redefined history to reflect more of the Native American point of view, albeit as seen through the eyes of Caucasian Jack Crabb. As such, *Little Big Man* was a key entry in the history of the presentation of Native Americans on the Hollywood screen.

A historian questions 121-year-old Crabb on the amazing events of his life and his search for his identity, whether among whites or Native Americans. The story flashes back to when he was ten years old and he and his sister were orphaned in a raid by hostile braves. While she escapes the CHEYENNE, Jack is raised by them, in particular Old Lodge Skins. A few years later, the tribe gives him the name Little Big Man for his bravery in battle against the Pawnee. Through circumstances, he later rejects his tribal background and becomes part of the white world again. He is cared for by the strange Rev. and Mrs. Pendrake, with the lascivious wife seducing him. His sojourns take him from medicine side-show hawker to becoming the gunfighter known as the Soda Pop Kid, who becomes a temporary friend of Wild Bill Hickok. Still later, Crabb weds the Swedish Olga, loses her to tribal warriors, and for a time is a scout in General Custer's cavalry unit. Next, Crabb moves onto a reservation with Sunshine and Old Lodge Skins, but Custer and his men massacre the village and Sunshine is killed. Tired of being a hermit after that, Jack becomes a scout again for Custer and this time is caught at the battle at Little Big-horn. Thanks to Younger Bear whose life Crabb once saved in the Cheyenne camp, Jack is spared being killed. After escorting Old Lodge Skins to the mountains to die, the two men reminisce and then both come down to the flatlands. The narrative jumps to the present, where a historian wonders how much of Crabb's ramblings are facts and what is fiction.

Within its construction of Native American life much was modified to make the scene appealing to a hipper young America. Yet, there were times within the picture when the braves were presented as objects of ridicule (e.g., the effeminate Little Horse or even Crabb's Little Big Man) or treated as quaint figures (e.g., the elderly Old Lodge Skins). Despite its excesses and faults (e.g., the discursive episodic nature of the satirical chronicle), the Old West was never the same again after this film, in particular such "noble" icons as Custer or even Will Bill Hickok.

One of the top box-office attractions of 1970, *Little Big Man* won an Oscar nomination for Best Supporting Actor (GEORGE).

Littlefeather, Sacheen (1947–) She was most known for having been the proxy in accepting Marlon Brando's Oscar at the 1973 Academy Awards festivities. When Brando was announced the Best Actor winner for *The Godfather*, Littlefeather, bedecked in white buckskin and much native jewelry, stepped out in front of 80 million TV viewers and read Brando's impassioned speech about the mistreatment of Native Americans by both the U.S. government and by Hollywood moviemakers. The stunned studio audience sat in silence as Littlefeather refused the proffered Oscar for Brando.

As Brando had predicted, the gesture created tremendous publicity and brought Native American issues front and center. But the notoriety of her TV appearance affected Littlefeather for years, especially when it was suggested erroneously by a national tabloid that she was not, perhaps, Native American after all.

Born Marie Littlefeather of an APACHE father and a Caucasian mother, she grew up in California where her white grandparents had her dress and act like an Anglo. Depressed by that situation and by the later death of her father, she suffered a nervous breakdown. Later, in San Francisco, she turned to acting, and filmmaker Francis Ford Coppola brought her to the attention of Brando. After the Oscar night event, she found work in a few films: *The Trial of Billy Jack* (1974), *Johnny Firecloud* (1975), and the following year's *WINTERHAWK*. Thereafter, upset by the movie-industry backlash directed at her, she went into seclusion for years. More recently, besides speaking on Native American matters, she occasionally was a participant in events dealing with ecology.

Lloyd, E. James See LAUGHLIN, TOM.

Lone Ranger, the See TONTO.

***Lone Ranger, The* (1949–1957)** ABC-TV series, b&w, 30 minutes. **Cast:** Clayton Moore (the Lone Ranger: 1949–52, 1954–57), John Hart (the Lone Ranger: 1952–54), Jay Silverheels (Tonto).

The Lone Ranger was still a popular radio show (1933–54) when it came to television in 1949. Beginning with an episode devoted to the retelling of how John Reid of the Texas Rangers became the masked Lone Ranger and of his faithful friend, TONTO, a member of the Potawatomi tribe, whom he had befriended as a child. The latter promised to remain with *Kemo Sabe* (i.e., "faithful friend" or "trusted scout") and help him to right wrongs in the Old West. The Lone Ranger's horse was Silver; Tonto's mount was Scout. They survive on the income from Reid's secret silver mine, which he had owned with his late brother. As they complete each good deed and ride off into the sunset, the Lone Ranger intones his famous "Hi-Yo Silver."

While SILVERHEELS—he of the serious demeanor—played Tonto for the TV show's entire run of 221 episodes, Moore dropped out for two seasons over conflicts with the producers and was replaced in those years by film actor Hart (who later had a small role in the theatrical release, *THE LEGEND OF THE LONE RANGER*, 1981). As the TV series drew to and end, Moore and Silverheels appeared in two theatrical adventures: *THE LONE RANGER* (1956) and *The Lone Ranger and the Lost City of Gold* (1958).

As was true in all incarnations of *The Lone Ranger*, loyal Tonto was a man of few words who deferred to his white friend in all matters. Tonto invariably wore buckskin trousers and a fringed shirt and was always seen wearing his dark headband. Similarly to the other media appearances of Tonto through the decades, this was one of the few occasions where a Native American had a positive and enduring (albeit secondary) screen role.

***Lone Ranger, The* (1956)** Warner Bros., color, 86 minutes. **Director:** Stuart Heisler; **Screenplay:** Herb Meadow; **Cast:** Clayton Moore (the Lone Ranger), Jay Silverheels (Tonto), Lyle Bettger (Reece Kilgore), Bonita Granville (Welcome Kilgore), Perry Lopez (Ramirez), Michael Ansara (Angry Horse), Frank de Kova (Red Hawk).

After years as a radio and a TV series, the adventures of the masked hero along with his faithful Potawatomi companion TONTO were adapted to the big screen.

The Lone Ranger and Tonto investigate recent tribal uprisings and discover that avaricious rancher Reece Kilgore is responsible for the problem. By laying the blame on the warriors, Kilgore hopes to unearth silver on Native American lands, not caring that mining the rich deposits would violate sacred tribal lands.

Nothing in this successful theatrical release disturbed the formula of the TV series. Tonto was on the side of the law, but he still remained subordinated to his white cohort. By the time of the follow-up feature, *The Lone Ranger and the Lost City of Gold* (1958), the television program had concluded its first run. In this new theatrical presentation, the Lone Ranger and Tonto discovered that three murdered tribesmen were each wearing a special medallion. The duo tracked another two men—still alive—whose pendants, when added to the first three, provided a treasure map to an amazing stash of riches. The Lone Ranger and Tonto outwitted the outlaw gang after the spoils, and the ancient treasure trove was returned to its rightful Native American owners.

In 1981, the expensively mounted misfire *THE LEGEND OF THE LONE RANGER* was released with new leading players in the time-tested roles.

***Lone Ranger, The* (1966–1969)** CBS-TV series, color, 30 minutes. **Voices:** Michael Rye (the Lone Ranger), Shep Menken (Tonto).

When there was no longer a radio or live-action TV series version of *The Lone Ranger*, the property came back as a Saturday late-morning TV animated cartoon show aimed at the children's marketplace. The premise remained the same, with the Lone Ranger and TONTO chasing bad guys. However, now there were several villains per episode rather than the standard one per segment of the 1949–56 television series. Also, being a cartoon show, the bad guys were far more offbeat compared to the relatively staid outlaws of the live-action version. Relying on the example of TV's *Batman* (1966–68), which used campy guest villains, the animated *The Lone Ranger* did likewise (e.g., the voice of Agnes Moorehead as the Black Widow).

Several years later, a new edition of *The Lone Ranger* cartoon series aired as a supporting product in the *Tarzan/Lone Ranger Adventure Hour* (1980–81) and then as part of the *Tarzan/Lone Ranger/Zorro Adventure Hour* (1981–82). Following much the same format as the prior animated version of the Masked Man and his friend Tonto, the new entry utilized the voices of William Conrad (the Lone Ranger) and Ivan Naranjo (Tonto).

Advertisement for *The Lone Ranger* (1956), the first full-length feature about the Masked Man and Tonto. (JC ARCHIVES)

***Lone Star* (1916)** Mutual, b&w, 5 reels. **Director:** Edward Sloman; **Screenplay:** Kenneth B. Clarke; **Cast:** William Russell (Lone Star), Charlotte Burton (Helen Mattes), Harry Von Meter (John Mattes), Alfred Ferguson (Jim Harper), Ashton Dearholt (Jefferson Mattes).

More so than with most other ethnic minorities (e.g., African American, Hispanic, and Jewish) but on a par with Asian Americans, there was a recurring theme in literature, theater, and film concerning HALF-BREED and full-blooded Native Americans finding love in the white world and whether it could endure. The topic was at odds with the general bias of Caucasian Americans toward "Indians" as savages who were not fit to mingle with the white race. (Later, as actual massacres against the whites became a faint memory from the past and reservation life had taken its toll of generations of Native Americans, the unfit aspect switched to different negative stereotypes: lazy, alcoholic, and uneducated.)

Disliking the archaic practices of tribal medicine men, Lone Star goes East to become a physician. Once there, he finds love with Helen Mattes, who had already rejected her family's social lifestyle for the sake of her medical profession. Her father is against her marrying Lone Star, a decision he revokes when the man saves his daughter's life after she is involved in an accident. By now, however, Lone Star realizes that, although his newfound knowledge of medicine will be useful to his people, Helen cannot be part of his life. They part, and he returns to his community.

The silent photoplay *Lone Star* followed the established Hollywood precepts that: (1) the Native American was to be played by a Caucasian actor and (2) the racially mixed couple split apart before miscegenation can occur.

***Lost Child, The* (2000)** CBS-TV, color, 100 minutes. **Director:** Karen Arthur; **Teleplay:** Sally Beth Robinson;

Cast: Mercedes Ruehl (Rebecca), Jamey Sheridan (Jack), Irene Bedard (Grace), Dinah Manoff (Helen), Tantoo Cardinal (Aunt Mary), Julia McIlvane (Caroline), Ned Romero (Yazzi), Michael Greyeyes (Eddie).

Based on the book *Looking for Lost Bird* (1999) by Yvette Melanson with Claire Safran, this TV movie tread the same ground as *SIOUX CITY* (1994): a Native American infant being adopted by a Jewish couple and belatedly discovering his/her strikingly different actual heritage. In this case, the infant was stolen from her parents and sold to an unknowing Jewish couple. The role of Rebecca, who learns that she is a full-blooded Navajo, was played by half-Cuban actress Ruehl.

Upon hearing from her blood sister (BEDARD), the Jewish Rebecca flies to Arizona to visit her kin on the NAVAJO reservation. She almost immediately feels a sense of belonging that she never had growing up or even as a wife and the mother of two daughters. The enthusiastic Rebecca embraces her new lifestyle and urges her husband and girls to follow. However, they are not so charmed by the culture clash.

At times plodding, at moments overly sentimental, *The Lost Child* barely tapped into its full potential. Filmed in Arizona, the drama was promoted with the catchphrase "A woman's quest for her missing past is about to lead her to an amazing discovery." (Other recent films dealing with white people who belatedly discovered that they had Native American heritages were *SIOUX CITY*, 1984, and *The Hi-Line*, 1999.)

***Lost Legacy: A Girl Called Hatter Fox* (1977)** CBS-TV, color, 100 minutes. **Director:** George Schaefer; **Teleplay:** Darryl Ponicsan; **Cast:** Ronny Cox (Dr. Teague Summer), Conchata Ferrell (Nurse Rhinehart), John Durren (Claude), Joanelle Nadine Romero (Hatter Fox), Donald Hotton (Dr. Levering), S. John Launer (Mr. Winton), Mona Lawrence (Native American nurse), Virginia Bird (old Native American woman).

At issue here is the life of a young Native American woman (Romero) who is sent to a state reformatory as unredeemable. Yet, she is in need of life-saving medical treatment that conflicts with the "superstitions" and "witchcraft" of her people. Dr Teague Summer is the concerned physician who is trying to help her.

This telefeature was based on Marilyn Harris's novel *Hatter Fox* (1973).

M

Magic Stone, The See *KILIAN'S CHRONICLE*.

Mala, Ray (1906–1952) One of the early NATIVE ALASKANS to make a name for himself in the Hollywood film industry, he also played on screen a variety of other ethnic types, including a South American native (*Green Hell*, 1940), a Mexican (*Hold Back the Dawn*, 1941), and an Hawaiian (*Honolulu Lu*, 1942).

Born in the Alaska Territory, Ray Mala came to Hollywood in the early 1930s, hoping to find work in the movie business in the area of cinematography. His first screen assignment was the lead in the quasi-documentary *ESKIMO* (1933). This was followed by parts in such entries as *The Jungle Princess* (1936), *Robinson Crusoe of Clipper Island* (1936—movie serial—as a Polynesian in the employ of the U.S. Intelligence Service), *Wild Bill Hickok* (1938—where he played a Native American brave), *Zanzibar* (1940), and *The Tuttles of Tahiti* (1942—as a Polynesian local). After a gap of nearly ten years, he returned to the screen in the Alaskan-set *RED SNOW*. That same year, he died in Los Angeles of a heart attack.

Man Called Horse, A **(1970)** National General, color, 114 minutes. **Director:** Elliot Silverstein; **Screenplay:** Jack DeWitt; **Cast:** Richard Harris (Lord John Morgan), Judith Anderson (Buffalo Cow Head), Jean Gascon (Batise), Manu Tupou (Chief Yellow Hand), Corinna Tsopei (Running Deer), Dub Taylor (Joe), Eddie Little Sky (Black Eagle), Lina Marin (Thorn Rose), Iron Eyes Cody (medicine man).

Like the same year's *LITTLE BIG MAN*, *A Man Called Horse* was a well-intentioned vehicle designed to let the white majority culture in America participate in the pro–Native American groundswell of the late 1960s as the ethnic minority made its presence, culture, and complaints much better known to the nation. In the name of quasi-authenticity, this film, according to such sources as Ward Churchill in *Fantasies of the Master Race* (1998) and Jacquelyn Kilpatrick in *Celluloid Indians* (1999), blended together traits of the Lakota SIOUX (in whose tribe the action took place) with other tribes, as well as an infusion of Hollywood myth/fiction, a celluloid mixture that frequently confused viewers as to actual Sioux traditions and customs. (The movie never overcame Hollywood's standard problem of how to convey Native American dialects without resorting to subtitles, pantomime, grunts, or the disconcerting practice of having the villagers speak English.)

Despite its positive aims, once again the point of view in *A Man Called Horse* was that of a white man (here both a British nobleman and a French mixed-blood captive). Thus, such a plot event as the movie's highly promoted and much-discussed Sun Vow ritual became *not* a spiritual experience as the Sioux regarded it but one in which the Caucasian hero can gain a woman and status. Moreover, having a key Sioux role played by veteran Australian white actress Anderson won no endorsements for this movie from Native Americans.

Based on Dorothy M. Johnson's story "Man Called Horse," which appeared in *Collier's* magazine in January 1950, the movie was set in the Dakota Territory of the early nineteenth century. After the Sioux massacre his hunting party companions and he is captured, British nobleman Lord John Morgan is taken to their village where Chief Yellow Hand makes him the property of the old squaw, Buffalo Cow Head. She uses him as a beast of burden to do her chores. As time passes, Morgan learns the Sioux language and customs and gains status when he acts bravely in a skirmish with the Shoshone. Meanwhile, Morgan hopes to wed Yellow Hand's daughter, Running Deer. To do so, he endures the Sun Vow ritual that occurs within a huge tepee. He survives the extreme ordeal and marries Running Deer. Later, however, the pregnant woman is killed in a Shoshone raid. After staying with Buffalo Cow Head as her son until she passes on, Morgan leaves the Sioux and returns—somewhat sadly—to England.

For a mixture of reasons—including the much-hyped gore and the extensive Sun Vow ritual sequence—*A Man Called Horse* was a commercial success. It led to *The Return of a Man Called Horse* (1976) in which the British lord (again played by Harris) helped the Sioux who were being abused by the whites. Veteran actress Gale Sondergaard took on a role similar to the one done by Anderson in the original entry. The disappointing *The Triumphs of a Man Called Horse* (1983), a U.S.–Mexican coproduction, focused on the half-breed son (played by Michael Beck) of the English aristocrat (again performed by Harris). With this production, the series ended.

***Manitou, The* (1978)** Avco Embassy, color, 104 minutes. **Director:** William Girdler; **Screenplay:** Girdler, Jon Cedar, and Tom Pope; **Cast:** Tony Curtis (Harry Erskine), Michael Ansara (Singing Rock), Susan Strasberg (Karen Tandy), Stella Stevens (Amelia Crusoe), Jon Cedar (Dr. Jack Hughes), Ann Sothern (Mrs. Kramann), Burgess Meredith (Dr. Ernest Snow), Tenaya (Singing Rock's wife), Joe Gieb (Misquamacas)

Based on one (1975) of Graham Masterston's Manitou book series, the film told of a four-century-old medicine man who has been discovered growing on the spine of Karen Tandy. Seeking help from her former boyfriend—a fake psychic (Curtis)—and physicians, the victim finally turns to a modern-day medicine man (ANSARA) to combat the evil spirit captured within her body.

The mysticism potential of the premise was sidetracked by the veteran cast—especially Curtis who played his corny role for high camp. In essence, the movie trivialized the topics of medicine men and spiritualism, subjects that would be a recurring theme of Hollywood films dealing with Native Americans in the decades to come (e.g., *THE DARK WIND*, 1991).

***Map of the Human Heart* (1993)** Miramax, color, 107 minutes. **Director:** Vincent Ward; **Screenplay:** Louis Nowra and Ward; **Cast:** Jason Scott Lee (Avik), Robert Joamie (young Avik), Anne Parilaud (Albertine), Annie Galipeau (young Albertine), Patrick Bergin (Walter Russell), Clotilde Courau (Rainee), John Cusack (Clark), Jeanne Moreau (Sister Banville), Mayko Pitseolak (Avi's grandmother), Rebecca Vevee (Inuit woman—cook), Josape Kopalee (Inuit elder).

This visually stunning screen romance concentrated on the Inuit (members of ESKIMO groups inhabiting the area from Greenland to West Arctic Canada).

This drama traced the life of part-white Inuit Avik who lives in Nunataaq in the early 1930s. The HALF-BREED becomes friends with visiting British cartographer Walter Russell, the latter helping Avik when the boy contracts tuberculosis. Recuperating at a Montreal clinic Avik is attracted to Albertine, a mixed-breed Canadian. Their romance is halted by the stern mother superior in charge of the facility. Later in the 1930s, Russell returns to Nunataaq, this time on a secret mission for his country.

During World War II, the adult Avik becomes a bombardier in the Canadian Air Force. He reencounters Albertine, only to discover she has become Russell's mistress. Nevertheless, the couple have a liaison, which leads Russell to seek vengeance by having Avik sent on a dangerous bombing raid over Dresden. Devastated by the damage done to that city, Avik eventually returns to Canada, becomes a cartographer, and turns to drink. More years pass, and his daughter Rainee—from his relationship with Albertine—asks him to attend her coming wedding. En route, his snowmobile crashes into the waters, and as he lays dying, he fantasizes about Albertine. His body later washes ashore. Found among his possessions is a note to his offspring.

Helmed by New Zealand director Ward, *Map of the Human Heart* was both a miniature documentary of life among the Inuit as well as an intelligent love story, grounded by LEE's charismatic performance. This movie unfortunately prompted mixed reviews and grossed less than $3 million in its domestic release.

***Massacre* (1934)** Warner Bros., b&w, 74 minutes. **Director:** Alan Crosland; **Screenplay:** Ralph Block and Sheridan Gibney; **Cast:** Richard Barthelmess (Joe Thunder Horse), Ann Dvorak (Lydia), Dudley Digges (Elihu P. Quissenberry), Claire Dodd (Norma), Henry O'Neill (Mr. Dickinson), Sidney Toler (Thomas Shanks), Arthur Hohl (Dr. Turner), Clarence Muse (Sam), James Eagle (Adam).

In 1925's *THE VANISHING AMERICAN*, the plight of modern-day Native Americans was addressed on camera; it was readdressed in this feature. But the presentation suffered from being forced into the standard Warner Bros. ripped-from-the-headlines exposé format that had worked better with such celluloid projects as *I Am a Fugitive from a Chain Gang* (1932). It should be noted that for many reformers of the period, improving the Native American' situation was focused on (or limited to) financial considerations (e.g., better living conditions, schools, medical facilities). Blending the races or sharing each other's culture never seemed to be part of the white majority's viewpoint.

As a stunt rider at the Chicago World's Fair, Joe Thunder Horse is a big success, and he enjoys an acculturated lifestyle. When his father is taken ill, Joe returns to the SIOUX reservation and discovers that his parent is not receiving proper care. Egged on by Lydia, a college-educated Sioux, Joe uncovers corruption at the administration level, involving INDIAN AGENT Quissenberry and mortician Shanks. Later, Joe's father dies, and at the funeral, Shanks finds the opportunity to rape Joe's sister, Jenny. Beating up her assailant, Joe is arrested but flees to Washington, D.C., where he pleads his case to the head (O'Neill) of the Bureau of Indian Affairs.

Later Shanks dies, and at his trial, Joe proves his motive for having attacked the deceased. Now freed, Joe and Lydia plan to wed, and he accepts a job with the Indian Affairs department.

As remained Hollywood's custom for several decades thereafter, the key Native American roles in *Massacre* were played by Caucasians. Here, for a change, they were handled respectfully by both Barthelmess and Dvorak.

***McMasters, The* (aka: *The Blood Crowd; The McMasters . . . Tougher Than the West Itself*) (1970)** Chevron, color, 90 minutes. **Director:** Alf Kjellin; **Screenplay:** Harold Jacob Smith; **Cast:** Brock Peters (Benjie), Burl Ives (Neal McMasters), David Carradine (White Feather), Nancy Kwan (Robin), Jack Palance (Kolby), Dane Clark (Spencer), John Carradine (preacher), Jose Maranio (Indian Joe), Richard Martinez (Black Fox), Joseph Duran (Black Cloud).

Coming at the very start of what would become the black exploitation film cycle in Hollywood, *The McMasters* did not find its proper market upon its initial release. It offered a controversial, and (at times) gory, presentation and featured topics such as the idea of two ethnic minorities working hand-in-hand to defeat bigoted white people.

After the Civil War, African-American Benjie who had fought for the North, returns to the South where his childhood benefactor, Neal McMasters, offers him half-interest in the farm. The hard-working Benjie discovers that no one in the area will work for him. Fortunately, a Native American, White Feather, whom Benjie had helped, offers the assistance of tribe members. This rouses the ire of local racists, especially the one-armed Kolby. The latter instigates an attack on the farm, during which White Feather's sister Robin is raped. Later, Kolby leads another assault on the farm, during which McMasters is killed and the farmhouse burned. Just as Benjie is to be lynched, White Feather's people launch their own assault, and Kolby is killed. Benjie and Robin remain on the farm together to build for the future.

The casting for this unusual movie was quite offbeat, with Caucasian Carradine and Asian Kwan as the two lead Native Americans. When initially distributed, the film hedged its bets by releasing two versions: one in which the African Americans and Native Americans triumphed, the other in which they did not.

McMasters . . . Tougher Than the West Itself, The See *MCMASTERS, THE*.

Means, Russell (1939–) As a staunch Native American activist, he organized protests against the U.S. government's treatment of his people and was a noteworthy figure in the American Indian Movement (AIM). He gained international attention for heading the takeover of Wounded Knee, South Dakota, in 1973. In the 1990s, he became a frequent and well-known screen performer.

Born on the Prine Ridge Reservation in South Dakota, he was the oldest son of a mixed-blood Oglala SIOUX father and a full-blood Yankton Sioux mother. His education was at the Bureau of Indian Affairs school on the reservation and later in the public schools of Vallejo, California. He attended several colleges but always dropped out. Thereafter, he worked in an assortment of jobs (including as a cowboy) as he traveled around the West.

In 1969, Means transferred from his post as a tribal council member at the Rosebud Reservation in South Dakota to assume directorship of the American Indian Center, a government-funded organization in Cleveland, Ohio. Becoming an increasingly prominent spokesperson and demonstrator for Native American causes, in February 1973, he led the occupation of Wounded Knee where, in 1890, many Sioux (including women and children) had been massacred by the U.S. military. The new protest was stirred up by a court decision in favor of a Caucasian who had killed a Native American man. (Russell's strong activism continued thereafter, despite the physical harm he endured over the years because of his political activities and in spite of being sentenced to prison for "rioting" on behalf of his beliefs.) In 1981, he was among those who occupied federal land at Yellow Thunder Camp in South Dakota, hoping to reclaim the Black Hills for the Lakota tribe. Means also involved himself in Native rights issues in other parts of the world (and later became involved in New Mexico politics).

His first screen role was the important one of CHINGACHGOOK in the 1992 remake of *THE LAST OF THE MOHICANS*. When asked if his new career meant the end of his activism, Means told *Entertainment Weekly* (October 23, 1992), "I see film as an extension of the path I've been on for the past 25 years—another avenue to eliminate racism." His follow-up screen parts included *Natural Born Killers* (1994), the TV movie *Buffalo Girls* (1995) in which he played SITTING BULL, *POCAHONTAS* (1995—as the voice of Powhatan), *Wind River* (1998), *Thomas and the Magic Railroad* (2000), the thriller *Ragged Point* (2001), and the comedy *29 Palms* (2002).

Means's autobiography, *Where White Men Fear to Tread*, written with Marvin J. Wolf, appeared in 1996. In the made-for-cable movie *LAKOTA WOMAN: SIEGE AT WOUNDED KNEE* (1994), actor Lawrence Bayne portrayed activist Means on screen.

mixed-blood See HALF-BREEDS.

musicals—feature films Putting aside tribal war dances performed by actual Native Americans or by actors, one of the earlier examples of an American movie having a Native American-themed dance number was Fanny Brice repeating one of her comedic stage numbers ("I'm an Indian") in the film *My Man* (1929). Eddie Cantor's *WHOOPEE!* (1930) offered a Busby Berkeley-choreographed precision dance performed at the reservation by a chorus of comely women dressed in colorful feathered headdresses and short revealing outfits. As the production moved onward, the showgirls—in *Ziegfeld Follies* style—rode horses as famed stager Berkeley maneuvered different geometric formations for the performers. *Rose-Marie* (1936), the second of three film versions of the 1924 Broadway operetta, boasted an elaborate "Totem Tom-Tom" number extravagantly staged by Chester Hale. (It was redone for the 1954 version of *Rose Marie*—with Joan Taylor in the dancing lead—but without the excitement or creativity of the original.) In the campus-set musical *Life Begins in College* (1937), featuring the Ritz Brothers, Joan Davis, and Tony Martin, there were several Native American-themed songs with titles such as "Our Team Is on the Warpath," "Big Chief Swing It," and "Indian Nuts." In *Happy Landing* (1938), starring Norwegian ice skating star Sonja Henie, one of the musical interludes—a tap routine to "War Dance of the Wooden Indians"—was performed by the agile Condos Brothers. In *Wolf Call* (1939), an entry from low-budget Monogram Pictures, hero John Carroll sang a pretty duet with Movita, she cast as a Native American maiden.

Moon Over Miami (1941) featured Betty Grable, Robert Cummings, and Charlotte Greenwood; one of the musical numbers was "Solitary SEMINOLE." Also in 1941 came the low-budget *Melody Lane* starring rubber-legged comedian Leon Errol, and one of its musical intervals was "Cherokee Charlie." Within *Riding High* (1943), starring Dorothy Lamour, Dick Powell, and Victor Moore, which was set partially at an Arizona dude ranch, there was the production number, staged by Danny Dare, entitled "Injun Gal Heap Hep."

Hyperenergetic Betty Hutton did an extremely exuberant rendition of "Doctor, Lawyer, Indian Chief" in the hit film *The Stork Club* (1945). For *Where Do We Go from Here?* (1945), a historical fantasy with musical numbers, leading man Fred MacMurray imagined himself back in several historical moments, including being one of the shipmates on Columbus's voyage to the New World. In Manhattan (before the tribal elders sold it to the Dutch), he encountered a curvaceous Native American maiden (played by June Haver). The couple had a song "Woo Woo Woo Manhattan," but it was deleted before the movie was released.

In *Good News* (1947), the second screen version of the old Broadway hit, the scene was a college-campus soda shop where Joan McCracken and other players performed "Pass the Peace Pipe." For the comedic western *THE PALEFACE* (1948), teaming Bob Hope, Jane Russell, and several Native American characters (played by such actors as CHIEF YOWLACHIE and IRON EYES CODY), one of its musical moments, "Buttons and Bow," won the Academy Award as Best Song. Also in 1948, in *Isn't It Romantic?*, Veronica Lake, Billy De Wolfe, and Mona Freeman did a spoof routine called "At the Nickelodeon" that contained a miniature satire on a warrior's war dance.

For the 1950 screen adaptation of Irving Berlin's *ANNIE GET YOUR GUN*, Betty Hutton as Annie Oakley was indoctrinated into a Native American tribe, leading into her performing "I'm an Indian Too." The comedy western with songs, *A TICKET TO TOMAHAWK* (1950), pairing Dan Dailey and Anne Baxter, dealt with the extension of a railroad through Native American territory. In the musical *Two Tickets to Broadway* (1951), costars Janet Leigh, Ann Miller, Gloria De Haven, and Barbara Lawrence performed "Big Chief Hole in the Ground." In this routine, they played on-camera squaws to the oil-rich leading man (played by Tony Martin). They wore abbreviated Native American maiden garb, set off by fur stoles and diamond earrings. For *About Face* (1952), starring Gordon MacRae, Eddie Bracken, and Virginia Gibson, one of the numbers in this musical remake of *Brother Rat* (1938) was "Wooden Indian." In 1957's *The Girl Most Likely*, leading lady Jane Powell and child actors executed the "Crazy Horse" number—a dream sequence concerning Chief Cliff Robertson (the leading man). In the screen version of *The Music Man* (1961), the mayor's wife (played by Hermione Gingold) and her townswomen put on a musical pageant involving "dancing" squaws.

Jumping ahead to the 1990s, the full-length animated feature *POCAHONTAS* (1995), retelling the legend of the seventeenth-century maiden, boasted several songs, including "Color of the Wind" by Alan Menken and Stephen Schwartz, which won an Academy Award as Best Song. The movie also won an Oscar for Best Musical or Comedy Score. The direct-to-video animated sequel, *Pocahontas II: Journey to a New World* (1998), also featured ethnic musical numbers.

Most of the above on-camera representations of Native Americans in song-and-dance were conceived and executed by non-Native Americans.

***Mystic Warrior, The* (1984)** ABC-TV miniseries, color, 250 minutes. **Director:** Richard T. Heffron; **Teleplay:** Jeb Rosebrook; **Cast:** Robert Beltran (Ahbleza), Devon Ericson (Heyatawin), Rion Hunter (Tonweya), Victoria Racimo (Napewaste), Nick Ramus (Olepi), James Remar (Pesla), Ned Romero (Wisa), Ron Soble (Wanagi), Will Sampson (Wambli), Roger Campo (young Pesla), Ivan Naranjo (Ogle), Branscombe Richmond (Miyaca).

When Ruth Beebe Hill's epic-length *Hanta Yo* was published in 1979, a controversy sprang up about the alleged authenticity of this multigenerational study of nineteenth-century Lakota SIOUX. With the modern-day Lakota community generally decrying the book and Hill employing a Native American to validate her tome's accuracy, the volume maintained a high visibility with the book-buying public. Television rights to the property were acquired by David L. Wolper and Stan Margulies, who had treated the African-American experience in their excellent TV miniseries *Roots* (1977). They planned to make *The Mystic Warrior* a ten-hour television offering, but with continued criticism from Native American PRESSURE GROUPS as to the authenticity and interpretations of the book, the project was not only delayed for several years but also cut back to a more manageable five-hour time slot.

Using a largely Native American cast, the made-for-television saga told of Ahbleza and his Sioux followers in the nineteenth century who utilized mystic powers entrusted to them by their ancestors to save their tribe from annihilation by the white settlers and the U.S. cavalry. The high-profile miniseries received four Emmy Award nominations in the area of costume design, hairstyling, makeup, and music score (for part one).

N

***Nakia* (1974)** ABC-TV series, color, 60 minutes. **Cast:** Robert Forster (Dep. Nakia Parker), Arthur Kennedy (Sheriff Sam Jericho), Gloria DeHaven (Irene James), Taylor Lacher (Dep. Hubbel Martin), John Tenorio Jr. (Half Cub).

In April 1974, an ABC-TV movie entitled *Nakia* served as the pilot for this short-lasting TV series. The telefeature revolved around Nakia Parker, a Native American deputy sheriff in New Mexico becoming involved in a tribal effort to prevent a historic mission from being torn down by a housing developer. The series continued Forster in the lead role, with Kennedy as the Caucasian sheriff and Lacher as another deputy repeating their assignments. Here, the culture clash was represented by Parker being torn between his tribe's roots and the conflicting methods and lifestyle demanded by his life as a law enforcer. One thing he did not do was to use a squad car; instead, he traveled about either on horseback or in his own truck. The series was shot in and around Albuquerque, New Mexico.

Nakia reminded reviewers and critics of Burt Reynolds's equally short-enduring police drama *HAWK* (1966) as well as the pro-Native American ambiance of *BILLY JACK* (1971).

***Nanook of the North* (1922)** Pathé, b&w, 79 minutes. **Director/Screenplay:** Robert Flaherty; **Cast:** Nanook (himself), Allee (Nanook's wife), Alle and Allegoo (Nanook's children).

This superior documentary introduced the filmgoing public to the life of NATIVE ALASKANS, tracing the ESKIMOS in their nomadic existence in the Arctic governed by their search for food and in their daily existence within the igloos they build. The unglamorous production depicted well the customs of their society.

This silent movie was reissued in 1948 with a narration written by Ralph Schoolman and voiced by actor Berry Kroger. A score composed by Rudolf Schramm in 1945 was incorporated into the reissue.

Native Alaskans Long before Alaska became the forty-ninth of the United States, U.S. moviemakers were featuring on screen both its exotic, often Spartan locales and its inhabitants, the Eskimos. At first, the great cold wastes were explored in silent documentaries such as *The Alaska-Siberian Expedition* (1912) and *Alaska Wonders in Motion* (1917). Then came dramas that were set, but usually not filmed, in the northern tundra, such as *LAUGHING BILL HYDE* (1918), *The North Wind's Malice* (1920), and *The Girl from God's Country* (1921). In 1922 there was *NANOOK OF THE NORTH*, a documentary filmed on location, using a slight story line to make the footage more entertaining to viewers. It presented the Eskimos in a dramatic way and made a deep impression on audiences. This led to such features as *THE ALASKAN* (1924) and later *Igloo* (1932) and *ESKIMO* (1933), which provided more detailed accounts of the cultural lifestyle of the far north. These were followed by entries such as *TUNDRA* (1936), *Girl from God's Country* (1940), *Northern Pursuit* (1943), *The Great Alaskan Mystery* (1944—movie serial), *Arctic Manhunt* (1949), *The Wild North* (1952), *RED SNOW* (1952), and *Alaska Seas* (1954).

By the time of *ICE PALACE* (1960), Alaska was part of the United States, and its sweeping chronicle included the problems faced by HALF-BREEDS in that frozen expanse. More recently, there was *THE WHITE DAWN* (1975), *Shadow of the Wolf* (1992), *MAP OF THE HUMAN HEART* (1993), and *Mystery, Alaska* (1999).

Through the decades, a few U.S. TV series have been situated in the north country. While *Sergeant Preston of the Yukon* (1955–58) and *The Alaskans* (1959–60) were bound by

Mikel Conrad and Carol Thurston in *Arctic Manhunt* (1949), one of several features dealing with Native Alaskans. (ECHO BOOK SHOP)

sound-stage, conventional action, the quirky *NORTHERN EXPOSURE* (1990–95) dealt with Native Alaskans on a more dimensional basis.

Navajo, the Best known today for their fine art and religious spiritualism, the Navajo (pronounced NAH-vuh-ho) were based largely in what is today northern Arizona and New Mexico, as well as a section of southern Utah and Colorado. Through the centuries, they too were pushed into warlike responses as Spanish (and later Mexican) forces came northward and pillaged their land, as did white settlers in their move westward.

Far fewer Hollywood films of the pre-1970s dealt with the Navajo people. Usually, stories set in their territory and featuring their people as characters were geared more to emotional dramas (e.g., *THE VANISHING AMERICAN*, 1925; *REDSKIN*, 1929; *LAUGHING BOY*, 1934) than more conventional cavalry-versus-"redskins" action entries (e.g., *RIO GRANDE*, 1950; *Fort Defiance*, 1951).

Yet, there was already an American film trend in the 1950s to explore the cultural and mystic side of Navajo life, as represented in *CALL OF THE NAVAJO* and *NAVAJO*, both 1952 releases. This interest led, in decades to come, to a small cycle of films of varying genres dealing with Navajo culture, religion, and especially mysticism. These included such entries as *NIGHTWING* (1979), *THE DARK WIND* (1991), *SHADOWHUNTER* (1993), and *THE SUNCHASER* (1997). More recently, and in another direction, John Woo's *Windtalkers* (2002) dealt with Navajo marines (one of whom was played by ADAM BEACH) during World War II being in danger because the enemy wants to break the Allied code based on the Navajo language.

***Navajo* (1952)** Lippert, b&w, 71 minutes. **Director/Screenplay:** Norman Foster; **Cast:** Francis Key Teller (Son of the Hunter), John Mitchell (Grey Singer), Mrs. Kee Teller (Good Weaver), Billy Draper (Billy, the Ute guide), Hall Bartlett (Native American school counselor).

An unvarnished view of NAVAJO life, this independently made feature was filmed entirely at the Navajo reservation in northeastern Arizona. It captured the dilemma of a youngster stuck between two opposing worlds: his traditional Native American life and the puzzling white world.

With his father, a railroad worker, long gone (and later found to have a new wife, a HALF-BREED), the seven-year-old Son of the Hunter stays with his mother (Good Weaver) and his sisters. He is instructed in his people's traditions by Grey Singer, once a medicine man. The boy and the old man visit Great Rock Canyon (aka: Canyon de Chelly) where the Navajo once held out against U.S. soldiers until starved into submission. Later, the pair camp at Rock Standing Up.

Then life changes. Grey Singer dies of old age, leaving his horse to the youth. (Before Grey Singer expired, he urged his young friend to avoid evil thoughts about white men and to "follow the path of light.") Later, Good Weaver and one of her daughters die from sickness, and the other girl is sent to stay with nuns. The frightened Son of the Hunter is caught and sent to school, which he hates, and he runs away to the wild. While at the Canyon of Death, he remembers the words of Grey Singer and decides that he must adjust to his new life (including the helpful efforts of a white school counselor with a positive viewpoint).

Made at a cost of $51,000 the picture received Oscar nominations for Best Cinematography and Best Documentary. The school counselor was played by Hall Bartlett, the actor-turned-film producer who packaged this personal project.

***Navajo Blues* (1997)** Pix Entertainment, color, 87 minutes. **Director:** Joey Travolta; **Screenplay:** Richard Dillon; **Cast:** Steven Bauer (Nicholas Epps), Irene Bedard (Audrey Wyako), Charlotte Lewis (Elizabeth Wyako), Barry Donaldson (Robert), Ed O'Ross (Not Lightning Struck), George Yager (Stevens), Tom Fridley (Joey Pinapolo Jr.), Michael Horse (Begsy), Billy Dayhedge (Grandfather Wyako).

When Joey Travolta, the brother of actor John, coproduced and directed this R-rated entry, a viable ambiance (i.e., the NAVAJO culture) was wasted in an amateurish cop drama. Native American actress BEDARD had little to work with as the tribal police officer investigating several murders tied to stolen Navajo artifacts. There was no comparison between this effort, which had a witness hiding out from the mob on the Navajo reservation, and *THE DARK WIND* (1991) or *THUNDERHEART* (1992)—two flawed but culturally intriguing genre pieces.

***Nightwing* (1979)** Columbia, color, 103 minutes. **Director:** Arthur Hiller; **Screenplay:** Steve Shagan, Bud Shrake, and Martin Cruz Smith; **Cast:** Nick Mancuso (Deputy Youngman Duran), David Warner (Phillip Payne), Kathryn Harrold (Anne Dillon), Stephen Macht (Walker Chee), Strother Martin (Selwyn), George Clutesi (Abner Tasupi).

Nightwing (1977) was the Edgar Award-nominated first novel by Native American author Smith who coadapted his screenplay for this pedestrian picture. The book effectively explored the eerie cave where the vampire bats clustered and their voracious eating activity (as well as detailing the low-key life on the NAVAJO reservation), but the movie version settled for a nature-upended approach. Thus, another opportunity to explore Native American culture went amiss.

When police deputy Youngman Duran investigates the death of mares on a Maski reservation ranch, he questions the shaman, Abner Tasupi. The mystic not only foresees his own death but also speaks of the end of the world in which Duran has a role to play. Later, a shepherd boy and several sheep are killed mysteriously, as well as Tasupi. By now, an English scientist on the scene informs Walker Chee, a local entrepreneur who plans to mine the oil shale in the tribe's sacred canyon, that plague-carrying vampire bats caused the deaths. Before the drama concludes, the petroleum-rich cave has been exploded, and, in true Hollywood fashion, Duran and nurse Anne Dillon have fallen in love. With the troublesome canyon destroyed, the tribe's supernatural curse vanishes.

Nightwing was filmed in New Mexico at Laguna Pueblo, Bonanza Creek Ranch, and in Albuquerque.

Nobody Loves a Drunken Indian See *FLAP*.

***Northern Exposure* (1990–1995)** CBS-TV series, color, 60 minutes. **Cast:** Rob Morrow (Dr. Joel Fleischman), Janine Turner (Maggie O'Connell), Barry Corbin (Maurice Minnifield), John Corbett (Chris Stevens), Darren E. Burrows (Ed Chigliak), John Cullum (Holling Vincouer), Cynthia Geary (Shelly Tambo), Elaine Miles (Marilyn Whirlwind), Peg Phillips (Ruth-Anne Miller).

Set in the tiny, inland Alaskan town of Cicely, this frequently wacky drama captured the public's fancy with its cast of eccentrics who were caught up in daily life within this quaint hamlet. (Some, such as pampered Fleischman, often wished they were elsewhere.) While the narrative focused on Jewish New Yorker Dr. Joel Fleischman and his off-and-on romance with gentile air-taxi pilot Maggie O'Connell, the other regulars were always in full view. Among the ensemble were two

Darren E. Burrows, Rob Morrow, and Elaine Miles in the TV drama *Northern Exposure* (1990–95). (ECHO BOOK SHOP)

NATIVE ALASKANS. One of them, Marilyn Whirlwind, had chosen to become Fleischman's office helper in his medical practice. A woman of few words, she remained seemingly emotionless in the toughest of situations, but little escaped her attention. Then there was young, impressionable Ed Chigliak, a jack-of-all-trades helper to retired astronaut Maurice Minnifield. He fantasized about life in a much bigger city but was always drawn back by his ethnic roots. At times, he was not certain if he would like to be a filmmaker or a shaman. Like Marilyn, he was part of the contemporary world, but Ed also maintained cultural ties to his heritage and rituals, which no amount of cynicism on the part of the Caucasian locals could shake.

The major success of this series reflected a great deal of interest in Alaska—its geography, its people, and its customs. This show was far more authentically Alaskan (albeit filmed in the state of Washington) than, for example, *The Alaskans* (1959–60), which betrayed its sound-stage settings.

O

***Old Overland Trail* (1953)** Republic, b&w, 60 minutes. **Director:** William Witney; **Screenplay:** Milton Raison; **Cast:** Rex Allen (Rex Allen), Slim Pickens (Slim Pickens), Roy Barcroft (John Anchor), Virginia Hall (Mary Peterson), Gil Herman (Jim Allen), Leonard Nimoy (Chief Black Hawk), Joe Yrigoyen (Pete).

There had already been many westerns—including those like this entry with a singing cowboy—dealing with INDIAN AGENTS and white villains leading tribal warriors astray. But this programmer boasted Nimoy (the future Mr. Spock of TV's *Star Trek*, 1966–69) as the weak-willed, troublemaking APACHE chief who undertook a variety of illegal activities on behalf of villainous John Anchor.

What was offensive about such formula entries as this were its clichéd assumptions, which, unfortunately, the filmgoing public seemed to believe to be mostly true: The Apache were always merciless killers, Native Americans should/must remain quietly on the reservations to which they have been relegated, "Indians" could be easily bent to the will of a white man—no matter how crooked—and, when all is said and done, the tribespeople should consider it a wonderful opportunity to work with the white settlers to develop land that once belonged to the Native Americans.

***One Flew Over the Cuckoo's Nest* (1975)** United Artists, color, 129 minutes. **Director:** Milos Forman; **Screenplay:** Lawrence Hauben and Bo Goldman; **Cast:** Jack Nicholson (Randle Patrick McMurphy), Louise Fletcher (Nurse Mildred Ratched), William Redfield (Harding), Will Sampson (Chief Bromden), Michael Berryman (Ellis), Brad Dourif (Billy Bibbit).

In 1963, Kirk Douglas starred on Broadway in Dale Wasserman's gripping adaptation of Ken Kesey's novel, *One Flew Over the Cuckoo's Nest* (1962). Unable to get it transferred to the screen, Douglas turned the property over to his actor/producer son, Michael. Under Forman's direction, the project became an impressive film. It provided a brilliant star turn for Nicholson and an excellent showcase for several of the cast, including Creek tribesman SAMPSON in his feature-film debut.

To forego being sent to a tough prison farm, Randle Patrick McMurphy—imprisoned for assault and statutory rape—pretends to be crazy and is reassigned to the state mental institution. He soon finds that under the tight-fisted control of Nurse Ratched, life is far more severe here than he had experienced previously. The rebel tries to revive his zombielike fellow inmates with his crazy schemes. At each step, he and the others are punished by the stern Ratched, who does her best to quash the patients' spirit.

In a rambunctious mood, McMurphy sneaks two girls into the ward for a late-night party. He arranges for one of the women to have sex with the highly disturbed young Billy Bibbit. When Ratched catches Bibbit with one of the females, she threatens to tell his mother, which leads the patient to commit suicide. McMurphy goes on a rampage, trying to strangle the head nurse. The latter retaliates by ensuring that McMurphy is lobotomized, and when he returns to the ward, he is nearly comatose. Taking pity on his now-vegetable friend, Chief Bromden suffocates him with a pillow. Then the enraged Native American breaks out on his way to freedom.

Made on a budget of $3 million, *One Flew Over the Cuckoo's Nest* grossed $112 million in domestic distribution. It won five Academy Awards: Best Actor (Nicholson), Best Actress (Fletcher), Best Adapted Screenplay, Best Director, and Best Picture. It received four additional Oscar nominations: Best Cinematography, Best Film Editing, Best Original Score, and Best Supporting Actor (Dourif). This important production was an illustration of how, slowly,

Native Americans were being drawn into mainstream cinema so that now they were occasionally represented in such character dramas as this one. Here Sampson's Chief Bromden was seemingly deaf-and-dumb, but the morose patient tells McMurphy that he is in the institution to avoid dealing with the world that destroyed his father.

O'Rourke of the Royal Mounted See *SASKATCHEWAN*.

Outlaw Josey Wales, The **(1976)** Warner Bros., color, 135 minutes. **Director:** Clint Eastwood; **Screenplay:** Phil Kaufman and Sondra Chernus; **Cast:** Clint Eastwood (Josey Wales), Chief Dan George (Lone Watie), Sondra Locke (Laura Lee), Bill McKinney (Terrill), John Vernon (Fletcher), Paula Trueman (Grandma Sarah), Sam Bottoms (Jamie), Geraldine Keams (Little Moonglow), Will Sampson (Ten Bears).

One of the last great U.S.-made westerns, *The Outlaw Josey Wales* was as much about the dying sagebrush genre as it was about the changing American frontier and the diminished status of Native Americans in the country.

In the early years of the Civil War, Missouri farmer Josey Wales loses his family and farm when they are attacked by the Redlegs, a group of Union guerrillas. The embittered man joins Confederates heading to Kansas to fight the Yankees. When the war ends, Wales is wanted by the Yankees for having killed Union soldiers who were responsible for murdering his maverick pals. He goes on the run.

As Wales migrates farther West, he inadvertently gains several loners as his traveling companions. They include Lone Watie, an elderly Cherokee who bemoans the loss of the old days when his tribe was a proud race. As they intersect a covered wagon being attacked by Comancheros, Wales intervenes and saves young Laura Lee from being raped by the warriors. The pack finally reaches its destination—the farmhouse owned by Grandma Sarah, another of the travelers—only to have Wales's old enemies, the Redlegs turn up in the area. The newcomers are dispatched by Wales and the farmers, and now Josey can begin life anew.

Two of the more intriguing characters in this western were Lone Watie, a man who once bargained (unsuccessfully) with the Secretary of the interior to regain his tribe's land. He was a man of wisdom, some of which he imparted to Wales. Another was the Comanchero chief, Ten Bears, with whom Wales discussed the toughness of life as ways of living changed and the open country was gobbled up by the white settlers. Again, as had become traditional in Hollywood films, the Native American characters (GEORGE and SAMPSON) were men of knowledge, passing on their insights to white men. Thus, these Native American elders were on-screen good guys, a big change from the hackneyed bloodthirsty "savages" depicted in earlier Hollywood movies.

The Outlaw Josey Wales was a critical and box-office success. The film received an Oscar nomination for Best Original Score.

Outsider, The **(1961)** Universal, b&w, 108 minutes. **Director:** Delbert Mann; **Screenplay:** Stewart Stern; **Cast:** Tony Curtis (Ira Hamilton Hayes), James Franciscus (Jim Sorenson), Gregory Walcott (Sergeant Kiley), Bruce Bennett (Major General Bridges), Vivian Nathan (Nancy Hayes), Charles Stevens (Joseph Hayes).

As *JIM THORPE—ALL AMERICAN* (1951) depicted the downfall (and regeneration) of a heroic modern-day Native American, so *The Outsider* detailed another less fortunate individual. Based on William Bradford Huie's article, "Torture Execution of a Hero Marine," which appeared in *Cavalier* magazine (December 1958), it traced the life of shy Pima tribesman Hayes. At age seventeen, having never left his impoverished reservation, he enlists in the U.S. Marine Corps to fight in World War II. There, he is discriminated against and/or ignored. Eventually, he makes one quasi-friend, a white man named Jim Sorenson. During combat action, Hayes and Sorenson are among the marines who raise the U.S. flag on Mount Suribachi during the fierce battle against the Japanese on Iwo Jima. Soon thereafter Sorenson is killed, leaving Hayes devastated. The photo taken of the symbolic flag-raising becomes world famous, and Hayes and the others are made into national heroes. Unable to deal with the fame, he turns to drinking and disgraces his unit.

After the victory, Hayes returns to the reservation but is unable to live quietly. The tribal elders use his notoriety to send him as a spokesman to Washington, D.C., regarding an irrigation project. He fails in his task, gets drunk, and lands in jail. Later, at the dedication of the Iwo Jima Memorial (in Arlington, Virginia), he gains the courage to reshape his life. Back at the reservation, when he is deliberately overlooked in the tribal-council election, he breaks down. He sneaks off to a desolate mountain with a cache of liquor, and there, at age thirty-two, he dies of exposure.

Giving one of his strongest screen performances, Jewish-American Caucasian Curtis was effective as the Native American who had unwanted fame heaped on him and could not cope with the notoriety. That the actor cannot get fully inside the hero's persona was mostly a problem of the shallow script and the Hollywood conventions of the period that guided this project. Location scenes for *The Outsider* included filming at the Pima-Maricopa Native American Reservation.

In real life, Hayes appeared in two film entries: the documentary short subject *To the Shores of Iwo Jima* (1945) and the John Wayne combat feature *SANDS OF IWO JIMA* (1949). In the latter, he played himself in a recreation of the raising of the U.S. flag at Mt. Suribachi during World War II.

It was several years before there was another major Hollywood biography of a real-life, contemporary Native American figure: *RUNNING BRAVE* (1983), the unsuccessful, contrived biography of Olympic runner Billy Mills, with, once again, a Jewish-American Caucasian (Robby Benson) cast in the central assignment.

P

Paleface, The (1948) Paramount, color, 91 minutes. **Director:** Norman Z. McLeod; **Screenplay:** Edmund Hartmann and Frank Tashlin; **Cast:** Bob Hope ("Painless" Peter Potter), Jane Russell (Calamity Jane), Robert Armstrong (Terris), Iris Adrian (Pepper), Joseph Vitale (scout), Chief Yowlachie (Chief Yellow Feather), Iron Eyes Cody (Chief Iron Eyes), Henry Brandon (Wapato, medicine man), Rolando Barrera (Native American).

A key Hollywood motion picture in demystifying the Old West for modern audiences was this rip-roaring Bob Hope comedy. It took the western genre for a satirical ride in its hilarious account of "Painless" Peter Potter, a cowardly, mail-order dentist who finds himself wed to buxom Calamity Jane. Unknown to the naïve quack, the fearless, sharpshooting legend was released early from prison to ferret out the renegades who are smuggling guns to Native Americans. She marries Potter as a cover for her government assignment but eventually falls in love with this wisecracking lug.

In the course of the celluloid hijinks, Calamity kills almost a dozen rampaging warriors in assorted skirmishes. Her casual attitude to her lethal target practice is a reflection of Hollywood's continued reluctance at that time to regard Native Americans as human beings rather than formulaic bloodthirsty savages. On a different level, the comical nature of Potter and Calamity's misadventures when captured by the warriors and sentenced to death turned the seemingly sadistic captors into buffoons, variations of animated cigar-store wooden "Indians."

The Paleface grossed a huge $4.5 million in domestic film rentals. The song "Buttons and Bows" from the comedy sold an estimated 3 million copies as a recording (and 700,000 copies in sheet-music form). "Buttons and Bows" won an Academy Award as Best Song. This huge film hit led to the sequel *Son of Paleface* (1952) and to the original movie being remade—to far less acclaim—as *The Shakiest Gun in the West* (1968) starring Don Knotts and Barbara Rhoades.

Phillips, Lou Diamond (1962–) His heritage was truly multicultural—he was born part-Cherokee, Filipino, Scottish-Irish, Hawaiian, Chinese, and Spanish. He became one of the busiest and most earnest of the younger actors in the 1990s, having made his show-business mark earlier with his charismatic performance as Chicano musical talent Ritchie Valens in *La Bamba* (1987).

He was born Louis Upchurch at the Subic Bay Naval Station in the Philippines, where his father was stationed, and was raised in Arlington, Texas. At the University of Texas, he became interested in both acting and filmmaking technique, later studied with actor Adam Roarke, and appeared in Roarke's *Trespasses* (1983), as well as other independent film ventures. After *Stand and Deliver* (1987), Phillips joined with "Brat Pack" members for the hip western *YOUNG GUNS* (1988) in which he played a NAVAJO-Mexican mystic.

In the 1990s, Phillips continued to act in a large output of movies, although few were of notable quality. With his mixed-blood heritage, he was frequently asked to play ethnic types in such films as *THE DARK WIND* (1991—as a Navajo reservation policeman), *Shadow of the Wolf* (1992—as an Inuit ESKIMO), and *SIOUX CITY* (1994—as a Lakota Sioux in this drama which he directed). The actor received critical kudos for his performance in *Courage Under Fire* (1996) starring Meg Ryan. In the late 1990s, Phillips played the monarch of Siam in the Broadway revival of the musical *The King and I* and continued with such features as *A Better Way to Die* (2000), *Knight Club* (2001), and *Lone Hero* (2002). He had the lead in the short-lived supernatural TV series *Wolf Lake* (2001), in which he portrayed a Seattle police officer whose girlfriend disappears.

***Pillars of the Sky* (1956)** Universal-International, color, 95 minutes. **Director:** George Marshall; **Screenplay:** Sam Rolfe; **Cast:** Jeff Chandler (1st Sgt. Emmett Bell), Dorothy Malone (Calla Gaxton), Ward Bond (Dr. Joseph Holden), Keith Andes (Capt. Tom Gaxton), Lee Marvin (Sgt. Lloyd Carracart), Michael Ansara (Kamiakin), Orlando Rodriguez (Malachi), Frank de Kova (Zachariah).

CHANDLER, so frequently cast as COCHISE in films (e.g., *BROKEN ARROW*, 1950) here played a taciturn U.S. Army officer in the Oregon country of 1868. In this setup, he had loyalties both to the military and to the Native Americans, including the Nez Percé scouts who were serving under him in his capacity as chief of the cavalry's tribal police force. While doing his duty as an officer, the brooding man—who loves a married woman (Malone)—has sympathy for Kamiakin, chief of the Palouse tribe. The latter are rebelling because the government broke its treaty by building roads within their territory.

There was much discussion within this well-honed movie of the Native Americans living in peace with the white men, which translated to their being pliable to any demands placed on them by the fickle U.S. government. And although there was a great deal of killing by the soldiers in the course of this picture, it was the Native Americans who were depicted as committing the more bloodthirsty (barbaric) murders, which stuck in viewers' minds. Lebanese-American ANSARA had another of his patented roles as a bellicose warrior leader

Pillars in the Sky was based on Will Henry's novel *To Follow a Flag* (1953).

***Pioneers, The* (1941)** Monogram, b&w, 61 minutes. **Director:** Al Herman; **Screenplay:** Charles Anderson; **Cast:** Tex Ritter (Tex Ritter), Arkansas "Slim" Andrews (Slim), Red Foley (Red Foley), Doye O'Dell (Doye O'Dell), Wanda McKay (Susanna Ames), Del Lawrence (Ames), Chief Many Treaties (Warcloud), Chief Soldani (Lonedeer).

Anything was possible in Hollywood, including taking the classic James Fenimore Cooper novel *The Pioneers, or the Sources of the Susquehanna* (1823) and transforming it into a budget screen vehicle for singing-cowboy star Ritter, abetted by an assortment of country music personalities. (The settings were updated from a distinct historical period to the Old West, and the inclusion of such musical numbers as "Wild Galoot from Tuzigoot" made it impossible to take the proceedings too seriously.)

Borrowing plot threads from some of Cooper's *The Leatherstocking Tales*, this makeshift production was one of many westerns to use the ploy of having the white crooks frame the Native Americans for attacks on settlers. In this instance, the villains were careless, and the hoofprints of the supposed "savages" revealed that the horses were shod, which was *never* the custom of Native Americans.

***Plainsman, The* (1936)** Paramount, b&w, 115 minutes. **Director:** Cecil B. DeMille; **Screenplay:** Waldemar Young, Harold Lamb, and Lynn Riggs; **Cast:** Gary Cooper (Wild Bill Hickok), Jean Arthur (Calamity Jane), James Ellison (Buffalo Bill Cody), Charles Bickford (John Lattimer), Helen Burgess (Louisa Cody), Paul Harvey (Yellow Hand), Victor Varconi (Painted Horse), John Miljan (George Armstrong Custer), Frank McGlynn Sr. (Abraham Lincoln), Anthony Quinn (a Cheyenne brave), Chief Thundercloud (fifth brave).

With history bent to the will of filmmaker DeMille, the grandeur of the spectacle in *The Plainsman* helped to compensate for its continued wavering from actual fact. To personalize the western epic, the narrative, set in the post-American Civil War era, focused on the legendary WILD BILL HICKOK and BUFFALO BILL CODY and their respective women, Calamity Jane and Louisa. Among the events depicted were the massacre of the garrison at Fort Piney by the SIOUX, the capture of Calamity and Hickok by CHEYENNE who torture them for information about Cody's whereabouts, and the activities of gun-runner Lattimer, who is selling firearms to the tribes. The annihilation of CUSTER and the cavalry at Little Bighorn (shot at the Cheyenne Indian Reservation at Lame Deer, Montana) is also enclosed into this action-packed excursion. In an unusual twist for an epic, the heroic Hickok meets his fate while playing a game of poker.

Clearly regarding the Native Americans as backdrop to portraying the acclaimed exploits of rugged white men Hickok and Cody, DeMille used the mass of on-camera braves as mere set dressing for his stars' turns. The highly successful *The Plainsman* was remade in 1966 to far less effect as a TV movie that first had theatrical release.

Pocahontas (ca. 1595–1617) Perhaps the most famous of all Native American females, she was the daughter of Wahunsonacock (whom the English called Powhatan), who ruled over a confederacy of villages and bands in the area now called Virginia. As legend had it, Pocahontas saved the life of British adventurer Capt. John Smith, who had led an exploration trip for the Virginia Company across the Atlantic Ocean in 1607 to what became Jamestown. In 1613, the English captured and held Pocahontas captive, hoping to exchange her for Caucasian prisoners whom Powhatan had taken. During her captivity, Pocahontas converted to Christianity and married a settler named John Rolfe. While visiting England with her husband, she contracted the "European disease" of smallpox and died.

Pocahontas figured as a character in several movies. She was played by Dolores Cassinelli (*Jamestown*, 1923), Jody Lawrence (*CAPTAIN JOHN SMITH AND POCAHONTAS*, 1953), voice of IRENE BEDARD (*POCAHONTAS*, 1995), singing voice of Judy Kuhn (*Pocahontas*, 1995), Sandrine Holt (*Pocahontas: The Legend*, 1995), voice of Bedard (*Pocahontas II: Journey to a New World*, 1998), and the singing voice of Kuhn (*Pocahontas II: Journey to a New World*, 1998).

***Pocahontas* (1995)** Buena Vista, color, 87 minutes. **Director:** Mike Gabriel and Eric Goldberg; **Screenplay:** Carl Binder, Susannah Grant, and Philip LaZebnik; **Super-**

vising Animator: Richard Bazley; **Voices:** Irene Bedard (Pocahontas—speaking voice), Judy Kuhn (Pocahontas—singing voice), Mel Gibson (Captain John Smith), Russell Means (Chief Powhatan), David Ogden Stiers (Gov. John Ratcliffe/Wiggins), Linda Hunt (Grandmother Willow), Billy Connolly (Ben), Christian Bale (Thomas), Michelle St. John (Nakoma), Gordon Tootoosis (Kebata).

In the politically correct 1990s, it was only a matter of time before the Walt Disney Studio turned to the settling of the United States and its affect on Native Americans. The vehicle chosen for this full-length animated movie was the commercially safe and familiar tale of noble love between the young tribal maiden POCAHONTAS and John Smith, a tolerant Englishman/Indian fighter. This was the first Disney animated feature to be based on real-life personalities.

In 1607, a British ship arrives in the New World carrying Governor Ratcliffe and his crew, which includes Indian fighter John Smith. Ratcliffe hopes to make his fortune in America tapping into its treasures. Once they land, it is not long before Smith encounters Pocahontas, the exuberant daughter of Chief Powhatan. Although she has already been promised in marriage to young warrior Kocoum, the maiden is quickly entranced with Smith. When Kocoum discovers the romance, he prepares to fight the interloper. Pocahontas intervenes, hazarding her life to save her beloved. By the finale, the unsullied lovers conclude that each should return to his/her own people. Smith sails back to England.

On the plus side, *Pocahontas* utilized the voices of several Native American actors including BEDARD and MEANS. Unusually slow-moving for a Disney animated feature and filled with several unremarkable songs, the film was made at a cost of $55 million and grossed more than $141 million in domestic distribution. It won Academy Awards for Best Musical or Comedy Score and Best Original Song ("Colors of the Wind").

The same year as this feature, there was the Canadian-made, live-action *Pocahontas: The Legend*, which featured Sandrine Holt as Pocahontas, Miles O'Keeffe as John Smith, Tony Goldwyn as Sir Edwin Wingfield, and Billy Merasty as Prince Kocoum. In 1998 came the direct-to-video animated feature with music entitled *Pocahontas II: Journey to a New World*. Bedard repeated her role as the voice of the young maiden who traveled abroad with her husband to meet the king of England and hopefully to bring peace between England and the colonies.

police dramas—motion pictures and television To date there have been few recurring roles of substance on TV series for Native Americans, but a few shows featured mixed-blood Native Americans as law enforcers. On *LAW OF THE PLAINSMAN* (1959–60) set in the New Mexico Territory of 1880, MICHAEL ANSARA, a non-Native American who frequently played warriors on camera, was cast as a college-educated U.S. marshal. Part-Cherokee BURT REYNOLDS starred in the short-lasting *HAWK* (1966), working the New York City night beat while assigned to the New York district attorney's office. His character was a full-blooded Iroquois. In *NAKIA* (1974), Robert Forster was a Native American employed as a contemporary deputy sheriff in New Mexico. On the 1990–91 *Twin Peaks*, among the cast of quirky characters in that strange town near the Canadian border was Deputy Tommy "the Hawk" Hill, played by Michael Horse.

Modern-day bounty hunters were not part of the police force, but they often worked in conjunction with same, and their efforts, when successful, helped to bring wrongdoers to justice. As such, *Renegade* (1993–97) costarred Branscombe Richmond as Bobby Sixkiller, the head of his own high-tech bounty-hunter agency. Part-Aleutian Indian (and part-French, Tahitian, English, Hawaiian, and Spanish), Richmond had previously played a Hawaiian law enforcer on the TV police drama *Hawaiian Heat* (1984). As a former stuntman (turned stunt coordinator, actor, director), Richmond had also been involved with *Danger Theatre* (1993), a half-hour comedy/adventure television offering. One portion of the weekly summer show was called "Tropical Punch" and was a take-off of the *Hawaii Five-O* (1968–80) cop series.

On the big screen, part–Native American LOU DIAMOND PHILLIPS had the lead role in *THE DARK WIND* (1991), the first of what was planned to be a movie series based on the detective books by Tony Hillerman about NAVAJO tribal policeman Jim Cree. (To date only that one entry was made.) The next year, part–Native American Val Kilmer headlined *THUNDERHEART* as a one-quarter SIOUX FBI agent who was assigned to a murder case on an Oglala Sioux reservation. He worked with a local law enforcer on the reservation, a role played by Native American actor GRAHAM GREENE. In 2001, there appeared the short-lasting supernatural TV drama, *Wolf Lake*. The TV series featured Lou Diamond Phillips as a Seattle police detective who is of Native American heritage.

***Poltergeist II* (1986)** United Artists/Metro-Goldwyn-Mayer, color, 90 minutes. **Director:** Brian Gibson; **Screenplay:** Mark Victor and Michael Grais; **Cast:** JoBeth Williams (Diane Freeling), Craig T. Nelson (Steve Freeling), Heather O'Rourke (Carol Anne Freeling), Oliver Robins (Robbie Freeling), Zelda Rubinstein (Tangina Barrons), Will Sampson (Taylor), Julian Beck (Rev. Henry Kane), Geraldine Fitzgerald (Gramma Jess), John P. Whitecloud (old Native American).

Four years after the highly popular *Poltergeist* came this adequate sequel, which was far less scary or original. Before, diminutive clairvoyant Tangina Barrons had been the mysterious mystic force who helped the overwhelmed Freeling family cope with menacing spirits who sucked their little girl (O'Rourke) through the TV set into another world. In this go-around, it was a soft-spoken Native American named Taylor who was the life and soul saver. He arrives unannounced at Gramma Jess's house in Arizona where the Freelings have fled after the devastation of their California home. Explaining that Tangina told him to come to their aid, he instructs the bewildered group on how to deal with the evil spirits that beckon to them through the dimensions. Eventually, Taylor, joined by Tangina, leads the Freelings back to California to confront their other-worldly tormentor.

Reflecting how Native American mysticism—albeit an unknown discipline to most filmgoers—had crept into popular culture, now it was Taylor who was the Freelings' interpreter, guide, and protector as they battled vengeful specters. *Poltergeist II* grossed more than $40 million in domestic distribution.

***Powwow Highway* (1989)** Warner Bros., color, 91 minutes. **Director:** Jonathan Wacks; **Screenplay:** Janet Heaney and Jean Stawarz; **Cast:** A Martinez (Buddy Red Bow), Gary Farmer (Philbert Bono), Joanelle Nadine Romero (Bonnie Reed Bow), Geoff Rivas (Sandy Youngblood), Roscoe Born (Agent Jack Novall), Wayne Waterman (Wolf Tooth), Margo Kane (Imogene), Wes Studi (Bull), Sam Vlanos (Chief Joseph Mahtasooma), Rodney [A.] Grant (brave on horseback).

Based on David Seals's 1987 novel and financed by British backers, this well-regarded feature was an example of the buddy movie genre being grafted onto a drama of acculturation.

Living on the Northern CHEYENNE Reservation in Lame Deer, Montana, Buddy Red Bow is a volatile political activist who is deeply involved in tribal matters. His sister alerts him that she and her daughters are being held in Santa Fe, New Mexico, on a drug charge with a $2,000 bail fee. Preoccupied with negotiations with a mining company, Red Bow is torn as to whether or not to help his estranged sister. Already having $2,000 from Chief Joseph Mahtasooma to use in a pending cattle buy, Red Bow accepts a ride from pal Philbert Bono in his '64 Buick. As the impatient Red Bow learns belatedly, the mentally slow Bono is making a spiritual trek along the "Powwow Highway" and intends to stop at tribal landmarks to gain inspiration.

Eventually, they reach Santa Fe where they learn that the FBI ensnared his sister to stall, hopefully, Red Bow's negotiations with the mining firm. Later, while Red Bow fights it out with Sandy Youngblood, the key to his sister's problems, Bono uses his own vehicle to break out the prisoners. Thereafter, Bono crashes his beloved car over a mountain top, but he and his passengers are thrown clear.

A Martinez and Gary Farmer in *Powwow Highway* (1989). (ECHO BOOK SHOP)

With the combination of the fast-acting Red Bow and the slow-moving Bono, the film created its own unique buddy team caught in a road movie. Much was also made of the spiritual voices that Bono heard that led him onward, while hot-headed Red Bow was quicker to use his fists than to rely on logic. It was a shame that more was not done to contrast these two disparate individuals as to how each coped with the pressures of modern American life as it tried to force them to "conform" to the white man's culture.

While *Powwow Highway* won a prize (the Filmmakers Trophy) at the Sundance Film Festival, it grossed only $283,747 in its limited American theatrical distribution. Later, it became a semi-cult favorite in the home-video marketplace.

pressure groups Organizations (beyond such broad-based groups as the American Civil Liberties Union and Common Cause) involved in specifically protecting the rights of Native American talent and in helping to integrate the entertainment media further have included the American Indian Anti-Defamation League, the American Indian Arts Council (AIAC), the American Indian Center, the American Indian Movement (AIM), the Association on American Indian Affairs (AAIA), the First Americans in the Arts, the Indian Heritage Council (IHC), the National Film Committee for the Association of American Indian Affairs, the Native American Policy Network (NAPN), the Native American Rights Fund (NARF), and the Native Congress of American Indians (NCAI).

***Prophecy, The* (aka: *God's Army*) (1995)** Dimension, color, 96 minutes. **Director/Screenplay:** Gregory Widen; **Cast:** Christopher Walken (Angel Gabriel), Elias Koteas (Thomas Dagget), Eric Stoltz (Angel Simon), Virginia Madsen (Katherine), Moriah Shining Dove Snyder (Mary), Adam Goldberg (Jerry), Viggo Mortensen (Lucifer), Nik Winterhawk (John), Albert Nelson (Grey Horse).

This horror film was cast as a modern parable of John Milton's *Paradise Lost* with the evil angel Gabriel battling angel Simon over the soul of a now-dead general who was guilty of Korean War atrocities. Simon has turned his corrupt essence into the spirit within Mary, a young Native American. With a wry Lucifer joining the struggle as well as ex-priest-turned-police-officer Thomas Dagget, the scene shifts to Mary's village in Arizona where the tribal elders seek to exorcise the evil spirit that has taken hold of her.

Mixing theology with Native American mysticism and the conventions of a contemporary horror film, the movie revolved around the tongue-in-cheek performance of Walken's cynical fallen angel. This production was part of a continuing trend in which Native American theology was blended into movies of terror. Made in 1993, *The Prophecy* grossed more than $16 million in its domestic release, leading to two sequels: *The Prophecy 2: Ashtown* (1997) and *The Prophecy 3: The Ascent* (2000).

Q

Quinn, Anthony (1915–2001) A two-time Academy Award-winner in the Best Supporting Actor category (*Viva Zapata!* 1952; *Lust for Life*, 1956), Mexican-born Quinn frequently played characters of different ethnic backgrounds, including an Asian hero in *Island of Lost Men* (1939) the barbarian in *Attila the Hun* (1954), the pope in *The Shoes of the Fisherman* (1968), and Zeus, the Greek mythological god, in several mid-1990s TV movies. For a time, one of the versatile star's specialities was taking on Native American screen roles, and on one occasion he played a NATIVE ALASKAN.

Born in Chihuahua, Mexico, he was of Mexican-Irish parentage. He grew up in the United States and was a prizefighter briefly before turning to acting. One of his first screen assignments was for veteran filmmaker Cecil B. DeMille (whose daughter Katherine he was married to for a time) in *THE PLAINSMAN* (1936). Quinn had a flashy cameo as a Northern CHEYENNE warrior in that western epic. In *Texas Rangers Ride Again* (1940), he was a HALF-BREED ranch foreman, and in *THEY DIED WITH THEIR BOOTS ON* (1941), the story of GEORGE ARMSTRONG CUSTER's defeat at Little Bighorn, he played CHIEF CRAZY HORSE.

One of Quinn's less-seen but best movie roles of the 1940s was as Charley Eagle in *BLACK GOLD* (1947). In 1953's *SEMINOLE*, set in Florida, he took the part of Chief Osceola. In succeeding years, during which he won Best Actor Oscar nominations for *Wild Is the Wind* (1957) and *Zorba the Greek* (1964), he was Inuk in *The Savage Innocents* (1959) set in Alaska. The star returned to playing a Native American in *FLAP* (1970), a drama with comedic sidelights.

R

***Ramona* (1916)** Clune/State Rights, b&w, 10–14 reels. **Director:** Donald Crisp; **Screenplay:** Not available; **Cast:** Adda Gleason (Ramona), Mabel Van Buren (Ramona, in the prologue), Anna Lehr (Ramona, as a child), Monroe Salisbury (Alessandro Assis), Nigel de Brulier (Felipe Moreno), Richard Sterling (Angus Phail), Princess Red Wing (his wife), Lurline Lyons (Señora Moreno), Alice Morton Otten (Starlight), James Needham [Donald Crisp] (Jim Farrar).

Helen Hunt Jackson's idyllic romance novel *Ramona: A Story* was first published in 1884. Four U.S. screen versions of this popular love tale, all came at a time when Native Americans were generally being portrayed as bloodthirsty savages on camera. The title figure was a HALF-BREED, a type of screen character that led Hollywood to two generalizations: Either they were extremely virtuous and worthy (i.e., better than a full-blooded Native American), or they were unpredictable, undependable, hot-blooded individuals who were not to be trusted. The lead character in *Ramona* fell into the former category.

The initial screen adaptation of *Ramona* was a two-reel silent entry directed by D. W. Griffith for Biograph in 1910. Shot in California (at Peru, Camulos, and Los Angeles), it featured Mary Pickford in the title role of the nineteenth-century half-breed who weds a full-blooded Native American. Henry B. Walthall, Francis J. Grandon, and Kate Bruce were also in the cast. The picture was reissued in 1914.

The 1916 silent edition was an expansive version, shot at California locations authentic to Jackson's story. Once again Caucasian actors played the leads. Gleason was the half-Native American and half-Scot who weds full-blooded Mission Native American Alessandro. As in the book original, the young couple are treated with contempt by most of the locals, and they find themselves moving from village to village to escape the prejudice. Eventually, one of the settlers murders Alessandro.

With the scenario having star-crossed lovers of somewhat different heritages, it was still a necessary convention to have the couple separated by death. This not only appeased audiences of the era who felt that mixed marriages were evil, but also it gave the idealized love tale a satisfying maudlin ending, guaranteed to appeal to many quixotic moviegoers.

Director Crisp appeared in this screen adaptation under the pseudonym of James Needham. The cast included a few actual Native Americans (e.g., Princess Red Wing and Chief Standing Bear). The feature was released in varying lengths.

***Ramona* (1928)** United Artists, b&w, 7,650′. **Director:** Edwin Carewe; **Screenplay:** Finis Fox; **Cast:** Dolores Del Rio (Ramona), Warner Baxter (Alessandro), Roland Drew (Felipe), Vera Lewis (Señora Moreno), Michael Visaroff (Juan Canito), John T. Prince (Father Salvierderra), Mathilde Comont (Marda), Rita Carewe (baby).

In this third silent-screen adaptation of Helen Hunt Jackson's 1884 novel, the drama became a full-blown tearjerker with Mexican actress Del Rio as the ill-fated Ramona and Ohio-born Baxter as her luckless husband. Again, it was the account of nineteenth-century Ramona, a HALF-BREED whom Señora Moreno has adopted. The mother, a Spanish sheep rancher, treats the girl maliciously; the wealthy woman's son, Felipe, shows compassion to her. When it is time for sheep shearing, the wandering Native Americans appear at the ranch to help with the chore. It is then that Ramona learns her true heritage and also falls in love with full-blooded Native American Alessandro. She and this young chieftain elope, much against the wishes of Señora Moreno. After the birth of their daughter, their joy is spoiled when the little girl dies during a bandit attack. Grieving and still dealing with local prejudice against their marriage, they escape to the mountains. There, Alessandro is falsely accused of horse thievery and is killed. Unnerved by the double tragedies, a distraught Ramona becomes a wanderer, an outcast wherever she goes. Faithful Felipe eventually finds her but is unsuccessful in snapping her out of her amnesia. Eventually, when Ramona hears a song attached to her childhood, her memory revives.

The theme song "Ramona," with music by Mabel Wayne and lyrics by L. Wolfe Gilbert, became extremely popular at the time, with Del Rio recording one version. This edition of Ramona was directed by Carewe (1883–1940), born Jay Fox in Texas and of Chickasaw descent.

***Ramona* (1936)** Twentieth Century-Fox, color, 84 minutes. **Director:** Henry King; **Screenplay:** Lamar Trotti; **Cast:** Loretta Young (Ramona), Don Ameche (Alessandro), Kent Taylor (Felipe Moreno), Pauline Frederick (Señora Moreno), Jane Darwell (Aunt Ri Hyar), Katherine DeMille (Margarita), Victor Kilian (Father Gaspara), John Carradine (Jim Farrar), J. Carrol Naish (Juan Can).

This was the fourth and final (to date) American adaptation of Helen Hunt Jackson's 1884 novel, *Ramona.* The new version had the advantages of sound dialogue and Technicolor over its predecessors. It reconstructed the familiar account of HALF-BREED Ramona who, this time around, was the ward of Señora Moreno at her southern California hacienda in the 1870s. As before, Moreno's son Felipe has known Ramona since childhood and adores her, but his mother disapproves, as does Margarita the servant who is in love with him. Tribal chief Alessandro and Ramona wed and have a child, but in this edition the offspring does not die. The infant is still alive after the tragic end of Alessandro, a reminder—says the loyal Felipe—that a part of Alessandro is still on earth with her.

Whether because the film had talking dialogue that made the idealistic romance seem coy and dated or because everyone in the cast came to the project with sensibilities attuned by the Great Depression, the 1936 *Ramona* came across as an antique piece. Despite the lush panoramas (filmed partially at Warner Hot Springs and the Mesa Grande Indian Reservation in San Diego County, California) of this more than $600,000 production, there was a condescending tone throughout, as seen in the way Señora Moreno treated the itinerant Native Americans come for the shearing or the undercurrent of superiority in which Father Gaspara regarded the simple native workers. In addition, there were biased undertones taken from the original book and infused into the new screenplay. For example, once Ramona discovered that she was part-Native American, then her love for a full-blooded tribesman was portrayed as not only understandable and correct by most people's standards but also as her only alternative (i.e., she could not be part of the white world).

Although Young gave an overly sweet and pure interpretation to her characterization, she was somewhat acceptable as the half-breed. On the other hand, Ameche as Alessandro not only looked foolish in his makeup, wig, and costume but also sounded ill at ease. He was one of the most uncomfortable impersonators of a Native American character on screen, a fact partly due to his fledgling status as a screen performer.

Don Ameche in *Ramona* (1936). (JC ARCHIVES)

***Rango* (1967)** ABC-TV series, color, 30 minutes. **Cast:** Tim Conway (Rango), Guy Marks (Pink Cloud), Norman Alden (Captain Horton).

This silly, unsuccessful series was set in the Old West. Conway, as a bungling Texas Ranger, is assigned to Deep Wells Ranger Station, where hopefully he can not (but does) get into trouble. At the post, his assistant is Pink Cloud, who prefers the white man's lifestyle, especially because it is less dangerous than roaming the wide open ranges.

Marks's Pink Cloud is both a butt of jokes (based on clichés of his Native American image) and the instigator of sly remarks. With his statements, he proves that he is well aware of how the whites see him as a preconceived type and not as an individual. As such, he plays to their biases to win his own way. In the politically *incorrect* style of that era, the TV show allowed the viewer to laugh with the ethnic minority figure while laughing at him.

***Ravenhawk* (1996)** HBO cable, color, 89 minutes. **Director:** Albert Penn; **Teleplay:** Kevin Elders; **Cast:** Rachel McLish (Rhyia Shadowfeather), John Enos III (Marshal Del Wilkes), Ed Lauter (Sheriff Daggert), Matt Clark (Ed Hudson), Michael Champion (Gordon Fowler), William Atherton (Philip Thorne).

Wrongly accused of killing her parents, Native American Rhyia Shadowfeather is locked away in a maximum-security institution. A dozen years later, she escapes to prove her innocence. She discovers that sleazy corporate businessmen—including Philip Thorne—framed her because they wanted the family's land for a nuclear-waste dump. The plant has been built over the objections of the Shoshone elders, and the muscular victim plots her revenge.

Pushing ecology/Native American justice themes (as used in *BILLY JACK*, 1971) up a few notches, this sleazy action entry utilized an ethnic minority heroine to gain viewer sympathy for its formula plotting.

***Red, Red Heart, The* (1918)** Bluebird Photoplays, b&w, 5 reels. **Director:** Wilfred Lucas; **Screenplay:** Bess Meredyth; **Cast:** Monroe Salisbury (Kut-le), Ruth Clifford (Rhoda Tuttle), Val Paul (Jack Newman), Gretchen Lederer (Katherine Newman), Allan Sears (John De Witt), Monte Blue (Billy Porter).

Based on the novel *The Heart of the Desert* (1913) by Honore McCue Willsie Morrow, this silent feature veered from the norm in its presentation. It had the familiar plot of a college-educated Native American (Salisbury), superintendent on a local irrigation project, falling in love with a Caucasian (Clifford). She is the orphaned Rhoda Tuttle, who is still grieving for her dead parents. While she is recuperating with friends in Arizona, Kut-le whisks her away to the desert to live an entirely different type of existence and helps her to overcome her depression. Her pals eventually put up a fight to make her return to "civilization." She refuses, preferring to remain with her new-found love. Allowing the mixed-blood couple to remain together was a rarity at this point in the American cinema.

Red Ryder See LITTLE BEAVER.

***Redskin* (1929)** Paramount, b&w with color sequences, 7,643′. **Director:** Victor Schertzinger; **Screenplay:** Elizabeth Pickett; **Cast:** Richard Dix (Wing Foot), Gladys Belmont (Corn Blossom), Jane Novak (Judy), Larry Steers (John Walton), Tully Marshall (Navajo Jim), George Rigas (Chief Notani).

Having succeeded with his ethnic portrayal in *THE VANISHING AMERICAN* (1925), Dix returned to playing a Native American in *Redskin.* More conventional in story content, this film boasted a music score and sound effects, as well as Technicolor sequences—all considered solid selling points as Hollywood converted from silents to talkies.

This time, the love conflict was not between a white and a Native American but rather between two Native Americans of different tribes. Having been educated back East, Wing Foot returns to his NAVAJO homelands, only to renounce their old-fashioned ways. As a result he becomes a pariah among his people. Adding to his problems, he loves Corn Blossom, a member of a rival tribe. Later, he discovers oil deposits in the desert that prove useful when he stops a brewing war between the two tribes by explaining that they are both wealthy now. Now back in emotional touch with his people, he and Corn Blossom can wed.

With his regal bearing and strong profile, Dix provided a more apt representation of a Native American than most Caucasian Hollywood stars of the period.

***Red Snow* (1952)** Columbia, b&w, 75 minutes. **Directors:** Boris L. Petroff and Harry S. Franklin; **Screenplay:** Tom Hubbard and Orville Hampton; **Cast:** Guy Madison (Lieutenant Johnson), Ray Mala (Sergeant Koovuk), Carole Mathews (Lieutenant Jane), Gloria Saunders (Alak), Robert Peyton (Major Bennett), Philip Ahn (Tuglu), Robert Bice (Chief Nanu).

During the early years of the cold war, there was great concern that the Russians might attack the United States through Alaska, then a U.S. territory and not yet a state. Playing on that fear, this minor production weaved a tale of pilot Lieutenant Johnson of the U.S. Air Force base in Alaska interacting with NATIVE ALASKANS—including Sergeant Koovuk, who is part of the U.S. military, and Tuglu, who is a Soviet spy. Involved in the narrative is the Russians' testing of nuclear bombs in Siberia and the Native-Alaskan soldiers being sent back to their northern tribes to investigate what is going on beyond the Bering Strait.

To blend in footage from the 1931 drama/documentary *Igloo* (1931), which had featured actor MALA (under his Native-Alaskan name of Chee-ak), Mala was cast as the heroic northerner in *Red Snow.* He is the one who risks all to save his village from starvation and to capture the undetonated nuclear bomb from the crashed Russian plane.

The reused material from *Igloo* contained a good deal of Native-Alaskan customs and rituals, which were incorporated into this espionage actioner. The opening credits to this movie acknowledged that Native Alaskans' "skill and courage have long been unheralded."

***Red Woman, The* (1917)** World, b&w, 5 reels. **Director:** Unknown; **Screenplay:** H. R. Durant; **Cast:** Gail Kane (Maria Temosach), Mahlon Hamilton (Morton Deal), Ed F. Roseman (Sancho), June Elvidge (Dora Wendell), Charlotte Granville (Mrs. Wendell), Gladys Earlcott (Chica).

In contrast to the screen dramas—especially in the silent era—that featured an Eastern-educated Native American male falling in love with a white woman, this time the focus was on a female.

Maria Temosach graduates from college and returns home to New Mexico to avoid bigoted snobs such as the ones who populated her school campus. Quickly, she falls in love with Morton Deal, a visiting Easterner. When she becomes pregnant, she is unsure who the father is as Sancho, a cattle thief, had forced his attentions on her. Once the blond-haired and white-skinned baby is born, she knows that Deal is the father. By now, he has rejected his East Coast socialite girlfriend and returns to New Mexico to be with Maria and their infant.

As in *THE RED, RED HEART* (1918), the miscegenation factor was ignored in this drama so that the plot could have the maiden and her idolized man be together at the fade out. But in this pre-feminist item, Maria revered her wealthy Caucasian friend Morton Deal as "her god," and his every wish was her command. Thus, she was almost a slave to him, which put her in a special category and softened the mixed-blood aspect of the story.

Renegade **(1992–1997)** Syndicated TV (then USA cable) series, color, 60 minutes. **Cast:** Lorenzo Lamas (Vince Black [Reno Raines]), Branscombe Richmond (Bobby Sixkiller), Kathleen Kinmont (Cheyenne Phillips: 1992–96), Stephen J. Cannell (Lt./Marshal Donald "Dutch" Dixon), Sandra Ferguson (Sandy Caruthers: 1996–97).

Renegade was an overly macho adventure/action series that relied heavily on the charisma of star Lamas. He was the good law enforcer who was framed for murder by bad cops, and his ongoing mission was to avoid capture by the sadistic perpetrator (Cannell) of the homicide and to prove his innocence. While searching for clues, he works for high-tech bounty hunter Bobby Sixkiller, who is assisted in his lucrative enterprise by his half-sister Cheyenne, the latter a computer genius.

While it was very clear that Lamas was the focus of the weekly proceedings, the plot premise did have him employed by his buddy Sixkiller. This was a rare instance on a nationally shown TV series for the Native American to be the boss of a willing Caucasian. To make sure that no one forgot Sixkiller's heritage, he wore sharp outfits, a mixture of contemporary Native American garb intermingled with hip mainstream accessories, including lots of jewelry.

Renegades **(1989)** Universal, color, 105 minutes. **Director:** Jack Sholder; **Screenplay:** David Rich; **Cast:** Kiefer Sutherland (Buster McHenry), Lou Diamond Phillips (Hank), Jami Gertz (Barbara), Rob Knepper (Marino), Bill Smitrovich (Finch), Floyd Westerman (Red Crow), Joe Griffin (Matt), Gary Farmer (George), Kyra Harper (Nema).

Previously, Native Americans had been pigeonholed on screen as the war-whooping "savage." Now, in the last years of the twentieth century, in turnabout, they were becoming stereotyped by Hollywood as overly noble individuals. This nonstop action entry, which had little plot logic, utilizes PHILLIPS'S standard on-camera persona as Hank, the force of good, who is paired with out-of-control undercover cop Buster McHenry (who is investigating police corruption). As the Lakota SIOUX tribesman who vows to revenge his brother's murder and retrieve an ancient, sacred tribal lance, stoic Hank becomes enmeshed in a diamond robbery gone bad.

In this buddy/cop picture, besides the righteous modern-day brave, was a full range of trite typecasting, including pasta-loving Italians, African-American drug dealers, and Asian-American police-hunting street gangs.

Renegades, with scenes filmed in Philadelphia, grossed slightly more than $9 million in domestic distribution. Sutherland and Phillips had previously costarred in the westerns *YOUNG GUNS* (1988) and *Young Guns II* (1990).

Reynolds, Burt (1936–) With a roller-coaster acting career that began in the 1950s, Reynolds amassed a huge number of performance credits through succeeding decades as actor, producer, and occasionally screen director (e.g., *Gator*, 1976; *Sharky's Machine*, 1981). Part-Cherokee, he sometimes took advantage of his ethnic heritage in choosing characters to portray on screen.

Born in Waycross, Georgia, he grew up in Palm Beach, Florida, where his father, a one-time cowboy, was the local police chief. His mother was Italian, and his father was part Cherokee. When Reynolds had to drop a promising football career because of a knee injury and an auto accident, he turned to acting. Having already costarred in the TV series *Riverboat* (1959–60), he returned to the format on *GUNSMOKE*, where he played half-breed blacksmith Quint Asper from 1962 to 1965. The next year, he starred as another part-Native American in the short-lasting TV cop entry, *HAWK*. On the big screen, he had the title role in *Navajo Joe* (1966) and was Yaqui Joe in the western *100 Rifles* (1969).

By the time of *Deliverance* (1972), Reynolds was a major star. He received a career push from *Smokey and the Bandit* (1977) and its two sequels (1980 and 1983). With his career in the doldrums, he returned to TV series work with the detective entry *B. L. Stryker* (1989–90) but had better luck with the TV sitcom *Evening Shade* (1990–94). His career received another needed boost when he was Oscar nominated for his supporting role as the pornography filmmaker in *Boogie Nights* (1997). Later pictures included *Big City Blues* (1999), *The Last Producer* (2000), *Tempted* (2001), and *Time of the Wolf* (2002).

Ride 'Em Cowboy **(1942)** Universal, b&w, 86 minutes. **Director:** Arthur Lubin; **Screenplay:** True Boardman and Johnny Grant; **Cast:** Bud Abbott (Duke), Lou Costello (Willoughby), Dick Foran ("Bronco" Bob Mitchell), Anne Gwynne (Anne Shaw), Johnny Mack Brown (Alabama Brewster), Ella Fitzgerald (Ruby), Jody Gilbert (Moonbeam), Linda Brent (Sunbeam), Lee Sunrise and Carmela Cansino (Native American women), Chief Yowlachie (Chief Tomahawk).

If the Marx Brothers could *Go West* (1940), so could Abbott and Costello. In this zany comedy filled with musical interludes (including one by Fitzgerald), the action was set at the Lazy S Ranch where the duo have been hired as ranchhands. When not confounding the romance between singing cowboy "Bronco" Bob Mitchell and Anne Shaw, the daughter of the ranch owner, Willoughby is being chased by local Native Americans. By error, he has become engaged to hefty Moonbeam, and her tribe insists that he follow through with the marriage ceremony.

This comic send-up of the Old West, cowboy heroes, and menacing "Indians" proved successful at the box-office and led to such later genre satires as *THE PALEFACE* (1948) and to the further demystification of Native Americans as fearful warriors. One of the comedic scenes in this film that was censored by the Breen Office took place at the "Indian village" where the braves have Willoughby about to be burned at the stake. The planned sequence was cut because of sexual innuendoes involved in the dialogue exchange regarding Moonbeam and her grandfather rather than for any desire to be politically correct.

***Ride Out for Revenge* (1957)** United Artists, 79 minutes. **Director/Screenplay:** Norman Retchin; **Cast:** Rory Calhoun (Sheriff Tate), Gloria Grahame (Amy Porter), Lloyd Bridges (Captain George), Joanne Gilbert (Pretty Willow), Frank de Kova (Yellow Wolf), Vince Edwards (Little Wolf).

This sometimes-clumsy B western attempted to be a thoughtful presentation of Native Americans interacting with the whites in the Old West.

The U.S. government commands the CHEYENNE to leave their ancestral homelands and to relocate to an Oklahoma reservation. Their chief (DE KOVA) offers gold nuggets to Captain George of the Sand Creek Army Post if he will disregard the order. Instead, George has Yellow Wolf killed, hoping that without guidance the tribe will go to the reservation peacefully. (This would leave George free to discover the gold for himself.) But Little Wolf, the new chief, vows to revenge his father's murder. Local sheriff Tate, who loves Little Wolf's sister Pretty Willow, is asked to intercede on George's behalf with the tribe. Before the finale, George and Tate have squared off for a shoot-out, while the Cheyenne are doomed to reservation life.

***Riders of the Whistling Skull, The* (1937)** Republic, b&w, 56 minutes. **Director:** Mack V. Wright; **Screenplay:** Oliver Drake and John Rathmell; **Cast:** Robert Livingston (Stony Brooke), Ray Corrigan (Tucson Smith), Max Terhune (Lullaby Joslin), Mary Russell (Betty Marsh), Roger Williams (Rutledge), Yakima Canutt (Otah), Chief Thundercloud (high priest), John Van Pelt (Professor Marsh), Iron Eyes Cody (Indian).

Part of the popular Three Mesquiteers western film series, this superior entry was based on the 1934 novel by William Colt MacDonald. It created an intriguing air of mystery as Betty Marsh searched for her missing father; he was hunting for the lost city of Luckachakai that was inhabited by an ancient Native American tribe. The Three Mesquiteers volunteer to join Betty, her native guide Otah, and others as they trek through the desert. Before the resolution, one of their number is branded by members of the Sons of Anatazia and, later, in the cave of the skull, the HALF-BREED Rutledge leads an attack of warriors against them.

It was a rarity in Hollywood of the 1930s to have Native Americans as part of a revered ancient culture, even if their ancestors were hated for being hostile and brutal. *The Riders of the Whistling Skull* was remade in 1949 as the Charlie Chan Chinese-detective series entry *The Feathered Serpent.*

***Rio Grande* (1950)** Republic, b&w, 105 minutes. **Director:** John Ford; **Screenplay:** James Kevin McGuinness; **Cast:** John Wayne (Col. Kirby Yorke), Maureen O'Hara (Mrs. Kathleen Yorke), Ben Johnson (Trooper Travis Tyree), Claude Jarman Jr. (Trooper Jefferson "Red" Yorke), Harry Carey Jr. (Trooper Boone), Chill Wills (Dr. Wilkins), J. Carrol Naish (General Sheridan), Victor McLaglen (Sgt. Maj. Tim Quincannon), Chuck Roberson (Native American).

This was the third and final entry in FORD's cavalry trilogy (*FORT APACHE*, 1948; *SHE WORE A YELLOW RIBBON*, 1949) and was based on James Warner Bellah's short story "Mission with No Record" (1947). Many of the Ford stock company who had been in *Fort Apache* were in this entry as well, with Wayne's character called Kirby Yorke this time, whereas it was Kirby York in *Fort Apache. Rio Grande* contained several songs sung by the Sons of the Pioneers.

In post-Civil War days at a cavalry stockade not far from the Rio Grande and Mexico, the troopers have been fighting renegade APACHE on both sides of the river/border. Back at the fort, Col. Kirby Yorke finds that his son Red has left West Point because of academic problems and is now a new recruit under Yorke's command. Later, Yorke's estranged wife Kathleen arrives at the fort ostensibly to buy her son's way out of the cavalry but also to perhaps patch up her marriage. The marauding Apache attack the fort, capture a wagon train filled with women and children, and kidnap the youngsters as hostages; the cavalry lays siege to the Apache village. Wounded, Yorke is helped by his son Red, who later is awarded a medal for his bravery in action.

Shot in Utah at Mexican Hat, Moab, and Monument Valley, the film was seen by some critics as a parable to the ongoing Korean War. (It was perceived that there was a correlation between the Apache darting across the Mexican border that U.S. troops were not supposed to cross and the then current situation where the thirty-eighth parallel had been established as the border between North and South Korea.) As he did frequently, Ford utilized NAVAJO tribesmen to play the warring Apache. Unlike the same year's *BROKEN ARROW*, no attempt was made to humanize the Apache or to present any of the skirmishes/battles from their point of view. The tribesmen were "merely" the enemy. Produced at a cost of $1.2 million, the movie earned a net profit of almost $216,000.

***Rose of the Yukon* (1949)** Republic, b&w, 59 minutes. **Director:** George Blair; **Screenplay:** Norman S. Hall; **Cast:** Steve Brodie (Maj. Geoffrey Barnett), Myrna Dell (Rose Flambeau), William Wright (Capt. Tom Clark), Emory Parnell (Tim MacNab), Jonathan Hale (Brig. Gen. Craig Butler), Francis McDonald (Alaskan), Lotus Long (Native-Alaskan woman), Charles Soldani (Native Alaskan).

This minor film boasted atmospheric Alaskan settings and several NATIVE-ALASKAN characters. Its plot revolved around Alaska's annual Nenana Ice Classic in which contestants guessed when the ice on the Tanana River would break. The programmer also includes a plot point about a U.S. Army deserter from World War II and a Japanese-drawn map leading to huge deposits of pitchblende (which are loaded with gold and uranium).

***Running Brave* (1983)** Buena Vista, color, 105 minutes. **Director:** D. S. Everett [aka: Donald Shebib]; **Screenplay:** Henry Bean and Shirl Hendryx; **Cast:** Robby Benson (Billy Mills), Pat Hingle (Coach Easton), Claudia Cron (Pat Mills), Jeff McCraken (Dennis), August Schellenberg (Billy's father), Denis Lacroix (Frank), Graham Greene (Eddie), Margo Kane (Catherine), Barbara Blackhorse (young Catherine).

Based on a true-life account, this was the narrative of Billy Mills, a SIOUX Native American from South Dakota who earned a Gold Medal for winning the 10,000-meter race at the 1964 Tokyo Olympics. Despite the sports genre clichés and the use of Caucasian actor Benson (born Robin David Segal) in the lead role (which garnered loud protests from Native American PRESSURE GROUPS), the movie had an earnestness that was *almost* endearing. On the other hand, mainstream Hollywood was not yet willing to make a honest study of how a Native American adapted to life off the reservation (e.g., in college, in the marines, in the Olympics) with all the culture shock and bigotry that included.

Running Brave was one of the first film credits for Native Canadian GREENE of the Oneida tribe. Made at a cost of $12 million, *Running Brave* went through many production problems, causing director Shebib to have his name removed from the screen credits.

Runningfox, Joseph (1955–) Best known for his role as the renegade APACHE leader in the TV movie *GERONIMO* (1993), he began acting professionally in the late 1970s. Like many other Native American talents, his show-business options were limited by the narrow confines of typecasting and racial bias.

He was born on the Pueblo Reservation in Santa Fe, New Mexico, in 1955. His father was a former football coach turned auto mechanic. The family moved to Utah where Runningfox graduated from high school in 1974. He was a student at Brigham Young University when he was discovered for the TV movie *Ishi: The Last of His Tribe* (1978). He played the mystical leader as a teenager. After that, he abandoned college (and baseball) for acting, appearing on episodes of such TV series as *Quincy, M. E.*, *Charlie's Angels*, *The Love Boat*, and *Sword of Justice*.

Robby Benson in *Running Brave* (1983). (JC ARCHIVES)

Runningfox played a car thief named Thomas Jefferson Wolf Call in the comedy *Seems Like Old Times* (1980) and was among the cast of *Porky's III: The Next Day* (1983). He was an Iroquois in the American colonial history epic *Revolution* (1985) and enacted Wanchese in the three-part PBS-TV production of *Roanoak* (1986). He rose to greater prominence in the 1990s when he starred in *GERONIMO* (1993), a well-received made-for-cable drama of the famed Apache—this time told from the Native American perspective. This led to *LAKOTA WOMAN: SIEGE AT WOUNDED KNEE* (1994) and more recently to *Ravenous* (1999), a drama dealing with cannibalism.

***Run of the Arrow* (1957)** Universal, color, 1957. **Director/Screenplay:** Samuel Fuller; **Cast:** Rod Steiger (O'Meara), Sarita Montiel (Yellow Moccasin), Brian Keith (Captain Clark), Ralph Meeker (Lieutenant Driscoll), Jay C. Flippen (Walking Coyote), Charles Bronson (Blue Buffalo), H. M. Wynant (Crazy Wolf), Frank de Kova (Red Cloud), Col. Tim McCoy (General Allen).

Filmmaker Fuller, who displayed a fascination with Japanese culture in *House of Bamboo* (1955) and *The Crimson Kimono* (1959), revealed his intrigue with Native American lore in this probing and often gory entry.

During the Civil War, O'Meara, an Irish American in the Virginia infantry, fires the last bullet of the war. Frustrated by the South's loss, he heads westward to join the SIOUX nation, a culture that has long fascinated him. He is made to run the torturous (and potentially fatal) arrow ordeal to be accepted by them. Thanks to the help of Yellow Moccasin, he survives the challenge and they wed, adding an orphaned mute boy to their household. Their peaceful life is disrupted when the U.S. cavalry violates treaties with the Sioux, leading to bloody attacks by both sides, with O'Meara firmly on the side of his Native American brethren. One of the interfering soldiers is Lieutenant Driscoll, the man O'Meara wounded on the last day of the Civil War. At the end, encouraged by Yellow Moccasin, O'Meara renews his attachment to the white man's way of life, and he and his wife head to the army fort.

Putting aside such items as Steiger's thick brogue, the dubbing of Montiel's dialogue (by actress Angie Dickinson), and the use of mostly Caucasian actors to portray the Sioux, *Run of the Arrow* was one of the more revealing screen studies of a white man situated among an alien culture. In some ways, it foreshadowed *A MAN CALLED HORSE* (1970).

S

Sampson, Will (1935–1987) As a result of his acting debut in the widely acclaimed and popular *ONE FLEW OVER THE CUCKOO'S NEST* (1975), Sampson quickly rose to prominence as a key Native American performer. He substantiated his talent with roles in such follow-up films as *THE OUTLAW JOSEY WALES* (1976) and *Buffalo Bill and the Indians, or Sitting Bull's History Lesson* (1976).

He was born William Sampson Jr. in Okmulgee, Oklahoma, on the Creek Nation Reservation. After a stint in the U.S. Navy, Sonny (as he was known to everyone) worked in an assortment of jobs, including forest ranger, rodeo cowboy, and oil-field worker. He also became a recognized painter with many exhibits through the years.

Sampson turned to acting at the age of forty in 1974. Through a friend, he learned that actor Michael Douglas (serving as producer) was casting the role of a "big Indian" in his new picture. At six feet, seven inches, Sampson qualified and was soon cast in *One Flew Over the Cuckoo's Nest*. As Chief Bromden, he was the alienated soul and a patient at an austere mental institution, where he developed a rapport with Jack Nicholson's character as they coped with the sadistic head nurse. This success led to TV work (e.g., episodes of *The Yellow Rose*, *Vega$*, and *Born to the Wind*), and the actor appeared on stage in *Black Elk Speaks* for the American Indian Theater Company of Oklahoma.

While Sampson continued to paint and have exhibitions, he was on screen in *From Here to Eternity* (1979—TV miniseries and the 1979–80 follow-up series), in *Fish Hawk* (1979) as Corporal Cheney, on the TV miniseries *THE MYSTIC WARRIOR* (1984) as Wambli, and as Taylor in *POLTERGEIST II: THE OTHER SIDE* (1986). With his art-world and show-business prominence and income, he gave of his time, knowledge, and money to Native American causes (In the mid-1980s he hosted a five-part series *Images on Indians* on PBS-TV. It traced the stereotyping of Native Americans by western dime-novels and Hollywood sagebrush tales.) His last movie was Chuck Norris's *Firewalker* (1986) in which Sampson played Tall Eagle.

Having long suffered from scleroderma, Sampson underwent heart and lung transplants. Complications led to kidney failure, and he died in Houston, Texas, in June 1987. His actor son Tim appeared in such film and TV projects as *WAR PARTY* (1989), *The Cherokee Kid* (1996), and *Backwoods* (2000). Tim also played his father's role of the broom-pushing Native American in a 2000 Broadway revival of *One Flew over the Cuckoo's Nest*.

Saskatchewan **(aka: *O'Rourke of the Royal Mounted*) (1954)** Universal-International, color, 87 minutes. **Director:** Raoul Walsh; **Screenplay:** Gil Doud; **Cast:** Alan Ladd (Sgt. Thomas O'Rourke), Shelley Winters (Grace Markey), J. Carrol Naish (Batoche), Hugh O'Brian (Marshal Smith), Robert Douglas (Inspector Benton), Jay Silverheels (Cajou), Antonio Moreno (Chief Dark Cloud), Anthony Caruso (Spotted Eagle).

Although this feature was shot in Canada (at Banff National Park in Alberta) and concerned the Cree tribe of that country, it was totally Hollywood in its sensibilities. It transferred the cavalry-versus-"Indians" plot to northern America where the soldiers in Canadian red (rather than the blue coats of the U.S. Army) were fighting the agitated braves. To its credit, *Saskatchewan* did point out that all tribes were not the same rampaging fighters, that some were peaceful and willing to coexist with the white invaders.

In the late 1870s, Ladd is a member of the North West Mounted Police and also is blood brother with Cajou of the Cree. The police come across a wagon-train massacre, the only survivor being Grace Markey. Before long, O'Rourke discovers that the tribe responsible for the slaying was the SIOUX, who cross the U.S. border northward, hoping to incite the peace-loving Cree into joining them in a war against the white man. Marshal Smith is the law enforcer from Montana who claims that Markey is wanted for murder; Inspector Benton is the martinet in charge of the Mountie outpost who is very reluctant to provide the Cree with firearms.

Of the lead warriors, SILVERHEELS was one of the few Native American/Native-Canadian actors used to play a brave, here cast once more as the white man's faithful friend.

***Savage, The* (1952)** Paramount, color, 95 minutes. **Director:** George Marshall; **Screenplay:** Sydney Boehm; **Cast:** Charlton Heston (Warbonnet [Jim Aherne Jr.]), Susan Morrow (Tally Hathersall), Peter Hanson (Lt. Weston Hathersall), Joan Taylor (Luta), Richard Rober (Capt. Arnold Vaugant), Donald Porter (Running Dog), Ted De Corsia (Iron Breast), Ian MacDonald (Chief Yellow Eagle), Iron Eyes Cody (warrior).

As the white/Native American warrior, Heston played an outsider (in a role similar to James Stewart in 1950's *BROKEN ARROW*) who perceived that there were good people among the Native Americans. He believed that there had to be a way for the two opposing groups to exist in peace. But within this moralizing framework (always from a conventional Caucasian point of view), the feature included all the set pieces expected from the genre: war councils assembled, battle strategies chewed over, skirmishes, attacks, and the aftermath to the bloody encounters.

After the Civil War, a Virginian schoolteacher heads westward for a new life. En route, in the Black Hills of Dakota, he and most of the others in the group are massacred by Crows. The only survivor is the teacher's eleven-year-old son Jim Jr. who is rescued by Yellow Eagle of the Miniconjou SIOUX. The latter names the brave boy Warbonnet and brings him up in his village as his own. Years later, when rumors of war with the U.S. cavalry rumble through the land, Warbonnet is dispatched to Fort Duane to learn the government's actual intent. Between being attracted to Tally (the sister of Lieutenant Hathersall at the fort), competing with jealous Running Dog at the Sioux camp, dealing with prowling Crow, and handling arrogant soldiers, Warbonnet is always on the run. The finale, part of the new Hollywood's more politically correct thinking, has Warbonnet/Jim and the perceptive Corporal Martin agreeing that there must be room for both sides in the new West.

***Savage Sam* (1963)** Buena Vista, color, 103 minutes. **Director:** Norman Tokar; **Screenplay:** Fred Gipson and William Tunberg; **Cast:** Brian Keith (Uncle Beck Coates), Tommy Kirk (Travis Coates), Kevin Corcoran (Arliss Coates), Dewey Martin (Lester White), Jeff York (Bud Searcy), Royal Dano (Pack Underwood), Marta Kristen (Lisbeth Searcy), Rafael Campos (young warrior), Rodolfo Acosta (Bandy Legs), Pat Hogan (Broken Nose).

Geared as a sequel of sorts to Walt Disney's very successful family film *Old Yeller* (1957), this "wholesome" feature treated the subject of unrelenting revenge against "redskins" who have captured white people. Although certainly far less gruesome and vituperative than John Wayne's *THE SEARCHERS* (1956), *Savage Sam* had to struggle to keep a virtuous quality to this chase drama. Again it was the APACHE who were used as catch-all villains for this piece, based on the 1962 novel by Gipson.

In 1870s Texas, eighteen-year-old Travis Coates loses track of his younger brother, Arliss. While he, his dog Savage Sam, and neighbor's girl Lisbeth Searcy hunt for the boy, renegade Apache capture them. Travis later escapes and is joined by his Uncle Beck and others in the hunt to retrieve the captured teenagers. Thanks to persistence, ingenuity, and the help of Savage Sam, they succeed in their mission.

***Savage Seven, The* (1968)** American International, color, 94 minutes. **Director:** Richard Rush; **Screenplay:** Michael Fisher; **Cast:** Robert Walker Jr. (Johnnie Little Hawk), Larry Bishop (Joint), Joanna Frank (Marie Little Hawk), John Garwood (Stud), Adam Roarke (Kisum), Max Julien (Grey Wolf), Mel Berger (Fillmore), John Cardos (Running Back), Penny Marshall (Tina).

Despite the contemporary ambiance of motorcycle gangs, punks, and their chicks, this was still a tale of whites against Native Americans.

In a rundown California desert town, the local Native Americans are bullied by Kisum and his motorcycle gang and cheated by local businessmen. Because Kisum takes an interest in reserved Marie Little Hawk, he befriends her brother Johnnie. But the truce between the Native Americans and the bikers is short lasting, exacerbated by the dirty dealings of storekeeper Fillmore involving the rape of a Native American woman from the local reservation and the murder of one of Kisum's followers. The showdown is as bloody as any cavalry confrontation with warrior braves.

The violent *The Savage Seven* became a minor cult entry, despite the lack of credibility of its trio of lead actors—including Frank, the sister of TV producer Steven Bochco—as Native Americans.

***Scalphunters, The* (1968)** United Artists, color, 103 minutes. **Director:** Sydney Pollack; **Screenplay:** William Norton; **Cast:** Burt Lancaster (Joe Bass), Shelley Winters (Kate), Telly Savalas (Jim Howie), Ossie Davis (Joseph Winfield Lee), Armando Silvestre (Two Crows), Dan Vadis (Yuma).

In this rollicking free-for-all that was filmed in Mexico, Caucasians, African Americans, Mexicans, and Native Americans grapple with one another, with no one having the final word. In some ways *The Scalphunters*—with its late 1960s political sensibilities—was setting the tone for the black exploitation movie cycle of the 1970s where African-American characters were no longer the subservient figures in Hollywood films and for the building empathy for Native American causes that was spearheaded on camera by *BILLY JACK* (1971).

A band of Kiowa warriors force grizzled trapper Joe Bass to swap his cache of furs and his mule for runaway slave Joseph Winfield Lee. Bass pursues them, witnessing their ambush by scalphunters, with only Two Crows escaping. Later, Lee is captured by these scalphunters, led by Jim Howie whose over-the-hill mistress is the raucous Kate. As the gang heads for Mexico, enterprising Bass picks them off one by one. At a crucial juncture, Lee saves Bass's life, but it does not stop them from arguing with each other (including a huge fight in a mudhole that symbolically leaves both men dark-skinned). Their quarreling is interrupted when Kiowa braves decimate the remaining scalphunters, taking the victims' women and pelts with them. Bass and Lee plot to retrieve their furs.

***Scarlet West, The* (1925)** First National, b&w, 8,390′. **Director:** John G. Adolfi; **Screenplay:** Anthony Paul Kelly; **Cast:** Robert Frazer (Cardelanche), Clara Bow (Miriam), Robert Edeson (General Kinnard), Johnny Walker (Lieutenant Parkman), Helen Ferguson (Nestina), Ruth Stonehouse (Mrs. Custer).

In the 1870s, Cardelanche, the son of a tribal chief, returns from being educated in the East. Many on the reservation think that he has abandoned their culture. Meanwhile, Cardelanche intervenes when renegade warriors attack a detachment of the U.S. cavalry. As a result of his heroic deeds, he is designated a captain in the army. Soon, he falls in love with Miriam, the daughter of the commandant at Fort Remington. (Brooklyn-born Bow was still several months away from becoming a major movie star as the result of *It*, released in 1927.) It leads to a rivalry with Lieutenant Parkman, who also adores Miriam. After Cardelanche's tribe participates in the massacre of GEORGE ARMSTRONG CUSTER and his soldiers at Little Big-horn, he realizes that he must be with his people. Abandoning Miriam, he returns to the hills.

Based on a short story (publication undetermined) by A. B. Heath, this assembly-line silent entry utilized the famous 1876 Battle of Little Big-horn as a linchpin for its plot. More importantly, it presented a Native American who, despite the temptations of the white culture, chooses—out of pride—to be with his own people. (At the same time this served as a plot contrivance to avoid having Cardelanche and Miriam go off into the sunset as a then taboo interracial couple at the film's fadeout.)

science fiction—feature films and television On *Star Trek: Voyager* (1995–2001), the fourth of the *Star Trek* TV series, ROBERT BELTRAN appeared as First Officer Chakotay, under the command of Capt. Kathryn Janeway. Originally this Native American had been captain of a Maquis assault ship being pursued by the USS *Voyager* when both were caught in a temporal anomaly and thrust into another part of the galaxy. When the Maquis craft was destroyed, its crew came aboard the Starfleet ship and were absorbed into the existing *Voyager* staff. One of the episodes on *Star Trek: Voyager* was devoted to exploring Chakotay's cultural roots. In the 1999 video game *Star Trek: Voyager—Elite Force*, Chakotay is among the cast of characters.

In the 1998 cable TV movie *A TOWN HAS TURNED TO DUST*, in a futuristic desert town, a Native American youth was lynched leading to a bloody revolt. This sci-fi channel entry was based on a 1958 Rod Serling script for the TV anthology drama show *Playhouse 90*. John Carpenter's *Ghosts of Mars* (2001), a theatrical release about human colonists on the red planet who must be rescued after becoming possessed by Martian ghosts, included a Native American character among the multi-ethnic mix of colonists.

***Searchers, The* (1956)** Warner Bros., color, 144 minutes. **Director:** John Ford; **Screenplay:** Frank S. Nugent; **Cast:** John Wayne (Ethan Edwards), Jeffrey Hunter (Martin Pawley), Vera Miles (Laurie Jorgensen), Ward Bond (Capt. Rev. Samuel Johnson Clayton), Natalie Wood (Debbie Edwards), John Qualen (Lars Jorgensen), Olive Carey (Mrs. Jorgensen), Henry Brandon (Chief Scar), Dorothy Jordan (Martha Edwards), Pippa Scott (Lucy Edwards), Hank Worden (Mose Harper).

One of the best-regarded American westerns ever made, *The Searchers* was a complex tale of hatred, with the venom directed fully at Native Americans. As the embittered frontiersman with burning revulsion for "Indians," the character Ethan Edwards is seen doggedly devoting many months to searching for his kidnapped niece who has been living among the COMANCHE. In his opinion, the only fit thing to do is to kill this white squaw.

In 1868, Edwards comes to Texas to visit relatives after fighting for the South in the Civil War. Soon, a war party of Comanche kill his brother and family, except for their two girls (Debbie and Lucy) whom they take as prisoners. Joining up with Martin Pawley, the half-breed Comanche whom the Edwardses had adopted, Ethan pursues clues to locate Chief Scar who took the sisters. Later, Edwards acknowledges that he had come across Lucy's mutilated body and that it has fueled his deep anger against "redskins." A year later, the trail leads first to a Texas merchant and thereafter to slow-witted Mose Harper, who refers them to a Mexican who takes Edwards and Pawley to Scar's camp. There, they find Debbie living as a squaw. She says that she is now a Comanche and they should leave. The two men escape, but some time later, Martin rescues her from Scar's tent, killing Scar in the process. Meanwhile, the cavalry is fighting it out with the Comanche, and Ethan ensures Debbie's safety as they all return home.

With ferocity, hatred, and brutality on both sides, it was hard to determine who was the real savage in this stark picture. For example, there was the moment when Ethan Edwards uncovered a recently buried Comanche and shoots out the corpse's eyes so it cannot—according to tribal beliefs—enter the next world. Then there was the brutality of the Comanche braves as they torture and kill their enemies, keeping the scalps as trophies of their murderous accomplishments.

Throughout the disturbing *The Searchers*, Wayne's character was consumed by his abhorrence for "Indians." It was this same detestation that caused Edwards to reject the half-breed Pawley, whom he had actually rescued as a child when his parents were murdered by warring braves. Throughout the lengthy movie, Edwards's beliefs (including his sexual tensions over lost/ungained loves) battled his sense of kinship as he debated whether or not to kill his Comanche-captive niece when he finally retrieved her. It created part of his character's ongoing tension throughout the film, which was resolved only near the finale when he scooped her up into his arms and said "Let's go home, Debbie."

Based on Alan LeMay's novel (1954), with many changes made by FORD and scripter Nugent, *The Searchers* grossed almost $6 million during its worldwide distribution.

Seminole, the The Seminole (pronounced SEM-in-ole) gained their name, which meant "runaway," because they had splintered off from the Creek and other tribes living in what became Georgia and Alabama and moved southward to Florida. In the decades before the Civil War, the Seminole were noted for harboring runaway slaves and welcoming them into their communities. One of the American generals who mounted a war against the Seminole that led to the First Seminole War (1817–18) was General Andrew Jackson. After Jackson took office as U.S. president in 1829, he ordered the Seminole to be relocated to the Indian territory (i.e., west of the Mississippi River). Many of the 3,000 Seminole who went died en route; others refused to leave and hid in the swamps. This led to the Second Seminole War (1835–42). One of the important leaders of the Seminole in this period was Osceola. The so-called Third Seminole War lasted from 1855 to 1858.

With such a history and the contrast of the Florida swamps and so on to the usual plains or mountain locales of most cavalry-versus-"savage-warriors" movies, Hollywood utilized the Seminole in several movies; among them were *Diane of the Green Van* (1918), *Drums of Destiny* (1937), *Key Largo* (1948), *DISTANT DRUMS* (1951), *SEMINOLE* (1953), *War Arrow* (1954), *Seminole Uprising* (1955), *Naked in the Sun* (1957), *Yellowneck* (1957), *JOHNNY TIGER* (1966), and *JOE PANTHER* (1976).

***Seminole* (1953)** Universal-International, color, 89 minutes. **Director:** Budd Boetticher; **Screenplay:** Charles K. Peck Jr.; **Cast:** Rock Hudson (Second Lt. Lance Caldwell), Barbara Hale (Revere Muldoon), Anthony Quinn (Osceola [John Powell]), Richard Carlson (Maj. Harlan Degan), Hugh O'Brian (Kajeck), Russell Johnson (Lieutenant Hamilton), Lee Marvin (Sergeant Magruder).

In the mid-1830s, the U.S. government pushed to move the SEMINOLE out of Florida, wanting the land for agricultural development. Lance Caldwell, freshly graduated from West Point, is dispatched to Fort King, Florida, where Maj. Harlan Degan orders him to expedite the government's policy. Because Caldwell grew up with Osceola, a half-breed Seminole chief, it is hoped that he can arrange a treaty to accomplish the move. But Osceola's rebellious son Kajeck undermines the efforts, eventually killing his father and putting the blame of a murdered sentry on Caldwell. The drama is told through flashback at Caldwell's court-martial, with Revere Muldoon, Caldwell's childhood sweetheart and who later falls in love with Osceola, saving the day.

Along with the APACHE, the COMANCHE, and the SIOUX, Hollywood was particularly intrigued with the Seminole tribe of Florida and frequently used them as characters for its screen fiction, allowing for the introduction of such offbeat non-western film scenery as the Everglades.

serials—motion pictures With its trademark action and excitement, the movie serial was particularly advantageous for chapterplays dealing with the Old West and the conflict between settlers/cowboys and Native Americans. Among the many dealing with tribes (frequently shown as on the warpath) were such silent entries as *Winners of the West* (1921), *White Eagle* (1921), *In the Days of Buffalo Bill* (1922), *The Oregon Trail* (1923), and *Hawk of the Hills* (1927). The sound era got off to a rousing start with the highly successful *The Indians Are Coming* (1930), followed by such genre pieces as *Battling with Buffalo Bill* (1931), *The Lightning Warrior* (1931), *Heroes of the West* (1932), *The Last Frontier* (1932), *Fighting with Kit Carson* (1933), *The Miracle Rider* (1935), *Custer's Last Stand* (1936), *Wild West Days* (1937), *Flaming Frontiers* (1938), *The Great Adventures of Wild Bill Hickok* (1938), *Hawk of the Wilderness* (1938), *The Lone Ranger* (1938), *The Lone Ranger Rides Again* (1939), *The Oregon Trail* (1939), *Overland with Kit Carson* (1939), *Adventures of Red Ryder* (1940), *Winners of the West* (1940), *White Eagle* (1941), *King of the Mounties* (1942), *Overland Mail* (1942), *Daredevils of the West* (1943), *Black Arrow* (1944), *The Scarlet Horseman* (1946), *Ghost of Zorro* (1949), *Roar of the Iron Horse* (1951), *Son of Geronimo* (1952), and *Man with the Steel Whip* (1954). In Republic's western cliffhanger, *The Phantom Rider* (1946), star Robert Kent had a dual role, one of which was as an Indian-masked avenger.

***Shadowhunter* (1993)** Republic, color, 98 minutes. **Director/Screenplay:** J. S. Cardone; **Cast:** Scott Glenn (Lt. John Kane), Angela Alvarado (Ray), Benjamin Bratt (Two Bear), Robert Beltran (sheriff), Beth Broderick (Bobby Cain), George Aguilar (Daniel Nez).

As part of the growing subgenre of thriller movies (e.g., *THE DARK WIND*, 1991) set in the American Southwest, this feature utilized NAVAJO characters and folklore to dress up its (conventional) drama.

Veteran Los Angeles homicide cop Lt. John Kane is burned out from his job and his life. He is assigned to a "simple" case of retrieving a murderer, Two Bear, captured by local police officers at the Navajo reservation in Arizona.

What Kane refuses to understand is that this mystic "coyote man" has the power to get under a person's skin and subordinate the individual to his will. Playing on Kane's frailties, the vicious Two Bear, who thinks only of murdering anyone in his way, outmaneuvers the law enforcer and escapes. This leads to a chase across the Sonora desert as Kane attempts to recapture his prey and regain his soul. Aiding him is his Native American guide Ray (whose parent was killed by Two Bear).

Filled with tribal customs/mystic beliefs and gorgeous Arizona scenery, *Shadowhunter*, a direct-to-video release, did not live up to its potential. Despite Bratt's crafty performance, the narrative was overloaded with expository dialogue and an unsubtle supporting cast.

***She Wore a Yellow Ribbon* (1949)** RKO, color, 104 minutes. **Director:** John Ford; **Screenplay:** Frank Nugent and Laurence Stallings; **Cast:** John Wayne (Capt. Nathan Brittles), Joanne Dru (Olivia Dandridge), John Agar (Lt. Clint Cohill), Ben Johnson (Sergeant Tyree), Harry Carey Jr. (Lt. Ross Pennell), Victor McLaglen (Sergeant Quincannon), Mildred Natwick (Mrs. Abby Allshard), George O'Brien (Maj. Mack Allshard), Harry Woods (Karl Rynders), Chief John Big Tree (Chief Pony-That-Walks), Chief Sky Eagle (Native American).

Coming after *FORT APACHE* (1948) and before *RIO GRANDE* (1950), this was the second of FORD'S cavalry westerns and was far gentler in its approach to Native Americans. It featured Wayne as the mature Capt. Nathan Brittles awaiting retirement from the military and still not adjusted to the death of his wife.

The time is 1876 at a fort in the Southwest as the restless CHEYENNE and the Arapaho lead war parties against the settlers and soldiers. Within the narrative, INDIAN AGENT Karl Rynders is selling guns to the warriors, who are eager to attack the white men. Meanwhile, Chief Pony-That-Walks tells Brittles when the latter boldly rides into his village that they each are too old to lead their men anymore and that the new generation is in charge. Later, Brittles scatters the warriors' horses to avoid a threatened raid on the whites, which forces the braves to retreat on foot back to their reservation. As for Brittles, his retirement is short-lived for the War Department reassigns him, now as chief of scouts.

Based on James Warner Bellah's short stories "The Big Hunt" (1947) and "War Party" (1948), the film was shot in and around Monument Valley, Utah, and cost almost $2 million; its worldwide gross was more than $4 million. The movie earned an Academy Award for Best Cinematography (Color).

***Silent Enemy, The* (1930)** Paramount, b&w, 84 minutes. **Director:** H. P. Carver; **Screenplay:** Richard Carver; **Cast:** Chief Yellow Robe (Chief Chetoga), Chief Long Lance (Baluk), Chief Akawanush (Dagwan, the medicine man), Spotted Elk (Neewa), Cheeka (Cheeka).

As an offshoot of an expedition mounted by New York City's Museum of Natural History, this quasi-documentary was shot mostly in the Temagami Forest Reserve in northern Ontario, Canada.

The prologue has Chief Yellow Robe stating, "This is the story of my people. Now the White Man has come; his civilization has destroyed my people. . . . But now this same civilization has preserved our traditions before it was too late; now you will know us as we really are."

Chetoga, chief of the Ojibwa, worries how his tribe will survive the winter. At Baluk's suggestion, the hunters search for food to the south. When that fails, they follow Dagwan's original plan, which is to move northward hopefully to intercept migrating caribou. Later, Chetoga passes away, and Baluk is made the tribe's chief. When Dagwan, his rival for Neewa's love, performs a medicine dance, it begins to snow. This is considered a sign of his special powers, and he orders that Baluk be sacrificed. Just before Baluk is to die on a funeral pyre, several caribou are sighted. Dagwan is exiled without provisions or weapons. Baluk and Neewa plan to wed.

***Silent Tongue* (1994)** Trimark, color, 101 minutes. **Director/Screenplay:** Sam Shepard; **Cast:** Richard Harris (Prescott Roe), Sheila Tousey (Awbonnie/ghost), Alan Bates (Eamon McCree), River Phoenix (Talbot Roe), Dermot Mulroney (Reeves McCree), Jeri Arredondo (Velada McCree), Tantoo Cardinal (Silent Tongue).

The final film of actor Phoenix, this bizarre movie was released after the young star's death from a drug overdose, having sat on the shelf for several months. It was a confused drama set in the Texas Panhandle of the early 1870s in which spirits of deceased Native American characters came "alive" to set things right by leading others on Earth to doing the right thing.

It focuses on Prescott Roe, a harried frontiersman, who has bought one of the HALF-BREED daughters of medicine-show owner Eamon McCree for his son, Talbot. Time passes, and the half-Kiowa woman dies during childbirth. This event leaves Talbot so distraught that he refuses to bury her according to her tribe's custom, thus entrapping her spirit. Now Prescott negotiates to bring McCree's other half-breed daughter, Velada, as a replacement for the near-crazed Talbot. Overlooking the personal dramas on Earth is the spirit of McCree's Kiowa wife, Silent Tongue.

Filled with mysticism that supposedly governed both the Native Americans and whites in this abstract drama, which was lensed in muted tones, the movie had extremely limited theatrical release where it grossed only slightly more than $61,000.

Silverheels, Jay (aka: Harry J. Smith, Silverheels Smith) (1912–1980) Perhaps one of the most famous Native American actors, he gained his acclaim as TONTO, the ever-loyal companion of the masked man known as the Lone Ranger. Throughout his long career, Silverheels played a wide variety of warrior braves and occasionally a contemporary Native American. But because of his long stint as Tonto, he created a then-new (and not always appreciated by some PRESSURE GROUPS) image of the benign "Indian" who was deferential to the white man.

A full-blooded Mohawk, he was born Harold J. Smith on the Six Nations Reserve in Brantford, Ontario, Canada. By 1933, he had moved to the United States and visited Hollywood as part of a touring pro lacrosse team. When he later returned to the movie capital, he was a professional boxer—in 1938, he qualified as a Golden Gloves contender. That same year, he entered movies as a stunt man. One of his first acting bits was as an extra in Lucille Ball's *Too Many Girls* (1940). By 1947, he was playing an Indian prince in *Captain from Castile* (1947), and the next year he was part of the gangster drama, *Key Largo*.

In 1949, he was hired to be Tonto opposite Clayton Moore (and for a time John Hart) as the masked man in *THE LONE RANGER* TV series, which lasted till 1957. The hugely successful show spawned two theatrical features (1956 and 1958) and a host of stereotypical images of the subservient Native American who spoke in (movie-style) broken English. On the other hand, Silverheels was always credited for playing the role with dignity and professionalism.

Silverheels had first played the renegade APACHE GERONIMO in the 1950 feature *BROKEN ARROW*, a role he repeated in *THE BATTLE AT APACHE PASS* (1952) and *WALK THE PROUD LAND* (1956). (He continued that characterization in episodes of the "Texas John Slaughter" segments on TV's *Disneyland* series in 1959 and 1960.) By the 1960s, as westerns faded from TV and films, he found acting jobs scarce, a situation not helped by his close identification with Tonto. He played the role of Great Bear on segments of the 1966–67 TV series *Pistols 'n' Petticoats* and had a small featured role in *SMITH!* (1969). His last acting roles were *SANTEE* and *One Little Indian*, both 1973 releases.

With his spare time, Silverheels had founded the Indian Actors Workshop in Hollywood in 1963 and, as a member of the Screen Actors Guild ethnic minority committee, became an activist for Native Americans receiving better roles in films. He noted to the *Hollywood Reporter* (March 23, 1972): "You take the blacks—they are an economic entity. Indians are so few in number that they are not an economic entity. If they were to boycott a picture they wouldn't even dent the box office." In the same trade-paper interview, he observed about the Hollywood power structure: "They're purely motivated by what they can sell. Their knowledge is very limited about Indians."

In the mid-1970s, the actor became licensed for harness racing and was a professional in that sport from 1974 to 1977. In 1979, he was the first Native American actor to have his star placed on the Hollywood Walk of Fame. Having suffered a stroke in the later 1970s, he died of complications from pneumonia at the Motion Picture and Television Country House in March 1980. A sports recreation center was later built in his honor on his reservation in Ontario, Canada. In 1998, Silverheels was inducted into the First Americans in the Arts' Hall of Honor.

One of his four children, Jay, did voiceovers for TV cartoons in the 1970s.

Sioux, the Also known as the Dakota, there were four branches of the Sioux, of which the largest was the Teton Sioux (who called themselves Lakota), which had seven bands: Brule, Hunkpapa, Itazipco, Miniconjou, Oglala, Oohenonpa, and Sihaspaa. The Santee Sioux (who called themselves Dakota) was composed of Mdewkanton, Sisseton, Wahpekute, and Wahpeton. The third branch (who like the Yanktonai called themselves Nakota) was the Yankton Sioux. The fourth was the Yanktonai Sioux, composed of Assiniboine, Hunkpatina, and Yanktonai.

Originally, the Sioux lived along the area of the upper Mississippi River but spread out during the eighteenth century across the Missouri River. The Teton, called the western Sioux, moved to the Black Hills area of what became parts of South Dakota, Wyoming, and Montana.. The Santee, known as the Eastern Sioux, remained in what is now Minnesota. The Yankton took root along the Missouri River in what became part of South Dakota, Minnesota, and Iowa. The Yanktonai settled in what became the eastern portions of North and South Dakota. The Yankton and Yanktonai are often referred to as Middle Sioux.

The Sioux were regarded as the most "stubborn" fighters against white expansion into their territory, leading to years of raids and retaliations on both sides from approximately 1850 to 1890. This warfare was highlighted by the Gratton Affair in the mid-1850s, SITTING BULL and CRAZY HORSE's wars to regain the Black Hills in 1876–77 (which led to the defeat of Lt. Col. GEORGE ARMSTRONG CUSTER and his cavalry troops at Little Big-horn in 1876), and ended in the Massacre at Wounded Knee Creek in South Dakota. There, more than 150 Native American men, women, and children were massacred by the U.S. cavalry.

With so many branches, so much fierce pride, and so much history, it is little wonder that Hollywood so frequently turned to the Sioux, often used generically by filmmakers as subjects for feature films. Among the many entries on the American screen featuring Sioux, Dakota, or one of the subdivisions were *The Indian Wars* (1914), *Custer's Last Fight* (1925), *A Daughter of the Sioux* (1925), *Red Love* (1925), *Warrior Gap* (1925), *With Sitting Bull at the Spirit Lake Massacre* (1927), *The Red Raiders* (1927), *Sioux Blood* (1929), *MASSACRE* (1934), *Custer's Last Stand* (1936—movie serial), *THE PLAINSMAN* (1936), *Western Union* (1941), *THEY DIED WITH THEIR BOOTS ON* (1941), *BUFFALO BILL* (1944), *The Prairie* (1949), *LITTLE BIG HORN* (1951), *Warpath* (1951), *Buffalo Bill in Tomahawk Territory* (1952), *The Great Sioux Uprising* (1953), *The Black Dakotas* (1954), *SASKATCHEWAN* (1954), *SITTING BULL* (1954), *The Gun That Won the West* (1954), *CHIEF CRAZY HORSE* (1955), *THE INDIAN FIGHTER* (1955), *WHITE FEATHER* (1955), *The Last Frontier* (1956), *7th Cavalry* (1956), *Westward Ho the Wagons!* (1956), *The Lawless Eighties* (1957), *Revolt at Fort Laramie* (1957), *RUN OF THE ARROW* (1957), *Shoot-Out at Medicine Bend* (1957), *TONKA* (1958), *Flaming Frontier* (1958), *Gun Fever* (1958), *Yellowstone Kelly* (1958), *The Great Sioux Massacre*

(1965), *The Hallelujah Trail* (1965), *Custer of the West* (1967), *A MAN CALLED HORSE* (1970), *LITTLE BIG MAN* (1970), *JOURNEY THROUGH ROSEBUD* (1972), *The Return of a Man Called Horse* (1976), *CENTENNIAL* (1978–79—TV miniseries), *RUNNING BRAVE* (1983), *The Triumphs of a Man Called Horse* (1983), *THE MYSTIC WARRIOR* (1984—TV miniseries), *Kenny Rogers as The Gambler, Part III: The Legend Continues* (1987—TV movie), *RENEGADES* (1989), *DANCES WITH WOLVES* (1990), *SON OF THE MORNING STAR* (1991—TV movie), *THUNDERHEART* (1992), *LAKOTA WOMAN: SIEGE AT WOUNDED KNEE* (1994—TV movie), *SIOUX CITY* (1994), *CRAZY HORSE* (1996—TV movie), and *STOLEN WOMEN, CAPTURED HEARTS* (1997—TV movie). The 1967 TV series *Custer* featured Sioux chieftain Crazy Horse and his tribesmen versus the U.S. Army cavalry.

***Sioux City* (1994)** IRS Releasing, color, 100 minutes. **Director:** Lou Diamond Phillips; **Screenplay:** L. Virginia Browne; **Cast:** Lou Diamond Phillips (Jesse Rainfeather Goldman), Ralph Waite (Chief Drew McDermott), Melinda Dillon (Leah Goldman), Salli Richardson (Jolene Buckley), Lise Cutter (Allison McDermott), Adam Roarke (Blake Goldman), Tantoo Cardinal (Dawn Rainfeather), Gary Farmer (Russell Baker), Apesanahkwat (Clifford Rainfeather).

This well-meaning, if sometimes plodding, entry was the feature film directing debut of PHILLIPS, the Philippines-born one-eighth Cherokee actor. Although its premise of a Native American baby being adopted by a Jewish couple—in this case in Beverly Hills—seemed a fanciful plot twist, a later TV movie (*THE LOST CHILD*, 2000) had a similar theme, indicating that this practice was not uncommon decades ago. (In the little seen theatrical release, *The Hi-Line*, 1999, Rachael Leigh Cook played a naïve young woman who belatedly discovers information about her real parents and goes in search of her actual mother—played by TANTOO CARDINAL—a Blackfoot living in a desolate part of Montana.)

On his birthday, Jesse Rainfeather Goldman, an emergency room intern who lives in Beverly Hills with his adoptive parents, receives a birthday gift of an unusual necklace from his biological mother (a Lakota SIOUX Native American) whom he has never known. He traces the package back to Sioux City, Nebraska. There he learns that she died a few days ago, supposedly in a fire. He starts to investigate despite the protestations of the sheriff. While seeing the sights, Goldman experiences racial bias, something to which he is unaccustomed back in L.A. He is helped in his investigation by a reporter (Cutter), has an encounter at the reservation with an old medicine man (Apesanahkwat) who is his grandfather, and becomes attracted to Jolene Buckley, a politically savvy Native American. After Goldman is nearly killed by the sheriff's deputies, he performs a tribal ritual so that in his hallucination he can perceive the truths of what is happening to him. It leads to a showdown with his mother's killer.

Sitting Bull (Chief) (ca. 1835–1890) The main chief of the Hunkpapa Teton SIOUX grew up in what is now South Dakota. Son of Tatanka Psica, a Sioux war chief, the boy was known as Hunkesni (i.e., "slow"), but later, after a battle, he assumed the name Sitting Bull. Later, he was a guiding force in rallying tribes to combat GEORGE ARMSTRONG CUSTER and his cavalry troops at the battle of Little Big-horn in 1876. As a result of having predicted the victory, he won great acclaim from his people. From 1886 to 1890, he lived on the Standing Rock Reservation in South Dakota. In December 1890, his arrest was ordered by an agent of the Bureau of Indian Affairs for his purported involvement in the Ghost Dance religion. During the confrontation with U.S. troops, several hundred people were killed, including Sitting Bull (supposedly by two members of the tribal reservation police).

Especially because of his leadership and victory over Custer, Sitting Bull who, for a time, traveled with BUFFALO BILL CODY's Wild West Show, was a favorite character for representation in movies. He was played on the American screen by Noble Johnson (*Hands Up!* 1926), Johnson (*The Flaming Frontier*, 1926), CHIEF YOWLACHIE (*Sitting Bull at the Spirit Lake Massacre*, 1927), CHIEF THUNDERCLOUD (*Annie Oakley*, 1935), Howling Wolf (*Custer's Last Stand*, 1936—movie serial), J. Carrol Naish (*ANNIE GET YOUR GUN*, 1950), Michael Granger (*Fort Vengeance*, 1953), Naish (*SITTING BULL*, 1954), John War Eagle (*TONKA*, 1958), Michael Pate (*The Great Sioux Massacre*, 1965), Frank Kaquitts (*BUFFALO BILL AND THE INDIANS, OR SITTING BULL'S HISTORY LESSON*, 1976), George American Horse (*Kenny Rogers as The Gambler, Part III: The Legend Continues*, 1987—TV movie), FLOYD "RED CROW" WESTERMAN (*Son of the Morning Star*, 1991—TV movie), RUSSELL MEANS (*Buffalo Girls*, 1995—TV movie), and August Schellenberg (*Crazy Horse*, 1996—TV movie).

***Sitting Bull* (1954)** United Artists, color, 105 minutes. **Director:** Sidney Salkow; **Screenplay:** Jack DeWitt and Salkow; **Cast:** Dale Robertson (Maj. Bob Parrish), Mary Murphy (Kathy Howell), J. Carrol Naish (Chief Sitting Bull), John Litel (General Howell), Iron Eyes Cody (Chief Crazy Horse), Douglas Kennedy (Lt. Col. George Armstrong Custer), Felix Gonzalez (Young Buffalo).

This was yet another (historically inaccurate) retelling of the slaughter of GEORGE ARMSTRONG CUSTER and his troops at Little Big-horn in 1876. Because this independent production could not compete with the visual grandeur of *THEY DIED WITH THEIR BOOTS ON* (1941)—except that color and wide-screen CinemaScope was now available to this production, which was shot in Mexico—it devoted much of its attention on contrived plot intricacies leading up to the massacre.

Maj. Bob Parrish, based at a fort in Black Hills area of the Dakota Territory, is sympathetic to the plight of SIOUX tribe, as prospectors violate treaties made with the U.S. government and invade their sacred lands. In contrast, self-aggrandizing Custer is anxious to subjugate the Sioux to improve his career. Eventually, Parrish meets with SITTING BULL and gains approval that the chief will meet with President Ulysses S. Grant. But the flamboyant Custer provokes a Sioux attack, which, in turn, leads to Custer's fateful stand at Little Bighorn. Following that annihilation, Sitting Bull and his followers run from the U.S. cavalry. Yet, per this film, he takes time to heed the plea of Parrish's girlfriend, Kathy Howell, and speaks directly with President Grant on behalf of Parrish, who stands accused of misconduct. That done, Sitting Bull returns to his people.

Naish, who had played Sitting Bull in the musical *ANNIE GET YOUR GUN* (1950), here returned to the character in a role intended originally for veteran horror film star Boris Karloff.

situation comedy series—television In the era before political correctness became effective, TV comedy series occasionally turned to Native Americans as a stereotype to provide easy laughs for undemanding viewers. In *GUESTWARD HO!* (1960–61), the cagey soul Hawkeye (played by J. Carrol Naish) ran a local store near a dude ranch in New Mexico. The enterprising modern-day brave devoted himself to finding peaceful, crafty ways to restore what had been taken away from his people. The contradictions between what the dude ranch's new Caucasian owners thought a "savage" should be and what Hawkeye actually was provided the "comedy." The western farce *F TROOP* (1965–67) offered a dumb bunch of soldiers at Fort Courage who thought they could outwit the local tribes but were constantly being outmaneuvered by the Native Americans. A parade of veteran comedians (e.g., Milton Berle, Paul Lynde, and Don Rickles) guested on this lowbrow series, playing "funny" versions of tribal figures.

In the entry *Pistols 'n' Petticoats* (1966–67) starring Ann Sheridan, three generations of a family faced all that life had to offer in Wretched, Colorado, in the 1870s. Along with a bumbling local sheriff, there were brave braves (played by Lon Chaney Jr. and others) who were the butt of rarely funny humor. *Rango* (1967) revolved around a bumpkin Texas Ranger (enacted by Tim Conway) who was attempting to keep peace in the quiet town of Deep Wells. He was abetted by an acculturated brave named Pink Cloud who much preferred to laze, read a book, and then go on the warpath. The character, performed by Guy Marks, talked in Hollywood version of broken English/Native American.

More recently, *Harts of the West* (1993–94) had Beau Bridges as a former Chicago department store salesman who moved his family to Sholo, Nevada, to what proved to be a broken-down ranch. Among the show's regulars was Auggie Velasquez (played by Saginaw Grant) who operated the local store.

***Skins* (2002)** First Look Pictures, color, 87 minutes. **Director:** Chris Eyre; **Screenplay:** Jennifer D. Lyne; **Cast:** Eric Schweig (Rudy), Graham Greene (Mogie), Gary Farmer (Verdell), Noah Watts (Herbie), Lois Red Elk (Aunt Helen), Michelle Thrush (Stella).

Based on the 1995 novel by Lakota tribe poet and novelist Adrian C. Louis, *Skins* is set at the poverty-stricken Pine Ridge Indian Reservation in South Dakota. There two brothers with disparate lifestyles are in constant conflict: Rudy is part of the local police force, while Mogie, a cynical Vietnam War veteran, exists in a drunken haze. The latter's alcoholism prevents him from being a proper father to his teenage son, Herbie. Meanwhile, Rudy, frustrated by dealing with the unruly results of his tribespeople's loss of dignity and spirituality, becomes a one-man vigilante force (fighting the bad element on the reservation and burning down a nearby liquor store that preys on the vulnerable Native Americans).

While praising the storytelling abilities of filmmaker Eyre (who directed 1998's *SMOKE SIGNALS*), *Daily Variety* (January 28, 2002) noted of the entry, which debuted at the January 2002 Sundance Film Festival: "while it avoids strident preaching, the film's historical and socio-cultural agendas are poorly integrated with its dramatic aims." The *Hollywood Reporter* (January 18, 2002) judged, "Technically, *Skins* is a riveting blend of styles that lets loose its personal stories with highest dignity." However, the trade paper noted, "While a wondrously good-spirited amalgamation, it's also intermittently wobbly, and when it loses the strength of its humor and falls into sociology . . . [it] loses its most embracing power."

***Smith!* (1969)** Buena Vista, color, 102 minutes. **Director:** Michael O'Herlihy; **Screenplay:** Louis Pelletier; **Cast:** Glenn Ford (Smith), Nancy Olson (Norah), Dean Jagger (judge), Keenan Wynn (Vince Heber), Warren Oates (Walter Charlie), Chief Dan George (Ol' Antoine), Frank Ramirez (Gabriel Jimmyboy), Jay Silverheels (McDonald Lasheway).

This low-keyed, at times naïve explication of the predicaments of modern-day Native Americans was told on a small-scale by the Walt Disney studio. It was based on Paul St Pierre's novel, *Breaking Smith's Quarter Horse* (1966).

Gabriel Jimmyboy, a young Native American accused of murder, takes refuge on Smith's small ranch. Smith tries to convince his blood brother, Ol' Antoine, who has a shack on the property where Jimmyboy is hiding, to have the fugitive surrender and to use the reward money to hire a good lawyer. After Jimmyboy is turned in, determined Smith and his family do their best to change the adverse situation, including having the unscrupulous Walter Charlie replaced as interpreter at the trial. As the case progresses, Ol' Antoine spells out for the court the many unjust things done to the Native Americans over the years. The old man's testimony helps to free Jimmyboy. Pleased with the outcome, the local tribe members return to working on Smith's farm to cut the hay.

One of the film's highlights was Ol' Antoine's courtroom speech. It was a version of the one delivered in 1877 by the esteemed Nez Percé chief, Joseph. Because DAN GEORGE spoke Squamish, not Nez Percé, he spoke in his native tongue.

Smith, Harry J. See SILVERHEELS, JAY.

Smith, Silverheels See SILVERHEELS, JAY.

***Smoke Signals* (1998)** Miramax, color, 89 minutes. **Director:** Chris Eyre; **Screenplay:** Sherman Alexia; **Cast:** Adam Beach (Victor Joseph), Evan Adams (Thomas Builds-the-Fire), Gary Farmer (Arnold Joseph), Tantoo Cardinal (Arlene Joseph), Irene Bedard (Suzy Song), Cody Lightning (young Victor Joseph), John Trudell (Randy Peone), Leonard George (Lester Fallsapart), Michael Greyeyes (Junior Polatkin), Elaine Miles (Lucy), Tom Skerritt (police chief).

A prize winner on the independent film circuit, *Smoke Signals* was a prime example of the new-era Native American-themed film. Directed by Eyre (of CHEYENNE-Arapaho descent) and based on stories in Alexia's book *The Lone Ranger and Tonto Fistfight in Heaven* (1993), this low-budget road drama allowed for a full-bodied, wry depiction of modern day Native American sensibilities.

Victor Joseph and Thomas Builds-the-Fire are two Couer d'Alene young men living on a reservation in Idaho. They are diametrically opposed individuals: Joseph, who lives with his single parent (CARDINAL) since his father Arnold deserted the family a decade ago, is cool and detached; in contrast, Joseph's former classmate, Builds-the-Fire, is a pleasant nerd. He stays with his grandmother since his parents died in a fire ten years ago and is an instinctive storyteller who believes in mystical powers.

When Builds-the-Fire learns that Arnold has died in Phoenix, he suggests that he and Joseph go to Arizona to collect his ashes. Because Builds-the-Fire is paying for the trip and it means so much to him (it was Arnold who saved his life in that long-ago fire), Joseph agrees to go along, hoping perhaps finally to put the past behind him. After traveling by bus to Phoenix, they meet Arnold's neighbor (Bedard) who relates that the long-ago fire was caused by a drunken Arnold and that the guilt from the tragedy has haunted him thereafter. As they drive home in Arnold's truck, the duo must deal with the bigotry of a local sheriff (Skerritt) who is convinced that the two Native Americans are guilty of a roadside accident they encounter. Finally reaching home, they scatter Arnold's ashes on the reservation, having come to a better understanding about themselves and each other.

Smoke Signals grossed more than $6 million in domestic distribution. Its cast, including BEACH, FARMER, Cardinal, BEDARD, and GREYEYES, represented some of the strongest Native American talent in the contemporary film industry. Miles had been featured in the popular TV series, *NORTHERN EXPOSURE* (1990–95).

soap opera series—television As in so many other areas of the entertainment arts, there was scant representation of Native American performers on TV soap operas. In the field of daytime dramas, *As the World Turns* (1956–), set in Oakdale, Illinois, had a subsidiary story line in 1992–93 about Lyla Peretti (played by Anne Sward) taking in a Native American boarder, college student Simone Bordeau (played by Katheri Walker). Simone's lawyer sister Leslie (played by Kim Snyder) later sued Peretti's wealthy oilman boyfriend Cal Stricklyn (played by Patrick Tovatt) when the latter intended to drill for oil on sacred tribal land. Once that story arc concluded, the Native American characters disappeared from the program. (This story arc came about because actress Sward had personally become involved with the plight of Native Americans and wished to bring their cause to the public's attention. In addition, the performer utilized her celebrity status to raise money for Native American scholarship funds.) Through the years, *One Life to Live* (1968–) used Native American characters in brief story arcs to provide a touch of the supernatural or to give sage advice. In the late 1980s, a Native American medicine man was involved in a time-travel story line.

On nighttime (soap) drama, *The Yellow Rose* (1983–84) dealt with life on a modern, 200,000-acre ranch in west Texas, operated by the late rancher's two sons. Orbiting in the weekly drama was the late rancher's widow (played by Cybill Shepherd), the man's ex-convict, illegitimate son (played by Sam Elliott), and toughened ranch hand John Stronghart (played by WILL SAMPSON). On *Twin Peaks* (1990–91), among the show's many odd characters was the town's deputy, Tommy "the Hawk" Hill, played by Native American actor Michael Horse.

***Soldier Blue* (1970)** Avco Embassy, color, 112 minutes. **Director:** Ralph Nelson; **Screenplay:** John Gay; **Cast:** Candice Bergen (Cresta Marybelle Lee), Peter Strauss (Pvt. Honus Gant), Donald Pleasence (Isaac Q. Cumber), Bob Carraway (Lt. John McNair), Jorge Rivero (Spotted Wolf), Dana Elcar (Captain Battles), Jorge Russek (Running Brave).

With scenes of extremely graphic violence, this R-rated feature, like *LITTLE BIG MAN* (1970), was pro–Native American as it reflected on the frequently extreme barbarism of the "civilized" white man in his treatment of "savages." For many commentators, this film bore a parallel to the Vietnam War and the repeated atrocities reportedly carried out by U.S. forces against civilian populations in Southeast Asia. There were other reviewers who cited such movies as *Soldier Blue* as a convenient way for Caucasians to put the blame for the decimation of many Native American tribes on the unwarranted cruelty of just a few white perpetrators over the decades.

In the Old West, Cresta Marybelle Lee and Pvt. Honus Gant are the only survivors of a Cheyenne massacre of their group. As they head back to Fort Reunion, Cresta confesses that Spotted Wolf (who led the war party) had been her husband during her two years of captivity among the CHEYENNE. She now intends to wed her fiancé, Captain McNair. After surviving an encounter with Kiowa, they meet up with greedy gun runner Isaac Q. Cumber. To prevent him from selling firearms to warriors, Gant burns the cache, and Cumber wounds the soldier. Lee rushes to the fort to bring help for Gant. There, she learns that the cavalry plans to attack the Cheyenne. Cresta warns Spotted Wolf, who wants to bring peace to the area. A horrendous slaughter occurs as the soldiers overrun the Cheyenne village. The once naïve Gant, who is a witness to the butchery, is arrested for speaking out on behalf of the victims. Cresta decides to remain with the Cheyenne survivors.

To bolster the box-office appeal of this gruesome polemic, a good deal of footage was expended on the budding romance of Lee and Gant. For later distribution of the film to television, much of the excessive gore from the massacre sequence was excised.

Solti, Mary Rose See LAUGHLIN, TOM.

***Sonny and Cher Comedy Hour, The* (1971–1974; 1976–1977)** CBS-TV series, color, 60 minutes. **Cast:** Sonny Bono and Cher Bono (themselves).

After an up-and-down career in the 1960s in the recording, club, and movie businesses, the unique husband-and-wife team of Sonny and Cher came to TV with their flashy, hip, and sometimes foolishly funny variety hour. Both played up to the public's image of them as the oddball couple who were opposites in so many ways.

One of their several differences was their heritage. He was Italian, she was part-Cherokee (on her mother's side) and part-Armenian (on her father's side). Several times over the tenure of their weekly musical variety outing, Cher—noted for her ostentatious and often outlandish but chic costumes designed by Bob Mackie—played into her Native American heritage. She might appear in a musical number garbed in an elaborate Native American outfit, complete with a fantastic feathered headdress, or she would sing one of her ethnic-tinged songs, such as "HALF-BREED," which also was the title of her 1973 album. She made her Native American roots work for her, and it raised the public's consciousness of this minority ethnic group just as part-Cherokee BURT REYNOLDS did in his choice of acting roles.

During the break between the run of their series, Cher divorced Bono and had her own one-hour variety show entitled *Cher.* It lasted for only one season (1975–76).

***Son of the Morning Star* (1991)** ABC-TV, color, 200 minutes. **Director:** Mike Robe; **Teleplay:** Melissa Mathison; **Cast:** Gary Cole (George Armstrong Custer), Rosanna Arquette (Libby Custer), Stanley Anderson (Ulysses S. Grant), Edward Blatchford (Lieutenant Cooke), George Dickerson (General Sherman), Rodney A. Grant (Crazy Horse), Nick Ramus (Red Cloud), Buffy Sainte-Marie (voice of Kate Bighead), Dean Stockwell (Gen. Philip Sheridan), George American Horse (Stone Forehead), Rion Hunter (Sioux interpreter), Sheldon Wolfchild (Bloody Knife), Floyd "Red Crow" Westerman (Sitting Bull).

This handsomely mounted production, shot mostly in Montana, relied on the 1984 book by Evan S. Connell and other historical documents for its factual data. It presented a far more balanced view of the fateful encounter between GEORGE ARMSTRONG CUSTER's Seventh Cavalry and the forces of Chief CRAZY HORSE and Chief SITTING BULL at the battle of Little Big-horn than did the overly romanticized and Caucasian-slanted *THEY DIED WITH THEIR BOOTS ON* (1941). Opening after the carnage had occurred, the narrative flashed back to 1866 and brought Custer, a Civil War hero, up to his battlefield death a decade later.

Custer was presented as a vainglorious, somewhat half-mad, but always charismatic officer who disobeyed or "reinterpreted" military orders through much of his career. To balance this perspective, detailed attention was paid to the Plains Indians, tracing the forces that led the CHEYENNE, the SIOUX, and other tribes to plotting the massacre in Montana, with Crazy Horse shown as a mystical soul. Part of the Native American perspective was offered by the native maiden Kate Bighead (narration by Sainte-Marie). Members of the various Native American tribes (e.g., Arikara, CHEYENNE, Crow, and SIOUX) speak in their own languages (part of the effort to make this project more authentic).

Coming after the hugely popular *DANCES WITH WOLVES* (1990), *Son of the Morning Star* reflected the new Hollywood where minority groups, such as Native Americans, were finally being given a (small) voice in the presentation of American history and where the "redskins" were not automatically the vicious wrongdoers.

***Squanto: A Warrior's Tale* (1994)** Buena Vista, color, 101 minutes. **Director:** Xavier Koller; **Screenplay:** Darlene Craviotto and Bob Dolman; **Cast:** Adam Beach (Squanto), Eric Schweig (Epenow), Michael Gambon (Sir George), Nathaniel Parker (Thomas Dermer), Mandy Patinkin (Brother Daniel), Alex Norton (Harding), Donal Donnelly (Brother Paul), Irene Bedard (Nakooma), Leroy Peltier (Pequod).

Perhaps in preparation for its upcoming animated feature *POCAHONTAS* (1995), the Walt Disney studio released this thoughtful and often stirring family feature. It traces the history (some factual, other areas of his life filled in) of a Native American (BEACH) who is forced aboard a British ship in the early seventeenth century and carted back to England to be displayed as a curiosity. He escapes from his captors, taking refuge at a monastery. Slowly, the monks find ways to communicate with this stranger in a strange land. With the encouragement of the religious men Squanto keeps out of the grasp of shipping entrepreneur Sir George and eventually is returned to America where he left his new bride. He is on hand when the Pilgrims come ashore and does his best to keep the peace between the tribes and the white settlers.

Filmed in Nova Scotia, *Squanto: A Warrior's Tale* grossed only slightly more than $3 million in domestic distribution.

***Squaw Man, The* (1914)** Jesse L. Lasky Feature Play Co./State Rights, b&w, 6 reels. **Directors/Screenplay:**

Oscar C. Apfel and Cecil B. DeMille; **Cast:** Dustin Farnum (Capt. James Wynnegate/Jim Carston), Monroe Salisbury (Earl of Kerhill), Winifred Kingston (Diana, Countess of Kerhill), Mrs. A. W. Filson (Dowager Lady Kerhill), Dick La Reno (Big Bill), Billy Elmer (Cash Hawkins), Princess Red Wing (Nat-U-Ritch), Joseph E. Singleton (Tabywana).

Edwin Milton Royle's play *The Squaw Man* (1905) ran on Broadway for 222 performances, starring William Faversham in the title role and Mabel Morrison as the obliging maiden. It was revived twice more (1911 and 1921) on Broadway and was turned into the stage musical *The White Eagle* (1927) by Rudolph Friml. This screen adaptation was a hit with its melodramatic theme of the self-sacrificing squaw who gave all for the white man she loved.

When his cousin, the Earl of Kerhill, embezzles money reserved for widows of regiment members, the earl's wife, Diana, persuades Wynnegate to take the blame. He departs England and comes to the United States where, as Jim Carston, he buys a ranch in Wyoming. Thanks to Nat-U-Ritch, the scheming Cash Hawkins is dispatched before he harms Carston. When she becomes pregnant, Wynnegate weds her. Time passes, and Diana arrives in the West with news that her husband is dead and that he confessed to his crime before dying. Rather than see her son Hal sent away, and knowing that she will be charged now for Hawkins's murder, Nat-U-Ritch commits suicide.

This overromanticized melodrama was unfolded strictly from the white man's point of view, with the maiden an object revolving around his needs and whims. Red Wing, born on the Winnebago Reservation in Nebraska in 1873, had been making movies as early as 1909. (She was also in the later *RAMONA*, 1916.) Made at a cost of $15,450, *The Squaw Man* grossed a sizable $244,700. Besides two remakes (1918 and 1931), the feature led to a sequel, *The Squaw Man's Son* (1917). For that five-reel silent feature, released by Paramount and directed by E. J. Le Saint, Edwin Milton Royle's novel *The Silent Call* (1910) provided the plot basis. Nat-U-Ritch's son, Hal (Wallace Reid), an adult, leaves both his wife (Dorothy Davenport) and England to return to his mother's land. Once there, he works on behalf of tribal rights against the cunning Indian agent David Ladd (C. H. Geldert) and falls in love with Wah-na-gi (Anita King) who is teaching at the reservation school. However, it is not until his drug-addicted wife dies that he is free to wed her.

***Squaw Man, The* (1918)** Famous Players-Lasky, b&w, 5,897′. **Director:** Cecil B. DeMille; **Screenplay:** Beulah Marie Dix; **Cast:** Elliott Dexter (Jim Wynnegate), Ann Little (Naturich), Theodore Roberts (Big Bill), Katherine MacDonald (Diana, Countess of Kerhill), Thurston Hall (Henry, the Earl of Kerhill), Jack Holt (Cash Hawkins), Tully Marshall (Sir John Applegate), Noah Beery (Tabywana).

In this more sophisticated remake of Edwin Milton Royle's play *The Squaw Man* (1905) and the 1914 movie, the basic story was better contrived than previously. After sacrificing his good name for the sake of Diana, his cousin's wife, Jim Wynnegate comes to Wyoming, where Naturich, the maiden girl, saves him from the dastardly Cash Hawkins. Wynnegate weds the pregnant Native American, and they enjoy life with their son Hal. Then Diana shows up with news of her husband's confession to the embezzlement and his death. Diana convinces Wynnegate that Hal should be raised in England so that he can assume his place in society. Hearing this news, Naturich commits suicide. Thereafter, Wynnegate and Diana marry.

***Squaw Man, The* (1931)** Metro-Goldwyn-Mayer, b&w, 106 minutes. **Director:** Cecil B. DeMille; **Screenplay:** Lucien Hubbard and Lenore Coffee; **Cast:** Warner Baxter (Capt. James Wyngate/Jim Carsten), Lupe Velez (Naturich), Eleanor Boardman (Lady Diana), Charles Bickford (Cash Hawkins), Roland Young (Sir John Applegate Kerbill), Paul Cavanaugh (Henry, Earl of Kerhill), Mitchell Lewis (Tabywana), Dickie Moore (little Hal).

By the time of this third and most-recent-to-date remake of Edwin Milton Royle's 1905 play, the subject matter had passed from quaint to antiquated. White U.S. views regarding the "savage" Native Americans had not especially changed, the heavily melodramatic structure of the original drama had become a cliché. Now as a talkie, the stilted dialogue of noble behavior, mother's love, and the duty of an Englishman seemed anachronistic to moviegoers who were more concerned with the Great Depression that they were enduring. This time around, the key role of Naturich was given to Mexican actress Velez, who had the beauty but not the dramatic acumen to make the cardboard role credible. In addition, there was no chemistry between her and costar Baxter. As for DeMille, he used this film to end his onerous working relationship with MGM.

In this rendition, which followed much of the plot line of the two earlier (silent) photoplays, there was more attention given to the nobility and feelings of Naturich. Rather than have her as a mere pawn in the white man's life, she came across this time as more self-sufficient. Yet, per the confines of the drama, she commits suicide rather than face life without her beloved boy. This time, the tale ends with Wyngate cradling his dying wife in his arms.

Filmed on location at Hot Springs Junction, Arizona, the poorly received feature lost more than $150,000 in its distribution.

***Stagecoach* (1939)** United Artists, b&w, 96 minutes. **Director:** John Ford; **Screenplay:** Dudley Nichols; **Cast:** Claire Trevor (Dallas), John Wayne (Ringo Kid), Andy Devine (Buck), John Carradine (Hatfield), Thomas Mitchell (Doc [Dr. Josiah Boone]), Louise Platt (Lucy Mallory), George Bancroft (Marshal Curley Wilcox), Donald Meek (Peacock), Tim Holt (Lieutenant Blanchard), Chief Big Tree (scout), Yakima Canutt (cavalry scout), Chief White Horse (tribal leader).

During Hollywood's revival of the big-budgeted western film in the late 1930s, *Stagecoach* emerged a landmark for several reasons: It was the movie that finally pushed veteran actor Wayne into stardom, and it was the start of his long working relationship as a leading man with director FORD. This was the filmmaker's first screen use of Monument Valley, Utah, which would become his favorite location site for sagebrush tales. It also introduced Ford to the Navajo residing in the Monument Valley area whom, whenever possible, he used thereafter in his westerns.

Based on the 1937 short story "Stage to Lordsburg" by Ernest Haycox, *Stagecoach* followed the personal stories of several people aboard the overland stage traveling from Tonto to Lordsburg in 1855. Besides the driver Buck and Marshal Curley Wilcox, there is alcoholic Doc Josiah Boone, Dallas (a prostitute who has been tossed out of town), the gambler Hatfield, Gatewood the banker who has a bag full of stolen money, pregnant Lucy Mallory on her way to meet her cavalry-officer husband, and meek whiskey salesman, Peacock. En route they take aboard the Ringo Kid, a prison escapee out to get revenge on the Plummers who not only killed his family but also got the Kid sent to jail on false evidence.

Stagecoach was much praised over the years for its structure, its intricate relationships between characters, its momentum, and its wonderful cinematography; the movie was also memorable for its thrilling chase sequence in which the warring APACHE attack the stagecoach as it crosses a dry lake bed. During the skirmish, Hatfield is killed, and both Buck and Peacock are wounded. At the crucial moment, the cavalry rides into sight and, having chased off the warriors, escorts the bedraggled passengers into Lordsburg where the climactic shootout between the Ringo Kid and the Plummers occurs.

Once seen, it is impossible to forget the pacing and choreography of the Apache assault on the fast-moving stagecoach. The footage encompassed close-up shots of the beleaguered passengers, glimpses of the marauding Native Americans drawing nearer, and then the gorgeous panoramas of the terrain as the cavalry swept into sight and dispersed the attackers.

On the other hand, the Apache in *Stagecoach* remained depersonalized enemies, horsemen to be feared as they galloped closer with their bloodcurdling cries, and targets to be cheered at as they were killed. Clearly in this movie, as in most Hollywood film products of this era, there was little recognition that (1) the attacking "savages" were human beings, (2) in many instances, the raids were provoked by greedy, untrustworthy white men, and (3) a great many of these celluloid contests between the two races were fanciful elaborations of myths or previously established genre ingredients for western movies.

Made on a budget of more than $500,000, *Stagecoach* grossed more than $1 million in distribution, producing a net profit of almost $300,000. The movie won Academy Awards for Best Score and Best Supporting Actor (Mitchell). (It also received Oscar nominations for Best Black-and-White Cinematography, Best Director, Best Film Editing, and Best Picture.) *Stagecoach* was remade to far less advantage in 1966 with Alex Cord and Ann-Margret starring and as a 1987 TV movie featuring Willie Nelson and Kris Kristofferson. This newest version, made in a more politically correct era, was far more pro–Native American than any of the earlier editions of *Stagecoach*, and as so, it lessened much of the tension of the warriors' attack.

***Stalking Moon, The* (1969)** National General, color, 109 minutes. **Director:** Robert Mulligan; **Screenplay:** Alvin Sergeant and Wendell Mayes; **Cast:** Gregory Peck (Sam Varner), Eva Marie Saint (Sarah Carter), Robert Forster (Nick Tana), Nolan Clay (boy), Frank Silvera (major), Lonny Chapman (Purdue), Nathaniel Narcisco (Salvaje).

All the elements were here for a mature study about the feelings of a white woman held captive for ten years by the APACHE, who is suddenly freed with her nine-year-old HALF-BREED son. However, more intent on capturing the silent interaction between the two leads and filming the landscape, the drama focused too much on the thriller aspect, as the murderous renegade Native American sought to regain possession of his son. This misfire was based on Theodore V. Oslens's 1965 novel.

In 1881 Arizona, the army captures several Apache who have escaped from the reservations. Among the contingent is white woman Sarah Carter and her mixed-blood young boy. She convinces Sam Varner, an army scout who is retiring, to accompany them out of the territory because she fears reprisals from the youth's father, Salvaje. Eventually, Varner suggests that they return to his ranch in New Mexico. Later, they are joined by Varner's half-breed friend, Nick Tana. Before long the stalking, vengeful Salvaje arrives on the scene, leaving death and destruction in his path. There is an eventual showdown between him and Varner, with the survivor returning to the ranch cabin to claim Sarah and the boy.

***Stay Away, Joe* (1968)** Metro-Goldwyn-Mayer, color, 101 minutes. **Director:** Peter Tewksbury; **Screenplay:** Michael A. Hoey; **Cast:** Elvis Presley (Joe Lightcloud), Burgess Meredith (Charlie Lightcloud), Joan Blondell (Glenda Callahan), Katy Jurado (Annie Lightcloud), Thomas Gomez (Grandpa).

One of Presley's lesser vehicles, this comedy with very little music suffered from sloppy construction that even the veteran supporting cast could not disguise. As in the superior *FLAMING STAR* (1960), Presley, who had Native American blood in his heritage, again played a mixed-blood individual. Unfortunately, in *Stay Away, Joe*, everyone, including Presley's trouble-prone HALF-BREED NAVAJO, came across as cardboard types with no in-depth characterizations or examination of their situation on the reservation. The movie derived vaguely from Dan Cushman's 1953 novel.

Scrappy rodeo champ Joe Lightcloud wants to do right by his parents. He convinces an Arizona official to have the government subsidize his father, Charlie, with a bull and

Elvis Presley as the half-breed in *Stay Away, Joe* (1968). (JC ARCHIVES)

twenty heifers so that he can start a herd on the Navajo reservation. Unfortunately, the bull is soon killed by drunken friends of Joe. Meanwhile, Joe is reacquainted with feisty Glenda Callahan, a past romance and, later, courts the spunky woman's daughter, Mamie. As for Joe's half-sister Mary, she is pursuing a relationship with a Caucasian. Her mother, Annie, needs money to redo the house to impress the suitor—so she sells off the heifers to pay for the alterations. Eventually Joe salvages the situation by earning enough money at a big rodeo to buy his father a new herd.

***Stolen Women, Captured Hearts* (1997)** CBS-TV, color, 100 minutes. **Director:** Jerry London; **Screenplay:** Richard Fielder; **Cast:** Janine Turner (Anna Brewster-Morgan), Jean Louisa Kelly (Sarah White), Patrick Bergin (Daniel Morgan), William Shockley (George Armstrong Custer), Michael Greyeyes (Tokalah), Rodney A. Grant (Waxanhdi).

Despite its soap-opera structure, *Stolen Women, Captured Hearts* generated interest in its narrative of two white women, Anna Brewster-Morgan and Sarah White, who are captured by SIOUX tribesmen in 1868 and held prisoners for a year. Sarah loathes her captors and seeks only to return to the white world. In contrast, the more self-sufficient Anna finds herself drawn to Tokalah the warrior, and they share a romantic passion that she did not have in her civilized life. Playing to the fantasies of exotic excitement among the savages, this romantic drama nevertheless imparted a degree of believability, especially due to the charismatic performance by GREYEYES. On the other hand, bringing U.S. calvary officer GEORGE ARMSTRONG CUSTER into the narrative—to give the tale historical bite?—was one of the clichés under which this project labored.

Studi, Wes (1947–) Making his screen debut in *POWWOW HIGHWAY* (1989), a watershed movie for many Native American performers, Studi gained prominence in the lead role of *GERONIMO: AN AMERICAN LEGEND* (1993). In contrast to some other ethnic minority actors who made a splash in show business and then quickly disappeared, Studi maintained his show-business momentum through the years.

This full-blooded Cherokee was born Wesley Studie at Nofire Hollow, Oklahoma, the eldest of four sons. His father was a ranchhand and often took Wes with him to teach him to be a cowboy. (Before he began his schooling, the youth spoke only his native dialect.) For high school, he attended the Chilocco Indian School, a boarding institution in northern Oklahoma. In 1967, he was drafted into the army and served eighteen months in Vietnam with the Ninth Division. After returning to civilian life and taking a few years to experience life, he attended the National Junior College where he further developed his interest in Native American activism. (Regarding his Cherokee heritage, Studi told *Entertainment Weekly* for its December 24, 1993, issue: "It's all about arrested development. I feel, we all feel, a certain resentment because my people will never know what we could have been because of the invasion of Europeans.")

In 1974, married for the second time, he began to work as a reporter for the *Tulsa Indian Times*. He and his schoolteacher wife purchased a ranch where they raised their two children. When that union failed in 1982, he turned to acting.

In the mid-1980s, he was involved in several stage productions, including the American Indian Theater Company's 1984 presentation of *Black Elk Speaks* in Tulsa, Oklahoma. He also worked on a number of short subjects filmed in 1985 for Nebraska Public Television, and thereafter, for PBS-TV, he participated in the full-length picture *The Trial of Standing Bear*.

Moving to Hollywood in the late 1980s, he made his screen debut in *Powwow Highway* followed by a small part as a Pawnee warrior in *DANCES WITH WOLVES* (1990) and a bit in *The Doors* (1991). During this slow professional period, he helped to create a one-man stage show for himself entitled *Coyote Chew His Own Tail*, which was performed in Los Angeles and in Santa Fe, New Mexico.

His acting breakthrough came with the role of the vengeful Huron Magua in *THE LAST OF THE MOHICANS* (1992). This led to *Geronimo: An American Legend*, where he made a sharp impression. Thereafter, Studi was Famous Shoes in the

TV miniseries *Larry McMurtry's Streets of Laredo* (1995), played One Horse in *Lone Justice 2*, and was part of *Deep Rising* and *Wind River* (with RUSSELL MEANS), both 1998 releases. Continuing to remain active, he was next in the superhero get-together *Mystery Men* (1999) and later in the action comedy *Road to Redemption* and the science-fiction entry *Ice Planet*, both 2001. He was among the cast of the prison drama *Undisputed* (2002) and featured in the TV movies *Superfire*, *Skinwalkers*, and *Undisputed* (all 2002).

Besides having written two children's books and sculpting, Studi the musician was a member of the band Firecat of Discord. In May 1999, Studi was honored by the Cherokee National Historical Society.

***Sunchaser* (1996)** Warner Bros., color, 121 minutes. **Director:** Michael Cimino; **Screenplay:** Charles Leavitt; **Cast:** Woody Harrelson (Dr. Michael Reynolds), Jon Seda (Brandon "Blue" Monroe), Anne Bancroft (Dr. Renata Baumbauer), Alexandra Tydings (Victoria Reynolds), Matt Mulhern (Dr. Chip Byrnes), Talisa Soto (Navajo woman).

This NAVAJO-mysticism movie was made in the manner of *SHADOWHUNTER* (1993). This time, the entry was constructed on a grander scale in production values, running time, emotional claptrap, and cast—all the ingredients except for a viable story or exciting characterizations. It used Navajo spirituality not so much to explicate cultural beliefs but as window dressing to patch over a paltry narrative.

Dr. Michael Reynolds, an oncologist at UCLA Medical Center, is kidnapped by sixteen-year-old killer Brandon "Blue" Monroe, a barrio gang banger who is on medical leave from prison. Monroe suffers from terminal cancer and is determined to reach the Navajo reservation in Colorado to test out the special curative powers of a mountaintop lake he once read about. As they proceed on the journey, hard-bitten Reynolds becomes compassionate about the dying teenager. Later, they are encouraged in their quest by a New Age physician, Renata Baumbauer, who believes in medical experimentation. By now Reynolds has become so involved in his captor's fate that he steals medications from a hospital to stabilize his patient's deteriorating condition. Once on the reservation, they climb the mountain to the healing lake where they encounter a medicine man. Blue walks on alone to the lake where he disappears into its waters.

T

***Taza, Son of Cochise* (1954)** Universal-International, color, 80 minutes. **Director:** Douglas Sirk; **Screenplay:** George Zuckerman; **Cast:** Rock Hudson (Taza), Barbara Rush (Oona), Gregg Palmer (Captain Burnett), Bart Roberts (Naiche), Morris Ankrum (Grey Eagle), Gene Iglesias (Chato), Ian MacDonald (Geronimo), Robert Burton (General Crook), James Van Horn (Skinya), Robert Hoy (Lobo), Jeff Chandler (Cochise).

Two years earlier, CHANDLER had portrayed COCHISE in *THE BATTLE AT APACHE PASS*, reprising the screen role he began in *BROKEN ARROW* (1950). In the intervening year, another Caucasian, Polish-American John Hodiak, had played the warrior leader in *CONQUEST OF COCHISE* (1953). Chandler's Native American chief made a guest appearance in this feature, a fabrication of history (e.g., there was no such offspring as Taza) to suit this efficient western, which was originally filmed using the 3-D process.

In the early 1870s, the U.S. government and the Chiricahua APACHE have signed a treaty, and the latter live peacefully on their mountain reservation in Arizona. When Cochise dies, the leadership falls to his older son Taza. This offends Taza's war-loving brother, Naiche, who fears that the new chief is too friendly with the whites. Meanwhile, the siblings compete for the love of Oona, the daughter of War Eagle, who would like to wed Naiche. Later, Naiche and his followers massacre settlers, which arouses the cavalry to action. Thereafter, the infamous GERONIMO escapes from the reservation and joins forces with other Apache to attack the whites. Thanks to Taza, Geronimo and most of his renegades surrender to the soldiers—all except Naiche who meets his fate at the hands of Geronimo.

There were a great many platitudes spoken here in pseudo-formal Native American language, and Hudson looked ill at ease in his wig and ethnic garb. In addition, Rush was unconvincing as a Native American maiden.

Rock Hudson (left) and Jeff Chandler (center) in *Taza, Son of Cochise* (1954). (JC ARCHIVES)

***Tecumseh: The Last Warrior* (1995)** TNT cable, color, 94 minutes. **Director:** Larry Elikann; **Teleplay:** P. F. Edwards; **Cast:** Jesse Borrego (Tecumseh), David Morse (Galloway), Tantoo Cardinal (Turtle Mother), David Clennon (William Henry Harrison), Douglas Spain (Tecumseh, as a teen), Holt McCallany (Blue Jacket), August Schellenberg (Black Hoof), Lorne Cardinal (Loud Noise), Gregory Norman Cruz (Chiksika).

Born in approximately 1768 in a village on the Mad River near what is now Springfield, Ohio, the future chief of the Shawnee devoted years to organizing several tribes (from Canada to Florida) in resistance to the white invaders, especially in the Indiana Territory and notably against the formidable future U.S. president, William Henry Harrison. Despite Tecumseh's efforts, his plan failed. Later, he allied with the British during the War of 1812 and died in October 1813 at the Battle of the Thames (in Canada). This well-photographed entry in TNT cable's Native American TV series *(Behind the Legends, Beyond the Myths)* recounted events in the life of this great warrior.

Based on James Alexander Thom's *Panther in the Sky* (1989), *Tecumseh*, filmed in North Carolina, benefited from the performance of part-APACHE Borrego in the lead. Like so many of these movies, the scripters were at a loss how to make the characters convincing when they were conversing in English rather than their native tongue. Then too there was the problem of avoiding having their dialogue loaded with the clichés used by Hollywood for Native American characters. Executive produced by Francis Ford Coppola, this telefeature was promoted with the tag line: "Born to lead. Determined to survive."

***Tell Them Willie Boy Is Here* (1969)** Universal, color, 97 minutes. **Director/Screenplay:** Abraham Polansky; **Cast:** Robert Redford (Christopher Cooper), Katharine Ross (Lola), Robert Blake (Willie Boy), Susan Clark (Liz Arnold), Barry Sullivan (Ray Calvert), John Vernon (Hacker), Charles Aidman (Benby), Mike Angel (Old Mike).

Relying on Harry Lawton's *Willie Boy, a Desert Manhunt* (1960), which retold a true-life event that occurred on the Banning, California, reservation in 1909, Polansky shaped this heavily dramatic feature film. Because Polansky had been blacklisted in Hollywood during the communist witch hunt of the late 1940s, and because the highly controversial Vietnam War was still in everyone's mind at the time, much would be written about the hidden messages and/or parallels within this movie to Polansky's political views about the U.S. participation in Vietnam. Other commentators found a veiled tie between this picture and America's treatment of African Americans who were then slowly emerging out of their total minority status.

On the other hand, experts examining this movie from the Native American perspective (e.g., Jacquelyn Kilpatrick in *Celluloid Indians*, 1999; Peter C. Rollins and John E. O'Connor, editors of *Hollywood's Indian: The Portrayal of the Native American in Film*, 1998) have detailed many factual errors about Paiute heritage and customs. More importantly, such sources pointed out how the motion picture essentially interpreted everything through the white man's perspective.

In usual Hollywood fashion, of course, the two key Native American roles in this feature were played by Caucasians: New Jersey-born Blake who, as a child actor in the 1940s costarred in a series of Red Ryder western movies playing the Native American sidekick, LITTLE BEAVER; and Los Angeles-born Ross, best known for portraying Dustin Hoffman's girlfriend in *The Graduate* (1967).

In the narrative, Willie Boy returns to the Paiute reservation at Banning, California, in the year 1909 after a spell in the white world. He has come home not only for the annual fiesta but also to see Lola, the girl he loves, whose father (Angel) has broken off their romance. Making a date with her at midnight in the woods, his tryst is interrupted by Lola's father and brothers. In the scuffle, Willie Boy kills her dad. Under tribal custom, she is now his woman. The two flee, with cynical Willie Boy convinced that the indifferent whites will not follow them.

Meanwhile, the reservation agent/doctor, Liz Arnold, a snobbish Bostonian, is having a sexual encounter with the not-so-swift undersheriff, Christopher Cooper. She thinks of him only as a sexual toy, much as she treats her Paiute charges as objects to be bent to her views and standards. She forces Cooper to form a posse of ranchers to pursue the fugitives. The group is composed of racial bigots who are eager to have another "Indian" hunt and relive the old days when they massacred the "redskins." As the chase continues through the Mojave Desert, Lola is worn down. The next morning, the pursuers come across her corpse. In the finale, Cooper sneaks up on Willie Boy in the mountains, and when Willie Boy aims his rifle at the lawman, Cooper shoots him dead. He soon discovers that Willie Boy's rifle was empty. Disgusted by the pursuit and all it stands for, Cooper insists that Willie Boy's body be given the tribal respect he deserves and that his body be burned according to tribal funeral custom.

When *Tell Them Willie Boy Is Here* was finally released in 1969 after sitting on the shelf for many months, it received far more critical attention than moviegoer interest.

***They Died with Their Boots On* (1941)** Warner Bros., b&w, 140 minutes. **Director:** Raoul Walsh; **Screenplay:** Wally Klein and Aeneas MacKenzie; **Cast:** Errol Flynn (George Armstrong Custer), Olivia de Havilland (Elizabeth "Libby" Bacon), Arthur Kennedy (Ned Sharp), Charley Grapewin (California Joe), Gene Lockhart (Samuel Bacon, Esq.), Anthony Quinn (Crazy Horse), Stanley Ridges (Maj./Gen. Romulus Taipe), John Litel (Gen. Phil Sheridan).

This lavish action drama about highly controversial military officer GEORGE ARMSTRONG CUSTER was one of Flynn's most elaborate screen adventures. It reflected the full-blown talents of director Curtiz and the craft of second-unit director B. Reeves Eason, who supervised the intricacies of the film's highlight—the massacre of Custer and his men at the battle of Little Big-horn in 1876. With a hefty budget that allowed all-out production values, the footage of CRAZY HORSE and his warriors overwhelming the Seventh Cavalry (of 250 men) was stunning.

On the other hand, as history, *They Died with Their Boots On* turned Custer into a near paragon of heroic virtues as the narrative followed him from his West Point days in 1857 through his years of fighting for the North in the Civil War and on to his encounters with the Plains tribes that led to his death. Within this saga, Custer's self-aggrandizement and breaking of military rules was interpreted so chivalrously by Flynn on camera that they became bad-boy hijinks that everyone must forgive because the character was so charming and handsome. As for the details leading up to Custer's disaster at Little Big-horn, they were twisted to suit the purpose of screen drama, which over the decades bothered historians but not the average film watcher.

Then there was the matter of the treatment of SIOUX on camera. According to director Walsh's autobiography (*Each Man in His Own Time*, 1974), "I tried to show [the Native American] as an individual who only turned vindictive when his rights as defined by treaty were violated by white men." Yet, despite this protestation, the overall feeling of the movie was still negative toward the Sioux, for, after all, look at what the savage warriors did to the noble Custer and his troopers. All the dashing officer wished to do was to prevent the warring Sioux from murdering General Terry's unsuspecting regiment. This was substantiated in the movie's emotional closing scenes when Mrs. Custer forced the government to complete the noble work her husband began (i.e., protecting the Black Hills for the Sioux and dismissing Taipe, the duplistic military officer).

It was such elaborate screen fare as this highly successful film that cemented the image of the murderous "redskins" into the minds of moviegoers for generations to come. It would take such demystifying films as *LITTLE BIG MAN* (1970) to begin to put a proper perspective on George Armstrong Custer (1839–76).

***They Rode West* (1954)** Columbia, color, 84 minutes. **Director:** Phil Karlson; **Screenplay:** DeVallon Scott and Frank Nugent; **Cast:** Robert Francis (Dr. Allen Seward), Donna Reed (Laurie MacKaye), May Wynn (Manyi-ten), Phil Carey (Capt. Peter Blake), Onslow Stevens (Col. Ethan Walters), Stuart Randall (Satanta), Eugene Iglesias (Red Leaf).

So many Hollywood westerns in the 1950s were still settling for the tried-and-true formula of the cavalry versus the "Indians" that this efficient adventure was refreshing because it depicted human beings, not cardboard characters, within its plot. *They Rode West* was coscripted by Nugent whose screenplay output included such genre pieces as *SHE WORE A YELLOW RIBBON* (1949), *Two Flags West* (1950), *THE SEARCHERS* (1956), and *GUNMAN'S WALK* (1958—also directed by Karlson).

Dr. Allen Seward is the new physician at Fort McCullough. Not only does the young doctor care for the soldiers meticulously, but he also takes an interest in the plight of the local Kiowa tribe existing on a reservation where the water is bad and malaria is spreading through the community. Although Seward's partiality to the Native Americans impresses Laurie MacKaye, the niece of the post's commandant (Stevens), it infuriates the troops who are biased against any "Indians." Later, Seward violates orders by revisiting the Kiowa reservation to minister to the ailing son of Manyi-ten, the white wife of the chief's son Red Leaf. The easterner even listens respectfully to the advice of the tribe's medicine man. Thereafter, because of Seward's positive relationship with the Kiowa and the success of his operating on Spotted Wolf, the chief's other son, a full-out war with the Kiowa is avoided.

Thorpe, Jim (1888–1953) This famed Native American Olympic athlete had a lifetime of tragedies that went far beyond the sanitized account presented in the movie *JIM THORPE—ALL AMERICAN* (1951) starring Burt Lancaster.

Born James Francis Thorpe in Prague, Indian Territory (later Oklahoma), he and his twin brother Charles grew up on the Potowatomi Reservation. (His Irish grandfather had moved to Oklahoma where he had married a Fox-Sac squaw. One of their six children was the father of the Thorpe twins.) Jim's brother Charles died of smallpox in 1896, and his mother, a descendant of Chief Black Hawk, passed away in 1901. Deeply upset, he ran away from school, later worked on a Texas ranch, and thereafter attended the Carlisle Indian School in Pennsylvania. There the hulking student became a famed athlete in track and football. During the summer of 1909, he played baseball in the East Carolina League at $15 a week. Having dropped out of Carlisle, he was urged by his college coach to try out for the 1912 Olympics, and he attained legendary status at the games in Stockholm, winning medals for the pentathlon and the decathlon. The next year, because of his past baseball salary, he had to return his medals.

Thereafter, his life dipped through marriage, divorce, and heavy drinking. During this period, he played professional baseball and football. By the end of the 1920s, he was broke. He sold his life story to MGM for $1,500 but the film never was made there. In desperation, he turned to movie acting. He began in 1931 with the twelve-chapter serial, *Battling with Buffalo Bill* as Swift Arrow and in the succeeding

Jim Thorpe in *Knute Rockne—All American* (1940). (JC ARCHIVES)

years played a variety of small roles, often as Native-Americans chiefs (e.g., *Wild Horse Mesa*, 1932; *Behold My Wife*, 1935) and occasionally as a tropical native (e.g., *King Kong*, 1933). He continued making mostly westerns through the mid-1940s. (For a time during World War II he worked in a defense plant.) His final screen roles were in the gangster drama, *White Heat* (1949) and playing a NAVAJO in JOHN FORD's *WAGONMASTER* (1950).

Thorpe died of a heart attack in his trailer home in Lomita, California, in March 1953. Years later, his Olympic records were restored and his medals returned to his family. In May 1984, the U.S. government issued a postage stamp with the likeness of Thorpe on it.

***Three Warriors* (1977)** Fantasy Films, color, 109 minutes. **Director:** Keith Merrill; **Screenplay:** Sy Gomberg; **Cast:** McKee "Kiko" Red Wing (Michael), Charles White Eagle (grandfather), Randy Quaid (Quentin Hammond), Lois Red Elk (mother), Christopher Lloyd (Steve Chaffey), Mel Lambert (horse dealer), Raydine Spino (older sister).

Young Native American Michael has been messing up his life. His concerned single mother—the father died when the boy was small—takes him back to the reservation to meet his wise granddad. At first, Michael refuses to deal with the tradition-bound relative, having only contempt for the old fashioned, but the patient grandfather buys the young man a lame horse, telling him that the animal can be healed if he follows the traditional wisdom of the tribe. The skeptical young man, who has grown attached to the horse, pursues his people's ways for the sake of the horse and, in the process, develops respect for his heritage.

This unpretentious film was shot in the Oregon wilderness.

Thundercloud (Chief) (1899–1955) One of the earlier Native American performers to gain recognition in the entertainment industry, he is extremely active in films in the 1930s and 1940s. He is not to be confused with screen and radio actor Scott T. Williams (1898–1967), who also performed as Chief Thundercloud and played TONTO on the radio in the 1930s.

He was born Victor Daniels in Muskogee, Indian Territory (later Oklahoma), and was Cherokee, with German, Scotch, and Irish in his background. Working in Hollywood, first as a stuntman and then, by 1931, as an actor in *99 Wounds*, he made his mark playing TONTO in two serials, *The Lone Ranger* (1938) and *The Lone Ranger Rides Again* (1939). Also notable as an APACHE renegade leader in the title role of *GERONIMO* (1939), a characterization he repeated in *I KILLED GERONIMO* (1950), his final movie assignments included *THE HALF-BREED* (1952) and *THE SEARCHERS* (1956). During his last years, he lived on the Corriganville movie ranch, operated by western performer Ray "Crash" Corrigan in southern California, where the chief ran the photo shop and sold Native American memorabilia. He died of stomach cancer in Ventura, California, in December 1955.

***Thunderheart* (1992)** TriStar, color, 118 minutes. **Director:** Michael Apted; **Screenplay:** John Fusco; **Cast:** Val Kilmer (Ray Levoi), Sam Shepard (Frank "Cooch" Coutelle), Graham Greene (Walter Crow Horse), Fred Dalton Thompson (William Dawes), Fred Ward (Jack Milton), Sheila Tousey (Maggie Eagle Bear).

In the same year that *Thunderheart* was released, British-born (documentary) filmmaker Apted directed *Incident at Oglala*. It concerned itself with the June 1975 event at the Pine Ridge Reservation in South Dakota where two FBI agents were murdered in a gun battle with several distraught Native Americans. Although multiple defendants were charged with slaying the government men, only Leonard Peltier was found guilty. *Thunderheart* dealt in a fictional way with events covered in *Incident at Oglala*.

Ray Levoi, one-fourth SIOUX, is a know-it-all FBI operative. He is unhappy when he is assigned to help investigate a politically motivated murder on an Oglala Sioux reservation in North Dakota. When the bullheaded Levoi arrives at the site, he works with local agent Frank "Cooch" Coutelle, who insists he knows what happened and that it is just a matter of cleaning up the pieces. Within the Native American community, Levoi finds himself relying on help from brusque law enforcer Walter Crow Horse and attractive Maggie Eagle Bear, the latter a savvy teacher and political activist. He also must cope with the reservation's supervisory council, run by Jack Milton, which finds it expedient to work with the U.S. government. As the "Washington Redskin"—as some call Levoi—becomes more enmeshed in the case, he begins to embrace his Native American heritage. Levoi digs into the situation and finds that there is a secret U.S.-backed program to dig for uranium on the reservation. He also discovers that dour Coutelle is not the man he thought he was.

Grossing more than $22 million in domestic distribution, *Thunderheart* was far more successful in maintaining suspense than the police procedural/mysticism drama, *THE*

Marvin T. Thin Elk (left) and Val Kilmer (right) in *Thunderheart* (1992). (ECHO BOOK SHOP)

DARK WIND (1991). The problem with *Thunderheart* was its overstuffed screenplay that strained from encompassing too wide a range of Native American political and ecological issues. In addition, Levoi's change-of-heart about dealing fully with his ethnic minority roots was not always convincingly handled.

***Ticket to Tomahawk, A* (1950)** Twentieth Century-Fox, color, 90 minutes. **Director:** Richard Sale; **Screenplay:** Mary Loos and Sale; **Cast:** Dan Dailey (Johnny Jameson), Anne Baxter (Kit Dodge Jr.), Rory Calhoun (Dakota), Walter Brennan (Terrence Sweeny), Charles Kemper (Chuckity Jones), Connie Gilchrist (Madame Adelaide), Arthur Hunnicutt (Sad Eyes Tatum), Chief Yowlachie (Pawnee), Chief Thundercloud (Crooked Knife), Marilyn Monroe (Clara).

This pleasant musical took place in 1876 and concerned the narrow-gauge Tomahawk and western Railroad running through the Colorado Rockies. Because the new line will put stagecoach operators and others out of business, there is a concerted effort to make the new franchise fail. Helping to restore justice is traveling salesman Johnny Jameson, along with tomboyish Kit Dodge Jr. whose grandfather is the local marshal. Mixed into the proceedings are a tribe of Arapaho whose chief, Crooked Knife, is acquainted with Jameson and who eventually allows the train safe passage through his territory.

Once planned as a Betty Grable vehicle, this lesser song-and-dance entry portrayed the Native American characters as one-dimensional figures, just as the Caucasian villains were etched in the proceedings.

***Tin Star, The* (1957)** Paramount, b&w, 93 minutes. **Director:** Anthony Mann; **Screenplay:** Dudley Nichols; **Cast:** Henry Fonda (Morgan Hickman), Anthony Perkins (Sheriff Ben Owens), Betsy Palmer (Nona Mayfield), Michel Ray (Kip Mayfield), Neville Brand (Bart Bogardus), John McIntire (Dr. Joe McCord), Mary Webster (Millie Parker), Peter Baldwin (Zebe McGaffey), Lee Van Cleef (Ed McGaffey).

Frequently, as in this case, the western genre was utilized to discuss topics considered too controversial at the time to be handled in a contemporary setting where the subject matter might be considered too threatening to moviegoers. Often, such serious themes virtually could be ignored by those moviegoers who were interested only in the standard action ingredients of a sagebrush drama. Yet, by testing the boundaries of censorship and public acceptance in this way, many such subjects were first introduced on the screen. If public reaction was not noticeably severe, they were often moved into screen dramas in which they became a central issue. Here the divisive topic was racial tolerance involving HALF-BREED Native Americans.

Ben Owens, the temporary sheriff of a western town, is unsure if he has the qualifications to handle the potentially dangerous job. The timid soul is given counsel by former sheriff and veteran bounty hunter Morgan Hickman. The latter's no-nonsense approach to dealing with outlaws helps Owens grow into his position, particularly when dealing with a deadly set of brothers (Baldwin and Van Cleef). By the denouement, Owens's girlfriend Millie Parker—whose sheriff-father died in the line of duty—has accepted that her husband-to-be, now more confident about life and career, will remain a lawman.

In *The Tin Star*, a good deal of bigotry toward Native Americans was displayed. For example, there was Nona Mayfield, whose late husband was a Native American who was killed for standing up for his rights; she refuses to give up her farm, despite the prejudice heaped on her and her half-breed son Kip. At first, interacting with her and Kip, bounty hunter Hickman is as bigoted as the others, but as he gets to know her and her son as individuals, he modifies his intolerance for all "Indians." In fact, by the movie's end, he, Nona, and her son leave town together to start anew. In the plot, there is also the half-breed who was shot by vicious Bart Bogardus, allegedly an act of self-defense but, in actuality, prompted by racial prejudice.

The Tin Star was Oscar nominated for Best Story and Screenplay (written for the screen).

Tom Sawyer See INJUN JOE.

***Tonka* (1958)** Buena Vista, color, 97 minutes. **Director:** Lewis R. Foster; **Screenplay:** Foster and Lillie Hayward; **Cast:** Sal Mineo (White Bull), Philip Carey (Capt. Myles Keogh), Jerome Courtland (Lt. Henry Nowlan), H. M. Wynant (Yellow Bull), Joy Page (Prairie Flower), Britt Lomond (Lt. Col. George Armstrong Custer), John War Eagle (Chief Sitting Bull), Slim Pickens (Ace), Rafael Campos (Strong Bear).

At the time of release, New York-born Mineo was at the peak of his popularity as a teenage heartthrob. His role as the SIOUX brave allowed him to parade through the film bare chested, titillating his fan base. That he was unsuited for such ethnic casting was not considered a hindrance by the filmmakers. Based on the novel *Comanche* (1951) by David Appel, the picture was shot partially in Bend, Oregon.

In 1987, in the Montana Territory, White Bull is a contented Sioux brave who does not always live up to the expectations of his uncle, Chief SITTING BULL. White Bull tries to prove himself by capturing and training a wild horse whom he names Tonka Wakan (i.e., "The Great One"). White Bull's cousin, Yellow Bull, demands the animal through his seniority in the tribe. When Yellow Bull mistreats the horse, White Bull sets him free, only for the animal to be captured by horse traders and sold to Capt. Miles Keogh of the U.S. cavalry at Fort Lincoln. Meanwhile, military officer GEORGE ARMSTRONG CUSTER has been fomenting trouble between the troops and the Sioux, unmindful that the warriors are joining with other tribes to combat him. At the fateful battle of Little Big-horn, White Bull is knocked unconscious and is later taken back to the fort along with Tonka (whose master, Keogh, has been killed at the massacre). There, Tonka is declared officially the only survivor of Little Big-horn, and White Bull is appointed his official exercise boy.

Tonka was heavily promoted as the first Hollywood film to deal with the battle of Little Big-horn from the Native Americans' point of view. Nevertheless, as constructed, the family-oriented feature treated the Sioux community as quaint, rambunctious, and vindictive. Aside from the fact that the ultimate fate of Tonka and White Bull is a plot device to provide the movie with a happy ending, it is, to a larger degree, demeaning to the dignity of this young Sioux brave to be made an exercise boy, with no promise that his future will ever expand beyond this.

Tonto One of the most enduring fictional teams in American pop culture was the Lone Ranger and Tonto, a duo who roved the Old West righting wrongs. *The* hero of the proceedings was the masked man (John Reid), who rode a white horse named Silver and *never* accepted payment for his good deeds. His faithful companion, the Potawatomi tribesman Tonto, whose horse was named Scout, was always a subordinate figure in the proceedings. He was Reid's childhood friend who called his pal *Kemo Sabe* (meaning "Trusted Scout" or "Faithful Friend"). As an adult, he was the one who rescued the wounded Reid, the only one of six Texas Rangers to survive an ambush by the Cavendish gang. Nursed back to health by Tonto, Reid donned—at Tonto's suggestion—a black mask and with Tonto's help captured the Cavendish outlaws. The rest became show-business history.

For many, through the decades, Tonto was the most famous Native American in contemporary American culture. On the other hand, for a long time, jokes circulated about the friendship of the Lone Ranger and Tonto, suggesting that because of their ethnic differences, Tonto would not be such an obliging, subservient helper if, for example, they found themselves in the middle of rampaging warriors. As the era of political correctness dawned in the 1960s, more vocal forces suggested that the character of Tonto was no different from an African-American domestic as depicted in films, television, and so on—that is, one who served his "master" and had no independent life of his own. Be that as it may, Tonto remained a famous pop-culture icon.

As created and produced by George W. Trendle and scripted by Frank Stryker, *The Lone Ranger* began as a radio serial in January 1933 on the Mutual radio network. Although the program changed networks over the years, it remained on the airwaves until mid-1955. Those playing the Lone Ranger over the years were George Seaton, Jack Deeds, Earl Graser, Brace Beemer, and Jim Jewell. During the lengthy run, John Todd was the voice of Tonto.

The Lone Ranger first came to the screen as a fifteen-chapter Republic serial, *The Lone Ranger* (1938), starring Lee Powell as the masked man, with CHIEF THUNDERCLOUD as Tonto. It was popular enough to prompt *The Lone Ranger Rides Again* (1939), another fifteen-chapter cliffhanger from Republic Pictures; this time, Robert Livingston was in the title role, and Chief Thundercloud was again his faithful companion. In 1941, Republic released *Hi-Yo Silver*, a condensation of the first serial, adding actors Raymond Hatton and Dickie Jones to provide narration for the flashbacks, using footage from the serial.

In 1949, *The Lone Ranger* became a thirty-minute TV series with Clayton Moore as the key figure and JAY SILVERHEELS as Tonto. From 1952 to 1954, because of contract disputes with Moore, John Hart took over the lead role of the masked man. Moore returned to the fold in 1954 and remained with the series until it ended in 1957. Meanwhile, Jack Wrather purchased all rights (including cartoon and merchandising) to the Lone Ranger property for $3 million. Wrather produced two feature films for Warner Bros.; *THE LONE RANGER* (1956) and *The Lone Ranger and the Lost City of Gold* (1958), both costarring Moore and Silverheels in their TV parts. Several years later, the Lone Ranger returned to the big screen in the unpopular *THE LEGEND OF THE LONE RANGER* (1981). Klinton Spilsbury, with his voice dubbed, was the heroic ranger, while Michael Horse played Tonto.

Meanwhile, on television, *The Lone Ranger* became a Saturday half-hour cartoon show on CBS (1966–69), featuring the voice of Michael Rye as the Lone Ranger and Shep Menken as Tonto. In 1980, a new cartoon version of *The Lone Ranger* became part of *The Tarzan/Lone Ranger Adventure Hour* on CBS-TV, and the following year, the show added a third component and the series became known as *The Tarzan/Lone Ranger/Zorro Adventure Hour*. During the two-season run (1980–82), William Conrad was heard as the voice of the Lone Ranger, with Ivan Naranjo as Tonto. In spring 2002, Columbia Pictures announced plans to make a new feature film based on the adventures of the Lone Ranger. Tonto was still being described as the masked man's trusty companion.

***Town Has Turned to Dust, A* (1998)** Sci-Fi cable, color, 91 minutes. **Director:** Rob Nilsson; **Teleplay:** Rod Serling; **Cast:** Ron Perlman (Jerry Paul), Stephen Lang (Sheriff Harvey Denton), Gabriel Olds (Hannify), Judy Collis (Ree), Barbara Jane Reams (Maya), Frankie Avina (Tooth).

Relying on a western script that Serling wrote for a 1958 episode of the TV series *Playhouse 90*, the new adaptation sets the action in the future in the rundown desert town of Carbon. A falsely accused Native American youth is lynched by wily town boss (Perlman), the man who ruthlessly runs the local mining operation and controls the hamlet's water supply. The hanging finally prompts the drunken sheriff (Lang) to take constructive action.

This unassuming drama continued the more recent trend of presenting Native Americans as society's victims, just as a few decades earlier African Americans had been cast in such a posture.

***Trooper Hook* (1957)** United Artists, b&w, 81 minutes. **Director:** Charles Marquis Warren; **Screenplay:** Martin Berkeley, David Victor, and Herbert Little Jr.; **Cast:** Joel McCrea (Sgt. Clovis Hook), Barbara Stanwyck (Cora Sutliff), Earl Holliman (Jeff Bennett), Edward Andrews (Charlie Travers), John Dehner (Fred Sutliff), Susan Kohner (Consuela), Terry Lawrence (Quinto), Rudolfo Acosta (Nanchez).

In *THE SEARCHERS* (1956), the virulent hatred of Native Americans was matched by the belief of many of the movie's white characters that if a Caucasian woman was taken captive by "redskins," she should kill herself rather than submit to the "beasts." This thought was strongly echoed in *Trooper Hook*, a far less expensively mounted feature directed by Warren, who had helmed such earlier genre pieces as *LITTLE BIG HORN* (1951) and *ARROWHEAD* (1953).

Trooper Hook came under critical attack by some reviewers at the time of its release because of the picture's strikingly sympathetic attitude both to the captured white woman who surrendered herself to an APACHE chief and came to accept their ways and to the film's positive viewpoint regarding the HALF-BREED child she refused to abandon. The picture was based on Jack Schaefer's short story "Sergeant Houck" (1951).

Sgt. Clovis Hook escorts Cora Sutliff and her mixed-blood son back to the town where her husband (Dehner) resides. With the murderous Apache Nanchez pursuing his white "squaw" to regain possession of their boy, every one in the group voices strong opinions on what this stoic woman should do about her offspring. Most devastating, but not unexpected, is Sutliff's reaction when he is reunited eventually with his wife: Get rid of the boy or else. By the finale, Cora and Hook find a resolution to the situation that pleases even her child.

***Tulsa* (1949)** Eagle Lion, color, 90 minutes. **Director:** Stuart Heisler; **Screenplay:** Frank Nugent and Curtis Kenyon; **Cast:** Susan Hayward (Cherokee "Cherry" Lansing), Robert Preston (Brad "Bronco" Brady), Pedro Armendáriz (Jim Redbird), Lloyd Gough (Bruce Tanner), Chill Wills (Pinky Jimpson/narrator).

This was a spirited and sprawling saga of the Oklahoma oilfields set in the 1920s at the start of the big oil boom there. An undercurrent of this rousing action drama was the fact that the heroine was one-fourth Native American. This plot thread was used in Hollywood's usual manner to characterize the mixed-blood leading female character as wild and sensual. (She was also ruthless, a quality she learned to contain by the film's wrapup.)

In contrast, the moments devoted to her father's friend—fellow rancher Jim Redbird—dealt with the fact that he, as a Native American, was a ward of the state and thus had diminished capacity to act on his own behalf. This other theme of Native Americans being second-class citizens legally who had less rights in the court system or in free enterprise than whites was also evident throughout *Tulsa*.

***Tundra* (1936)** Burroughs-Tarzan, b&w, 75 minutes. **Director:** Norman Dawn: **Screenplay:** Norton S. Parker; **Cast:** Del Cambre (Dr. Jason Barlow, the Flying Doctor), William Merrill McCormick and Wally Howe (trappers), Earl Dwire (storekeeper), Jack Santos (a half-breed), Fraser Acosta (Native-Alaskan father), Mrs. Elsie Duran (Native-Alaskan woman).

Although there were several films through the years dealing with Alaska and the Arctic, most used the territory and the NATIVE ALASKANS as backdrops to their genre tales A few others like *NANOOK OF THE NORTH* (1922), *Igloo* (1931), and *ESKIMO* (1933) were quasi-documentaries that delved into the lifestyle and traditions of the Native Alaskans. *Tundra* fell in the middle, with its slight tale of a "flying doctor" who covered vast expanses in his plane to administer to the medical needs of the locals. The highlight of this episodic feature was Dr. Jason Barlow's adventure with two bear cubs he protected on the tundra and whom he eventually returned to the care of their mother.

This project, originally begun at Universal Pictures, utilized stock footage from the studio's *S.O.S. Iceberg* (1933) and other such Alaskan-set entries like *Igloo*. *Tundra* was remade as RKO's *Arctic Fury* (1949) and reused a lot of its footage, especially that involving actor Cambre.

***Two Rode Together* (1961)** Columbia, color, 108 minutes. **Director:** John Ford; **Screenplay:** Frank Nugent; **Cast:** James Stewart (Sheriff Guthrie McCabe), Richard Widmark (Lt. Jim Gary), Shirley Jones (Marty Purcell), Linda Cristal (Elena de la Madriaga), Andy Devine (Sgt. Darius P. Posey), John McIntire (Major Frazer), Henry Brandon (Chief Quanah Parker), David Kent (Running Wolf), Jeanette Nolan (Mrs. McCandless), Woody Strode (Stone Calf).

For many viewers, this leisurely entry was filled with too many unrewarding comic moments that were painted with a broad stroke, and its ambition to be an adult psychological western went unrealized. Others found this production too much of a rehash of FORD's *THE SEARCHERS* (1956)—also scripted by Nugent—but without the greatness of that classic feature. Moreover, despite the sensitivity of Ford's approach, the downbeat nature of this movie, along with the unpleasant (i.e., corruptness) aspects of Stewart's on-screen character diminished its appeal to many filmgoers.

U.S. Army Lt. Jim Gary approaches small-town sheriff Guthrie McCabe to join him in a mission into COMANCHE territory to rescue white prisoners who were kidnapped years ago. Lazy and dishonest, McCabe is content to reap rewards from the illicit activities in his domain, but he is persuaded to go along when a $500 reward is established for each captive retrieved. Their trek into the lands of Chief Quanah Parker results in the freeing of a white boy known as Running Wolf, whom the Comanche have brought us as one of their own, and Elena de la Madriaga, a Mexican who has been the enforced "squaw" of Stone Calf. The latter doesn't want to lose his woman, and McCabe has to fight him to the death to retrieve her. As for Running Wolf, once back in civilization, no one claims him except the deranged Mrs. McCandless, whom the savage boy later kills. As a result, he is lynched. Elena is disillusioned by staying at the fort where she is shunned because of her life with Stone Calf. By the finale, she and McCabe (who has lost his profitable job) are left to console one another.

Two Rode Together registered a nearly $1 million loss for Columbia Pictures.

U

***Ulzana's Raid* (1972)** Universal, color, 103 minutes **Director:** Robert Aldrich; **Screenplay:** Alan Sharp; **Cast:** Burt Lancaster (McIntosh), Bruce Davison (Lt. Garnett DeBuin), Jorge Luke (Ken-Ni-Tay), Richard Jaeckel (Sergeant), Joaquin Martinez (Ulzana), Lloyd Bochner (Captain Gates), Dran Hamilton (Mrs. Riordan), Aimee Eccles (McIntosh's Native American woman).

Having collaborated on *APACHE* and *Vera Cruz*, both from 1954, star Lancaster and director Aldrich reteamed for this surprisingly brutal and regressive, R-rated western. Just when it seemed that political correctness had altered Hollywood's take on Native Americans, this rugged tale emerged. On the other hand, the film did offer a rationale/apology for the APACHE'S barbarous conduct within the story line. As ethnic scout Ken-Ni-Tay explained to Lt. Garnett DeBuin, it was tribal belief that the torturer drew strength from his captive's torment.

Ulzana's Raid focused on grizzled old Indian fighter McIntosh assigned to work with greenhorn cavalry officer DeBuin. The latter is an idealistic young man charged with pursuing Ulzana and his band of renegade Chiricahua APACHE who are attacking homesteads in the vicinity. As each side maneuvers to outwit the other, the Apache leave gory mementoes of their murderous encounters with white settlers. By the finale, both McIntosh and Ulzana have fallen in the field of battle, while the now seasoned and disillusioned DeBuin leads his surviving troops back to the fort.

***Unconquered* (1947)** Paramount, color, 146 minutes. **Director:** Cecil B. DeMille; **Screenplay:** Charles Bennett, Frederic M. Frank, and Jesse Lasky Jr.; **Cast:** Gary Cooper (Capt. Christopher Holden), Paulette Goddard (Abby Hale), Howard Da Silva (Martin Garth), Boris Karloff (Guyasuta, chief of the Seneca), Cecil Kellaway (Jeremy Love), Ward Bond (John Fraser), Katherine DeMille (Hannah), Henry Wilcoxon (Captain Steele), Marc Lawrence (Sioto, the medicine man), Iron Eyes Cody (Red Corn), Robert Warwick (Pontiac, chief of the Ottawa).

On the surface, *Unconquered* was another rousing, if overstuffed, DeMille epic, this time dealing with the American colonies of 1763 as they sought to keep their frontier outposts and settlements from being destroyed by unfriendly tribes. Noble Christopher Holden (the staunch Virginia militia officer) and curvaceous Abby Hale (the flirtatious British indentured servant sold to Martin Garth, an unscrupulous gun trader) were the focal points of this expansive narrative. The picture followed the two lead characters as they struggle to help the colonies, to stay alive, and to consummate their on-again, off-again romance (which encompassed Goddard's famous barrel both scenes).

Nevertheless, a good deal of plot attention in *Unconquered* was drawn to warring Native American tribes in the East who were plotting to join forces to drive the colonists off the North American continent. As their leaders, Karloff (chief of the Seneca) and Warwick (chief of the Ottawa) were never convincing in their sizable ethnic roles; they looked and acted like staunch stage performers when orating to their warriors and/or their British collaborators. Supposedly, they were coached for this production to speak occasionally in dialects appropriate to their tribes, but such passages came across as fake as the sound-stage sets that were used for many of the movie's outdoor scenes.

More importantly, as had been the case with most past DeMille extravaganzas (e.g., *THE PLAINSMAN*, 1936; *UNION PACIFIC*, 1939), the Native Americans here were highlighted as being vicious not only to their male foes but also to the enemy's women and children. As portrayed in *Unconquered*, these primitive warriors tortured and killed their victims often just for the pure sport of it, thus becoming stereotypes of the wilderness "savage." This emphatically negative on-screen representation of Native Americans prompted the *New York Times* (October 19, 1947) to observe (in what later could be defined as politically incorrect terminology): "it is deplorably evident that *Unconquered*, in this year of grace, is as viciously anti-redskin as *The Birth of a Nation* [1915] was anti-Negro long years back."

Based on Neil H. Swanson's *Unconquered: A Novel of the Pontiac Conspiracy* (1947), DeMille's saga had a then-huge budget of more than $4 million. *Unconquered* earned more than $5 million in rentals in domestic distribution. The movie received an Oscar nomination for Best Special Effects.

***Unforgiven, The* (1960)** United Artists, color, 125 minutes. **Director:** John Huston; **Screenplay:** Ben Maddow; **Cast:** Burt Lancaster (Ben Zachary), Audrey Hepburn (Rachel Zachary), Audie Murphy (Cash Zachary), John Saxon (Johnny Portugal), Charles Bickford (Zeb Rawlins), Lillian Gish (Matilda Zachary), Carlos Rivas (Lost Bird).

In his genre study *Fantasies of the Master Race* (1998), Ward Churchill ranked *The Unforgiven* as "arguably the most venomously racist of all Hollywood's treatments of native people." Based on a 1957 novel by Alan LeMay (who authored the fiction on which *THE SEARCHERS*, 1956, was constructed), this western remained the director's least favorite project for many years, partly because he wanted to make the feature even more a tale of frontier racism than the box-office conscious producers allowed him to do.

Filmed in Durango, Mexico, *The Unforgiven* with its bizarre choice of talent (in particular, decorous continental Hepburn) was set in post–Civil War Texas. Rumors circulate in the small settlement that free-spirited Rachel Zachary is actually a Kiowa, adopted by Matilda and her late husband when she was a tiny baby. Matilda eventually acknowledges its truth. Meanwhile, the locals, who despise all Native Americans (for their murderous, devilish ways), shun Rachel, calling her a "red-hide nigger." Even her brother Cash turns against her, and he regards his family as "Injun lovers." By now Lost Bird, a Kiowa brave from the neighboring hills, comes repeatedly to the Zachary property wanting the return of his sister, Rachel. When peaceful methods fail, the Kiowa lay siege to the Zachary household. In the stand-off, Matilda is killed, and the others seem doomed until Cash returns in time to shoot most of the attackers. Lost Bird confronts Rachel, and her response is to shoot him dead with her rifle. The battle ended and their house burned to the ground, Rachel, Ben, and the others must start anew.

With its grim, overriding tone of frontier bigotry, *The Unforgiven* was not a commercial success.

***Union Pacific* (1939)** Paramount, b&w, 135 minutes. **Director:** Cecil B. DeMille; **Screenplay:** Walter DeLeon, C. Gardner Sullivan, Jesse Lasky Jr., and Jack Cunningham; **Cast:** Barbara Stanwyck (Mollie Monahan), Joel McCrea (Jeff Butler), Akim Tamiroff (Fiesta), Robert Preston (Dick Allen), Lynne Overman (Leach Overmile), Brian Donlevy (Sid Campeau), Anthony Quinn (Jack Cordray), J. M. Kerrigan (Monahan), Noble Johnson, Sonny Chore, Iron Eyes Cody, James P. Spencer, Tony Urchel, Chief Thundercloud, Greg Whitespear, and Ray Mala (warrior braves).

DeMille's *Union Pacific* was oversized, unsophisticated entertainment. Not since *The Iron Horse* (1924) of Hollywood's silent era had there been such a sprawling Hollywood epic dealing with the building of the railroad across the American continent. But the ramifications of the completion of the transcontinental railroad went beyond the grandeur of the entrepreneurial feat and the engineering and physical challenges.

With the ending of the gap between the East and West Coast via trains, the old American West was essentially finished, and with that came the founding of new cities across the United States that led to the end of the buffalo roaming the plains and to the renewed urge to push more Native Americans onto reservations. Thereafter, there were further problems as the Native Americans attempted to acculturate or reacted against the process that was eroding their ethnic roots. None of these dire consequences to Native Americans were part of DeMille's historical saga. For him, the Native Americans were integral in *Union Pacific* to supply exciting conflict as their war parties raided the builders of the iron track across the prairies and through/over mountains.

Filling out the lead characters of this colorful entry were Jeff Butler as the railroad troubleshooter, combating marauding warriors and Caucasian saboteurs, aided by his sidekicks (Tamiroff and Overman). Their arch enemies are gambler Sid Campeau and his assorted henchmen (including QUINN). There is also the tough-willed heroine (Stanwyck), the postmistress and the offspring of a long-time railroad engineer (Kerrigan). To make the on-camera love triangle complete, there is the rival (Preston) for the leading lady's affection.

Union Pacific, which was based on Ernest Haycox's novel *Trouble Shooter* (1937), received an Academy Award nomination for Best Special Effects.

Untamed West See *FAR HORIZONS, THE.*

V

***Valley of the Sun* (1942)** RKO, b&w, 1942. **Director:** George Marshall; **Screenplay:** Horace McCoy; **Cast:** Lucille Ball (Christine Larson), James Craig (Jonathan Ware), Sir Cedric Hardwicke (Warrick), Dean Jagger (Jim Sawyer), Tom Tyler (Geronimo), Antonio Moreno (Chief Cochise), Chris Willow Bird (Apache brave).

In post-Civil War Arizona, Jim Sawyer, the corrupt government agent handling APACHE matters, is cheating the tribe of their rightful dues. Combating his ploys, which stirs up the Apache leaders (Tyler and Moreno), is jocular frontier scout Jonathan Ware who has been court-martialed for helping a trio of innocent braves escape from an army stockade. Mixed into the shrieking attacks on the cavalry and settlers was the romance between Ware and feisty Christine Larson, who owned the Busy Bee Café in Desert Center.

In this decade, it was still rare for a western to be so pro-Native American.

***Vanishing American, The* (1925)** Paramount, b&w, 9,916′. **Director:** George B. Seitz; **Screenplay:** Ethel Doherty; **Cast:** Richard Dix (Nophaie), Lois Wilson (Marion Warner), Noah Beery (Booker), Malcolm McGregor (Earl Ramsdale), Nochi (Native American boy), Guy Oliver (Kit Carson), Charles Stevens (Shoie).

Based on Zane Grey's 1925 novel, this impressive silent film was a milestone in the history of the presentation of Native Americans in the U.S. cinema. Although the tribulations of the noble savage coping with the modern white world was part of Grey's romanticized theme, it was the pro-Native American presentation and the dimensional characterizations of the tribe members that made this production so unique for its time. It was also an exposé about the mistreatment of Native Americans over the decades.

The drama opens with a prologue recounting the history of the NAVAJO, especially with the defeat of the cliff dwellers by the onslaught of warrior tribes and then, in turn, the subduing of the Native Americans by the white man who forced the losers onto reservations.

The focus then switches to modern times where Nophaie, the son of a chief, does his best to protect his people in their dealings with the white world. Optimistic Nophaie has great faith in white schoolteacher Marion Warner who is bright and quite sympathetic to her students. Meanwhile, when America enters World War I, Nophaie and several others from the reservation join the army, serving bravely in France. When the survivors return to the reservation, however, they discover that the crooked Booker is the new government agent and that ownership of their homes has been taken away from them and their families have been dispersed to the desert. This eventually leads the Navajo to revolt. At the crucial moment, Marion arrives with news from Washington that Booker has been ousted. By now, the braves have surrounded the blockhouse where the Caucasians are gathered. Before long, Booker is killed by an arrow, while Nophaie is downed by a stray bullet as he goes outside to calm his people. A grieving Marion later finds happiness with a white army officer.

The enthusiastic reviewer from the trade paper *Harrison's Report* (October 24, 1925) noted, "the most pathetic scenes are the ones that show Naphaie [sic] dying; it will be hard for one to suppress his emotions in those scenes—the scenes of the passing away of the brave son of a fast vanishing race."

Before its 1925 book publication, *The Vanishing American* had been serialized in the *Ladies Home Journal* in 1923. Because the publication received so many outraged responses from readers both about the story's interracial romance and the unflattering portrayal of a Christian missionary, the book publisher demanded that author Grey revamp the novel's ending—which he did, having Nophaie die. The 1925 movie adaptation was filmed partially in Monument Valley and the Betatkin Cliff Dwellings of Arizona.

***Vanishing American, The* (1955)** Republic, b&w, 90 minutes. **Director:** Joe Kane; **Screenplay:** Alan LeMay; **Cast:** Scott Brady (Blandy), Audrey Totter (Marian Warner), Forrest Tucker (Morgan), Gene Lockhart (Blucher), Jim Davis (Glendon), Julian Rivero (Etenia), Gloria Castillo (Yashi), Jay Silverheels (Beetaia), James Millican (Marshal Joe Walker).

Much had changed in the thirty years since the release of the original screen version of *The Vanishing American.* Films such as *BROKEN ARROW* (1950) and *THEY RODE WEST* (1954) had displayed a new sensitivity toward Native Americans. Concerns over miscegenation issues—while still unresolved in many jurisdictions and for many people—were not the hotbed issues they had been in the 1920s. On the other hand, this 1955 remake—which changed several of author Zane Grey's plot points—lacked the production values or caliber of cast to make it special to moviegoers. In fact, today, its existence is hardly recalled while the original is still well regarded.

Marian Warner arrives in New Mexico to take over ownership of the ranch left to her by her uncle. She encounters Blandy, the embittered NAVAJO who is a much-decorated veteran of the Spanish-American War. Since returning home, he has been ignored by his own people because he was brought up by whites and has been shunted aside by the Caucasians, even though he came back from the war a hero. As time passes, the two unite to combat the corrupt trading-post owner (Tucker) and the dishonest reservation agent (Lockhart) who have been cheating the Navajo for years and sexually abusing their young women. The duo gain the trust of a U.S. marshal (Millican), and both scoundrels are eventually arrested. As a result, there is promise of better advocacy for the Navajo rights. Blandy and Marian plan a future together.

***Villain, The* (aka: *Cactus Jack*) (1979)** Columbia, color, 93 minutes. **Director:** Hal Needham; **Screenplay:** Robert G. Kane; **Cast:** Kirk Douglas (Cactus Jack), Ann-Margret (Charming Jones), Arnold Schwarzenegger (the handsome stranger), Paul Lynde (Nervous Elk), Foster Brooks (bank clerk), Ruth Buzzi (damsel in distress), Robert Tessier (Anxious Beaver).

This western spoof was essentially a live-action Roadrunner cartoon. Scoundrel Cactus Jack is released from jail and hired by a banker to prevent Charming Jones from reaching her father with the funds that will save his silver mine from foreclosure. Charming is accompanied on her buggy ride by a handsome stranger, a courtly man who refuses to take advantage of her. Meanwhile, the bumbling Cactus fails to delay Jones's progress. Finally, he confronts her, and she, bored with her tame companion, settles for the leering outlaw.

Among the unreal characters in this unsuccessful film were the uptight Nervous Elk and his companion Anxious Beaver, who were ordered by the banker to keep a check on Cactus Jack. As the frenetic surveillance team, they were as over-the-top and as unfunny as the rest of the struggling cast. In contrast, another spoof of the same year, *The Frisco Kid*, starring Harrison Ford and Gene Wilder, took its Native Americans far more seriously. But in either case, the definitive screen image of this ethnic minority group as merely tomahawk-wielding savages was long over.

W

***Wagon Master* (1950)** RKO, b&w, 86 minutes. **Director:** John Ford; **Screenplay:** Frank S. Nugent and Patrick Ford; **Cast:** Ward Bond (Elder Wiggs), Ben Johnson (Travis Blue), Harry Carey Jr. (Sandy Owens), Joanne Dru (Denver), Jane Darwell (Sister Ledeyard), Movita Castenada (Navajo woman), Jim Thorpe (Navajo).

The lyrical *Wagon Master* was one of FORD's less-splashy movies but one of the director's favorites and was based on his own screen story. It reflected the emerging tolerance for minorities after World War II. Made at a cost of $1 million, *Wagon Master* studied a group of Mormons who were pushed out of Crystal City in the nineteenth century by the bigoted sheriff and the townsfolk and their decision to move on to Utah. During the course of their hazardous trek, they learn to be more broadminded in accepting others of different lifestyle, whether it be the traveling medicine-show folk or their face-to-face encounter with Native Americans.

Practical-minded Wiggs, the Mormon elder, persuades two horse traders, Travis Blue and Sandy Owens, to help him deliver the wagon train of Mormons safely to Utah. En route, the religious but narrow-minded flock contend with the medicine-show troupe (including the attractive Denver) who many of the group feel are a moral threat to them. In actuality, it is the evil Clegg family—robbers and killers led by Uncle Shiloh—that the Mormons have most to fear. As the wagon train nears its destination, the Mormons intersect with a band of NAVAJO. The gun-happy Cleggs want to fight it out, but Wiggs tries a peaceful approach. It works and the two disparate groups share the evening together, the Mormons and the Native Americans each enjoying their own version of dancing. Disaster is averted when Wiggs punishes the Clegg gang member who has raped a Navajo maiden. Thereafter, as the Mormons approach their destination—a peaceful valley—the inevitable showdown with the Cleggs occurs.

Wagon Master was a sturdy exercise in racial and moral tolerance. Its inclusion of the Navajo—many of whom had been Ford's friends for years—was another example of the growing albeit very slow trend in U.S. moviemaking to utilize minorities for more than negative stereotypes.

Wagon Master provided the impetus for the later TV series *Wagon Train* (1957–65), which featured Bond for its first several seasons.

***Walk the Proud Land* (1956)** Universal-International, color, 88 minutes. **Director:** Jesse Hibbs; **Screenplay:** Gil Doud and Jack Sher; **Cast:** Audie Murphy (John P. Clum), Anne Bancroft (Tianay), Pat Crowley (Mary Dennison), Charles Drake (Tom Sweeny), Tommy Rall (Taglito), Robert Warwick (Chief Eskiminzin), Jay Silverheels (Geronimo), Eugene Mazzola (Tono).

INDIAN AGENTS were a fact of life once the Native Americans were relegated to reservations beginning in the late nineteenth century; as such, the government representatives were frequently portrayed in movies typically as corrupt people (e.g., *THE VANISHING AMERICAN*, 1925; *THE HALF-BREED*, 1952). In contrast, *Walk the Proud Land*, based on the book *Apache Agent* (1936) by the subject's son Woodworth Clum, told of a real-life, dedicated government official who worked earnestly on behalf of the Native Americans.

In the 1870s, John P. Clum begins his task as Indian agent/adviser to the San Carlos APACHE Reservation near Tucson, Arizona. Contrary to current practices, he is compassionate to the tribe members, who have surrendered and are being made to work the fields at the reservation. He even gains permission to have the Apache establish their own law-enforcing and judicial structure. Later, when GERONIMO and other renegade Apache threaten the peace, Clum first tries negotiation and then trickery to subdue the outlaw warrior. Successful in compelling Geronimo and his men to surrender, Clum considers quitting his post but is persuaded to continue his fight for the Native American cause. Meanwhile, he regains the support of his Caucasian wife, Mary, who had been unforgiving about the "squaw" widow Tianay and her son Tono who had been living with Clum previously.

***War Party* (1989)** TriStar, color, 99 minutes. **Director:** Franc Roddam; **Screenplay:** Spencer Eastman; **Cast:** Billy Wirth (Sonny Crowkiller), Kevin Dillon (Skitty Harris), Tim Sampson (Warren Cutfoot), Jimmy Ray Weeks (Jay Stivic), Kevin M. Howard (Calvin), M. Emmet Walsh (Detweiler), Cameron Thor (Lindquist), Tantoo Cardinal (Sonny's mother).

This gimmicky, bloody, and ultimately feeble venture made clear that racial discrimination was still alive and well in the United States. It starts in 1889 with a band of Blackfoot warriors being wiped out. A century later, in the same area, the town of Binger, Montana, is staging a Labor Day pageant reenacting the massacre, which appeals to the white racists in town. During the recreation, a drunken lout fires live ammunition at one of the Native American performers, and a real-life battle begins. Before long the National Guard and a local posse are chasing the survivors. Adding to the mayhem and bigotry is the arrival of a bounty hunter.

As handled by British director Roddam, the unsubtle *War Party* was more an exercise in gore than in racial tolerance and was a device to bring back the cavalry-versus-"redskins" action that had supposedly become outmoded in Hollywood's new political era of the late twentieth century.

Wars of Civilization, The See *INDIAN WARS, THE.*

Westerman, Floyd (Red Crow) (1935–) Most recognized by the general public for his role as Ten Bears in *DANCES WITH WOLVES* (1990), he earlier had been known as an outstanding Native American folksinger and activist. Among his most famous recordings were "Custer Died for Your Sins," "The Land Is Your Mother," and "Indian Country."

He was born on the Sisseton-Wahpeton SIOUX Reservation in South Dakota. At the age of ten, he went to a government boarding school some eighty miles off the reservation. Later, he attended high school on the Flandreau South Dakota Sioux Reservation. At Northern State College (in South Dakota), he majored in speech, theater, and art and earned a degree in secondary education. Thereafter, he began his career as an entertainer, performing on the country- and folk-music circuit. In 1969, he signed his first recording contract; his debut album, *Custer Died for Your Sins*, was released in 1970. His songs often poked fun at and/or ridiculed the treatment of Native Americans. As a performer, he toured both North and South America and Europe. His next album was *The Land Is Your Mother* (1982); by then, his concerts were performed in support of Human Rights of Indigenous People of the World. He had also become deeply involved in the North American Indian Movement as well as other antidiscrimination causes (e.g., in 1999, he was elected national cochair of the Coalition Against Racism in Sports).

Westerman made his motion picture debut in RENEGADES (1989), playing Red Crow, the Lakota Sioux father of LOU DIAMOND PHILLIPS. He appeared as a shaman/spiritual guide in *The Doors* (1991), the biography of rock musician Jim Morrison. For TV's SON OF THE MORNING STAR (1991), he was cast as SITTING BULL, who helped to defeat GEORGE ARMSTRONG CUSTER and the Seventh Cavalry. In the made-for-cable move *THE BROKEN CHAIN* (1993), he was a tribal elder, and he was especially memorable as No Ears in the television movie *Buffalo Girls* (1995). Later films included *The Brave* (1997) and *Naturally Native* (1998). Through the years, he guest-starred on such TV series as *Northern Exposure*, *The X-Files*, and *Dharma & Greg*. He was a regular on the *Walker, Texas Ranger* show from 1993 to 1994, playing the star's Uncle Roy Firewalker.

At the October 1997 fifth annual Diversity Awards held in Beverly Hills, California, Westerman received the Integrity Award for "the actor or actress who has brought credibility and dignity to several of their roles."

In 2000, Westerman formed the Red Crow Creations, a production company to develop Native American-oriented, film/TV/new media projects. His first entry was a 90-minute docudrama, *Exterminate Them! America's War on Indian Nations—The California Story*. In promoting his projects, he told the *Hollywood Reporter* (September 6, 2000): "The people of Indian nations have always agonized over the way history is written. Every time we hear about the Jewish Holocaust, we think about what happened in America. In the early 1900s, the reservations were nothing more than concentration camps that summarily snuffed out the Indian voice." Most recently, he appeared in the theatrical release *Grey Owl* (1999) and the TV feature *Dream Keeper* (2003).

western series—television Although quite a number of features through the decades dealt with Native Americans (usually in cowboys vs. Indian format), not that many U.S.-made western TV series encompassed this ethnic minority as recurring characters or themes.

One of the first such TV westerns to feature a Native American was *THE LONE RANGER* (1949–57), which traced the weekly adventures of the masked rider and his loyal pal TONTO. In the mid-1950s, as the sagebrush genre was going through an upswing on TV network programming, there were a few entries to deal with the ethnic minority: *BRAVE EAGLE: CHIEF OF THE CHEYENNE* (1955–56), *Buffalo Bill Jr.* (1955–56), *Cheyenne* (1955–63), *GUNSMOKE* (1955–75), and *BROKEN ARROW* (1956–60). At the end of the decade came *LAW OF THE PLAINSMAN* (1959–60), which was set in the New Mexico Territory in the 1880s as white men and warrior braves competed for control of the land, while a college-educated deputy U.S. marshal (played by MICHAEL ANSARA) struggled with his duty.

In the 1960s there were *DANIEL BOONE* (1964–70), *The Monroes* (1966–67), *CUSTER* (1967), and *Hondo* (1967), with most of these entries dealing with pathfinders and settlers moving westward and confronting Native Americans. A decade later came *The Quest* (1976), which dealt with two Caucasian brothers (played by Kurt Russell and Tim Matheson) in the 1890s West, one of whom had been raised by the CHEYENNE. *The Chisholms* (1979–80) sprang from a 1979 TV miniseries dealing with a family (whose patriarch was played by Robert Preston) who moved westward in the 1840s and coped with rampaging braves along the way.

Lasting only a few weeks on the air in late summer 1982, *Born to the Wind* was a western adventure set in the early nineteenth century in which a North American tribe was dealing with the elements, each other, and their moral code—all before the white man arrived on the scene. The group's leader was Painted Bear (played by WILL SAMPSON). *The Young Riders* (1989–92) was a hip revisionist version of the Old West dealing with the Pony Express, and the adventures sometimes involved marauding "redskins."

An oddball entry was the supernatural western *Ned Blessing—The Story of My Life & Times* (1993) with WES STUDI as the sidekick of the title figure (played by Brad Johnson). *DR. QUINN, MEDICINE WOMAN* (1993–98), set in 1860s Colorado, had the newly arrived Boston physician (performed by Jane Seymour) dealing with various local Native Americans, including a medicine man (played by Larry Sellers). The contemporary western *Walker, Texas Ranger* (1993–2001) featured for its first season FLOYD (RED CROW) WESTERMAN as Uncle Ray Firewalker, the Native American elder who had raised the show's hero (played by Chuck Norris). *Harts of the West* (1993) was a contemporary western that had a Native American character (played by Saginaw Grant) operating the general store in a small Nevada town. *The Magnificent Seven: The Series* (1998–99), based on the 1960 movie hit, opened its premise with the focal group of gunslingers helping SEMINOLE tribesmen deal with a vicious ex-Confederate officer.

***Western Union* (1941)** Twentieth Century-Fox, color, 95 minutes. **Director:** Fritz Lang; **Screenplay:** Robert Carson; **Cast:** Robert Young (Richard Blake), Randolph Scott (Vance Shaw), Dean Jagger (Edward Creighton), Virginia Gilmore (Sue Creighton), John Carradine (Doc Murdoch), Barton MacLane (Jack Slade), Chief Big Tree (Chief Spotted Horse), Chief Thundercloud (warrior leader).

If the building of the transcontinental railroad helped to close the American frontier, so did the stringing of telegraph wire across the midcontinent that further connected both sides of the sprawling country. This historical drama, on a lesser (but still impressive) scale than *THE IRON HORSE* (1924) and *UNION PACIFIC* (1939), was another pageant of the development of the United States. For a change, the Native Americans depicted herein were not merely bloodthirsty savages. This feature was based on novelist Zane Grey's final novel, published in October 1939, three days before his death.

In 1861, as the Civil War erupts, Western Union is stringing telegraph wire between Omaha, Nebraska, and Salt Lake City, Utah, a distance of 1,100 miles. Edward Creighton is in charge, and his staff includes engineer Richard Blake as well as ex-bank robber Vance Shaw, who is hired as the project's scout. When Native Americans supposedly attack the supply camp and run off the cattle, Shaw, suspicious that the "Indians" were actually whites, discovers that outlaw Slade and his men masqueraded as warriors to grab the livestock. Later, when Blake shoots a drunken Dakota brave, there is almost trouble with Chief Spotted Horse, the father of the injured man. Creighton negotiates a truce, and after other near disasters are averted, the line is completed.

This lavish western was produced at a cost of $1 million. Under the direction of German-born Lang, this romanticized entry displayed sensibilities to Native Americans even if the director didn't utilize local (Piute) tribesmen because their stature and look did not match moviegoers' conception of "redskins."

***When the Legend Dies* (1972)** Twentieth Century-Fox, color, 107 minutes. **Director:** Stuart Miller; **Screenplay:** Robert Dozier; **Cast:** Richard Widmark (Red Dillon), Frederic Forrest (Tom Black Bull), Luana Anders (Mary Redmond), Vito Scotti (Meo), Herbert Nelson (Dr. Wilson), John War Eagle (Blue Elk). Tillman Box (young Tom Black Bull).

This sterling drama concerned the kinship between an old rodeo champion and a Native American newcomer to the circuit. This was among several Hollywood features of the early 1970s that utilized the rodeo environment as a symbol of the Old West. In that posture, it depicted how rugged, freewheeling individualists were being forced to cope with changing times in a more sophisticated environment. It also dealt with contemporary Native Americans as they balanced the value of acculturation with maintaining traditional values.

Grizzled, alcoholic Red Dillon is coming to the end of his rope in the rodeo business, but he gains a new financial lease on life by promoting promising young Tom Black Bull. The crass veteran, however, blows his and Bull's money on reckless drinking binges and wagering on fixed events. A disgusted Black Bull goes out on his own and becomes a major success in his profession but is injured during a wild spree in the ring. Later, he reunites with the dying Dillon, who revives enough to fleece Dillon for one more giant bender. After Dillon dies, Black Bull returns to his reservation to instruct the young folk on their Native American roots and customs. He has met the elders' requirements that he observe and understand the ways of the white world.

When the Legend Dies was based on the 1963 novel by Hal Borland.

***White Dawn, The* (1974)** Paramount, color, 109 minutes. **Director:** Philip Kaufman; **Screenplay:** James Houston, Tom Rickman, and Martin Ransohoff; **Cast:** Warren Oates (Billy), Timothy Bottoms (Daggett), Lou Gossett

(Portagee), Simonie Kopapik (Sarkak), Joanasie Salomonie (Kangiak), Pilitak (Neevee), Sagiaktok (shaman), Munamee Sako (Sowniapik).

In the tradition of *NANOOK OF THE NORTH* (1922) and *ESKIMO* (1932), this absorbing drama was filmed on the northern tundra. Based on Houston's 1971 novel, it depicted in starkly dramatic terms how the Caucasian civilization could infect and diminish a traditional society such as that of the NATIVE ALASKANS and lead to a culture's meltdown.

In the 1890, a trio of whalers (Oates, Bottoms, and Gossett) are marooned in the bleak Arctic and find refuge with a Native-Alaskan tribe. As the weeks drag on, the newcomers introduce their assorted vices (gambling, drinking, sexual abandon) to the village, causing tremendous changes to the locals.

With its careful replication of life at the end of the nineteenth-century and its contrast of the two quite divergent societies, the well-photographed *The White Dawn* was an important entry in Native–Alaskan-themed films produced by Hollywood. A good deal of the film's dialogue was spoken in native dialect, with subtitles providing an English translation.

***White Eagle* (1932)** Columbia, b&w, 67 minutes. **Director:** Lambert Hillyer; **Screenplay:** Fred Myton; **Cast:** Buck Jones (White Eagle [John Harvey]), Barbara Weeks (Janet Rand), Robert Ellis (Gregory), Jason Robards Sr. (Dave Rand), Ward Bond (Bart), Robert Elliott (Captain Blake), Frank Campeau (Gray Wolf), Jim Thorpe (warrior chief).

White Eagle was one of nine 1932 releases made by popular cowboy star Jones. It combined several plot elements that were becoming frequently repeated themes in westerns featuring Native Americans but that hardly ever blended together as here.

As Janet Rand heads to Virginia City to stay with her brother, she encounters Pony Express rider White Eagle. The two are attracted to one another, but Gray Wolf tells his son White Eagle that he should return to his own people and not begin a romance with the white woman. Meanwhile, White Eagle discovers that crooked Gregory, Bart, and their henchmen are posing as braves to rob stages and cause other problems with the citizens. When White Eagle conveys this information to the townsfolk, they don't believe him. Later, because settlers have wiped out a tribal village, there is retaliation by the local warriors, but White Eagle, who finds himself caught in the middle between the opposing cultures, negotiates a peace. By now, he has learned that he is actually a Caucasian who was found by Gray Wolf in the remains of a burning fort and was brought up as a Native American. He and Janet are free to marry.

For some reason, the plot ploy of outlaws masquerading as Native Americans to throw the blame off themselves appealed mightily to scriptwriters of westerns, especially in low-budget items as this. Typically, in an interracial romance plot, one of the two parties would renounce the romance in the name of logic—another script strategy that would keep the film within the industry censorship guidelines and avoid offending officials in states that had miscegenation laws. Here, White Eagle's discovery that he was a Caucasian resolved that problem and magically allowed the picture to have its desired happy ending.

Jones again played the same-named Native American warrior in the 1941 fifteen-chapter Columbia Pictures serial, *White Eagle.*

***White Feather* (1955)** Twentieth Century-Fox, color, 102 minutes. **Director:** Robert Webb; **Screenplay:** Delmer Daves and Leo Townsend; **Cast:** Robert Wagner (Josh Tanner), John Lund (Colonel Lindsay), Debra Paget (Appearing Day), Jeffrey Hunter (Little Dog), Eduard Franz (Chief Broken Hand), Noah Beery (Lieutenant Ferguson), Hugh O'Brian (American Horse).

The mid-1950s witnessed a strong revival of cavalry-versus-"redskins" movies prompted by the fact that such action genre pieces photographed well in color (which had finally become the industry standard) and looked impressive in the new wide-screen processes, especially CinemaScope. Putting aside some of the unfortunate casting of Caucasians as Native Americans (e.g., Paget and O'Brian), *White Feather* benefited from the thoughtful script coauthored by Daves, who directed such Native–American-themed films as *BROKEN ARROW* (1950), *Drum Beat*, (1954), and *THE LAST WAGON* (1956). (*White Feather* was adapted from John Prebble's 1952 short story "My Great Great-Aunt Appearing Day.")

In this handsome feature there was a concerted effort to present CHEYENNE warriors (both old and young) as men of dignity and worth. The picture also treated the growing interrelationship among surveyor Josh Tanner, rebellious Little Dog, and the latter's comely sister Appearing Day in a relatively mature manner.

In 1877, Josh Tanner arrives at Fort Laramie, Wyoming, carrying the body of a white man shot by a Cheyenne arrow. Colonel Lindsay warns his men not to break the treaty with the Cheyenne, or they will likely suffer the same fate as this victim. In the coming days, Tanner encounters Little Dog, who invites him to his Cheyenne village. There, Appearing Day makes known her affection for the white man, while her father, Chief Broken Hand, asks Tanner's counsel regarding the tribe's projected relocation to a reservation—a plan that upsets the chief's proud son, Little Dog. During the coming weeks, minor incidents on the part of both the Cheyenne and cavalry lead to deaths and recriminations. Nevertheless, Chief Broken Hand persists in signing the peace treaty, even though it prompts his prideful son and the latter's friend, American Horse, into a deadly confrontation with the soldiers. Tanner tends to Little Dog's corpse, showing his respect for his fallen friend. Now, with peace between the two opposing forces, the surveyor weds Appearing Day.

It was most unusual in the mid-1950s for a script to allow an interracial marriage, but it reflected the more liberal thinking of Hollywood as old mores slowly (and occasionally) gave way to the goals of a more politically correct society.

***Whoopee!* (1930)** United Artists, color, 94 minutes. **Director:** Thornton Freeland; **Screenplay:** William Conselman; **Cast:** Eddie Cantor (Henry Williams), Eleanor Hunt (Sally Morgan), Paul Gregory (Wanenis), Jack Rutherford (Sheriff Bob Wells), Ethel Shutta (Mary Custer), Chief Caupolican (Black Eagle).

Based on the successful stage comedy *The Nervous Wreck* (1923) and the hit musical *Whoopee!* (1928), Cantor recreated his song-and-dance role as the superhypochondriac at an Arizona dude ranch who found himself the dupe of beautiful Sally Morgan. The heroine loved Wanenis, a Native American young man who was currently being educated at white institutions. Meanwhile, lustful sheriff Bob Wells wants to marry Sally. To avoid the law enforcer, she convinces nervous Henry Williams to help her escape the demanding sheriff and her bigoted father. Williams's car breaks down near a reservation where they hide out. By the (contrived) joyful finale, it is discovered that Wanenis is actually Caucasian, so his marriage to Sally can take place.

With its blatant racial demeaning of African Americans (e.g., the scenes in which Cantor's character pranced about in the star's traditional blackface guise) and Native Americans, *Whoopee!* was a prime example of old-fashioned racial intolerance and cultural chauvinism. On the plus side, it boasted pleasing two-strip Technicolor cinematography and the choreography of Busby Berkeley, which included his precision dance numbers including one featuring a bevy of comely "Indian maidens" wearing revealing shorts and colorful headdresses.

The Nervous Wreck, which had been filmed as a silent photoplay in 1926, was remade as the Danny Kaye screen comedy *Up in Arms* (1944).

***Winchester '73* (1950)** Universal, b&w, 92 minutes. **Director:** Anthony Mann; **Screenplay:** Robert L. Richards and Borden Chase; **Cast:** James Stewart (Lin McAdam), Shelley Winters (Lola Manners), Dan Duryea (Waco Johnny Denan), Stephen McNally (Henry "Dutch" Brown [Matthew McAdam]), Will Geer (Wyatt Earp), Rock Hudson (Young Bull), Tony Curtis (Doan), Chief Yowlachie (warrior).

One of the best westerns of the 1950s and one of the first of a new breed of psychological sagebrush tales, *Winchester '73* was a multiple-episode tale as the characters vied to become the latest owner of a rare Winchester '73 rifle. In the shifting sands of possession, in 1876, cowboy Lin McAdam arrives in Dodge City, Kansas, where he is a contestant in the Centennial Rifle Shoot. He wins the prized firearm from his competitor, Dutch Brown (who is actually the elder brother whom McAdam believes killed their father). By a series of happenstances, the coveted weapon continues to switch ownership. One individual to acquire the rifle is Young Bull, who kills a trader and grabs the Winchester. Later, when the cavalry attacks Young Bull's band, the warrior is killed by Lin, who does not know that his opponent has the sought-after rifle. Eventually, the round-robin ends when Lin and his brother engage in a final shootout with the much-sought-after rifle going to the victor.

In this action drama, the scene and mood shifted frequently. Interestingly, the sections involving the Native American trader and then Young Bull meeting his fate are not downplayed, thus placing the Native Americans on equal footing with the Caucasian characters. It was a muted sign of a changing moral viewpoint in still racially bigoted and divided Hollywood.

Winchester '73, which was extremely successful at the box office, was converted into a lackluster TV movie in 1967 starring John Saxon and Tom Tryon.

***Windwalker* (1980)** Pacific International, color, 108 minutes. **Director:** Keith Merrill; **Screenplay:** Ray Goldrup; **Cast:** Trevor Howard (Windwalker), Nick Ramus (Smiling Wolf/Twin Brother/narrator), James Remar (Windwalker, as a young man), Serene Hedin (Tashina), Dusty Iron Wing McCrea (Dancing Moon), Silvana Gallardo (Little Feather), Billy Drago (Crow scout).

A tribute to Native American heritage, this feature with a largely Native American cast was shot in the CHEYENNE and Crow languages with English subtitles provided. As he lays dying, aged Windwalker recalls for his grandchildren his history. When he was a young brave, his wife (Hedin) was murdered by Crow warriors, and one of his twin boys was kidnapped. After Windwalker passes on, he is compelled to return from the grave to set matters right with his family and his tribe. As a reward, he can join his wife in the spirit world.

Putting aside the miscasting of Britisher Howard in the pivotal role, this unusual feature was unique for being a "Western" with *no* cowboys and *no* cavalry. Based on the 1979 novel by Blaine M. Yorgason, *Windwalker* grossed more than $18 million in domestic distribution.

***Winterhawk* (1976)** Howco International, color, 98 minutes. **Director:** Charles B. Pierce; **Screenplay:** Pierce and Earl E. Smith; **Cast:** Michael Dante (Chief Winterhawk), Woody Strode (Big Rude), Leif Erickson (Elkhorn Guthrie), Denver Pyle (Arkansas), L. Q. Jones (Gates), Dawn Wells (Clayanna), Sacheen Littlefeather (Paleflower).

Shot in Montana, this adventure featured Dante as Winterhawk, the legendary Blackfoot leader who asked white settlers to assist his people who were dying of smallpox. Thereafter, he is misled by a pair of settlers who murder two of his warriors; as payback, he kidnaps a white woman and her brother. Following the filmmaking trend of the 1970s, Native American points of view were favored here, and there was also a dash of ethnic mysticism blended into the proceedings.

***Wolfen* (1981)** Warner Bros., color, 115 minutes. **Director:** Michael Wadleigh; **Screenplay:** David Eyre and Wadleigh; **Cast:** Albert Finney (Dewey Wilson), Diane

Verona (Rebecca Neff), Edward James Olmos (Eddie Holt), Gregory Hines (Whittington), Tom Noonan (Ferguson), Dick O'Neill (Warren), Dehi Berti (old Native American), Joaquin Rainbow, John Ferraro, Rino Thunder, and Julie Evening Lilly (Native Americans).

Unlike many contemporary horror tales that utilized Native Americans as a gimmick (e.g., *POLTERGEIST II*, 1986), the underrated *Wolfen*, based on Whitley Strieber's 1978 novel, was a sterling genre piece. It not only provided tension, violence, and shocks but also contained thoughtful concepts within its plot premise. As such, *Wolfen* was anything but a standard werewolf movie.

New York Police Department homicide detective Dewey Wilson is assigned to investigate the murder of three individuals in Manhattan's Battery Park. The victims' throats were ripped out. As he pieces together clues with the help of coroner Whittington and criminal psychologist Rebecca Neff, Wilson is given useful information from a contingent of Native American construction workers. They explain that the Wolfen, whose lair has been an abandoned South Bronx church, are a pack of supersmart wolves who once roamed the New York City area. As civilization encroached on the land, they were driven to the slum part of town where they now feed off the human garbage of society—that is, victims who no one really cares about. These fierce creatures have great compassion for Native Americans who, in the settlement of the United States, suffered the same fate as the wolves.

Made at a cost of $15 million, the hard-to-categorize *Wolfen*, with its visually stunning cinematography and effects, was not successful in its initial release but became a cult favorite in later years.

Y

***Young Dan'l Boone* (1977)** CBS-TV series, color, 60 minutes. **Cast:** Rick Moses (Daniel Boone), Devon Ericson (Rebecca Bryan), Ji-Tu Cumbuka (Hawk), John Joseph Thomas (Peter Dawes), Eloy Phil Casados (Tsiskwa).

Hoping to capture a share of the youth market, this series centered not on the mature Kentucky woodsman as had been played by Fess Parker in *DANIEL BOONE* (1964–70) but on the adventures of the frontiersman when he was twentysomething. In this premise, the unmarried pioneer had an assortment of ethnically diverse pals: twelve-year-old Peter Dawes, the runaway-slave Hawk, and Tsiskwa, a Cherokee. Boone's patient girlfriend waiting by the hearth was Rebecca Bryan.

The public was unimpressed by the series, which left the airwaves after only four installments.

***Young Guns* (1988)** Twentieth Century-Fox, color, 97 minutes. **Director:** Christopher Cain; **Screenplay:** John Fusco; **Cast:** Emilio Estevez (Billy the Kid [William H. Bonney]), Kiefer Sutherland (Josiah "Doc" Scurlock), Lou Diamond Phillips (José Chavez y Chavez), Charlie Sheen (Dick Brewer), Dermot Mulroney ("Dirty Steve" Stephens), Casey Siemaszko (Charley Bowdre), Terence Stamp (John Henry Tunstall), Jack Palance (Lawrence G. Murphy), Alice Carter (Yen Sun), Brian Keith (Buckshot Roberts).

In this high-concept western starring Estevez, his brother Sheen, and several young actors of the Hollywood scene, Phillips played a NAVAJO-Mexican mystic caught in gunplay in New Mexico. He was one of the gunslingers who was involved with Billy the Kid and their mentor, rancher John Henry Tunstall, in the Lincoln County war against vicious beef tycoon Lawrence G. Murphy. Rather than developing distinctive characterizations, the young stars traded on their personas that were enhanced by the quirkiness of their screen alter egos. The pseudo gunfights in this entry were filled with MTV rock soundtrack music and proved to be no more believable than the film's synthetic ambiance.

Because of the popularity of its young lead players, *Young Guns* grossed more than $44 million in domestic release. It led to *Young Guns II* (1990), in which Phillips repeated his characterization of José Chavez y Chavez.

Yowlachie (Chief) (1891–1966) Although he performed in more than sixty movies during his thirty-five-year film and TV career, he was also known as a concert baritone, had two guest appearances at the White House, and saw his six-feet, two-inch figure immortalized in stone in a London, England, square.

Born Daniel Simmons at the Yakima Indian Reservation, Washington, at age twenty-one, he enrolled at the Cushman Trade School in Tacoma. It was during his four years there that he began his voice training. So that he could continue his musical instruction, he worked at the institution for the next six years. It was during this period that he began his concert appearances.

In 1923, he moved to Hollywood, hoping to become an actor to pay for further vocal coaching. He made his debut in the silent feature *Wanderer of the Wasteland* (1924). In the next few years, he continued acting in pictures, as well as serving as technical director and then casting director (for Native Americans) on movies.

In 1927, he undertook further study in New York, and by 1930, he made his official concert debut. He performed two tribal operas at the Metropolitan Opera. Through the 1930s, he toured as a featured artist with the Columbia Concert Bureau, singing in Italian, French, German, English, and his native dialect. In Los Angeles, he performed at the Hollywood Bowl and was a soloist with the Philharmonic Orchestra. He sang at the White House for Presidents Herbert

Top row: Ji-Tu Cumbuka, Rick Moses, Devon Ericson, and Eloy Phil Casados; bottom row: John Joseph Thomas in the TV western series *Young Dan'l Boone* (1977). (VINCENT TERRACE)

Hoover and Franklin Delano Roosevelt. Also during this period he posed for the statue of "A Noble Indian," which was erected in a London city square.

In the 1940s, he returned to pictures, including: *North West Mounted Police* (1940), *RIDE 'EM COWBOY* (1942), *Bowery Buckaroos* (1947), *Red River* (1948), and *THE PALEFACE* (1948). In the 1950s, he was in such entries as *The Last Outpost* (1951—as COCHISE), *Son of Geronimo* (1952—as GERONIMO), and *The Spirit of St. Louis* (1957). His final movie was *Heller in Pink Tights* (1960).

He died in Los Angeles in March 1966 at age seventy-five.

Bibliography

Newspapers and Periodicals

Among the publications consulted were: *Boxoffice, Cineaste, Classic Images, Cowboys and Indians, Creative Screenwriting, Daily Variety, DGA, Ebony, Entertainment Today, Esquire, Fade In, Film Comment, Film Quarterly, Filmmaker, Films in Review, Films of the Golden Age, Hollywood Reporter, Interview, Jet, Journal of Popular Film and Television, LA New Times, LA Weekly, Los Angeles Daily News, Los Angeles Herald Examiner, Los Angeles Times, Monthly Film Bulletin, Movieline, New York Daily News, New York Observer, New York Post, New York Times, Newsweek, People, Premiere, Rolling Stone, Script, Sight & Sound, Time, Total Film, TV Guide, US, USA Today, Vanity Fair.*

Books

Altman, Susan. *The Encyclopedia of African-American Heritage.* New York: Facts On File, 1997.

Armstrong, Richard B., and Mary Willems Armstrong. *Encyclopedia of Film Themes, Settings and Series.* Jefferson, N.C.: McFarland, 2000.

Baxter, John. *Woody Allen: A Biography.* New York: Carroll & Graf, 1999.

Berkhofer, Robert F., Jr. *The White Man's Indian.* New York: Vintage, 1979.

Bernardi, Daniel, ed. *The Birth of Whiteness: Race and the Emergence of U.S. Cinema.* New Brunswick, N.J.: Rutgers University Press, 1996.

———. *Classic Hollywood, Classic Whiteness.* Minneapolis, Minn.: University of Minnesota Press, 2001.

Bernheimer, Kathryn. *The 50 Greatest Jewish Movies: A Critic's Ranking of the Very Best.* Secaucus, N.J.: Citadel, 1998.

Bernstein, Matthew, and Gaylyn Studlar, eds. *Visions of the East: Orientalism in Film.* New Brunswick, N.J.: Rutgers University Press, 1997.

Berumen, Frank Javier Garcia. *The Chicano/Hispanic Image in American Film.* New York: Vantage, 1995.

Birchfield, D. L., gen. ed. *The Encyclopedia of North American Indians.* Tarrytown, N.Y.: Marshall Cavendish, 1997.

Bogle, Donald. *Blacks in American Films and Television: An Illustrated Encyclopedia.* New York: Garland, 1988.

———. *Prime Time Blues: African Americans on Network Television.* New York: Farrar, Straus and Giroux, 2001.

———. *Toms, Coons, Mulattoes, Mammies, & Bucks: An Interpretive History of Blacks in American Films* (rev. ed.). New York: Continuum, 1989.

Bradley, Edwin M. *The First Hollywood Musicals: A Critical Filmography of 171 Features: 1927 through 1932.* Jefferson, N.C.: McFarland, 1996.

Bronner, Edwin J. *The Encyclopedia of the American Theatre: 1900–1975.* San Diego, Calif.: A. S. Barnes, 1980.

Brooks, Tim. *The Complete Directory to Prime Time TV Stars: 1946—Present.* New York: Ballantine, 1987.

Brooks, Tim, and Earle Marsh. *The Complete Directory to Prime Time Network and Cable TV Shows: 1946—Present* (7th ed.). New York: Ballantine, 1999.

Capsuto, Steven. *Alternate Channels: The Uncensored Story of Gay and Lesbian Images on Radio and Television: 1930s to the Present.* New York: Ballantine, 2000.

Churchill, Ward. *Fantasies of the Master Race: Literature, Cinema and the Colonization of American Indians.* San Francisco, Calif.: City Lights, 1998.

Cisco, ed. *Dictionary of Indian Tribes of the Americas* (2nd ed.). Newport Beach, Calif.: American Indian, 1993.

Cline, William C. *In the Nick of Time: Motion Picture Sound Serials.* Jefferson, N.C.: McFarland, 1984.

Cotter, Bill. *The Wonderful World of Disney Television: A Complete History.* New York: Hyperion, 1997.

Craddock, Jim, ed. *VideoHound's Golden Movie Retriever: 2002.* Detroit, Mich.: Visible Ink, 2001.

Curtis, Sandra. *Zorro Unmasked: The Official History.* New York: Hyperion, 1998.

Daniels, Roger. *Asian America: Chinese and Japanese in the United States Since 1850.* Seattle, Wash.: University of Washington Press, 1988.

Davis, F. James. *Who's Black? One Nation's Definition.* University Park, Penn.: Pennsylvania State University Press, 1991.

Davis, Natalie Zemon. *Slaves on Screen: Film and Historical Vision.* Cambridge, Mass.: Harvard University Press, 2000.

Desser, David, and Lester D. Friedman. *American-Jewish Filmmakers: Traditions and Trends.* Urbana, Ill.: University of Illinois Press, 1993.

Dockstader, Frederic J. *Great North American Indians: Profiles in Life and Leadership.* New York: Van Nostrand Reinhold, 1977.

Druxman, Michael B. *Play It Again, Sam.* South Brunswick, N.J.: A. S. Barnes, 1977.

Dunning, John. *On the Air: The Encyclopedia of Old-Time Radio.* New York: Oxford University Press, 1998.
Ehrenstein, David, and Bill Reed. *Rock on Film.* New York: Delilah, 1982.
Emery, Robert J. *The Directors: Take One.* New York: TV Books, 1999.
Epstein, Lawrence J. *The Haunted Smile.* New York: Public Affairs, 2001.
Erens, Patricia. *The Jew in American Cinema.* Bloomington, Ind.: Indiana University Press, 1984.
Eyman, Scott. *Print the Legend: The Life and Times of John Ford.* New York: Simon & Schuster, 1999.
Faung, Joann, and Jean Lee. *Asian American Actors: Oral Histories from Stage, Screen and Television.* Jefferson, N.C.: McFarland, 2000.
Ferber, Abby L. *White Man Falling: Race, Gender, and White Supremacy.* Lanham, Md.: Rowman & Littlefield, 1998.
Friedman, Lester D. *Jewish Image in American Film.* Secaucus, N.J.: Citadel, 1987.
Furmanek, Bob, and Ron Palumbo. *Abbott and Costello in Hollywood.* New York: Perigee, 1991.
Garber, Neil, Frank Rich, and Joyce Antler. *Television's Changing Image of American Jews.* Los Angeles, Calif.: The American Jewish Committee and the Norman Lear Center, 2000.
Gevinson, Alan, ed. *The American Film Institute Catalog of Motion Pictures: Within Our Gates: Ethnicity in American Feature Films: 1911–1920.* Berkeley, Calif.: University of California Press, 1997.
Gonzalez, Juan. *Harvest of Empire: A History of Latinos in America.* New York: Viking, 2000.
Green, J. Ronald. *Straight Lick: The Cinema of Oscar Micheaux.* Bloomington, Ind.: Indiana University Press, 2000.
Grossman, Mark. *The ABC-CLIO Companion to The Native American Rights Movement.* Santa Barbara, Calif.: ABC-CLIO, 1996.
Hadley-Garcia, George. *Hispanic Hollywood: The Latins in Motion Pictures.* Secaucus, N.J.: Citadel, 1990.
Hammond, Stefan, *Hollywood East: Hong Kong Movies and the People Who Make Them.* Lincolnwood, Ill.: Contemporary, 2000.
Hanke, Ken. *Charlie Chan at the Movies: History, Filmography, and Criticism.* Jefferson, N.C.: McFarland, 1989.
Hanson, Patricia King, exec. ed. *The American Film Institute Catalog of Motion Pictures: Feature Films: 1911–1920.* Berkeley, Calif.: University of California Press, 1988.
———. *The American Film Institute Catalog of Motion Pictures: Feature Films: 1941–1950.* Berkeley, Calif.: University of California Press, 1999.
———. *The American Film Institute Catalog of Motion Pictures: Feature Films: 1931–1940.* Berkeley, Calif.: University of California Press, 1993.
Hyatt, Wesley. *The Encyclopedia of Daytime Television.* New York: Billboard, 1997.
James, Darius. *That's Blaxploitation!: Roots of the Baadasssss 'Tude.* New York: St. Martin's, 1995.
Jones, William. *Black Cinema Treasures: Lost and Found.* Denton, Tex.: University of North Texas Press, 1991.
Katz, Ephraim. *The Film Encyclopedia* (4th ed.). Rev. ed. by Fred Klein and Ronald Dean Nolen. New York: HarperPerennial, 1998.
Keller, Gary D. *A Biographical Handbook of Hispanics and United States Film.* Tempe, Ariz.: Bilingual, 1997.
Kilpatrick, Jacquelyn. *Celluloid Indians: Native Americans and Film.* Lincoln, Neb.: University of Nebraska Press, 1999.
Kim, Hyung-Chan, ed. *Distinguished Asian Americans.* Westport, Conn.: Greenwood, 1999.
Krafsur, Richard P., exec. ed. *The American Film Institute Catalog of Motion Pictures: Feature Films 1961–1970.* New York: R. R. Bowker, 1976.
Kranz, Rachel, and Philip J. Koslow. *The Biographical Dictionary of African Americans.* New York: Facts On File, 1999.
Leab, Daniel J. *From Sambo to Superspade The Black Experience in Motion Pictures.* Boston, Mass.: Houghton Mifflin, 1976.
Lee, Spike, with Ralph Wiley. *By Any Means Necessary: The Trials and Tribulations of the Making of* Malcolm X. New York: Hyperion, 1992.
Lenburg, Jeff. *The Encyclopedia of Animated Cartoons.* New York: Facts On File, 1999.
Logan, Rayford W., and Michael R. Winston. *Dictionary of American Negro Biography.* New York: W. W. Norton, 1982.
Lyman, Darryl. *Great African-American Women.* Middle Village, N.Y.: Jonathan David, 1999.
———. *Great Jews in the Performing Arts.* Middle Village, N.Y.: Jonathan David, 1999.
———. *Great Jews on Stage and Screen.* Middle Village, N.Y.: Jonathan David, 1987.
Malinowski, Sharon, and Simon Glickman. *Native North American Biography.* Detroit, Mich.: Gale Research, 1996.
Malossi, Giannino. *Latin Lover: The Passionate South.* Milan, Italy: Charta, 1996.
Maltin, Leonard, ed. *Leonard Maltin's Movie and Video Guide, 2002 edition.* New York: Signet, 2001.
Mapp, Edward. *Directory of Blacks in the Performing Arts* (2nd ed.). Metuchen, N.J.: Scarecrow, 1990.
Marill, Alvin H. *Movies Made for Television: 1964–1986.* New York: Baseline, 1987.
Martinez, Gerald, Diana Martinez, and Andres Chavez. *What It Is ... What It Was!: The Black Film Explosion of the '70s in Words and Pictures.* New York: Hyperion, 1998.
Moon, Spencer. *Reel Black Talk: A Sourcebook of 50 American Filmmakers.* Westport, Conn.: Greenwood, 1997.
Munden, Kenneth W., exec. ed. *The American Film Institute Catalog of Motion Pictures: 1921–1930.* New York: R. R Bowker, 1971.
Ng, Franklin, ed. *The Asian American Encyclopedia.* Tarrytown, N.Y.: Marshall Cavendish, 1995.
Nowlan, Robert A., and Gwendolyn Wright Nowlan. *Cinema Sequels and Remakes: 1903–1987.* Jefferson, N.C.: McFarland, 1989.
Null, Gary. *Today's Black Hollywood: From 1910 to Today.* Secaucus, N.J.: Citadel, 1993.
Okuda, Michael, and Denise Okuda. *The Star Trek Encyclopedia: A Reference Guide to the Future* (expanded ed.). New York: Pocket Books, 1997.

O'Neil, Thomas. *The Emmys* (2nd ed.). New York: Perigee, 1992.
———. *Movie Awards: The Ultimate, Unofficial Guide to the Oscars, Golden Globes, Critics, Guild & Indie Honors.* New York: Perigee, 2001.
Oseary, Guy. *Jews Who Rock.* New York: St. Martin's, 2001.
Owens, Louis. *Mixedblood Messages: Literature, Film, Family, Place.* Norman, Okla.: University of Oklahoma Press, 1998.
Parish, James Robert. *Gays and Lesbians in Mainstream Cinema.* Jefferson, N.C.: McFarland, 1993.
———. *Great Combat Pictures.* Metuchen, N.J.: Scarecrow, 1991.
———. *Great Cop Pictures.* Metuchen, N.J.: Scarecrow, 1990.
———. *The Hollywood Book of Death.* Lincolnwood, Ill.: Contemporary, 2001.
———. *Let's Talk! America's Favorite Talk Show Hosts.* Las Vegas, Nev.: Pioneer, 1993.
———. *Today's Black Hollywood.* New York: Pinnacle, 1995.
———. *Whoopi Goldberg: Her Journey from Poverty to Mega-Stardom.* Secaucus, N.J.: Birch Lane, 1997.
Parish, James Robert, and Leonard DeCarl, with William T. Leonard and Gregory W. Mank. *Hollywood Players: The Forties.* New Rochelle, N.Y.: Arlington House, 1976.
Parish, James Robert, and George H. Hill. *Black Action Films.* Jefferson, N.C.: McFarland, 1989.
Parish, James Robert, and William T. Leonard. *Hollywood Players: The Thirties.* New Rochelle, N.Y.: Arlington House, 1976.
Parish, James Robert, and William T. Leonard, with Gregory W. Mank and Charles Hoyt. *The Funsters.* New Rochelle, N.Y.: Arlington House, 1979
Parish, James Robert, and Michael R. Pitts. *Hollywood Songsters: A Biographical Dictionary.* New York: Garland, 1991.
———. *The Great Detective Pictures.* Metuchen, N.J.: Scarecrow, 1990.
———. *The Great Hollywood Musical Pictures.* Metuchen, N.J.: Scarecrow, 1992.
———. *The Great Science Fiction Pictures.* Metuchen, N.J.: Scarecrow, 1977.
———. *The Great Science Fiction Pictures II.* Metuchen, N.J.: Scarecrow, 1977.
———. *The Great Western Pictures.* Metuchen, N.J.: Scarecrow, 1976.
———. *The Great Western Pictures II.* Metuchen, N.J.: Scarecrow, 1988.
Parish, James Robert, and Don Stanke. *Hollywood Baby Boomers.* New York: Garland, 1992.
Parish, James Robert, and Vincent Terrace. *The Complete Actors' Television Credits: 1948–1988: Volume 1—Actors* (2nd ed.). Metuchen, N.J.: Scarecrow, 1989.
———. *The Complete Actors' Television Credits: 1948–1988: Volume 2—Actresses* (2nd ed.). Metuchen, N.J.: Scarecrow, 1990.
Pearl, Jonathan, and Judith Pearl. *The Chosen Image: Television's Portrayal of Jewish Themes and Characters.* Jefferson, N.C.: McFarland, 1999.
Phelps, Shirelle, ed. *Contemporary Black Biography.* Detroit, Mich.: Gale Research, 1992.
———. *Who's Who Among African Americans* (11th ed.). Detroit, Mich.: Gale Research, 1998.
Pickard, Roy. *Who Played Who on the Screen.* New York: Hippocrene, 1988.
Quinlan, David. *Quinlan's Film Directors* (revised ed.). London, England: B. T. Batsford, 1999.
Quinlan, David, ed. *The Film Lover's Companion: An A to Z Guide to 2,000 Stars and the Movies They Made.* Secaucus, N.J.: Citadel, 1997.
Reyes, Luis, and Peter Rubie. *Hispanics in Hollywood: A Celebration of 100 Years in Film and Television.* Los Angeles, Calif.: Ifilm, 2000.
Richard, Alfred Charles, Jr. *Censorship and Hollywood's Hispanic Image: An Interpretive Filmography, 1936–1955.* Westport, Conn.: Greenwood, 1993.
———. *Contemporary Hollywood's Negative Hispanic Image: An Interpretive Filmography, 1956–1993.* Westport, Conn.: Greenwood, 1994.
———. *The Hispanic Image on the Silver Screen: An Interpretive Filmography from Silents into Sound, 1898–1935.* Westport, Conn.: Greenwood, 1992.
Rogin, Michael. *Blackface, White Noise: Jewish Immigrants in the Hollywood Melting Pot.* Berkeley, Calif.: University of California Press, 1996.
Rollins, Peter C., and John E. O'Connor, eds. *Hollywood's Indian.* Lexington, Ky.: Kentucky University Press, 1998.
Rovin, Jeff, and Kathy Tracy. *The Essential Jackie Chan Sourcebook.* New York: Pocket Books, 1997.
Ryan, Joal. *Former Child Stars: The Story of America's Least Wanted.* Toronto, Canada: ECW, 2001.
Samberg, Joel. *Reel Jewish: A Century of Jewish Movies.* Middle Village, N.Y.: Jonathan David, 2000.
Sampson, Henry T. *Blacks in Black and White: A Source Book on Black Films* (2nd ed.). Metuchen, N.J.: Scarecrow, 1995.
Savada, Elias. *The American Film Institute Catalog: Film Beginnings: 1893–1910.* Metuchen, N.J.: Scarecrow, 1995.
Schutz, Wayne. *The Motion Picture Serial: An Annotated Bibliography.* Metuchen, N.J.: Scarecrow, 1992.
Silverman, Stephen M. *Funny Ladies: 100 Years of Great Comediennes.* New York: Harry N. Abrams, 1999.
Smith, Ronald L. *Who's Who in Comedy.* New York: Facts On File, 1992.
Smith, Valerie, ed. *Representing Blackness: Issues in Film and Video.* New Brunswick, N.J.: Rutgers University Press, 1997.
Soutenbrugh, John, Jr. *Dictionary of the American Indian: An A-to-Z Guide to Indian History, Legend, and Lore.* Avenel, N.J.: Wings, 1990.
Stokes, Lisa Odham, and Michael Hoover. *City on Fire: Hong Kong Cinema.* London, England: Verso, 1999.
Straub, Deborah Gilan, ed. *Native North American Voices.* Detroit, Mich.: Gale Research, 1997.
Swish, Karen Gayton, ed. dir. *Native North American Firsts.* Detroit, Mich.: Gale Research, 1998.
Tardiff, Joseph C., and L. Mpho Mabunda, eds. *Dictionary of Hispanic Biography.* Detroit, Mich.: Gale Research, 1996.
Teo, Stephen. *Hong Kong Cinema: The Extra Dimension.* London, England: British Film Institute, 1997.

Terrace, Vincent. *Fifty Years of Television: A Guide to Series and Pilots: 1937–1988.* Cranberry, N.J.: Cornwall, 1991.

———. *Radio Programs, 1924–1984: A Catalog of Over 1800 Shows.* Jefferson, N.C.: McFarland, 1999.

———. *Television Character and Story Facts: Over 110,000 Details from 1,008 Shows: 1945–1992.* Jefferson, N.C.: McFarland, 1993.

———. *Television Sitcom Factbook: Over 8,700 Details from 130 Shows: 1985–2000.* Jefferson, N.C.: McFarland, 2000.

Thomas, Victoria. *Hollywood's Latin Lovers: Latino, Italian and French Men Who Make the Screen Smolder.* Los Angeles, Calif.: Angel City, 1998.

Tibbetts, John C., and James M. Welsh. *The Encyclopedia of Novels into Film.* New York: Facts On File, 1998.

Unterburgre, Amy L., ed. *Who's Who Among Asian Americans: 1994–95.* Detroit, Mich.: Gale Research, 1994.

Waldman, Carl. *Encyclopedia of Native American Tribes.* New York: Facts On File, 1988.

Watkins, Mel. *On the Real Side: A History of African American Comedy from Slavery to Chris Rock* (2nd ed.). Chicago, Ill.: Lawrence Hill, 1999.

Weiss, Ken, and Ed Goodgold. *To Be Continued. . . . : A Complete Guide to Sound Movie Serials.* Stratford, Conn.: Star Tree, 1981.

Weisser, Thomas. *Asian Cult Cinema.* New York: Boulevard, 1997.

Xing, Jun. *Asian America Through the Lens: History, Representations, & Identity.* Walnut Creek, Calif.: AltaMira, 1998.

Zia, Helen, and Susan B. Gall, eds. *Notable Asian Americans.* Detroit, Mich.: Gale Research, 1995.

Zinman, David. *Saturday Afternoon at the Bijou.* New Rochelle, N.Y.: Arlington House, 1973.

INTERNET SITES

All Movie Guide: www.allmovie.com

E!Online: www.eonline.com

Epguide.com: www.epguide.com

Internet Movie Database: www.imdb.com

About the Author

JAMES ROBERT PARISH, a former entertainment reporter, publicist, and book series editor, is the author of numerous major biographies and reference books on the entertainment industry, including *Gus Van Sant, The Hollywood Book of Death, Jason Biggs, Whoopi Goldberg, Rosie O'Donnell's Story, The Unofficial "Murder, She Wrote" Casebook, Let's Talk—America's Favorite TV Talk Show Hosts, The Great Cop Pictures, Ghosts and Angels in Hollywood Films, Prison Pictures from Hollywood, Hollywood's Great Love Teams*, and *The RKO Gals*. Mr. Parish is a frequent on-camera interviewee on cable and network TV for documentaries on the performing arts. Mr. Parish resides in Studio City, California.

Index

Boldface page numbers indicate major treatment of a subject. Page numbers followed by an *f* indicate a photograph.

B

D

F

M

N

O

P

Q

S

W